K

FOR REFERENCE
NOT TO BE TAKEN FROM THE ROOM

Twentieth-Century
Literary Criticism

Guide to Thomson Gale Literary Criticism Series

For criticism on	Consult these Thomson Gale series
Authors now living or who died after December 31, 1999	**CONTEMPORARY LITERARY CRITICISM (CLC)**
Authors who died between 1900 and 1999	**TWENTIETH-CENTURY LITERARY CRITICISM (TCLC)**
Authors who died between 1800 and 1899	**NINETEENTH-CENTURY LITERATURE CRITICISM (NCLC)**
Authors who died between 1400 and 1799	**LITERATURE CRITICISM FROM 1400 TO 1800 (LC)** **SHAKESPEAREAN CRITICISM (SC)**
Authors who died before 1400	**CLASSICAL AND MEDIEVAL LITERATURE CRITICISM (CMLC)**
Authors of books for children and young adults	**CHILDREN'S LITERATURE REVIEW (CLR)**
Dramatists	**DRAMA CRITICISM (DC)**
Poets	**POETRY CRITICISM (PC)**
Short story writers	**SHORT STORY CRITICISM (SSC)**
Literary topics and movements	**HARLEM RENAISSANCE: A GALE CRITICAL COMPANION (HR)** **THE BEAT GENERATION: A GALE CRITICAL COMPANION (BG)** **FEMINISM IN LITERATURE: A GALE CRITICAL COMPANION (FL)** **GOTHIC LITERATURE: A GALE CRITICAL COMPANION (GL)**
Asian American writers of the last two hundred years	**ASIAN AMERICAN LITERATURE (AAL)**
Black writers of the past two hundred years	**BLACK LITERATURE CRITICISM (BLC)** **BLACK LITERATURE CRITICISM SUPPLEMENT (BLCS)**
Hispanic writers of the late nineteenth and twentieth centuries	**HISPANIC LITERATURE CRITICISM (HLC)** **HISPANIC LITERATURE CRITICISM SUPPLEMENT (HLCS)**
Native North American writers and orators of the eighteenth, nineteenth, and twentieth centuries	**NATIVE NORTH AMERICAN LITERATURE (NNAL)**
Major authors from the Renaissance to the present	**WORLD LITERATURE CRITICISM, 1500 TO THE PRESENT (WLC)** **WORLD LITERATURE CRITICISM SUPPLEMENT (WLCS)**

Volume 177

Twentieth-Century Literary Criticism

Criticism of the
Works of Novelists, Poets, Playwrights,
Short Story Writers, and Other Creative Writers
Who Lived between 1900 and 1999,
from the First Published Critical
Appraisals to Current Evaluations

Thomas J. Schoenberg
Lawrence J. Trudeau
Project Editors

Detroit • New York • San Francisco • New Haven, Conn. • Waterville, Maine • London • Munich

Twentieth-Century Literary Criticism, Vol. 177

Project Editors
Thomas J. Schoenberg and Lawrence J. Trudeau

Editorial
Jessica Bomarito, Kathy D. Darrow, Jeffrey W. Hunter, Jelena O. Krstović, Michelle Lee, Russel Whitaker

Data Capture
Frances Monroe, Gwen Tucker

Indexing Services
Laurie Andriot

Rights and Acquisitions
Margaret Abendroth, Lori Hines, Emma Hull

Imaging and Multimedia
Dean Dauphinais, Robert Duncan, Leitha Etheridge-Sims, Mary Grimes, Lezlie Light, Michael Logusz, Dan Newell, Kelly A. Quin, Denay Wilding

Composition and Electronic Capture
Tracey Matthews

Manufacturing
Rhonda Dover

Associate Product Manager
Marc Cormier

© 2006 Thomson Gale, a part of The Thomson Corporation. Thomson and Star Logo are trademarks and Gale is a registered trademark used herein under license.

For more information, contact
Thomson Gale
27500 Drake Rd.
Farmington Hills, MI 48331-3535
Or you can visit our Internet site at
http://www.gale.com

ALL RIGHTS RESERVED
No part of this work covered by the copyright herein may be reproduced or used in any form or by any means—graphic, electronic, or mechanical, including photocopying, recording, taping, Web distribution, or information storage retrieval systems—without the written permission of the publisher.

This publication is a creative work fully protected by all applicable copyright laws, as well as by misappropriation, trade secret, unfair competition, and other applicable laws. The authors and editors of this work have added value to the underlying factual material herein through one or more of the following: unique and original selection, coordination, expression, arrangement, and classification of the information.

For permission to use material from the product, submit your request via the Web at http://www.gale-edit.com/permissions, or you may download our Permissions Request form and submit your request by fax or mail to:

Permissions Department
Thomson Gale
27500 Drake Rd.
Farmington Hills, MI 48331-3535
Permissions Hotline:
248-699-8006 or 800-877-4253, ext. 8006
Fax 248-699-8074 or 800-762-4058

Since this page cannot legibly accommodate all copyright notices, the acknowledgments constitute an extension of the copyright notice.

While every effort has been made to secure permission to reprint material and to ensure the reliability of the information presented in this publication, Thomson Gale neither guarantees the accuracy of the data contained herein nor assumes any responsibility for errors, omissions or discrepancies. Thomson Gale accepts no payment for listing; and inclusion in the publication of any organization, agency, institution, publication, service, or individual does not imply endorsement of the editors or publisher. Errors brought to the attention of the publisher and verified to the satisfaction of the publisher will be corrected in future editions.

LIBRARY OF CONGRESS CATALOG CARD NUMBER 76-46132
ISBN 0-7876-8931-9
ISSN 0276-8178

Printed in the United States of America
10 9 8 7 6 5 4 3 2 1

Contents

Preface vii

Acknowledgments xi

Literary Criticism Series Advisory Board xiii

André Gide 1869-1951 1
French novelist, poet, essayist, playwright, and critic
Entry devoted to the novel The Immoralist *(1902)*

Randall Jarrell 1914-1965 122
American poet, critic, novelist, translator, essayist, and children's writer

Rose Wilder Lane 1887-1968 264
American novelist, short story writer, biographer, essayist, journalist, travel writer, and historian

Jean Shepherd 1921-1999 290
American radio performer, novelist, screenwriter, short story writer, essayist, and television scriptwriter

Literary Criticism Series Cumulative Author Index 327

Literary Criticism Series Cumulative Topic Index 433

TCLC Cumulative Nationality Index 447

TCLC-177 Title Index 453

Preface

Since its inception *Twentieth-Century Literary Criticism* (*TCLC*) has been purchased and used by some 10,000 school, public, and college or university libraries. *TCLC* has covered more than 1000 authors, representing over 120 nationalities and over 40,000 titles. No other reference source has surveyed the critical response to twentieth-century authors and literature as thoroughly as *TCLC*. In the words of one reviewer, "there is nothing comparable available." *TCLC* "is a gold mine of information—dates, pseudonyms, biographical information, and criticism from books and periodicals—which many librarians would have difficulty assembling on their own."

Scope of the Series

TCLC is designed to serve as an introduction to authors who died between 1900 and 1999 and to the most significant interpretations of these author's works. Volumes published from 1978 through 1999 included authors who died between 1900 and 1960. The great poets, novelists, short story writers, playwrights, and philosophers of the period are frequently studied in high school and college literature courses. In organizing and reprinting the vast amount of critical material written on these authors, *TCLC* helps students develop valuable insight into literary history, promotes a better understanding of the texts, and sparks ideas for papers and assignments. Each entry in *TCLC* presents a comprehensive survey on an author's career or an individual work of literature and provides the user with a multiplicity of interpretations and assessments. Such variety allows students to pursue their own interests; furthermore, it fosters an awareness that literature is dynamic and responsive to many different opinions.

Every fourth volume of *TCLC* is devoted to literary topics. These topics widen the focus of the series from the individual authors to such broader subjects as literary movements, prominent themes in twentieth-century literature, literary reaction to political and historical events, significant eras in literary history, prominent literary anniversaries, and the literatures of cultures that are often overlooked by English-speaking readers.

TCLC is designed as a companion series to Thomson Gale's *Contemporary Literary Criticism,* (*CLC*) which reprints commentary on authors who died after 1999. Because of the different time periods under consideration, there is no duplication of material between *CLC* and *TCLC*.

Organization of the Book

A *TCLC* entry consists of the following elements:

- The **Author Heading** cites the name under which the author most commonly wrote, followed by birth and death dates. Also located here are any name variations under which an author wrote, including transliterated forms for authors whose native languages use nonroman alphabets. If the author wrote consistently under a pseudonym, the pseudonym is listed in the author heading and the author's actual name is given in parenthesis on the first line of the biographical and critical information. Uncertain birth or death dates are indicated by question marks. Single-work entries are preceded by a heading that consists of the most common form of the title in English translation (if applicable) and the name of its author.

- The **Introduction** contains background information that introduces the reader to the author, work, or topic that is the subject of the entry.

- The list of **Principal Works** is ordered chronologically by date of first publication and lists the most important works by the author. The genre and publication date of each work is given. In the case of foreign authors whose works have been translated into English, the English-language version of the title follows in brackets. Unless otherwise indicated, dramas are dated by first performance, not first publication. Lists of **Representative Works** by different authors appear with topic entries.

- Reprinted **Criticism** is arranged chronologically in each entry to provide a useful perspective on changes in critical evaluation over time. The critic's name and the date of composition or publication of the critical work are given at the beginning of each piece of criticism. Unsigned criticism is preceded by the title of the source in which it originally appeared. All titles by the author featured in the text are printed in boldface type. Footnotes are reprinted at the end of each essay or excerpt. In the case of excerpted criticism, only those footnotes that pertain to the excerpted texts are included. Criticism in topic entries is arranged chronologically under a variety of subheadings to facilitate the study of different aspects of the topic.

- A complete **Bibliographical Citation** of the original essay or book precedes each piece of criticism. Source citations in the Literary Criticism Series follow University of Chicago Press style, as outlined in *The Chicago Manual of Style,* 15th ed. (Chicago: The University of Chicago Press, 2003).

- Critical essays are prefaced by brief **Annotations** explicating each piece.

- An annotated bibliography of **Further Reading** appears at the end of each entry and suggests resources for additional study. In some cases, significant essays for which the editors could not obtain reprint rights are included here. Boxed material following the further reading list provides references to other biographical and critical sources on the author in series published by Thomson Gale.

Indexes

A **Cumulative Author Index** lists all of the authors that appear in a wide variety of reference sources published by Thomson Gale, including *TCLC*. A complete list of these sources is found facing the first page of the Author Index. The index also includes birth and death dates and cross references between pseudonyms and actual names.

A **Cumulative Topic Index** lists the literary themes and topics treated in *TCLC* as well as other Literature Criticism series.

A **Cumulative Nationality Index** lists all authors featured in *TCLC* by nationality, followed by the numbers of the *TCLC* volumes in which their entries appear.

An alphabetical **Title Index** accompanies each volume of *TCLC*. Listings of titles by authors covered in the given volume are followed by the author's name and the corresponding page numbers where the titles are discussed. English translations of foreign titles and variations of titles are cross-referenced to the title under which a work was originally published. Titles of novels, dramas, nonfiction books, and poetry, short story, or essay collections are printed in italics, while individual poems, short stories, and essays are printed in roman type within quotation marks.

In response to numerous suggestions from librarians, Thomson Gale also produces a paperbound edition of the *TCLC* cumulative title index. This annual cumulation, which alphabetically lists all titles reviewed in the series, is available to all customers. Additional copies of this index are available upon request. Librarians and patrons will welcome this separate index; it saves shelf space, is easy to use, and is recyclable upon receipt of the next edition.

Citing *Twentieth-Century Literary Criticism*

When citing criticism reprinted in the Literary Criticism Series, students should provide complete bibliographic information so that the cited essay can be located in the original print or electronic source. Students who quote directly from reprinted criticism may use any accepted bibliographic format, such as University of Chicago Press style or Modern Language Association (MLA) style. Both the MLA and the University of Chicago formats are acceptable and recognized as being the current standards for citations. It is important, however, to choose one format for all citations; do not mix the two formats within a list of citations.

The examples below follow recommendations for preparing a bibliography set forth in *The Chicago Manual of Style,* 15th ed. (Chicago: The University of Chicago Press, (2003); the first example pertains to material drawn from periodicals, the second to material reprinted from books:

Morrison, Jago. "Narration and Unease in Ian McEwan's Later Fiction." *Critique* 42, no. 3 (spring 2001): 253-68. Reprinted in *Twentieth-Century Literary Criticism.* Vol. 127, edited by Janet Witalec, 212-20. Detroit: Thomson Gale, 2003.

Brossard, Nicole. "Poetic Politics." In *The Politics of Poetic Form: Poetry and Public Policy,* edited by Charles Bernstein, 73-82. New York: Roof Books, 1990. Reprinted in *Twentieth-Century Literary Criticism.* Vol. 127, edited by Janet Witalec, 3-8. Detroit: Thomson Gale, 2003.

The examples below follow recommendations for preparing a works cited list set forth in the *MLA Handbook for Writers of Research Papers,* 5th ed. (New York: The Modern Language Association of America, 1999); the first example pertains to material drawn from periodicals, the second to material reprinted from books:

Morrison, Jago. "Narration and Unease in Ian McEwan's Later Fiction." *Critique* 42.3 (spring 2001): 253-68. Reprinted in *Twentieth-Century Literary Criticism.* Ed. Janet Witalec. Vol. 127. Detroit: Thomson Gale, 2003. 212-20.

Brossard, Nicole. "Poetic Politics." *The Politics of Poetic Form: Poetry and Public Policy.* Ed. Charles Bernstein. New York: Roof Books, 1990. 73-82. Reprinted in *Twentieth-Century Literary Criticism.* Ed. Janet Witalec. Vol. 127. Detroit: Thomson Gale, 2003. 3-8.

Suggestions are Welcome

Readers who wish to suggest new features, topics, or authors to appear in future volumes, or who have other suggestions or comments are cordially invited to call, write, or fax the Associate Product Manager:

Associate Product Manager, Literary Criticism Series Thomson Gale
27500 Drake Road
Farmington Hills, MI 48331-3535
1-800-347-4253 (GALE)
Fax: 248-699-8054

Acknowledgments

The editors wish to thank the copyright holders of the criticism included in this volume and the permissions managers of many book and magazine publishing companies for assisting us in securing reproduction rights. Following is a list of the copyright holders who have granted us permission to reproduce material in this volume of *TCLC*. Every effort has been made to trace copyright, but if omissions have been made, please let us know.

COPYRIGHTED MATERIAL IN *TCLC*, VOLUME 177, WAS REPRODUCED FROM THE FOLLOWING PERIODICALS:

The Centennial Review, v. 17, summer, 1973. Copyright © 1973 by *The Centennial Review.* Reproduced by permission.—*French Forum,* v. 2, January, 1977; v. 4, September, 1979. Copyright © 1977, 1979 by the French Forum, Inc. All rights reserved. Both reproduced by permission of the University of Nebraska Press.—*The French Review,* v. 43, winter, 1970; v. 76, December, 2002. Copyright © 1970, 2002 by the American Association of Teachers of French. Both reproduced by permission.—*The Great Lakes Review,* v. 5, summer, 1978. Copyright © 1978 by Central Michigan University. Reproduced by permission.—*The International Fiction Review,* v. 21, 1994. Copyright © 1994 International Fiction Association. Reproduced by permission.—*The Iowa Review,* v. 5, spring, 1974 for "Randall Jarrell's 'Eland': A Key to Motive and Technique in His Poetry" by Russell Fowler. Copyright © 1974 by The University of Iowa. Reproduced by permission of the author.—*The Journal of Men's Studies,* v. 14, winter, 2006. © 2006 by the Men's Studies Press, LLC. Reproduced by permission.—*Journal of Popular Culture,* v. 16, summer, 1982. Copyright © 1982 by Ray B. Browne. Reproduced by permission of Blackwell Publishers.—*The Mississippi Quarterly,* v. 39, winter, 1985-86. Copyright © 1985-86 Mississippi State University. Reproduced by permission.—*New York Times Book Review,* v. 87, February 28, 1982 for review of Jean Shepherd's *A Fistful of Fig Newtons* by Martin A. Jackson. Reproduced by permission of the author.—*Nottingham French Studies,* v. 23, May, 1984. Copyright © The University of Nottingham 1984. Reproduced by permission.—*The Old Northwest,* v. 2, December, 1978 for "Memoryscape: Jean Shepherd's Midwest" by Joseph F. Trimmer. Reproduced by permission of the author.—*Parnassus: Poetry in Review,* v. 16, 1991 for "Randall Jarrell" by Sven Birkerts. Copyright © 1991 Poetry in Review Foundation, NY. Reproduced by permission of the author.—*PMLA,* v. 120, January, 2005. Copyright © 2005 by the Modern Language Association of America. Reprinted by permission of the Modern Language Association of America.—*Romance Quarterly,* v. 37, August, 1990. Copyright © 1990 by Helen Dwight Reid Educational Foundation. Reproduced with permission of the Helen Dwight Reid Educational Foundation, published by Heldref Publications, 1319 18th Street, NW, Washington, DC 20036-1802.—*The Romanic Review,* v. 57, December, 1966; v. 64, 1973. Copyright © 1966, 1973 by the Trustees of Columbia University in the City of New York. Both reproduced by permission.—*Southwest Review,* v. 81, summer, 1996. Copyright © 1996 by Southern Methodist University. Reproduced by permission.—*The South Atlantic Quarterly,* v. 86, spring, 1987. Copyright, 1987, Duke University Press. All rights reserved. Used by permission of the publisher.—*South Atlantic Review,* v. 50, May, 1985. Copyright © 1985 by the South Atlantic Modern Language Association. Reproduced by permission.—*The South Carolina Review,* v. 17, fall, 1984. Copyright © 1984 by Clemson University. Reproduced by permission.—*South Dakota Review,* v. 30, summer, 1992. Copyright © 1992, University of South Dakota. Reproduced by permission.—*The Southern Review, Louisiana State University,* v. 20, April, 1984 for "Randall Jarrell: The Paintings in the Poems" by Jeffrey Meyers. Copyright © 1984 by Jeffrey Meyers. Reproduced by permission of the author.—*Studies in 20th Century Literature,* v. 2, 1977-78. Copyright © 1977-78 by *Studies in Twentieth Century Literature.* Reproduced by permission.—*Studies in Short Fiction,* v. 26, fall, 1989. Copyright © 1989 by *Studies in Short Fiction.* Reproduced by permission.—*Sub-Stance,* v. 26, 1980. Copyright © 1980 by the Board of Regents of the University of Wisconsin System. Reproduced by permission.—*Symposium,* v. 28, winter, 1974. Copyright © 1974 by Helen Dwight Reid Educational Foundation. Reproduced with permission of the Helen Dwight Reid Educational Foundation, published by Heldref Publications, 1319 18th Street, NW, Washington, DC 20036-1802.—*Texas Studies in Literature and Language,* v. 46, spring, 2004 for "Randall Jarrell's Answerable Style: Revision of Elegy in 'The Death of the Ball Turret Gunner'" by Marc D. Cyr. Copyright © 2004 by the University of Texas Press. All rights reserved. Reproduced by permission of the publisher and the author.—*Twentieth Century Literature,* v. 40, fall, 1994. Copyright 1994, Hofstra University Press. Reproduced by permission.

COPYRIGHTED MATERIAL IN *TCLC*, VOLUME 177, WAS REPRODUCED FROM THE FOLLOWING BOOKS:

Apter, Emily S. From *André Gide and the Codes of Homotextuality.* ANMA Libri, 1987. Copyright © 1987 by ANMA Libri and Department of French & Italian, Stanford University. All rights reserved. Reproduced by permission of the publisher and the author.—Babcock, Arthur E. From *Portraits of Artists: Reflexivity of Gidean Fiction, 1902-1946.* French Literature Publications Company, 1982. Copyright © 1982 French Literature Publications Company. Reproduced by permission.—Bergmann, Eugene B. From *Excelsior, You Fathead! The Art and Enigma of Jean Shepherd.* Applause Theatre & Cinema Books, 2005. Copyright © 2005 by Eugene B. Bergmann. All rights reserved. Reproduced by permission.—Bryant, J. A., Jr. From *Understanding Randall Jarrell.* University of South Carolina Press, 1986. Copyright © University of South Carolina 1986. Reproduced by permission.—Burt, Stephen. From *Randall Jarrell and His Age.* Columbia University Press, 2002. Copyright © 2002 Columbia University Press, New York. All rights reserved. Republished with permission of the Columbia University Press, 61 W. 62nd St., New York, NY 10023.—Campbell, Donna. From "'Written with a Hard and Ruthless Purpose': Rose Wilder Lane, Edna Ferber, and Middlebrow Regional Fiction," in *Middlebrow Moderns: Popular American Women Writers of the 1920s.* Edited by Lisa Botshon and Meredith Goldsmith. Northeastern University Press/University Press of New England, 2003. Copyright © 2003 Northeastern University Press/University Press of New England, Hanover, NH. Reprinted with permission.—Cordle, Thomas. From *André Gide, Updated Edition.* Twayne Publishers, 1993. Copyright © 1993 by Twayne Publishers. Reproduced by permission of Thomson Gale.—Ehrhardt, Julia C. From *Writers of Conviction: The Personal Politics of Zona Gale, Dorothy Canfield Fisher, Rose Wilder Lane, and Josephine Herbst.* University of Missouri Press, 2004. Copyright © 2004 by The Curators of the University of Missouri. All rights reserved. Reprinted by permission of the University of Missouri Press.—Freedman, Ralph. From *The Lyrical Novel: Studies in Hermann Hesse, André Gide, and Virginia Woolf.* Princeton University Press, 1963. Copyright © 1963 by Princeton University Press, 1991 renewed by Princeton University Press. Reprinted by permission of Princeton University Press.—Guerard, Albert J. From *André Gide.* Harvard University Press, 1951. Copyright © 1951 by the President and Fellows of Harvard College. Renewed 1970 by Albert Joseph Guerard. Reproduced by permission of the Literary Estate of Albert J. Guerard.—Hagenbüchle, Helen. From *The Black Goddess: A Study of the Archetypal Feminine in the Poetry of Randall Jarrell.* Francke Verlag Bern, 1975. Copyright © A. Francke AG Verlag Bern, 1975. Reproduced by permission.—Hathcock, Nelson. From "'Standardizing Catastrophe': Randall Jarrell and the Bomb," in *Jarrell, Bishop, Lowell, & Co.* Edited by Suzanne Ferguson. The University of Tennessee Press, 2003. Copyright © 2003 by The University of Tennessee Press. Reproduced by permission of The University of Tennessee Press.—Humphrey, Robert. From "Randall Jarrell's Poetry," in *Themes and Directions in American Literature: Essays in Honor of Leon Howard.* Edited by Ray B. Browne and Donald Pizer. Purdue University Studies, 1969. Copyright © 1969 by Purdue University Press. Reprinted by permission. Unauthorized duplication not permitted.—Jarrell, Randall. From *The Complete Poems.* Farrar, Straus and Giroux, LLC., 1969. Copyright © 1969 by Randall Jarrell, renewed 1997 by Mary von S. Jarrell. Reprinted by permission of Farrar, Straus and Giroux, LLC. In the UK by Faber & Faber Ltd.—Nachman, Gerald. From *Seriously Funny: The Rebel Comedians of the 1950s and 1960s.* Pantheon Books, 2003. Copyright © 2003 by Gerald Nachman. Used by permission of Pantheon Books, a division of Random House, Inc.—Quinn, Sister Bernetta. From *Randall Jarrell.* Twayne Publishers, 1981. Copyright © G. K. Hall & Co. Reproduced by permission of Thomson Gale.

Thomson Gale Literature Product Advisory Board

The members of the Thomson Gale Literature Product Advisory Board—reference librarians from public and academic library systems—represent a cross-section of our customer base and offer a variety of informed perspectives on both the presentation and content of our literature products. Advisory board members assess and define such quality issues as the relevance, currency, and usefulness of the author coverage, critical content, and literary topics included in our series; evaluate the layout, presentation, and general quality of our printed volumes; provide feedback on the criteria used for selecting authors and topics covered in our series; provide suggestions for potential enhancements to our series; identify any gaps in our coverage of authors or literary topics, recommending authors or topics for inclusion; analyze the appropriateness of our content and presentation for various user audiences, such as high school students, undergraduates, graduate students, librarians, and educators; and offer feedback on any proposed changes/enhancements to our series. We wish to thank the following advisors for their advice throughout the year.

Barbara M. Bibel
Librarian
Oakland Public Library
Oakland, California

Dr. Toby Burrows
Principal Librarian
The Scholars' Centre
University of Western Australia Library
Nedlands, Western Australia

Celia C. Daniel
Associate Reference Librarian
Howard University Libraries
Washington, D.C.

David M. Durant
Reference Librarian
Joyner Library
East Carolina University
Greenville, North Carolina

Nancy T. Guidry
Librarian
Bakersfield Community College
Bakersfield, California

Heather Martin
Arts & Humanities Librarian
University of Alabama at Birmingham, Sterne Library
Birmingham, Alabama

Susan Mikula
Librarian
Indiana Free Library
Indiana, Pennsylvania

Thomas Nixon
Humanities Reference Librarian
University of North Carolina at Chapel Hill, Davis Library
Chapel Hill, North Carolina

Mark Schumacher
Jackson Library
University of North Carolina at Greensboro
Greensboro, North Carolina

Gwen Scott-Miller
Assistant Director
Sno-Isle Regional Library System
Marysville, Washington

The Immoralist

André Gide

The following entry presents criticism on Gide's novel *L'immoraliste* (1902; *The Immoralist*). For discussion of Gide's complete career, see *TCLC,* Volumes 5 and 12; for discussion of his novel *Les faux monnayeurs* (1925; *The Counterfeiters*) see *TCLC,* Volume 36.

INTRODUCTION

Published in 1902, *The Immoralist* is the first and, for many critics, the most accomplished of Gide's *récits,* a term he used to describe his short first-person narratives written during the early decades of the twentieth century. As Gide proclaimed, the *récit* is different from the novel in its close delineation of a psychological flaw—often an obsession over an ideal—in the story's protagonist, as opposed to the broader scope of the novel. Critics also recognize *The Immoralist* as the founding work in which Gide developed his detached and ironic method as a writer. In terms of plot, characterization, and style, *The Immoralist* is classic in its formality and precision; the narrative explores complex themes such as the conflict between radical individualism and social morality, the dangers of excessive will and idealization, and the constructed nature of personal identity. The book is also praised as a landmark achievement in the development of the French psychological novel because of its concise and circumspect realism and its skillful use of the first-person narrator. As J. C. Davis has noted, "Gide's view is essentially that of the classical artist, whose aim is to present characters in action, who reveal themselves sufficiently by what they say or do, without any need for the author to intervene and explain motives or draw conclusions." Though it was initially dismissed as a scandalous work by many critics, *The Immoralist* was championed by a later generation of French readers and thinkers, influencing the existentialist movement in literature and paving the way for such writers as Albert Camus and Jean-Paul Sartre.

PLOT AND MAJOR CHARACTERS

Gide employs a formal narrative device in *The Immoralist*: the story is "framed" within a letter written by the protagonist's friend who, with two other "dearest" friends, has been summoned by the hero to hear the account of his tragic experience and offer counsel. The letter itself is a verbatim record of events as described by Michel, the protagonist and narrator. The story within this framing device begins when Michel, a twenty-four-year-old archaeologist, marries Marceline, a family friend, at the request of his dying father. Their marriage is based more on a sense of duty than on romantic love. On their honeymoon trip to Biskra in North Africa, Michel's health deteriorates and he develops tuberculosis and almost dies. Marceline nurses him back to health, and as he recovers he is filled with a new desire for life. Marceline brings Bachir, an attractive Arab boy, into Michel's sickroom to help with his recovery. Michel becomes enamored of Bachir and the other native boys, which he attributes to their youthful energy and its positive effect on his own recuperating health. But he soon begins inventing excuses for seeing the boys alone. He particularly favors Moktir, who is robust and unruly. When he has recovered, Michel and Marceline leave Biskra for France. Michel feels his love for his wife growing but still keeps his inner thoughts hidden from her. In Italy, on the return voyage, he has a fight with a coachman, and later that night consummates his marriage with Marceline.

When they return to La Morinière, his estate in France, Michel struggles with the duality of his desires. On the surface he enjoys success. He holds a college professorship and takes an apartment in Paris. Marceline discovers she is pregnant. Despite his good fortunes, Michel becomes increasingly agitated with the hypocrisy of his academic life and loses interest in maintaining his estate. He begins associating with the uneducated and primitive farmhands, and in one notable scene takes part with some of the workers in poaching from his own estate. Michel is suddenly overcome with a desire to destroy everything he has worked to create. It is during this time that he develops a friendship with Ménalque, a well-traveled intellectual who forces him to face his ambivalent tendencies. One night while he is away conversing with Ménalque, Marceline miscarries. In an ironic parallel to Michel's experience, she begins to show symptoms of tuberculosis. Michel resigns his professorship and sells La Morinière. As Marceline's health declines, they move to St. Moritz. Marceline begins to recover, but Michel becomes restless in Switzerland and continues to move them further south, all the while recklessly spending money. In each new city,

Michel neglects his ill wife and seeks company with questionable members of society. In Taormina, he is attracted to a Sicilian boy and kisses him. In Syracuse, he abandons his wife and spends time with sailors. Finally, they travel back to Biskra, but this time it is Marceline who is on the verge of death. In the two years since they have been away, the native children have changed in Michel's eyes, except for Moktir, who has just gotten out of prison. Michel moves his wife to Touggourt and brings Moktir with them. In a perverted attempt to satisfy his unconscious desires, Michel sleeps with Moktir's mistress while Moktir is present in the room. After this act, he returns to his hotel just before Marceline dies. Unable to help her, Michel descends into a moral weariness and restless state. Three months pass after Marceline's death before he contacts his friends to hear his story.

MAJOR THEMES

At the thematic forefront of *The Immoralist* is Michel's existential struggle between responsibility and personal freedom. Throughout the story, Michel's ambivalence is revealed as he chooses between these two forces in his life. After his illness, he makes a commitment to both his marriage and his financial and professional success, but as the story progresses, he gradually undermines these commitments and chooses individual freedom instead. Michel is away all night, talking with Ménalque when Marceline delivers their still-born baby. And later in the story he takes part in poaching on his own estate, thereby contributing to his financial ruin. Writing in 1963, Ralph Freedman drew connections between Michel's longing for freedom and "North Africa, Arab boys, lush gardens, and implied homosexuality," while he associated restraint "with womanhood, marriage, France, bourgeois order, and religion." When Marceline becomes ill with tuberculosis, Michel takes them first to Switzerland, where she makes a partial recovery. However, Michel's boredom and quest for absolute freedom leads them further south, despite the negative effect this has on Marceline's health. Some critics have interpreted his desire to return to Africa as an effort to expedite Marceline's death and provide for himself the ultimate release from responsibility. Indeed, in relating the events to his friends, Michel equates her death with his own liberation.

Other critics have defined the protagonist's ambivalence and search for personal freedom as a struggle against morality. Michel's upbringing is characterized as austere, morally rigid, and even puritanical. His marriage to the conservative and Christian Marceline further ensnares him in the conventional moral trappings of his society. Many scholars have cited Michel's attraction to lawlessness, his latent homosexuality, and his destructive tendencies toward himself and Marceline as evidence of his longing to escape the moral restrictions placed on him. Michel is attracted to the young Arab boys he meets in Biskra, especially Moktir. When Moktir steals Marceline's scissors, Michel not only looks the other way but delights in being complicit in the act. His participation in poaching, as well as his determination to sleep with Moktir's mistress while Marceline is dying, become acts against the rigid moral system to which he is bound.

Rebirth of the self is another important theme of Gide's *The Immoralist*. Many scholars interpret Michel's illness and return to health in Biskra as a kind of regeneration for the protagonist. Michel sees the world differently after his recovery, and he is determined to experience life in a new way by living in the present moment. To symbolize this rebirth, Michel shaves his beard. He is attracted to anything that symbolizes health and vitality for him, including the Arab boys, the sun, and his own growing strength. As Michel struggles to define his new sense of self, Gide employs the "palimpsest" as a metaphor for his transformation. Marshall Lindsay has argued that this metaphor supports Michel's theory that his newfound identity represents not an entirely new being but an authentic self, or "the survival of a kind of primitive self within him." When Michel returns to France, he is faced with the artifacts and responsibilities of his old life. To preserve his authentic self, Michel initially leads a dual existence upon his return home, but he ultimately pursues an extreme and destructive course under the delusion of nurturing and preserving his new identity.

CRITICAL RECEPTION

Upon its publication *The Immoralist* received a mixed response from reviewers and the reading public. Although the novel was praised by Gide's friends and literary acquaintances, others regarded it as a scandalous work for its open treatment of sexuality and social hypocrisy, and for its stark depiction of its protagonist's single-minded pursuit of sensual experience and individual freedom. Complicating reactions to the book was the fact that the story closely paralleled events in Gide's own life, which led many critics to read it as an autobiographical work. This opinion was so strong that the author was compelled to disavow, in a preface to the second edition, any endorsement of his hero's narrative. Even those critics who praised *The Immoralist* disagreed over the nature of Gide's treatment of his central theme. Some saw in the depiction of Michel and his personal quest a clear warning against the dangers of unrestrained egoism and the pursuit of absolute will. Others argued that *The Immoralist* was, in fact, a sympathetic story of one man's desire to strip away cultural decay and hypocrisy and achieve self-knowledge.

Since the 1950s *The Immoralist* has won increasing praise, and today it is considered one of Gide's greatest *récits* and among the best examples of psychological realism in French literature. It is also regarded as an important work in the development of Gide's literary aesthetics and concept of "disponibilité"—his moral philosophy based on sincerity, integrity, and self-awareness. Modern commentators have emphasized the complexities in Gide's treatment of his themes of personal freedom, human will, social responsibility, and morality, and in the narrative structure of *The Immoralist*. Whereas previous readers saw in the work either an endorsement of or attack against Friedrich Nietzsche's philosophy of the superiority of individual will over social order, later twentieth-century and twenty-first-century critics have discerned a more ambiguous message. Many have debated the exact nature of Michel's immorality and the role his homosexuality plays in his personal quest. One line of enquiry, such as that voiced by Albert J. Guerard, Germaine Brée, Laurence M. Porter, and Marshall Lindsay, maintains that Michel is "immoral," not because of his selfish pursuit of absolute will and personal freedom, but because he is a flawed figure, a person "too weak intellectually to comprehend the forces with which he was playing, too weak morally to make a choice," according to Brée.

Other commentators have stressed the presence of religious myth and symbol in *The Immoralist*, arguing that Michel's quest for physical gratification and freedom represents a rejection of Christian salvation. One of the most prevalent trends in recent criticism of the novel is to praise Gide's skillful use of irony and first-person narration, which, in the assessment of Allan H. Pasco, complicates simple readings of the work and undercuts the sincerity of Michel's account of his experience. Such metafictional interpretations have also been made by John T. Booker, Nathaniel Wing, Arthur E. Babcock, Emily S. Apter, Louis A. MacKenzie, Jr., and James T. Day. In fact, MacKenzie has asserted that one of the "basic themes" of *The Immoralist* is the process by which the reader "dis-covers" Gide's ironic textual strategies in the story. In a similar vein, Day has maintained that "theater itself" is a key theme in the novel, and that "one of the least explored sources of ambiguity that saturates *L'Immoraliste* is the interplay of performance-based and textual models, and the failure of the former to offset the inadequacies of the latter."

Although a number of current critics fault aspects of *The Immoralist*, particularly the artificiality of Gide's frame story and his characterization of the Wildean figure of Ménalque, most consider it a positive example of his skills as an author, especially his craftsmanship of the first-person novel. As Thomas Cordle concluded in 1993: "Gide's artistry is abundantly displayed in *L'Immoraliste,* and nowhere more impressively than in the narrative style. The story that he invents is a romantic one in all essential respects—in its glorification of self, of desire, and of will; in the excesses of action and thought that it depicts; and in the ironies that it sustains from start to finish, the irony of Michel and the irony of freedom."

PRINCIPAL WORKS

Les cahiers d'André Walter [*The Notebooks of André Walter*] (novel) 1891

Le traité du Narcisse [*Narcissus*] (verse and prose poetry) 1891

Les poésies d'André Walter (prose poems) 1892

Le voyage d'Urien [*Urien's Voyage*] (novella) 1893

Paludes [*Marshlands*] (novella) 1895

Les nourritures terrestres [*The Fruits of the Earth*] (prose poetry) 1897

Le Prométhée mal enchaîné [*Prometheus Illbound*] (novella) 1899; also translated as *Prometheus Misbound*

Le Roi Candaule (play) 1901

L'immoraliste [*The Immoralist*] (novel) 1902

Prétextes: Réflexions sur quelques points de littérature et de morale [*Pretexts: Reflections on Literature and Morality*] (essays) 1903

Amyntas (journals) 1906

Le retour de l'enfant prodigue [*The Return of the Prodigal*] (dialogues) 1907

La porte étroite [*Strait Is the Gate*] (novel) 1909

Oscar Wilde (reminiscences) 1910

Isabelle (novella) 1911

Les caves du Vatican. 2 vols. [*The Vatican Swindle*] (novel) 1914; also translated as *Lafcadio's Adventures*

Philoctète (play) 1919

La symphonie pastorale [*The Pastoral Symphony*] (novella) 1919

Si le grain ne meurt. 2 vols. [*If It Die*] (autobiography) 1920-21

Saäl (play) 1922

Dostoïevsky [*Dostoevsky*] (criticism) 1923

Corydon (dialogues) 1924

Les faux monnayeurs [*The Counterfeiters*] (novel) 1925

Les journal des faux monnayeurs [*Logbook of the Coiners*] (journal) 1926

Numquid et tu . . . ? (journal) 1926

Voyage au Congo [*Travels in the Congo*] (travel essays) 1927

*Le retour de l'enfant prodigue (play) 1928

L'école des femmes [*The School for Wives*] (novella) 1929

Oedipe [*Oedipus*] (play) 1931

Œuvres completes d'André Gide. 15 vols. (novels, novellas, plays, prose poems, dialogues, travel essays) 1932-39

†*Les caves du Vatican* (play) 1933
Perséphone (libretto) 1934
Le treizième arbre (play) 1935
Retour de l'U.R.S.S. [*Return from the U.S.S.R.*] (travel essays) 1936
Journal, 1889-1939 (journal) 1939
Thésée [*Theseus*] (novella) 1943
Robert ou l'intérêt général (play) 1946
Et nunc manet in te [*The Secret Drama of My Life*] (journal) 1947
Paul Valéry (criticism) 1947
Le théâtre complet. 8 vols. (plays) 1947-49
The Journals of André Gide. 4 vols. (journals) 1947-51
Journal, 1942-1949 (journal) 1950
My Theatre (plays and essays) 1951
Ainsi soit-il; ou, les jeux sont faits [*So Be It; or, The Chips Are Down*] (memoir) 1952
Correspondence, 1896-1950 (letters) 2004

*This work is an adaptation of Gide's dialogues published in 1907 under the same title.

†This work is an adaptation of Gide's novel by the same name.

CRITICISM

Albert J. Guerard (essay date 1951)

SOURCE: Guerard, Albert J. "The Early Novels." In *André Gide,* pp. 93-138. Cambridge, Mass.: Harvard University Press, 1951.

[*In the following essay, Guerard considers* The Immoralist *"a study of latent homosexuality, of repression and compensation, of the effect preconscious energies may have on a man's acts, feelings, and ideas."*]

L'Immoraliste, finished in 1901, is the first, the most autobiographical, and the best of Gide's "récits." Certainly it is the most frequently misunderstood of his novels, partly because its deceptive simplicity of surface invites casual and very literal reading. Like the unread *Voyage d'Urien,* the misread *Immoraliste* demands a fuller analysis than books as well or better known. Historically, it is an important moment in the development of the French psychological novel—which threatened to become, in the hands of Bourget, a lucid pondering of abstract problems and a vehicle for transparent instruction. *L'Immoraliste* brought to the French novel all the seriousness and much of the complexity of Dostoevsky's short novels—and did so first of all through its successful use of the "imperceptive" or self-deluded narrator as subject of the story he tells. *L'Immoraliste* is not, to be sure, *The Possessed,* or even *Crime and Punishment.* But it exists as a touchstone for shorter and less ambitious fiction. It helps us to define a level of achievement which autobiographical and subjective fiction can rarely hope to surpass: fiction which concentrates on one man's destiny (a shadow of the author's own) and which offers no comprehensive understanding of society. Michel's revolt reflects his age (the age of Nietzschean hopes and destructions) but reflects even more the timeless conflict of the unconscious life and the conscious. Already the psychological realism of *L'Immoraliste* seems more important than its critique of individualism; its anticipation of Freud more valid than its oblique reflection of Nietzsche. Its more personal triumph lies in the successful avoidance of lyricism, of confused or angry self-justification, of special pleading—of all the evasions, in fact, to which autobiographical fiction is tempted. The precarious balance of the author's sympathy and detachment remains to the end under minute control.

Gide readily admitted the part which symbolic action played. He told Francis Jammes he had spent four years on the book, not writing but living it. He had struggled through the novel as through a disease, in order "to go beyond."¹ In a letter to Scheffer he reduces such symbolic action to an aesthetic principle:

> That a germ of Michel exists in me goes without saying . . . How many germs we carry in us, which will burgeon only in our books! They are what the botanists call "sleeping eyes." But if, by an act of will, you suppress them, *all but one*—how it springs up at once and grows! How it seizes at once upon the sap! My recipe for creating a hero is simple enough. Take one of these germs; put it in the pot by itself—and you soon obtain an admirable individual. Advice: choose preferably (if it's true one can choose) the germ that most disturbs you. By doing so you rid yourself of it at once. Perhaps that is what Aristotle meant by the purgation of the passions. Purge ourselves, Scheffer, purge ourselves! There will always be passions enough.²
>
> [Undated letter to Scheffer]

However, the process was not as simple as this letter implies. A fragment on Ménalque preceded *Les Nourritures terrestres,* and in the completed book only Ménalque has a personal history of any significance. Was Gide long determined to fix the lesson and personality of Oscar Wilde for posterity, or did he imagine once again a fictional blend of Wilde and himself? *L'Immoraliste,* in any event, appears to have been planned as a "life of Ménalque," to be told from the outside.³ But Gide could not, in 1897 or later, tell a detailed story of subjective torment except in the first person and from the inside. For this or for some other reason a separation occurred. The Ménalque of *L'Immoraliste* is no longer a blend of Wilde and Gide, but a walking manual of hedonism who recalls only too obviously the recorded personality and recorded epigrams of Wilde. He is as sprightly and as unreal as the Protos of *Les Caves du Vatican,* and is therefore out of place in a somber realistic novel. But Michel, transposed to a plane and life of tragic failure, is a potential or suppressed self, a refashioned image of the young André Gide.

There are differences, such differences as made the writing of *L'Immoraliste* possible. The fictional Michel is a latent and frustrated homosexual even after his marriage with Marceline, and is paralyzed by the freedom he has won. The freedom is of course incomplete, since to the very end he does not satisfy his pederast inclinations. Otherwise, the resemblances between the hero and his creator are striking and too obvious to insist on: the double oppression of childhood Huguenot teachings and an isolated bookish adolescence; an ill-advised marriage and the first fascinated observation of the children in Biskra; tuberculosis, convalescence, and the fierce egoism which accompanies it. Later, the dual impulses to concentration and dissolution of the self; the sense of estrangement on returning to the artificial Paris salons; the crucial meeting with a notorious hedonist. And at last the reckless unrest of the journeys to Switzerland and Italy, in roundabout obedience to the ineluctable pull of North Africa, where the last discoveries must be made. Gide thus "used" extensively his first two trips to North Africa and their surrounding moral complication, though the poachers of the second part derive from much older memories.[4]

Not everything was so retrospective, however. Gide also used certain more recent events: memories of ice-skating in St. Moritz on his honeymoon, of his wife's illnesses in Switzerland and North Africa in 1897 and 1898, of her carriage accident in 1900.[5] A brief 1897 letter to Jammes from Switzerland—mentioning both his wife's illness and Athman—reminds us of the very dilemma which Michel could not define.[6] Weighed against such living forces and memories, the influence of Nietzsche on the novel scarcely seems worth mentioning. This other "source" was in any event negative. The translation of Nietzsche's books into French freed Gide from the obligation to theorize on individualism at length.[7] We can only regret that he did not feel free to dispense with Ménalque as well. But this is perhaps the hardest thing for any novelist to do: to cut away all traces of what he had once (and wrongly) supposed to be his real subject.

In personal terms, *L'Immoraliste* was a symbolic act of dissociation from Michel. Had Gide not discovered himself so fully, he too might have been driven to such a harsh and aimless individualism. This is the book's "personal" subject. *L'Immoraliste* is also, of course, a critique (not rejection) of Nietzschean individualism. But most of all it is a study of latent homosexuality, of repression and compensation, of the effect preconscious energies may have on a man's acts, feelings, and ideas. It is no wonder, since the book was all these things, that it was little read and little understood at first. A very few early readers—and readers as different as Madame Rachilde and Francis Jammes—saw that the conflict was a sexual one. Yet Lilian Neguloa's valuable census shows that a large majority of the book's critics (including some very recent ones) have considered *L'Immoraliste* to be a novel "about individualism" and have not seen Michel's homosexuality at all.[8] Some, to be sure, may have simply refused to acknowledge what they saw. Thus Charles du Bos candidly admits that he could not take up "le problème Wilde" with the particular audience of his early lecture on the book.[9] Unlike French biography, French criticism has long resisted the influence of psychology and has also remained curiously discreet.

There is the further fact that Michel's revolt against repression and conformity may be transferred to any plane of experience, and so may invite the sympathy of a critic differently repressed. But the strongest obstacle to understanding has probably been the inveterate tendency of critics to take a narrative told in the first person at its face value and to confuse the narrator's consciousness with the author's. It is nevertheless hard to understand why so few critics (including those who return constantly to "intention") have referred to Gide's statement that Michel was an unconscious homosexual.[10] Miss Neguloa's article reminds us that nearly all readers are casual readers, and that most criticism of fiction is inexpert to an unsuspected and scandalous degree. It also suggests that any new commentary on *L'Immoraliste* must, to counteract established misconception, provide an old-fashioned summary of plot.

Michel, a precocious and withdrawn archaeologist of twenty-four, marries Marceline to please his dying father. At first he hardly realizes that she is a human being, with an inner life of her own. He feels at most tenderness and pity, and the honeymoon is loveless in every sense. Michel's long accumulated fatigue brings on tuberculosis. He begins to spit blood while crossing the desert and arrives at Biskra more dead than alive. His first surrender to sickness is followed by a violent craving to live. To consider as "right" only what contributes to health is the first phase of his "immoralism." And as health returns he begins to suspect that life has unexplored joys, that he carries within him a precious and unrealized self. He determines to discover this self by a ruthless elimination of everything factitious and acquired.[11] The self is a palimpsest. All the false superscriptions of education and moral training must be erased before he can discover the "occult text."

Marceline unwittingly takes the first important step toward revelation. She brings Bachir, a handsome native child, to Michel's sickroom. Michel interprets his affection for the boy as a love of animal health. But when he is able to go outside and watch the children at play, he is irritated by his wife's presence. He is "frightened" by the weak, sickly, and well-behaved boys she brings to their rooms but fascinated by the unruly Moktir. He says nothing when he sees Moktir steal a pair of scissors. And now he invents various pretexts for seeing the boys alone: Ashour, Lassif, and Lachmi with his "golden nudity." He wanders into one particular enchanted garden which will haunt his memory, and perhaps account for the attraction shaded places are to hold for him in Ravello and Normandy. But as the hot days approach they leave Biskra and the children behind. Michel feels that his love for Marceline is increasing, yet he takes pleasure in concealing from her his sense of a hidden, undefined self. In Italy, on the way back to France and a resumption of his studies, he has a fight with a drunken coachman. That night he possesses Marceline for the first time.

Michel leads a curiously divided life during the months that follow. On the one hand he tries to impose order on La Morinière, his Norman estate. He guards against "vagabond inclination" by tying himself down to an expensive Paris apartment, and by accepting a lectureship at the College de France. But he is attracted in his studies only by barbarism and indiscipline; by such figures as the fifteen-year-old Athalaric, in revolt against his mother and his Latin education. His lectures become an "apology and eulogy of non-culture." His friend Ménalque (who had visited Biskra after him and had heard of his liking for the native children) demands an explanation of these contradictions. Is Michel one of those who, out of a fear of isolation, refuse to be themselves? Before leaving on another of his fabulous journeys, Ménalque preaches the joys of dangerous living; that is, of the acceptance of life as it comes.

The balance between anarchy and discipline wavers during the months which separate the two visits to La Morinière. Something, seemingly Ménalque's lessons, tips it sharply toward anarchy. On the first visit Michel had spent his days supervising his estate with the prudent and orderly Charles, the caretaker's seventeen-year-old son. But now he is fascinated by the most primitive and irresponsible of the farmhands; feels an "evil curiosity" concerning them. He takes up with Bute, a demoralized army veteran, and listens avidly to his stories of the incestuous Heurtevents. He catches the boy Alcide poaching, and joins him in poaching on his own estate. He now feels a strange urge to destroy the harmony and order he had helped establish. He tries in vain to spend more time with his wife, who had lost a child, and who has begun to show tubercular symptoms. His pity struggles against a deepening sense that she is tainted by this illness. Her weakness seems contemptible.

Michel sells La Morinière and takes Marceline to St. Moritz. But he is intolerably bored by the honest mediocrity of the Swiss. His "reverence" for his wife increases simultaneously with a now demonic urge to spend all his money; to move always farther to the south; to seek out and observe, in each Italian city, the "lowest dregs of humanity." In Taormina he feels an irresistible attraction for a coachman—a Sicilian boy "as beautiful as a line of Theocritus"—and kisses him. A few days later they leave for Syracuse, and here too Michel neglects his dying wife to seek out the sailors and vagabonds in the port cafés. But Syracuse is only a last and futile detour. Their destination is Biskra. This time when they arrive it is Marceline who is more dead than alive.

In the two years, the native children have changed horribly. Only Moktir, just out of prison, remains "superb." In his vague restlessness Michel drags his wife on to Touggourt, taking Moktir with them. On the first night there he sleeps with Moktir's mistress in the boy's presence, seeking peace in highly cerebral perversion. He returns to the hotel in time to see Marceline die. Only then, freed from conscious restraint yet still restless, he sends for the three friends to whom he tells his story. Can they advise him? Tell him what to do with his objectless freedom? Even Michel is aware that this freedom is not truly complete. "Sometimes I am afraid that what I have suppressed will avenge itself." In the months since Marceline's death he has spent an occasional night with an Ouled Naïl prostitute. But the girl suspects it is really her little brother Ali he desires. "Perhaps she is not altogether wrong . . ."

L'Immoraliste is one of the first modern novels to deal at all seriously with homosexuality. But it is most important to keep in mind that Michel never participates in a homosexual act. The reader who assumes that such acts occur but are not mentioned, for reasons of discretion, is likely to misinterpret everything else. One can imagine Gide's exasperation when Paul Bourget asked him, as late as 1915 (and as soon as Edith Wharton had left the room) whether Michel was a "practicing pederast."[12] Through many pages of a first reading we have every right to share Michel's bewilderment. We explore him with the same curiosity that he explores himself. And how much would be lost if the last revealing lines of the novel were its first ones! But on second and subsequent readings the ambiguities should dissolve. Not till then, perhaps, does the reader notice that Michel possesses Marceline only after fighting with the drunken coachman; that he felt "obliged" (in an hour of frustration) to caress a strangely textured shrub; that his period of tranquility at La Morinière ends abruptly with the coming of the boy Charles; that he longs to sleep in the barn because the boy Alcide sleeps there; that, in fact, he never proceeds beyond the stage of longing for these boys. The important fact about Michel is not that he is a homosexual, but that he is a latent homosexual, a homosexual without knowing it.

Thus *L'Immoraliste* is not a case study of a particular and manifest neurosis, but a story of unconscious repression. In the light of this, but only in this light, various unexplained ritual acts take on meaning: the shaving of the beard, or the ceremonial undressing, sunbathing, and immersion in the pool near Ravello. The vengeance of what has been suppressed touches every fiber of Michel's intellectual and moral life; determines his self-destructiveness and his anti-intellectualism alike. Restrained from sexual satisfaction and even from self-discovery by an unconscious force, Michel rebels in other ways. The outburst may be sudden and specific, as when he leaps into the draining lake and takes a savage excitement in catching eels with Charles. More generally, Michel rebels against his early intellectual training in his philosophical defense of barbarism; against his inherited Norman prudence in trying to destroy the harmony and order of his farm. *L'Immoraliste* dramatizes as clearly as Dostoevsky's *Gambler* the compulsion to risk—and lose. Payment must eventually be made to the internalized parental authority. But the first impulse is to destroy not appease this superego. The harshness of Michel's individualism—and this, in general terms, is no less than the "subject" of the novel—is determined by the harshness of the repression.

The hidden victim of this hidden restraint reveals itself in a curious hostility toward the convention-bound and in an abnormal sympathy for the free. Michel's acts seemed to many early readers (and even at times to himself) unmotivated and "Satanic." Like *The Secret Sharer, Heart of Darkness,* and parts of *Lord Jim, L'Immoraliste* dramatizes unconscious or half-conscious identification.[13] The lawless buried self is attracted to all whom the superego and the waking conscience deem guilty, and repelled by all the well-behaved. Even when he is most determined to lead a regulated life, Michel's affections go out to the unmoral, the corrupt, the unrestrained. He has a "horror of honest folk," but is paralyzed by "joy" when he sees Moktir steal the scissors, when he learns that Alcide is a poacher—or when he uncovers, in the lifeless pages of his research, the youthful savagery of Athalaric. He envies Pierre's drunken brutality as he envies Ménalque's refined selfishness. The movement toward discovery is not, to be sure, uninterrupted. The alternating and sometimes simultaneous impulses to concentrate and to destroy the ego—to use Baudelaire's terminology rather than Freud's—increase or weaken according to the self at the moment dominant and the self at the moment suppressed. The frustrated Huguenot as well as the frustrated homosexual may demand satisfaction. In the final chapters, however, the inward aggressions become frenzied as the "authentic self" nears the surface.

Not all of Michel's feelings may be so simply explained. Does he resent the dying Marceline because he fears a return of his own tuberculosis, or because he has equated weakness and virtue, or simply because he longs to be rid of her? One strength of *L'Immoraliste* lies in its awareness of the close interdependence of Michel's health, his degree of sexual adjustment, his moral heritage, and his intellectual interests. The novel's over-all "meaning" is reducible to the barest Freudian terms, but Michel as a character is not. His intelligence and will, however weak, do play some part. His tenderness toward Marceline develops into love at the same time as his cruelty toward her—and at the same time as his homosexual impulses. And if his ideas are determined by unconscious needs, his arguments still demand attention. The problem of individualism, though provoked in this instance by a specific sexual situation, nevertheless transcends neurosis.

For Gide knew that the problem of the emancipated individualist goes on, even after sexual adjustments have been made. Must one choose between a refusal to live and an individualism which makes others suffer? Marceline justly observes that Michel's doctrine may be a "fine one," but that it threatens to suppress the weak. And can the individualist cut himself off to be free, yet live in that rarefied air? "To know how to free oneself is nothing; the arduous thing is to know what to do with one's freedom." It is here, in its critique of Nietzschean individualism, that *L'Immoraliste* is necessarily imperfect—and first of all because Michel is an imperfect Nietzschean. Gide agreed with Michel and Nietzsche that the world is divided into the strong and the weak, and many of Michel's arguments are transcribed from *Les Nourritures terrestres.* But Michel was incapable of the solution Gide elsewhere proposed: to become fully conscious of the inner dialogue between order and anarchy, and to suppress by an act of will whichever voice threatens to become too strong. The very fact that makes Michel so interesting dramatically and psychologically—his imperfect understanding of himself—makes him a poor vehicle for Gidean and Nietzschean ideas. His story could not answer the question raised in the Prologue: how is society to use the energies of the free man? "I fear the failures of individualism," Gide wrote in 1898.[14] Michel is such a failure; he is not a free man.

Thus the aspect of *L'Immoraliste* most emphasized by critics is in fact unsatisfactory. The novel's strength lies rather in its art and psychological understanding, and in its controlled transposition of personal experience. For it is a "fruit filled with bitter ashes,"[15] a novel written severely from memory, but also out of mind and nerve. The triumph of intelligence reveals itself in the close pressure of form. Not a single irrelevant memory has survived this pressure, other than the memory of Wilde's epigrams. This required a conscious separation of the author's consciousness from Michel's, and a careful use of the "imperceptive" narrator as a technical device. We shall see in Rivière's *Aimée* and Chardonne's *Eva* (two books possibly derived from *L'Immoraliste*) to what diffuseness and incoherence this device may lead (see Chapter 5). Yet it remains one of the few ways of saving psychological fiction from pedagogical abstractness, and perhaps the best way to convey (rather than "explain") a conflict between conscious and unconscious energies. The problem for the novelist is to keep his narrator (or Jamesian "fool" and observer) self-deluded, imperceptive, blind; incapable of accurate self-analysis—yet have that narrator supply all the evidence necessary to the reader's understanding. He must say enough to convey his daily suffering and betray his true difficulties, but not say too much more.

Critics have more and more come to realize that a novelist's "technique" has some intimate relationship with his understanding of his characters, as well as a more obvious bearing on the mobility, energy, and persuasiveness of his books. But it is nearly impossible to demonstrate these relationships specifically, and even discussions of "point of view" are often disappointingly vague. The device of the obtuse narrator or observer is, however, a particular and definable one, and Gide's major success in using it deserves close analysis. *L'Immoraliste* also demands extensive comparison with other novels, short novels especially. *Great Expectations* prolongs a central imperceptiveness over many hundreds of pages, but does so primarily for dramatic suspense. The technique (which demands unusual and continued alertness on the reader's part) seems particularly suited to the short novel. To measure Gide's success in exploiting this "point of view" we should look to certain familiar short novels of Melville and of Joseph Conrad and Thomas Mann. How did they, faced by such a problem as Gide's, exploit the resources of this technique? The comparisons may seem digressive, but only such comparisons can establish *L'Immoraliste* in its proper place as one of the formal triumphs of the modern novel.

Melville's *Benito Cereno* is certainly one of the more conspicuous successes. Captain Delano is literally a "fool," wholly incapable of interpreting experience or of seeing evil, because of his benign temperament and Emersonian optimism. But for various reasons his story had to be more diffuse than Michel's. Melville wanted to involve the reader in Delano's error, and not merely for the sake of suspense or melodramatic surprise. "You too, optimistic and complacent reader," he might have said; "this is the way you too would have calumniated innocence and rationalized evil!" Following such an intention, and conceiving such a drama of appearance and reality, Melville had to provide much misleading or irrelevant appearance. His grave prose rhythms and mortuary similes promise tragedy, but the reader has little opportunity to detect what this tragedy will be. Only the long legal deposition fully corrects Delano's distortions and reconstructs the events in detail. It provides a retrospective irony and horror, and ultimately proves that even the truth cannot shatter Delano's optimism. The deposition is very effective in its cold phraseology and abstract summation of death; only the lazy reader would want to see it go. But it suggests one of the ways in which the technique of the obtuse narrator or observer may thwart economy.

Dostoevsky, of course, provides several close analogues. *The Gambler* is as autobiographical as *L'Immoraliste,* but offers a much slighter separation of the character's consciousness from that of the author—who, incidentally, returned to his compulsive gambling immediately after finishing his book. *The Double,* however, dramatizes an unconscious conflict with great care, and anticipates the Freudian categories astoundingly: Golyadkin, Sr., as the menaced ego, while Golyadkin, Jr., acts out in turn the obscene id, the successful ego-ideal and the accusing superego. *The Double* is nevertheless the story of a neurotic descending into psychosis, as the early visit to the doctor warns us. Thus an alert reader separates himself from the character almost at once and accepts no evidence at face value. But in *Notes from Underground* Dostoevsky undertook a formal task very similar to Gide's. Like Gide, he understood that his narrator was neurotic, yet he shared some of his feelings and attitudes: his hatred of deterministic psychology and his longing to act gratuitously, his disgust with positivist ethics. The problem was to write a psychological novel which would yet raise certain ideas provocatively. But Dostoevsky's blending of the two interests was less satisfactory than Gide's. The isolated and self-destructive "underground mouse," compelled to reënact a few experiences of childhood and adolescent rejection, does not understand why he acts as he does. He long bemuses us with his circular diatribe against determinism, but this essay is really irrelevant.

Five pages—and five pages more clearly dissociating author and subject—would have sufficed. For it is the body of the novel that proves man can act against his own interests, and does so not freely but compulsively. In this second part too, the formal difference from *L'Immoraliste* is enormous. Dostoevsky offers us not only obtuseness but the "original," chaotic, diffuse experience of the neurotic. He gives the full stenographic report of a patient's confession—from which we may, if we are sufficiently alert, deduce our clear conclusions. And there is much evidence that Dostoevsky knew he was doing just this. The narrator is diffuse only when what he says is irrelevant. He reveals the important facts of his story (his schoolboy experiences, for instance, or his onanism) in begrudging, bitter, and very brief asides. Thus *Notes from Underground* is in one sense a more authentic "report" than *L'Immoraliste,* and certainly takes us closer to the lived experience of neurotic suffering, the actual impression of hourly damnation. But for these very reasons it may offer less psychological understanding and achieve a rarer impression of tragedy. Tragedy is not mere suffering, but suffering delimited and ordered, understood with finality.

Conrad's *Heart of Darkness* has much of *Benito Cereno*'s density of atmosphere and calculated ambiguity of appearance, and at times it may recall the evasiveness of *Notes from Underground*. The author's purpose here as in his longer novels was to involve the reader minutely, and at whatever tiring of his patience. But other short novels by Conrad, told in the first person or seen by an obtuse observer, show an economy as impressive as Gide's. Conrad's general impulse was the same: to dramatize compulsive inward journeys, the very processes of self-exploration and self-discovery. And he too dramatizes unconscious identification—Marlow allying himself with the atavistic Kurtz, or the young captain of *The Secret Sharer* with the fugitive from the "Sephora," or the crew of the "Narcissus" with the malingering James Wait. But only *The Smile of Fortune* presents the kind of sexual self-delusion which would have interested Gide, and did interest him in **Isabelle**. Conrad's usual practice was to universalize such particulars and to see the conflict with the unconscious or preconscious in large symbolic terms. A few very slight changes could give *The Secret Sharer* a localized and even homosexual meaning. But the story as it stands has no such primary meaning. The captain's double is instead the whole of the unconscious, to be explored and recognized—including that area of the unconscious which may provoke unreflective action and unpremeditated crime. Technically, *The Secret Sharer* shows the same formal control as **L'Immoraliste**. The narrator describes an experience of extreme incoherence, and even manages to convey a state of mind bordering on madness. Yet his cool report, like Michel's, contains very little that is irrelevant. It seems to move with the casualness and waste of unselective realism, but nearly every word counts. Much of Conrad's success here, and in the still more generalized *Shadow-Line*, lies in his full evocation of a plausible speaking voice. This is also one of the reasons for Gide's success with Michel. Extreme economy of narrative is masked by these calm and casual tones.

The closest approach to Gide's novel, in subject and technique, is Thomas Mann's *Death in Venice*, which was written a few years later. It is essentially the same story of latent and unrecognized homosexuality leading to self-destruction—though the reader who finds only theorizing on individualism in Gide may find only theorizing on the artist in Mann. Like Michel, Gustav von Aschenbach goes on a journey, not realizing that it is a journey within nor understanding the reasons for his restlessness. He too pays severely for his years of discipline and excessive restraint. The same alternating impulses to concentrate and to dissolve the self control these two destinies, and both men—frightened by their new anarchy—make one last strong effort to recover self-control. Both rationalize their aggressive inward drives in philosophical terms. But their real objective is the restraining superego, which must be destroyed before Tadzio and Ali can be enjoyed. Gustav von Aschenbach's homosexual reactions are fewer than Michel's, though Mann had read Freud and Gide had not. Mann's hero is repelled by the old and painted homosexual on the boat from Pola to Venice, that exact image of his future self, as Michel is repelled for a time by Ménalque. But his most characteristic pederast reaction—a delighted recognition that Tadzio will die young *and therefore never be a mature man*—comes later in the story than Michel's resentment of Charles's growing-up. The two men are most strikingly alike in the way they externalize their inward conflicts. Michel's frenzied effort to probe and uncover the secrets of the Heurtevents is a symbolic attempt to uncover his own secret. In precisely the same way Gustav von Aschenbach, only dimly aware of his inner plague, combats the efforts of the Venetian authorities to conceal the cholera epidemic (after a brief period of pleased complicity). These things, all things, must be brought to the surface.

We have thus the same minute drama of self-delusion and self-discovery, and roughly the same separation between the author's consciousness and his character's. The great initial difference is that Michel is an obtuse narrator and Gustav von Aschenbach an obtuse observer, whose observations are rephrased by the author's ironic detachment. But the separation is at first unclear. How much of this sophisticated weary irony (and how many of these reflections on the "artist") are shared by Mann and Gustav von Aschenbach? Mann's technique most closely resembles Gide's after Tadzio has entered the story. At this point we are offered ample evidence of the latent homosexuality. But Mann does not "explain" why Gustav von Aschenbach acts as he does until the victim can explain it himself. Both stories, incidentally, show the same technical flaw. These wholly inward stories need no outside pressures to achieve their tragic ends. Yet Mann brings in an outside force—the misdirection of the baggage—to "tip the scales toward anarchy," as Gide brings in Ménalque. Of the two, Gide's mistake is the more serious one. For it suggests that Michel's inward debate needed pedagogical support from without.

These are some of the resemblances. But there are differences in conception, which are reflected closely in structure and technique. **L'Immoraliste** is the purer Freudian drama of the two, since both the homosexual urge and the tyrannical repressive force long remain unconscious. But in *Death in Venice* the restraining force is often conscious—a conscious longing for dignity and order—and the hero is not merely an intellectual but himself a psychological novelist. No doubt he too could interpret his love of the ocean as a yearning "for the unorganized, the immeasurable, the eternal—in short, for nothingness." His more conscious struggle therefore demands more explicit analysis than Michel's—even though much of that analysis may be deliberately misleading.

Beyond this, Mann offers a grand over-all "explanation" which Gustav von Aschenbach could not have made. This is the four-part equation of homosexuality, plague, unconsciousness, and death; the hero approaching one is approaching them all. Thus the daydream in Munich anticipates that atavistic dream in Venice which "left the whole cultural structure of a lifetime trampled on, ravaged, and destroyed." And the tiger in the bamboo thicket of the daydream is a real tiger in the "primeval island-jungle" of the Ganges Delta where the cholera epidemic began. Here already the author has "added something" to nature, for the sake of explanation and for dramatic effect. But how much more he adds in the occult appearance of the three strangers: the man standing near the funeral hall in Munich; the lawless gondolier with his gondola black as a coffin; the entertainer with his homosexual gestures, his unprovoked hysteria, and his heavy carbolic smell.[16] For Gustav von Aschenbach does not see what author and reader see—that they are the same man, with the same facial characteristics, alike beckoning the hero to self-discovery, unconsciousness, and death. They are, simply, his destiny.

The texture of *Death in Venice* is realistic—and Mann, like Melville and Dostoevsky, offers a great deal of irrelevant detail (the description of Tadzio's sisters, for instance) to make his story more plausible. But the over-all structure is symbolist in a manner as traditional as Chaucer's in *The Pardoner's Tale*. *L'Immoraliste* confines itself, instead, to our only too natural world. Against the ingenious symbolist connections of *Death in Venice* it offers the structural firmness and inward connections of a fully dramatized psychic situation. Most obvious are the falling then rising line of Michel's health, as Marceline's line rises and declines; the balance of the two visits to La Morinière as Michel preserves then destroys his estate, and the vast circular movement from Biskra back to Biskra. Even these unities (if we accept the common view that tuberculosis is often a neurotic illness) seem psychologically necessary. More specifically, each step in Michel's journey looks forward to some future step: the fight with the drunken coachman near Positano to the kissing of the coachman in Taormina; the gardens of Biskra to the gardens of Ravello; the daylight rides with Charles to the nighttime poaching with Alcide. Yet these anticipations are never fortuitous, as the gondolier's anticipation of the entertainer is fortuitous. The changed Michel is compelled to return to the same places and experiences, if only to discover how he has changed.

Still more challenging, to the student of realism, is the fact that nearly everything Michel says and nearly everything he sees has a direct bearing on his sexual problem. He keeps Moktir's theft secret not merely because he sees in it an acting-out of his own longing to rebel against accepted decencies, but because he here enters into a first clandestine relationship with a child. A large psychological situation is thus perfectly dramatized in the action or inaction of a moment; the "gratuitous act" of sympathetic identification is in no sense gratuitous. Yet Michel's prolonged compulsive need to spend all his money is, to the reader of Menninger and Freud, fully as convincing. The novel offers very little "neutral" or innocent imagery. Lassif's canals and Lachmi's gourd for collecting the sap from palm trees are images as primary, for this latent homosexual, as the eels he caught with Charles; clay and shrub alike have a fleshy texture. How could Gide, using so much significant imagery, yet contrive to give an impression of real life, of unselected experience? The question poses itself when we recall the amount of "wasted" imagery in Mann and Dostoevsky, wasted for the sake of realism. One answer is that Gide's significant images also serve as casual images—*and so serve because never explained.* No single image or experience, but the cumulative effect of them all, drives us very slowly to an awareness of Michel's trouble. Everything in Michel's story leads to his revelation in the last line, yet no particular page seems to lead there in an obvious way. The minutiae of style and technique thus disguise an economy as extreme as any in modern fiction. Could Gide achieve a latent homosexual's vision of experience so exactly and so economically only because he had been, himself, a latent homosexual? To ask this is to take a very naïve view of the art of fiction—and to forget the imperfections of certain earlier books. In *L'Immoraliste* he reduced a most confused personal experience to an order which even the best-adjusted writers rarely achieve.

It is hardly the intention of this book to defend realism as such, and the anti-realism of **Les Faux-Monnayeurs** may have done more for the modern novel. But **L'Immoraliste** is a great realistic novel, and perhaps the best novel Gide would write. It demanded a fairly extended analysis because it shows us, at the outset, the characteristic tactics and strategy of Gide's other "récits." Beyond this it proves that even the realistic and subjective psychological novel may be economical. The neurotic experience of a Michel can be more than neurotic experience; it can reflect a universal conflict. And it requires, to be told, neither the diffuseness of *Notes from Underground,* nor the confusion of *The Double,* nor the superimposed intellectualism of *Death in Venice.* These are great works, and perhaps more astonishing at a first reading than **L'Immoraliste.** But

Gide's novel belongs with them. And, like a great poem, it deserves and can survive repeated readings.[17]

Notes

1. Undated letter to F.J., *OC* Andre Gide, [*Oeuvres complètes,* edited by Louis Martin-Chauffier, 15 vols. (Paris: Nouvelle Revue Frangaise, 1932-39). Henceforth abbreviated *OC*], III, 562.

2. Undated letter to Scheffer, *OC,* IV, 616-617.

3. Letter to Jammes of July 1897, Francis Jammes et André Gide, *Correspondance, 1893-1938* (Paris, 1948), pp. 117, 330.

4. "Jeunesse," *OC,* XV, 83.

5. See Jean Schlumberger, *Eveils,* p. 144; Jammes et Gide, *Correspondance,* pp. 109-110, 144, 158.

6. Jammes et Gide, *Correspondance,* pp. 109-110.

7. Gide was aware of this negative influence as early as 1898: "Nous mêmes, plus personnellement, nous risquions de laisser s'encombrer toute notre oeuvre par d'informes mouvements de pensées—de pensées qui maintenant sont dites" ("Lettres à Angèle," *OC,* III, 236). "Mon *Immoraliste* était à moitié écrit déjà et tout composé dans ma tête lorsque j'ai rencontré Nietzsche. Je puis dire que d'abord il m'a beaucoup gêné; mais grâce à lui j'ai pu expurger mon livre de toute sortes d'idées adventices qui me tourmentaient confusément, qui n'avait plus besoin d'être dites, puisque je les trouvais exprimées par lui bien mieux que je n'aurais su faire" ("Feuillets," *OC,* XIII, 441). On another occasion Gide felt, wrongly no doubt, that his book had been impoverished because of his unwillingness to restate these ideas (*Journal,* August 4, 1922). In 1927 he recalled again that discovering Nietzsche had proved a handicap at first, but had served to free the book from a theorizing "qui n'eût pas manqué de l'alourdir" (*Journal,* November 4, 1927).

   The Nietzsche in whom Gide found his own ideas is perhaps best represented by *The Birth of Tragedy,* with its attack on inertia and its insistence on the value of inner contradictions and antagonisms: ". . . tous ses futurs écrits sont là en germe" ("Lettres à Angèle," *OC,* III, 232). *The Birth of Tragedy* is one of the most striking nineteenth-century analyses of the impulses toward concentration and dissolution of self. Henri Drain's *Nietzsche et Gide* (Paris, 1932) is an interesting but unreliable study, depending too exclusively on a one-volume selection from Gide's work and on *Also Sprach Zarathustra*—which, as we know, Gide tried on several occasions to read and could not. Drain does make a valuable distinction between Nietzsche's desire to absorb the cosmos and Gide's to be absorbed by it (p. 94). We must recall, in any consideration of this problem, that the influence of Nietzsche generally preceded a real knowledge of his books, and that Nietzsche was admired especially for the openness of his attack on Christianity. In the light of these facts, Renée Lang's attempt to prove that Gide read Nietzsche earlier than he said he did, and to prove a particularized influence on *L'Immoraliste,* seems irrelevant (see *André Gide et la pensée allemande* [Paris, 1949], pp. 81-120, 177-185). Even a few catch-phrases from an author who is "in the air" may influence us. By 1901 Gide had not fully assimilated Nietzsche, whom he had read at least in part, but he had thoroughly assimilated Freud, whom he had not read!

8. In an article, not yet published, on forty-seven years of criticism on *L'Immoraliste*. D. L. Thomas' *André Gide: The Ethic of the Artist* (London, 1950), the most recent book on Gide, offers a long and sympathetic account of *L'Immoraliste* which makes no mention of homosexuality. It similarly ignores the conscious sexual background of *La Porte étroite* and, of course, the unconscious or half-conscious sexual background of *Le Voyage d'Urien.* The reader will be forewarned by Thomas' prefatory praise of Charles du Bos. Several of Thomas' dates are wrong; he even suggests that *La Symphonie pastorale* (1919) was written before *Philoctète* (1899). His book is nevertheless one of the best written yet published on Gide; it has a Victorian innocence and grace.

9. Du Bos, *Le Dialogue avec André Gide* (Paris, 1947), p. 218.

10. *Journal,* November 26, 1915.

11. Michel's sickness and convalescence recalls Nietzsche's as well as Gide's, as this striking parallel shows: "After that touch from the wing of Death, what seemed important is so no longer; other things become so which had at first seemed unimportant, or which one did not even know existed. The miscellaneous mass of acquired knowledge of every kind that has overlain the mind gets pulled off in places like a mask of paint, exposing the bare skin—the very flesh of the authentic creature that had lain beneath it" (*The Immoralist* [New York, 1930], p. 64). "Illness likewise gave me the right to a complete reversal of my mode of life; it not only allowed, it actually ordered me to forget; it enforced the necessity of repose, of idleness, of waiting, of patience . . . And all that meant thinking! . . . The state of my eyes was enough to stop all book-wormishness, or, in plain English, philology: I was delivered from books; for years I read nothing—the greatest boon I have

ever conferred upon myself! That essential self, which had been buried, as it were, which had lost its voice under the pressure of being forced to listen to other selves continually (which is what reading means!), awakened slowly, timidly, doubtfully—but at last it *spoke again*" ("Ecce Homo," translated by Clifton Fadiman, *The Philosophy of Nietzsche* [Modern Library edition], pp. 84-85).

12. *Ibid.*

13. See my introduction to the Signet Book edition of *Heart of Darkness and The Secret Sharer* (New York, 1950).

14. For Gide's intellectual conclusions at this time, we must look to the "Lettres à Angèle" (*OC*, III, 222-241). In 1898 Gide failed to distinguish clearly between the final affirmation of Nietzsche and the final renunciation of Dostoevsky, and brought them too close together by verbal legerdemain. If the individualist's energies are stifled, they may break out in some violent antisocial way. A universally accepted individualism, on the other hand, would ruin both the strong and the weak. The true "exceptional" man would be lost in the crowd of "meaningless eccentrics." There is no rule of thumb, Gide observes, by which we may distinguish the successes from the failures, the Nietzsches from the Stirners. We should therefore repudiate "individualism," out of respect for the individualist. Gide argued in much the same terms during his communist period.

15. Gide's Preface to *L'Immoraliste*.

16. Charles Neider's excellent essay on *Death in Venice* detects five men "with odd features in common," and calls the second and the third (the sailor with the goatee, the ancient dandy) "secondary symbols." See *Short Novels of the Masters,* ed. Neider (New York, 1948), p. 49.

17. After reading an earlier but roughly similar study of *L'Immoraliste*, Gide commended my analysis of its "freudisme latent et précurseur," but felt I exaggerated its value as compared with that of his other short novels. "Quant à moi-même, je ne parviens à considérer mon *Immoraliste* comme supérieur aux autres sous aucun rapport, littéraire, moral, psychologique . . ." (See Gide's letter, at end of this book). Authors are, to be sure, imperfect judges of their own books, and *L'Immoraliste* has been a great favorite among my Harvard students, even among those who had read no criticism and heard no lectures on the novel. On the other hand, no published criticism has valued the book as highly as mine.

Ralph Freedman (essay date 1963)

SOURCE: Freedman, Ralph. "The Mirror of Narrative." In *The Lyrical Novel: Studies in Hermann Hesse, André Gide, and Virginia Woolf,* pp. 143-56. Princeton, N.J.: Princeton University Press, 1963.

[*In the following essay, Freedman explores the symbols, both Christian and otherwise, that make up the moral theme of* The Immoralist, *stating that the novel "enacts the conflict between an 'immoralist' and a symbolic 'woman' as the bearer of Christian love."*]

1

The disjunction between personal experience and an objective form besets any novelist who seeks to reconcile his craft with a compulsion to reflect variations of himself. The Gidean solution, particularly successful within its limits, rested on a balance between the poet, mirroring the perceptions and moral crises of a self in the work, and the dramatist, playing his role upon the stage of himself. Yet, despite his success, Gide resented the bonds within which his achievement was contained. His drive for different forms was motivated by his dissatisfaction with the limits of his art, by his search for an external reality through which, he felt, his work could be justified.

The egocentric predicament, which shaped Gide's epistemological point of view, sharply limits his scope. The hero's vision, whether continuous or momentary, had to remain a focal point of each scene or work. The problems raised in Gide's imaginative writing, as distinct from his critical essays, therefore tend to resolve themselves into particular forms of awareness and self-expression. The self seeks to break the fetters of external control or it submits to its requirements. This theme of expression or abnegation of the self in the service of superior commandments (God or *l'autrui*) pervaded Gide's writings from **Les Cahiers d'André Walter** to **Le Voyage d'Urien** until, in **Les Nourritures terrestres,** it is actually narrowed to pure sensation and perception. In **L'Immoraliste** (1902), designed to refute the latter's spirit and form, the introduction of an explicit moral situation unifies sensations and lends them a particular narrative direction.[1]

This moral theme is introduced through a dramatic conflict which is substantially absent in **Les Nourritures.** The hero of **L'Immoraliste** is not just an obvious reproduction of the *moi* in **Les Nourritures**; he is also given a specific personality and a place in the social world. Michel is a promising scholar, an unworldly archeologist who spent his life in unbelievable purity and devotion to his studies until, after the death of his father, he promises to take a resigned and devoted wife. In the course of the novel, he undergoes a series of transformations occasioned by well-delineated episodes. Although these episodes often mirror the loose collection of scenes in *Les Nourritures,* they are marshaled around a theme which is easily recognizable and fully explored. For it is one thing to exclaim about the self's need for absolute expression, for an absolute destruction of puritanical bonds, for total exultation in sensual freedom, and it is quite another to test the strength of such convictions against the contingent need to commit an immoral act.

The foil against which the hero's morality can be measured is created in the beatific wife Marceline. She is one of the few important figures in *L'Immoraliste* who is almost wholly absent in *Les Nourritures.* Although in his early work Gide usually assigned to the feminine figure a restrictive role, in an aesthetic as well as in an ethical sense, in this full-length *récit* she assumes a Christian role of renunciation as a person. This "rounding out" of the problem might be partially explained by Gide's marriage, which occurred after the experiences recorded in *Les Nourritures.* The change in his life, which involved at least the problem of social *engagement,* invited this new heroine through whom personal tragedy is converted into formal melodrama. For Marceline sets up the moral debate which introduces characters, however ephemeral, and the semblance of dramatic action.

Michel is the key to this action as a percipient. Indeed, in one sense he is wholly the focal point, in whose consciousness and conscience the action is embedded. This position is assured him through the frame-story device. He tells the substance of the novel to his friends after Marceline's death and at the same time establishes himself in his present way of life. This device ensures both immediacy of personal experience and formal detachment. It is reinforced by an artificial structure within the envelope which seems to arise from the author's compulsion to force a rigid coincidence of symbolic form and a content of ideas and experience. In *L'Immoraliste,* as in *Les Nourritures,* freedom of sensation is identified with North Africa, Arab boys, lush gardens, and implied homosexuality, while restraint is associated with womanhood, marriage, France, bourgeois order, and religion. Between these two poles Michel's choices are made to fluctuate in a pendulum movement. Recognition of illness is accompanied by a heavy burden of guilt and resentment for his dependence on his wife and, simultaneously, by an expanding awareness of the preciousness of sensation for its own sake. Having stated the double nature of his theme, Gide neatly carries his hero from one crisis to the next in which he first chooses morally acceptable solutions while entertaining morally reprehensible desires, and later chooses complete surrender to his desires, forsaking his wife and, with her, his moral force of control.

Inside the frame, a rigorous architecture mirrors Michel's choices and perceptions. Ostensibly divided into three parts, the novel actually unfolds in five movements and two parallel interludes. The first and last movements take place exclusively in North Africa. Despite their disproportion in length (the first sequence takes up nearly all of Part 1, while the last one encompasses only a few pages), they are obvious *pendants,* inversely mirroring one another. The book opens with Michel's discovery of his illness, his near-death, and recovery; it closes with Marceline's similar illness and her death. The first movement poses problem and conflict; the conclusion enacts their consequences.

Between this frame-within-a-frame, however, there exists a further triadic constellation. Two lengthy episodes describe Michel's attempt to become a respectable landowner in Normandy. North Africa, with its gardens and Arab boys, and Normandy farms, with their animal smells and rustic fellows, are both sketched in *Les Nourritures.* But in *L'Immoraliste* they are dramatized because they are identified with the protagonist's choices. The romantic compulsion to penetrate to the seamier side of life upsets Michel's precarious escape from his true feelings. Perceiving animal warmth beneath the settled rural exterior of his farm, he turns to the intellectual atmosphere of his Paris apartment. This phase forms the center and turning point of the book. As in *Les Nourritures,* so in *L'Immoraliste* the diabolic Ménalque appears and forces the issue indirectly. Preenacting the denouement, Michel deserts his wife to spend the night talking with Ménalque during the very time that Marceline falls seriously ill and is delivered of her still-born child. The book's cycle henceforth mirrors in a downward slope the upward slope that had led to its apex. Betrayal follows upon betrayal, and a helpless Marceline must suffer the obverse of her own solicitude. The second phase in Normandy permits the hero to act out his repressed desires: he joins poachers on his own estate to contribute to his own ruin. This phase is eventually followed by Marceline's death in Africa. Moreover, two intervening passages of *vagabondage* (also reminiscent of *Les Nourritures*) describe the hero's ambivalence. The first sequence of travels intervenes between Africa and Normany and includes the consummation of his marriage which cements the temporary decision for a moral commitment. The second phase, just before the end, acts out the opposite decision. Although at first Michel heeds the doctor's advice for a sojourn in Switzerland, later he insists on returning to Africa with a dying Marceline. Such a rigid scheme indicates less the choices of rounded characters dramatically impelled than artificially imposed movements ideologically propelled.

2

The structure of *L'Immoraliste* is determined by forms which transmute epistemological into moral awareness.

Such a change is made credible by the hero's persistent conversions of visual and tactile experience into moral meanings, a method which continues the tendencies of **Les Nourritures terrestres.** But in *L'Immoraliste* the moral implications of the hero's perceptions are introduced, not through a narrator's sign-post statements, but through the verbal and physical development of the novel. For example, Michel's ambivalence between sickness and health at the moment of convalescence is expressed in an awareness which shapes his life:

> I was unable to sleep that night, so much was I disturbed by these new virtues. I had, I think, a slight temperature; a bottle of mineral water lay close by; I drank one glass, two glasses; the third time I drank I emptied the bottle in a single draught. I exercised my will, like a lesson one goes over; I understood my hostility; I directed it towards all things; I had to combat everything: my health depended upon myself alone.
>
> At last I saw the night's passing; the day arose. This had been my night of taking up arms.
>
> ([*Oeuvres complètes*] IV, 35)

This passage shows the conversion of perception into an articulated morality. The heightened perception of the self alone in the night becomes the self struggling to define itself in combat against all others. In a Baudelairean fashion, moral implications emerge from sensual awareness. The conclusion of these scenes portrays the dual point of the first movement of the book:

> . . . the wall before me bore the streak of oblique shadow; the regular palm trees, without color or life, seemed to be forever immobile. . . . But one finds in such a slumber once more the palpitation of life. . . .

His awareness issues in supplication:

> One day will come, I thought, one day will come when I shall not have the strength even to bear this same water to my lips. . . .
>
> (IV, 51-52; 40)[2]

The hedonism of *The Song of Songs,* which underlies *Les Nourritures,* is translated into a counterpoint associated with *Ecclesiastes*. Through the medium of perception—palm trees, shadows, feelings for sensations suggesting a capacity for life—Gide explores the equation of naïve hedonism and moral value as a further dimension of his attempt "to glimpse through the gaps of culture." Picking up the Bible, Michel reads in the moonlight from St. Matthew: "When thou wast young, thou girdest thyself and walkedst whither thou wouldest: but when thou shalt be old, thou shalt stretch forth thy hands. . . ." (IV, 52) This counterstatement to *Les Nourritures* arises from a sensuous recognition of inevitable decay. Sin and death involve one another, for the latter is the moral ground of the former. Decay perceived, therefore, becomes sin perceived, and the connection of morality and awareness is established.

This idea of sense perception as moral perception defines a passive hero. A prone Michel observes the small Arab boy Bachir, whose health and vivacity become symbolic of health. Similarly, throughout all the stages of Michel's convalescence he views the children passively, whether he sits with Marceline on a bench in the public gardens or whether he wanders in the parks. They appear to him essentially through their beauty or color (Ashour is "as black as a Sudanese"). (IV, 40-41) Michel observes the "golden glow of nudity," as one of the boys climbs down from a tree.

The early episodes carefully intertwine the hero's penetration to the depth of his sensuous life with the approach of a climax in the novel's theme. The key is found in the public gardens and especially in the forbidden "oasis." Obvious allusions to Eden and the Fall emphasize the symbolic impact of these scenes. The experience of the oasis is passive and perceptual. As Michel, in the company of Marceline, approaches the riverbed leading up to it, he notes: ". . . the walls are made of the same earth as the path—the same as that of the whole oasis—a pinkish soft gray clay, which the burning sun crackles, which hardens in the heat and softens with the first shower so that it becomes a plastic soil that keeps the imprint of every naked foot." (IV, 44; 33-34) Readers familiar with **Les Nourritures terrestres** and the extreme sensuousness conveyed by the image of bare feet touching the sand realize the direct appeal to which the fleshly color of the clay has been turned. Moreover, the walk into the oasis proceeds wholly by visual and auditory discoveries. Michel hears a flute behind branches moved by a gentle wind and, entering the sensual sanctum through a breach in the wall, he perceives:

> It was a place full of light and shade; tranquil; it seemed beyond the touch of time; full of silence, full of rustlings—the soft noise of running water that feeds the palms and slips from tree to tree, the quiet call of pigeons, the song of the flute the boy was playing. He was sitting, almost naked, on the trunk of a fallen palm-tree, watching the herd of goats. . . .
>
> (IV, 45; 34)

Michel's response to this sight is one of extraordinary peace. Passively, he lies on the ground and places his head in Marceline's lap. As he feels the burning sun and rejects thoughts, he begins to visualize his new self—*le vieil homme* or Adam before the Fall, as he calls it later. (IV, 55-57) Henceforth, he returns to the oasis alone whenever possible, reveling in taste, sound, and sight.

The moral consequences of the oasis are depicted in the scene with Moktir. One of the older and more criminal types among the Arab boys, Moktir (whose dubious character is revealed by his looks) is the very antithesis of Marceline, whose favorite he had been. The decisive scene is portrayed through observation, very much as the decisive scene in *Les Nourritures* is portrayed through Ménalque's observation of the boy. Michel views the Arab boy's theft of Marceline's scissors through a reflection in the mirror. The sight itself turns into an immoral act which delights him and moves him toward a decision in favor of self-expression at all cost. The contrary decision is also conveyed through perception. It has been much commented that the covert homosexual theme of the novel is made blatantly obvious in the first and probably only consummation of Michel's marriage. Showing his newly found strength by beating up a coachman on their *vagabondage* (the postillion of *Les Nourritures*), he evokes in Marceline, rather incredibly, the supreme admiration that sweeps them into their passionate bed and in himself the ability to consummate their union. But the conclusion of the sequence is more significant. Michel watches his sleeping wife at dawn, contrasting his pity for her great fragility with an awareness of his own strength, and bestows on her the most gentle and "pious" of kisses. The actual consummation lies in this deliberate act of perception and in the condescending kiss. (IV, 66-67) Moreover, this "picture" foreshadows two further occasions when Michel comes upon his wife: her first illness and her death. The passive hero is led to his choices, not by deliberate acts, but by the subtle intertwining of inclination and perception that involves moral consequences.

Perceptual images and sign-post statements (mostly Michel's lectures and Ménalque's monologues) depict the hero's gradual estrangement from any sense of obligation or care for others. In the first Normandy sequence, perceptions develop into pictures of sensual temptation. Michel's unconscious attraction for Charles Bocage, for example, is shown through extremely suggestive tactile sensations. Fishing for eels with their hands, he "called to [Charles] after a moment to hold a big eel; we joined hands in trying to hold it." Michel notes naïvely that he is pleased that Marceline had not yet come "as though she would have a little spoiled our pleasure." (IV, 79-80) Although, as the estate manager's efficient son, young Bocage belongs in the sphere of restrictive civilization, the actions which appeal to Michel suggest the uncivilized freedom of the self. In a revealing scene, Charles superbly imposes his will on a wild colt while Michel and Marceline *look on*. (IV, 84-87) In the second Normandy sequence, on the downward slope of the novel, Michel's far more explicit yearning for freedom, sensuality, the criminal side of life is also portrayed through sense perception. Indeed, here his penchant for observation brings on his ruin. He is drawn into the criminal activities of the Heurtevent brothers by watching their poaching on his own estate and eventually becoming their accomplice. For the passive hero, the very fact of viewing becomes a moral act.

Even in the narrative form of the *récit*, Gide cannot quite manage without "sign-post statements." Here most of these explanations are contained in Michel's professional lectures, which he gives during the sojourn in Paris. Rationalizing his own instincts, he seeks to show in these lectures that a parallel exists between the individual's search for health and the development of cultures. Civilizations grow by their secretions of health; they decay when life diminishes, when barriers are put up between mind and nature. But these statements, too, are converted into visually accessible motifs. The idea of the sick culture—the diminution of life under the appearance of life—is of course suggested by Marceline's disastrous pregnancy and its denouement viewed by an impotent husband. But it is also shown in the parties at Michel's Paris apartment. Following him from room to room we see a vivid demonstration of the false cultural life that covers a decaying civilization by watching with him his lounging friends amid littered furniture and ash-trays. Ménalque's appearance, which gives the novel its occult twist, introduces further verbal explanations—discussions in detail of the ideas heretofore pictured in image-scenes—but it also introduces visual motifs. In the first instance, Ménalque mysteriously produces the scissors Moktir had stolen in Africa as evidence of Michel's unconscious immoralism. In the second case, Michel's night of talk with him issues in the scene of Marceline's illness that pictures its consequences.

The brief conclusion, which matches Part I of the novel, concerns Michel's compulsive search for Moktir, a symbolic return to the "oasis." Significantly, both his betrayal and Marceline's death are shown through perceptions. Coming upon Moktir just out of prison, Michel feels as if he had reached the end of his pilgrimage. In the climactic scene, he takes Moktir's mistress in the former's presence. The importance of this scene lies not only in the further displacement of obvious homosexuality but in the way in which Gide chose to cast his transparent veil. Michel sinks passively into the mistress' arms while Moktir plays impassively with a white rabbit whose anxiety he tames. Echoing Michel's observations of Charles' taming the horse, it reverses the perceivers while it retains the theme of taming as an act of the strong or liberated self. The inversion of the percipient's roles is similarly important—Moktir's indifferent presence makes possible Michel's release—because it reenacts his view of Moktir's theft with opposite roles and so completes the novel's cycle. But chiefly this scene vivifies Gide's method: through the reflection of a vision in the consciousness of another, the hero's own action is observed, mirrored, and objectified.

3

Among the images in *L'Immoraliste* which involve moral consequences, those concerned with blood are especially pertinent to the formal and dramatic development of the novel. In the early phases, Michel's illness is ushered in with a profusion of blood. During a coach journey in Africa—echoing the coach scene in *Les Nourritures*—he suffers the novel's first hemorrhage. Napkins, shawls, nothing can stop the blood from draining his body except a miracle and Marceline's devotion which save him. (IV, 24-25) During his convalescence, blood appears again, this time introducing a growing life. He *observes* Bachir at play as the boy cuts his finger, and he is impressed by the rich flowing of the child's *living* blood. (IV, 30-32)

After the novel's reversal, the blood motif is transferred to Marceline. Indeed, her decline and death are portrayed through perceptions of blood. In the first scene, Michel penetrates the semi-darkness of her room until his glance is finally arrested by the crucial, blood-stained object:

> The room was darkened and at first I could make out nothing but the doctor who signed to me to be quiet; then I saw a figure in the dark I did not know. Anxiously, noiselessly I drew near the bed. Marceline's eyes were shut; she was so terribly pale that at first I thought she was dead; but she turned her head towards me, though without opening her eyes. The unknown figure was in a dark corner of the room, arranging, hiding various objects; I saw shining instruments, cotton wool; I saw, I thought I saw a cloth stained with blood. . . .
>
> (IV, 116; 97)

In the final scene, there is no such gradual revelation. Lighting the room, Michel sees her half raised in agony, covered by the blood of her hemorrhage. If in the early scene Marceline's devotion had arrested Michel's flow of blood, no such devotion saves her in the conclusion. As blood streams from her, the helpless husband only searches for an unsullied spot to kiss. The experience of her death, and the flow of her blood, are conveyed as a cruelly vivid sense perception. And with penetrating irony, the hero's search for a place to "put the horrible kiss" recalls the pious kiss of their night of love.

The scene of Marceline's melodramatic death unfolds the novel's theme through its action as an image. Lighting up the figure of renunciation bathed in blood, it also illuminates the hero's liberation. The irony of the novel is shown in this double-edged conclusion. Death is revealed to Michel's senses with the intensity of those visual and tactile sensations he had learned in the service of the joys of life. Within the progression of the novel, it also signifies Michel's successful quest for the sensualist's "oasis." But Michel is not only freed by Marceline's death, he has also scored his most outrageous point. The rosary which he had refused Marceline in her first illness, and which had been her weapon against his incredible hedonism, now seems to be useless. She appears to be stripped even of her God.[3] The epilogue, in which Michel combines his somber confession with unmistakable references to a "liberated" life, opens this resolution to further questioning.

The scheme of *L'Immoraliste* is presented through a passive hero's creation. It portrays Gide's obsession with the moral implications of sense experience and creates a philosophical tale from a constellation of image-scenes held together by rapid transitions. Through such scenes and perceptions within an artificial structure, it enacts the conflict between an "immoralist" and a symbolic "woman" as the bearer of Christian love. For Dostoyevsky, the outcome would have been a foregone conclusion, but Gide's hero succeeds in his quest and even destroys the heroine's confidence in her values. This resolution is portrayed through sensuous awareness, in which the reader is invited to share.

4

Both the movement and the ideas of *L'Immoraliste* are viewed in symbolist as well as in Christian terms. For the symbolist, the evanescence and inadequacy of the senses necessitate their transcendence and eventual denial through artifice. For the Christian, sensations entail their obverse, decay, sin, and death—the fruits of the Fall. These two implications are telescoped in *L'Immoraliste* as the lover's kiss, celebrated in *Les Nourritures,* becomes the kiss of death. Something of this sort touched the tortured conscience of Huysmans' Des Esseintes, who recognized that the degeneracy attendant upon a surfeit of sensation signifies the bankruptcy of the world of sense but who refused the Christian sacrament with which to transcend it.

Whatever may have been the psychological significance of Gide's vision, either for himself or his hero, the key to his method in *L'Immoraliste* is a skillful exploitation of his protagonist's visual compulsion. In his quest for the "oasis"—a pilgrimage past symbolic way stations suggested by the gardens and the scenes of *vagabondage*—Michel alludes to the transcendental hero. He also recalls Rimbaud's *Voyou* in the literal sense of the term. He is essentially a prototype of the passive hero who transforms the universe of nature and social relations into an inner world and converts inaction into tragedy. Despite its concern with events, Gide's novel retains many distinguishing characteristics of his symbolist *traités*. The protagonist creates a world of his own, whose images bear a primary relation only to his passive choices.

Although he had rejected the thinking of Mallarmé, Gide retained crucial features of the symbolist hero: the passive apprehension, the deformation of the world, and the conversion of perception into symbolic ideas. Gide sought to avoid the artifice and intellectual insularity of the symbolist novel by establishing a universal moral scheme as part of his culture. But in narrowing this scheme to the passive hero's orbit, he vitiated his critique of symbolism and retained the artificial framework he had sought to avoid. Mirroring both ideas and narrative in a design of significant perceptions, he created not only a well-made *récit* but also a form in which a hero's inner life is rendered with the immediacy of a lyrical poem.

Notes

1. Gide himself felt that, with *L'Immoraliste,* he had finally achieved a vision of a world outside himself. Curtius, moreover, saw this attitude as a culmination of a drive which began with Gide's early work; "the breakthrough to life" starts in the early *traités* and in *Les Nourritures,* but in *L'Immoraliste* it is not only symbolically stylized or presented in abstract discussion but also treated in the narrative of a concrete human fate. Ernst Robert Curtius, *Französischer Geist im Zwanzigsten Jahrhundert* (Bern: A. Francke, 1952), pp. 46ff. Generally, *L'Immoraliste* is identified with the appearance of *l'autrui*. See, for example, Ramon Fernandez, *André Gide* (Paris: Corrêa, 1931), p. 95. On the other hand, Rivière clearly perceived that in the last analysis Gide still exposed himself: the hero of *L'Immoraliste* discovers the lives of others, but as he does so, he also discovers his own; *Études,* p. 234.

2. Page references given here are to both the French edition and, following the semicolon, the English translation used by the author, which was Dorothy Bussey, trs., *The Immoralist* (New York: Vintage Books, 1959). Subsequent references to this translation in this section will be treated similarly.

3. For the first rosary scene, see *Œuvres,* [Andre Gide, *Oeuvres complètes,* edited by Louis Martin-Chauffier, 15 *vols.* (Paris: Nouvelle Revue Française, 1932-39)] IV, 117-119; for the second, *ibid.,* pp. 167-168.

Robert Goodhand (essay date December 1966)

SOURCE: Goodhand, Robert. "The Religious Leitmotif in *L'Immoraliste*." *Romanic Review* 57, no. 4 (December 1966): 263-76.

[*In the following essay, Goodhand discusses the importance of the Christian leitmotif in* The Immoralist, *comparing Michel's repeated rejections of Christian salvation offered by his wife, Marceline, to Peter's three denials of Christ.*]

In order to communicate the wonder and delight he feels at the time of his physical and psychic rebirth, Michel, the protagonist of André Gide's ***L'Immoraliste,*** resorts to an intriguing analogy: "Et je me comparais aux palimpsestes; je goûtais la joie du savant, qui sous les écritures plus récentes, découvre, sur un même papier, un texte très ancien infiniment plus précieux. Quel était-il, ce texte occulté? Pour le lire, ne fallait-il pas tout d'abord effacer les textes récents?"[1] Michel's glimpse of a dormant and authentic self likened to the scholar's discovery of only partially erased writing on a palimpsest is an image which has multiple connotations. First of all, as the narrator unfolds his story, it becomes more and more obvious to the reader that the content of one "texte" is latent homosexuality. Since Michel proves to be incapable of comprehending this writing which he uncovers, his entire narration is deeply tinged with irony. This aspect of ***L'Immoraliste***—the revelation that underneath the hero's fervent embracing of emancipation and individualism lurk ambiguous motives—has already been thoroughly elucidated.[2] There is, however, compelling reason to believe that, despite the wealth of critical commentary bestowed upon the novel, a second text has been ignored, a text perhaps more appropriately qualified by the adjectives "ancien" and "occulté." The structure, the implicit significance of certain scenes, a number of images (particularly images of light and shadow) infuse the work with a symbolic import centering around Michel's repeated rejections of his wife Marceline and the possibility of religious salvation which she holds out to him. If these elements are closely examined, they strongly suggest an interpretation of the Christian leitmotif which has as its source the New Testament accounts of Peter's three denials of Christ.

Biblically inspired themes in Gide's works always retain a distinctly Gidian flavor and ***L'Immoraliste*** is obviously no exception to this; the religious text hidden below the literal narrative becomes bitterly ironic as soon as the nihilistic tone of Michel's rebellion and the futility of Marceline's self-sacrifice are taken into account. Michel is the fictional embodiment of a Peter who denies three times but who never experiences faith; by the same token, Marceline's agony in the final part of the novel constitutes a somber dramatization of the triumph of satanic forces.

As far as the structure of this novel is concerned, Burleigh T. Wilkins has taken note of the fact that, in a work of art with an underlying religious motif, the hauntingly persistent recurrence of the number three serves to underscore the Christian implications present in the work. There are three parts to the novel; there are three principal characters (if one concedes that Ménalque's episodic but, nonetheless, important role places him in this category); Michel's narration covers a period of three years and he relates his story to three friends.[3] A scrutiny of the text reveals that there are additional examples of Gide's preoccupation with the ternary. Michel takes care to mention that nearly three weeks separate his first meeting with Ménalque and the second (p. 429). The last lines of Michel's story place in relief the fact that three months have elapsed between the death of his wife in April and the visit of the three friends who have come to listen to his tale: "C'est à El Kantara qu'elle repose, dans l'ombre d'un jardin privé qu'elle aimait. Il y a de tout cela trois mois à peine. Ces trois mois ont éloigné cela de dix ans" (p. 470).

For Wilkins the connection between the novel's ternary composition and the religious content can be found by tracing the evolution of the protagonist's behavior with specific reference to the trinity of Christian virtues: "Part One of *L'Immoraliste* shows Michel's rejection of faith, Part Two traces the disappearance of hope, and Part Three is concerned with Michel's failure to practice charity."[4] As valid as this explanation seems, two questions should be posed with regard to the possibility of a more synthetic analysis of the Christian leitmotif. Has Gide himself not explicitly indicated the symbolic import of the Michel-Marceline relationship by twice emphasizing within the novel the importance of a verse of the Gospel of John which relates the words of Jesus to Peter at the time of the Risen Christ's appearance in Galilee? And has he not structurally reinforced the impression that Michel-Peter parallels are drawn in *L'Immoraliste* by inserting within each of the three parts of the novel one scene of emphatic rejection of Marceline by Michel? If these two questions could, in fact, be taken as rhetorical, then the many allusions to the number three would appear as a formal device which is completely integrated with the depiction of a thrice-denied wife and, at the religious level of meaning, the novel would reflect the degree of artistic integrity which was of primordial importance to the author when he embarked upon the literary form of the *récit*. Before expanding this idea of increased aesthetic harmony, the two "rhetorical questions" must be elaborated through analysis of the text.

The first of the two specific references to Christ and Peter in *L'Immoraliste* appears in the section of Part One which records the end of Michel's convalescence in North Africa. On the eve of his departure from Biskra the hero leaves his wife whom he believes is asleep and goes out into a moonlit courtyard where the deathly stillness prompts him to dwell upon the "tragic sense" of his life. The night lends itself to Baudelairian *recueillement*, to sensory awareness of past and future, of present life and mortality, and culminates days marked by Michel's compulsive preoccupation with his body and with robust health. The scene is carefully constructed to evoke a mood of emotional tension and of momentary reflexion impregnated with religious overtones; it terminates abruptly and dramatically with a brief notation concerning the couple's departure at dawn.

Je touchai mon front, mes paupières. Un frisson me saisit. Un jour viendra—pensai-je—un jour viendra où même pour porter à mes lèvres même l'eau dont j'aurai le plus soif, je n'aurai plus assez de forces. . . . Je rentrai, mais ne me recouchai pas encore; je voulais fixer cette nuit, en imposer le souvenir à ma pensée, la retenir; indécis de ce que je ferais, je pris un livre sur ma table—la Bible—la laissai s'ouvrir au hasard; penché dans la clarté de la lune, je pouvais lire; je lus ces mots du Christ à Pierre, ces mots, hélas! que je ne devais plus oublier: "Maintenant tu te ceins toi-même et tu vas où tu veux aller; mais quand tu seras vieux, tu étendras les mains. . . ." Tu étendras les mains. . . .

Le lendemain, à l'aube, nos partîmes.

(pp. 396-97)

Injected into the last part of a scene which attains a relatively high peak of dramatic intensity, the biblical passage paraphrased by Michel takes on an intensified suggestiveness. In addition, this position of emphasis within the first section of the novel is buttressed by the fortuitous manner in which Michel stumbles upon these lines and by his assertion that Christ's words will remain indelibly imprinted in his mind.

Obviously, the verse of the Fourth Gospel has certain personal implications for Michel and it is significant that he fails to complete the quotation which he repeats to himself.[5] For this reason the complete verse should be quoted: "Amen, amen, I say to thee, when thou wast young thou didst gird thyself and walk where thou wouldst. But when thou art old thou wilt stretch forth thy hands, and another will gird thee, and lead thee where thou wouldst not." (John 21:18). Here Jesus warns Peter that the impetuous zeal of his youth will be put to a severe test in later years. There is an allusion to the possibility of crippling infirmities which Peter might have to endure in old age; taken in this very literal sense and placed within the context of the whole scene in which it appears, Christ's warning becomes for Michel a kind of clarion call to unshackle himself from his lifeless past and cultivate the joys of the present.

However, it is also true that in the phrase "stretch forth thy hands" there is a reference to Peter's future martyrdom and the fact that he will be obliged to prove in this ordeal his fidelity to Christ. When the verse is taken in this sense, Michel's inability to finish the quotation constitutes a sobering foreshadowing of his continued failure to accept the Christian ethic which Marceline incarnates (at this point he has already brutally rejected the "aid of God" which she has sought for him through her prayers) and a portent of the spiritual void which will haunt Michel as soon as he ends his head-long flight towards complete liberation of an authentic self. Peter will be taken where he does not want to go but will be sustained by loyalty to his Master and by faith; Michel, on the other hand, will be led where he does not want to go, will find himself suspended there in a state of aimless negation, and this will be due, in part, to his deliberate repudiation of his wife and the Christian ideals which she espouses. This is made eminently clear in a scene near the end of the novel which echoes in many striking respects the description of Michel's initial discovery of the biblical passage: Marceline, now gravely ill, is sleeping and, despite her condition, Michel has stubbornly decided to leave Biskra and continue his frantic journey south to Touggourt; again the awesome illumination provided by the moon provokes introspection and soul-searching; and again the scene ends with a short mention of a dawn departure, although this time the couple is accompanied by Moktir who is "heureux comme un roi."

> A présent elle dort dans la chambre voisine. La lune, depuis longtemps levée, inonde à présent la terrasse. C'est une clarté presque effrayante. . . . Son flot entre par la fenêtre grande ouverte. Je reconnais sa clarté dans la chambre, et l'ombre qu'y dessine la porte. Il y a deux ans elle entrait plus avant encore . . . oui, là précisément où elle avance maintenant—quand je me suis levé renonçant à dormir. J'appuyais mon épaule contre le montant de cette porte-là. Je reconnais l'immobilité des palmiers. . . . Quelle parole avais-je donc lue ce soir-là? . . . Ah! oui; les mots du Christ à Pierre: "Maintenant tu te ceins toi-même, et tu vas où tu veux aller. . . ." Où vais-je? Où veux-je aller?
>
> (p. 467)

Thus, the similarities and dramatic qualities present in the two scenes serve to focus the reader's attention upon a revelation which is of paramount importance in bringing to the surface of the "palimpsest" the underlying religious connotations: the hero of *L'Immoraliste* perceives an affinity between his situation and that of Christ's disciple. Moreover, in Christ's admonition it is easy to detect the voice of Marceline—a muted voice, to be sure, but one which is heard, nevertheless, throughout the book as the voice of a Christian conscience.

It is upon the background of the identification of Michel with Peter that the ternary elements in the novel and the religious theme reach a point of convergence. References to the number three are, of course, ubiquitous in the Bible, but rare are the occasions when these allusions are as dramatically accentuated as they are in those verses which treat Christ's concern with the loyalty and devotion of his Apostle Peter. In fact, the Risen Christ's words cited by Michel from the Fourth Gospel (incidentally this appearance of the Risen Christ marks the *third* time he appeared to his disciples after rising from the dead) are preceded by a singular conversation in which Jesus asks Peter three times if he loves him and, with each affirmative reply, commissions Peter three times to look after his flock, i.e., to prove his love by becoming the principal shepherd of the Christian flock. These repeated demands by Christ for a profession of love are significant because they are a reminder that the Apostle has disowned his Master three times. In summary, the following points relevant to religious symbolism should be stressed: 1) An inordinate amount of emphasis is placed upon the ternary in the novel. 2) An identification, oblique as it may be, is made between Michel and Peter. 3) The number three has heightened associations in regard to the relationship of Jesus and Peter, particularly in light of the fact that Peter's thrice-repeated disowning of Christ before the crowing of the cock is one of the most universally familiar incidents in the New Testament. Gide's reworking of this incident will be explored after a glance at the elements in the characterization of Marceline and Michel which provide a foundation for the transposition of the biblical episode.

The Christian qualities of the heroine are by no means dynamic and forceful. However, the subdued aura of piety which envelops her, the self-effacing willingness to give of herself (both in regard to Michel and, significantly enough, in regard to the weak and sickly Arab children), the stoic resignation to physical and mental anguish, all these traits serve to define her role in the novel: she offers to Michel the example of a Christian way of life. Her tender care and self-denial are alone responsible for saving her husband's life and the eventual consequence of her self-sacrifice—tuberculosis and death—connotes most emphatically a Christ-like acceptance of Michel's sins with its culmination in suffering and death. This connotation is amplified by Michel's avowal of repressed guilt feelings concerning his wife's illness: ". . . je fis venir un docteur de Lausanne. Il s'inquiéta . . . de savoir si déjà, dans la famille de ma femme, je connaissais d'autres cas de tuberculose. Je répondis que oui; pourtant je n'en connaissais pas; mais il me déplaisait de dire . . . qu'avant de m'avoir soigné Marceline n'avait jamais été malade" (p. 454).[6]

As far as the characterization of Michel is concerned, it certainly can't be asserted that he is a fisherman by vocation as was the case of Peter. Nevertheless, there is a scene in the second part of Gide's work which contains the description of Michel's precipitous transformation into an enthusiastic fisherman. A stagnant pool at La Morinière is drained and Michel, excited by "la partie de plaisir d'une pêche," suddenly decides to wade into the water with the son of the overseer of the estate in order to help with the catch. In relating this episode, the narrator registers the fact that "les poissons abondaient au-delà de toute espérance . . ." (pp. 412-13) and one could very well link this notation to the miraculous draught of fish which Peter catches on the two occasions he encounters Jesus by the Sea of Galilee (Luke 5:1-9 and John 21:1-11). However, if parallels are obliquely indicated, ironic divergences are also underlined by Gide: at the outset of this scene Michel is greatly disturbed that Marceline is not present to watch the extraordinary catch; he starts out to get her but soon becomes so involved in "l'ardeur du jeu" that he no longer misses her and, in fact, finally realizes that her presence would vitiate his pleasure.

The sketch of Peter's personality is quite consistent in all four Gospels and, if this portrait is compared to that of Michel, certain resemblances appear quite striking. The Apostle reflects in his attitude towards his Master an inconsistency and impulsiveness which are manifested in wavering of fidelity and outright failure, feelings of remorse and repentance, and bursts of affection and devout returns to faithfulness; this comprises a succinct description of Michel's mercurial behavior in regard to his wife—with the significant exception that Peter's constant return to allegiance to Christ is ironically inverted in the case of Michel. The quintessence of this attitude which is so similar to Peter's is stated by Michel in a passage immediately preceding his first encounter with Christ's warning to Peter. At this moment he is remorseful about his neglect of Marceline during their stay in Biskra and he resolves to make amends in the future: ". . . je retournai vers Marceline l'exaltation de mon esprit et de mes sens. A la joie qu'elle en eut, je m'aperçus qu'avant elle était restée triste. Je m'excusai comme un enfant de l'avoir souvent délaissée, mis sur le compte de ma faiblesse mon humeur fuyante et bizarre, affirmai que jusqu'à présent j'avais été trop las pour aimer, mais que je sentirais désormais croître avec ma santé mon amour. Je disais vrai; mais sans doute j'étais bien faible encore, car ce ne fut que plus d'un mois après que je désirai Marceline" (pp. 395-96).

It is worth noting that the consummation of the marriage to which Michel refers in the last line of this quotation is brought about in a spontaneous and unexpected manner. Michel's violent attack upon the drunken coachman who endangers Marceline's life is a prelude to an expression of selfless love by Michel and to the one and only experience of complete union shared by husband and wife: "Le danger n'avait pas été grand; mais j'avais dû montrer ma force, et cela pour la protéger. Il m'avait aussitôt semblé que je pourrais donner ma vie pour elle . . . et la donner toute avec joie . . ." (p. 405). The impetuosity of Michel's act and his feeling of exultant loyalty recall the rash and impulsive nature of Peter's displays of fidelity (e.g., his cutting off the ear of Malchus at the time of Christ's arrest—recorded in John 18:10).

Many facets of Michel suggest, then, that Gide has endowed his principal character with traits reminiscent of Peter. With the dramatization of three distinct denials of Marceline the parallels become more apparent and, at the same time, diverge from the biblical source. This paradox is explained by the fact that the progressively increasing vehemence and cruel finality of Michel's three rebukes preclude redemption for him and lead to doubt and despair in Marceline.

An examination of the three sections of *L'Immoraliste* uncovers one scene of rejection in each part which is distinguished by the intensity and directness with which the narrator expresses his feelings. In Part One the scene which clearly evokes a first denial occurs during Michel's period of recovery. Marceline's supplication on behalf of her husband elicits a response in Michel which, although somewhat attenuated by a tone of "douceur," constitutes an insensitive rebuke of Marceline and an explicit abjuration of the spiritual life which she represents.[7]

> Le lendemain, c'était dimanche. Je ne m'étais jusqu'alors pas inquiété, l'avouerai-je, des croyances de Marceline; par indifférence ou pudeur, il me semblait que cela ne me regardait pas; puis je n'y attachais pas d'importance. Ce jour-là, Marceline se rendit à la messe. J'appris au retour qu'elle avait prié pour moi. Je la regardai fixement, puis, avec le plus de douceur que je pus:
>
> —Il ne faut pas prier pour moi, Marceline.
>
> —Pourquoi? dit-elle, un peu troublée.
>
> —Je n'aime pas les protections.
>
> —Tu repousses l'aide de Dieu?
>
> —Après, il aurait droit à ma reconnaissance. Cela crée des obligations; je n'en veux pas.
>
> Nous avions l'air de plaisanter, mais ne nous méprenions nullement sur l'importance de nos paroles.
>
> (p. 385)

This conversation is alluded to in a crucial scene of the second part of the novel and its reintroduction gives rise to the idea that Gide intentionally linked the three scenes of denial. The second instance is marked by such violent hostility on the part of Michel and by such ringing finality that it can well be considered the climax of the *récit*. This second rejection occurs shortly after Michel's narration of two events which are most decisive in shaping the course of his life: his exposure to Ménalque's mode of existence and iconoclastic code of ethics and the shocking loss of Marceline's baby. Ménalque nefariously brings to the surface nebulous impulses of revolt deep within his young and impressionable friend: ". . . toutes ses phrases . . . mettaient à nu brusquement ma pensée; une pensée que je couvrais de tant de voiles, que j'avais presque pu l'espérer étouffée" (p. 437). The loss of the baby completely shatters Michel's hopes for a promising and stable future: ". . . devant moi n'était plus qu'un trou vide où je trébuchais tout entier" (p. 438). These two incidents are preparation for a scene of rebellion which brings to an end a period of precarious equilibrium realized at La Morinière and announces the almost unimpeded acceleration of the hero's moral disintegration. It is this climactic scene which places in bold relief the denial of Part Two of *L'Immoraliste*:

. . .—que veut-elle? J'apporte près du lit la boîte; je sors un à un chaque objet. Est-ce ceci? cela? . . . non; pas encore; et je la sens qui s'inquiète un peu.

—Ah! Marceline! c'est ce petit chapelet que tu veux!

Elle s'efforce de sourire.

—Tu crains donc que je ne te soigne pas assez?

—Oh! mon ami! murmure-t-elle.

Et je me souviens de notre conversation de Biskra, de son craintif reproche en m'entendant repousser ce qu'elle appelle "l'aide de Dieu." Je reprends un peu rudement:

—J'ai bien guéri tout seul.

—J'ai tant prié pour toi, répond-elle.

Elle dit cela tendrement, tristement; je sens dans son regard une anxiété suppliante . . . Je prends le chapelet et le glisse dans sa main affaiblie qui repose sur le drap, contre elle. Un regard chargé de larmes et d'amour me récompense—mais auquel je ne puis répondre; un instant encore je m'attarde, ne sais que faire, reste gêné: enfin, n'y tenant plus:

—Adieu, lui dis-je—et je quitte la chambre, hostile, et comme si l'on m'en avait chassé. . . . La maladie était entrée en Marceline, l'habitait désormais, la marquait, la tachait. C'était une chose abîmée.

(p. 439)

At the risk of some repetition, it should be stated that nowhere in this section is there an avowal of antipathy so pronounced and straightforward as this confession by the narrator. In this respect, the passage takes its place alongside the repulsing of Marceline's entreaty for God's protection and the third and last sharply defined scene of denial: Michel's desertion of his mortally ill wife in a hotel room in Touggourt near the end of the novel. Moreover, the mention of Marceline's rosary (in the passage quoted above) helps make the leap to the final scene of renunciation since this religious object reappears there in a most symbolic context. This fortifies the impression that Gide consciously attempted to fuse the three rather widely spaced scenes of denial in order to render more discernible the connotations implicit in the three taken together.

The action which comprises the final episode in Michel's narration unfolds against the suggestive background of the arid desert village of Touggourt. Michel, whose conduct now borders on the inhuman, prefers this sterile landscape and doggedly insists upon bringing his wife to this wasteland where she will wither and die. He spends the early part of one evening with her but, despite the gravity of her condition, he cannot resist the impulse to roam the streets of Touggourt in search of distraction. Thus, this act of appalling neglect stands as an ironic counterpart to Marceline's constant vigil over her tuberculosis-stricken husband during the first trip to North Africa. Later in the evening Michel encounters Moktir and he compounds the enormity of his third flagrant rejection of Marceline by giving himself to Moktir's mistress. The events which commence with this act should be extensively quoted and juxtaposed with citations from the Gospels in order to illuminate the Peter-Michel parallels and the Christ-like agony of Marceline. Although the parallels in this scene do not chronologically correspond at all times to the biblical incidents which appear to inspire them, the similarities still remain unmistakably salient. First, let us consider the seduction scene in **L'Immoraliste** and the account of Christ's agony in Gethsemane:

> Nous entrons tous les trois dans l'étroite et profonde chambre où l'unique meuble est un lit . . . Un lit très bas, sur lequel on s'assied . . . cette femme m'attire à elle et je me laisse aller à elle comme on s'abandonne au sommeil.
>
> (p. 469)

> Then he came to the disciples and found them sleeping. And he said to Peter, "Could you not, then, watch one hour with me? Watch and pray, that you may not enter into temptation. The spirit indeed is willing, but the flesh is weak."
>
> (Matt. 26:40-41)

The qualifying phrase that Michel offers himself to the Arab girl "as one abandons oneself to sleep" is a most startling one; it can, of course, be explained in terms of Michel's basic unresponsiveness to the carnal attraction of the opposite sex. However, it is equally true that this is the hour that he should be watching over Marceline. With the figurative reference to Michel's peculiarly "somnolent" betrayal of his wife his weakness of the flesh becomes implicitly linked to Peter's lapse of fidelity. Moreover, the words "the spirit indeed is willing, but the flesh is weak" can be regarded as a fitting epigraph for the novel from the point of view of the religious and homosexual themes. Spiritually, Michel is drawn at times to his saintly wife despite the more dominant protestations of physical and intellectual liberation; physically, his weakness of the flesh is magnified by a failure to recognize the darker instincts which isolate him from his wife.

While Michel is "sleeping," Marceline is in acute agony and, when he finally comes to her bedside, he finds her drenched in blood and sweat. The graphic notations made by the narrator are echoed by the description of the agony which Christ experienced while Peter slept:

> Marceline est assise à demi sur son lit; un de ses maigres bras se cramponne aux barreaux du lit, la tient dressée; ses draps, ses mains, sa chemise, sont inondés d'un flot de sang; son visage en est tout sali; ses yeux sont hideusement agrandis; et n'importe quel cri d'agonie m'épouvanterait moins que son silence.—Je cherche sur son visage transpirant une petite place où poser un affreux baiser; le goût de sa sueur me reste aux lèvres.
>
> (pp. 469-470)

And there appeared to him an angel from the heaven to strengthen him. And falling into an agony he prayed the more earnestly. And his sweat became as drops of blood running down upon the ground.

(Luke 22:43-44)

Insofar as this night of betrayal represents Michel's third explicit repudiation of Marceline, it is illuminating to go back an instant in time and compare the passage which describes his return to the hotel and the account of Peter's distress when he perceives that he has fulfilled the prophecy of Jesus.

Je retourne seul à l'hôtel, Moktir restant là-bas pour la nuit. Il est tard. Il souffle un siroco aride; c'est un vent tout chargé de sable, et torride malgré la nuit. Au bout de quatre pas, je suis en nage; mais j'ai soudain trop hâte de rentrer, et c'est presque en courant que je reviens.—Elle s'est réveillée peut-être . . . peut-être elle a besoin de moi? . . .

(p. 469)

Then he began to curse and swear that he did not know the man. And that moment a cock crowed.

And Peter remembered the word that Jesus had said, "Before a cock crows, thou wilt deny me three times." And he went out and wept bitterly.

(Matt. 26:74-75)

As the torrid "siroco" blows across the town Michel is suddenly seized by apprehension and by the chilling realization that he has failed Marceline at a time of dire need; as the cock crows Peter suddenly becomes aware that he has thrice disowned Jesus.

The rosary is reintroduced into the scene depicting Marceline's agony; Michel stumbles upon it near his wife's bed and, when he gives it back to her, "sa main aussitôt s'abaisse et le laisse tomber de nouveau." He picks it up again; ". . . mais de nouveau elle le laisse—que dis-je? elle le fait tomber" (p. 470). Thus, she has dropped it a total of three times and this symbolic gesture conveys all the tragic irony of her situation. Not only does she now rebel against her religion but the three times she drops the rosary can be interpreted as an anguished and ironic reprise of her husband's threefold denial, a reprise which ineradicably underlines the religious connotations brought to mind by the ternary structure of the work and the specific allusions to Christ and Peter.

The prospect of religious salvation for the hero and of fulfillment for the heroine is, of course, inexorably doomed practically from the outset. The religious theme is nothing more than a leitmotif clearly subordinated to the author's presentation of the pitfalls present in an unenlightened and irresponsible revolt against all conventions. It goes without saying that the stress laid upon depicting the nihilistic corruption of Nietzschean thought—the primary and surface text of the "palimpsest"—precludes any religious statement of a positive nature. But it should be also pointed out that the ironic and non-Christian twist which Gide gives to the Christian aspects of the Michel-Marceline relationship is perfectly consonant with aesthetic views which he formulated during the time of composition of *L'Immoraliste*.

In a lecture delivered in 1903, a year after the publication of the novel, Gide questioned the existence of a truly Christian art: "L'art chrétien en tant qu'art chrétien, n'existe guère, peut-être y a-t-il contradiction dans les termes."[8] In this statement there is a reflection of Gide's unshakeable adherence to the primacy of literary values over all others; the struggle of good and evil and the triumph of Christian forces in a work of fiction tend to destroy any chance of attaining complexity and fullness of characterization.[9] His meaning is clarified in a lecture on the theatre given in 1904 and, despite the fact that Gide is speaking of the drama, his remarks can be validly applied to the novel: "Qui dit drame, dit: caractère, et le christianisme s'oppose aux caractères, proposant à chaque homme un idéal commun. Aussi le drame purement chrétien, à vrai dire, n'existe pas. Les Saint-Genest, les Polyeucte peuvent bien s'intituler, s'ils veulent, drames chrétiens. Ils sont chrétiens en effet par tout l'élément chrétien qui y entre, mais ne sont drames qu'en raison de l'élément non chrétien que l'élément chrétien combat."[10]

Applied to *L'Immoraliste*, this reference to a combat between Christian and non-Christian elements is of particular interest since the recurring images of light and shadow in the work play a contributing role in the dramatization of such a combat and extend the religious parallels which I have sought to bring to the surface. The broader spiritual dimensions created by the stylistic accentuation of chiaroscuro are, in fact, a logical and well integrated extension of the association of Marceline with Christian ideals. The significance of the imagery in this regard is crystallized in a verse of the Fourth Gospel: "Again, therefore, Jesus spoke to them saying, 'I am the light of the world. He who follows me does not walk in the darkness, but will have the light of life'" (John 8:12).

The first salient antithetical reference to sun and shadow occurs in one of the very rare passages where verb tense changes from the past to the more dramatic present. In this passage Michel is talking of his long and inactive convalescence and of Marceline's patient vigil: "Là coulèrent des jours sans heures. Que de fois, dans ma solitude, j'ai revu ces lentes journées! . . . Marceline est auprès de moi. Elle lit; elle coud; elle écrit. Je ne fais rien. Je la regarde. O Marceline! . . . Je regarde. Je vois le soleil; je vois l'ombre; je vois la ligne de l'ombre se déplacer; j'ai si peu à penser, que je l'observe" (p. 381). The feeling of immediacy imparted by the sudden switch to present tense, the emotional invocation of Marceline's name, and, above all, the strikingly concise opposition of light and dark, these factors prompt speculation regarding the implicit meaning of these few lines. The implications begin to take shape a few pages later when Michel gives prominent attention to sun and shadow in relating his visit to the park in Biskra. Parenthetically, the incidental examples of Gide's preoccupation with the number three should be noted: "Marceline m'accompagnait, portant un châle. Il était trois heures du soir. Le vent, souvent violent dans ce pays, et qui m'avait beaucoup gêné depuis trois jours, était tombé. La douceur d'air était charmante. . . . Des bancs, à l'ombre de ces arbres. . . . Presque pas d'étrangers, quelques Arabes; ils circulent, et, dès qu'ils ont quitté le soleil, leur manteau blanc prend la couleur de l'ombre. Un singulier frisson me saisit quant j'entrai dans cette ombre étrange; je m'enveloppai de mon châle; pourtant aucun malaise; au contraire . . . Nous nous assîmes sur un banc. Marceline se taisait" (p. 387).

Here the shadow imagery becomes strongly associated with the dark-skinned Arab boys and Michel symbolically enters the shadows with "un singulier frisson." Marceline, who is described as a blond at the outset of the novel, not only stands as a contrast to the Arabs who come and surround the couple but also her presence eventually makes Michel feel uncomfortable. The conflict is delineated: Michel's attachment to Marceline is menaced by satanic forces, by shadowy impulses deep within him. Thus, two themes—latent homosexuality and the symbolic import of the couple's relationship—intertwine at this point and Christ's words to Peter—"The spirit indeed is willing, but the flesh is weak"—appear even more relevant to the situation of Michel.

The chiaroscuro imagery recurs persistently enough to assume uncontrovertible symbolic proportions in the subsequent descriptions of the public gardens which Michel visits with more and more relish. By and large, the images of Part One appear to evoke a tenuous balance of the contradictory forces within the hero: "J'ai dit que le jardin touchait notre terrasse; j'y fus donc aussitôt. J'entrai avec ravissement dans son ombre. L'air était lumineux. . . . L'ombre était mobile et légère; elle ne tombait pas sur le sol, et semblait à peine y poser. O lumière!" (p. 390); on a later visit, drawn by the melody of a flute, Michel and his wife go through a breach in a wall of the gardens and find themselves in "un lieu plein d'ombre et de lumière"; lulled by the music they remain in this spot and Michel absorbs "le soleil ardent doucement tamisé par les palmes . . ." (p. 392).

At other times the notations of blackness and moonlight provide a highly suggestive setting for Michel's sobering reflections upon death and upon the consequences of a life lived without the kind of Christian ethic embodied by his wife. In this respect two scenes already discussed should be reconsidered. The night Michel first stumbles upon the important verse of Saint John he reads it "penché dans la clarté de la lune" (p. 397). The next time he remembers the quotation, it is too late to retrace the course of his life and the moonlight dazzles him with what could certainly be called a vindictive force: "La lune . . . inonde à présent la terrasse. C'est une clarté presque effrayante. On ne peut pas s'en cacher. . . . Son flot entre par la fenêtre grande ouverte. . . . Il y a deux ans elle entrait plus avant encore. . . . Quelle parole avais-je donc lue ce soir-là? . . . Ah! oui; les mots du Christ à Pierre. . . ." (p. 467). Thus, the warning and the prophecy fulfilled are symbolically highlighted by the moonlight.

The precarious harmony evoked by the blend of sun and shadow in the first section of the novel is ultimately shattered and darkness prevails in *L'Immoraliste* from the moment of the second denial in Part Two to the conclusion. After the second repudiation Michel is in the grip of inner anarchy; this is, in part, revealed by the fact that he poaches upon his own estate—but *only* after nightfall: "Mais quand la nuit tombait—et la nuit à présent déjà, tombait vite—c'était notre heure, dont je ne soupçonnais pas jusqu'alors la beauté; et je sortais comme entrent les voleurs. Je m'étais fait des yeux d'oiseau de nuit. J'admirais l'herbe plus mouvante et plus haute, les arbres épaissis. La nuit creusait tout, éloignait, faisait le sol distant et toute surface profonde. Le plus uni sentier paraissait dangereux. On sentait s'éveiller partout ce qui vivait d'une existence ténébreuse" (p. 449).

There is one slight glimmer in the darkness which enshrouds Michel's escapades. When his young poaching companion leaves him, Michel feels "affreusement seul" and looks to La Morinière for a light to guide him. It is certainly no coincidence that a lamp is lit in Marceline's room "comme un paisible phare" (pp. 449-50) since she *is* the earthly representative in this novel of the forces of light.

Despite the occasional light in the darkness supplied by Marceline, the appeal of an "existence ténébreuse" becomes stronger as Michel's obscure impulses towards anarchy become more imperious. Marceline grows more seriously ill and the tragic end is foreshadowed (the verb "foreshadow" is most appropriate here) during the couple's trip to St. Moritz in the opening pages of Part Three: "Comme elle paraît faible et changée; dans l'ombre, ainsi, je la reconnaîtrais à peine" (p. 455). At this advanced stage of his moral deterioration Michel believes that he has been born to pursue "recherche ténébreuse, pour laquelle . . . le chercheur devait abjurer et repousser de lui culture, décence et morale" (p. 457).

The predominance of shadows is broken by the reappearance of an all-consuming sun in the final stages of the trip back to North Africa; paradoxically, light at this point is associated with the way of darkness since it saps Marceline's strength and increases Michel's craving for gratification of the senses: "Tunis. Lumière plus abondante que forte. L'ombre en est encore emplie. L'air lui-même semble un fluide lumineux où tout baigne, où l'on plonge, où l'on nage. Cette terre de volupté satisfait mais n'apaise pas le désir, et toute satisfaction l'exalte" (p. 464).

Finally, Michel's anguished cry upon remembering Christ's words to Peter proclaims the victory of "l'élément non chrétien" over "l'élément chrétien" (embodied in the novel by the thrice-denied Marceline) and reaffirms the religious implications of the imagery of light and dark: "L'art s'en va de moi, je le sens. . . . Ce n'est plus, comme avant, une souriante harmonie. . . . Je ne sais plus le dieu ténébreux que je sers" (p. 467).[11]

Notes

1. *L'Immoraliste* in *Romans, Récits, et Soties* (Paris: Gallimard, 1958), p. 399. Page references in parentheses are to this edition.

2. For the most extensive discussion of this question, see A. J. Guérard, *André Gide* (Cambridge, Mass., 1951). Note also in this regard Germaine Brée's comment in "Form and Content in Gide," *FR* [*The French Review*], XXX (1957), 424: "Much has been said about his (Michel's) latent homosexuality, a great deal too much. Yet it is of slight importance in the story."

3. "*L'Immoraliste* Revisited," *RR* [*The Romanic Review*], LIII (1962), 113.

4. Wilkins ["*L'Immoraliste* Revisited"], p. 119.

5. Any suggestion of specific implications beyond the text in regard to Gide's use of biblical sources should be prefaced by a reaffirmation of his thorough familiarity with the New Testament. Sec, for example, his remarks in *Si le Grain ne Meurt.* . . . in *Journal d'André Gide (1939-1949), Souvenirs* (Paris: Gallimard, 1954), p. 499.

6. In respect to the symbolic overtones of Marceline's illness, note Germaine Brée's reading: "Dans cet être pieux et fragile . . . comment ne pas voir un reflet de l'âme chrétienne de Michel, âme qui, après son corps, tombe malade et meurt désespérée?" See *André Gide, l'insaisissable Protée* (Paris: Belles-Lettres, 1953), p. 177.

7. It might be argued that Michel's tacit approval of the theft of Marceline's scissors constitutes an equally emphatic denial in this section. However, that particular incident offers only an oblique reflection of Michel's sentiments; there is no explicit expression of rejection; moreover, the religious leitmotif does not enter into play in that scene.

8. "De L'Importance du Public" in *Nouveaux Prétextes* (Paris: Mercure de France, 1921), p. 38.

9. Concerning the question of faith in its relation to art, see Catharine H. Savage, *André Gide, L'Evolution de sa pensée religieuse* (Paris: Nizet, 1962), pp. 96-97.

10. "L'Evolution du Théâtre" in *Nouveaux Prétextes*, pp. 20-21.

11. Michel's capitulation to internal disorder and the satanic realm of shadows suggests two more notes of irony: his name is etymologically linked to the Archangel Saint Michael, the vanquisher of chaos and the forces of darkness; equally ironic is the fact that Peter, whose three denials are fictionally transposed to Michel's life, was surnamed the "Rock" by Christ (Matt. 16:17-19) and that Michel aimlessly distracts himself after Marceline's death with "des cailloux blancs": "J'ai là, voyez, des cailloux blancs que je laisse tremper à l'ombre, puis que je tiens longtemps dans le creux de ma main, jusqu'à ce qu'en soit épuisée la calmante fraîcheur acquise. Alors je recommence, alternant les cailloux, remettant à tremper ceux dont la froideur est tarie" (p. 471).

Frieda S. Brown (essay date winter 1970)

SOURCE: Brown, Frieda S. "*L'Immoraliste*: Prelude to the Gidian Problem of the Individual and Society." *French Review* 43, no. 1 (winter 1970): 65-76.

[*In the following essay, Brown contends that critics have directed too much attention to "the moral question of individualism" when analyzing* The Immoralist.]

> Qui ne vit aucunement à autruy, ne vit guere à soy.
>
> Montaigne (*Essais*, III, x)

I

On 25 October 1901, André Gide completed his first *récit*, a work which upon its publication some months later received little laudatory criticism[1] and which since has been both vilified and praised as his greatest achievement.[2] *L'Immoraliste* scandalized many of Gide's contemporaries, thanks largely to the allegedly immoral and anti-religious qualities of its subject and its hero and to its underlying suggestions of sexual deviation. Bias and religious prejudices certainly played their roles in early criticism of the novel,[3] but it is equally true that there was much to support the arguments of Gide's antagonists in Michel's virtual murder of his wife, his refusal to accept the help of God, his hostile rejection of Marceline's prayers for him, and his dubious attachment to young Arab boys. Recent critics have succeeded in viewing the novel more objectively than a Paul Claudel or a Francis Jammes and have placed these specific elements within a more appropriate perspective not only to the entire book but to Gide's writings as a whole. Yet, for the most part, they have persisted in analyzing *L'Immoraliste* in a manner almost exclusively directed toward the moral question of individualism, paying little or no attention to the social implications inherent in that very problem. By his repeated admission that he was for a long time—perhaps always—far more interested in moral than in social questions, Gide himself supports that approach. It is also evident that at the time he wrote *L'Immoraliste,* which he tells us in his *Journal* had been developing in his mind for almost fifteen years (12 July 1914, p. 437), he was well on the way to becoming a moralist in the best French tradition. But, if by 1896, he had already recognized the precedence of the moral problem, he had also acknowledged the social one: "Question sociale?—certes. Mais la question morale est antécédente,"[4] and it is this acknowledgement that critics have either ignored or failed to consider sufficiently when examining Gide's first *récit*.[5]

L'Immoraliste is indeed a novel of individuality, but in the light of Gide's early comment and, more particularly, in view of the evolution of his works and thought, it is an oversimplification to separate so sharply the domain of individual ethics from that of social existence. Or perhaps the affinity between the two is so close as to account at least in part for the essentially one-sided view of this particular work. Nevertheless, critical concentration on the moral aspects of the problem of individual liberty tends to limit the novel's scope of interest, particularly when that novel was written by a man whose later works were to reflect deep concern and even personal involvement in the most agonizing social problems and whose own relationship to the society in which he lived was perpetually complicated by his constant anxiety over freedom and individualism.

To what extent is man free to do as he alone wills? Is he answerable to society or responsible only to himself? Are restraint and belief in the rule of law fundamental to the very concept of freedom in any meaningful sense? These, it seems to me, are among the vital questions posed by the novel. They are clearly no less important as social questions than as moral ones, and to the extent that Gide both asks them and answers them in *L'Immoraliste,* this work contains the seeds of his intense concern with the individual's role in society. If, then, we are to appreciate this first *récit* as the work of a man to whom duty was always more readily acceptable than freedom: "Au fond j'ai toujours aimé le *devoir,* et m'y sens plus valeureux que dans la liberté" (*JAG* [*Journal 1889-1939*], 18 Jan. 1929, p. 908),[6] the same man who, in 1934, in a typically Gidian attempt to justify his own actions,[7] was to declare that "Celui qui demeure contemplatif, aujourd'hui, fait preuve d'une philosophie inhumaine, ou d'un aveuglement monstrueux" (*JAG,* 25 July, p. 1211);[8] if we are to realize more fully the evolution in his writings of an ever-increasing concern with the relationship between the individual and society, between the moral and the social; if, finally, we are to understand Gide's work as an integral whole, we must re-examine *L'Immoraliste* for the indications it may offer of the author's early thinking on these problems.

II

Two short months after the publication of the *récit,* Gide indicated in a letter to Jammes that *L'Immoraliste* was essentially the same story he had told in *Les Nourritures terrestres* in 1897.[9] No conscientious reader of the two books would fail to note the accuracy of that statement. Indeed, Michel might well be the Nathanaël who heeded not his mentor's advice to throw away his book (*OC* [*Oeuvres complètes*], II, 223) but followed him all too closely in quest of "une vie palpitante et déréglée" (*OC,* II, 90),[10] forgetting, too, the important admonition to follow his bent, provided it be *upward* (*OC,* XII, 495). But the lyrical dithyramb which celebrated an unrestrained liberty now gives way to the more realistic account of a borning Nietzschean figure in search of his individuality. No longer are we lured by the lyrical, spontaneous outpourings of a symbolistic and somewhat illusory narrator; rather we are repulsed and frightened by the overt actions of a flesh-and-blood hedonist, by "personnages réels (c'est-à-dire qui aient une réalité),"[11] and it is perhaps that very realism which makes apparent a significant step in Gide's social orientation.

It is quite a bit more serious for a "real" Michel to seek his happiness and individuality by casting everything aside with a simple "tant pis" as the narrator of *Les Nourritures terrestres* advocates (*OC,* II, 85), and it is eminently more dangerous for him to try to throw off the past and to judge his right to do something solely by the pleasure he alone finds in doing it (*OC,* II, 83).[12] Professional responsibility, the possession of property, and a devoted wife can, as Michel sees it, only thwart his pursuit, so he will make a fiasco of his lectures,[13] willfully destroy much of his estate, and—"Ah! qu'aurais-je besoin de tant, une fois seul!" (*OC,* IV, 152)—bring about the death of Marceline, to whose "soins passionnés [et] amour seul" he owes his own life (*OC,* IV, 28). This is hardly the "dénuement" Gide celebrated all his life and by which he defended *Les Nour-*

ritures terrestres in the preface to the 1927 edition of that book (***OC***, II, 229). We are far—and the novel makes it explicit—from the "oubli de soi" which he maintained would lead to the most perfect self-realization (***OC***, II, 229). As the theme is traced in ***L'Immoraliste***, it is not privation and self-denial that we find but the grossest debauchery and self-indulgence. If, as both the earlier paean and the *récit* make abundantly clear, the material possessions of life have nothing to do with true happiness and in no way contribute to individuality, if even those people to whom our lives are most attached impede Gidian fervor and freedom, what has Michel denied himself by relinquishing his position, by ridding himself of his property, and by destroying his wife? On the other hand, what sensual gratification, what real or less tangible pleasure is he prepared to sacrifice for any but his own appetites and desires? Not one. Nor, of course, was his predecessor of 1897. But another new element in the novel makes its hero different from the earlier narrator: Michel himself finally comes to fear the ultimate consequences of his unrestrained pursuit of personal pleasure and individuality, and with that expression of anxiety, the total glorification of an uncommitted individualism, as it was extolled in ***Les Nourritures terrestres***, is past. Gide has, as we shall see, already moved toward a position which he was to take in 1932: "l'individualisme lui-même, bien compris, doit servir à la communauté" (***JAG***, 9 Feb., p. 1113).[14]

Another important development in this direction is revealed by the altered portrayal of Ménalque, who had been the complete immoralist of ***Les Nourritures terrestres***. In 1935, Gide himself was quite prepared to join his friend, Jef Last, in condemning the ethical code of Ménalque as it had been expounded in 1897:

> Jef Last blâme l'éthique de Ménalque. Il a raison. Moi-même je la désapprouve et en ce temps déjà, ne la donnant que sous réserves, j'avais soin de la faire endosser par autrui. Il est vrai; mais la désapprobation partielle reste presque imperceptible et le peu d'ironie que je crus mettre dans certaines phrases . . . n'est pas assez marqué. La figure de Ménalque est mieux dessinée dans *l'Immoraliste*. Ici, dans les *Nourritures,* se confondant sur certains points avec la mienne, elle risque de fausser ma ligne et contrevient à ce qui reste de plus précieux dans l'ouvrage: l'apologie du dénuement.

(***JAG***, 24 March 1935, p. 1222)

The "confusion in certain respects" with himself, at least that self which almost a decade before ***L'Immoraliste*** had lived the experience recounted in the novel,[15] had apparently burgeoned sufficiently for Gide to see more clearly and to fear more profoundly the dangers in Ménalque's doctrine. But if, as he declared, he had written the *récit* to purge himself of the risk of becoming a Michel,[16] it would also appear that the Ménalque of 1901 marks a transition in Gide's social thinking. As Justin O'Brien correctly observed, "the new Ménalque had equilibrium without sacrificing anyone else to his ends . . . *he was making a positive contribution to society* and finally . . . he possessed admirable virtues."[17] The thoroughly undisciplined, unconstructive Ménalque is gone, and if Michel is closer to the old Ménalque than to the new, we should remember that his story appears to have been planned originally as "la vie de Ménalque"[18] and that no one has yet contested the fact that the novel contains a direct critique of ***Les Nourritures terrestres***.

III

The hero (or anti-hero) of ***L'Immoraliste*** elicited the denunciation of his own creator who described him as a sick and vile man, a failure and an anarchist rather than as a healthy and free man.[19] Yet we scarcely need Gide's own attack on Michel to appreciate the failure of his path to freedom. It is inherent in the story as it is told to us and in that story's uncertain conclusion. Michel falls too easily, completely selfishly, and, as it were, randomly (his only acts of will are the initial efforts he makes to be cured and to divest himself of the past) into the trap already set by the narrator of ***Les Nourritures terrestres***:

> Je tombai malade; je voyageai, je rencontrai Ménalque, et ma convalescence merveilleuse fut une palingénésie. Je renaquis avec un être neuf, sous un ciel neuf et au milieu de choses complètement renouvelées.

(***OC***, II, 71)

This, in fact, is the very myth that prevents Michel from becoming a free man in any meaningful sense of that word. The palingenesis of a man already molded, as is the protagonist of ***L'Immoraliste***, by tradition, education, moral and religious training, indeed by biological factors, can never be as complete as Michel would have it. And a man is not a palimpsest![20] The dilemma had already been posed in ***Les Nourritures terrestres***:

> Il y a d'étranges possibilités dans chaque homme. Le présent serait plein de tous les avenirs, si le passé n'y projetait déjà une histoire. Mais hélas! un unique passé propose un unique avenir—le projette devant nous, comme un point infini sur l'espace,

(***OC***, II, 67)

and that Gide became increasingly aware of this problem is amply demonstrated by the recurrence of the theme in his works (why else his later fondness for bastards?),[21] by all that he will eventually say on the question of the individual and society, and by his own personal inability to free himself satisfactorily from the unwanted bonds of his early training and background.[22]

Moreover, there is much evidence within the novel itself which prepares us for Michel's specific actions as an *immoraliste* and which therefore gives the lie to the concept of complete palingenesis. Even before Michel becomes ill, he has not only revealed his delicate state of health but has provided us with a markedly clear indication of his uneasiness over the possession of wealth:

> A mon père et à moi des choses simples suffisaient; nous dépensions si peu tous deux, que j'atteignis mes vingt-cinq ans sans savoir que nous étions riches. J'imaginais, sans y songer souvent, que nous avions seulement de quoi vivre . . . je fus presque gêné quand je compris que nous possédions beaucoup plus.
>
> (*OC,* IV, 18)

In the light of the manner in which this sentiment is exploited later, it does not seem unreasonable to suggest that such an attitude on Michel's part represents a rejection or fear of social responsibility rather than a sincere "dénuement". More than once he acknowledges the mastery and permanence of "cette première morale d'enfant" (*OC,* IV, 17; 24-25). He remains even in his twenty-fifth year unaware of his friends, unaware of himself (but cherishing *in himself* "chaque beau sentiment" [p. 18]), unaware even of the woman he marries. Up to the time of his marriage, he had lived for himself or at least, as he explains, "selon moi" (p. 21), and not loving Marceline (or not knowing what to love her means)[23] when he marries her, he is, even more significantly, surprised to learn that his wife had "sa vie propre et réelle!" (p. 21). We are thus well prepared for his pure egoism which Gide skillfully underlines by the use in less than two pages of the text of "pour la première fois." It is worthwhile to look again at those crucial passages:

> Le loisir obligé du bord me permettait enfin de réfléchir. C'était, me semblait-il, pour la première fois.
>
> Pour la première fois aussi je consentais d'être privé longtemps de mon travail.
>
> (p. 19)
>
> . . . . .
>
> Elle [Marceline] était assise à l'avant; je m'approchai, et, pour la première fois vraiment, la regardai.
>
> (p. 20)
>
> . . . . .
>
> Pour la première fois je m'étonnai, tant cette grâce me parut grande.
>
> (p. 20)
>
> . . . . .
>
> Marceline sentit-elle à cet instant que je la regardais pour la première fois d'une manière différente?
>
> (p. 21)

At Tunis, their first debarkation point, we are already introduced to Michel's sensuality:

> Au toucher de nouvelles sensations s'émouvaient telles parties de moi, des facultés endormies qui, n'ayant pas encore servi, avaient gardé toute leur mystérieuse jeunesse.
>
> (p. 22)

Consistent with his not really knowing his wife as another human being with a life and feelings of her own, he is more flabbergasted than pleased at her delight (p. 22), and his supreme selfishness will again come to the fore when he shows himself incapable of suppressing his *instinct* to tell her he has had a hemorrhage.[24] Even the tract which casts him into the scholarly world is a "supercherie" and if he is confounded by its success, he nonetheless accepts it (p. 18).[25]

Thus, all of Michel's actions after the alleged palingenesis have their roots in an already formed, ego-involved, socially uncommitted individual who, in attempting to discover his individuality by stripping away the layers imposed by his background and by the society in which he lives (can they, particularly in Michel's case, be anything but protective?), can succeed only in making "de son désir sa loi."[26] The tendencies toward immoralism and a-social behavior are present in Michel from the beginning; they will only be carried to excess, for Michel, as has often been noted, will try to surpass himself. Moreover, whatever reasons Gide's protagonist may offer and however "renewed" he may feel, the people and things he had known before his rebirth remain *there* where they were before and during his illness. The interdependence which existed between them and him does not cease on their part—Marceline, on her death bed, gives up God but clings to her husband—[27] and for Michel to attempt to achieve freedom without them, without anybody, is to conceive of liberty in a vacuum. (One wonders if an appreciation of Donne and Montaigne would not have served him better at twenty than writing an *Essai sur les cultes phrygiens*!). *L'Immoraliste* points specifically to that conclusion, and Gide himself will again affirm it in a letter of 19 May 1911 to Georges Deherme: "je ne mets pas en doute, si vous relisez un jour *L'Immoraliste,* que, éclairé par mes livres suivants, loin d'y voir une attitude dont j'eusse été dupe d'abord, vous saurez y découvrir la critique latente de l'anarchie" (*OC,* VI, 469-470).

IV

In his *Lettres à Angèle,* written during the same period Gide was working on *L'Immoraliste,* the author had already expressed his awareness of the dangers of complete individualism (*OC,* III, 225). Now in his first realistic novel, Gide recognizes the need, which will continue to be filled in his subsequent works, for the antithesis or antidote to the problem to be contained within the book itself.[28] Michel's appetites are excessive, his crimes are grotesque, and his actions, void of any real meaning even for himself finally, become absurd. In seeking an answer to "Qu'est-ce que l'homme peut encore?" (*OC,* IV, 148), he has only learned what man *cannot* do. He cannot completely ignore the world in which he lives and which has formed him; he cannot find happiness by sacrificing everything and everybody to his own selfish ends; he cannot attain freedom in isolation. Michel has gone mad, or very nearly so, trying to do just that. Failing to respond to the signs of danger in his way of life, a response which is necessary for survival itself; devoid of all restraint and a rule of law fundamental to the very existence of society, and therefore of the individual, Michel completely loses his equilibrium. His "cri d'alarme" to his friends is the specific testimony of his apprehension, his mental atrophy, and his spiritual deterioration. His imperative appeal contradicts his assertion that he has called them from so great a distance "pour vous voir uniquement, et pour que vous puissiez m'entendre. Je ne veux pas d'autre secours que celui-là: vous parler" (*OC,* IV, 15).

Before beginning his tale, Michel announces, in one of the most frequently quoted statements in all of Gide, "Savoir se libérer n'est rien; l'ardu, c'est savoir être libre" (*OC,* IV, 15). It would appear, then, that he sees himself at this point as a free man. Yet, having related his story and perhaps with that last strain of sanity which has made him call for help, his apparent confidence seems to have diminished at least slightly, and he seems closer to acknowledging only the possibility that he has achieved freedom.

> Arrachez-moi d'ici à présent, et donnez-moi des raisons d'être. Moi je ne sais plus en trouver. Je me suis délivré, c'est possible; mais qu'importe? je souffre de cette liberté sans emploi. . . . Arrachez-moi d'ici, je ne puis le faire moi-même. Quelque chose en ma volonté s'est brisé . . . Parfois j'ai peur que ce que j'ai supprimé ne se venge.
>
> (*OC,* IV, 169-170)

At an earlier stage in his recovery, Michel had read these words of Christ to Peter: "Maintenant tu te ceins toi-même et tu vas où tu veux aller; mais quand tu seras vieux, tu étendras les mains" (*OC,* IV, 52). The questions he poses to himself later upon recalling that text: "Où vais-je? Où veux-je aller?" (*OC,* IV, 163), are but a preamble to his confused and frightened plea. In the end, he is indeed stretching out his hands to plead for help, and to that very society without which there is neither freedom nor survival.

It is true that Michel does not acknowledge his error. He is not, he admits, weary of his crime ("s'il vous plaît de l'appeler ainsi" [p. 169]), but he urgently seeks to convince himself—and given his state of mind and his complete lack of will, we understand *be convinced*—that he has not "outre-passé [son] droit" (p. 169); he refuses to judge his actions and is fully aware that exotic splendor and voluptuousness persist in holding him, but he knows too that he no longer possesses that "grande fixité de pensée . . . qui fait les vrais hommes" (p. 160). All that lingers and continues to attract him to self-indulgence, as well perhaps as the suggestive final, incomplete allusion to his sexual anomaly, may make it impossible for Michel ever to return to the world he selfishly sacrificed to his own appetites, but his fear and urgent need to return, given there is still a semblance of sanity in him, underlines the certain impossibility of complete social alienation for the truly free man. Michel has not found his individuality; he has rather lost his identity. Clearly he does not know where he is going or where he wants to go, but neither does he know who or what he has become. His last ties to society are his friends. He calls them.

That his only hope lies in finding a way back to an orderly social structure is conveyed by the letter which forms the introduction to the novel. Having heard Michel's story, one of his friends writes to a highly-placed and apparently influential brother:

> En quoi Michel peut-il servir l'état? J'avoue que je l'ignore . . . Il lui faut une occupation. La haute position . . . le pouvoir que tu tiens, permettront-ils de la trouver?—Hâte-toi. Michel est dévoué: il l'est encore; il ne le sera bientôt qu'à lui-même.
>
> (*OC,* IV, 10)

In Gide's original manuscript, this passage dealt at greater length with the role of the state itself. Such significant lines as "Sous notre triste république, notre France appauvrie, lassée, pleurerait moins ses pertes d'énergie, si de chaque homme de valeur elle faisait directement son redevable . . . Que si de telles énergies n'ont pas de raison d'être en l'État c'est que l'État n'a pas raison d'être pour elles. Ce qui tuera la République, disais-tu, c'est ce dont elle n'aura pas su tirer parti,"[29] have been struck from the present version. Their suppression may have been attributable to Gide's reading of Nietzsche, which, he reports in his *Journal,* helped him to purge his book "de toute une part de théorie qui n'eût pas manqué de l'alourdir" (4 Nov. 1927, p. 859). On the other hand, such statements, in placing the greater burden if not the blame on the state, would surely have reduced the responsibility of Michel and, coming closer to glorifying him, would have diminished the power of the *récit* as a critique of absolute individualism. In either case, the original text would seem to attest once again, if in a somewhat reverse fashion, to Gide's fundamental recognition of the social question, and the passage as it now stands retains its emphasis on the necessary interrelationship between the individual and society.

In the final analysis, Michel's failure is not only that of a weakling who is intrinsically incapable of attaining freedom, but the result of his choice of method and his utter disregard of predetermined laws which we may call moral but which must be viewed equally as fundamentally social. Gide will continue in later works to toss an esthetic coin alternately, as it were, between the moral and the social, between the demands of individual freedom and those of social existence, but with *L'Immoraliste,* he has already started on the road, which nevertheless always discomfited and bewildered him, to appreciating that freedom for the individual lies neither in the abandonment to self nor in the isolated, vacuous quest for individuality but in some well-balanced relationship between the individual and society.

Notes

1. That Gide expected the book to have a poor reception is clear in his comment of 8 Jan. 1902: "Pourquoi je tire *l'Immoraliste* à trois cents exemplaires? . . . Pour me dissimuler un tout petit peu ma mévente," *Journal 1889-1939* (Paris: Bibliothèque de la Pléiade, 1939). Hereafter references to the *Journal,* cited in the text as *JAG,* will be to this edition. Wherever possible, the date of entry will be given to facilitate its location in other editions. References in the text to *OC,* followed by the volume and page number, are to the 15-volume edition of *Œuvres complètes* (Paris: Gallimard, 1932-1939).

2. For such opposing views, see the letters of Claudel, dated 29 Feb. 1912 and 2 March 1914, in Paul Claudel et André Gide, *Correspondance 1899-1926,* 18ᵉ éd. (Paris: Gallimard, 1949), pp. 194, 216-217; and Albert J. Guérard, *André Gide* (Cambridge: Harvard University Press, 1951), pp. 99-118.

3. See, for example, Francis Jammes et André Gide, *Correspondance 1893-1938,* 10ᵉ éd. (Paris: Gallimard, 1948), pp. 195-200; and Claudel-Gide, *Corr.,* p. 194.

4. *Réflexions sur quelques points de littérature et de morale,* in *OC,* II, 423, and *JAG,* p. 93. These *Réflexions* appeared in 1897.

5. Among others, Georges I. Brachfeld, *André Gide and the Communist Temptation* (Geneva: Droz; Paris: Minard, 1959), whose primary concern seems to be with establishing Gide's social orientation in the years leading to his Communist adventure, goes only so far as to acknowledge that, in some of the works from *L'Immoraliste* to *La Symphonie pastorale* in 1919, Gide's moral positions "may point to social and even political attitudes" (p. 89).

6. Gide recognized quite correctly that it was in this way that he differed most from Montaigne, always one of his favorite authors. The resemblance of an essential theme in *L'Immoraliste* to the epigraph above is therefore of special interest.

7. Gide was at this time in the midst of his Communist interlude. The question of his need for self-justification has been discussed at varying lengths by almost all Gide scholars and there is scarcely reason to elaborate on it here.

8. It is interesting once again to see how close on occasion Gide comes to Montaigne's thought. Cf. "De se tenir chancelant et mestis, de tenir son affection immobile et sans inclination aus troubles de son pays et en une division publique je ne le trouve ny beau ny honneste," in *Œuvres complètes* (Paris: Bibliothèque de la Pléiade, 1965), III, i, 770, and quoted by Gide in *OC,* XV, 8.

9. Jammes-Gide, *Corr.,* letter of 7 July 1902, p. 197.

10. Cf. Michel's comment, "Je devais faire de la vie la palpitante découverte" (*OC,* IV, 28).

11. L. Martin-Chauffier, *Notices,* in *OC,* IV, vii. See also Pierre Lafille, *André Gide, romancier* (Paris: Hachette, 1954), pp. 2-27.

12. In *L'Immoraliste,* it is Ménalque who states, "pour chaque action, le plaisir que j'y prends m'est signe que je devais la faire." The result of Michel's use of this principle simply demonstrates the truth of his response that "Cela peut mener loin" (*OC,* IV, 107).

13. ". . . au long de mon cours je m'occupais, avec une hardiesse que l'on me reprocha suffisamment dans la suite, d'exalter l'inculture et d'en adresser l'apologie" (*OC,* IV, 87).

14. In his preface to *L'Immoraliste,* Gide affirmed that his book was intended neither as an accusation nor as an apology and that he had avoided making any judgment. "Au demeurant, je n'ai cherché de rien prouver, mais de bien peindre et d'éclairer bien ma peinture" (*OC,* IV, 6-7). In later statements, as we shall see, he seems to have reversed his position significantly and recognized the critical aspect of his novel.

15. How much *L'Immoraliste* owes to Gide's experiences during his African trip of 1893-1894 is clearly discernible in *Si le grain ne meurt,* in *Journal 1939-1949-Souvenirs* (Paris: Bibliothèque de la Pléiade, 1960) pp. 549-615.

16. Jammes-Gide, *Corr.,* letter of 6 Aug. 1902, p. 199. Cf. the undated letter to Scheffer in *OC,* IV, 615-617.

17. *Portrait of André Gide: A Critical Biography* (New York: McGraw Hill, 1953), p. 176. The italics are mine. Cf. Guérard, *André Gide,* p. 101.

18. Jammes-Gide, *Corr.,* [July 1897], p. 117, and see p. 330.

19. In a letter to Arthur Fontaine, dated 8 July 1902, quoted by Yvonne Davet in the introduction to *L'Immoraliste* (Lausanne: La Guilde du Livre, 1951), p. 16.

20. It is worthwhile to note that Gide had at first erased from his manuscript the entire passage in which Michel compares himself to palimpsests. See *Notice,* in *Romans, récits et soties, œuvres lyriques* (Paris: Bibliothèque de la Pléiade, 1958), pp. 1525-1526. I have relied on this edition for all variants.

21. For examples, see *Les Caves du Vatican* and *Les Faux-Monnayeurs.*

22. These difficulties which seemed to Gide to limit the possibilities of individual growth and progress within a fixed social structure are too complex to enter into here, but certainly this problem contributed greatly to Gide's inability to accept freedom easily.

23. While this comment obviously conveys more significance than simply a sexual one, the indications that the marriage is not consummated until after the carriage incident are, of course, sufficiently present at the beginning to allow for Michel's latent homosexuality. In this connection, we note again Gide's care in clarifying situations. To the manuscript which read, "nous couchions dans mon appartement de Paris," Gide later added, "où l'on nous avait préparé deux chambres," *Romans, récits,* p. 1520. See *OC,* IV, 21, 23. For a detailed discussion of Gide's own unconsummated marriage and its parallels in *L'Immoraliste,* see Jean Delay, *La Jeunesse d'André Gide* (Paris: Gallimard, 1956), II, 557-592. Cf. Guérard, *André Gide,* pp. 102-108.

24. "Je me sentais injuste, il est vrai, me disais: si elle n'a rien vu c'est que je cachais bien; n'importe; rien n'y fit; cela grandit en moi comme un instinct, m'envahit . . . à la fin cela fut trop fort; je n'y tins plus; comme distraitement je lui dis:

—J'ai craché le sang, cette nuit" (*OC,* IV, 25-26).

25. The hoax is, of course, the idea of Michel's father, and one may well wonder what implications that may have in the social, moral and psychological formation of his son.

26. See Gide's letter of 27 Nov. 1927 to R. P. Victor Poucel, in *OC,* XIV, 404-410.

27. Marceline's final casting away of the rosary and her clinging "désespérément" to Michel (*OC,* IV, 167-168) are not without parallel in Alissa's desperate recognition, in *La Porte étroite,* that she needs Jérôme in order to love God (*OC,* V, 230-231) and in her final realization that she has been deserted even by God (*OC,* V, 238).

28. Gide himself felt that *Les Nourritures terrestres* contained its own critique. See *JAG,* 26 Aug. 1926, pp. 825-826, and 18 April 1928, p. 880.

However, compared to *L'Immoraliste,* the antithesis to a hedonistic, a-social individualism in the earlier work is at best indirect. For differing views on this subject, see O'Brien, *Portrait,* p. 125, and Klaus Mann, *André Gide and the Crisis of Modern Thought* (New York: Creative Age Press, Inc., 1943), p. 95.

29. *Romans, récits,* pp. 1519-1520.

Allan H. Pasco (essay date 1973)

SOURCE: Pasco, Allan H. "Irony and Art in Gide's *L'Immoraliste.*" *Romanic Review* 64, no. 3 (1973): 184-203.

[*In the following essay, Pasco comments on the numerous ironic devices Gide employs in* The Immoralist, *which serve to complicate simple readings of the work, undercut the sincerity of Michel's story, and self-consciously affirm that the novel is not real life but art, intentionally artificial.*]

When Albert Sonnenfeld recently proclaimed that "Gide loved the calculated effect," that "he was obsessed with technique, preferred himself to all other readers of his work (their interpretations might not be sufficiently complex),"[1] Sonnenfeld points, strangely enough, to what is perhaps a reason for the continuing interest in *L'Immoraliste.* Even though the modern novel has taught us to be more sensitive to meaningful nuance in structure and style, Gide's *récit* remains capable of satisfying our new demands. Gide was indeed obsessed with his art. But, then, perhaps that explains why the self-conscious *Immoraliste* represents an outstanding precursor of the *noveau roman.*

On the most accessible level, *L'Immoraliste* is just a good story, resembling many nineteenth century works which the reader may enjoy passively or accept as a realistic portrayal of a possible adventure. He may act as a distant observer, or join Michel's friends while they listen to the account, or even to some degree identify with Michel. Gide's fictional audience did the latter: "Nous nous taisions aussi, pris chacun d'un étrange malaise. Il nous semblait hélas! qu'à nous la raconter, Michel avait rendu son action plus légitime. De ne savoir où la désapprouver . . . nous en faisait presque complices. Nous y étions comme engagés."[2] Some readers have been similarly affected. François Porché, for example, wrote to Gide, "*L'Immoraliste,* lui ne transpose rien. Il ne dit pas, il laisse entendre, mais, roman ou confession lyrique, l'ouvrage tout moderne s'adresse directement à nous, d'une voix chuchotante. *L'Immoraliste* peut troubler. *Saül,* point."[3] For Porché, the work was a tempting, convincing defense of irresponsible egotism and sensualism.

However common this reading may be, it is nonetheless unacceptable, for irony undermines it on every level of the text. Especially after having followed the program of reading Gide suggested in 1902 ("Je lis comme je voudrais qu'on me lise; c'est-à-dire: très lentement. Pour moi, lire un livre, c'est m'absenter quinze jours durant avec l'auteur"—*J* [André Gide, *Journal*], I, p. 132), it seems certain that to feel complicity is to have abandoned a rational, critical sense of reality and to have committed Michel's crime, that is, to have given in to instinct and sensation. Hytier reminds us of what *L'Immoraliste* says so clearly: "Pour Gide, l'intelligence est une valeur essentielle, c'est que l'esprit critique est à la base du vrai progrès et, sans doute aussi, du véritable amour."[4] Gide was not at all reticent about calling attention to his irony. In one widely quoted passage, for example, he says: "A la seule exception de mes *Nourritures* [*Les Nourritures Terrestres*], tous mes livres sont des livres ironiques; ce sont des livres de critique. . . . *L'Immoraliste,* d'une forme de l'individualisme. (Ceci dit sommairement.)" (*O.C.* [*Oeuvres complètes d'André Gide*], XIII, 439-40). But, as Gide suggests parenthetically, neither this statement, nor others (e.g., *J* I, p. 437), do justice to the depth and implications of his irony.

As Grahame C. Jones pointed out in his study, *L'Ironie dans les romans de Stendhal* (Lausanne: Grand Chêne, 1966), any irony presupposes an ironic attack against one of two assumed types of readers: not against those who understand the deeper significance that the more accessible levels of the text belie, but against those who are oblivious to anything but the surface, thus falling victim, in a sense, to the author. Because of the subtlety of the ironic processes, "C'est . . . surtout aux lecteurs avertis que l'ironiste destine son œuvre: ceux-ci constituent un public raffiné auquel il adresse des clins d'œil que les autres n'apercevront pas" (Jones, p. 66). Those devices which undermine Michel and reveal his unreliability join with others to destroy the verisimilitude of *L'Immoraliste.* The "reality" of "art" is called into question. By making sure that this work would not be taken either as "life" or as idealistic abstractions removed from reality,[5] Gide affirmed the reality of *L'Immoraliste* as art, that is, as a "compromission" between the two opposing poles.[6]

I

If the first level of *L'Immoraliste* consists of the straightforward account of a moral crisis, the second is the realization of the unreliability of the narrator. Not only does Michel not tell the truth, he uses his listeners in the same way he used Marceline—to prove his freedom. Through an ironic device common to farce, he gives himself away. Like Jérôme in *La Porte étroite,* like Gérard in *Isabelle,* and like the somewhat too obvious pastor in *La Symphonie pastorale,* he unwittingly lets slip the truth he elsewhere denies. After having said, "Je ne veux pas d'autre secours que celui-là: vous parler" (*Im* [*L'Immoraliste*], p. 372), he gives a skillful exposition that succeeds in making his companions feel the already mentioned guilty complicity. Only then does Michel finally reveal his true reasons for telling the story: he wants them to take him away, and he feels the necessity of proving "to himself" that he has not exceeded his rights (*Im,* p. 471). It is left for us to see that this self-justification consists partly, perhaps wholly, perhaps unconsciously, in swaying his friends.

Earlier, at the beginning of his account, Michel tells his friends that he will tell his story simply (*Im,* p. 372). This claim is essential, for simplicity has long been considered the guarantee of sincerity. Roy Pascal goes so far as to maintain that excessive rhetoric warns readers to suspect the sincerity of autobiographers.[7] He makes the mistake of using a stylistic convention of autobiographies as a means of judging truth. We know, for example, that Rousseau labored over at least three, and possibly four, versions and an unknown number of *brouillons* to give *Les Confessions* an air of spontaneity and artlessness.[8] Of course, whether or not Rousseau was sincere is beside the point. It is pertinent, however, to recognize his cognizance of the need to adhere to a convention of simplicity if his readers were to believe in his sincerity. By Gide's time, the convention was firmly established, and it becomes increasingly important to note that while Michel is well aware of the need to convince his listeners of his artlessness and, thus, insists that he is going to "raconter ma vie, simplement," his style gives him the lie and impugns his sincerity.[9]

There are a number of indications that Michel's story lacks the unstudied, unaffected, guileless qualities he claims for it. Considering that organization requires planning if not art, the presence of *L'Immoraliste*'s excessively rigorous composition serves to sound the alarm. And when Gide has Michel obliquely admit the structure of his story, the irony becomes even more piquant. Michel's statement: "En vain chercherais-je à présent à imposer à mon récit plus d'ordre qu'il n'y en eut dans ma vie" (*Im,* p. 464), is particularly damaging when seen in conjunction with his claim of simplicity, for he implicitly admits to having "imposed order." Furthermore, at this point in the account, the "disorder" to which he calls attention is already both well-established and necessary to communicate the feeling that the narrator was unable to control himself. As town after town flashes precipitously by, the impression arises that Michel is driven, that he cannot make rational decisions, that he is, therefore, not responsible. Because one can scarcely fail to perceive the artificially rigid structure of Michel's story and to note the discrepancy between it and his pretensions to simplicity, the structure becomes an ironic device for betraying the untrustworthiness of this most unreliable narrator.

Even without the roman numerals marking the various divisions in the book, the structure of *L'Immoraliste* is nothing if not obvious. Michel implicitly admits his share in the effort when he says at the end of part I, "Que serait le récit du bonheur? Rien que ce qui le prépare, puis ce qui le détruit, ne se raconte. Et je vous ai dit maintenant tout ce qui l'avait préparé" (*Im*, p. 408). Formally, the book breaks into three main divisions: "une ascension, un palier, une chute,"[10] the first major part having nine chapters, the second three, and the third only one. This movement from nine to one supports Michel's growing isolation and finds further support in the motifs of travel and time. In part I, concerned with Michel's spiritual embarcation, both the marriage and the voyage highlight the importance of his rebirth and renewal. The phrase "nouvel être" (*Im*, p. 403) further suggests the importance of time to Michel's quest. He like Ménalque realizes that he must "tourner la page" (*Im*, p. 431) and forget the past.

In part II, despite the move to Paris and back to La Morinière, the emphasis rests on immobility since Michel is primarily concerned with putting down roots. While attempting to come to terms with his life, he struggles to integrate an aspiration for "l'être authentique" (*Im*, p. 398) with the claims of his past. The study of Athalaric apparently represents an attempt to make his background serve the new inclinations. Whereas part I centers on aspiration for the being he wishes to become, part II recounts the effort to synthesize past, present and future, although it gradually narrows to Michel's dissatisfaction with the present. Unfortunately, he forgets Ménalque's warnings: "Les plus délicats [souvenirs] se dépouillent, les plus voluptueux pourrissent; les plus délicieux sont les plus dangereux dans la suite" (*Im*, p. 436), for in part III, Michel attempts to retrieve his past, perhaps because he seeks the "*vieil* homme" (*Im*, p. 398; italics mine). After having asked, "Qu'est-ce que l'homme peut encore?" (*Im*, p. 457), he scurries to Biskra, the scene of former joys, and finds that the children "ont affreusement grandi. . . . Ménalque avait raison: le souvenir est une invention de malheur" (*Im*, p. 466). As Davies points out, the symmetry of parts I and III emphasizes the change from joyous discovery to despair and dispersion.[11] Only Moktir leads him on. At the conclusion of the book the future has ceased to exist; Michel is enslaved to present sensation; and the past lives on through his need to tell: "Je suis à tel point de ma vie que je ne peux plus dépasser. . . . J'ai besoin . . . J'ai besoin de parler, vous dis-je" (*Im*, p. 372).

Another motif, as Roy Jay Nelson suggested to me, turns the work into a quinquepartite structure.[12] Part I takes place primarily in the *pays d'abondance ordonnée*. In part III, the concluding section, the "orle désir" (*Im*, p. 464). Of part II's three chapters, the first is situated in Normandy, the land of "cette abondance ordonnée, de cet asservissement joyeux" (*Im*, p. 410). The second, the formal center of the book in which Ménalque appears, is set in Paris, the land of the dead and of masks where people only seem to live. The third takes the reader back to the *pays d'abondance ordonnée*. In part III, the concluding section, the "order" of La Morinière finds an echo in Switzerland, but for the most part, the activity takes place once again in Italy and the *pays sauvages* of North Africa.

Statements about the tripartite and quinquepartite structure of *L'Immoraliste* must not obscure the more forceful movement that changes direction in part II. Where in part I Michel seems to be ascending hesitantly towards self-integration, later, at La Morinière in part II, he begins to take advantage of his wife's generosity and pays less attention to her. Soon he finds himself with "plus de cent hectares sur les bras" (*Im*, p. 419). Then, in the second chapter of part II, after leaving his seriously ill wife to visit Ménalque, after the miscarriage, after angrily giving Marceline the requested rosary and storming from the room, the disintegration becomes so pronounced that even Michel recognizes it. He speaks of his "vie défaite" (*Im*, p. 441, 453). Where Ménalque knew that "il faut choisir" (*Im*, p. 435), Michel tries to live with opposites. When Charles says, "Vous ne pouvez protéger à la fois le garde et le braconnier," Michel responds for example, "Pourquoi?" (*Im*, p. 452). Not even his decision to sell La Morinière reflects an attempt to unify his life, rather a desire for more dispersion. The will power that drew him from his sick bed and created his healthy body gradually gives way, and, as Marceline weakens physically, he loses self-control to those dark forces of the "vieil homme" he has sought and found.

Because the formal structure emphasizes external factors over which Michel has little conscious control, it stresses his lack of responsibility. As he moves north he gains control, confidence and happiness. After North Africa, Italy and La Morinière produce the desired self-integration, but Paris destroys the fine balance. The capital city appears to be the fulcrum for the lever of Ménalque and the miscarriage to reverse Michel's direction. Even a return to La Morinière has no effect, and the voyage south causes him to return to his original state of helplessness. The clearly tendentious structure functions with other devices to increase distance.

Michel's style works a similarly destructive magic. People simply do not talk the way he does, unless they have carefully prepared. In fact, if the works of such contemporary, established novelists as Barrès, Bourget, Zola, Anatole France or Huysmans are any indication, neither do literary creations. Michel's speech is overly artificial and unrealistic, as a number of critics have suggested.[13] Not only does Michel use the pluperfect subjunctive, but his periods reveal syntax which, if not convoluted, is scarcely common. He begins his exordium, for example, by saying, "Mes chers amis, je vous savais fidèles. A mon appel vous êtes accourus, tout comme j'eusse fait au vôtre. Pourtant voici trois ans que vous ne m'aviez vu. Puisse votre amitié qui résiste si bien à l'absence, résister aussi bien au récit que je veux vous faire." And a few lines farther on, after the apothegm, "Savoir se libérer n'est rien; l'ardu, c'est savoir être libre," which is preceded and highlighted by three successive negative clauses, two "j'ai besoin" 's, and the single "parler," Michel adds, "Souffrez que je parle de moi; je vais vous raconter ma vie, simplement, sans modestie et sans orgueil, plus simplement que si je parlais à moi-même" (*Im,* p. 372). The sentence forcefully contradicts the claimed simplicity through the smooth, carefully modulated members, the amplification, the repeated use of *parler,* the conduplication of *simplement.* Though such extended and dense clusters of rhetorical devices do not occur from this point on, the narrator's style continues to be of sufficient quality to cause considerable doubt about its "simplicity," hence about Michel's reliability. Michel's style joins the structure of his story as an ironic device which encourages the suspicion that he has carefully planned and rehearsed his account, that it is therefore tendentious, and that we must consequently stay on our guard.

But it has another, and I think more important, result. It seriously damages whatever verisimilitude the book as a whole may have. J. C. Davies puts it this way: "If we demanded strict authenticity, we might ask Gide how it is that an archaeologist without especial literary pretentions, however brilliant he might be, could relate his story in a style so rich in literary merit, so full of excellent lyrical and dramatic qualities and containing such a wealth of suggestive images. Or we might wonder how a man so disillusioned and broken in spirit as Michel appears to be, could rise at times to such lyrical heights as does the narrator in telling his story to the friends who have come to rescue him. Michel's tone is not always strictly in harmony either with his professional interests or with the mood of extreme dejection in which he appears before his friends" (*Gide,* p. 43). Michel, in short, is *invraisemblable,* and because of this fact, the work is as well. Today, applying the criterion of verisimilitude to a work of art may seem both out-of-date and naive. As Ullmann suggests, "It could of course be argued that the novelist . . . could legitimately aim at a . . . style which would correspond to the narrator's character but would be transposed into a purer and more artistic key" (*Image* ["The Development of Gide's Imagery"], p. 30). Since we present-day readers know that no work can ever be truly realistic, that a certain amount of artifice is unavoidable, we tend to accept artificialities without question. It is worth recalling, however, that whenever an artist pushes the style of his characters beyond credence, "such a solution, whatever its advantages, is bound to affect verisimilitude, 'that willing suspension of disbelief for the moment, which constitutes poetic faith'" (*ibid.*). Furthermore, when Gide was working on ***L'Immoraliste,*** the canon of *vraisemblance* was very much alive, though not universally adhered to. Gide could not have failed to know of the dangers of Michel's style. Why did he nonetheless allow his character to speak in a fashion that would not only undermine the speaker, but the work as well? I would hesitate to put it down to inexperience or bad judgment, for Gide was in no sense a beginner. By the time of ***L'Immoraliste,*** he had already authored a considerable body of work which shows a mastery of the writer's trade. Furthermore, because he elsewhere suggested that such artificiality was inherent, indeed, essential to art and because the artificiality extends beyond the portions for which Michel is putatively responsible, one begins to suspect that Gide intended his *récit* to be unrealistic.

Even the introductory letter employs a style at least as rhetorical as Michel's, and it swarms with clichéd devices, any one of which could certainly increase a reader's distance. As Germaine Brée has suggested, the letter presenting Michel's account is "artificial." It relies "on the conventional and rather awkward narrative device by which the story purports to be told by a witness. . . . [and] as a way of setting his story in motion, Gide uses another well-worn device, the adolescent pact."[14] Although less knowing readers might not go so far, surely even the most susceptible, trained by nineteenth century fiction and ready to experience the illusion of "real life" while reading, must find it at least somewhat difficult to believe in the introductory letter to the scribe's brother, the Premier. The letter appears to guarantee the reliability of Michel's story, which is to follow. But it is an ironic document where style joins with the worn-out devices noted by Brée to vitiate any verisimilitude it may have. The only indication that the scribe destines the letter for a close relative appears in the familiar address and in the colloquial turn of a very few sentences, for example, the first which begins *in medias res*: "Oui, tu le pensais bien: Michel nous a parlé, mon cher frère" (*Im,* p. 369). Otherwise, an author of a handbook of rhetoric could well mine it for a multitude of examples. The style is periodic and polished. It makes frequent use of antitheses, binary and ternary constructions, and repetitive sounds, words and phrases. "Le récit qu'il nous fit, le voici. Tu l'avais demandé; je te l'avais promis" (*ibid.*). This compar, the first of several alexandrines, leads directly into another equally artificial clause marked by anaphora: "Mais à l'instant de l'envoyer, j'hésite encore, et plus je le relis et plus il me paraît affreux" (*ibid.*). The two binary constructions are then followed by three rhetorical questions, and the paragraph ends with a summary alloiosis: "Saura-t-on inventer l'emploi de tant d'intelligence et de force—ou refuser à tout cela droit de cité?" The letter subsequently tells the Premier what he already knows: "Tu sais quelle amitié de collège, forte déjà, mais chaque année grandie, liait Michel à Denis, à Daniel, à moi." It further introduces the major images and sets the scene. Then, without further ado, the scribe turns the podium over to Michel. Should the reader still be willing to suspend his disbelief (as was the judge at the obscenity trial of *Jurgen,* after having read James Branch Cabell's similarly artificial introduction), Michel's highly polished presentation and unbelievably stylized account should at the very least impede involvement with the characters and events.

"If we demand strict authenticity," says J. C. Davies, and that, it seems to me, is precisely what we must do. The text leaves little choice. To become so deeply involved in Michel's story that one consistently identifies with him is not only to ignore but to deny the obvious. Gide, of course, pointed to *L'Immoraliste*'s lack of verisimilitude in a widely quoted letter: "Non, je ne pense pas que Michel puisse jamais écrire. . . . Croyez bien, cher Scheffer, que ce n'est que parce que je ne suis pas Michel que j'ai pu raconter son histoire aussi 'remarquablement bien' que vous dites" (***O.C.,*** IV, 616). I would go further and suggest that the reader must recognize the structural and rhetorical games in the work; he must sense that these devices, developed long ago by other writers to increase verisimilitude, function ironically in *L'Immoraliste* to achieve the opposite result. At the same time that the text explicitly promises to give us the exact words spoken by Michel, implicitly it says the contrary: "I, the text, am not real; I am not even lifelike; I am art." Of course, not every reader would sense this ironic message, nor did Gide expect them to. As Justin O'Brien pointed out, *L'Immoraliste* was "published in May 1902 in an edition of 300 copies, the number at which the young author then estimated [his] potential public."¹⁵ Gide was writing for a very specific kind of reader, a reader he did not expect to find, and he was willing to settle for himself until such time as a future audience appeared.¹⁶

I do not wish to overemphasize this irony, however, for it is not sufficiently strong to negate the undeniable attraction the work exerts. Even when an expert reader like Martin Turnell has recognized the artificiality, he nonetheless admits to being under the sway of *L'Immoraliste*'s insidious enchantment (*Art of French Fiction,* p. 257). For such people a particular kind of reading results: "Le plaisir d'art alterne avec le choc de vérité. C'est une des sources de la jouissance spéciale que procure le récit gidien, que ce trouble spirituel, cet envoûtement, cet état d'existence objective et d'irréalité artistique. Le lecteur éprouve parfois le besoin de faire le point de sa propre position et de celle de ses personnages. Où en est-on? Qui parle? Que fait-on de moi? Voilà questions qui s'imposent souvent, au cours du récit où la vérité la plus dénudée alterne avec l'artifice et le hors-d'œuvre littéraire."¹⁷ The reader participates on two levels. While subjectifying the account, thus "living" it, he objectifies it, thus judging it. This kind of a reading correlates exactly with the first two steps of Gide's description of creation and art, as expounded during the summer of 1901 while he was working on ***L'Immoraliste.***

> "L'homme propose et Dieu dispose," nous a-t-on dit; ceci est vrai dans la nature;—mais . . . dans l'œuvre d'art au contraire, *Dieu propose et l'homme dispose*; et tout prétendu producteur d'œuvres d'art qui n'est pas conscient de ceci est tout ce que l'on veut: pas un artiste.
>
> Coupez la phrase en deux, ne prenez pour credo qu'un des deux membres de la formule, et vous aurez les deux grandes hérésies artistiques qui toujours à neuf s'entrecombattent pour ne vouloir comprendre que c'est de leur union même et de leur compromission seulement que l'art peut naître.
>
> *Dieu propose*: c'est le naturalisme, l'objectivisme, appelez-le comme il vous plaît.
>
> *L'homme dispose*: c'est l'à-priorisme, l'idéalisme . . .
>
> *Dieu propose et l'homme dispose*: c'est l'œuvre d'art.
>
> . . . . .
>
> L'art est une chose tempérée. Et certes je ne veux non plus dire par là que l'œuvre d'art la plus accomplie serait celle qui se tiendrait à la plus égale distance de l'idéalisme et du réalisme; non certes! et l'artiste peut bien se rapprocher autant qu'il osera d'un des deux pôles, mais à condition qu'il ne quittera pas du talon le second; un sursaut de plus, il perd pied.
>
> (***O.C.,*** III, 407-409)

Gide had previously produced works that conform to the first two categories. For what he calls naturalism or objectivism, *Dieu propose,* there is **Les Nourritures terrestres**—a strange sort of naturalism, perhaps, but, as he points out elsewhere, the work satisfies his definitions: "Quand ont paru mes **Nourritures,** on était en plein symbolisme; il me paraissait que l'art courait de grands risques à se séparer ainsi du naturel et de la vie. Mais mon livre était beaucoup trop naturel pour ne point paraître factice à ceux qui n'avaient plus de goût que pour l'artificiel; et précisément parce qu'il s'échappait de la littérature on n'y vit d'abord que de la quintessence de littérature" (***O.C.,*** XIII, 440). For a prioristic idealism or *l'homme dispose,* perhaps the best example is **Le Prométhée mal enchaîné,** excellently studied by Holdheim (*Theory [Theory and Practice of the Novel]*, pp. 190-212). In neither case, however, do we find the "compromission" he mentions in 1901. **Les Nourritures terrestres** leans too much toward an indiscriminant recording of impressions to satisfy the category of "l'homme dispose," and **Le Prométhée** tends in the other direction toward a contortionist's mannered, though amusing, *tour de force.* An early attempt at concession might be found in **Paludes.** Nonetheless, one must wait until **L'Immoraliste** to find a clear, and successful, example of all three levels. There, while suggesting life (a point I shall make in more detail), he simultaneously undermines it with irony and prepares the third level—art.

II

After having noticed the ironic function of the letter-document, the style, and the structure and having, as well, grown distrustful of what Albert J. Guérard has aptly called the "deceptive simplicity of surface [that] invites casual and very literal reading,"[18] numerous unanswered questions remain. If, for example, Michel was progressing toward spiritual and physical regeneration in North Africa, how did he go wrong? Perhaps this question will incite the reader to go beyond the stage of alternating participation and judgment to find the final stage: *Dieu propose et l'homme dispose*. It seems to me that this *sustantificque mouelle* is in the subsurface pattern of coherent imagery Gide employed as a major conveyor of meaning in *L'Immoraliste*. A system of images metaphorically climbing from darkness through various levels of water to light accentuates the protagonist's struggle toward spiritual and physical health; whereas his subsequent psychic disintegration reverses the symbolic movement and descends to darkness.

Although Robert Goodhand has argued convincingly that Gide employed allusions to the New Testament story of Peter, suggesting that images of light and darkness symbolize Christian and non-Christian elements respectively,[19] it seems to me that allusions to the Bible and to Christian practice appear as only one part of the system of imagery serving to highlight the conflict between Michel's conscious rational mind and his unconscious. No one would deny that Gide's Protestant heritage was important both to him and to *L'Immoraliste*,[20] but it is far from being the only influence or his only preoccupation.[21] I would prefer to say that the chiaroscuro represents the conscious and unconscious mind or, in other terms, the forces of Apollo (representative of light, integration, heroism, activity, good judgment, and will power) and Dionysus (associated with the infernal, a lack of control, the unleasing of desire, chaos, dissolution, passivity, and the unconscious). This opposition appears very early in the narrative sequence. The introductory letter names the listeners: "Denis, Daniel et moi." Lest the reader make the mistake of ignoring them, the names are repeated five times in thirty-three lines (*Im*, p. 369-70). The attitude required in confronting the story is partially defined with the recognition that Denis derives from Dionysus, and Daniel from the Hebrew Dan for judge, thus related to the qualities of Apollo. Within these same lines, other names—Silas and Will—reiterate the theme. "Will" comes from a Teutonic word meaning "resolute," and "Silas" derives from Silvanus, the Latin sylvan deity (traditionally related to the dark forces, hence the unconscious and Dionysus). These names join the light and darkness imagery in suggesting the major conflict in *L'Immoraliste* between Apollo and Dionysus.[22]

No reader of Gide's early work can seriously doubt that the author had a wide knowledge of traditional symbols. Although he no longer adhered to the narrow Symbolist doctrine by the time of *L'Immoraliste*, he continued to use symbols, both private and traditional, throughout his literary career. He did mock the device in *Paludes* and *Les Caves du Vatican*,[23] but the counterfeit coin of *Les Faux-Monnayeurs* and the precious stones in *Thésée*, for example, show that he was not denying the effectiveness of symbols in literature. The difference between the symbolism of *Le Traité du Narcisse* or *El Hadj* and that of *L'Immoraliste* resides in degree of subtlety. In *L'Immoraliste* the symbols are attributes inherent to the fictional world; they are neither incongruous nor exotic and, thus, do not call attention to themselves. The realistic objects gradually take on symbolic significance by reason of context and repetition.[24]

Even if the reader were not aware that the night traditionally represents the demonic, *L'Immoraliste* emphasizes its fearsome nature through insistent association with destruction. It is at night that Michel begins coughing blood, that Marceline begins to cough and finally that she dies. When Michel begins to open his windows (in contrast to the narrator of *Paludes*, who spends his time closing them), it is to the night: "Je ne sais comment j'avais fait jusqu'alors pour dormir avec les vitres closes; sur les conseils de T . . . j'essayai donc de les ouvrir la nuit; un peu, d'abord; bientôt je les poussai toutes grandes; bientôt ce fut une habitude, un besoin tel que, dès que la fenêtre était refermée, j'étouffais. Avec quelles délices plus tard sentirai-je entrer vers moi le vent des nuits, le clair de lune . . ." (*Im*, p. 387). Windows traditionally represent penetration, transcendence. It seems significant that with a few notable exceptions the windows of *L'Immoraliste* open wide to the night and to the moon (*Im*, pp. 387, 396, 467). After two such instances, Michel quotes portions of the Biblical passage: "Maintenant tu te ceins toi-même et tu vas où tu veux aller; mais quand tu seras vieux, tu étendras les mains . . ." (*Im*, pp. 397, 467) which ends: "and another shall gird thee, and carry *thee* wither thou wouldest not" (John 21:18). Only once does the text explicitly state that the sun entered his window—the morning after his marriage was finally consummated (*Im*, p. 406). By the time of the second visit to La Morinière, Michel has come under the domination of the night. Although the alluring daytime sounds enter through his open window, he resists the temptation to go out until nightfall. And in the little house at Sidi b.M., his absolute freedom finds support through the "vastes trous dans les murs" (*Im*, p. 370) instead of windows, and his incapacity to make use of this freedom through the low wall surrounding the property.

Michel is a night creature when his friends arrive. Appropriately, he begins his story only when "ce fut la nuit" (*Im,* p. 371). The importance of this statement becomes clear on noting that in the first half of the book after the couple's arrival in Biskra, images of light predominate, even in the shadow: "J'entrai avec ravissement dans son ombre. L'air était lumineux. . . . L'ombre était mobile et légère; elle ne tombait pas sur le sol, et semblait à peine y poser. O lumière!" (*Im,* p. 390). Twice as many references to the night occur in the second half of the *récit* as in the first, and at the end of *L'Immoraliste,* although there is sunlight in the desert, Michel only comes alive at night.

Michel's room in Biskra provides a related supporting image which Gide exploited more fully in *La Porte étroite*: "Une petite porte menait à la chambre de Marceline; une grande porte vitrée ouvrait sur la terrasse" (*Im,* p. 381). Michel chooses the large door and penetrates farther and farther into the world, to the terrace (*Im,* p. 383), to the public garden (*Im,* p. 387), to the "merveilleux vergers de l'oasis" (*Im,* p. 391), and "plus loin" (*Im,* p. 393).

As Michel moves from his room and from the garden, he and Marceline follow the river which may be a reference to time, for when the couple pause beneath some palm trees, Michel says, "C'était un lieu . . . qui semblait comme à l'abri du temps" (*Im,* p. 392). At this point in the narrative sequence, his need for water has already been emphasized: "Une bouteille d'eau minérale était là; j'en bus un verre, deux verres; à la troisième fois, buvant à même, j'achevai toute la bouteille d'un coup" (*Im,* p. 385). Michel's health improves, and they leave Biskra and the river for Ravello in Italy where Michel finds a spring located high above the plain. After suitable exposure to the sun—"J'offris tout mon corps à sa flamme" (*Im,* p. 401)—and three trips to the spring, he plunges in (three symbolizes spiritual synthesis).[25] "Vite transi, je quittai l'eau, m'étendis sur l'herbe, au soleil. Là, des menthes croissaient, odorantes; j'en cueillis, j'en froissai les feuilles, j'en frottai tout mon corps humide mais brûlant. Je le regardai longuement, sans plus de honte aucune, avec joie. Je me trouvais, non pas robuste encore, mais pouvant l'être, harmonieux, sensuel, presque beau" (*Im,* p. 402). Here, Michel seems close to becoming a well-integrated person. The forces of nature (Dionysus) and of rationality (Apollo) are in harmonious balance. He cuts his beard, protects Marceline, and while begetting his child begins a new life free of the limitations of his former existence. "Notre bonheur, durant cette fin de voyage, fut si égal, si calme, que je n'en peux rien raconter" (*Im,* p. 408). Perhaps it is significant that the plant with which Michel dries himself is mint, Jupiter's plant, for Jupiter is normally considered to correspond to the virtues of judgment and will.

The happiness and equilibrium established when he consummates his marriage appears as the apex of his moral and physical development. He experiences a moment of happiness so intense that it can never again be equaled: "Rien n'empêche le bonheur comme le souvenir du bonheur. Hélas! je me souviens de cette nuit" (*Im,* p. 405). Nonetheless he maintains a sort of plateau, characterized by happiness (*Im,* pp. 406, 408), tranquility (*Im,* pp. 406, 408, 410), and confidence (*Im,* p. 410). In addition, both Marceline and Michel are fruitful—he begins to work and she is pregnant (*Im,* p. 410). Unfortunately, a hint soon appears that the equilibrium established in Italy and maintained in Normandy is about to go out of balance. Michel looks at the Normandy land, where "de cette abondance ordonnée, de cet asservissement joyeux, de ces souriantes cultures, une harmonie s'établissait, non plus fortuite mais dictée, un rythme, une beauté tout à la fois humaine et naturelle" (*Im,* p. 410), and he begins to imagine not just order, but perfect order: "Je me construisais une éthique qui devenait une science de la parfaite utilisation de soi par une intelligente contrainte" (*Im,* p. 411).

His desire for perfection spills out onto the farm, and he decides to repair a leaking pond. As the workers drain it, Michel considers leaving to seek Marceline. But suddenly the eels are sighted. He forgets his wife, enters the water, joins hands with Bocage's son Charles, addresses the latter in the familiar form, and allows himself to be covered with mud. The eels suggest an erotic attraction, and the mud adumbrates the eventual end of the unconscious choice Michel makes at the pond. He does not go after his wife, and "déjà je ne regrettais plus son absence; il me semblait qu'elle eût un peu gêné notre joie" (*Im,* p. 413).

The image of the pond's *eau fuyante* reappears somewhat farther on: "Je me penchais sur elle [i.e., Marceline] comme sur une profonde eau pure, où, si loin qu'on voyait, on ne voyait que de l'amour. Ah! si c'était encore le bonheur, je sais que j'ai voulu dès lors le retenir, comme on veut retenir dans ses mains rapprochées, en vain, une eau fuyante; mais déjà je sentais, à côté du bonheur, quelque autre chose que le bonheur, qui colorait bien mon amour, mais comme colore l'automne" (*Im,* p. 420). This passage recalls the images discussed above. We have the pure water which appeared in the spring near Ravello related to Marceline. The leaking water reminds us of the episode in the pond at La Morinière, and the reference to time already noted in relation to running water is clear. The passage also prepares Ménalque's image: "Ah! Michel! toute joie est pareille à . . . l'eau de la source Amélès qui, raconte Platon, ne se pouvait garder dans aucun vase . . . Que chaque instant emporte tout ce qu'il avait apporté" (*Im,* pp. 436-37).

Given Gide's later public stance on homosexuality, perhaps I should insist that the episode at the pond provides no indications that Michel is on the right track. To the contrary, the mud puts him back to the beginning of what we shall see to be a metaphorical evolution. Further, where Marceline has been clearly associated with his equilibrium and with the pure water of the spring of Ravello, here, after the water has escaped, he begins to reject her. The following day, a new movement begins. In the company of Charles, "Nous nous dirigeâmes tous deux vers les bois" (*Im,* p. 413). Soon, "nous gagnions la limite des bois" (*Im,* p. 417), and when he actually enters the woods to poach (prepared by the already mentioned etymological relationship of Silas to the forest), he reveals a new preference for water near the ground: "Je rentrais à travers champs, dans l'herbe lourde de rosée, ivre de nuit, de vie sauvage et d'anarchie, trempé, boueux, couvert de feuilles" (*Im,* p. 449).

To return to the first stay at La Morinière, the watchword is order, excessive order that runs in the face of reality. Simultaneously, he pushes in the other direction by exalting the wild and untutored ethic of the Goths: "Par une sorte de réaction naturelle, tandis que ma vie s'ordonnait, se réglait et que je me plaisais autour de moi à régler et à ordonner toutes choses, je m'éprenais de plus en plus de l'éthique fruste des Goths" (*Im,* p. 418). The order, which stays only on the surface, affecting his external life and everything surrounding him, is nothing but apparent order. Naturally, because of his unwillingness to recognize the availability of farm labor, when he departs for Paris he leaves La Morinière in worse shape than he found it. In Paris, empty formulations are the rule. Art occurs at the opposite extreme from life since most novelists and poets "ne vivaient point, se contentaient de paraître vivre et, pour un peu, eussent considéré la vie comme un fâcheux empêchement d'écrire" (*Im,* p. 423). Writing and teaching are but empty words: "Ah! que je compris bien, dès lors, que l'enseignement presque tout moral des grands philosophes antiques ait été d'exemple autant et plus encore que de paroles!" (*Im,* p. 429). Encouraged by the example of Ménalque, he begins to undermine the forms of his life, by poaching, by deciding to sell the farm, and finally by attacking Marceline herself. The willed abandonment to sensation eventually leaves him helpless, like flotsam after the water has receded.

The trip south, which has "tous les vertiges d'une chute" (*Im,* p. 458), ends only in the midst of the desert at Touggourt. During this trip, Michel repeatedly leaves bodies of water, despite the fact that they seem beneficial to Marceline. Not only did he leave the Engadine valley, but he leaves Palermo ("La baie de Palerme est clémente et Marceline s'y plaisait"—*Im,* p. 462) and the sea ("Sur mer, Marceline alla mieux . . ."—*Im,* p. 464). Rain and humidity, on the other hand, prove harmful to Marceline (*Im,* p. 459, 465), but in Naples we find Michel enjoying it: "Je humais l'humidité de la nuit" (*Im,* p. 461). Finally, at Touggourt, they drink some tea, "auquel l'eau salée du pays a donné son goût détestable" (*Im,* p. 468). Then, with the wind stirring up the sand which appears repeatedly in the last pages (*Im,* pp. 467, 468, 469, 470), Michel cannot resist the night and leaves his dying wife alone.

When one considers the earth, sand and water imagery, the various references support what is actually happening to Michel in much the same way as do light and darkness. Indeed, there seems to be a value distinction between the types of water. While Michel's body and mind gain strength in Biskra, he follows a river in which "l'eau lourde est couleur de la terre" (*Im,* p. 387). The metaphorical progression continues to a reasonably healthy state and to what might be called "upper waters," the spring of pure water near Ravello. "Lower waters" appear in conjunction with Michel's unconscious rejection of Marceline and his homosexual tendencies at La Morinière. Michel likes the swampy lake at Neuchâtel, "ce lac aux rives glauques . . . sans rien d'alpestre, et dont les eaux, comme celles d'un marécage, longtemps se mêlent à la terre et filtrent entre les roseaux" (*Im,* p. 454), and describes the little lake high in the Alps as "un hideux lac bleu" (*Im,* p. 456). At sea-level, in Palermo (*Im,* p. 462) and Syracuse (*Im,* p. 463), he joins "la société des pires gens" (*ibid.*). When he finally reaches the desert, there is only the vilest of drinking water and sand. At this point Michel has lost control to the forces of "le dieu ténébreux" (*Im,* p. 467), a state of helpless disintegration which becomes almost complete by the time his friends arrive at Sidi. There, he tells his friends, he likes to play with "des cailloux blancs" (*Im,* p. 471). If names have importance, as I have suggested in reference to Denis, Daniel and Will, it may be significant, in respect to the pebbles, that Pierre, the farmhand at La Morinière, is a brute "uniquement mené par l'instinct" (*Im,* p. 442).

Coming back to the water imagery, humidity, as distinct from bodies of water, appears in conjunction with transition. At the spring when Michel approaches integration, his body is "humide mais brûlant" (*Im,* p. 402); moistness, dew or humidity occurs at La Morinière during his comradery with Charles (*Im,* p. 417), when he goes to visit Ménalque (*Im,* p. 435), when he joins the poachers (*Im,* p. 449), and as Marceline dies (*Im,* pp. 453, 459, 461, 465). One might summarize by saying that Michel's progression from sickness and near death to health and happiness is highlighted by a system of images that moves concomitantly from earth-laden water to pure water at high altitudes. The spiritual disintegration is accompanied by a movement to low water, and finally to sand, pebbles and night. This complex of imagery closely follows the traditional symbolic divisions between darkness, a state of destruction or of unrealized potential, and light, the gold of wisdom and self-integration. Earth, the lowest symbolic level of evolution, signifies disintegration when it occurs as sand or pebbles, while water, a transitional element, has more freedom and may be transformed into air by fire, which is related to light and gold. Those seeking salvation and the light traditionally turn to the flaming aridity of the desert. Michel also seeks the desert in the final portion of *L'Immoraliste,* but he refuses the sun, taking instead the easy path in the shadow of the night. If, as Goodhand has reasonably suggested, Marceline "*is* the earthly representative in this novel of the forces of light" ("Religious," p. 276), Michel should have sought his salvation through her. Significantly, as already mentioned, it was only when he was attending to his husbandly duty that the sun entered his window.

The system of imagery contradicts what Michel attempts to make his listeners believe. Despite his assertion to Marceline—"Oh! Marceline! . . . partons d'ici. Ailleurs je t'aimerai comme je t'aimais à Sorrence. Tu m'a cru changé, n'est-ce pas? Mais ailleurs, tu sentiras bien que rien n'a changé notre amour . . ." (*Im,* p. 453)—the frantic voyage south does not mean a search for the values he espoused during his first visit to North Africa. Nor is it the quest for a new, future-oriented ethic ("Qu'estce que l'homme peut encore?"), for in seeking the "vieil homme" he voyages to the places where past joys occurred. And finally, his night is not like Ménalque's *veillée des armes,* it represents almost total incapacity. He can do nothing but ask for help. At La Morinière, in willfully relaxing the control over his sensations, in neglecting to continue the balanced self-discipline he developed in North Africa, in abandoning his future-oriented ethic, Michel makes the fatal error which results in his final helplessness. Enslaved to the night, to his unconscious, to sensualism, incapable of conscious choice, he follows the whim of the moment as his disintegration increases in velocity. Michel and, consequently, Marceline are doomed.

III

As we follow the covert structure of significant images, an interesting thing occurs. The overt structure is subverted. Neither the three main parts, nor the thirteen chapters are related to what are actually the formative developments of Michel's life. Michel approaches integration in chapter 6 when he plunges into the spring of pure water. Only in chapter 8, when he makes love to his wife, do happiness and equilibrium arrive. The "plateau" of happiness is recounted in chapter 9 (the last chapter of part I) and in the first few pages of part II. Where, earlier, while under the seductive sway of Michel's accounts, it seemed that the death of the child and the meetings with Ménalque (which occur, as mentioned, at the "center" of the book's formal structure—chapter 2, part II) are responsible for Michel's rejection of all restraints, in fact, they only emphasize his already well-established tendency. The formal structure, then, corresponds to what Michel wants his listeners to believe. But it is far removed from having anything to do with what actually happened. In that sense, it corresponds to the kind of "art" Michel finds in Paris, that is, it reflects a preconceived idealization which ignores reality.

The disparity between the formal divisions of *L'Immoraliste* and the reality of the events as they happened provides an astonishingly powerful support for one pole of Michel's moral dilemma. It is an extreme, exactly as was Michel's decision to make his life and La Morinière conform to his idea of perfection: "la parfaite utilisation de soi par une intelligente contrainte." In the light of what Michel subsequently does, it is clear that by "intelligente" he does not mean "constraint based on understanding." He means "constraint that reveals the working of the intelligence." It is intellection run wild, without any regard for the realities of farming in Normandy or of his own capacities. He, thus, presents vivid proof that culture can kill life, as he prophetically suggests in his course (*Im,* p. 424). By the time Michel reaches Paris, he conforms to his image of its inhabitants. However much he disdains them for being and living empty forms, for guiding their lives according to appearance, for writing "art" that has nothing to do with life, the plain truth is that when he rejects all constraints, whether self-imposed or not, he attempts to conform to his intellectual ideal of an unrestrained Gothic leader. If logic or directness were the standards of judgment, one would have difficulty faulting Michel's actions. As he systematically attacks every restraining bond, all fall, even will power and the orderly use of his mind that successfully overcame the effects of his sickness. His intellectual goal leads to control by unconscious sensation.

When this occurs, Michel coincides with the quality he sees in North Africa: "Terre en vacance d'œuvres d'art. Je méprise ceux qui ne savent reconnaître la beauté que transcrite déjà et toute interprétée. Le peuple arabe a ceci d'admirable que, son art, il le vit, il le chante et le dissipe au jour le jour; il ne le fixe point et ne l'embaume en aucune œuvre. C'est la cause et l'effet de l'absence de grands artistes . . ." (*Im,* pp. 464-65). Michel, like his conception of the North Africans, accepts his lot and floats with the current. "L'art s'en va de moi, je le sens" (*Im,* p. 467). One minute follows another, the expected effect always follows the cause, and since there is no attempt to overcome chronological or causal relationships, nothing is fixed, everything flows. "Ici toute recherche est impossible, tant la volupté suit de près le désir. Entouré de splendeur et de mort, je sens le bonheur trop présent et l'abandon à lui trop uniforme" (*Im,* p. 471). Michel has left Paris to become North Africa, a development that is structurally supported by what appears at first glance to be the artlessness of Michel's account. On the surface, the *récit* is of the simplest variety, ordered only by the normal sequence of cause and effect and by chronology. It appears perfectly natural and ineluctible when, from innocent beginnings, the events concentrate and, with a vertiginous rush, turn into tragedy. This aspect of *L'Immoraliste* perhaps best satisfies the demands of the *récit*. A reader is encouraged, after all, to read in a linear fashion, line by line, page by page, from beginning to end, accepting each word as an ordered event and as it comes. Michel's *récit* superficially resembles "life" and not "art." While Michel touches two opposing extremes: a straitjacket and anarchy, Paris and North Africa, *L'Immoraliste* incorporates artificial, non-linear order and unilinear *récit*. In respect to Michel, the first visits to both Italy and Normandy also serve as a middle term. There he attained happiness and fruitful activity, a situation that seems to be echoed structurally by the integration of those verisimilar, unobtrusive elements which serve as the primary conveyance of meaning and as the most important means for providing *L'Immoraliste* with the equilibrium Gide expected of art.

Art, as Gide clearly understood, must be natural. "Savez-vous ce qui fait de la poésie aujourd'hui et de la philosophie surtout, lettres mortes? C'est qu'elles se sont séparées de la vie" (*Im*, p. 435). Carried to an extreme, however, nature can be destructive. "Le vrai retour à la nature, c'est le définitif retour aux éléments: la mort" (*O.C.*, III, 405). In the work of art, nature must be balanced by order (a sort of Maxwell E. Perkins for a Thomas Wolfe). Gide put it this way in "Les Limites de l'art": "Dans la nature, rien ne peut s'isoler ni s'arrêter; tout continue. L'homme y peut essayer, proposer la beauté; la nature aussitôt s'en rend maîtresse et en dispose. Et voici bien l'opposition que je disais: Ici, l'homme est soumis à la nature; dans l'œuvre d'art au contraire, il soumet la nature à lui" (*ibid.*, p. 407). In *L'Immoraliste,* not only does *Dieu propose,* not only does *l'homme dispose,* but also "*Dieu propose et l'homme dispose*: c'est l'œuvre d'art" (*ibid.*, p. 408). This happens to Michel and to the book. When Michel's seemingly sincere outpouring confronts evidence that the expression of his thoughts and feelings is rigorously controlled in an apparent attempt to influence his listeners, when the lifelike *récit* confronts schematic structure, when "life" confronts artifice, both terms are ironically subverted and the reader is forced to the third level of "compromission" or art. *L'Immoraliste* then becomes something more than a good story; it is also a magnificent aesthetic demonstration in which every element fulfills multiple functions.

As irony undermines the credibility of Michel's account and the realism of the work as a whole, it stimulates the reader's alternating involvement and rejection, participation and judgment and consequently provides a pleasurable experience similar to gazing down into a pool of pure water, where the wind-caused ripples and the shifting angle of light make widely varying visions of what is essentially the same object. In the end, although I should not like to slight *L'Immoraliste* insofar as it provides insights into one form of individualism (*O.C.,* XIII, 439-40), it seems to me that its primary success resides in permitting readers to see multiple levels of meaning integrated into one significant work where Gide has succeeded in what he attempted: to "bien peindre et d'éclairer bien [sa] peinture" (*Im,* p. 368).

Notes

1. "André Gide," *ConL*, 10 (1969), 118-19.

2. *L'Immoraliste,* in *Romans, récits et soties, œuvres lyriques,* ed. Yvonne Davet and Jean-Jacques Thierry (Paris: Pléiade, 1958), p. 470; further references to this edition will be cited as *Im*. References to the *Œuvres complètes d'André Gide,* ed. L. Martin-Chauffier, 15 vols. (Paris: NRF, 1932-1939), will be preceded by *O.C.*; and those to *André Gide, Journal: 1889-1939* (Paris: Pléiade, 1951), by *J* I.

3. Published in *O.C.,* IX, 331.

4. Jean Hytier, *André Gide* (Paris: Charlot, 1945), p. 170.

5. W. Wolfgang Holdheim has brilliantly argued that this opposition resides at the center of Gide's artistic theory and practice: *Theory and Practice of the Novel: A Study on André Gide* (Geneva: Droz, 1968).

6. I summarize from Gide's important discussion of this problem in "Les Limites de l'art" (1901), *O.C.,* III, 399-409.

7. *Design and Truth in Autobiography* (Cambridge, Mass.: Harvard Univ. Press, 1960), pp. 189-90.

8. Hermine de Saussure, *Rousseau et les manuscrits des Confessions* (Paris: Boccard, 1958), pp. 265-69; cf. Jean Starobinski, *Jean-Jacques Rousseau: La Transparence et l'obstacle* (Paris: Plon, 1957), p. 216; P. Moreau, "Remarques sur le style du 6e livre des *Confessions*," *Revue Universitaire,* 66 (1957), 81; and Charly Guyot, "Du Manuscrit de Neuchâtel au manuscrit de Genève: Etude de quelques variantes du texte des *Confessions*," in *Jean-Jacques Rousseau et son œuvre: Problèmes et recherches: Commémoration et Colloque de Paris (16-20 octobre 1962) organisés par le Comité National pour la Commémoration de J.-J. Rousseau* (Paris: Klincksieck, 1964), pp. 33-46.

9. *Im,* p. 372. The claim by itself is enough to arouse suspicions, as Boris Tomashevsky pointed out: "A system of realistic motivation quite often includes a denial of artistic motivation. The usual formula

is, 'If this had happened in a novel, my hero would have done such and such, but since it really happened, here are the facts . . .' But the denial of the literary form in itself asserts the laws of artistic composition"—"Thematics," in *Russian Formalist Criticism,* tr. Lee T. Lemon and Marion J. Reis (Lincoln, Neb.: U. of Nebraska Press, 1965), p. 85.

10. Pierre Lafille, *André Gide romancier* (Paris: Hachette, 1954), p. 23.

11. J. C. Davies, *Gide: "L'Immoraliste" and "La Porte étroite,"* Studies in French Literature (London: Edward Arnold, 1968), pp. 34, 57.

12. I am deeply indebted to Professors Nelson and David Lee Rubin for the helpful suggestions they made on reading an early version of the present study.

13. E.g., Davies, *Gide,* pp. 40-51; Martin Turnell, *The Art of French Fiction: Prévost, Stendhal, Zola, Maupassant, Gide, Mauriac, Proust* (New York: New Directions, 1959), pp. 272-82; and Stephen Ullmann, 'The Development of Gide's Imagery," *The Image in the Modern French Novel: Gide, Alain-Fournier, Proust, Camus* (Cambridge: Cambridge Univ. Press., 1960), esp. pp. 2-4, 24, 30.

14. *Gide* (New Brunswick, N.J.: Rutgers Univ. Press, 1963), p. 125.

15. *Portrait of André Gide* (New York: Knopf, 1953), p. 169.

16. See, for example, his "Préface," *Im,* p. 368, and "De l'importance du public" (1903), *O.C.,* IV. 187.

17. Lafille, *André Gide,* p. 23.

18. *André Gide* (Cambridge, Mass.: Harvard Univ. Press, 1951), p. 99.

19. "The Religious Leitmotif in *L'Immoraliste,*" *RR* [*The Romanic Review*], 57 (1966), 274-76.

20. See Gide's comments, e.g., *J* I, pp. 1051-52. In a letter to Pastor Ferrari, Gide talked of the dissolution of Saul's personality in *Saül* and Michel's "abandon à soi, qui est précisément à l'opposé de cet abandon *de* soi que nous enseigne l'Evangile"—*O.C.,* XV, 532.

21. Gide returns again and again to the question of "influence"—e.g., *J* I, p. 739; *O.C.,* XIII, 440-43. Before the publication of *L'Immoraliste,* Gide became acquainted with the work of Nietzsche and Dostoevski, to name but two. Affinities with these and others are evident in *L'Immoraliste* (see, e.g., n. 24). One even wonders whether the influence of the Greek and Latin tradition has not been as important in this *récit* as his religious training.

Gide himself suggested: "La grande influence que peut-être j'ai vraiment *subie,* c'est celle de Gœthe, et même je ne sais si mon admiration pour la littérature grecque et l'hellénisme n'eût pas suffi à balancer ma première formation chrétienne" (*J* I, p. 859).

22. For a more comprehensive study of Gide's names, see: A. H. Pasco and Wilfrid J. Rollman, "The Artistry of Gide's Onomastics," *MLN* [*Modern Language Notes*], 86 (1971), 523-31.

23. E.g., the discussion between the narrator-protagonist and Angèle about symbols in *Paludes,* in *Romans, récits et soties,* p. 94, and Carola's delightful ubiquitous cuff-links emblazoned with four encircled cats' heads. From Lafcadio, after going full circle, one of them returns to him.

24. For the symbology in the following pages, the most helpful references have been: Carl G. Jung, et al., *Man and His Symbols* (New York: Doubleday, 1964); Jung, *Psychology and Alchemy,* vol. 12 of *The Collected Works of C. G. Jung,* tr. R. F. C. Hull (London: Routledge, 1953); J. E. Cirlot, *A Dictionary of Symbols,* tr. Jack Sage (New York: Philosophical Library, 1962); Paul Diel, *Le Symbolisme dans la mythologie grecque* (Paris: Pagot, 1952); Ernst and Johanna Lehner, *Folklore and Symbolism of Flowers, Plants and Trees* (New York: Tudor, 1960); Harold Bayley, *The Lost Language of Symbolism,* 2 vols. (London: Williams and Norgate, 1912); and, of course, the extremely important works by Nietzsche, esp., *The Birth of Tragedy, Beyond Good and Evil, On the Genealogy of Morals,* and *Thus Spoke Zarathustra,* all in Walter Kaufman's translations.

Nietzsche's reverberating echoes are especially difficult to ignore in conjunction with the light and darkness imagery and Michel's adhesion to the night. Consider Zarathustra's temptation, thirst, rather, for the night: "Light am I; ah, that I were night! But this is my loneliness that I am girt with light. Ah, that I were dark and nocturnal! How I would suck the breasts of light! . . . But I live in my own light; I drink back into myself the flames that break out of me. I do not know the happiness of those who receive; and I have often dreamed that even stealing must be more blessed than receiving. This is my poverty, that my hand never rests from giving; this is my envy, that I see waiting eyes and the lit-up nights of longing. Oh, wretchedness of all givers! . . . A hunger grows out of my beauty: I should like to hurt those for whom I shine; I should like to rob those to whom I give; thus do I hunger for malice"—*Thus Spoke Zarathustra: A Book for All and None* (New York: Viking, 1966), pp. 105-106.

25. Critics have made a great deal of the number three in *L'Immoraliste*. There is no question about its importance, but it should also be noted that one and two appear more frequently. Four, five, six, eight, twelve, fifteen, twenty and one hundred occur a significant number of times. Gide's use of numerology deserves more attention. His understanding of the symbolic import of numbers is revealed throughout his work. Lafcadio says, for example, "Trente-quatre rue de Verneuil, . . . quatre et trois, sept: le chiffre est bon" (*Les Caves du Vatican*, in *Romans, récits et soties,* p. 732). Indeed it is. Seven, the number Lafcadio reaches through mystic addition, symbolizes perfect order. As Germaine Brée pointed out, this number occurs frequently in *Le Voyage d'Urien* (*Gide*, p. 147).

Robert F. O'Reilly (essay date winter 1974)

SOURCE: O'Reilly, Robert F. "Ritual, Myth, and Symbol in Gide's *L'Immoraliste*." *Symposium* 28, no. 4 (winter 1974): 346-55.

[*In the following essay, O'Reilly examines the elements of ritual, myth, and symbol that Gide uses in* The Immoralist *"to enlarge Michel's story and to convey certain archetypal patterns constituting a mythopoeic vision of human life."*]

Studies of ***L'Immoraliste*** have usually centered on the main character's personal drama.[1] However, Michel's story remains essentially incomplete unless viewed in its mythological context.[2] By merging the day to day realism of Michel's story with a mythological backdrop,[3] Gide created the double perspective of a character who is both agent and victim of life and announced an important structure of his subsequent works where psychological and natural laws have to be considered to understand the actions of his characters and the events confronting them.[4] The present study examines the elements of ritual, myth, and symbol Gide has used in ***L'Immoraliste*** to enlarge Michel's story and to convey certain archetypal patterns constituting a mythopoeic vision of human life.

The mythopoeic underpinnings of ***L'Immoraliste*** have their source in Western literary traditions.[5] Biblical themes and symbolism and motifs from mythology and folklore disclose the shifting relationship of Michel's inner life and reveal the fundamental archetypal configuration created by the Marceline-Menalcas antipathy. Gide has structured the novel around the archetypal dialogue of the angelic and demonic aspects of a man's nature, a quasi-Biblical conception of human nature which enlarges the demonic through association with pagan elements. Through stylized characters who may be expanded into psychological archetypes, Gide expressed a life process which goes beyond Michel's personal story. The Biblical conflict of angel and devil (two natures descended from the same source) and the psychological archetypal debate of the spirit and the shadow (two aspects of a man's character) are manifested in the opposition of Marceline's spirituality and Menalcas' paganism. The interaction and integration of characters with symbolic rituals of death and revival, ceremonial ablutions, and blood sacrifices, enhanced by contrasting images of light and darkness, frequent references to the periodicity of day and night, and natural seasonal cycles, reveal Gide's mythopoeic intention of extending Michel's experience into the realm of the archetypal.

The novel's suggestive ternary structure delineates the cyclical movement of the life process through the rise of the hero, his maturity, and his decline and describes his psychological evolution in the three major divisions of the novel. The numerous repetitions of the number three and its multiples has a traditional Biblical meaning of wholeness and completeness in diversity intimating the wholeness yet individuality of the three major phases of Michel's psychic life. Part I examines Michel's withdrawal from the dominance of the Marceline influence and the beginning of his quest, Part II, the integration of conflicting psychic forces, and Part III, the Menalcas' influence and Michel's decline. The repetition of the number three provides a poetic incantation for the novel's cyclical movement and its ritualistic patterns. There is the traditional literary device of a gathering of a small group of friends (likened to the three friends of Job) to hear an intimate tale recounted in tranquility. The three friends have been separated for three years and are reunited three months after Marceline's death. It requires three days for the ailing Michel to arrive in Biskra, and he takes his first walk during his convalescence at 3:00 P.M. after a three-day wind storm subsides. To further reinforce the interrelated aspects of Michel's inner life, the names of the three principal characters begin with *M*.

Gide encouraged a symbolic reading of Marceline and Menalcas by portraying them as forces in a Judaeo-Christian cultural tradition by which Michel will feel alternately attracted and repulsed. They are forces which are both inside and outside Michel, and Gide slides back and forth between these characters as exteriorized symbolic aspects of Michel's psyche and the characters as real agents who cause Michel to reveal aspects of his psyche. The struggle of Marceline and Menalcas for possession of Michel's inner life constellates an informing psychological structure by polarizing the work between warring archetypes. The decline in Marceline's influence occurs in inverse proportion to the increase in Menalcas' influence. A significant though brief social encounter of the two moral opposites manifests the growing tension of the psychological archetypes and ushers in Marceline's decline: "Marceline commença d'aller moins bien."[6] Literally the Menalcas' force of Michel's psyche overwhelms the Marceline aspect. This shift in moral influences is symbolically portrayed in Marceline's illness. In contrast to Michel's illness which is externalized and purged figuratively by "un gros affreux caillot que je crachai par terre" (p. 383), Marceline's disease is internalized and lodged permanently in her lungs by a fatal embolism, an "affreux caillot de sang" (p. 439).

Marceline is the single most important link between Michel and his past, and it is only through diminishing her importance that he can attempt a liberation from that past. As the pregnant wife she is integrated into the nature cycle as expressed through the descriptions of fertility and abundance of the Norman countryside and its animals: "Marceline me confia qu'elle était enceinte[. . .]. J'admirais quel tranquille avenir promettaient ces robustes bœufs, ces vaches pleines dans ces opulentes prairies" (p. 410). She embodies social and domestic responsibilities which oblige Michel to begin his teaching again (p. 408). Back in Paris Marceline exercises a frugality offending Michel's desire to free himself from material dependencies (p.421), and she opens the door to a society which no longer interests her husband (p. 430). Marceline is identified with certain Pauline virtues which Michel rejects (pp. 459-60) particularly her charity to the weak and sick Arab boys (p. 389). Above all, Marceline is spiritualized through association. She is the devout Christian who turns to her Bible, prayers, and rosary at a time when Michel's instinctual life is being aroused (pp. 385-86). The decline in Marceline's physical state and moral influence coincides with the movement of the novel away from the moistness and greenery of Normandy back towards the deserts of North Africa. That land which prompted Michel's lower drives becomes an appropriate site for her death. Marceline is the victim to be sacrificed in order for Michel to develop fully his primitive instincts. Despite his sincere protests of love and devotion, an opposing compulsion towards the demonic encourages and receives a symbolic slaughter, a bloody *rite de passage,* which gives a finality to the struggle between archetypes: "ses draps, ses mains, sa chemise, sont inondés d'un flot de sang; son visage en est tout sali[. . .]. Vers le petit matin, un nouveau vomissement de sang . . ." (pp. 469-70).

Gide was clearly not concerned with presenting Menalcas as a realistic character. He was interested rather in the dramatic contrast he would make with Marceline: "Il me pria de le présenter à ma femme; la flamme froide de son regard indiquait plus de courage et de décision que de bonté. Il ne fut pas plutôt devant Marceline que je compris qu'il ne lui plaisait pas" (pp. 430-31). The appearance of Menalcas at the very center of the novel, though unexpected, is not entirely unprepared. The enchanted flutes of the shepherd boys near Biskra, the deserts of North Africa, and the reference to Theocritus loosely introduce Menalcas, the admired singer of the *Idylls* of Theocritus and the *Eclogues* of Virgil where Menalcas' scandalous behavior is mentioned as it is in **L'Immoraliste.** The suggestive nature of this poetically sonorous name is easily recognizable. Michel's slavish imitation of certain aspects of Menalcas' life style and his unquestioning acquiescence to the demonic archetype are heightened by Menalcas' association with the mythological shepherd who is followed blindly by his flock of sheep.

Menalcas provides a convenient occasion for Michel to project into the real world hidden psychic contents. He incarnates an ideal of absolute freedom. As an *outsider* whose morals have been condemned by society in an "honteux procès à scandale," he lives life spontaneously and dangerously. Abhorring property and material restraints of any kind, he approaches life purely, naturally, and lucidly. He does not choose his acts in view of some higher value but for the pleasure of exercising his freedom. He possesses no ethics. While Menalcas precipitates a whole series of latent tendencies in Michel, he also issues a warning. He combines both negative and positive sides of Michel's psyche and forewarns Michel of the possible dangers of listening too exclusively to those resonant echoes of the primal man: ". . . pour quelqu'un qui n'a pas le sens de la propriété, vous semblez posséder beaucoup, c'est grave" (p. 428).

The novel's threefold pattern traces the relative importance of the archetypes in Michel's life. In Part I Gide stressed the importance of Michel's early moral and social consciousness through reference to his "grave enseignement huguenot" and implied the continuing influence of this austere morality throughout Michel's life. By contrasting Marceline's physical strength with Michel's fraility, Gide emphasized Marceline's dominant influence early in the novel: ". . . j'étais d'une santé délicate . . . Marceline au contraire, semblait robuste" (p. 374). When Michel gives up hope, Marceline becomes his source of life: "J'étais las. Je m'abandonnai" (p. 379). "Je revois Marceline, ma femme, ma vie, se pencher" (p. 380).

The Moktir episode is one of the more crucial events of Part I since it portends symbolically the direction of Michel's development.[7] Michel's tacit approval of the theft of the scissors suggests antisocial tendencies, a cavalier attitude with respect to property, and a fascination with the criminal. Though the full meaning of this episode is hidden from Michel, the fact that these scissors belong to Marceline and that the thief is one of her favorites is significant. By allowing the theft and by protecting Moktir, Michel figuratively begins a process of cutting himself off from the social and moral authority which his wife represents.[8] The expanded archetypal meaning of the symbol of separation is achieved in Part II of the work when the shadowy figure of Menalcas, Marceline's opposite, emerges with the stolen scissors in his possession.

The novel attains a *détente* early in Part II as Michel's evolution levels off between a tranquil though somewhat sterile past and a possibly ominous future.[9] A particularly felicitous combination of events brings the archetypes into a natural balance for the first and only time in the novel. Marceline's pregnancy, the inspirational fertility of the land, and an interest in the management of his farms provide a harmonious framework in which Michel renews his interest in scholarly work. His study of primitive cultures and of the debauched barbarian king, Athalaric, allows a harmless and therapeutic projection of the demonic archetype. This ambiance of a judicious, productive, and orderly complicity between civilized man and raw nature is conveyed through descriptions of natural phenomena: "Un rythme, une beauté tout à la fois humaine et naturelle où l'on ne savait plus ce que l'on admirait, tant étaient confondus en une très parfaite entente l'éclatement fécond de la libre nature, l'effort savant de l'homme pour la régler. Que serait cet effort sans la puissante sauvagerie qu'il domine? Que serait le sauvage élan de cette sève débordante sans l'intelligent effort qui l'endigue et l'amène en riant au luxe?" (pp. 410-11).

This spontaneous equilibrium of the archetypes is conditioned through ceremonial patterns containing elements of both Christian and pagan religious rites and affording Michel a *rite de passage* between stages of life. Michel undergoes a ritualistic death and rebirth transformation symbolized by his illness and recovery. This rebirth is accompanied by traditional signs of initiation. Michel engages in a pagan-like cleansing ceremony in which sun, water, and a variation on tonsuring are used.[10] Exposed naked to the warm rays of the sun and immersed in water, he undergoes a physical and spiritual rejuvenation and purification:" . . . je me dévêtis lentement. L'air était presque vif, mais le soleil ardent. J'offris tout mon corps à sa flamme" (p. 401) Michel's dive into a pool of water and the shaving of his beard are additional preconditions of leaving the past and of advancing further in pursuit of his new self:

> . . . j'avançai, résolu d'avance, jusqu'à l'eau plus claire que jamais, et sans plus réfléchir, m'y plongeai d'un coup tout entier. Vite transi, je quittai l'eau, m'étendis sur l'herbe, au soleil.
>
> (p. 402)
>
> Sentant sous les ciseaux tomber ma barbe, c'était comme si j'enlevais un masque.
>
> (p. 403)

This *rite d'entrée* is completed by a trial by strength. The act of violently subduing a reckless and drunken coachman and thereby protecting Marceline provides Michel with a test similar in meaning to the ordeals of the knights of romance. In a primitive manner he has proven his manhood through courage and is worthy of possessing his wife physically: "Ce fut cette nuit-là que je possédai Marceline" (p. 405). This complex initiation ceremony reveals possibilities of psychic wholeness for Michel who masters his impulse to kill the coachman through moral controls: "l'étrangler paraissait légitime et je crois bien que seule l'idée de la police m'arrêta." However, the psychic meaning of these symbolic patterns is never raised to the level of Michel's consciousness. Consequently the integration of the archetypes remains latent.

Gide portrays the tenuousness of this harmony through suggestive clusters of images, a recurring horse image and water and fish imagery. Working within a literary tradition which has often used wild horses in mythology and folklore to symbolize the sub-animal side of man,[11] Gide was able to disclose through the taming of a young horse, the problems of individuation in Michel's life. Michel's early praise for the barbarian king Athalaric, who rejects his culture "comme un cheval entier fait un harnais gênant" (p. 407), implies the potential revolt which remains controlled in Michel's admiration of Charles breaking a wild horse: "c'est un de mes plus vifs souvenirs" (p. 416). Michel's appreciation of this restraint of bestial nature appears to maintain the archetypes in a harmonious relationship for a brief moment. However, the subsequent refusal to ride on horseback among his workers demonstrates the disruption of this balance, a figurative descent towards the primitive, and Michel's incipient revolt (p. 441).

The scene in which Charles and Michel empty a carp pool discloses also Michel's difficulty in reconciling the contradictory aspects of his inner life.[12] The fixity of Michel's past is revealed in the form of a stagnant pond: "la mare[. . .]terreuse et d'instant en instant plus opaque" (p. 412) whose "vase" threatens to hold him and to prevent his progress: "parfois on enfonçait jusqu'aux cuisses" (p. 413). On the other hand, certain psychic contents take shape in the image of the "carpes et tanches[. . .]qui ne quittaient plus les bas-fonds" (p. 412) and that are fished out of their obscure hiding places. Michel's inability to firmly fix the evanescent quality of his new self is disclosed by the image of those eels that resist capture and slip readily off the fingers: "elles glissaient entre les doigts. Je l'appelai bientôt pour m'aider à cerner une grosse anguille" (p. 413). This symbolic representation of Michel's emerging inner life is completed appropriately by a hostile reference to the spiritual archetype: "Marceline n'était pas encore venue et ne vint pas, mais déjà je ne regrettais plus son absence; il me semblait qu'elle eût un peu gêné notre joie" (ibid.).[13]

Following the appearance of Menalcas, Michel projects vigorously the demonic archetype. He suppresses the social aspect of the self by withdrawing from his wife and job. The poaching on his own land and the selling of the farm are concrete examples of the denial of property latent in the North African scissors episode. No longer concerned with Charles, Michel's interests have moved to disreputable people, the thieving carousing Bute and the debauched primitive Heurtevent family. This perverse side of Michel's psyche emerges with greater rapidity and intensity during the final third of the novel as he selfishly drags his ailing wife across Europe and back to Africa on the pretext of caring for her health. His behavior develops along the lines of certain criminal and aberrant tendencies. Disillusioned with his former young friends who have matured and become useful members of society, Michel cultivates lower types (p. 463). His criminal inner drive, for example, is flattered by an unchanged Moktir: "Celui-là sort de prison" (p. 466).

Gide has delicately paced the development of the homosexual theme to coincide with Michel's withdrawal from his wife. Miss Brée has pointed out correctly that Michel's initial reaction to the youths is gauged by their degree of healthiness and by his state of convalescence (*André Gide*, p. 160). However, Michel's interest in young boys towards the end of the book cannot be explained away by the desire to regain his health. His enthusiasm for a Sicilian boy "beau comme un vers de Théocrite" (p.462), whom he embraces significantly in front of Marceline and his preference of young Ali to his Ouled-Naïl sister form a sharp contrast with the archetypal union of man and woman. The appearance of Ali at the beginning and end of the récit seems to imply a sexual conflict, not to disclose the urges of a "latent and frustrated homosexual" as Guerard says (*André Gide,* p. 160) but to dramatize Michel's opposition to everything Marceline represents. For Michel this emerging homosexual archetype is the unconscious impulsion of a man who rejects all traditional dependencies by seeking self-sufficiency in his own sex and thus within himself.[14]

Gide has carefully calculated the seasons of the year to coincide with Michel's symbolic death and rebirth in order to convey the total rhythm of the life process. Thus Michel's illness takes on the character of the Dionysian nature myth. Just as the god's life describes a death and birth cycle which corresponds to the seasons of the year, so, too, Michel's illness and symbolic death reach a climax during the fall and winter seasons while his resurrection occurs in the spring.[15] In the archetypal context of Michel's immerging instincts, there is a similarity between Nietzsche's substitution of the Dionysian myth for the Christian mystery and the ascendancy of Menalcas' influence over that of Marceline in Michel's life.[16]

L'Immoraliste begins as a quest to balance certain primal forces in a man's life and develops into an exaggerated program of subduing the spiritual side of life: "je prétendis découvrir l'être authentique, celui dont ne voulait plus l'Evangile; celui que livres, maîtres, parents, et que moi-même avions tâché d'abord de supprimer" (pp. 398-99). Michel's story becomes a descent into an inner hell. A complete shift from the spiritual to the demonic brings Michel face to face with a dark frightening instinctual life which he projects into own life and which he does not understand:

Un démon me possédait.

(p. 459)

En chaque être le pire instinct me paraissait le plus sincère.

(p. 464)

Je ne sais plus le démon ténébreux que je sers.

(p. 467)

The geographical return to North Africa at the end of the novel highlights the power of the demonic archetype. That land which prompted Michel's rebirth becomes an external landscape of a wasted life and of a barren arid soul. Michel's spiritual isolation is rendered graphically by a house physically separated from the regularly traveled routes, accessible only with difficulty, and shut off by a wall: "La route cesse loin du village. Nous montâmes à pied; deux mulets avaient pris nos valises. La maison de Michel est la première du village. Un jardin de murs bas, ou plutôt un enclos l'entoure" (p. 370).

Michel's freedom at the end of the novel is clearly more apparent than real. Each step forward in his search for the archaic man is accompanied by a backward glance towards that which he has suppressed. Michel's greatest error, Gide suggests, rests in believing that freedom exists solely in the exploitation of the instincts. "Parfois, j'ai peur que ce que j'ai supprimé ne se venge" (p. 471), is an understated and ironic lamentation. If the beginning of *L'Immoraliste* represents the revenge of the flesh on an overdeveloped spirit, Michel's "cri d'alarme" and the confession form of the récit substantiate Michel's fear of a spontaneous and natural revenge of the spirit on an overemphasized shadow. Yet, nowhere, does Michel seem to have clear knowledge of the reasons for his dilemma. The récit is the appeal of a tormented soul yearning for an authority outside of the self and follows Michel's pattern of questioning others for the answer to his life.

In *L'Immoraliste* Gide has created a fictional structure reminiscent of ancient tragedy. He suggests the importance of psychological and natural laws in a person's life, and he portrays his characters ironically without depriving them of choice. However, Michel is by no means a tragic victim, and his innocence is constantly called into question by the numerous warnings Gide places along his path. Michel chooses to exaggerate the instinctual side of life to the exclusion of the social and spiritual and consequently freely elects to set himself outside of society. Michel's situation remains pathetic rather than pitiful because he is unwilling to understand or accept that he has overreached his own limits and the boundaries of good sense.

Gide has conceptualized in *L'Immoraliste* a collective phenomenon through a metaphorical language of ritual, myth, and symbol to convey those ancient and obscure signs which we intuit even though we may never fully comprehend or know them. Gide warns that unless the demonic side of a man's nature can be integrated with its spiritual opposite, man will remain, as we find Michel at the end of the novel, a confused distorted and isolated person incapable of pursuing a well-balanced and civilized life.

Notes

1. Germaine Brée emphasizes the role of the unconscious in shaping the direction of Michel's life, *André Gide: L'Insaisissable Protée* (Paris: Société d'édition "Les Belles-Lettres," 1953), p. 158, p. 162, p. 178. Albert Guerard studies the novel in terms of such traditional categories as "psychological novel" and "realistic novel," *André Gide*, 2nd ed. (Cambridge: Harvard University Press, 1969), pp. 99, 101.

2. Recent criticism which has studied Gide's use of myth and symbol has been too narrow in scope to include any complete discussion of *L'Immoraliste*. As the title of her book indicates, *André Gide and the Greek Myth* (Oxford: Oxford University Press, 1967), Helen Watson-Williams does not treat any of Gide's works which are not taken directly from the mythology of Greece. Vinio Rossi deals primarily with the development of Gide's art up to *Paludes* in *André Gide: The Evolution of an Aesthetic* (New Brunswick: Rutgers University Press, 1967) and can only suggest the pattern which myth and symbol take in Gide's later writings. Rossi feels that the terminology "modern parable" more accurately describes a tendency in Gide's novels than the word myth.

3. Northrop Frye's observation on the reappearance of myth in the irony of modern literature applies particularly well to *L'Immoraliste*: "Irony begins in realism and dispassionate observation. But as it does so, it moves steadily towards myth, and dim outlines of sacrificial rituals and dying gods begin to reappear in it," *Anatomy of Criticism* (Princeton: Princeton University Press, 1957), p. 42.

4. The tendency of Gide's characters to be victimized by unfathomable natural laws is most pronounced in his *soties*.

5. A number of critics have remarked that Gide's novels are among the first important examples of a mythopoeic tendency of many modern books. Cf. Wallace Fowlie, *André Gide* (New York: Macmillan, 1965), pp. 48-49 and Rossi, *André Gide*, p. 160.

6. André Gide, *Romans, Récits et Soties, Œuvres lyriques,* ed. Nadeau, Davet, and Thierry (Paris: Gallimard, 1958), p. 433. Subsequent parenthetical page references are to this edition.

7. Brée, *André Gide,* p. 172 sees the Moktir episode as a "révolte sournoise contre l'ordre moral que représente Marceline."

8. "Marceline aimait beaucoup cet enfant; pourtant ce ne fut pas, je crois, la peur de la peiner qui me fit quand je la revis, plutôt que dénoncer Moktir, imaginer je ne sais quelle fable pour expliquer la perte des ciseaux. A partir de ce jour, Moktir devint mon préféré" (p. 395).

9. Gide commented on this "plateau" in the novel, *Romans,* p. 1514.

10. A similar though much briefer lustral ceremony occurs shortly before the expanded version. The process of purification and of subsequent passage are symbolically conveyed through the rather grandiose gestures of washing and of exiting rhrough an open door: "Je me souviens de la dernière nuit. La lune était à peu près pleine dans ma chambre. Je me levai, trempai dans l'eau mes mains et mon visage, puis, poussant la porte vitrée, je sortis" (p. 396).

11. Carl G. Jung, *Modern Man in Search of a Soul,* trans, Dell and Baynes (New York: Harcourt, 1933), p. 25, comments on this traditional meaning of the horse image in literature.

12. Jung's thoughts on the archetypal images of water and fish as symbols of the unconscious have suggested certain of my observations on Gide's use of the images. Cf. Carl G. Jung, *The Archetypes and the Collective Unconscious,* trans. R. F. C. Hull. 2nd ed. (Princeton: Princeton University Press, 1968), IX, 24. Cf. also Northrop Frye, *Anatomy of Criticism,* p. 146.

13. The image of water and the mysterious creatures which inhabit the depths exercised a fascination for Gide in a number of his works, esp. *Le Voyage*

d'Urien, Paludes, and *Les Faux-Monnayeurs.* Sometimes the symbol provides an exterior landscape of a character's inner life and possesses such numerous qualities as translucence, fluidity, or purity as in the "eau lustrale" of *Les Poésies d'André Walter* and opaqueness, stagnancy, or foulness in the case of *Paludes.*

14. For a discussion of this particular interpretation of the homosexual archetype as a retreat towards some primeval hermaphroditic state, cf. Frye, *Anatomy,* p. 149 and Jung, *Archetypes,* p. 71.

15. The marriage trip begun at the end of October marks a decline in Michel's health (p. 22). The illness is intensified during the winter months (p. 48), and Michel regains his strength and experiences his rebirth during the middle of April (p. 60).

16. It has become somewhat commonplace to see affinities between Nietzsche's and Menalcas' Dionysian tendencies. Renée Lang, "Gide and Nietzsche," *Romanic Review* 34 (April 1943), 139-49), and Jean Delay, *La Jeunesse d'André Gide* (Paris: Gallimard, 1956), II, 623-37, have attempted to clear up some of the mystery surrounding Gide's relative knowledge of Nietzsche at the time he wrote *Les Nourritures terrestres* and *L'Immoraliste.* However, W. Wolfgang Holdheim wisely cautions that "Nietzsche, like Freud and Dostoevsky, did not inspire Gide's ideas but merely confirmed them" (p. 59) in *Theory and Practice of the Novel: A Study on André Gide* (Geneva: Droz, 1968), pp. 58-65.

Laurence M. Porter (essay date January 1977)

SOURCE: Porter, Laurence M. "The Generativity Crisis of Gide's *Immoraliste.*" *French Forum* 2, no. 1 (January 1977): 58-69.

[*In the following essay, Porter traces Michel's inability to replace his "imposed identity" with a mature and responsible self. Instead, according to the critic, Michel regresses, unwilling or unable to free himself from parental influences.*]

> Nombreux sont ceux qui attendent que l'écueil les soulève, que le but les franchisse, pour se définir.
>
> René Char, «A la santé du serpent»

The problem of defining personal identity consistently preoccupied Gide. When the naive hero of his early work, *Le Prométhée mal enchaîné,* asks why the Parisians are hurrying about so, his café waiter explains, «ce qu'ils cherchent c'est leur personnalité»[1]. And forty-seven years later, Gide's *Thésée* announces that the essential thing in life is to know exactly who one is. Such knowledge, combined with self-acceptance, was initially not easy to come by for the historical Gide, a Protestant homosexual of genius in what was officially a heterosexual, Catholic society. «Je sens en moi,» he wrote in his *Caractères,* «toujours assemblée, une foule contradictoire; certaines fois, je voudrais agiter la sonnette, me couvrir et quitter la séance» (*OC* [*Oeuvres complètes*] XII, 5-6). And there were times, he confesses, when he found himself unable to write unless he sat next to a mirror, in which he could repeatedly recapture his own elusive image[2].

Gide's typology of identity is neoromantic. It derives from a faith in the self-determined perfectibility of the individual, reflected, for example, in Bergson's contrast between inner self and social self in his 1889 *Essai sur les données immédiates de la conscience*; in Jung's and in Maslow's notions of «self-actualization»; and, in American popular culture, in David Riesman's distinction between «inner-directed» and «other-directed» in *The Lonely Crowd*. Gide contrasts identity, conceived as the object of a quest to fulfill all one's potentialities, with the imposed identity consisting of our family's, friends' and associates' expectations concerning our behavior. In *Le Retour de l'enfant prodigue,* the prodigal explains, «Moi-même je ne suis pas tout entier dans celui que vous vouliez que je fusse. J'imaginais malgré moi d'autres cultures, d'autres terres, et des routes pour y courir, des routes non tracées; j'imaginais en moi l'être neuf que je sentais s'y élancer. Je m'évadai.» And his censorious elder brother replies: «Mais ce que tu ne sauras jamais, c'est la longueur du temps qu'il a fallu à l'homme pour élaborer l'homme. A présent que le modèle est obtenu, tenons-nous-y» (*OC* V, 12-13). The tragedy of Jérôme and Alisse in *La Porte étroite* is to confuse these two modes of identity: each perceives as the goal of his self-fulfillment the exalted image which the other has of him. As Edouard later expressed it in *Les Faux-Monnayeurs,* «involontairement, inconsciemment, chacun des deux êtres qui s'aiment se façonne à cette idole qu'il contemple dans le cœur de l'autre» (*OC* XII, 108).

But as the protagonists of *Le Retour de l'enfant prodigue, La Symphonie pastorale* and *L'Immoraliste* discover to their sorrow, one cannot define oneself merely by recognizing one's imposed identity and then destroying it: «Savoir se libérer n'est rien; l'ardu, c'est savoir être libre»[3]. How others should use their freedom, Gide does not claim to know. The way of self-actualization is different for each person. Nor need it entail the total rejection of the imposed identity, provided that no part of that identity is accepted without having been scrutinized.

At the outset of the narrative in *L'Immoraliste* itself, Michel's imposed identity has been tightly circumscribed. His father has trained Michel to emulate him as an historian and has published one of Michel's essays in his own name to show that their professional abilities are indistinguishable. As he dies, he urges Michel to marry a childhood acquaintance, Marceline, so that he will not be alone. Michel unquestioningly accepts. «Ainsi, j'engageai ma vie sans savoir ce que pouvait être la vie . . . je m'ignorais moi-même. Pas un instant ne me survint l'idée que j'eusse pu mener une existence différente ni qu'on pût vivre différemment» (pp. 373-74).

That his father has made Michel's choices for him posponses but also intensifies his identity crisis. Erik Erikson pithily explains that this «time of breakdown» and of «acute identity diffusion» «usually becomes manifest at a time when the young individual finds himself exposed to a combination of experiences which demand his simultaneous commitment to *physical intimacy,* . . . to decisive *occupational choice,* to *energetic competition,* and to *psychosocial self-definition*» (emphasis Erikson's)[4]. During the honeymoon voyage to North Africa, Michel fleetingly feels a protective pity for Marceline, an awareness of her needs which reveals the possibility of his achieving a transition from narcissism to nurture. «J'avais vécu pour moi ou du moins selon moi jusqu'alors,» he realizes. But the responsibilities of caring for another, although as yet only imagined, overwhelm Michel, deprived as he is of the support of his father's guidance and of his scholarly routines (pp. 375-76). Promptly, before consummating the marriage, he withdraws into an illness which he himself will later admit to be at least in part psychosomatic, although he does not understand its cause[5].

As soon as Michel begins to convalesce, Marceline invites Arab children to come play in their apartment, ostensibly to entertain him (pp. 389-90). «Maternelle et caressante» towards them, she actually wishes to show Michel that she is eager to become a mother and to join him in the enterprise of raising a family. She puts forward the one primal, universal expectation of the imposed identity for humans and other animals: we shall perpetuate the species as our parents did before us. There are other ways of moving from self-absorption towards maturity, but to conceive and care for children *is* the most obvious way[6]. From this perspective, Michel's marriage has raised the question whether he will remain like a child, or follow his parents in orderly succession by raising children of his own.

Facing this decisive issue of early adulthood has been characterized by Erikson as the «generativity crisis.» (Unfortunately for Michel, it comes on top of his identity crisis, rather than, as is more usual, afterwards.) He explains that sexual mates who achieve true mutuality

> will soon wish . . . to combine their personalities and energies in the production and care of common offspring [or in other forms of creativity and altruistic concern which absorb the energies of parental responsibility]. The pervasive [personal] development underlying this wish I have termed *generativity*. . . . Generativity is primarily the interest in establishing and guiding the next generation. This is a stage in the growth of the healthy personality . . . Individuals who do not develop generativity often begin to indulge themselves as if they were their one and only child. The mere fact of having or even wanting children does not of course [necessarily] involve generativity.
>
> (Erikson, «The Healthy Personality,» *op. cit.,* p. 97)

During Michel's convalescence his physical recovery is a legitimate preoccupation: he lacks the energy to devote himself to others. The presence of the Arab children, rather than inspiring him with paternal feelings, stimulates the revival of the impulsive, egotistical child in himself. «Du fond du passé de ma première enfance se réveillaient enfin mille lueurs, mille sensations égarées» (p. 390). At length Michel vicariously rebels against adult restraints when he surreptitiously allows the child Moktir to steal Marceline's little sewing scissors. For the scissors symbolize what could be whimsically called the castrating claims of marriage upon childhood irresponsibility.

As Michel leisurely returns to France, he becomes clearly aware of the distinction between his imposed identity, and identity as the object of a quest. His inherited profession of historian now seems to have only «un rapport tout accidentel et conventionnel» with himself. «Pouvais-je m'intéresser à moi, sinon comme à un être perfectible?» With all the forces of his will, he drives himself towards «cette perfection inconnue et que j'imaginais confusément» (pp. 398, 400).

At first it appears that his search for selfhood can be reconciled with the claims of marriage and of generativity. He finally makes love with Marceline. When they arrive at the Normandy estate he inherited from his mother, she is pregnant. He busies himself with tending that estate and consciously sublimates his revolt against civilized restraints by studying the self-destructive adventures of Athalaric, a teenage Gothic king (p. 407). But Gide underlines several enduring obstacles to Michel's maturation. First of all, Michel had been unconsciously stimulated to have intercourse with Marceline by his fight with a drunken coachman earlier the same day. The homosexual implications of this juxtaposition of events are stressed by the parallel scene in Italy, during Michel's return voyage to Africa, when he kisses a coachman impulsively[7]. Second, Michel suspects that his estate manager Bocage is conspiring with the tenant farmers to cheat him by replacing his healthy livestock with their sick animals. Whether or not this suspicion—never definitely confirmed—is justified, it points to Michel's underlying resentment: having possessions with their attendant responsibilities makes him feel exploited by others. And finally, Michel's experience of severe illness and the threat of death have left him with a child's instinctive, self-centered horror of any physical blemish or weakness. This horror and resentment flow together when Michel's friends abuse his furniture in Paris. He complains: «Meubles, étoffes, estampes, à la première tache perdaient pour moi toute valeur; choses tachées, choses atteintes de maladie et comme désignées par la mort» (p. 430). Desperately, Michel multiplies his commitments in an attempt to subdue the desire to forswear them. But such repression only makes his intermittent outbursts of egotism the more violent. When Marceline's health fails, Michel callously observes: «la maladie était entrée en Marceline, l'habitait désormais, la marquait, la tachait. C'était une chose abîmée» (p. 439).

Meanwhile, Michel's lectures at the Collège de France anticipate the thesis of Freud's *Civilization and Its Discontents,* but go further by lauding *l'inculture* with evangelistic enthusiasm. Thus he argues against the very institution which provides a *raison d'être* for his imposed identity, but he lacks an alternative self-concept. «Qu'entendais-je par: vivre?—C'est précisément ce que j'aurais voulu qu'on m'apprît» (p. 423). His lectures constitute an unwitting appeal for the surrogate father who will provide such guidance. And the adventurer Ménalque (who had disappeared from France shortly before Michel's marriage, and about when Michel's father died) promptly materializes to fill this role. That Ménalque is inherited from Vergil, La Bruyère, and Gide's own **Nourritures terrestres** makes him appear more allegorical than real. Because he has followed on Michel's traces in Africa, asking questions, he seems in part to represent Michel's own mind looking back on his recent experiences and pondering what meaning the convictions expressed in his lectures might have for his life. Michel at once feels himself strongly drawn to Ménalque «par une secrète influence» (p. 425).

Shortly before publishing **L'Immoraliste,** Gide had written the perspicacious essay «De l'influence en littérature.» There he declared that the power of an influence «vient de ceci qu'elle ne fait que me révéler quelque partie de moi encore inconnue à moi-même; elle n'a été pour moi qu'une explication . . . Les influences agissent par ressemblance» (*OC* III, 256-57). And indeed Michel recognizes, in Ménalque's words during their second conversation, an echo of his own desire—thus far suppressed—to attack his imposed identity[8]. Ménalque defines the latter lucidly: «chacun se propose un patron, puis l'imite; même il ne choisit pas le patron qu'il imite; il accepte un patron tout choisi . . . Lois de l'imitation; je les appelle: lois de la peur. On a peur de se trouver seul; et l'on ne se trouve pas du tout. . . . Ce que l'on sent en soi de différent, c'est précisément ce que l'on possède de rare, ce qui fait à chacun sa valeur» (pp. 431-32).

The eve of Ménalque's departure from France, Michel stays out all night to have a third and similar conversation with him. On the way home, Michel's weakening impulse towards generativity appears to be struggling successfully against his destructive impulses: «je me cramponnais à mon douteux bonheur . . . je ne pouvais, hélas! en écarter l'inquiétude, mais prétendais que cette inquiétude servît d'aliment à l'amour. Je me penchais vers l'avenir où déjà je voyais mon petit enfant me sourire; pour lui se reformait et se fortifiait ma morale» (p. 437). But as Freud pointed out in «Mourning and Melancholia»[9], unspecified anxiety («inquiétude» above) concerning loved ones often derives from repressed hostility towards them. By the defensive strategy of reaction-formation—that is, by opposing an inadmissible feeling with its exaggerated contrary—one unconsciously transforms a desire to kill one's encumbering family into a solicitous desire lest they be killed. One assumes an overly-protective role. Michel will later come to understand this psychic mechanism well: «comme d'autres ravivent leur foi en en exagérant les pratiques, ainsi développai-je mon amour» (p. 455. One thinks of Emma Bovary's sporadic, melodramatic episodes of parenting and praying). But the requirements of such roles augment one's feeling of being trapped and feed the very anger against which they were intended to defend. Here in the magical world of the novel, Michel's secret wishes have had a real effect: Marceline has a miscarriage during his absence. Thus Michel forfeits his opportunity for developing generativity by raising a child.

Subconsciously, Michel sees no gains in renouncing adolescence for adulthood. Childhood, when healthy and non-conformist, seems to him a period of limitless potentiality. He clings to it by associating with boys whom he rejects when they begin to mature. His manager's son Charles, a constant companion during his first summer on the Normandy estate, strikes Michel as oppressively formal and dignified the next year. So he seeks out Charles' criminal younger brother Alcide instead. He poaches off his own land (metaphorical self-destructiveness and auto-eroticism); neglects his estate; puts it up for sale; and sets off for Africa. There he seeks unawares the children he had played with two years earlier. But their having grown up dismays him. «Ils ont affreusement grandi . . . Quels travaux vils ont déjeté si tôt ces beaux corps? . . . Que les carrières honorables abêtissent» (p. 466). His «intolérable tristesse» at this encounter is the counterpart of the protagonist's joy in Thomas Mann's *Death in Venice,* when he realizes that Tadzio will never survive to manhood. For Michel's unconscious pederasty is rooted in a regressive narcissism and the vain hope of recapturing lost childhood. (Such feelings, of course, often help motivate our interests in those of either sex much younger than ourselves—children and students as well as paramours.)

I do not wish to imply that Michel's fascination with childhood energy is intrinsically undesirable. On the contrary, his African sun-baths and Normandy horseback rides reflect a wholesome vitality. Only when Michel directs this force against his own commitments does it become self-destructive and decline through anarchy (see p. 449) to a final entropy. He believes that through the magic of similarity and contagion, his return to the natural wildness of the African landscape, to a sterile place free from the obligation to grow things, will foster his personal freedom. But Gide himself knew better. The same year he published *L'Immoraliste,* he wrote: «Le vrai retour à la nature, c'est le définitif retour aux éléments: la mort. . . . Comment, pourquoi, ne pas comprendre que ces deux 'naturels'—extérieur et intime—s'opposent?» («**Les Limites de l'art,**» *OC* II, 405).

Among the Arab boys Michel rejoins, only the former scissors-stealer Moktir, unemployed and just released from prison, still corresponds to Michel's ideal of independence. When Michel again abandons his wife overnight, to talk with Moktir and to sleep with Moktir's mistress (latent homosexual sharing), Marceline has a fatal hemmorhage. Her death ends his opportunities for unselfish commitment. Release from responsibility for her consummates his loss of identity. Alone, he spends his days holding cool pebbles in his hands until they become warm, and then replacing them with others. This metaphor of fragmentation and aimless repetition, like the peas shifted from pan to pan in Camus's *La Peste,* or like the incoherent heapings evoked by Baudelaire's Spleen poems, symbolizes dispersion of the forces of Michel's personality. After telling his friends his story, he exclaims: «Quelque chose en ma volonté s'est brisé. . . . Arrachez-moi d'ici à présent, et donnez-moi des raison d'être. Moi, je ne sais plus en trouver» (p. 471).

The confessional compulsion which serves as *prétexte* for the novel is inherently narcissistic: it shows Michel trapped in the past[10]. He never has really freed himself sufficiently from his father's disproportionate influence, embodied in the imposed identity, and from his mother's influence, embodied in his nostalgia for childhood, sufficiently to be able to elaborate an alternative but positive ideal. Therefore his drive towards autonomy assumes a destructive and self-destructive form. He seeks a surrogate father to tell him what to believe; he becomes a sorcerer's apprentice to Ménalque; he is pathetically vulnerable to his idol's self-assured assertions of value. But, more often than not, Michel feels too weak to try to live by these values: from Ménalque's example he derives mainly self-contempt: «la vie, le moindre geste de Ménalque, n'était-il pas plus éloquent mille fois que mon cours?» (p. 429). When the energy of his revolt has dissipated, the outcome of his generativity crisis is a regression, to an inverted, fixated version of the father-son relationship. Through his indulgent cherishing of the Arab child who keeps him company at the end of the novel, Michel tries futilely and unwittingly both to exorcise and to perpetuate his parents' influence. Impelled by misdirected paternal instincts and vicarious narcissism, Michel tries to re-enact under more favorable circumstances his own childhood. He attempts to undo his father's domination by reversing the roles in retrospect. *He* will be the person who influences; a younger person will become the one influenced; but *he* unlike his father will allow this young person to develop freely, without the oppressive expectation that his quasi-child will imitate *him.*

Such regression need not inevitably assume the overtly homosexual form it comes to assume in Michel. Gide himself, who displays a much greater imaginative range in character portrayal than that with which he has usually been credited, depicts a heterosexually-oriented retreat from generativity quite clearly in **La Symphonie pastorale.** The pastor's enthusiastic endorsement of Christ's saying that one must become like a little child in order to enter the kingdom of heaven functions to justify his self-indulgence in devoting himself to Gertrude: and it is placed in the text shortly before the pastor's impatient expression of lack of interest in his own small children (*OC* IX, 63, 66-69, especially 68)[11]. But Gide of course more frequently discusses homosexual feelings in his writing; in part because social condemnation transformed them into a continual irritant and an insoluble problem.

The process through which a homosexual orientation like Michel's can develop has been cogently analyzed by Freud, who says that at some point in childhood «the boy represses his love for his mother; he puts himself in her place, identifies himself with her, and takes his own person as a model in whose likeness he chooses the objects of his love. In this way he becomes a homosexual.» Michel's unnatural compliance to his father's wishes suggests that such a substitution of son for mother has occurred. And Michel reveals this progression in himself clearly when he says that he assimilated his mother's Puritan religious fervor (itself sublimated eroticism) and assiduousness only to redirect it to his studies, and later to the restoration of his body (pp. 373, 401). Freud continues:

> What he has in fact done is to slip back to autoeroticism; for the boys whom he now loves as he grows up are after all only substitutive figures and revivals of himself in childhood—boys whom he loves in the way in which his mother loved *him* when he was a child. He finds the objects of his love along the path of *narcissism* . . . [and] remains unconsciously fixated to the mnemic image of his mother. By repressing his love for his mother he preserves it in his unconscious and from now on remains faithful to her.
>
> [«Leonardo da Vinci and a Memory of His Childhood»]

One remembers that this tendency was explicitly encouraged by the mother of André Walther. As she lay dying, she asked André to renounce Emmanuèle to T*** (*OC* I, 29-30). Likewise, the horrified reaction of Gide's own mother put an end to his sleeping with an Arab prostitute, shortly before his initiation to homosexual practices[12]. Freud continues:

> While he seems to pursue boys and to be their lover, he is in reality running away from the other woman, who might cause him to be unfaithful . . . [He] is in fact attracted by women in the same way as a normal man; but on each occasion he hastens to transfer the excitation he has received from women on to a male object[13]

In fact this pattern appears at the end of ***L'Immoraliste***: Michel begins by sleeping with an attractive courtesan, but then becomes more interested in her jealous little brother, Ali, and sends her away.

Some critics tax Michel with hypocrisy, claiming that his elegant language and the pervasive structuring of the tale betray his calculated, conscious attempt to evade responsibility for his actions by implying a fatality beyond his control. But this accusation makes a naive confusion between the implied author and the protagonist granted narrative authority. «The problem for the novelist [in the confessional novel] is to keep his narrator . . . self-deluded, imperceptive, blind; incapable of accurate self-analysis—yet have that narrator supply all the evidence necessary to the reader's understanding» (Guérard [*André Gide*], p. 110).

The point is that fiction simultaneously serves two opposing purposes: to express fantasies and to control them. To put it another way, fiction mediates between the pleasure-principle and the reality-principle. Gide, perhaps more complexly than any author of a confessional novel since Goethe in *The Sorrows of Young Werther,* multiplies distinctions between the two resulting viewpoints, with a rich repertory of devices: the ironic detachment of the title (imagine it with a Voltairian twist: «Michel: ou l'immoralisme»); overt structural divisions dissociated from the narrator's control; glaring contradictions in the narrator's self-judgments; consciously unmotivated shifts in the linguistic encoding of the tale; changing tastes and changing friendships of the narrator, tracing a descent from order to anarchy; the ironic juxtaposition of the narrator's description and advocacy of his own life-plan, with its trivial, base, or disastrous outcome; and a narrative frame of preface and epilogue.

Obviously Michel does deceive himself. Despite his protestations to the contrary, he suffers from a guilt he would prefer to evade: «A présent que, dans mon désœuvrement, le passé détesté reprend sa force . . . parfois j'ai peur que ce que j'ai supprimé [culture, décence, morale] ne se venge» (pp. 458, 471). But the structural ordering principles of the *récit* express the inexorable logic of unconscious drives rather than Michel's defensive creation of a simulated fatality which can be blamed for his misdoings. For example, the division of the tale into three sections and twelve chapters cannot plausibly be attributed to Michel, who is telling the story out loud in the course of a single night. Those divisions are the creation of the implied author, who is suggesting that beneath Michel's genuine confusion lies an implacable inner deterioration of which he is unaware. Michel's self-contradictory reaction to his own account of himself forces us to acknowledge the coexistence of two levels, conscious and unconscious: «En vain chercherais-je à présent à imposer à mon récit plus d'ordre qu'il n'y en eut dans ma vie . . . Ah! désembarrasser mon esprit de cette insupportable logique» (p. 464)[14].

Without Michel's intending it, frequent shifts from past to present tense reveal his rising excitement as he relives those moments in the past where his instinctual life became dominant: his discovery that «being is occupation enough» as he recovers from his sickness; his rescue of Marceline; his overt rejection of her religious beliefs; his trapping the poacher Alcide; his decision to sell La Morinière; his cruel remark that «only the strong deserve sympathy»; his fury when Marceline becomes too sick to enjoy flowers; and his yielding himself up to the delights of sun and barbarism upon his return to Africa. All these are impulsive moments when he is «living in the present» with full spontaneity.

As soon as Michel attempts to formulate a justification of his unreflective, self-indulgent life-style, however, Gide's implied author undercuts it. To write a new chapter in his life, Michel returns to Tunis, «terre de volupté,» dragging along after him the sick and exhausted Marceline. He justifies the failure of his own creativity and generativity, and his amoral unconcern for her, with the *topos* that life should resemble a work of art. «Tunis . . . Terre en vacance d'œuvres d'art. Je méprise ceux qui ne savent reconnaître la beauté que transcrite déjà et toute interprétée. Le peuple arabe a ceci d'admirable que, son art, il le vit, il le chante et le dissipe au jour le jour; il ne le fixe point et ne l'embaume en aucune œuvre» (pp. 464-65). In other words, forcefulness and originality, rather than a sense of human solidarity, gives actions their merit: one admires «un beau crime.» But Gide's next paragraph deflates Michel's pretensions. He puts his philosophy into action by sleeping on mats outdoors among the Arabs, and comes home in the morning covered with vermin. Similarly, the degeneracy and premature death of the barbarian Athalaric passes judgment on Michel's newfound preference for him rather than for classical Roman civilization[15].

In the course of his liberation, Michel sacrifices all that embodies the demands of maturation and responsibility—wife, career, possession. He gains nothing in return. He thought that abandoning Europe for Africa was the supreme expression of his will, but its freedom has become a prison: «je souffre de cette liberté sans emploi» (p. 471). Uneasy with the outcome, he reactivates an adolescent pact and summons three school friends from distant lands to hear him. This narrative framework has been called awkward and artificial[16]. On the contrary, it is in keeping with the situation for Michel to revive adolescent relationships, dominant in his emotional life before his marriage, shortly after his wife dies. For he returns to an earlier stage of his development. True to his practice of underlining the meaning of crucial episodes by reduplicating them, Gide reinforces the meaning of the frame situation by having Michel and Ménalque also spend a night talking as the result of a pact. And the association of night with regression and with Michel's preferring men to Marceline recurs in his escapades with Alcide, with the Arabs outside the café, and with Moktir.

The revival of adolescent friendships conceals a layer of deeper regression. Michel wishes his friends to absolve and counsel him. His self-absorbed confessional ritual is essentially an appeal to his hearers to replace the lost or rejected parents (see note 10). Michel's friends play along: they appeal to an influential father-figure back in France to find a worthwhile occupation for Michel and to tell him what to do. No doubt their well-meaning intervention, with which *L'Immoraliste* chronologically ends (p. 369), will be ineffectual. They don't understand Michel's need for a quest-identity. They can only imagine a new imposed identity for Michel, «something to do» to serve society and justify his existence in others' eyes. But Michel's problem is precisely to reconcile the service of self with the service of others[17]. Michel's salvation would have to come from within. He has moved from a compliant to an aggressive to a withdrawn strategy for relating to others[18]. But his dramatically-changing styles of behavior are all unbalanced and betoken no actual progress towards maturation.

Gide knew that to define a problem was not to solve it. His later works continue to struggle with the question of personal identity. «Se connaître,» he wrote in 1922 (***Journal*** for February 10th), «c'est bien la dernière chose à laquelle l'artiste doit prétendre; et il ne peut y arriver que par ses œuvres, qu'en les produisant»[19]. Not till twenty-five years after ***L'Immoraliste*** did Gide fully actualize his own impulses towards generativity. His courageous self-disclosure in ***Si le grain ne meurt*** aimed in part, altruistically, at fostering more tolerant social attitudes towards sexuality; he at last became a father; and in his African travel journal he protested eloquently and effectively against an oppressive paternalism writ large, the abuses of French colonialism. The later Gide lucidly defended individual freedom against authoritarian ideologies—Catholic, Communist, and Fascist. The vehement reactions of the spokesmen for those ideologies reveal that Gide, self-centered as he at times appears, nevertheless had a broad influence on society. «C'est une mesure du sens très particulier qu'avait Gide d'une sorte de mutation de la société visible dans de nouveaux 'styles de vie' qu'il réaffirme la place de l'individu et de la vie quotidienne comme élément moteur de l'aventure collective. D'où son pouvoir d'irritant malgré l'aspect en apparence marginale de son œuvre à une époque de 'grande histoire'»[20]. For Gide, social concern came increasingly to supplant the inner stage of prose fiction as a place to perform and to witness the quest for identity: and for his last twenty-five years, he could virtually abandon writing novels.

Notes

1. André Gide, *Oeuvres complètes,* edited by Louis Martin-Chauffier, 15 vols. (Paris: Nouvelle Revue Française, 1932-39). III, 104. Henceforth abbreviated *OC.*

2. Gide, *Journal, 1939-49* (Paris: Gallimard, 1954), p. 514 (*Si le grain ne meurt*).

3. Gide, *Romans; récits et soties; œuvres lyriques* (Paris: Gallimard, 1966), p. 372. This sentence comes from *L'Immoraliste* (pp. 367-472), henceforth referred to by page numbers alone. Many important passages omitted from the final version are found on pp. 1519-36. Note that the recently-published *Récit de Michel* (Neuchâtel: Ides et Calendes, 1972) has nothing to do with *L'Immoraliste.* It relates the debauchery of a shop-girl as told to Gide by his friend Michel Yell (pseudonym for Jules Iehl).

4. Erik H. Erikson, «The Problem of Ego Identity,» in his *Identity and the Life Cycle. Selected Papers* (in *Psychological Issues* I, no. 1, 1959), p. 123.

5. «Je pense, quand j'y réfléchis aujourd'hui, qu'un trouble nerveux général s'ajoutait à la maladie; je ne puis expliquer autrement une série de phénomènes, irréductibles, me semble-t-il, au simple état tuberculeux» (p. 386). As late as the return journey to France, says Michel, «mon état nerveux amenait des troubles fréquents» (p. 397). Cf. Thomas Cordle, *André Gide* (New York: Twayne, 1969), pp. 85-86.

6. Twenty years later, less afraid of disclosing his sexual orientation, Gide suggests in *Les Faux-Monnayeurs* an idealistic homosexual relationship across generations—that of Olivier and Edouard—as a possible substitute for biologically-determined parenting.

7. Albert Guérard mentions several such parallels and observes that «the changed Michel is compelled to return to the same places and experi-

ences, if only to discover how he has changed,» *André Gide* (Cambridge: Harvard University Press, 1969), p. 116.

8. Concerning Ménalque, cf. Justin O'Brien, *Portrait of André Gide* (New York: Knopf, 1953), pp. 171-72. With regard to the hypothesis that Michel seeks outside support for what he wishes to do anyway, compare Gide's self-revealing comments concerning Flaubert's composition of *Salammbô*: «Il me paraît que Flaubert, dans les textes sur lesquels il s'appuie, n'a jamais tant cherché une documentation qu'une autorisation. Par horreur de la réalité quotidienne, il s'est épris surtout de ce qui en différait. Croit-il vraiment avec Théophraste que les escarboucles soient 'formés de l'urine de lynx?' Certes non! mais il se réjouit de ce qu'un texte de Théophraste l'autorise à feindre d'y croire; et ainsi du reste,» *Journal, 1889-1939* (Paris: Gallimard, 1948), p. 266—entry for April 9, 1908.

9. *The Standard Edition of the Complete Psychoanalytical Works of Sigmund Freud,* edited by James Strachey, 23 vols. (London: Hogarth Press, 1953-66): XIV, 243-58. Henceforth abbreviated *SE*.

10. I discuss this idea at length in the companion article «Autobiography versus Confessional Novel: Gide's *Immoraliste* and *Si le grain ne meurt*,» *Symposium,* 30 (1976), 144-59.

11. Concerning praise of childlikeness as a symptom of emotional regression, see the detailed, compellingly-argued article by M.D. Faber on «The Suicide of Young Werther,» *Psychoanalytic Review,* 60 (1973), 239-76.

12. Jean Delay offers a penetrating psychologically oriented account of the period in Gide's life reflected in *L'Immoraliste,* in his *La Jeunesse d'André Gide,* 2 vols. (Paris: Gallimard, 1956-57): II, 128-592 (in the one-volume English edition, pp. 289-482).

13. Freud, «Leonardo da Vinci and a Memory of His Childhood,» *SE* XI, 100. See also «The Sexual Aberrations,» in *Three Essays on the Theory of Sexuality, SE* VII, 145, note 2; and «Some Neurotic Mechanisms in Jealousy, Paranoia and Homosexuality,» *SE* XVIII, 230.

14. See Göran Schildt's sensitive *Gide et l'homme* (Paris: Mercure de France, 1949): chapter six, «La Psychologie de Gide,» pp. 169-98. Gide's major accomplishment as a writer, Schildt argues convincingly, was that he learned how to depict protagonists whose consciousness is only an embroidery on the surface of their being.

15. Shortly after *L'Immoraliste* appeared, Gide categorically condemned the behavior of its protagonist as anarchical, childish, cruel, and vile (letter to Arthur Fontaine, 8 July 1902, cited by O'Brien, pp. 175-76). This judgment may have been influenced by Gide's strenuous attempt at self-discipline at the outset of his marriage.

16. By Pierre Lafille in *Gide romancier* (Paris: Hachette, 1954), p. 23.

17. Camus neatly epitomized this dilemma in his story «Jonas, ou l'artiste au travail,» in *L'Exil et le royaume*. The artist's last painting is one small, blurred word. No one can tell whether it reads «solidaire» or «solitaire.»

18. See Karen Horney, *Our Inner Conflicts: A Constructive Theory of Neurosis* (New York: Norton, 1945); her *Neurosis and Human Growth: The Struggle toward Self-Realization* (New York: Norton, 1950); and Bernard J. Paris, *A Psychological Approach to Fiction* (Bloomington: Indiana University Press, 1974), chapter two.

19. Cited by Daniel Moutote, *Le Journal d'André Gide et les problèmes du moi (1889-1925)* (Montpellier: Imprimerie Universitaire, 1968), p. 637. Moutote's fine conclusion (pp. 637-41) inspired mine here.

20. Germaine Brée, «Gide et l'histoire,» *ECr* [*L'Esprit Créateur*], 15 (1975), 317-18. For similar views, see Jean Hytier, «André Gide et l'esthétique de la personnalité,» *RHL* [*Revue d'Histoire Littéraire de la France*], 70 (1970), 230-43.

John T. Booker (essay date 1977-78)

SOURCE: Booker, John T. "*The Immoralist* and the Rhetoric of First-Person Narration." *Studies in 20th Century Literature* 2 (1977-78): 5-22.

[*In the following essay, Booker argues that the formal structure of* The Immoralist *needs to be assessed from the perspective of time, not just in terms of the architecture of the novel. In doing so, the critic shows that Gide's narrative is not nearly as symmetrical as critics contend.*]

Published in 1902, Gide's **The Immoralist** seems almost to straddle two centuries without belonging clearly to either, a position analogous to its place in a long line of short first-person novels in France. By its general form and plot, it is inevitably compared to *Manon Lescaut* and *Adolphe,* earlier memoir-novels in which a troubled narrator relates from retrospect a liaison or marriage that ended unhappily in the death of the woman, and in that sense Gide's novel belongs to a fictional cycle that dates from the early eighteenth century. From our perspective today, on the other hand, **The Im-**

moralist appears to open a series of modern novels in which the narrator's awareness of the impact of his story upon reader or listener—and hence his own sincerity or credibility—are questions of central importance; in that respect, Michel's narration can be seen as a very subtle preview of that of Clamence in *The Fall*.

The Immoralist owes this pivotal place in a certain line of French fiction to its narrative structure, which marks it unmistakably as a work of our century. Michel's story shows the essential characteristics of "discourse," as Emile Benveniste has defined and studied it: "any enunciation involving a speaker and a listener, and on the part of the former the intention of influencing the other in some way."[1] The rhetorical bias to which Benveniste calls attention has in fact come to be recognized as one of the real points of interest in ***The Immoralist*** and the question of the narrator's reliability is raised very early in the story by Michel's claim to speak in an open and straightforward manner: "I am going to tell you my life simply," he assures his three friends, "without modesty and without pride, more simply than if I were talking to myself."[2] What has not been pointed out, however, is just how clearly the development of Michel's story calls into question the traditional basis of the narrative process itself, the conditions and limitations—and even the temptations—faced by anyone who undertakes to recount from hindsight his own experiences. A close look at the structure of Michel's account, and in particular the way it evolves to reflect the shifting temporal relationship between the past of events narrated and the present of their narration, provides insight not only into his own self-interested motives, but also into the very rhetoric of first-person narration.

Michel's story is framed in a rather standard way: after a period of three years during which he has not seen his three close friends, he calls them to his side, according to the terms of a pact to which all had subscribed as schoolmates, and in the course of one evening he tells them what has happened since they last saw him at his wedding. One of the three listeners, having apparently (if implausibly) transcribed Michel's account, addresses it, along with his own ambivalent reactions, to his brother, and it is this transcription that we read as the core of the novel.

Michel's story itself is an eventful one. The marriage to Marceline, one autumn, is followed by an extended trip to North Africa, in the course of which Michel falls seriously ill. Through Marceline's care and his own fierce determination to live, he not only recovers, but experiences something of a rebirth, a new awakening to the sensual side of life. The following spring, Michel's recuperation complete, the couple decides to pass the coming summer and autumn at La Morinière, his property in Normandy, where he can finish preparations for a course on the last years of the Gothic Empire that he is to give at the Collège de France. The summer and fall at La Morinière form a period of contentment and stability, as Michel, supervising the working of the property, pursues a balance between the "fecundity of nature and the wise effort of man to regulate it" ([***The Immoralist***] p. 61) and formulates a corresponding code of personal ethics "which should institute the scientific and perfect utilization of a man's self by a controlling intelligence" (p. 61). At the same time, however, he acknowledges a growing admiration for the "rude ethics of the Goths" (p. 71), an admiration that surfaces in the course he gives in Paris during the winter. It is at Paris as well that he comes to have a series of philosophical discussions with an old acquaintance, Ménalque, who espouses a Nietzschean ethic of the strong, an ethic to which Michel himself is already inclined. While Michel is spending a night in such discussion with Ménalque, Marceline loses the child she was carrying and falls ill herself. In the spring, they move back to La Morinière, but Michel, instead of cultivating the property, now spends the summer and autumn roaming with poachers of his own game whose "Gothic" nature he clearly admires, and finally puts the farm up for sale. He then takes Marceline on a hectic trip, through Switzerland and Italy, back to North Africa, in what he wants to believe is an effort to restore her health. She finally dies the following spring—from the illness, from the rigors of the trip, and from Michel's brutal attitude—and he remains a pathetic, spiritless man, appealing to his friends to help him pull together the pieces of his life and make a new start.

The symmetrical movement of the story—from North Africa to La Morinière to Paris to La Morinière and back to North Africa—is reinforced by the formal structure of the narration. Michel's account is divided into three parts: the first, broken into nine chapters, recounts the initial trip to Africa; the second is composed of three chapters which relate respectively the periods spent at La Morinière, Paris, and again La Morinière; the third part, not divided into chapters—which is of some significance, as we shall see—recounts the return trip to North Africa. The result is what critics commonly cite as the ternary division of the work into an ascent, a levelling-off or plateau, and a fall, which can be represented this way:

I	II	III
	Paris	
	La Morinière La Morinière	
North Africa		North Africa

Just how to reconcile the general symmetry of this formal structure with the fact that Michel is supposed to tell his story orally and at a single sitting is an interesting question. Actually, it is difficult not to attribute the division into parts and chapters to the implied author or to Gide himself (depending on the frame of reference chosen), unless one grasps at the unlikely possibility that they are introduced by the listener who sends the story on to his brother. The real significance of the formal structure continues to be debated by critics. Albert Sonnenfeld sees "the fearful symmetry of *L'Immoraliste*" undermining the verisimilitude of the novel itself and argues that "Michel's uninterrupted and excessively symmetrical narrative, while admirable in its perfection of composition, does not come to grips with the problematic of creation and reading . . ."[3] For Allan H. Pasco, the "excessively rigorous composition" indicates instead the unreliability of the narrator: "Because one can scarcely fail to perceive the artificially rigid structure of Michel's story and to note the discrepancy between it and his pretensions to simplicity, the structure becomes an ironic device for betraying the untrustworthiness of this most unreliable narrator."[4] Pasco's contentions have been countered by Laurence M. Porter, who maintains that the glaringly obvious structure of the work is to be attributed, not to the narrator, but to the implied author, and that it serves to highlight, not conscious deception on the part of Michel, but rather motives (and a resulting "destiny") of which Michel himself is not entirely aware: "the structural ordering principles of the *récit*," argues Porter, "express the inexorable logic of unconscious drives rather than Michel's defensive creation of a simulated fatality which can be blamed for his misdoings."[5]

While these critical approaches are all well argued, they share the common limitation of considering formal structure only in an "architectural" sense, independent of the temporality inherent in Michel's narration—and in the reader's experience of that narration. Such arguments provide a synchronic overview (or "picture," as in the diagram above) that may be quite helpful in grasping the general form of the work once it has been read, but they do not take sufficiently into account the fact that narration and reading are essentially diachronic in nature, unfolding progressively in time. In fact, when we examine more closely the way Michel's narration actually develops, we find important indications that it is *not* as symmetrical as has often been claimed.

In order to appreciate not only what we come to reconstruct from retrospect as the novel's formal structure, but the gradual development of the narration itself, we should begin by looking closely at the temporal relationships set up in Michel's story. He tells his story on what must be July 18th or thereabouts, since the listener's letter to his brother, dated July 30th, states that they have been with Michel for twelve days (p. 3) and that Michel related his story the night of their arrival (pp. 5-6). Although both the listener (p. 4) and Michel himself (p. 7) mention three years as the period of time since the wedding, it would seem that the marriage must have taken place in October, not July, for the couple leaves directly for the trip and arrives in Tunis the last day of October (p. 13). The events of Michel's story take place, then, over some thirty-three months of fictional time.

Within this span of fictional time, the events recounted in Part I (the first trip to Africa) occupy nine months, the couple returning to France to settle down at La Morinière "in the first days of July" (p. 59). The events of Part II run over a period of about sixteen months, from that July to what must be early November over a year later, for when the following mid-January is eventually mentioned in Part III, Michel and Marceline have already been in Switzerland for two months (p. 126), at the start of the return trip to North Africa. The fictional time represented in Part III then runs from that November to Marceline's death in April (p. 136), an event separated in turn from the moment of Michel's narration by "barely three months" (p. 143).

This span of fictional time, with the division into parts in the formal structure, can be represented quite simply (to scale, in this case):

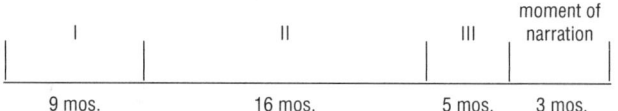

One might argue at this point that the periods of fictional time comprising Michel's story still form a roughly symmetrical pattern—the two trips framing the longer period of La Morinière and Paris—but the very perception of that pattern depends once again on one's perspective. While the symmetry may seem apparent from a detached point of view—that normally assumed by the omniscient narrator of a third-person novel, for example, and represented by the eye of anyone looking down at the time line above—it may not be obvious at all to the first-person narrator whose viewpoint is anchored in a particular moment of fictional time and hence quite limited. Michel, obliged to look "back along" that time line, as it were, rather than down on it, can hardly share the synchronic perspective enjoyed by the detached observer.

What makes Michel's narration particularly interesting, in fact, is the shrinking interval between the fictional time of the events he relates and his own moment of narration. More than two years have elapsed since his own illness and recovery, for example, while barely three months separate him from the death of Marceline. In spite of his assertion that "Those three months have put a distance of ten years between that time and this" (p. 143), one would expect his narration to reflect quite a difference in effect between the events of such a recent period and those of a much earlier one. In short, the events of Parts I and III, which might seem to the privileged observer to fall into such a neat pattern, are likely to be far from "symmetrical" in their impact upon Michel.

Theoretically speaking, a shifting interval between time of events and the moment at which they are related would seem to affect the resulting narration in two different ways. The longer the interval, on the one hand, the less the narrator should be able to recall of the past; intervening time should act as a filter, screening out unexceptional incidents and leaving only the more striking events around which to build a story. On the other hand, an increased interval should allow the narrator to reflect upon his past experiences with more detachment and perspective, to see himself more objectively, and to evaluate his actions in a more disinterested manner. Should the resulting image prove too distasteful, however, it may well prompt the narrator to arrange his version of events with a view to presenting himself to listener or reader in a better light. While a longer interval between past and present would seem to favor a narrator's lucidity, then, it does not necessarily assure his sincerity or credibility.

In the case of *The Immoralist*, Parts I and III—for all of their apparent symmetry—reflect quite clearly the effects of such a shrinking interval between the narrator's past and his present. Michel himself acknowledges at several points the varying degree of control he exercises over his story. In Part I, for example, he notes his careful reflection on early developments: "I think, when I come to reflect on it today, that, in addition to my illness, I was suffering from a general nervous derangement" (p. 27). He also admits at times, if only in passing, that he has consciously ordered this part of his account: "I am going to speak at length of my body. I shall speak of it so much you will think at first I have forgotten my soul. This omission, as I tell you my story, is intentional; out there, it was a fact" (p. 26), or again, quite simply: "I shall not speak of every stage of the journey" (p. 41). These early comments are certainly innocuous enough; there is little to suggest at this stage that the ordering of the story reflects Michel's desire to sway the reader's interpretation of events. The one remark in the first part that may make the attentive reader uneasy is Michel's admission that he has embellished his account of certain thoughts reported from the early days of his recovery: "I did not think all this at the time, and my description gives a false idea of me. In reality, I did not think at all . . ." (p. 44). But the most revealing indications of just how carefully Michel has organized the first part of his story come only much later and indirectly, in Part III, when he seems no longer able to make the necessary effort: "It would be useless for me to try at present to impose on my story more order than there was in my life. Long enough I've sought to tell you how I became who I am. Ah, to rid my mind of this unbearable logic! I feel nothing in me that isn't noble."[6] This brusque revelation is echoed by a second, a few pages later: "Oh, here I might deceive you or be silent—but what use can this story be to me if it ceases to be truthful?" (p. 141). These "explosions" of pent-up feelings, amounting to indirect admissions that Michel *has* carefully ordered portions of his story, should make the reader wonder at that point if he has accepted too naively or too unquestioningly the narrator's version of earlier events.

If these last comments seem to mark a point in his story where Michel's conscious control gives way rather suddenly to impulsive feelings, that process is actually much more gradual and subtle, and much more difficult to plot in exact terms. It is nevertheless apparent that Part I, by its general composition and tone, is in fact more controlled and ordered than Part III. Part I is marked, for instance, by numerous cases of foretelling, where the narrator, from his present vantage point, offers the listener or reader momentary insights into developments yet to be related: "The excessive tranquility of the life I led weakened, while at the same time it protected, me. Marceline, on the contrary, seemed strong—that she was stronger than I we were very soon to learn" (p. 10); "I read Christ's words to Peter—those words, alas, which I was never to forget . . ." (p. 40); "I passed by the beautiful temple of Paestum, in which Greece still breathes, and where, two years later, I went to worship some God or other—I no longer know which" (pp. 44-45); and especially Michel's ominous comment at the close of that opening part: "What would there be in a story of happiness? Only what prepares it, only what destroys it can be told. I have now told you what prepared it" (p. 57). This kind of foretelling, prevalent only in Part I, signals the narrator's conscious manipulation of the portion of his story covering events that took place more than two years earlier.

The detached perspective enjoyed by Michel on those early events is also discernible, if not quite so visible at first sight, in any number of passages of Part I where the narration of events or feelings from the past is "overlaid," as it were, with parenthetical comments or phrases that come from his present state of mind. A good composite example of this subtle interplay of temporal levels is the final paragraph of Chapter 8, where Michel conveys in general terms his attitude towards Marceline during the later stages of his recuperation:

> For the time being, therefore, my relationship with Marceline remained the same, though it was every day getting more intense by reason of my growing love. My dissimulation (if that expression can be applied to the need I felt of protecting my thoughts from her judgment), my very dissimulation increased that love. I mean that it kept me incessantly occupied with Marceline. At first, perhaps, this necessity for falsehood cost me a little effort; but I soon came to understand that

the things that are reputed worst (lying, to mention only one) are only difficult to do as long as one has never done them; but that they become—and very quickly too—easy, pleasant and agreeable to do over again, and soon even natural. So then, as is always the case when one overcomes an initial disgust, I ended by taking pleasure in my dissimulation itself, by protracting it, as if it afforded opportunity for the play of my undiscovered faculties. And every day my life grew richer and fuller, as I advanced toward a riper, more delicious happiness.

(p. 50)

This passage might actually be considered characteristic of any first-person narration in which enough time has elapsed between events and the moment of their narration to allow the narrator to reflect upon them and order his account accordingly; were it not for the particular details mentioned, the passage might just as well be from *Adolphe* or *The Fall*. The token expression of concession ("perhaps"), the efforts to downplay the importance of certain key words ("if that expression can be applied . . ." or "I mean that . . ."), the suggestion that individual actions are in fact only typical of general patterns of human behavior ("as is always the case . . .") and therefore excusable—all are quite characteristic of the narration of someone who has clearly reflected in advance on what he has to say, has considered the potential impact on listener or reader, and who then makes subtle efforts to soften that impact or at least present himself in a more favorable light than the facts themselves would otherwise suggest. What makes this passage particularly interesting in the present context is the preoccupation with perversion of the truth—"dissimulation," "falsehood," "lying"—and the possibility that Michel, having overcome long ago the "initial disgust" to which he refers and ended up "taking pleasure" in "dissimulation itself," is now enjoying that same pleasure at the reader's expense.

Another subtle but real measure of the way the diminishing temporal lag between past and present is reflected in the narrator's gradual loss of control over his story is the shifting tone of Michel's frequent allusions to his listeners. From start to finish he is aware of their presence, naturally enough, and conscious of their possible reaction to his narration. His references to them in Part I tend to be stylized or rhetorical (and in that respect, once again, similar in tone to those of Clamence in the early portions of *The Fall*): "I will confess my folly" (p. 13); "Shall I confess that I felt not the least shock?" (p. 17); "Must I confess that so far I had paid very little attention to Marceline's religious beliefs?" (p. 25); "But must I confess that what made me most uncomfortable was not the children's presence—it was Marceline's" (p. 28); "I will tell you, however, about one other action of mine, though perhaps you will consider it ridiculous . . ." (p. 48); "But shall I confess that the figure of the young king Athalaric was what attracted me most?" (p. 55). The formal tone of these expressions (conveyed in particular by the rather affected inversion, *avouerai-je*, in French) indicates the polished nature of Michel's narration of these early events from which he is now quite detached. He does not really engage the participation of his listeners by such remarks, he simply acknowledges in a rhetorical manner their presence and possible reaction.

In Part III, by contrast, his references to the friends are quite different in tone: "And Marceline, I tell you, began forthwith to recover hope" (p. 121); "Yes, I tell you, I cared for her tenderly" (p. 129);[7] "Oh, perhaps you will think I did not love Marceline. I swear I loved her passionately" (p. 129); "It is not, believe me, that I am tired of my crime—if you choose to call it that . . ." (p. 145). Michel clearly feels compelled in instances such as these to defend himself against the anticipated reaction of his listeners, and his appeals to them, personal and emotional now, reflect his defensive posture in this part of his narration. It is true that he has reason indeed to feel much more vulnerable in relating this part of the story, but beyond that, it also seems that he simply lacks the temporal perspective necessary to bring the end of his narration to the same point of refinement and polish evident in the first part. One suspects—quite hypothetically, to be sure—that if Michel were more removed in time from the events at the end of his story, his narration of them would be much smoother, much more detached in tone, than it is in fact in its present state.

If Michel's diminishing control over his narration can be traced in a number of rather subtle ways, it is no doubt most obvious in the ease or difficulty with which he actually recalls the past. To judge from his narration, he remembers the earlier events of his story more clearly than the recent ones. He himself seems to suggest that the loss of the baby (related towards the end of the second chapter of Part II) is the decisive point in this respect: "My recollections here are lost in dark confusion," he remarks, and then adds two paragraphs later, "My memory of this time is blurred; I have forgotten how the weeks passed" (p. 98). He confirms this trend—his memory of recent events being the least sure—near the end of his story: "It is this last part of the journey, though it is still so near me, that I remember least" (p. 139).

While Michel's conscious recall of events seems to diminish as his narration progresses, his retention of sensations or impressions appears to follow just the opposite course (which is not entirely surprising, given his reawakening to the primitive, sensual side of life recounted in Part I). The ease with which he calls up particular impressions, already apparent in the latter chapters of Part I, is confirmed indirectly in the first chapter of Part II by his *inability* to say much about that stable time of his life: "If no distinct memory of this period of my life stands out for me, it is not because I am less deeply grateful for it—but because everything in it melted and mingled into a state of changeless ease, in which evening joined morning without a break, in which day passed into day without a surprise" (p. 60). His narration of the return trip to North Africa, on the other hand, is filled with impressions that have lost none of their immediacy. Early in Part III, for example, he notes: "I remember every sensation of that journey as vividly as if they had been events," and he elaborates a few lines later: "I remember it all, hour by hour; I remember the strange, inclement feeling of the air; the sound of the horses' bells; my hunger; the midday halt at the inn; the raw egg that I broke into my soup; the brown bread and the sour wine that was so cold" (p. 122). In fact, he later claims to be absolutely haunted by the memory of certain sensations, such as those of the two months spent (so impatiently, on his part) in Switzerland: "And yet now, when in my idleness the detested past once more asserts its strength, those are the very memories that haunt me. Swift sledge drives; joy of the dry and stinging air, spattering of the snow, appetite; walks in the baffling fog, curious sonority of voices, abrupt appearance of objects . . ." (p. 126). In this last example, the impressionistic notation, without verbs, effectively erases the distinction between the past of events related and the present of their narration.

The immediacy with which Michel calls up from the past certain sensory experiences is further underlined by their narration in the *present* tense, an effect that has received less attention than one would expect from critics (and which, even more surprisingly, has often been simply ignored—or "corrected"?—by translators). From very early in his story, Michel slips briefly into the present tense to relate certain moments of a particularly striking nature. In recounting how he began to spit up blood during a coach ride on the first trip, for example, he recreates a few isolated lines of monologue without setting them off as such from the rest of his narration in the past:

> My handkerchief was very soon used up. My fingers were covered with it. Should I wake up Marceline? . . . Fortunately I thought of a large silk foulard she was wearing tucked into her belt. . . . Then, there suddenly came over me a feeling of extreme weakness; everything began to spin round and I thought I was going to faint. Should I wake her up? . . . No, shame! . . . My first thought was to hide the blood from Marceline. But how? I was covered with it; it seemed to be everywhere; on my fingers especially . . . My nose might perhaps have been bleeding . . . That's it! If she asks me, I shall say my nose has been bleeding . . .
>
> (pp. 15-16)

What he can recall of his fight for life is also introduced in the present: "I see again only Marceline, my wife, my life, bending over the bed where I lay agonizing" (p. 19).[8] The sketchy memories of the initial stages of his recuperation are likewise given in the present: "Marceline sits beside me. She is reading, or sewing, or writing. I am doing nothing—just looking at her. O Marceline! Marceline! . . . I look. I see the sun; I see the shadow; I see the line of shadow moving; I have so little to think of that I watch it. I am still very weak; my breathing is very bad; everything tires me—even reading; besides, what should I read? Existing is occupation enough" (p. 20). Michel then goes on to use the present tense sporadically through the rest of Part I, recreating scenes that apparently remain vivid for him, such as the visit of the Arab boy, Bachir (pp. 20-21), descriptions of the garden outside his terrace (p. 28) and of the oasis beyond (pp. 33-34), and a few lines from the altercation with the drunken coachman (p. 52).[9]

From the end of the second chapter of Part II on, however, Michel uses the present tense with increasing frequency, as Martine Maisani-Léonard has pointed out,[10] until it comes to dominate his narration. The critical point in this respect seems once again to be the loss of the baby; it is at that moment in Michel's story that conscious and orderly recall of events gives way more and more to direct re-living of the past.[11] A first notation on the initial period of Marceline's convalescence—"I see myself again leaning over her . . ."[12]—echoes a passage seen earlier (p. 19) and underlines the reversal of roles that has taken place. Michel then recreates at the end of that chapter the entire scene where his wife asks for her rosary: "It's one morning, shortly after the embolism; I'm right by Marceline; she seems to be a little better . . ."[13] Disdainful of her weakness in seeking God's help while he got well alone," he rushes out of the room and the chapter ends on his incredibly cruel observation that disease had "stained" Marceline: "she was a thing that had been spoiled" (p. 100). While much of the third chapter of Part II is recounted once more in the past tense, Michel slips into the present again to relate, or re-live, the scenes of poaching that make up the last quarter of the chapter (scenes that neither translation conveys in the present tense).

The initial events of Part III are recounted in the past tense, as if Michel were making a final effort to keep past and present separate and to bring his story once more under control. Although there are periodic notations in the present tense (pp. 122-23, 126-27, 129-30—the last not rendered in the present by either translation, however), the past tense prevails for more than half of Part III, until Michel, in the middle of a paragraph, slips definitively into the present: "We left Syracuse at last. I was haunted by the desire and the memory of the past. At sea, Marceline's health improved . . . I see again the color of the sea. It is so calm that the ship's track in it seems permanent. I can still hear the noises of dripping and dropping water—liquid noises;

the swabbing of the deck and the slapping of the sailors' bare feet on the boards. I see again Malta shining white in the sun—the approach to Tunis . . . How changed I am!" (pp. 134-35).[14] The rest of Michel's story is told in the present, with only an occasional vestige of the narrative past tense used originally.[15]

What makes this definitive shift to the present all the more significant is that it is followed at once my Michel's admission, noted earlier, that he is henceforth abandoning the effort to impose more order on his story than there was in his life. What has been up to this point an occasional recreation in the present tense of experiences from earlier parts of his story (experiences further in Michel's past, more removed from his moment of narration) now becomes a general surrender to the dramatized re-living of the very recent past: "Biskra! That then is my goal . . . Yes; here are the public gardens; the bench . . . I recognize the bench on which I used to sit in the first days of my convalescence. What was it I read there? . . . Homer; I have not opened the book since. Here's the tree with the curious bark I got up to go and feel. How weak I was then! Look! here are some children! . . . No; I recognize none of them. How grave Marceline is! She is as changed as I. Why does she cough so in this fine weather? Here's the hotel! Here are our rooms, our terrace!" (p. 136).[16]

It seems clear that the movement from the detached tone and well-ordered format of Part I to this kind of direct re-experiencing of recent events can in fact be tied to the shrinking interval separating Michel's moment of narration from his past.[17] Whereas he could look back on the developments related in Part I from a comfortable perspective of more than two years, he must deal in Part III with a past that is still very fresh; when he finally slips once and for all into the present tense, he is, after all, relating events that are only some four months past, events recent enough to interfere with his efforts to mold them into the finished format of a traditional narration. In spite of his assertion that the three months since Marceline's death have seemed like ten years, that interval is obviously too short to allow him to treat the final incidents of his story with the same degree of detachment he shows in narrating his earlier experiences.

It is this same general movement from well-structured narrative to direct re-living of the recent past that underlines the increasing *reliability* of Michel as narrator. The very contrast in tone and composition between Parts I and III should be enough to make the reader wonder if the polished format of the first part does not in fact betray the rhetorical slant of discourse emphasized by Benveniste. But if that does not prompt the reader to reconsider his reaction to earlier portions of Michel's narration, the re-creation of later events should certainly do so. For in re-living scenes such as the return to Biskra, Michel lays bare his insensitivity to Marceline's worsening health and invites the blame he clearly deserves for not calling a halt to the exhausting ordeal of the trip to which he impetuously and selfishly subjects his wife. In that sense, Michel's gradual surrender to an unstructured re-creation of scenes in the present tense strips away the smooth veneer of his earlier narration and reveals the real Michel; in the final analysis, it is only in the latter stages of his story that he fulfills his early promise to tell his life "simply."

More generally speaking, what might be called the "deterioration" of Michel's narration has turned out to be a remarkable preview of the course followed by much of first-person fiction in the twentieth century. Part I of his account remains essentially faithful to the formula of the short memoir-novel, such as *Manon Lescaut* or *Adolphe,* in which enough time separates the past of the story from the present of narration to insure that the two do not interfere with each other. Because narrator and character are one and the same, there are of course emotional ties between the two levels, yet the lapse of time allows a narrator like Michel to look back and see himself almost as someone else. Moreover, the retrospective viewpoint itself tends to lend a definitive, even fatalistic, quality to the story; events that were originally experienced as unrelated are selected and seen from hindsight as steps in an inexorable progression towards an outcome that seems inevitable simply because it is already known. The resulting order of the story and the predominance of the narrative past tense then create, in a narrative like the first part of **The Immoralist,** something analogous to what Roland Barthes has termed, in the context of the third-person novel, the "euphoria" of traditional narration,[18] the creation of a fictional world where events seem frozen in time, fixed once and for all in a past that is cut off definitively from the present of narration.

In Part III, however, where the interval between Michel's past and his present is drastically reduced, the stability of this world of fiction begins to break down, as it does in so many modern novels. In that respect, **The Immoralist,** like Gide's **The Pastoral Symphony** in a diary format, subtly calls into question the very conception of the traditional first-person novel. Both illustrate initially, and then undermine progressively, the privileged status of a narrator reviewing events from a comfortable hindsight and presenting an account of them that is inevitably more structured—and thereby more reassuring, no doubt, to reader as well as narrator—than his original experience could possibly have been. While there are, to be sure, later first-person novels which continue to observe the convention of a past that can be re-created virtually intact and held up as authentic in its own right—*Remembrance of Things Past* is a notable example—more often the past is presented as fragmented, incomplete, at least partially irretrievable or "lost," and almost always as a function of the narrator's ongoing present. Michel's narration is in that sense a sign of things to come, a very early and indirect forerunner of works such as *Nausea*, where Roquentin arrives at the conclusion that any re-creation of the past—and storytelling in particular—is indeed artificial, or Claude Simon's *The Flanders Road*, in which the past is depicted as an unstable, evanescent image of a memory in action, or Butor's *Passing Time*, which amounts to a systematic demonstration that the past can never be recaptured at all, in large part because the present will not "stand still" long enough to permit it.

In undermining the story as it is traditionally conceived, the progressive deterioration of Michel's narration also highlights the inherent temporality of the narrative process itself, the simple fact that it takes time to tell a story. In the traditional first-person account, the narration is in a certain sense atemporal, situated outside the normal flux of time. Nothing happens, for example, during the hours it must take Des Grieux or Adolphe to relate their experiences—or the much longer period necessary in the case of Proust's narrator—to affect the story as it is originally projected; between the moment the story is begun and the moment it is completed, the present of narration plays no active role and has, for all practical purposes, no duration of its own.[19] In the modern first-person novel, by contrast, the real duration of the storytelling process, made visible in **The Immoralist** by the gradual breakdown of Michel's narration, has come to be of central concern. This interest no doubt explains in part the renewed popularity of the diary or journal form in the twentieth century, for the journal-novel is by nature a narration drawn out over time, where the narrator's original purpose in keeping a diary is subject to changes that may take place even as he writes. In novels as different in many respects as **The Pastoral Symphony,** Mauriac's *The Knot of Vipers, Nausea,* and *Passing Time,* the narrator's original intention to note, review, and understand certain experiences is deflected or even completely thwarted by developments (including the re-reading itself of earlier entries) that arise during the course of his narration. **The Immoralist** would seem to represent, in that sense as well, one of the first steps towards denying the narrator his privileged, artificial status and recognizing instead the fundamental temporality of narration.

From our vantage point today, then, **The Immoralist** not only belongs very clearly to our century, but provides an excellent point of reference from which to view the developments of an entire line of short first-person novels in France. By its temporal structure, it is—like **The Pastoral Symphony,** again—a hybrid work, the first part faithful to the traditional narration of earlier centuries, the third part a preview of much later novels. If the first part looks back, so to speak, to the reassuring world of conventional storytelling, where events seem securely classified and ordered in a fictional world no longer subject to change, the third part looks forward to the unsettled (and often unsettling) world of the contemporary novel, where the emphasis on the present of narration is designed to reflect the unorganized quality of life as it is lived. **The Immoralist** is, in short, a remarkable image of the evolution of a long line of fiction, of the distance, and yet underlying continuity, between such disparate works as *Manon Lescaut* and *Passing Time.*

Notes

1. *Problèmes de linguistique générale* (Paris: Gallimard, 1966), p. 242 ("toute énonciation supposant un locuteur et un auditeur, et chez le premier l'intention d'influencer l'autre en quelque manière").

2. André Gide, *The Immoralist,* trans. Dorothy Bussy (New York: Vintage Books, 1954), p. 7. References throughout are to this edition, which is generally more faithful to the original than the more recent translation by Richard Howard (New York: Knopf, 1970). In certain cases, as noted, I have modified Bussy's translation in order to come closer to the original.

3. Albert Sonnenfeld, "On Readers and Reading in *La Porte étroite* and *L'Immoraliste*," *Romanic Review,* 67 (1976), pp. 172, 182.

4. Allan H. Pasco, "Irony and Art in *L'Immoraliste*," *Romanic Review,* 64 (1973), pp. 186, 187.

5. Laurence M. Porter, "The Generativity Crisis of Gide's *Immoraliste*," *French Forum,* 2 (1977), 66. Porter makes the same point in another article, "Autobiography Versus Confessional Novel: Gide's *L'Immoraliste* and *Si le grain ne meurt*," *Symposium,* 30 (1976), pp. 152-53.

6. My translation; Bussy's rendering of this key passage is not as faithful to the original.

7. "I tell you" is my translation of the original "vous dis-je"; Bussy's translations ("as I tell you," p. 121, and "I say," p. 129) do not fully convey the defensive, argumentative tone of Michel's remarks.

8. "I see again only" is my translation of the original "Je revois seulement"; Bussy's "I can only see," while a smoother translation, does not convey the key idea of seeing *again.*

9. Neither Bussy nor Howard translates the last passage in the present.

10. *André Gide ou l'ironie de l'écriture* (Université de Montréal, 1976), p. 172. Porter's contention that Michel's use of the present is "episodic" ("Autobiography," 153-54) is inaccurate.

11. Both Maisani-Léonard, p. 180, and Porter, "Generativity," p. 66, come to similar conclusions.

12. "I see myself again" is my translation of "Je me revois," which Bussy renders simply as "I remember" (p. 98).

13. My translation; Bussy translates this in the past tense (pp. 98-99).

14. "I see again" is my translation of "Je revois," which Bussy renders as "I can still see." With few exceptions, Bussy is faithful to Michel's use of the present tense through the balance of his narration; Howard, on the other hand, transposes it into the past tense.

15. Maisani-Léonard points out very well (pp. 161-66) how Michel comes to use the *passé composé*, with its implicit references to the present of narration, in passages where the present tense now forms the basis of his account.

16. Bussy translates the initial verb in the past tense and the "voici" that recurs through the passage as "there are."

17. Maisani-Léonard, while underlining Michel's increasing use of the present, does not relate it directly to the circumstances of his narration.

18. Roland Barthes, *Le Degré zéro de l'écriture* (Paris: Seuil, 1953), p. 48.

19. Both Jean Pouillon, in "Les Règles du je," *Les Temps Modernes,* 12 (1957), p. 1592, and Gérard Genette, *Figures III* (Paris: Seuil, 1972), p. 234, refer in passing to this convention of traditional narration.

Manfred Kusch (essay date September 1979)

SOURCE: Kusch, Manfred. "The Gardens of *L'Immoraliste.*" French Forum 4, no. 3 (September 1979): 206-18.

[*In the following essay, Kusch examines the "central and important" role of the garden in* The Immoralist, *claiming that Michel's "discovery of, preference for, and, finally, residence in, a particular type of garden" corresponds closely to the novel's three-part structure and its formation of an ideology.*]

Among all spatial entities in Gide's fiction, the garden occupies a place of special importance. Not surprisingly, its frequent recurrence, especially in his *récits,* has attracted the attention of several critics. The best of these studies, Georges Poulet's "L'Instant et le lieu chez André Gide"[1], offers an excellent synoptic analysis of the dominant structures of Gidian time and space among which the garden plays a central role. But while the general nature of his study helps us to perceive the elementary orientations and characteristic preoccupations of Gide's vision, it does not deal with the specificity of these structural assumptions in particular works. An investigation into the concrete features of a specific actualization of a very general model such as the garden can, however, produce very interesting insights not only into the concept and role of physical space within the signifying system of a particular fiction, but also into its implicit ideological assumptions.

Robert Goodhand is at least partially aware of this when he states in the introduction of his study of "Locale as Thematic Expression in *L'Immoraliste*":

> The various locales in which the action takes place constitute an important component of the pattern of images. In fact, it is surprising that the critics have not taken a closer look at the passages which create the work's physical ambience, since locale not only acts as a kind of moral landscape mirroring and foreshadowing the phases of Michel's internal crisis, but it also provides some valuable insight into the fundamental and unchanging nature of the protagonist[2].

However, Goodhand restricts the role of space to that of "locale" and "ambience," a limitation which results in a relatively simplistic symbolical interpretation of the different places the protagonist visits during his voyage of self-realization. As the naming of moral attributes of particular spatial entities such as springs, gardens, deserts, etc., assumes more importance than a detailed analysis of the concrete spatial structures themselves, it is not surprising that landscape (in the widest sense of the term) is associated with the personality of the protagonist rather than being related to the ideological assumptions that would account for both. This is especially true of his short interpretation of the gardens in *L'Immoraliste*[3]. The garden occupies, however, a very central and important place in this, perhaps the most programmatic of all Gidian *récits*. Indeed, I think it would not be exaggerated to claim that the programmatic character of ***L'Immoraliste***—the title itself announces not an individual identified by his name, but rather the representative of a certain ideology—becomes most apparent in the prominent role the garden and its interpretation play in the story.

As the garden is among the most systematic of all spatial structures in literature—it constitutes a closure containing a meaningful microcosm radically separated and protected from an amorphous and limitless space outside it—its description in a text always deserves special attention. For while, in their basic form, most gardens are structurally related, they do not all carry the same message. Their potential meanings can, in fact, vary immensely. It is rather in the concrete detail of the particular actualization of the basic model, as well as in its relationship to the surrounding space, and in the manner the garden is experienced by the protagonist(s) that we may find the concrete expression of a narrative's generating assumptions (desires, principles). This, I feel, can be shown particularly well in Gide's *L'Immoraliste.*

Despite the apparently informal character of Michel's narration—the hero of *L'Immoraliste* recounts his story orally, at night, to a group of friends who in turn submit a transcript of his report to "Monsieur D.R., président du conseil"—Gide's *récit* is very consciously and systematically structured. Its division into three parts suggests a classically-balanced and complete movement: a beginning, a middle, and an end. On the level of the plot (action), the three divisions may be characterized as exposition (preparation), crisis, and catastrophe (resolution)[4]. But since Gide's *récit* is above all a story dealing with conflicting attitudes or ideologies—the negative prefix *im-* of the title implies a rebellion against, or at least the negation of, a positive standard—it would, I think, seem more appropriate to view the three segments of the story as stages in the formulation of an ideology: an ideology intuitively arrived at in part one, consciously defined in part two, and radically applied in part three. As we shall see, these stages of awareness correspond to the discovery of, preference for, and, finally, residence in, a particular kind of garden.

The oasis of Biskra is the central geographical setting of the first part of Michel's story. It is the spatial environment in which he recovers from his near-fatal disease and awakens to a new awareness of life and a new concept of himself. But despite the obvious symbolic implications of an insular oasis surrounded by desert, especially in a story dealing with the definition and creation of self, Gide does not dwell on the concept of the oasis as a symbolic entity. Indeed, the oasis as such is never described comprehensively. It serves instead mainly as an enveloping closure for parallel, but more specific, smaller spatial entities which the hero progressively explores and which, as we shall see, assume the role of structural models shaping and reflecting his perceptions of himself[5].

Michel's initial situation at Biskra is in many ways that of a newborn. Confined to his bed in an unfamiliar room, he appears to be ignorant both about his past and his situation in the present: "Je ne savais plus ni qui, ni où j'étais"[6]. But as he gains strength and becomes increasingly aware of his own existence, his room, too, seems to come into sharper focus. It appears spacious; a wide glass door "opens" onto a terrace overlooking the town and its public gardens:

> Je fus complètement séduit par notre home. Ce n'était presque qu'une terrasse. Quelle terrasse! Ma chambre et celle de Marceline y donnaient; elle se prolongeait sur des toits. L'on voyait, lorsqu'on en avait atteint la partie la plus haute, par-dessus les maisons, des palmiers; par-dessus les palmiers, le désert. L'autre côté de la terrasse touchait aux jardins de la ville; . . . Ma chambre était vaste, aérée; murs blanchis à la chaux, rien aux murs; une petite porte vitrée ouvrait sur la terrasse.
>
> ([*Oeuvres complètes*] pp. 28-29)

During the initial stage of his recovery-discovery ("Je devais faire de la vie la palpitante découverte" [p. 28]), this room and its terrace remain Michel's only habitat. Within the seclusion of this minimal world, to which young children are admitted like medicine, Michel forms his new credo of self-sufficiency, of selfhood, of independent strength. Its empty, whitewashed walls become emblematic both of a radical new beginning and, in their austerity, of single-minded determination and discipline.

From the closure of his room, protected behind transparent glass doors, Michel gazes out over the terrace beyond which, beyond roofs and treetops, the desert signals a space of unlimited possibilities. Between the two "empty" spaces of the *chambre/terrasse,* on the one hand, and the distant desert, on the other, lies the "full" space of collective and individual immersion, the city and the garden. The city (and its society), only briefly alluded to as *maisons* and *toits,* do not, however, attract Michel's interest. The roofs remain opaque, the many interconnected rooms of society unexplored; and the only door leading from Michel's to his wife's room is small, functioning only to admit Marceline to his room, but not to provide access to hers.

Beyond the large and transparent door leading onto the terrace, and at the opposite end of the terrace overlooking the city, lies, however, the less complex and more clearly structured space of the garden. As soon as Michel has gained enough strength, physically and ideologically, to leave the airy solitude of his room and terrace, he continues his parallel explorations of space and identity (*où? qui?*) by entering, or more accurately, by *descending* into the garden:

> Jusqu'alors craignant l'essoufflement de l'escalier, je n'avais pas osé quitter la terrasse; dans les derniers jours de janvier, enfin, je descendis, m'aventurai dans le jardin.
>
> Jardin public . . . Une très large allée le coupait, ombragée par deux rangs de cette espèce de mimosas très hauts qu'on appelle là-bas des cassies. Des bancs à l'ombre de ces arbres. Une rivière canalisée, je veux dire plus profonde que large, à peu près droite, longeant l'allée; puis d'autres canaux plus petits, divisant l'eau de la rivière, la menant, à travers le jardin, vers les plantes; l'eau lourde est couleur de la terre, couleur d'argile rose ou grise. Presque pas d'étrangers, quelques Arabes; ils circulent, et, dès qu'ils ont quitté le soleil, leur manteau blanc prend la couleur de l'ombre.
>
> (p. 38)

Among the features that strike Michel during his first visit to the garden (the features described in his narrative) are its linear design, its public character, its opaque, canalized river, and its shade. Only the latter aspect impresses him favorably: "Un singulier frisson me saisit quand j'entrai dans cette ombre étrange; je m'enveloppai de mon châle; pourtant aucun malaise; au contraire . . ." (pp. 38-39), whereas the controlled river and the wide, straight avenue intersecting the garden seem to accentuate a lack of seclusion and independence[7], an impression reinforced by Marceline's caring and watchful presence. Quickly fatigued by a space so obviously connected to the social world, a space which has to be shared with others, Michel soon returns to his elevated and secluded room, but only in order to visit the garden a short time later alone: "Rentrons, lui dis-je; et je résolus à part moi de retourner seul au jardin" (p. 39).

During subsequent visits, the garden appears progressively in a different light. When Michel returns to it—this time he is accompanied only by a young boy ("fidèle et souple comme un chien" [p. 39])—the garden is nearly deserted: "Nous étions presque seuls dans l'allée" (p. 39). During his next visit, Michel is entirely alone, the garden completely deserted, and its most salient features are now no longer the rational linearity of its design, but rather such immaterial and vague aspects as light, shade, sound, and silence. Gradually, the garden becomes, thus, a space of personal and sensual immersion, a luminously shady closure within which Michel descends through the layers of his "inauthentic being" to make contact with the deepest (and, therefore, truest) level of his personality:

> J'ai dit que le jardin touchait notre terrasse; j'y fus donc aussitôt. J'entrai avec ravissement dans son ombre. L'air était lumineux. Les cassies, dont les fleurs viennent très tôt avant les feuilles, embaumaient—à moins que ne vînt de partout cette sorte d'odeur légère inconnue qui me semblait entrer en moi par plusieurs sens et m'exaltait. . . . L'ombre était mobile et légère; elle ne tombait pas sur le sol, et semblait à peine y poser. O lumière!—J'écoutai. Qu'entendis-je? Rien; tout; je m'amusais de chaque bruit. . . .
>
> J'avais oublié que j'étais seul, n'attendais rien, oubliais l'heure. Il me semblait avoir jusqu'à ce jour si peu senti pour tant penser, que je m'étonnais à la fin de ceci: ma sensation devenait aussi forte qu'une pensée.
>
> (pp. 42-43)

While Michel's immersion in the sensual present and in the asocial solitude of the garden abolishes his dependence on the past (his acquired knowledge) and frees him of his anxiety about the future (*j'avais oublié, je n'attendais rien*), it also connects him—I should say, reconnects him—with a past of a different kind. This other past is in no way comparable to a linear and progressive, historical evolution that would explain Michel's present as the result of a coherent chain of events, but is more like a state, a persistent and unchanged personal capacity which, while always present, had lain buried half-dormant under the accumulation of rational, impersonal constructs. In short, the concept of horizontally-oriented time and space (history and continuous geographical space) is negated or, at least, de-emphasized in favor of a vertical model in which time and space are above all discontinuous and repetitious[8].

Michel's descent into the garden is indicative of a fundamental reorientation; indeed, a reorientation aiming at uncovering the foundation of his being. Thus, the movement of descent is paralleled by other vertically-oriented movements such as *oubli,* immersion, exaltation, *reconnaissance,* and *découverte*:

> . . . du fond du passé de ma première enfance se réveillaient enfin mille lueurs, de mille sensations égarées. La conscience que je prenais à nouveau de mes sens m'en permettait l'inquiète reconnaissance. Oui, mes sens réveillés désormais, se trouvaient toute une histoire, se recomposaient un passé. Ils vivaient! ils vivaient! n'avaient jamais cessé de vivre, se découvraient, même à travers mes ans d'étude, une vie latente et rusée.
>
> (p. 43)

But even if Michel experiences his rebirth ("Était-ce enfin ce matin-là que j'allais naître?" [p. 43]) within the space of the public garden, clearly it is not because its structural features guide his thoughts or feelings; they do not even form a parallel reinforcing them. Indeed, Michel's selective transformation of the open and geometrical *jardin public* into a personal and intimate space through emphasis on such relatively unstructured elements as sound, fragrance, and luminosity, only points to the deficiency of this particular spatial model[9].

The public garden is, however, only the first stage in a continuing movement of descent and discovery, and it serves, in its deficiency, to underscore the importance of the next garden Michel visits: "les merveilleux vergers de l'oasis" (p. 44). These gardens, actually a whole system of gardens, are peaceful and shady like the earlier *jardin public,* but offer, in addition to these immaterial properties indicating seclusion and stasis, a concrete spatial structure perfectly in harmony with the structural assumptions of Michel's new ideology. The attraction for Michel of its non-linear design, its closure, solitude, "timelessness," "depth"[10], and lack of perspective, confirms his option for immersion (descent) rather than progression, for repetition rather than linear continuity, and for selfhood rather than community:

> Elle [Marceline] me précéda dans un chemin bizarre et tel que dans aucun pays je n'en vis jamais de pareil. Entre deux assez hauts murs de terre il circule comme indolemment; les formes des jardins, que ces hauts

murs limitent l'inclinent à loisir; il se courbe ou brise sa ligne; dès l'entrée un détour nous perd; on ne sait plus ni d'où l'on vient, ni où l'on va.

(p. 44)

J'oubliais ma fatigue et ma gêne. Je marchais dans une sorte d'extase, d'allégresse silencieuse, d'exaltation de sens et de la chair. . . . Une brèche au mur, nous entrâmes.

C'était un lieu plein d'ombre et de lumière; tranquille, et qui semblait à l'abri du temps; plein de silences et de frémissements, bruit léger de l'eau qui s'écoule, abreuve les palmiers, et d'arbre en arbre fuit, appel discret des tourterelles, chant de flûte dont un enfant jouait.

(p. 45)

The central generating concept determining the spatial structure both of the individual garden and of the total system of gardens, is very explicitly that of *la ligne brisée*. The perspectiveless sinuosity of the path leading into the maze of individual gardens, the sinuosity of the river flowing parallel to the path ("L'eau fidèle de la rivière suit le sentier" [p. 44])—we remember that in the public garden the linearity of the *allée* was repeated by the straight line of the canalized river—and the walled closure of the garden accessible only through a *brèche* (literally: a break), are all actualizations of this structural principle. Their main function is the affirmation of the positive value of discontinuity—i.e., the valorization of a present nourished not by a teleological past, but rather by a fundamental truth which reveals itself only in an ahistorical encounter between man and nature in the accommodating seclusion of the garden[11].

Discontinuity is also the structuring principle on the social level. The garden functions not only as a "break" in the continuity of space and time, but also as a defensive and protective closure against social cohesion and dependence. It is a space to be enjoyed in solitude: "Le lendemain matin, dans ce même jardin je revins avec Marceline; le soir du même jour j'y allai seul" (p. 46); a space also in which the dominant mode of relating to the world is that of unmediated sensation rather than the linear mode of *la pensée*: "je sentais le soleil ardent doucement tamisé par les palmes; je ne pensais à rien; qu'importait la pensée? je sentais extraordinairement . . ." (p. 46). And even the water system within the garden reflects the principle of discontinuity: "l'eau, sagement et parcimonieusement répartie, satisfait à la soif des plantes, puis leur est aussitôt retirée" (p. 46).

In all of its aspects, then, the ideal garden in *L'Immoraliste* represents a spatial entity radically different and offset from the world beyond its enclosure. A "sunken" refuge[12], hidden behind high walls, it functions as a space in which the protagonist can assert his independence of all "linear" forces—i.e., forces which would integrate him into metapersonal systems and processes such as history, society, rationality, and even geography[13]. Thus, the garden is, in large measure, a negative structure, a spatial system directed not so much against the content of the world outside its enclosure as against its structural orientation. The sinuous and intimate structure of the gardens seems to confirm the authenticity, depth, and independence of the self Michel claims to discover in them.

In his pursuit of identity and authenticity, Michel is in many ways comparable to the romantic hero who seeks in the communion with nature a redefinition of man's role and destiny outside the confining and burdensome complexities of society[14]. Michel's preference for, and use of, a particular kind of garden reminds us, however, even more of one of the prototypes of the Romantic hero and of the symbolic power of his favorite garden. I am thinking, of course, of Saint-Preux and the *Élysée* garden of his beloved Julie. As we remember, Saint-Preux's description of the garden at Clarens forms one of the central and most important passages in Rousseau's *La Nouvelle Héloïse*. Just like Michel's garden, Saint-Preux's is closed and accessible only through a narrow opening (gate); it is a place of immersion, of "timelessness," a place in which the principle of sinuosity and of *la ligne brisée* is consciously contrasted with the negative principle of linearity[15].

Yet, while the comparison between the two garden systems reveals many similarities, it also makes us more clearly aware of the important differences between them. It also demonstrates why a mere subsumption of Michel's garden (or of any garden) under the label of pastoral or the topos of the *locus amoenus* does not do justice to its specificity. While Michel's and Saint-Preux's gardens share pastoral features, they nevertheless represent very clearly two fundamentally different systems.

Saint-Preux's garden is above all a utopian structure, an ideal space, emblematic of ideal relationships, on all levels, between man and his fellow men as well as between man and nature. Its closure, while directed against the corruption of the world at large, is, nevertheless, productive and positive as it seeks to propose a comprehensive new world built on the principles integrated into its very design. The singularity and centrality of Saint-Preux's garden underline its programmatic character and its role as an enduring alternative system.

Michel's garden, on the other hand, is characterized by its small size and multiplicity. In fact, one might claim that his garden is composed of many small sub-gardens, almost room-like closures accessible only through hidden and surprising openings. Although he visits gardens often, no particular one of them serves as his preferred personal space. So long as they fulfill the abstract, structural criteria I have enumerated earlier, all gardens are equally inviting, none can claim his permanent attachment. In this sense, Michel's attitude towards gardens is not very different from his attitude towards the young boys he encounters in them and, in a more general sense, his attitude towards any other person. As soon as he becomes familiar with one, he feels the need to move on in the hope of encountering another, of the same kind, yet slightly different: "Il se nommait Ashour. . . . Quelque plaisant que me parût Bachir, je le connaissais trop à présent, et j'étais heureux de changer. Même, je me promis, un autre jour, de descendre tout seul au jardin et d'attendre, assis sur un banc, le hasard d'une rencontre heureuse" (p. 41). Referring to the gardens of the oasis, he comments: "Les jours suivants j'allai plus loin; je vis d'autres jardins, d'autres bergers et d'autres chèvres. Ainsi que Marceline l'avait dit, ces jardins étaient tous pareils; et pourtant chacun différait" (p. 47).

Thus, the almost endless labyrinth of small and sensuous gardens strung out along Michel's path comes to signify two different, even conflicting, tendencies in Michel's ideology. While the seclusion and depth of the individual garden seem to imply immersion—i.e., commitment to a specific space and to a specific way of being (the process I have described in the earlier part of this essay)—this commitment is never definitive or permanent. It is, indeed, very much like Michel's quick immersion in the pool below a waterfall during his return voyage through Italy:

> Dans une anfractuosité des rochers dont je parle, une source claire coulait. Elle retombait ici même en cascade, assez peu abondante, il est vrai, mais elle avait creusé sous la cascade un bassin plus profond où l'eau très pure s'attardait. . . . Ce quatrième jour, j'avançai, résolu d'avance, jusqu'à l'eau plus claire que jamais, et, sans plus réfléchir, m'y plongeai d'un coup tout entier. Vite transi, je quittai l'eau, m'étendis sur l'herbe, au soleil.
>
> (p. 60)[16]

Even while inside the garden, Michel is implicitly always aware of the inviting existence of other gardens, of other possibilities on the same level. The plurality of the garden thus becomes, in the signifying system of the *récit,* the structural expression of Michel's desire for absolute freedom and his horror of permanence and commitment. It is revealing that the gardens are always situated below a terrace which serves as a kind of viewing platform from where their plurality and availability are simultaneously visible. Drawn towards the depth of their enveloping closure and at the same time aware of their paratactic coexistence, Michel remains, as it were, suspended above them, just like the shadow he had observed in the public garden: "L'ombre était mobile et légère; elle ne tombait pas sur le sol, et semblait à peine y poser" (pp. 42-43). The open space of the desert, visible beyond the maze of multiple gardens, is, in this context, only the ultimate confirmation of the endless repetition of gardens, of repeated immersions, of a freedom that is never invested and which thus remains the promise of more promises.

That the model of the garden(s) I have sketched above is not an arbitrary abstraction of an accidental local setting is confirmed by the repetition of its structural features in subsequent descriptions of other garden systems Michel visits during his return voyage through Italy. Thus, at Syracuse, when he speaks of his dissatisfaction with the historical studies that had occupied him in the past, he contrasts his former interest in ruins with his new preference for a system of "deep" gardens: "J'en viens à fuir les ruines; à préférer aux plus beaux monuments du passé ces jardins bas qu'on appelle les Latomies . . ." (p. 54). While, in this instance, only depth and plurality are emphasized, the description of his situation at Ravello repeats all the structural features I have pointed out in my analysis of Michel's situation at Biskra. A room with a terrace overlooks a system of gardens beyond which an infinitely open space seems to prolong the freedom implied in the varied sameness of the garden's repetition:

> Une ancienne maison religieuse, à présent transformée en hôtel, nous hébergea; sise à l'extrémité du roc, ses terrasses et son jardin semblaient surplomber dans l'azur. Après le mur surchargé de pampres, on ne voyait d'abord rien que la mer; il fallait s'approcher du mur pour pouvoir suivre le dévalement cultivé qui, par des escaliers plus que par des sentiers, joignait Ravello au rivage . . . plus bas, des citronniers près de la mer. Ils sont rangés par petites cultures que motive la pente du sol; ce sont jardins en escalier, presque pareils; une étroite allée, au milieu, d'un bout à l'autre les traverse; on y entre sans bruit, en voleur. On rêve, sous cette ombre verte; le feuillage est épais, pesant; pas un rayon franc ne pénètre; comme des gouttes de cire épaisse, les citrons pendent, parfumés; dans l'ombre ils sont blancs et verdâtres; ils sont à portée de la main, de la soif; ils sont doux, âcres; ils rafraîchissent.
>
> (pp. 57-58)

At Sorrento, Michel's room and balcony are again situated directly adjacent to, and above, the gardens of the hotel: "Notre hôtel était hors la ville, entouré de jardins, de vergers; un très large balcon prolongeait notre chambre; des branches le frôlaient. L'aube entra librement par notre croisée grande ouverte" (p. 66).

Thus, we might design the following graphic model of Michel's gardens and their relationship to his room, on one side, and infinite space, on the other:

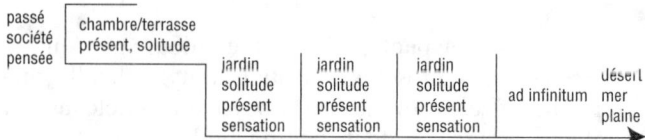

Seen in the context of this model, Michel's effort (during the second part of the *récit*) to become a *pro-*

priétaire is to be interpreted as an attempt to reduce the theoretically infinite number of gardens awaiting his visit to just one garden, domestic and productive, a garden not to be visited, but to be cultivated. But as his attempt fails, his role as *propriétaire* changes—indeed, reverts—to that of "thief." Michel's poaching on his own land clearly portends the transformation of his domestic "garden" into an anonymous garden of pleasure, one he may visit secretly and alone (at night) like a thief. As we remember, Michel had used this term already in describing his visit to the gardens of Ravello: "On y entre sans bruit, en voleur" (p. 58).

The contradiction between Michel's desire to establish himself—to have a family, a profession, to own land—and at the same time to remain permanently undefined, to be, like Ménalque, "toujours en passage" (p. 98), is well expressed in Charles's observation: "Vous ne pouvez pas protéger à la fois le garde et le braconnier" (p. 138). It is the same contradiction we had observed in the garden model of Biskra and all subsequent garden systems, the contradiction between immersion and timeless stasis (*descente au fond*), on the one hand, and, on the other, limitless plurality merging into infinite space.

This contradiction was, however, less urgent at Biskra, as Michel was primarily concerned with liberation and less with the application of his newly gained freedom. But even then, the desert beyond the many intimate and sensuous gardens signaled not only the immensity of this freedom, but also its emptiness. It indicated that the new transitive mode of relating to the world Michel had discovered in the depth of the garden had as yet no concrete object: "je sentais extraordinairement" (p. 46). The principle of discontinuity which dominated the structure of the garden system functioned not only to separate Michel from his past, but also to block his view from a concretely defined future. Thus, the garden was, despite its apparent abundance of vegetation and animal life, a strangely vague and, in a sense, an empty space: the lack of a concrete internal structure—here again, a comparison between Michel's and Saint-Preux's gardens is most instructive—suggested that the garden itself was not a model for a new world, but rather only a staging area for secretive new encounters beyond its walls. The repetition of the garden—Gide uses almost always the plural form *les jardins*—devalues, in the end, the programmatic potential of *le jardin,* and its plurality tends to merge instead with the infinity and emptiness of the desert.

This, I think, is the logic and meaning of Michel's final situation in the *récit*. From a house with a terrace above an almost empty garden enclosed by only a low wall, Michel overlooks, perched high above it, an infinite and desert-like plain:

> Michel le [le récit] fit sur sa terrasse où près de lui nous étions étendus dans l'ombre et dans la clarté des étoiles. A la fin du récit nous avons vu le jour se lever sur la plaine. La maison de Michel la domine, ainsi que le village dont elle n'est distante que peu. Par la chaleur, et toutes les moissons fauchées, cette plaine ressemble au désert.
>
> (p. 11)
>
> Quand on y vient par ce chemin, la maison de Michel est la première du village. Un jardin fermé de murs bas, ou plutôt un enclos l'entoure où croissent trois grenadiers déjetés et un superbe laurier rose.
>
> (p. 12)

The plurality, hermetic closure, and intimacy of *les jardins* have been reduced to little more than symbolic remnants. Of the model I have sketched earlier, only the *chambre/terrasse,* an almost empty garden, and the empty space of the desert are left. Expressed in spatial terms, Michel's immoralism is manifest in his failure to give an internal structure to his garden, to make it emblematic of a coherent world view. In the end, the refusal to invest the freedom discovered in the depth of the garden leads to its atrophy. The desert invades the garden(s) and its vast sterility proves a more stifling prison than the closure of the garden: "Arrachez-moi d'ici à présent, et donnez-moi des raisons d'être. Moi je ne sais plus en trouver. Je me suis délivré, c'est possible; mais qu'importe? je souffre de cette liberté sans emploi" (p. 169).

Notes

1. *La Revue des Lettres Modernes,* 331-335 (1972), 56-66.

2. *French Review,* 43 (1970), Special Issue, no. 1, 77.

3. Goodhand [*French Review, ibid.*], p. 78.

4. See, for example, Jean Hytier, *André Gide* (London: Constable, 1963), p. 140.

5. The question whether the spatial environment in *L'Immoraliste* is primary or secondary, whether it creates or reflects the identity of the protagonist, cannot be clearly resolved. It may, in fact, be an inappropriate question. If we remember that the story is not an impersonal account of random activities by a random individual, but rather the expression of certain authorial desires/principles—not Michel, but Gide is telling the story—it should not surprise us that these desires should be manifest isomorphically on different levels of the narrative. On this subject, see also Hippolytus Dority and Réal Ouellet, "Les Images de la nature dans *L'Immoraliste*," *Études Littéraires,* 2 (1969), 313.

6. André Gide, *Oeuvres complètes* (Paris: N.R.F., 1933), IV, 28. Page numbers in parentheses after quotations from *L'Immoraliste* will refer to this edition.

7. The linearity of the river and avenue emphasizes destination and origin more than the situation in the present.

8. See also Poulet, pp. 58-59.

9. For Gide's preference, in general, for intimate gardens and his dislike for open and public gardens, see the comments by Gérard Defaux, "Sur des vers de Virgile: Alyssa et le mythe gidien du bonheur," *La Revue des Lettres Modernes*, 331-335 (1972), 117.

10. ". . . le vent ne descendait pas jusqu'à nous, n'agitait que les palmes hautes" (p. 46).

11. R. Goodhand, eager to prove that Gide ironically undermines the "insane" and "inhuman" ideology of his hero, interprets the sinuous and discontinuous gardens differently, but, I think, incorrectly: "It is also most plausible to interpret the labyrinthine 'chemin bizarre' as the equivalent of the maze of ambiguous instincts through which Michel wanders during the course of the novel. He overturns the old tables of morality, replaces them with a set of provisional tenets, and then follows a serpentine path until he becomes hopelessly lost" (Goodhand, p. 79). It is, however, quite obvious that Michel does not get "hopelessly lost" in the garden, but that, on the contrary, he loses himself sensuously and blissfully in the depth of its closure.

12. As I have pointed out earlier, the impression of depth is mainly due to the height of the walls surrounding the garden, to its location below Michel's room and terrace, and less to an actual difference in elevation between the garden and the space outside it. In what follows, it will, however, become quite clear that the concept of depth is, in fact, a very important and real feature of Michel's gardens.

13. Michel's rebellion against the "rigidity" of history and against his role as historian is, of course, one of the central topics of the *récit* (see in particular pp. 53-55). His refusal or inability to become part of society is the main subject of part two of the story. The flight from rationality is obvious in the passages I have just quoted and becomes even more evident in the frantic third part of Michel's narration. And lastly, the devaluation of coherent and continuous space (geography) is most apparent in his paratactic enumeration of unconnected localities. His voyage is less a continuous movement than a series of jumps from one closure to the next. See on this point the article by Poulet cited earlier.

14. Not surprisingly, Michel has often been compared with Werther and Adolphe.

15. The similarities between Saint-Preux's and Michel's gardens are in some instances quite striking. In what follows, I juxtapose only a few of the more important features:

"Dès l'entrée un détour nous perd; on ne sait plus ni d'où l'on vient, ni où l'on va."
L'Immoraliste (p. 44)

"A peine fus-je dedans, que, la porte étant masquée . . . je ne vis plus . . . par où j'étois entré, . . . je me trouvai là comme tombé des nues"
La Nouvelle Héloïse (p. 471)

"Je marchais dans une sorte d'extase, d'allégresse silencieuse, d'exaltation des sens et de la chair."
L'Immoraliste (p. 45)

"Je me mis à parcourir avec extase ce verger ainsi métamorphosé."
La Nouvelle Héloïse (p. 472)

"Entre deux assez hauts murs de terre, le chemin circule comme indolemment; . . . il se courbe ou brise sa ligne."
L'Immoraliste (p. 44)

"Mais les deux côtés de ses allées ne seront point toujours exactement parallèles; la direction n'en sera pas toujours en ligne droite."
La Nouvelle Héloïse (p. 483)

"C'était un lieu plein d'ombre et de lumière; tranquille et qui semblait à l'abri du temps; plein de silences et de frémissements, bruit léger de l'eau qui s'écoule, . . . appel discret des tourterelles, chant de flûte dont un enfant jouait."
L'Immoraliste (p. 45)

"En entrant dans ce prétendu verger, je fus frappé d'une agréable sensation de fraîcheur que d'obscurs ombrages, . . . un gazouillement d'eau courante et le chant de mille oiseaux porterent à mon imagination. . . ."
La Nouvelle Héloïse (p. 471)

Quotations from *La Nouvelle Héloïse* are from the second volume of the Pléiade edition of Rousseau's *Oeuvres complètes*.

16. It is interesting to observe that in Rousseau's novel, where the garden functions also as a space of immersion, the concrete act of immersion in water which corresponds to the function of the garden is Saint-Preux's intended permanent submersion in the nearby lake. Thus, the more comprehensive size and definitive character of Saint-Preux's garden is repeated and confirmed by the size and stasis of the lake, whereas Michel's more intimate and elusive garden—elusive in the sense that Michel's experience is not linked to one concrete garden, but may be repeated in any number of similar gardens—is emblematically represented

by a small hybrid *source,* composed of the dynamic elements of the *cascade* and the deep static element of the *bassin* hidden in a rocky recess.

Nathaniel Wing (essay date 1980)

SOURCE: Wing, Nathaniel. "The Disruptions of Irony in Gide's *L'Immoraliste.*" *Sub-Stance* 26 (1980): 76-85.

[*In the following essay, Wing analyzes the interrelation between the frame-story—Michel's discourse to his friends—and the actual story of Michel's experience in order to demonstrate the manner in which the text of* The Immoralist *is ironic and undermines "the self-identity which is the* telos *of the narrative."*]

> J'aime . . . que chaque livre porte en lui, mais cachée, sa propre réfutation et ne s'assoie pas sur l'idée, de peur qu'on n'en voie l'autre face. J'aime qu'il porte en lui de quoi se nier, se supprimer lui-même; qu'il soit un tout si clos qu'on ne puisse le supprimer que tout entier, qu'il ne laisse après lui pas de déchets, de résidus, pas de cendres, . . .
>
> Postface pour la deuxième édition de **Paludes** (1895)

> J'ai fini de vous raconter mon histoire.
>
> Michel, in *L'Immoraliste*

The two statements which I have quoted above pose the problematic of the work as a finite entity. Michel, the narrator hero of ***L'Immoraliste,*** arriving at the juncture of the recounting of his past (*mon histoire*) and the act of narration, states simply that the story is finished, that there is nothing to add ("Qu'ajouterais-je de plus?").[1] The work of the telling has ended and the story as a completed work has been constructed; the narrator sets himself clearly "outside" of the history he has reconstructed:

> Il y a de tout cela trois mois à peine. Ces trois mois ont éloigné cela de dix ans.[2]

This passage at the conclusion of the *histoire* is a necessity of narrative structure; it marks the fulfillment of the narrative contract, by the shift from the dual first person of the story, which includes both the narrated and the narrating *je,* to the single *je* of the *discours,* and by the shift from the *passé simple* of the *histoire* to the present of the *discours.* The break is further confirmed by the return to the voice of the preamble, that of the friend who introduced the narrator and his story.

This is not the only way the passage functions, however. The moment of conclusion is presented as a moment of both deliverance and anguish:

> Je me suis délivré, c'est possible; mais qu'importe: je souffre de cette liberté . . . je sens le bonheur trop présent et l'abandon à lui trop uniforme.
>
> (p. 471)

The term *délivré* alludes to the ontological status of the narrator in a context which necessarily relates it to the structure of the narrative. The malaise articulated here undermines the very notions of completeness which the juncture of *histoire* and *discours* seem to call forth.[3]

The postface to **Paludes,** quoted above, alludes to the completeness of the text as a necessity for the very subversion proposed. Within its own system, the work will contain elements which will suppress its apparent sense ("se supprimer lui-même"), or generate opposite meanings ("ne s'assoie pas sur l'idée, de peur qu'on n'en voie l'autre face"). A similar statement can be found in the preface to ***L'Immoraliste***: "C'est à contre-coeur que j'emploie ici le mot 'problème'. A vrai dire, en art il n'y a pas de problèmes—dont l'oeuvre d'art ne soit la suffisante solution" (p. 367). Meaning would be dislocated from within, but the displacement is nonetheless localizable within the limits circumscribed by the work. My effort in this paper will be to affirm what no reader of Gide's *récit* would seriously doubt: that the text *is* ironic, that it subverts its own meanings in the manner proposed by the passages quoted above. I would like to suggest, however, that the "problem" of the work of art is more problematic than is generally assumed, since the processes of this subversion of meanings put in question the notions of completeness articulated in Gide's comments and imposed by Michel as he attempts to emerge from his *histoire.* In this reading of ***L'Immoraliste*** I will first discuss narrative structure, the interrelation between *discours* and *histoire* in Michel's narration of his own story as that interaction inscribes the protagonist's desire and as it undermines the self-identity which is the *telos* of the narrative. I will then examine certain semantic aspects of the text, specifically passages dealing with reading and writing, and finally reconsider the problems of closure, self-reflexivity and irony.

The end point of the protagonist's history is *une liberté sans emploi* in which the "I" of the speaking voice assumes an identity in the present of the *discours,* "outside" the double relationship between the narrating and the narrated "I," imposed by the *histoire.* That moment is described paradoxically as both a plenitude and an absence. Desire and pleasure are almost simultaneous, and Michel speaks of that satisfaction as a debilitating continuity:

> Ici toute recherche est impossible, tant la volupté suit de près le désir. Entouré de splendeur et de mort, je sens le bonheur trop présent et l'abandon à lui trop uniforme.
>
> (p. 471)

It will be my purpose to show that the relationship to language by which the hero arrives at this assertion of plenitude subverts its very possibility and that the moment of self-presence, which provides the ethical and ontological motivation of the narrative, is undercut by the discursive processes of the text in which it is articulated. Having arrived at its goal, the self, it will be seen, is displaced by language which is the *only* means by which it can articulate its instance. In the attempt to set itself outside of the *histoire,* the self in the *discours* is no less excluded from origin; the dilemma is simply shifted to another linguistic level and the predicament must be reformulated.

Before further discussing this displacement, I would like to show that it is prepared in the prologue and affirmed again in the conclusion by passages which undermine the identity of the listener (*tu*) as a stable entity able to assume the burden of judgment. In both the preamble to the *récit* and the pages which follow Michel's statement that the story has been completed, several passages raise questions concerning the narrative contract and concerning a certain complicity between the speaker and the listener. The question of complicity established by the act of listening is first presented in an unresolved but hardly startling manner in the preamble. Michel's friend conveys the story which he has just "heard" to his brother M. D. R., *Président du conseil,* in the traditional manner of a pseudo-mémoire or a pseudo-autobiography, in which the novel is "naturalized" by formulae which camouflage its status as fiction. The story is transmitted to a representative of the viewpoint of order, as the ethical question on the first page indicates clearly: "En quoi Michel peut-il servir l'Etat?" The ease with which this preamble can be read according to a traditional pattern is cause for concern, however, for the assessment of the truth of Michel's story is here called into question in a manner which finally undermines the identity of the *tu* which poses the problem:

> Michel nous a parlé, mon cher frère. Le récit qu'il nous fit, le voici. Tu l'avais demandé, je te l'avais promis; mais à l'instant de l'envoyer, j'hésite encore, et plus je le relis et plus il me paraît affreux. Ah! que vas-tu penser de notre ami: D'ailleurs qu'en pensé-je moi-même?
>
> (p. 369)

The passage from judgment to complicity is indicated here in the oscillation between "plus je le relis et plus il me paraît affreux" and "qu'en pensé-je moi-même?" This eclipse of judgment by complicity is articulated less equivocally in the conclusion following the story, spoken by the same friend:

> Michel resta longtemps silencieux. Nous nous taisions aussi, pris chacun d'un étrange malaise. Il nous semblait, hélas, qu'à nous la raconter, Michel nous avait rendu son action plus légitime. De ne savoir où la désapprouver, dans la lente explication qu'il en donna, nous en faisait presque complices. Nous y étions comme engagés.
>
> (p. 470)

The issues of judgment and complicity are considerably more complex than the earlier assertions introducing the story had indicated. Here the earlier detachment of a sympathetic listener is undercut by acknowledgment that the role of the listener is not an innocent one. The narrative/narration constructs on several levels, and that process includes the listener. The story is not a simple and faithful reproduction of the past which can be perceived and judged from a detached otherness; the *tu* of the *je/tu* dyad consequently is a mobile instance, one which is inevitably modified through its assimilation by the narrative performance. The question of judging the *histoire* and the protagonist is shifted by the syntax of the narrative from the stable ground of established value, that of the preamble, with its guarantee in a pseudo-referentiality, *le Président du conseil,* to the indeterminacy of the conclusion. That shift has been established more by the telling than by the narrated "events" themselves. The pseudo-referential actions recounted are eclipsed in their importance by the relation between *discours* ("à nous la raconter . . . la lente explication . . .") and *histoire* ("son action"), wherein *discours* acquires the greater significance. The malaise expressed at these critical junctures of the text is not exclusively or even primarily ethical, for it relates not only to the signified of the *histoire,* but to telling as a performative act. The independence of the signified of the *histoire* ("son action") is thus undermined as it is incorporated by the telling; the "place" of action is no longer unequivocally "outside" narration/listening: "de ne savoir *où* la désapprouver, *dans* la lente explication qu'il en donna . . ."

I turn now to a discussion of the protagonist's relation to language as it is articulated on different levels of the text, in the *discours,* through comments about the telling of the story, and on the level of the *histoire* in several passages in which the protagonist recounts his past activities as a writer, lecturer, reader or listener. I will examine the relations between dispossession and desire as they structure the logic of the narrative, specifically, the way in which the desire to possess is made manifest by a process of *dis*possession. On a thematic level dispossession can be seen as Michel's efforts to divest himself of an academic culture; to free himself from his Norman estate, after actively contributing to its ruin; to free himself from his sick wife Marceline by dragging her from Paris to Switzerland, to Italy and to North Africa in a cruel reenactment of their wedding trip, which ends in her death; and finally to reject heterosexuality. This thematics has been repeatedly discussed and needs no analysis here.[4] Dispossession as the function of desire also operates in the subject's relation to language, which is less accessible to reductive thematic readings and appears in several variants throughout the text.

The narration begins in the present tense with remarks by Michel about his *need* to tell the story. These statements are clearly necessitated in part by the diegetic situation, for they effect the transition from the first person of the prologue, the voice of Michel's friend, to the *je* of the principal narrator, who in turn takes responsibility for establishing the temporal gap and the doubling of the first person which will constitute the autobiographical narration/narrative.[5] The statements also function as phatic utterances, which establish contact between the narrator and his listeners. Both of these functions are consistent with the diegetic situation, but the statements themselves extend their reference to the speaker and his attitude toward his story and, in Jakobson's terms, thus combine the phatic and the emotive functions.[6] The passage sets the act of telling in relation to desire ("J'ai besoin . . . J'ai besoin de parler") and states its *telos* as an ontological quest:[7]

> . . . si je vous appelai brusquement, et vous fis voyager jusqu'à ma demeure lointaine, c'est pour vous voir, uniquement, et pour que vous puissiez m'entendre. Je ne veux pas d'autre secours que celui-là: vous parler. Car je suis à tel point de ma vie que je ne peux plus dépasser. Pourtant ce n'est pas lassitude. Mais je ne comprends plus. J'ai besoin . . . J'ai besoin de parler, vous dis-je. Savoir se libérer n'est rien; l'ardu, c'est savoir être libre.—Souffrez que je parle de moi; je vais vous raconter ma vie, simplement, sans modestie et sans orgueil, plus simplement que si je parlais à moi-même. Ecoutez-moi . . .
>
> (p. 392)

The narrator states that the narration is motivated by a desire to know ("Savoir se libérer n'est rien; l'ardu, c'est savoir être libre."); cognition will dissipate present ignorance ("je ne comprends plus") and will emerge from the telling itself. The impetus for narration is marked by a shift in the meanings of the term *savoir*. In the first instance here ("savoir se libérer") it refers to the completed process of dispossession, which provides the content of the *histoire* and which implicitly includes all actions up to the present moment of narration. Paradoxically, however, *savoir* here indicates a deficiency of knowledge. In the second instance ("savoir être libre") the term *savoir* suggests the possibility of knowing as the acquisition of an undivided self-knowledge. From its outset, however, the "knowing" which is posited as the *telos* of the narration is undermined by the strategies of desire, which are those of language. Knowledge is not to be acquired by judgment operated through a process of distancing the present from the past, an "état actuel de connaissance récapitulative," in Starobinski's phrase.[8] It is to be achieved through the narration, whose motivation, paradoxically, is not primarily the will to know, but desire: "J'ai besoin . . . J'ai besoin de parler." The act of understanding is thus linked at the outset of the story to a *deferral* of the moment of awareness, displaced toward an atemporal present ("savoir être libre") which will be arrived at through the performance itself and is to be located at the convergence of *histoire* and *discours*. The cognitive is thus secondary to a desire which will function as a process of deferral. The convergence of *histoire* and *discours* is a mythical moment of self-possession in language; it "has been" arrived at through dispossession of the past self, that of the *histoire*. Michel's blindness at the beginning of the story is apparent in his confusion of knowledge and desire and in his situating the quest for fulfillment of desire in the very structure of language, which will necessarily defer its attainment indefinitely, beyond the juncture posited as the moment of fulfillment. As the *je* of narration and the *je* of *histoire* meet at the conclusion of the story, the displacement of self-possession, presence, plenitude will simply be reinscribed at a different level in a self-perpetuating *mise en abîme*.[9]

The possibility of language as the form and substance of mastery and self-appropriation is suggested in the first pages of the story by an anecdote which is the first mention of writing in the narrative itself. As a young man, Michel distinguishes himself by his erudition and brilliance; in a substitution designed to prove his equality to his father, Michel publishes under his father's name a treatise on Phrygian religion which Michel himself has composed. In terms of the problematic described above in which writing is a liberating exercise which will lead to self-possession, this episode can be seen as the negative moment which makes possible the subsequent efforts of undoing. This appropriation of the name and language of the father confirms Michel's successful access to erudition as the discourse of mastery, but the episode can be read ironically since the "independence" is purchased by an unacknowledged submission to the father. By extension, all of Michel's erudition, his reading, his lectures delivered in Paris, his lessons derived from conversations with Ménalque are marked by the original subservience. Throughout the first and second parts of the *récit*, writing, lecturing, and even the lesson of the famous anecdote of the stolen scissors recounted by Ménalque will be seen as exercises in imitation which recall ironically the earlier imitation of the father. Even in denying a certain mastery over truth in language—a kind of possession—the denial reinstates the same mastery through the rhetoric in which it is articulated, through metaphors of unveiling, of the book, of the palimpsest and in various other figures.

Michel's discovery of his senses during his convalescence marks the present by the inscription of an almost lost but more authentic past; the figure of self-discovery as the reading of a more concealed text occurs throughout the account of his recovery:

> La conscience que je prenais à nouveau de mes sens m'en permettait l'inquiète reconnaissance. Oui, mes sens, réveillés désormais, se retrouvaient toute une histoire, se recomposaient un passé.
>
> (p. 390)

Michel's growing mistrust of his erudition as what separates him from the present ("J'en vins à mépriser en moi cette science qui d'abord faisait mon orgueil . . . ," p. 398) incites him to seek his yet hidden authentic being in a process described by the figures of unveiling and of deciphering. The origin is ironically not a self-sufficient presence, but a text, as the figure of the palimpsest indicates:

> Et je me comparais aux palimpsestes; je goûtais la joie du savant, qui, sous les écritures plus récentes, découvre sur un même papier un texte très ancien infiniment plus précieux. Quel était-il ce texte occulte? Pour le lire, ne fallait-il tout d'abord effacer les textes récents?
>
> (p. 399)

The erudite choice of deciphering the palimpsest as a figure for self discovery and relating the pleasure of doing so to that of a *savant* contribute to establishing the irony of the passage, for in its use of figural language the passage reinscribes the very terms it would undermine, origin as trace or text.

The course which Michel offers at the Collège de France, the content of which is alluded to briefly at the end of Part One and presented in a series of maxims in the second chapter of Part Two, offers a eulogy of primitive European culture. The young king Athalaric, who revolts against his Latin training in favor of the barbarous Goths, serves as an analogon of Michel's own revolt. Michel uses the occasion to explore his own self-analyzing discourse. In his search for origins, he simultaneously dispossesses himself of a classical European culture and seeks to "unveil" a more authentic, more primitive being. This quest is undermined here also by the rhetoric in which it is articulated, first by the obvious situational irony established by the academic setting, but more significantly by the figure of truth as accessible through a process of unveiling, which simply reinstates truth as a possession attainable through an act of mastery. Once again, Michel is writing/speaking in subservience to the law of the father.

The sequences with Ménalque, Michel's moral double, in the very center of the *récit*, are structured according to a similar figural logic. Here the figures are those of substitution, in which Ménalque serves as a metonym for Michel, and of allegory, which is the structure of the anecdote of the scissors as it is related by Ménalque. Both figures undermine the apparent message of this sequence, not by their semantic values but by their function as figures. Ménalque's ethic of authenticity is grounded in a rejection of what he calls "laws of imitation":

> . . . la plupart d'entre eux [ceux qui nous entourent] pensent n'obtenir d'eux-mêmes rien de bon que par la contrainte; ils ne se plaisent que contrefaits . . . Chacun se propose un patron, puis l'imite; il accepte un patron tout choisi. Il y a pourtant, je le crois, d'autres choses à lire, dans l'homme. On n'ose pas. On n'ose pas tourner la page. Lois de l'imitation je les appelle . . .
>
> (p. 431)

Insofar as Ménalque doubles for Michel, the example ironically reinscribes the process of imitation it would escape. Similarly, the use of the metaphor of the book ironically undermines Ménalque's message, for he offers yet another embodiment of truth to be possessed, if one would only turn the page. The famous anecdote of the stolen scissors, in which Ménalque recalls Michel's complicity when he observed an Arab boy, Moktir, stealing Marceline's scissors and yet failed to intervene, is presented as an allegory of Michel's lack of a sense of property. In its own rhetoric, however, the moral anecdote reinstates truth as property, the signified of the allegory, accessible again through unveiling:

> [ces phrases] . . . mettaient à nu brusquement ma pensée; une pensée que je couvrais de tant de voiles, que j'avais presque pu l'espérer étouffée.
>
> (p. 437)

A final example of a story which rejects culture, decency and morality reveals a hidden truth far more somber in its primitive irrationality than any of the others. Returning in the second part of the *récit* to his farms in Normandy, Michel establishes relations with the sons of the woodcutter, Heurtevent, and listens to the stories told by one of them, Bute:

> J'interrogeais Bute, comme j'avais fait les informes chroniques des Goths. De ses récits sortait une trouble vapeur d'abîme qui déjà me montait à la tête, et qu'inquiètement je humais.
>
> (p. 446)

The stories are of incest and rape and they offer an extreme example of the denial of culture. Unlike the proleptic allegory of Ménalque's conversation, which finds its apparent fulfillment in Michel's casting off of his material possessions, this story evokes no response, however deluded. The truth ultimately unveiled in the protagonist's quest to know finally is revealed as truly subversive of the father's law. The narrator's silence suggests that the "truth" of these stories is not susceptible to a domesticating imitation, for the pattern proposed undermines the pact which is constitutive of culture and which Michel refuses to know. The truth appropriated from this primitive chronicle is considerably attenuated, in fact; for it awakens in Michel a more anodyne desire for anarchy, that of poaching his own land, which, not surprisingly in this context, had formerly belonged to his mother.

The third section of the *récit*, in its few references to textual work and its use of the variants *travail, écrire*, reiterates the structure of dispossession/unveiling/possession:

> Il me semblait alors que j'étais né pour une sorte inconnue de trouvailles; et je me passionnais étrangement dans ma recherche ténébreuse, pour laquelle je sais que le chercheur devait abjurer et repousser de lui culture, décence et morale.
>
> (p. 457)

In the same passage Michel explicitly rejects history in a gesture which is a "final" refusal of culture and which will then permit him to turn to an exclusively self-reflexive search: "A présent, le jeune Athalaric lui-même pouvait pour me parler, se lever de sa tombe; je n'écoutais plus le passé" (p. 457). Remarks on the level of discourse, however, reinscribe the narrator, in spite of himself, in a relation with the past which has just been rejected and indicate a continuing malaise about a culturally determined logic, hostile, in Michel's terms, to the authenticity of the story. In the first passage, the narrator speaks of the persistence of logic, which continues to control the formulation of his story:

> En vain chercherais-je à présent à imposer à mon écrit plus d'ordre qu'il n'en eut dans ma vie. Assez longtemps j'ai cherché de vous dire comment je devins qui je suis. Ah! désembarrasser mon esprit de cette insupportable logique!
>
> (p. 464)

The narrator strives to obliterate any rhetorical control over the *histoire,* since that control would reinstae the cultural order from which he seeks to escape.[10] We may read the term *ordre* here as connoting esthetic conventions which would obtain in the telling of stories and which would govern the selection and combination of what can properly take place in the *histoire.* The dispossession to be operated is now clearly located in the linguistic relation between *discours* and *histoire*: "L'art s'en va de moi, je le sens. C'est pour faire place à quoi d'autre" (p. 172). And further on: "Ah! je pourrais ici feindre ou me taire; mais que m'importe à moi ce récit, s'il cesse d'être véritable?" (p. 175). At the conclusion of the narrative, the ethical values of good and evil are superceded by the values of truth and falsehood, thereby locating the problematic within the text.[11] The ethical ideal of authenticity is dependent on the erasure of any rhetoric (*logique, art*) which would maintain control over and therefore distance between what is told and the act of telling. Michel's narrative is controlled by a *telos* which places the moment of truth at the juncture of *histoire* and *discours,* in a sort of atemporal present. That moment is a fiction, however, always already displaced by its reliance on language. Any *discours* through its articulation constitutes the instance of the first person, which in Michel's mystified quest would be self-sufficient; yet that "person" exists only in a discursive relation to others in a signifying chain, a *mise en abîme* which effects an inevitable displacement of an impossible presence.

The impossibility of reactivating a lost origin in a moment of pure presence is figured also at the end of the *récit* by the anecdote of Michel's efforts to kill time by playing an apparently innocent game in which he places white pebbles in the shade, then holds them in his hand:

> jusqu'à ce qu'en soit épuisée la calmante fraîcheur acquise. Alors je recommence, alternant les cailloux, remettant à tremper ceux dont la fraîcheur est tarie. Du temps s'y passe . . .
>
> (p. 471)

The results of the game are hardly innocent, though the narrator remains unaware of their ironic effect. In fact, Michel has constructed a clock, since the apparently gratuitous play must depend on his following the moving demarcation between light and shadow. Time is thus reintroduced at that very point of the narrative which was to mark the emancipation from time.

The main point of this reading has been to show that **L'Immoraliste** is indeed a self-reflexive ironic text, which contains within itself its own refutation and thus conforms to Gide's statement quoted at the beginning of my paper. I have traced many of the numerous references in the *récit* to writing, reading and listening; it has been possible to show that the protagonist's quest of freedom from laws of imitation which function in writing/speaking by duplication of the mastery of the father simply reproduces that system in the metaphors which figure its rejection. Irony results from the reader's perception of this similarity in apparent difference and the narrator/protagonist's blindness to it. Irony operates as well in this text, however, to undermine Gide's definition of the critical function of his works, with its comfortable notion of closure. The narrator's dilemma at the end of his *histoire,* at the junction of *histoire* and *discours,* is that he is still a prisoner of the language which was to have produced his freedom; the need which initiated the telling remains unfulfilled, for the moment which it posits as the moment of fulfillment, a moment of presence of the self in its own discourse, is a fiction, infinitely deferrable. The language in which the quest is articulated is unable to know what it needs most to understand, the process of its own production.

Notes

1. My use of the terms *histoire* and *discours* is derived from E. Benveniste's well-known studies on subjectivity in language, verb tense structure and shifters, and informed by distinctions clarified by G. Genette in *Figures III*. See E. Benveniste, "L'Homme dans le langage" in *Problèmes de linguistique générale* (Paris: Gallimard, 1966), pp. 225-288; Gérard Genette, *Figures III* (Paris: Seuil, 1972), esp. pp. 71-78, 225-243, 261-265. *Histoire,* throughout this study, will refer to the narrated "events" situated by the narrator in the past and which constitute the content of the story to be related; *discours* will refer to the act of narration in

the fictional present. *Récit* is not used in the technical sense, such as that elucidated by Genette in *Figures III,* but refers to Gide's own use of the term to classify his prose works. For an extensive analysis of verb tenses, and other temporal markers and of personal pronouns in Gide's *récits,* see Martine Maisani-Léonard, *André Gide ou l'ironie de l'écriture* (Montréal: Les Presses de l'Université de Montréal, 1976). On Benveniste's unexamined presuppositions regarding presence in language, see Jacques Derrida, "Le Supplément de la copule," in *Marges de la philosophie* (Paris: Les Editions de Minuit, 1972), pp. 211-246.

2. Gide, *L'Immoraliste* in *Romans* (Paris: Gallimard, Bibliothèque de la Pléiade, 1958), p. 470. All references to *L'Immoraliste* are taken from this edition.

3. Departing from Gide's famous statement that all his *récits* are ironic works, critical of certain moral positions, many commentators have analyzed the functions of irony within the textual enclosure. See, for example, Jean Hytier, *André Gide* (Paris: Charlot, 1945), pp. 159-193; Allan Pasco, "Irony and Art in Gide's *L'Immoraliste*," *Romanic Review,* 64 (1973), 184-203. Albert Sonnenfeld's excellent study "On Readers and Reading in *La Porte étroite* and *L'Immoraliste*," *Romanic Review,* 67, No. 3 (May 1976), 172-186, deals principally with Gide's ironic manipulation of supposedly unformed confession in *La Porte étroite*. Although the study contains suggestive remarks on the structure of the prologue in *L'Immoraliste* and on the thematics of dispossession, to which I refer below, its focus is on *La Porte étroite*.

4. See J. C. Davies, *Gide: "L'Immoraliste" and "La Porte étroite"* (London: Arnold, 1968), pp. 56-59; Jean Hytier, *André Gide,* p. 184; Henri Maillet, *"L'Immoraliste" d'André Gide* (Paris: Hachette, 1972), pp. 31-50; Allan Pasco, "Irony and Art in Gide's *L'Immoraliste*," esp. pp. 186-189; Sonnenfeld, "On Readers and Reading in *La Porte étroite* and *L'Immoraliste*," p. 185.

5. Léonard, *André Gide ou l'ironie de l'écriture,* in the section "Aux frontières du récit: fonction du préambule," pp. 38-64, discusses the linguistic elements which constitute the shift in this text and in Gide's other récits.

6. Roman Jakobson, "Linguistics and Poetics," in *Style in Language,* Thomas A Sebeok, ed. (Cambridge, Mass.: M.I.T. Press, 1960), pp. 350-377.

7. On the interaction between the desire to know, the desire to excuse and the desire to tell I have found Paul deMan's recent study of Rousseau's *Confessions* to be most suggestive. See Paul deMan, "The Purloined Ribbon," *Glyph,* 1 (*Johns Hopkins Textual Studies,* Baltimore and London: The Johns Hopkins University Press, 1977), pp. 28-49.

8. Jean Starobinski, "Le Style de l'autobiographie," *Poétique,* 3 (1970), 257-265; v.p. 261.

9. I use this expression to indicate a process of infinite deferral, inscribed by language as the structure of desire. See deMan, "The Purloined Ribbon," p. 34. *Mise en abîme* as the use of a story within a story, a structure which is considerably different from the process I am discussing, is analyzed in a suggestive article on *Paludes*: Graeme Watson, "Gide's Construction 'en abyme'," *Australian Journal of French Studies,* 7 (1970), 224-233. See also Lucien Dällenbach, *Le Récit spéculaire. Essai sur la mise en abyme* (Paris: Seuil, 1977). Dällenbach defines the narrative figure as: ". . . la *réduplication simple* (fragment qui entretient avec l'oeuvre qui l'inclut un rapport de similitude), la *réduplication à l'infini* (fragment qui entretient avec l'oeuvre qui l'inclut un rapport de similitude et qui enchâsse lui-même un fragment qui . . . , et ainsi de suite) et la *réduplication aporistique* (fragment censé inclure l'oeuvre qui l'inclut)" (p. 51). The author studies the structures in Gide's *La Tentative amoureuse, Paludes* and *Les Faux-monnayeurs*.

10. On "over-writing" as a narrative strategy in Gide's autobiographical *Si le grain ne meurt,* see Philippe Lejeune, "Gide et l'espace autobiographique," in *Le Pacte autobiographique* (Paris: Seuil, 1975), pp. 165-196, esp. 189-193.

11. See deMan, "The Purloined Ribbon," p. 29.

Arthur E. Babcock (essay date 1982)

SOURCE: Babcock, Arthur E. "*L'Immoraliste.*" In *Portraits of Artists: Reflexivity of Gidean Fiction, 1902-1946,* pp. 15-28. York, S.C.: French Literature Publications Company, 1982.

[*In the following essay, Babcock questions the purpose of Michel's transcribed narrative in* The Immoralist, *contending that "Michel's* récit *attempts to serve its own end; rather than being an appeal to external authority, it turns inward upon itself as an act of self-creation through language."*]

Et que l'on parle bien, tant qu'on parle dans le désert!

—André Gide, *Journal*

Although simplicity is often held to be one of the traits of the Gidean *récit*, **L'Immoraliste** (1902) has given rise to widely divergent, often contradictory interpretations. In his preface, Gide alludes to the mystification felt by the book's earliest readers: neither apologia nor accusation, *L'Immoraliste* frustrates those who seek unequivocal answers to the questions raised by Michel's narrative. Even when the reader abandons any hope of finding a clear moral lesson, he is still faced with many difficulties: to understand Gide's expressed desire to "bien peindre et d'éclairer bien ma peinture" ([*Oeuvres complètes*] p. 368), one needs to know that his notion of light in painting was that of Rembrandt, for whom, according to Gide, shadow is as important as light.[1]

So it is with the aspect of Gide's fiction that this study proposes to examine: it is not at all obvious upon first reading that *L'Immoraliste* is reflexive. The first of the *récits* to be published sets the pattern for the later examples of the sub-genre: reflexivity is present, but only latently. Unlike *Les Caves du Vatican* and *Les Faux-Monnayeurs*, *L'Immoraliste* and the other *récits* reveal their reflexive dimension only upon very close examination.

One such examination is that of Allan Pasco, whose argument for *L'Immoraliste* as reflexive fiction is based on elements of the book that are, according to Alter's definition, self-conscious.[2] Whereas Michel's expressed aim is to "raconter ma vie, simplement" (p. 372), Pasco argues, his narrative is entirely too well structured to bear out this claim.[3] Divided into three parts of nine, three, and one chapters, *L'Immoraliste*'s "fearful symmetry," as Albert Sonnenfeld puts it,[4] clashes with Michel's professed artlessness. Behind his claimed simplicity is an artifice that puts the reader on his guard, saying "I, the text, am not real; I am not even lifelike; I am art" (Pasco ["Irony and Art in *L'Immoraliste*"] p. 192).

Indeed, the very context of Michel's monologue strikes one as *invraisemblable*: as G. W. Ireland points out, the writer of the letter (one of the three listeners whom Michel calls to his side and who subsequently sets down his story) must have been supplied with vast quantities of paper and pencils to write down Michel's story, told in a single night.[5] Pasco sees this device as an ironic signal (flaunted artifice, Alter would say) that Michel's narrative is not what it appears to be, even going so far as to suggest that the *récit* is not spontaneous, but carefully rehearsed (Pasco, p. 189). At first glance, at least, the argument is attractive: to provide listeners for Michel and a setting for his narrative is to naturalize his discourse, to make it plausible. The very implausibility of the device, however, counteracts its ostensible intent: *L'Immoraliste* moves in the direction of verisimilitude, but so feebly that the effect upon the reader is quite the opposite.

To this line of reasoning, other readers reply that it is the implied author, not Michel, who supplies the rigid order and refined style of *L'Immoraliste*.[6] Interestingly, the manuscript text of *L'Immoraliste* supports this view (the portion of the text in italics was removed by Gide and does not appear in the published edition):

> Je t'adresse donc ce récit, tel que Denis, Daniel et moi l'entendîmes. *tel que tous trois nous l'avons dû récrire, hélas! le déformant parfois par oubli, tâchant surtout de lui garder son accent même. Ce furent les récits de trois mois, Michel les fit sur sa terrasse.*
>
> (p. 1520)

Even though the three scribes sought to preserve the "accent" of Michel's narrative, the admission of editorial deformation has been made: in the manuscript version, Michel is not solely responsible for the text of *L'Immoraliste*.

Nonetheless, comparison of the manuscript and the published text of *L'Immoraliste* confirms Pasco's view. It is always dangerous to attempt to reconstruct an author's intentions, but it seems fair to say, given the more *vraisemblable* variant reproduced above, that Gide cannot have failed to consider the question of plausibility as he determined the circumstances of Michel's narrative. If the context of Michel's tale lacks verisimilitude, the likely supposition is that Gide intended it. In any case, the text of *L'Immoraliste* with which one must deal—the published version—supports the argument that an air of falsity is established at the beginning of the book, and that the reader must be on his guard for further evidence that Michel's narrative is not what it first may seem.

Whatever Michel's intentions may have been in calling his three friends to his side, it is clear that the letter-writer's ambition, initially at least, is to rehabilitate his errant friend. His letter is addressed to his brother, the Premier, a symbol of authority, whom he asks how Michel might best serve the State (p. 369). Yet after having heard Michel's story and reread his own transcription of it, the writer has doubts: "Ah! que vas-tu penser de notre ami? D'ailleurs qu'en pensé-je moi-même?" (p. 369). This abstention from judgment is echoed by the writer's vague exaltation produced by the Algerian climate: he is able to feel neither "triste" nor "gai" (p. 369). Conventional names for emotional states seem no longer to apply, which means that conventional value systems no longer function. Whereas the writer has no difficulty in characterizing the old Michel, he cannot *name* the new one: "Ce n'était plus le puritain très docte de naguère [. . .] C'était . . . mais pourquoi t'indiquer déjà ce que son récit va te dire" (p. 370). Yet the *récit* specifically fails to provide the promised judgment. Thus, the preamble of *L'Immoraliste* at first promises a moral decision and the submission of Michel's case to a politically and socially constituted authority, but the judgmental nature of the letter is undermined from the very beginning. Moreover, there is doubt whether the letter ever reaches its destination: "[. . .] mais à l'instant de l'envoyer, j'hésite encore [. . .]" (p. 369). If the letter containing Michel's *récit* is never to be sent to the Premier, that figure of authority and judgment will remain forever absent, and Michel's narrative will exist only by itself, never submitted to the opinion of conventional morality.[7] The writer's preamble concludes: "Quand ce fut la nuit, Michel dit:" (p. 371), the colon serving to introduce Michel's long monologue. In this case, it must be concluded that the verb *dire* is intransitive. What at first appears to be a confession may be quite different.

Perhaps significantly, Gide's preface reveals a similar independence from moral and political systems: "A vrai dire, en art, il n'y a pas de problèmes—dont l'oeuvre d'art ne soit la suffisante solution" (p. 367). External evidence at best—though it should be noted that, unlike many of Gide's works, no edition of ***L'Immoraliste*** but the first has appeared without the preface—Gide's emphasis of the text's primacy echoes the letter-writer's retreat from judgment and reluctance to send his letter, and makes the reader wonder what function Michel himself sees in his own narrative. Is it a confession, an appeal for help from outside, or does it somehow respond to its own needs? Michel says to his friends:

> Car si je vous appelai brusquement, et vous fit voyager jusqu'à ma demeure lointaine, c'est pour vous voir, uniquement, et pour que vous puissiez m'entendre. Je ne veux pas d'autre secours que celui-là: vous parler.
>
> (p. 372)

In the remaining pages of this chapter I will argue that ***L'Immoraliste*** is reflexive fiction in that Michel's *récit* attempts to serve its own end; rather than being an appeal to external authority, it turns inward upon itself as an act of self-creation through language.

If at the outset of his narrative Michel says that speaking is the only succor he needs, the conclusions of ***L'Immoraliste*** shows why: "Il nous semblait hélas! qu'à nous la raconter, Michel avait rendu son action plus légitime" (p. 470). In between these two points is other evidence that for Michel, telling his story is not a means to an end, but an end in itself; throughout the *récit*, Michel evolves toward his final compulsion to speak. Michel's narrative is not simply the vehicle of his action, but part of that action itself. And in a sense, he ends in language, precisely where he begins. The old, pre-Biskra Michel is already intimately concerned with words. He knows several ancient languages and has already written, under his father's name, a well-received study of Phrygian religious customs that has gained him entry into his father's circle of professional friends. Yet he appears to reject all this when his illness and the example of Bachir's health imbue him with the exalted feeling of being alive in the present. However, Michel's initial revulsion with book-learning, subsequent attempt to return to his scholarly pursuits, and final collapse do not begin to describe his changing (but unchanged) involvement with language. Nearly every phase of his metamorphosis is reflected in his attitude toward speaking, reading, and writing.

To some extent, Michel's rebirth is accompanied initially by a rejection of language: "[. . .] tout me fatigue, même lire; d'ailleurs que lire? Etre, m'occupe assez" (p. 381). Bachir, who has "de grands yeux silencieux" (p. 381), at first does not speak and elicits no speech from Michel: "je ne dis rien" (p. 381); "je fais signe qu'il doit me passer son sifflet" (p. 382). Later, however, the boy's charm is linked to his voice: "'Malade?' dit-il gentiment; le timbre de sa voix était exquis" (p. 383). This small example is but the first to show that Michel's rebirth is accompanied not so much by a rejection of language as by a newly acquired preference for a certain kind of language at the expense of the sort he previously favored. Following his sudden awakening to life, his first reading is not of a scholarly text, but of poetry:

> [. . .] je sortis de ma poche un petit Homère [. . .], relus trois phrases de l'Odyssée, les appris, puis, trouvant un aliment suffisant dans leur rythme et m'en délectant à loisir, fermai le livre et demeurai, tremblant, plus vivant que je n'aurais cru qu'on pût être, et l'esprit engourdi de bonheur.
>
> (p. 391)

Michel has rejected scholarly, scientific language, which is essentially referential in that it seeks to describe the world. In its place he selects poetry, whose referentiality is at best problematical. To suggest further that what interests him in poetry is that it is an end in itself, Michel notes that it is the "rythme" of Homer's verse, not its tenor, that delights him. Moreover, that he should find "un aliment *suffisant*" in the three lines implies that there are other nourishments to be found in Homer but which do not interest him. Indeed there are: the story, for one, but Michel here seems to prefer pure language to language whose chief purpose is to represent. Another significant aspect of the passage is that life is here associated with art: through Homer, Michel feels vibrantly alive. Furthermore, art is non-intellectual, depending upon and affecting the senses alone: Michel's "esprit" is "engoudi." Finally, there is some irony in Michel's choice of the *Odyssey* as his *texte de jouissance*: so ancient a text clashes with his professed rejection of the past. And while he claims that he was not interested in reading, it appears that he has been carrying it about in his pocket. These factors suggest that the operant variable of his "rebirth" is not past/present but non-fiction/fiction.

Similar reflections on poetry are found when Michel begins his return voyage to France, seeking a renewal of productivity but failing to find it in his old preoccupations: "Les grands faits politiques devaient donc m'émouvoir beaucoup moins que l'émotion renaissante en moi des poètes, ou de certains hommes d'action" (p. 398). He rejects objective fact as he has already rejected the language that represents it, but Michel's new interests are not so much a rejection of the real as its redefinition. That "poets" should be in apposition to "men of action" suggests once again that Michel is beginning to associate life with art. The Greek etymon of "poetry" means "creation," and Michel's approach to the real is no longer one of revealing it, as does a conventional historian, but of "l'imaginant au présent" (p. 398). Once in Paris, he finds his old associates, philologists and archaeologists, about as interesting as those most referential of books, "de bons dictionnaires d'histoire" (p. 423), and finds the company of novelists and poets more attractive (p. 423). Finally, Michel uses a significant image of rebirth that reveals his changing preoccupation with texts: that of the palimpsest (p. 399). Comparing himself to a parchment containing two texts, one obscured in order to make room for the other, Michel is interested in recovering his original self ("le vieil homme"), that is, the original text. One must wonder if in fact he will not ultimately be led to "rewriting" himself, providing a *new* text to replace the old: the *récit*.

For that is the direction in which Michel's evolution is leading: self-creation through language. In an interesting passage in Part III, Michel tells his listeners that he has not completely abandoned his work, yet it is not at first very clear what the subject of his work is. He is no longer interested in history, nor even in the young king Athalaric in whom he had been interested in an attempt to modernize history by emphasizing his own similarity to an historical personage. Now, it appears that he is interested only in "man," and, especially, in man's use of language: "Ce que l'homme a dit jusqu'ici, est-ce tout ce qu'il pouvait dire? N'a-t-il rien ignoré de lui? Ne lui reste-t-il qu'à redire?" (p. 457). And since the passage begins "Cependant je ne renonçais pas à tout travail et trouvais chaque jour plus d'une heure où méditer sur ce que je sentais devoir *dire*" (p. 457, emphasis added), it becomes apparent that the "man" he wishes to investigate is named Michel, and that his investigations will concern what "man" must *say*.

That to speak is to create oneself is shown in Michel's attitude toward conversation. Having married Marceline with no great affection for her, no real sense of her existence, Michel discovers his wife when she begins to speak: "Nous commençames à parler. Ses propos charmants me ravirent. [. . .] Ainsi donc celle à qui j'attachais ma vie avait sa vie propre et réelle!" (p. 376). Later, Marceline again affirms her existence through language: "Brusquement, je songeai qu'à côté, dans une chambre pareille, était ma femme, Marceline; et je l'entendis qui parlait" (p. 379). Discovery of Marceline's autonomous existence is, in effect, the interruption of Michel's voice:

> [. . .] je m'étais marié sans imaginer en ma femme autre chose qu'un camarade, sans songer bien précisément que, de notre union, ma vie pourrait être changée. Je venais de comprendre que là cessait le monologue.
>
> (p. 376)

It is, of course, an irony (and a self-conscious element) that "là cessait le monologue" occurs in a monologue. The point is that Michel will go from one monologue to another. In between, his search for "la parfaite utilisation de soi par une intelligente contrainte" (p. 411) will be characterized by an apparent search for dialogue. Dialogue for Michel is associated with productivity; once his marriage is consummated he takes a special joy in talking with Marceline, whereas in his Narcissistic self-discovery he relished being silent (p. 407). But he fails to find a suitable interlocutor, for he is really seeking monologue.

It has already been shown that he has no taste for conversation with his former associates and friends of the family. And it is not simply that they speak from within a bourgeois ethic that Michel can no longer accept, for even Ménalque, who scarcely represents the moral code against which Michel is rebelling, is far from being an ideal interlocutor: "[. . .] rien ne me montre encore que je puisse vous parler plus qu'aux autres" (p. 427). The point is that Ménalque has his own axe to grind and is far too aggressive for Michel to accept him as a partner in conversation. Indeed, Michel does not seek conversation at all, but an association with others that will not fetter his own imagination.

The few satisfying relationships that Michel finds in France support the hypothesis that he does not seek real conversation but the illusion of it, in order to objectify his own feelings. The Norman peasants of La Morinière, with whom he speaks little but enjoys "une sorte de sympathie" (p. 441), are for him "un immédiat écho de chaque sensation étrangère" (p. 441). Even Bute, with whom Michel is glad to talk, is valued principally because he knows about the mysterious Heurtevent family; and that mystery is important to Michel because it reflects his own obsessions, not because he is genuinely interested in an exterior phenomenon: "[. . .] poursuivre un médiocre mystère qui reculait toujours devant moi? peut-être même *inventer* le mystère [. . .]" (p. 449). Bute's testimony is important not so much for itself but because it enables Michel to externalize his own consciousness.

Michel's quest for dialogue fails because he wants it to. His ideal is not the free exchange of ideas but a silent background for his own thoughts. Silence, for him, is not obscure, but of crystalline clarity: "Quand la diligence s'arrête, on plonge jusqu' au coeur dans la nuit et dans le silence limpide; limpide . . . il n'y a pas d'autre mot. Le moindre bruit prend sur cette transparence étrange sa qualité parfaite et sa pleine sonorité" (p. 455). So it is with his *récit*: delivered in silence, Michel's narrative will form a closed universe of sonority. When his friends arrive, they do so in silence: "Jusqu'à la nuit nous n'échangeâmes pas dix paroles" (p. 371); when he has finished telling his story, "nous nous taisions aussi" (p. 470). In between, a single voice dominates the silence and creates itself: Michel's.

It has thus been shown, in a hypothetical sort of way, why for Michel "parler" is "secours": for him, to speak is to create himself—to reduce the world to an interiorized space. Rejecting dialogue in favor of monologue, Michel never rejects language at all, but simply evolves from one use of language—scholarly, mimetic—to another—the poetic *récit*. When he gives the list of foreign languages that he has learned as a philologist—Latin, Greek, Hebrew, Sanskrit, Persian and Arabic (p. 373), it is curious that all are dead, or at least ancient, tongues, and that he admits to knowing no modern foreign languages. German, for instance, would be a logical choice for so accomplished a scholar, yet he does not mention knowing it. Whether or not he has learned German, it is clear that his list, as long as it is, is incomplete, for he knows one modern foreign language, Italian, at least well enough to flirt with an attractive coachman (p. 462). That he should associate the foreign languages that he knows with his rejected past is misleading, for Michel's rebirth is not at all a rejection of language, but an evolution from ancient tongues, which for him are associated with mimesis, for he learns them in order to describe the ancient world, to a modern language, French, in which he will not imitate the exterior world, but will articulate the inner, in his *récit*. It remains to be shown, however, exactly how, on a more practical level, Michel benefits from language. Exactly what profit does he obtain in speaking? If his evolution is indeed from archaeology to fiction, in what way is his *récit* fictional?

First, it is not accurate, and the inaccuracies serve to justify Michel's behavior. On at least three occasions, he admits that the *récit* omits certain episodes of the part of his life that he is supposedly recounting. In each case, what he fails to tell would have cast Marceline in a good light, making Michel's ultimate rejection of her more difficult to excuse. The first episode is their arrival in Biskra, when Michel's health is at its lowest point. Although he cursorily notes Marceline's tender devotions to him, Michel denies her the advantage of existing in the *récit*: "Pourquoi parler des premiers jours? Qu'en reste-t-il? Leur affreux souvenir est sans voix" (p. 380). Significantly, the role of memory is not quite clear here: is it that Michel cannot remember these days, or that he chooses not to recount them? The "souvenir" exists, after all, but it has no voice; the voice that has been denied it is Michel's. At best, Michel's memory is selective, but the more likely supposition is that the exigencies of the *récit* do not allow the narration of episodes that do not serve the *récit*'s purposes. Once Michel has mentioned Marceline's devoted nursing, he adds, as though to show that his memory is not the determining factor in his choice of what to tell, "pourquoi la conter tout cela? L'important, c'était que la mort m'eût touché, comme l'on dit, de son aile" (p. 380). Thus Marceline has been banished from the *récit*: what matters is Michel, especially his suffering, which will excuse his self-centered quest for liberation. Moreover, in this passage life (the actual events of those first days in Biskra) begins to yield to art; what matters is that "la mort m'eût touché de son aile," a stock literary image.

The second omission confirms the suggestion that Michel's narrative eschews aspects of reality in the name of art. Referring to their return voyage to France, Michel again deprives the episode of its status in the *récit*: "Notre bonheur [. . .] fut si égal, si calme, que je n'en peux rien raconter. Les plus belles oeuvres des hommes sont obstinément douloureuses. Que serait le récit du bonheur?" (p. 408). there is no suggestion at all that this period cannot be remembered; it simply has no place in a "belle oeuvre," the *récit*. Michel here implies, quite openly, that his narrative is art, and that art has the right, even the obligation, to separate itself from life.

A third example shows the subtlety of Michel's self-justification. Having announced her pregnancy, Marceline enjoys with Michel a time of "uniforme bien-être" (p. 410). Michel claims that he has no distinct recollection of this period in his life and, accordingly, glosses over it in a short passage. Nonetheless, even though he is hasty in his account of it, "ce n'est point que j'en garde une moins vive reconnaissance" (p. 410). Thus, Marceline has fulfilled her role as a sexual partner in a way that conforms perfectly to conventional morality, even to the extent that their first lovemaking results in pregnancy. Michel pays lip service to Marceline and society by expressing his gratitude, but denies them any real status in the *récit*. In this instance as in others, Michel can, through his narration, reject his society's values while appearing to remain within their framework.

Surely this is one reason why *parler* is *secours*, but, although it is the most immediate and precise explanation of Michel's motivation in speaking, it is not the most profound. For if Michel's need is to speak and speaking is art, it is through art itself that he will try to save himself. To select a single example of this process—or twenty—is to weaken the hypothesis, for the process is everywhere present. For the sake of argument, however, attention may be paid to a particular instance in which Michel distinguishes between his past attitude as character and his present attitude as narrator. Describing his new passion for life, Michel adds: "Toutes ces pensées je ne les avais pas alors, et ma peinture ici me fausse" (p. 399). Yet some of his "thoughts" are less ideas than lyricism:

> Il y avait ici plus qu'un convalescence; il y avait une augmentation, une recrudescence de vie, l'afflux d'un sang plus riche et plus chaud qui devait toucher mes pensées, les toucher une à une, pénétrer tout, émouvoir, colorer les plus lointaines, délicates et secrètes fibres de mon être.
>
> (p. 399)

The content of this passage (that Michel's recovery changed his thinking) makes less impression than its form; indeed, the lyrical form *is* the content. "Peinture" is exactly the right word to use; Michel's portrait of himself is no photograph, but a retrospective influenced by the art of the narrator. Michel's ambition is to convince his listeners through beauty:

> J'ai toujours cru les grands artistes ceux qui osent donner droit de beauté à des choses si naturelles qu'elles font dire après, à qui les voit: «Comment n'avais-je pas compris jusqu'alors que cela aussi était beau . . . »
>
> (p. 465)

Such is Michel's aim: to normalize through revealed beauty a behavior otherwise unacceptable to the society represented by his three listeners. Few readers, whatever their sexual orientation, could be immune to his description of Bachir's beauty, for example.

Thus the motivation of Michel's enterprise seems clear: through monologue, selective memory and the power of art itself his *récit* will create a blameless Michel. Yet *L'Immoraliste* also contains expressions of failure and contrition. While Marceline lies dying, for example, Michel stays with her for a while "par un dernir semblant de vertu" (p. 468). While a great many of these admissions are not genuine—as has been shown, Michel pays lip service to a morality that he rejects—others are less easily dismissed. At the end of his narrative, for instance, Michel says "Arrachez-moi d'ici à présent, et donnez-moi des raisons d'être" (p. 471), suggesting that the *récit* may not be the complete salvation it was perhaps intended to be. To resolve this difficulty, one needs to examine Michel's attitude toward art; therein lies the true sense of his *récit* and the fullest reflexive meaning of *L'Immoraliste.*

Michel's commentaries on art are complex, if not ambiguous. It has been shown that in his discovery of life at Biskra he turns to Homer, yet when he returns there, seeking to recapture his original sense of vitality, he takes along a copy of Homer but never opens it (p. 465).

His course at the Collège de France is a step toward art, in the sense that he "modernizes" Athalaric and seeks justification in his example, yet Ménalque's life, his slightest gesture, seems "plus éloquent mille fois que mon cours" (p. 429). He despises the Swiss, "sans crimes, sans histoire, sans littérature, sans arts" (pp. 457-458), but revels in North Africa, "terre en vacances d'oeuvres d'art" (p. 464).

The point is that if art is Michel's attempted solution, it is a solution that has been forced upon him. His unattainable ideal is the perfect fusion of life and art that so delighted him when he read the three lines of Homer. Ménalque, too, furnishes a model in his description of Greek art: "[. . .] la vie de l'artiste était elle-même une réalisation poétique [. . .]" (p. 436), an ideal that Michel also finds in North Africa: "Le peuple arabe a ceci d'admirable que, son art, il le vit, il le chante et le dissipe au jour le jour; il ne le fixe point et ne l'embaume en aucune oeuvre" (pp. 464-465). Michel fails to live his life as an artistic experience; the *récit* is an attempt retroactively to fuse art and life. In Parts I and II, Michel's artfulness accomplishes this with some degree of success, as in the case of Bachir's description and the first meeting with Charles, for example. In Part III, however, Michel the character becomes increasingly aware that his circular odyssey will fail to recapture the past, and Michel the narrator finds it increasingly difficult to compress lived experience into an artistic vision. He makes more and more admissions of guilt. His contrition is not real, however; his passion is still present, but emerges only when he detaches the *récit* from events, when *histoire* becomes *discours*:

> Il faut chaud. Il fait beau. Tout est splendide. Ah! je voudrais qu'en chaque phrase, ici, toute une moisson de volupté se distille . . . En vain chercherais-je à présent à imposer à mon récit plus d'ordre qu'il n'y eut dans ma vie [. . .] Je ne sens rien que de noble en moi.
>
> (p. 464)

Ironically, this outburst contradicts Michel's notion of art. The Arabs know that they cannot "embalm" art, but Michel desperately seeks a "harvest of voluptuousness" that will be "distilled" into his *récit,* spoken three months after Marceline's death. The latter terms have more positve connotations than the first, but the three have the same meaning here: to preserve in art the passion of lived experience. This Michel can no longer do; only when he interrupts the *histoire* does his passion still have its full force. Art is fused with present life, in narrative time, but not with the past.

Michel concludes his narrative with this appeal: "Arrachez-moi d'ici à présent, et donnez-moi des raisons d'être. Moi je ne sais plus en trouver" (p. 471). Readers who see in *L'Immoraliste* a straightforward confession cite these lines as proof that Michel concedes guilt and welcomes rehabilitation. Yet their meaning may be quite different, for at the end of his *récit* he also says, "L'art s'en va de moi, je le sens" (p. 467). It is quite literally true that art is taking its leave, for the *récit* is coming to a close, Michel having realized that art, however powerful it may be, cannot become one with his life.

Thus Michel's *récit* is partly a failure and partly a success. A failure because art cannot do all Michel asks of it, the *récit* succeeds as a mediator between Michel's consciousness and his life. For if **L'Immoraliste** ends on an unmistakable note of paralysis and statis as Michel endlessly warms pebbles in his hand only to let them cool in the shade in order to repeat the process (p. 471),[8] it cannot be said that his case will be submitted to society's judgment. The isolated, closed setting of Michel's nocturnal monologue suggests that his action has been removed from a social setting and transposed to another: that of art. For if art cannot wholly subsume the real, neither can the real intrude upon and annihilate the world of art. Indeed, as Gide says in his preface, in art, there are no problems—except the problem of art itself.

Notes

1. André Gide, *Oeuvres complètes* (Paris: Gallimard, 1932-1939), XI, pp. 220-221.

2. Allan H. Pasco, "Irony and Art in *L'Immoraliste*." *Romanic Review,* 64 (1973), pp. 184-203. Only page numbers will be given, within the body of the text, for further references to this article.

3. Martine Maisani-Léonard in *André Gide ou l'ironie de l'écriture* (Montreal: Presses de l'Université de Montréal, 1976), p. 79, argues that the word *simplement* is ambiguous, being readable as *avec simplicité* or as *uniquement*. In the latter sense of the word, Michel will *simply tell* his story, not *tell it simply*: the *énonciation* is independent from the *énoncé*. There seems to me to be little doubt that *simplement* should be read as *avec simplicité*, but the slight ambiguity may indeed put the alert reader on his guard, and rightly so.

4. "On Readers and Reading in *La Porte étroite* and *L'Immoraliste*." *Romanic Review,* 67 (1976), pp. 172-186.

5. Quoted by Sonnenfield, *ibid*.

6. Laurence M. Porter, "The Generativity Crisis of Gide's *Immoraliste*." *French Forum*, 2, No. 1 (1977), p. 65. Porter's argument, which is persuasive, does not depend upon his point that the implied author is responsible for the order and style of the *récit*.

7. Sonnenfeld ("On Readers and Reading . . .") offers a different view of Michel's possible reinsertion into bourgeois society.

8. As pointed out by Porter, p. 63.

Marshall Lindsay (essay date May 1984)

SOURCE: Lindsay, Marshall. "Gide's Ethic of the Moment: *L'Immoraliste*." *Nottingham French Studies* 23, no. 1 (May 1984): 24-36.

[*In the following essay, Lindsay examines the impact of time on the development of Michel's emerging desire and commitment "to live in and for the present moment."*]

"L'insupportable instant!"

"A la seule exception de mes **Nourritures** [*Les Nourritures Terrestres*], tous mes livres sont des livres *ironiques*; ce sont des livres de critique."[1] As enlightening as Gide's comments on his own works are, what he said about them is nearly always incomplete. In this famous distinction between **Les Nourritures terrestres** and the later *récits,* he failed to add that the earlier work is not altogether affirmative, that it carries an implicit criticism of its own doctrine.[2] Although lyrical and fervently enthusiastic, the speaker of the **Nourritures** seems secretly aware of the dangers lurking in his poetic of the instant. He risks losing his time, running out of instants, never finding himself outside the limits of the moment. Yet the risk in that book is the speaker's alone, moments are his alone to grasp or lose. There are other characters, to be sure, but they are hardly more than shadows; the Nathaniëls, the Alcides, the Myrtils, without sex or individuality, are there to participate in the rituals of the speaker's discovery of life and to receive his teaching. Although they are the objects of his momentary awareness, they have no real existence elsewhere or at another time. They are not opaque or real enough to be endangered by the speaker's creed. **L'Immoraliste** and the fiction that followed it add two new dimensions to the world of Gide's imagination. The first is that other people as separate entities with all the attributes of the self begin to inhabit these books. Secondly, time is perceived as problematical, and the uses one puts it to, the choices one makes as to how to live it become an essential part of an overall moral question.[3]

Another characteristic, the frame, is a formal element that distinguishes the *récits* of Gide's maturity from his other works of fiction. It is true that the *récits* from *L'Immoraliste* to *Thésée* differ from the novel and the *sotie* in their economy of means, their use of a single perspective, and their exploitation of one aspect of a personality. But that each one is composed with a frame is of major structural significance.[4] The frame encloses the story, limits its duration, and restricts the development of the characters. But unlike so many frame stories of the nineteenth century, the return of the frame at the end of Gide's *récits* does not put the world back together or suggest that any disorder in the action is illusory. The time of the telling and the time of the action are not separated but form a continuum; if the time of the frame is a present, that of the events within the frame is a completed past whose purpose is to show how the present became unstable and the future in jeopardy. The conflict is not resolved; the past has brought about a present that cannot endure. Something will change, must change, yet since we are in the domain of fiction, nothing can change. Hence the uneasiness one often experiences in reading these short works.

Gide took particular care in the opening section of the frame to establish the voice of the narrator and constitute the fictional audience for whom the story, from within, is intended, both of which become basic structural values. He made it a practice, also, in the opening of a *récit* to focus a moral perspective that will infuse the rest of the story, providing a specific environment for the characters to move in. It is an Old Testament atmosphere that the frame of ***L'Immoraliste*** creates in the desert setting, the allusion to the Book of Job, the solemn *passé simple* of the verbs, and the repeated demands for judgment. "Ah! que vas-tu penser de notre ami?"[5] Michel's friend asks his brother to whom he sends the story, adding: "D'ailleurs qu'en pensé-je moi-même?" (369), suggesting already the moral ambiguity of Michel's behaviour. The distant judge is "Monsieur D. R., Président du Conseil", the highest secular authority in the French Third Republic. Jehovah has become Prime Minister, and the values appealed to are those of friendship, social class, and state. "En quoi Michel peut-il servir l'Etat?" To this question no answer is given at the closing of the story's frame; the divinity remains silent. Michel puts his fate in the hands of others insofar as he, too, awaits the judgment of the Prime Minister. But for the moment he wishes only to speak: "Je ne veux pas d'autre secours que celui-là: vous parler" (372). For to articulate one's past can be to deliver oneself of it or to assume it fully; we do not yet know which value Michel assigns to his act of confession.

Michel's story is one of new beginnings. Even before his symbolic rebirth at Biskra, where he arrives "comme mort", he confronts new situations in complete innocence. "Pour la première fois", he often says when he is not working, when he looks at his new wife, when travel awakens fresh sensations within him. Neither his twenty years of scholarship nor twenty centuries of Judeo-Christian culture have touched the virgin world that opens constantly before him. His discovery of it comes in sudden realisations:

> Brusquement, avec une évidence effarante, il m'apparut que . . . brusquement ma vie m'apparut . . .
>
> (384)

and a similar abruptness characterises his acts. Life has for him a kind of immediacy that will permit no delay: he insists on instant realisation of his decisions to avoid any lag between the world and his thought. Once his mind is made up, delay of any sort irritates him. With increasing impatience, he wishes to sweep away the old moment, to hurry up time, and to place himself in the next moment which will be open again to infinite possibilities. Every new moment is a beginning and encloses a new consciousness. The discovery of life and life itself spring forth constantly in the next moment. If Michel should attempt, out of judgement or tact, to delay or suppress the moment, it comes all the more suddenly and violently for his efforts:

> rien n'y fit; cela grandit en moi comme un instinct, m'envahit . . . à la fin cela fut trop fort; je n'y tins plus . . .
>
> (379)

For Michel to become fully conscious of the immediacy of his existence requires a shock, an upheaval. His near death from tuberculosis provides the shock, but his return to health brings a new awareness of the world in a way full of turns and detours. Early in his recovery, the segments of time vanish from his consciousness; time becomes an invisible duration: "Là coulèrent des jours sans heures" (381). When he rediscovers sensation, it comes to him within a nonarticulated time; sensations themselves are indistinguishable from each other, and he registers only their intensity:

> Combien de temps nous y restâmes? je ne sais plus—qu'importait l'heure? . . . je sentais extraordinairement.
>
> (392)

Time as chronology and time as change have disappeared. In the gardens of Biskra, the world becomes pure presence to his sensation, and that sensation is joy and light. Michel is aware of his joy, but he does not conceptualize it; his contact with the world is felt not as momentary but as full, immediate, and eternal.

But contentment in the present as duration does not satisfy Michel for long. It is interrupted by a moment when something happens, by a moment of excitement, as when Marceline brings in an Arab boy to play in Michel's presence. After this intrusion of an intensely felt moment, the enduring present returns, but it brings no longer happiness but boredom, and Michel longs for the arrival of another experience that is isolated in the present moment:

> Le lendemain, pour la première fois, je m'ennuie; j'attends; j'attends quoi? je me sens désœuvré, inquiet. Enfin je n'y tiens plus:—Bachir ne vient donc pas, ce matin, Marceline?
>
> (382)

The vision of Bachir and the other children is one of health. Michel had trusted that his cure would come of its own accord, that "il ne restait qu'à l'attendre" (383), that time itself would eventually make him well. But within a time that does not change he could wait eternally for health to return. He thus puts his mind and will at work to make himself strong, to promote what he calls an "effort vers l'existence". This obliges him to view time as a duration that brings change, as a progression. Happiness no longer inhabits the present but is located at the far end of a finite series of present moments:

> j'avançais chaque jour, dans une vie plus riche et plus pleine vers un plus savoureux bonheur.
>
> (404)

Progression is a continuity, a bond between moments that relates present to past and future, and it satisfies for a time Michel's need for a certainty in a world that has shown itself, when he nearly dies, to be unstable. What he discovers on his rebirth to life is the principle of change. As he has changed so has the world around him. History, once his sole reason for being, has now taken on the odour of death, and in its place Michel experiences something new to him, "le sentiment du présent".

But at this stage Michel is not prepared to recognise a fundamental change in himself. When he seeks to determine what his reborn identity is, he formulates the theory of *l'être authentique*, which is not a new being but the survival of a kind of primitive self within him. It lets him change while remaining basically the same, as the metaphor of the palimpsest suggests:

> Et je me comparais aux palimpsestes; je goûtais la joie du savant, qui, sous les écritures plus récentes, découvre, sur un même papier, un texte très ancien infiniment plus précieux. Quel était-il, ce texte occulté? Pour le lire, ne fallait-il pas tout d'abord effacer les textes récents?
>
> (399)

The psychology implied in Gide's description of the authentic self was to become a fundamental element of his thinking during the years that produced his most important fiction; that there is a kernel of intelligent personality covered over by layers of pseudo-selves imposed by culture and institutions is essential to his humanism. But in Michel's formulation, it is still a hesitant and cautious way of permitting a "lente transformation", of letting him cry "Un nouvel être! Un nouvel être!" on the route from Taormina to the Castel Mola without having to acknowledge in himself a radical change of being.

But ultimately the slow transformation does become a radical change. Several factors bring this about. To begin with, Michel dissimulates, he resolves to live two lives: to be his authentic self for himself and for Marceline to continue being as she had known him. His two lives become independent of each other, and his *nouvel être,* set free from the disapproving glances of another person, develops unchecked on its own. Through dissimulation Michel becomes free also of the influence of Marceline's view of time. From what little insight he provides into Marceline's thought and attitudes, it is evident that she lives a temporality of hope. Her marriage was based on it, as was her devotion in caring for Michel during his illness.[6] For Marceline it is time which will ultimately bring a blessing hoped for and prayed for in the present; time itself will produce change through the intervention of a miracle. The attitude of the hopeful person is patience, and what characterises patience is that it lasts, that it can last indefinitely. The single moment is without importance since any number of them can be accumulated without exhausting patience. The only moment that counts is that of divine action, a moment so full that it recuperates all those moments of waiting and gives the plenitude of happiness to all those that follow. For Marceline that moment never comes. Her prayers were, in her view, answered when Michel recovered; but Michel usurped them, attributing his cure to the power of his will alone.

In Paris Michel continues to conceal his *être authentique,* not only from his wife but from a larger number of social and professional acquaintances. This sets him apart, encourages him to see himself as unique, somehow superior to the others who appear to live empty lives. In a passage remarkably similar to a page in *Paludes* but more sinister, Michel describes his alienation from casual acquaintances and from members of his social and intellectual set:

> Ils vivent, ont l'air de vivre et de ne pas savoir qu'ils vivent. D'ailleurs, moi-même, depuis que je suis auprès d'eux, je ne vis plus. Entre autres jours, aujourd'hui, qu'ai-je fait? J'ai dû vous quitter dès neuf heures; à peine avant de partir ai-je eu le temps de lire un peu; c'est le seul bon moment du jour. Votre frère m'attendait chez le notaire, et après le notaire . . .
>
> (423)

After a long list of the day's activities Michel concludes:

> et quand le soir, maintenant, je repasse toutes les occupations du jour, je sens ma journée si vaine et elle me paraît si vide, que je voudrais la ressaisir au vol, la recommencer heure après heure et que je suis triste à pleurer.
>
> (424)

This is the time of the inauthentic self—the chronological succession of instants without depth or fervour, a social time that can be articulated and communicated. It is superficial precisely because it belongs to everyone:

it cannot contain unique experiences, it cannot bring any sensation but that which can easily fall into words understood by all.

The time of the authentic self is opposed to social time as authenticity is to the "faux personnage" Michel is forced to assume in the company of his acquaintances. Unique and uncommunicable, it can be experienced in depth only by that part of an individual which is most truly himself. Its segments are not chronological, for each moment is unlike and unrelated to any other. Such moments appear similar only to those who do not know how to savour each one in its particularity. More than anything else, they resemble Michel's description of the gardens of Biskra: "ces jardins étaient tous pareils; et pourtant chacun différait" (393). Like the speaker of *Les Nourritures terrestres,* Michel has found that sensation is located in the present moment and that each sensation or moment is unique and totally detached from all others.

But for each moment to be an event within itself, to be experienced as an absolute, all tenses but the present must be eliminated, for every other tense presupposes the succession of moments and their similarity. Once again Michel's evolution is far from sudden. His return to Normandy puts him in contact with a past of childhood sensations he had forgotten. He begins to prepare lectures for the Collège de France and becomes concerned again with history. Furthermore the time of Normandy and the rhythm of agricultural life are ordered toward the promise of harvest. There Michel no longer passively receives sensations from nature, he dominates it for a purpose that lies ahead in time. Marceline is pregnant and Michel's life is oriented toward his child's birth. Time becomes a continuity that passes from the past through a present into a future that will eventually become present only if the present is put to good use. Michel enjoys again a present that consists of a blissful and indistinct continuity of like moments:

> Nous allions nous asseoir près du bois, sur le banc où jadis j'allais m'asseoir avec ma mère; là, plus voluptueusement se présentait à nous chaque instant, plus insensiblement coulait l'heure. De cette époque de ma vie, si nul souvenir distinct ne se détache, ce n'est point que j'en garde une moins vive reconnaissance— mais bien parce que tout s'y mêlait, s'y fondait en un uniforme bien-être, où le soir s'unissait au matin sans saccades, où les jours se liaient les uns aux autres sans surprises.
>
> (410)

Michel breaks with this temporality when, again in Paris, he renews acquaintance with Ménalque, who showers him with aphorisms about the need of escaping the past for the present to attain perfection:

> C'est du parfait oubli d'hier que je crée la nouvelleté de chaque heure. Jamais, d'avoir été heureux, ne me suffit. Je ne crois pas aux choses mortes, et confonds n'être plus, avec n'avoir jamais été.
>
> (436)

> Que chaque instant emporte tout ce qu'il avait apporté.
>
> (437)

And the future is destroyed when Marceline's child is miscarried. The Michel who narrates his story with the knowledge of what is to come warns his listeners of the fragility of happiness based on the future:

> Ah! combien dangereusement déjà notre bonheur se reposait sur l'espérance! et sur quel futur incertain!
>
> (434)

Now the future suddenly passes into the memory of a hope; it is replaced as future by sheer emptiness:

> Ah! subit avenir! . . . devant moi n'était plus qu'un trou vide où je trébuchais tout entier.
>
> (438)

Michel has been reduced to living in the present; from this point on his existence will be located in the moment.

What is the quality of the moment as Michel lives it? He describes it as it appeared to him during his travel in Italy:

> . . . souvenirs ou regrets, espérance ou désir, avenir et passé se taisaient; je ne connaissais plus de la vie que ce qu'en apportait, en emportait l'instant.—O joie physique! m'écriais-je; rythme sûr de mes muscles! santé!
>
> (404)

This is the temporality of hedonism in the refined form Gide had given it in *Les Nourritures terrestres* where, in fact, it is defined with more precision than in *L'Immoraliste.* Here the moment of fervour comes out obliquely, as when Michel describes a wine he drinks in Switzerland:

> Je me souviens d'un bizarre barba-grisca, dont il ne restait plus qu'une bouteille, de sorte que je ne pus savoir si le goût saugrenu qu'il avait se serait retrouvé dans les autres.
>
> (456)

The image suggests that the moment-experience is without precedent and cannot be repeated, and it implies that from continually dissimilar experiences no knowledge can come forth, that pleasure and sensation are limited to themselves, offering no possibility of accumulation in such a way as to provide for growth. The experience of the present moment is vividly described in the pages dealing with Michel's poaching on his farms and his bizarre friendship with the animalistic Bute and the elusive Alcide during his second stay in

Normandy. Even earlier there are moments that stand out from the surrounding time by reason of the intensity with which they are lived. Passages such as the one describing a night in Biskra when Michel decides on a plan of action to achieve his cure (his "veillée d'armes") and the one in which he watches without interfering an Arab boy steal Marceline's scissors communicate above all moments of intensified awareness. Another such moment occurs when Michel beats up a drunken coach driver; he experiences the event so strongly that it prompts him the next night to possess Marceline for the first time after several months of marriage.

The evocation of the night of love provides a lucid formulation of the ethic of the moment:

> Avez-vous bien compris ou dois-je vous redire que j'étais comme neuf aux choses de l'amour? Peut-être est-ce à sa nouveauté que notre nuit de noces dut sa grâce . . . Car il me semble, à m'en souvenir aujourd'hui, que cette première nuit fut la seule, tant l'attente et la surprise de l'amour ajoutaient à la volupté de délices,—tant une seule nuit suffit au plus grand amour pour se dire, et tant mon souvenir s'obstine à me la rappeler uniquement. Ce fut un rire d'un moment, où nos âmes se confondirent . . . Mais je crois qu'il est un point de l'amour, unique, et que l'âme plus tard, ah! cherche en vain à dépasser; que l'effort qu'elle fait pour ressusciter son bonheur, l'use; que rien n'empêche le bonheur comme le souvenir du bonheur. Hélas! je me souviens de cette nuit . . .
>
> (405)

Though he has warned his listeners that he intends to speak at length about his bodily functions, Michel here adopts the idealistic language of **Les Cahiers d'André Walter.** The moment is above all pure: it transcends the sensation it brings and can be translated only in spiritual terms. Unanticipated and never to be repeated, it is a plenitude which excludes all that is not itself; just so it will be excluded from subsequent moments that will bring joys of a different sort. That nothing prevents happiness so much as the memory of happiness and that Michel still remembers that night with sorrow is the first admission of the failure of his temporality. He has not been able to surpass the night of love; the principle of *dépassement,* which holds that moments must be of increasing order of intensity, has been unable to provide another still more fervently felt experience. This description of the perfect moment reveals indirectly the insufficiency of that moment in its need to be negated by an even better one. If the laughter of a moment is not surpassed, it will remain in the past as a bitter reminder that the present is empty.

> Tout cela est absurde.
>
> (453)

It is to this absurdity that Michel's ethic of the moment leads. During his second summer at La Morinière he exists for sensation only, in immediate contact with nature and in pursuit of the mystery he senses in the lives of the peasants and labourers. It is as if his mind were left behind, unable to catch up with the rapid pace of his body's frantic activity. When his mind does come to grips with the situation he has created, as when he announces to Charles that he will sell his farms, he becomes aware of a total breakdown of the familiar world:

> Décidément tout se défait autour de moi, de tout ce que ma main saisit, ma main ne sait rien retenir.

This is what comes from *disponibilité,* from life within the moment, from the constant desire to surpass each experience with another more fervent one. Present moments, unrelated to past or future, without continuity, are unorganised, incapable of making sense.

Michel becomes aware ultimately that the instant is not so much a way of embracing life as it is of constantly losing it. Any attempt to retain what he loves is in conflict with his desire for novelty:

> Je tâchai donc, et encore une fois, de refermer ma main sur mon amour. Mais qu'avais-je besoin de tranquille bonheur?
>
> (454)

Once already, while Marceline was pregnant and still apparently healthy, Michel saw her as escaping him:

> Comme un souffle parfois plisse une eau très tranquille, la plus légère émotion sur son front se laissait lire; en elle, mystérieusement, elle écoutait frémir une nouvelle vie; je me penchais sur elle comme sur une profonde eau pure, où, si loin qu'on voyait, on ne voyait que de l'amour. Ah! si c'était encore le bonheur, je sais que j'ai voulu dès lors le retenir, comme on veut retenir dans ses mains rapprochées, en vain, une eau fuyante; mais déjà je sentais, à côté du bonheur, quelque autre chose que le bonheur, qui colorait bien mon amour, mais comme colore l'automne.
>
> (420)

Already his happiness with Marceline and indeed Marceline herself are felt as unstable, as belonging to the cycle of planting, growth, and harvest. The objects on which happiness is founded are in flight, and the image of water tells not only of purity and fecundity, but also, in its depth, of the unknown and change. Her beauty, like that of autumn, is enhanced by its very instability. Later when Michel sees Marceline as spoiled, worn out by sickness, his love for her is enhanced by her paleness and frailty, by the fact that he feels her slipping from his grasp. The paradox between Michel's love for Marceline during the final part of the book and his frantic race to destroy her is only apparent:

> Ah! peut-être allez-vous penser que je n'aimais pas Marceline. Je jure que je l'aimais passionnément. Jamais elle n'avait été et ne m'avait paru si belle. La maladie avait subtilisé et comme extasié ses traits.
>
> (460)

Her approaching death is essential to his love; it is her inevitable passing that gives to Michel's instants their immense value.

To live fully is to live in and for the present moment, to be open to all the possibilities that moment has to offer, regardless of past or future, without memory or anticipation. Such is Michel's creed. But what is that but to lose constantly the moment which comes *ex nihilo* and immediately dissolves into nothingness. The self is left experiencing a series of unrelated and meaningless pulsations of fervour. Ultimately it is reduced to momentary sensations, and there it ceases to be a human reality. Michel does not advance that far, but it is evident as the story progresses that he becomes depersonalised and undergoes a slow process of fragmentation. Increasingly he has to acknowledge that he has become divided from himself, that the various parts of his personality operate separately:

> Mais étais-je maître de choisir mon vouloir? de décider de mon désir?
>
> (462)

His will and desire, both free, have splintered from his self, acting independently of and without communication with it. At one point, in order to reassure Marceline and to give her new hope, he explains:

> Tu m'as cru changé, n'est-ce pas? Mais ailleurs, tu sentiras bien que rien n'a changé notre amour.
>
> (453)

Thus the self and love are independent entities, and Michel grants Marceline his love but keeps the rest of his being for himself. Furthermore, he seems to think that a simple shift in place can restore what time has destroyed. At another point he even feels separated from his own sensations:

> Je sors. Devant la porte de l'hôtel, la place de Touggourt, les rues, l'atmosphère même sont étranges au point de me faire croire que ce n'est pas moi qui les vois.
>
> (468-469)

There, in Touggourt, where he has gone as a final *dépassement*, Michel finds only passive release in the back room of a Moorish café:

> Un lapin blanc, enfermé dans la chambre, s'effarouche d'abord, puis s'apprivoise et vient manger dans la main de Moktir. On nous apporte du café. Puis, tandis que Moktir joue avec le lapin, cette femme m'attire à elle, et je me laisse aller à elle comme on s'abandonne au sommeil.
>
> (469)

Without will or desire, Michel lets himself be drawn into the sensation of a moment. By now his senses are numb, and instead of fervour he feels only a gradual loss of awareness. It is as if he were indifferently observing another person experience the woman, vaguely, as from a great distance. Thus Michel, the individualist, ends his career in near anonymity.

Michel's attitude towards his own story is characteristically ambivalent; even the friend who wrote it down cannot tell whether or not he is moved by it. That he is still in bad faith is evident in his desire to justify himself:

> Ce n'est pas, croyez-moi, que je sois fatigué de mon crime, s'il vous plaît de l'appeler ainsi; mais je dois me prouver à moi-même que je n'ai pas outrepassé mon droit.
>
> (471)

The only evidence of real progress in self-understanding occurs in the last line when he admits, cautiously, to a strong liking for an Arab boy.

Although the moral question is left in the air at the end of the *récit*, the closing of the frame clearly delineates how Michel's sense of time evolves after Marceline's death:

> Il y a de tout cela trois mois à peine. Ces trois mois ont éloigné cela de dix ans.
>
> (470)

It would seem that Michel's moments have been emptied of fervour; they no longer contain distinct sensations; they have lengthened into indefinite duration. Time has become hollow, and Michel suffers from continuous ennui. The cause of his ennui, he explains to his friends, is the climate, the

> persistance de l'azur. Ici toute recherche est impossible, tant la volupté suit de près le désir. Entouré de splendeur et de mort, je sens le bonheur trop présent et l'abandon à lui trop uniforme.
>
> (471)

Time as duration has become an obstacle, Michel's only enemy, and he is ultimately brought to devising means of killing it:

> Je me couche au milieu du jour pour tromper la longueur morne des journées et leur insupportable loisir. J'ai là, voyez, des cailloux blancs que je laisse tremper à l'ombre, puis que je tiens longtemps dans le creux de ma main, jusqu'à ce qu'en soit épuisée la calmante fraîcheur acquise. Alors je recommence, alternant les cailloux, remettant à tremper ceux dont la fraîcheur est tarie. Du temps s'y passe, et vient le soir.
>
> (471)

Here Michel himself creates the divisions of time in order to offer himself the illusion of its passing.[7]

> Car je suis à tel point de ma vie que je ne peux plus dépasser.
>
> (372)

As unlike as Michel was from Marceline in all respects, his life needed hers as something to go beyond, and her death was his last *dépassement*. For her to die was a necessary part of his project; but once she was dead, his project, and his life with it, collapses for lack of a goal. This is the impasse created by the contradictions inherent in the way of life he had adopted. At the end he lives an empty present that provides no sensations, excitement, or new experiences; the future is dead for him unless he can be given, by someone else, reasons to live. The only part of time that has any content for him is the past, the hateful past he so strove to eliminate:

> Je me souviens de tout, heure par heure . . .
>
> (455)

He is in a kind of inferno where precisely that part of his life he had wished most to destroy returns to torture him.

The only real fear Michel had expressed during his story was of dependence. He was able to throw off any need he might feel for Marceline, for God, for other people, but he realised, as an early passage shows, that time itself would ultimately destroy his strength:

> Un frisson me saisit. Un jour viendra—pensai-je,—un jour viendra où même pour porter à mes lèvres même l'eau dont j'aurai le plus soif, je n'aurai plus assez de forces . . . Je rentrai, mais ne me recouchai pas encore; je voulais fixer cette nuit, en imposer le souvenir à ma pensée, la retenir; indécis de ce que je ferais, je pris un livre sur ma table,—la Bible,—le laissai s'ouvrir au hasard; penché dans la clarté de la lune, je pouvais lire; je lus ces mots du Christ à Pierre, ces mots, hélas! que je ne devais plus oublier: "Maintenant tu te ceins toi-même et tu vas où tu veux aller; mais quand tu seras vieux, tu étendras les mains . . ." Tu étendras les mains . . .
>
> Le lendemain, à l'aube, nous partîmes.
>
> (396-397)[8]

Fearing above all the dependence of old age, Michel is at the end of *L'Immoraliste* forced to stretch forth his hands and cry for help, and this happens not after many years but while he is still young. Michel shares with Gide's other heroes this inability to accept a time that means becoming and brings change and ultimately age and death. Each escapes time by means of a strategy of his own and adopts another mode of living, a time of his own invention that provides him with an illusion of eternity. Michel in this instance wishes to hurry time along, and by departing at dawn, he is in effect annihilating it.

Michel has gone full circle. After a courageous effort to live within the moment, he has finally lost the moment, as he has lost the other objects he had valued: his studies and career, his farms, his wife. At the end he has survived in a state of almost total *dénuement*. But *dénuement*, as extolled by Ménalque and the speaker of ***Les Nourritures terrestres***, was a condition for happiness, it made possible living eternity within the confines of the instant. The hero of ***L'Immoraliste*** has reversed the order of an ascent to happiness: he has chosen sensation first. Before self-purification, before throwing out possessions, he opted for the instant and then let the instant destroy everything he had been unwilling to give up freely. Ultimately the instant, for him, destroyed itself, leaving Michel with nothing. Moments have now no content; they are simply strung together in an empty sameness within a world without fervour or joy. Haunted by the past, Michel is helpless in the present, and he awaits a future that will be determined by others.

Yet others can do nothing for him. To be sure, the Prime Minister could appoint him to a position with responsibility, send him on a mission to the colonies. But in terms of Michel's conception of his own story, no one can grant him moments, fervour, or the energy to surpass himself. No one but Michel, who is exhausted and without inner resources. Perhaps he was right in saying to his friends, at the beginning, that the only help he wanted was to speak. Now that he has spoken, he can expect nothing more.

Notes

1. André Gide, "Feuillets," *Œuvres complètes,* Paris (N.R.F. [Nouvelle Revue Française]), n.d., XIII, 439. I am deeply indebted to my colleague Professor Richard N. Coe for reading this study and making most helpful suggestions.

2. On the temporality of *Les Nourritures terrestres* see George Poulet, "L'instant, le lieu et les nourritures gidiennes." *Etudes Franciscaines,* Oct. 1965, pp. 93-96 (reprinted and expanded in *La Revue des Lettres Modernes,* 331-335, 1972, 57-66), and my own "Time in Gide's Early Fiction," *Symposium,* 26, 1972, 39-56.

3. In recent years a considerable number of studies of *L'Immoraliste* have been published. Some of these offer thematic analyses: Hippolytus Dority and Réal Ouellet, "Les Images de la Nature dans *L'Immoraliste*," *Etudes Littéraires,* 2, 1969, 313-334; Allan H. Pasco, "Irony and Art in Gide's *L'Immoraliste*," *Romanic Review,* 64, 1973, 184-203 (see the discussions of the "covert structure of significant images", 193-201); Pierre Petit, "L'Eau, structure fondamentale de l'imagination gidienne. Essai d'analyse bachelardienne de

L'Immoraliste," *French Studies in Southern Africa*, 5, 1976, 64-70; Manfred Kusch, "The Gardens of *L'Immoraliste*," *French Forum*, 4, 1979, 206-218. John T. Booker, "*The Immoralist* and the Rhetoric of First-Person Narration," *Studies in Twentieth-Century Literature*, 2, 1977, 5-22, writes on the "fundamental temporality of narration" in relation to the events narrated (20).

4. For a detailed discussion of the "préambule" of Gide's *récits*, see Martine Maisani-Léonard, *André Gide ou L'Ironie de l'écriture*, Montréal (Les Presses de l'Université de Montréal), 1967, pp. 33-64.

5. André Gide, *Romans, récits et soties, œuvres lyriques*, Paris (Gallimard: Bibliothèque de la Pléiade), 1958, p. 371. Subsequent citations from *L'Immoraliste* are to this edition. Page numbers are given parenthetically after each quotation; when the same page is cited more than once consecutively, reference is given only after the first quotation.

6. As Marceline herself grows sick, it is hope that keeps her alive: "Et je ne guéris pas encore sa tristesse, mais déjà, comme elle se raccroche à l'espoir!" (453). Her last significant gesture before dying is to drop voluntarily her rosary, and in so doing she delivers herself to despair, thus belying a life based on hope.

7. Another interpretation of the temporality of this passage is offered by Nathaniel Wing, "The Disruptions of Irony in Gide's *L'Immoraliste*," *Substance*, 26, 1980, p. 83.

8. For a discussion of this passage in relation to the other biblical allusions in the *récit*, see Andrew Oliver, "Michel, Job, Pierre, Paul: Intertextualité de la lecture dans *L'Immoraliste* de Gide," *Archives des Lettres Modernes*, 183, Archives André Gide, no. 4, Paris (Lettres Modernes), 1979, pp. 18-20, 33.

Emily S. Apter (essay date 1987)

SOURCE: Apter, Emily S. "The Etiology of the Unspoken: Negation and Gender in the *Récits*." In *André Gide and the Codes of Homotextuality*, pp. 105-50. Saratoga, Calif.: ANMA Libri, 1987.

[*In the following essay, Apter focuses on the textual and subtextual significance of ellipses, unfinished thoughts, and unspoken implications in the narratives of Gide's* récits—*which she compares to Freud's concept of* Fehlleistung, *or "the Freudian slip"—arguing in the case of* The Immoralist *that these indicate Gide's desire for his text to subvert its own intentions and to question the reliability of Michel's discourse, namely that surrounding his latent homosexuality.*]

> Le récit, construction médiate, retardée: Freud ne fait pas autre chose en écrivant ses "cas."
>
> Roland Barthes, *L'Obvie et l'obtus*

In 1901, just one year prior to the redaction of Gide's first *récit*, **L'Immoraliste,** Freud published his *Psychopathology of Everyday Life*. In this work, Freud introduced the concept of *Fehlleistung*, translated with the English neologism "Parapraxis" (for there as yet existed no precise English equivalent), in turn devised as a synonym for the literal sense of "faulty function." What is now loosely alluded to with a host of interrelated designations ranging from "the Freudian slip" or "lapsus" to the "misreading," possessed in Freud's native tongue a more unified frame of reference. "The German language," as Laplanche and Pontalis point out, "brings out the common denominator of all these mistakes by giving the prefix 'ver-' to many of the words which describe them: *das Vergessen* (forgetting), *das Versprechen* (slip of the tongue), *das Verlesen* (misreading), *das Verschreiben* (slip of the pen), *das Vergreifen* (bungled action), *das Verlieren* (mislaying)."[1]

Although other linguists and psychoanalysts (Meringer and Meyer, Ruths, Ernest Jones) had already identified significant theoretical aspects of the slip, it was Freud who interpreted them inventively as psychical phenomena, explicable as indications of suppressed motives, intuitions or neuroses. Commenting on the corrections of detail made by friends and former patients to his own reports of their analyses (errors that he may have made subconsciously to enhance the ingenuity or credibility of his case studies), Freud unabashedly noted: "*Here once again we find an unobserved error taking the place of an intentional concealment or repression*" (Freud's emphases).[2]

In an analysis of Gide's *récits*—the most unequivocally classical and rhetorically understated of his writings—Freud's concept of the slip or "unobserved error" is particularly useful, especially in interpreting the psychosexual implications of yet another form of negative writing—*the unspoken*. Though the theory of the slip applies ostensibly to what is said rather than to what is not stated, Freud leaves open the specification of the possible forms such "verbal disturbances" can take. One can thus assume that inadvertent omissions or ellipses qualify as legitimate slips of the tongue just as easily as figures of spoken language, such as accidental obscenities, unintentional puns, or mispronounced names. Using this category of the inadvertent omission, we might even add to Freud's list of errors governed by the prefix 'ver-' a new term: *das Verschmieren* ("to smear, daub, to waste paper in writing"), a term that could be stretched to mean "a slip of the text." Unlike Freud's "slip of the pen," which focuses on the writer's personal motives for committing an error, the "slip of the text" would refer to a purely *textual* stratum of unintentionality, the *un*written implications of what is pointedly implied by the *un*spoken. We will be looking then not only at what Gide's narrators seem to be withholding from their confessions, but also at specific moments in the *récit* where what is said by these fictional narrators is belied by what the text, as a narrative system, "accidentally" suggests (and we put accidental in quotations because these unwritten implications may in fact be fully intended by the author).

An incompletely formulated yet nonetheless coherent definition of the slip or lapsus can be discovered *in nuce* within Gide's oeuvre, not in relation to his *récits* (where we intend to resituate it), but in the context of his critical remarks on the nature of myth and his efforts to transpose classical myths into the idiom of modern theater. As Walter Benjamin noted in his review of Gide's ***Oedipe*** (staged in 1930), this was a theater of language—of excessive "bavardage" in which archetypal heroes (Oedipus, Saul, Theseus) were allowed to define themselves as *myths* in an outburst of anger, a flash of tenderness, or a slip of the tongue. Benjamin emphasized in his essay entitled "Oedipe ou le mythe raisonnable," that unlike the Sophoclean Oedipus who remains a mute pawn of Fate, Gide's Oedipe dares to speak out, to interpret his destiny subjectively. During the second act of the play, he angrily refuses Tiresias' orthodox recourse to the Gods' will as a means of explaining the origin of his personal and political tribulations: "Que chercher près d'un Dieu? Des réponses. Je me sentais moi-même une réponse à je ne savais encore quelle question."[3] The fact that Gide's Oedipe is allowed to "answer back" to the supercilious prophet is, according to Benjamin, a long overdue settling of accounts:

> Le drame de Sophocle a cinq actes; c'est à la fin du second que le voyant Tirésias quitte la scène. Oedipe aura dû attendre deux millénaires pour engager avec lui, chez Gide, le grand débat au cours duquel il exprime ce que, chez Sophocle, il n'eût pas même osé penser.[4]
>
> ["Oedipe et le mythe raisonnable"]

As willful author of both question and answer, this Oedipus reserves the right to define his own fate even when this necessitates the recognition of his own inner "monstrosity": "Engourdi dans la récompense, je dors depuis vingt ans. Mais à présent, enfin j'écoute en moi le monstre nouveau qui s'étire. Un grand destin m'attend, tapi dans les ombres du soir. Oedipe, le temps de la quiétude est passé. Réveille-toi de ton bonheur."[5] Oedipe's premonition of his future monstrosity (as a myth) gives him the right to both define the crime and determine the nature of his punishment. No longer is his guilt the result of parricide and incest; it resides instead in the realization that his twenty years of "bonheur" were purchased through ignorance of the power-hungry motives of his family. He chooses to blind himself not because he aims to do penance for crimes that were accidents of fate, but because he can no longer endure contemplating the ignominious scheming of Etéocle, Polynice, Créon, Ismène and Antigone.

In his reading of Oedipus, Gide seems intent on traveling beyond Freud. Where Freud stops at a psychological allegory of mother-loving and father-killing (the inherent drama of which is heightened by theatrical representation), Gide gravitates towards the more prosaic moment of the subject's verbal cure—often brought on by a slip of the tongue. In ***Thésée***, Gide's final *récit* (1946), it is the "bêtise" lodged in pure "bavardage" that dismantles the protective facade of repression. Here, in the course of his uncontrollable chatter to himself, Theseus stumbles unwittingly on the explanation for his "forgetting" of the black sails (thereby provoking his father's suicide):

> . . . J'ai regret d'avoir causé sa mort par un fatal oubli: celui de remplacer par des voiles blanches les voiles noires du bateau qui me ramenait de Crète, ainsi qu'il était convenu si je revenais victorieux de mon entreprise hasardeuse. On ne saurait penser à tout. Mais à vrai dire et si je m'interroge, ce que je ne fais jamais volontiers, je ne puis jurer que ce fût vraiment un oubli. Egée m'empêchait, vous dis-je, et surtout lorsque, par les philtres de la magicienne, de Médée, qui le trouvait, ainsi qu'il se trouvait lui-même, un peu vieux en tant que mari, il s'avisa, fâcheuse idée, de repiquer une seconde jeunesse, obstruant ainsi ma carrière, alors que c'est à chacun son tour. Toujours est-il qu'à la vue des voiles noires . . . j'appris en rentrant dans Athènes, qu'il s'était jeté dans la mer.[6]

In the colloquial expressions and commonplaces littered throughout Theseus' monologue, phrases such as "On ne saurait penser à tout," "il se trouvait lui-même, un peu vieux en tant que mari," "repiquer une seconde jeunesse" or "c'est à chacun son tour" one can locate instances of verbal lapsus. To carefully attuned post-Freudian ears, it is painfully obvious that "à chacun son tour" is a euphemism for patriarchal displacement—an act the violence of which is elided yet conveyed by the gap in the last sentence. In addition to euphemisms that have the effect of blocking out unpleasant truths, Theseus exhibits (and even admits to) the same tendency towards resisting self-questioning as do typical patients in analysis ("si je m'interroge, ce que je ne fais jamais volontiers . . ."). But as resistance erodes and the unconscious ploy of the "oubli" is abandoned, Theseus approaches the verge of speaking the unspeakable—acknowledging his parricide outright. By catching him at this pivotal moment in his "talking cure" Gide rewrites the legend of Theseus as Freud might have rewritten it—as a symbolic rendering of "dénégation," or the function of resistance in the affirmation of repression. Indeed, it is this rationality of repression (explicated so brilliantly by Freud in psychoanalytical terms) that constitutes what Benjamin identified as the "reasonableness" of the Gidean myth, noting how his characters "speak" the logic of their unconscious desires and fears. Gide himself, long before writing *Thésée,* had given theoretical expression to this notion in a brief essay on Greek mythology (1919):

> Et l'on a rien compris au caractère de Thésée, par exemple, si l'on admet que l'audacieux héros
>
> *Qui va du dieu des morts déshonorer la couche,*
>
> a laissé par simple inadvertance la voile noire au vaisseau qui le ramène en Grèce, cette "fatale" voile noire qui, trompant son père affligé, l'invite à se précipiter dans la mer, grâce à quoi Thésée entre en possession de son royaume. Un oubli? Allons donc! Il oublie de changer la voile comme il oublie Ariane à Naxos. Et je comprends que les pères n'enseignent pas cela aux enfants; mais pour cesser de réduire l'histoire de Thésée à l'insignifiance d'un conte de nourrice, il n'est qu'à restituer au héros sa conscience et sa résolution.[7]
>
> ["**Considérations sur la mythologie grecque**"]

Insisting on the implausibility of Theseus' plea of "not guilty" on the grounds of faulty recollection, Gide insinuates that the metonymy of the fatal black sails is itself the equivalent of a textual lapsus in the Greek version of the myth, thinly concealing yet exposing Theseus' underlying wish-fulfillment. In his modern adaptation of the myth, Gide, following the implied prescription of his argument, devised linguistic corollaries for the black veil—the insipid blunders, horrendous clichés and maladroit euphemisms that festoon Theseus' speech.

One of the major differences between the use of the lapsus in *Thésée* (Gide's final *récit*) and its uses in the early *L'Immoraliste,* lies in the fact that Theseus is a far less intelligent, hence less manipulative, narrator than Michel. The latter reveals himself as constantly on guard against the reader's powers of supposition, which means that Michel's slips of the tongue, like the author's slips of the text, are more difficult to localize. Frequently, evidence of Michel's narratorial circumspection is registered through anacoluthon, technically defined as "the failure, accidental or deliberate, to complete a sentence according to the structural plan on which it was started" and used more loosely by Barthes to signify "a break in sense or construction."[8] The first instance of this rupture occurs when Michel, having summoned his friends to North Africa to listen to his story, finds himself unable to articulate precisely why he needs them or what he wishes to say: "Car je suis à tel point de ma vie que je ne peux plus dépasser. Pourtant ce n'est pas lassitude. Mais je ne comprends plus. J'ai besoin . . . J'ai besoin de parler, vous dis-je."[9] Here, the verb "parler" is ironically substituted for the "faille" or temporary failure of speech on Michel's part. As in the discourse of Theseus, it is the impromptu utterance or uncontrolled pause that signals the speaker's fear of disclosure.

What is it that Michel fears to disclose? Initially it appears to be the ambivalence of his sentiments towards his new bride Marceline: "j'étais habitué à sa grâce . . . Pour la première fois je m'étonnai, tant cette grâce me parût grande" (*I* [*L'Immoraliste*], 33). Here, the gap records the shock as he recognizes his former indifference to Marceline. Suddenly, he senses her presence and though he claims at this moment to welcome it, assuring the reader of his pleasure, the ellipsis foreshadows the awkward moments of silence that will occur when communication between them deteriorates, and Marceline's presence resented as an imposition. This begins to happen soon enough during what turns out to be a grotesque travesty of a conventional wedding night. The blood which is shed comes not from Marceline's deflowering, but from Michel's diseased lungs, and, as if to add to the horror, it is staunched by a scarf that Marceline wears around her waist (a symbolic chastity belt), stealthily procured by Michel while she sleeps. Throughout this scene, Michel engages in a debate with himself marked by hesitations and ellipses, which themselves signal the textual spaces of transgression:

> Pourtant je me sentais très faible et fis monter du thé pour nous deux. Et tandis qu'elle l'apprêtait, très calme, un peu pâle elle-même, souriante, une sorte d'irritation me vint de ce qu'elle n'eût rien su voir. Je me sentais injuste, il est vrai, me disais: si elle n'a rien vu, c'est que je cachais bien; n'importe; rien n'y fit; cela grandit en moi comme un instinct, m'envahit . . . à la fin cela fut trop fort; je n'y tins plus: comme distraitement, je lui dis:
>
> —J'ai craché le sang, cette nuit.
>
> (*I,* 37)

Michel's "irritation" at Marceline escalates rapidly into rage as he struggles inwardly against uttering the unspeakable revelation of his illness. Here the rupture in his narration, directly following the allusion to an "invading instinct," provides a clue, perhaps, to what he fears to divulge for it is this very instinct, so strong as to defy constraint, that will ultimately impel him away form his wife and towards members of his own sex.

If Michel's latent homosexuality is *pre*-figured in the "creux" or hollows of a spoken sentence, it also emerges after his return to health, as a *sub*-text in the analogy drawn between himself and a palimpsest:

> Et je me comparais aux palimpsestes; je goûtais la joie du savant, qui, sous les écritures plus récentes, découvre sur un même papier un texte très ancien infiniment

plus précieux. Quel était-il, ce texte occulte? Pour le lire, ne fallait-il pas tout d'abord effacer les textes récents?

(*I,* 60)

The palimpsest is used as a metaphor of the quest for lost origins, both in the historical sense (Adamic man, the Greek pagans) and in the personal sense (childhood, freedom from social inhibitions, the novelty of sensual experience). All this seems laudable in the context of Michel's renewed resolve to live and fortify himself until one recalls that the "textes récents" of the life that he would so eagerly "effacer" include his marriage to Marceline. Moreover, as we gradually learn, references to "origins" are encoded as the original nature of the "vieil homme," which, like the palimpsest, has been submerged in artificial layers of civilization. It is for this reason that the new Michel no longer devotes his intellectual energies to abstract, philological research, but rather to studying the periods in history where political authority is undermined (as when Altharic, a young Italian king, rebels against his mother and aligns himself with the wicked Goths) or when high culture begins to degenerate. In the course that he offers at the Collège de France, he delights in focusing on the most decadent phase of the late Roman empire for it permits him to fashion a thesis with Nietzschean and Spenglerian overtones in its prophecy of decline and fall in the West.

In Michel's description of the public's reaction to his lectures, Gide may be seen not only to be alluding to the unstated subtext of homoeroticism, but also to be committing a slip of the text in relation to his own narrative control over the reader. Implying that only the inferior scholar is capable of enthusiasm ("Les historiens blâmèrent une tendance, dirent-ils, aux généralisations trop rapides. D'autres blâmèrent ma méthode; *et ceux qui me complimentèrent furent ceux qui m'avaient le moins compris*" [*I,* 93; my emphasis]), Michel places the scholar-reader in a double bind. If, like the historians in relation to Michel's interpretation of history, we discern in **L'Immoraliste** a certain "tendency," then we reveal ourselves as morally prudish and narrow-minded. If, on the other hand, we admit to being moved by the text, then we betray our ignorance of its subversive content. The work apparently falls at this point into its own trap: Michel's scorn of the sympathetic reader parallels Gide's, who, by implication, exhorts the reader to relinquish his naïveté and adopt an attitude of suspicion towards the ruses of writing. But by rendering the reader less susceptible, **L'Immoraliste** undoes a measure of its reader-manipulation. Is this accident or plan? Certainly it can be interpreted as a version of the Freudian "unobserved error."

A comparable example of textual lapsus occurs in the treatment of a hallowed (even hackneyed) Gidean theme: the relationship between truth and sincerity. After an extenuating soirée during which he has been compelled to "feign his feint," that is, disguise the fact that he is pretending to share the views of his colleagues, Michel concludes: "On ne peut à la fois être sincère et le paraître" (*I,* 90). Whether this is interpreted as a statement of fact or a moral admonition, the axiom unwittingly drives a wedge between the reader and the text, for **L'Immoraliste** is replete with instruments of literary artifice specifically chosen for their effectiveness in making the text *appear* sincere. From the frame conceit of multiple prefaces (with each narrator echoing the sincerity claims of the other), to the use of the gaze as a mirror of the lie (a kind of "regard regardé," as when Moktir watches Michel watch him steal Marceline's scissors), to an inverted rhetoric of self-exposure that grotesquely ranks dissimulation as the highest expression of truth, these techniques are in evidence. The last is particularly well exemplified in one of Michel's reports on the evolving patterns of his married life:

> Mes rapports avec Marceline demeurèrent donc, en attendant, les mêmes—quoique plus exaltés de jour en jour, par un toujours plus grand amour. Ma dissimulation même (si l'on peut appeler ainsi le besoin de préserver de son jugement ma pensée), ma dissimulation l'augmentait. Je veux dire que ce jeu m'occupait de Marceline sans cesse. Peut-être cette contrainte au mensonge me coûta-t-elle un peu d'abord: mais j'arrivai vite à comprendre que les choses réputées les pires (le mensonge, pour ne citer que celle-là) ne sont difficiles à faire que tant qu'on ne les a jamais faites; mais qu'elles deviennent chacune, et très vite, aisées, plaisantes, douces à refaire, et bientôt comme naturelles. Ainsi donc, comme à chaque chose pour laquelle un premier dégoût est vaincu, je finis par trouver plaisir à cette dissimulation même, à m'y attarder comme au jeu de mes facultés inconnues.

(*I,* 66)

According to this convoluted logic, dissimulation "protects" from the truth, and the artifice of dissimulation—the tricks that forge the appearance of sincerity—are perversely valorized as a labor of love. Even the lie is naturalized ("comme naturelle"), presented as a vice which, like tobacco or alcohol, becomes through force of habit a sophisticated, acquired taste. If one rejuxtaposes this passage to the previously cited axiom—"one cannot be sincere and appear to be so at the same time"—it would seem that the narrator is deceiving us with the appearance of appearances, craftily substituting an ethic of falsehood for what seems to be a version of the noble lie. The axiom, however, belies the lie—like a slip or mistake, it signals the aesthetics of mimetic truth that undermine Michel's courageous avowals of duplicity and render his entire discourse of sincerity a kind of preamble or founding text for the postmodernist practice of dissemblance. As Alice Jardine, expanding on Deleuze's post-Nietzschean reflections on the modern status of falsehood has surmised:

In effect, for many contemporary theorists and writers, to be radical in our culture may require new kinds of mental acrobatics: for example, to be radical may no longer be to work for the side that is "right," speaks the "truth," is most "just." It may in fact be to work rather for the *Pseudos,* for "the highest power of falsehood"; it may be to opt for overwhelming falsehood, thereby confusing and finally destroying the oppressive system of representation which would have us believe not only in its sub-systems of models (the real, the first) versus simulacra (the unreal, inauthentic), good versus bad, true versus false; but would also have us believe in a world ultimately obsessed with self-destruction.[10]

[*Gynesis*]

Examined thus from the hindsight of our own critical climate, Michel emerges as the prototypically Nietzschean king of the "Pseudos," even more than Ménalque, Michel's sinister mentor, whose characterization parodies and oversimplifies the stereotypical essentials of Nietzsche's thought. Privileging the simulacrum or semblance of truth over truth itself by means of such techniques as the partial avowal, the withheld inference, or the deceptive sign, Michel makes of the error a textual precondition.

In the cat and mouse encounters between Michel and Ménalque, the latter stalks the former and eventually traps him through the rhetorical manipulation of silence. As if to emphasize this point, Ménalque's persona is introduced under the sign of the unspoken; in his first words to Michel, he indicates his fundamental antipathy to idle chatter: "Je ne cause pas volontiers, mais voudrais causer avec vous" (*I,* 94). By breaking his habitual "code of silence," Ménalque begins his initiation of Michel into a secret society whose members recognize each other by their reserve in conversation. For this reason, Ménalque's discourse, with its pregnant pauses and pointed omissions, serves a didactic function as a model of the coded language that Michel has yet to master. The first lesson posits the necessity of indiscretion (foreshadowing the voyeurism in which Michel will later indulge after learning of the bestial sexual practices of some of his laborers). In the ellipsis into which Ménalque's speech trails, Michel receives his first prodding to respond in code:

> Je n'ai coutume d'être discret que pour ce qu'on me confie; pour ce que j'apprends par moi-même, ma curiosité, je l'avoue, est sans bornes. J'ai donc cherché, fouillé, questionné partout où j'ai pu. Mon indiscrétion m'a servi, puisqu'elle m'a donné désir de vous revoir; puisqu'au lieu du savant routinier que je voyais en vous naguère, je sais que je dois voir à présent . . . c'est à vous de m'expliquer quoi.
>
> Je sentis que je rougissais.
>
> (*I,* 95)

Michel's blush—the biblical sign of shame—shows that he is beginning to divine the missing texts of his interlocutor. When he reddens for a second time, it is because the unspoken comes dangerously close to enunciation; but ironically, what is revealed is yet another silence—Michel's silence as, on that fatal day, he watched Moktir furtively pocket Marceline's scissors:

> Vous aviez vu le vol et vous n'avez rien dit! Moktir s'est montré fort surpris de ce silence . . . moi aussi.
>
> —Je ne le suis pas moins de ce que vous me dites: comment! il savait donc que je l'avais surpris!
>
> Là n'est pas l'important; vous jouiez au plus fin; à ce jeu, ces enfants nous rouleront toujours. Vous pensiez le tenir et c'était lui qui vous tenait . . . Là n'est pas l'important. Expliquez-moi votre silence.
>
> —Je voudrais qu'on me l'expliquât.
>
> Nous restâmes pendant quelque temps sans parler.
>
> (*I,* 96)

Here it becomes evident that in remaining silent in the face of Moktir's theft, Michel was giving the sign of his assent to the tacit contract that will in future hold between them. The contract is grounded in a masochistic paradigm described by Fredric Jameson as "stealing from oneself."[11] Jameson identifies the pattern in relation to a later episode in which Michel is portrayed poaching on his own land, an accomplice to his most brutish farmhands. For Jameson, the travesty of the trope lies in its perversion of capitalism, and indeed, this is the explicit reproof communicated by the young manager of Michel's estate, Charles Bocage: "Il faut prendre ces devoirs au sérieux et renoncer à jouer avec . . . ou alors c'est qu'on ne méritait pas de posséder" (*I,* 125). Taken as a figure, however, this "stealing from oneself" may be interpreted in its wider ramifications as a synonym of the self-undermining text; the text that robs itself, depleting its stock of moral integrity just as Michel deplete his own territories of valuable game, because he simply is unable to resist the temptation to "jouer avec . . ."

What is it about these games that excites Michel so profoundly? More than just the risk of being caught, his reputation tarnished by scandal, his name (and that of his wife) the object of public ridicule, it is the delight in being duped that spurs Michel towards danger. Having learned that Alcide, the wildest of the poachers, has tricked old Bocage into paying him to destroy illegal traps which he himself has laid, Michel confesses:

> Et ce qui me dépite en cette affaire, ce n'est pas le triple commerce d'Alcide, c'est de le voir ainsi me tromper. Et puis que font-ils de l'argent, Bute et lui? Je ne sais rien; je saurai jamais rien de tels êtres. Ils mentiront toujours, me tromperont pour me tromper.
>
> (*I,* 122)

Like both Swann and Marcel in *A la Recherche du temps perdu,* Michel reveals his vulnerability to the seductive powers of what Deleuze has called the "deceptive sign," a sign which, by "concealing what it expresses" alludes to those mysterious "possible worlds" of concupiscence and coquetry from which the jealous lover is excluded by the beloved.

Alcide, through his transparent lies, draws Michel deeper into the underworld of deception, a world governed, as Deleuze has advanced, by its own inverted "system," of rules and "laws":

> Si le mensonge obéit à des lois, c'est parce qu'il implique une certaine tension dans le menteur lui-même, comme un système de rapports physiques entre la vérité et les dénégations ou inventions sous lesquelles on prétend la cacher: il y a donc des lois de contact, d'attraction et de répulsion, qui forment un véritable "physique" du mensonge. En effet, la vérité est là, présente dans l'aimé qui ment; il en a une connaissance permanente, il ne l'oublie pas, tandis qu'il oublie vite un mensonge improvisé. La chose cachée agit en lui de telle manière qu'il extrait de son contexte un petit fait vrai destiné à garantir l'ensemble du mensonge. Mais c'est précisément ce petit fait qui le trahit, parce que ses angles s'adaptent mal avec le reste, révélant une autre origine, un appartenance à un autre système. Ou bien la chose cachée agit à distance, attire le menteur qui ne cesse de s'en rapprocher.[12]
>
> [*Proust et les signes*]

When Michel covers for Alcide, fabricating excuses that will in turn signal his complicity to the young criminal even at the expense of putting his own credibility into question, he discovers the magic point of contact that connects him to that "autre système," that society of marginals tainted by poverty, incest and rape ("la famille Heurtevent"). But as Alcide is to Michel, so Michel is to Marceline: her point of intersection with the shady, mediated world of middle-class deception: her prevaricating beloved. Often, as Deleuze points out in relation to Proust's Marcel, Michel's "mensonge improvisé" is forgotten, as when he pretends to Marceline during the period of his malady that she should continue to engage young Arab companions, only in order to keep the enviable example of their health (rather than their animal sensuality) before him. Alternatively, in some of the subtle, almost imperceptible shifts in his interior monologues, one can discern the "petit fait vrai" which according to Deleuze gives away the lie. At one point, after exclaiming selfishly over the cost of a proper apartment for his ailing wife, he cunningly reverses his position: "D'ailleurs, qu'ai-je besoin d'argent? Qu'ai-je besoin de tout cela? Je suis devenu fort, à présent . . . Marceline, elle, a besoin de luxe; elle est faible" (*I*, 131). The sudden change in attitude from respect to scorn for private property acts as a disguise for Michel's shift in allegiance from the weak to the strong, the strong being the unbridled clan instructed by Ménalque, deserting responsibility, sleeping in barns, and heaping contempt on bourgeois moral protocol.

In his gradual withdrawal from Marceline, Michel saturates his own discourse with deceptive signs, as he progressively bankrupts the discourse of Marceline, and it is in this rhetorical negation of the female signifier, that one can begin to observe the broader relationship between negation and gender. Although he would never be so brutal as to voice openly the complaint that Marceline's conversation amounts to little more than a tissue of moral platitudes, the complaint is nonetheless communicated through textual juxtaposition, the requotation of her phrases in a hostile context. Shortly after one of their habitual evening "causeries," Michel remarks angrily on the conformity of opinion that appears to prevail among their friends, to which his wife replies: "Mais, mon ami, . . . vous ne pouvez demander à chacun de différer de tous les autres." "Plus ils se ressemblent entre eux," he retorts, "et plus ils diffèrent de moi" (*I*, 91). The manifest vehemence of this rebuke renders what happens later in the course of his discussion with Ménalque all the more astonishing:

> Je laissais Ménalque parler; ce qu'il disait, c'était précisément ce que, le mois d'avant, je disais à Marceline; et j'aurais donc dû l'approuver. Pourquoi, par quelle lâcheté l'interrompis-je, et lui dis-je, imitant Marceline, la phrase mot pour mot par laquelle elle m'avait alors interrompu:
>
> —Vous ne pouvez pourtant, cher Ménalque, demander à chacun de différer de tous les autres.
>
> (*I*, 101)

Repetition of the trivial phrase brings on swift and exigent punishment. Ménalque turns his back abruptly on Michel and only subsequently relents on the condition that Michel disown his words. Michel capitulates, condemning the phrase as a worthless commonplace, then furthering condemning its speakers ("Je hais tous les gens à principes"), thereby implicitly repudiating his wife. This seems to be what is understood by Ménalque who concurs, with satisfaction, that "Les gens à principes" qualify as "ce qu'il y a de plus détestable au monde" (*I*, 102). Marceline's words, read metonymically for her entire person, are thus radically negated, but with impunity, for Michel has not actually uttered a single word against her directly. Indeed, he even allows himself the luxury of "forgetting" the slip, as he masquerades as the most devoted of husbands after she has lost her child. The only overt signs of his betrayal can be found in the silent recrimination of the dead infant (a ghoulish metaphor of absence) and in the prohibition of all speech pertaining to the miscarriage: "Pas un mot ne fut échangé, au sujet du triste accident qui meurtrissait nos espérances" (*I*, 108). Here, Barthes's concept of the "Inter-dite," as that which is linguistically forbidden or taboo, as well as "read between the lines," appropriately describes the new mode of censorship to which all future exchange between them will be subjected.

If on one level, Marceline's discourse is rhetorically negated (judged to be conformist, "detestable," and finally unspeakable by Michel), on another and even more sinister level, the representation of her diseased and decomposing body merges horrifically with the textual figuration of the "abîme" or abyss. The association between the feminine body and the "abîme" as hole or gap acquires further semiotic dimensions with the help of its secondary meaning, the verb "abîmer" denoting the process of rotting, spoiling, or deterioration. It is in this sense that Michel initially uses the word in conjunction with Marceline's metonymical scissors after their theft by Moktir: "Et pourquoi les avait-il volés," he wonders, "si c'était aussitôt pour les *abîmer,* les détruire?" (*I*, 100; my emphasis). Michel's perplexity in regard to the motives of a thief who defaces the booty which he has run such risks to procure is left unresolved, but perhaps, as is intimated, Moktir's perversely destructive gesture was guided by the unconscious wish-fulfillments of Michel. Is it simply a slip of the text that as Marceline's condition worsens, her body becoming the mirror of her husband's growing immoralism, it is as "une chose abîmée" that she appears to Michel? "La maladie était entrée en Marceline, l'habitait désormais, la marquait, la tachait. C'était une chose abîmée," he observes with chilling detachment (*I*, 109). The semantic links implicit in the verb "abîmer" between organic decay (the body as transitively decomposed, reduced to the holes of the death's head), are luridly personified in the description of Marceline's face as it reflects the advanced stages of the disease: "Comme elle paraît faible et changée; dans l'ombre, ainsi, je la reconnaîtrais à peine. Que ses traits sont tirés! Est-ce que l'on voyait ainsi les deux *trous noirs* de ses narines?" (*I*, 131; my emphasis).

Michel's projected vision of the "black holes" in Marceline's head is prefigured several times in ***Les Cahiers d'André Walter,*** conforming with the alarming exactitude of a classic case history, to the Freudian description of fetishism. The curious gaze that travels from below to above, pruriently investigating beneath a woman's skirt, is duly recorded by the tormented narrator of *André Walter*: "Oh! me blottir auprès de toi, m'asseoir à tes pieds, dans ta chaleur enveloppante, ma tête sur tes genoux, dans le pli profond de ta robe," And if here the "pli profond" evokes the dark space of the absent female phallus, so terrifying to the fetishist, it later develops into the even more redoubtable apparition of a "nothingness," featured as "noir comme un trou":

> Cauchemar:
>
> Elle m'est apparue, très belle, vêtue d'une robe d'orfroi qui jusqu'à ses pieds tombait sans plis comme une étole; . . .
>
> Sous la robe, il n'y avait rien; c'était noir, noir comme un trou; je sanglotais de désespoir. Alors, de ses deux mains, elle a saisi le bas de sa robe et puis l'a rejetée jusque par-dessus sa figure. Elle s'est retournée comme un sac. Et je n'ai plus rien vu; la nuit s'est refermée sur elle . . .[13]

André Walter's nightmare of the womb shockingly emptied like a bag (another figure of female castration) foreshadows the placement in later works of the female signifier "en abyme." The text of Marceline's body becomes the site of gaps, disfigurations, and defamiliarizing anatomical displacements. Most sinister is the grotesque displacement of the eyes, and by implication the spiritual value of her gaze, to the nostrils, which encircle the black hollow of physical dematerialization:

> O goût de cendres! O lassitude! Tristesse du surhumain effort! J'ose à peine la regarder; je sais trop que mes yeux au lieu de chercher son regard, iront *affreusement* se fixer sur les *trous noirs* de ses narines; l'expression de son visage souffrant est atroce. Elle non plus ne me regarde pas.
>
> (*I*, 146; my emphases)

In addition to the "trous noirs," the adverbial qualifier "affreusement" (denoting "horror" from the root *affre,* but also, significantly enough, that which is "détestable") serves to underscore the fine line between Michel's sympathy and contempt for his wife. The repressed significance of "détestable" (the very word used by Ménalque in reference to people like Marceline) resurfaces in the ambivalent word "affreux." The adverb is even carried over as an adjective in the description of Marceline's death-throes, in which the awful silence between husband and wife is transferred back from the gaze to the lips, just as the abyssal signs of lifelessness are redisplaced back to the eyes from the nose:

> Marceline est assise à moitié sur son lit; un de ses maigres bras se cramponne aux barreaux du lit, la tient dressée; ses draps, ses mains, sa chemise, sont inondés d'un flot de sang; son visage en est tout sali; *ses yeux sont hideusement agrandis*; et n'importe quel cri d'agonie m'épouvanterait moins que *son silence.* Je cherche sur son visage transpirant une petite place pour poser un *affreux baiser*; le goût de sa sueur me reste aux lèvres.
>
> (*I*, 147; my emphases)

The transfixed expression of Marceline's cavernous eyes is harrowingly transcribed yet again a moment before her death ("mais ses yeux restent grands ouverts" [*I,* 148]), as if to punctuate the end-point in the abyssal chain stretching from the dark patches of discoloration on her body, to the blank spaces in dialogue, to the black orifices of nose and eyes.

Without imputing a vulgar misogyny to Michel, or for that matter to Gide, we are nonetheless left with the dilemma of how to interpret this censorship of the feminine—of the woman's body and the woman's "parole." Has Marceline simply been sublated, interred and inscribed in the homotextual "inquiétude" that reverberates in each of the *récit's* elisions? Or can her negation, her disappearance into the "abîme," be read as a protofeminist fable in which masculine and feminine "jouissance" are presented as mutually exclusive? Perhaps it is only in the slips of the text, in those flashes of simultaneous concealment and disclosure that the full complexity of these unspoken issues can be glimpsed.

Notes

1. J. Laplanche and J.B. Pontalis, *The Language of Psychoanalysis,* tr. Donald Nicholson-Smith (New York: Norton, 1973), p. 300.

2. Sigmund Freud, *The Psychopathology of Everyday Life,* tr. Alan Tyson (same as Vol. VI of Standard Edition) (New York: Norton, 1965), p. 220.

3. André Gide, *Oedipe* in *Théâtre* (Paris: Gallimard, 1942), p. 288.

4. Walter Benjamin, "Oedipe et le mythe raisonnable," *Walter Benjamin: Oeuvres,* II, tr. Maurice de Gandillac (Paris: Denoël, 1971), 47.

5. Gide, *Oedipe,* p. 289.

6. Gide, *Thésée* in *Romans, récits et sôties,* pp. 1416-17.

7. André Gide, "Considérations sur la mythologie grecque," *Incidences* (Paris: Gallimard, 1924), p. 129.

8. [Roland] Barthes, "Pierre Loti," *Nouveaux Essais* [*Critiques* in Le Degrézéro de l'écriture (Paris: Seuil, 1972)], p. 173 (my paraphrase).

9. André Gide, *L'Immoraliste,* ed. Elaine Marks and Richard Tedeschi (Toronto: Macmillan, 1963), p. 29. All further references to this work will appear in the text abbreviated *I.* I have used this edition because of its useful notes.

10. Alice Jardine, *Gynesis* (Ithaca: Cornell University Press, 1985), p. 146.

11. Fredric Jameson, *The Prison-House of Language* (Princeton: Princeton University Press, 1972), p. 178. Jameson writes: "Vice, said Sartre once is a taste for failure; and it is in Gide (think of the situation in which Michel ends up helping the poachers steal from himself) the penalty for an allegiance to the myth of some absolute and original presence."

12. Gilles Deleuze, *Proust et les signes* (Paris: PUF, 1964), pp. 93-94.

13. André Gide, *Les Cahiers d'André Walter,* in *Oeuvres complètes,* ed. L. Martin Chauffier, I (Paris: Editions de la Nouvelle Revue Française, 1932-1938), 144, 169-70.

Selected Bibliography

Rhetoric, Stylistics, Narrative Theory

Barthes, Roland. *L'Obvie et l'obtus.* Paris: Seuil, 1982.

Critical Theory, Psychoanalysis, Feminism

Deleuze, Gilles. *Proust et les signes.* Paris: PUF, 1964.

Freud, Sigmund. *Dora: "Negation." Standard Edition of the Complete Works of Sigmund Freud.* 24 vols. Ed. James Strachey. 24 vols. London: Hogarth Press, 1953, vol XIX, pp. 234-36.

———. *The Psychopathology of Everyday Life.* Tr. Alan Tyson. New York: Norton, 1965.

Jardine, Alice. *Gynesis*. Ithaca: Cornell University Press, 1985.

Laplanche, J. and Pontalis, J.B. *The Language of Psychoanalysis.* Tr. D. Nicholson-Smith. New York: Norton, 1973.

Works by Gide consulted which are not included in the Gallimard (Pléiade) edition

"Considérations sur la mythologie grecque." In *Incidences.* Paris: Gallimard, 1924.

L'Immoraliste. Ed. Elaine Marks and Richard Tedeschi. Toronto: Macmillan, 1963.

Théâtre. Paris: Gallimard, 1942.

Articles on Gide

Benjamin, Walter. "Oedipe ou le mythe raisonnable." In *Oeuvres* II. Tr. Maurice de Gandillac. Paris: Denoël, 1971.

Louis A. MacKenzie, Jr. (essay date August 1990)

SOURCE: MacKenzie, Jr., Louis A. "The Language of Excitation in Gide's *L'Immoraliste*." *Romance Quarterly* 37, no. 3 (August 1990): 309-19.

[*In the following essay, MacKenzie considers "discovering" a central theme of* The Immoralist, *and he examines the process by which the reader dis-covers Gide's textual strategies in the book.*]

L'Immoraliste is a book that slips deftly through the fingers of outrage. The reader's instinctive—or unconsidered—sense of the scandal lacing Michel's narration seems to be blocked either by an inability to define just what constitutes that scandal, or by an uncertainty as to whether or not there is indeed anything scandalous in what has just been read.[1] There is all the same something that tends to make readers uneasy about Michel's confession. Indeed, as one of the internal interlocutors admits: "Il nous semblait hélas! qu'à nous la raconter, Michel avait rendu son action plus légitime. De ne savoir où la désapprover, dans la lente explication qu'il en donna, nous en faisait presque complices."[2] That the fictive witnesses, these faithful and concerned friends, are made to confront their own inability to judge serves two closely related purposes: first, it signals to subsequent witnesses, that is, to readers of the *récit,* that the notion of judgment is, if by indirection, an important issue for Gide; and secondly, it stands as a sign-post referring back to the rhetorical and stylistic features of the narrative in ways that underscore the artfulness of Michel the narrator and, hence, the artistry of Gide the writer. One could in fact assert that the "scandal" of *L'Immoraliste* resides specifically in the friction between a tale of arrogance, ego-centrism, dissipation, and decadence and a style that tends to thwart the rush to judgment by cloaking such unsavory traits and actions in language that is as refined as it is clever.

The reader of *L'Immoraliste* is confronted with a discursive strategy designed to ensure that the off-putting aspects of the confession are in fact put off, are hidden by the mechanisms and motives of Michel's own hypersensitivity. The reader is to be seduced, or to use Barthes's term, "picked-up" (*dragué*);[3] he is to be cajoled into looking for the erotic part of the body/text; that is, the parts where the garment/language gapes intermittently. This "flashing," what Barthes calls the staging of an "appearance-as-disappearance," will constitute an important part of the pleasure to come from Gide's text. This type of pleasure is the pleasure of discovering, of pulling aside semantic and stylistic veils in order to peek at, to reveal, and revel in, the intimate gifts that Gide clothes in the classical modesty of his language. And while it can, of course, be maintained that the process of dis-covering is common to all serious reading, *L'Immoraliste* does all the same provide an especially rich example, in that the reader's discovering of Gide's strategies is refracted by the discovery process functioning as one of the basic themes of the book.

As Michel's sexual awakening and its *seemingly* disastrous consequences are at the heart of what in his preface the author refers to as the "problem" of the book, it is on the question of the erotic that Gide's artful dodging is most evident and crucial. The intent of the present essay will be, then, to excavate the various instances where, in a book that teems with the erotic, the author manages to talk sexual excitation without ever explicitly coming out of the closet of strict linguistic *bienséance*. It can be noted, and not in a wholly incidental way, that the stylistic limits the author imposes on himself, and the almost prudish way he treats sexuality, are fully consonant with the psychography of his main character. If, as we shall see, Michel speaks in metaphors, images and other linguistic detours that hide (and thus highlight) the significant moments of his psycho-sexual itinerary, it is precisely because, having had no experience of the erotic, he does not really possess the appropriate words with which to speak explicitly of his desires and, ultimately, of his deviancy.[4]

Until the time of his malady, Michel had led the effete life of a scholar whose brilliance and creative energies were, in large part, expropriated by a domineering father (his study on Trojan culture appeared under his father's name). Moreover, in deference to that same father he marries a woman for whom he feels no intense passion. On this point he is characteristically, if cloyingly, frank: "Si je n'aimais pas, dis-je, ma fiancée, du moins n'avais-je jamais aimé d'autre femme" (p. 16). And on another occasion: "J'ai dit que je ne l'aimais point—du moins n'éprouvais-je pour elle de ce qu'on appelle amour, mais je l'aimais, si l'on veut entendre par là de la tendresse, une sorte de pitié, enfin une estime assez grande" (p. 17). In both instances, Michel feels compelled to qualify or justify his love for Marceline. As a consequence, the reader comes away with the sense of a dispassionate, polite affection expressing little more than a conventional or institutional relationship.

That Michel will describe himself as "ravi"—ravished, swept away—by the charm of what Marceline has to say to him after he makes what he considers to be the important discovery of her autonomy, anticipates and enhances the shock to his complacency that he is soon to receive in Tunis. To use the term dear to the Gide of the *Nourritures terrestres,* Michel is psychologically "disponible": he is poised for the "new sensations" he is about to experience. And even if on the heels of his *ravissement,* he and Marceline sleep in separate berths,[5] the "surprise" of Tunis, the "new sensations," have to be seen as correlated to the sexual content, however fragile or deferred, of a kiss Michel places on Marceline's forehead. At this point in the tale, Michel's sexual side is beginning to stir; it is opening up to the urges of its yet unexpressed desire and need. Not unlike Proust's narrator who, under the charms of a first, light sleep, took on the forms and features of the books he had been reading, Michel's "dormant faculties," which are at once his drives and his awareness of them, became animated precisely because, never having been called to action, they still contain a "mystérieuse jeunesse," that is, their sense of wonder, their freshness, flexibility and naivete.

Youthfulness is, of course, the swing term that will legitimize for Michel his association with the unfettered vitality and eroticism of the youthful objects of his desire. He will become fascinated and obsessed with youth—his own, which he had forgotten and is now discovering intact, and that of the Arab boys orbiting around him and taking shadowy places in the folds of his psyche. An especially clear example of this occurs when Marceline introduces a boy named Bachir into Michel's room. At first Michel is "gêné"—annoyed and embarrassed—by the boy's presence, but after a short while his uneasiness wanes. What transpires between the original feeling and its dissipation is significant.

Michel's cool, if not overtly hostile, reaction to Bachir's presence causes the boy to recoil towards Marceline. Furthermore, at the precise moment when Bachir takes Marceline's hand and kisses it, Michel catches a glance of the boy's nakedness. Important here is a convergence of details which in isolation would surely have been less significant. What is in fact revealed here, what Michel discovers—implicitly at the time, much less innocently in the recounting—is a link between the boy, the boy's nudity and the kiss. Bachir does not simply interpose himself between Michel and his wife. Rather, he takes the husband's place: in kissing Marceline, he is, if only in a fragile way, eroticised for Michel, whose perception of the boy's nudity and through it, his own, takes on a special and logical significance.

This scene contains other details that further punctuate Michel's nascent sexual desires and excitation. For example, Bachir passes his time carving a whistle; that is, manipulating two objects, the knife and the wood, with latent phallic connotation. Once again Michel remarks the boy's nudity, but this time perception begets a measure of appreciation: "Je le regarde. . . . Ses pieds sont nus; ses chevilles sont charmantes" (p. 31). Michel then has the boy pass him the whistle. He pretends to admire it, but has no explicit sense of why the whistle appeals to him; he is not consciously aware that the whistle is a direct and palpable extension of the boy, of his call and of his maleness. What he is to know, and what he reveals, is his impatience for Bachir's return: "Le lendemain pour la première fois je m'ennuie; j'attends; j'attends quoi. Je me sens désœuvré, inquiet. Enfin je n'y tiens plus: "Bachir ne vient donc pas ce matin?'" Michel's wait, his *attente,* is at once indicative of the *attention* which almost in spite of himself he is now paying to the boy and of the psychological *tension* attending his waiting. The following day the boy does return and, in an almost ritualistic way, sets again to whittling. It is, however, specified that he is working "un bois trop dur." Now, the notion of hardness might in another context be of less or little interest, but here the ramifications are particularly significant: "Il voulut tailler un bois trop dur, et fit si bien qu'il s'enfonça la lame dans le pouce. J'eus un frisson d'horreur; il en rit, monta la coupure brillante et s'amuse de voir couler son sang. Quand il riait, il découvrait des dents très blanches" (p. 32). The erotic symbolism of this sequence is literally less wooden than in the earlier encounter with Bachir. The whistle of the day before has been transformed—suddenly, but perhaps not surprisingly—into a more vital symbol, the boy's thumb. In bringing the thumb to life, by arranging for it to spill forth the liquid it contains, Gide can logically invest the symbolic ejaculation and deflowering with an appropriate dose of pleasure. Bachir's expression of pleasure, his laughter (which in showing off his white teeth evokes the nudity that had earlier impinged itself on Michel) is accompanied by an act that intensifies the erotic component: "il lécha plaisamment sa blessure; sa langue était rose comme un chat."

The interest here lies not just in the act of licking the bleeding thumb, but also in the fact that the word "plaisamment" is applied to the act. Now this term fits perfectly both into the thematic and the stylistic handling of Michel's psycho-sexual condition. On one level, "plaisamment" is synonymous with "drôlement," that is, in a funny, unexpected way. As such it jibes with Michel's own naiveté, with the "innocent," social pleasure, already announced in his profound disappointment over Bachir's absence the day before and in his "frisson d'horreur" at the sight of the boy's blood. But "plaisamment" also signifies "in a pleasurable way." On this level, the erotic flows more visibly: the uninhibited pleasure Bachir takes in licking his wound reflects and intensifies the pleasure Michel himself takes in watching him. Clearly, this sort of complicity will be amplified in the most famous scene in the book; that is, when Michel watches himself watch Moktir steal a pair of scissors, an act which can be seen as figuratively violating the notion of domesticity and of marriage, as well as a sense of property and propriety. Recalling the earlier moment when Michel witnessed Bachir's intimacy with Marceline—he not only kisses her hand, but also snuggles up to her—a simple algebra will allow for the extrusion from this apparently innocent, but clearly titillating scene an even more intense erotic element. If, in the earlier moment, Bachir had symbolically taken Michel's place as Marceline's sexual partner, in a sense becoming Michel, it can then be inferred that when Bachir takes and *gives* pleasure by licking his thumb, it is as if Michel himself were performing the act and taking his own pleasure from it. At the risk of oversimplifying what is clearly a highly complicated problem, it could be said that this coalescence of Michel and Bachtir exemplifies one of the determining factors of homosexuality; namely, the narcissistic urge to find a partner who most closely resembles oneself.

Now, while Michel may not yet be fully conscious of a manifest sexual attraction towards the boy, he is, nonetheless, powerfully attracted to him. The attraction is, however, "sanitized" by the detour of aestheticization: "Ah, qu'il se portait bien. C'était là ce dont je m'éprenais en lui: la santé. La santé de ce petit corps était belle" (p. 32). Significantly, when Michel valorizes the "health," which is also to say the healthy sexuality, of Bachir and his playmates, he does so at the expense of his relationship with his wife. Indeed, he comes to realize that when he is in the company of the Arab boys, Marceline's presence annoys him. "Mais ce qui me gênait, l'avouerai-je, ce n'étaient pas les enfants, c'était elle. Oui, si peu que ce fût, j'étais gêné par sa présence" (p. 41). On one level, Michel's annoyance is linked to his manifest and stated desire for self-sufficiency in his cure. His *prise de conscience/santé* is to be a personal journey. On another, it has everything to do with a first rejection of Marceline, of the autonomous adult female. So, "malgré [lui-même] mais par parti pris," Michel admits to preferring the boys not under Marceline's protection. The hostility of this "parti pris" is underscored in the text when Michel, recalling that Marceline had to go out on an errand, adds, "j'en profitai." This verb implicitly but clearly directs the reader's attention to something illicit in Michel's deep intentions, if not in his explicit acts.

This "j'en profitai" serves also to cast the terms with which Michel qualifies his psychic state upon Bachir's arrival into a specific light: "Le petit Bachir, qui manquait rarement de venir le matin, prit mon châle; je me sentais alerte, le cœur léger" (p. 41). The profit Michel takes from Bachir's presence/Marceline's absence is somehow linked to alertness. But what is the sense of this somewhat unexpected term? On the surface, the term expresses Michel's impatience, his mental and physical openness with regard to the day ahead of him. On a less obvious, but certainly more meaty level, this same term actually signals Michel's sexual alertness, his excitation. Indeed, as it turns out, "alert" benefits from a fascinating etymological heritage. The term itself comes directly from *à l(h)erte,* an adverbial expression meaning "to be on one's guard," itself deriving from an earlier Italian phrase *all'erta* (*sur la hauteur* in French) which, in effect, was the call for the sentry to take his post "up high." The *erta* of this command comes from *erto* which meant an escarpment, that is, a sharp, almost vertical incline characteristic of a fortification. Now, this *erto* is itself a derivative of the Latin verb *erigere,* the past participle of which is nothing less than *erectus.*[6]

To infer from this that Gide has put Michel in a state of explicit sexual excitation would, of course, violate rather clearly drawn semantic boundaries. On the other hand, the *apparent* gap between the term "alert" and the notion of arousal is precisely the point. At this moment in the tale, Michel is just beginning to understand his own sexual leaning. On a psycho-sexual level, Michel is in many respects an adolescent, and, like an adolescent, he is only partially aware of what is happening to him. He is aware of going through profound physical, psychic and social changes, but he is sufficiently inhibited by convention and inexperience to come to full grips with those changes. This is not, of course, to minimize the semantic suggestiveness of the term "alert." To the contrary, it highlights the coherent elegance of Gide's artistry. Given the fact that Michel is a philologist and historian, it is altogether possible to argue that on some level he is aware of the connotations of the word he uses after the fact, that is, in what the reader intuitively takes to be a sanitized version of the event. So this alertness is an index, however fragile or latent, both of Michel's growing excitement and his awareness of it.

At the same time, it underscores a resistance to, and a deferring of, self-definition. Michel's state of alertness is not only a call to duty, to the ancient and difficult duty of faithfulness to oneself, it is also a call to ascend the heights ("all'erta") of duty and pleasure, an ascent that will demand a special and arduous reconciliation with the social pressures consequent to the call itself. As one critic has observed, "les héros de Gide sont attirés par les routes difficiles, les chemins qui montent. . . . Grimpeurs, ou plongeurs, navigateurs ou explorateurs, ils sentent en eux, comme Urien, leur vaillance appeler les prouesses."[7]

This notion of verticality, associated metonymically with male excitation, is highlighted a short time later in the text. On his way to visit one of the orchards of the oasis, Michel recounts: "Je marchais dans une sorte d'extase, d'allégresse silencieuse, d'exaltation des sens et de la chair. A ce moment, des souffles légers s'élevèrent; toutes les palmes s'agitèrent et nous vîmes les palmiers les plus hauts s'incliner;—puis l'air entier redevint calme, et j'entendis distinctement, derrière le mur, un chant de flute.—Une brèche au mur; nous entrâmes" (p. 48). The richness of the scene derives from the intimate connection between the physical environment (the walls and the trees) and Michel's psychosexual state. There operates here a kind of hermeneutic circling between environment and stimulation, between perception and excitation. Michel describes himself as caught up in ecstasy, *allégresse* and exaltation. The three terms are significant, as is the distinction among them. Ecstasy has to do with a special kind of joy. It is, quite literally, a movement away from stasis; in this case, away from a static and bookish world devoid of real experience. For Michel, the ecstasy he feels has everything to do with the rejection of an earlier worldview and the anticipation of a new one. The joy expressed in *allégresse* is slightly, but meaningfully, different in that it carries a nuance of public display.[8] Michel's burgeoning sexuality, however indeterminate, instills in him a kind of euphoria, both mental and physical, which, in turn, will impel him to give it some sort of public expression.

The final term of Michel's semantic triad, "exaltation," brings back into focus the underlying, but hardly ancillary, connotations of the term "alerte." Like that term, "exaltation," which appears with telling frequency over the course of ***L'Immoraliste,*** points upward to the heights (*ex/altus*). The image of height (of arousal and heightened sensuality) is refracted in Michel's evocation of the tallest palm trees. These trees, concrete extensions of Michel's increasing awareness of, and commitment to, the sensuality that surrounds him, bend and beckon. This action (*s'incliner*), already suggestive of a sexual advance—in classical French discourse, the term *inclination* refers to sexual attraction[9]—is punctuated by the sound of a flute rising directly from behind the wall of the garden. The song itself—one thinks instinctively, if associatively, of Debussy's "Prélude à l'après-midi d'un faune" and of Mallarmé's poem celebrating sexual wantonness—may, however, be less significant than the instrument upon which it is produced; for, in a sense, the flute (and its call) is a more evolved, more seductive, avatar of Bachir's rudimentary and childish *sifflet*. The palm trees will also be endowed with a more explicitly sexual charge when one of the Arab boys, Lachmi,[10] climbs one of them. This act, already vaguely sexual, provides Michel with a privileged view of the "nudité doré" under the boy's flowing robe. That Lachmi makes Michel taste the sap of the tree, a syrupy and bitter liquid that is not (yet) to Michel's liking, adds to the sexual information flowing just under the surface of the prose.

Michel's erotic itinerary reaches a kind of climax when he has to come to the rescue of his wife. Michel starts out alone on the road to Sorrento and soon finds himself in a state of near ecstasy as he thrills to the beauty of the surroundings. His reverie is interrupted in a brutal way by Marceline's carriage. Careening out of control, it transforms a scene of beauty and calm into one of noise, terror, fear, flight, fury and frenzied violence. Michel's heightened energies are put directly to the service of counter-aggressive action. The beating he gives the coachman who had provoked the incident is invested with an implicit eroticism. In **L'Immoraliste** the erotic, the manly, the robust, and the healthy are coextensive. Such is surely the case when Michel sits on the coachman's chest and administers a drubbing that draws blood, and thus reminds the reader of the more innocent and youthful blood that had issued from Bachir's thumb. Even more significant is the fact that this expression of manliness is followed by the most direct expression of sexual activeness in the book. "Ce fut cette nuit-là que je possédai Marceline" (p. 73). The bluntness of the declaration serves to punctuate this night as the consummation of a perfect day, a day in which an explosion of virility comes on the heels of spiritual/sensual exaltation, all of which climaxes in sexual action. And the verb used to express this action must be understood in both a literal and a figurative sense. Michel has "possessed" his wife sexually and in so doing has taken possession of her. He has appropriated her, rendered her his own (*propre*) and, to use an expression, cleaned up his sexual act (has rendered it and himself "propre"). He has reached a personal climactic point, the high point of the *altus* of "exaltation" and the *erta* of "alerte," a point of exaltation and manliness, of sexual potency, satisfaction—in a word—normalcy. It is a wholly privileged moment: "Car il me semble, à m'en souvenir aujourd'hui, que cette première nuit fut la seule, tant l'attente et la surprise de l'amour ajoutaient à la volupté des délices,—tant une seule nuit suffit au plus grand amour pour se dire, et tant mon souvenir s'obstine à me rappeler uniquement. Ce fut un rire d'un moment, où nos âmes se confondirent . . . Mais je crois qu'il est un point de l'amour, unique, et que l'âme plus tard, ah! cherche en vain à dépassser . . ." (p. 73). Being privileged, however, it marks the point after which things take something of a downhill turn. In this sense, the "possession" of Marceline represents an orgasmic moment after which come secondary, waning spasms and ultimately a kind of weariness.

In the second part of the narrative, which begins just after this incident, Michel and Marceline have left the warmth of the Mediterranean for Normandy, "le pays le plus ombreux et le plus mouillé" that Michel can imagine. The Norman wetness will constitute an essential element of a scene that carries an especially blatant—and banal—sexual symbolism: the scene in which Michel joins Charles in the muddy waters of a pond that is being drained. As the water level goes down, fish begin to appear. The thrashing of the fish causes the water to turn muddy and thick. In the earthy water the number of fish seems to multiply, exceeding the wildest hopes of the onlookers. The scene is of frantic, frenzied life, of something primitive and excessive. There is an evident movement away from the "cleanliness," the *propreté* and the propriety represented in the text by Michel's proper appropriation/possession of his wife. This embrace of that which is dirty can be related to Freud's thought that the development of civilization has always entailed a rejection of that which is dirty, disorderly, and improper: "Dirtiness of any kind seems to us incompatible with civilization."[11] As becomes increasingly evident over the course of the narrative, the pattern and evolution of Michel's actions underscore a movement away from the strictures of society and the values of propriety (and property) upon which it is constituted. On the level of Michel's psyche, this is to be paralleled by a movement away from the tyranny of the superego towards the no less tyrannical demands of the id and the libidinal energy it carries.

In the scene we examine here, an even more manifest erotic aspect is figured by the appearance of eels. The phallic connotation is obvious enough. More interesting is the reaction that the eels provoke first in Charles, then Michel: neither can resist the urge to jump into the muddy turbulence. "Charles, qui jusqu'alors était resté près de son père sur la rive, n'y tint plus; il ôta brusquement ses souliers, ses chaussettes, mit bas sa veste et son gilet, puis relevant très haut son pantalon et les manches de sa chemise, il entra dans la vase résolument. Tout aussitôt je l'imitai" (p. 87). Especially significant here is the attention paid by Gide and Michel to Charles's disrobing. The persistent and otherwise superfluous descriptive detail suggests something not too far removed from a strip-tease; and if such is not Charles's intention, it certainly seems to be part of Michel's perception, playing as it does such an important part in his memory of the incident.

Once together in the muddy water, Michel and Charles form something of a couple in their effort to catch an especially large eel: "Nous unissions nos mains pour la saisir . . ." (p. 88). The ellipsis at the end of the sentence serves to underscore the suggestive quality of Michel's memory. The patina of sexuality becomes even clearer when Michel first specifies that the eels cause the muddy water to splash up in their faces. It can be suggested that this scene represents a kind of hinge between the generally antiseptic and sublimated sexuality of the first part of the story and the earthiness and depravity that will mark the second; not that it is any more explicit, but rather that there is something vaguely off-putting about it. That quality lies assuredly in the coming together of the elements mentioned above: inability to resist, disrobing, the eels, the splash of the mud, the coupling of Charles and Michel. All of which is then linked to a final detail, one that the reader had seen earlier on, namely, that Marceline comes to represent a troubling, constraining force. "Marceline n'était pas encore venue et ne vint pas, mais déjà je ne regrettais plus son absence; il me semblait qu'elle eût un peu gêné notre joie" (p. 88).

The erotically charged notions of wetness and joy will also mark the celebrated scene where Michel fights wind and snow as well as his own anxiety to keep a rendezvous with the mysterious and diabolically irresistible Ménalque. The psycho-sexual interest of the scene resides in Michel's association of his anxiety and Marceline herself: "Marceline allait un peu mieux ce soir-là, et pourtant j'étais inquiet; une garde me remplaça près d'elle. Mais sitôt dans la rue, mon inquiétude prit une force nouvelle; je la repoussai, luttai contre elle, m'irritant contre moi de ne pas mieux m'en libérer" (p. 128). The primary antecedent of the personal pronoun "elle" is, of course, *inquiétude* (or its "new strength"). It can, and probably should, be argued also that it is Marceline herself who is targeted in Michel's willful struggling. "I push *her* away. I struggle against *her*." At the very minimum, Marceline incarnates the source of Michel's anxiety, representing as she does the features of the super-ego: social and sexual normalcy, family values, virtue. Michel's own struggle—that is, the expressing of his manliness and a sense of self—bring him to a state of *surtension* and of a special sort of *exaltation*. Indeed this state of hyperstimulation derives in part from the anxiety itself. It is not a rejection either of *mauvaise conscience* or of the anxiety attending it. It is, rather, an incorporation—a second level of appropriation by which Michel digests and annihilates Marceline—that in itself defines the peculiar kind of happiness Michel feels in the boldness of his act.

In the final pages of the tale, Michel's rejection of the social orderliness that had defined his previous life view, and the acceptance of the demands of the body, will move ever further into what might be termed the "dirtier" elements of the world in which he locates and defines himself. His desire leads him deeper into the streets, the darkness, and the dirt. Michel's moral trajectory will take him from nights spent poaching on his own land, that is, stealing from himself; to sneaking out "comme un voleur" in Naples, where he spends a night of "débauche vagabonde" (pp. 169-70); to Syracuse, where he finds the company of "les pires gens" to be "délectable" (p. 172); to Kairouan, where, having slept the night outside a café, he returns home "couvert de vermine" (p. 175). This descent, all the while part of the ineluctable logic of a journey of self-enlightenment, is devoid of the kind of enthusiasm, exaltation and excitation that had marked earlier instances of sexual dallying, implied, stylized or sublimated though they might have been. Indeed, in the end, it all comes across as rather mechanical. When, for example, he gives himself to Moktir's mistress, he does so as if he were "letting himself fall asleep." And in the final lines of the *récit*, where pederasty is most clearly alluded to, there is a weariness and a lack of enthusiasm in Michel's response to the quip that it is for one of the local boys that he stays on in the isolated desert town of Sidi b. M. This tone of weariness, linked though it is to the original call for help that had triggered the confession, does not necessarily signal a retreat from the relentless trajectory and consequences of Michel's quest. To the contrary, the demure quality of the confession ends up injecting Michel's resignation with the kind of legitimacy that the internal interlocutor finds troublesome. It is this apparent legitimization that pulls the reader of the *Immoraliste* into an intellectual modality, one in which judgment of Michel's sexual practices and their social corollaries has to be suspended. Indeed, as if to underscore the point in a graphic way, Gide ends the text with an ellipsis, with these *points de suspension* marking indeterminance, playfulness and provocation.

Notes

1. Maurice Blanchot makes the point that the ensemble of Gide's work is marked by this slipperiness and that public reaction to it has been ambivalent on an almost historical scale: "[Gide] always ends up by discovering, at the very brink of self-forgetfulness, the moment that brings him back to himself; at the extremist point of innovation, the guarantee of some traditional rule; in his moment of greatest risk, a longing for, a sudden taste for propriety and balance. The century has been such that, for one whole part of his life Gide saw himself rejected because of his audacity; for another, because of his *lack* of audacity." "Gide and the Concept of Literature as Adventure" in *Gide,* ed. David Littleton (Englewood, New Jersey: Prentice Hall, 1970), p. 60. On *L'Immoraliste* itself, Albert Sonnenfeld writes that "Gide may be revealing his [own] pederasty, his infidelity and his pseudo-Nietzschian and Whitmanian penchants

in *L'Immoraliste,* but his real psychography is hidden behind the guilt-covering of the philosophical dialect between Marceline's Christian ethic and Ménalque's Virgilian paganism which Michel's hesitant middle position fails to synthesize." See "On Readers and Reading in *La Porte étroite* and *L'Immoraliste,*" *Romanic Review* 67, 3, (1976), 184.

2. André Gide, *L'Immoraliste,* Collection Folio (Paris: Mercure de France, 1902), p. 184.

3. See Barthes, *Le Plaisir du texte* (Paris: Seuil, 1973), p. 10.

4. I use this term in a nonjudgmental way. I have chosen it in light of what we know about Gide's own anguish over his sexual tendencies during the gestation of *L'Immoraliste.* On this point see Jean Delay's chapter on Gide's own premarital consultation with a specialist on the subject of his sexual "problem," in *La Jeunesse d'André Gide* (Paris: Gallimard, 1957), pp. 516-56. Of course, one has to be careful in making too close a connection between Gide and his fictional hero. It would, nonetheless, be overly fastidious to ignore parallelisms that seem to offer themselves logically to an understanding of a work that does in fact beg such autobiographical consideration.

5. "Ainsi donc celle à qui j'attachais ma vie avait sa vie propre et réelle! L'importance de cette pensée m'éveilla plusieurs fois cette nuit; plusieurs fois je me dressai sur ma couchette pour voir, sur l'autre couchette, plus bas, Marceline, ma femme, dormir" (p. 22).

6. See *Dictionnaire Robert,* entry *alerte.*

7. Maurice Maucuer, *Gide: L'Indécision passionée* (Paris: Editions du Centurion, 1969), p. 135.

8. *Le Petit Robert,* "allégresse: joie très vive qui d'ordinaire se manifeste publiquement."

9. The term is especially popular in classical French writing, e.g., *La Princesse de Clèves.* The evocation of classical literature is made *en connaissance de cause*: perhaps more than any other modern writer Gide is dubbed a classical stylist. Indeed, his treatment of sexuality generally rings of classicism where sexuality was more often than not cloaked in elegant language that at once purifies and draws attention to the erotic content. Serge Doubrovsky makes the point: "Il ne faut pas oublier, habitué que l'on est de nos jours à l'exhibitionism littéraire, que la discrétion coutumière du langage, chez Corneille autant que chez Racine, atteste non pas l'absence, mais le présence contenue d'une sensualité puissante." See *Corneille et la dialectique du héros* (Paris: Gallimard, 1963), p. 106.

10. Gide has, it seems, been purposefully playful in his choice of names, a significant number of which tend towards sexual connotation. Lachmi suggests a kind of playful, sexual pursuit ("Lache-moi"/"let me go"), while Lassif suggests the French term *lascif* = lascivious.

11. Sigmund Freud, *Civilization and Its Discontents* (New York: Norton, 1961), p. 40.

Thomas Cordle (essay date 1993)

SOURCE: Cordle, Thomas. "Romantic Resurgence." In *André Gide: Updated Edition,* pp. 48-98. New York: Twayne Publishers, 1993.

[*In the following essay, Cordle describes* The Immoralist *as "the first representative of that most remarkable category of Gide's work, the psychological novel" and claims that its central strategy is the gradual replacement of the main charecter's heterosexual relationship with a homosexual one.*]

L'Immoraliste (*The Immoralist*) (1902) is the first representative of that most remarkable category of Gide's work, the psychological novel. Gide did not invent the genre, but he did revive it in a period when prose fiction was more or less divided between the pseudosociological chronicles of the Naturalists and the delicately perverse romances of the Decadents. Gide's models, we may reasonably presume, were *La Princesse de Clèves, Manon Lescaut, René, Adolphe,* and *Dominique.* But there was something in this type of fiction that was more important for him than any model, and that was the kind of action that the narrative represented. In **"Un Esprit non prévenu"** (An unbiased mind) Gide made a distinction between two sorts of novels, "or at least two ways of depicting life":

> The one, exterior and commonly called "objective," which visualizes first of all the other person's gesture, the event, then explains and interprets it.
>
> The other, which seizes first of all emotions and thoughts, then creates the events and characters most fitted to bring these out and runs the risk of being powerless to depict anything that the author has not first felt himself. His inner riches, his complexity, the antagonism of his too diverse possibilities, will allow the greatest diversity in his creations. But everything comes out of him. He is the only guarantee of the truth he reveals, the only judge. The hell and the heaven of his characters is in him. It is not himself that he depicts, but what he depicts he could have become if he had not become precisely himself.[1]

What the psychological novel offered Gide was a means of dramatizing his inner turbulence in terms appropriate to it. The *action* of these books is in the conflict between desire and inspiration on the one hand and the restrictive force of pain and obligation on the other hand. Physical encounters and displacements are to be interpreted as symbolic inventions employed to reflect and enrich the psychological action. This does not make them any less important: indeed, one of the outstanding qualities of Gide's psychological novels is to be found in the suggestive power of these secondary effects of scene and situation. (Such effects, we must remember, were the *primary* value of his symbolist tales.)

The central strategy of **L'Immoraliste** is one that we have already seen in Gide's work: the dissolution of a heterosexual relationship and its replacement by a homosexual one. The difference here is that the strategy is neither concealed nor abbreviated; it is the subject of the story from beginning to end, and the course of its development is punctuated with peripeties and discoveries. Gide found the way to involve all the motives and countermotives of his personality in this one plot. The result is a story that is at once direct and clear in its depiction of the growth of a desire and complex and ambiguous in its thought about the demands of that desire.

The attack upon heterosexuality (which for Gide was always an attempt to be rid of the frustrating oedipal relationship) begins on the first page of Michel's story when he says of his bride Marceline: "I had married her without love, mainly to please my father, who, dying, was worried at leaving me alone" (**RRS** [**Romans, récits et soties**] 372). The illness that strikes him on their wedding journey to North Africa is not an accident but rather a defense against the undesired relationship.

Michel begins his recovery by refusing Marceline's attentions. He avoids her and seeks health in the company of a band of Arab boys. When he sees one of these steal Marceline's sewing scissors he is delighted to be a silent accomplice in the theft. He does not understand his joy, but its reason is not to our eyes impenetrable: the scissors are an emblem of feminine power, an instrument of castration. When the child takes them he disarms Marceline and displaces her as an object of erotic interest.

Michel not only recovers from his illness, he becomes a new man whose strength and vitality are based upon his acknowledgment of the claims of his fundamental being—what he calls, in biblical language, "the old man." As a sign of rebirth he shaves his beard. (So did Saül, and so did Gide.) At this point there occurs a reversal in the process of homoeroticism. In southern Italy, on the way home, he finally accomplishes his conjugal duty to Marceline—but it is of the utmost importance to note that this act takes place after he has wrestled with and thrashed a drunken coachman.

At home on his Norman farm Michel puts his new strength to work practicing in all things what he calls "a science of the perfect utilization of self through an intelligent restraint" (**RRS**, 411). He is relieved of his marital obligations by Marceline's pregnancy, and he enters into a warm virile relationship with the 17-year-old son of his farm manager. Together they plan to carry out certain projects in agricultural economy. Michel's latent homosexuality finds a sort of symbolic expression and a partial satisfaction when, one day, he paddles around barefoot in a pond helping Charles catch the eels that have been exposed by draining the pond.

The next major episode of the novel is the turning point in Michel's history. He meets Ménalque, a godlike figure who manifests and professes a doctrine of risk, expenditure, and egoism. Ménalque is a notorious homosexual. (His name, of course, recalls **Les Nourritures terrestres,** and still more pertinently Virgil's *Bucolics.*) In token of his authority over Michel he brings the scissors that Moktir stole from Marceline. In a single conversation he undermines the prudent plan of Michel's life and teaches him to despise his possessions and his expectations. On the night of their meeting Marceline suffers a miscarriage and becomes very ill. The accident marks the end of her ascendancy in Michel's life. Ménalque plays no other role in the story than this one of being the means through which Michel discovers a little more of his hidden and repressed nature. He is a kind of demonic intercessor who could better be called a force, or an idea, than a character.

When Michel and Marceline return to the farm, Michel no longer has any thought for productive economy. He poaches game on his own lands with the disreputable young son of his farm manager. This relationship has the same homoerotic character as the one with Charles, but the setting of Michel's encounters with Alcide endows them with an illicit and clandestine value. Finally, restlessness overcomes him and, abandoning the farm, Michel drags the ailing Marceline away on a journey that leads them step by step back to Africa.

Michel's conduct this time is the reverse of what it was coming north out of Africa. He is no longer prudently building his health and strength but recklessly expending and risking both by drinking with the riffraff of Naples and Sicily, and sleeping in their company on tavern floors. On one occasion he frankly embraces and kisses his carriage driver. Back in Africa, he seeks out his former companions and, freeing them from want and subservience, he indulges their appetite for pleasure, as well as his own. Marceline, weakened by his demonic pursuit of satisfaction, dies; Michel consoles himself with the little boy Ali. It is in this manner that the heterosexual marriage is definitively destroyed and the homosexual encounter put in its place.

The essential action of the story is this protracted conversion from the normal, socially sponsored sexual relationship that is inimical to Michel's nature to the forbidden relationship that satisfies his native desires. The knowledge of who and what he is, and of what he must do to become who he is, comes in the form of impulses rather than decisions. The powers of clear vision and determination are stifled in him by his moral and intellectual culture, which has proscribed the solution that he is unconsciously striving to find.

It is in the conflict between the hero and his culture that Gide develops his accompaniment to the main action. This secondary conflict seems at times to override the major one because its terms are clearer and franker. Being more verbal than imagistic, and conscious rather than unconscious, it tends to seize tonal control of the narrative.

At the very beginning of the novel Michel is referred to as "the very learned Puritan," and as he begins to tell his story he mentions "the grave Huguenot teaching" given him by his mother. This is his moral capital: a stock of austere, inflexible precepts. To his father he owes a similarly dogmatic training in classical philology, which has taught him to regard Athens and Rome as the two foci of human history.

Michel's bondage to his culture is symbolized by his marriage to Marceline, who represents the Christian ideal at its most excellent. Her virtues of devotion, abnegation, restraint, and pity are all expressions of the triumph of human weakness. To complete the image of submission Gide makes her a Catholic.

In going to North Africa, Michel crosses the frontier of his culture, and when he loses its protection and guidance he falls ill. His recovery is owed entirely to the assertion of a primitive power within him that is independent of traditional and collective values. This "authentic being" is discovered only when the veneer of acquired knowledge peels off. "There was more here than a convalescence; there was an augmentation, a recrudescence of life, the inflow of a richer, warmer blood which was to touch my thoughts, touch them one by one, penetrate everything, stir, color the most remote, delicate, and secret fibers of my being" (***RRS***, 399).

Michel's first task is to create physical strength, but concurrently he must reshape his moral and intellectual being to conform to that strength. The first stage in his moral revolution culminates in that "perfect utilization of self through an intelligent restraint" that he formulates in the midst of work on the farm and the preparation of the course that he will give at the Collège de France. This course entails a complete revision of his historical studies. He is no longer interested in the "abstract and neutral knowledge of the past." Philology is now a means of approaching the human personality of an earlier time. He is drawn more and more to the rough, uncultured Goths and especially to the rebellious and debauched young King Athalaric (A.D. 516-534). The thesis that he subsequently proposes is that culture, born of life, ends by stifling life and preventing the contact of mind with nature.

Michel's critical thought has in fact preceded and opened the way to a new conduct. His prudent, economical way of living is in conflict with this new conception of man. When he meets Ménalque after his first lecture his thought is: "The life, the least gesture of Ménalque, was it not a thousand times more eloquent than my course?" (***RRS***, 429). This new man enunciates a doctrine of radical individualism, sensualism,[2] and consumption that makes the ground give way under Michel's feet, as he puts it. From that moment forward, his thought and conduct are directed toward a new end: to discover what man is yet capable of. "And each day there grew in me the obscure feeling of untouched riches, covered over, hidden, smothered by cultures, decencies, moralities" (***RRS***, 457).

When Marceline says to him: "I understand your doctrine—for it is a doctrine now. It is fine, perhaps . . . but it suppresses the weak," Michel replies: "That is what is needed" (***RRS***, 459-60).

Up to this point, Michel's "immoralism"—his rejection of conventional Christian, middle-class morality and his effort to found a vital and authentic ethic on the acknowledgment and pursuit of desire and possibility—bears a close resemblance to the Nietzschean "revaluation of all values." Gide was familiar with Nietzsche's work and had written about it in 1898 in his **"Letters à Angèle"** ([*Oeuvres complètes*] 12). In later years he attempted to minimize the influence of Nietzsche on the book,[3] and in a sense he may have been justified in doing so. Ménalque could be called a genuine Nietzschean hero: his life is a risky pursuit of his own unrealized possibilities; he refuses the restraint of principles and retrospective judgments; and still he sublimates his more aggressive instincts, finding in ascetic self-denial a pleasure superior to that of indulgence and satisfaction. Michel is another matter. He is very unsure about the grounds of his revolt. With Marceline very near death, he reflects: "Ah, perhaps there would still be time. . . . Shall I not stop?—I have sought, I have found what makes my value: a sort of stubborn commitment to the worst" (***RRS***, 467). And to the friends who have answered his call for aid after his wife's death he says: "It seems to me sometimes that my real life has not yet begun. Drag me away from here now and give me reasons for existing. I no longer know how to find them. I have freed myself, possibly, but what difference does it make? I am suffering from this unutilized freedom. Believe me, it is not that I am overcome by my crime, if you choose to call it that—but I must prove to myself, that I have not overstepped my rights" (***RRS***, 471).

This speech, and indeed the whole development of the moral countercurrent in the novel, imply that Michel's erotic impulse has not been able to conquer altogether his moral resistance. The erotic has achieved its end but at the cost of painful division within the hero's soul. He feels that he was right to follow his own desire and Ménalque's teaching, but the puritan in him is still alive, and he has not been proven wrong. It is on this ambiguous note that Gide ends his story.

The erotic conflict provides the basic energy of the novel. That is the problem that has to be solved. Unlike Gide, Michel is unable to create and play two lovers' roles. One has to be sacrificed to the other. But there is ambiguity in this, for Michel never fully recognizes that he is a homosexual, and that his conduct is inspired by *distaste* for the heterosexual relationship he has passively accepted and by *desire* for love with a boy. Instead of seeing his problem for what it is, he does something extravagant: he poses it in terms of the entire moral and intellectual order of his world. He effects a transference that makes his personal dilemma appear, in the first place, to be directly related to the revolution in Western moral thought that is represented principally by Friedrich Nietzsche, and in the second place he assimilates it to the revolution in historical thinking that established philosophical anthropology as a rival to antiquarian historiography (another development in which Nietzsche played a primary role).

It is this elevation and expansion of his personal anomaly that makes Michel a hero. He attacks the very heart of the ideology of his society, and he offers himself as an example of the new thought that he is advancing. But his heroic rebellion, by its very vigor and honesty, turns Michel into a satanic figure, for it leads him to destroy a gentle and unprotesting victim who is sacrificed as a representative of her culture. The immolation of Marceline casts a deep shadow over Michel's entire venture, obscuring its value and making it profoundly questionable.

The result is, as we have seen, a downcast hero, one who has asserted his notion of the truth and had it strike back at him in its consequences. However, there is no inscrutable fate working against him, nor any vengeful god. His difficulty is located entirely in the human condition, and more specifically in the fact of human freedom. The problem is one of conflicting rights among persons, and Michel's action in attempting to resolve it becomes an episode in a continuing drama within Western civilization. He illustrates with great force and clarity the manner in which the conflict may appear to a particular man in a set of particular historical circumstances.

Gide's artistry is abundantly displayed in *L'Immoraliste,* and nowhere more impressively than in the narrative style. The story that he invents is a romantic one in all essential respects—in its glorification of self, of desire, and of will; in the excesses of action and thought that it depicts; and in the ironies that it sustains from start to finish, the irony of Michel and the irony of freedom. But the narrative is the work of a symbolist who foregoes all rhetorical effects in order to make his language a purely descriptive instrument. The voice that recounts is that of Michel, not that of Gide. The haughty tone, so often stiff and artificial, is precisely that of a scholarly puritan who is trying to set forth his turbulent inner experience without knowing quite what it is all about. This austere, insensitive voice is Gide's primary means in making the character of Michel. It is an unceasing evidence of what he is, a man whose action and thought are governed by impulses that he either fails to comprehend or misrepresents to himself.

The symbolical representation of ideas in the story is extraordinarily rich, and so too are the symbols that reveal the constant presence of the erotic motive. The composition of the narrative mirrors both the Gidean personality division and the antithetical character and action of Michel. Half the story is allotted to the productive, or angelic, phase of Michel's reform and half to the consumptive, or demonic, phase. The encounter with the mythical, archangelic Ménalque stands at the midpoint. The effect of this perfect division can hardly be overestimated. It gives the book an air of equilibrium and resolution that is at odds with the ambiguous sense of the story. Perhaps it is to this aspect of his work that Gide was alluding when, after declaring in his preface that he had intended to pose a problem and not to judge it or solve it, he added: "I use the word 'problem' here with reluctance. To tell the truth, in art there are no problems—of which the work of art is not a sufficient solution" (**RRS,** 367).

However important a work *L'Immoraliste* may appear to be today, at its publication it found few readers, and among those few some greeted it with hostile indignation. Gide felt that this reaction was wholly unjustified since he had not sought to make Michel's excesses seem anything but ignoble. The indignation, however, was probably provoked by something deeper than Michel's *conduct.* What he *does* is easy enough to judge and condemn. What he *is* would have been harder for Gide's indignant readers to get at. Michel's arrogance, anarchism, and insensitivity are essentially class attributes, and the readers of the novel were mostly of Michel's class. Their outcry was provoked really by Gide's association of their guilty being, which they had felt was adequately hidden, with guilty deeds that could not be concealed.

Notes

1. "Un Esprit non prévenu" (1929), in *Divers* (Paris, 1931), 61-62.

2. Gide gave the following definition of sensuality in 1898: "Sensuality . . . consists simply in considering as an end and not as a means the present object and the present minute." ("Lettres à Angèle, 10," *OC* [*Oeuvres complètes*] 3:220).

3. "My *Immoraliste* was already half-written and entirely composed in my head when I encountered Nietzsche. I can say that at first he bothered me a lot; but thanks to him I was able to rid my book of all sorts of adventitious ideas which were obscurely tormenting me, which no longer had any need to be expressed, since I found them much better said by him than I should have been able to do," (*OC*, 13:441).

Selected Bibliography

COLLECTIONS

Oeuvres complètes. 15 vols. Paris: Gallimard, 1932-39. (Referred to in the text as *OC*, 1-15.)

Romans, récits et soties: Oeuvres lyriques. 1958. Reprint. Paris: Gallimard, (Bibliothèque de la Pléiade, 1980.) (Referred to in the text as *RRS*.)

The edition cited for individual works listed below is generally the first edition. If the work is included in one or more of the collections given above, a brief parenthetical indication of where it may be found follows the entry. The parenthetical English translation cited after the entry is the most recent known to me.

NOVELS, TALES, LYRICAL WORKS IN PROSE

Les Faux-Monnayeurs. Paris: Gallimard, 1926. (*OC*, 12; *RRS*.) (*The Counterfeiters.* Translated by Dorothy Bussy. New York: Random House, 1973.)

Geneviève. Paris: Gallimard, 1936. (*RRS*.) (In Bussy, trans., *The School for Wives*.)

L'Immoraliste. Paris: Mercure de France, 1902. (*OC*, 4; *RRS*.) (*The Immoralist.* Translated by Richard Howard. New York: Bantam Books, 1970.)

Isabelle. Paris: Gallimard, 1911. (*OC*, 6; *RRS*.) (In *Two Symphonies.* Translated by Dorothy Bussy. New York: Random House, 1977.)

Les Nourritures terrestres. Paris: Mercure de France, 1897. (*OC*, 2; *RRS*.) (*Fruits of the Earth.* Translated by Dorothy Bussy. New York: Knopf, 1949.)

ESSAYS; SOCIAL AND LITERARY CRITICISM

Divers. Paris: Gallimard, 1931. (A selection from this work appears in *Pretexts*. Edited by Justin O'Brien, translated by Angelo Bertocci and others, New York: Delta Books, 1964.)

Ben Stoltzfus (essay date 1994)

SOURCE: Stoltzfus, Ben. "Gide's *Immoraliste*: Orientalism Against the Grain." *International Fiction Review* 21, nos. 1-2 (1994): 20-4.

[*In the following essay, Stoltzfus applies Edward Said's concept of "Orientalism" to an interpretation of* The Immoralist, *stating that the novel "fits into two Orientalist categories: the accumulation of knowledge about the region and sexual freedom."*]

Over the years, since its publication in 1902, André Gide's novel *L'immoraliste* has elicited a variety of responses. Paul Claudel denounced the book by saying that Gide was personally responsible for leading French youth astray both morally and sexually. Although avoiding Claudel's peremptory denunciation, some readers have emphasized the homosexual component of the novel, whereas others have stressed Michel's quest for liberation from religious and social constraints. Indeed, until discussions of metafiction and self-reflexive art became fashionable, *L'immoraliste* was read as an example of that "monstrous rose" (Gide's own term)—Michel's unbridled licentiousness and self-interest—the dialogic opposite of Alissa's renunciation in *La porte étroite* (1909). It was customary, and Gide himself encouraged the coupling, to read *L'immoraliste* and *La porte étroite* together as typical examples of the Gidean dialog.[1]

When Jean-Paul Sartre wrote that Gide was one of the four coordinates of twentieth-century thought, the other three being Marx, Hegel, and Kierkegaard, readers were quick to see in Michel's quest for freedom the beginnings of existential emancipation.[2] After the passing of existentialism and the advent of the nouveau roman the audience could emphasize *L'immoraliste*'s specular levels—the novel within the novel, its self-consciousness, and the shifting narrative voices. A recent addition to Gideana stresses the centrality of homosexuality to everything he wrote. These varied responses attest to *L'immoraliste*'s multileveled richness and yet, despite his good fortune, Gide is no longer as popular or, it seems, as relevant as he once was. Nonetheless, his work continues to address important issues of the 1990s.

Gide has always championed the rights of women, children, and homosexuals. Indeed, he was acutely aware of alterability, difference, and marginality. *L'école des femmes* (1929) did for women what *Si le grain ne meurt* (1926) and *Corydon* (1924) had done for children and gay men. *L'école des femmes* (1929) dramatizes the plight of a woman whose identity is being snuffed out by the paternalistic rhetoric of society, marriage, and the church. These works, with another special place for *Les faux-monnayeurs* (1926), continue to be topical, and they can be taught in ways that stress their usefulness, if indeed social relevance, rather than art, defines literary standards.

Fortunately, Orientalism as a topic encompasses both aesthetic values and social concerns, and it is recent enough to shed new light on Gide's works, particularly *L'immoraliste.* This essay will therefore focus on Orientalism, the title of a book published in 1978, by Edward Said. As a concept, Orientalism concerns itself with the discourse of the West about the East. This discourse is made up of a vast body of texts that has been growing since the Renaissance and it deals with literary, topographical, anthropological, historical, and sociological matters. Said focuses on writing about the Near East and argues that the discourse is self-validating and tautological. Orientalism, he says, constructs certain stereotypes that become accepted as self-evident facts—facts that dovetail both consciously and unconsciously with Western political and economic imperialism. In his introduction Said says that "taking the late eighteenth century as a very roughly defined starting point Orientalism can be discussed and analyzed as the corporate institution of dealing with the Orient—dealing with it by making statements about it, authorizing views of it, describing it, by teaching it, settling it, ruling over it: in short, Orientalism as a Western style for dominating, restructuring, and having authority over the Orient."[3] Said goes on to demonstrate that the books about the Orient have determined the West's perception of it, that the West's discourse about the Orient is a hegemony of enormous proportions. Orientalism is, in fact, a striking example of the postmodern dictum that language structures reality, that the West's representation of the Orient becomes the Orient, that the West is not dealing with reality but with a representation of reality. Although we might argue that all language distorts because the signifier is not the signified, Said's point is that Orientalism is synonymous with the West's imperialism because it is based on a self-serving definition of Europe in relation to the rest of the globe. Moreover, it was knowledge of the Orient that created the Orient, the Oriental, and his world.

In view of the fact that Gide was one of many French writers to incorporate the Orient into his writings, the interesting question is whether *L'immoraliste,* either consciously or unconsciously, reflects the Western stereotypes that Said describes. Napoleon, Sylvestre de Sacy, Chateaubriand, Lamartine, Nerval, Hugo, Renan, Flaubert, Gauthier, Baudelaire, Huysmans, and Lotti, among others, have a great deal to say about the Orient, and all of them, in one way or another, in their writings, reflect Western stereotypes of conquest, knowledge, control, proselytizing, fantasy, the femme fatale, and exotic sex.

According to Said, the Orient provoked a writer to his vision but very rarely guided it. Indeed, "the history of Orientalism has both an internal consistency and a highly articulated set of relationships to the dominant culture surrounding it" (*O* [*Orientalism*] 22). Chateaubriand believed that "the Oriental Arab was 'civilized man fallen again into a savage state,'" and he advocated a redemptive Christian mission to revive a dead world (*O* 171-72). Lamartine believed that the Orient was "waiting anxiously for the shelter" of European occupation (*O* 179). Renan took it for granted that the Occidentals were superior to the Orientals (*O* 15). "In contrast to Nerval's negative vision of an emptied Orient," Flaubert's view was full and corporeal (*O* 184). Whereas Nerval sought for "the traces of his personal sentiments and dreams," Flaubert's most celebrated moments were with Kuchuk Hanem, a famous Egyptian dancer and courtesan, whose "learned sensuality, delicacy, and . . . mindless coarseness" were to flesh out the characters of Salammbô and Salomé (*O* 186-87). For all of these writers the Orient was an archive of information (*O* 41) and for some, such as Nerval and Flaubert, a place of déjà vu (*O* 180). The Orient gave them what they brought to it.

Although Gide differs markedly from his predecessors, his **Immoraliste** fits into two Orientalist categories: the accumulation of knowledge about the region and sexual freedom. Despite the philosophical veneer that he imposes on Michel's choices, it may be useful to look at his anarchic conduct in the light of these two categories, because, in due course, Michel's Orientalism reverses itself. He becomes the living embodiment of an Orientalism *à rebours*: instead of proselytizing for Western values, he espouses the immediate sensuality of the Orient and incorporates it into his life as he begins to subvert the order, logic, measure, and control of European ideology (or what it was alleged to be)—the very ideology that invented Orientalism. But I am getting ahead of myself. What are the characteristics that define Michel as an Orientalist?

A professional scholar by the age of twenty-five, Michel knows Greek, Latin, Hebrew, Sanskrit, Persian, and Arabic, and he is an expert on the cult of the Phrygians ([*L'Immoraliste*] 373), the people who lived in Phrygia, an ancient region of central Asia Minor (now central Turkey) that was settled about 1200 B.C. It was later occupied by the Romans and most of it was assigned to the province of Asia. Despite Michel's background and training, however, when he goes to Tunisia, he does not, as many of his countrymen before him, from Chateaubriand to Huysmans, impose a ready-made vision of the Orient on that country, but succumbs, instead, to those sensuous elements of the Arab world that have become clichés in the Orientalist's lexicon, "qu'importait la pensée? je sentais extraordinairement" (392). He does not try to change the Orient, it changes him. He internalizes the alleged "weaknesses" of the Arab world (as defined by Orientalism) and uses them to subvert the core of Western ideology. His course at the *Collège de France* is on the Goths and Athalaric's rebellion against his mother, Amalasuntha. What attracts Michel to Athalaric, is his revolt against his Latin education and the wisdom of Cassiodorus in favor of barbarism and debauchery. Michel, like Athalaric is also rejecting the civilizing elements of the Roman empire in favor of the vandalism and anarchy that led to the dark ages.

Earlier, while in Syracuse, on his way back to France, Michel rereads Theocritus as he contemplates the shepherds in the fields, and he imagines that they are the same ones he had loved in Biskra (398). We need to remember that the history of the pastoral begins with Theocritus, the Alexandrian Greek poet born in Syracuse (c. 270 B.C.). In this connection, it is interesting to note that Michel imposes the memory of the inhabitants of Biskra on the landscape of Syracuse, but it is an association that he now finds cumbersome. "Mon érudition qui s'éveillait à chaque pas m'encombrait, empêchant ma joie. . . . J'en vins à fuire les ruines" (398).

He used to read Homer, but he has not read him since his departure from Biskra. He now admires the Arab people because "son art, il le vit, il le chante et le dissipe au jour le jour; il ne le fixe point et ne l'embaume en aucune oeuvre" (464). Clearly, Michel is devaluing Europe's culture and exalting the Orient. But Michel's admiration for the Arab people is not without mixed blessings: he trades the monuments of the past for spontaneity and immediate freedom, but, ironically, it is his sexual liberation that undermines his moral discipline.

Instead of judging Moktir's theft of Marceline's scissors, Michel is overcome with joy, and from that moment on Moktir becomes his favorite Arab boy (394-95). This is a lesson in dishonesty that Michel will use on his estate at La Morinière. In due course he not only questions all authority, he also divests himself of his belongings (La Morinière, Marceline, God, France) by rejecting the very idea of property. In Paris he renews contact with former colleagues, archeologists and philologists, "mais ne trouvai à causer avec eux guère plus de plaisir et pas plus d'émotion qu'à feuilleter de bons dictionnaires d'histoire" (423). What Michel really wants is "life," not books or bookish people, and he will go to any lengths to find it. He abandons his wife periodically for the company of Arab boys, he rejects essentialism in favor of existential choices, and he embarks on a quest for absolute freedom. When he returns to France, the landscape and the values of North Africa are internalized as a home away from home. Indeed, the memory of place is the impetus that challenges marriage, religion, and tradition. A reverse exile lifts the veil of opportunity even as it foregrounds the differences between opposing ideologies.

The violence that attracted Michel to the Goths is also manifest in the behavior of the farmers at La Morinière, Michel's country estate. In the Heurtevant household the father sleeps with his daughter and he encourages his son's rape of a servant girl by holding her down. Michel questions Bute, one of his associates, about these events with the same pleasure he had displayed earlier in researching the Goths. "De ses récits [Bute's] sortait une trouble vapeur d'abîme qui déjà me montait à la tête et qu'inquiètement je humais" (446). While roaming his fields and his woods, Michel carries the memory of Africa with him, and when he hears one of the Heurtevant boys singing he says: "je ne puis dire l'effet que ce chant produisit sur moi; car je n'en avais entendu de pareil qu'en Afrique" (445). Africa has become a home away from home and, because of Michel's clandestine behavior, La Morinière now seems more decadent than Tunisia. His subversion of law and order on his estate not only tests the limits of the possible, it undermines the values of French social propriety. In these endeavors Michel also embraces the heavy, sensuous collusion of nature; so much so that, after one of the poaching episodes, he says, "je rentrais à travers champs, dans l'herbe lourde de rosée, ivre de nuit, de vie sauvage et d'anarchie, trempé, boueux, couvert de feuilles" (449).

Gide explores the opposition between the values of Europe and the values of the Orient. Western ideals based on the acquisition of knowledge, dominion over others, the exploitation of land and property, and the proselytizing for Christianity—this is Said's Orientalism—are undermined by Michel's actions because the West's values are perceived as inimical to his physical well-being. Michel survives physically (he is dying of tuberculosis) perhaps because he rejects doxologies that are killing him. But the grand experiment that saves his life is also the cause of his wife's death. His two journeys into the Orient may mean life for him, but the second one is death for Marceline.

It is worth remembering that Orientalism coincides exactly with the colonial expansion of Western Europe in the nineteenth century, and that it was a movement of power, control, and exploitation. For France it began with Napoleon's campaign in Egypt and the subsequent occupation by later regimes of all of North Africa as well as the territories further south. There is an irony, therefore, in Gide's use of Arab values, as defined by Orientalism, to subvert an ideology that was part and parcel of France's hegemony. After his immersion in Tunisia, Michel refuses all homegrown values, disciplines, and practices. He accepts the temptation of the East, a condition he does not fully understand and from which, at the end, he cries out for help, but only after the stereotype of the Orient is evoked as a place of permissive sexual practices. Meanwhile, Marceline is dying and, after her death, Michel continues to live in the present, from day to day, sleeping alternately with Ali or his sister. Michel's will has been undermined and he is now the prisoner of his senses.

Although Michel's cry for help seems to reverse the novel's statement of faith, *L'immoraliste* has, nonetheless, cleared the way for a definition of freedom that remains topical for artistic, philosophical, and cultural reasons. It is a novel that refuses closure because Michel's quest is both a triumph and a failure. It is a work in which the origins of being are endlessly deferred because his search for the blueprint of human nature uncovers nothing. Michel rejects the cultural hegemony of Orientalism, incorporating a life-style and a way of life that, for a century, hard-core Orientalists had been denouncing as inferior. Michel's new life and professional activities veil an Orientalism *à rebours*. He frees himself from the tyranny of European thought, but his dilemma is that he does not know how to transcend the tyranny of the senses.

Michel may have begun as a young Orientalist—a man of great, singular, and youthful accomplishment—but, ironically, he ends up a prisoner, a person immobilized by events he can no longer control, and he calls for help because he is unable to manage his freedom or his bondage. Europe's culture almost killed him, physically, but the mores he discovers in Biskra atrophy his moral being. Nonetheless, it is in Tunisia that Michel finds the strength and the courage to reject the values and encratic language that had been stifling him. But Michel is in limbo, the casualty of a dual exile: a man caught between two cultures and two affective states, unable to reconcile the mind and the body or Europe and the Orient. He has found freedom, but freeing oneself, he says, is nothing. The most difficult part is knowing what to do with it (372). Freedom has become an ontological state, and exile is experienced as an alienation from self. Michel's cry for help is thus a tacit acknowledgment of moral failure. The corollary to despondency is exile from happiness and from authenticity. As an Orientalist in exile, Michel provides a useful corrective to the stereotype despite, or perhaps because of, his flawed behavior.

Notes

1. André Gide, "L'immoraliste," in *Romans Récits et Soties. Oeuvres Lyriques* (Paris: Gallimard, 1958) 365-472. Subsequent references to this edition will appear in the text.

2. Jean-Paul Sartre, "Gide vivant," *Les temps modernes* 65 (March 1951): 1538.

3. Edward Said, *Orientalism* (New York: Putnam, 1978) 3. Subsequent references to this work will appear after the abbreviation *O*.

James T. Day (essay date December 2002)

SOURCE: Day, James T. "Theater, Texts, and Ambiguity in Gide's *L'Immoraliste*." *French Review* 76, no. 2 (December 2002): 332-45.

[*In the following essay, Day contends that "theatricality and performance" play a central role in* The Immoralist *and that "theater itself" is a key theme in the novel.*]

In the years just prior to the publication of *L'Immoraliste* in May of 1902, Gide had been devoting enormous energy to the composition of some theatrical pieces that never enjoyed much popularity. Dramatic works such as **Philoctète, Saül,** and **Le Roi Candaule,** as Germaine Brée observes, were condemned to a lukewarm reception because of their unfamiliar innovations ([*André Gide, l'insaissable Protée*] 122) and enigmatic endings ("Elles sont chargées d'un sens ambigu que le dénouement n'éclaire pas" [123]). In addition, they presented considerable problems for staging—early critics declared that **Saül** and **Le Roi Candaule** were "injouables" (Martin [*La Maturité d'André Gide, de Paludes à L'Immoraliste*] 402)—but at least they allowed Gide to explore moral crises in characters driven by destructive desires.[1] Accordingly, critics have tended to follow Brée's example and link the plays to *L'Immoraliste* and other of Gide's novels with respect to themes, action, and character development. In the process, what has generally gone unnoticed is the importance of theater itself as a key theme in Michel's story. Indeed, one of the least explored sources of the ambiguity that saturates *L'Immoraliste* is the interplay of performance-based and textual models, and the failure of the former to offset the inadequacies of the latter.

Since the work stands as a piece of narrative fiction, readers have naturally attended to its textual dimension without necessarily taking note of its numerous allusions to modes of performance. Jean Claude's recent "Écriture théâtrale, théâtralité de l'écriture" does acknowledge the importance of theatrical elements such as dialogue, setting, and what might be called narrative stage directions in Gide's fictional works, but his study does not mention *L'Immoraliste* specifically. Georges Vidal has admired the novel's tragic efficiency ("son étonnante composition en cinq Actes, comme la plus classique des tragédies de Racine" [(*De L'Immoraliste à la Porte étroite*) 90]), but this observation refers only to Gide's structuring of the action. In fact, theatricality and performance enrich the novel on other levels as well and compete with the more obvious themes of reading and writing in such a way as to raise thorny questions about moral authority.

Thematization of the theater begins with the preface that has accompanied *L'Immoraliste* in all editions following the first limited printing of 300 copies. In this short prologue, Gide explicitly associates ambiguity, or at least equivocation, with theatrical models. Having referred to his novel several times as "ce livre" while observing that it is neither a defense nor an indictment of its hero, Gide takes an unexpectedly theatrical turn: "Le public ne pardonne plus aujourd'hui que l'auteur, après l'action qu'il peint, ne se déclare pour ou contre; bien plus, au cours même du *drame* on voudrait qu'il prît parti, qu'il se prononçât nettement soit pour Alceste, soit pour Philinte, pour Hamlet ou pour Ophélie [. . .]" (367, emphasis added). In the context of these precedents from theater, the word *drame*, which is repeated a few lines later as a synonym for Michel's *problème*, recovers a good bit of the theatrical legacy that is normally lost in the metaphorical use of *drame* in French. Gide's use of exemplary characters from theater was no doubt based on the perception that there is a greater distance between characters and author in a play than in a novel (cf. Claude, *André Gide* 2: 312, 318)—especially a novel with a first-person narrator, whose voice invites identification with that of the author. In seeking to disengage himself from Michel by likening his protagonist to a stage character, Gide also initiates an association between moral dilemmas and matters of performance.

If Gide had not added the preface, thematization of the theater would have begun with the stage-like setting in which Michel begins his long narration. As if in obedience to an established ritual, Michel awaits nightfall before beginning his dramatic monologue. He leads his trio of friends not to an actual stage and its constructed backdrop, but to a terrace with a splendid view ("la terrasse d'où la vue à l'infini s'étendait" [371]). While a terrace presents no automatic analogy to a theatrical space, in this case the analogy is compelling, for the house lights have dimmed, thus eliminating distractions and focusing attention on the performer, who is about to speak. The outdoor scene includes elements that suggest the image of a rather small ancient proscenium. Moreover, in the larger context of Gide's work, one finds in his play **Saül** a somewhat similar setting, indicated in the initial stage directions as being part of the king's palace: "Entre les colonnes la vue se prolonge sur une terrasse [. . .]" (**Théâtre** 11).

If we look only for narrative precedents, we might, like Albert Sonnenfeld, account for the structure of Michel's *récit* by pointing out generic affinities with the traditional frame tale (["On Readers and Reading in *La Porte étroite* and *L'Immoraliste*"] 181). On the other hand, to the extent that Michel's account is carefully set up as an oral performance, we might just as easily see his dramatic monologue as evoking early Greek plays before Aeschylus, when a single actor directed his narration to the chorus. Through songs, dances, and responses, the chorus would express their reaction to the events reported (Loomis [*Aristotle*] 425 n). Michel's chorus of three friends updates the formula by replacing the songs and dances with the portentous letter to Monsieur D. R., président du Conseil. As readers we are Michel's ultimate audience, with his friends being part of the spectacle we hope to enjoy. This perspective on Michel's narratorial performance is not incompatible with the structure of frame tales such as the *Thousand and One Nights,* in which Scheherazade's very life depends on the skill of her performance. But Michel, unlike Scheherazade and the narrators of most ancient frame tales, is telling his own story.[2] His verbal display as teller is quickly subordinated to his performance as protagonist, and so it is in this dimension that the thematization of performance becomes most significant.

Yet while our narrator cannot lay claim to the inventiveness of other storytellers with respect to plot, since story constraints allow him to report little else than the events in which he participated, he is still at liberty to choose the verbal style that suits his narrative ends. In various ways, the style he chooses contributes to the theatrical dimension of the novel. Michel's formal, stilted discourse, with a remarkable density of imperfect subjunctives, is clearly not that of spontaneous spoken French. It is the prose of a writer—and a fussy one at that—who is reproducing the sort of language he has encountered in books and the dialogues of classical drama. His stylized language at times displays poetic and theatrical qualities by virtue of the numerous alexandrines he uses.[3] One of the most "classical" of these occurs as part of Michel's reminiscence on the youthful Ashour:

Il m'aurait paru beau s'il n'avait été borgne.

(389)

Here the symmetry of "il [. . .] aurait / il [. . .] avait" draws attention to the alliterative pairing of *beau* and *borgne*. Despite similarity in sound, the two adjectives present a violent semantic contrast. *Beau*, which Michel uses to characterize so many males he encounters, represents the ideal pursued by the beholder's gaze, while *borgne* carries the unflattering freight not only of disfigurement, but also of flawed vision, of defective perception. Metaphorically, this line sums up with Racinian concision the moral situation in which Michel later will find himself.

Further down on the same page of the novel, there are two additional alexandrines:

Un peu craintivement, Marceline me dit:

[—Le pauvre petit est malade.]

—Ce n'est pas contagieux, au moins? Qu'est-ce qu'il a?

There are several others here and there in the text.[4] What, one may legitimately wonder, might these scattered alexandrines signify? That Michel's speaking style reflects speech patterns absorbed in the course of a refined education? That Gide freely flouts the convention according to which you do not allow distracting alexandrines to infiltrate your prose? That Michel's theatrical mindset will inevitably influence his interpretation of experience? Probably all of these. In addition, we should observe that while the dialogues in **Saül** stand as prose, those of **Le Roi Candaule** are presented as lines of free verse, in which there are many alexandrines. Moreover **Proserpine,** published as a "Fragment d'un drame" in 1899, was composed in alexandrines that Martin qualifies as "fort réguliers" (404). Gide's fictional imagination appears, then, to have been tainted with the language and conventions of theater as he set about composing **L'Immoraliste.**

Because of this, Michel's oral performance as narrator in the dramatic setting of his terrace prepares us to accept his world as but a stage. To confirm the pertinence of the theatrical metaphor, his narrative offers up a cluster of related images over the space of a few pages. In Biskra, where Michel is to undergo an existential epiphany ("Je devais faire de la vie la palpitante découverte" [381]), he will observe this world from the strategic vantage point of a lodging that delights him because it is little more than a terrace ("Ce n'était presque qu'une terrasse. Quelle terrasse!" [381]). Before taking an active role himself, Michel must first be a spectator in the theater of society. and indeed, even before reprising in Biskra the terrace of his own *récit,* Michel, as a man newly married and newly ill, begins to attune his observations to ethnographic and social performance. Modern everyday life becomes much more stimulating than thoughts of ancient spectacles such as those that took place in the huge Roman amphitheater in El Djem. The monument disappoints him, perhaps because of the dreary weather, as he surmises (377; Michel's indifference is eloquent if we recall that this well-preserved structure represents the third-largest amphitheater of the Roman Empire and the largest in Africa). Later, in Syracuse, he will consciously associate monumental ruins with death, and his historical knowledge will diminish his joy in the present: "Je ne pouvais voir un théâtre grec, un temple, sans aussitôt le reconstruire abstraitement" (398). These images signal quite effectively Michel's horror of the past, of his past, but the juxtaposition of *théâtre* and *temple* in this remark also provides a useful reminder that theatrical performance has its origins in religious ritual.

Such evocations of the sites of ancient spectacle shed light on Michel's growing concern with performance in the present. At first, he instinctively connects the North Africa he sees with the ancient past he has studied. When he catches sight of Bachir's mother, for example, he places her in a historical context: "C'était une femme admirable, pesante, au grand front tatoué de bleu, qui portait un panier de linge sur la tête, pareille aux canéphores antiques [. . .]" (388). A "canéphore," as the *Petit Robert* prompts us to recall, carried baskets on special occasions ("jeune fille qui portait les corbeilles sacrées dans certaines fêtes"). Michel admires the costume and bearing of this washerwoman, whom he likens to participants in ancient rituals. So his perception of this mute but picturesque supernumerary depends, in fact, not only on a historical connection, but also on inchoate principles of a kind of performance ethnography, a mode of inquiry that establishes its main point of observation at the intersection of ritual, theater, and the customs of a given society.[5] Everyday life in North Africa is not merely an exotic spectacle for our scholarly young French observer; it is a reenactment of earlier practices.[6]

Trained as a historian, Michel does not find it easy to shift from a diachronic to a synchronic perspective on life in society. He comments in the first paragraphs of part 1, chapter 6, on his sense of personal change and the accompanying revulsion for the past (e.g., "A présent, si je pouvais me plaire encore dans l'histoire, c'était en l'imaginant au présent" [398]). Yet his historian's habits do not leave him quickly: he cannot help seeing a connection between the boys recently met in Biskra and the shepherds encountered in a rereading of Theocritus (398). Even so, he has already begun to take notice of patterns of sameness and difference in the present. This is the significance of his observations in Biskra: "[J]e vis d'autres jardins, d'autres bergers et d'autres chèvres. Ainsi que Marceline l'avait dit, ces jardins étaient tous pareils; et pourtant chacun différait" (393).

Before his awareness of personal change and of the rift between historic past and existential present, Michel's sense of social performance evolves on a subconscious level. On the ship that carries Michel and Marceline from Marseille to Tunis, Michel has understood the meaning of marriage: "que là cessait le monologue" (376).[7] If dialogue, then, is the essence (not only of theater but also) of marriage, it is time to talk. After bestowing upon Marceline a chaste but emotional kiss, Michel feels a spasm of pity that induces involuntary tears; he reports the words that accompany his wife's reaction: "—Qu'as-tu donc? me dit Marceline." Dialogue begins, but the narrator gives us only a summary: "Nous commençâmes à parler. Ses propos charmants me ravirent. Je m'étais fait, comme j'avais pu, quelques idées sur la sottise des femmes. Près d'elle, ce soir-là, ce fut moi qui me parus gauche et stupide" (376).

Since the words Marceline speaks are not very prominent in Michel's *récit,* this initial quotation, "Qu'as-tu donc," is important in establishing a link between her speech and her role as concerned caregiver. Despite his acknowledgment of the dangers of stereotypes ("Je m'étais fait [. . .] quelques idées sur la sottise des femmes" [376]), Michel quotes Marceline very selectively and reduces her social performance to the role of nurturer. Other examples: "Tu ne guériras pas tout seul, pauvre ami" (386); "Tu n'as pas froid?" (388; Michel cites these words in a context that indicates his growing irritation with her solicitude); "Le pauvre petit est malade" (389); all of which prepare for the highly charged: "[M]ais [votre doctrine] supprime les faibles" (460). While it may be true, as Wilkins suggests, that Marceline "seems fitted by nature to play the role of ministering angel" (115 ["*L'Immoraliste* Revisited"]), it is not her natural role that we encounter, but Michel's perception and selective representation of her as conforming to a stereotyped mode of social performance.

With the waning of his interest in historical materials and the past in general, Michel looks increasingly to theatrical models to help him value the present. This is no doubt why he feels a strange kind of joy when he sees in a mirror the reflected image of Moktir stealing Marceline's sewing scissors (394-95). In stealing "the woman's tiny weapon," as Naomi Segal puts it, the boy takes a symbolic swipe at Michel's unsatisfying marriage bonds as he becomes Michel's "new master" ([*André Gide*] 174). But Moktir's fine performance as petty thief also reveals that he has a hidden, perhaps more authentic side that is not apparent in his everyday persona, which has been virtuous enough to allow him entrance to the club of Marceline's favorites. Between diligent schoolboy and sly thief, which is the actor, which the character? Michel's own role in the incident is no less ambivalent, for, as Roger Pensom observes, he is both victim and accomplice, and thus in a situation that allows him to indulge his contradictory impulses (["Narrative Structure and Authenticity in *L'Immoraliste*"] 837). Michel does not reflect on the source of his joy in such precise terms, but these terms are in keeping with the theatrical dimension that is implied by the illusionary space of the mirror.

The scissors in this scene link it to a later one, when Michel has his beard cut off. "Sentant sous les ciseaux tomber ma barbe," he states, "c'était comme si j'enlevais un masque" (403). Michel is making progress in the discovery of new possibilities of social performance. The idea of a mask introduces an established theatrical association, and intertextually it reprises a scene in Gide's play *Saül* [3.6, 8] in which the king has his beard removed so he will feel less locked into his kingly role.[8] The autobiographical inspiration behind these two scenes is of course well known, but this does not diminish the power of their theatrical imagery. Michel's beard also problematizes the relations between nature and social convention. Removing a beard does not restore a man's face to its natural state, since the beard grows naturally; indeed, cutting it undoes the work of nature. But Michel's beard has come to seem inauthentic ("je la sentais comme postiche" [402]), and it signals his place in society all too effectively: "[J]'avais l'air de ce que j'avais été jusqu'alors: un chartiste" (403). Since naturalness is not just there, but like social identity depends at least in part on a process of construction, Michel has his work cut out for him if he is to establish an authentic self in society.

To this end, he experiments. In physically subduing the drunken coachman who has endangered Marceline's life, Michel summons a level of masculine performativity that might have embellished an adventure story.[9] He reflects with self-satisfaction on his display of strength: "[J]'avais dû montrer ma force, et cela pour la protéger" (405; note the striking evolution of Michel's role when the scene is replayed later in Taormina and he deals his coachman not a blow but a kiss [462]). Caught up in the exhilaration of this masculine triumph, Michel experiments with the conventions of heteronormativity: he consummates his marriage that very night. Later, on their farm in Normandy, he finds himself envying young Charles, who has just subdued the unbroken colt. Michel will then ride the colt himself and will share with Charles, also mounted, characteristically masculine pleasures of domination: "[N]ous savourions cette joie fière, de précéder et dominer les travailleurs" (417). While engaged in a mode of social performance that depends on subjugation, he will continue his research into the rough mores of the Goths (418), but, paradoxically, he will be mindful to limit, in and around himself, the unrefinement that so intrigues him (418; Michel's words are "dominer" and "inculture"). He can thus deplore the incompetence of some tenant farmers while describing relations with them in dramatic terms: "j'attendais résolument les fermiers." When they hesitate to accept his revised lease and threaten to leave the farms, his words suggest that he has *rehearsed* his rejoinder and has been waiting for the cue: "Moi *qui n'attendais que ce mot*: 'Eh! partez donc si vous voulez! Je ne vous retiens pas', leur dis-je" (418-19, emphasis added). And he concludes with the histrionic gesture of tearing up the leases in their faces. To throw maximum light on Michel's conception of the social performance that is expected of his gender and class, Gide has him say: "[J]e me promenais à cheval, surveillant, dirigeant les travaux, prenant plaisir à commander moi-même, à dominer" (419).

But Michel soon finds that social performance is difficult to sustain if it conflicts with one's nature, so that with his friends in Paris, as he says, "[J]e me vis comme contraint par eux de jouer un faux personnage" (422). Michel's sense of difference leads him to complain to Marceline that they all seem alike, but she lamely excuses them: "Mais, mon ami [. . .] vous ne pouvez demander à chacun de différer de tous les autres" (423). This is the sentence that Michel, in a subsequent conversation with Ménalque, is surprised to find himself parroting ("imitant Marceline [. . .] mot pour mot"

[432]). Ménalque, who has been restating Michel's position in that earlier conversation, offers a puzzled look before walking away. Why does Michel "play the role" of Marceline in this conversation with Ménalque? It is surely because Michel, still casting about for a stable persona, recognizes Ménalque as the superior performer. Not satisfied with his own response to Marceline's words, he repeats them and studiously awaits his mentor's rejoinder. Unfortunately, the desired acting lesson does not ensue. Theatrical models are not providing Michel with unequivocal solutions.

And his role-playing quandary only worsens when he returns to La Morinière with Marceline more than a year later, for now, in the presence of Bocage, he is obliged to play a part that no longer suits him ("il me fallait, quand il venait, *jouer* au maître, et je n'y trouvais plus aucun goût" [441, emphasis added]). At the end of the period during which he helps Alcide poach the game he ordered Bocage to protect, Michel describes his fear of performance breakdown in theatrical terms when the moment of explanation arrives: "Comme je vais jouer mal! Ah! je voudrais rendre mon rôle . . ." (451).

These words point to similarities linking social and theatrical performance. Both modes depend on a citational process, whether the recitation of a dramatic text or repetition of the clichés and formulas of social discourse, the familiar conventions of the theater or those of stereotyped social conduct. And the performance itself, involving a measure of display as well as sufficient observable fidelity to known conventions, naturally invites a reaction in spectators or witnesses that is likely to include judgment.[10] When imagining the inept performance suggested by the words "Comme je vais jouer mal," Michel fears especially his own negative judgment of his attempt to display the skills of clever individuals who use their wits to get out of a tight spot. He fears he will not measure up to familiar models of performativity in this sort of situation.

But Michel does not judge himself only. In one of his most uncharitable observations on Marceline, he judges her performance in the area of tubercular coughing, and his standard of judgment is his own past performance: "Il me semble que je toussais mieux que cela: Elle fait trop d'efforts . . ." (455; Wilkins stresses the "perversity" of this observation [120]). Ultimately, Michel's performance as narrator will be judged by his three friends, who, during a prolonged narrative silence near the end, conclude that they feel like accomplices merely from having heard his story (470). This is testimony to Michel's narrative efficacy. They report, moreover, that Michel's apparent lack of emotion in recounting Marceline's burial gives rise to at least three competing interpretations of his mental state.[11] Performative models, in other words, are as likely to create ambiguity as to resolve it. Michel's theatrical allusions and metaphors have furnished engaging and subtle analyses of the problem of autonomous individual behavior in a society governed by conventional norms, but without reaching any resolution.

Throughout his progressive discovery that theatrical models tend to complement rather than resolve his own uncertainties and inner contradictions, Michel often seeks the solace of authority in textual models. His story unfolds, after all, not as a play but as a work of fiction, so one might expect the numerous internal images of reading and writing in ***L'Immoraliste*** to point to texts as a source of intellectual and moral legitimacy. But instead, allusions to texts in the novel furnish additional sources of ambiguity by clouding the notion of authority. In "Drama, Performativity, and Performance," W. B. Worthen argues that both literary studies and performance studies have unjustly viewed drama as a somewhat derivative art that is slavishly bound to a prior text. Social performance, however, as theorized by performance studies, is distinct from dramatic performance in that it "appear[s] to depart from the authority of texts" (1093). Seeking acknowledgment of the originality and autonomy of dramatic interpretations, he calls for a reassessment of the "relations of authority that inform texts and performance" (1246). Worthen's subtle arguments in this study afford evidence of the precarious connection between written texts and a certain notion of authority, on the one hand, and between the presumed constraints of custom and liberating social performance, on the other. Gide's Michel, trained as a scholar to attach great importance to the production and reception of texts, nonetheless finds himself irresistibly drawn to the theater of life. These competing orientations defeat his search for a principle of authority that might have dispelled the moral ambiguities that accumulate around him.

His search may have been compromised from the beginning, as we discover within the first three pages of Michel's narration. After much reading and study of ancient languages, Michel reports, he published a treatise that his father had encouraged him to write: "L'*Essai sur les cultes phrygiens,* qui parut sous son nom, fut mon œuvre; à peine l'avait-il revu; rien jamais ne lui valut tant d'éloges. Il fut ravi. Pour moi, j'étais confus de voir cette supercherie réussir" (373). With this brief anecdote, Gide deftly tarnishes the notion of textual authority while revealing the conventions of society and family to be untrustworthy. Ambiguity of expression makes us uncertain as to whether "Il fut ravi" means that the father was delighted with his son's brilliant success, or delighted with his own enhanced prestige. Disconcerted by the success of the fraudulent authorial attribution, Michel endures an assault on his youthful idealism as he encounters society's eagerness to trust false appearances.

Yet even if the authority of texts, fathers, and social values is not absolutely reliable, the writing of others *can* be inspiring and instructive, and Michel's relation to texts will remain essentially positive during the first stage of his moral evolution. It is after reading a letter and some documentary works on tuberculosis sent by a certain T . . . , for example, that Michel musters the will to battle his illness (383-84). Literary writing is valuable, too, for it can appeal to the senses and enhance one's feeling of vitality, as Michel experiences in the park in Biskra while reading and memorizing three lines from the *Odyssey* (391). The Bible, in which he reads a prophetic verse found at random the night before leaving Biskra, serves to solemnize a moment he wants to retain in memory (396-97). A rereading of Theocritus in Syracuse provides, as we have seen, a reassuring link between past and present, as Michel muses on the agelessness of the poet's shepherd boys in this timeless region ("ses bergers au beau nom étaient ceux mêmes que j'avais aimés à Biskra" [398]). Those of us who have chosen to read Michel's story are likely to identify with his belief in the value of literary and documentary texts. As fellow readers, we admire his commitment to scholarship and reading. So Gide's portrayal of Michel as a reader and writer in the early part of the novel, especially in the context of his illness, disposes us favorably toward the protagonist and leaves us with ambivalent feelings toward him, rather than purely negative ones, after we have witnessed the selfish and destructive aspects of his project of personal liberation.

Michel's relation to texts partially redeems him in the eyes of the reader and thus contributes to his ambiguity as a character. This relation will also offer him a metaphor—although undoubtedly an inadequate one—for self-discovery, as he compares himself, in a famous passage, to palimpsests containing a hidden but precious initial layer of writing: "Quel était-il, ce texte occulté? Pour le lire, ne fallait-il pas tout d'abord effacer les textes récents?" (399). Robert W. Greene has observed that Michel presents himself as both the layers of writing and as the cryptographer; that is, "as both the texts read and the texts' reader" (["Fading (Sacred) Texts and Dying (Guiding) Voices in Gide's Early Récits"] 77). For Greene, this conjunction of disparate functions reflects the interplay of story and discourse in the novel. By the same token, the unusual combination is clearly consistent with the interchanging of performative and textual tropes. Michel longs for the legitimacy of an original text, even as he seeks performative freedom. Much of the novel's ambiguity derives precisely from this tension.

Although seductive, the palimpsest image is not entirely compelling, for why should the initial layer be more authoritative than one of the others? Moreover, to compound uncertainty, as Charles O'Keefe has observed, the image of overlaid texts of indeterminate authority mirrors the overlaid narrative voices found in the frame of the novel: those of Michel and the scribe, the second of these being, technically, the primary narrator ([*Void and Voice*] 79). The authenticity of Michel's own story is thus problematized, and all the more so in that the narrative frame encloses the thematically related issue of his first published book, for which he was denied authorship (O'Keefe 94). The palimpsest image, then, and its variants, drive a wedge between authorship and authority, and in so doing call into question the process of self-discovery that the metaphor was supposed to illustrate.

In a more advanced phase of Michel's progressive immoralism, he has considered turning his Collège de France lectures into a book (418), but he is increasingly disenchanted with books and with those who write them. He claims derisively that his fellow scholars are about as engaging as "de bons dictionnaires d'histoire," while novelists and poets appear to view living as an obstacle to writing (423). Ménalque, conversely, sees writing as an obstacle to living; this is why he has no interest in publishing his memoirs or an account of his travels (436). For a while, Michel manages to stifle his restlessness by caring for Marceline during her convalescence: "Près d'elle je lisais, j'écrivais [. . .]" (438). But Ménalque's example and his discomfiting curiosity about what such an inveterate reader as Michel ("ce liseur" [426]) might have been doing in Biskra finally lead our scholar to embrace the flawed conclusion that books are antithetical to life.

To learn about life, he will study people instead of texts: "Et j'interrogeais Bute, comme j'avais fait les informes chroniques des Goths" (446). Near the end of his story, the demons within him are so successful that he acknowledges not having opened a single time the trunkful of books he packed for the final tortuous journey with Marceline (459). Upon his return to Biskra, it occurs to him that he has not reopened the volume of Homer he had read in the park during his first stay there (465). The mental charms of reading have yielded to the physical and ego-centered pleasures of action and performance. Reading has in fact borne the stain of inaction since very early in the novel. If Marceline's first reported words—"Qu'as-tu donc"—identify her as a nurturing caregiver, her second response a few pages later ("Non: tu vois: je lis" [377]) betokens a kind of passivity that her husband will soon hope to transcend.

Thus reading and writing in the novel give rise to numerous questions about sources of authority and authentic modes of existence. Reading may entail passivity (Marceline, the younger Michel), or it may provide the will to live (Michel's medical reading) or contact with the dynamic lives of authors removed in time or space (Homer, Theocritus). Writing may be an avoidance of life, as for those who "remain true to that Symbolist ideal of the Word and the Book" (Sonnenfeld 186), or it may suggest an intense engagement with life (the book Michel planned to write). It can both establish authority and problematize it.

To the extent that Michel's basic dilemma is how to navigate between the constraints of society and the exhilaration of personal freedom, it is tempting to associate texts (and the attendant notions of origins, legitimacy, and authority) with the codification of social order. Performance, if perceived "as a mode of resistance to textual authority" (Worthen 1099, in the context of his critique of Dwight Conquergood), then squares with the pursuit of individual freedom. But as Worthen's analyses indicate, such a view is simplistic, and indeed Gide in *L'Immoraliste* does not leave us with the equations "text=authority" and "performance=freedom." Tension between the lofty themes of authority and freedom is assuredly a fertile source of ambiguity in the novel, but Gide creates further indeterminacy by exploring the negative sides of both of these highly regarded concepts.

By the end of his story, Michel has seen that performative models are no more reliable for understanding an individual's relation to others than are the texts in whose authority he has lost faith. With no resolution in sight, Michel's thinking about the individual has remained closest to a generalized image of the palimpsest. He clings to what he calls "le confus sentiment de richesses intactes, que couvraient, cachaient, étouffaient les cultures, les décences, les morales" (457). Layers of conventional values, in other words, repressively obscure the riches of an individual's unique first layer. The notions of text and performance merge in the palimpsest metaphor, which suggests the existence of two competing scripts for an individual's behavior, or general performance in society: the genetic script (later assimilated to "nature" in *Corydon*) and the social script. A man of extremes, Michel is not disposed to negotiate between these two scripts. After his experiments with the social script do not produce enduring contentment, he chooses to act out the genetic script instead, and this leads to isolation and a plea for assistance. Gide of course assigned his own contradictory tendencies to Michel's character. Preferring to revel in dichotomies rather than resolve them, Gide has earned such apt labels as proto-structuralist (Kadish ["Meaning in *L'Immoraliste* and *La Symphonie pastorale*"] 385), Dionysiac Catharist (Cordle [*André Gide, Updated Edition*] 10-14), and homosexual moralist (Pollard [*André Gide*]). The opposition Gide created in *L'Immoraliste* between theater/performance and text/reading/writing joins other dichotomies to support a general rhetoric of ambiguity that, paradoxically, is essential to his elaboration of the theme of authenticity.[12]

Curiously, or perhaps appropriately, Michel's meandering between the authority of writing and that of performance produces a reversal of the usual order of things. Now that his friends have come and heard his story, they have sought the intervention of Monsieur D. R., président du Conseil, who is then the reader of the transcription Michel's friends have made of his oral performance. Although a text—a script—generally precedes dramatic performance, it is the other way around in *L'Immoraliste*: text has the last word.

Postscript: In the late 1940s, Gide authorized August and Ruth Goetz to adapt *L'Immoraliste* for the American stage. The theatrical version was performed in Philadelphia and New York in 1954 (Claude, *André Gide* 1: 229).

Notes

1. Gide's own words associate *L'Immoraliste* with the plays in this regard: "Jusqu'à présent, j'ai su donner un nom à mes maladies, appeler l'une Candaule, l'autre Saül, l'autre Michel [. . .]"; cited by Martin (533) from a letter written by Gide to Marcel Drouhin on July 15, 1901. Is it just a coincidence that in the two plays and the novel, a man's wife is put to death?

2. Or at least he *appears* to be telling his story. As Fortier points out, we cannot be certain that the transcribed version of Michel's oral account contains no inaccuracies, since the scribe admits that he and the other two friends had a strong emotional response to the story they heard. This enhances the novel's pervasive ambiguity by turning the frame into "un principe générateur d'incertitude" (34).

3. At the turn of the century, Gide was fully aware of the dominance of prose over verse, but, as Martin puts it, "Le vieil alexandrin lui apparaît encore bien vivant" (404).

4. A few examples: "Le jour suivant je vis un frère de Lassif" (393); "L'air était presque vif, mais le soleil ardent" (401); [following a semicolon] "elle attend tout de moi, et moi je la délaisse! . . ." (406); "Le plus uni sentier paraissait dangereux" (449).

5. In this regard, Cordle offers the useful observation that Michel frames his dilemma in terms of "the revolution in historical thinking that established philosophical anthropology as a rival to antiquarian historiography (another development in which Nietzsche played a primary role)" 72.

6. Social identity, following the reasoning of Judith Butler on gender, operates in the context of "ritual social dramas" and "requires a performance that is *repeated*" (*Gender Trouble* 178, her emphasis). Validation of identity depends on approval of "the

mundane social audience," which includes "the actors themselves" (179). Butler acknowledges that her theorization "sometimes waffles between understanding performativity as linguistic and casting it as theatrical," but she has concluded that "the two are invariably related" (xxv). In *Bodies That Matter*, Butler lays additional stress on performativity as citationality (see especially 12-16). W. B. Worthen's subtle critique of Butler and others who have written on performance and the performative argues that citationality does not preclude interpretative autonomy in the theatrical and cinematic context. A common theme in such studies is the interdependence of social and theatrical performance, a notion that is confirmed by Gide's incorporation of theatrical conventions and allusions in his treatment of social performance in *L'Immoraliste*.

7. Michel's term here may suggest a theatrical perspective on marriage. Claude praises Gide for his skill in using "les ressources du dialogue théâtral" ("Écriture" 182) and for his composition of certain "monologues d'une puissance magistrale" (183). Ifri's comments on the thematic use of dialogue in the novel—for example, to suggest Michel's level of isolation (492)—are insightful. The difference between monologue and dialogue is problematic in Gide's "essais dialogués" such as *Corydon* where, as Claude observes, "s'entretiennent deux instances de sa pensée comme deux voix autonomes" (*André Gide* 2: 405).

8. In his 1904 lecture, "De l'évolution du théâtre," Gide outlines an inverse relation between social and theatrical masks: "Les plus splendides époques de l'art dramatique, celles où le masque triomphe sur la scène, sont celles où l'hypocrisie disparaît de la vie. Au contraire, celles où triomphe ce que Condorcet appelle 'l'hypocrisie des mœurs' sont celles mêmes où l'on arrache le masque à l'acteur, où on lui demande, non plus tant d'être beau que d'être naturel [. . .]" (440).

9. Robert F. O'Reilly identifies this scene as a "trial by strength" and sees it as an initiatory "test similar in meaning to the ordeals of the knights of romance" (350). The ritual or ceremonial actions, generally rooted in myth, that O'Reilly identifies in the novel suggest a theatrical dimension while contributing to "a fictional structure reminiscent of ancient tragedy" (353).

10. In the anthropological perspective of Bauman, performance supposes a "display of competence" that is "marked as subject to evaluation" by the audience (11). If a performer explicitly appeals to tradition, this "implies a standard of judgment against which one's performance is evaluated" (21). In social performance, the criterion of citationality suggests at least an implicit appeal to recognizable conventions, and likewise the inevitability of judgment on the part of observers.

11. "Il avait achevé ce récit sans un tremblement dans la voix, sans qu'une inflexion ni qu'un geste témoignât qu'une émotion quelconque le troublât, soit qu'il mît un cynique orgueil à ne pas nous paraître ému, soit qu'il craignît, par une sorte de pudeur, de provoquer notre émotion par ses larmes, soit enfin qu'il ne fût pas ému" (470-71).

12. Jean-Michel Wittmann has argued that ambiguity in *L'Immoraliste* owes much to Gide's ironic use of contradictory symbols, as well as to his overall rhetorical stance. The reader, forced to collaborate with the author, assumes a share of the author's moral responsibility along with the burden of making free interpretative choices.

Works Cited

Bauman, Richard. *Verbal Art as Performance*. With supplementary essays by Barbara A. Babcock et al. Rowley, MA: Newbury, 1977.

Brée, Germaine. *André Gide, l'insaissable Protée*. Paris: Les Belles-Lettres, 1953.

Butler, Judith. *Bodies that Matter*. New York: Routledge, 1993.

———. *Gender Trouble: Feminism and the Subversion of Identity*. Tenth anniversary edition. New York: Routledge, 1999.

Claude, Jean. "Écriture théâtrale, théâtralité de l'écriture." *Revue des Lettres Modernes* 1362-70 (1998): 163-89.

———. *André Gide et le théâtre*. 2 vols. Paris: Gallimard, 1992.

Cordle, Thomas. *André Gide, Updated Edition*. New York: Twayne, 1993.

Fortier, Paul A. *Décor et Dualisme*: L'Immoraliste *d'André Gide*. Stanford French and Italian Studies 56. Saratoga, CA: ANMA Libri, 1988.

Gide, André. *Corydon*. Paris: Gallimard, 1924.

———. "De l'évolution du théâtre." Conférence prononcée le 25 mars [1904] à la Libre esthétique de Bruxelles. *Essais critiques*. Ed. Pierre Masson. Paris: Pléiade-Gallimard, 1999. 433-44

———. *L'Immoraliste*. 1902. *Romans, soties et récits, œuvres lyriques*. Ed. Yvonne Davet and Jean-Jacques Thierry. Paris: Pléiade-Gallimard, 1958. 365-472.

———. *Théâtre*. Paris: Gallimard, 1942.

Greene, Robert W. "Fading (Sacred) Texts and Dying (Guiding) Voices in Gide's Early Récits." *French Forum* 12 (1987): 75-91.

Ifri, Pascal A. "Focalisation et récits autobiographiques: l'exemple de Gide." *Poétique* 72 (1987): 483-95.

Kadish, Doris Y. "Meaning in *L'Immoraliste* and *La Symphonie pastorale*." *Romance Quarterly* 32 (1985): 383-91.

Loomis, Louise Ropes, ed. *Aristotle: On Man in the Universe*. Princeton, NJ: Van Nostrand, 1943.

Martin, Claude. *La Maturité d'André Gide, de Paludes à L'Immoraliste (1895-1902)*. Paris: Klincksieck, 1977.

O'Keefe, Charles. *Void and Voice: Questioning Narrative Conventions in André Gide's Major First-Person Narratives*. Chapel Hill, NC: U of North Carolina P, 1996.

O'Reilly, Robert F. "Ritual, Myth, and Symbol in Gide's *L'Immoraliste*." *Symposium* 28 (1974): 346-55.

Pensom, Roger. "Narrative Structure and Authenticity in *L'Immoraliste*." *Modern Language Review* 84 (1989): 834-41.

Pollard, Patrick. *André Gide: Homosexual Moralist*. New Haven and London: Yale UP, 1991.

Segal, Naomi. *André Gide: Pederasty and Pedagogy*. Oxford: Clarendon, 1998.

Sonnenfeld, Albert. "On Readers and Reading in *La Porte étroite* and *L'Immoraliste*." *Romanic Review* 67 (1976): 172-86.

Vidal, Georges G. "De *L'Immoraliste* à la *Porte étroite*: Étude pour les masques de Gide." *Revue des Lettres Modernes* 688-92 (1984): 87-115.

Wilkins, Burleigh Taylor. "*L'Immoraliste* Revisited." *Romanic Review* 53 (1962): 112-27.

Wittmann, Jean-Michel. "Responsabilité de l'écrivain et légitimité de l'écriture dans *L'Immoraliste*." *Lettres Romanes* 51 (1997): 75-83.

Worthen, W. B. "Drama, Performativity, and Performance." *PMLA* 113 (1998): 1093-1107. Abstract, 1246.

Robert M. Fagley (essay date winter 2006)

SOURCE: Fagley, Robert M. "Narrating (French) Masculinities: Building Male Identity in André Gide's *The Immoralist*." *Journal of Men's Studies* 14, no. 1 (winter 2006): 79-91.

[*In the following essay, Fagley reads* The Immoralist *as "an expression of an alternative masculinity," opposed to that based on bourgeois morality.*]

Men's studies and, more specifically, the study of masculinities evidently owe much to feminism and feminist criticism. As Stephen M. Whitehead (2001) remarks, "The critical interrogation of men and masculinities is a relatively recent phenomenon, emerging out of the second-wave feminism of the 1970s and 1980s" (p. 355). Given the central position of French feminists in the foundation of feminist theory, it seems surprising that we have heard little from theorists of masculinities in France, with a few important exceptions including Michel Foucault and Pierre Bourdieu, who were not essentially theorists of masculinity or men's studies per se. This is not, however, the primary concern of this study, but what will be directly addressed is the representation of masculinity in French literary works, specifically in André Gide's most read novel, **The Immoralist.** To date, and despite the extensive development of feminist criticism, no comprehensive methodology has been established for the analysis of literary texts from a masculinities perspective. One may argue that criticism has, until a few decades ago, been largely from a male perspective (which is true) and that any new criticism claiming a textual reading of masculinities is merely a male appropriation of the feminist project. Although the former is true, I consider that men's/masculinity studies is an essential parallel to, not continuation of or replacement for, women's studies. Therefore, it is crucial to orient literary criticism toward the inclusion of male subjectivity in new ways. Some feel that men are simply incapable of genuine feminist analyses, in part due to their inability to experience female subjectivity. Although one may disagree, it is perhaps time to create new opportunities for men to contribute to gender-based criticism without posing the threat of colonizing female subjectivity as they have in the past. This is why male feminists must build their own branch of criticism; this complimentary methodology must incorporate the basic beliefs of feminism while offering the insight needed for a holistic theory of gender study. Just as male feminists cannot claim to understand the female experience without the contribution of women, female feminists will benefit from the study of masculinity to better understand the male experience. This work, targeting one version of French hegemonic masculinity and one possible counter current, represented in Gide's work, is a short step on a long path of experimenting with such a methodology.

What makes Gide and his work of particular interest to studies of masculinities is not only the writer himself, for he is a rich source for study, but also the period during which he lived and wrote. In this study I place the period from the Franco-Prussian War (1870) to the time of the First World War into a context that brings light to the French conception of masculinity during this period. Second, I place Gide within this framework. The goal of this work will then be to examine **The Immoralist** as an expression of an alternative masculinity at a time when a much different one was recognized as the norm in mainstream French society: modern French hegemonic masculinity as instituted through a bourgeois morality. The analysis of this particular novel holds rich possibilities, not only for its value as a socioliterary document but also because it is not a work primarily about men, and it therefore becomes necessary to read beyond the intentional discourse of the author. It is through such a reading that one discovers in Gide the possibility for a new branch of criticism of his unique variation of masculine writing.

Gide and *The Immoralist*: Origins of Problematic Masculine Identity

In his book, *Masculinity and Male Codes of Honor in Modern France,* Robert A. Nye (1998) writes about "a male code of honor that survived the destruction of the Old Regime in 1789" (p. 8). This code of honor involved a strong value being placed on courage and self-sacrifice for the greater national good, both concepts of masculinity that survived long beyond the period of this present study. The code manifests itself in the duel of honor between men, especially those of the bourgeoisie, which Nye describes in detail. Male honor at the turn of the century perpetuated a long tradition, described by Nye as "the transition experienced by all European societies from a feudal world shaped over centuries by the values of noble warriors to an industrial order dominated by the commercial and professional bourgeoisie" (p. 8). The French defeat in the Franco-Prussian War brought with it a fear of depopulation that added to a growing national consciousness of common values, specifically marriage, family, and courage, of which the latter Nye describes as "indistinguishable from manliness." Nye's particular examination of masculinity within the bourgeois class is crucial to any study of Gide such as the present one. Because both Gide and the principal character of *The Immoralist* are members of the bourgeois class, let us keep in mind these words from Nye as we proceed: "In effect, honor was *embodied* in bourgeois men as a set of normative sexual characteristics and desires that reflected the strategies of bourgeois social reproduction" (p. 9). Honor is gained and retained through one's social respectability and responsibility, both reflected by one's reputation, relations, and actions, especially with regard to protecting women's virtue and thereby one's own honor. Both Gide and his Michel were born into a milieu where such a sense of honor was privileged, and they struggled with the possibility of damaging it through the expression of their individuality.

André Gide was born in 1869 into this same bourgeois class. Gide was 11 years old at the time of his father's death, after which his mother raised him according to a strict Protestantism. He married his cousin Madeleine after the death of his mother in 1895, despite the protestation of the family and his then realized homosexuality. His extensive travels, especially throughout North Africa, brought Gide a new realization of diverse sexual identities. This is a common theme in many of his novels, in which male characters are often portrayed as ambiguous sexual beings.[1] This consciousness or coming into consciousness of one's sexuality is an important theme in *The Immoralist* as it is in other works by the author.

Michel, the principal character of the novel, is a historian by profession. At the death of his father, Michel marries Marceline, a woman he barely knows but who is a member of another bourgeois family with social connections to that of Michel. Their extensive honeymoon across Europe and into Africa reveals to Michel the personal qualities of Marceline, whom he begins to love. Their voyage is interrupted by Michel's violent struggle with tuberculosis. In Algeria, Marceline takes charge of Michel's convalescence. After his recovery, Michel takes Marceline to live for a short time on some family farm lands he had inherited, around which time Marceline realizes that she is pregnant. They soon relocate to Paris, where Michel takes a teaching position. Marceline miscarries, and they quickly return to the farms. Soon Marceline's health declines, and Michel must in his turn care for her. When she is eventually consumed by the same tuberculosis suffered by Michel, he returns to Algeria to live. It is there where Michel summons his friend, who introduces the novel and to whom Michel recounts the story summarized above.

Although Michel's realization of his homosexuality is intimated throughout the novel and is important to the narrative, this novel is neither a justification of nor an apology for homosexuality.[2] In this respect, Gide rejects all judgment of his *personnage*, and rather treats an even greater and more pervasive theme. Although Gide's anti-hero must be considered with regard to his slowly developing sexuality, I hold that the novel brings to light a wider consideration: the struggle of a man, representative of a collective, to shed the guilt and constraints accumulated since his childhood, reflective of a strictly enforced and monolithic morality. This struggle is also an effort to reveal in himself his "authentic being," not primarily to others, but to himself. For Michel, this identity discovery is as much a revelation as a rebirth. As previously stated, the subject of the novel is not simply homosexuality, although it is an important element. Its subject is a rejection of a fixed moral hegemony, a socially constructed set of rules that manifests a behavioral dogma, an artificial ontology that Michel refuses. Nationalistic bourgeois morality in France reaches far beyond a simple system of ethics. It equally produces and reproduces (gendered) identity in the interest of a rigid national identity. Social *being* appears as fixed and immutable through the institutions that create the masculine identity prescribed for Michel. In his

1897 *Fruits of the Earth*³ Gide wrote his famous dictum "Families, I hate you" (p. 58), spoken through his character, Ménalque, who reappears to play an important role in *The Immoralist*. The family, marriage, patriarchy, religion, and other national hegemonic values are examined by Gide as obstructions to the authentic self. Here the intention is to focus on one key aspect of these institutional values that is inextricably linked to them all: hegemonic masculinity. Although the hegemonic structures I will discuss may be observed in either the public or the private sphere, they are all part of a social identity composed of many qualities considered to be proper to the masculine sex. I will treat them all in turn in order to establish a clear image of this particular masculinity that Michel faces. It will thereby become clear how this individual eventually arrives at an alternative, yet problematic, masculine identity.

The Value of a Man: Masculinity as Strength

The introductory letter that initiates the novel also serves as an introduction to one of the important themes of the work: social responsibility. The author of the letter, like Denis and Daniel who are mentioned within, is a longtime friend of Michel. The main body of the novel is Michel's retelling of his own story to his three friends who come to visit him at his residence in Algeria. One of the more revealing expressions of the letter writer is conveyed when he asks of a certain Monsieur D. R., *Président du Conseil,* how Michel, as a man, might possibly fulfill his role in society.

> Can we accommodate so much intelligence, so much strength—or must we refuse them any place among us?
>
> How can a man like Michel serve the state? I confess I do not know. . . . He must have an occupation. Will the high position your great merits have gained you and the power you hold permit you to find it?
>
> (Gide, 1970, p. 3)

The letter, written by a man of the established bourgeois class to readers of the same milieu, gives evidence already of four values held in high esteem for men in French bourgeois society: intelligence, strength, a strong work ethic, and respect for one's duty to the state. Michel is assigned a value; he has typically masculine virtues, intelligence, and strength. The authority of the male addressee, the *Président du Conseil,* is also invoked: "the power you hold. . . ." Before his marriage, Michel was considered an ideal model of the values mentioned. His intelligence and work ethic were incontestable, as evidenced by his fervent devotion to his studies from a young age and his secret authorship of a book published under his father's name. His devotion to academics will continue through the gravest moments of his illness. At a certain moment when he seems to lose hope and gives himself up to his disease, Michel makes this statement, a projection perhaps of an unwritten auto-obituary: "After all, what did life have in store for me? I worked to the end, did my duty resolutely, devotedly. The rest . . . what does it matter?" (p. 19). As one begins to examine Michel as a masculine subject, one must not forget to touch upon, however briefly, the feminine. R. W. Connell (2000) indicates that gender identities do not develop in isolation and only meet afterward but "are produced together, in the process that makes a gender order" (p. 40). The same can be said of gender perceptions. Michel indicates that he had previously, before his marriage, considered the virtue of intelligence proper of men, a sign of masculinity. "I had somehow acquired ideas about the stupidity of women," (p. 13). He comes to appreciate his wife's own intellect. Marceline, the only female character developed in any depth, gives the reader a gauge of femininity by which to judge the masculinity that Michel is supposed to perform. Michel's observations of her intelligence, and her value in general, inform the reader of gender relations as imposed by sociocultural conditions. Intelligence is not the only masculine virtue addressed, and it is perhaps a minor one in the novel. One of the more important such virtues is strength, held in equal esteem throughout the novel.

Strength functions both as a physical attribute and a trait of the will: perseverance. On the physical level, strength appears through demonstrations of courage, manifested as heroism. It also appears as a personal characteristic, especially important in one's appearance. Michel, during his convalescence, occupies himself with the development of his bodily strength. In this way he lays claim to this particular quality indexically linked to the masculine sex, whereas he will soon deny others, as will become evident. In his reflections upon his own strength and that of his wife, Michel displays much hypocrisy throughout the novel. This emerges most strikingly after his convalescence. As he describes his impressions of Marceline just after their wedding, Michel remarks how strong she appears and "that she was stronger than I we were soon to learn" (p. 11). Later, he notes that since he grew stronger, she seemed more delicate. Perhaps Marceline, who is portrayed as a very "proper" French wife, consciously reappropriates her "feminine" role as Michel has less need of her strength. Unfortunately, this is impossible to determine given Gide's often superficial development of female characters. When Marceline later becomes ill herself, Michel describes, on more than one occasion, his displeasure with her poor constitution. To him it seemed that he "had coughed better than that" (p. 143). It seems clear that Michel's devaluation of his wife's strength is a reaction to his own weakness. He fears being seen as weak, especially after his illness, which filled him with a sense of impotence.

After Michel's illness and while he is developing his strength, he performs a heroic act uncharacteristic of his "old self." While walking to visit the Italian town of Positano, where he would rejoin Marceline traveling by carriage, Michel recognizes her driver from along the road, the latter evidently intoxicated and driving recklessly. At the collapse of the man's horse, Michel drags the man from his carriage, strikes him, drawing blood, and ties him up. It seems that this show of courage and his regained physical strength reawakens in Michel his sense of honor, typically masculine and, as Nye describes it, displayed in the defense of "helpless" women. This realization is conveyed in Michel's statement, "The danger had not been great; but I had had to show my strength, and in her defense," (p. 62). He remarks that that night he "possessed" Marceline,[4] apparently for the first time since their wedding night; he credits the occasion of the latter to its "novelty." It seems that the conflict with the carriage driver awoke in Michel a deep feeling of what could seem to the reader as "manliness," which in turn precipitated another such act, that of making love to his wife. It seems that the ordeal had a similar effect on Marceline, as is implied when Michel notes, "What glances, after that, Marceline and I exchanged!" (p. 62). The choice of expression for the love act is revealing. Though it may be ascribed to the conventionality of the term "possession" for love-making, this aggressive image of taking possession follows logically from the violent encounter that precedes it. Previously, Michel had apologized to his wife, explaining his lack of desire for her as attributable to his exhaustion. Well after his full recovery, however, this custom continued. Through his physical rehabilitation, Michel's (masculine) preoccupation with strength entails a certain concern with virility.

Tailored Masculinity

Although Michel is shown to subvert certain aspects of French hegemonic masculinity (patriarchal authority, social responsibility), he, in fact, embraces other aspects of this masculinity like strength and independence. This provides evidence that he does not reject masculinity in a wholesale fashion but rather rejects it as predetermined by society; he creates his own masculinity, tailored to his self image and to his developing sexual identity; he invents. While his sexual interests are now directed toward young men, his sense of honor and responsibility with regard to his wife remains intact. It is here that the multiplicity of masculinities must be recalled. In the introduction to his book, *Writing Masculinities: Male Narratives in Twentieth-Century Fiction,* Ben Knights (1999) explains that, in narratives of classic masculinity, men "are themselves victims of patriarchy and the heterosexual presumption" (p. 6). It is not certain that this should be phrased in such a manner, that men are victims. More aptly, they are subject to patriarchy and heterosexual presumption. Gide, however, does not write such a "classic" narrative of masculinity, but rather it is against that prescribed masculinity that Michel struggles. Knights also explains the limits of the male narrative: "Inasmuch as masculinity too is a rhetorical construct, our choice of masculinities has been limited by the narratives addressed to us" (p. 23). In Gide we see that he proposes another option; he creates a new choice of masculinity that is not proffered to replace the accepted paradigm but as one possibility of masculine identity as constructed by the individual from an infinite pool of masculinities.

As Michel becomes more occupied with the care of his body, he ignores, in a certain sense, the mind: "I am going to speak at length of my body. I am going to speak of it so much that it will seem to you, at first, I am forgetting the mind's share," (p. 30). For him, being preoccupied with both the body and the mind was to live a "double life," which he could not sustain in his illness. This concern with the body runs counter to many essentialist views of gender that oppose the mind (considered the domain of men) with the body (that of women). Such an essentialist view, in fact, contradicts popular conceptions of masculinity, in which men must be both intelligent and physically powerful. This only further illuminates the contradictions of hegemonic masculinity, often in conflict with itself.

Salvation Through the Self

As Michel's health and strength are restored, he seems to take much pleasure and even pride in improving his appearance. He grows to disdain his old self, not only for its devotion to study, but for its utter denial of the body. He devotes his energy to improving his body through his diet, exercise, and sunbathing. Marceline, on the other hand, is described throughout as appropriately delicate and pale.

In reflecting upon how Marceline resists her illness, Michel shows, as has been stated, a certain disdain for her lack of strength and determination. As Michel develops his new morality, even Marceline in her illness cannot help but be aware of her exclusion from it. She recognizes the beauty of his "doctrine," "but it eliminates the weak," as she says. Callously, and perhaps without thinking, Michel responds, "As it should" (p. 150). Here again his hypocrisy hides not only his guilt for not caring for his wife as well as she had cared for him but a fear of weakness or inadequacy in himself. In describing the first days of his illness, he admits "that her devoted care, that her love and nothing else" (p. 21) had saved him. But later, as he regains his strength, he forgets his debt to her. After the worst period of his illness has passed, Michel begins to distance himself from Marceline, both physically and in terms of his dependence upon her. Though she has saved his life, he esteems that his "salvation" depended solely on himself. This implies not just his survival but the recovery and rediscovery of his identity.

The religious image recalled by the word "salvation" is appropriately used. It appears in the text just before a scene in which Michel denies God's help, sought in prayer by Marceline, herself a devout Protestant. He says that he does not like to be indebted and wants no obligations presumably to God or to anyone. Marceline's religious devotion is a weakness in Michel's eyes. That Marceline and, in fact, all women of her class were required to be chaste and spiritually clean is understood, whereas Michel denies any such supposition for himself. This does not necessarily deviate, however, from the prescriptions of hegemonic masculinity. The inconsistency of prescribed moral standards between the sexes was common enough in late 19th century France, a continuation of the same moral double standards throughout French history, similar to those of Greek society discussed by Foucault in his *History of Sexuality*. That religion be left for the woman and the so-called "important" tasks for the man is implied in Michel's attitude. Michel's manner of brushing off Marceline's religiosity may be one way for him to cast off his mother's Huguenot moral teachings. His anti-religiosity may also be read as a rejection of the feminine, conveyed through the mother, and the search for the masculine, as recalled through reestablishing the atheism of Michel's father.[5] Although religion in France at the time cannot be considered solely the domain of women, it does become relegated to an inferior female sphere within Michel's construction of his masculine self. This discussion brings up the central theme of the novel as inferred by the title: morality.

Michel's refusal of his mother's morality, which represents that of the wider society,[6] is the driving force behind his newly discovered being. Despite this, or perhaps because of it, he makes more than one reference to passages from the Bible,[7] which he relates to his own spiritual journey, tailoring them to his secular world view. His convalescence is alluded to on several occasions as a rebirth, and one cannot help recognizing the biblical significance of his plunge into a pool of water at Ravello in Italy, an important moment of baptism and personal rebirth. Just previous to this baptism scene, he refers to his quest for "authentic being,"

> ... "the old Adam" whom the Gospels no longer accepted; the man whom everything around me—books, teachers, family and I myself—had tried from the first to suppress.
>
> (p. 51)

All of the suppressive forces mentioned may be regarded as social apparatuses for the reproduction of a hegemonic masculinity. For now, let us focus on the importance of the family as an agent of homogeneous gender enforcement.

Birth of the *Immoraliste*

As mentioned earlier, procreation had considerable importance in France at the time. Although Michel does little in the way of increasing his odds of paternity, he seems to attach a particular importance to the prospect of having a child. He was still quite wealthy at the time and no doubt was expected to produce an heir. The doubts that had begun to accumulate concerning his happiness and future were dispelled by the thoughts of a child. "I yearned toward the future where already I saw my new baby smiling at me; because of that child my spirits were strengthened, renewed" (p. 113). After the loss of the baby, Michel also loses hope of finding happiness in the life that he had fashioned with his wife. The child may have been his last incentive to seek contentment with Marceline, whom he had married, admittedly, without loving and in order only to please his father. Just as men of his time and station were expected to marry a woman of similar social rank in order to produce a respectable family and children with her, undoubtedly they were expected to want to do so. Michel struggles with these social expectations, the goal of which is to perpetuate the family as well as the gender order. Michel seeks to transgress the morality that depends on such institutions. In these next several pages, focus will be directed toward Michel's unorthodox moral identity as that of an alternative masculinity.

If one reflects upon the title of the novel, one remarks that the word "immoralist" does not mean, at least in the original language, "immoral person." The moralist is, according to Webster,[8] "a teacher of or writer on morals" or "one who seeks to impose personal morals on others." Michel is then *not* these things, as the prefix implies. The concept of "moralist" has somewhat passed out of usage in America, so it is important to point this out. Although "immoralism" does not often appear in English dictionaries, "immoralist" is occasionally defined as an "advocate of immorality,"[9] but this does not seem to fit the intentions of the author. In French, quite differently, "*immoralisme*" is defined as a "doctrine which proposes rules of action different, inverse of those admitted by the common morality."[10] Here the intended meaning of the title becomes clearer.

Gide himself wished to remain neutral in regard to his novel, to avoid being a moralist. As he states in his preface, "I wanted to write this book neither as an indictment nor as an apology, and I have taken care not to pass judgment" (Preface, p. xiii). In his book, Ben Knights (1999) explains that one of the first steps in reading a narrative from a "gender-aware position" is "to place in question much that is considered normal, exposing as profoundly ideological the tyranny of so much that passes for natural" (p. 12). In Gide's narrative, the author attempts to do this for us. He does not, as he states, write an apology for Michel or for homosexuality; it is actually rather easy for the reader to condemn the protagonist, given the stark contrast between his egotism and the many virtues of Marceline. What Gide reluctantly refers to in his preface as the "problem" in the novel is indeed unclear. He rather leaves it to the reader to determine it and to contemplate it but warns that to judge is to oversimplify the issue. The "problem" could be his search for authentic being, or perhaps even homosexuality. I will suggest replacing the word "problem" with "masculinity," for this too is problematic in the novel. In Michel's case, sexuality is only one aspect of his morality, albeit an important one.

Though Christian doctrines such as that taught by Michel's devout Huguenot mother accept that people may sin and be redeemed, it is nevertheless implied that they are meant to be moral creatures. For Michel, this moral doctrine is incompatible with his "new being." One finds in Gide's religious language, used in reference to Michel's self-discovery, remnants of Gide's own religious upbringing. While its use may be considered irreverent by morally conservative critics, it is unlikely that Gide uses such language ironically. He may be seen to create a new religion for himself, just as many men, certainly some gay men, create a religion of masculinity. Shortly before his "baptism" at Ravello, referred to earlier, Michel states his mission in these terms: "My sole effort, a constant effort then, was therefore systematically to revile or suppress whatever I believed due merely to past education and to my early moral indoctrination" (pp. 52-53). The earliest sign of Michel's new morality comes when he notices one of Marceline's favorite guests in Biskra, a local child named Moktir, stealing a pair of her scissors. Michel, rather than denouncing him, pretends not to have noticed and remarks his own utter delight at the sight of the theft. Moktir then becomes his favorite. Another moment of inverted morality occurs when Michel must justify hiding his newly discovered identity from his wife. The following statement can be applied to an understanding, not only of Michel's new comprehension of lying to protect his loved one but also of his latent homosexuality.

> Perhaps the need to lie cost me something, at first: but I soon realized that what are supposedly the worst things (lying, to mention only one) are hard to do only when you have never done them; but that each of them becomes, and so quickly! easy, pleasant, sweet in each repetition, and soon a second nature. . . . And I advanced every day into a richer, fuller life, toward a more delicious happiness.
>
> (p. 60)

Here one encounters a typical response to one's own homosexuality, still today, but to a much greater degree when the novel was written. Rather than openly embracing his new identity, Michel hides it, lies about it, and takes pleasure in the game of dissimulation. As his newly discovered identity develops, hiding it becomes more difficult and problematic.

Salon Masculinity: Social Performance

Earlier, as Michel attempts to improve his body, he shaves his beard. Whether facial hair is a sure sign of masculinity in France at the time is difficult to say, although photos from the period show that beards and moustaches were a popular trend. What is worthy of note is Michel's reaction to having shaved his beard, his "final garment." "No, the fear grew out of my sense that others could read my thoughts now, thoughts which to me seemed suddenly fearful" (p. 59). Let us compare his response with these words from Nye. "For the discreet homosexual male, there was little need to fear direct police intervention in his private life; he had much more to fear, however, from the judgments of his fellow citizens about the *quality* of his masculinity" (p. 107). The fear of judgment is a constant burden for Michel; though he never expressly shows concern for his masculinity, it may be implied. Michel admits to his friends at the end of the novel, "When you first knew me, I had a great steadfastness of mind, and I know that's what makes real men—I have it no longer" (p. 170). To be seen as a respectable man, a "real man," by polite society is one of Michel's preoccupations throughout much of the book.

Michel's reputation and social status earlier involved his frequentation of the many Parisian *salons,* which only served to bore and sadden him. After his travels, Michel returns to Paris only to feel even more out of place in the social circles that he and his wife had the habit of frequenting. Despite his feelings of alienation, he feels obliged to play his former role in society. For fear of discovery, and perhaps for convenience, he performs the role expected of him, counterfeiting the steadfastness he knows that he lacks. In this way, his new identity includes an aspect of espionage, which surfaces again later on his family farmlands, where he secretly poaches animals on his own lands rather than occupying himself with the respectable landowner role. In Paris, however, his artifice is employed as a cover, a protection of his new identity, which he explains in the following manner. "From our very first conversations, I was more or less obliged by them to act a part—either to resemble the man they thought I still was, or else appear to be pretending; so to make things easier, I acted as if I had the thoughts and tastes they attributed to me" (pp. 89-90). It is not the case, in fact, that Michel disliked being dishonest; he affirms later that he had nearly grown "to regard honesty itself as no more than restriction, convention, timidity" (p. 146). Rather, he seeks to surround himself with individuals in whose presence he can achieve his own happiness and in whom he sees his own values reflected: the children in Biskra, the workers around his farms, and in Paris, Ménalque.

The character Ménalque is widely considered to be one of Gide's representations of Oscar Wilde. It was after Michel's first lecture in Paris that he first sees Ménalque, an individual whom he had before rather disliked, after a long absence. This time he establishes a very different understanding of him. Ménalque, who had attended the lecture, approaches him. Michel remarks that the traits that had earlier repelled him in Ménalque now please him. What characterizes Ménalque as an individual is his complete disregard for the conventions of society, its opinions of him, and his own respectability. He remarks on the profound changes in Michel, invites him to dinner, and gently slights his status as a married man. Michel, who by this point is much less concerned with his reputation in society, still seeks to please this newly discovered ally. He admits: "I was afraid of seeming weak even more than of having offended him, and I promised I would join him after dinner" (p. 95). This after-dinner visit is the first of three crucial scenes of confession and revelation for both men. Ménalque tells Michel that he himself had recently visited Biskra and had made several discoveries about the latter. Michel, embarrassed, inquires as to what he had learned. Ménalque then retells the story of the stolen scissors as he had heard it from the boy Moktir, who in fact knew that Michel had seen him commit his petty theft. Both men admit their incomprehension of Michel's inaction upon witnessing this. After a short silence, the following exchange ensues:

> "There is," he continued, "a 'sense,' the others would say, a 'sense' you seem to be lacking, my dear Michel."
>
> "You mean a 'moral sense,'" I said, trying to smile.
>
> "No, just a sense of property."
>
> (p. 98)

Michel then points out that Ménalque seems to lack such a sense. Ménalque then professes that he has a horror of comfort and embraces a life of risk: "I want life to demand of me, at every moment, all my courage, all my happiness, and all my health" (p. 99). The doctrine expressed by this statement is not counter to any concept of masculinity, but it is how he, and eventually Michel, realize it that subverts hegemony. When Michel becomes defensive of these implications, Ménalque clarifies: "All I meant was that for a man without a sense of property you seem to own a great deal; that's a serious matter" (p. 99). For Ménalque, Michel's prestigious lecturer's position, his Normandy estate, his luxurious Paris apartment, even his marriage and, at the time still expected, child are all unlikely "possessions" for someone with no sense of property. Thus ends their evening together, rather uncomfortably. As Ménalque points out this contradiction, one sees that Michel has not entirely given himself up to his own morality. While in his mind he rejects the symbols of respectable men (social responsibility, respectability, property), he has yet to put this ideology into practice.

Their next meeting is at a soirée at Michel's home. Their conversation turns to the constraints imposed on their "friends" by society. What follows may easily be read as Ménalque's condemnation of the social restrictions that render him "a man of discredited tastes" and that chain Michel to the life he feels forced to continue.

> If there's one thing each of them claims not to resemble it's . . . himself. Instead he sets up a model, then imitates it; he doesn't even choose the model—he accepts it ready-made. Yet I'm sure there's something more to be read in a man. . . . I hate all this moral agoraphobia—it's the worst kind of cowardice.
>
> (p. 104)

Part of the ready-made model he describes, arguably the most important part, is masculine identity. Ménalque's description of "moral agoraphobia" as cowardice must have had quite an effect on Michel, who despises being seen as weak or cowardly. This provides further evidence that Michel values many of the virtues characteristic of hegemonic masculinity. Although it is not expressly stated, as it rarely is in Gide's work, Ménalque's homosexuality is strongly implied. When he must leave the country for an extended period, he asks Michel to spend the last night with him and prove that he is not "a man of principles." When the night arrives, two weeks later, Marceline's health has worsened. Michel goes nonetheless, and the two men discuss their respective plans for the future. Ménalque seems to regret that he must leave while Michel remains behind, but Michel remains determined to content himself with, as Ménalque calls it, the "fireside happiness" that he has made for himself. Ménalque sees in his friend contradictions and counsels him to leave his past behind, or risk losing his future happiness. "A man has to choose" he says. "What matters is to know what he wants" (p. 108). Ménalque embodies the masculinity sought by Michel. He has no familial obligations, is unmarried, has few possessions to tie him down, and can sustain a nomadic existence, constantly feeding his desire for the new. We see at the end of the novel that Michel adopts a similar lifestyle; Marceline's death and that of his parents release him from all obligations to the family. The sale of La Moriniere, the family farm, as well as all of his substantial possessions frees him of the social constraints tied to owning property. Michel's constant relocation allows him the liberty of movement and free existence often hindered by a national consciousness of what is required of "real men" and true republicans. Michel's self-exile to Algeria is, in a sense, his escape from the pressures of hegemonic masculinity. It is interesting to note, however, that Michel is portrayed in the book's final pages as somewhat trapped at his residence in Biskra. As he notes to his confidant, the letter writer, it may be his new friend Ali who prevents his moving on; his ensnarement indicates that he is perhaps trapped in a land where he is free to embrace his new masculine identity, though he is only beginning, at the close of the novel, to openly announce it to the world.

Though this brief study of a unique alternative masculinity in Gide's narrative is far from exhaustive, it does offer a few indications of what was considered "normal" and acceptable for men of the privileged bourgeois class at the time; it also demonstrates some ways by which Gide envisions possibilities of overcoming this rigid model, which consists of both an immutable morality and hegemonic gender identities. As Michel combines his own discoveries with the many insights he gains from Ménalque, we see the creation of a new subjectivity. This subjectivity will be recreated many times over in Gide's various works, the fruit of what one may venture to call, while not a universal one, at least a new masculine writing.

Notes

1. See Gide's Edouard of *The Counterfeiters* (1973) and Lafcadio of *Lafcadio's Adventures* (1960).

2. Gide does write such an apology in *Corydon*, which first appeared in 1911.

3. Originally in French, *Les Nourritures Terrestres*.

4. "Ce fut cette nuit-là que je possedai Marceline."

5. The figure of the father is another important element in Gide's work with bearing on the study of masculinity. The "bastard" character is well developed in his work, especially Bernard of *The Counterfeiters* and Lafcadio of *Lafcadio's Adventures*.

6. Although Protestantism is far from the unique religious order in France at the time, it represents, as one component of it, a wider national morality, with its roots in the broader Christian Church.

7. This is not uncommon to Gide. See also *Strait is the Gate* and *La Symphonie Pastorale*.

8. *Webster's New World Dictionary*, 1990.

9. *Merriam-Webster Online*, 2003.

10. My translation, original in *Le Petit Robert*, 1969, "Doctrine qui propose des règles d'action différentes, inverses de celles qu'admet la morale courante."

References

Connell, R. W. (2000). *The men and the boys*. Berkeley: University of California Press.

Foucault, M. (1978). *The history of sexuality* (3 Volumes; Robert Hurley, Trans.). New York: Random House.

Gide, A. (1931). *Pastoral symphony* (Dorothy Bussy, Trans.). New York: Knopf. (Original work published 1919)

———. (1948). *Strait is the gate*. (Dorothy Bussy, Trans.). London: Secker & Warburg. (Original work published 1909)

———. (1949). *Fruits of the earth* (Dorothy Bussy, Trans.). London: Secker & Warburg. (Original work published 1897)

———. (1960). *Lafcadio's adventures* (Dorothy Bussy, Trans.). New York: Random House. (Original work published 1914)

———. (1970). *The immoralist* (Richard Howard, Trans.). New York: Random House. (Original work published 1902)

———. (1973). *The counterfeiters* (Dorothy Bussy, Trans.). New York: Random House. (Original work published 1926)

———. (1985). *Corydon* (Richard Howard, Trans.). London: GMP Publishers Ltd. (Original work published 1924)

Knights, B. (1999). *Writing masculinities*. Great Britain: Macmillan Press Ltd.

Nye, R. A. (1998). *Masculinity and male codes of honor in modern France*. Berkeley: University of California Press.

Whitehead, S. M. (2001). Man: The invisible gendered subject? In S. M. Whitehead & F. J. Barrett (Eds.), *The masculinities reader* (pp. 351-368). Cambridge: Polity Press.

FURTHER READING

Criticism

Brée, Germaine and Margaret Guiton. "The Masters." In *An Age of Fiction: The French Novel from Gide to Camus,* pp. 11-56. New Brunswick, N.J.: Rutgers University Press, 1957.

    Interprets *The Immoralist* as a story of a man who re-molds his life according to a destructive ideal.

Callen, A. "*L'Immoraliste* as a Modern *Adolphe*." *Modern Language Quarterly* 31, no. 4 (December 1970): 450-60.

    Draws attention to the similarities between Benjamin Constant's novel *Adolphe* and *The Immoralist*.

Clark, Phyllis. "Gide's Africa." *South Central Review* 14, no. 1 (spring 1997): 56-73.

    Traces Gide's "idealization of Africa" in *The Immoralist*.

Cohn, Robert Greer. "Man and Woman in Gide's *The Immoralist*." *Romanic Review* 80, no. 3 (May 1989): 419-33.

    Investigates male-female relations in *The Immoralist*.

Davies, J. C. *Gide: L'Immoraliste and La Porte Étroite*, London: Edward Arnold, 1968, 80 p.

    Offers a comparative analysis of *The Immoralist* and *Strait Is the Gate*.

Day, James T. "The Structure of Education in Gide's *L'Immoraliste*." *Symposium* 46, no. 1 (spring 1992): 23-33.

    Describes *The Immoralist* as a work derived from "the novel of education."

Fowlie, Wallace. "*L'Immoraliste* (1902) and the Problem of Freedom." In *André Gide: His Life and Art*, pp. 46-56. New York: The Macmillan Company, 1965.
:   Focuses on the problem of freedom as a central theme in *The Immoralist*.

Golden, Kenneth L. "Archetypes and 'Immoralists' in André Gide and Thomas Mann." *College Literature* 15, no. 2 (1988): 189-98.
:   Applies C. G. Jung's concept of the "child archetype" and Friedrich Nietzsche's theories of the Apollonian and Dionysian forces in life to *The Immoralist*.

Goodhand, Robert. "Locale as Thematic Expression in *L'Immoraliste*." *French Review* 43, no. 1 (winter 1970): 77-86.
:   Discusses Gide's use of imagery as thematic expression in *The Immoralist*.

Hellerstein, Nina S. "The Problematic Couple in *L'Immoraliste, Partage de midi* and *Le Grand Meaulnes*." *Australian Journal of French Studies* 27, no. 2 (May-August 1990): 155-72.
:   Compares the treatment of the theme of self-definition, as enacted in the male protagonist's confrontation with his sexual nature and with the female Other, in *The Immoralist*.

Ireland, G. W. "*L'Immoraliste, La Porte Étroite*." In *Gide*, pp. 22-44. Edinburgh: Oliver and Boyd, 1963.
:   Compares *The Immoralist* to *Strait Is the Gate*.

Kadish, Doris Y. "Meaning in *L'Immoraliste* and *La Symphonie pastorale*." *Kentucky Romance Quarterly* 32, no. 4 (1985): 383-91.
:   Demonstrates the crucial role binary opposition plays in *The Immoralist* and *The Pastoral Symphony*.

Nelson, Roy Jay. "Gidean Causality: *L'Immoraliste* and *La Porte Étroite*." *Symposium* 31, no. 1 (spring 1977): 43-58.
:   Compares Gide's treatment of the principle of causation in *The Immoralist* and *Strait Is the Gate*.

Nettelbeck, Colin W. "*L'Immoraliste* Turns Ninety; Or What More Can Be Said about André Gide? An Essay on Cultural Change." *Australian Journal of French Studies* 29, no. 1 (January-April 1992): 102-24.
:   Defines *The Immoralist* "as an exemplar of modernist creation."

Newton, Joy. "Zola and Gide, a Reflection: *La Faute de l'Abbé Mouret* and *L'Immoraliste*." *Nottingham French Studies* 24, no. 2 (October 1985): 55-60.
:   Traces the influence of Émile Zola's *La Faute de l'Abbé Mouret* on Gide's *The Immoralist*.

Porter, Laurence M. "Autobiography versus Confessional Novel: Gide's *L'Immoraliste* and *Si le grain ne meurt*." *Symposium* 30, no. 2 (summer 1976): 144-59.
:   Compares and contrasts *The Immoralist* and *Si le grain ne meurt*.

Segal, Naomi. "Male Chains." In *André Gide: Pederasty and Pedagogy*, pp. 169-209. Oxford: Clarendon Press, 1998.
:   Interprets *The Immoralist* in the context of Gide's formation of "a chain modeled on the structure of pederastic desire."

Stoltzfus, Ben. "The Immoral Gate." In *Gide's Eagles*, pp. 24-37. Carbondale: Southern Illinois University Press, 1969.
:   Maintains that the dominant theme of *The Immoralist* is Michel's pursuit of absolute freedom.

Turnell, Martin. "André Gide and the Disintegration of the Protestant Cell." *Yale French Studies* 7 (1951): 21-31.
:   Discusses Gide's treatment of the theme of the prodigal son in *Strait Is the Gate*, *The Immoralist*, and *The Pastoral Symphony*.

Walker, David H. "First-Person Narratives." In *André Gide*, pp. 21-79. London: Macmillan, 1990.
:   Assesses the ironic and self-reflexive qualities in the first-person narrative structure of *The Immoralist*.

Additional coverage of Gide's life and career is contained in the following sources published by Thomson Gale: *Contemporary Authors*, Vols. 104, 124; *Dictionary of Literary Biography*, Vols. 65, 321; *DISCovering Authors*; *DISCovering Authors: British Edition*; *DISCovering Authors: Canadian Edition*; *DISCovering Authors Modules: Most-studied Authors* and *Novelists*; *DISCovering Authors 3.0*; *Encyclopedia of World Literature in the 20th Century*, Ed. 3; *European Writers*, Vol. 8; *Guide to French Literature: 1789 to Present*; *Literature Resource Center*; *Major 20th-Century Writers*, Eds. 1, 2; *Major 21st-Century Writers*; *Novels for Students*, Vol. 21; *Reference Guide to Short Fiction*, Ed. 2; *Reference Guide to World Literature*, Eds. 2, 3; *Short Story Criticism*, Vol. 13; *Twayne's World Authors*; *Twentieth-Century Literary Criticism*, Vols. 5, 12, 36; and *World Literature Criticism*.

Randall Jarrell
1914-1965

American poet, critic, novelist, translator, essayist, and children's writer.

The following entry presents criticism on Jarrell from 1969 to 2005. For additional discussion of Jarrell's career, see *CLC*, Volumes 1, 2, 6, 9, 13, and 49.

INTRODUCTION

A multifaceted writer and one of the foremost figures of the "Middle Generation" of American poets, Randall Jarrell is best known today for his literary criticism and his seven volumes of poetry published during his lifetime. As a literary critic, Jarrell is lauded for his metaphoric and witty style of writing, as well as for his keen insights into the verbal gifts of other poets. Often acerbic and impatient with what he viewed as uninspired work, he was also highly supportive of many promising poets and helped establish the careers of a number of writers. His insightful and admiring assessments of such poets as Robert Frost, William Carlos Williams, Walt Whitman, and W. H. Auden turned out to be prescient and set the tone of much subsequent criticism of these figures. As a poet, Jarrell is often praised for his exploration of the mundane yet essential aspects of human experience, and for his depiction of the chaos, isolation, and uncertainty of American life in the years following World War II. His poems, which are often narrative and colloquial in style, evoke the experiences of multiple personae—such as soldiers, children, and women—and reflect, as critic Suzanne Ferguson noted, "the ironic incongruity of men's ideals with their way of living." The Fugitive poets—John Crowe Ransom, Robert Penn Warren, and Allen Tate—were mentors early in Jarrell's career, but his major influences were Auden, Frost, Ezra Pound, and the German Rainer Maria Rilke. Perhaps most influential was Frost, who informed the tone and structure of Jarrell's poems, as well as his attention to the rhythms of American speech. Regarding this last attribute, the poet Karl Shapiro, a contemporary of Jarrell's, asserted that "Jarrell is the one poet of my generation who made an art of American speech as it is. . . . Here Jarrell is unique and technically radical. No other poet of our time has embalmed the common dialogue of Americans with such mastery. And because he caught our bourgeois speech he caught our meaning."

BIOGRAPHICAL INFORMATION

Jarrell was born May 6, 1914, in Nashville, Tennessee. Much of his formative childhood experience took place in California, near Hollywood, where he spent time with his paternal grandparents after his parents, Anna Campbell and Owen Jarrell, divorced. Later, Jarrell attended Vanderbilt University, where he earned an undergraduate degree in psychology. During this time, he began studying under the Fugitive poets John Crowe Ransom and Robert Penn Warren and shifted his focus to literature and writing. In 1937, Jarrell followed his mentor Ransom to Kenyon College and, until 1939, worked there part-time as a teaching assistant. It was during this time that he met the poet Robert Lowell, who would remain an important colleague and friend throughout his life. After receiving a graduate degree in 1939, Jarrell accepted a teaching position at the University of Texas in Austin and began publishing poetry in literary journals, such as *The American Review* and *Kenyon Review*. In 1942, he published his first significant volume of poetry, *Blood for a Stranger*. That same year, he enlisted in the U.S. Air Force and served as a flight and navigation instructor during World War II. Jarrell's next volumes of poetry, *Little Friend, Little Friend* (1945) and *Losses* (1948), deal primarily with his World War II experiences.

In 1946, Jarrell resumed his career writing poetry and teaching, first at Sarah Lawrence College and then at Woman's College at the University of North Carolina at Greensboro. He continued writing, and his reputation as an astute critic of poetry grew. Jarrell's next volumes of poetry, including *The Seven-League Crutches* (1951) and *The Woman at the Washington Zoo* (1960), reflect his growing interest in German culture, particularly the folklore and fairy tales that came out of that tradition. Jarrell won the National Book Award in 1962 for *The Woman at the Washington Zoo*. Jarrell's last volume of poetry, *The Lost World,* was published in 1965, shortly before his death. In his later years, Jarrell was beset by physical and emotional problems that resulted in at least one suicide attempt. He was killed on October 14, 1965, when struck by a car while walking near his home in Chapel Hill, North Carolina.

MAJOR WORKS

Jarrell's poetry is generally divided into three categories: his early poems, including those collected in *Blood for a Stranger*; his elegiac war poetry of *Little Friend,*

Little Friend and *Losses*; and his later work, including *The Seven-League Crutches, The Woman at the Washington Zoo,* and *The Lost World,* which rely heavily on German folklore and display Jarrell's keen interest in psychology, philosophy, and children's literature.

The war poems of *Little Friend, Little Friend* and *Losses* have been praised for their vivid depictions of the effects of war and their individual insights into life as a soldier. Many of these poems emphasize the theme of lost childhood—a thematic concern that recurs throughout Jarrell's later work—and focus on the young soldiers and their attempts to understand the meaning of their lives and deaths. *Little Friend, Little Friend* contains some of Jarrell's best known war poems, including "A Pilot from the Carrier," "Losses," "Siegfried," and "The Death of the Ball-Turret Gunner." This last work is the most anthologized of Jarrell's poems on the subject of war. Here, Jarrell connects a soldier's death with images of the womb and birth. In "Eighth Air Force," from *Losses,* Jarrell broaches the subject of mass bombing. The poem explores the ideas of guilt and complicity in the killing that takes place during war, and at different points refers to the soldiers as both children and murderers. It ends with an allusion to Pontius Pilate, "Men wash their hands, in blood, as best they can: / I find no fault in this just man."

In his next collections, *The Seven-League Crutches* and *The Woman at the Washington Zoo,* Jarrell delved more deeply into mythical and psychological themes. Rilke's influence on Jarrell's poetry is especially evident in the first of these two works. In fact, one of the most critically praised poems from the collection, "Seele im Raum," borrows its title from Rilke's work. The poem explores themes of misery, obsession, and loss of self in its sympathetic portrait of a lonely, middle-aged woman. It is also considered one of Jarrell's most effective uses of the dramatic monologue. Another famous poem in the volume, "A Girl in a Library," employs a female persona, through whom Jarrell structures a dialectic between educated and uneducated states of mind, and between past and present cultures. In *The Seven-League Crutches* and *The Woman at the Washington Zoo,* Jarrell established his technique of using speakers, especially women and children, and monologue, dialogue, and everyday conversation to reveal his themes of human suffering, loneliness, and mortality. Many critics regard the title poem of *The Woman at the Washington Zoo* as Jarrell's greatest work of verse.

Jarrell's last volume of poetry, *The Lost World,* is considered the most confessional of his oeuvre. The book, which is divided into three sections, deals mainly with memory and childhood, and takes place in Los Angeles. Jarrell utilizes Hollywood movie imagery to highlight the fantastic aspects of childhood. The overarching mood of *The Lost World* is one of melancholy, driven mainly by a nostalgia for the past. The inevitability of adulthood and mortality are also ideas that inform the poems of this book, such as the piece "Next Day," which presents the monologue of an aging woman shopping for laundry detergent in a grocery store. In the last section of the book, the innocence of childhood is threatened by the potential destructive violence of the adult world. Although *The Lost World* is considered a departure from Jarrell's early work because of its autobiographical slant, its themes of lost childhood, dream, and mortality are sympathetic with the body of his work.

Although Jarrell's poetry is most prominent among his literary achievements, his contributions to fiction, for both adults and children, as well as to critical studies are significant. In addition to his novel, *Pictures from an Institution* (1954), Jarrell wrote three books for children, *The Bat-Poet* (1964), *The Animal Family* (1965), and *Fly by Night* (1976), which have come to be respected not only as enduring works for children but as interesting self-portraits of the writer. *Poetry and the Age* (1953), Jarrell's most important critical work, focuses on the state and trajectory of poetry in the modern age. Rather than attacking the poetry of the past generation, Jarrell approaches the period from a different perspective. Adam Kirsch describes the essays in *Poetry and the Age* as "acts of rehabilitation, pointing out the virtues in poets whom other critics have denigrated or ignored—especially Walt Whitman, Robert Frost, and William Carlos Williams."

CRITICAL RECEPTION

For many critics, Helen Vendler's statement that Jarrell "put his genius into his criticism and his talent into his poetry" is a fair assessment of the author's contribution to American literature. As a poet, Jarrell won praise for his ability to translate abstract ideas into direct, simple, and colloquial language, and for creating vivid characters and voices in his verse. Indeed, many commentators consider among Jarrell's greatest strengths his ability to delineate his themes and reveal the psyche of his narrators through dialogue, conversation, and the use of everyday speech in his poems. Critic Charlotte H. Beck referred to this technique as Jarrell's "sweet uses of personae," which she considered essential to his art and "to his delineation of truth as he perceived it." While recognizing Jarrell's skills at creating characters that capture the essence of modern life, other critics have faulted the poet for the sentimentality, directness, and simplicity of his verse. In an often-quoted review of Jarrell's *Selected Poems* (1990), James Dickey described the collection as "the most untalentedly sentimental, self-indulgent, and insensitive writings that I can remember," claiming that Jarrell lacked "the power, or the genius, or the talent, or the inclination, or whatever, to make experience rise to its own most intense, concentrated, and meaningful level." In his defense, Jarrell had earlier stated that he'd rather have "the child in the chimney-corner" moved by one of his poems, "in spite of his ignorance of its real meaning, than to have the poem a puzzle to which that meaning is the only key." Other critics have derided Jarrell for his uncritical acceptance of Freudian psychology and, more often, for his failure to reconcile the conflict in his poems between the ultimate futility of language, on the one hand, and the spoken word, on the other—what Karl Shapiro described as the tension between the "High Culture" of his modernist predecessors and the language of "ordinary life." As a result, many scholars maintain that Jarrell deserves a place, if not among the great poets of the twentieth century, certainly among the very good and representative ones.

Jarrell's reputation as a critic is less ambivalent. Indeed, many commentators regard his criticism as his most significant contribution to twentieth-century literature. Although his assessments of the work of other poets were often acerbic and harsh, Jarrell also promoted many good writers and demonstrated a keen judgment of literary talent. Many of his critical opinions, such as his praise of contemporaries Elizabeth Bishop and Robert Lowell and his criticism of e. e. cummings, William Carlos Williams, and W. H. Auden, have been confirmed with the passing of time. Writing in 1986, J. A. Bryant, Jr., claimed that, despite the overly vitriolic tone of Jarrell's early reviews, "his judgments from the beginning had a significant effect on the taste of the American reading public—and perhaps an effect on the direction of letters in postwar America as well." Suzanne Ferguson wrote in her *Poetry of Randall Jarrell* that Jarrell's criticism would "ask always, both explicitly and implicitly, whether the poem tells the truth about the world; whether it helps the reader see a little farther, a little more clearly the dark and light of his situation."

Ultimately, critics generally agree that Jarrell was among the best of his generation to create poetry and meaning out of the chaos of mid-century America. In his famous lecture on Jarrell, presented shortly after the poet's untimely death in 1965, Karl Shapiro maintained that he "tried to do the impossible: to observe and make poetry of a chaos, without being either inside or outside of it. He did it better than anyone else, better than it can be done." Shapiro concluded that Jarrell "died, you might say, because his heart was in the right place and his heart was even stronger than his intellect. Jarrell was split between his heart and his mind. He was modern, which means hating being modern. He was born after Humpty-Dumpty fell off the wall, and he knew that T. S. Eliot scotch tape couldn't put anything back together again."

PRINCIPAL WORKS

Blood for a Stranger (poetry) 1942
Little Friend, Little Friend (poetry) 1945
Losses (poetry) 1948
The Seven-League Crutches (poetry) 1951
Poetry and the Age (criticism) 1953
Pictures from an Institution (novel) 1954
Selected Poems (poetry) 1955
The Woman at the Washington Zoo (poetry) 1960
The Golden Bird and Other Fairy Tales of the Brothers Grimm [translator] (fairy tales) 1962
The Rabbit Catcher and Other Fairy Tales of Ludwig Bechstein [translator] (fairy tales) 1962
A Sad Heart at the Supermarket (essays) 1962
The Bat-Poet [with Maurice Sendak] (juvenilia) 1964
The Gingerbread Rabbit [with Garth Williams] (juvenilia) 1964
Selected Poems (poetry) 1964
The Animal Family [with Sendak] (juvenilia) 1965
The Lost World (poetry) 1965
The Complete Poems (poetry) 1969
The Third Book of Criticism (criticism) 1969
Snow-White and the Seven Dwarfs [translator] (fairy tales) 1972
Fly by Night [with Sendak] (juvenilia) 1976
Goethe's Faust: Part I [translator] (novel) 1976
A Bat Is Born [with John Schoenherr] (juvenilia) 1977
Kipling, Auden & Co.: Essays and Reviews, 1935-1964 (essays) 1980
Randall Jarrell's Letters: An Autobiographical and Literary Selection (letters) 1985
Selected Poems [edited by William H. Pritchard] (poetry) 1990
No Other Book: Selected Essays [edited by Brad Leithauser] (essays) 1995

CRITICISM

Robert Humphrey (essay date 1969)

SOURCE: Humphrey, Robert. "Randall Jarrell's Poetry." In *Themes and Directions in American Literature: Essays in Honor of Leon Howard*, edited by Ray B. Browne and Donald Pizer, pp. 220-33. Lafayette, Ind.: Purdue University Studies, 1969.

[*In the following essay, Humphrey identifies a number of recurring themes in Jarrell's poetry, such as necessity and pain, dreams and hope, and the psychological theories of Sigmund Freud and Carl Jung. The critic argues that Jarrell's straightforward grappling with human emotion sets him apart from other contemporary poets, saying that few "of the successful poets of our time have been as unashamedly sad, angry, and sympathetic toward fear and loneliness."*]

Although "literary history is ruthless toward the unsuccessful,"[1] we have to grapple with the paradox that literary history, and the critics who write it, give us the understanding and perspective with which we determine literary success. Very recent writers who may deserve some space in future literary histories may be judged failures simply because critics were too late in transmitting their understanding. This is a greater risk nowadays than at any time previously—especially with American poets—since there have been many very good ones in the past thirty or forty years.

The significance of Randall Jarrell's poetry, particularly the poems first published between 1944 and 1951, has not been recognized widely.[2] No chronicler of recent American poetry has written the proper chapter with which to give literary history a basis for being "ruthless" (or not) towards Jarrell's poetry.[3] The fact is that no other American poet published so many excellent poems during the period of the late 1940's. Few have published so many since. It is the excellence of these poems that I hope to identify here.

The unchanging base of all of Jarrell's poetry is the group of abstractions that concerned him: Necessity and Pain, Dreams and Hope—those compass points of twentieth century psychology. Jarrell's ideological framework, the source of his symbols, was the Necessity of Freud and the Universal Unconscious of Jung; yet this frame is denied by the specific attitudes of the poems which reject all faith in the reality of abstractions, not only religions and politics, but also semi-sciences, including psychoanalysis. Nevertheless, the dream-world and its mechanisms and the perennial story of the unconscious as it is realized in fairy tales and legend ("Sleeping Beauty" and "Hansel and Gretel" providing recurring symbols in Jarrell's poetry) are as useful to Jarrell as Dante's "Comedy" was to Eliot and as Yeats' Vision was to himself. Although Jarrell would have winced at the thought, he is the only poet of significance who, philosophically, depends on psychoanalytical theory. (Yet there are only two or three times that he ever gives overt recognition to this involvement—as, for example, in the late poem **"Woman"**—and then only within context of his remarkable knowledge of nearly all "culture" pertinent to the human condition.)

In his **Selected Poems** (Knopf, 1955), Jarrell arranges his poems by subject matter. The subject headings are effective rhetoric, but they are misleading, for the categorizations of "Lives," "Dream-Work," "The Wide Prospect," "Once Upon a Time," etc., are all attributes of almost all the poems. Jarrell's subjects are all "lives," usually children's or soldiers' or prisoners' or invalids'. It is, too, the very widest prospect of dreamwork and of fairy tales that his characters look out upon. The best of the poems are peopled by the most vulnerable of beings: Lady Bates, the motherless girl of **"The Night Before the Night Before Christmas"**; the sister of the dead girl of **"The Black Swan"**; the boy who is sick in bed in **"A Quilt Pattern"**; the wounded man **"In the Ward"**; the ragged and displaced girl of **"A Game at Salzburg"**; and many more, including all of the battlesick, wounded, captured and dead soldiers of the war poems—all of those who escape the Pain through dreams, fantasies, or under quilt covers, or in death.

Jarrell's attitude toward those cornered beings who inhabit his poems is invariably sympathetic; he never mocks them; he is never impatient. His indignation is directed—when it is present—at the causes of the Pain, which are those unrequited monsters: the State, War, Loneliness, Poverty and Illness.

Jarrell is as sympathetic as Wordsworth and as outraged as Shelley. Few of the professional and successful poets of our time have been as unashamedly sad, angry, and sympathetic toward fear and loneliness. It takes masterful technique to succeed with such a tone in our anti-sentimental time. The heart of Jarrell's artistry is in his precise control of rhetoric and rhythm and in the dramatic tension often found in the best of the poems. This can be suggested even out of context of a complete poem by the opening lines of **"The Sleeping Beauty: Variation of the Prince,"** a poem terrifying in its sense of frustration:

> After the thorns I came to the first page.
> He lay there gray in his fur of dust:
> As I bent to open an eye, I sneezed.

The poem plunges into its own world of fairy tales and dreams, with a teasing pun ("page"), a rhetorical tension ("thorns"), a kinetic force ("I bent to open an eye") and a disarming, gentle humor ("I sneezed"). Later in the poem, when the heart-breaking lines come: "When the world ends—it will never end—/ The dust at last will fall from your eyes"—and later, "When they come for us—no one will ever come—," we have been able to remember, because of the texture of the opening, that we were in Wonderland all the time. Almost all of Jarrell's poems, like this one, are charged with physical activity. People seem constantly to move: A hand curls and uncurls; fingers wander; bodies bend, stretch and arch; legs curl; eyes close or open; hands seize; a child sniffles; a child holds a cat "so close he pants;" one crushes a petal; another plunges home. This kinetic life in the poems is, strangely the typically, most often found in the context of the dream.

In Jarrell's poetry to dream is to change; it is to escape from one pain to another, for dreams are wider prospects of life and in them metamorphosis is natural. But

Jarrell is a twentieth century realist who understands not only the functions of myths and dreams, but also that they cruelly end in an awakening and another pain.

The pain of war in Jarrell's world most often leads to a permanent release, i.e., vegetation or death, but the living remain to endure the anguish. Jarrell has written the best poems to come out of World War II. Anthologies and literary histories thus tend to give the impression that he was exclusively a war poet. Although Jarrell has a body of fine poetry relating to the war, it is a distorted view to label him "war poet," because his war poems are no different from his other poems in viewpoint, tone, method and themes; and it is a misleading label chiefly because Jarrell has written some better poems than his war poems. These, at their best, are as general in their truth as are his poems with other locales or with un-uniformed yet lost souls speaking. The anthologies have, unfortunately, popularized a few of the more melodramatic and clever poems (**"The Death of the Ball Turret Gunner,"** first published in 1945, had been, up to 1958, published in sixteen places[4]). Actually, the best of the poems relating to the war are those less frequently anthologized: **"A Front," "A Camp in the Prussian Forest," "Second Air Force," "Burning the Letters,"** and **"Eighth Air Force."**

"Eighth Air Force" (published first in 1947) represents Jarrell's skill in a more lyrical mode than he usually employs. Its tone and the poet's attitude, nevertheless, are characteristic of almost all the war subjects. In spite of the absence of a dramatic super-structure (there is no dialogue), the poem springs forth with a concrete dramatic setting and with actors moving—the almost always present choreography of Jarrell's poetry. The first eight lines demonstrate this movement, this brilliantly "staged" setting that the poet knows how to use so well:

> If, in an odd angle of the hutment,
> A puppy laps the water from a can
> Of flowers, and the drunk sergeant shaving
> Whistles *O Paradiso!*—shall I say that man
> Is not as men have said: a wolf to man?
>
> The other murderers troop in yawning;
> Three of them play Pitch, one sleeps, and one
> Lies counting missions, lies there sweating

Jarrell's "creatures" are as prominent in the war poems as in the fairy tales and dreams; the puppy that "laps the water" becomes, in the third stanza, the airmen who ". . . play, before they die, / Like puppies with their puppy; . . ." This is one of the earlier uses of the "furry things" that repeats itself throughout Jarrell's poetry as the soft assurance, the infantile comforter, the last hope against pain.

This poem is no more, or less, bitter than the other war poems, but it is much less brutal and *just* better than some of the better known ones. As he does in later, more psychologically involved poems, in his best war poems Jarrell identifies his own ambiguity. The last stanza, which crystallizes this in the speaker's identification with Pilate's dilemma, must be given in full:

> I have suffered, in a dream, because of him,
> Many things; for this last saviour, man,
> I have lied as I lie now. But what is lying?
> Men wash their hands, in blood, as best they can:
> I find no fault in this just man.

Another successful poem emanating from the war, but of the kind that anthologies of "poems of social protest" will treasure for many decades, is **"A Camp in the Prussian Forest."** The poem reminds one of the horror of Wilfred Owen's poetry, although its irony is noticeably more removed from the moment of horror. A brief passage will convey this:

> I paint the star I sawed from yellow pine—
> And plant the sign
> In soil that does not yet refuse
> Its usual Jews

The Audenesque metrical control is one of the factors in this and other war poems that keeps us from sighing with discomfort at the burden of knowledge the poet carries.

Not only do the war poems project the attitudes of sympathy and indignation for those who suffer easily and helplessly (soldiers, children, the ill and deprived) that are characteristic of the later, more highly developed themes, but they also often use a similar, strong dramatic method.[5] Among the poems with war subjects that are forerunners of the later, more substantial dramatic narrations are **"Burning the Letters,"** and **"Second Air Force."** The first of these is a monologue. The wife of a pilot who has been killed is speaking—the **"Second Air Force"** is a narrative suggesting the internal monologue of the mother who is visiting her son, a bomber pilot, at his base. In each of these poems, the central sufferer is the helpless, bewildered one who is only an observer, an object of the necessity and pain of war. Both poems have the material of pathos, but both transcend this to become works of knowledge and perspective; and they do it because they are successful dramatic projections—the poet gives you the objective reality and neither he nor you are more involved than observers ever are. If you react by wanting to "wail at the world's wrong," it is not because the poet is wailing; nor because he, like Shelley, tells you to; he is a reporter of the limits he observes of human understanding—his own, the pilot's wife's, the bombardier's mother's and the reader's.

Not all of these poems of the war, even those chosen for the ***Selected Poems,*** avoid the final effect of sentimentality. (This limitation is likely to appear noticeably in the poems that do not have dramatic structure, such as **"New Georgia"** and **"The Dead in Melanesia."**) We might as well consider the limitations of Jarrell's poetry all at once, for there are some recurring ones, and even sentimentality is found in poems other than the ones with war subjects. These occasional flaws are those found in all "romantic" poets, for part of being a romantic is being willing to take risks with the unsettled and unsorted emotional extremes of one's self or one's subjects. But romantic, in this latter sense, Jarrell was, and he did not always extricate himself from the artistic danger of sentimentality, of imitativeness and, finally, of cleverness. Never, however, in the poems of the period 1949-1951, was the poet less than a skilled professional; seldom was he ridiculously sentimental or trivial as Wordsworth was sometimes and even Frost was occasionally.

The sentimentality has been cited above in the war poems; it is also found in some of the poems centering on children. Although his gift for capturing a child's view often protects the sentimental in Jarrell from becoming sentimentality—as is illustrated at its best in the poem **"Moving"**—in a few of the poems (**"A Sick Child"** is a notable example), there is a lack of the saving humor and the necessary whimsical correlative to carry the sentiment.

A few of the poems in *Selected Poems* are relatively trivial (**"Nollekans," "The Boyg, Peer Gynt, The One Only One"**); some are too imitative to take seriously (**"Jonah"** of Ezra Pound; **"Song: Not There"** of Auden; **"The Snow Leopard"** and **"Loss"** of Rilke) and several that have superb sections are too full of the whims and manners of the author; for example: **"An English Garden in Austria,"** where one has to try to reconstruct a good deal of the poet's own vast knowledge, not only of the subtleties of the plot of *Der Rosenkavalier*, but also some of the lesser social details of the European Enlightenment. Unfortunately the result is not a powerful poem, as in the best of Ezra Pound and almost all of Eliot—those poems where allusions to the world's knowledge enhance a theme and are submerged to it.

Jarrell was one of the many poets who emerged in the forties determined, it seems, not to be influenced by Eliot, although stylistic elements indicate he had learned much from Pound. His respect for, if not direct influence by, Pound's methods is reflected in their common emphasis on images of metamorphosis and, even more, their concept of a poem as a dramatic event. Pound's *tenson* from Provençal verse is Jarrell's "All my poems are meant to be said aloud; many of them are dramatic speeches or scenes."[6] (The differences between Pound's and Jarrell's position toward a poem are more significant than the technical devices Jarrell may have learned from Pound. Perhaps the basic difference is the positioning of the reader that the poets demand; in Pound, since his "personae" are named and placed in history, the reader has no need to identify himself with the character; in Jarrell, the anonymity of the characters encourages the reader to enter into an emotional bond with them.)

The American poet who most clearly stands behind the poetry of Randall Jarrell is Frost, in spite of the many differences between the two men in background, temperament, and in the subject matter of their poems. It is the tone and his sense of structure that reflects Jarrell's precise knowledge of Frost's poetry. (Interestingly, there is no feeling of imitation of Frost anywhere in Jarrell—except once, perhaps, in the first part of **"A Country Life."**)

The most significant parallels between the work of these two poets need mentioning. There is, for example, the tone of the poems that lies in wait underneath the simple exterior (in Frost) and the clever one (in Jarrell). Jarrell pinned down this tone, or attitude, when he wrote about Frost's poems: ". . . many of these poems are extraordinarily subtle and strange, poems which express an attitude that, at its most extreme, makes pessimism seem a hopeful evasion; they begin with a flat and terrible reproduction of the evil in the world and end by saying: It's so; . . ."[7] Substitute Jarrell's poems for Frost's and leave out the emphasis on subtlety and there is an exact description of Jarrell's attitude in such a tense and dramatic monologue as **"In the Ward: The Sacred Wood."** The speaker in this poem is a wounded man who has "lain so long" in the ward. His thoughts, as he contemplates the crèche he has cut from paper, carry him from innocence to death. The sick man thinks of the paper trees as rising ". . . to me from the world / That made me, I call to the grove / That stretches inch on inch without one God: / 'I have unmade you, now; but I must die.'"

The secret of Jarrell's control of such complex material reflects again what he shares with Frost—his sense of the spoken poem in the rhythm of American speech. Neither poet is heard unless he is heard aloud. With both poets the listener can know the poem and a good deal of its subtlety (with Frost) or complexity (with Jarrell) by *hearing* it. The techniques involved include a firm control of rhythm and a playwright's ear for speech patterns.

At least one other poet left his mark on Jarrell's best poetry as much as did Frost, but differently. Rainer Marie Rilke was, in many respects, nearly the opposite of the poet Robert Frost. Both were, of course, completely devoted to the demands of poetry and both were master craftsmen. The mark of these poets is on Jarrell's work, but Frost's mark is blended into the whole of Jarrell's technique whereas Rilke's usually is still

Rilke. Several of Jarrell's very fine poems sound more like Rilke than Jarrell; an outstanding example is **"La Belle au Bois Dormant."** It is not imitative—too much of the unique Jarrell is in it—but it is an attack on a theme in the manner of Rilke, and the imagery and the rhetoric could sometimes be mistaken for translations from Rilke's poetry.

Rilke's approach is comparable to photographic stills (or more accurately to "expressionistic" portraits) whereas Frost's is cinematic. Although Jarrell captured for his own the method of presenting movement, he often is like a fluent user of a language not his own when he presents stills. Nevertheless, **"La Belle au Bois Dormant"** is a perfect poem. It opens with a startling and bare image: "She lies, her head beneath her knees, / In their old trunk . . ." This is, after a few lines, transformed into the Rilkean expressionism of, ". . . she coils breathlessly / Inside his wish and is not waked." The third stanza is pure symbolic imagery:

> Yet where is the hunter black enough to storm
> Her opening limbs, or shudder like a fish
> Into the severed maelstrom of her skull?
> The blood fondles her outrageous mouth;
> The lives flourish in her life, to alienate
> Their provinces from her outranging smile.

If this is not great poetry, it is only because we may hear too clearly echoes of another poet.

Like Rilke, Jarrell seldom writes (in his poems before 1955) about relations among people as individuals or as members of a social order. It is significant, too, that certain abstractions which have traditionally concerned poets do not often appear directly in Jarrell's work; for example, "sin," "beauty," "love" (romantic, sexual or religious on the adult level) are not Jarrellian subjects. These concepts are present only as masks for other things and the unmasking and the resultant terror is the true subject. Jarrell's purpose appears to be to project his understanding of what awful things man must know about himself to live with himself. This, in turn, suggests his method and themes: at any point at which he, or we, can penetrate the dark barrier of myth and dream to the submerged consciousness, we are closer to understanding. In those many fine poems in which only the attempt to penetrate is the whole poem—where not even shadowy answers are forthcoming, the *understanding* is still conveyed; that is, the failure and frustration in *trying* to understand are the concrete truths of the human condition that the poet is expressing.

No one does it better, partly because nobody has dared risk the deadly pitfalls: negativism, sentimentality, incompleteness, obscurity. To verbalize and formalize the confused terror of psychological reality, and then to "universalize" it, to apply it to an expanded knowledge of man's fate, is to set a task for himself as terrifying as the nightmare subject itself. That Jarrell often accomplished it in poems of clarity and a kind of overwhelming beauty has earned him his place in American poetry.

To approach an understanding of Jarrell's art, it is necessary to look at a whole poem. Not only one of the best, but also one of the most typical of all the major attributes of his craft is **"A Quilt Pattern,"** first published in 1950. It is not practical in this essay to give the whole poem nor to analyze it in depth, yet it may be possible to study a few of its significances. I quote the first eighteen lines:

> The blocked-out Tree
> Of the boy's Life is gray
> On the tangled quilt: the long day
> Dies at last, after many tales.
> Good me, bad me, the Other
> Black out, and the humming stare
> Of the woman—the good mother—
> Drifts away; the boy falls
> Through darkness, the leagues of space
> Into the oldest tale of all.
>
> All the graves of the forest
> Are opened, the scaling face
> Of a woman—the dead mother—
> Is square in the steam of a yard
> Where the cages are warmed all night for the rabbits,
> All small furry things
> That are hurt, but that never cry at all—
> That are skinned, but that never die at all.

The dramatic situation is immediate and clear: A sick boy is lying in bed covered by a quilt, which has on it, ironically and symbolically, the "Tree of Life" pattern. The boy is weary of hearing stories read to him and sinks into a dream. Here, then, is Jarrell's basic setting; a concrete and familiar world, but a painful and negative one (in this poem it is illness—often it is war, or simply bewildered childhood). The psychoanalytical apparatus of the dream takes over with the fusing of personalities, with the blacks and whites of good and bad, and with the drifting of characters. But this is no clinical process, for the terms are still the child's and the individual dream becomes the collective nightmare—"the oldest tale of all."

In the opening of the second stanza, we are in the forest of Grimm. From this point, the Hansel and Gretel drama of terror and the boy's dream life merge into a new drama in an old setting. The rhetoric and the "things," the symbols, are unmistakably Jarrell's: "All small furry things / That are hurt, but that never cry at all—/ That are skinned, but that never die at all."

The reader is never allowed to lose the boy's point of view. The third stanza begins:

> Here a thousand stones
> Of the trail home shine from their strings

> Like just-brushed, just-lost teeth.
> All the birds of the forest
> Sit brooding, stuffed with crumbs.

There is no adult, stilted abstracting here! Yet, yet (to use a Jarrellian rhetoric) there is; for the Freudian allusion is unmistakable: the vision of stones (the crumbs of the fairy tale) as "like just-brushed, just-lost teeth" has to suggest a weakening bond to his mother ("the dead mother"), for brushing teeth is an act of submission for a boy and when he loses them he is almost a man, a rival to his father. The symbolic imagery even expands from there, for the birds have eaten the crumbs-stones-teeth and childhood is irretrievable. Yet, through the license of the dream and the availability of the myth's symbols, the rhetoric is as "easy as pie," which to Jarrell's everlasting credit, it always is in his poems.

The rest of the poem can be read in the same multiple story fashion, although the distorted forms of the dream become more intense and closer to the moment of no escape from terror: "His whole dream swells with the steam of the oven / Till it whispers, 'You are full now, mouse.'" Characteristically—for the poet, for the poem, for dreams and for märchen—there is a metamorphosis, which is the escape mechanism:

> If something is screaming itself to death
> There in the oven, it is not the mouse
> Nor anything of the mouse's. Bad me, good me
> Stare into each other's eyes, and timidly
> Smile at each other: it was the Other.

The scapegoat ("it was the Other") of the collective unconscious has appeared. But in all of those poems of Jarrell's where suffering is thwarted by the scapegoat of the myth or dream, we are not allowed to partake of the redemption, for we awake into the pain of necessity: the poem ends—

> But they are waking, waking; the last stair creaks—
> Out there on the other side of the door
> The house creaks, "How is my little mouse? Awake?"
> It is she.
> He says to himself, "I will never wake."
> He says to himself, not breathing:
> "Go away. Go away. Go away."
>
> And the footsteps go away.

One hates to end on this solemn and psychoanalytical note, for this mid-twentieth-century American poet who dared to be emotional was neither solemn nor doctrinaire in his poems. He was, however, fully involved in his art and thus was deeply serious toward every poem, even those with a quantity of fun in them. Jarrell was also a gifted critic of the poetry of his contemporaries. Like many poets who also write criticism, he apparently lacked that fine perspective on himself that he could take toward, among others, John Ransom, Wallace Stevens, Marianne Moore and, particularly, Frost, but not usually toward Robert Lowell, to whom, perhaps, he stood too close. I say "apparently lacked" above, because I do not know whether Jarrell also thought his best poetry was, with possibly two or three later poems excepted, those published in the mid- and late forties and early fifties.

In an essay on Wallace Stevens, in that precise language he was so capable of, Jarrell wrote of the special existential predicament of the poet: ". . . it is (necessary) to think of the poet as somebody who has prepared himself to be visited by a daemon, as a sort of accident-prone worker to whom poems happen—for otherwise we *expect* him to go on writing good poems, better poems, and this is the one thing you cannot expect even of good poets. . . . A man who is a good poet at forty *may* turn out to be a good poet at sixty; but he is more likely to have stopped writing poems. . . . A good poet is someone who manages, in a lifetime of standing out in thunderstorms, to be struck by lightning five or six times; a dozen or two dozen times and he is great."[8] Jarrell was struck by lightning a number of times, whether eight, twelve or fourteen will be determined by readers henceforward, and since the purpose of this essay is to state the writer's conviction that Jarrell was so struck, he would like to name some of those points at which he is quite sure it happened. The poems that are the works of, at the very least, an exceedingly good poet are: **"Lady Bates," "Seele im Raum," "A Quilt Pattern," "In the Ward: The Sacred Wood," "The Orient Express," "A Game at Salzburg," "The Sleeping Beauty: Variation of the Prince," "The Carnegie Library, Juvenile Division," "Eighth Air Force," "Burning the Letters," "A Front,"** the late poem **"The Lost World"** and large sections of **"A Conversation with the Devil."**

In **"A Conversation with the Devil"** the poet comes closest—in his verse—to presenting the basis of his contract with readers:

> Indulgent, or candid, or uncommon reader
> —I've some: a wife, a nun, a ghost or two—
> If I write for anyone, I wrote for you;
> So whisper, when I die, *We was too few*;
> Write over me (if you can write; I hardly knew)
> That I—that I—but anything will do,
> I'm satisfied . . . And yet—
>   and yet, you *were* too few:

Perhaps we have taken the agreement too literally (and he hardly knew), but Jarrell *did* write for us, and we will not assume that "anything will do."

Notes

1. According to that admirable evangelist of contemporary poetry, J. Isaacs.

2. For example, Miss Babette Deutsch wrote 449 pages about *Poetry in Our Time* (in the second edition of 1962), but devoted exactly one paragraph of less than a page to Jarrell's poetry.

3. This gap in recorded history has been filled to a modest extent by a memorial volume published as this essay is being drafted: *Randall Jarrell 1914-1965* (Farrar, Straus & Giroux). Editors Robert Lowell, Peter Taylor and Robert Penn Warren have given us a bright and sad collection of essays and reminiscences mostly by Jarrell's colleagues and friends. With only a few exceptions, these pieces—even the most moving and readable ones—do little to secure Jarrell's rank as a poet. The occasion of the volume was one for praise and regret, and the implied protest in many of the essays that Jarrell's poetry had heightened in quality in the years after the *Selected Poems* of 1955 will not, I believe, be convincing under more objective consideration. Among the exceptions mentioned are the very fine essays by Sister M. Bernetta Quinn, O. S. F., and Karl Shapiro, and the last part of Robert Watson's, which is excellent.

4. An excellent bibliography was prepared by Charles M. Adams and published in that year (*Randall Jarrell, A Bibliography,* Chapel Hill, the University of North Carolina Press).

5. Jarrell's mastery of dramatic techniques in poems is rivalled only by two or three twentieth-century poets. It is no accident that Jarrell wrote penetrating appreciations of Robert Frost's poetry and almost single-handedly placed that poet's work in the proper perspective, for Jarrell not only gave us the best analysis of Frost's confrontation with reality but also explained the power of his dramatic technique.

6. "Answers to Questions," *Mid-Century American Poets,* ed. John Ciardi (New York, Twayne Publishers, Inc. 1950).

7. "The Other Robert Frost," *Nation* (Nov. 29, 1947), 590-592.

8. *Poetry and the Age* (New York: Vintage Books, 1955) p. 134.

Robert Weisberg (essay date summer 1973)

SOURCE: Weisberg, Robert. "Randall Jarrell: The Integrity of His Poetry." *Centennial Review* 17, no. 3 (summer 1973): 237-55.

[*In the following essay, Weisberg focuses on what he describes as "the two Jarrell's": "the congenial, readable poet, and the dark, obsessive poet." Weisberg contends that the former can be seen in Jarrell's later poetry, where the poet addressed "mundane" subjects, while the latter is reflected in the poems of childhood.*]

I

Karl Shapiro wrote a rhapsodic and often beautiful eulogy for Jarrell in which he praises him in explicit comparison to Robert Lowell.[1] Shapiro denigrates Lowell for being too vain and ambitious in his poetry, too concerned with making himself a major poet and thereby twisting and forcing experience to fit his monumental designs. Jarrell's poetry is lauded for its modesty before experience, for humbly accommodating itself to the common world. And certainly Shapiro, despite his idiosyncratic antipathy to Lowell, rightly characterizes at least part of Jarrell the poet. For Jarrell, and this most noticeably in his later poetry, was so in love with the world as it simply appeared to him that he always wrote on the brink of banality. Who but Jarrell would write a poem to a professional football player? Here is part of his offering on the death of Gene "Big Daddy" Lipscomb of the Baltimore Colts:

> Big Daddy, who found football easy enough, life hard
>   enough
> To—after his last night cruising Baltimore
> In his yellow Cadillac—to die of heroin;
> Big Daddy, who was scared, he said: "I've been scared
> Most of my life. You wouldn't think so to look at me.
> It gets so bad I cry myself to sleep—" his size
> Embarrassed him, so that he was always helped by
>   smaller
>   men,
> And hurt by smaller men; Big Daddy Lipscomb
> Has helped to his feet the last ball carrier, Death.[2]
>
> [*The Complete Poems*]

So much of Jarrell is revealed in this little passage—the interest in mundane things like American football, the loose, conversational verse, the unfortunate triteness of the last line. But Jarrell was always concluding poems with lines like "Life, well, is life." He called one section of his *Selected Poems* "The World is Everything That is the Case," and his own "Life Studies" in *The Lost World* seem so mild and artless next to Lowell's.

This quality of acceptance in Jarrell became most apparent after the war. Like most of the bright young poets of his generation, when he started writing in the late thirties he was excessively influenced by certain modernist models, especially, of course, Auden and Ransom and Tate. He wrote heavily ironic poems about war and politics, bitter and pessimistic poems that often reflected the harsh formality of *Lord Weary's Castle*. And still Jarrell wrote some of his best poems about the war. But even more than others of his generation, Jarrell relaxed in the nineteen-fifties, acted more like what seemed to be his natural self, something of a dilettante, fond of opera and German mythology, and if not a lover certainly not a hater of the America that many poets thought complacent and materialistic. He wrote witty but sympathetic satire on American character types, like "A Girl in a Library." All this adds up to a poet of congenial personality, appealing, very readable, rarely obscure, a poet, in fact, usually in good possession of his material, but almost never possessed by it, never really powerful or verbally or psychologically exciting.

Which of course is only half of Jarrell. For throughout his career one subject did possess him—even haunt him: childhood. This may surprise readers of his light and charming poems for and about children. But I refer here to an interest in childhood in terms of an absolutely obsessive need to return to an almost psychoanalytic figure of the infantile and pre-infantile human state. And I believe that the two Jarrell's, the congenial, readable poet, and the dark, obsessive poet, are not ultimately separable, but are two sides of a man whose writing, for all its apparent looseness and dilettantism, achieved a subtle but real unity.

The obsessive womb image is of course apparent in the war poem that probably remains his most famous, the one poem known to people who know nothing else of Jarrell:

> From my mother's sleep, I fell into the State,
> And I hunched in its belly till my wet fur froze.
> Six miles from earth, loosed from its dream of life,
> I woke to black flak and the nightmare fighters.
> When I died they washed me out of the turret with a hose.

"The Death of the Ball-Turret Gunner" was and is a feast for New Criticism. The moment of death for the gunner is the moment of a new birth. His life is seen as a pre-natal sleep and then a kind of death-in-life. The airplane is his mother and also the cold machinery of the political state: almost endless permutations of states of being appear. But the important thing is that the usually un-visionary Jarrell creates a truly timeless vision, an ultimate figure of modern man, a stillborn fetus, although the emphasis is not on its death but on the flash of revelation at the split second before death. And what is revealed for modern man is the infantile core of his life, the child that is father to him.

Jarrell revered Wordsworth and in a way shares Wordsworth's basic quest—to isolate the child within the man—or woman. And here we can begin to grasp the unity of Jarrell's disparate poetic interests. His light poems about the mundane things of life show Jarrell writing "childishly"—he would have seen this as a compliment. That is, once he recovered from the bitter and almost life-reviling ironies of his early poetry, he strove to see the world through the believing eyes of a child.

A child has no consciousness of his own consciousness. He believes the world to be just what it appears to be. This is the faith Jarrell sought in his poetry, and indeed it is virtually religious, since its goal is the discovery of absolute truth. Jarrell places no limits on the validity of human perception or imagination—the point is to believe in the fundamental reality of everything one senses, thinks, imagines, or dreams. It is almost a kind of mental polymorphous perversity—only the neurotic adult mind presumes a hidden dimension beyond its perceptions and the consequent falsehood of those perceptions. All Jarrell wanted was to be at peace with the world, and this peace required this undoubting fundamental belief; and so, ironically, the ideal world for Jarrell is one-dimensional. The mere existence of anything or anyone is reason enough to accept it. Even the satire on the girl in the library turns to affection at the end; unrelenting satire contradicts the childish belief.

This belief, of course, means that Jarrell's imagination does not work vast upheavals on the emotional or psychological or natural phenomena he perceives—presumably Shapiro meant this, and meant it as a virtue. Rather, for Jarrell imagination is a matter of the poet almost passively making himself susceptible to the changes that dream and fantasy work on whatever the senses record. Hence his interest in metamorphosis, and the dreamy poems like **"The Black Swan,"** in which the poet indulges in the fluidity of reality—the world is *everything* that is the case—the fictions as well as the facts. Coleridge might have objected, "That's not imagination, that's only fancy!" True, but that is Jarrell. He always lacked, as Shapiro implies correctly, the imaginative aggressiveness to create grand designs. But we have to appreciate the poetry for what it is, not for what it never was.

II

The "charming, readable" Jarrell, the daylight Jarrell, comes out, therefore, when the conventional child within him speaks and believes and enjoys what he sees about the world. But then there is the darker, more profound poet, who cannot rest at the daylight level of perception, but must delve farther into himself to discover, let us say, the meta-child within the man. Certainly **"The Death of the Ball-Turret Gunner"** is Jarrell's first real glimpse of, or more rightly through, this meta-child, but I think his most interesting penetrations occur in the later poetry. A virtual gloss on this poetry is the aptly titled "The Grown Up," perhaps Jarrell's finest translation—from Rilke. It appears in the 1960 volume, ***The Woman at the Washington Zoo.***

> All this stood on her and was the world
> And stood on her with all things, Pain and Grace,
> As trees stand, growing and erect, all image
> And imageless as the ark of the Lord God,
> And solemn, as if set upon a State.

> And she bore it; bore, somehow, the weight
> Of the flying, fleeting, far-away,
> The monstrous and the still-unmastered,
> Unmoved, serene as the water-bearer
> Stands under a full-jar. Till in the midst of play,
> Transfiguring, preparing for the Other,
> The first white veil fell smoothly, softly,
>
> Over her opened face, almost opaque,
> Never to raise itself again, and giving somehow
> To all her questions one vague answer:
> In thee, thou once a child, in thee.

The "all" is a wonderfully ambiguous word for "grown-up" experience, which she bears like a rock of dignity. Then in the "midst of play" (the "mist" of play?), play as childlike pleasure and therefore a sense of unity and peace, the "first white veil" falls, a kind of divine filter or lens of the childhood imagination. The poem, then, describes the spiritual strength of the adult in enduring the pain of conscious existence, a strength which becomes a more apparent ideal in later poems. And the grown-up achieves salvation, or better yet epiphany, through the blossoming of the child within her. Epiphany for Jarrell is the return of the childhood perspective.

I believe that Jarrell's best poems are epiphanies in this sense, though the concept must be kept very broad to include poems that without this unifying principle may seem together a hodgepodge of many different kinds of writing. And I further believe that Jarrell's deepest, most mature poetry comes in his last book, where more clearly than anywhere else, the two Jarrell's meet. The creator of the often fragmentary and formally weak poems of childhood from **The Seven-League Crutches,** the creator of light fairy tale poems, dense and obscure mythic poems, the Freudian dilettante, and the witty and sympathetic observer of **"A Girl in a Library,"** all the many Jarrell's, in fact, merge in **"The Lost World,"** not into any one kind of poem, since this book is as varied as any other, but into an overall confidence and control and depth. We have to examine a few of the major poems in this last book to demonstrate this exhilarating synthesis.

Part of his late success is stylistic, and Jarrell in this last book can be now prosaic and now write *terza rima*, but as **"A Well-to-do Invalid"** demonstrates, either way he is far more in control of his material than ever before. The poem at first glance looks like one of his talkative, prosaic "character poems," but it turns out to be a powerful statement of his central theme, powerful especially because the seemingly slack verse is underlined by its embittered and fully controlled irony. The chief character, one of several frustrated adult characters who have lost all their vitality, is the wife of the invalid friend whom the poet addresses, having observed how the woman has subtly destroyed herself:

> You are a natural
> Disaster she has made her own. Meanly
> Clinging to you, taking care—all praise
> And understanding outside, and inside all insurance—
> She has stood by you like a plaster Joan of Arc.
> Prematurely tired, prematurely
> Mature, she has endured
> Much, indulgently
> Repeating like a piece of white carbon paper
> The opinions of that boisterous, sick thing, a man.
> I can see through her, but then, who can't?
> Her dishonesty is so transparent
> It has about it a kind of honesty.
> She has never once said what she thought, done what
>   she wanted
> But (as if invented by some old economist
> And put on an island, to trade with her mate)
> Has acted in impersonal self-interest.
>
> Never to do one thing for its own sake!

The woman has wasted her life because she has never experienced the world for its own sake, never simply believed in her own actions or thoughts, never been unconscious of motive. She has "matured" in the worst sense, by destroying the child within her. The surety of tone in the poem indicates, I think, that Jarrell has made this "loose" style his own very distinctive style. Indeed the poem is almost harrowing in the coolness of its statement, though the awfulness of it blends with compassion at the end:

> It was a terrible shock to me when she died.
> I saw her cheeks red for the first time
> Among the snowdrifts covering her coffin;
> And you were up and talking, well with grief.
> As I realized how easily you'd fill
> This vacancy, I was sorry
> For you and for that pale self-sufficient ghost
> That had tended so long your self-sufficiency.

The first line ironically implies his surprise at her ever having lived, like Fredric Henry at the end of *A Farewell to Arms* "kissing a statue." And the "vacancy" is both her absence and her life itself. The woman seems to die just as her husband gets well, as if she had no inner core of life, and so the final irony and despair of this poem are wholly unrelieved. And they continue through several other poems in this book, other "character" poems, many of them dramatic monologs. I do not think Jarrell is a very successful dramatic poet. I do not even think that the monologs, like the earlier **"The Woman at the Washington Zoo,"** achieve convincing and individuated voices. Rather Jarrell's character poems are mood-pieces, and variations on themes of frustrated sexuality and bourgeois malaise, themes that devolve back into the basic theme of the smothered child within the adult. As such, these poems can become, not monotonous, but repetitive; each new situation is touching or interesting in its own way, but Jarrell can go only the same distance with one after the other. Jarrell now demands of himself the deeper "penetrations" I spoke of before, and he achieves this depth in a handful of last poems, first, because he finally confronted the truths of his personal past, and second, because after earlier obscure and fragmentary efforts, he was able to probe farther and more lucidly into the almost mythical mysteries of psychic life.

In another "character" poem, **"The One Who Was Different,"** Jarrell recalls the face of a dead woman and asks:

> Is a smile like life,
> A way things look for a while,
> A temporary arrangement of the matter?
>
> I feel like the first men who read Wordsworth.
> It's so simple I can't understand it.

I find this passage a perfect epigraph for the long autobiographical poem **"The Lost World,"** not just because it summarizes the basic theme of simplicity and unity beyond intellectual comprehension, but because that one phrase, "a temporary arrangement of the matter," defines so nicely the structure of the whole poem. For the poem is not so much a recollection as a re-enactment of his childhood, and the childhood is perceived not as a secure but distant paradise, but a fragile and inspired condition, a "temporary arrangement," and yet at the same time a glimpse of something divine. In a way, then, the phrase links Jarrell with Stevens, who also chose to be content with the transient patterns he acknowledged as the only knowable order in the universe of his sensations and experience. But again Jarrell is really a more religious poet, in that this temporary arrangement is still a reflection of a divine order, a peace and unity, that the adult is alien to.

The poem of course deals with Jarrell's life in Los Angeles, near Hollywood, when he was a young boy. The brilliant opening epitomizes the poem because it captures the subtle frailty of the arrangement.

> On my way home I pass a cameraman
> On a platform on the bumper of a car
> Inside which, rolling and plunging, a comedian
> Is working; on one white lot I see a star
> Stumble to her igloo through the howling gale
>
> Of the wind machines. On Melrose a dinosaur
> And pterodactyl, with their immense pale
> Papier-mâché smiles, look over the fence
> Of *The Lost World*.

The inescapable fact is that Hollywood is false and artificial, a place where dreams are packaged for sale. But the passage shows how the reconstructed childhood mind can move so easily, so unselfconsciously, so unbitterly, between artificial illusions and reality. The dinosaurs are artificial but still cherished fantasies, and look with the boy over the fence that protects them like the catcher in the rye out over a dreamless adult world. The boy simply believes all he sees. Jarrell's technical skill is vital here, as deft juxtaposition of phrases reflect how the boy acknowledges and even embraces the falsity. The star in line 4 is a real star for a moment's linebreak hesitation and then becomes a clumsy movie star in a laughable but not derisory turn of image. So in the next line we have a real howling gale until the line after proves it machine-made. No irony: we constantly oscillate between artifice and reality, and this tenuous stance is central to the poem. And so "Melrose" is casually linked with "dinosaur," for only in the lost world of childhood can such things meet without clash. The comedian is depicted in raucous action, at once comic and yet an act of "working." Here we have another aspect of the central theme, the merging of work and play, the substitution of one for the other. Adult "play" is painful work. A child's "work" is delightful play.

The chief element I have so far overlooked is, of course, the *terza rima*. Apparently Jarrell, Frost's most avid admirer and incisive critic, has decided to play tennis with the net this time, and much of the poem scans like *North of Boston*, the flow of the apparently casual speech encountering the regular iambic pattern and rhyme scheme to mirror the tension in the poet's mind between illusion and reality. The tight interlocking of end-rhymes, enhanced by plenty of internal rhyme, modulated by phase-breaking line-length, gives the poem great vigor precisely where it might have lapsed into sentimentality:

> O dead list, that misunderstands
> And laughs at and lies about the new live wild
> Loves it lists! that sets upright in the sands
> Of age in which nothing grows, where all our friends
>   are old,
> A few dried leaves marked THIS IS THE GREEN-
>   WOOD—
> O arms that arm, for a child's war, the child!

The tight rhyming, the assonance that connects to the end-rhymes, makes the passage humorous and even mock-heroic.

A finer distinction has to be made about the structure of the poem. John Crowe Ransom complains of the over-intelligence and cultivation of the child's mind.[3] But there is *recollection* in the poem, in the usual sense of the word, as well as *re-enactment*. Jarrell recollects or remembers when the adult mind overtly shapes or evaluates the childhood experience. But most of the recollections in the poem serve to frame the re-enactments, the central visions of the fragile, temporary arrangements of the child's world. We have, then, spots of time within spots of time, and the poem drifts between these two elements, always swelling to the point of reenactment when the child-father is isolated. Most of the events of the poem are the rituals of childhood, the daily customs that "habit itself makes holy," the reassuring patterns in the boy's life that acquire religious significance. The obvious rituals are meals and good-night embraces, but a more complex ritual becomes the climax of the poem. The boy's grandmother, the "Mama" of the poem, sacrifices a chicken for supper, and for a moment the chicken's headless body reels around in mad circles, and the boy's world is threatened by his fear that his pet rabbit will also be sacrificed. The boy is finally reassured, not by words of reassurance, but by a gradual restoration of the daily ritual, a restoration of the "temporary arrangement," signalled by Pop's return from work:

> My universe
> Mended almost, I tell him about the scientist. I say,
> He couldn't really, could he, Pop? My comforter's
> Eyes light up, and he laughs. "No, that's just play,
> Just make-believe," he says. The sky is gray.
> We sit there at the end of our good day.

The chicken incident recalls another nagging threat—a story he has heard about a scientist's plan to blow up the world. Pop assures him, but the adult's dismissal of anything make-believe ironically reveals his own limitations to the boy—the one sure thing in the poem is the very blurry line between reality and "make-believe." Only a temporary and fragile security is achieved under gray skies. But still the poem ends in a rhythmic peace, for the temporary, threatened pattern is as much as the poet can or will find, and though adult despair is omened, there is consolation in the simple, if transient, existence of such a holy order in the boy's life.

III

"The Lost World" is not the only "arrangement" in the book, and the others are not so homely. Probably the two most striking poems in the book—**"A Hunt in the Black Forest"** and **"The House in the Wood"**—deal with much darker psychological mysteries. They may superficially resemble the "mythic" poems of earlier years, poems like **"The Märchen"** that seemed too dislocated, too subjective, too lacking in context. But if seen as expressions of this final thrust towards epiphany, they stand as the apex of the, let us say, "darker" Jarrell; they are the two poems in which he is most impressively "possessed."

Like **"The Lost World," "A Hunt"** is a projection of the childhood imagination, but it is a concentrated nightmare rather than a sensitive re-enactment, and in its lucid, chiseled language, a great advance on earlier dream poems. A young boy enters the threatening forest of his mind as his mother leaves his bedroom:

> The wind roars in the leaves: his cold hands, curled
> Within his curled, cold body, his blurred head
> Are warmed and tremble; and the red leaves flow
> Like cells across the spectral, veined,
> Whorled darkness of his vision.

The child feels as if dead and cold and yet curled like a fetus—we return once more to the quintessential simultaneity of **"The Death of the Ball Turret Gunner."** The almost ritualized return to this condition is prolog to the strange and frightening story that makes up the rest of the poem, a story more comprehensible by the senses than the interpretive mind:

> A horn calls, over and over, its three notes.
> The flat, gasped answer sounds and dies—
> The geese call from a hidden sky.
> The rain's sound grows into the roar
> Of the flood below the falls; the rider calls
> To the shape within the shades, a dwarf
> Runs back into the brush.

Among the threatening and enchanting noises are the three characters—a dwarf, a hunter-king, and a mute. The hunter's horse follows a scent of smoke into a hut inhabited by a friendly, frenetic, tongueless mute. The mute shows a crown branded on his shoulder, as if he in some way represented the destiny of the king. The hunter-king questions the mute, then eats the stew as the mute scuttles away. The hunter-king immediately suffers a weird paroxysm:

> . . . and something catches at his heart,
> Some patient, senseless thing
> Begins to squeeze his heart out in its hands.
> His jerking body, bent into a bow,
> Falls out of the hands onto the table
> Bends, bends further, till at last it breaks.
> But, broken, it still breathes—a few whistling breaths
> That slow, are intermittent, cease.

This metamorphic death is rendered in gracefully musical syllable:

> Now only the fire thinks, like a heart
> Cut from the breast. Light leaps, the shadows fall
> In the old alternation of the world . . .

The morning star brings the end of the dream, and we are left to consider the simple fire that remains. The bubbling pot is overturned a pile of ashes, and as the poem ends the mute and dwarf jostle each other for a look back into the child's window, the eye of the dreamer:

> The pane is clouded with their soft, slow breaths,
> The mute's arms tire; but they gaze on and on,
> Like children watching something wrong.
> Their blurred faces, caught up in one wish,
> Are blurred into one face: a child's set face.

They stare at him and he must stare at them in self-reflection, for he is dreaming of what he really is. That is the point of this poem, though it leaves almost everything to explain. Jarrell has moved beyond conventional memory and reverie to a confrontation between child and the meta-child within him, and the child's mysterious dream therefore stands together with the vision of the ball-turret gunner. The difficulty of course lies with the mythic material of the dream.

Several Germanic folk myths involving king-hunters are likely sources for the poem. One has the king-hunter, the quester, ensnared and killed by an ogre; another has the disguised king aided or fed by the humble peasant who is rewarded by his unmasked guest. Jarrell, in apparently synthesizing at least two stories, makes a parable of the quest into one's past and one's psychic core of dreams and fears, a quest resulting in an unmasking, a self-discovery, The self, oddly enough, is transmuted here only into the vision of the quest, and finally into the face of the real quester—the child—as if the answer to the identity question were circular—"thee, thou once a child, thee." As such the poem seems ultimately perplexing. The problem, I think, is that the reader almost unconsciously senses near the end that the poem has been a kind of allegory of psychoanalysis. This it certainly is, but it is not a coherent drama of the process of analysis. Rather it is chiefly an impressionistic poem illuminating the sensations of self-discovery as a quest after an inner mystery. The king-hunter of course can be the ego that meets the id in the babbling, manic mute and undergoes a ritual death in the encounter, presumably to be reborn. But the poem does not depict the substance of the discovery. Rather, it expresses its emotional effect, the way it feels to undergo this quest. The parable is fairly ambiguous because it expresses the irrational mystery of the quest, depicts what it feels like to encounter something one's intellect cannot grasp alone. Another critic might object that deliberate ambiguity or obscurity is a fault in the poem, but I think the reader is too absorbed in the excitement of a poet on the verge of a great self-discovery to be bothered by this. Jarrell is out to find the uncontrollable mystery of his bestial floor, and **"A Hunt in the Black Forest"** is one of his best reconnaissance missions.

Again, Jarrell's solutions to the question of man's ultimate identity are imagistic rather than logical. The vision of the ball-turret gunner and the gaze of the child's set face and even the tenuous picture of the lost world are variant images, variant answers to the question. Jarrell asks it again in **"The House in the Wood,"** another childhood dream of self-confrontation, and another imagistic answer. Jarrell tries a new verse form here—he did so many things so well in this last book—a series of unrhymed couplets of regular iambic feet. We are in the woods as always, but the poet says that the woods are seasonal; the "summer" woods are of the daylight world, and represent the daylight imagination:

> At the back of the house there is the wood.
> While there is a leaf of summer left, the wood
>
> Makes sounds I can put somewhere in my song,

> Has paths I can walk, when I wake, to good
>
> Or evil;

But then:

> . . . after the last leaf
> The last light—for each year is leafless,
>
> Each day lightless, at the last—the wood begins
> Its serious existence: it has no path,
>
> No house, no story; it resists comparison . . .

In the summer-daylight the poet, the "readable" Jarrell, easily converts his sensations and experience into poetry, but at night, the time of "serious existence," he must deal with the difficult truths. The poet-child-dreamer continues the again-repeated quest, passing a brook of "fouled" water, and reaches the mystery again, here encased in the House in the Wood and seen as "something covered, something humped / Asleep there, awake there—but what? I do not know?" The turret-gunner is obviously revived in this mysterious fetal hump. "Time has struck, / All the clocks are stuck now." "Numbed, wooden, motionless, / We are far under the surface of the night." And then the beautifully restrained ending, probably the most powerful image-answer yet:

> Then someone screams
> A scream like an old knife sharpened into nothing.
>
> It is only a nightmare. No one wakes up, nothing happens,
> Except there is gooseflesh over my whole body—
>
> And that too, after a little while, is gone.
> I lie here, like a cut-off limb, the stump the limb has left . . .
>
> Here at the bottom of the world, what was before the world
> And will be after, holds me to its black
>
> Breasts and rocks me: the oven is cold, the cage is empty,
> In the House in the Wood, the witch and her child sleep

The quest is again a painful ritual death and birth, an agonizing shucking off of the daylight world, passing into a postpartum calm. The whole pattern of the ball-turret gunner is repeated here. The witch is the forest and the mother and the state and the World War II bomber—the image of the humped body embraced by a demonic mother recapitulates all the psychic insights of Jarrell's poetry. The end is calm, and yet also cold, like the ashes of **"A Hunt"** [**"A Hunt in the Black Forest"**] and the hose water that washes out the dead gunner. The core of the man here, the meta-child, is a preconscious creature and yet again a still-born fetus, stillborn because it cannot survive in the self-conscious adult world. The paradise Jarrell reaches for is really a terrifying thing because it contains feelings the sentimentalist of childhood cannot imagine, and because it shows life to be an abortion. **"A House in the Wood"** is in its own way an allegory of psychoanalysis, but still essentially a tactile and imagistic poem about a great mystery that Jarrell does not rhapsodize or analyze, but approach and recognize.

In the volume's last poem, **"Thinking of the Lost World,"** Jarrell comes up for air—the polluted air of the new Los Angeles. He returns to the daylight world, and writes like the first Jarrell, the readable, conversational poet who wants to make peace with the world. But now he has glimpsed the darker side of things, and he will have to make peace with the daylight and the night world. This is a poem that tries to tether the lost connections, to reconcile the deeper epiphanies: it is aptly titled, because it is an evaluation, an adult perspective, not a re-enactment. And yet, like the two previous poems, its conclusion is really imagistic. Like them, it is orchestrated toward a final focus on an image of the child within the man.

The poem is of course about loss, but puzzled and bemused, rather than anguished loss.

> . . . I have already traveled
> Through time to my childhood. It puzzles me
> That age is like it.
>
> Come back to that calm country
> Through which the stream of my life first meandered,
> My wife, our cat, and I sit here and see
> Squirrels quarrelling in the feeder, a mockingbird
> Copying our chipmunk, as our end copies
> Its beginning.

Age has found a secure domestic unit to replace the lost family; the lost values endure. Yet the real loss is undeniable.

> Back in Los Angeles, we missed
> Los Angeles. The sunshine of the Land
> Of Sunshine is gray mist now, the atmosphere
> Of some factory planet;

Los Angeles, like the poet, is and is not the same thing it was. We then get a series of affectionate memories:

> *Twenty Years After,* thirty-five years after,
> Is as good as ever—better than ever,
> Now that D'Artagnan is no longer old—
> Except that it is unbelievable.
> I say to my old self: "I believe. Help thou
> Mine unbelief."

He longs for the faith in the things of this world that defines the childhood and creativity and salvation, and this poem's focal image becomes the "old self." It is envisioned in the intense, packed, distilled passage that seems, in relation to his career, as useful a poetic conclusion as "Under Ben Bulben" and as moving a poet's self-elegy as Crane's "The Broken Tower."

> I wave back. When my hand drops to the wheel,
> It is brown and spotted, and its nails are ridged
> Like Mama's. Where's my own hand? My smooth
> White-bitten-fingernailed one? I seem to see
> A shape in tennis shoes and khaki riding pants
> Standing there empty handed; I reach out to it
> Empty-handed, my hand comes back empty,
> And yet my emptiness is traded for its emptiness,
> I have found that Lost World in the Lost and Found
> Columns whose gray illegible advertisements
> My soul has memorized world after world:
> LOST—NOTHING. STRAYED FROM NOWHERE.
>   NO REWARD.
> I hold in my own hands, in happiness,
> Nothing: the nothing for which there's no reward.

Jarrell plays a complicated game with the crucial words "lost" and "empty" as if his life were a puzzle and his poetry a game he finally learned to play. He waves back to the old Los Angeles and to his old self, his former child-self, an empty-handed figure, and I suppose that the empty-handedness is related to the stump-like condition of the image in **"The House in the Wood."** Now all this seems a contradiction. If the salvation of a man is to find his meta-child, why is the old self empty-handed, offering nothing? Jarrell implies here that ultimately an adult must simply acknowledge his condition, that though he may glimpse the divine and terrifying child within him he can never return to that state—indeed that state, psychologically, is really anterior even to childhood. The child is closer to it, but still lost to it—recall the ominous ending of **"The Lost World."** And so Jarrell's vision at the end is toughened by his refusal to sentimentalize childhood as paradise. In poems like **"The Death of the Ball Turret Gunner"** and **"A House in the Wood"** Jarrell glimpses some absolute truth, some elemental fact, of his existence. That truth cannot be finally or completely expressed. "The Lost and Found Columns" are a brilliant figure for the poems in which he has searched for his identity "world after world" and which have turned up no easy answer. But Jarrell is still tougher, for he accepts the insoluble sense of loss and separation as a fact of adult life. Like Yeats in "A Dialogue of Self and Soul" he accepts all the futility. He even accepts Los Angeles, rejects bitterness towards modern America, as if he and it had aged together.

Jarrell, at his most mature, has come as close as poetry can bring him to salvation by at least clarifying the relationship between childhood and adulthood. The object of his life-long search is the terrifying mystery of the timeless condition from which he emerged and towards which he can reach only in death. Life for him is a sad state caught in between. But he makes a new beginning in this revelation that ends his poem.

Notes

1. Karl Shapiro, "The Death of Randall Jarrell," in *Randall Jarrell: 1914-1965,* Robert Lowell, Peter Taylor, and Robert Penn Warren, editors (Noonday Press: New York, 1967).

2. All poetry quotations are from Randall Jarrell, *The Complete Poems* (Farrar, Straus, and Giroux: New York, 1965).

3. John Crowe Ransom, "The Rugged Way of Genius," in *Randall Jarrell: 1914-1965*.

Russell Fowler (essay date spring 1974)

SOURCE: Fowler, Russell. "Randall Jarrell's 'Eland': A Key to Motive and Technique in His Poetry." *Iowa Review* 5, no. 2 (spring 1974): 113-26.

[*In the following essay, Fowler considers Jarrell's poems as specific answers to dilemmas of human existence, such as life, authority, war, power, conformity, and death.*]

The growing critical interest in the work of Randall Jarrell reveals two things: his reputation as one of the most perceptive and helpful literary critics of the last three decades continues to flourish, while his own poetry remains the center of intense controversy. Judgments of its overall value and place alongside the work of contemporaries like Robert Lowell and Theodore Roethke vary radically, and even his admirers seem unable to relate his poetry conclusively to any of the major critical or methodological "schools" of this century. For friend and foe alike he is the most "idiosyncratic" of modern poets, for the one consistent element in the diverse collection of strategies and subjects found in the poems from *The Rage for the Lost Penny* (1940) to *The Lost World* (1965) is an insistence on unfettered improvisation, an absolute refusal to be systematic or provide a theoretical or symbolic paradigm for his own work. This attitude is also clearly operative in his criticism, and, ironically, is chiefly responsible for its fresh and innovative approaches to writers like Whitman and Frost. Nothing like Stevens' "Supreme Fiction," Frost's characteristic idioms and landscapes, or Pound's consistent use of private sources is available to the reader of Jarrell, for the core of his work, the announced *purpose* for its existence, is emotional and quasi-mystical rather than theoretical or aesthetic.

What unifies the poems modeled after German Märchen and dreams, the dramatic monologues on war and supermarkets, and the tortuous, syntactically dense considerations of life and death in the "Modern Age" is the attitude behind them, the belief that they all provide specific answers for the same vague question and sponsor recognition (not necessarily understanding) of the human condition in its primal form. Necessary manifestations of this belief in the poetry are an ongoing, painfully sympathetic tone and an overt hostility toward absolute definition of any kind or "that traumatic passion for Authority, any Authority at all, that is one of the most unpleasant things in our particular time and our particular culture."[1] Once one recognizes the fundamental character of Jarrell's sensibility and its insistence that poetry function as a "location" where the effects of experience are most dramatically presented, the common purpose behind much of Jarrell's experimentation with the dramatic monologue and the vital presentation of scenes of childhood, warfare, and modern culture becomes clearer. His characteristic use of syntactically complex stanzas, heavy with apposition and qualification, his love of paradox and his "muscular identification with his subject matter" (a phrase Jarrell used to explain his special admiration for Rilke's lyrics), are all designed to show the "real and difficult face" of human experience *and* to promote sympathy for those who suffer its effects.

Many critics have either failed to recognize the importance of this emotional nexus or dismissed it as sentimental and self-indulgent. The latter is an easy judgment often applied to the work of recent poets, but it is particularly damaging to Jarrell's since the intensity of tone and underlying plea for emotional recognition are not simply poetic devices or alternatives but recurring indications of the vague yet constant aims behind all his poetry. Stephen Spender feels, "Jarrell is very difficult to 'place' or even describe as a poet," because he "seems to complain against most of the human condition without . . . much discrimination."[2] His critique is predicated on what he sees as a lack of selectivity, of "self-control," in subject matter joined with a tedious, unchanging tone and approach. "B.," the "Opposing Self" of James Dickey's article on Jarrell, sharply dismisses his poetry on more theoretical grounds as lacking conscientious "technique" and too dependent on mere presentation of a generalized, domesticated reality.[3] Both critics quarrel as much with the intentions of Jarrell's poetry as with its aesthetics or how successfully those intentions are realized, and base their major objections on personal views of what poetry "should do." Jarrell partisans have tended to reply in kind, proclaiming how well Jarrell creates direct, moving visions of modern life free of personal prejudices and the pointless verbal gymnastics of more formal poetry.

It is my intention not to join in this general debate about the "true function" of poetry, but to define as precisely as possible that central attitude behind all of Jarrell's poems responsible for both their diversity of content and consistency of approach. One can at least gain a clearer understanding of Jarrell's real aims and accomplishments by briefly charting his development of a mature technique which he felt best expressed the basic motivations and themes behind all his work and then examining in more detail one of the finest examples of his mature verse, a dramatic monologue entitled **"Seele im Raum."**

Jarrell's earliest work, the poems published in *The Rage for the Lost Penny*[4] and *Blood for a Stranger* (1942), encompasses an astonishing variety of subjects, strategies, and influences. Clearly the young poet was searching among the various methods and idioms of his contemporaries for those he could best adapt to his own themes and poetic needs. The early poetry of W. H. Auden seems to have had the most dramatic effect on Jarrell's own experimentation. Early efforts like **"A Little Poem"** and **"On the Railway Platform"** adopt Auden's conversational, economical mode of address and also employ the domestic and travel imagery associated with much of Auden's best early poetry. Above all, Auden's ability to build a complex mood with a progression of concrete images, often vigorously idiomatic in nature, seems to have impressed Jarrell. He explained his special admiration for Auden's language in a critical essay on the poet:

They [Auden's images] gain uncommon plausibility from the terse understated matter-of-factness of their treatment, the insistence (such as that found in the speech of children, in Mother Goose, in folk or savage verse, in dreams) upon the "thingness" of the words themselves.[5]

Jarrell continued to use concrete, descriptive imagery in his dramatic poetry in order to "locate" their events and themes in scenes with their own sense of dramatic immediacy and "uncommon plausibility." His development of the dramatic monologue in the war poems of *Little Friend, Little Friend* (1945) and *Losses* (1948) and his ceaseless revision of earlier poems suggest a common impulse, an insistence on poems with their own autonomous settings and internal developments, on a total elimination of the didactic authorial voice. Jarrell's subsequent rejection of his early Audenesque models seems an outgrowth of this same basic concern, for although he first adopted Auden's brusque, declarative mode of authorial address along with his sharp, idiomatic imagery, he later abandoned it as too didactic and "omniscient" in tone and perfected a narrative approach that is more conditional, iterative, and often mildly rhetorical in its general assertions and "judgments." Auden's allegorical landscapes and his occasional tendency toward straightforward social commentary are too one-dimensional and declarative for Jarrell's purposes in his later, more investigative verse.

His rejection of the early, more assertive tone of his own poetry is clearly a factor in his personal selection of the poems to be included in the *Selected Poems* edition of 1955. Of the forty-odd poems of *Blood for a Stranger,* only ten were included, and most of those had either been revised structurally or were similar in strategy and tone to Jarrell's later poems. Perhaps the best poem from that first volume, **"Children Selecting Books in a Library,"** is the most instructive of all in indicating the motives and effects of Jarrell's revisions. A quick comparison of the first stanzas of the original and revised versions will show what Jarrell was about:

> The little chairs and tables by a wall
> Bright with the beasts and weapons of a book
> Are properties the bent and varying heads
> Slip past unseeingly: their looks are tricked
> By our fondness and their grace into a world
> Our innocence is accustomed to find fortunate.
>
> Our great lives find the little blanched with dew;
> Their cries are those of crickets, dense with warmth.
> We wept so? How well we all forget!
> One taste of memory (like Fafnir's blood)
> Makes all their language sensible, one's ears
> Burn with the child's peculiar gift for pain.[6]

* * *

> With beasts and gods, above, the wall is bright.
> The child's head, bent to the book-colored shelves,
> Is slow and sidelong and food-gathering,
> Moving in blind grace . . . Yet from the mural, Care,
> The grey-eyed one, fishing the morning mist,
> Seizes the baby hero by the hair
>
> And whispers, in the tongue of gods and children,
> Words of a doom as ecumenical as dawn
> But blanched, like dawn, with dew. The children's cries
> Are to men the cries of crickets, dense with warmth
> —But dip a finger into Fafnir, taste it,
> And all their words are plain as chance and pain.[7]

The second version not only has a greater complexity and ease of rhythm and imagery but also transforms the comparatively stiff personal address of the original into a more lyrical, direct observation of characters who are involved in a process rather than serving as mere "illustrations" for a series of declarative, general remarks. The first line of the revision is more syntactically complex and manages to convey most of the raw information of the first two lines of the original. This movement toward more complex and condensed phrasing and syntax is perhaps the most consistent and characteristic stylistic development in all of Jarrell's poetry. As in these lines, the use of syntactical pauses and inverted phrases became a favorite device of Jarrell's, for they allowed syntactical rhythms that were sonorous while remaining conversational in tone. In the words of Denis Donoghue, Jarrell had a special understanding of "the relation between silence and speech, the flow of feeling between them," and could do "wonderful things with a full stop, a colon, a question mark."[8]

But even more important for our purposes is the abrupt change in the mode of address, for it is a sure technical clue to the motives behind Jarrell's mature style. The speaker in the original, who seems to control so insistently the "meanings" of his narration, withdraws to a greater distance in the revised version and refuses to generalize about the scene until it has worked itself out. The imagery likewise moves toward greater specificity and dramatic autonomy. The general category of "bent and varying heads" becomes "The child's head . . . / Moving in blind grace." The rather stuffy commentator disappears, and the "wordly wisdom" he supplied is expressed by another "character" involved in the drama, by the fantastic figure of "Care," who belongs to the scene itself and does not intrude upon it with extraneous generalizations. In short, Jarrell transforms a mere "example" into a self-realized and dramatically intact scene. The change partially relieves the author of his responsibilities as an omniscient interpreter, a stance Jarrell finds particularly uncomfortable. The worst examples of such awkward commentary and "public" imagery occur in the following lines and explain their total deletion from the revised poem:

> They are not learning answers but a method:
> To give up their own dilemmas for the great
> Maze Of The World—to turn in all their gold
> For the bank-notes of the one unwithering State.

Such major revisions throughout the poem show the key technical effects of Jarrell's later revolt against the relatively complacent moralizer who often narrates Auden's early poetry and much of Jarrell's own. The ever-increasing use of personae and dramatic scenes in the war poems of Jarrell's middle period and the adoption of the dramatic-monologue strategy almost exclusively in his most mature poetry seem a direct consequence of the attitudes and aims behind the extensive revision of **"Children Selecting Books in a Library."** Although Jarrell never overtly defined these aims in philosophical or critical terms, we have clear evidence of consistent and intense motives behind his revisions and the characteristic strategy he develops in his later poetry. His "speakers" become participants in concrete, dramatic situations—as wounded fighter pilots, tired housewives, or aging government employees—and Jarrell speaks *for* them if he speaks at all. Increasingly he expresses general themes *through* specific personae or the confusing, "unexplainable" circumstances which often entrap them. The ponderous "explanations" in early lines, like "Our great lives find the little blanched with dew," are strenuously avoided, are changed through a less declarative approach to specific subject matter.

Jarrell channels his general themes into intricate symbolic and syntactical patterns that express their "own" meanings through the interaction of characters and key phrases, producing less didactic but more subtle and complex expressions of emotional themes that are themselves often vague, intricate, and paradoxical. The more successful war poems, like **"Eighth Air Force,"** where the moralizing speaker is inevitably drawn into his own judgment of soldiers who are both children and murderers at the same time, are those where the distinct, often bizarre scenes of World War II and its participants are allowed to sort out the paradoxical, absurd meanings of their own actions and machinations. The combatants, as unique representatives of human kind, are usually the real subjects of such poems and are always shown to be both victimizers and victims with equal cogency.

A wide reading of Jarrell's work begins to reveal a recurrent attitude behind the diverse events and scenes, the sense that explanation itself, as a pat, logical generalization about what human life "means," is the greatest absurdity of all. The motives behind Jarrell's own movement away from the didactic voice are best explained by the constant undercutting (and often downright parodies) of the didactic, positivist approach to experience in the later poems themselves. In his best criticism, the praise of poets like Whitman and W. C. Williams for courageously *presenting* the world of human experience with all its contradictions and absurdities intact helps us understand his own attitude. Ultimately his poetry seems designed to present specific examples of the "human condition," not in general, abstract terms, but through the direct, often consciously colloquial description of individual lives. Jarrell's final development of a personal style can best be understood as an attempt to find an approach which best *allows* such presentations. In one of his finest essays, **"Some Lines from Whitman,"** Jarrell almost certainly speaks for his own poetics as well:

> There is in him almost everything in the world, so that one responds to him, willingly or unwillingly, almost as one does to the world, that world which seems both evil beyond any rejection and wonderful beyond any acceptance. We cannot help seeing that there is something absurd about any judgment we make of its whole—for there is no "point of view" at which we can stand to make the judgment, and the moral categories that mean most to us seem no more to apply to its whole than our spatial and temporal or causal categories seem to apply to its beginning or end.[9]

Jarrell's avoidance of absolutes or "categorical judgments" in the few comments on his own poetry and his frequent dismissal of them as useless within the poems themselves is surely related to such critical praise of the same attitudes in the work of other poets. Although I have only been able to give the most cursory attention to the development of Jarrell's mature style, it is clear even from the briefest examination that the strategies related to the dramatic monologue so widely and effectively used in Jarrell's final collections, ***The Seven-League Crutches*** (1951), ***The Woman at the Washing-***

ton Zoo* (1960), and *The Lost World* (1965), are designed to permit the most direct, concrete presentation of "things and lives" as they are in the modern world *and* thereby sponsor recognition of the human predicament. The latter can only be "judged" by the sum of its parts, and the particular characters and scenes of the final volumes compose a "gallery" of unique instances which defy logical summation.

I would now like to turn to one of the finest examples of these later poems, an interior monologue entitled **"Seele im Raum,"** for it also expresses, perhaps more overtly than any other poem, the essential emotional motivation and quasi-mystical "beliefs" responsible for its own form. Like so many of the better late poems, it describes a persona's confused yet concrete sense of personal being and its apparent fate in a hostile culture and environment. Yet, unlike most of her "fellows," the protagonist of **"Seele im Raum"** manages to prevail rather than submit to "the world's one way" of defining public reality. Thus her tale becomes one of the few encouraging instances of human existence among other more despondent portrayals of personal failure like **"A Girl in a Library," "The Face,"** and **"Next Day."** And in expressing those feelings and the awareness of personal being which allow her to escape the common fate, the speaker becomes especially useful to us. She becomes one of the few effective "spokesmen" for an attitude consistently fostered in Jarrell's poetry and their true "raison d'etre." In short, **"Seele im Raum"** enunciates Jarrell's completed vision of ideal human consciousness. If there is a unifying element in all of his poetry, it is the emotional plea for this comprehensive awareness of life and the sense that it must be protected and encouraged (and especially by poetry itself) with special care in a harsh, impersonal, mechanistic age.

"Seele im Raum" begins with a typical, domestic dinner scene. Yet the setting is also "like a dream" since a place is set for a mysterious visitor who is materially invisible yet seen:

> It sat between my husband and my children.
> A place was set for it—a plate of greens.
> It had been there: I had seen it
> But not somehow—but this was like a dream—
> Not seen it so that I knew I saw it.
> It was as if I could not know I saw it.
> Because I had never once in all my life
> Not seen it. It was an eland.[10]

The halting, contorted syntax is, as I have noted, characteristic of Jarrell's later verse. It is designed to function dramatically as well as structurally and usually denotes a sense of desperation and helplessness in the speaker who attempts to explain away the absurdities of his own actions and experiences. Yet here the confusion is less desperate, for the speaker wishes to describe a familiar yet fantastic vision. She shows all the apprehension of people who fear their listeners will think them insane. Yet her "vision" is not that of a schizophrenic, for she "sees" and doesn't see a part of her own being precisely because it is so familiar to her. She characterizes it as an "eland," a part of her earliest consciousness of self, and "feels" its presence at her table without undue alarm. Her "eland" seems strange, not because it is unfamiliar, but because it is an eland.

As in **"Children Selecting Books in a Library,"** Jarrell presents rather than defines his concept of **"Seele"** by making the exotic creature an active participant in the scene. The woman recalls, "Many times / when it breathed heavily (when it had tried / A long useless time to speak")" and she "touched it" and found the eland "of a different size / And order of being." And this is really the animal's function as a concrete image in the poem. It represents directly a subliminal awareness of human life that is both organic and mystical; incapable of logical articulation, it simply "breathes." In his introductory notes for the *Selected Poems* Jarrell explained that the title, **"Seele im Raum,"** is taken from "one of Rilke's poems; 'Soul in Space' sounded so glib that I couldn't use it instead."[11] Yet it is clear that Jarrell is attempting to present with special conclusiveness his own sense of that spiritual entity in this poem, and the eland serves as its dramatic representative. A paradox, it embodies both an expansion and a reduction of human consciousness. In the context of the poem it serves as a "domesticated incarnation," mystical yet innately personal, rather than as the traditionally fearsome manifestation of a deity. Its condition invokes sympathy rather than reverence. Its exotic nature is also intentional. In the same introductory notes Jarrell suggests his reasons for choosing the animal:

> An eland is the largest sort of African antelope—the males are as big as a horse, and you often see people gazing at them, at the zoo, in uneasy wonder.

Its "wondrous" identity is important, for, like other such fabulous characters in Jarrell's poems, its physical form expresses the strange yet concrete nature of the "other self" it embodies. Jarrell's personae, like "die alte Marschallin" in **"The Face"** and the narrator of **"A Ghost, a Real Ghost,"** often see in their mirrors the image of another being, comparable to the mysterious "Doppelgänger" of German Märchen, who incorporates "wraithlike" elements of human existence from which they feel estranged. For Jarrell such apparitions embody personal senses of self most evident in the child's imagination and clearly operative in dreams, myths, and imaginative literature. As such, they are no less "real" as expressions of human reality than more empirical, objective descriptions. Such "beings" appear in the poems not as mere poetic devices but as literal representatives of deeper, more irrational levels of human consciousness.

Mrs. Mary Jarrell recalls that "Randall (so it seemed to me) had an affinity for what he thought of as his Other: that One he saw in ponds and photographs and mirrors."[12] So for Jarrell, children's "tales are full of sorcerers and ogres / Because their lives are." In this sense, the woman's fantasy is "childlike," but in Jarrell's view this marks her as exceptionally fortunate. She has not lost her "soul," her sense of complete and mystical being, like most of the "adults" of Jarrell's poetry.

The dramatic conflict of **"Seele im Raum"** does not spring from the woman's own doubts but from the necessary relationships with "the others," with her family, who make jokes about her setting a place for the beast, and "my whole city," which, "after some years . . . came / And took it from me—it was ill, they told me." The persona of **"Seele im Raum,"** like the mother in **"Second Air Force,"** the **"Woman at the Washington Zoo,"** or Jarrell himself in **"Thinking of the Lost World,"** wrestles with the disparity between public reason and private vision, and the essential conflict responsible for the intensely sympathetic tone and air of advocacy in most of Jarrell's poetry is overtly dealt with in her internal debate. After the loss of her eland the woman's tone becomes elegiac, and in the remainder of the poem she attempts to generalize about its "meaning." In so doing she expresses precisely, not what the eland "was" (again, such generalizations are avoided in Jarrell's late poetry), but what it meant *to her*, and her ruminations assume the quality of a personal credo.

Jarrell's use of the repeated subjunctive in the following passage reinforces the conditional, uncertain tone already established in the syntax, for the woman struggles with the absurdity of her "faith":

> It is as if someone remembered saying:
> "This is an antimacassar that I grew from seed,"
> And this were true.
>
>   And, truly,
> One could not wish for anything more strange—
> For anything more. And yet it wasn't *interesting* . . .
> —It was worse than impossible, it was a joke.
>
> And yet when it was, I *was*—
> Even to think that I once thought
> That I could see it is to feel the sweat
> Like needles at my hair-roots, I am blind
>
> —It was not even a joke, not even a joke.

The issue remains unresolved, as such issues must in Jarrell's poetry, but the woman's remarks indicate a strength of belief and, even more important, of imagination which hold the world's rationality and derision at arm's length. Jarrell's organization of the first sentence in the second group helps show this, for the last prepositional phrase quite suddenly asserts a general attitude about the value of the "strange" beast which remains unshakable. The woman's tenacity in defending her private vision becomes the main subject of this poem and certifies her status as one of Jarrell's heroines. She defends a form of subjective mysticism, for the martyr she worships is neither "holy" in the conventional sense, nor public, but a destroyed part of her own psyche. Her faith is completely private and presumes nothing beyond itself; it is simply both an indication and a fulfillment of personal needs. The woman's imaginative memory, which allows her to *feel* the eland's presence at the slightest suggestion, saves her from the dull, lonely "reality" of less open and responsive personae in Jarrell's poems.

It would also seem at this point that she comes as near as one can to expressing Jarrell's own feelings. A prose passage describing his favorite elements of John Crowe Ransom's poetry also illuminates in remarkable detail the purposes of **"Seele im Raum"**:

> His poems are full of an affection that cannot help itself for an innocence that cannot help itself—for the stupid travellers lost in the maze of the world, for the clever travellers lost in the maze of the world. The poems are not a public argument but personal knowledge, personal feeling; and their virtues are the "merely" private virtues.[13]

In such a context, the woman's "blind" persistence in defending her "merely private" and terribly fragile vision is both courageous and a rallying point for the "honestly defenceless." Her very admission of personal confusion is a sign of her special enlightenment. In the following passage she states her case in terms that sum up Jarrell's own fundamental attitudes as well as one could hope:

> Yet how can I believe it? Or believe that I
> Owned it, a husband, children? Is my voice the voice
> Of that skin of being—of what owns, is owned
> In honor or dishonor, that is borne and bears—
> Or of that raw thing, the being inside it
> That has neither a wife, a husband, nor a child
> But goes at last as naked from this world
> As it was born into it—
>
> And the eland comes and grazes on its grave.
>
>   This is senseless?
> Shall I make sense or shall I tell the truth?
> Choose either—I cannot do both.

The key alternatives of self-definition are stated here, and the "normal," factual, social self is seen as "that skin of being," a material shell for "that raw thing, the being inside it." The former is finite, visible, and easily categorized by referring to its organic and practical activities in time, whereas the latter is unaffected by the temporal realm, is a "naked" and "raw thing," untouched by the abstract dualisms of human society and its impersonal "definitions." Inspired by its example, the woman puts a very Jarrellian ultimatum to the reader, for she distinguishes between "making sense" (in normal, rational, empirical terms) and "truth." They are judged mutually exclusive, and she, like a child or a mystic, must deal in fantastic beings and paradoxes to explain what is most important to her. Her comprehensive awareness of two opposed levels of existence keeps her, like most of Jarrell's enlightened personae, in a state of constant indecision. Yet the conclusion of **"Seele im Raum"** shows how well the integration of her "eland self" has helped her both judge and live with her life, and *that* is the real purpose and succor of such awareness in Jarrell's poetry. She also understands the folly of didacticism and egotism, even when defending the existence of a personal "Daemon," and that too makes her "tale" one of the most optimistic in tone among Jarrell's poems and one of the surest indications of the motives behind his own distrust of the declarative mode. She concludes, not with a logical proof, but with an enthusiastic, "childlike" cry of faith:

> I tell myself that. And yet it is not so,
> And what I say afterwards will not be so:
> To be at all is to be wrong.
>   Being is being old
> And saying, almost comfortably, across a table
> From—
>   from what I don't know—
>   in a voice
> Rich with a kind of longing satisfaction:
> "To own an eland! That's what I call life!"

What sits, or sat, at her table remains beyond identification, yet her awareness of "owning" it allows her to be old "almost comfortably." One does not encounter the word "satisfaction" very often in Jarrell's poetry unless it is used ironically, but here the atmosphere and the woman's voice are "rich" with it.

It is the plea for this special awareness of personal being which lies behind most of Jarrell's poetry; his mature technique is designed to present "plausible" scenes and characters in which either its presence or, more often, its loss is shown to have specific existential consequences. The desperate tone this underlying plea promotes in many poems, along with its vague emotional outlines and Jarrell's refusal to give it conclusive theoretical or aesthetic definition, is what seems to annoy the critics who consider Jarrell's approach either too unvaried or effusively sentimental. Yet, as Douglas Dunn notes in a recent essay on Jarrell, "When poets are accused of sentimentality it is sometimes an indication that feeling in their poems has been misunderstood."[14] Such objections are based more on taste than on direct analysis of technique or the aesthetic realization of emotional yet definite intentions. Jarrell's own aims in his poetry seem remarkably constant, as we have seen in the ceaseless development of a personal style over a twenty-five-year period, and in terms of its own goals, **"Seele im Raum"** works extremely well. Its dramatic strategy integrates the fantastic figure of the eland and the normal, domestic setting so well in the woman's mind that they seem to bear out her final judgment and exist in a precarious but natural union. One must either judge **"Seele im Raum"** as the charming confession of a genuine neurotic or see it as a remarkably comprehensive explanation of the self by one who has learned to straddle its two worlds simultaneously. Jarrell characteristically refuses to step in and decide for the reader; in fact the poem's technique is designed to make such an intrusion appear artificial and unnecessary. Like so many of Jarrell's late poems, **"Seele im Raum"** is intended as a parable, and assessments of the speaker's "case" must themselves be subjective. Of course, by adopting a persona whose sense of the "facts" of daily life is consistently strong and who undercuts any charge of general insanity with her thoughtful, understated, self-analytical mode of address, Jarrell slants the argument in his protagonist's favor. The real intention of the poem, in both its form and content, is the direct involvement of the reader in a dilemma he may recognize as his own, and in this it succeeds admirably.

In any case, it is clear that Jarrell is often more interested in the emotional impact of his poems than in their formal artistry, and that this places him at odds with much of the practice of recent years. His increasing use of the dramatic monologue and straightforward, descriptive imagery in his last years seems a natural outgrowth of this demand for recognizable, accessible "portraits" of modern life in America. His developed style is clearly intended as a means to an end, and **"Seele im Raum"** suggests with special clarity the philosophical source of this shift in emphasis from "objective technique" and general assertion toward more subjective, impressionistic explorations of "private lives" and personal experiences. The concrete experience is primary; its aesthetic articulation is evaluated by its ability to *transmit* the physical and emotional outlines of a "single life" as directly and comprehensively as possible.

In developing a style capable of expressing such attitudes in the poems themselves, Jarrell drew on a wide variety of sources he felt shared his intense concern for non-rational, intuitive states of awareness. His poetry and criticism are filled with references to Freudian psychology, American Transcendentalism (of the "applied" Whitmanian school), German Märchen, and Proust's analysis of memory in *Remembrance of Things Past,* to cite only a few examples. Jarrell's extensive allusions to such diverse and wide-ranging sources, despite their single-mindedness of purpose, are a new phenomenon and suggest more about the wide-open, cross-cultural eclecticism and the explosion of "subjective" poetic conventions and systems of the last three decades than they do about the "purer," more codified theories of the Imagists or Surrealists. But because Jarrell's emotional description of ideal human awareness demands the inclusive vision of all mystical systems and feeds on paradox and unchecked observation, it is extremely difficult to define with any precision or selectivity. I have seized upon Randall Jarrell's "eland" simply because it is a distinct manifestation of this attitude with the temerity to express it literally and in precise language.

Jarrell's "eland self," as a soul or source of being, cannot be related to the Christian conception of that entity, for the Judeo-Christian soul is involved in its own linear, temporal progress toward some finite moment of redemption and is subject to all kinds of moral and existential categories and judgments. As Jarrell's speaker tells **"A Girl in a Library,"** "The soul has no assignments . . . / it wastes its time."[15] Its functions and value for each individual must be *recognized* rather than understood; as the woman in **"Seele im Raum"** explains, she had "Not seen it so that I knew I saw it." These are some of the reasons I have identified Jarrell's "Soul in Space" as essentially mystical in conception; it defines enlightenment as a state of comprehensive and intuitive awareness rather than as the complex organization of logical and empirical hypotheses. In fact, the latter are impediments to a direct and unified recognition of true self. Near the end of **"Seele im Raum,"** the speaker can only suggest the nature of her eland by defining what it "is not." In so doing she employs the process of "negative definition" found in the writings of many mystics when they describe the character of God or the soul. In like manner, Jarrell's own refusal to provide a theoretical definition for his aesthetic or philosophical intentions should not be judged as irresponsible or self-indulgent, but as a necessary extension of the attitudes expressed in the poems themselves. Attempts to objectively define rather than simply present the "beliefs" behind such feelings are always self-defeating, like the speaker's attempt to define what he seeks in **"A Sick Child"**: "If I can think of it, it isn't what I want."[16] But in **"Bamberg,"** a short poem written the year of his death, Jarrell uncharacteristically employs simple religious imagery to suggest the depth of his belief in the unifying "powers of concentration":

> You'd be surprised how much, at
> The Last Judgment,
> The powers of concentration
> Of the blest and damned
> Are improved, so that
> Both smile exactly alike
> At remembering so well
> All they meant to remember
> To tell God.[17]

As Jarrell's "representative," the eland mocks the world's logical dichotomies (visible and invisible, material and spiritual, life and death) by adopting both alternatives simultaneously and timelessly; it "grazes on its own grave." It expresses the insistently emotional, anti-logical view of human life around which Jarrell's poetry must be unified. The varied interests and sources which influenced his own practice, his intense interest in Freud and the nature of dreams, his admiration for Rilke's surrealistic imagery, and his insistence on dealing with contemporary American scenes in American idioms, all relate to the subliminal nature yet concrete personal relevance of a "state of mind" his poetry is designed to encourage. His poems are instructional without being prescriptive or undercutting the responsibility for personal recognition of one's own condition. His tone is often desperate and painfully sharp because he feels modern culture besets his enlightened personae on all sides, insisting on a lobotomy of the consciousness and fragmented, unfocused perceptions. The world defines "real knowledge" only as the accumulation of objective, impersonal data—"divides itself into facts," according to Jarrell's positivist Satan[18]—and demands that one "make sense." Yet, as the persona of **"Seele im Raum"** knows, such knowledge is fundamentally *useless* in helping her live her life. It is, in fact, destructive to the soul, to the emotional, imaginative sense of being that is her birthright. In a poem called **"The Lost World,"** one of Jarrell's last works, he makes clear his own feelings about the world's wisdom with images similar to those of **"Seele im Raum"**:

>   In my
> Talk with the world, in which it tells me what I know
> And I tell it, "I know—"how strange that I
> Know nothing, and yet it tells me what I know!—
> I appreciate the animals, who stand by
> Purring. Or else sit and pant. It's so—
> So *agreeable*.[19]

And in an essay from ***Poetry and the Age*** Jarrell provides an effective description of those embattled beings he wishes his poetry might encourage and protect:

> Children are playing in the vacant lots, animals are playing in the forest. Everything that the machine at the center could not attract or transform it has forced out into the suburbs, the country, the wilderness, the past: out there are the fairy tales and nursery rhymes, chances and choices, dreams and sentiments and intrinsic aesthetic goods—everything that doesn't pay and doesn't care.[20]

Again, the ultimate "utility" Jarrell strives for in his verse is akin to that of the parable or the spiritual exercise. The poems of his late period, the products of endless technical experimentation and revision, are intended as psychic "catalysts," and their direct, often highly emotional approaches to their subject matter are part of their design. We, of course, are still faced with the ongoing controversy about them, yet it seems that Jarrell's critics must at least deal with those elements of his work they find excessive as integral components of an overall method. It seems too easy to react to any consistently strong emotion in modern poetry as mere lack of artistic control, and this is certainly not the case in Jarrell's practice. Sister Bernetta Quinn, in discussing Jarrell's last book, *The Lost World,* suggests the real source of the debate over Jarrell's poetry:

> There is a great tenderness here, with a willingness to present emotion without apology, unique among poets today.[21]

Perhaps, ironically, Jarrell simply worked his design too well. We must be content, like so many of his personae, to take sides. Yet it is hoped that both Jarrell's advocates and his detractors will at least know what they are fighting about. In yet another of his critical essays Jarrell probably described the best criteria for those who would judge his own poetry:

> To have the distance from the most awful and most nearly unbearable parts of the poems to the most tender, subtle, and loving parts, a distance so great; to have this whole range of being treated with so much humor and sadness and composure, with such plain truth; to see that a man can still include, connect, and make humanly understandable so *much*—this is one of the freshest and oldest of joys.[22]

Notes

1. Randall Jarrell, *Poetry and the Age* (New York, 1955), p. 90.
2. Stephen Spender, "Randall Jarrell's Complaint," *New York Review of Books,* ix, No. 9 (Nov. 23, 1967), p. 28.
3. James Dickey, "Randall Jarrell," *Randall Jarrell / 1914-1965,* ed. Robert Lowell et al. (New York, 1967), pp. 33-48.
4. *Five Young American Poets* (Norfolk, Conn., 1940), pp. 81-124.
5. Randall Jarrell, *The Third Book of Criticism* (New York, 1969), p. 155.
6. Randall Jarrell, *Blood for a Stranger* (New York, 1942), p. 15.
7. Randall Jarrell, *Selected Poems* (New York, 1955), p. 97.
8. *Randall Jarrell / 1914-1965,* p. 55.
9. *Poetry and the Age,* p. 114.
10. *Selected Poems,* p. 27.
11. *Ibid.,* p. x.
12. *Randall Jarrell / 1914-1965,* p. 279.
13. *Third Book of Criticism,* p. 313.
14. Douglas Dunn, "An Affable Misery: On Randall Jarrell," *Encounter,* xxxix, No. 4 (October, 1972), p. 43.
15. *Selected Poems,* p. 4.
16. *Ibid.,* p. 43.
17. Randall Jarrell, *The Complete Poems* (New York, 1969), p. 490.
18. *Ibid.,* p. 31.
19. *Ibid.,* p. 287.
20. *Poetry and the Age,* p. 99.
21. *Randall Jarrell / 1914-1965,* p. 147.
22. *Third Book of Criticism,* p. 302.

Helen Hagenbüchle (essay date 1975)

SOURCE: Hagenbüchle, Helen. "The Horrid Nurse." In *The Black Goddess: A Study of the Archetypal Feminine in the Poetry of Randall Jarrell,* pp. 10-25. Zurich: Francke Verlag Bern, 1975.

[*In the following essay, Hagenbüchle examines the theme of the hostile or absent mother in Jarrell's poetry, stating that this negative mother-image reflects the broader concern in Jarrell's work of the absoluteness of "man's isolation and insecurity."*]

Jarrell's poetic oeuvre is eminently concerned with the precariousness of human existence. It is with indignation, pity, or resignation that the poet points out, time and again, man's dependence on "Necessity", that mysterious power behind the phenomenal world which seems to be totally blind in its own activity, its creative urge being neutralized by the equally strong impulse to destroy. Man's existence is therefore marked by insecurity, ignorance, homelessness, helplessness, and especially by the fear of death. The social restraints imposed upon the individual turn out to be an extrapolation of this existential Necessity. The soldier caught in the merciless grip of the omnipotent state and the child domineered by its authoritarian parents represent prototypes of dumbly suffering man.

This unusual aspect of the child may bewilder a reader to whom childhood represents that blessed state of carefree security which all grown-ups look back to with longing. The child is commonly thought to have at least one refuge of ultimate security, protection, and help: his mother. In Jarrell's poems, however even this most fundamental of all human relationships is disrupted; man's isolation and insecurity is absolute. It is astonishing that among his many poems about children or their dreams there is not one which describes a boy or girl feeling safe in the presence of the mother.[1] In Jarrell's poetic world no child can rely on maternal help in a moment of distress or danger, for she is invariably represented as either absent, dead, fainting, crazy, or thoroughly hostile to the child.

One is tempted to look for biographical reasons of such a consistently negative mother-image. A glance at the rather lengthy poem **"Hope,"** (***CP*** [***The Complete Poems***] 305-12) which is largely based on Jarrell's own childhood memories, is instructive. We notice that "the parents of the apartment fight like lions" (***CP*** 305). The poet then remembers "a recurrent / Scene from [his] childhood. / A scene called Mother Has Fainted" (***CP*** 308).[2] This scene confronted young Jarrell with the painful discovery that what had seemed the center of life could suddenly stop moving, could breathe "as if it no longer breathed;" the same face which before had sanctioned or reproved the child's actions with smiles or frowns might unexpectedly become a mere blank to him: "Her face no longer [. . .] did anything to us" (***CP*** 308). Mother who was to him a figure of unquestioned authority could fall deathly silent: "It was as if God were taking a nap." This reference to God projects the crippling experience onto an ontological level.[3] Clearly, his mother's recurring physical weakness was to be of incalculable consequences for a child who, as a result, would completely lose his bearings; without a mother's guiding presence life is likely to lose its sense of direction.[4] Her shortcomings were all the more keenly felt as Jarrell's father left the home and re-married when Randall was about five or six years old. As a consequence the boy was raised by his mother and had only her to rely on.

There was yet another incident in the poet's childhood which must have upset his childish trust in life and in the mother-figure in particular: the slaughtering of a hen by his grandmother, whom he used to call "Mama." The high frequency of this motif in Jarrell's work indicates the strong effect which this experience produced on his imagination.

> Mama comes out and takes in the clothes
> From the clothesline. She looks with righteous love
> At all of us, her spare face half a girl's.
> She enters a chicken coop, and the hens shove
> And flap and squawk, in fear; the whole flock whirls
> Into the farthest corner. She chooses one,
> Comes out, and wrings its neck. The body hurls
> Itself out—lunging, reeling, it begins to run
> Away from Something, to fly away from Something
> In great flopping circles. Mama stands like a nun
> In the center of each awful, anguished ring.
> The thudding and scrambling go on, go on—then they fade,
> I open my eyes, it's over . . . Could such a thing
> Happen to anything? It could to a rabbit, I'm afraid;
> It could to—
>   "Mama, you won't kill Reddy ever,
> You won't ever, will you?" The farm woman tries to persuade
> The little boy, her grandson, that she'd never
> Kill the boy's rabbit, never even think of it.
> He would like to believe her . . . And whenever
> I see her, there in that dark infinite,
> Standing like Judith, with the hen's head in her hand,
> I explain it away, in vain—a hypocrite,
> Like all who love.
>
>   (***CP*** 292)

The killing of the hen seems to mark the beginning of the child's death-consciousness. For, by analogically linking the hen with his beloved rabbit, it dawns on him that the same fate might eventually be in store for himself. In the manuscripts to **"The Lost World"** the meaning of the ambiguous dash, "It could to—", is made explicit: "chickens along with rabbit at back of backyard (✓ could happen to rabbit, I'm afraid, could happen to Randall, I'm afraid ✓) wring neck or chop off head . . ." (Mss to **"The Lost World,"** Berg Collection, New York).

Two things should here be noted: First, the boy thinks of death as being administered by the mother-figure; secondly, death is associated with having one's neck wrung or one's head chopped off.[5] Accordingly, his young and impressionable mind identifies "Mama" with impersonal Fate, an indefinable "Something" that is vaguely reminiscent of the God of the Old Testament: "She looks with righteous love at all of us." Even before grandmother kills the hen she lacks that warmth one is wont to attribute to a mother, extending a sort of cold justice based on a sense of upright moral behaviour to the animals and the boy in the yard. This may partly account for the curious blending of mother, fate, and nun in the child's fancy. The virginal life of a nun and her seclusion from an unjust and immoral world gives her a touch of the numinous. It is this quality which relates her in the poet's mind to Mama's indisputable power over life and death.[6] Obviously, the act of killing is sanctioned by God, an observation which finds expression in the description of Judith holding the hen's (i. e. Holofernes') head in her hand. The association of "Mama" with both Judith and the nun as well as with the mysterious circling of the hen round its own slayer, raise the slaughtering of the chicken to a symbolical level.[7] The reader finds himself reminded of a ritual, where the victim is slain by a priestess who, after the sacrifice, lifts the bleeding head up, for God and the believers to witness. Thus, death acquires that aura of a sacred rite which is noticeable in poems such as **"The Prince," "A Hunt in the Black Forest,"** or **"Orestes at Tauris."** Already early in Randall's childhood this experience must have merged with visions of an archetypal mother-goddess who is at the core of the poet's terror and fear of death. We shall revert to this aspect of the poet's mother-image in the subsequent chapter.

In the poem **"Thinking of the Lost World,"** however, the motif of "Mama" killing the chicken acquires an almost cosmic significance. Musing on the California of his childhood, "that calm country / Through which the stream of [his] life first meandered" (*CP* 336), Jarrell states how sadly everything has changed in the past twenty-five years. All the people of his youth, he realizes,

> "are gone
> Except for me; and for me nothing is gone—
> The chicken's body is still going round
> And round in widening circles, a satellite
> From which, as the sun sets, the scientist bends
> A look of evil on the unsuspecting earth."
>
> (*CP* 337)

Jarrell seems to look upon memory as a way to preserve the past. For good or worse nothing of what once happened in "Mama's" yard is forgotten. However, the subsequent metamorphosis of the dead chicken into the satellite, which is in fact still going round the "unsuspecting earth" makes us aware that Jarrell is speaking of a particular kind of memory. There is a radical difference between the slaughtering of the chicken and his other, more ordinary childhood experiences, which can be resuscitated from memory at any time. The poem opens up with the description of such an associative reminiscence in an almost Proustian way:

> "This spoonful of chocolate tapioca
> Tastes like—like peanut butter, like the vanilla
> Extract Mama told me not to drink.
> Swallowing the spoonful, I have already traveled
> Through time to my childhood."
>
> (*CP* 336)

In contrast to the memories excited by the vanilla extract, Jarrell's first impression of dying does not need an accidental reminder to trigger it off; in fact, the traumatic awareness of death has never left him for a moment. Death is as imminent to him now as it was in Mama's yard, it has—with the orbital bomb circling the earth—only changed its outward appearance. Furthermore, Jarrell still feels as if he alone were "suspecting" death and he suffers from this depressing knowledge. When "Mama" cut the chicken's neck he was the only one present who consciously anticipated the hen's fate not only for himself, but also for his rabbit, and for all the other animals. This faculty of lonely insight seems to have remained with him unchanged: the poet is intensely aware of the danger of extinction which threatens mankind at every moment of its existence, while the scientists of "the unsuspecting earth" keep sending satellite after satellite into space. "Mama" killing the chicken has finally come to symbolize universal cosmic destruction. Standing in the middle of the doomed chicken's circles she merges with the scientist who explores the universe with the help of satellites spinning off in ever "widening circles" and who bends "a look of evil" on the earth. From the poem **"A Street off Sunset"** we know that the scientist, planning to destroy the world, is a figure that Randall happened to read about in a science-fiction book at the time of the unfortunate experience in Grandmother's yard. Although the boy's grandfather, Pop, tired to waive his fears about an impending annihilation of the earth by that villainous scientist, the end of the poem nevertheless indicates, that Randall could not quite believe in Pop's comforting words; nor was he reassured by Mama's promise never to kill his own rabbit:

> My universe
> Mended almost, I tell him [i. e., Pop] about the scientist. I say,
> "He couldn't really, could he, Pop?" My comforter's
> Eyes light up, and he laughs. "No, that's just play,
> Just make-believe," he says. The sky is gray,
> We sit there, at the end of our good day.
>
> (*CP* 293)

Here Jarrell is referring not only to the end of a particular "good day" but to the end of innocent childhood as such, when he was still "unsuspecting" that death was waiting to catch up with him. On the evening of that memorable day the blue sky of his light-hearted youth turned "gray" and finally merged into the dark night of that death-consciousness with which all his great poems are informed.[8]

Experiences like these may have contributed to shake young Randall's inner poise in its foundation.[9] In fact, he could never quite regain his trust once it was lost. His relation to his mother became extremely ambiguous, as can be gathered from his notes to the poem **"Hope."** There we find statements such as, "anti-Mother as much in her Terms, as little free from her, indifferent to her, as apron-strings." [. . .] "everywhere on surface magazines radio television making conversation at parties and trying to escape" [. . .] "back far enough, down deep enough, one comes to the mothers (snuggle against, beat against) what difference?" (Mss to **"Hope"**, Berg Collection, New York) The contradictory feelings of repulsion and attraction are conspicuous in the final version of the poem, where he describes how, out of love, he would do anything to help her whenever she fainted: "Put a pillow under her head (or else her feet) / To make the blood flow to her head (or else away from it)" (*CP* 308-09); yet, at the same time he nourished a subconscious hatred for her, because she either appeared too weak or too overpowering, and was finally linked up with the idea of death.

In a way, all the children in Jarrell's work reflect the poet's disturbed mother relationship. In **"The State"** the Nazis do away with a boy's mother who is "crazy." Since a crazy mother cannot give a child the warmth and safety he needs the boy does not get upset about her death, ironically he even admits that the régime was right. His unconscious hatred sanctions the murder. The beginning of **"The Prince"** describes the frustration of a boy whose mother walks away while he feels helplessly exposed to the grip of a hair-raising dream-figure: "after the door shuts, and the footsteps die, / I call out, 'Mother?' No one answers. [. . .] the floor creaks, someone stirs / In the other darkness—and the hairs all rise / Along my neck, I whisper: 'It is he!'" (*CP* 97). Jarrell here uses a pronoun without a referent. "He" is the child's dream-fantasy of nothingness, a hypostatization of his dead rabbit which demands the boy's voluntary surrender in a sort of death-ritual. "I cannot breathe / But inch my cold hand out to his cold hand" (*CP* 97). Awaking to reality, however, he must recognize that death has not even the terrible beauty of a rite, but that "A man dies, like a rabbit, for a use." He himself is in the situation of the animals which Mama used to kill almost as mechanically as she picked the "clothes from the clothesline."

The poem **"A Hunt in the Black Forest"** opens in much the same way: "After the door shuts, and the footsteps die, / He calls out: 'Mother?'" (*CP* 319). Left alone, the child starts dreaming his gruesome dream. In **"London,"** too, the baby finds it hard to adjust to the reality of this world. "He tumbles all unwilling from the womb / He reaches for a breast and gets a bone" (*CP* 360). Once it has left the womb a child remains utterly helpless and can no longer rely on his mother to provide the necessary feeling of security. The widely differing publication dates of the poems mentioned above[10] show that the traumatic loss of confidence in the mother remained for Jarrell the most powerful symbol of the basic insecurity of existence.

In the poem **"Protocols"** the alternating voices of the two children who died in the concentration camps of Birkenau and Odessa sum up their experience of "how you die." Characteristically, both of them suffered death in the arms of their helpless mothers:

"And I said to my mother, 'Now I'm washed and dried,'
My mother hugged me, and it smelled like hay
And that is how you die. And that is how you die."

(*CP* 193)

The repetition of the last sentence gives special emphasis to the idea that it is normal to die in the arms of one's mother. She is thereby depersonalized and acquires an archetypal meaning. The smell of hay, furthermore, stresses her symbolic function as Mother Earth embracing the dead. Her womb has become a tomb.

For the child in **"Variations III"** life is made utterly miserable by a seemingly endless "all day" toilet-training in a nursery that makes for a horribly automatic monotony.

"I lived in a room full of bears and porridge,
My mother was dead and my nurse was horrid.
I sat all day on a white china chamber
And I lay all night in my trundle bed.
And she wasn't, she wasn't, O not a bit dead!

The boy said, the girl said—and Nurse she said:

"I'll stew your ears all day, little hare,
Just as God ate your mother, for you are bad,
Are bad, are bad—" and the nurse is the night
To wake to, to die in: and the day I live,
The world and its life are her dream.

(*CP* 122)

The second line allows of two different interpretations. Either the mother is dead because the child in his abysmal hatred of her has killed her in his imagination, which would explain the bitter disappointment, "And she wasn't, she wasn't, O not a bit dead!" This interpretation can be supported by Jarrell's commentary on the same motif in the poem **"The Quilt Pattern."**[11] While the "dead" mother in that poem is replaced by the witch, she is substituted in **"Variations"** by the "horrid" nurse. In both poems, moreover, the children feel frightened by their mother-substitutes who threaten to eat them up. The alternative, however, that the child who feels ill at ease in the nursery longs to be back in the womb cannot be ruled out. Yet, this amniotic refuge is now absolutely irretrievable; the boy's mother is, indeed, "dead" as far as his secret wishes are concerned. His actual mother, on the other hand, whose educational methods are the cause of the boy's discomfort, is called "nurse," for she does not give the child the warmth he requires and remains as indifferent as a hired babysitter. Her main purpose seems to consist in implanting in the child's mind an early and unnecessary guilt-complex— "for you are bad"—whose result seems to be the fear of being eaten up, itself an archetypal symbol, that is in turn connected with death through the dead mother. Since the loss of the womb is for the child a fatal and irreversible disaster Jarrell has the nurse say: "God ate your mother." Similar symptoms of an Oedipus complex occur in several poems where the child-mother relationship plays a part. They transcend, however, as will be demonstrated, the merely sexual level.[12]

Mutatis mutandis the poet describes a girl in **"The Night Before the Night Before Christmas"** who— after having lost her mother—dreams of her as possessing all the love, beauty, clothes, and social success which the girl herself now lacks:

"The girl would still dream of the mother
Who, two years dead,
Looks more like her sister than her mother
—So they had said—
And lays, slowly, a dark shining head
On the dark, stooped shoulder
Of the girl's new teacher.
Is there any question?

> The girl has forgotten to answer
> And watches him open the door of the cab
> That is bringing an Invitation to the Dance:
> Till Mother disappears in fur,
> The girl trails toward the house
> And stares at her bitten nails, her bare red knees—
> And presses her chapped, cold hands together
> In a middy blouse."
>
> (*CP* 40)

The obvious use of the Cinderella-motif makes it quite clear that the girl does not endow her imaginary mother with all the things she herself lacks merely out of love or admiration. She rather sees in her mother an enemy and rival whom she envies and therefore hates. This woman who "looks more like her sister than her mother" is a dream condensation of both the stepmother and the sisters in the fairy-tale. The girl's hatred for her mother is supposedly the fruit of her frustrated love for her father. In the fairy-tale the father-image is represented by the Prince for whose love Cinderella yearns in vain as long as her stepmother and her sisters go to the ball without her. The dream as told in the poem, however, mixes up the girl's new teacher with the Prince or father-image. The poem is evidently a conscious adaptation of Freudian dream-analysis, the girl's dream being a classical example of an Electra-complex.[13]

The root of such an abnormally strong resistance of a child against its mother is usually to be found in an unnaturally strong possessiveness on the part of the latter. In the autobiographical poem **"Hope"** the poet, in fact, refers to such an imperious behaviour on the mother's part:

> "As the child starts into life, the woman dies
> Into a girl—and, scolding the doll she owns,
> The single scholar of her little school,
> Her task, her plaything, her possession,
> She assumes what is God's alone, responsibility."
>
> (*CP* 311)

Jarrell makes it quite clear that mother wrongly appropriates this godlike authority in treating her child like a doll. Randall himself seems to have deeply suffered from such a crippling relationship. Whenever his mother fainted, he and his brother, while helplessly waiting for her to come round,

> "[. . .] looked out, shyly, into the little lanes
> That went off from the great dark highway, Mother's Highway,
> And wondered whether we would ever take them—"
>
> (*CP* 309)

"The little lanes" obviously refer to the process of individuation, as all children must eventually break away from the original symbiosis with their mothers. With Mother lying on the floor the boys immediately feel a faint urge to decide for themselves and to go their own ways. This budding initiative, however, withers away as soon as Mother regains consciousness and is back in control: "And she came back to life, and we never took them."

"The Quilt Pattern" is one of Jarrell's most intricate poems about this ambiguous relationship between mother and child. It appears to be an ingenious synthesis of a great number of symbols taken from psychological studies. Indeed, Jarrell admitted in a letter to Sr. Bernetta Quinn that the **"Quilt Pattern"** was "the most carefully Freudian, best worked-out child's dream" he had ever done.[14] He even gives the clues to many details that may not be immediately clear to a reader unfamiliar with the Freudian interpretation of dreams: "[. . .] you know, the mother in Hansel and Gretel is the real mother, not a stepmother—so in my poem. When I say the dead mother in the dream that's because the boy's made her dead in the dream; she is demanding and completely possessive and awful to him and he hates her. [. . .] What the poem is, in its simplest terms, is the child's redreaming of Hansel and Gretel (presumably it was one of the many tales he got told that afternoon) in terms of his mother and himself. There's nobody else in the dream; everything is either himself or his mother (presumably there is no father in this family).[15] Many commentators on Hansel and Gretel say that the wicked mother is in some sense the witch; after the witch is killed they come home to see the mother dead. The mother is the house (a common symbol for women in dreams, all psychoanalysts say) and the witch too; and partly so in the fairytale—the witch can tell when somebody nibbles on her house just as though it were part of her. The fact that the house is the mother who used to nurse him is alluded to in house of bread, the finger he sucks at, and the taste of the house / Is the taste of his—he won't admit this to himself even in the dream, but it thinks, 'No, I don't know!' (Later, very unexplicitly—I wanted to have it far under the surface) there is a sort of sexual symbolism, since the child does at first conceive of sexual things in terms of his mother, and this mother has made this child her whole emotional life [. . .] the scaling face / of a woman—the dead mother, a reference to the dead real mother; but you can just as well take it as being a second reference to the same woman, made dead now in the child's dream. Even in the dream the child cannot bear to know, to be conscious of and face the guilt of, his feelings toward his mother; after he pushes her into the oven and kills her both parts of him deny that it's anything of theirs that they've done it to—and they deny they've done it, say, timidly smiling at each other, 'It was the Other.' Of course the child is helpless in reality, triumphs only in the dream to which he escapes, and has a most pathetic tiny triumph (pretending to be asleep and 'willing' her away) to be a tiny happy ending for the poem."[16]

The reader surely wonders how much of this material might partly be biographical, but he may also ask himself, if the psychologically trained poet has here not overshot his objective.

Throughout his life Jarrell was painfully conscious that his character was largely determined by his childhood experiences and the subsequent formation at the hands of his parents. Yet, since his father left the family when Randall was still a little boy, the chief influence was actually his mother's. It is, in fact, only late in life that the poet found the strength to forgive his parents for the capital mistake of not allowing him to branch off from "Mother's Highway." In the poem **"The Player Piano"** he protests, "I don't blame you, / You weren't old enough to know any better" (*CP* 354). It is in this very poem, however, that he also discloses by means of metaphors, how terribly handicapped he feels as a result of his parents' educational incompetence. The main point as expressed in the self-pitying outcry "If only, somehow, I had learned to live'." does not, at first, seem to be in keeping with the overall theme of the poem, which turns on his inability to play the piano. In "The Group of Two"[17] Mrs Jarrell has this to say about the biographical background to the poem: "Just before he wrote **'The Player Piano'** and forgave his parents everything, we were listening to the Richter record of Pictures at an Exhibition. Randall was sitting with his eyes closed and his face turned upward and was playing chords on his knees. When the music finished, he said with sudden vehemence, 'You'd have thought somebody would have given me piano lessons!'" It is characteristic of the poet's metonymic manner of association that he should treat this actually insignificant shortcoming in his education as a synecdoche for not having learned to live. The associative links in question are obvious: His "playing chords on his knees" evidently reminds him of the player piano which the Jarrells owned when he was a child. He feels again the old frustration at being condemned to passivity since his "waltz [played] itself out a half-inch from [his] fingers." The small but decisive distance between mechanical aping and creative activity, indicated by "a half-inch" would have been easy to bridge in his youth, providing his parents had had the necessary understanding. However, such was their spiritual apathy that they were totally unable to see through the inauthenticity of their own existence; for them to play at playing was enough.

Unfortunately Jarrell only realized what he had missed when it was already too late to make up for it. Playing the real piano, therefore, became a sort of unattainable ideal for him. The interpretation of a piece of music presupposes a harmonious relationship between the work of art and the player. If the player piano was used as an emblem for the automatic and predetermined "running down" of life, the pianoforte, by contrast, allows or even demands a creative activity or realization and is therefore an apt symbol of the potentiality of life. Jarrell, however, only rarely reached such an agreement with the world. In the above poem all this is hinted at by the suggested correspondence of play or creative work and life: "I [. . .] play I play—If only, somehow, I had learned to live!" If he knew how to play not only the chords of the instrument but the chords of life, as it were, living would no longer be an imaginary make-believe, but might become an authentic performance in which life would be art and artistic creativity life. Instead, existence in general and creative work in particular were rather like a rusty pump, "hard to move and absurd, a squirrel-wheel / A sick squirrel turns slowly, through the sunny / Inexorable hours" (*CP* 300).

Before writing **"The Player Piano"** Jarrell obviously used to blame his parents for giving him only a player-piano which forced him into a merely passive existence. After listening to the record "Pictures at an Exhibition", however, he came to the conclusion: "You weren't to blame." For, as he notes in poems such as **"Washing," "Eighth Air Force,"** or **"Siegfried,"** man's individual guilt is always secondary to that "primal fault" of the universe: "It happens as it does because it does" (*CP* 149).[18] In **"The Player Piano"** accordingly, Mother, Father, and the child come to represent the family of Man who are forced to watch life's player-piano play itself out "a half-inch from [their] fingers."[19] Nobody in particular is to blame for this human predicament. It is, furthermore, useless to try and shape one's destiny by playing one's own tune, since this does not affect the mechanism of the fateful player-piano in the least. Man can at best "hold [his] hands out" and pretend to play the same melody like the player-piano in a sort of Spinozist acquiescence with Necessity.

The seemingly authoritative parents are thus shown to be as powerless as the child itself. When we compare this statement with the "Blind Mother," Jarrell's metaphorical representation of the dumb life-force behind all existence, which is both creative and self-destructive, the "figure in the carpet" of Jarrell's world begins to emerge. We may, therefore, conclude that, despite his critical attitude to his mother, his blame is not primarily directed against her. The poem makes use of the parental relationship to describe man's universal situation, his impotence in the grip of irrational forces and his imprisonment in an absurd chain of events that even includes the "Great Mother" herself and all she stands for in his poetry.

Thus the personal child-mother relationship assumes archetypal dimensions. Although Jarrell asserts, time and again, that a man cannot escape his own mother whose image he carries for ever with him, it is clear that his very image by far transcends the memory of the personal mother: "Back far enough, down deep enough, one comes to the Mothers" (*CP* 310). The mysterious agency of this archetypal power (cf. Goethe's "Mütter") manifests itself in various ways:

> "Just as, within the breast of Everyman,
> Something keeps scolding in his mother's voice,
> Just so, within each woman, an Old Woman
> Rocks, rocks, impatient for her kingdom."
>
> (*CP* 310)

Deep down within his unconscious "mother" is scolding "Everyman" for his separation from her. This, Jarrell concludes, makes it next to impossible for men ever to be happy and content with women even though they might consider them "their type." For "a woman never is a man's type."

> "Possessed by that prehistoric unforgettable
> Other One, who never again is equaled
> By anyone, he searches for his ideal,
> The Good Whore who reminds him of his mother."
>
> (*CP* 326)

She always falls short of "the Good Whore," that projection of man's yearning for an uroboric suspension of opposites, "good" and "bad" in particular, and, as a result, for a state without guilt. In fact, the more a woman resembles this "prehistoric unforgettable Other One" the more he succumbs to the illusion of having found his type. However, the realities are "too much one or the other, / Too much like Mother or too bad . . . Too bad" (*CP* 326). This realization might hinder man from marrying at all and thus would interfere with Nature's urge to bring forth new life. Man's self-delusion about "his own type" is therefore part of the general plan of nature. In the poem **"A Man Meets a Woman in the Street"**—the woman being his own wife, Mary—Jarrell exclaims:

> "Since I can call her, as Swann couldn't,
> A woman who is my type, I follow with the warmth
> Of familiarity, of novelty, this new
> Example of the type,
> Reminded of how Lorenz's just-hatched goslings
> Shook off the last remnants of the egg
> And, looking at Lorenz, realized that Lorenz
> Was their mother. Quacking, his little family
> Followed him everywhere; and when they met a goose,
> Their mother, they ran to him afraid.
>
> Imprinted upon me
> Is the shape I run to [. . .]"
>
> (*CP* 351)

Thus, the "imprinted" mother image is to the individual what the archetype of the Magna Mater is to man in general.

Notes

1. The little bats and owlets in the poems "Bats" and "The Owl's Bedtime Story" may be considered the only exceptions. However, the little bat clinging to its mother's belly has not yet really left the foetal stage. We must remember, moreover, that the alienation of mother and child, which is so conspicuous in many of Jarrell's poems, is also a result of consciousness and as such characteristic of the human predicament. Owl and owlet, by contrast, represent an ideal "natural" mother-child relationship having the character of a fairy-tale. The poem "The Owl's Bedtime Story" accordingly begins: "There was once upon a time a little owl. / He lived with his mother in a hollow tree" (*CP* [*The Complete Poems*] 348).

2. This incident is clearly autobiographical. In her essay, "The Group of Two," Mrs. Randall Jarrell tells us that she and Randall must—unknowingly—have met as children in the reception room which her father "shared with another doctor, Dr. von W., who was treating Mrs. Jarrell for that recurrent / Scene from my childhood, / A scene called Mother Has Fainted." Mrs. Randall Jarrell, "The Group of Two," in Randall Jarrell 1914-1965, ed. Robert Lowell, Peter Taylor, and Robert Penn Warren (New York: Farrar, Straus, and Giroux, 1967) p. 283.

3. Cf. for example, "A Game at Salzburg" where the relation of child to grown-up is compared to the relation of man to God. What is only hinted at in "Hope" as a possibility ("it was as if") is here made more explicit: God really seems to take a nap. Whereas the child, venturing a playful "Hier bin i'" is answered "Da bist du," the world is left in uncertainty and loneliness, without ever getting an answer. Jarrell's imaginary conversation between the world and God is actually reduced to a dramatic monologue. There is no comfort or help to be expected from the "parent" in heaven.

4. One is well-advised, however, to heed Jung's caveat concerning the etiological significance of the personal mother: "The [. . .] traumatic effects produced by the mother must be divided into two groups: 1) those corresponding to traits of character or attitudes actually present in the mother, and 2) those referring to traits which the mother only seems to possess, the reality being composed of more or less fantastic (i. e. archetypal) projections on the part of the child. [. . .] This is not to deny that such a development can be traced back to disturbing influences emanating from the mother. I myself make it a rule to look first for the cause of infantile neuroses in the mother, as I know from experience that a child is much more likely to develop normally than neurotically, and that in the great majority of cases definite causes of disturbances can be found in the parents, especially in the mother. The contents of the child's abnormal

fantasies can be referred to the personal mother only in part, since they often contain clear and unmistakable allusions which could not possibly have reference to human beings. This is especially true where definitely mythological products are concerned, as is frequently the case in infantile phobias where the mother may appear as a wild beast, a witch, a specter, an ogre, a hermaphrodite, and so on. It must be borne in mind, however, that such fantasies are not always of unmistakably mythological origin, and, even if they are, they may not always be rooted in the unconscious archetype but may have been occasioned by fairytales or accidental remarks." C. G. Jung, "Psychological Aspects of the Mother Archetype," [1954], The Collected Works of C. G. Jung, translated from the German by R. F. C. Hull, New York, 1959. Quoted in The Modern Tradition: Backgrounds of Modern Literature, ed. Richard Ellmann and Charles Feidelson, Jr. (New York: Oxford University Press, 1965), pp. 658-59.

5. See ch. 8, "Blood for the Muse," especially p. 154-155.

6. In mythology Mother-Goddesses usually appear simultaneously as both mothers and virgins. Cf. Erich Neumann, The Origins and History of Consciousness, p. 52: "The Great Mother is a virgin, too, in a sense other than that intended by the patriarchate, which later misunderstood her as the symbol of chastity. Precisely in virtue of her fruitfulness, she is a virgin, that is, unrelated and not dependent upon any man. In Sanskrit, 'independent woman' is a synonym for a harlot. Hence the woman who is unattached is not only a universal feminine type but a sacral type in antiquity." Jarrell's association of Mama, fate, and nun closely corresponds to the mythological synthesis of autonomous virginity, fruitful motherhood, and godlike power over life and death.

7. The choice of the word "flock" instead of the generic "fowl" evokes connotations with "sheep," and as a result, with the animal of sacrifice. Cf. "An Essay On The Human Will":

> The lambs wring nothing: they are wrung.
> It is simply pathetic: the tragic flaw
> May lead to stockyards, but the flawless too
> Are swept in the common current of their kind
> To the Pole's indifferent and stunning hand.

8. Cf. the end of "The Old and the New Masters," where the scientist merges with "the last master."

9. This loss of confidence in his mother must have contributed to shake his faith in "God." Cf. "A Sick Child" (*CP* 53), "A Game in Salzburg" (*CP* 67), etc.

10. "London" was first published in Blood for a Stranger, 1942. "The State" in Selected Poems, 1955. "Hope" and "The Hunt in the Black Forest" in The Lost World, 1965.

11. See below, p. 20.

12. My view differs here significantly from that of Schwarz, whose thesis despite its many insights is somewhat impaired by the rigid schema of Freudian psychology. J. M. Schwarz, "An Introduction to the Poems of Randall Jarrell," Diss. University of California, L.A., Ph. D., 1969.

13. Mrs Randall Jarrell has confirmed this interpretation in a letter to me. Randall told her "that his mother had been young and trim and pretty enough when he was at High School to be mistaken for his sister. At that time of his life he felt close to her again after having lost her when his younger brother was born and became her favourite. He lost her again, however, when she remarried while he was still at school."

14. Letter to Sr. Bernetta Quinn (Dec. 15, 1951), Berg Collection (New York Public Library).

15. It may not be irrelevant in this context that Jarrell was without a father when he grew up.

16. Letter to Sr. Bernetta Quinn (Dec. 15, 1951), Berg Collection (New York Public Library).

17. Mrs. Randall Jarrell, "The Group of Two," in Randall Jarrell 1914-1965, p. 296.

18. Cf. John Steinbeck's realistic concept of society as expressed in the novel In Dubious Battle: "Things are as they are because they must be."

19. In one of his handwritten notes to the poem "Hope" Jarrell goes even further: "Dad, the wife, and the child, and apartment eleven / I am them all. We are a way for each other to be." Insofar as man's thusness (Sosein) is determined by "family relationships" everybody is a threat to the other's self-consciousness (Selbstbewusstsein) but at the same time he can only discover his own self in the other: "We are a way for each other to be."

Jarrell's holograph of this and most other notes and sketches cited are in the Berg Collection, New York Public Library. I wish here to express my thanks to the director of the Berg Collection, Dr. Lola Szladits, for permission to consult the manuscripts and supplying helpful information.

A Selected Bibliography

This list includes all books and articles cited in my text. It also includes those additional works which, in my opinion, may contribute significantly to the reader's understanding of Jarrell. The first section below is arranged thematically, the other sections alphabetically.

I. Primary Sources: Books and Articles by Randall Jarrell

1. Poetry

Jarrell, Randall. *The Complete Poems.* New York: Farrar, Straus & Giroux, 1969.

———. *Blood for a Stranger.* New York: Harcourt, Brace and Co., 1942.

———. *Selected Poems.* New York: Alfred A. Knopf, 1955.

———. *The Lost World.* New York: Macmillan Co., 1965.

2. Manuscripts and letters

Jarrell, Randall. Manuscripts and letters. The Berg Collection, New York City Public Library.

II. Secondary Sources: Biographical and Critical Works

Arendt, Hannah. "Randall Jarrell," *Randall Jarrell 1914-1965,* ed. Robert Lowell et al. New York: Farrar, Straus & Giroux, 1967, 3-9.

Jarrell, Mary. "The Group of Two," *Randall Jarrell 1914-1965,* op. cit., 274-298.

Schwarz, John Moritz. "An Introduction to the Poems of Randall Jarrell." Unpublished dissertation, University of California, Los Angeles, 1969.

III. Other Works and Background Studies

Jung, C.G. *Gesammelte Werke.* ed. Marianne Niehus-Jung et al. Zürich: Rascher Verlag und Co., 1964.

Neumann, Erich. *The Origins and History of Consciousness.* Translated from the German by R. F. C. Hull. Bollingen Series XLII. 1st. ed. 1954. Princeton: Bollingen Paperback Printing 1971.

Sister Bernetta Quinn (essay date 1981)

SOURCE: Quinn, Sister Bernetta. "The Original Bat-Poet." In *Randall Jarrell,* pp. 92-109. Boston: Twayne Publishers, 1981.

[*In the following essay, Quinn offers close readings of Jarrell's three books of poetry for children:* The Bat-Poet, The Animal Family, *and* Fly by Night, *emphasizing the autobiographical element in these works.*]

The preceding chapters on Jarrell's poetry intimate rather than exhaust his multifaceted genius. A third could readily follow on those lyrics that involve the Old and the New Testaments, the most interesting being the autobiographical mask entitled **"Jonah,"** as well as others on different themes. Since he himself constructed list after list of preferences in his reviews, there is excuse for singling out some favorites not treated in detail ahead: **"Losses," "Hohensalzburg: Fantastic Variations on a Theme of Romantic Character," "The Carnegie Library, Juvenile Division," "The Woman at the Washington Zoo," "The Sleeping Beauty: Variation of the Prince," "The Girl Dreams that She Is Giselle," "A Soul," "A Sick Child," "Cinderella," "Nestus Gurley," "The Black Swan," "Deutsch durch Freud," "The End of the Rainbow."** Like his own "top-billings," the catalog is no sooner ended than seen as flawed by omissions. Yet its concreteness highlights the power of this poet to change.

On *The Nashville Tennessean*'s literary page, where fifty years earlier Donald Davidson was acquainting the South with the Fugitives, Thomas Inge has called for a study to reveal Jarrell as the supreme poet he was: "But the time is ripe for someone to come forth and state with the proper justification and support—a careful analysis of his style and technique as an inspired craftsman—that Randall Jarrell was one of the two or three at the very top of his generation as a contemporary American poet."[1]

Meanwhile, a self-portrait of Jarrell the poet emerges from the triad of children's books on which he had the good luck to collaborate with another "poet," Maurice Sendak.

Sendak, in his remarks to a session of the National Council of Teachers of English, meeting in New York in November 1977, made the same suggestion, recognizing how self-revelatory of the writer was this triad for which they had planned the "decorations." He reported that his own original books, especially *Where the Wild Things Are,* were "super-personal"; so he regarded Randall's, unified by the theme of the search for a mother and rising from that "primitive place," the subconscious, locus of a child's paradise which is "truer than time." Despite the war lyrics, Jarrell by temperament was no hawk, but "a small, furred animal," like the little brownish bat he chose as his symbol in the best-known of his children's books.

No partnership could have been more felicitous than that of Jarrell and Sendak. At first, the artist objected to the proposal that he illustrate Randall's **The Bat-Poet,** feeling that the lyrics were illustration enough entirely apart from the exquisitely pictorial effects in the prose. Finally he agreed, but only on the terms that his contributions be announced as "pictures by Sendak," as they are on the dust jacket. In Jarrell he found a keen graphic sense (in his earlier years, the poet had executed representational paintings in warm colors), together with that music which he confesses most stimulates his own work.[2] Their business relationship grew into friendship, shared by Mary Jarrell, with whom they went places in New York when not working: "I loved Randall Jarrell," Sendak told the English teachers at the meeting mentioned above.

After the poet died, Maurice Sendak continued "decorating" (his own word) Jarrell's books. An example is his posthumous designs for **The Golden Bird and Other Tales from Grimm.** Four stories had appeared in 1962 in a volume also containing Lore Segal's renditions of others. Introducing a different version of the Grimm tales, that by Sandro Nardini, Jarrell noted: "I know a poet who has written poems about Hansel and Gretel, Sleeping Beauty, the Frog Prince, and Cinderella."[3] The poet was, of course, himself.

Jarrell used at least thirty-six of the Grimm fairy stories in his lyrics. **"Cinderella"** casts into symbol an unhappy marriage in the way that moderns tend to use the Medusa myth, as Samuel French Morse did in "Beyond Medusa."[4] Had Sendak decorated Randall's prose translation of **"Cinderella,"** he might have put in an enormous cat with fierce eyes, glowering from the hearth at the maiden and her newly met godmother, a pair who, smiling like two old women, "lapped in each other's looks, / Mirror for mirror, drank a cup of tea." In the tales he did do, the images seem suggested by Jarrell: the dog with his stern disapproving stare at the witch in "Hansel and Gretel" (more prominent than the children); the owl as ominous center of Snow White's story; the puppy in bed with his fisherman-master as the greedy wife stands over them to pronounce her final wish. In fact, Maurice Sendak affirms he can still hear Randall Jarrell's voice in the room with him whenever he works on one of the stories.

I. THE BAT-POET

No one knew more intimately than Mary Jarrell the blessedness of the Sendak-Jarrell team. Reviewing **The Animal Family,** she comments thus:

> Mr. Sendak's unique illustrations are a kind of music you hear while you read. It is a strange music made of pines and shells and misshapen cliffs and it comes from moonlight and ocean waves and deserted places. They belong with the book as much as the book belongs with the sentence of Gogol's that my husband quotes for the preface: 'Say what you like, but such things do happen—not often, but they do happen.'[5]
>
> [*Greensboro Daily News*]

And no one guessed more wrongly about children's reactions to the initial book, **The Bat-Poet,** than Hayden Carruth: "The kids won't like it and I don't blame them."[6] The fact that it is still going strong in paperback as well as hard cover editions is proof enough of his error. While the charm and depths of **The Bat-Poet** dawned gradually on reviewers, some acclaimed it at once, such as Lavinia Ross, who attributes to it the immortality that Ingmar Bergman felt his films to possess: she quotes Bergman as saying, "After seeing my pictures, I hope people will see a little more—the light will change—the landscape will look a little different."[7] It did, after Jarrell.

When **The Bat-Poet** appeared, dust jacket and frontispiece showed a "solitary singer," not the thrush with which Whitman identified himself in "Out of the Cradle Endlessly Rocking," but a small creature "like a furry mouse with wings." The simple adventures of this "little light brown bat" are those of Jarrell himself, in their essence. No sensitive child or adult would mistake the Bat-poet for just a bat, any more than the Mole as only mole in *The Wind in the Willows*. Shortly after Jarrell's death, this identity was acknowledged by a North Carolina journalist: "But '**The Bat-Poet,**' like 'Alice in Wonderland,' is more than a children's story. It is the story of the Bat-Poet who for a long time to come, will remain one of America's greatest living poets,"[8] the second adjective ironical but accurate.

Beginning the bat-parable "Once upon a time" lifts it out of the ordinary. As Thomas Noesen says in "Fairy Tales and the Gospels," this standard opening causes time to disappear in favor of an eternal dimension: "Whether we say 'once upon a time' as in the fairy tale or 'in the beginning' as in John's gospel, we have expressed the same point in history: no point."[9] The story goes beneath sequential "facts" into something more important: a totality of message. The use of "you" introduces an auditor, perhaps Mary, to whom the book is dedicated. Like a *doppelgänger*, Jarrell goes in and out of the little house, studying the bats over his head and occasionally turning a flashlight on them to watch them screw up their faces in the painful glare. His presence as character and audience in the drama achieves aesthetic distance.

When the fable begins, the coffee-colored bat is as wingless in daylight as the others in the bunch hanging upside-down from the porch rafters, but gradually, unlike the rest, he experiments with the sun. With summer's end, the other bats having retreated to the barn, he finds himself alienated; pleading with them to return but meeting refusal, he no more succumbs to following them than did his creator to following the popular tastes he deprecated in **A Sad Heart at the Supermarket.** Like Jonathan Seagull, he decides to "go it alone."[10] Loneliness often afflicted Randall Jarrell. Autumn having arrived, the bat-poet is seized with this emotion: "So he had to sleep all alone. He missed the others." But he bravely accepts his fate of nonconformist.

In the hitherto unknown daytime world, he makes friends with other animals and birds, the most satisfactory being the chipmunk, a parallel to Mary Jarrell in its appreciation of his poetry. Jarrell's interest in Marianne Moore, translator of La Fontaine and deviser of many original fabulae, shines forth in the types of persons represented by the bat's new acquaintances." In *Poetry and the Age,* he compares her lyrics to animals that rescue "the foolish heroes of fairy tales—which can save only the heroes, because they are too small not to have been disregarded by everyone else" (p. 166).

As the bat-poet admits into his ken the squirrels, chipmunks, possums, and owls whose lives he has previously slept through, his vision is extended, as poets' must be before their readers' vision can be. He comes to "see" in the sense of "understand" how shadows can be "bright as moonlight" and how the "black-and-gray turns to green-and-gold-and-blue," knowledge locked away from his somnolent bat-relatives. In the "blurred and golden" light he perceives how the chipmunk's tail is rosy and in his poem likens the color to maple leaves and fox fur. In short, as he comes to live a multicolored existence, his poetic ability strengthens ("the sunlight and the shadows and the red and yellow and orange branches made a kind of blurred pattern . . ."). Arrived at the gift of thinking in landscapes ("In the west, over the gray hills the sun was red"), he discovers the sunset forever hidden from the other bats.

In **"The Obscurity of the Poet"** Jarrell laments over how most persons of his age, having read neither the poetry of yesterday nor of today, cannot understand "the mockingbird's song," nor have they any wish to try (*Poetry and the Age,* p. 3). The bat-poet's plea to the polite but uninterested other bats that they listen to the mockingbird (a good poet, despite a difficult personality) reminds one of Jarrell's desire that everyone enjoy the poetry *he* enjoyed: "Once you get used to [the mockingbird's song] it sounds wonderful." In real life, whether in a conference with a student or in letters to friends like Taylor and Lowell, he would say about their original verse "It's wonderful . . . Wonderful!" just as the little bat does, listening to the virtuosity of the mockingbird. In the fable, the mockingbird, possibly representing the New Critics, offers only dry comments on line-lengths and metrical dexterity as response to the timid bat's first song.

The bat's imitative period, patterned on a number of poets as recapitulated in the mockingbird's music (Auden, Yeats, Tate, Warren), coincides with ***Blood for a Stranger,*** its words often too derivative to be united in an original "tune." As his apprenticeship continues, he sees in a flash of insight that "If you get the words right you don't need a tune." The poetic career of the bat-poet is not all advances, any more than was Jarrell's: there were times when only translations were possible and when the dread of never recovering poetic powers was heavy upon him. His own misgivings appear in *The Bat-Poet*: "But sometimes the poem would seem so bad to him that he'd get discouraged and stop in the middle, and by the next day he'd have forgotten it." Sometimes too he began a prose work he found impossible to complete: the way the cardinal resisted the bat-poet's Muse as a subject has its parallel in Hart Crane, on whom Jarrell once undertook to do a small book, financed by a Guggenheim grant. Though he greatly admired Crane, difficulty after difficulty intervened, until finally he had to give up the project and return the money. In *The Bat-Poet* his friend the chipmunk encourages him about the verse-portrait he is struggling to do on the cardinal: "Why, just say what he's like, the way you did about the owl and me," yet try as best he can the bat-poet cannot put into words the beauty of the cardinal.

The villain of this Jarrellian fable enters the action early, in an episode which almost resulted in the demise of the "hero": one night an owl swoops toward him, coming so close that the little bat would have been caught had not a refuge offered itself in the hole in the old oak growing beside the little house in the wood, a symbolic salvation by the Sacred Wood of Sir James Frazer and Robert Graves. This owl provides the subject for **"The Bird of Night,"** possibly the most suitable lyric in *The Complete Poems* for introducing Randall Jarrell to high school or college students. Its context, *The Bat-Poet,* while helping as motivation, is not indispensable: the lyric floats free from the fable, as free as its owl-hunter floats over and through the woods. Robert Penn Warren's "The Owl," one of his lesser-known pieces, and his "Time as Hypnosis" make excellent comparative studies, since all three are initiations into the problem of evil, along with Warren's "Blackberry Winter." **"Thinking of the Lost World"** is another such initiation, the grandmother attacking the chicken taking the place of the owl.

Jarrell's traumatic exposure to the "murder" of that chicken haunted him throughout life, nor is it absent from the owl-poem (p. 12) that the bat-poet, inspired by the mockingbird, composes:

> A shadow is floating through the moonlight.
> Its wings don't make a sound.
> Its claws are long, its beak is bright.
> Its eyes try all the corners of the night.
>
> It calls and calls: all the air swells and heaves
> And washes up and down like water.

As in Warren's "Bearded Oaks," an Atlantis metaphor prevails: *floating, swells, heaves, washes, water.* The liquidity of the consonants heightens the effect, as does the undulating imitative not only of the ocean but also of easy flight. The moonlight itself is the "water."

Moonlight is used so often in Jarrell that it might be thought of as a character binding the lyrics together in a narrative way, just as the same person appears throughout thirty feet of a Chinese scroll on life along a river. In **"Hohensalzburg: Fantastic Variations on a Theme of Romantic Character,"** the invisible vampire, who says *"I am here behind the moonlight,"* may be nothing but the moonlight. Other examples that significantly employ moonlight are **"A Girl in a Library," "The Märchen," "The Rising Sun," "Windows," "A Ward in the States," "Mother, Said the Child," "Hope," "Dreams," "A Ghost Story."** Sendak's double-page picture (pp. 6-7) closest to **"The Bird of Night"** shows owl and moon prominently in conjunction.

To imagine the bird as a floating shadow with wings is original and beautiful. In the line drawing opposite the poem, Maurice Sendak suggests in the wings the headdress of an Indian chief, silhouetted against the disc of moon and centered in the only clear area in the wilderness, with its ivy, gnarled trees, leafy branches, ferns, grasses. The polysyllabic meter of "A shadow is floating in the moonlight" gives way in the second line to the retardation of the three strong stresses "wings don't make." In the third, the shadow has not only wings but claws and beak; the doom of small furry creatures hiding below is not ameliorated by the adjective *bright*, alliterating with *beak*, since the brightness may be blood. The caesura, part of the leisurely flight, helps the hunter to scrutinize his terrain.

Besides claws and beak, this shadow is equipped with eyes that "try" all the corners of the night, turning the forest from huge seaweed clusters and coral to a new metaphor, a prison from which there is no escape, the "corners" implying its rectangular shape. The onomatopoeic identical rhyme—"It calls and calls: all the air swells and heaves"—is common in Jarrell. When the mockingbird evaluates the bat's poem he does not mention the repetition of the letter *l* here, leading up to and away from *all,* that word so common in Jarrell lyrics, though it is the sort of thing he does notice, to the author's dismay, instead of the fright at the heart of the composition.

No ear, of itself, believes in death; to say so is metonymy. But poets do and none more so than Randall Jarrell, from ***Blood for a Stranger*** through ***The Lost World.*** Although not specifically occurring in this stanza, as in **"Lady Bates,"** the hooting of the owl vibrates so threateningly through the air that it seems to own it: the night becomes "the owl's air," meant on a secondary level as mournful melody ("If you get the words right you don't need a tune"). "Still as death" could be trite, but next to "stone" and when attributed to the scared little mouse and the even more scared (because more aware) bat, it is no cliché. The quiet ocean of moonlight become a prison, now as if in a Charles Burchfield painting, turns into a living creature that can hold its breath in terror, the cutting off of the final line dramatizing this fear, as the mockingbird notes: "And it was clever of you to have that last line two feet short" (p. 14). The mood is unlike the calm acceptance of the companion-piece (**"The Breath of Night"**) from a 1947 *Kenyon Review,* though even this poem detects beneath the joy of the forest's beauty at night "the Strife that moves the stars." The universe itself in **"The Bird of Night"** trembles before the owl.

Maurice Sendak's theory, alluded to above, is that the "search for a mother" ties together ***The Bat-Poet, The Animal Family,*** and ***Fly by Night.*** This motif was already present in ***The Gingerbread Rabbit,***[12] illustrated by Garth Williams. Its most direct elucidation in the first Sendak volume is the fourth poem: "Sleepily, almost dreaming, the bat began to make up a poem about a mother and her baby." Like W. C. Williams, Jarrell believed the unconscious to be the place where poems are born: in **"Dreams"** "The darkness puts to its lips its finger. / The children spell in their sleep." In the magical state of dream the bat recalls the story of his own infancy: "It was easier than the other poems somehow: all he had to do was remember what it had been like and every once in a while put in a rhyme," like Wallace Stevens striking the silver chime of a rhyme at will.

Jarrell's mother died shortly after he did, early in 1966, the following year. Although very close when he was a child, they grew apart. Yet there was a time when as a young boy in California he wrote affectionate, funny, "sharing" letters to her in Tennessee, enjoying a relationship he idealizes in that of the little bat and his mother, one quite different from the estrangement described as early as **"The Bad Music,"** which must have been written in the 1930s. Here, he remembers his mother as crying; the son asks, ". . . how many know or love at all / You, Anna?" about her present status and answers himself, "Enough." ***The Animal Family*** underscores that happy memories of Anna were not dead; in fact, one is recalled in **"The Player Piano,"** where Jarrell, disguised as a feminine speaker, writes, "I remember how I'd brush my mother's hair / Before she bobbed it."

The bat's birth is in human terms, "Naked and blind and pale." The poem he makes up about himself, like **"The Bird of Night,"** simulates flight: "Doubling and leaping, soaring, somersaulting. . . ." The baby bat hangs on underneath the mother's body. About a third of the thirty-four lines rhyme, and about a third are in pentameter, but shorter line-lengths dominate to give the illusion of flying. The figures of speech—for example, "Like shining needlepoints of sound"—make up in quality for quantity. In the embroidery image (the synesthetic needle of the "high sharp cries" of the mother bat weaving in and out of the moonlight-and-shadow fabric) the poet "complicates" in the way that the original bat-poet loved to: it is a compass reference, a variant of the Christ Child toward which everything is pointed in **"The Old and the New Masters"** ("The naked, / Shining baby, like the needle of a compass"). The seventeenth line is followed by a pivot, the "echo" trick Jarrell had praised in *Paterson,* here "In full flight; in full flight." In Sendak's picture for the poem, love stands in antithesis to death: "Their single shadow, / printed on the moon / Or fluttering across the stars, / Whirls on all night." Home again, the mother like a guardian angel "folds her wings about her sleeping child."

In H. W. Suber one sees a reviewer who early detected the personal revelation that Sendak was to note: "Randall Jarrell, in his book **The Bat-Poet,** left an autobiography of sorts."[13] But this children's tale also serves as a literary memoir, Suber believes, a critique of the age itself, alluding obliquely to Robert Frost ("After Apple Picking"), to Dylan Thomas ("Fern Hill"); besides being "an annotated anthology of the Bat-Poet's [Jarrell's] own poems" and "a textbook on contempoetics," it can also be taken as "an introduction to Ezra Pound." The author of *Personae* may well be the mockingbird, assuming one voice after another (Daniel, Browning, Villon). In the lyric on the mockingbird which the bat sings to the chipmunk, he may be satirizing Pound's youthful role among fellow-writers from his posts as foreign editor in Europe: "On the willow's highest branch, monopolizing / Day and night, cheeping, squeaking, soaring," and again, "All day the mockingbird has owned the yard" and "fighting hard / To make the world his own" (p. 28). If this be true, the genuine admiration with which Jarrell regarded *The Cantos* nevertheless comes through at the end:

> A mockingbird can sound like anything.
> He imitates the world he drove away
> So well that for a minute, in the moonlight,
> Which one's the mockingbird? which one's the world?

If Randall Jarrell wrote little about *il miglior fabbro* ("the better maker"), he did consciously benefit from Poundian technique in such dramatic monologues as **"Jonah."** As a teacher Jarrell thought each of his Greensboro students better than they were. Similarly he may have been presenting in his generous and persistent eulogies of the mockingbird (Pound?) to the other bats, as well as in his bat-poet discipleship, a much more positive than negative estimate of the poet whom some critics were accusing of vanity, arrogance, over-concern with technique.

II. THE ANIMAL FAMILY

Despite its title, the protagonist of **The Animal Family** is a human being, a hunter who finds a mermaid by following a mysterious song to the ocean near a cabin made of logs which he, like Robinson Crusoe, has chopped down himself. Yet even before he begins to collect his "family" about him, this hunter's garments identify him with animals: deerskin trousers, shirt, and shoes; cloak of a mountain lion's hide; cap of a sea-otter's skin. Moreover, he has ornamented the walls and chairs of his house with foxes, seals, a lynx, a mountain lion, as if to prepare the right kind of home for those who will occupy it. This classic has often been likened to *The Little Prince,* its central character at home amidst the nonhuman. Margaret Sherwood Libby wrote "Not since St.-Exupèry's *Little Prince* have I found a book of this kind that I wanted to share with everyone."[14]

Mary Jarrell relates the setting to their residence on South Lake Drive in Greensboro, though at the same time picturing it as a collage of Randall's memories of drives along the Pacific, scenes from Coos Bay to Big Sur.[15] Mixed in with these recollections are visits to Rock Creek Park in Washington, D.C. But more important than these is the ivied Greensboro house, present also as setting in the other two Sendak books, with its seat under the large eastern window made of stained and clear glass combined. The hunter's possessions in **The Animal Family** were actually Randall's: the brass horn, ship's figurehead, animal pelts, wooden table utensils. The fireplace is the fireplace of the home where this prose-poem dream was dreamed, in the tranquility of the North Carolina evenings.[16]

The projected essay mentioned above on Randall Jarrell and music could deal not just with the operatic and orchestral, but also with nameless melodies like the one that brings out the mother-motif as the hunter, warm under his bearskin, hears it in the song of the waves: "the great soft sound the waves made over and over. It seemed to him that it was like his mother singing." When he falls off to sleep, it really *is* the mother, sitting by his bed singing. In **The Animal Family,** which opens with the same four words that **The Bat-Poet** does, one is conscious that this lullaby is "once upon a time, long, long ago," partly through the reference to his dead father, who sits repairing bow and arrow at the fireplace. The same dream returns in the summer: when sleep comes, "his thoughts changed to dreams, and his mother was singing to him." When he awakens in the moonlight the mother-figure singing changes to the seal-like creature in the waters, not yet classified as a mermaid. It might be the moonlight itself: in that strange little design by Sendak on the title page the moon is wreathed in leaves, the symbol of the mermaid whose hair and skin Jarrell describes as "the same silvery blue-green, the color of the moonlight on the water." As if she were truly only the moonlight, the mermaid, unlike the personalities in **The Bat-Poet,** never appears in the decorations.

The bat, once he has discovered the joy of poetry through the mockingbird, goes on to original composition; the hunter remains a "mockingbird." He courts the mermaid by memorizing a tag of the song from the sea and interspersing it among all the other tunes he can recollect. The speech of human and ondine are mutually unintelligible, but not hopelessly so, any more than the children's after a taste of dragon's blood in **"Children Selecting Books in a Library"**:

> . . . The children's cries
> Are to men the cries of crickets, dense with warmth
> —But dip a finger into Fafnir, taste it,
> And all their words are plain as chance and pain.
>
> (**C. p.** [*The Complete Poems*], p. 106)

Gleefully they begin to teach each other, she making many an amusing mistake in language though a quicker learner than he. When she asks what "mistakes" are, Jarrell the hunter replies in a manner applicable to his own poetic practice: "The wrong word—the wrong sound, one you don't mean to make." She puzzles over the ambiguities in human speech, such as "legs" in reference to the hunter and to his table, but readily adds the word *leg* to her vocabulary, like the mermaid in "A Soul," who touches the man's legs as she and her lover sit near the shore: "Yes, here is one, / Here is the other . . . *Legs* . . . / And they move so?"

"A Soul" features in its initial line a bat as nonconformist as the furry winged protagonist of the child's tale: "It is evening. One bat dances / Alone, where there were swallows." These sentences could serve as epigram for the entire Sendak "trilogy." Written ten years earlier than the fable about the mermaid, it is a tender little dialogue in six stanzas, in which the mermaid's *thou* approximates the German *du*. That happy "dailiness of life" with which **"Well Water"** ends characterizes this couple, the "once more" disclosing their habit of meeting at night even though the "thin air" is dangerous to her. Exceptional among mermaids as the bat-poet among bats, she has scales on her breast as well as tail, unlike the ondines of art, but she is even more exceptional in that she has gained a soul by winning the love of a human. The same legend, out of Hans Christian Andersen, forms the groundwork of *The Animal Family,* and as implied in her domestication, the same blessing comes to its mermaid, as their love (the love of friendship) matures.

From time to time the sea-creature of *The Animal Family* returns to her former home under the waves, where she finds it as difficult to tell the other mermen and mermaids about a fire as the bat-poet did to communicate to the other bats what bright shadows were. Their problem can be related to **"The Obscurity of the Poet."** Like the chipmunk, she has a natural understanding of poetic images, shown by her reaction to the branch of red maple leaves the hunter gives her: "The mermaid looked at it as if she couldn't believe it; she carried it, and stroked it, and said to him lovingly, 'It's the best thing I've ever had in all my life.'" Reading *The Animal Family,* Jarrell's former student Sylvia Wilkinson recalled the day she and others brought him a gift: "I remember how excited he was when we carried him a bunch of red berries we had stolen off a campus branch."[17] If he is the Hunter in the fable, he is also the Mermaid.

The fire, after it burns her, becomes an object of fear like the owl to the chipmunk, bewildering but beautiful. She compares it to a red shell just as she has the meadow flowers to white shells. Sendak has chosen for his cover a shell ringed with leaf-tendrils, as the moon is inside the book. The necklace of gold and green and blue stones from the bottom of the sea that the mermaid presents to the hunter is a "poem," received as such when he repeats to her what she has said to him about the red maple branch.

The theme of the lost mother never vanishes: "The hunter would tell her about his father and mother and the years the three of them had lived there, showing her a little square of lace, his mother's handkerchief; to the hunter and the mermaid it was a great treasure" (p. 49). Since the mermaid is not able to imagine a woman, he carves a statue of his mother for her, and she exclaims at once: "'Why, she's like me!'" (p. 50). Thus through fantasy the hunter recovers the mother for whom has he never ceased to shed invisible tears.

The wealth of fairy tales that the hunter shares with his mate (if one can call her that) comes from his dead mother. It is the mother remembered so fondly from boyhood that Jarrell intends in the wish: "Whenever anything reminded him of his father and mother, you could see that he missed them and longed to have them alive again." (In the last of the series, *Fly by Night,* he does resurrect them.)

Since they cannot be parents without a child, the man and mermaid add to their household a bear cub. Sendak's leafless branches reach out as if in love, under the title of Chapter Three, "The Hunter Brings Home a Baby." As always in his decorations for this book, the members of the animal family do not appear. Nothing seems unusual about the bear's entrance into their household circle, though his coming occasions some funny incidents, such as the mermaid's consternation at his hibernation, which recalls to her the mother's Sleeping Beauty story as told her by the hunter. In Chapter Five the man steals a lynx as brother for their son, no doubt a compliment to Elfie, Jarrell's tortoise-shell cat, to whom this volume is dedicated. The newcomer destroys with his sharp claws the mother's lace handkerchief, but it is marvelously repaired, as if in a Hawthorne myth. At the end of this chapter comes a deft foreshadowing of the next when the hunter tells the mermaid how his mother used to admonish their cat "Velvet" to get him to tuck in his claws: "That's what my mother used to say on the boat.'"

The child Jarrell is externalized in the shipwrecked boy found one day by the lynx: "A woman was lying at the other end [of the unlucky vessel], half in and half out of the water that filled the bottom of the boat": huddled against her was a little boy who was crying. Between lynx and bear the boy is installed in the seaside Eden which the cabin has become. When the mermaid and hunter return, they seem scarcely even surprised at finding the sleeping child snuggled up to the bear beside the fireplace. The child's first word to the mermaid when he awakens is "Mama." The burial of the mother that same day by the hunter reawakens in him his own desolation at being parentless. Suspense continues to build as to whether the mermaid will go back to the ocean, as Matthew Arnold's does in "The Forsaken Merman," a poem referred to in **"The End of the Rainbow,"** where a cynic calls mermen only seals and mermaids manatees (aquatic animals with rounded tails). When the mermaid chooses the land as her home, Jarrell uses the decision to say something important about Life, that it is struggle as indeed it is for her—just the opposite of the convent in Hopkins's "Heaven Haven," which is "out of the swing of the sea," where "storms not come."

The Animal Family ends in a lie, told to the child by his parents, who have so confused dream and reality in their own minds that they believe their insistence he has always been their child; it is a lie in the sense that art itself is a lie. "We've had you always," are the last words of the book, said by the mermaid to the boy. The symbolic source of this "lie," standing in Jarrell as in Yeats for the creative process, is the seashell and the strange music dwelling within its ivory spiral.

This story offers details from Jarrell's life in the manner that *trobar clus* poetry did in regard to the troubadours. Its most profound autobiographical sense is the whole enchanted world that the family inhabits, the straw of reality spun into gold: "It is not a sentimental happiness. The lynx is stolen from his mother, the boy is cast up by a storm in which *his* mother has died; each of the characters in the fable knows the meaning of pain, and sadness, and fear. But the happiness is there, all the same, though it has to be won."[18] The mermaid must exert effort beyond the usual as she travels without legs to and from the ocean and so does the husband as he tries to decipher her tongue or puts up with her ineptitude in cooking, but somehow they manage, like the young couple in Steinbeck's *The Pearl* who have been driven out of their first paradise only to enter into a more realistic one.[19]

In **The Complete Poems,** the nearest analogue to their marriage is **"A Man Meets a Woman in the Street."** Sunlight, gingko trees, the wife's hair of coarse gold above her champagne-colored dress all conspire to make the husband happy, though he recognizes mutability. ("if only . . . If only . . ."), especially toward the end:

> After so many changes made and joys repeated,
> Our first bewildered, transcending recognition
> Is pure acceptance. We can't tell our life
> From our wish. Really I began the day
> Not with a man's wish: "May this day be different,"
> But with the birds' wish: "May this day
> Be the same day, the day of my life."
>
> (*C. p.*, p. 353)

If Jarrell's tales begin "Once upon a time," they do not finish "And they lived happily ever after." Yet, as in this poem celebrating conjugal love, they are illuminated with what Robert Penn Warren calls delight.

III. Fly by Night

Fly by Night, concluding the "spiritual autobiography" decorated by Maurice Sendak, did not appear until 1976. The dust jacket shows a mother-figure holding a huge placard on a pole which announces title, author, artist; later in the volume the same woman cradles against herself a child, in the forest "where the wild things are." Never having met Anna Campbell Jarrell Regan, Sendak constructed her out of recollections of his own mother as he drew the dreams of this third "chapter." Also on the jacket, high over the mother's head, the floating David, whose story it is, is pictured face down resting against the air, as if it were the water implied in **"The Bird of Night."**

The locale is Greensboro, as in the other two books: "If you turn right at the last stoplight on New Garden Road," *Fly by Night* begins. The Jarrells had lived on Spring Lake Drive, which does turn off the New Garden Road cutting through Greensboro. The hero's chow dog is Reddy, the name of the pet rabbit Jarrell had in California as a child (the poet in Part III of **"The Lost World"** begs his grandmother, "'Mama, you won't kill Reddy ever, / You won't ever, will you?'" but cannot believe her when she says she would never even think of such a thing). Reddy's worried expression in his prominent righthand corner of the Sendak frontispiece is a transference of the owner's anxiety. David also has a cat named Flour; cats were always indispensable to Jarrell, even in his Nashville days, as remembered by the Breyers.

Nocturnal flying is just the opposite of the accomplishment of the bat-poet, who learns to fly by day, but of course that a boy should fly at all is amazing, like a tree walking. The fact that David is naked, Sendak told the NCTE [National Council of Teachers of English] audience, is to emphasize that there is nothing between him and the experience. After Randall's death, Sendak used the same symbolism in his book *In the Night Kitchen* (New York, 1970) where on the third page Mickey falls through the dark, "out of his clothes," jumping back into them at the end. Randall's devotion to Wordsworth's "Intimations" Ode accords with David's conviction when beginning to float that could he only remember he would have the power always, by day as well as night. The visualization as in comic strip balloons of the dreams of father, mother, dog, sheep is a touch any child-reader would adore. **"The End of the Rainbow,"** possibly Jarrell's own favorite among his lyrics,[20] closes with a similar effect in Su-Su's dream, where like one sheep in *Fly by Night* the animal dreams that he is dreaming:

> The little black dog sleeping in the doorway
> Of the little turquoise store, can dream
> His own old dream: that he is sleeping
> In the doorway of the little turquoise store.
>
> (*C. p.*, p. 229)

The father's dream, wherein he is "running back and forth with David on his back, only David is big as ever, "hints that the son during waking hours may have felt a burden to his father. But it also symbolizes how the child within Jarrell never died. The mother dreams of making pancakes, in a snow of pillow feathers.

As in a Grimm story, or the Acts of the Apostles, the door opens of itself for the hero, who does not seem in the least surprised to have the cat address him in poetry: "Wake by night and fly by night, / The wood is black, / the wood is white." Circling within view but out of reach of the cat, three mice also talk in rhyme: "What's that great big black thing in the sky? . . . / It's little David—he can fly." Menaced by the cat, they scamper away into a hole, calling back in an echo of Tatyana's farewell to the girl in the library: "It's time to go—goodbye, goodbye!"

The hypnotic trance of **"Lady Bates"** returns in the boy's inability to say a word or move, even to yawn or close his eyes. Both trance and dream also recall **"Hohensalzburg."** Floating over the sheep, he is mingled in image with the girl and her brother of **"The Night before the Night before Christmas"** ("She and her brother float up from the snow"), though here the only "snow" is fleece in the moonlight.

The main character, outside of David, in the fable is the owl: "It glides towards him silently—then it gives two big slow strokes of its wings, but not a single feather makes a sound." Though the description tallies with the *Bat-Poet*'s ("Its wings don't make a sound"), the bird's symbolism is no longer sinister, as if death were taking on a less terrible significance for Jarrell. A silvery fish writhes in its beak, no longer bright with blood but "yellow," the hunter's booty here nothing but a good mother's provision for her nestlings. (The fish as sketched by Sendak for the back cover of the jacket does not look too resigned; rather, it does for the tri-part tale what the skull does for a medieval painting.)

The "search for a mother" motif receives further evidence in the first of the owl's songs, an invitation to David to become for the night one of her offspring. When they arrive at the tree home where the two owlets are waiting and the big silvery fish has been disposed of, the mother owl tells them and David an irregularly rhymed story which takes up five pages of the slender book. This is a fantasy-autobiography of the author, based on the need for a mother: "He'd stand on tiptoe / Staring across the forest for his mother / And hear her far away"; the desire for a brother or sister must also have existed in the poet (though Randall did have a brother, Charles, the relationship was severed, except for rare occasions, once their Tennessee boyhood passed, and he had no sister). **"The Owl's Bedtime Story"** crystallizes remembered loneliness—"Sometimes it seemed to him his heart would break." The cycle comes around to the beginning, the poet as night-creature, bat or owl, in the dreamed white owl's promise of a sister-friend (the mermaid?) if he will fly from the nest "into the harsh unknown / World the sun lights."

After a series of severe trials, as in the fairy tales, his perseverance in daylight-flying is rewarded by a real owl-sister, not a blood-sister but a beloved substitute (". . . her face looked dear / As his own sister's, it was the happiest / hour of his life." Now he must teach her too to fly in the bright sun. Relevantly, Mary Jarrell is rather clearly meant by "The Meteorite": "Breathe on me still, star, sister";[21] according to her own account she read poems avidly under his tutelage. Imperiled by crows, they wait in a tall tree for rescue by the mother owl: "How strong, how good, how dear / She did look! 'Mother!' they called in their delight."

The poem about bats in *The Bat-Poet* (p. 37) ends with a mother as guardian angel: "She folds her wings about her sleeping child"; and so does **"The Owl's Bedtime Story"**: "She opened her wings, they nestled to her breast." The next morning David realizes that the shining eyes of the dreamed-owl, as he had suspected the night before, are those of his human mother. The eyes fade into the daylight world, a world in which "his mother looks at him like his mother," the end of *Fly by Night*. It is an echo of "They look back at the leopard like the leopard" in **"The Woman at the Washington Zoo."**

Sendak's autobiography through his work for children also has its "David" in Max of *Where the Wild Things Are,* who after a night of wild dreams, begun in a bedroom transformed into a forest, sails "back over a year and in and out of weeks and through a day and into the night of his very own room." In Sendak the longing to be the object of a unique affection is phrased thus in the last line of his fantasy: "And Max the king of all wild things was lonely and wanted to be where someone loved him best of all." Being loved "best of all" was more important to Jarrell than it is to most of us. In the "Jerome" worksheets at UNCG [The University of

North Carolina at Greensboro],[22] the doctor reaches out for one patient, just one, who will love him for himself and not as surrogate. One likes to think that the poet's loneliness is over now, like the dog Jennie's in a Sendak story "Higgelty Piggelty Pop," published in 1967 two years after Randall's death. Arrived in the Castle Yonder, Jennie sends back a letter to her former master: "As you probably noticed, I went away forever. But if you ever come this way, look for me" (p. 69). The subtitle for this book is "There Must Be More to Life." That "more" was what Randall Jarrell always wanted.

Notes

1. November 2, 1967. Inge himself is well qualified to undertake such a study for he was already published, with Vanderbilt's Thomas Young, a book-length examination of worksheets of Donald Davidson, Jarrell's graduate mentor.
2. "Randolph Caldecott: An Appreciation" in *The Randolph Caldecott Treasury.* Selected and edited by Elizabeth L. Billington. (New York and London: Frederick Warne, 1978), p. 12.
3. *The Golden Bird, and Other Fairy Tales of the Brothers Grimm.* New York, Macmillan, 1962.
4. "Rehearsal against Time" in *Poetry* 48, no. 3, June, 1936, 124-25.
5. *Greensboro Daily News,* November 28, 1965. In his Caldecott tribute Sendak writes: ". . . this, of course, is what the illustrator's job is really about—to interpret the text as a musical conductor interprets a score" (p. 13).
6. *Poetry,* December, 1964, p. 105.
7. *Publisher's Weekly,* December 13, 1965, p. 63.
8. *Durham Morning Herald,* October 31, 1965.
9. *The Religion Teacher's Journal,* April, 1978, p. 15.
10. Loneliness as a Jarrell affliction is explored in my *Shenandoah* essay (Winter, 1969, 49-78) listed above; as well as in "Jarrell's Desert of the Heart," *Analects,* Spring, 1961, pp. 24-28.
11. Jarrell prefaces his 1942 parody of Marianne Moore, "The Country Was": "*I hope that it is accurate, admiring, and a little critical.*" The poem is a witty personification of sheep, imitating Miss Moore.
12. In a more pessimistic manner, Rosenthal interprets "The Skaters" and "The Death of the Ball Turret Gunner" as "the symbolic search for the irretrievably lost mother," p. 369.
13. *Durham Morning Herald,* October 31, 1965.
14. *Book Week,* April 17, 1966.
15. *Greensboro Daily News,* November 28, 1965.
16. The young lawyer, L. Richardson Preyer, who shortly after passing the bar took a course from Jarrell, writes in an elegy a year after the death: "He loved Greensboro, and it was interesting to find references to our town in his work" (*Greensboro Daily News,* October 31, 1965).
17. Letter to author, May 21, 1979.
18. Alan Pryce-Jones "More than Just Child's Play," *Book Week,* October 31, 1965, p. 7.
19. What Sendak attributes to Caldecott in the eulogy cited above is equally true of Jarrell's children's books: "There is no emasculation of truth in his world," p. 14.
20. *Higgelty Piggelty Pop!* (New York, 1967).
21. Cf. 152.
22. As reproduced in *The Biography of a Poem: Jerome* (New York, Grossman, 1971), pp. 58-84. These worksheets hold fascinating revelations, for instance, that "A War," mentioned by at least one critic as his nomination for the best war poem by Jarrell, is included in them, although it was published in a volume earlier than *The Woman at the Washington Zoo,* which contained "Jerome."

Selected Bibliography

Primary Sources

1. Collected Works

The Complete Poems. New York: Farrar, Straus & Giroux, 1969.

2. Poems

Blood for a Stranger. New York: Harcourt, Brace and Co., 1942.

Losses. New York: Harcourt, Brace & Co., 1948.

The Lost World. New York: Macmillan, 1968.

The Woman at the Washington Zoo: Poems and Translations. New York: Atheneum, 1960.

3. Editions and Translations

The Golden Bird, and Other Fairy Tales of the Brothers Grimm. Translated and introduced by Randall Jarrell. Illustrated by Sandro Nardini. New York: Macmillan, 1962.

4. Children's Books

A Bat Is Born, from *The Bat-Poet* by Randall Jarrell. Illustrated by John Schoenherr. New York: Doubleday, 1977.

The Animal Family. Pictures by Maurice Sendak. New York: Pantheon Books, 1965.

The Bat-Poet. Pictures by Maurice Sendak. New York: Macmillan, 1964.

Fly by Night. Pictures by Maurice Sendak. New York: Farrar, Straus & Giroux, 1976.

The Gingerbread Rabbit. Pictures by Garth Williams. New York: Macmillan, 1964.

SECONDARY SOURCES

1. BOOKS AND MAGAZINES

Analects I (Spring, 1964). A short-lived periodical but famous for this issue dedicated to Randall Jarrell, and including tributes by Glauco Cambon, Inigo Seidler, and several more.

Rosenthal, M. L. *Randall Jarrell.* Minneapolis, Minnesota: University of Minnesota Press Pamphlets, 1972. A rather biased handling of Jarrell, reprinted in Denis Donoghue's *Seven American Poets from MacLeish to Nemerov: An Introduction,* as well as in *American Writers: A Collection of Literary Biographies,* II, for which Leonard Unger, once at Greensboro, acted as editor-in-chief. It would seem that a writer as significant as Jarrell should have inspired Mr. Rosenthal to different research.

2. ARTICLES AND CHAPTERS IN BOOKS

Carruth, Hayden. "Daylight." *Poetry* 105 (December, 1964), 194-95. Review of *The Bat-Poet.* Despite a few kind statements, cruel in a way Jarrell was not: "*The Bat-Poet* is only Remus again: sugar-coated esthetics instead of sugar-coated morality. What a bloody bore!"

Preyer, L. Richardson. "A Friend Remembers." *Greensboro Daily News,* October 31, 1965. The recollections of a local lawyer, banker, and tennis player who discovered in Jarrell's modern poetry course the best teacher he was ever to know.

Pryce-Jones, Alan. "More than Just Child's Play." *Book Week,* October 31, 1965, p. 5. Review of *The Animal Family.* The title indicates a recognition of serious fiction, as Jarrell himself did in regard to a children's story, telling his cousin Bitsy's daughter: "It really isn't just about *cats.*"

Quinn, Sister M. Bernetta.

———. "Jarrell's Desert of the Heart." *Analects* I (Spring, 1964), 24-28.

———. "Randall Jarrell: Landscapes of Life and *Life.*" *Shenandoah* 20 (Spring, 1969), 49-78. As in *Analects* article, the lyrics are read in terms of symbolic-landscape imagery.

Jeffrey Meyers (essay date April 1984)

SOURCE: Meyers, Jeffrey. "Randall Jarrell: The Paintings in the Poems." *Southern Review* 20, no. 2 (April 1984): 300-15.

[*In the following essay, Meyers draws parallels between the poems "The Knight, Death, and the Devil," "Jerome," and "The Old and the New Masters" and the four paintings by Albrecht Dürer, Georges de La Tour, and Hugo van der Goes on which they are based.*]

I

Auden and Rilke, the two modern poets who had the greatest influence on Jarrell's early and later poetry, both wrote poems that were directly inspired by specific paintings.[1] Jarrell followed their admirable example and was preeminent among his contemporaries in his use of aesthetic analogies.[2] He was an intensely visual poet, for as Suzanne Ferguson notes: "His imagery . . . enforces attention to the subject rather than to itself; what lingers in the mind after reading Jarrell is rarely the verbal icon, more often it is a picture, tellingly detailed: a girl asleep in a college library; a woman at a zoo."[3]

Jarrell, who was drawn to Germanic rather than to Latin culture, was attracted to the superbly detailed draftsmanship of North European painters, whom Wölfflin characterized as linear rather than painterly. Four religious pictures by Albrecht Dürer, Georges de La Tour, and Hugo van der Goes (Hugo appears in the diary of Dürer, who saw his work in Brussels) linked Jarrell to a passionate tradition of learning, culture, craftsmanship, and commitment to art as well as to a faith he could no longer sustain.[4]

Jarrell discussed the relation of meaning and difficulty in his poems by alluding to Sidney's *Defence of Poesy*: "It is better to have the child in the chimney-corner moved by what happens in the poem, in spite of his ignorance of its real meaning, than to have the poem a puzzle to which that meaning is the only key. Still, complicated subjects make complicated poems, and some of the best poems can move only the best readers. . . . I have tried to make my poems plain, and most of them are plain enough; but I wish that they were more difficult because I had known more."[5] The interest in his essentially direct and tangible poetry lies more in ideas than in technique; and he often fortified his work by allusions to military experience, contemporary events, cultural history, fairy tales, and opera. He became interested in these paintings for personal and aesthetic reasons and discovered their technique and meaning by analysis and interpretation. The analogous process of creation stimulated his mind and inspired his imagination. The paintings increased and intensified his intellectual and emotional range by providing suggestive visual allusions and added significant texture and substance to his poetry. Jarrell mastered and transformed these paintings, which became his by right of plunder.

Wallace Stevens observed: "To a large extent, the problems of poets are the problems of painters, and poets must often turn to the literature of painting for a discussion of their own problems."[6] In three of his best poems, **"The Knight, Death, and the Devil," "Jerome,"** and **"The Old and the New Masters"**—published in three consecutive volumes: *The Seven-League Crutches* (1951), *The Woman at the Washington Zoo* (1960), and *The Lost World* (1965)—Jarrell described and interpreted these paintings and used them to illustrate his themes. His poems, at once a meditative description and incisive analysis of the details of the pictures, adapted their presentation of the external world to reveal his own vision.

Jarrell believed: "Between the object and its representation there is an immense distance: within this distance much of painting lives."[7] He therefore mediated between the paintings and their meaning by interpreting their complex symbols and allegory. For Jarrell, iconography represented ideas. He was drawn to paintings that both embodied abstractions and made them more tangible. The ideal poetry, writes Walter Pater, should be "exquisite pauses of time" arrested so that "we seem to be spectators of all the fullness of existence."[8] Jarrell's poems add a visual element to a verbal art, and transform static images into dramatic narratives. They realize their meaning by combining Auden's sympathetic interpretation with Rilke's passionate exaltation of art.

II

Jarrell employed art in many of his poems. **"The End of the Rainbow"** concerns the tragic life of an aging woman painter; **"In Galleries"** describes a guard in an Italian art museum; **"Nollekens"** is based on the life of an English sculptor; in **"Jamestown,"** "Power, golden as a Veronese, / Showers her riches on the lovers"; **"The Head of Wisdom"** is "the maned and erring head" of Beethoven, who dazzles with "the great stare / Of the magnificent eyes." **"The Bronze David of Donatello," "The Augsburg Adoration"** and **"Bamberg"**[9] were inspired by the famous statue in the Bargello of Florence and by the sculpture on the façades of two German cathedrals. But the poems of art with the greatest range and depth meditate on Dürer's engravings in **"The Knight, Death, and the Devil"** and **"Jerome"** and on de La Tour and van der Goes in **"The Old and the New Masters."**

"The Knight, Death, and the Devil" is much more than a "very simple recreation and reshaping of the subject,"[10] as in Williams' *Pictures from Brueghel*. It is both a tour de force of precise description (which Jarrell's Introduction invites us to compare with the work of art) and an interpretation of Dürer's enigmatic allegory of 1513—the favorite engraving of Nietzsche.[11] The mounted, moving, monumental Knight, armored with belief, dominates the center of the work. He is modeled on Verocchio's equestrian statue of *Colleoni* in Venice, Donatello's *Gattamelata* in Padua, and Leonardo's *Sforza* in Milan. In the background, beyond the craggy slopes and stripped trees, is the refuge and fortress that symbolizes the strength of God in Psalm 91 (later translated by Luther as "Ein feste Burg ist unser Gott"). The eager long-haired setter points the way to the distant castle, a goal that requires an arduous spiritual quest but is not beyond reach.

Death is portrayed as a repulsive, half-decomposed corpse, entwined with serpents. He has no nose or lips and (like the Fourth Horseman in Dürer's *Apocalypse*) rides a jaded nag, which sniffs at a skull. The Devil is a hoofed figure with horned boar's head and leering eyes, who follows limply behind on foot. The Knight's unwavering belief in God—the invisible fourth figure in the engraving—gives him the same firm strength as the castle. His faith allows him to resist diabolical temptation, to oppose the admonitory hourglass with an eternal concept of time, and to achieve a moral victory over Death. Dürer reveals "the idea of a Christian faith so virile, clear, serene and strong," writes Panofsky, "that the dangers and temptations of the world simply cease to be real. . . . They are not foes to be conquered but, indeed, 'spooks and phantoms' to be ignored. The Rider passes them as though they were not there and quietly pursues his course, 'fixing his eyes steadily and intensely'" forward.[12]

Jarrell aims at an exact verbal delineation of the engraving, but his alliterative description—though convincing—is not always accurate. For Death wears an iron crown with four sharp points (not a "cowhorn") and the comparison of Death to a wavering "teetotum," or single die, seems forced and inappropriate:

> Cowhorn-crowned, shockheaded, cornshuck-bearded,
> Death is a scarecrow—his death's-head a teetotum
> That tilts up toward man confidentially
> But trimmed with adders; ringlet-maned, rope-bridled,
> The mare he rides crops herbs beside a skull.
> He holds up, warning, the crossed cones of time:
> Here, narrowing into now, the Past and Future
> Are quicksand.[13]
>
> [*The Complete Poems*]

Though Jarrell's verbal compounds clearly capture the phantasmagoric Devil, his horn is not "pocked" (concave) but spiny at the base, like a lobster.

> A hoofed pikeman trots behind.
> His pike's claw-hammer mocks—in duplicate, inverted—

The pocked, ribbed, soaring crescent of his horn.
A scapegoat aged into a steer; boar-snouted;
His great limp ears stuck sidelong out in air;
A dewlap bunched at his breast; a ram's-horn wound
Beneath each ear; a spur licked up and out
From the hide of his forehead; bat-winged, but in
    bone;
His eye a ring inside a ring inside a ring
That leers up, joyless, vile, in meek obscenity—
This is the devil. Flesh to flesh, he bleats
The herd back to the pit of being.

Once again, in the detailed description of the self-sufficient Knight, Jarrell calls the setter a "sheep-dog" and has the porcine Devil "moo" (rather than grunt) in ironic amity:

In fluted mail; upon his lance the bush
Of that old fox; a sheep-dog bounding at his stirrup,
In its eyes the cast of faithfulness (our help,
Our foolish help); his dun war-horse pacing
Beneath in strength, in ceremonious magnificence;
His castle—some man's castle—set on every crag:
So, companioned so, the knight moves through this
    world.
The fiend moos in amity, Death mouths, reminding:
He listens in assurance, has no glance
To spare for them, but looks past steadily
At—at—
    a man's look completes itself.

The last lines of each stanza move from a forceful realism to a weaker abstraction to suggest the immediate threat of death, the temptations of the body, and (with a characteristically unfinished "At—at—") the Knight's resistance to both.

Though the threats of Death and the Devil are not equal—the former must inevitably conquer the Knight—Jarrell equates them in the fourth and final stanza of the poem. He subtly notes the slight contemptuous smirk on the face of the Knight, who knows his body must die but is confident about the fate of his soul. He rides steadily forward, believing "a man does what he must," which echoes the epigraph to **Blood for a Stranger** (1942) from Beethoven's F Major Quartet: "Muss es sein? / Es muss sein! / Es muss sein!" and reinforces his own "preoccupation with the 'Kingdom of Necessity.'"[14]

III

According to Butler's *Lives of the Saints*, St. Jerome, overwhelmed by his sense of sin,

> withdrew into the wilderness of Chalcis, a barren land to the southeast of Antioch [in Syria], where he spent four years alone. He suffered much from ill health, and even more from strong temptations of the flesh.

> "In the remotest part of a wild and stony desert," he wrote years afterwards to St. Eustochium, "burnt up with the heat of the scorching sun so that it frightens even the monks that inhabit it, I seemed to myself to be in the midst of the delights and crowds of Rome. . . . In this exile and prison to which for the fear of Hell I had voluntarily condemned myself, with no other company but scorpions and wild beasts, I many times imagined myself witnessing the dancing of the Roman maidens as if I had been in the midst of them. My face was pallid with fasting, yet my will felt the assaults of desire: in my cold body and in my parched-up flesh, which seemed dead before its death, passion was able to live. Alone with this enemy, I threw myself in spirit at the feet of Jesus, watering them with my tears, and I tamed my flesh by fasting whole weeks. I am not ashamed to disclose my temptations, but I grieve that I am not now what I then was. I often joined night to day crying and beating my breast till calm returned."[15]

The legend relates that a lion once came to Jerome with a thorn in its paw, and after the saint had extracted it, followed him about like a faithful domestic pet.

Jarrell, who was noted for his sharp and satiric wit, may have become interested in Jerome because of their similar personalities. Butler speaks of Jerome's "intemperateness in controversy, his contempt for opponents, the virulence of his tongue and pen, his savage and insulting invective. . . . Looking at a picture which showed Jerome beating his breast with a stone, [Pope] Sixtus V is said to have observed, 'You do well thus to use that stone: without it you would never have been numbered among the saints.'"[16]

Dürer did more paintings, drawings, studies, engravings, and woodcuts of Jerome than any other saint. Since no single work precisely matches Jarrell's description in **"Jerome,"** it seems that the poet has conflated several engravings of the penitential and scholarly saint, who translated the Bible into Latin. *St. Jerome Penitent in the Wilderness* (1496) portrays Jerome with savage landscape and snarling lion as he struggles inwardly, tests his doubt, questions his error, and repents his sin. *St. Jerome by the Pollard Willow* (1512) shows the scholar, fortified by a solid boulder and sleeping lion, leaning on the Bible and praying for inspiration.[17]

In **"Jerome,"** as Helen Hagenbüchle says, Jarrell "portrays himself as a combination of analyst, 'Father,' and Saint Jerome (writer in the desert), a triple persona, who at night turns into his own patient, 'Son,' and lion."[18] In the poem, the lion describes the saint, who is always portrayed as an aged man, though he was only thirty-two when he first became a hermit:

—There is an old man, naked, in a desert, by a cliff.
He has set out his books, his hat, his ink, his shears
Among scorpions, toads, the wild beasts of the desert.
I lie beside him—I am a lion.
He kneels listening. He holds in his left hand
The stone with which he beats his breast, and holds

> In his right hand, the pen with which he puts
> Into his book, the words of the angel:
> The angel into whose face he looks.
> But the angel does not speak.
>
> (*Complete Poems,* p. 271)

The hat symbolizes (according to traditional belief) Jerome's later elevation to the rank of cardinal; the scorpions and wild beasts (which echo Deuteronomy 8:15) are a direct quote from St. Jerome's *Letters.* ("Toads" recalls the metaphor for dreams in the first line.) In the engravings, Jerome holds the stone in his *right* hand and prays to a crucifix: no angels are visible.

"Jerome" begins in the daytime and moves through gloaming, midnight, late night, dawn, and back to daytime. The old Freudian analyst, a Father Confessor who talks to patients, identifies with the aged Church Father who talks to God (his lion is at the zoo, not at his feet). He spends all day listening to dreams, in the form of toads and dragons that boil up from the unconscious of his clients, rather than to the demons that tempt the saint.

When the last patient is gone, the ascetic analyst boils an egg under his version of the Cross: a Pompeiian plaque of *Gradiva,* "a fully-grown girl stepping alone with her flowing dress a little pulled up so as to reveal her sandalled feet,"[19] which inspired Wilhelm Jensen's German novel of 1903. Jarrell's Freudian poem, inspired by a work of art, alludes to a work of art which inspired a novel that was analyzed by Freud. As the patients' monologues continue to reverberate in the analyst's memory, he lies down on their couch and listens to the night. The Id or "it"—described as an armored dragon-lion—*reverses* and "changes" Freud's belief that civilized man must control his instinctual impulses, and declares: "Where Ego was, there Id shall be."[20] The doctor is like the saint because both men, though learned, are tormented by their own weakness, inadequacy, and inability to penetrate psychological problems and spiritual dilemmas.

When night has passed, and the analyst has slept and achieved a kind of catharsis, his soul is revitalized in the day-world where the Ego is dominant. In this respect, he is like the saint whose prayers have been answered and who has experienced the grace of God. In the heavily alliterated last lingering lines, the analyst goes to the grocer to buy meat for his pet, walks placidly to the zoo, and makes the final identification with the saint by feeding his favorite feline—who thanks the doctor with his tongue:

> [He] walks on . . .
> To a lynx, a leopard—he has come:
>
> The man holds out a lump of liver to the lion,
> And the lion licks the man's hand with his tongue.

IV

"The Old and the New Masters" has a tight logical structure: a premise, two concrete examples based on paintings, and a conclusion. In "Musée des Beaux Arts," written in December 1938 at the end of "a low dishonest decade," Auden alludes to the tragic position of Brueghel's Icarus and the commonplace events of Flemish genre paintings. He bitterly asserts great painters show that human beings have always been indifferent to the suffering of their fellow men:

> About suffering they were never wrong,
> The Old Masters: how well they understood
> Its human position; how it takes place
> While someone else is eating or opening a window or
>   just walking
>   dully along.

Jarrell takes a less absolute, more optimistic view; states the essential subject of his two paintings in the opening line; describes the immobility of the figures; and claims, in opposition to Auden:

> About suffering, about adoration, the old masters
> Disagree. When someone suffers, no one else eats
> Or walks or opens the windows—no one breathes
> As the sufferers watch the sufferer.
>
> (*Complete Poems,* p. 332)

Jarrell's brilliant example of suffering is de La Tour's *St. Sebastian Tended [Soigné] by Irene* (Louvre, 1649), which was discovered in a French provincial church as recently as 1945.[21] Butler relates that St. Sebastian, an officer in the imperial guard, "having sent so many martyrs to Heaven before him, was himself impeached before Diocletian; who, after bitterly reproaching him with his ingratitude, delivered over to certain archers of Mauretania, to be shot to death." The tragic painting does not, of course, suggest that "Irene, the widow of St. Castulus, going to bury [Sebastian], found him still alive and took him to her lodgings, where he recovered from his wounds."[22]

The strong vertical line of the oak tree on which the saint had endured his martyrdom is paralleled by the high white flames of the torch, held upright by Irene, by the figures of the four grieving women who are bathed in its brilliant light and deep shadows, and by the four linked hands (of Sebastian, Irene, and two of the grieving women) that rise, above and below Irene's left arm, through the center of the painting. The parallel figures, leaning toward the fallen saint, reinforce the strict geometrical design and form a diagonal, moving from top right to bottom left. This angle is strengthened by the saint's left arm and right leg, by the single arrow that pierces his chest and expels a single drop of blood, and by the two tendrils wrapped around the trunk of the tree.

The woman in white, on the far right, has abandoned all hope and buried her face in her handkerchief. The next woman, in black dress and red mantle, leans forward with open hands in a gesture of supplication. The third woman, whose face is almost obliterated by the deep blue of a thick nun's cowl that hangs in heavy folds, has woven her fingers together in silent prayer. The kneeling Irene, with shining forehead, dangling curls and splendid red dress over a full-sleeved blouse, holds the pulse of the wounded martyr and feels the life ebb out of his beautiful body. The suffering, dying saint, in a *Pietà* position—head thrust back, eyes closed and mouth half-open—has his smooth chest burnished by the glow of the torch. The four frozen, static, sculpted ladies are isolated in their individual grief and pity. But that silently weeping chorus is also unified: for the first and third women have buried faces and closed hands while the second and fourth have exposed faces and open hands. As Malraux observes: "No other painter, not even Rembrandt, can so well suggest this elemental stillness; de La Tour alone is the interpreter of the serenity that dwells in the heart of darkness."[23]

In an essay published in 1957, eight years before the poem appeared in **The Lost World,** Jarrell gave a profound and moving Freudian interpretation of the abstract element in the expressive woven fingers of Irene's companion. He suggested why he was attracted to the painting and contrasted the spiritual gesture in de La Tour with the lack of meaningful content in the abstract New Masters:

> In Georges de La Tour's *St. Sebastian Mourned by St. Irene* there is, in the middle of a dark passage, a light one: four parallel cylinders diagonally intersected by four parallel cylinders; they look like a certain sort of wooden fence, as a certain sort of Cubist painter would have painted it; they are the hands, put together in prayer, of one of St. Irene's companions. As one looks at what has been put into—withheld from—the hands, one is conscious of a mixture of emotion and empathy and contemplation; one is moved, and is unmoved, and is something else one has no name for, that transcends either affect or affectlessness. The hands are truly like hands, yet they are almost more truly unlike hands; they resemble (as so much of art resembles) the symptomatic gestures of psychoanalysis, half the expression of a wish and half the defence against the wish. But these parallel cylinders of de La Tour's—these hands at once oil-and-canvas and flesh-and-blood; at once dynamic processes in the virtual space of the painting, and spiritual gestures in the "very world" in which men are martyred, are mourned, and paint the mourning and the martyrdom—these parallel cylinders are only, in an Abstract-Expressionist painting, four parallel cylinders: they are what they are.[24]
>
> [Art News]

Jarrell's description of the painting in his poem contains several significant errors, caused by his subjective interpretation and desire to intensify the tragic content—as de La Tour did to the history of Sebastian:

> In *St. Sebastian Mourned by St. Irene*
> The flame of one torch is the only light.
> All the eyes except the maidservant's (she weeps
> And covers them with a cloth) are fixed on the shaft
> Set in his chest like a column; St. Irene's
> Hands are spread in the gesture of a Madonna,
> Revealing, accepting, what she does not understand.
> Her hands say: "Lo! Behold!"
> Beside her a monk's hooded head is bowed, his hands
> Are put together in the work of mourning.

By making the compassionate but secular Irene into a saint (which she was not) and changing the title from "Tended" to "Mourned," Jarrell adds a superfluous saint and suggests that Sebastian has already died. Another inexcusable error (since Jarrell was noted for his learning) was his mistaken identification of the second woman, in the black dress and red kerchief, with Irene. This weakens the force of the physical connection between the principal comforter (clearly distinguished by her magnificent dress) and the dying martyr. Jarrell also confuses the sex of the figure in the cowl and claims the woman is a monk. This error also weakens Jarrell's connection of Sebastian's *imitatio Christi* with the seven last words of the Redeemer in Matthew 27:46, for the weeping women in the painting suggest the two Marys at the foot of the Cross.

> It is as if they were still looking at the lance
> Piercing the side of Christ, nailed on his cross.
> The same nails pierce all their hands and feet, the same
> Thin blood, mixed with water, trickles from their sides.
> The taste of vinegar is on every tongue
> That gasps, "My God, my God, why hast Thou forsaken me?"
> They watch, they are, the one thing in the world.

The *Nativity* portrays adoration just as *St. Sebastian* represents suffering. "On a trip to Florence," writes Bernetta Quinn of Hugo van der Goes' magnificent *Nativity* (1476), "Jarrell found a good copy [reproduction?] of this Uffizi altar-triptych which, displayed thereafter on a metal stand in his Greensboro home, provided increasingly illuminating detail under the magnifying glass."[25] Jarrell, especially at the end of his life, may have been interested in the inner life of the artist as well as in the painting. For Hugo's illness, "a feverish compulsiveness that may be regarded as both a cause and a consequence of his illness . . . came on abruptly and catastrophically. . . . He kept on complaining that he was delivered to eternal damnation and wanted to do away with himself."[26] In 1481 he suffered an acute attack of suicidal mania, which he survived by only one year.

The huge altarpiece (8½ by 19½ feet) was commissioned by Tommaso Portinari, one of the Medici representatives at Bruges, who presented it to the Church of Santa Maria Nuova in Florence. The interior wings of the triptych (not shown in the illustration) depict, on the left, Portinari and his two sons kneeling beneath a rather austere St. Thomas and St. Anthony; on the right, his wife and daughter praying below St. Mary Magdalene and St. Margaret. Panofsky, in an expert analysis of the painting, writes:

> In the background of the donors' wings are seen, as prelude and epilogue to the Nativity which occupies the center of the altarpiece, the Holy Parents and the three Magi on their way to Bethlehem. . . . The Virgin Mary, no longer able to ride, has descended from her donkey and seeks support in the arms of St. Joseph as she will lean on the huge column seen in the central panel [during the birth of Christ]. The outrider of the Magi has dismounted and asks directions from a pious shepherd who, in more ways than one, belongs to those who dominate the central panel on the right. Thus streams of energy seem to converge towards the Nativity scene; but in the center of this whirlwind there is calm.[27]
>
> [*Early Netherlandish Painting*]

Hugo portrayed his *Nativity*, contrary to tradition, in the day rather than in the night. In the white center, encircled by a halo, lies the naked Christ child. He is surrounded, at an awed distance, by the adoring Virgin Mary and the dignified St. Joseph, nine kneeling and six hovering angels, an ox and an ass nibbling the hay in the manger,[28] and three intensely realistic (though divinely illuminated) shepherds, who violate traditional iconography and clash with the highly stylized angels. Hugo was perhaps the first painter to introduce "coarse and low-born men to the sacred and supernatural circle . . . [and to] give vehement expression to their devotion, equal in prominence to the angels and the Holy Family."[29]

All the details of the painting have symbolic significance. The columbine in the jar represents the Sorrows of the Virgin; the column prefigures the Flagellation; "the scarlet lily signifies the blood of the Passion; the iris, the sword that pierces the heart of the Mater Dolorosa. . . . While the flowers announce the Lord's Passion, the sheaf of grain, placed behind the two vessels, refers to the ideas centered around His birthplace. Its name, Bethlehem, means 'House of Bread.' Hugo's attempt to combine a maximum of spatial depth and plastic energy with a maximum of surface detail resulted in a terrific tension."[30]

Jarrell's description, which has two simple but effective similes in the first six lines, stresses the contrasting sizes of the figures: the huge shepherds and domestic beasts, the small angels and newborn infant, and the tiny people approaching from the distant background, who do not yet know their Saviour has been born. He does not mention the symbolic meaning of the objects in the foreground; and emphasizes the fixed concentration ("no one breathes," as in de La Tour) on the helpless baby, destined to save the donors' family and all Christian believers:

> So, earlier, everything is pointed
> In van der Goes' *Nativity,* toward the naked
> Shining baby, like the needle of a compass.
> The different orders and sizes of the world:
> The angels are like Little People, perched in the rafters
> Or hovering in mid-air like hummingbirds;
> The shepherds, so big and crude, so plainly adoring;
> The medium-sized donor, his little family,
> And their big patron saints; the Virgin who kneels
> Before her child in worship; the Magi out in the hills
> With their camels—they ask directions, and have pointed out
> By a man kneeling, the true way; the ox
> And the donkey, two heads in the manger
> So much greater than a human head, who also adore;
> Even the offerings, a sheaf of wheat,
> A jar and a glass of flowers, are absolutely still
> In natural concentration, as they take their part
> In the salvation of the natural world.
> The time of the world concentrates
> On this one instant: far off in the rocks
> You can see Mary and Joseph and their donkey
> Coming to Bethlehem; on the grassy hillside
> Where their flocks are grazing, the shepherds gesticulate
> In wonder at the star; and so many hundreds
> Of years in the future, the donor, his wife,
> And their children are kneeling, looking: everything
> That was or will be in the world is fixed
> On its small, helpless, human center.

The adoration of Christ in Hugo's painting leads ineluctably to the suffering and martyrdom of Sebastian in de La Tour's.

The final section of the poem describes the diminution of religious art, of the painter, and even of the earth itself as representation eventually surrenders to abstraction. This section moves away from the compassion and ecstasy of de La Tour and van der Goes to a peripheral depiction of tragedy—as in Piero della Francesca's *Flagellation* (1456) or Brueghel's *Fall of Icarus* (c. 1567)—which was noticed by Auden. Veronese, who secularized religious themes, was forced to appear before the Tribunal of the Inquisition in 1573 and explain that the dwarfs and fools (not the dogs) in *The Supper in the House of Levi* were not meant to disparage religion.[31] The discovery by Copernicus in the early sixteenth century changed man's conception of the earth from the center of the universe to a mere "planet among galaxies."

The last five lines are related to Jarrell's attack in the essay on de La Tour on the lack of content in abstract art, and to his sadness when religious feeling was extinguished in the work of the New (and Last) Masters, who reduce the now radioactive earth to a spot of color. The loss of faith and belief in a humanistic ideal has led to the disappearance of man in abstract art and, ultimately, to the atomic destruction—rather than the religious salvation—of the world.

Jarrell's three poems about paintings become increasingly complex, and their effectiveness is directly related to the way he used works of art. The vivid (if sometimes inexact) description of **"The Knight, Death, and the Devil,"** which is very close to Dürer's complex images, is not sufficiently balanced by a substantial explication of the meaning of the allegory. **"Jerome,"** a much more difficult poem, uses several of Dürer's engravings as a starting point for a series of parallels between the saint and the analyst rather than as a visual center, and by diffusing the focus weakens the effect of the aesthetic analogy. An analysis of the paintings by de La Tour and van der Goes and an understanding of how Jarrell used them to illustrate his ambitious themes in **"The Old and the New Masters"** illuminate the creative process in one of his finest and most elaborately structured poems. Though he ignores the symbolism and is mistaken about certain important details, he brilliantly combines the verbal description of **"The Knight, Death, and the Devil"** with the visual significance of **"Jerome."** These deeply moving paintings become a perfect vehicle for Jarrell's union of Auden's and Rilke's great themes about the modern world: the loss of faith, the indifference to suffering, and the transcendent power of art.

Notes

1. See Auden's "Musée des Beaux Arts" (on Brueghel's *Fall of Icarus*) and "Woods" (on Piero di Cosimo's *Hunting Scene* and *Return from the Hunt*); and Rilke's "St. Sebastian" (on Mantegna), "The Mountain" (on Hokusai's views of Mt. Fuji) and the "Fifth Duino Elegy" (on Picasso's *Les Saltimbanques*).

   For a discussion of how paintings are used as symbolic centers of modern novels, see the following works by Jeffrey Meyers, *Painting and the Novel* (Manchester and New York, 1975); "Brueghel and *Augie March*," *American Literature,* 49 (March 1977), 113-119; "Velázquez and 'Daisy Miller,'" *Studies in Short Fiction,* 16 (Summer 1979), 170-178; and "Van Gogh and Lewis's *Revenge for Love,*" *Modern Fiction Studies,* 29 (Summer 1983), 234-239.

2. Jarrell's friend Robert Lowell also wrote poems inspired by Grosz, Cuyp, Giorgione, and Cranach in *Notebook* (1969); by Holbein, Titian, and Rembrandt in *History* (1973); and by Vermeer in *Day by Day* (1977). Their American contemporaries—John Berryman, Howard Nemerov, Richard Wilbur, Anthony Hecht, W. D. Snodgrass, Adrienne Rich, and Joseph Langland—also wrote poems about paintings.

3. Suzanne Ferguson, *The Poetry of Randall Jarrell* (Baton Rouge, 1971), p. 4.

4. In the "Notes" to his translation of *The Three Sisters* (New York, 1969), pp. 105-106, Jarrell compares Chekhov's "spot-surface" with its visual counterpart in the paintings of Vuillard.

5. Randall Jarrell, "Answers to Questions," in *Mid-Century American Poets,* ed. John Ciardi (New York, 1950), p. 183.

6. Wallace Stevens, *Opus Posthumous* (1957), (New York, 1966), p. 160.

7. Randall Jarrell, "The Age of the Chimpanzee" [an argument against abstract art], *Art News,* 56 (Summer 1957), 34.

8. Walter Pater, "The School of Giorgione," *The Renaissance* (1873), (London, 1922), pp. 149-150. See also Vladimir Nabokov, *Lectures on Literature* (New York, 1980), p. 3:

   "When we look at a painting we do not have to move our eyes in a special way even if, as in a book, the picture contains elements of depth and development. The element of time does not really enter in a first contact with a painting. In reading a book, we must have time to acquaint ourselves with it."

9. Critics have discussed "Bamberg" without noticing the crucial allusion to Samuel Johnson. Compare James Boswell, *The Life of Johnson* (London, 1961), p. 849:

   "Depend upon it, Sir, when a man knows he is to be hanged in a fortnight, it concentrates his mind wonderfully"

   and:

   You'd be surprised how much, at
   The Last Judgment,
   The powers of concentration
   Of the blest and damned
   Are improved.

10. Ferguson, p. 112.

11. There is a fine photograph of Jarrell examining Dürer's engraving in the memorial volume, *Randall Jarrell, 1914-1965,* ed. Robert Lowell, Peter Taylor and Robert Penn Warren (New York, 1967).

12. Erwin Panofsky, *The Life and Art of Albrecht Dürer* (1945), (Princeton, 1971), p. 152.

13. Randall Jarrell, *The Complete Poems* (New York, 1969), p. 21.

14. Ferguson, p. 10, discusses Jarrell's use of Beethoven's epigraph. See also Robert Clements, "Dürer's *Knight, Death and the Devil*: Five Liter-

ary Readings," *Canadian Review of Comparative Literature,* 6 (1979), 1-8, a comparative rather than an analytical study.

15. Butler's *Lives of the Saints,* ed. Herbert Thurston and Donald Attwater (New York, 1966), 3.687.

16. Donald Attwater, *The Penguin Dictionary of Saints* (London, 1965), p. 186.

17. See *The Complete Engravings, Etchings and Drypoints of Albrecht Dürer,* ed. Walter Straus (New York, 1972), pp. 17, 21. *Jerome: The Biography of a Poem* contains an interesting essay on the genesis of the work by Mary Jarrell, fifty of Jarrell's worksheets, and seven engravings and woodcuts by Dürer. This volume does not include Dürer's painting, *St. Jerome* (Panofsky 252); four studies for the painting (Wilhelm Waetzoldt, *Dürer and His Times,* London, 1950, 77-80); and a drawing, *St. Jerome in His Study* (Panofsky 255).

18. Helen Hagenbüchle, *The Black Goddess: A Study of the Archetypal Feminine in the Poetry of Randall Jarrell* (Berne, 1975), p. 4.

19. Sigmund Freud, "Delusions and Dreams in Jensen's *Gradiva,*" *Standard Edition of the Complete Psychological Works,* trans. and ed. James Strachey (London, 1959), 9.10.

20. Critics have completely missed the irony of Jarrell's reversal of Freud. See Ferguson, p. 172:

    "Like a true psychologist, the dragon thinks in Freudian terms of the freedom of the libido: 'Where Ego was, there Id shall be.'"

    Frances Ferguson, "Randall Jarrell and the Flotation of Voice," *Georgia Review,* 28 (1974), 433, repeats this error:

    "The cyclical movement of the poem establishes an interpenetration of figures so that they reflect mutually in a release of individuality. Where Ego was, there Id shall be."

    See Freud, "The Dissection of the Psychical Personality," *New Introductory Lectures on Psychoanalysis* in *Standard Edition,* 22.80.

21. Wilde, D'Annunzio, Mann, Proust, and Mishima have all recreated the figure of St. Sebastian in their art. See Jeffrey Meyers, *Homosexuality and Literature, 1890-1930* (London, 1977), pp. 44, 168-169.

22. Butler's *Lives of the Saints,* 1.129.

23. André Malraux, *The Voices of Silence* (1953), trans. Stuart Gilbert (London, 1974), p. 391.

24. Jarrell, *Art News,* p. 34.

25. Sister Bernetta Quinn, "Randall Jarrell: Landscapes of Life and LIFE," *Shenandoah,* 20 (1969), 69. Quinn, pp. 75-78, discusses Jarrell's interest in Uccello, Piero della Francesca, Carpaccio, Bosch, Brueghel, Cézanne, Vuillard, and Kokoschka.

26. Max Friedländer, *Hugo van der Goes* in *Early Netherlandish Painting* (1924-37), trans. Nicole Veronee-Verhaegen (Leyden, 1969), 4.14-15. See also Rudolf and Margot Wittkower, *Born Under Saturn* (New York, 1963), pp. 108-113.

27. Erwin Panofsky, *Early Netherlandish Painting* (Cambridge, Mass., 1953), p. 333.

28. *Ibid.,* p. 470, note 1:

    "On the strength of Isaiah 1:3 ('The ox knoweth his owner and the ass his master's crib') . . . the two animals attending the Nativity were always presumed to have been aware of Christ's divinity."

29. Friedländer, p. 17.

30. Panofsky, *Netherlandish Painting,* pp. 333-334.

31. John Ruskin, *Guide to the Principal Paintings in the Academy at Venice* (1877), in *Works,* ed. E. T. Cook and Alexander Wedderburn (London, 1903-12), 24.187-190, prints, with his commentary, the transcription of Veronese's trial.

Suzanne Ferguson (essay date fall 1984)

SOURCE: Ferguson, Suzanne. "Narrative and Narrators in the Poetry of Randall Jarrell." *South Carolina Review* 17, no. 1 (fall 1984): 72-82.

[*In the following essay, Ferguson describes Jarrell's use of first-person narrators in his poetry—such as children, combat pilots, women, and fairy-tale beings—that speak both of and to other characters in the poems. The critic asserts that in his use of such narrators, Jarrell's work is closer to modernist fiction than to dramatic poetry.*]

I: Jarrell's Narrative Poetry

Among poets of the second generation of American modernists, Randall Jarrell is unusual in having written poetry in a predominantly narrative mode from the beginning of his career. While a number of his poems have first-person narrators who tell "stories" of themselves that could be construed as Jarrell's own story, these are less prominent than poems with narrators who are ostensibly not "Jarrell-the-poet"—children, women, combat soldiers and flyers, fairytale characters and others—or than poems using omniscient or "central intelligence" narrators to relate stories of others' rather than of the poet's own experience. Even Jarrell's shortest poems are rarely lyric in the traditional sense, and description and meditation are more likely to appear in the context of a poetic story than on their own. While one might be tempted to analyze a number of these poems as dramatic monologues,[1] I find the manipulation of narrative voices, the use of interior monologue, and the loose, impressionist plotting of the poems much closer to that of modernist fiction than to earlier dramatic poetry. (It can also be argued that Browning's own dramatic monologues are steps in the direction of modernist fiction rather than examples of a generically dramatic art, since they do not anticipate production in a theatrical setting, but an audience of readers.)

In view of the strong narrative values in his poetry, Kathe Davis Finney's rhetorical question, in her essay on Jarrell's fictions, "What need prompts a poet to write a story instead of a poem?"[2] seems almost inappropriate: we might better ask, why didn't he write more stories? Why, indeed, write poems at all? "And yet, . . ."—in Jarrell's favorite transition—we have to concede that the poems, however narrative their structure or prosaic their style, rarely suggest that they could have or should have been prose stories. Like other short verse narratives, they lack what Jarrell, in his essay, **"Stories,"** called "the flesh of ordinary fiction," at least quantitatively.[3] What can we usefully say, then, about the place of narrative in Jarrell's poetry?

To start with, Jarrell's own notion of narrative will take us some way into the problem. From **"Stories,"** originally an anthology introduction, two fundamental critical notions emerge. One, that stories are "truth" modified by art, is essentially glossed by the other, that stories originate in wishes, and that they often develop and close in response to contradictory wishes. The idea of stories as wish fulfilment for their authors and readers is Freudian, and Jarrell clearly subscribes to it as an article of faith in other essays and poems as well as in **"Stories."** In the two early "library" poems, for example, **"Children Selecting Books in a Library"** (1941) and **"Carnegie Library, Juvenile Division"** (1944), Jarrell's history of the child's experience with books is a history of seeking to transform life, by "trading another's sorrow for our own" or by acquiring "knowledge for a life" if not the will to use that knowledge to change our lives, always seemingly "so different from the books.'"[4] The theme of stories as wishes is even more baldly put forward in **"The Märchen"** (1946). Moreover, the wish and the dream (the wish-in-disguise) are frequently explicitly present in Jarrell's poetic narratives as turning points, epiphanic moments in the plots.

Wish fulfilment can thus be seen as both a structural and semantic component of the story, oriented toward solving problems for author and reader. In addition, we can discern in Jarrell's poetic stories corresponding rhetorical strategies for problem solving, in which themes are treated discursively and directly, side by side or concurrently with their narrative treatment. In my essay, "To Benton, with Love and Judgment: Jarrell's ***Pictures from an Institution***,"[5] I argue that Jarrell's long prose narrative is in part an attempt to resolve his own ambivalence about teaching in an "institution." It is an ambivalence also exactly demonstrated in the 108-line poem, **"A Girl in a Library."** In both the novel and the poem, Jarrell uses the narrative mode rhetorically, to work out a problem by creating characters who represent and speak to several aspects of the problem and by creating plots that, in their exposition, complication, and dénouement, can readily be seen to correspond to an essayistic structure of exposition, analysis of the problem, solutions, objections and confutations, and a conclusion. (Oddly enough, Jarrell's essays are rarely so tidily organized.)

In both novel and poem, as in many other Jarrell poems, dialogue frequently sets up the terms of a dialectical opposition, or of something analogous but more amorphous, as multiple characters speak for ideas that cannot be resolved into binary oppositions. In the main action of ***Pictures from an Institution*** a series of characters confront each other in situations that call into question the values of progressive education and the effect of progressive education on the character of individuals and on the society. Postwar America is seen in microcosm in the world of Benton College, where social consciousness and self-development are stressed at the expense of scholarly discipline and aesthetic standards. In the end, however, inspired by a dazzling statue created by a "potato bug" sculptress, the novel's narrator decides to make "a separate peace" with his institution, which can occasionally produce a wonder despite its principles. A similar conflict in miniature takes place in **"A Girl in a Library,"** where the girl, sleeping, "studying" home economics and physical education, is ridiculed, first by the narrator, then by an apparition of Pushkin's character, Tatyana Larina. The image of Tatyana Larina, herself the very type of romantic heroine, is seemingly invoked by the narrator to be an antithesis to the girl, but he soon finds himself defending the girl to her. Gradually, the girl is revealed to the narrator as a figure comparable to Helen, Brünnhilde, Salome, and, ultimately, archetypal Woman. In a sense, he makes peace with her in the closing lines of the poem: "I have seen / Firm, fixed forever in your closing eyes, / The Corn King beckoning to his Spring Queen" (18).

While the plots of ***Pictures from an Institution*** (1954) and **"A Girl in a Library"** (1951) unfold toward an act of judgment, other Jarrell plots are more oriented toward an understanding of the situation, but they follow trajectories similar to the judgmental plots. A protagonist—child, soldier, woman—is caught in a bad situation: loss, illness, a wound, alienation or isolation, aging, dying. He or she meditates, or an omniscient narrator meditates, on the meaning of the situation. How can it be understood, justified? Has the character deserved this fate? How so? Can s/he transcend it? Oppositions are weighed, imponderables pondered. Something happens: a dream, a discovery; or perhaps the narrator finds an analogue in myth or märchen. Somehow, a point of equilibrium is reached.

These are contours of plot—or deliberative essay—which also resemble those of the modernist story in a psychological-realist mode. In a sense, "nothing happens" in a Jarrell narrative poem, and that is the point of it, as in a Chekhov story. The typical Jarrell plot is established early, for example in the compact **"90 North,"** (1941; 32 lines) in which the narrator dreams, or recalls a dream, of going to the North Pole while a child supposedly sleeping in bed. In the dream he sails all night "up the globe's impossible sides" until he arrives at the pole:

> There in the childish night my companions lay frozen,
> The stiff furs knocked at my starveling throat,
> And I gave my great sigh: the flakes came huddling,
> Were they really my end? . . .
>
> —Here, the flag snaps in the glare and silence
> Of the unbroken ice.
>
> (113)

This amount of detail is sketchy for a story, though not for the narrative of a dream, always so elusive in the telling. But the interpretation is present, if cryptic, in the poem's surface. The Pole is a serious goal, something that will give life meaning, but once the narrator gets there, "The dogs bark, my beard is black, and I stare / At the North Pole . . . And now what? Why, go back." "Nothing" has happened, but the narrator has had an illumination, or, to use the term fixed for the modern short story by Joyce, an "epiphany," which differs from the traditional climax of a plot in being a psychological event determined by unconscious intuitions rather than "real world" cause and effect. The speaker's insight is an existential one: "I see at last that all the knowledge / I wrung from the darkness—that the darkness flung me—/ Is worthless as ignorance: nothing comes from nothing. / The darkness from the darkness." A number of Jarrell's most distinctive and memorable poems follow closely this basic plot—a journey, physical or mental; a dream or dreamlike vision; a recognition; an acceptance of nothingness. See, for example, from the forties, **"Siegfried"** and **"Burning the Letters"**; from the fifties, **"Seele im Raum," "The Woman at the Washington Zoo," "Jerome"**; from the sixties, **"Thinking of the Lost World."**

The proportion of discursive "moralizing" to story in **"90 North"** and the other short narrative poems is quite large. Indeed, one of the differences between such narrative poems and the stories they might have been is the large amount of openly meditative reflection which accompanies the action. We can generalize as we do about prose fictions: the more mimetic material in the narrative, the greater the emphasis on the experimental element of the reader's response; and the less the mimetic material, that is, the more skeletal the narrative, the greater the emphasis on the idea or theme. Thus, Jarrell's primary interest is ordinarily upon the interpretation of an event; an attenuated narrative will do. It is not that we are expected to fill in the gaps in the narrative with more "action," as in the "inferential walks" Umberto Eco sees us as taking in the novel or other narrative,[6] but rather that we are to focus upon the essential, the typical in the situation: a lyric, or traditionally poetic, rather than a narrative value.

As the narrative poems get longer, Jarrell exploits the interplay of setting and theme to call upon the reader's capacity for entering the situation imaginatively, but the plots do not necessarily become more extensive in terms of action. In **"Seele im Raum"** (1950; 75 lines), after a section of exposition in which the narrator—a woman who has apparently had some sort of breakdown involving the hallucination of an eland in her house, at her table—describes the history of her experiences, the crucial incident in the plot is the woman's discovery of the word *elend* (misery) in a German dictionary. She immediately connects it with the eland that haunts her in her mental illness. Like the achieved North Pole, this revelation is a disappointment: "it wasn't *interesting* . . . /—It was worse than impossible, it was a joke." Even in such long poems as **"The Night before the Night before Christmas"** (1949; 375 lines) or **"The End of the Rainbow"** (1954; 315 lines), the plots are similarly minimal (though the narration of dreams within or extending from the plots gets more elaborate).

As in prose stories with brief fabulae, setting is the major contributor to the substance of the longer narrative poems, and it functions to increase verisimilitude so that the implications of a theme can be tested in a "real life" situation. What distinguishes the settings of Jarrell's narrative poems from the early work of the other leading poets of his generation—Roethke, Lowell, Berryman—is their relentless middle-class urban or suburban ambiance. There is little or no distance in the world of the Jarrell narrative poem from the domestic world of apartments and supermarkets and hospital waiting rooms, schoolteachers, psychiatrists, and newspaper boys, in which the implied reader actually lives. The fictional space in which Lowell suprisingly arrives in "Skunk Hour," Jarrell had been occupying since the forties.

I think it can be argued, too, that his characters, even those explicitly identified as mythic or fairy-tale characters, are not mythologized to the extent that Roethke's parents or "Frau Bauman, Frau Schmidt, and Frau Schwartze," or Berryman's Anne Bradstreet or Lowell's Arthur Winslow are; rather, they are compared to mythic or literary figures while remaining stubbornly in the real, contemporary world, sleeping in a library or shopping in a supermarket. Myth and fairy tale are paradigms to help us understand and cope with "life." In the world that we share with Jarrell's characters, we ourselves walk past displays of "Cheer," "Joy," and "All" with never a thought of how strange, how meaningless these words are as names for laundry detergents; in the poems Jarrell insists that we feel both the strangeness and absurdity, and our own complicity in it. Such are the verbal/material artifacts of contemporary, daily life that make Jarrell's narrative poetry so typically Jarrellian, attractive and true to some readers, while banal and anti-poetic to others. Jarrell's tone, his attitude toward his settings and characters, is itself ambivalent and ambiguous. As in his consideration of progressive education, he feels both attraction to the things and terms of the world and impatience and repugnance against them. Can a woman who grows old in the ambiance of station wagons and supermarkets and suburban funeral parlors be a tragic figure? Is she to be taken seriously at all? Clearly, Jarrell thinks so, for he returns to her, to her problem and her story, in many poems.

One of the early treatments of this female protagonist on her home turf is **"The Night before the Night before Christmas,"** in which the plot again turns on a dream, in this case a dream of transcendence which reveals to the adolescent protagonist, a Jamesian "central intelligence," that her sick brother is "dying," seemingly, as her mother died, as the friendly squirrel who lives outside her home in "the Arden Apartments" has died. With its detailed descriptions of the family's life in their apartment, the school activities, the books the girl reads to her brother, the Christmas present she wraps for a friend ("And ties it, one gold, gritty end / Of the string in her mouth, and one in her left hand; / Her right forefinger press[ing] down the knot"), it comes perhaps closest of any Jarrell narrative to being a candidate for "story" rather than poem. Even so early, radiators, angora bed socks, and "Rexall's Theatrical Cold Cream" take their places in the poem with Hansel and Gretel and phrases from Marx, Dickens, and Jack London. Such "props," acceptable, even expected in the short story at least from Joyce forward, still disturb the equilibrium of the poem. What does Jarrell mean by introducing them?

In American literature it is Whitman who first insists on the immanence of spirit in the commonplace, but I imagine Whitman himself stopped short by "Rexall's Theatrical Cold Cream." Details of the mundane enter French poetry in Baudelaire and Corbière, and English poetry through them, and the intent, in such poems as Eliot's "Preludes" or "The Waste Land," is to jar the conventional expectations of the reader and, often, to inspire disgust at the sordidness or banality of the images. Jarrell's aim seems more nearly to parallel Whitman's, and it is a calculated risk he takes to import such trivia, such "misplaced concreteness," into the poem. Even Williams takes plums from the icebox, not the Frigidaire or the Amana.

In the case of **"The Night before the Night before Christmas,"** as in a few other of the longer poems, one might well ask, what is the virtue of having written this subject as a poem rather than as a story, where its wealth of commonplace detail would be more "natural"? The answer is not self-evident. It brings us to a juncture of fiction and poetry; it raises a question of genre and function, of the relation of theme to medium. Jarrell at this point in his life did clearly think of himself as a poet, and not a writer of fiction. (And, even then, a critic only on the side.) But there must have been a compelling reason to treat this narrative material in verse. While the poem could readily be seen as a "stream of consciousness" form of narration, indirect interior monologue because it maintains the third-person pronoun in speaking of the girl, it observes two important conventions typical of poetry rather than prose narrative: the freedom to leave the gaps in the narrative quite large, gaps which the reader does not need to fill in or take "inferential walks" from in order to make sense of the text; and, more significantly, the requirement of presenting the themes and situations in rhythmic, poetically adorned language.

These are narrative poems, but their emphasis is a traditional poetic one; the working through of conceptual or emotional conflicts by formalizing them in the language and structure of the poem. The narrative structure, I have argued, is homologous with a deliberative or meditative discursive structure, but it is finally the play of language that marks the poem as poem rather than story. Syntax is freed, alliteration and assonance are encouraged, repetition is acceptable, and the lines of the verse estrange the commonplace by foregrounding both the images themselves and the aural aspects of the language. One can only assume that, for Jarrell, this aspect of poetic language was the overriding consideration in his choice of genres, that the stylistic choices subsumed by the genre "poem" were necessary to his "transformation" of truth into art. In this transformation, the poet's self is deeply involved; although he casts his experience in narratives of other personae, the very fact of their appearing in poems, with the language in which they are embodied calling attention to itself as an individual poetic "style," tangles them inextricably with his most fundamental self-concept. It is through study of Jarrell's poetic narrators that this unity of self and the work of art becomes most apparent.

II: The Narrators

In his poetic narratives, Randall Jarrell uses the full range of modern narrative techniques and narrative personae, from the omniscient, self-projecting narrators who speak not only of but to the characters of the poems ("**Siegfried**," "**Lady Bates**," "**A Girl in a Library**"), through third-person "central intelligence" narrators of Jamesian decent ("**The Night before the Night before Christmas**," "**The End of the Rainbow**"); first-person monologists who are to be seen with irony ("**Sears Roebuck**," "**Money**"); serious, sympathetic, first-person protagonist narrators ("**The Woman at the Washington Zoo**," "**Seele im Raum**," "**Next Day**," so many others); first-person narrators who seem to be the "poet" ("**Jamestown**," "**A Rhapsody on Irish Themes**," "**A Conversation with the Devil**"); to those who seem to be not just the poet but the private person, Randall Jarrell ("**The Lost World**," "**A Man Meets a Woman in the Street**"). It is the presence of this last type which calls into question the relation of author to narrator in the other poems.

In a 1974 *Georgia Review* essay, Frances Ferguson tried to pinpoint Jarrell's characteristic poetic "voice" by way of his interest in narrative, citing in particular his essay "**Stories**," in which she found "two dialogues . . . Jarrell's dialogue with the storytellers whose stories he recounts, and (probably more importantly) the dialogue which emerges as the divided consciousness of the text itself. . . . Throughout '**Stories**' we encounter a . . . conflation of third person and first person that makes it appear that the search for individual identity is somehow at issue."[7] This same conflation is to be found, as Ferguson shows, in the poems, and there too we sense a search "for individual identity." The slippage between narrative voices that characterize such a poem as "**Eighth Air Force**," where we cannot tell for certain whether the "I" is one of the flyers or the observer figure of the poet, is typical, and once noted, it begins to create problems in our understanding of the narrative voice of other poems. In *Pictures from the Institution* and "**A Girl in a Library**," the narrators are readily acceptable as spokesmen for the poet, and the similarity of their style to that of the Jarrell of the essays—especially the polemical essays such as "**Poetry and the Age**" and "**A Sad Heart at the Supermarket**"—reinforces our identification of that fictional and poetic narrative voice with that of "Randall Jarrell," the writer of the essays, the professor, if not the private person.

Even in the poems in which the nominal narrator differs in age, gender, or condition of life from Randall Jarrell, we often encounter many of the same concerns, attitudes, and problems as those in which the narrator seems comfortably to fit the authorial persona. "**90 North**" is indubitably narrative, and by itself it seems obviously enough a "character" monologue, like a number of other Jarrell narratives of children ("**A Sick Child**," "**A Story**"). Yet the voice is remarkably like that of a number of the poems we would likely classify as autobiographical poems, in particular, "**The Lost World**." The last section of *The Complete Poems* includes "unpublished" poems, a number of which are much more obviously personal poems than those he chose to include in the published collections. They encourage one to look at other poems as more personal expressions than they may seem at first to be. Returning to Jarrell's idea of the story as a "cure" for pain, a vicarious experience that transforms life, we reconsider the narrative poems as episodes of the macro-narrative of Jarrell's life.

Looking backward from "**The Lost World**," for example, we read such poems as "**90 North**" and "**A Story**" rather differently than we read them in the chronological order of Jarrell's published poems. "**A Story**" (1939), in particular, with its narration of homesickness that cannot quite admit itself, is one that teases with its lack of differentiation between narrator and poet. The narrator is a boy, to be sure, lonely, resentful at being sent away to school, rationalizing, fearing that he has been forgotten, plotting his revenge: he'll disappear, "they'll wake up one day / And find *my* bed's the one that's empty" (132). He fantasizes a "lost" boy whose absence the matron and dean try to cover up. That "story" is literally untrue, we presume, but it is a projection of the boy's own feeling of separation and isolation.

The resolution of the plot is only the boy's resolution to turn his pain outward, to cause the others—the parents—pain by disappearing as they have disappeared, and he comes to this resolution not through any decisive action or event but as a product of accumulated grief. It is only when we read, in "**The Lost World**," "the little girl is crying / Because I didn't write. Because—/ of course, / I *was* a child, I missed them so" (291), and learn that in fact Jarrell never wrote to his father's family in California after being sent back to Tennessee in 1926, that "**A Story**" begins to reverberate with a personal tone overtly denied in its narrative voice.

Other first-person narrators seem more distinctively separate. In a number of dramatic monologues, the narrators are women and children apparently far removed from Jarrell's station or situation: children dying or bereaved in the war, a war widow, various middle-class, unintellectual women. The usual way of explaining why Jarrell invented so many women and children narrators is that adult male narrators couldn't "get away with" the kinds of statements that are made in these poems.[8] The implication is that in these narrators Jarrell is projecting his own feelings but masking himself with a persona who could, in contemporary American society, acceptably express the emotions, perceptions, and judgments found in the poems, the sensations of loss, grief, isolation, and bewilderment. Women and children are supposed to be emotional, intuitional, even sentimental. The children's views, too, are by their directness or "innocence" a way of "making strange" the dreadful ordinariness of war and psychic destruction. This explanation seems to me accurate, as far as it goes, but, following up on Frances Ferguson's phrase, I think that we are justified in seeing as well a divided self-seeking identity within itself and common cause with the world outside. A Jungian reading of these personae as aspects of the self-seeking integration also seems warranted.[9]

Like a novelist, Jarrell uses different types of narration for different signifying purposes. The story-poems with third-person narration allow Jarrell to speak from "outside" the narrative as well as inside the characters' consciousness. This type of narration is used to "get behind" speech with characters who couldn't or wouldn't plausibly speak for themselves. James's "method of the central intelligence" allows Jarrell to explore life both with these characters and apart from them. "Content," the heroine of **"At the End of the Rainbow,"** is one who couldn't tell her own story; she has repressed its meaning, like Joyce's Maria in "Clay," who leaves out the potentially painful lines of her song. The psychiatrist of **"Jerome"** is a narrative center who most likely wouldn't tell his own story (except perhaps in analysis). The poem has a strangely bland surface which suggests that, even with the third-person narration, something is being held back, repressed, hidden from us. In the end we are left with "pure" narration of action: "The man holds out a lump of liver to the lion, / And the lion licks the man's hand with his tongue" (272).

In general, the "dramatic" narrative poems in both third and first-person narration tend to place their protagonists in positions of what my colleague, poet Edward Hirsch, has called "no exit." Seeing mostly the horror of life, Jarrell nonetheless drew back from putting himself squarely in the nihilistic center by projecting his fear onto characters who *can* express it and need not be rescued from its consequences: the woman of **"Seele im Raum,"** the protagonist of **"The Woman at the Washington Zoo,"** the child who has lost his family or his own life in the war in **"The State"** or **"Come to the Stone."** The dread of annihilation at the heart of such poems is made bearable by the distance created by the narrative situation.

The first-person narrator who stands in for the poet, however, is a more hopeful character, and it is interesting that this narrator appears more frequently in the later rather than earlier poetry. Whether the direct influence of Lowell's *Life Studies* convinced Jarrell that a more autobiographical poetry was possible for him, or that milestone book was simply one of a number of factors, the "I-who-am-Randall Jarrell" rather than the "other" or the more formal "I-am-the-poet," becomes more prominent in Jarrell's work after 1957.

A premonition of this movement is seen in **"Nestus Gurley"** (1956), a poem of great charm which appears unobtrusively in **The Woman at the Washington Zoo,** as a kind of counter to the "no-exit" situation of other poems in the volume. Ostensibly a description of the Jarrells' paper boy in Greensboro, it turns out to be a narration-cum-meditation on the possibilities for happiness we have in a world threatened by nuclear holocaust or just ordinary death. In his triumphant individuality and matter-of-fact optimism, Nestus would be, for the poet, an acceptable announcing angel of the Last Judgment. Details of Jarrell's life on South Lake Road—his cat, his stepdaughter, their domestic and church-going preparations for Christmas, Nestus' derby hat, and the precise amount of the monthly bill—blend with his global fears and speculations.

> Sometimes I only dream him. He brings then
> News of a different morning, a judgment not of men.
> The bombers have turned back over the Pole,
> Having met a star. . . .
>
> (236)

After nearly two decades of poems about others—other people, other fictional characters—in which the first-person appears only as a character or a fictionalized, often detached and supercilious narrator, this is a fairly surprising poem. Hardly "confessional," it nevertheless is a movement in the direction of self-revelation that was uncharacteristic. The reception of his last book, **The Lost World** (1965), suggests that Jarrell was perhaps right in remaining disguised in his earlier poetry, for the chief objection to its title poem, in particular, was sentimentality, and, recovering from an emotional breakdown in the spring of 1965, he was devastated by the ferocity and apparent personal animus of several of the reviews. That the poem, and its companion poem, **"Thinking of the Lost World,"** have since found an increasingly appreciative audience is both sad irony and an interesting comment on the changing critical reception of contemporary poetry. Over the years, critics have come to understand and expect the introspective and confessional voice, consequently effecting a revision of the valuation of Jarrell's later work.

The history of the genesis of **"The Lost World"** is worth rehearsing: in 1962 Jarrell's mother returned to him a number of letters he had written to her when he was twelve and on a summer visit to his grandparents in Los Angeles, after his parents had separated and he had already resettled with his mother and brother in Nashville. The return of these letters was the catalyst that set him free to deal with that wrenching, beautiful time of his life. A return visit to Southern California with his wife in the summer of 1963 sharpened the contrasts, so that the narrator of the poems is clearly doubled (in the tradition of Wordsworth and Proust): the boy, reclaimed from the past, and the man, looking back. The detail of the letters was essential to Jarrell in his reconstruction of that past, deliberately excluded or totally disguised up to this point in his career, as in **"A Story."**

That the child who wrote such eloquent letters to his mother about his love for the California family, that the man who would write with such love of that family, never wrote *to* the family is nearly impossible to credit. Yet it is a fact, once comprehended, that fits in with other suppressions of Jarrell's life from his public persona. The separation was quite literally too difficult for him to cope with, and he both consciously suppressed and unconsciously repressed it for over thirty years.[10] Projecting onto his grandparents a rejection of himself that was, so far as one can tell, completely unfounded, he reproached them, in disguise, in poems from several periods of his career. (We must not think that Jarrell's interest in the Freudian notion of poetry as "dreamwork" was purely academic or theoretical.)

In **"The Lost World"** and **"Thinking of the Lost World,"** for the first time dealing openly with this separation, he found the psychological courage to confront his own fear and resentment, to reveal the so-long hidden love. Speaking in the first person of himself, poet and person, he is able to recover and welcome back the child-that-was, along with the whole family, the entire magical ambiance of the Hollywood childhood, and—hardest of all—its pastness and his present. The end of this story takes us back through Jarrell's career to that other story of a quest, **"90 North,"** which ended with a bitter recognition of the nothingness at the base of life. But at the end of **"Thinking of the Lost World,"** happiness, not "nothing," comes from nothing. Wisdom has somehow transcended pain, and the exchange of the *story* of his own past for the youth that is gone is now acceptable, worthy of gratitude. It is its own reward. Thus does the story, at least temporarily, triumph over life's pain.

There is no exit from what Jarrell the poet, Jarrell the personal narrator, confronts at the end of **"Thinking of the Lost World."** Yet the creative act that forms the poem out of those real bits of the past, the childhood letters, can, this time, use the personal narrator, can bring together the divided self into one self, an "I" connected to its own past and accepting of its own future annihilation. Of course, the story doesn't end with **"Thinking of the Lost World."** There are other, later poems to consider: on the one hand, the precarious happiness of personal narrative in **"A Man Meets a Woman in the Street,"** and on the other, the rueful dramatic monologue of **"The Player Piano,"** in which the character-narrator has never learned to live but only to pretend to live, as she pretends to play the player piano. Yet the contours of a conclusion are solidly present, and reaffirmed in the ending of **"A Man Meets a Woman in the Street"** when a man and woman "can't tell our life / From our wish," and discover their wish to be not the "human" wish for variety, but "the birds' wish: 'May this day / Be the same day, the day of my life'" (353). By trading his own sorrows in the composition of narrative poems, Jarrell gained the knowledge to make at once a body of poetry and a life: the knowledge, finally, that the only real, successful change we can make in our lives is precisely the transformation that makes the truth of our wishes into art.

Notes

1. As does Charlotte Beck in her *Worlds and Lives: The Poetry of Randall Jarrell* (Port Washington, N.Y.: Associated Faculty Press, 1983).
2. "The Poet, Truth, and Other Fictions: Randall Jarrell as Storyteller," in *Critical Essays on Randall Jarrell*, ed., Suzanne Ferguson (Boston: G. K. Hall, 1983), p. 284.
3. *A Sad Heart at the Supermarket* (New York: Atheneum, 1967), p. 148.
4. *The Complete Poems* (New York: Farrar, Straus & Giroux, 1969), pp. 106-07, 98-99; further references appear within the text.
5. In *Critical Essays on Randall Jarrell*, pp. 272-83.
6. See *The Role Of the Reader* (Bloomington and London: Indiana University Press, 1979), pp. 31-33.
7. Frances C. Ferguson, "Randall Jarrell and the Flotations of Voice," in *Critical Essays of Randall Jarrell*, p. 165.
8. See Mary Jarrell, "Ideas and Poems," *Parnassus*, 5 (Fall-Winter 1976), 218-19; and Beck, *Worlds and Lives,* pp. 35-37.
9. Looking at the poems historically, we can also see the postwar prevalence of female narrators as a peacetime adaptation of the soldier-victim protagonists of the war poems.
10. See Mary von Schrader Jarrell, "The Group of Two," in Robert Lowell, Peter Taylor, & Robert Penn Warren, eds., *Randall Jarrell, 1914-1965* (New York: Farrar, Straus & Giroux, 1967), pp. 284-85.

Charlotte H. Beck (essay date May 1985)

SOURCE: Beck, Charlotte H. "Randall Jarrell's Modernism: The Sweet Uses of Personae." *South Atlantic Review* 50, no. 2 (May 1985): 67-75.

[*In the following essay, Beck contends that Jarrell's use of various "masks," or narrators, in many of his poems was essential to his art and his "delineation of truth as he perceived it."*]

Randall Jarrell once wrote, "We never step twice in the same Auden." His own readers might ask, "Will the *real* Randall Jarrell please stand up?" Searching the poems, M. L. Rosenthal finds that Jarrell's typical speaker is "at once himself or herself *and* Randall Jarrell; not, of course, Jarrell the wit, translator of Rilke and edgily competitive poet, but the essential Jarrell" (["Between Two Worlds"] 31). The many Jarrells are as difficult to classify as to define. Jerome Mazzaro places him "between [the] two worlds" of modernism and postmodernism ([*Randall Jarrell*] 83), and Rosenthal praises *The Lost World* as Jarrell's vehicle of entry into a confessional period wherein he "finally treats intimate realities of his own actual life and memory" (41). These efforts to postmodernize Randall Jarrell, to prefer the confessional poet of *The Lost World,* is to devalue much if not all that precedes, as well as much that is in that climactic volume of poetry. It was the other Jarrell, the reluctant heir of modernism, who created monologues, dialogues, and scenes so central to his achievement. This was the poet who discovered and turned to his advantage one of modernism's chief strategies, "the sweet uses of personae."

I have adapted that phrase, "the sweet uses of personae," from Mary Jarrell's article "Ideas and Poems," wherein she describes how for Randall Jarrell, "the idea of altering the gender of his feelings" enabled him to avoid "the maudlin effects of a man's self-pitying confessions." She relates how first in **"The Face"** and afterwards in **"The Woman at the Washington Zoo"** and **"The End of the Rainbow,"** he "established how sweet the uses of the persona could be for him" (218-19). Not only with female personae, but with a procession of soldiers, children, and an assortment of other male speakers, Jarrell found in the dramatic poem an effective distancing strategy. The use of personae in well over half of his poems places Randall Jarrell among the modernists, whose poetic he alternately admired and deplored but fully understood.

My intention is not to define such protean terms as "modern" and "postmodern" except insofar as they imply a judgmental contrast between Jarrell's dramatic and his so-called "confessional" poems. Rather, I would argue that for Jarrell, the use of many masks—of critic, novelist, children's storyteller, satirist, and translator, as well as all those that appear in his poetry—was necessary to his art and to his delineation of truth as he perceived it. For Mazzaro, this "insist[ence] on dramatic monologues" as "one alternate to shaping his views into a single voice" makes him a relativist, even a modern skeptic (87). The same charge can, of course, be leveled at Jarrell's predecessors in the genre—Browning, Tennyson, Frost, and Eliot, to name a few—who, like Jarrell, saw reality as composed of many differing perceptions coexisting in one multifaceted world. For such poets, the dramatic monologue and related forms become the way to allow each self its version of truth; and relativism becomes the only viable philosophy.

I

Does Jarrell's use of the dramatic monologue make him a modernist? To answer this question one need only recall how he consistently, throughout his career, defined modernism. In his 1942 essay, **"The End of the Line,"** Jarrell anticipates modern critics' efforts to merge modernism with romanticism by labeling the former an "extension" and "end product" of the latter. For the first time, also, Jarrell calls the dramatic monologue a form which began as a "departure from the norm of ordinary poetry" but which "in modernist poetry . . . itself becomes the norm" (79). And although he proceeds to pronounce modernism's death, thereby separating himself and his generation from a spent tradition, Jarrell gives to modernist poetry thirteen characteristics—including experimentalism; heightened emotional intensity to the point of violence; obscurity and inaccessibility; lack of restraint; emphasis on detail; preoccupation with the unconscious, with dreams; irony of every type; primitivism; isolationism; and condemnation of the present for an idealized past (79)—all of which, with the possible exception of primitivism, might be used to describe Jarrell's own poetry. For Randall Jarrell, both modern poetry and its most characteristic form, the dramatic monologue, had become a cliché which had yet to be replaced by any major kind of innovation. In a sense, then, to follow in the modern tradition was for Jarrell and his generation a compromise and a delaying strategy.

Jarrell's critics have often mirrored his ambivalence toward the dramatic mode by asking, with Frances Ferguson, "Why did he have so many 'characters' populating his poems" (["Randall Jarrell and the Flotations of Voice"] 163)? Others have objected, along with James Dickey, to the nameless, faceless quality of Jarrell's personae (["Randall Jarrell"] 44). To begin, it must be said that Jarrell's dramatic monologues and dialogues are not, like Browning's, said aloud to a listener; rather, they resemble Tennyson's monodramas and Eliot's interior monologues, Laforguian utterances of a mind looking inward. Jarrell's dramatic poems resemble Shakespearean soliloquies, wherein the speaker puts into words those unutterable truths he or she would tell no one; they are, for their lyrical qualities, like operatic arias that capture the speaker's emotions at an epiphanic moment. What makes Jarrell's dramatic poems come alive for the reader is their realization of a concrete situation in time and place. Although most of his speakers do represent types, as critics have complained, they are made unique by their particular relationships to the worlds around them. "What," Jarrell once asked (in a letter to Amy Breyer), "shall it profit a man if he gain his own soul and lose the whole world?" So much do

Jarrell's speakers depend for their identity on their situation that the titles of the dramatic poems often name, not the speaker, but a place occupied by the speaker. One immediately recalls **"In the Ward: The Sacred Wood," "A Camp in the Prussian Forest," "A Girl in a Library,"** and **"The Woman at the Washington Zoo."** Other titles fuse speaker with temporal and spatial situation so that separation is inconceivable; consider **"The Death of the Ball Turret Gunner," "Next Day," "A Street off Sunset,"** and **"A Man Meets a Woman in the Street."** Still others, like **"Burning the Letters"** and **"The Player Piano,"** connect the persona in a Proustian manner with the object that precipitates the monologue. Surely Jarrell's "dramatic lyrism," as Parker Tyler early phrased it (["The Dramatic Lyrism of Randall Jarrell"] 140), has its earliest antecedent in the Wordsworthian and Keatsean dramatic lyric, wherein the speaker and landscape are interdependent. Add the Laforguian irony that gives the modern interior monologue its distinctive tone and one has the main ingredients of Jarrell's dramatic poems, themselves recapitulating the tradition and further extending it into the middle of the twentieth century, when, in Jarrell's own words, the "reign of the dramatic monologue" was finally at an end (*Stevens* [**"The Collected Poems of Wallace Stevens"**] 66).

II

Because Jarrell's personae are typical rather than individual, his critics have from the beginning enjoyed classifying the poems according to similar personae. Tyler's 1952 groupings of soldiers, children, and fairy princes (141) have to give way to include the women who, after the publication of *A Woman at the Washington Zoo,* became his most frequently employed personae. To these classes I add the observers, Jarrell's most transparent masquers, who, though present throughout his career, come to prominence in *The Lost World.* Here I will illustrate briefly four groups of Jarrell's personae—soldiers, children, women, and observers—by focusing on one characteristic poem and, in typical Jarellian manner, naming a few equally characteristic poems that every Jarrell reader ought to know. To survey Jarrell's personae in this order is to recapitulate the approximate succession in which they became the central concern of his monologues. The soldiers (or airmen) dominate Jarrell's second and third volumes: *Little Friend, Little Friend* and *Losses.* The children have their domain in the fairytale world of *The Seven-League Crutches,* his first postwar collection. The women and observers, though represented in Jarrell's earlier volumes, come to prominence in his latter collections, *The Woman at the Washington Zoo* and *The Lost World.*

The war poems came out of Jarrell's indirect involvement with the nightmare world in which he participated, first as pilot trainee and then as flight instructor. A long letter to Allen Tate, dated 1944, provides an astonishingly complete gloss on these war poems. Jarrell reports having had "a pretty good time when I was flying," but, since most of his fellow pilots were training for combat, he had to conclude that being "washed out" was "a very great piece of luck." Had he failed as pilot and then been assigned to Sheppard Field, he almost certainly would have been made a gunner. Such are the sweet uses of personae: two of Jarrell's best poems, **"Gunner"** and **"The Death of the Ball Turret Gunner,"** resulted from his relief at not occupying that most vulnerable position in a combat plane. The composite voice in **"Losses"** intones, "In bombers named for girls, we burned / The cities we had learned about in school." Jarrell writes in the same letter that "your main feeling about the army, at first, is just that you can't believe it; it couldn't exist, and even if it could, you would have learned what it was like from all the books, and not a one gives you even an idea." The speaker of **"Eighth Air Force,"** who judges himself along with the other "murderers" who sit around him playing pitch or trying to sleep, is but one remove from the flight instructor who describes to Tate how he would "sit up at night in the day room . . . writing poems, surrounded by people playing pool or writing home, or reading comic-strip magazines." Jarrell's enthusiastic description of the celestial navigation tower where, "in a tower about forty feet high, a fuselage like the front of a bomber—the navigator . . . sits . . . and navigates by shooting with his sextant the stars that are in a star dome above his head" is answered, in **"Losses,"** by the complaints of those who "died on the wrong page of the almanac" because star data was misinterpreted. Neither the confessional poems of a washed-out pilot nor the objective observations of a non-combatant could achieve the force of these dramatic poems spoken by the victims. It is not surprising that these two war volumes established for Jarrell a reputation for war poetry that he did not easily exchange for a more timely label.

Jarrell's child speakers have caused much controversy among his readers. Robert Lowell compared Jarrell with Wordsworth for making of the child's world a "governing and transcendent vision" (["Randall Jarrell"] 109). James Dickey's "B"—half of his divided opinion on Jarrell—accuses Jarrell of maudlin sentimentality of a James Fieldian variety (45). Certainly, Jarrell's children constitute for him a less successful distancing strategy than his soldiers or women. One is conscious of the painful memories that created such poems as **"A Story"** and **"The Truth,"** although the situations in which Jarrell places his child-speaker are fictional. The most successful solution to this tonal problem is to be observed in two poems, **"90 North"** and **"The Lost World."** In these, Jarrell achieves distance through the use of a double persona, by which the adult and child together recreate two levels of consciousness: the powerless innocence of the past and painful experience of the present. Neither is superior to the other; both are simultaneously real. In a 1945 letter to Allen Tate, Jarrell reacts to the marriage of Tate's daughter Nancy by saying that to him she will always be "a fat little girl who surely can't have ceased to exist, but is waiting somewhere for you to discover that the other is an impostor." Thus did Jarrell's children exist on a causeway between past and present, easily traversed when an impulse from memory stimulated the mind to return.

Between **"90 North"** and **"The Lost World"** Jarrell wrote his more conventional dramatic monologues wherein the child speakers are placed in a fictional temporal and spatial setting. In addition to **"The State,"** **"A Story,"** **"The Truth,"** and **"Protocols,"** grounded in the terrible realities of the Second World War, there are the fantasy settings of **"The Prince"** and **"The Black Swan."** In the latter, as well as in the extended narrative with dialogue, **"The Night before the Night before Christmas,"** the speaker has the dramatic advantage of being a girl rather than a thinly concealed version of young Randall. Even the most obviously biographical of these personae are given the objective detachment of fictional settings and time-frames necessary for the dramatic monologue. Among Jarrell's uncollected poems, until recently unpublished, is a case in point. **"The New Ghost"** is the dramatic monologue of a child newly separated by death from parents who, he believes, have always considered him an outsider. From his vantage point beyond life, he looks in on the world of the living. His "scratchy wool gown and shoes that squeak" represent his new condition, while comfortable in the lighted living room that has always excluded him, the ghost's parents appear happy to be rid of his unwanted presence:

>   Father and mother are sitting there
>   To mean that I'm not really theirs
>   So that they don't say a word to me
>   To pretend to me that I'm not there.
>
>   In a dream there's no one there at all . . .
>   But—but there it *is* a dream.
>
>   (Beck [*Worlds and Lives*] 101)

The child's confused speech mirrors the predicament of one who, like Rilke's dead children, is a stranger in the world inhabited and controlled by unfeeling adults. These children, crippled either physically or emotionally, are obvious objectifications of the fears and hostilities that marred Jarrell's childhood as well as our own. For several of these children, the only comforter is a beloved pet, the only escape the seven-league crutches of fantasy, dreams or death. Such monologues make Jarrell's readers uncomfortable, because they strike too close to aspects of reality we would like to forget and because the tone in such poems cannot be other than pathetic, even bathetic.

Jarrell's feminine personae represent his highest achievement in the dramatic monologue. As versions of the Jarrellian *anima,* these speakers are based on personal experience ironically masked; as products of Jarrell's reading of Rilke and Frost, they achieve classical status. Jarrell translated Rilke's "Faded" and "The Widow's Song" at about the time he was writing **"The Woman at the Washington Zoo"** and **"The End of the Rainbow."** Added to the Rilkean theme of isolation and rejection is the Frostian character of the mad or apparently mad speaker whom Jarrell so much admired in "A Servant to Servants" and "The Witch of Coös." Jarrell's feeling of ambiguity toward women, so brilliantly apparent in the non-dramatic poem **"Woman"** and in the essay **"A Sad Heart at the Supermarket,"** provides the ironic seasoning that such poems as **"Seele im Raum"** and **"Next Day"** require. The first of these personae must have been the bereaved wife of **"Burning the Letters,"** but they reach their height of dramatic realism in **"Next Day"** and **"The Lost Children,"** which sit alongside the supposedly confessional poems included in and coming after *The Lost World.*

Perhaps none of Jarrell's dramatic monologues so successfully combines authenticity with self-displacement as **"Gleaning,"** written in 1963 and one of his last poems. The catalyst is a childhood memory, one contiguous with those that account for the three semi-autobiographical poems in **"The Lost World."** On the Sunday drives that the boy Randall Jarrell took with his California grandparents, he observed some aged persons patiently looking for beans left by the pickers. Later, when the recollection merged with the Biblical story of Ruth and Boaz, Jarrell was once again aware of the sweet uses of personae. The speaker, sensing the allegorical implications of her gleaning, becomes, in a compression of her entire existence, a "grown-up-giggling, grey-haired girl" who has begun to "glean seriously." Like Ruth, she has "lain / At midnight with the young men in the field"; at the evening of her life, she now awaits death, "A last man, black, gleaming / To come to me." Coming at the end of Jarrell's career, **"Gleaning"** establishes better than any other poem how personal experience may be universalized through the use of personae. The modern gleaner could have been the subject of a dramatic lyric poem with the observer as persona; instead, Jarrell has given her particularly archetypal significance. Jarrell had discussed with his publisher a volume entitled *Woman,* which would have displayed his best speakers in a more advantageous context than does their sporadic appearance in all his earlier volumes (M. Jarrell, interview). Without such an arrangement, Jarrell's readers still have evidence, both early and late, that the use of women as personae was always for Randall Jarrell a useful way to universalize his own experience.

Jarrell's observer-personae demonstrate his residual romanticism more than his modernism; but if one can believe the Jarrell of **"The End of the Line,"** there is no reason why a poet cannot be both romantic and modern at the same time. In poems like **"The Sick Naught,"** appearing with the early war poems, and in much later ones, **"The Well-to-do Invalid"** and **"Three Bills,"** Jarrell becomes a dramatic lyricist—like Wordsworth, Keats, or Arnold—who places himself, as surrogate both for the reader and the poet, at the periphery of a dramatic situation centered around someone who has arrested his attention. The observer is a rather transparent version of the poet, but the fact that the action of the poem takes place in the present in a fully realized spatial framework does, in fact, make it a dramatic poem. A much-admired product from the middle of Jarrell's career, **"A Girl in the Library,"** may serve as an illustration. Herein, the speaker, almost surely a professor of literature, is found at a safe distance leisurely observing "an object among dreams" sitting "with [her] shoes off" as her "face moves toward sleep." Not content with his status as an observer, the speaker conjures up an image of Tatyana (from *Eugen Onegin*) to serve as the girl's antithesis in sophistication. He, refusing to accept Tatyana's arrogant dismissal of the girl as a "poor fat thing" who is never to realize her potential, mentally changes her to his "Spring Queen," symbolizing all feminine potentiality. As her "Corn King," the observer successfully penetrates the closed world of her psyche without even disturbing her nap. A by-product of such poems is, of course, an opportunity to observe the observer, to gain insight into the poetic consciousness caught in the act of transforming life into art. These observer poems stand as evidence that the poet may indeed play a role in his dramatic poem, if only as a supporting actor.

Robert Pinsky has commented that, although the use of a borrowed voice or alter-identity ". . . partly distinct from the poet, constitutes one of the most widely noted . . . and fundamental aspects of modernism," certain recent poets have employed "a speaker or protagonist who is not only dramatic, but somewhat eccentric [to] present a statement about oneself" ([*The Situation of Poetry*] 14). In his use of personae, Randall Jarrell is able, as Pinsky implies, to be both dramatic and confessional and realize the full benefits of both poetic strategies. The Jarrell who saw no discontinuity between romanticism and modernism would no doubt summarily dismiss Procrustian barriers between modernism and post-modernism. By the end of his career, Jarrell had begun, on occasion, to write directly from experience; but he had not—as **"Gleaning"** and **"The Player Piano"** prove—abandoned the sweet uses of personae. The brilliance of Jarrell's monologues, dialogues, and scenes lies not in what they say, or do not say about the poet himself; rather, their value resides in that shock of recognition the reader experiences upon discovering, in one of Jarrell's speakers, not only a portrait but a mirror.

Works Cited

Beck, Charlotte H. *Worlds and Lives: The Poetry of Randall Jarrell.* Port Washington, NY: Associated Faculty P, 1983.

Dickey, James. "Randall Jarrell." *Randall Jarrell, 1914-1965.* Ed. Robert Lowell, *et al.* New York: Farrar, Straus and Giroux, 1967. 33-48.

Ferguson, Frances. "Randall Jarrell and the Flotations of Voice." *Critical Essays on Randall Jarrell.* Ed. Suzanne Ferguson. Boston: G. K. Hall, 1983. 163-75.

Jarrell, Randall. "The Collected Poems of Wallace Stevens." *The Yale Review* (Spring 1955). Rpt. *The Third Book of Criticism.* New York: Farrar, Straus and Giroux, 1969. 55-73.

———. "The End of the Line." *The Nation,* 21 February 1942. Rpt. *Kipling, Auden and Company: Essays and Reviews, 1935-1964.* New York: Farrar, Straus and Giroux, 1980. 76-83.

———. Letter to Amy Breyer, undated. Henry W. and Albert A. Berg Collection, New York Public Library, Astor, Lenox and Tilden Foundations. Quoted with permission of Mrs. Randall Jarrell and the New York Public Library.

———. Letter to Allen Tate, 1944. The Allen Tate Papers, Princeton U, Princeton, NJ. Quoted with permission of Mrs. Randall Jarrell and Princeton University Library.

———. Letter to Allen Tate, 1945. The Allen Tate Papers, Princeton U, Princeton, NJ. Quoted with permission of Mrs. Randall Jarrell and Princeton University Library.

Jarrell, Mary von Schrader. "Ideas and Poems." *Parnassus Poetry in Review,* 5 (1976): 213-30.

———. Personal Interview. 2 September 1984.

Lowell, Robert. "Randall Jarrell." *Randall Jarrell, 1914-1965.* Ed. Robert Lowell, *et al.* New York: Farrar, Straus and Giroux, 1967. 101-112.

Mazzaro, Jerome. "Between Two Worlds; The Post Modernism of Randall Jarrell." *Critical Essays on Randall Jarrell.* Ed. Suzanne Ferguson. Boston: G. K. Hall, 1983. 82-100.

Pinsky, Robert. *The Situation of Poetry.* Princeton: Princeton UP, 1976.

Rosenthal, M. L. *Randall Jarrell. University of Minnesota Pamphlets on American Authors,* no. 103. Minneapolis: Jones Press, 1972.

Tyler, Parker. "The Dramatic Lyrism of Randall Jarrell." *Poetry,* 79 (1952): 335-46. Rpt. *Critical Essays on Randall Jarrell.* Ed. Suzanne Ferguson. Boston: G. K. Hall, 1983. 140-48.

Patricia Rodgers Black (essay date winter 1985-86)

SOURCE: Black, Patricia Rodgers. "The Atom Bomb: Jarrell's Dream-Work in *The Lost World.*" *Mississippi Quarterly* 39, no. 1 (winter 1985-86): 31-40.

[*In the following essay, Black contends that* The Lost World *expresses Jarrell's "dream-wish" to "protect and establish the permanence of this world," but the wish is "distorted by displacement" into a book of "children's fantasies."*]

While working on his book *The Lost World,* Randall Jarrell told his friend Robert Watson that he was writing a book of poems about the atom bomb. After reading *The Lost World* one can only be puzzled by this statement, for the three poems entitled **"The Lost World"** that form the core of the collection appear to be only about the author's childhood, and the remainder of the poems in the collection form a world of other characters, other voices.

For Jarrell, the craft of poetry bore a striking resemblance to the dream-work described by a man he admired very much, "the poet Sigmund Freud";[1] according to Mary Jarrell, her husband believed that what enables the poet to write a good poem is "the Unconscious, that is the *help* of the Unconscious."[2] The dream-motif is found throughout his poetry. Perhaps if we regard **"The Lost World"** as a dream, Jarrell's mystifying statement about this book will have more meaning for us.

According to Freud a dream is a way in which the Unconscious can get a message to the Conscious, a way in which the Unconscious can make itself heard. But because of the nature of the message the dream must be distorted by what Freud calls the censor before it is allowed access to the Conscious; this distortion is termed the dream-work. The identification of dreams with works of art is found throughout Jarrell's writings. To **"A Girl in a Library"** he says, "So many dreams! And not one troubles / Your sleep of life?"[3] The poet's frustration is audible—in Jarrell's own words, "the tone of someone accustomed to helplessness,"[4] accustomed to not being heard. The artist has a message for us, just as the Unconscious has a wealth of messages for the Conscious, and so a work of art, a dream, is created in an attempt to give voice to this message.

In *The Interpretation of Dreams* Freud says that "two separate functions may be distinguished in mental activity during the construction of a dream: the production of the dream-thoughts, and their transformation into the content of the dream."[5] The dream-thoughts are the essence, the origin of the dream; their transformation is the dream-work. If we are to believe what Jarrell told Bob Watson, the dream-thoughts from which *The Lost World* originates concern the threat of atomic annihilation. This view can be substantiated by a closer look at Freud's theory and at what we know of Jarrell through his writings. Freud tells us that "our dream-thoughts are dominated by the same material that has occupied us during the day and we only bother to dream of things which have given us cause for reflection in the daytime."[6] Reading Jarrell's essays we gain an insight into his daytime thoughts: In an essay from his book *Poetry and the Age* we hear him say, "The World of the Future! . . . where, above the concrete cavern that holds a General Staff, the rockets are invisible in the sky . . . Of this world I often think."[7] In the title essay of *A Sad Heart at the Supermarket* he says:

> One imagines as a characteristic dialogue of our time an interview in which someone is asking of a vague gracious figure, a kind of Mrs. America: "But while you waited for the intercontinental ballistic missiles what did you do?" She answers: "I bought things." She reminds one of the sentinel at Pompeii.[8]

Notice how Dr. Helen Caldicott of the anti-nuclear movement reiterates Jarrell's vision:

> Superimposed on this passive state of psychic numbing is an active pathology—labeled by an English psychiatrist as "manic denial." This requires redirection of the uncomfortable energy induced by the subconscious fear of nuclear war into diversionary activities such as an immoderate interest in material possessions. . . . It is imperative that Americans face reality and start grieving . . . for their families, their country, and their planet.[9]
>
> [*Nuclear Madness*]

Those at the National Poetry Festival in 1962 heard Jarrell say:

> Most poets, most good poets even, no longer have the heart to write about what is most terrible in the world of the present: the bombs waiting beside the rockets, the hundreds of millions staring into the temporary shelter of their television sets, the decline of the West that seems less a decline than the fall preceding an explosion.[10]
>
> [**"Fifty Years of American Poetry"**]

Freud's theory tells us that in the second part of the construction of the dream, "the dream work . . . restricts itself to giving things a new form. . . . The thoughts have to be reproduced . . . in the material of visual and acoustic memory-traces."[11] Freud names the four aspects of the dream-work: condensation, displacement, representation, and Secondary Revision. Jarrell's dream reflects these four activities.

As a child Jarrell lived for a year or so with his grandparents and great-grandmother in Hollywood, California, the setting of **"The Lost World."** This world was very dear to Jarrell, but his time there was abruptly ended when he had to return to his parents in Tennessee. The three separate parts of **"The Lost World"**—**"Children's Arms," "A Night with Lions,"** and **"A Street off Sunset"**—are unified by Freud's theory: "Separate and successive dreams . . . may have the same meaning, and may be giving expression to the same impulses in different material."[12] Each of the three poems is filled with "visual and acoustic memory-traces" from that time of his life.

"On my way home I pass a cameraman." So opens the first poem, **"Children's Arms."** For us, Jarrell is the cameraman now, and we are watching his home-movies, those dreams a family creates together. He will make us love his life so that we, too, cannot bear to see it vanish.

Hollywood is the factory of America's fantasies. But what are fantasies? Again we turn to Freud and realize that they are day-dreams, wish-fulfillments, an arsenal against the disappointments of the reality over which one has no control. Hollywood provides arms against reality for all the children who have grown up to become Americans. In the list Jarrell makes of the child's weapons, he mentions a small biplane that takes off and lands on "the counterpane"—a word to help explain the purpose of children's arms, and the purpose of fantasies and dreams. Dreams are the mind's attempt to counteract the psychic stress created by the divergence between what we desire and what reality offers us.

> A certain relief comes from the island:
>   Across the seas
> At the bottom of the world, where Childhood
> Sits. . . .
> The island sang to me: *Believe! Believe!*

Jarrell situates the island "at the bottom of the world" and in the first stanza of this poem he mentions the dinosaurs of **The Lost World,** a movie version of Conan Doyle's novel about the discovery of a site of prehistoric life in South America: both island and dinosaurs are images, parallels of the deep source the poet draws upon, the Unconscious. To believe in something is very similar to the process of creating.

Condensation is the first aspect of the dream-work described by Freud: "The construction of collective and composite figures is one of the chief methods by which condensation operates in dreams."[13] The poet must make these condensations visible to us through words. The dream-work can visually fuse these images but in reading a poem we must merge them in accord with the author's intention. After reading **"The Lost World"** one can see the super-imposed images. The Hollywood movie sets are repeated by the high-school play about "The island that the children ran." The "dinosaur / And pterodactyl, with their immense pale / Papier-mâché smiles" looking over the fence of the movie set in the beginning of **"Children's Arms"** are superimposed on the concluding image:

> We press our noses
> To the glass and wish: the angel—and devilfish
> Floating by on Vine, on Sunset, shut their eyes
> And press their noses to their glass and wish.

A scene in the high-school play—"Chatting over their fruit, / Their coconuts, they relish their stately feasts"—repeats a breakfast scene: "We eat in the lighted kitchen / . . . Happiness / Is a quiet presence, breathless and familiar." That description of happiness reminds one of the eland in Jarrell's **"Seele in Raum"**—an evocation of that aching loss of something beloved and irreplaceable.

The second aspect of the dream-work is displacement. Freud says:

> A transference and displacement of psychical intensities occur in the process of dream-formation, and it is as a result of these that the difference between the text of the dream-content and that of the dream-thoughts comes about. . . . The consequence of the displacement is that the dream-content no longer resembles the core of the dream-thoughts and that the dream gives no more than a distortion of the dream-wish which exists in the unconscious.[14]
>
> [*The Interpretation of Dreams*]

The poet's dream-wish, to protect and establish the permanence of this world, is distorted by displacement to become a poem of children's arms, children's fantasies. The "psychical intensity" of the poem lies in the fragile images of the child's everyday life. The power of the dream is the juxtaposition of the insufficiency of the child's arms in confrontation with the core of the dream-thoughts: the threat of atomic devastation hovering over the child's cherished world. With displacement, the manifest content of the dream is created, though it covers "a latent content . . . which is of far greater significance."[15]

Representation is the third step in the mind's creation of the manifest content of the dream. Freud speaks of this selection of dream material: "Dreams can select their material from any part of the dreamer's life, provided only that there is a train of thought linking the experience of the dream-day (the 'recent impressions') with the earlier ones."[16] In **"The Lost World"** it is not until the third and final poem that "the experience of the dream-day" (that is, the day preceding the dream) is mentioned. In the first two poems we are given only earlier material from the dreamer's life, material released by the "recent impression" we find beginning the third poem. **"Children's Arms"** is a collage of images from the poet's youth; toys, tree-house, adventure magazines, dinosaurs, grandparents, a dog named Lucky, and much more.

The final aspect of the dream-work, what Freud calls Secondary Revision, is that distortion that makes the dream take on a sensible appearance, makes the dream appear to be about one thing when it is really about something else. Freud speaks of the process as "building up a façade for the dream."[17] The poet can use the techniques of Secondary Revision just as the Unconscious does: to cover what could be an alarming message with a less threatening communication.

Part II of **"The Lost World"** is entitled **"A Night with Lions."** Very short in comparison with the first and third poems of the trilogy, it is almost entirely a poetic elucidation of Freud's concept of condensation. Though Tawny is the only "real" lion in the poem, it is a night with *lions*. The first stanza tells of the child visiting "my aunt's friend / Who owned a lion, the Metro-Goldwyn-Mayer / Lion." Then there is a break, and the second stanza shows the poet as a man with a "dream-discovery" that he's made into a poem for us: The woman beside him in bed is there because she is the condensation of the lion Tawny, the "young, tall, brown aunt," and Jane from the Tarzan movies. The lion of the first stanza bears a strong resemblance to the portrait Jarrell devises of **"Woman"** later in this collection, and to the woman beside him in the second stanza: "I'd play with him, and he'd pretend / To play with me. . . . / Till he got bored." In the second stanza the condensation of his perception of the lion's and the woman's personalities is expressed with the repetition: "you talk to me or pretend / To talk to me as grown-up people do." This aspect of the condensation lays the groundwork for the typical, fond, Jarrellian irony of the conclusion: "'You're my real friend.'"

This poem also elucidates another value of the dream: Past, present and future are united:

> I lie beside
> My young, tall, brown aunt, out there in the past
> Or future. . . .
> till in the end
> I think as a child thinks.

The dream-work of this poem aids Jarrell in his Proustian endeavor to recapture lost times, to add them to his present world and to insure them a life in the future.

The trilogy's third poem, **"A Street off Sunset,"** is the final dream of the night. Freud says, "The content of all dreams that occur during the same night forms part of the same whole."[18] He goes on to say that these successive dreams become progressively clearer in disclosing the true message of the Unconscious, and that the dream-thoughts can most easily be deciphered from the final dream of the series.

This third poem begins with the dream-day experience that triggered the cycle of dreams: The smell from the Vicks factory in the town where he now lives reminds the poet of the eucalyptus tree that held his tree-house in California. Freud tells us that the source of a dream can be "an internal significant experience (e.g. a memory or a train of thought), which is in that case invariably represented in the dream by a mention of a recent but indifferent impression."[19] The Vicks plant means nothing to the poet except that it provides the sensory stimulus that triggers the dream-material of his childhood. Once again he's back in Hollywood and we recognize all the elements that we grew to know in **"Children's Arms."**

"A Street off Sunset" is very much concerned with the coming of night; it shows that even the poet's idyllic childhood was lit by the ominous light of sunset. In **"Children's Arms"** the darkness was held at bay, but in this final dream the censor has been unable to keep the dark threat out of the manifest content of the California home.

The four elements of the dream-work are still operating in this poem despite the few cracks in the surface. Condensation works to merge an opening scene of the child reading about a mad scientist who intends to destroy the world with a scene even earlier in his childhood in which he was looking at the cover of the *Literary Digest*: "A poor two-seater being attacked by four / Triplanes. . . . / The colors of the afternoon would fade" and the small child would think "I'm not afraid."

The most remarkable condensation in this poem however is the unification of his grandmother's image (he calls her Mama) and the image of the evil scientist, that emissary from the dark dream-core:

> There off Sunset, in the lamplit starlight,
> A scientist is getting ready to destroy
> The world. "It's time for you to say good night,"
> Mama tells me. . . .

The humor is almost too black. Again:

> I read as I undress.
> The scientist is ready to attack.
> Mama calls, "Is your light out?" . . .
> Forced out of life into
> Bed, for a moment I lie comfortless
> In the blank darkness.

Forced out of life into . . . bed. As he listens to the earphones of the crystal set in bed "the uneasy tissue / Of their far-off star-sound, of the blue-violet / Of space" leads him to sleep and in the following instant to the sound of the hens "as Mama brings their chicken feed." This is a foreshadowing of the point of terror in the poem—when Mama wrings the neck of the chicken—and points even further to lines from the last poem in the book:

> The chicken's body is still going round,
> and round in widening circles, a satellite
> From which, as the sun sets, the scientist bends
> A look of evil on the unsuspecting earth.

With the condensation, displacement and representation unite to form a powerful transference of psychical intensity: The stanza that describes the sight of his grandmother killing the chicken turns the poem into a nightmare:

> The body hurls
> Itself out—lunging, reeling, it begins to run
> Away from Something, to fly away from Something
> In great flopping circles. Mama stands like a nun
> In the center of each awful, anguished ring.
> The thudding and scrambling go on, go on—

Following this stanza, as the dream draws to a close, Pop arrives home from work. It is at this point that the poet shows an exact knowledge of Freud's theory of Secondary Revision. Freud mentions that as a part of the effort of the censor to preserve the secrecy of the dream-thoughts, the manifest content of the dream will often contain the words "oh, it's just a dream." Freud cites this as "a prelude to waking up. . . . And still more frequently it has been preceded by some distressing feeling which is set at rest by the recognition that the state is one of dreaming."[20] So, as we are about to awaken from this poem, we hear the child ask for reassurance, not mentioning his grandmother, but rather the scientist he's been reading about:

> My universe
> Mended almost, I tell him about the scientist. I say,
> "He couldn't really, could he, Pop?" My comforter's
> Eyes light up, and he laughs. "No, that's just play,
> Just make-believe," he says.

And so we are released from the dream. The poet can only hope that his readers will analyze and come to understand the message he sends. In his essay **"Poets, Critics, and Readers"** Jarrell says, "Freud talks of the 'free-floating' or 'evenly-hovering,' attention with which the analyst must listen to the patient. . . . But this is quite as true of critics and the poems that are *their* patients."[21]

These three poems are a tribute to the "ways that habit itself makes holy." Just like his great-grandmother Dandeen, each of us is a miraculous time-capsule. **"The Lost World"** is of course a true celebration of Jarrell's childhood and not just the insignificant manifest content of a dream. The poet can fulfill many purposes in a poem; I have only focused on an intention that might be missed otherwise. Freud himself said that "it is in fact never possible to be sure that a dream has been completely interpreted. . . . It is impossible to determine the amount of condensation."[22] The atom bomb may be only an aspect of a deeper meaning.

In comparison to his earlier poems, those of this last book of Randall Jarrell's poetry are marked by a greater accessibility, a simpler language and more personal subject-matter. I believe that this difference is due to the poet's intention: He wanted to write about the worlds he shared with all men, those worlds we hold, and lose, in common. Throughout time dreams have had the power to warn, the power to awaken the dreamer to potential danger. By directing our attention to the danger of nuclear annihilation Jarrell establishes mortality as the undeniable bond that unites us all. In **"The Lost World"** Randall Jarrell expresses his love for the past, the present, and the uncreated and threatened future.

Notes

1. Randall Jarrell, "Love and Poetry," *Kipling, Auden & Co.: Essays and Reviews, 1935-1964* (New York: Farrar, Straus and Giroux, 1980), p. 250.

2. Mary Jarrell, "Ideas and Poems," *Parnassus,* 5 (1976), 215.

3. Randall Jarrell, "A Girl in a Library," *The Complete Poems* (New York: Farrar, Straus & Giroux, 1969), p. 16. All further quotations from Jarrell's poetry are taken from this edition.

4. Randall Jarrell, "The Obscurity of the Poet," *Poetry and the Age* (New York: The Ecco Press, 1980), p. 18.

5. Sigmund Freud, *The Interpretation of Dreams,* trans. and ed. James Strachey (New York: Avon Books, 1965), p. 544.

6. Freud, p. 207.

7. Randall Jarrell, "The Obscurity of the Poet," pp. 20-21.

8. Randall Jarrell, "A Sad Heart at the Supermarket," *A Sad Heart at the Supermarket: Essays & Fables* (New York: Atheneum, 1962), pp. 68-69.

9. Helen Caldicott, with the assistance of Nancy Herrington & Nahum Stiskin, *Nuclear Madness: What You Can Do!* (Toronto; New York: Bantam Books, 1980), pp. 111-112.

10. Randall Jarrell, "Fifty Years of American Poetry," *National Poetry Festival Proceedings* (Washington: Library of Congress, 1964), p. 137.

11. Freud, p. 545.

12. Freud, p. 369.

13. Freud, p. 328.

14. Freud, p. 343.

15. Freud, p. 196.

16. Freud, p. 202.

17. Freud, p. 529.

18. Freud, p. 369.

19. Freud, p. 213.

20. Freud, p. 526.

21. Randall Jarrell, "Poets, Critics, and Readers," *Kipling, Auden & Co.*, p. 307.

22. Freud, p. 313.

J. A. Bryant, Jr. (essay date 1986)

SOURCE: Bryant, J. A., Jr. "Jarrell as Critic and Essayist." In *Understanding Randall Jarrell*, pp. 69-101. Columbia: University of South Carolina Press, 1986.

[*In the following essay, Bryant traces Jarrell's development as a literary critic, asserting that "his judgments from the beginning had a significant effect on the taste of the American reading public."*]

During his lifetime Randall Jarrell published two books of essays and made a list of items to be included in a third. The first of these, ***Poetry and the Age*** (1953), established him as something more than a brilliant reviewer, and this is the collection by which Jarrell's stature as literary critic has been judged ever since. ***A Sad Heart at the Supermarket,*** which came out in 1962, is a collection of personal essays that ranges more widely, including one on the stories of Kipling; one on short stories generally; an enthusiastic account of the poetry of Eleanor Taylor, wife of his friend Peter Taylor; a review of André Malraux's *The Voices of Silence*; and an explanation of how he wrote **"The Woman at the Washington Zoo."** Other essays deal more or less directly with the decline of taste in mid-twentieth-century America. ***The Third Book of Criticism*** appeared four years after his death, in 1969, and contained two early and (and uneven) pieces on Auden; the introductions to his anthology *Six Russian Short Novels* and his collection of Kipling's English short stories; essays on Wallace Stevens, Robert Graves, Christina Stead's *The Man Who Loved Children* (a novel Jarrell championed enthusiastically for two decades), and Frost's "Home Burial"; and a lecture, **"Fifty Years of American Poetry,"** that he delivered at the National Poetry Festival in Washington in 1962. A fourth volume, entitled ***Kipling, Auden & Co.: Essays and Reviews*** (1980) made available virtually all of Jarrell's uncollected criticism, much of it first published in *The Nation, The New Republic, Vogue, The Partisan Review, The Yale Review,* and *The New York Times Book Review*. In addition, the volume reprinted five essays from ***A Sad Heart at the Supermarket*** (by that time out of print) and the essay on Kipling's English stories from ***The Third Book of Criticism*** ("so as to gather all of Jarrell's criticism of Kipling between the covers of one book").

Persons familiar with the work of Jarrell the reviewer, particularly the early Jarrell, though they admired his unflagging perceptiveness and his wit, admit to having winced frequently at the vitriol he seemed prepared to throw at almost anyone who asked the reader to give attention to work that was careless, professionally irresponsible, or untouched by genius. These older readers probably did not need to be reminded of what some of the early Jarrell reviews were like, and one suspects that the mature Jarrell would never have gone out of his way to make accessible much of the material that this last volume dropped so casually on the younger generation's bedside table. Even so, nothing in it diminishes Jarrell's stature as critic, and his judgments from the beginning had a significant effect on the taste of the American reading public—and perhaps an effect on the direction of letters in postwar America as well.

Jarrell's first essay for *The Southern Review* (Autumn, 1935), written when he was twenty-one, is a good example. It is an omnibus review of ten new works of fiction by a group of writers that included Ellen Glasgow, Erskine Caldwell, Stark Young, Willa Cather, and Rachel Field. Jarrell's judgments are remarkably consistent with those that prevail after fifty years of reflection and sifting. He found Glasgow's style and perceptions commonplace but not without occasional moments of power. He obviously admired Caldwell as a craftsman but found him sentimental in his undiscriminating use of brutality. Just as obviously, he did not care for Stark Young: "Sometimes . . . snobblish, sometimes sentimental, sometimes he shows a disquieting admiration for moral perceptions or stylistic effects which do not seem to the reader admirable at all." His four paragraphs on Willa Cather's *Lucy Gayheart* combine qualified praise for an unpretentious novel with a clear perception of the qualities that have kept Cather's work alive for more than half a century. Rachel Field was highly thought of by other critics at the time, but Jarrell summarized his opinion of *Time Out of Mind* with the observation that on a certain level it "is quite a good story; but this level is surprisingly low."

Understandably readers came in time to look for quips and cutting remarks in Jarrell's reviews, and sensitive authors came to fear them. He called Frederic Prokosch "a decerebrate Auden, an Auden popularized for mass consumption." He published a devastating essay on Archibald MacLeish's *The Fall of the City* in *The Sewanee Review* (Spring, 1943), in which he called it, among a great many other things, a "black-and-white political cartoon, plainly at variance with most of the facts." Irritated with Conrad Aiken's fluency and lack of substance, he wrote in *The New Republic* (February 17, 1941) that Aiken "seems as much at ease as Merlin pulling a quarter out of a schoolboy's nose." In time Jarrell came to regret some of his flippancies. Approaching his middle years he said that he had come to understand pain of the spirit and was increasingly reluctant to take pleasure in inflicting it, however justified the pain might be. Still, his honesty tended to redeem even the more outrageous sallies of his rambunctious youth. Painful or not, his judgments more often than not turned out to be right, and he made them all out of a deep concern for literary values. His reputation as a critic has, if anything, been enhanced by the republication of his more ephemeral pieces.

Jarrell's earliest essays also give evidence of an intellect that was flexible as well as formidable, one that he might have deployed successfully in any number of directions; but being congenitally disinclined to be a follower, he eschewed the route of apprenticeship and insisted from the outset on finding a direction that would allow him to be uniquely himself. He managed to maintain his indifference to the interests of some of his Fugitive mentors in the tradition of the American south and to their subsequent flirtation with agrarianism. He resisted attempts to make him set down his principles and thus came close to annoying James Laughlin of New Directions, who wanted a preface for the group of poems Jarrell contributed to *Five Young American Poets* (1940).[1] And he gave evasive answers to the series of questions posed by John Ciardi, who had included him in the anthology *Mid-Century American Poets* (1950).[2] Subsequently, in almost a quarter of a century of writing about literature, he never produced aesthetic statements or rationales comparable to those in Warren's "Pure and Impure Poetry" or the essays in Ransom's *The World's Body* or Tate's several volumes of criticism.

The closest he ever came to producing a set of principles was in **"The Age of Criticism,"** the fourth essay in his first collection, ***Poetry and the Age***. There he endorsed the commonplace that the present age is one of criticism and explained that this is so because most people can no longer read. The deficiency is just as conspicuous in university professors and scholars, he said, as it is among the general public. The latter read less because their leisure is increasingly filled with other occupations; the professors read less because they feel compelled to spend their time strengthening their specialties by reading books and articles *about* literature rather than literature itself. Hence the need for the critic, who properly is nothing more than a loving, self-effacing reader who seeks only to lead others to the monument and then disappear in the presence of the thing itself. If all of us were the readers we ought to be, he said, there would be no need for criticism.

Jarrell's own practice as critic was always just this and nothing more: to bring his readers to the monument and entice them, cajole them if need be, into seeing for themselves. Usually his strategy, whether writing reviews for *The Nation* or producing essays for *The Kenyon Review,* was to make a series of affirmations, punctuated by occasional quips (sometimes characterized by detractors as wisecracks), followed by a list, occasionally divided into best and second best, of the pieces under consideration that he preferred. In short reviews, poetry chronicles, and surveys like the one he delivered at the National Poetry Festival in Washington in 1962 he usually limited himself to judgments and quips; but in all of his critical writing he seemed to be implying that the work of the critic was an activity best summed up in a remark he made in 1959: "Art is long, and critics are the insects of a day."[3] During his lifetime more formal critics dismissed this procedure of Jarrell's as simplistic. Hindsight has compelled acknowledgment from both critics and general readers that many of the affirmations still stand as defensible critical perceptions, that the quips continue to charm as wit, and that the lists still serve admirably as guides to what is most characteristic of the subject's work.

For Jarrell criticism was, like his poetry and his fiction, simply one more extension of his person—normally an ephemeral extension, to be sure (like the song of an insect), but dignified in his case by the fact that he was himself a poet and a writer of fiction. In conversation the word he most often used to indicate his reason for a particular judgment was *taste*. It was taste, he said, that told him that a piece of clothing was or was not appropriate, that a musical selection was good (though he knew music mainly from records), and that one painting was preferable to another. He recognized the implication that his reliance on taste had for some. "Using such a word as *taste*," he wrote in "Poets, Critics, and Readers," "helps to make us believe that there is some passive faculty that responds to the new work of art, registering the work's success or failure."[4] *Passive* is the key word here. The faculty was real enough, he thought, but it was not some kind of aesthetic litmus, and it was not widely disseminated. In the same essay he went on to say that "the new work must call forth in us an active power analogous to that which created it." Here he was confident of his ground, for Jarrell believed in nothing if not his own gift of creativity. He might just as easily have been a painter, a composer, or a fashion designer, he felt; but by accident of circumstances he was a poet, and the creativity that had made him a poet, he was sure, qualified him to be a critic of other forms of art as well—a critic and an interpreter.

As a critic of writing Jarrell felt especially free to promote his personal enthusiasms, sometimes without very much explanation. Among the writers he praised virtually without qualification were Eleanor Taylor, Adrienne Rich, Cristina Stead (though mainly for one novel), Elizabeth Bishop, Katherine Hoskins, and Robert Graves. He also felt free—indeed obligated—to point out the shortcomings in certain established writers whose accomplishments might have been expected to intimidate a relatively young critic like himself, among them T. S. Eliot, Ezra Pound, his old friends and mentors Allen Tate and Robert Penn Warren, and his closest friend (aside from Peter Taylor) among contemporaries, Robert Lowell. Moreover, though he began and ended an ardent admirer of the poetry of W. H. Auden, he did not hesitate throughout his life to call the older poet to task for a variety of literary sins, including sentimentality, vagueness, and banality.

He could also recommend to public attention and admiration older authors who he felt had been neglected by fashionable writers and literary critics. The best example here is Walt Whitman, who in an age of Eliot, Pound and such journals as *The Southern Review* and *Scrutiny* had suffered the fate of being taken for granted.[5] Jarrell began by wittily postulating a war (not entirely imaginary) in which the partisans of Henry James were waging a life-and-death battle with the partisans of Whitman, and then he reflected that James had once given Edith Wharton a private reading of Whitman that left them both "shaken and silent." The source of Whitman's greatness, Jarrell insisted, lies, as greatness always does, in the "minute particulars" of the poetry, not in some nebulous cumulative excellence. "All the dead lines in the world," he observed, "will not make one live poem"; then he added that with Whitman's poetry one does not need to explain or argue this point but merely to quote. After that he proceeded to give a demonstration.

This took the form of a three-page mosaic, set in a single paragraph, of metaphors, epithets, and concrete detail, all illustrative of Whitman's lifelong preoccupation with things both static and active: men, women, children, plants, animals, insects, weather phenomena of various kinds, and such artifacts as scythes, drainpipes, and kitchen utensils, all set forth in nouns, active verbs, and (used sparingly) precise adjectives. Then dismissing some insensitive reader's inclination to detect a resemblance here to Thomas Wolfe (a writer much admired during Jarrell's formative years, though never by Jarrell), he pronounced Whitman even at his worst "ingeniously bad" and went on to say, "Only a man with the most extraordinary feel for language, or none whatsoever, could have cooked up Whitman's worst messes."

To substantiate his points further he provided several pages of extended quotation interspersed with brief comments suggesting possible comparisons with Berlioz; James at his best; Chekhov; and Tennyson ("the most skillful of all Whitman's contemporaries"), who suffered from the limitation imposed by the forms he used, a limitation Whitman happily was able to avoid.

As for Whitman's notorious contradictions, which Whitman himself acknowledged and airily accepted, Jarrell saw these as inherent in the comprehensive view of the world that was the supreme gift Whitman passed on to his readers. He admitted that Whitman did not give us "the controlled . . . contradictions of the great lyric poets," but he pointed out that Whitman should not be compared with the lyric poets at all but with Homer or the writers of the sagas or perhaps the Melville who wrote *Moby-Dick*. Where the qualities of a Walt Whitman are concerned, he wrote, the critic can only point "in despair and wonder" and call them by their names.

This is a good example of Jarrell the critic "coming clean," exposing the critic's pretensions, acknowledging the limitations of his role; for he firmly believed that in the end the critic when dealing with works that are truly great or that have a touch of greatness—Homer's, Shakespeare's, Goethe's, or Whitman's—can only stare in wonder and point out his discoveries to others. Being modest (or perhaps innocent as well), he did not say here (though he had elsewhere implied as much in his remarks about taste) that the critic who would write in this way and expect to be effective must have eyes and ears and imagination comparable to the eyes and ears and imagination that had produced the works under inspection. In one way, however, Jarrell failed to measure up to his own prescription: try as he would, he could not be self-effacing. His better critical essays almost inadvertently create the impression of classrooms with Jarrell presiding as teacher, exhorting, reassuring, explaining where necessary, occasionally indulging in witticisms. For those who expect their critics to maintain objectivity, with at least an illusion of distance, this can be disconcerting; but most agree that the dividends in illumination and insight more than compensate for indulging Jarrell in this regard.

Another neglected writer whom he helped to return to prominence was Rudyard Kipling. The project came about almost by accident when Doubleday asked him to select fifty of Kipling's stories for an anthology to be published under their Hanover House imprint. Jarrell's introductory essay, **"On Preparing to Read Kipling,"** subsequently found its way into *A Sad Heart at the Supermarket* and after that into *Kipling, Auden & Co.* as well. In the last collection it was accompanied by two more essays on Kipling that he had written for shorter anthologies in Doubleday's Anchor series. One of these, **"In the Vernacular,"** prefaced a collection of tales about India; the other, **"The English in England,"** prefaced a companion volume of stories about England. Jarrell's interest in Kipling had begun in childhood; it was still strong during his Vanderbilt days, when he once winced to hear his teacher Ransom speak disparagingly of *Plain Tales from the Hills.*[6] He had no illusions about Kipling's limitations and freely admitted that he was no Shakespeare—not even a Turgenev or a Chekhov. Even so, Jarrell pronounced him a great genius, a great neurotic, a great professional, "one of the most skillful writers who have ever existed," and unbeatable when it came to creating his own unique kind of story.

His defense of the man and his work was not unlike the defense he mounted on behalf of Whitman. Once more he began with a citation from Henry James, who, it turns out, was as appreciative of Kipling as he had been of the American poet. Then he asked readers to divest themselves of everything they had ever heard or believed about the man and take a fresh look for themselves. The Kipling who emerged in the next eight pages or so was a vastly talented reporter who put truth above rhetoric and (like Jarrell himself) produced a body of writing that was an extension of his own person and reflected his response to the specter of a collapsing world of presumably benevolent imperialism. In that vision, which he shared with all enlightened Anglo-Indians, Jarrell said, Kipling had recognized in Victorian England the truth of Thomson's City of Dreadful Night; and that knowledge, which he had tried futilely to communicate in his stories, made him sadly congenial with the debacle of the First World War ("the death and anguish of Europe") that took his own son.

In a sense Jarrell's three principal essays on Robert Frost constitute a rehabilitation of that literary figure also. Jarrell knew Frost fairly well and brought him to Greensboro on several occasions to give readings to the students. The first of these essays, **"The Other Frost,"** included in *Poetry and the Age,* contains sharp criticism of some of Frost's most popular poetry as well as of the man himself; and by comparison with the images that Jarrell presented of Whitman and Kipling, his picture of Frost seems almost diminutive. "A sort of Olympian Will Rogers out of *Tanglewood Tales,*" is only one of several disparaging epithets with which he begins the essay. Nevertheless, **"The Other Frost"** almost certainly places in focus the Frost that will command the interest and respect of knowledgeable readers in generations to come. This is the Frost of "The Witch of Coos," "A Servant to Servants," "After Apple-Picking," "Directive," "Design," "Provide Provide," and "Home Burial." Jarrell's second essay, also in ***Poetry and the Age,*** contains excellent readings of several of these poems, including "Provide Provide" and "Directive," which he calls "one of the strangest and most characteristic, most dismaying and most gratifying, poems any poet has even written." A detailed reading of "Home Burial" was reprinted in ***The Third Book of Criticism.*** Here he called Frost "a complete and representative poet," and by that he meant a poet who had looked at the world and attempted, with remarkable success, to set it forth, all of it, as it appeared to him. Frost's view was inevitably partial, but that was not entirely his fault; it was as comprehensive as Frost was capable of giving, and that was enough to leave most readers in wonder and awe and rejoicing.

Jarrell presents his homage to Wallace Stevens in two essays: **"Reflections on Wallace Stevens"** in ***Poetry and the Age*** and **"The Collected Poems of Wallace Stevens,"** which first appeared in *The Yale Review* in 1955, the year of Stevens's death, and later in ***The Third Book of Criticism.*** In the first Jarrell spends a good deal of time being witty (for example, he compares *Harmonium* to a travel poster); and he criticizes Stevens for philosophizing too much and avoiding figures of earth, "always swinging between baroque and rococo." Yet even as he criticizes, he pronounces Stevens one of the true poets of our age and concludes, somewhat condescendingly, with what is probably the most quoted sentence in all of his criticism: "A good poet is someone who manages, in a lifetime of standing out in thunderstorms, to be struck by lightning five or six times; a dozen or two dozen times and he is great." From the second essay one concludes that Stevens was more than great. There Jarrell retracts his earlier judgment that Stevens philosophized too much. He declares it a virtue that he wrote steadily with or without inspiration for most of his life, and was able at the end to put into poetry the rich insights that the end of a lifetime brought him. Then characteristically Jarrell provides a list of sixty or so poems, which as he puts it, is sufficient to give a "dazzlingly definite" idea of the things that are exceptional about Stevens's work.

Poetry and the Age contains two essays on Marianne Moore, both in part defenses against critics who persisted in saying that she was not really a poet at all. For Jarrell, as for T. S. Eliot, Moore was one of the finer poets of contemporary America; and he warmed to her work as he had been unable to warm to the austerities of Wallace Stevens. The things he especially admired in Moore's work were her use of particularities; her recognition that relationships are the realities in this world and that everything is related to everything else; her unembarrassed recourse to "expression in general" (that is, common discourse) as opposed to "poetic expression"; and her refusal to consider anything unpoetic or unfit for inclusion in her unpretentious but precise lines. Having said all this in three remarkable pages, Jarrell translates these virtues into a series of comparisons: as tersely conclusive as Grimm, as wise as Goethe, as beguiling as Beatrix Potter, as purely magical as Alban Berg, as elevated as the Old Testament, and as morally and rhetorically magnificent as St. Paul. Near the end of the second essay he clinches his points with the customary list of her best poems—pieces, he says, quoting Moore's own words, that make the reader feel "a life prisoner, but reconciled."

The reader of Jarrell's essay on John Crowe Ransom,[7] his onetime teacher and mentor, may detect behind the appearance of self-confident ease a note of diffidence that is rare in Jarrell's criticism. In the first sentence he says that Ransom's poems are "about everything from Armageddon to a dead hen," as indeed they are, though put thus baldly Ransom's range diminishes to the level of a wisecrack. Near the end he takes note of Ransom's influence on "at least three good poets"—Robert Graves, Allen Tate, and Robert Penn Warren; then he suggests that these were influenced "more by his accident than by his essence" and adds, "To expect Tate's and Warren's poems to be influenced by Ransom's is like expecting two nightmares to be influenced by a daydream." The list of best poems here comes at the middle, and the essay ends with a virtuoso performance that is more Jarrell than Ransom: "a recollected Breugelish landscape of the country of Ransom's poems," in which familiar images of the older man's poetry are recognizable but only as shapes translated into an alien mode. One is tempted to think that Jarrell never quite escaped a youthful intimidation by the confident tone of Ransom's poems (those written after *Poems About God*) and felt uncomfortable at realizing that while he could capture the accidents and even make sport with them, he still could not lay hand on the elusive essence.

He found the work of William Carlos Williams, a poet not attractive to Jarrell's early mentors, considerably more to his liking. Williams is the subject of two of the last essays in **Poetry in the Age**; he receives more than half of the space in a third and shares a fourth with Richard Wilbur and Robert Lowell. In all four Jarrell addresses a sophisticated public that, even as he wrote, was beginning to accord Williams the respect that since then it has more than amply confirmed. For Williams, Jarrell had such epithets as *generous, spontaneous, open, humanitarian, liberal,* and *democratic,* all signifying the qualities by which the young Jarrell had thought himself differentiated and distanced from the austerely formal Fugitives who had ignited but at the same time frustrated his youthful genius. Acknowledging that parts 2 and 3 of *Paterson* were discouraging, he declared part 1 a work of genius, a "microcosm which he has half-discovered, half-invented," narrower than Whitman's but strongly reminiscent of that older poet's world. Jarrell's most telling compliment is probably his suggestion that Williams has an unusual dislike and distrust of Authority (Jarrell's capital), a dislike that aroused sympathies which even the mature Jarrell may never have fully recognized in himself. Mere dislike of authority probably would not have been enough to win his approval; but Williams, in defiance of the "establishment" that had exalted Eliot for more than a generation, managed to produce a body of durable poetry of a radically different kind. He had challenged Goliath without losing either his life or his identity. "If you have gone to the moon in a Fourth of July rocket you built yourself," Jarrell quipped at the conclusion of **Poetry and the Age,** "you can be forgiven for looking askance at Pegasus." He may have been thinking of his own achievement.

He was almost certainly thinking about his own achievement and career in some of the things he wrote about Auden, the idol of his youth who never ceased to amaze, challenge, and frequently anger him. Writing in *The Yale Review* in 1955 (in one of the essays reprinted in **Kipling, Auden & Co.**) he could speak of the "flatness" of *Nones* and the "comfortable frivolity" of *The Shield of Achilles*; yet in the last sentence he could not forbear recalling nostalgically that in the thirties Auden had produced "some of the strongest, strangest, and most original poetry that anyone has written in this century." Anger triumphs over nostalgia, however, in essays that he wrote for *The Southern Review* in 1941 and for *The Partisan Review* in 1945. These were included in **The Third Book of Criticism** as **"Changes of Attitude and Rhetoric in Auden's Poetry,"** and **"Freud to Paul: The Stages of Auden's Ideology."** There Jarrell set forth the grounds for his disaffection at length, explaining in the first essay how Auden had abandoned his early preoccupation with the resources of English language in favor of a preoccupation with rhetoric. Thus, whereas in the beginning he had done what poets ought to do—namely, extend creatively the range of the language—midway in his productive career he had let his language go flat and resorted to rhetorical tricks that sometimes startle but never completely obscure the fact that his thought had slipped to a prosaic level commensurate with his diction. Even for readers who resist the evaluation, Jarrell's analysis of Auden's style here should be extremely valuable, particularly his account of the idiosyncratic language in Auden's early poetry. The results of what must have been a youthful and loving scrutiny of Auden's work is set forth in a remarkable list of salient characteristics, twenty-six in all. An alert reader will note that many of these are characteristics of Jarrell's own adventurous early poetry.

Equally remarkable in the same essay is a list of elements that went into the "world order" that Jarrell has Auden making to oppose to the world of "late-capitalist society in which [during the thirties] he found himself." These include Marxism, Freudian psychology, fairy tales and folklore, boyish sources of value (including flying and polar exploration), the world of the biological sciences, and homosexuality. Jarrell seems to have had no interest in the last of these, but he shared fully Auden's interest in the first four, and he understood Auden's interest in the fifth, it being at the time, as he said, practically incapable of being corrupted by capitalist culture. In any case this was a schema of the Auden Jarrell admired, and one finds echoes of it throughout his first four volumes of poetry, where it might almost serve as a schema of the Jarrell one sees there.

The second essay deals with Auden's shifts in ideology, "from Freud to Paul," and is if anything more disapproving than the first one. In Jarrell's view the later Auden ceased to be serious but adopted a pose of solemnity that masked his ingenious maneuvers to avoid confronting enemies far more formidable than capitalism. Jarrell's generation confronted them head-on by going to war; Auden had abandoned a decadent Europe for the relative tranquility of the United States, where he moved steadily toward the position of St. Paul (as Jarrell presents it), accepting our involvement in original sin and waiting passively to be saved by grace. Ten years later Jarrell was still paying lip service to the poet Auden might have been. "Auden's laundry list would be worth reading," he wrote," and then he added, "I speak as one who's read it many times, all rhymed and metered."[8]

Jarrell wrote on other contemporary poets, of course, but not at great length and not with the intensity that he displayed in writing about the ones that have been discussed here. Near the end of his life, in the fall of 1962, he delivered a lecture at the National Poetry Festival in Washington, **"Fifty Years of American Poetry."** This was published the following year in *Prairie Schooner,* and it was included as the last item in **The Third Book of Criticism.** This piece is literally a distillation of Jarrell's critical performances of a lifetime enclosed in a single vessel. In it he occasionally paraphrases earlier essays; sometimes he quotes verbatim without indicating that he is serving up older material.[9] No matter: everything seems fresh and perfectly appropriate in its new setting; and from this simple survey the reader can get a better sense of Jarrell's achievement in criticism than from any other single essay that he wrote. His procedure is also a distillation of past procedures; he begins at the beginning and reviews the poets roughly in chronological order, making judgments as he goes, occasionally enlivening the proceedings with a witticism, and providing lists so that the reader can go and confirm the judgments for himself. As always he presents himself as unpretentious teacher and guide, without apology, fully confident of the rightness of his own taste.

His judgments on Frost, Stevens, Ransom, Moore, and Williams remain essentially unchanged. These figures are still the larger stars in his firmament, and the mature Jarrell even enhances the luster of some of them—notably Frost, Stevens, and Ransom—by omitting most of the mildly disparaging qualifications he had recorded earlier. He begins by noticing with respect Edwin Arlington Robinson, Edgar Lee Masters, and Carl Sandburg, praising Robinson for his somber honesty, Masters for his historical truth about nineteenth-century American life, and Sandburg for his innocence. He becomes almost enthusiastic, however, in the page he devotes to Vachel Lindsay, who had the courage, or the eccentricity, to be a poet in a world that had little patience with artists. Lindsay's reward is to be remembered for having more imagination and more command of his art than most of his contemporaries.

Jarrell devotes three pages to Ezra Pound, whom he recognized as a true critic and a great poet, though one marred by his own obsessions ("a moral and intellectual disaster") and by his choice of a form, *The Cantos,* that permitted him much of the time not to write poetry at all. Yet Pound survives, he notes; for not even the worst in the man and his work or the worst in the age that produced him has been able to destroy *The Cantos* or obscure the beauties, lines, poems, resurrections of the past, that they contain.

Two pages are given to T. S. Eliot, and Jarrell apologizes, after a fashion, for presuming to write on one about whom so much has already been written. At the time of the essay Jarrell had in fact been talking among friends about an essay on Eliot that he planned to do. He never published such an essay, but he let his comments on Eliot in the 1962 survey suggest the direction the essay might have taken. Midway through his remarks he asks, "Won't the future say to us in helpless astonishment: 'But did you actually believe that all those things about objective correlative, classicism, the tradition, apply to *his* poetry'?"[10] Then, speaking for the future with characteristic sureness, he sweeps away all the academic talk and pronounces Eliot "one of the most subjective and daemonic poets who ever lived." Beneath Prufrock, "The Waste Land," *Murder in the Cathedral,* and *The Family Reunion,* he declares, lies a poetry that Eliot's own age, mistaking the personal struggle for a realistic photograph of the time, has never seen. Nevertheless, he concedes, the age has loved the right poet and the right poems, and for that it is entitled to take satisfaction.

E. E. Cummings gets two pages also, but Jarrell does not see him as the poet of the age. Cummings is the circus performer among poets, striving always for the limit of every possibility. Like all intelligent people he recognizes that words describe the world imperfectly at best; consequently he manipulates words in all the ways he can think of and teases his readers into guessing what they might mean. As a rule, however, they have only quasi-denotations in the use he makes of them and hence only vague or contradictory meanings. His poems amuse but do not often enlighten.

After thus dismissing Cummings, Jarrell turns briefly to Conrad Aiken, whom he had offended in an early review. He still allows him only second best in the rankings ("poems that come close to being good poems, without ever quite being so"), compares him to Frederick Delius ("undifferentiating wash of lovely sounds"), and pronounces his work nostalgic verse that "turns everything into itself." He also gives short shrift, but respectful praise, to the work of Allen Tate, Aiken's friend and the early mentor to whom Jarrell had dedicated his first volume of poetry, **Blood for a Stranger.** Tate's poems lack charm and human warmth, he says, but he names three of them—"The Mediterranean" and, somewhat oddly, "Mother and Son" and "The Cross"—for which the current state of neglect will "surely be temporary." Two other poets whom he dismisses with a paragraph of comment are Robinson Jeffers and Archibald MacLeish; these receive only faint praise.

As he comes closer to the current scene, Jarrell understandably resorts to broad sweeps, making a list of poets he would like to write favorably about if there were "room" and naming four groups of practicing poets for whom he had little use. Howard Nemerov and his old friends John Berryman and Delmore Schwartz head the list of the good poets ("interesting and intelligent") followed by fourteen others, about most of whom he had written favorable reviews at one time or another. The groups that he disapproved of were the beatniks (their method of writing precludes their ever producing poetry); the followers of Yvor Winters ("learned imbecility, a foolishness of the schools"); the academic, tea-party imitators of Richard Wilbur; and the writers of "feminine verse" (Edna St. Vincent Millay, Eleanor Wylie, Leonie Adams, and Louise Bogan), though these occasionally wrote good poems. He was careful to exclude from the last group his favorite women writers, Marianne Moore, Eleanor Taylor (for whose *Wilderness of Ladies* he had written an introduction), Adrienne Rich, Katherine Hoskins, and Elizabeth Bishop, whose *Poems* he called "one of the best books an American poet has written."

Of Hart Crane he has somewhat more to say, though he finds *The Bridge* unsuccessful as a unified work of art. Like Cummings, Crane was a manipulator of words, and like Auden he was a master of rhetorical strategies. But Jarrell counterpoises these shortcomings with such imprecise phrases as "magical successes" and "soaring rapture of something unprecedented, absolutely individual"; and he singles out "Black Tambourine," "Repose of Rivers," "National Winter Garden," and "Voyages II" as pieces of special distinction. He gives similar praise to the work of Robert Penn Warren and Theodore Roethke. The work of Warren's that most impresses him is the long poem *Brother to Dragons* with its "traumatic subject" of original sin in a world without a Savior and only raw nature and the shaky grace of custom to fall back on. In contrast, he finds Roethke's great distinction in the short lyric (for example, "My Papa's Waltz" and "I Knew a Woman") but notes that his style is still changing.

In conclusion Jarrell comments on three poets with whom he had often been compared by other reviewers. The first of these is Karl Shapiro, who had recovered quickly and with good grace from drubbings that Jarrell had given him in early reviews. Jarrell takes note of Shapiro's "visual and satiric force," his precision and "memorable exactness of realization," and his honesty. The second poet is Richard Wilbur, whom Jarrell here describes with a wit that rises above mere cleverness, calling him one who "obsessively sees, and shows, the bright underside of every dark thing" and noting his "lyric calling-to-life of the things of this world."

It was inevitable that Jarrell should conclude with a poet who had been his friend from Kenyon days, who had had a notable influence on his own work, and who had reached a level of achievement more remarkable, perhaps, than that of any other contemporary poet: Robert Lowell. Lowell's poetry, Jarrell says at the outset, is the poetry of shock; but crude or magnificent, what shocks us is almost always fact, "the live stumbling block that we fall over and feel to the bone." Moreover, it is always the only fact that Lowell or anyone else can write about truthfully, the fact personally perceived, seen, and felt. In the beginning Lowell sometimes "bullied" his facts, forced them to submit to a preconceived order. In his later work he has allowed facts to lead their own lives, and his poetry accordingly has gone on developing in grandeur and in power.

Jarrell's **"Fifty Years of American Poetry"** turned out to be the final statement by an observer of remarkable authority and perception. In the histories of formal literary criticism Jarrell will probably occupy at most a modest paragraph or two. As has been noted, he never devised a system to incorporate his insights or articulated a set of principles to explain them. Yet his judgments have already proved to have extraordinary staying power, and the reasons for that are not difficult to understand. He was, first of all, endowed with genius, which for a variety of reasons he chose to deploy in the study and creation of literature. Second, though he recognized that any vision or insight he might have would necessarily be personal, he accepted the integrity of the external world on faith and proceeded on the assumption that he possessed sufficient means at least to touch that world with his senses and perceive its reality. Third, he respected what he saw, heard, and touched, and early in his career decided that anything he might create could at most be a window on the world that he had been gifted by luck or grace to know somewhat better than his fellows. He thought of his poems as such windows, and he thought the same of his fiction and his essays—different devices, but all serving the same objective. And the objective, for Jarrell, was always to know the world and make it known.

It is understandable that Jarrell should have been accused of arrogance throughout most of his life. Being human and therefore limited he saw, as does everyone with partial vision. Hence he was often mistaken in his judgments, sometimes in ways that observers with less acute vision saw before he did. Again, being human he sometimes bristled when others challenged him. Nevertheless, Jarrell's basic stance never changed: he loved the world and the creatures in it. He respected the right of all things to be themselves; and as he would not tolerate gladly or for long anyone's attempt to make him submit to authority, so he resisted any move to impose restrictive authority on others, whether by rule or by custom or by art. He lived by the conviction that all things, animate and inanimate, should be freed of inhibitions and left to fulfill their own natures; and for this categorizing historians in time to come may well label him an American romantic. By implication he advocated the same freedom in his own poetry, and he praised other poets, provided they possessed a modicum of genius, in proportion as they freed themselves of the temptation to make displays of virtuosity and simply let their work stand as uninhibited but self-effacing pointers to the world of common experience.

Jarrell's essays did not always deal with literary criticism. *Poetry and the Age* deals exclusively with literary matters, as does *The Third Book of Criticism*; but Jarrell wrote about American culture too, about education, and about art. From time to time he also wrote about music, though he played no instrument and had only a listener's knowledge of it. Readers of *Pictures from an Institution* are properly impressed by the authority with which he created a professional musician to serve as one of the central characters of that novel, but this was authority of the kind that enabled a Shakespeare to create credible Macbeths and Cleopatras. Music for Jarrell, like language, was a medium for the exploration of the world of human feelings and perceptions; and the same thing was true of the graphic and plastic arts. In his view the world of things must be the primary object of any artist's attention, his art a secondary concern—as in poetry, a means to know the world and make it known.

He made his point in an essay reprinted in *Kipling, Auden & Co.,* "Against Abstract Expressionism." Painting, he said there, is a kind of metaphor for the reality it stands for. Sometimes the relationship is a rigorously mimetic one, and sometimes it is much less so, but the relationship is always present. Abstract expressionism removes half of the equation, the half that is the world, and so removes from art the necessity of imitation. In Jarrell's view such a development could only be deplored, but no art, he observes optimistically, regardless of its pretensions, will ever be able to hold out against nature indefinitely.

Abstract expressionism as he saw it, was simply one consequence of pursuing to a logical conclusion the American ideal of purity, which derives from a dangerously limited view of human nature and the world, one that in the end could destroy man—or dehumanize him—just as readily as the bombs and other war machines that same ideal had created. Throughout his career Jarrell continued to be concerned about this and other things that he considered aberrations of the American spirit, and in some of the early poems his concern took the form of sharp indictments. By the time he came to put together his second collection of essays, *A Sad Heart at the Supermarket*, he had mellowed considerably, and the indictments there were muted with the sadness that the title refers to. The first essay, "**The Intellectual in America**," serves as a preface to all the others. The specific object of its attack is the disease of anti-intellectualism that swept the United States in the decade and a half following World War II. Anti-intellectualism, as he recognized, was not something new; and it was not a simple malady but a complex disease that even de Tocqueville in the early days of the republic had seen as endemic in the nation. Jarrell was not prepared to offer either an explanation of the problem or a remedy for it, but he could and did continue to provide eloquent laments that its existence was continuing to vitiate American life. Nevertheless, in spite of his strictures Jarrell never ceased to love his country or mankind generally or to nourish the hope that both might somehow see the need to change.

Jarrell's capacity for love is best demonstrated in an essay that he never saw fit to reprint, or perhaps never found an opportunity to do so. This was the piece that he wrote for *The Nation* on Ernie Pyle shortly after that popular correspondent's death in 1945.[11] Jarrell was a poet, and even then a prose stylist of considerable accomplishment. Writing for a sophisticated magazine, he might have found it easy to ignore the passing of a mere journalist or to say condescending things about him. But Pyle, as Jarrell saw, was no mere journalist, and the qualities that made him special happened to be the same qualities that almost made Jarrell unique in his time. Pyle cared about facts, Jarrell said; and he did not care about style so much if he could just make the reader see and feel as he did. Moreover, what Pyle looked at and responded to as he went from one combat theater to another was precisely what Jarrell looked at and responded to all his life. "His affectionate amused understanding and acceptance of all sorts and levels of people [derived] from his imaginative and undeviating interest in [and] observation of . . . people." These were the words of Jarrell that best summarized his view of Pyle's greatness and claim to truth. They constitute a garland that in his better moments (that is to say, in most of them) Jarrell himself deserved to wear.

Notes

1. See *Randall Jarrell's Letters*, ed. Mary Jarrell (Boston: Houghton Mifflin, 1985) 25-26.

2. *Kipling, Auden & Co.: Essays and Reviews 1935-1964* (New York: Farrar, Straus, 1980) 170-71.

3. *A Sad Heart at the Supermarket* (New York: Atheneum, 1962) 103; *Kipling, Auden & Co.* 312. This essay, "Poets, Critics, and Readers," reprinted in both volumes, was first published in *The American Scholar* (Summer 1959).

4. *Kipling, Auden & Co.* 312-13; *Sad Heart* 105.

5. "Some Lines from Whitman," *Poetry and the Age* (New York: Knopf, 1953) 112-32.

6. *Letters* 43.

7. *Poetry and the Age* 96-111.

8. *Kipling, Auden & Co.* 246.

9. At the outset Jarrell had announced that he would sometimes summarize or quote from things he had written previously.

10. *The Third Book of Criticism* (New York: Farrar, Straus, 1969) 314.

11. Reprinted in *Kipling, Auden & Co.* 112-21.

Mark I. Goldman (essay date spring 1987)

SOURCE: Goldman, Mark I. "The Politics of Poetry: Randall Jarrell's War." *South Atlantic Quarterly* 86, no. 2 (spring 1987): 123-34.

[*In the following essay, Goldman contends that Jarrell's war poetry depicts a central conflict, that of the young soldier who longs for childhood, but who is "caught in the tentacles of the state" and must act out a role "for which he is ill-suited."*]

Having washed out as a pilot trainee, Randall Jarrell spent his war years as an instructor of aviation, including, appropriately for a poet, classes in celestial navigation. Though Jarrell did not get overseas and into combat, his war poems are a sustained and impassioned attempt to understand the nature of war, especially air war, and the experience of being a soldier during World War II.

Since World War II was what we might call a "justifiable" or at least necessary or inevitable war, unlike Vietnam, Jarrell is impressive in his ability to go beyond the historical or political perspective to the individual, universal horror of war as an expression of man's inhumanity to man.

In **"Eighth Air Force,"**[1] Jarrell tries to resolve the dilemma of a war that turns boys into "murderers" by asserting their sacrificial, Christ-like innocence that is itself a martyrdom for the historical brutality of the state. The portrait of the bomber crew emphasizes their casual, boyish behavior as "they play, before they die / Like puppies with their puppy." In his essay on Ernie Pyle, Jarrell quotes Pyle's ironic view of these boy-men, who "talked about their flights and killing and being killed exactly as they would discuss girls or their school lessons."[2] In the last two stanzas, the speaker of the poem, a survivor, plays Pontius Pilate in offering up the young men as the man,[3] Christ, sacrificed to the will of the people or mob. The real complexity of the poem is in the last stanza, with the speaker's emphasis on lying. He says that he has lied for the "last saviour, man," and then adds, "But what is lying?" If man is the real savior sacrificed again and again in history, then in this necessary war, where men "wash their hands, in blood, as best they can," the speaker finds no fault in the "just man," pilot or bombardier; each is an innocent murderer.

For sympathetic critics of Jarrell's war poetry, such as Suzanne Ferguson, Sister Bernetta Quinn, and Cleanth Brooks, **"Eighth Air Force"** is a poem of reconciliation, or recognition of the dilemma of "the modern Pilate who would like to evade judgment."[4] Even harsh critics of Jarrell's poetry, however, such as Richard Fein and M. L. Rosenthal, concede that **"Eighth Air Force"** is a successful war poem by virtue of its moral complexity. In Fein's words, "This is a poem of forgiveness for man as murderer, and forgiveness remakes the image of man . . . and succeeds in the attempt to place him above us." For Rosenthal, the poem is a "rare instance" of Jarrell's "being out of his usual orbit to deal with the moral issue of mass bombing."[5]

In the majority of his war poems, however, instead of trying to resolve the dilemma implicit in **"Eighth Air Force,"** Jarrell turns to the innocent airman caught in the tentacles of the state, who plays a role for which he is ill-suited while he yearns to escape to his prewar, paradisiacal world. In this emphasis on dreams, escape, longing for the primal world of childhood, one recognizes the familiar themes of Jarrell's peacetime poems of fairy tales and the **"Lost World."** In the war poems, Jarrell repeatedly places the individual soldier at the mercy of the impersonal state, the Moloch-like machine for destroying cities and devouring men. While critics like James Dickey have accused Jarrell of writing about abstractions instead of individual soldiers,[6] Karl Shapiro sees Jarrell's impersonality as the natural legacy for the World War II poet: "We inherited an historical perspective which was denied our fathers. We foresaw and witnessed the whole world turning into the state."[7] Jarrell's *Letters* [*Randall Jarrell's Letters*] reveal a deliberate concentration on the impersonal nature of war and on himself as a detached yet compassionate observer or voice, rather than as the center or subject of the poem. In a letter to Robert Lowell he writes, "If you'll notice, I've never written a poem about myself in the army or war, unless you're vain or silly you realize that you, except insofar as you're exactly in the same boat as the others, aren't the primary subject of any sensible writing about the war."[8]

In **"Losses,"** the speaker assumes the role of the collective we of the bomber crews trained to kill. At first they die in training crashes, "like aunts or pets or foreigners." Fresh out of high school, they have had no experience of death, but wake up one morning over England "operational." Now if they die, it is no longer an accident but a "mistake," though they are still boys burning cities they learned about in school: "Till our lives wore out; our bodies lay among / The people we had killed and never seen." The tired, resigned voice of the speaker is at last absorbed into the mindless world of missions and a vast impersonal death: "They said, 'Here are the maps'; we burned the cities." At the end, which repeats the opening lines of the poem, it is not dying that possesses him; but the night he dreams of his own death, he hears the cities speak to him, asking, "Why are you dying? / We are satisfied, if you are; but why did I die?" This is a far cry from trying to find a justifying answer, as in **"Eighth Air Force."** While the poetry is in the pity, as Wilfred Owen has said, it is a universal pity for mankind, which kills for some mindless purpose forgotten in the ashes of every war.

In the first paragraph of his prose interlude, **"1914,"** Jarrell declares that the First World War is no longer "THE WAR, but a war: our own has taken its place." Yet for twenty years of looking at photographs of the Great War, "while the wire and trenches in the mud were everybody's future, how could any of it seem old-fashioned to us?—it was our death. But when we died differently we saw that it was old."[9] Paul Fussell, in *The Great War and Modern Memory,* has emphasized the persistence of the myth of the Great War in the literature of World War II.[10] But as Jarrell demonstrates in his war poems, the point is more complex and ironic, since each soldier in every war experiences what is old and timeless, yet always new. It is this terrible paradox that allows men or states to make wars and send young boys to fight and die. In **"1914,"** the paradox of the fall into history, the fall of man into time and death is old, timeless, yet always new. And now, after Korea and Vietnam, Jarrell's Second World War is old, and civilization and states go on blindly trying to make it new.[11] We move, then, from history into history, or the real, though for Jarrell reality is always mixed with dreams, the dream of home and peace or the nightmare dream assumed by reality in time of war.

In **"Transient Barracks,"** an airman just back from overseas looks out over the causal details of the barracks and the bombers on the runway and hears a voice from the dayroom radio saying, "The thing about you is, you're real." Staring into the shaving mirror, he sees his face, and "it is *real.*" Surveying the field, its pattern of "light and darkness," he thinks of all the times he has dreamed of being back in the States and, in a moment of pure joy, murmurs to himself, "*I'm back for good. The States, the States!*" He then puts out his hand to "touch it—/ And the thing about it is, it's *real.*" But in **"Siegfried,"** the very next poem in the section called **"Bombers,"**[12] an aerial gunner in his turret looks at the fighter he has just shot down and at the pattern of bombs on the ground and feels that under the "leather and fur and wire" it is a dream and he is an actor watching himself play soldier. Inside the machine of death, there is only himself, the one whose sole wish is to return to the past, to be "what I was." Like the gunner in **"Transient Barracks,"** he is granted his wish, but at a price, for he returns home for good "almost as you wished." He has lost a leg, and wakes again to the dream that is the old dream, repeating in italics lines from the first part of the poem: "*It happens as it does, it does, it does.*" This is the impossibly cold comfort of war, no longer acceptable to the civilian missing a leg. In the end, Jarrell drives home the point that this is the reality of war and of man's knowledge of himself and death in war:

> You look at the people who look back at you, at home,
> And it is different, different—you have understood
> Your world at last: you have tasted your own blood.

Jarrell entitled the second section of war poems "The Carriers," and the first two poems, **"A Pilot from the Carrier"** and **"Pilots, Man Your Planes,"** are remarkable achievements for a poet with no first-hand experience of aircraft carriers or war in the Pacific. In **"A Pilot From the Carrier,"** a pilot bails out of the fire and blood in his cockpit and falls into the apparent safety of the sky, "to warmth, to air, to waking." It is almost an escape to wholeness, to childhood, to "the great flowering of his life," as he dangles slowly in the air and sees the world under him and the smoke and flames from his own carrier. But the strange sense of aloneness and well-being are soon shattered by the sudden approach of a "sun-marked plane" and the spurting flame that will end, in midair, his life.

"Pilots, Man Your Planes" is a long, more detailed account of a carrier in battle that combines the dense rhetoric of Lowell's "Quaker Graveyard in Nantucket" with the visual drama of World War II films. Jarrell first describes the giant organism of the sleeping carrier, then, in vivid colors, the battle itself: a Japanese plane diving and crashing near the ship; an American pilot attacking an enemy fighter ("the Jill") through the flames and flak from his own ship, then being hit and crashing into the sea.[13] From his life raft the downed pilot gets another view of the carrier firing, itself in flames, and finally sinking into the sea. Through the oil and smoke and fire we see the rescue of the men from the carrier and our lone pilot, who sits in shock on the rescue ship, "drugged in a blanket," and "knows, knows at last" what the gunner in **"Siegfried"** knows before he succumbs "sobbingly" to sleep.

In **"The Dead Wingman,"** Jarrell follows the dream of a pilot who has lost his friend and wingman, a dream that searches obsessively for a lost friend in "the circles of that worn, unchanging *No*—/ The lives' long war, lost war." Jarrell's recurrent themes of loss, of the dream of home and the nightmarish separation from childhood or the womb, are repeated in the **"Carrier"** poems, which, like **"A Front"** and other Army Air Force poems, dramatize "situations of disaster" and the "flier's inability to return to home base."[14]

"Burning the Letters" is a dark, moving example of Jarrell's ability to bring to his war poetry the depth and complexity of his later work. This dramatic monologue of a woman whose pilot-husband has been killed in the Pacific anticipates the fine poems spoken by and about women in the later volumes, *The Woman at the Washington Zoo* (1960) and *The Lost World* (1965). In the opening lines the wife contrasts her world of change with the changeless world of the carrier, planes, and corpses that disappeared into the sea. She repeats the words *head* and *hands,* for only in her head is "the home that is left" for her, and only in her hands the letters that float from the sea. And yet she must finally burn her husband's letters in order to go on living herself. He has remained a child in the "unchanging country" of his death, while she has aged and changed in a few short years into her own "troubled, separate being." In a parenthesis under the title, Jarrell explains that the wife was once a "Christian, a Protestant." Religious overtones and allusions run through the poem as the wife tries to understand her husband's death but cannot see any transcendence or redemption in secular terms: "By man came death / And his Life wells from death, the death of Man."[15] Cain struggles with Christ in her head as she rejects her religious faith: "The dying God, the eaten Life / Are the nightmare I awaken from to night." As in **"Eighth Air Force,"** Christ becomes the symbol of man as murderer and secular martyr to the mystery of life and death. In the end, the death of her husband is a mystery and a sacrifice, even a victory over those who, like herself, must go on living the life granted by the dead. "Because of you," she cries out, "I have not died, / By your death I have lived." While the husband remains in his "great green grave," forever young, she must finally choose between his life and hers:

> Bound in your death,
> I choose between myself and you, between your life
> And my own life: it is finished.

In a variation on the opening lines of the poem, the echoing words of Christ's end lead to her release in the living world. Now that she has let go of her husband, she can make room for him in her head. In Whitmanesque lines and gestures she gives up the letters to the grave—"great grave of all my years"—and the life of her husband is now completed with the final fragments of his "accepting" and "accepted" words.

In a letter to Margaret Marshall, literary editor of *The Nation,* Jarrell provides a critical gloss on the religious implications of the poem: "This part about her belief and her gradual loss of it ends with 'The dying God, the eaten Life / Are the nightmare I awaken from to night.'" Thinking of the early Christians and their total belief, the woman then thinks about "the antithetical death and burial of her husband and those like him: she thinks that he and they literally died for her . . . just as Christ is supposed to have died for her; it's because of this that I used 'it is finished' for the climax of what she says. So far as I can see this is all literally true: they died for us just the sort of atoning death, a death not for their own sins but for ours (after all, most of them were kids out of high school) . . . that Christ is supposed to have died."[16]

In the section called **"Camps and Fields,"** Jarrell returns to the less dramatic world of stateside army posts and airfields, a world of dreary daily service to the state, where the individual is subservient, anonymous, lost in the larger order and disorder of the machine.

Reading Jarrell's *Letters,* written during the years he was in the Air Force (1943-46), one gets the taste and feel of the soldier's world, the strange mix of tedium and tyranny that was the lot of all stateside soldiers. In a letter to Allen Tate, for example, he explains: "Your main feeling about the army, at first, is just that you can't believe it: it couldn't exist, and even if it could you would have learned what it was like from all the books, and not a one gives you even an idea."[17] And in another letter, to Robert Lowell, he goes on in the same vein: "The main feeling you have about most people in the army—and in the war, too—is that you're sorry for them; everything else comes after. But the next feeling, I imagine, is one of wonder: the size and impossible lunacy of everything in the war and army are beyond everything."[18]

In **"A Lullaby,"** the soldier learns to fight for "freedom and the State" in a round of trivial, mindless details, his life a "dull torment" ignored or lost in the "lying amber of histories." In **"Mail Call,"** he is again an object waiting for a letter that will identify him in the anonymous mass. The last line clearly dramatizes his need: "the soldier simply wishes for his name." In **"Absent**

Without Leave," as in so many Jarrell poems, the soldier escapes by dreaming of his past civilian life, while in **"Leave"** the airman does manage to get away to the mountain above his base, only to look down at the army world to which he must return. In **"The Sick Nought,"** the speaker imagines a frail wife traveling to visit her sick soldier-husband and the soldier himself as a poor cipher in military annals. The speaker's voice is full of consternation and despair as he tries to give substance and meaning to the individual soldier's life but cannot: "But you are something there are millions of." Lost in the poet's attempt to humanize him, the soldier is simply swept aside by history:

> I see you looking helplessly around, in histories,
> Bewildered with your terrible companions, Pain
> And Death and Empire: what have you understood, to
>   die?

The soldier becomes all soldiers, whose purpose is to survive; but against the reality of war and history, the individual's natural will to live becomes "nonsense"—for "what is demanded in the trade of states / But lives, your lives?—the one commodity." In **"The Range in the Desert,"** the speaker meditates again on the historical meaning of war, on the scrawled landscape of an airfield in the midst of war and after:

> Profits and death grow marginal:
> Only the mourning and the mourned recall
> The wars we lose, the wars we win;
> And the world is—what it has been.

This is from *Losses* (1948) and, like *Little Friend, Little Friend* (1945) and *The Seven-League Crutches* (1951), was published just after World War II. With the publication of *The Letters* we are now able to discover, to some degree, which poems were written during the war, rather than from the perspective of a postwar world.

In **"A Front"** and **"Second Air Force,"** we have a similar view of an Air Force training field, but these poems are closer to the mood and meaning of **"Eighth Air Force"** and **"Losses."** Here, as in **"Eighth Air Force,"** the landscape and conditions, the training and crashes are "dry runs" for the bombing raids and losses in actual combat. In **"A Front,"** as Jarrell explains in the introductory notes, fog has closed down the bomber base; but one plane, whose radio has gone bad and can only transmit, tries to land, a voice from the plane eerily "rising: *Can't you hear me? Over. Over*" before it crashes, as "all the air quivers, and the east sky glows."[19]

"Second Air Force" is the most successful of the training-base poems. In it Jarrell moves from the observer's eye to the inner thoughts of a mother visiting her son at a large airfield in the Southwest. Just as the soldiers in the various camps and field have been exiled from their previous lives, so the mother has to have "a pass / To what was hers," and she thinks "heavily: My son is grown." She also sees what the speaker and we see of the wartime base: tarpaper barracks, roads, runways, and the western desert rising to a range of mountains. As late afternoon changes to dusk, she and her soldier-son watch the crews climb into their B17s or Flying Fortresses and take off into the twilight: "And the green, made beasts run home to air. / Now in each aspect death is pure." Mother and son move off in the evening light, and the woman sees the soldiers also pass, "like beasts, unquestioning," as she suddenly understands the shadowy nature of their world and the world they are being trained to enter: "The shadows learning in their shadowy fields / The empty missions." Here Jarrell's notes help us again. The woman remembers having read about a conversation between a bomber in flames over Germany and one of the fighters protecting it. Jarrell quotes the entire conversation on the title page of *Little Friend, Little Friend*:

> Then I heard the bomber call me in:
> "Little Friend, Little Friend, I got two
> engines on fire. Can you see me, Little Friend?"
>   I said "I'm crossing right over you.
> Let's go home."

The mother feels the flames eating "along the metal of the wing into her heart" and the lives of the bomber crew streaming out over the earth. Later, she and her son watch a squadron on parade before it ships out overseas. Again she identifies with the crews and feels for them "the love of life for life." But only she, a mother, can really imagine it all; feel the horror of having borne a child for the blind purpose of this world: "The years meant *this*?" Sadly, inevitably, only she can visualize and, like Teiresias, helplessly know all. For the soldiers, there is no other meaning or horizon than the present: "for them the bombers answer everything."

Lowell had apparently criticized the rhetoric of **"Second Air Force,"** which "obliterated" the mother and her situation. Jarrell defended the poem by explaining the role of the mother: "It's a descriptive poem to show what a heavy bomber training field was like; the mother is merely a vehicle of presentation, her situation merely a formal connection of the out-of-this-world field with the world."[20] But Lowell may be right in pointing to the focus of the poem. Jarrell's emphasis on the descriptive element ignores his other poems, such as **"The Death of the Ball Turret Gunner,"** where the mother-womb motif is dominant.

In the next section, **"The Trades,"** Jarrell presents a series of poems set in remote Pacific islands only remembered from World War II: New Georgia, New Britain, Melanesia. The settings recall some of Karl Shapiro's poems in *A V-Letter And Other Poems,* which are based on his service in the Pacific.[21] Jarrell's poems, however, seem more bitterly ironic, with a monologue by a dead Negro soldier ("**New Georgia**") and a description of the dead, including missionaries ("**The Dead in Melanesia**") who, sprawled in the "blood of an untaken beachhead," are confused with the island's "own black dead." In other poems, such as "**1945: The Death of the Gods**" and "**The Wide Prospect**," Jarrell again echoes Lowell's kind of rhetoric in an attack on the corrupt economic and political system responsible for the war:

> All die for all. And the planes rise from the years:
> The years when, West or West, the cities burn,
> And Europe is the colony of colonies—
> When men see men once more the food of Man
> And their bare lives His last commodity.

In the following section, "**Children and Civilians**," Jarrell extends his view of war to include the death of a child in an air raid ("**Come to the Stone . . .**"), the air raid inside Germany ("**The Angels at Hamburg**"), Jewish children going off to a death camp ("**Protocols**"), and a child orphaned by the blitz on London ("**The Truth**"). But Jarrell's attempt to examine the sins and suffering of war from many points of view, each showing the human cost exacted by blind obedience to the state, is not as successful as the less abstract poems on individual soldiers seen in the immediate context of the war.

In the last section of war poems, entitled simply "**Soldiers**," Jarrell returns to the earlier view of lonely figures lined up at a "**Port of Embarkation**" or being discharged finally from the regimentation of army life in "**The Lines**": "The lines break up, for good; and for a breath / The longest of their lives, the men are free."[22] In "**A Field Hospital**," a wounded soldier dreaming of home wakes only to be sent back into a drugged sleep by the orderly, while the less fortunate "**Gunner**," who has been killed in his turret, speaks, like so many of Jarrell's personae, from the grave:

> All my wars over? . . . It was as easy as that!
> Has my wife a pension of so many mice?
> Did the medals go home to my cat?[23]

Jarrell placed two poems at the end of the *Selected Poems* that were not included in any of his postwar volumes. One, "**The Survivor among Graves**," is a long poem about the meaning of the war for the guilty survivor, while the other, "**A War**," is an epigrammatic verse of four lines in Jarrell's best mordantly witty style. Summing up the world of soldiers who embark on the business of war, Jarrell changes the cliché to make his satiric point:

> There set out, slowly, for a Different World,
> At four, on winter mornings, different legs . . .
> *You can't break eggs without making an omelette*
> —That's what they tell the eggs.

"**The Survivor among Graves**" is a profoundly moving poem about the relationship between the living and the dead. The dream that was the war still holds the sleepers, but what is it for these dead, now that it has been numbered and lost? Ironically, the survivor has also lost something, the all-encompassing demands the war made only to live—"that left bare life / The sense life made, stripping from all there is / Its old, own sense." Simply to realize the dream of returning to civilian life and reading the Sunday papers seemed enough during the war. But now the speaker looks back on the existential life in war as paradoxically more real and timeless for being removed from the slow process of ordinary life and death. So he asks the dead where and how to live:

> For your lives are not lived
> But, there in mid-air, cease, and do not fall
> And are what is not, but that could have been.
> And ours are—what they are; and, slowly, end.

As in "**Burning the Letters**," the speaker recognizes that without the dead there would be no understanding of life; or, as Yeats said, one does not begin to live until one has conceived life as a tragedy. The speaker's response to the dead recalls Mrs. Dalloway's thoughts on the suicide of Septimus Warren Smith: "Death was defiance. Death was an attempt to communicate, people feeling the impossibility of reaching the centre which, mystically, evaded them; closeness drew apart; rapture faded; one was alone. There was an embrace in death."[24] And in Jarrell's poem, from the survivor's point of view:

> We endure to fulfillment; it is victory
> The living lose. And loss? The living lose
> All things alike; and, recompensed, in the survival
> That brings them, daily, that indifference, death,
> Ride in the triumph of the world in chains.

In the symbiosis of the living and the dead, the speaker also admits his guilt, since one must not forget that these young men died needlessly in battle:

> Your ignorance
> Is immortal in your deaths, a spring
> Of blood to which the living come, to bend
> In dry half-dreaming supplication.

But in the end, supplication comes from the dead who in "**Unison**" cry out to the survivors for confirmation that there is life beyond death, a consolation the speaker, tragically, cannot provide:

> *Say again,*
> Say the voices, *say again*
> *That life is—what it is not;*
> *That, somewhere, there is—something, something;*
> *That we are waiting; that we are waiting.*

It would be instructive to end by comparing the most famous of Jarrell's war poems, **"The Death of the Ball Turret Gunner,"** with a poem included in the first part of the *Selected Poems* but seemingly outside the canon of his war poems. The poem, **"A Game at Salzburg,"** was published in *The Seven-League Crutches* and seems to have come out of Jarrell's experience at the Salzburg Seminar in American Civilization in the summer of 1948.

We can understand **"The Death of the Ball Turret Gunner"** after having read the other war poems. As in **"Second Air Force,"** we have the image of the mother and the idea of the state as the false mother in whose womb the airman finds no dream of life but the nightmarish harbingers of death. As in so many of Jarrell's war poems, the speaker has died, and the shock of the celebrated ending derives from the further separation between the gunner's human voice and the final dehumanizing action of the state.

In contrast to Jarrell's other poems on the end of the war, **"A Game at Salzburg"** is a quiet, understated poem about the postwar world. In spite of its ironic, realistic details, it is Jarrell's lyrical affirmation of life after the death of the Wagnerian gods. The speaker is playing a makeshift tennis match against the backdrop of Austria's former empire, "Franz Joseph Park," "Maria Theresa's sleigh," and the broken statuary and stone horse that has "sunk in marsh to his shoulders." But it is this beauty and power—again the state—that is responsible for so many wars, the latest one recalled by his tennis partner, an "ex-Afrika Korps" soldier who feels privileged to have been a prisoner of war in Colorado. The ironies and madness of a postwar world pile up against the dark clouds and rain of the landscape. Against the desolate world of empire and war, however, there is Romana, a little girl of three who licks sherbet from a spoon and plays a game with the speaker in which she says, "Hier bin i'" and he replies, "Da bist du." After the tennis match, he goes home and walks through the dead leaves and overwhelming detritus of history. Finally, the sun comes out and "the sky / Is for an instant the first rain-washed blue / Of becoming." He looks away now from the state to nature, which, like the child, provides its own simple yet profound meaning: "In anguish, in expectant acceptance / The world whispers: *Hier bin i'*." In the notes Jarrell explains the little game played among Germans and Austrians with very young children and comments further that "if there could be a conversation between the world and God, this would be it."

But Jarrell added another note to the poem in a letter to Elizabeth Eisler, an artist he had met in the seminar at Salzburg: "The point at the end of the poem . . . is that when the world says in anguished longing acceptance, *Hier bin i'* there is no answering *Da bist du*, even though the world feels there is just about to be: this is meant to express our longing, worshipping, painful acceptance of things, a sort of question-and-waiting that has to be its own answer."[25]

Salzburg provided the setting and "psychological roots" for a number of other poems, such as **"Hohensalzburg: Fantastic Variations on a Theme of Romantic Character," "An English Garden in Austria," "A Soul," "The Orient Express," "Seele im Raum,"** and **"A Quilt Pattern."**[26] Though Jarrell did not get overseas during the war, postwar Europe had an extraordinary effect on him. Like Lowell, Jarrell tried to understand history in terms of the Second World War and wars in general.[27] In **"A Game at Salzburg,"** he moves beyond the war, though still in its shadows; moves from his dark view of General Moloch and the state to a persistent faith in the child's dream of another, better life on this earth.

Notes

1. Unless otherwise noted, the poems under discussion can be found in Randall Jarrell's *Selected Poems* (New York, 1955). In *The Complete Poems* (New York, 1969) the *Selected Poems* are printed at the beginning of the volume.

2. Randall Jarrell, "Ernie Pyle," *Kipling, Auden and Co.* (New York, 1980), 114.

3. Jarrell emphasizes the secular or humanist theme by repeating the word *man* six times in his five stanzas.

4. Suzanne Ferguson, *The Poetry of Randall Jarrell* (Baton Rouge, 1971); Sister Bernetta Quinn, *Randall Jarrell* (Boston, 1981); Cleanth Brooks, "Jarrell's 'Eighth Air Force'," *Randall Jarrell: 1914-1965,* ed. Lowell, Taylor, and Penn Warren (New York, 1967). The quote is from Brooks, 30.

5. Richard Fein, "Randall Jarrell's World of War," *Critical Essays on Randall Jarrell,* ed. Suzanne Ferguson (Boston, 1983), 161. M. L. Rosenthal, *Randall Jarrell* (Minneapolis, 1972), 181.

6. James Dickey, "Randall Jarrell," *Randall Jarrell: 1914-65,* 33-48.

7. Karl Shapiro, *Randall Jarrell* (Washington, D.C., 1967), 19.

8. *Randall Jarrell's Letters,* ed. Mary Jarrell (Boston, 1985), 151.

9. Also in the *Selected Poems,* 194.

10. [Paul Fussell, *The Great War and Modern Memory* (New York, 1975).] See especially chapter 2, "Persistence and Memory."

11. Shapiro, 19.

12. Jarrell arranged his *Selected Poems,* 1955, as parts I and II, with almost all the war poems in part II under separate headings: Bombers, The Carriers, Prisoners, Camps and Fields, The Trades, Children and Civilians, and Soldiers.

13. Jarrell's note to this poem (in the notes that precede the *Selected Poems*) suggests that the pilot is hit by fire from his own carrier.

14. Fein, 153.

15. Sister Quinn tries to salvage some form of belief for the wife. "Though Jarrell's headnote and the lyric itself show her as a person who no longer adheres to Christianity, the paradoxes of death and life as embodied in the Passion and Resurrection event elicit from her a kind of unorthodox faith rather than complete disbelief" (*Jarrell,* 44).

16. Jarrell, *Letters,* 134.

17. Ibid., 119.

18. Ibid., 151.

19. "A Front," as mentioned earlier, is connected to the "Carrier" poems about pilots who are unable to return home, to their ships or airfields.

20. Jarrell, *Letters,* 132.

21. Such as "Full Moon, New Guinea," "Sunday, New Guinea," "Christmas Eve, Australia," "Hill and Parramatta," and others, in *V-Letter and Other Poems* (New York, 1944).

22. In a letter to Philip Rahv, an editor of *Partisan Review,* Jarrell refers to "The Lines" as the "armiest army poem I've written." *Letters,* 140.

23. In his book on the poets of the Second World War, Vernon Scannell praises Jarrell's satirical war poetry, such as "Gunner," and expresses his wish that he would have written more. *Not Without Glory* (London, 1976), 197.

24. Virginia Woolf, *Mrs. Dalloway* (London, 1925), 202.

25. Jarrell, *Letters,* 199.

26. See the notes and commentary by Mary Jarrell in *The Letters,* 195. While critics such as Suzanne Ferguson and Sister Bernetta Quinn interpret the Salzburg poems as symbolic fairy tales of change or metamorphosis, one can also read into them the anguished love for Elizabeth Eisler. As the editor tells us (197), the love affair was not consummated out of deference for Jarrell's marriage.

27. As in poems from *Life Studies* such as "Beyond the Alps" and "A Mad Negro Soldier Confined at Munich."

Sven Birkerts (essay date 1991)

SOURCE: Birkerts, Sven. "Randall Jarrell." *Parnassus: Poetry in Review* 16, no. 2 (1991): 78-93.

[*In the following essay, Birkerts examines Helen Vendler's assertion that Jarrell "put his genius into his criticism and his talent into his poetry." Birkerts ultimately agrees with Vendler's statement, but he tempers it somewhat by claiming that Jarrell's "critical genius was poetic."*]

Though I have recently read William Pritchard's literary biography of Randall Jarrell[1] and his selection of the poetry—and reread a number of Jarrell's own essays—I do not propose here to discuss his life or to assess in any depth the nature of his contribution to poetry and criticism. The magazines and quarterlies have been plump with just such assessments, suggesting that the publishing strategy of a tandem life and works was a good one; suggesting, too, that the time for a consideration of the career is nigh. But my interest just now is not with the big picture—of Jarrell's place among his contemporaries, of his legacy to practicing poets and critics—but with the sounding of a single pronouncement. I mean Helen Vendler's observation that Jarrell had "put his genius into his criticism and his talent into his poetry."

The phrase has an economy and aphoristic elegance—and authority—worthy of Jarrell himself. And indeed, it has stuck to the fine cloth of his posthumous reputation, at first like a natural burr, later like some laboratory hybrid that has grown and extended itself until the cloth appears half-obscured. While this may or may not prove the accuracy of the estimate, it certainly figures as an instance of "poetic" justice. How many writers of Jarrell's generation did not feel that the critic, in his terrible desire to be memorable, had pinned to their posterity some tag that no future attainment could pry away? Cleverness is deadly, especially in criticism and literary journalism; a well-turned line can storm the places of memory as a reasoned judgment seldom can, remaining there long after the other contents have faded away. If you live by way of the *mot,* be prepared to die by it.

But Vendler's formulation is not merely clever—it crystallizes what enough readers have registered for themselves to carry some of the weight of a lasting judgment. We shouldn't forget that the instincts of the many (comprising, in Jarrell's case, mainly serious readers) are an essential kind of balloting: They determine a consensus that often overrides and outlives subtler sorts of reckoning. That consensus, when ratified by a reasoned critical declaration like Vendler's, may then come to look very much like *the* truth. Before it does, however, it is one of the tasks of the critical community to attempt its overthrow; or, failing that, to set up baffles and roadblocks—to refuse it the uncontested status of a dogma.

This does not mean that I want to counter Vendler here, to argue the poetry over the criticism, or to somehow demote the latter and thereby dull the barb of the epigram. To the contrary—Vendler and I are finally in accord. But I do wish to apply a slight interrogative pressure to its neat symmetry, to look at its central assumption in a noon-hour light, to discuss its applicability with some reference to actual words on the page.

Jarrell, then, "put his genius into his criticism and his talent into his poetry." What does this mean? To begin, we have the implication that one can, if fortunate, possess the distinct natural endowments of "talent" and "genius." Moreover, that one can possess both along a single continuum, in this case that of the "literary." I have no doubt that one can be a thinker of genius caliber in applied mathematics and a talented weekend cellist. But can a writer, a user of words, be one *and* the other, depending upon the genre? It would seem possible. After all, the different genres—criticism and poetry, say—call upon different faculties. The former requires aptitudes of insight and analysis, though not exclusively; the latter asks more in the way of imagination and creativity. There may be, in other words, two very different ways of using language, involving separate faculties and being directed toward distinct ends. What this perspective suggests, however, is not so much that Jarrell had two levels of aptitude, which he directed ("put") into two (or more, if we recall that he was a translator and novelist also) sluices; rather, that he had a single, if highly complex, linguistic imagination which he refracted with greater and lesser success through the formal options of the various genres.

But let me stay with Vendler's phrase a moment longer, to look at it from another angle. Jarrell is said to have put his *genius* into his criticism. How shall we construe this? I mean: What is the place of genius in criticism? After all, criticism is not in most senses a creative endeavor. To be a critic means to read, understand, evaluate, analyze, and compare. The practitioner must be capable of insight and clarity of expression with regard to the work in question. This is, I realize, a limited definition, but one must set down the line somewhere. If the basic task of criticism is as I have outlined, then I would ask: Can one actually *be* a genius at criticism, and—if so—was Jarrell one?

Loosely speaking, I suppose that one can be a genius at anything, so long as one does the thing as well as it can possibly be done. But if we invoke a stricter criterion, if we hold that genius is an aptitude that naturally exceeds what a normally endowed individual might attain with all the hard work and determination in the world, then the business is a bit trickier. How can one be a genius at criticism? Not, I would say, merely through high proficiency at reading, understanding, evaluating, analyzing, or comparing—one may perform these functions very well, but never at the level of inexplicability. What possibilities for genius there are in being a critic seem to have a great deal to do with the narrower matter of the formulation and expression of unique insights. Here we are not so much concerned with accuracy or validity (for these are fully within reach of the non-genius) as with the unexpectedness of invention or synthesis. The genius critic would find and express that truth that no thousand merely excellent critics could have arrived at. And this unexpectedness (of connections or approaches), is this not finally more the product of the kinds of linguistic insight—inspiration—that are thought to be the poet's special property?

Jarrell, I would say, was in touch with this special something—power, gift, or ability—throughout his critical career. His critical reputation has everything to do with it. For he was not, strictly speaking, a remarkable critic in terms of the above job description. He knew the flash of lightning; he pushed the language out of its customary track incessantly, and in the process he found the unknown and unthought. He did not like, or attend to, the drudge work—did not pause, except in rare instances, to analyze and evaluate. He was not much interested in contexts and traditions. In other words, he worked at criticism with the spirit of a poet—his critical genius was *poetic*.

This does not mean that Jarrell should therefore have attained to genius in his poetry. For though his poetic genius was not lacking, it did not present itself to him as the form-making gift. Nor was he possessed in the least of the sort of negative capability essential to the feats of ventriloquism he attempted. Jarrell was Jarrell was Jarrell. His curse as a poet, very possibly, was that he did not recognize that fact; or that if he did, he made the mistake of fighting it. He insisted upon donning female masks, but one can always see the male lips moving through the mouth-opening. In his criticism, too, he tried every so often to bend to a different expectation; he tried to tame his associative brilliance, to adopt a more systematic approach, in certain of his longer essays (on Frost, on Auden). But to no avail. The tics and fidgets break through; the repressed gives way, if only momentarily, to the irrepressible. Jarrell trying to be other than he is is like a juvenile delinquent in a suit at a formal dinner: He is on his best behavior and everyone is nervous for him.

My point? That criticism—more properly, high-class reviewing—was finally the most hospitable home for a temperament and style like Jarrell's. Further, I would say that he achieved his best effects, and made his greatest contribution to the genre, when he brought his fundamentally anarchic sensibility up against poets of some formal rigidity (like Frost, Auden, Ransom), for it was only then that he could find some constraint upon the skittering play of his discriminations. The poetry is alive with the same cross fire of energies that animates the essays, but its rhythmic signature feels either insufficiently anchored or too determinedly willed. The poems, even the best of them, are like improvisations by a pianist who has never been schooled in Bach.

I have picked out two texts—Jarrell's well-known poem **"Next Day"** and the long opening paragraph of his essay **"John Ransom's Poetry."** My notion is to set them side by side in order to address again these elusive questions of talent, genius, temperament, and style. I don't plan to undertake this methodically—I don't know that there is a method I could discover—but will, instead, take my cue from Jarrell himself. My hope, of course, is that the associative momentum will, as it did so regularly for Jarrell, come to something.

I realize that any such culling of bits risks either the charge of arbitrariness, or the opposite: that I have selected with conscious, or unconscious, bias to making a case, and that other pairings would yield different results. About my choosing I can say only this, that I opened the volumes of poetry and prose with a single conscious design: to find in each a passage of which I could say, "This is the Jarrell I think of when I think of Jarrell." First the poem, then the prose.

> Moving from Cheer to Joy, from Joy to All,
> I take a box
> And add it to my wild rice, my Cornish game hens.
> The slacked or shorted, basketed, identical
> Food-gathering flocks
> Are selves I overlook. Wisdom, said William James,
>
> Is learning what to overlook. And I am wise
> If that is wisdom.
> Yet somehow, as I buy All from these shelves
> And the boy takes it to my station wagon,
> What I've become
> Troubles me even if I shut my eyes.
>
> When I was young and miserable and pretty
> And poor, I'd wish
> What all girls wish: to have a husband,
> A house and children. Now that I'm old, my wish
> Is womanish:
> That the boy putting groceries in my car
>
> See me. It bewilders me he doesn't see me.
> For so many years
> I was good enough to eat: the world looked at me
> And its mouth watered. How often they have undressed me,
> The eyes of strangers!
> And, holding their flesh within my flesh, their vile
>
> Imaginings within my imagining,
> I too have taken
>
> The chance of life. Now the boy pats my dog
> And we start home. Now I am good.
> The last mistaken,
> Ecstatic, accidental bliss, the blind
>
> Happiness that, bursting, leaves upon the palm
> Some soap and water—
> It was so long ago, back in some Gay
> Twenties, Nineties, I don't know . . . Today I miss
> My lovely daughter
> Away at school, my sons away at school,
>
> My husband away at work—I wish for them.
> The dog, the maid,
> And I go through the sure unvarying days
> At home in them. As I look at my life,
> I am afraid
> Only that it will change, as I am changing:
>
> I am afraid, this morning, of my face.
> It looks at me
> From the rear-view mirror, with the eyes I hate,
> The smile I hate. Its plain, lined look
> Of gray discovery
> Repeats to me: "You're old." That's all, I'm old.
>
> And yet I'm afraid, as I was at the funeral
> I went to yesterday.
> My friend's cold made-up face, granite among its flowers,
> Her undressed, operated-on, dressed body
> Were my face and body.
> As I think of her I hear her telling me
>
> How young I seem; I *am* exceptional;
> I think of all I have.
> But really no one is exceptional,
> No one has anything, I'm anybody,
> I stand beside my grave
> Confused with my life, that is commonplace and solitary.

The subject-matter of Ransom's poetry is beautifully varied: the poems are about everything from Armageddon to a dead hen. All their subjects are linked, on the surface, by Ransom's persistent attitude, tone, and rhetoric; at bottom they are joined, passively, by being parts of one world—joined, actively, by fighting on one side or the other in the war that is going on in that world. On one side are Church and State, Authority, the Business World, the Practical World, men of action, men of affairs, generals and moralists and applied mathematicians and philosophers you set your watch by—efficient followers of abstraction and ideals, men who have learned that when you know how to use something you know it. There is a good deal of rather mocking but quite ungrudging credit—if little fondness—given to this side of things, the motor or effector system which, after all, does run the world along its "metalled ways" of appetency (our version of Tennyson's "ringing grooves of change"). But Ransom's affection goes out to that other army, defeated every day and victorious every night, of so-lightly-armed, so-easily-vanquished skirmishers, in their rags and tags and trailing clouds, who run around and around the iron hoplites pelting them with gravel and rosemary, getting killed miserably, and—half the time, in the pure pleasure or pain of being—forgetting even that they are fighting, and wandering off into the flowers at the edge of the terrible field. Here are the "vessels fit for storm and sport," not yet converted into "miserly merchant hulls"—the grandfather dancing with his fierce grandsons, in warpaint and feathers, round a bonfire in the back yard, having "performed ignominies unreckoned / Between the first brief childhood and the second," but now "more honorable . . . in danger and in joy." In these ranks are children and the old, women—innocent girls or terrible beauties or protecting housewives, all above or below or at the side of the Real World—lovers, dreams, nature, animals, tradition, nursery rhymes, fairy tales, everything that is at first or at last "content to feel / What others understand." Sometimes the poems are—as Empson might say—a queer mixture of pastoral and childcult. Although the shepherds are aging and the children dead, half of them, and the foxhunters not making much headway against the overweening Platonism of the International Business Machine Company, it is all magical: disenchantment and enchantment are so prettily and inextricably mingled that we accept everything with sad pleasure, and smile at the poems' foreknowing, foredefeated, mocking, half-acceptant pain. For in the country of the poems wisdom is a poor butterfly dreaming that it is Chuang-tze, and not an optimistic bird of prey; and the greatest single subject of the romantics, pure potentiality, is treated with a classical grace and composure.

[1963]

I have read both selections many times now, brooding the way I do when I know that I am looking but when I am not sure what for. Some time after the sixth or seventh rereading, I found myself asking certain questions. Of the poem: Why does it seem to me very good but not great? Of the prose: Why, for all its excesses and flourishes and tail-pipe firings, does this paragraph strike me as brilliant? Asking the second question, I pause to recheck. *Is* it brilliant? I'm sure and then less sure. I know that at one point, and through several subsequent readings, it seemed that way. Whereas the poem never put me in such a quandary. From the start it kept saying: "I am only very good."

It's a funny business, this comparing. For the writing, as writing, in **"Next Day"** is in some ways more accomplished—more sure, more clear, more balanced in sense and syntax—than the writing in the Ransom paragraph. But I expect different, dare I say "higher," things of a poem; I set down different demands right from the threshold. In a poem of a certain type—a type I recognize instantly from certain salient features (repeating rhyme pattern, stanzaic regularity)—I wait for a motion that will be toward inevitability: the best words in the best order. And I expect, over and above the satisfactions of meaning, a consolidating rightness of rhythm and sound, an aesthetic lift that returns me, if only briefly, from the sensations of made art to those of life; that resonates, in other words, with the recognitions and feelings that I hoard within myself. The poem enticed me, held me poised, but it could not gratify that core desire.

The prose, on the other hand, labored under no such constraints. It was clear from the outset that Jarrell was not guiding me toward any experience of aesthetic inevitability; that he was, instead, actively attempting to liberate another poet from the fixed assumptions that so rapidly crystallize around such inevitable expression. In other words, this one long paragraph alerted me to a mission that was very different from the poetic mission. I was sprung from having to care, in that largest sense of caring that a poem requires, and I was released, instead, into a realm of freedom. Jarrell was playing with ideas, manipulating conceits, but I felt no pressure to believe him. His movements were more like those of a butterfly battering its way around a statue in the garden. But while the butterfly could not dislodge or in any way affect the statue, its tentative flutters brought out the materiality of the stone as the surrounding volumes of air never could. In that recognition I experienced an aesthetic transport; it is my warrant for calling the prose brilliant.

"Next Day" can be taken as a perfectly transparent window opening upon Jarrell's poetic procedure. It is, as much as any poem can be, representative. That is, it features the thematic and technical elements that recur throughout the *oeuvre*: the preoccupation with time, loss, and death; the play between oblique wit and declarative confession; the formal manipulation of time frames and subjective and objective vantages; the use of crescendo patterns where the rhythm rises to a pitch and abruptly breaks off; and, of course, the female mask, or persona. We see Jarrell at his best, or near-best; and we might also discover why the poetry falls short of greatness.

The ten six-line stanzas are arranged to present an unambiguous—and chilling—recognition. An older woman has gone out shopping. When the bag boy carries her purchases to her car, she realizes that he does not see her as a woman. She then remembers a time when she was desirable ("the world looked at me / And its mouth watered."); she starts to remember some former moment of sensual ecstasy, then represses the memory, thinks instead of her husband and children. Her days, she realizes, have become routine, but even so she fears the changes time will inevitably bring. The image of her face in the car mirror reminds her: "You're old." She now remembers the funeral of a friend held just the previous day (thus the poem's title). The face and body, she thinks, were hers, too. She tries to counter with happier thoughts: that she is exceptional, that much has been given to her. But the effort breaks down. The poem ends:

> But really no one is exceptional,
> No one has anything, I'm anybody,
> I stand beside my grave
> Confused with my life, that is commonplace and solitary.

The success or failure of **"Next Day"** ultimately depends upon these four lines, on whether or not they can fill the reader with the recognition—the shudder—of truth. I confess that I am only half-moved. I admire the poem as a linguistic artifact, but I do not feel it impinge upon my life. And this is not to say that I am not susceptible to realizations of the kind that Jarrell expresses. Alas, my reaction is quite typical of my response to Jarrell's poetry in general. My interest is compelled, but my engagement is blocked.

The biggest obstacle, so far as I am concerned, is the voice, the mask. I am willing to credit the woman's abstracting intelligence, her ironic detachment (she is the one who is punning with the detergent labels), her bookish way of citing William James in her thoughts. I grant as plausible the sequence of her thoughts and memories. But what defeats me is the imbalance between the rhythmic life of the poem and the sensibility presented. Which is precisely the point: The woman is *presented*, not enacted. And yet Jarrell would have us feel the final lines from within, as a direct consequence of our involvement with her inner process. Jarrell's woman is moving toward an important realization about her life, but the movement is finally all mind, not heart. This suggests to me that Jarrell himself was thinking his way through to the emotions he deemed necessary, almost as though the true feelings had been repressed. There is just no deeper signature of emotion in the linguistic rhythm of the poem. The transcription of the inward process feels almost staccato:

> I am afraid, this morning, of my face.
> It looks at me
> From the rear-view mirror, with the eyes I hate,
> The smile I hate. Its plain, lined look
> Of gray discovery
> Repeats to me: "You're old." That's all, I'm old.

In the absence of any momentum of discovery, with no rhythmic enactment of a deeper psychic affect, we are forced to conclude that these are familiar observations that are being rehearsed mechanically. This would not necessarily be a problem, except that the poem is building toward a stark epiphany that cannot seem formulaic if it is to compel the reader.

In this poem, as elsewhere (most notably in the poems of **"The Lost World"** sequence), Jarrell tries to create dynamic momentum through a tactic of dilation followed by sudden interruption. An interior swell of thought or memory is abruptly cut off, returning us to a more flattened—and by implication *truer*—diction. Jarrell enacts this reversal three times in the course of the poem. In the first instance, the woman has plunged into an emotional reverie about her former desirability:

> . . . How often they have undressed me,
> The eyes of strangers!
> And, holding their flesh within my flesh, their vile
>
> Imaginings within my imagining,
> I too have taken
> The chance of life . . .

The forward surge that has built up over the stanza enjambment breaks off with: "Now the boy pats my dog / And we start home."

The need to retrieve the past is strong in her, however. Almost immediately she takes up the reverie again, now incorporating the image of a burst soap bubble:

> The last mistaken,
> Ecstatic, accidental bliss, the blind
>
> Happiness that, bursting, leaves upon the palm
> Some soap and water—
> It was so long ago, back in some Gay
> Twenties, Nineties, I don't know . . . Today I miss
> My lovely daughter

I am persuaded by the recurrence of the memory, by the way that the woman hovers at the brink of a deeper recollection and then draws herself back. I am not convinced, though, by Jarrell's characterization of her thought process, that he would allow a woman remembering a past happiness to raise up so contrived a rhetorical shield: "It was so long ago, back in some Gay / Twenties, Nineties, I don't know . . ." Nor do I trust her use of the adjective "lovely" in the next line, for it suggests a self-consciousness—a socialized distancing—in a moment that is meant to be unguarded.

The final reversal comes right at the end of the poem:

> As I think of her I hear her telling me
>
> How young I seem; I *am* exceptional;
> I think of all I have.
> But really no one is exceptional . . .

Jarrell has not managed the moment of awakening very well. He has instigated a thought sequence wherein the woman remembers being told that she seems young, then tells herself that she *is* exceptional, then begins the presumably reflexive process of reminding herself of her good fortune. But the collapse of the initiative comes too swiftly. There is no pause or check, no scramble to sustain the illusion. We have no recourse but to read it as a step—very nearly a dialectical backswing—in a rational continuum. The emotion, the pity or the terror, that should accompany the awakening is not there. We end up stranded in another person's thought, deprived of the release of a felt response.

It is easy to see why Jarrell favored the persona poem. Freed from the subjective constraints of the "I" (such as Lowell grappled with), he could indulge his psychic scenarios by proxy. These scenarios were, by and large, written by his own obsessive need to work through loss, primarily the early loss of his parents. His fascination lay chiefly in the possibilities they offered for the exploration of the processes of memory. That he would so often choose women as masks hints at the degree of imaginative remove he required in order to handle the true subject matter of his life. (Others have suggested the opposite, I realize: that Jarrell adopted female masks because he felt a closer kinship with the feminine psyche.) But even by way of these gender masks, Jarrell proved unable to vent the emotions, the grief, of his loss. The repression was too strong. What we get instead are poems that probe the wounded area with the artifice of intellect. One consequence is that the poems lack a natural structure. In spite of Jarrell's intelligence and craft, the work has a willed quality that hampers the deepest kind of engagement.

The criticism is, by contrast, free from all constraints of enactment. The mind that in the poetry tries to make emotion can range among ideas and associations unhampered. Indeed, in reading Jarrell's prose one senses that here is a mind that knows the difference, that feels the adrenaline rush when the shackles drop away and injects that rush directly into the work. It is an adolescent friskiness; for all his sophistication of thought, Jarrell is forever mugging and miming and scurrying just out of reach with a "catch me if you can" expression on his face. But never mind. The combination of message and means is irresistible, and it becomes more irresistible still whenever the critic can batten onto a subject of four-square solidity. Jarrell is not half as good, or effective, when dealing with the type of a cummings, a Hart Crane, a Dylan Thomas. But with a Frost, Auden, or Ransom—with a poet, that is, whose language serves a vision or a metaphysics—he is in his element. With these poets, the underlying terms are manifest in the work; they need only be brought forward and clarified. The critic does not need to argue or debate. His job, rather, is to open the front door and take possession of the house. Which is precisely what Jarrell does: He leads the visitor from chamber to chamber, pointing out excellences.

Jarrell was, as I said, a poet-critic. By this I mean that his approach to criticism, his way of responding, was to write a kind of poem of association around the subject in question. The Ransom essay, especially the opening passage cited here, is a perfect instance. Jarrell begins with one simple observation about the poet's subject matter—that it is "beautifully varied"—and ends some hundreds of words later with another: that "the greatest single subject of the romantics, pure potentiality, is treated with a classical grace and composure." In between we find a veritable bazaar of ideas, discriminations, illustrations, and asides. Rationally—logically—it does not add up to very much. We learn that Ransom's poems enact a warfare between the worldly claims of authority and order and the more soulful, if frailer, forces of spontaneity, instinct, and feeling. But what a saying it is! By the time Jarrell has moved us from the first sentence to the last he has sold us, if not on the subtlety and depth of Ransom, then on subtlety and depth themselves. We do not really know where Jarrell leaves off and Ransom begins; we do not know which is about the poems and which about the critic's disorderly psyche. But we do not much care. For we have been made privy, in a way that almost never happens, to the actual ebb and flow of a refined and complex sensibility *in the act*. We have experienced, in effect, a poem of the mind's movement. The critic has shown us what it can be like to respond to a work of art. And though we cannot specify how or why, we know more about the world than we did when we started reading.

Though Jarrell's prose cannot be reduced to a system, it is possible to point to certain conspicuous features that contribute to its essential character. Most prominent, of course, is the Jarrell tone, which is authoritative and certain, but which can modulate in a split second into playfulness, excess, slapstick, or any one of a hundred slightly fey poses (like those "skirmishers . . . who run around and around the iron hoplites pelting them with gravel and rosemary . . ."). He is also proudly and wittily referential, in this one paragraph working in nods to Kant, Eliot, Tennyson, Wordsworth, Yeats, Empson, Chuang Tzu, and doubtless others that went right by me. And he makes a mighty virtue of what is many a lesser writer's failure: In Jarrell's hands the non sequitur and unprepared transition leave off being weaknesses and become, instead, instruments of unexpectedness. Tonally, thematically, even syntactically, one never quite knows where the critic will go from one sentence to the next.

Then there is Jarrell's sly way of making discriminations. In his hands—and who can say why?—distinctions made as afterthoughts acquire a metaphysical resonance. He writes, for example, characterizing his "skirmishers," that "half the time, in the pure pleasure or pain of being," they forget they are fighting. The extra beat of pause that accompanies "or pain" gives a simple statement a resonance of profundity. Similarly, when he writes later that "everything is at first or at last 'content to feel / What others understand,'" his addition of "or at last" amplifies the import of his statement tenfold.

I mention this because it gives some inkling about the workings of the mind that spins out this prose. The fact that Jarrell repeatedly modifies his assertions suggests to me that the special quality of the writing may be owing, at least in part, to a strain between two sides of his nature. He is horse and rider; he launches into a pronouncement, then hastily checks himself. The prose crackles with electrical crosscurrents. Within the sentence, but also writ large, Jarrell is forever dashing off on a spree and then rearing up to look proper.

This back-and-forth shifting among levels of diction and postures of regard is in some ways similar to the strategy of switching rhythms that Jarrell uses so often in the poems. Here we are talking not about dilations of memory so much as swerves into trope making, gratuitous witticism, or inspired but inessential brooding. In the poems the rhythm will suddenly break, bring us back to earth, to the facts of the present. In the criticism the gesture is back toward the more customary posture of the sober critic. Consider how the penultimate sentence of the paragraph builds up pressure (of insight mounting toward chaos), and how deftly we are brought back around to feel the restraints of a more balanced style in the clauses of the last sentence. The sense of achieved resolution is all the more striking for the riot that preceded it:

> Although the shepherds are aging and the children dead, half of them, and the fox-hunters not making much headway against the overweening Platonism of the International Business Machine Company, it is all magical: disenchantment and enchantment are so prettily and inextricably mingled that we accept everything with sad pleasure, and smile at the poems' foreknowing, foredefeated, mocking, half-acceptant pain. For in the country of the poems wisdom is a poor butterfly dreaming that it is Chuang-tze, and not an optimistic bird of prey; and the single greatest subject of the romantics, pure potentiality, is treated with a classical grace and composure.

I would say that the difference between the poetry and the prose is this: that in the poetry the shifts ultimately signal a war between the claims of feeling—the feeling that would prompt the writing—and the defensive structures of reason. It is a war that ended early on, as soon as intellect annexed the feeling and transformed it into thought. In the criticism, however, the split between one kind of tone and approach and another suggests something different: the constant struggle between the critic who would parse and analyze with an eye fixed on the demands of public and academy, and the *reader,* that mercurial creature who is all appetites and nerve endings. Out of this conflict comes a kind of poetry that is more challenging and less constrained than the lineated product that emerges from the opposition of feeling and intellect.

Talent and genius. Psychologist K. R. Eissler, in his book *Talent and Genius,* made this observation: "The talent usually never succeeds in harnessing the unconscious into the service of creativity, to an extent that would even approach that which genius is *compelled* to achieve." Applying this to Jarrell, while holding to the notion that he *did* come closer to attaining genius in the criticism than in the poetry, I would offer that Jarrell was best able to storm the fortifications surrounding his unconscious by reading; that, further, he was able to record—*needed* to record—some of that responsiveness in his critical prose. Or, to put it another way: Jarrell practiced criticism largely because he could thus indulge his reader's sensibility. The criticism is, in other words, a pretext, and this is what gives it its revolutionary character. It is not criticism at all, but poetry carried on by other means.

Note

1. The book is, I'm sad to say, a disappointment. For all Pritchard's elegance and acumen, one feels distanced further from an already distant individual. This may sound paradoxical, but it is not inexplicable. Reading Jarrell's prose and poetry one comes right up against the sensibility, if not the biographical self (and Jarrell, if anyone, put his genius into his sensibility and his talent into his life). At least, I feel that I know Jarrell in some way after reading his work. But the biography, in accounting for what little has been unearthed about the particulars of the life, sidesteps the man in the books in favor of the man who wrote them. And *he* is an altogether elusive creature. It is all but impossible to square the stray externals with the readerly intuitions. The sensibility—existing in spite of outward circumstance more than because of it—cannot be tracked in the sequential fashion that the footsteps can. Some biographies are better left unwritten.

Alan Williamson (essay date fall 1994)

SOURCE: Williamson, Alan. "Jarrell, the Mother, the Märchen." *Twentieth Century Literature* 40, no. 3 (fall 1994): 283-99.

[*In the following essay, Williamson argues that the "story" running throughout Jarrell's work has to do with loneliness of living in this world. The critic also examines how this story in Jarrell's poetry exemplifies Jarrell's superior understanding of "his time's definition of masculinity."*]

"There is one story and one story only," Randall Jarrell was fond of quoting, from Robert Graves, about those poets whose enabling obsessions he felt he had penetrated to their depths. It was true of many of them, but truest of all of himself. Appropriately, since he was the most consciously psychoanalytic even of the poets of the "confessional" generation, his is a story that resonates with the earliest, most forgotten experiences of life, and with the senses of identity, relationship, and gender that begin to be formed there. To understand it is to understand why Jarrell's poetry has been accused of sentimentality, and why, at its most incandescent moments, it completely transcends that accusation.

Jarrell's story is, first and foremost, a story about our loneliness in the world, or about the world's failure to keep us: how to see things is not to be joined with them; how close, beyond the little circle of warmth our bodies cast, begins the unimaginably dead space that does not know us; how all the beauties, the fables of return, the talking animals, are a web of illusion cast over these unacceptable, irrefutable facts. The aging Marschallin, looking at her own face in the mirror, says "If just living can do this . . . It is terrible to be alive." The bomber calls *"Little Friend!"* to the fighter it can already see going down in flames. The adolescent girl in **"The Night before the Night before Christmas,"** falling asleep "under the patched star-pattern / of the quilt,"

> warms a world
> Out slowly, a wobbling blind ellipse
> That lengthens in half a dozen jumps
> Of her numb shrinking feet,

but, beyond that world almost assimilated into the self, she feels the other "world . . . no longer hidden . . . By the day of the light of the sun," where

> nothing moves except with a faint
> Choked straining shiver;
> Sounds except with a faint
> Choked croaking sigh

and where "There is not one thing that knows / It is almost Christmas."[1]

Even a seemingly reportorial war poem like **"A Pilot from the Carrier"** derives much of its strength from its underlying metaphysical preoccupations. The airman, having ejected from his burning plane, finds in his narrow escape, its renewed guarantee of a complete future, a momentarily "steadie[d]" relation to reality. He

> falls, a quiet bundle in the sky,
> The miles to warmth, to air, to waking:
> To the great flowering of his life, the hemisphere
> That holds his dangling years. In its long slow sway
> The world steadies and is almost still

Though still "Slight, separate, estranged," he experiences the mastery of "Reading a child's first scrawl." But what he reads are, in fact, the signs of something he does not see and cannot control, that can still destroy him—first "The traveling milk-like circle of a miss," then the "little blaze" of the carrier's guns,

> Toy-like as the glitter of the wing-guns,
> Shining as the fragile sun-marked plane
> That grows to him, rubbed silver tipped with flame.

The beautiful world is, read correctly, the malign or indifferent one; toy-scale to the ego's false perceptives, it will soon reduce the ego itself to the dispensable toy.

The other story Jarrell tells obsessively—really it is only a variant of the first one—has to do with our failure to keep each other; our inability to find, even in our loved ones, even in ourselves, a trustworthy "good" that can be categorically opposed to evil. It comes up in the War, as the poet looks around at the lovable, frightened men who have destroyed cities:

> If, in an odd angle of the hutment,
> A puppy laps the water from a can
> Of flowers, and the drunk sergeant shaving
> Whistles *O Paradiso!*—shall I say that man
> Is not as men have said: a wolf to man?

It seems almost part of the nature of things that there are only semantic solutions to these problems: a "puppy" is good, but a "wolf" is evil; and there are only "men" to say which of these "man" resembles. The problem comes up earlier, in childhood, in one of the most memorable scenes in Jarrell's poetry—the grandmother of **"The Lost World,"** who "looks with righteous love / At all of us, her spare face half a girl's," then goes into the chicken coop and wrings a chicken's neck. As the chicken's body tries "to run / Away from something, to fly away from Something / in great flopping circles," the grandson thinks "Could such a thing / Happen to anything?" And the grandmother, the "farm woman," has to

> tr[y] to persuade
> The little boy, her grandson, that she'd never
> Kill the boy's rabbit, never even think of it.
> He would like to believe her.

And I think—without diminishing their reality as stories about the world—these are all, in a sense, stories about childhood. They take us back to the very earliest stages, when the knowledge of separateness does indeed bring "death into the world, and all our woe," but is necessary for the very existence of an individuated self. And then the complex angers of separation, as psychoanalytic writers from Melanie Klein to Jessica Benjamin have charted them: anger at the parent for abandonment, anger at the parent for being so powerful to begin with, anger coming from the parent but inextricably confused with the anger coming from the child—all that the "good" and "evil" of fairy tales try so hard, and unsatisfactorily, to sort out.

Jarrell knew his Freud thoroughly—and intuited much that object-relations theory was only beginning to explore—and I think we can see him, consciously or unconsciously, returning to these primary feelings for his deepest sense of the crises or the potential horror in life. Looking back at **"A Pilot from the Carrier,"** how inescapably "And falls, a quiet bundle in the sky" suggests birth, or "In its long slow sway / The world steadies" the sensuous blurring, and precarious triumph, of learning to walk. Or take Jarrell's most famous single poem, **"The Death of the Ball Turret Gunner"**:

> From my mother's sleep I fell into the State,
> And I hunched in its belly till my wet fur froze.
> Six miles from earth, loosed from its dream of life,
> I woke to black flak and the nightmare fighters.
> When I died they washed me out of the turret with a hose.

This poem may have succeeded so well as an elegy on the indifference of war precisely because it is really an elegy for the primal separation. The "State" itself is only a hopeful, if colder, womb (a fact, of course, that totalitarian States have known very well how to manipulate). But by the third line, the metaphor has become cosmic: the earth itself, in its capacity to support life, is, from the point of view of outer space, only another womb, another contingent "dream." Nothing ultimately cares for us; so that the waking to inevitable mortality, when it comes in the fourth line, is only the last in a series of destructive births. It is the grief and anger about this that give the brutal journalistic details—the loss of the shape that constitutes an "I," the body reduced to a thing—so much more power than the detailed brutalities of many war poems. The feeling about death, technology, the State, the Universe becomes the primal angry grieving of Wallace Stevens's great poem "Madame La Fleurie": "His grief is that his mother should feed on him, himself and what he saw."

In the German fairy tales, of course, Bad Mothers do eat their children. Jarrell was fascinated with the Märchen partly because they recall a harsher time in the history of the species, when we were more at the mercy of the surrounding forest, the conditions of being (see the poem **"The Märchen"**); but even more because they recall a harsher time in the history of the psyche. The child driven into exile or setting out on a heroic quest—it hardly matters which, at age one or two they are so profoundly the same event. The Good Mother, the stepmother, the Witch—that triangulation that so clearly suggests the way of handling very early feelings of anger that Melanie Klein calls "splitting." I quote Dorothy Dinnerstein's explanation, as more succinct than any I was able to find in Klein herself:

> [The child's] hateful feelings are sharply dissociated from its loving ones; the menacing, vengeful aspects of the mother (as she exists in the child's mind) are walled off from her comforting, providing aspects. The child comes to feel "that a good and a bad breast exist." The good breast remains intact, unsullied by badness, but it disappears from time to time and a bad breast is there instead.
>
> ([*The Mermaid and the Minotaur*] 97)

Hansel and Gretel was Jarrell's favorite of the Märchen, I think because in it the mechanisms of splitting are so perfectly articulated—as well as the transformation of the lost oral unity into an engulfing horror. Jarrell draws on the loneliness of the story for the girl's predicament in **"The Night before the Night before Christmas,"** and makes Hansel a type of questing humanity in **"The Märchen."** But the quirky *locus classicus* for his psychoanalytic understanding of the story is **"A Quilt-Pattern."**

The poem is taken from the point of view of a sick child—threatened with the ultimate abandonment of death, but also subjected to a level of maternal ministration which, in his healthy state, he would have outgrown. He falls into a troubled sleep, and redreams the fairy tale. The dream shows, among other things, how strong his longing is for the lost infantile unity:

> Here a thousand stones
> Of the trail home shine from their strings
> Like just-brushed, just lost teeth.

"Home" is the place the milk teeth lead back to, the original undifferentiation. The witch's house is the place where we go when that is not only no longer available, but has become a threat. There, to need the mother is to eat the mother—a guilty, dangerous act the child must deflect onto something smaller and weaker: "It is a mouse." But to accept that the mother wishes to feed is equally dangerous: no doubt she is fattening him up, to eat him in turn. Her yard is full of rabbits in cages. The reader who knows Jarrell's later work—as this poem's initial readers could not—will immediately make the connection to "Mama" 's rabbits and chickens in **"The Lost World."** And so the childhood issues open directly onto the largest moral issues, even of the war poems. Where does one find goodness, in this world of eaters and eaten? "His white cat eats up his white pigeon."

And so, both mother and child are split, in the child's mind. The "dead mother"—the unambiguously good mother of infancy—is buried underneath the witch's yard, her face "scaling." And the twins of the story become the compliant "good me," who represses his pain ("All small furry things / That are hurt, but that never cry at all"), and "bad me," whose oral aggressions are punished in kind: "My mother is basting / Bad me in the bath-tub."

Finally, splitting apart "good me" and "bad me" is not sufficient to contain these conflicts, and the terrible

"Other" is born, what consciousness cannot acknowledge at all—both the murderous mother who deserves to be killed, and the child who wants to kill her.

> If something is screaming itself to death
> There in the oven, it is not the mouse
> Nor anything of the mouse's. Bad me, good me
> Stare into each other's eyes, and timidly
> Smile at each other: it was the Other.

It is a disturbing poem, not least because the sources of the hatred of the mother remain mysterious. Jarrell himself, in a letter trying to explain the poem, seems unreasonably angry with her: "She is demanding and completely possessive and awful to him and he hates her."[2] This is so out of keeping with the data within the poem that one is tempted to put it down either to some unexpressed personal memory or to the ready availability (as many writers have noted) of misogynist mother-hatred in the culture in pre-feminist days. Within the poem, the worst thing the mother does is to wash the child's mouth out with soap—not good, but hardly enough, in the context of the 1910s, to qualify her as "awful to him." What we hear most about is her intrusive tenderness. Her "humming stare" becomes the "hum[ming]" voice of the "house of bread"; "mouse" turns out to be her nickname for the child. But his reaction is as extreme as the poet's: hearing her voice outside his door,

> He says to himself, "I will never wake."
> He says to himself, not breathing:
> "Go away. Go away. Go away."
>
> And the footsteps go away.

In D. W. Winnicott's terms, he has killed off his True Self, or at least its outward manifestation ("I will never wake"), to put it forever out of reach of the mother's infantalizing care ([*The Maturation Processes and the Facilitating Environment*] 140-52). "Never trust the teller, trust the tale," as D. H. Lawrence said. What Jarrell has written is not a story about an objectively "awful" mother, but about a child's fear of (and nostalgia for) maternal engulfment. For Melanie Klein such fears are nearly universal: the preoedipal mother is simply too powerful, the strength of the child's dependency on her, and consequent anger—which Klein calls "envy"—and guilt, are too great. But for later thinkers, from Winnicott to Alice Miller to Jessica Benjamin, there are less universal causes for the need to distance the mother so drastically.[3] What is crucial, they argue, is that the child should feel loved and "recognized" as he or she moves into, and acts on, the sense of being a separate self. When this link is not maintained, then the theme takes on the full, terrible force we have seen in Jarrell's work generally. Separation is cosmic lostness; unity is engulfment, loss of self. This happens, Jessica Benjamin argues, through a failure of the "paradox of recognition," the need to enjoy another's independent existence in order to receive his or her confirmation of one's own, which can so easily be thrown off by too much, or too little, control on the parent's part. Alice Miller, in a more famous, drastic formulation, speaks of the "narcissistically deprived" parent, who needs "a specific echo from the child," because she experiences herself, still, as "a child in search of an object that could be available to her" ([*The Drama of the Gifted Child*] 11). Such a parent is too involved in his or her own internal dramas to see the child as an other, and unconsciously forces the child to assume a role in those dramas—often with exquisite attunement, since it is the only way to get the parent's recognition at all.

Did Jarrell have such a childhood? William Pritchard's biography, though resolutely anti-psychoanalytic in tone, does provide some suggestive evidence. There was, first of all, the trauma of the loss of Jarrell's father, when his mother moved back from California to Nashville after the divorce. ("Presumably there is no father in this family," Jarrell writes in the letter about **"A Quilt-Pattern."**[4] This in itself might, in the Kleinian formulation, intensify resentment of the mother's power, by cutting off one of the traditional avenues of escape, identification with the father.) Pritchard's characterization of Jarrell's mother, though sketchy, does fit the broad outlines of Alice Miller's "narcissistically deprived" parent, needing always to "feel herself the center of attention":

> Anna Jarrell was not only young but pretty and petite, with dark eyes, curly hair, and a skin so sensitive she needed to wear silk next to it and used only non-allergenic soaps and creams. . . . Furniture and rugs, draperies and dishes were constantly replaced, and no leftovers were allowed to accumulate in the icebox. When she made her angel cake, said to have been delicious, she flushed a dozen egg yolks down the commode. But Owen's salary as a photographer's assistant was unequal to such extravagances. . . . With money tight and no family of her own or Owen's to turn to, her health suffered and she became, in the ladylike phrase, "delicate."
>
> [*Randall Jarrell*]

Pritchard applies the adjectives "'sensitive' and histrionic" to her, and suggests that the "recurrent . . . scene called Mother Has Fainted," from the late poem **"Hope,"** is autobiographical ([*Randall Jarrell*] 12-13).

It does seem clear that the happiest phase of Jarrell's childhood was the year he spent away from his mother, with his paternal grandparents. Pritchard quotes a long, quite literary letter from that year, in which Jarrell seems to be trying at once to convince his mother that "I wish I could see you" and that California is very "exciting" and he should be allowed to stay:

> We sure did see lots of buzzards on our trip. On one detour we saw four great big ones right in the road eating a dead chicken. They just stalked to the side of the

road when we passed and then stalked back again. They sure are mean, ugly-looking birds. They just sail around in the sky, looking for some carrion to eat. They seem to say, "We'll get *you* someday, get you get you. We'll getyouyet, getyouyet, getyouyet. Just like choruses of songs that seem to run together.

(17)

To Pritchard this letter, "natural, untroubled, happily alert to this or that circumstance and expressive possibility," is evidence against "the assumption that Jarrell endured a lonely, unhappy childhood." But, as Alice Miller points out, the need to perform in this way for a parent is not necessarily evidence that the child feels accepted as and for his or her self; often, quite the reverse. The adult Jarrell is described—by students, friends, readers, even wives and lovers—as a continuously, and consummately, brilliant performer. But the voice of unexpressed grief, the voice of the buzzard saying "getyouyet," is heard obsessively in his poetry; and seems to have dominated in the desperation of his final year.

If Jarrell did, in fact, feel the ambivalence toward his mother that **"A Quilt-Pattern"** and some of the biographical details suggest, it is an interesting question why he was so obsessively sympathetic to women in his poetry, writing so many poems either in a female persona or essentially from the woman's point of view. Undoubtedly he projected the fragile, wistful side of himself, inclined to blame the universe when its absolute yearnings were not met, onto female characters partly because these traits were simply not acceptably "male" in the climate of the 1940s and 1950s. But we need, here, to remember another insight of Alice Miller's: that the narcissistic mother has, helplessly, the same kind of fragile, wistful personality that she generates in her child, and that her child is used to, having spent much of childhood "understanding" it. In projecting the "inner woman," the son is projecting both a feelingful self *and* a feelingful mother, who can be rescued together. This element of pure wish-fulfillment accounts, I think, for the sense of sentimentality and lack of depth of character many readers have when faced with such famous, because very clear-cut, persona poems as **"Next Day," "The Face,"** or **"The Woman at the Washington Zoo."**

But could Jarrell write for very long about adult women without dredging up some of the resentments, the harsh judgments, directed, say, toward the mother of **"A Quilt-Pattern"**? The ungiving characteristics of this "real" mother will often reappear, subtly understood and apparently forgiven, in the inner woman of the poems. If the speakers of **"Next Day"** and **"The Woman at the Washington Zoo"** seem wounded innocents in their expectations of life, what of the mother in **"The Lost Children,"** whose sense of loss leads her to make no distinction between the child who has died and the child who has had the opportunity to distance herself in the normal way, by growing up? Is there no murderous undercurrent in this poem, simply because its manner is passive, wistful, metaphysical, the manner of the Marschallin saying "It is terrible to be alive"? Is it entirely an accident that, in **"A Girl in a Library,"** *both* the bovine Home Ec. major and the hypercritical (projected) "Tatyana Larina" are embodiments of female narcissism, and it is the task of the male speaker to mediate between the two of them with compassion?

It is in these tensions, I would argue, that Jarrell's poems pass beyond sentimentality to profound psychological truth. The person who experiences herself, since it is so clearly the poet—as weak, yearning, never getting enough from life, is the *same* person who will be perceived by others as self-involved, lacking the resources to give. One of the greatest moments of moral insight in Jarrell's poetry, therefore, comes in **"The Lost World,"** when he perceives himself as capable of inflicting the same kind of damage on the child-selves of others as they have inflicted on his. The story is, in a way, a classically Kleinian one—the Good Object punitively repudiated because it cannot be controlled. When Jarrell was forced to leave his grandparents and his great-grandmother to return to his mother in Nashville, he simply erased them from his memory: never answered their letters, never communicated with them again. In the poem, this memory intrudes into the present time of writing, just as he has finished recounting the story of how his great-grandmother was frightened by a Union captain during the Civil War:

> She cries . . . As I run by the chicken coops
> With lettuce for my rabbit, real remorse
> Hurts me, here, now: the little girl is crying
> Because I didn't write. Because—
>   of course,
> I *was* a child, I missed them so. But justifying
> Hurts too.

And so, when, a few lines later, the "rabbit" becomes the potential object of "Mama" 's murderous indifference, the speaker himself is implicated in the crime, the universal cycle of victimizers and victims.

The way of handling these problems that the persona poems suggest has potentially tragic consequences if carried over into life. The man who comforts his own weaker, yearning side by projecting it onto a woman—thereby failing to recognize its destructive potential—may find himself back in the same situation of not being heard, not being understood, facing insatiable demands, that created the sense of weakness to begin with. Jarrell's love letters to Elisabeth Eisler, and particularly to Mary von Schrader, have at once a teacherly, protective quality and a sense of twinship, almost of alter ego, paralleled only in Rilke's letters to Benevenuta. "Truly we are one and were always one. *As you know, there is no difference between us,*" he writes to Mary; and repeatedly addresses her as "sister" (Pritchard 201, 206). But in lasting relationships he never seems to have been quite sure whether he had gotten the Good Mother or the Witch. In his last year he apparently turned vehemently against Mary, wanting to divorce her, as he had his first wife, and to marry a younger woman. It is one of the grim, but not unfitting, ironies of his life that it is up to us to choose whether to believe Mary's conceivably self-serving account, that they were happily reconciled and that his death was an accident, or to believe with his close friends that he committed suicide.

There is one fairy-tale poem, **"Hohensalzburg,"** that particularly explores the dark side of alter-ego relationships, and the underlying identity of the wistful and the destructive selves. Jarrell tried to distance himself from this poem, by the subtitle ("Fantastic Variations on a Theme of Romantic Character"), and by all the jokes that remind us he is writing about German culture, tourist response. Yet its composition was intimately intertwined with the unconsummated affair with Elisabeth Eisler; that, and the sheer intensity of the writing, suggest that it may tell more of the truth about his inner erotic life than he was used to telling, or entirely comfortable with.

"Hohensalzburg" is a variant of the vampire story. The (female) vampire is imagined with great sympathy, as a tomboy who does not want to grow up, knowing that gender, sexuality, relationship will comprise her freedom. She does not want to be the object of perception, of desire. When the old woman who serves her tea chides her for having "run, all evening, by the shore / Naked, searching for your dress upon the sand," and then asks her "What would you be, if you could have your wish?", she answers, "*I would be invisible.*" And when the old woman says,

> "What you do will do,
> But not forever . . .
> What you want is a husband and
> children"

her reply speaks for all of the Jarrell characters who despair of, and therefore mystically see through, the world that would in any way delimit their yearnings: "*They will do, / But not forever.*"

And yet, for the male speaker of the poem, this elusive woman is so profoundly an alter ego—"Pure, yearning, unappeasable"—that she becomes the vehicle for a more primary, preoedipal, even Wordsworthian experience of cosmic interfusion:

> I should always have known; those who sang from the
>   river,
> Those who moved to me, trembling, from the wood
> Were the others: when I crushed on a finger, with a
>   finger,
> A petal of the blossom of the lime, I understood
> (As I tasted, under the taste of the flower, the dark
> Taste of the leaf, the flesh that has never flowered)
> All the words of the wood but a final word.

What both the speaker and the girl have in common, in short, is the impatience with phenomena, the longing to gain access to the essence beyond, the "final word" that includes all other words. But in relation to a finite other this longing has a vampiric potential. That this potential belongs to him as well as to her is made beautifully clear through the imagery of "taste," here and later in the poem:

> Your cold flesh, faint with starlight,
> Wetted a little with the dew,
> Had, to my tongue, the bloom of fruit—
> Of the flower: the lime-tree flower,
> And under the taste of the flower
> There was the taste of—

The unfinished sentence has to be completed, in the light of the earlier passage, by "the dark / Taste of the leaf," the "final word" it represents. But surely there is a burden of terror, guilt, repression in the incompletion. The reader who knows **"A Quilt-Pattern"** will remember that there virtually the same phrase was broken off, and asked to be completed with "his mother." Jarrell's canon remembers, if this particular poem does not, the connection both of the desire for oneness and of the guilt of vampirism to the infantile relationship.

The guilt of consuming the mother is, it would seem, both expiated and acted out by submission to the other person's "unappeasable" yearning. The broken sentence cuts directly to

> I felt in the middle of the circle
> Of your mouth against my flesh
> Something hard, scraping gently, over and over
> Against the skin of my throat.

It is a deeply disturbing scene, for more than just the obvious reasons. When he realizes that his blood is being sucked, he feels such a sense of sacrificial union, perhaps of goodness restored through punishment, that he assumes the posture of the crucified Christ:

> I used my last strength and, slowly,
> Slowly, opened my eyes
> And pushed my arms out, that the moonlight pierced
>   and held—

And this very action awakens his sexual desire, for the first and only time in the poem—a desire which the girl, in her perpetual virginity, must of course refuse.

> I said: "I want you"; and the words were so heavy
> That they hung like darkness over the world,

> And you said to me, softly: *You must not so.*
> *I am only a girl.*
> *Before I was a ghost I was only a girl.*

But if his desire is bound up with the need to consume or be consumed, hers, for all her elusiveness, includes the desire to be recognized—for Miller and Benjamin the fundamental desire of the narcissistically deprived child. She wants to be found out in her invisibility; and despairs that it can never happen.

> What shall I call you, O Being of the Earth?
> *What I wish you to call me I shall never hear.*

Why did Jarrell refigure the alter-ego relationship of his Salzburg period in terms of the vampire story? Perhaps he intuited (it is a common enough psychological insight) that the very sense of lack that made the two sympathetic could lead to forms of dependence destructive to each other's autonomy. In the poem, "Something light, a life / Pulse[s]" in her face only after she has absorbed his blood. And perhaps, too, he understood that to try to make up for childhood is always, in some sense, to repeat childhood. But beyond this, the vampire story is itself, in its odd way, a love story. Because the vampire has never learned how to connect with the earth, in mutuality, without loss of self, she/he can never leave the earth behind, like the souls that go on to Heaven or Hell. That is why her only accessible name is "a dweller of the Earth." And she/he kills, in part, to create another vampire, an immortal/earthly companion. Strangely—and yet not so strangely, since the female voice, in Jarrell, is always the voice of grieving—in the poem it is the woman who sees through the limitations of this project: "*In the end we wake from everything.*" And it is the male voice that continues to ignore its darkness in favor of its transcendent potential:

> And yet surely, at the last, all these are one,
> We also are forever one:
> A dweller of the Earth, invisible.

But in the end Jarrell too had to face the darkness of his own meanings. His last poem on the Hansel and Gretel story, **"The House in the Wood,"** is also the only poem that gives us an idea of how unendurable the depression of his last year must have been. It is a poem about the taking-back of projection; the moment when we see through the screens, splittings, denials that enable us to tell stories and live lives.

> At the back of the houses there is the wood.
> While there is a leaf of summer left, the wood
>
> Makes sounds I can put somewhere in my song,
> Has paths I can walk, when I wake, to good
>
> Or evil: to the cage, to the oven, to the House
> In the Wood.

But when the leafless winter wood "begins / Its serious existence," that has "no path . . . no story," and "resists comparison," the speaker makes the fundamental psychoanalytic discovery that the fairy tale was constructed to prevent:

> If I walk into the wood
>
> As far as I can walk, I come to my own door,
> The door of the House in the Wood.

Such recognitions—in which there is no more Good Me and Bad Me, or Good Mother and Witch—should be the beginning of psychic health. But, as E. M. Forster said in another context, wait till you have one, dear reader! In this poem, consciousness is not strong enough to endure either the horror of the discoveries or the implication that one has lived—and might live forever—in a solipsistic universe:

> On the bed is something covered, something humped
> Asleep there, awake there—but what? I do not know.
>
> I look, I lie there, and yet I do not know.

Instead of finding health, the self seems to fall out of adult time and space, into a primal amorphousness in which it is at once infinite and infinitely helpless:

> How far out my great echoing clumsy limbs
>
> Stretch, surrounded only by space! For time has struck,
> All the clocks are struck now, for how many lives,
>
> On the same second.

If this sounds like descriptions of infantile consciousness—in particular, the boundlessness, the seeming permanence, of infantile rage and despair—it is no accident.[5] For what is discovered on the bed ("covered," "humped"—deformed, copulating, and pregnant) is not just the self but the merging, both oedipal and preoedipal, of the self and the mother—what the self fears and, at some level, has never stopped desiring. The last line of the poem makes this explicit: "In the House in the Wood, the witch and her child sleep." In this boundaryless state, monstrous crimes occur—monstrous actualizations of (and confusions of sexuality with) anger and pain—but neither their agents nor their victims can be located:

> Someone screams
> A scream like an old knife sharpened into nothing.
>
> It is only a nightmare. No one wakes up, nothing happens,
>
> Except there is gooseflesh over my whole body.

All-powerful in one sense, the self is in another sense infinitely cut off, both from the male phallic identity that once enabled it to rise above the preoedipal needs and fears, and from the Good Mother whose almost organic continuity with the self could assuage them: "I lie here like a cut-off limb, the stump the limb has left." The continuity is rather with the Bad Mother, who, as so often in Jarrell's poetry, becomes reality itself, the reality that has permitted all this to happen:

> Here at the bottom of the world, what was before the world
>
> And will be after, holds me to its black
>
> Breasts and rocks me.

Perhaps it is only in hindsight that this union with the Dark Mother seems, as in Sylvia Plath's poems, a premonition of suicide. (Although, in the most chillingly premonitory passage in Jarrell's work, in **"Thinking of the Lost World,"** it is when the driver-poet turns around to look into the eyes of the "mad girl" in the back seat that he is killed.) And, in any case, the deathly implications of that concluding "sleep" are strong. The grim lesson of this poem seems to be that splitting and projection are necessary to life itself; their distinctions give the adult ego its existence and its powers.

Here we would have to leave Jarrell, were it not for the strange fact that, at almost exactly the same time in his life as **"The House in the Wood,"** he wrote his own fairy tale, in which these dark forces are conquered, in which mutuality between formed personalities does, just barely, hold the infinite expectations and fears at bay. His great children's book, ***The Animal Family,*** is a parable of what Benjamin calls the pleasure of recognizing the irreducible otherness of other people.[6] A hunter courts a mermaid, eventually persuades her to live with him on land, and they adopt first a bear cub, then a lynx, then a shipwrecked boy. A great deal of the fun of the book lies in resolving the comic, but potentially harrowing, mistakes creatures make about other creatures' worlds. The mermaid wants to pick up a coal from the fire, thinking it a pretty shell; the "parents" fear the bear is dying the first time he hibernates.

No doubt it is significant that what Jarrell imagines is almost, but not quite, a fully human erotic family. There is plenty of sexual, and even oedipal, tension in the book; but the fact that none of the characters have actually emerged from each other's bodies gives them an ontological equality—in poignancy and independence—that is surely partly wish-fulfillment. (It also rhymes, curiously, with Jarrell's life; he was devoted to his stepdaughters, and dedicated his ***Selected Poems*** to them, as well as to Mary, but he had no children of his own.)

The connection of the mermaid to the "oceanic" memory of the original mother is, however, made clear in the book. The hunter has a dream of his dead mother singing, from which there emerges, as he wakes, first the wave-sound, then the mermaid's voice from the reefs. And she has just enough of the Dark Mother about her to make her a sister of the women in Jarrell's poems, and to make loving her a significant moral accomplishment. She has the indifference of "Mother Nature," which, Dinnerstein suggests, is a projection of the infant's feelings about the mother's unpredictable fulfillment of its needs.[7]

> Whenever anything reminded the hunter of his father and mother, you could see that he missed them and longed to have them alive again. The mermaid would tell him about her childhood and her family and her sister, the dead one, but she never seemed to want any of it back. The hunter said, puzzled, "Don't you wish your sister were still here?"
>
> The mermaid answered: "She was then. Why do you want her to be now too?" The hunter remembered that he had never seen the mermaid cry; he thought with a little shiver, "Do mermaids cry?"
>
> (*Animal Family* 51-52)

Yet in other ways the mermaid's pure momentariness is a revivifying force in the hunter's life. And she, in turn, comes to realize that she loves her new family in a different way: "if you died, if he died, my heart would break" (170).

The theme of the lost mother does recur in its full darkness at one point in the book, when the boy is found in the lifeboat and has to be disentangled from the body of his dead mother. There is a dreamlike slow-motion quality to the passage, in comparison to the rapid conciseness of most of the book. Though the boy reaches out at once to the transitional object ("Nice kitty!"), the lynx, himself frightened, has to run back to the house, wake up the bear, and go through the whole approach all over again, before the boy will go with them, first falling, then taking "two or three uncertain steps" (137). Ambiguities of perception give the whole episode a haunted, a nightmarish tinge. "Inside the boat something was crying" (132). "The boy looked very small and pale and the bear dark as a mountain, as they went slowly up the beach; the lynx, gray-silver and shining, flowed back and forth ahead of them like the tide" (137). We are momentarily back to the dangerously unsteady, shifting world—the toddler's wavering steps, the ambiguity of good and evil—that runs through the poems, from **"A Pilot from the Carrier"** to **"The House in the Wood."** But here, instead of the Witch, the lost child finds the good-enough parents, who have faced the problem of separateness, and cannot be destroyed by it. Things regain their stable, though playful, shapes. The book ends with the boy accepting, and loving, his "parents'" difference ("The difference between the hunter and the mermaid was no greater, to the boy, than the difference between his father's short hair and trousers, his mother's long hair and skirts, is to any child" [157]); and even coming to believe that there is nothing to mourn for, no lack in his own ontological status, because he has "lived with them always" (158).

And so there are two stories: one in which "what was before the world / And will be after" has "black / Breasts," and one in which the only answer to "Do you like your life?" is "Can you not like it?" (162) Both are, in a way, perennial truths about life; and both depend, in another way, on different resolutions to very early psychological conflicts. Which was truer, for Jarrell, is an unanswerable a question as exactly what led to the events of his last day. The point is that he had the largeness, as an artist, to tell them both.

I am conscious, here, of having said far too little about why Jarrell seems to me a great poet, the equal, in his way, of his more famous contemporaries, Robert Lowell and Elizabeth Bishop. But surely a good part of "greatness" lies in giving some crucial nexus of general feeling, hitherto less fully explored, words that seem definitive. What some call sentimentality, and others human truth, in Jarrell is his closeness to areas our culture is anxious about: the "unappeasable" yearning, pity, and self-pity that are permissible in women but forbidden in men after the age of five, except in the protected wilderness of Romantic Love. Jarrell's poetry adumbrates the history of forgotten infancy behind these emotions, and suggests some of the consequences for the human psyche, and the male psyche in particular, when that history stays unresolved: the dread of female powers, the horror both of helplessly merged states and of isolation. The feminist implications of this state of affairs are beyond the scope of this essay. They are explored brilliantly in the books I have alluded to by Benjamin and Dinnerstein. Reading these books has only increased my respect for how much Jarrell got, intuitively and as an artist, by refusing, even in the limited, ambivalent way he did, his time's definition of masculinity; by continuing, throughout his work, to interrogate the "inner woman" and her grieving child. I hope this way of thinking about him may also rearrange his canon a little, away from the poems that merely act out these issues—the more naive of the war poems, **"Next Day," "The Woman at the Washington Zoo"**—and toward the ones that do, in a subtle, textured, troubled, at once richly metaphorical and reflective way, "interrogate" them, over a lifetime. These would include, besides the ones discussed in detail here, **"The Night Before the Night Before Christmas," "The Lost World," "The Bronze David of Donatello."** These poems make up, for me, one of the larger and more compelling of all those "one stories" American poetry has told.

Notes

1. All quotations follow the text of *The Complete Poems*.

2. Letter to Sister Bernetta Quinn, December 1951. Jarrell *Letters* 303.

3. Here I am, obviously, giving a mere gist of the arguments of some very complex thinkers. See Klein, Miller, and Benjamin (especially Chapter One, "The First Bond").

4. *Letters* 303.

5. On the "infinity" of infant despair, see Dinnerstein 165n.

6. See Benjamin 38-41 on Winnicott's concept of "destruction."

7. See especially Chapter 6, "Sometimes You Wonder if They're Human."

Works Cited

Dinnerstein, Dorothy. *The Mermaid and the Minotaur*. New York: Harper, 1976.

Benjamin, Jessica. *The Bonds of Love*. New York: Pantheon, 1988.

Jarrell, Randall. *The Animal Family*. New York: Knopf, 1965.

———. *The Complete Poems*. Boston: Faber, 1981.

———. *Letters*. Ed. Mary Jarrell. Boston: Houghton, 1985.

Klein, Melanie. *Envy and Gratitude and Other Works 1946-1963*. New York: Free Press, 1984.

Miller, Alice. *The Drama of the Gifted Child*. New York, Basic: 1981.

Pritchard, William H. *Randall Jarrell: A Literary Life*. New York: Farrar, 1990.

Winnicott, D. W. *The Maturation Processes and the Facilitating Environment*. New York: International Universities, 1965.

James Longenbach (essay date summer 1996)

SOURCE: Longenbach, James. "Randall Jarrell's Semifeminine Mind." *Southwest Review* 81, no. 3 (summer 1996): 368-86.

[*In the following essay, Longenbach examines the perceived "feminine" quality of Jarrell's verse.*]

As a boy, Randall Jarrell posed for the statue of Ganymede, loved by Zeus, adorning the replica of the Parthenon in Nashville's Centennial Park. Jarrell's adult friends were bemused by this anecdote, for it seemed almost too appropriate to their idea of Jarrell's sensibility: over and over again their memoirs return, more or less uncomfortably, to Jarrell's lack of manly virtues. Berryman remembered that Jarrell once had a hangover brought on by a poisoned canape: "He's the only poet that I've ever known in the universe who simply did not drink." Robert Watson (Jarrell's colleague at Greensboro) remembered that, in addition, Jarrell did not smoke, use profanity, or enjoy jokes about sex. To Robert Lowell, consequently, Jarrell never quite seemed one of the boys: "one felt, beside him, too corrupt and companionable."

Jarrell himself would not have denied these characterizations; teaching at Princeton, he complained openly about the "improper subjects" that marred conversations with his male colleagues. But Jarrell wasn't simply a prude. He took considerable delight in his transgressions of typically masculine behavior. Robert Fitzgerald remembered him as "one of the few men I have known who chortled. He really did. 'Baby doll!' he would cry, and his voice simply rose and broke in joy." These exclamations were spontaneous, but they weren't unselfconscious, at least after Jarrell had known Berryman, Lowell, and Fitzgerald for many years. A man who writes his publisher that he's coming into New York on the "choo-choo" is making practiced fun of professional solemnity. So is the newly bearded poet who says this to Robert Penn Warren, his old teacher: "When I look in the mirror it's just as if the fairies had stolen me away." There's not only something appropriate but something lovely in the fact that Jarrell's first encounter with high art was his posing for Ganymede.

But if Jarrell's friends were sometimes uncomfortable with this sensibility, his detractors were unsympathetic. The *New York Times* reviewer of **The Lost World** was downright mean, calling Jarrell's poems—among other things—corny, cute, folksy, infantile, pathetic, self-indulgent, sentimental, and tear-jerking. Jarrell was understandably upset by this notice (friends speculated that it contributed to the depression preceding his death) but he couldn't have been surprised, since these adjectives had been used for years to describe his poems (only not so many at once). Part of what Jarrell's male readers were complaining about was his repeated use of female speakers. And his female readers weren't fully convinced by these voices either: Elizabeth Bishop complained about "his understanding and sort-of-oversympathizing with the lot of women." As a more recent critic of both Jarrell's and Berryman's representations of female consciousness has said, "it is finally a narrow view of the feminine that he gives voice to."

Unlike Berryman, however, Jarrell was not so much interested in prescribing a voice for women as developing a socially respectable way of dramatizing his own divided sensibility. As a critic, Jarrell was certainly comfortable with the professional man's world of hardnosed reviewing (this may account, at least in part, for the common opinion that Jarrell's criticism is superior to his poetry). But the aggressive stance of his essays often seems defensive—a strategy that bolsters his ostensibly masculine credentials while allowing him to occupy a more marginalized position in his poems. Bishop once remarked to Lowell that Jarrell's women "seem to be like none I—or you—know," and she was right: the female speakers of Jarrell's poems are closer to a man who doesn't drink or participate in locker-room banter but who likes to read fairy tales and shout "Baby doll!"

But even if a compelling explanation of Jarrell's female personae could be mounted, the question of Jarrell's style (which also seemed feminine to many readers) would still remain. Close friends found Jarrell's poems formally wayward or—Allen Tate's word—limp. But just as Jarrell knew what he was doing when he cried "Peachy!" in the Princeton faculty club, he understood the implications of avoiding certain modernist tenets of good writing. As Langdon Hammer has suggested in an important reevaluation of Jarrell, the "manifest excesses" of his poetry are "evidence of his dissatisfaction with the boundaries within which he was obliged to work." Early in his career, Jarrell set out to write poems that would not always be well-read through the lens of Tate's version of modernism. The results were poems that to an eye trained to look for irony seemed sentimental—poems that to Allen Tate seemed feminine.

Jarrell was able to capitalize on this impression. "I like your poetry better than anybody's since the Frost-Stevens-Eliot-Moore generation," he told Elizabeth Bishop, "so I looked with awed wonder at some phrases feeling to me a little like some of my phrases, in your poems; I felt as if, so to speak, some of my wash-cloths were part of a Modigliani collage, or as if my cat had got into a Vuillard." Bishop was the contemporary poet to whom Jarrell felt closest. Despite her sense of the limitations of his female personae, Jarrell found not only his words but his life uncannily reflected her poems. And while Jarrell's own poems don't often resemble Bishop's, they do exemplify Bishop's stylistic ideal of "a mind thinking" rather than a finished thought. Jarrell associated that ideal, as Bishop did not, with certain notions of femininity. But unlike Bishop, whom Tate or Lowell never expected to write "like a man," Jarrell had to defend his stylistic choices. Just as a woman's voice allowed him to dramatize himself more openly, it also allowed him to publish poems that rubbed against the kind of modernism he learned from Tate, Ransom, and Warren. For Jarrell, the dramatization of a feminine sensibility became inseparable from the exploration of what might be possible in American poetry at the end of the line.

During his freshman year at Vanderbilt (1932-33), Jarrell was assigned to classes with both Ransom and Warren. Four years later, he and the slightly younger Lowell migrated to Kenyon College, continuing their studies with Ransom and Tate. Before he completed his M.A., Jarrell's poems appeared in the *American Review* (edited by Tate), the *Kenyon Review* (edited by Ransom), and the *Southern Review* (edited by Warren). But almost from the start Jarrell's teachers recognized that they had an uneasy disciple on their hands. "I like to talk shop, and aesthetics more or less is," said Jarrell of Ransom, "politics and freeing the slaves not much." Jarrell's politics kept him distant from Agrarian aesthetics as well. His early Marxism, fueled by Auden, gave him a more supple sense of poetry's historicity ("A poem, today, is both an aesthetic object and a commodity"), and his keen sense of the complexity of Tate's classicism allowed him to learn openly from his Romantic and Victorian predecessors: "the best modern criticism of poetry is extremely anti-romantic, and the change in theory covers up the lack of any essential change in practice."

While he questioned his teachers, Jarrell didn't want his opinions to eclipse theirs entirely. He never lost respect for the rigor of Tate's formalism. And he always insisted that Tate and Blackmur (as well as Kenneth Burke and Edmund Wilson) wrote the best criticism of his time. But Jarrell's loyalty was never confused with dogmatism. When Margaret Marshall asked him to take her place as literary editor of the *Nation,* Jarrell thought himself worthy of the job precisely because he wasn't associated with "any particular variety of literary opinion." Thinking of the *Kenyon* and *Southern* reviews, he explained that several of his friends were editors: "their dogmatic convictions and idiosyncrasies and general sectarian leanings hurt their work a lot."

Jarrell meant to criticize the editorial decisions of Ransom and Warren, but he might as well have been discussing Warren's poems—though not Ransom's, with which Jarrell did feel some affinity: "To expect Tate's and Warren's poems to be much influenced by Ransom's is like expecting two nightmares to be influenced by a daydream." Two nightmares: what bothered Jarrell most about Warren and Tate was their delight in violence and evil—a sensibility that Jarrell knew was deeply romantic, despite any gestures toward anti-romantic classicism. Tate's poems about the Second World War especially troubled Jarrell: "violence is to him, perhaps unconsciously, an intrinsic good," he told Lowell. His criticism of Warren's 1944 *Selected Poems* suggested the political dangers of this aesthetic position.

> [T]he only excuse you can find for doing nothing is to say that the world is essentially evil and incurable, that anything you did would only be a silly palliation to hide from yourself the final evil of existence; and so you believe in Original Sin, and dislike progress, science, and humanitarianism, and go in for religion and the Middle Ages, and so-on.

Ultimately, for Jarrell, this fascination with evil allowed Warren to avoid responsibility for the world's condition, however engaged with the social problems of the American South Warren's poems may have been.

Jarrell would sometimes be accused of maintaining too rosy an outlook on the modern world; but it was the dominance of Warren's sense of modernity's essential horror (present, Jarrell said, in the work of "thousands of others") that eventually made Jarrell's position seem sentimental. To save Jarrell from this fate, some of his admirers have tried to grant him the prestige sometimes associated with Lowell's or Berryman's public agonies, insisting that Jarrell's death was a suicide. Helen Vendler has more sensibly wondered if Jarrell became, after being separated from his beloved paternal grandparents, a chronically depressed child: "One could read the life . . . as a desperate one, heroic in its struggle against emptiness, as though a drowning man were to come up for air a hundred times rather than thrice." Like most people, Jarrell was not unacquainted with suffering; but his life-long effort to portray "difficult ordinary happiness" (a phrase he admired in Adrienne Rich's poetry) was fueled by his sense of the danger, so carefully avoided by Bishop, of idealizing human suffering.

Even when Jarrell was a student, he developed remarkably prescient terms to describe his distance from Tate's sensibility. In a 1939 letter he explained why he didn't feel any "abyss" of modern uncertainty opening up beneath him: "I think all in all I've got a poetic and semifeminine mind, I don't put any real faith in abstractions or systems; I never had any certainties, religious or metaphysical, to lose, so I don't feel their lack." Here Jarrell is relying, as Bishop would later point out, on a sexist idea of femininity (one that equates it with amorphous physicality and uncertainty), but he is freely offering to Tate the terms in which his own poems would be discussed for many years to come. The difference is that Tate would never use the word "feminine" in anything but a derogatory sense; Jarrell, in contrast, welcomes the appellation.

The Rage for the Lost Penny, Jarrell's first collection of poems, appeared in 1940 as part of a New Directions gathering of Five Young American Poets. When Tate offered the first of several uncomfortable criticisms of the "limpness" of the poems, Jarrell responded that the effect was intentional: "it's an occupational risk, a defect of quality. In other words, I'd rather seem limp and prosaic than false and rhetorical." **"A Story,"** which opens with these lines, was probably the object of Tate's censure.

> Even from the train the hill looked empty.
> When I unpacked I heard my mother say:
> "Remember to change your stockings every day—
> Socks, I mean." I went on walking past their

Buildings gloomy with no lights or boys
Into the country where the roads were lost.

This is the only poem from *The Rage for the Lost Penny* that Jarrell would include in his *Selected Poems* (half of **"For an Emigrant"** was also included, though heavily revised). And it is the only poem in which we can feel the presence of Jarrell's later fascination with the fragile state of childhood domesticity.

If **"A Story"** consequently seemed limp and prosaic, it was in contrast to far more rhetorical lines like these, from **"The Machine Gun."**

Our times lie in the welded hands,
Our fortune in the rubber face—
On the gunner's tripod, black with oil,
Spits and gapes the pythoness.

Some of Jarrell's earliest poems do veer closely to his teachers' apocalyptic sensibility (associated here, not coincidentally, with a threatening vision of femininity—the gaping pythoness): it was this side of the early Jarrell of which Tate approved. Even as late as 1985 Warren would say that some of Jarrell's best poems were written while Jarrell was still a student. But the attitude of those poems was learned behavior for Jarrell (his contemporaneous letters don't show it at all), and as soon as Jarrell found a way to express his own sensibility, his teachers were immediately dismayed. Reading Tate's or Warren's recollections of Jarrell, one feels that they saw him as they saw Hart Crane: the prodigiously talented young poet who never equalled his earliest successes, in part because of his suspicious sexuality.

The year after *The Rage for the Lost Penny* appeared, Edmund Wilson accepted a half dozen of Jarrell's poems for the *New Republic*: once again Tate expressed discomfort with some of their lines. The subsequently well-known **"90 North"** compares a childhood fantasy of discovering the North Pole with the adult realization of the meaninglessness of discovery. For the adult, there is nowhere to go but backwards; all steps are to the south. For the child, every night offers a new discovery.

In the child's bed
After the night's voyage, in that warm world
Where people work and suffer for the end
That crowns the pain—in that Cloud-Cuckoo-Land

I reached my North and it had meaning.

Tate wanted Jarrell to cut the first four of these lines, presumably because he once again found them limp and sentimental in contrast to the adult's confrontation with meaninglessness. The poem ends with lines much closer to Tate's sensibility ("Pain comes from the darkness / And we call it wisdom. It is pain"), but as William Pritchard has pointed out, **"90 North"** differs from Jarrell's earlier apocalyptic poems in that it "enacts its discovery of the world as pain within the poem, instead of laying it on from outside." Jarrell's childhood fantasy is essential to the process; he conceded to Tate that "the stanza may be bad" but assured him that "it's impossible just to remove it."

I doubt that Jarrell thought the stanza was bad, however, since its idealization of childhood once again foreshadows the preoccupations of his fully mature poems. But I suspect that Tate's continuing criticism helped to persuade Jarrell to cast his dramatizations of the "semi-feminine" mind in a different form: **"The Christmas Roses,"** published in the *New Republic* a few months after **"90 North,"** is the first poem Jarrell wrote in a woman's voice. Compared to other poems Jarrell wrote at the same time, there's nothing about the content of **"The Christmas Roses"** that particularly demands a female speaker; a dying woman speaks to her former lover from a hospital bed. But in **"The Christmas Roses"** Jarrell's idea of femininity is crucially different from his earlier vision of the gaping pythoness; it is much closer to his poems of childhood vulnerability. While Jarrell wrote poems about childhood from the very start of his career, his turn to female personae came somewhat later: it was a strategy that allowed Jarrell to present his own sensibility more fully. Mary Jarrell would call these poems "semi-self portraits." And she would remember that on at least one other occasion Jarrell wrote a poem in his own voice before changing it to a woman's: in **"The Face"** he simply replaced the word "handsome" with "beautiful" and added an epigraph from Strauss's *Rosenkavalier*, associating the poem with the Marschallin's lament over her aging face.

Jarrell must have suspected that Tate (or almost anyone else) wouldn't know how to read the overwrought final lines of **"The Christmas Roses."**

Come to me! Come to me! . . . How can I die without you?
Touch me and I won't die, I'll look at you
And I won't die, I'll look at you, I'll look at you.

These lines came to Jarrell naturally (like his cries of "Baby doll!"), but he was canny as well as sincere, aware that he "was writing in an age in which the most natural feeling of tenderness, happiness, or sorrow was likely to be called sentimental." Jarrell made this comment apropos of Ransom, who, he went on to say, "needed a self-protective rhetoric as the most brutal or violent of poets did not." Jarrell's **"Christmas Roses"** needed protection as well. He told the more violent Tate that the poem "is supposed to be said (like a speech from a play) with expression, emotion, and long pauses. It of course needs a girl to do it. I can do it pretty well for myself, to anybody else I get embarrassed." This explanation of **"The Christmas Roses"** is especially revealing of Jarrell's general predicament: given that he found his own sensibility "semifeminine" in contrast to Tate's glorification of the abyss, all of Jarrell's poems needed, as it were, a girl to do them. And since Jarrell was embarrassed by the sound of his own girlish voice, he enlisted female personae to speak for him. It was around the time he wrote **"The Christmas Roses"** that Jarrell also wrote his own epitaph in **"To Be Dead,"** a poem that remained unpublished until after his death: "'Woman,' men say of him, and women, 'Man.'"

It was also at this time that Jarrell was drafting **"The End of the Line,"** his declaration of independence from the antiromantic modernism he had absorbed at Vanderbilt and Kenyon. The contiguity of these efforts suggests that Jarrell was trying self-consciously to write poems that wouldn't reflect Agrarian values—poems that were at least in this limited sense "postmodern." For a brief time Auden offered an important example to Jarrell, but by 1946 Lowell seemed to Jarrell the legitimately postmodern poet (he first used the word "postmodernist" to describe Lowell's early poetry). And while Jarrell did try to write like Auden, he was not influenced by *Lord Weary's Castle,* even as he helped to canonize it as the decade's most important book of poems. Much modern poetry seemed to Jarrell primarily negative in impulse: it "rejects a great deal, accepts a little, and is embarrassed by that little." Writing poems like **"The Christmas Roses,"** Jarrell wanted to risk even more embarrassment by including a wider range of human emotion. Lowell wasn't embarrassed enough, and Jarrell helped to make his friend's poems more encompassing, more forgiving.

Corresponding about the manuscript of *Lord Weary's Castle,* the agnostic Jarrell found Lowell's explanations of Christianity "humane and sympathetic" but was dismayed that there was "almost no indication of this attractive Christian attitude" in the fire-breathing poems. Lowell's early poems too often seemed to Jarrell (to borrow the phrase he used to criticize his own work) "false and rhetorical" in their savoring of evil and damnation. Jarrell consequently helped Lowell to change the ending of "After the Surprising Conversions" from this—

> The multitude, once unconcerned with doubt,
> Once neither callous, curious, nor devout,
> Starts at broad noon, as though some peddler whined
> At it in its familiar twang: "My friend,
> Come, come, my generous friend, cut your throat.
>   Now;
> 'Tis a good opportunity. Now! Now!"

—to this, the version which Lowell would publish in *Lord Weary's Castle*:

> The multitude, once unconcerned with doubt,
> Once neither callous, curious nor devout,
> Jumped at broad noon, as though some peddler
>   groaned
> At it in its familiar twang, "My friend,
> Cut your own throat. Cut your own throat. Now!
>   Now!"
> September twenty-second, Sir, the bough
> Cracks with the unpicked apples, and at dawn
> The small-mouth bass breaks water, gorged with
>   spawn.

As Bruce Michaelson has shown, all that Jarrell did to provoke this revision (much like Pound, editing *The Waste Land*) was to criticize the diction, rhythm, and metrics of the earlier version. But his motive was to soften Lowell's tendency to emulate his teachers' delight in violence; having altered the earlier lines, casting the speech in past tense, Lowell realized that the poem could end with an image of natural continuity rather than apocalyptic horror. Its last three lines comprise one of the earliest manifestations of what Seamus Heaney has called Lowell's "less assertive voice," the voice that would distinguish many of the poems of *For the Union Dead*.

An even more revealing response to Lowell came in **"The End of the Rainbow,"** first published in 1954 and later included in ***The Woman at the Washington Zoo***. *Lord Weary's Castle* ends with "Where the Rainbow Ends," Lowell's apocalyptic vision of Puritan Boston: "I saw the sky descending, black and white, / Not blue, on Boston." Jarrell's much longer poem traces the thoughts of a female painter (named "Content") who has moved from Massachusetts to Southern California. She hasn't been able to abandon her heritage completely; among her possessions are pieces of Pilgrim Rock, a copy of Emerson's *Compensation,* and a miniature of her great-great-great-grandfather, "pressed to death in Salem / For a wizard." Content is aging, lonely, and obsessed with the ghosts of her past. Like Lowell, she almost sees the sky descending, "black and white":

> She looks around her:
> Many waves are breaking on many shores,
> The wind turns over, absently,
> The leaves of a hundred thousand trees.
> How many colors, squeezed from how many tubes
> In patient iteration, have made up the world
> She draws closer, like a patchwork quilt,
> To warm her, all the warm, long, summer day!
> The local colors fade:
> She hangs here on the verge of seeing
> In black and white,
> And turns with an accustomed gesture
> To the easel, saying:
> "Without my paintings I would be—
> why, whatever would I be?"

This turn from potential nightmare to the saving processes of daily life is quintessential Jarrell: not paintings, not even the act of painting, but the act of turning to the easel saves her, and the gesture is so much a part of her daily life that she can't imagine her existence without it. Her realization is almost empty of meaning ("whatever would I be?"), but it is crucial to the continuity of her life.

The realization also underwrites the poem's structure. **"The End of the Rainbow"** is typical of Jarrell's mature work in that it follows the turns and digressions of meditation, avoiding a clear sense of an ending or even of accumulated significance. And though the meditation is a woman's, Jarrell invites us to see **"The End of the Rainbow"** as a record of his own thoughts.

> If you look at a picture the wrong way
> You see yourself instead.
> —The wrong way?

Content looks at the glass covering her painting and sees herself in her own work. This is not the "wrong" way to view the painting or to read the poem: Jarrell suggests that he may similarly be found in what he has made. **"The End of the Rainbow"** focuses on a woman because Jarrell associated its healthy acquiescence with femininity, just as he associated Lowell's apocalypticism with masculinity. Explaining what troubled him about the heroine of "The Mills of the Kavanaughs," Jarrell said, "You feel, 'Yes, Robert Lowell would act like this if he were a girl'; but whoever saw a girl like Robert Lowell?"

At the same time that he was reading *Lord Weary's Castle,* Jarrell saw himself in the poems of a particular woman. In this passage from his review of Elizabeth Bishop's *North & South* (which appeared shortly before the review of *Lord Weary's Castle*), Jarrell seems to be describing the ideals of his own poems—as he does not even when writing admiringly of Lowell or Williams.

> Instead of crying, with justice, "This is a world in which no one can get along," Miss Bishop's poems show that it is barely but perfectly possible—has been, that is, for her. Her work is unusually personal and honest in its wit, perception, and sensitivity—and in its restrictions too; all her poems have written underneath, I have seen it. She is morally so attractive, in poems like "The Fish" or "Roosters," because she understands so well that the wickedness and confusion of the age can explain and extenuate other people's wickedness and confusion, but not, for you, your own; that morality, for the individual, is usually a small, personal, statistical, but heartbreaking or heart-warming affair of omissions and commissions the greatest of which will seem infinitesimal, ludicrously beneath notice, to those who govern, rationalize, and deplore.

For Jarrell, Bishop's poems offered a powerful corrective to the idealization of violence he found in Warren, Tate, Lowell, and "thousands of others." "It is odd how pleasant and sympathetic her poems are," he continued, "in these days when many a poet had rather walk down children like Mr. Hyde than weep over them like Swinburne, and when many a poem is gruesome occupational therapy for a poet who stays legally innocuous by means of it." In his own poems, Jarrell preferred to weep, even if he gave readers like Tate the chance of finding his poems sentimental. Bishop herself never weeps, but she never rails against the world's evil, exempting herself from responsibility to that world—keeping herself "legally innocuous."

The other words Jarrell uses to praise Bishop's work (sympathetic, personal, honest, sensitive, moral, heartbreaking) describe qualities Jarrell courted in his own. "Your poems seem really about real life," he told Bishop with calculated naivete, "and to have as much of what's nice and beautiful and loving about the world as the world lets them have." Jarrell used these grand terms (life, beautiful, loving) intentionally; they allowed him to describe the mysterious ways in which the formal qualities of Bishop's poems, in contrast to Moore's, made them seem like a part of human life, rather than an artistic record of it: "I've quite got to like your poems better than Marianne Moore's as much as I do like hers—but life beats art, so to speak, and sense beats eccentricity, and the way things really are beats the most beautiful unreal visions, half-truths, one can fix up by leaving out and indulging oneself." Jarrell admired exactly what Bishop tried hardest to capture in her poems: the process of thinking, rather than the completed thought—a formal structure that eschewed the contours of the well-wrought urn for a more wayward and self-questioning kind of poetry. With poems like **"The End of the Rainbow"** Jarrell would capture this ideal himself.

It would not be exactly right to say that Bishop was a crucial influence on Jarrell's poems; by the late forties his sensibility was fully formed. But as his letters to Bishop suggest, Jarrell felt that his mind was uncannily similar to hers: "It's a feeling I never have with anybody else," he told her, ". . . It's as if you were a color I see so easily I hardly have to look." Bishop's work provided him with a compelling example of his own aesthetic goals (one that he could write about more gracefully than he could write about himself), and in his review of *North & South* Jarrell easily enlists Bishop in his effort to undermine his teachers' values. In this regard, Bishop was especially useful to Jarrell because her poems did not overthrow those values completely. During the 1940s and 50s Jarrell would write appreciations of poets (Williams and Whitman most prominently) whose sensibility was far more capacious than Bishop's. Just as he never tried to write like Lowell, however, he never tried to write like Williams either. Poems like **"A Game at Salzburg," "A Girl in the Library,"** or **"The Night Before the Night Before**

Christmas" are loosened up in the way that Bishop's "bramble bushes" are; they retain an amount of formal clarity even as they trace the wayward action of a mind thinking.

Like Bishop's career, consequently, Jarrell's reveals a gradual development rather than a "breakthrough" to unprecedented formal or autobiographical openness. The early books offer suggestions of Jarrell's mature sensibility, and in *The Seven-League Crutches,* published in 1951, Jarrell perfected the formal strategies that would sustain his work until the end of his life. Reviewing the volume, Lowell praised **"A Game at Salzburg"** in terms that recall Bishop's way of talking about her own poems: it "has the broken, chanced motion of someone thinking out loud." Jarrell had taught in the Salzburg Seminar in American Civilization in the summer of 1948, and the poem is set in the Schloss Leopoldskron, where Jarrell lived. The setting provides the only link between the three "games" the poem describes. First, Jarrell plays a game of tennis with a German man. Next, he meets a three-year-old girl who initiates a game well known to German children: she says to Jarrell, "Hier bin i'" [Here I am], and Jarrell, aware of the rules, replies "Da bist du" [There you are]. Throughout these two games, arbitrary and pleasant in themselves, there are hints of some darker significance. The tennis partner had been a prisoner of war in Colorado; and while Jarrell sits on the veranda with the little girl, "a darkness falls, / Rain falls." The poem's third game takes place when the storm has passed.

> But the sun comes out, and the sky
> Is for an instant the first rain-washed blue
> Of becoming: and my look falls
> Through falling leaves, through the statues'
> Broken, encircling arms
> To the lives of the withered grass,
> To the drops the sun drinks up like dew.
>
> In anguish, in expectant acceptance
> The world whispers: Hier bin i'.

"A Game at Salzburg" is a definitively post-war poem: Jarrell remains conscious of the Second War World but explores the odd ways in which the world absorbs its own destructiveness, moving forward. Though he wants to accept the loveliness of the world, there can be no answer to the world's "Here I am": his acceptance is fragile, hesitant, like the associative structure of the poem itself.

A month after he published *The Seven-League Crutches,* Jarrell wondered about the "monotonous violence and extremity" of "The Mills of the Kavanaughs," likening it to "a piece of music that consisted of nothing but climaxes." In contrast, Jarrell's **"Night before the Night before Christmas,"** the longest poem in *The Seven-League Crutches,* seems like a piece of music with no climaxes at all: it embodies a process of almost constant variation or metamorphosis. Like **"A Game at Salzburg"** though on a much larger scale, **"The Night before the Night before Christmas"** traces the thoughts of a "wandering mind." But its prosody is looser. And the poem is even more characteristically Jarrell's in that its protagonist is a fourteen-year-old girl. She is (like Jarrell himself) a child of the thirties, and her mind is full of Marx and Engels, John Strachey's *The Coming Struggle for Power,* and Bertold Brecht's "In Praise of Learning." Throughout the night, the girl's mind wanders between the "real" world these books describe and a dream world populated by her mother and pet squirrel, both of whom have recently died.

Even as she wraps Christmas presents, the girl cannot accept religious consolation ("how could this world be / If he's all-powerful, all-good?"), but she does believe that Marxist education might save her family. In her dreams, Engels becomes an angel; her squirrel might not have died, she muses, half asleep, "if he were educated." Ultimately, however, her dreams won't protect her from her own life, from "the abyss that is her home." In her final dream, she imagines that she and her brother (who is sick and may be dying as well) are Hansel and Gretel and then John and Wendy from *Peter Pan.*

> Staring, staring
> At the gray squirrel dead in the snow,
> She and her brother float up from the snow—
> The last crumbs of their tears
> Are caught by the birds that are falling
> To strew their leaves on the snow
> That is covering, that has covered
> The play-mound under the snow. . . .
> The leaves are the snow, the birds are the snow,
> The boy and girl in the leaves of their grave
> Are the wings of the bird of the snow.
> But her wings are mixed in her head with the Way
> That streams from their shoulders, stars like snow:
> They spread, at last, their great starry wings
> And her brother sings, "I am dying."
>
> "No: it's not so, not so—
> Not really," She thinks; but she says, "You are dying."
> He says, "I didn't know."
>
> And she cries: "I don't know, I don't know, I don't know!"
>
> They are flying.

These lines offer a condensed version of the poem's almost constant process of metamorphosis; their force is centripetal, pushing the poem in several disparate directions at once. Instead of saying "I am flying" as the children do in *Peter Pan,* the girl's brother says "I am dying." Her dreams had been her only refuge from her mother's death, but death has intruded even there. She makes room for it, however, imagining death as one of childhood's delightful adventures: the word "flying" initially allowed the word "dying" into the dream, but now the acts of flying and dying merge in a fantasy of omnipotence. Yet the dream ends, as it must, and the poem itself ends with these lines.

> She feels, in her hand, her brother's hand.
> She is crying.

Given his friends' earlier responses to his poems, Jarrell must have known he was courting all the usual objections to his "semifeminine" sensibility. Bishop's example had helped him to write **"The Night before the Night before Christmas,"** but Bishop herself was uncomfortable with the poem. She told Jarrell that she liked it, but she also wondered if it were loose, overly long, and possibly self-indulgent. Jarrell replied cheerfully that "Rilke certainly is monstrously self-indulgent a lot of the time." Years earlier, he had told Tate that limpness was an "occupational risk," and Jarrell responded similarly to Bishop's charge of self-indulgence. **"The Night before the Night before Christmas"** represents his most ambitious effort to write against the grain of certain prejudices his teachers distilled from their strategically limited reading of modernism. And if the poem resists any effort to read it closely; if it violates Poundian strictures against Victorian sentiment; if it fits comfortably neither with the poems of Williams nor the poems of Tate; if it even seems mannered or self-indulgent in its preoccupation with children and fairy tales, then the poem has succeeded in the terms Jarrell valued most. Lowell seemed to recognize this when he wrote that **"The Night before the Night before Christmas"** was the "best, most mannered, the most unforgettable, and the most irritating poem" in *The Seven-League Crutches.*

Like Lowell, Bishop did admire Jarrell's poems, whatever her misgivings; she seemed genuinely dismayed when her second book won the Pulitzer instead of Jarrell's *Selected Poems,* and she praised Jarrell for avoiding (as she did herself) the "anguish-school that Cal [Lowell] seems innocently to have inspired." But given Jarrell's consistent admiration for Bishop, it isn't simply ironic that Bishop was particularly troubled by *The Seven-League Crutches.* Writing about **"A Girl in the Library,"** another poem from this volume, Langdon Hammer wonders if Jarrell's decision to address the girl "begins to look like a way of preserving male authority by making it appear benevolent." This charge might be brought against others of Jarrell's poems: their desire to speak to, for, and about women could be a way of appropriating (and thereby delimiting) the terms of femininity. After Jarrell's death, Mary Jarrell recalled that **"The Lost Children"** (spoken by a woman) grew from her account of one of her own dreams; the most famous lines in the poem ("I know those children. I know all about them. / Where are they?") were actually written by Jarrell's wife. What may initially seem like an act of appropriation and mastery on Jarrell's part is something more complicated, however, since Mary Jarrell recognized that her words echo lines that Jarrell himself had already written in **"Thinking of the Lost World."** To her, **"The Lost Children"** was as much about Jarrell's "happy-sad recollections of lost boyhood" as it was about "a woman's happy-sad remembrances of lost motherhood." Similarly, she felt that **"The Night before the Night before Christmas"** was the first of Jarrell's "lengthy semiautobiographical poems that culminated in the three-part *Lost World.*" There are some poems (Hammer is right to single out **"The Girl in the Library"**) in which Jarrell asserts male authority in the guise of sympathy for women; but other poems (like **"The Night before the Night"**) suggest that Jarrell sometimes occupied within our culture a legitimately and productively feminized position.

The importance of granting this possibility is suggested by the *New York Times* review of *The Lost World.* Dismissing most of the volume, Joseph Bennett wrote that there were four successful poems. Two of them (**"Woman"** and **"In Nature There Is Neither Right nor Left nor Wrong"**) are unique in The Lost World for their sexism: "Men are what they do, women are what they are," says the tough-talking female narrator of **"In Nature."** In contrast to these poems, **"The Lost World"** and **"Thinking of the Lost World"** are not spoken by women; nor do they concern women's experience. Having spent many years impersonating a woman, Jarrell seems to drop the mask, speaking openly of his love of childhood, fairy tales, and pets. Tellingly, Bennett found these poems to be infected by "an indulgent and sentimental Mama-ism." Jarrell had done something worse than pretend to be a woman: he had pretended to be himself.

Thematically, structurally, and prosodically, **"The Lost World"** and its pendant **"Thinking of the Lost World"** seem in retrospect to be the work Jarrell was always pushing toward. **"Thinking of the Lost World"** strikes a note that is not uncommon in Jarrell's poetry; in **"The End of the Rainbow"** or in **"The Lost Children"** there is a similar sense of emptiness transfigured into something palpable and dear. What is different about **"Thinking of the Lost World"** is that Jarrell openly associates these feelings not with women but with his own idiosyncratic sensibility. Judith Butler has argued that the act of female impersonation, even when it draws on unchallenging styles of femininity, "implicitly reveals the imitative structure of gender itself—as well as its contingency." **"Thinking of the Lost World"** may in this sense be the logical conclusion of Jarrell's life-long act of impersonation, since its effort of self-definition is no less dependent on masquerade—on the necessity of fabricating an identity, rather than taking it for granted.

At the end of **"Thinking of the Lost World,"** the bearded Jarrell drives past a boy who calls out "Hi, Santa Claus." Jarrell waves, willing to play along, but newly aware that he's now as old as his grandparents once were. He looks at his hand on the steering wheel, and the hand becomes his grandmother's, brown and spotted: "Where's my own hand?" To answer this question, Jarrell confronts a vision of himself as a child. He knows that the child has nothing to give him. But as in Stevens (and looking back to *King Lear*), "nothing" becomes a powerful presence. As Jarrell drives inexorably forward, into the future, nostalgia is revealed as a fool's game—a game of pretense and disguise that Jarrell plays lovingly, over and over again.

> I seem to see
> A shape in tennis shoes and khaki riding-pants
> Standing there empty-handed; I reach out to it
> Empty-handed, my hand comes back empty,
> And yet my emptiness is traded for its emptiness,
> I have found that Lost World in the Lost and Found
>
> Columns whose gray illegible advertisements
> My soul has memorized world after world:
> LOST—NOTHING. STRAYED FROM NOWHERE.
>   NO REWARD.
> I hold in my own hands, in happiness,
> Nothing: the nothing for which there's no reward.

Stephen Burt (essay date 2002)

SOURCE: Burt, Stephen. "Jarrell's Interpersonal Style." In *Randall Jarrell and His Age,* pp. 21-51. New York: Columbia University Press, 2002.

[*In the following essay, Burt contends that Jarrell's style derives from the "alienations" he delineates in his poems by "linking emotional events within one person's psyche to speech acts that might take place between persons."*]

Randall Jarrell's best-known poems are poems about the Second World War, poems about bookish children and childhood, and poems, such as **"Next Day,"** in the voices of aging women. **"Next Day"** begins in a supermarket, where its lonely shopper puns on brand names:

> Moving from Cheer to Joy, from Joy to All,
> I take a box
> And add it to my wild rice, my Cornish game hens.
> The slacked or shorted, basketed, identical
> Food-gathering flocks
> Are selves I overlook. Wisdom, said William James
>
> Is learning what to overlook. And I am wise
> If that is wisdom.
>
> (*CP* [*The Complete Poems*] 279)

If the henlike shoppers amount to "selves [she] overlook[s]," she too feels overlooked, and wishes "That the boy putting groceries in my car / See me. It bewilders me he doesn't see me." Feeling less than present to herself, she sees her face in the mirror as alien:

> Its plain, lined look
> Of gray discovery
> Repeats to me: "You're old." That's all, I'm old.
>
> And yet I'm afraid, as I was at the funeral
> I went to yesterday.
> My friend's cold made-up face, granite among its
>   flowers,
> Her undressed, operated-on, dressed body
> Were my face and body.
> As I think of her I hear her telling me
>
> How young I seem; I *am* exceptional;
> I think of all I have.
> But really no one is exceptional,
> No one has anything, I'm anybody,
> I stand beside my grave,
> Confused with my life, that is commonplace and solitary.
>
> (*CP* 280)

Several readers have found the poem representative.[1] Like many of Jarrell's protagonists—among them the **"Woman at the Washington Zoo"** in her "dull, null" uniform, the depressed child of **"The Elementary Scene,"** and the dead American airmen of **"Losses"**—the woman in **"Next Day"** seems confined by circumstance and fate to a deeply troubling typicality. This is the plot many of Jarrell's poems suggest, the story his characters suffer: no one else confirms their unique selfhood, and so they are given occasions to doubt it.

Everyone who reads **"Next Day"** acquires some idea of the sort of person who speaks and how she feels. It takes longer to see how Jarrell's stanzas contribute to our sense of her frustrations—to see in the poem Jarrell's verse style. Jarrell rhymes "exceptional" with "exceptional," the word with a later instance of itself; the buildup of other repeated words ("wisdom," "wish," "afraid," "body") suggests the woman's doubts that such words, for her, retain useful meanings. The rhyming of stressed with unstressed syllables helps produce the self-muffling, self-baffling tone she adopts. And the spaces and pauses the stanza form leaves (as if for replies) help make the poem as affecting as it is.[2]

Jarrell's stylistic particularities have been hard for critics to hear and describe, both because the poems call readers' attention instead to their characters and because Jarrell's particular powers emerge so often from mimesis of speech.[3] Jarrell's style responds to the alienations it delineates by incorporating or troping speech and conversation, linking emotional events within one person's psyche to speech acts that might take place between persons. This chapter will emphasize those interpersonal elements, which, taken together, create Jarrell's style. I begin by describing an early poem in which Jarrell seems to discover the interpersonal as a goal for his poems. I then show how that goal emerged from Jarrell's readings of modernism, of literary history, and of Wordsworth. These readings, in turn, let us see how his verse style works and what its elements achieve.

Randall Jarrell began to create his style in poems he finished between 1939 and 1942; the best-known among them is **"90 North."**[4] It is a poem of announcement, discovery, and self-dedication, analogous to other self-dedicatory poems (Keats's "On First Looking into Chapman's Homer," Heaney's "Digging") in which an extraliterary discovery stands for a poet's commitment to his work. The dreamer-explorer says he has reached a goal: "I sailed all night—till at last . . . I stood at the northern pole" (*CP* 113). Yet the dream quest, remembered from childhood, seems futile to the adult dreamer who completes it:

> The world—my world spins on this final point
> Of cold and wretchedness; all lines, all winds
>
> End in this whirlpool I at last discover.
> And it is meaningless.
>
> (*CP* 113)

The isolated, adult, his explorations "meaningless," seems to have discovered (to borrow Geoffrey Hartman's words about Wordsworth) "that to heighten consciousness [is] to intensify rather than assuage the sense of isolation" (*Wordsworth's* xvii). Like Wordsworth at Simplon Pass (*Prelude* [1805] 6: 580-585), Jarrell's dreamer expected sublimity, and wisdom, from a summit, but learns instead that he must go back down:

> There in the childish night my companions lay frozen,
> The stiff furs knocked at my starveling throat,
> And I gave my great sigh: the flakes came huddling,
> Were they really my end? In the darkness I turned to my rest.
>
> —Here, the flag snaps in the glare and silence
> Of the unbroken ice. I stand here,
> The dogs bark, my beard is black, and I stare
> At the North Pole . . .
>
> And now what? Why, go back.

The "huddling" flakes, and the dogs, are plural and alive; only the poet's "I" and his flagpole stand alone. The poem, in fact, pivots on the word "alone"—the only word that ends two lines, and those lines one after the other, as if the poem had then to retrace its steps:

> Here at the actual pole of my existence,
> Where all that I have done is meaningless,
> Where I die or live by accident alone—
>
> Where, living or dying, I am still alone;
> Here where North, the night, the berg of death

> Crowd me out of the ignorant darkness,
> I see at last that all the knowledge
>
> I wrung from the darkness—that the darkness flung me—
> Is worthless as ignorance; nothing comes from nothing,
> The darkness from the darkness. Pain comes from the darkness
> And we call it wisdom. It is pain.

Alan Williamson has written that Jarrell's poems tell a "story of our loneliness in the world" ("Märchen" 283). **"90 North"** may be said to propose—along with Jarrell's vocation—a dilemma central to that vocation: loneliness, in various guises, constitutes the problem, and the "pain," that the poems wish to remedy.

Jarrell's best critics have often overstated the poems' senses of futility by ignoring the ways in which his style contains and answers them.[5] Jerome Mazzaro has called Jarrell's corpus of poetry "a succession of efforts . . . to get rid of the 'aloneness' which he felt" (*CE* [*Critical Essays on Randall Jarrell*] 99). These efforts generate the fictions of speaking and listening with which he created his style. Even as it describes isolation, **"90 North"** thus imagines a listener. The poem flaunts devices that imply speech and response—deictics ("There," "Here"), rhetorical questions ("Were they really my end?"; "Now what? *Why* . . ."), self-corrections ("The world—my world"), and repetitions. These evocations of listeners became essential components of Jarrell's practice.

Jarrell developed that practice by attending at once to his own emotions and to literary history. **"90 North"** sets limits to unaided imagination. But its discovered terminus, where "all lines, and winds / End," also tropes a more specific limit—the end, not of wishes or poetry but of modernist poetry, what Jarrell in 1942 dubbed **"The End of the Line."** "Modernist poetry," he wrote, "appears to be and is generally considered to be a violent break with romanticism; it is actually . . . an end product in which most of the tendencies of romanticism have been carried to their limits" (***KA*** [*Kipling, Auden and Co.*] 77). "Poets can go back and repeat the ride," Jarrell continued, or "settle . . . along the railroad"; nevertheless "Modernism As We Knew It . . . is dead" (***KA*** 81). William Pritchard writes that "'**90 North**' is exactly the poem to illustrate the 'fairly solitary individuality' [Jarrell] predicted for the poet of the early 1940s, at the end of the line, just where the man in the poem finds himself" ([*Randall Jarrell*] 81). But **"90 North"** reflects the postmodernist poet's dilemma in more specific ways. The polar explorer who turns back to the real world points the way, not only for modern poetry to rejoin other poetry but also for modern poetry to face, and hence to rejoin, other people, whose speech can be heard and shared.[6]

Modernism can be distinguished *from* romanticism, in Jarrell's view, by its greater "specialization": the modernist poet is much less like nonpoets, modernist poetic language much farther from nonexpert speech and prose, than Romantics and their language were.[7] The early poem **"Esthetic Theories: Art as Expression"** mocks poems, like medical specimens, "preserved in jars, and certified / By experts" (*CP* 384). Jarrell wrote in 1950 that he intended his poems "for the audience that reads poetry from age to age, I believe, and not for the more specialized audience that reads modern poetry" (*KA* 170). Reviewing **Poetry and the Age,** Delmore Schwartz found that its essays "express the anguish of one who does not feel superior, but lonely; and the dismay of one who does not want to be cut off from other human beings by his love of literature" (*CE* 43). Against the "expert" or "specialist" models he deplored (models that chapter 2 will revisit), Jarrell's work attempts to reduce the distance between poets and the rest of the world.

The explicitly political poems of the thirties and forties sometimes see politics in the same terms in which other poems and letters see literary history and private life. How can Jarrell bring himself closer to the subjects and victims of politics? An unpublished poem, "The Patient Leading the Patient," asks what Jarrell can do for "The poor with their bad manners and bad bones . . . whom I do nothing for / Unless pity is something; and it is something, / Isn't it?" (Berg Collection). Alluding to Christ's "The poor ye have always with ye" (Matthew 26:11), **"The Soldier Walks Under the Trees of the University"** attacks the gaps in understanding between academia and the war effort, academia and the American poor, academia, and everything "real":

> The poor are always—somewhere, but not here;
> We learn of them where they and Guilt subsist
> With Death and Evil: in books, in books, in books.
> Ah, sweet to contemplate the causes, not the things!
>
> The soul learns fortitude in libraries,
> Enduring patience in another's pain,
> And pity for the lives we do not change:
> All that the world would be, if it were real.
>
> (*CP* 401)

Jarrell's early Marxism (recalled in the later poem **"The Tower"**) looks here like a desire for solidarity with the world outside literature, the contemporary world below the tower and its libraries.

Modernist specialization, modernist remove, were hardly Jarrell's discovery: he inherited (from Edmund Wilson, among others) the idea that poets after Pound and Eliot would have to reconnect themselves to the outside world. Auden's late-thirties work took on just these problems—one reason Jarrell followed it so intently and with such mixed feelings. By 1941 he had reached a judgment on it he was never to retract: "Auden has been successful," Jarrell wrote, "in making his poetry more accessible; but the success has been entirely too expensive. Realizing that the best poetry of the twenties was too inaccessible, we can will our poetry into accessibility—but how much poetry will be left when we finish?" (***Third*** [***The Third Book of Criticism***] 149).

Jarrell shared Auden's early Marxist sympathies, as his thirties and forties essays attest; he even wrote an admiring poem about Friedrich Engels (Berg Collection).[8] But the kind of poetry Jarrell developed did not find its answer to modernist isolation by turning (as Wilson recommended in *Axel's Castle,* as Auden had in poems such as "Spain") from the level of the solitary individual to the level of a whole society. Jarrell's mature poems would describe, and try to alleviate, the isolation of the modern poet, not by addressing a whole society but by recognizing other people one by one—seeking, with and for them, as notes for a 1958 essay put it, a "quiet private place where something can ripen"—whether or not such a place could be had (UNC-Greensboro).

This difference between the level of society (which Jarrell's lonely characters largely reject) and the level of the interpersonal (which Jarrell and his characters seek) might be understood in terms of the differing goods the philosopher Paul Ricoeur names "equality" and "solicitude."[9] For Ricoeur "*Equality . . . is to life in institutions what solicitude is to interpersonal relations.* Solicitude provides to the self another who is a face, in [Levinas's sense]. Equality provides to the self another who is an *each*" ([*Oneself as Another*] 202; italics Ricoeur's). The front pages of the *Nation* pursued "equality"; the poems and book reviews Jarrell published in the back of the same magazine pursued "solicitude" instead. Jarrell's literary-historical problem about modernism, his ethical problem about solidarity, and his more personal problem about loneliness, thus steered him toward the same goal: he would write poems that describe and alleviate isolation, imagining "other people" and their speech.

Jarrell found models for such poems in Wordsworth. From the early forties to the sixties, his prose constantly invokes Wordsworth as a standard of value and as a counterweight to current practice. **"The End of the Line"** mentions many poets but quotes only Wordsworth: "the very world, which is the world / Of all of us—the place where, in the end, / We find our happiness or not at all" (*KA* 81). Jarrell wrote Harry Ford in January 1955: "I'm working hard on Wordsworth right now—I mean to do four or five long articles, designed from the beginning to be a book"; the same year Jarrell "spent a month reading nothing but Wordsworth . . . and like him much better than ever, even" (Berg Collection; *Letters* [*The Letters of Randall Jarrell*] 404).[10] Jarrell told the readers of the *New York Times Book Review* in 1955 that "when I recommend the second book of *The Excursion,* or speak of Wordsworth as one of the three or four greatest of English poets, I don't mind having the remark thought either a truism or an absurdity" (*KA* 220). Three years later he treated the audience at the National Book Awards to quotations from the preface to *Lyrical Ballads,* from Book 7 of the *Prelude,* and from Wordsworth's sonnet to Toussaint L'Ouverture (**"About Popular Culture"** 9-10).

It took originality for a reader trained on New Critical practices to see Wordsworth as a usable model.[11] Robert Penn Warren wrote in *American Review* in 1934, "I had rather read [Archibald] MacLeish's *Poems, 1924-1933* than Wordsworth's *Prelude;* and I am prepared to accept whatever damnation that involves" ("Twelve Poets" 218). (The same issue contained Jarrell's first published poems.) Warren (and Brooks and Ransom and Tate) are the critics Jarrell described in 1941, who "have repudiated romanticism so wholeheartedly that they condemn in their criticism the vices that they exploit in their poetry" (*KA* 62). Jarrell's 1941 letter to Louise Bogan declares by contrast his own allegiances: "I was simply charmed by something you said (in *Partisan Review* I think) about the feel of early romanticism at its best; I feel so, too" (*Letters* 45).

What did Jarrell learn from Wordsworth? Occasionally his poems echo Wordsworth directly.[12] More often he invoked Wordsworth's example as oblique authorization for his own projects. Jarrell's poems take seriously Wordsworth's famous prescription of 1802: "the Poet must descend from [his] supposed height; and, in order to excite rational sympathy, he must express himself as other men express themselves" (261). Jarrell's **"The One Who Was Different"** exclaims (in lines Elizabeth Bishop admired), "I feel like the first men who read Wordsworth. / It's so simple I can't understand it" (*CP* 316). "When critics first read Wordsworth's poetry," Jarrell reminds us in **"The Obscurity of the Poet,"** "they felt that it was silly"—though many "*said,* with Byron," that it didn't make sense (*Age* [*Poetry and the Age*] 8; italics Jarrell's). The disarming flatness, the patches of very simple (and unironic) diction that have made Jarrell's critics so uncomfortable—these, too, seem learned from Wordsworth. Reviewing Jarrell's *Selected Poems* in 1956, James Dickey imagined a debate between two fictive readers, A and B:

> B . . . the poems are the most untalentedly sentimental, self-indulgent and insensitive writings I can remember; when I read them I cry and laugh helplessly all night, over the reputation that has come out of such stuff.
>
> A. I would say, in answer, that you have missed the entire point of Jarrell's contribution, which is that of writing about real things, rather than playing games with words. . . . His world is *the* World, and People, and not the cultivated island of books, theories, and schools.
>
> (*RJ* [*Randall Jarrell 1914-1965*] 34-35)

Dickey later sided with his "A" character, concluding that **"Next Day"** (for example) "is convincing as speech before it is convincing—or even felt—as 'Art'" (*Reader* [*The James Dickey Reader*] 299).

Jarrell took from Wordsworth the idea that poems had to be "convincing as speech" before they were anything else; to be, for him, "convincing as speech," the poem ordinarily had to imagine a listener. Barbara Schapiro has described Wordsworth's "continual reference to a personal other . . . in his most deeply introspective poems": as William turns to Dorothy in "Tintern Abbey" and to Coleridge throughout the *Prelude,* Jarrell and his personae also invoke projected listeners ([*Literature and the Relational Self*] 31-32). **"The Bad Music"** asks: "Of those millions, how many know or love at all / You, Anna?" (*CP* 368) **"The Player Piano"**—written over twenty years later—pivots on imperatives, asking its audience twice to "Look" and once to "Listen" (*CP* 354-355). Both Jarrell and Wordsworth quote other speakers in their poems, and both like to quote children—the children in **"The Truth"** and **"Protocols,"** numbed and half conscious of death, look like answers to the child of "We Are Seven," who knows nothing of it. Both Jarrell and Wordsworth can turn in mid-poem from one auditor to another; both can treat poems as occasions to resituate oneself in time, to contrast a remembered event with a present occasion.

All these poetic tactics cohere as one overarching project, a project inaugurated in **"90 North."** David Bromwich has shown how Wordsworthian vocation reappears in Frost and in Stevens stripped of the encounters with other people that Wordsworth requires. What Bromwich finds in Wordsworth's "Resolution and Independence" (but not in its modernist rewritings) is a quality he calls "sympathy," though (he writes), "Sympathy may be a misleading word for what I mean: 'acknowledgement' or 'recognition' might be better. But [sympathy's] very etymology includes what is central to my argument: a feeling that touches some second figure, and that could not come into being without it" (*Choice* [*A Choice of Inheritance*] 230-231).[13] Sometimes Jarrell's second person is an imagined listener or reader. Sometimes it is a character who is lost, or dead, or beyond hearing. And sometimes the second person appears and responds in the scene of the poem, an occurrence that corresponds to a "happy ending." It is such a turn to the intersubjective—to the quest for "acknowledgement" or "recognition"—that binds Jarrell's work most deeply to Wordsworth's poetry.

Jarrell's Wordsworthian turn towards the interpersonal created his characteristic verse style. Many readers see discontinuities between the war poems and later poems such as **"Next Day."** The first often feature an omniscient or impersonal narrator; the second tend to be spoken by characters. These differences make it easy to miss the persistence of Jarrell's goals: both the war poems and the later poems seek to establish a nexus of recognition between reader and speaker, speaker and listener, actor and observer.

The poet of the war poems seeks or wishes—often fruitlessly, as he realizes—to individualize soldiers and pilots who risk becoming mute, interchangeable objects. The convalescent serviceman in **"The Sick Nought"** disturbs Jarrell into heights of rhetoric because he seems not even to know his family:

> Do the wife and baby travelling to see
> Your grey pajamas and sick worried face
> Remind you of something, soldier? I remember
> You convalescing washing plates, or mopping
> The endless corridors your shoes had scuffed;
> And in the crowded rooms you rubbed your cheek
> Against your wife's thin elbow like a pony.
> But you are something there are millions of.
> How can I care about you much, or pick you out
> From all the others other people loved
> And sent away to die for them? You are a ticket
> Someone bought and lost on, a stray animal:
> You have lost even the right to be condemned.
>
> (*CP* 174)

As Paul Fussell suggests, this soldier's worn-down bewilderment gives Jarrell an especially vivid example of the facelessness the war poems, in general, fear. The ability to recognize other individuals, and to be recognized by them, seems to Jarrell a (even *the*) test of personhood; to be anonymous is not to have lived.[14]

The soldiers and airmen who are granted some measure of consciousness in the war poems seek (and only occasionally find) a particular, dead or departed or vulnerable individual amid the alienations of the war. The lost flier in **"A Front"** asks, *"Can't you hear me?"* before his plane crash-lands (*CP* 13; italics Jarrell's). **"A Pilot from the Carrier,"** falling slowly in his parachute (and perhaps to death by fire) recapitulates the trajectory of the explorer-poet in **"90 North"**: "He is alone; and hangs in knowledge / Slight, separate, estranged: a lonely eye / Reading a child's first scrawl" (*CP* 153). Another poem about a pilot, **"The Dead Wingman,"** deserves more attention than it has received. Its protagonist circles, in dreams, the space where his wingman died:

> Seen on the sea, no sign; no sign, no sign
> In the black firs and terraces of hills
> Ragged in mist. The cone narrows, snow
> Glares from the bleak walls of a crater. No.
> Again the houses jerk like paper, turn,

> And the surf streams by; a port of toys
> Is starred with its fires and faces; but no sign.
>
> In the level light, over the fiery shores,
> The plane circles stubbornly: the eyes distending
> With hatred and misery and longing, stare
> Over the blackening ocean for a corpse.
> The fires are guttering; the dials fall,
> A long dry shudder climbs along his spine,
> His fingers tremble; but his hard unchanging stare
> Moves unacceptingly: *I have a friend.*
>
> The fires are grey; no star, no sign
> Winks from the breathing darkness of the carrier
> Where the pilot circles for his wingman; where,
> Gliding about the cities' shells, a stubborn eye
> Among the ashen nations, achingly
> Tracing the circles of that worn, unchanging *No*—
> The lives' long war, lost war—the pilot sleeps.
>
> (*CP* 157)

Shifts in caesura placement and line length graph the feel of a moving airplane: lines seem to yaw, bank, turn. Jarrell's speaker seems at once a pilot bereaved of his companion and a poet looking for readers, sadly confined to his unstable aerial view. The horribly distant houses look like paper—it would be better to live in them than to see them from afar. By the same token, it would be better to see the faces as faces than as toys, but Jarrell's weary pilot can see no one face-to-face: no one answers or looks back.

Jarrell liked to define literature (following Freud's definition of a dream) as "a wish modified by a truth."[15] The description gains special force in **"The Dead Wingman,"** where the poem's false or avoided endings represent the pilot's wish ("I have a friend") and the actual end of the poem the truth (*SH* [*A Sad Heart at the Supermarket*] 140-141). Key words grow multivalent through repetition: the poem describes a *stare* in search of a *sign* that turns out to be a recurring *no*. The poem begins as a rescue mission, gives us to understand that the mission has failed, and ends as a dream of that mission: when the pilot's dream ends, the poem does too. The words "sign" and "no" and the rhyme on "stare" all return: nothing *will* change, no listener, no audience, no friend can ever be found.

Suzanne Ferguson has described **"The Dead Wingman"** as a poem of unrelieved fatalism: its final "no," she writes, "expands from the simple negation of the individual's search for his 'little friend' to [a] universal negation" (*Poetry* [*The Poetry of Randall Jarrell*] 96). Its attitudes become more complex, and more generous, once the pilot's actions are seen as models for reading and writing. Over the length of the poem the aerial remove of the poet-pilot-dreamer, the distance of the land, the inaccessibility of the missing partner, remain insistently "unaccepted," a hypothesis persisted in despite contrary evidence. The pilot and his chronicler end the poem without renouncing their desire to close the distance, to find the one person they mean to hear or see—they trace the circles of their ache even in sleep and give up only when exhausted. Jarrell's poem, circling its *no,* thus imagines a bereaved pilot to whom Jarrell offers his own poem in partial consolation, even solidarity: **"The Dead Wingman"** aches and strives, and sounds as if it aches and strives, to be a speech to and for its pilot, to become itself the sign of recognition he can't see.

Seen this way, the pilot of **"The Dead Wingman"** can look very much like the woman of **"Next Day,"** who also mourns her best, or only, "friend." Both poems seem to allegorize models of poetic reading like Allen Grossman's, in which poems model intersubjective relations. For Grossman, poems make their readers fictively intimate with persons who (by the end of the poem) have said to us all they can ever say: "the poem," he writes, "is, therefore, the dead friend" ([*The Sighted Singer*] 319).¹⁶ Like **"The Dead Wingman," "Next Day"** tries to pick out its nameless speaker and to alleviate her loneliness by individuating her to us, making for her a responsive poem (even a stanza form) of her own. And the graveside scene near the end of **"Next Day,"** like the pilot's dream in **"The Dead Wingman,"** gives us a model of "care" (as Grossman would put it) in that now-solitary speaker's memory, a model to which she wishes to return. As Jarrell offers his third-person poem to the pilot who mourns **"The Dead Wingman,"** the woman of poems such as **"Next Day"** offers her speech to us: in both, a reader may recognize the speaker and thus take the place of the absent friend.

"The Dead Wingman" and **"Next Day"** show how the wartime Jarrell and the author of his last poems shared stylistic devices and deeper goals. We have seen how those goals arose: the rest of this chapter will show how his style enacts them. Jarrell's 1948 letter to William Carlos Williams describes some of his favorite formal devices:

> the regular way I write now—forms I use, that is—is that in **"Lady Bates," "Moving,"** and the new poem [**"The Night Before the Night Before Christmas"**] I'm sending with this letter. I find that by having irregular line lengths, a good deal of irregularity of scansion, and lots of rhyming, not just perfect regular rhymes, musical forms, repetitions, "paragraphing," speech-like effects, and so on, you can make a long poem seem a lot shorter and liver. But of course you know this better than I do.
>
> (*Letters* 191)

These are all "speech-like effects," nor does Jarrell confine them to long poems: they are essential elements in his sometimes hopeful, sometimes desperate simulations of speaking and listening.

Though many nineteenth- and twentieth-century poets may be said to trope speech, Jarrell's speechlikeness far exceeds the norms of his era. Jarrell's meters (as Stephen Spender noticed) tend to evoke, but also to violate, accentual-syllabic pentameter norms in the name of varying kinds of speech.¹⁷ Karl Shapiro had those metrics in mind when he wrote that Jarrell "advanced beyond Frost in using . . . the actual rhythms of our speech" (*RJ* 215). Jarrell told Allen Tate that his 1940 poem **"The Christmas Roses"** "is supposed to be *said* (like a speech from a play) with expression, emotion and long pauses" (*Letters* 26).¹⁸ Its speaker's desperate garrulity belies her loneliness; the terminal patient speaks to her absent friend (or romantic partner), whose absence has made her feel unreal (and made her want to die):

> Why don't you write to me? . . . The day nurse sits
>   and holds
> The glass for me, but yesterday I cried
> I looked so white. I looked like paper.
> Whiter. I dreamt about the pole and bears
> And I see snow and sheets and my two nurses and the
>   chart . . .
>
> (*CP* 392)

The images' logic overlaps with that of **"90 North"**: seeing oneself, and only oneself, in the mirror resembles a visit to the cold, deathly North Pole.

The poem—probably Jarrell's first with a female speaker—has become a locus for discussion of Jarrell and gender.¹⁹ If **"The Christmas Roses"** was the first of Jarrell's poems to link speechlikeness and the feminine, it was also the first one to show how thoroughly speechlikeness could demonstrate loneliness, how much poems that sounded like speech could represent a speaker's need for response. The end of the poem leaves the hospital settings behind entirely, becoming a protest and plea to the absent beloved: "Touch me and I won't die, I'll look at you / And I won't die, I'll look at you, I'll look at you" (*CP* 393). That closure amounts to a tonal gamble, a bawl: either we react almost as if to a real acquaintance dying or we dismiss her pleas as sentimental, as failures of art.

Jarrell's craft—so involved in troping speech—required that he risk such sentimentality.²⁰ These risks turn up, often, in his endings, which can rely on tone, inflection, and the force of a speech act almost to the exclusion of images. If the poems begin (like **"Next Day"**) in concrete situations, they are often situations from which the recognized speakers wish to escape. The poems can thus end on abstract adjectives ("commonplace," "solitary"), as in **"Next Day,"** or in bizarre, affecting, abstract illocution, as in **"The Venetian Blind,"** whose speaker finds that inside or around him "something calls, as it has called, / But where am *I*? But where am *I*?" (*CP* 55). Jarrell's revealing notes for a talk on his own poems show that he knew the risks his work was taking: "poetry," the notes assert, is a process of decades not a craft: craftsmanship useless except as accompaniment, concomitant, ancillary: craftsmanship, technique useful for everything except what is essential and the great and original poets technique, craftsmanship, often look to the first generations like clumsiness, lack of technique, bad craftsmanship: Whitman, Wordsworth, Hardy, so many more—

(UNC-Greensboro)

Early in his career Jarrell began a lengthy essay called **"Why Particulars Are So Much More Effective Than Generalities"** (Berg Collection). In choosing generalities for his endings so often, Jarrell knew what he was doing. And what he was doing was choosing intonation, persona, pace—all the aspects of poems that make them like speech—over consistent symbols, proportions, and descriptions—the aspects of poems that make them like craft objects.

In many of the war poems the awkwardness of real speech becomes the chief stylistic goal. The child who speaks **"The Truth"** (Jarrell's note tells us) "has had his father, his sister and his dog killed in one of the early fire-raids on London" (*CP* 11):

> I used to live in London till they burnt it.
> What was it like? It was just like here.
> No, that's the truth.
> My mother would come here, some, but she would cry.
> She said to Miss Elise, "He's not himself";
> She said, "Don't you love me any more at all?"
> *I* was *my*self.
> Finally she wouldn't come at all.
> She never said one thing my father said, or Sister.
> Sometimes she did,
> Sometimes she was the same, but that was when I dreamt it.
> I could tell I was dreaming, she was just the same.

(*CP* 195)

Comparison of these lines with their source (Anna Freud and Dorothy Burlingame's *War and Children*) will demonstrate how far they are from mere transcription.[21] What matters in them is not raw verisimilitude but the sense of speaking and listening—the interpersonal nexus wished or hoped into being—for which realism in speech serves Jarrell as a proxy. In this case that nexus joins the mother and the shell-shocked boy; she returns at the end, when "she put her arms around me and we cried." As with **"The Christmas Roses,"** the apparent artlessness of **"The Truth,"** Jarrell's elimination from it of most kinds of specifically poetic organization, makes the devices peculiar to *his* work—the interruptions, the repetitions, the open spaces—clearer.[22]

All these devices ask us to imagine a speaker's vocalized, demonstrated need for others. Charles Taylor writes that "the self's interpretations [of itself] can never be fully explicit" since those interpretations are "part of, internal to, or constitutive of the 'object' studied" ([*Sources of the Self*] 34). If Taylor is right, poetic language should approach inarticulacy as it tries harder to distinguish the self (or the inner self, or interiority) from its social surround. And this is exactly what happens in Jarrell, whose hesitations, evasions, ellipses, and stutters (all present in **"The Truth"**) enact the difficulty of making one's own interiority present to others. His rhetorical questions, and the spaces his poems leave for answers, contribute to the same project, since, as Taylor also writes, "One is a self only among other selves. . . . My self-definition is understood as an answer to the question Who I am. And this question finds its original sense in the interchange of speakers" (35).

Jarrell often incorporates "interchange of speakers" in subgenres of poetry (such as the meditative or scenic lyric) that normally exhibit only one speaker. When he observes people with nothing to say, their silence (as in **"The Sick Nought"**) becomes the poem's subject; happier figures in Jarrell's war poems find themselves amid some sort of verbal interchange. His most accomplished war poem along these lines must be the intricately awkward **"Transient Barracks,"** which describes a gunnery instructor's return to America. **"Transient Barracks"** sets itself to make several overheard speakers, and their overlapping phrases, contribute to the creation of one lyric subject. Here is the first half:

> Summer. Sunset. Someone is playing
> The ocarina in the latrine:
> You Are My Sunshine. A man shaving
> Sees—past the day-room, past the night K.p.'s
> Bent over a G.I. can of beets
> In the yard of the mess—the red and green
> Lights of a runway full of '24's.
> The first night flight goes over with a roar
> And disappears, a star, among mountains.
>
> The day-room radio, switched on next door,
> Says, "The thing about you is, you're *real*."
> The man sees his own face, black against lather,
> In the steamed, starred mirror: it is real.
> And the others—the boy in underwear
> Hunting for something in his barracks-bags
> With a money-belt around his middle—
> The voice from the doorway: "Where's the C.Q.?"
> "Who wants to know?" "He's gone to the movies."
> "Tell him Red wants him to sign his clearance."
> These are. Are what? Are.

(*CP* 147)

With their quick scene-setting, their self-deprecating narrator and their reliance on the soldiers they quote, the lines mimic the chitchat we might overhear in an actual barracks. They owe much to the war reporter Ernie Pyle, whose columns about ordinary soldiers Jarrell admired unreservedly.[23] For Pyle, he wrote, the speaking soldiers' "scraps—jobs, families and states . . . are a bridge pushed back shakily to their real lives;

and [Pyle] understands and puts down what they tell him, always; and the foolish think it a silly habit of his" (*KA* 116).

As in the dispatches, so in the poem, the soldiers and flyers' lives, their continued being, matter more than any point an observer-author could make *about* them. It is in this populated, talky, milieu that the shaving soldier knows and claims himself as a speaking subject. The poem began when he looked at his face and can end when (answering somebody else's question) he realizes that he is "home for good" . . . (*CP* 148).

The instructor feels "real" and knows he is "back for good" when he can join in the conversation, answering a direct question: "This is my field." Repeated words at line endings (*field, real*), with their chiming long *e*, frame the key lines, almost all of them reported speech. Jarrell's ending thus makes a particular structural principle out of what for Grossman is a general rule: Grossman writes, "The achievement of that state of sociability in which interhuman acknowledgement is adequate to human need extinguishes lyric by putting an end to the trouble which gives rise to lyric" (277). This interhuman acknowledgement becomes the effect produced by Jarrell's closing phrases. The sick woman of **"The Christmas Roses"** dreamt of being listened to, of being heard: the conversation of the Stateside dayroom confirms the flyer's new safety, which seems to him a dream come true.

"For the confirmation of my identity," Hannah Arendt wrote in *The Origins of Totalitarianism,* "I depend entirely upon other people; and it is the great saving grace of companionship for solitary men that it makes them 'whole' again" (476).[24] The shaving man in **"Transient Barracks"** recognizes himself in the mirror because he is surrounded by companions who can speak to him. More usually, people in Jarrell's poems, like the patient of **"The Christmas Roses,"** try but fail to recognize themselves in mirrors, attempt to claim their faces as theirs.[25] Mary remembers Randall as playfully obsessed with mirrors: "He had favorite and unfavorite mirrors but I believe he looked into all he ever saw" (*Remembering* [*Remembering Randall*] 136). The fourteen-year-old girl in **"The Night Before the Night Before Christmas"** "looks at herself in the mirror / And thinks; 'Do I really look like *that*?' . . . 'What do I *really* look like? / I don't know" (*CP* 42). The woman in **"Next Day"** is "afraid, this morning, of my face," which "Repeats to me, 'You're old.'" Christopher Benfey has looked at Jarrell's poems and seen "a man seeing himself as a woman in the mirror"; for him, Jarrell's "mirror poems . . . mak[e] male narcissism and male identity relatively self-contained and self-justifying, while condemning women to exhibitionism, dependent on the gaze of others" (["The Woman in the Mirror"] 123, 128). If to be "feminine" in Jarrell's time and place meant depending on others to confirm one's own identity, then almost everyone in Jarrell's poems seems "feminine": not only the lonely woman of **"Next Day"** but also the soldier in **"Transient Barracks," "The Lonely Man"** in the poem of the same name, and the bearded Jarrell of **"Thinking of the Lost World"**:

> I hear a boy call, now that my beard's gray:
> "Santa Claus! Hi, Santa Claus!" It *is* miraculous
> To have the children call you Santa Claus.
> I wave back. When my hand drops to the wheel,
> It is brown and spotted, and its nails are ridged
> Like Mama's. Where's my own hand? My smooth
> White bitten-fingernailed one?
>
> (*CP* 338)

Jarrell is not really Santa Claus, nor is he the boy he remembers being. But he is glad when the boys call him "Santa Claus"—glad but also disturbed, since (like the boy in **"The Truth"**) he doesn't seem to others to be himself. As in **"Transient Barracks,"** the seed of the "miraculous" lies in others' speech. Encounters with mirrors, attempts to establish visual identity, end in anxiety; aural interchange has better results. And the poems' many exclamations and rhetorical questions—exclamations such as "Hi, Santa Claus!" or "The States!"; questions such as "Where's my own hand?"—thus become the simplest and most consistent of the many devices with which Jarrell imagines speech as interchange, testing or confirming the presence of somebody else.[26]

Fictions of imagined or real companions, of listeners answering and being answered, console Jarrell and his characters whenever anything can. These fictions of shared space, response, interchange extend outside Jarrell's own poems into their relations with other texts. When Mark Jarman writes that "Jarrell's characters seem to speak in quotations," he means not that they quote one another—though they do—but that they quote or allude to books they have read (["John and Randall, Randall and John"] 573). Thus the squirrels in **"The Night Before the Night Before Christmas"** "have nothing to lose but their lives" because the girl in the poem has read the Communist Manifesto, and the snow-loaded boughs near the end of the poem seem to read "*To End Hopefully / Is a Better Thing—/ A Far, Far Better Thing*" because the girl, falling asleep, conflates Sydney Carton's words with a motto from her father's office (*CP* 50). The woman in **"Next Day"** takes refuge in William James; the hermitlike painter of **"The End of the Rainbow,"** living alone on a California beach, quotes Goethe and Beddoes to her dog and rehearses, to herself,

> Proverbs of the night
> With the night's inconsequence, or consequence,
> Sufficient unto the night . . . *Every maid her own*

> *Merman*—and she has left lonely forever,
> Lonely forever, the kings of the marsh.
>
> (*CP* 221)

These chains of quotations and allusions might remind us of the chains of speakers in poems such as **"Transient Barracks"**—they trope them, in a sense.[27] Quotations connect Jarrell's stranded characters to a world more populous and more hospitable than one beach cottage or apartment or bedroom. In the logic of Jarrell's quotations, the more we can use or reuse others' words, the more we feel our world is theirs too, and the less lonely we become.

Jarrell's exchanges and quotations interact with his frequent forms of aposiopesis—trailing off, interruption, and self-interruption. All create moments and instances where (as Pritchard puts it) "words fail him, or just about"; these moments "implicitly ask . . . to be understood by the sympathetic reader as proof of true feeling" (198). These devices, too, evoke the intersubjective—the play between one speaker and the possibility of another. Jarrell's broken-off lines can imply that a conversation should have taken place but cannot: they indicate—sometimes quite literally—distress calls. The climactic speech act in **"A Front,"** a flier's "Over—," goes unanswered. His controllers "beg, order, are not heard; and hear the darker / Voice rising: *Can't you hear me? Over. Over*—/ All the air quivers, and the east sky glows" (*CP* 173). **"A Perfectly Free Association"** also ends on a distress call: its air traffic controller

> hears, from the homing fighter,
> The fairly scared, the fairly gay
> Voice saying, *Mayday! Mayday!*
> Then there is a position, static,
> And the voice ends on *May*—
>
> (*CP* 452)

Jarrell closes other poems with similar calls for assistance. More often, though (as in **"The Dead Wingman"**), he ends poems by following broken-off utterance with a brief closural gesture—mentioning, for instance, sleep or death. Evoking (in Barbara Herrnstein Smith's term) "nonliterary experiences" of closure, such devices allow the poems to end while leaving their problems of human communication unsolved ([*Poetic Closure*] 121).

If (as Grossman claims) a whole or integral line of poetry represents a whole speaking subject, Jarrell's interdependent, incomplete speech acts, his broken-up sentences, and his cut-off or wavering pentameter-based lines represent interdependent, relational selves. So often afraid they are "commonplace" and "solitary," the people in his poems are no more whole nor self-sufficient than their utterances: they say things such as "That I—That I—But anything will do," or "These are valued at—some value I forget, / Which I learned from—I cannot remember the source" (*CP* 306). These phrases make no sense, convey no information, until we have learned to hear the characters behind them. The characters, in turn, elicit our sympathy by trying and failing to say things: an unsympathetic character in Jarrell's novel "seemed very human and attractive" when, for once, "he lost his way in his sentence" (49-50).

The discipline known as sociolinguistics has devoted much attention to forms and devices of conversation, among them interruption, repetition, and incompletion. These devices often signal a change of speaker; they also distinguish conversation from recitation and scripted performance. As the sociolinguist Robin Lakoff explains,

> ordinary conversation makes much use of devices that signal, "I'm making this up as I go along": repetitions, corrections, hesitations, and "fillers" that play for time to compose one's thoughts. In part, these are literally necessary because speakers are constructing their talk as they go along; but they also figuratively signal, "This talk is spontaneous: you can trust me."
>
> ([*Talking Power*] 43)

These "conversational" features are those Jarrell's poems flaunt and depend on. The style of such "private discourse," Lakoff continues, implies

> at least the conventional expectation of parity among participants—if not social real-world equality at least equality of linguistic opportunity . . . a discourse type that is reciprocal is likely to be spontaneous, and one that is public, to be formal as well. . . . Power goes along with formality, non-spontaneity and nonreciprocity.
>
> (44)

Jarrell's talky, stuttery style could therefore mark his verse as informal and distant from public power.

It could also mark his verse as feminine. The same devices that mark speech as conversational, spontaneous, or shared can also mark particular speakers as women. Lakoff lists habits observers take to characterize women's spoken English as against men's: most of the features in her list also characterize Jarrell's poetry as against the work of his peers. One such habit is the use of "adjectives . . . expressing emotional not intellectual evaluation" (such as *lovely*)"; another involves "Forms that convey impreciseness: *so, such*," "hedges of all kinds" (204). Jarrell's poetry make copious use of these features: he writes, in one late poem, "It's so—/ So *agreeable*," and in another, "I saw that he resembled—/ That he *was*—/ I didn't see it" (*CP* 305, 287). Lakoff also describes "Intonation patterns that resemble questions, indicating uncertainty or need for approval" as stereotypically feminine; Pamela Fishman's empirical studies have in fact found that "women use tags and declarative questions much more often than men" (["Conversational Insecurity"] 204, 254). Jarrell uses these patterns at key points in his poems: "Don't signs, don't roads know any more than boys?"; "If things could happen so, and you not know / What you could do, why, what is there you could do?" (*CP* 132, 262). Other examples of feminine speech patterns include *being* interrupted (examples of which multiply above) and being indirect.[28]

All these "linguistic traits," Lakoff explains, "are directly connected not with their speakers' actual lack of power, but with their feelings about the possession of power. Women's language becomes a symbolic expression of distance from power, or lack of interest in power" (207). Jarrell took advantage of these associations, and his contemporaries noticed. Karl Shapiro's prose poem to Jarrell contrasts his "prose sentences—like Bernini graves, staggeringly expensive, Italianate, warm, sentences once-and-for-all" with "the verses you leave half-finished in mid-air—I once knew a woman who never finished a sentence" (*Bourgeois* [*The Bourgeois Poet*] 91). Shapiro seems to have mapped the difference between Jarrell's prose and verse onto purported masculine and feminine "sides"; later critics divided his work up in similar ways.[29]

If men tend to interrupt, and women to be interrupted, it is no wonder the poet who wrote of himself, "'Woman,' men said of him, and women, 'Man'" should tend to interrupt himself (*CP* 471).[30] At the same time Jarrell's linguistic habits—from his subjective adjectives to his abstract endings—emphasize "rapport" (in Lakoff's terms) over "facts," acknowledgement of persons over the sharing of information. (The final lines in both stanzas of **"Transient Barracks,"** for example, provide no concrete details, no "brute facts," at all: nor do the closing phrases of **"90 North."**) The apparent femininity of Jarrell's style (which led him to redraft a few poems by making their speakers clearly women) appears, at least in some poems, as a consequence of his concern to represent our need for the intersubjective. Langdon Hammer and James Longenbach have both shown how Jarrell's "semifeminine" tones and attitudes help him (in Hammer's phrase) "disengage literature from power" (*Letters* 19; "Who" ["Who Was Randall Jarrell?"] 392). His speech patterns and syntactical choices perform this separation in order to imagine selves and speakers who need one another—they imagine the interpersonal.

To evoke the interpersonal is in Jarrell's poems to fulfill a wish. The alienated modern man in **"Jamestown"** who asks a witch to "make me what I am" has been absorbed into the social and institutional, as against the interpersonal; he cannot assimilate difference, cannot change, and his imperviousness to enchantment reflects his lack of imagination (*CP* 257). But the man in the later **"A Man Meets a Woman in the Street"** who wishes to stay as he is describes an ideal condition, since he already has the intimacy he needs. His wish fulfillment is very literally a mutual recognition; at the end of the poem, the man's wife turns to see him catching up to her:

> A wish, come true, is life. I have my life.
> When you turn just slide your eyes across my eyes
> And show in a look flickering across your face
> As lightly as a leaf's shade, a bird's wing,
> That there is no one in the world quite like me,
> That if only . . . If only. . . .
>   That will be enough.
>   . . . . .
>
> Our first bewildered, transcending recognition
> Is pure acceptance. We can't tell our life
> From our wish. Really I began the day
> Not with a man's wish: "May this day be different,"
> But with the birds' wish: "May this day
> Be the same day, the day of my life."
>
>   (*CP*, 353)

The end of this poem (among the last Jarrell wrote) deploys all his stylistic devices in order to present a wish fulfilled—the wish for "recognition," which justifies a life and lets the poem end. The man's satisfaction consists in a series of equivalences: his wish is his life, his wife is the wife, his day the day, for which he had hoped. Jarrell's play among ordinary words establishes just those equivalences.

"Recognition" became in Jarrell's last poems his own word for what his characters seek. For the psychoanalytic thinker Jessica Benjamin, erotic love (as distinct from sexual desire) constitutes precisely an achievement of recognition, a fulfilled wish to be known and changed by another: "the desire for erotic union with another person who is endowed with the capacity to transform the self can be seen as the most intense version of the desire for recognition . . . the point is to contact and be contacted by the other—*apprehended as such*" (*Like* [*Like Subjects, Love Objects*] 184). Such a desire creates the whole form of a much shorter, earlier love poem. After Jarrell met Mary von Schrader in 1951, he wrote this poem, **"The Meteorite,"** for her:

> Star, that looked so long among the stones
> And picked from them, half iron and half dirt,
> One; and bent, and put it to its lips
> And breathed upon it till at last it burned
> Uncertainly among the stars its sisters—
> Breathe on me still, star, sister.
>
>   (*CP* 264)

The poem depends on the fiction it builds of a singular listener—her attentions, at first as unlikely and distant as starlight and then as close as the breath in a kiss, cue the whole speech. The poet-lover-stone called "One" rests solitary in the middle, until the female star and the noun "star" return in the last lines to elevate and embrace it.³¹ Stars in love poems normally keep their distance (Keats's "Bright Star," Auden's "The More Loving One"); this star comes close enough to heed a request. Like **"A Man Meets a Woman in the Street,"** **"The Meteorite"** imagines the relation between lovers as creating its own—in this case, extraterrestrial—shared space, a space as distinct as possible from the ordinary and alienating social world. Randall told Mary von Schrader, in a letter written soon after the poem's composition, "I'll be glad to move away from this society into Ours" (*Letters* 323). The experience of falling in love, of being loved, *meant* for Jarrell the creation of terms of intimate recognition, terms that set him (as they would set any lover) apart from the crowd, the larger "society," of stars or stones.

If the love poems embody recognition at its most joyful, its clearest instance has to be **"In Galleries."** The American museum guard at the start of this poem "has a right to despair"; in the sculpture he watches,

> The lines and hollows of the piece of stone
> Are human to people: their hearts go out to it.
> But the guard has no one to make him human—
> They walk through him as if he were a reflection.

(CP 298)

Nor does the guard see the visitors—he "stands / Blind, silent, among the people who go by / Indistinguishably," like the sad shopper in the supermarket or the soldier waiting in line. The Italian museum guard in the second verse-paragraph "speaks and smiles / And whether or not you understand Italian, / You understand he is human and still hopes": he evokes a minimal recognition (and gets a minimal tip). But the best kind of museum guard (also Italian) is piously enthusiastic. When he

> takes a magnifying glass
> From the shiny pocket of his uniform
> And shows you that in the painting of a woman
> Who holds in her arms the death of the world
> The something on the man's arm is the woman's
> Tear, you and the man and the woman and the guard
> Are dumbly one. You say *Bellissima!*
> *Bellissima!* and give him his own rapt,
> Dumb, human smile, convinced he guards
> A miracle. Leaving, you hand the man
> A quarter's worth of nickel and aluminum.

(CP 299)

The coins with which the American tips the guard are inadequate, as any recompense would be inadequate, to the experience of empathy the guard makes possible. He has, moreover, given the tourist that experience by showing him or her another depiction of empathy: a painted tear on a painted arm. "The visitor as well as the guard," Suzanne Ferguson writes, "must come alive to make the miracle happen" (*Poetry* 195). Jarrell highlights the pity involved in Christian religious awe in order to redescribe its virtues in human, secular terms. That guard's "gestures," the poem says, "are full of faith in—of faith"; but the painting (according to Mary Jarrell, a Verona *Pietá*—she does not say which one) inspires in Jarrell not an assent to religious faith but an experience of human community.³²

If **"In Galleries"** and **"A Man Meets a Woman"** demonstrate the recognitions the poems seek, **"Seele im Raum"** presents their more usual dilemma: a protagonist who can't be recognized or individuated by the other people she sees. Given pride of place in ***The Seven-League Crutches*** (1951), **"Seele im Raum"** describes a woman who for years had seen, or hallucinated, a friendly eland at her dinner table. The speaker's breakings- and trailings-off announce the reality of the eland, even if "they"—her family—cannot see it. The eland seems present inasmuch as it resists words:

> Many times
> When it breathed heavily (when it had tried
> A long useless time to speak) and reached to me
> So that I touched it—of a different size
> And order of being, like the live hard side
> Of a horse's neck when you pat the horse—
> And looked with its great melting tearless eyes
> Fringed with a few coarse wire-like lashes
> Into my eyes, and whispered to me
> So that my eyes turned backward in their sockets
> And they said nothing—
>   many times
> I have known, when they said nothing,
> That it did not exist. If they had heard
> They *could* not have been silent. And yet they heard . . .

(CP 37)

Jarrell's woman felt overlooked by her husband or children: the eland seemed to know her as they could not. (She learns later that "elend" in German means "wretched.") The eland comes into being in response to the state of mind Nancy Chodorow later named "lack of self, or emptiness. This happens especially when a person who has this feeling is with others who read the social and emotional setting differently but do not recognize this, nor recognize that the person herself is in a different world." Chodorow suggests, following the psychoanalyst Enid Balint, "that women are more likely to experience themselves this way. Women who feel empty of themselves feel that they are not being accorded a separate reality nor the agency to interpret the world their own way" (*Mothering* [*The Reproduction of Mothering*] 100).

It would be almost right to say (as other commentators have said) that the eland represents imagination, or the woman's "separate reality."³³ It would be truer to say that the eland is the companion, even the listener, the imagination creates so that it may be recognized: when the eland tried "a long useless time to speak" and "looked with its great melting tearless eyes . . . Into my eyes, and whispered to me," it acts out a desperate approximation of exchanges like the one at the end of **"In Galleries."** The woman suggests, and no one argues otherwise, that if the eland isn't real, isn't compatible with "real life," then real life may not be worth living. Later she asks, in lines rich with self-interruptions,

> Is my voice the voice
> Of that skin of being—of what owns, is owned
> In honor or dishonor, that is borne and bears—
> Or of that raw thing, the being inside it
> That has neither a wife, a husband, nor a child
> But goes at last as naked from this world
> As it was born into it—
>
> And the eland comes and grazes on its grave.
>
> (*CP* 39)

The "thing" that can be shown and remembered but not directly described is something like a soul; it is the part of her left over after she fulfills her social role. This soul or "thing" has summoned up (hallucinated, or created) the eland because souls require acknowledgement and do not get it: "And yet when it was, I *was*—[. . .] Yet how can I believe it?" As Hammer puts it, "The eland is the embodiment of her will to imagine another life, a full sensual life in which one's desire need not be postponed or dismissed as make-believe" ("Who" 405).

This desire can appear more specifically as a desire for interpersonal channels, a companionable remedy for her "lack of self." A husband who saw the eland would therefore see how wretched, *elend,* the woman has been. Part of **"Seele im Raum"** adapts Rilke's "The Unicorn," which Jarrell translated; Rilke's unicorn, like the housewife's eland, becomes real because human beings require its company:

> because they loved it
> One became an animal. They always left a space.
> And in the space they had hollowed for it, lightly
> It would lift its head, and hardly need
> To exist. They nourished it, not with grain
> But only, always, with the possibility
> It might be.
>
> (*CP* 482)

The eland, too, is summoned into being: it represents not the woman's soul but her soul mate, not the inner self but the companion whose presence makes innerness knowable. The eland becomes the occupant "of a different size / And order of being" who establishes the space ("raum") in which her soul ("seele") can know itself.[34]

And this is why we see the eland at dinner. In *Pictures from an Institution* a succession of dinner parties and household scenes offer models for good and bad kinds of sociability. One bad kind appears in the novelist Gertrude Johnson, who lacks empathetic imagination: Gertrude sees everyone, save her husband Sidney, as "material"—"she listened only As A Novelist" (131). Desperate for recognition and empathy, the woman of **"Seele im Raum"** imagines the eland as her friend and companion. Gertrude reverses **"Seele im Raum"** exactly, since she sees all her companions as elands: "'It's nice not to have to lie out at some water-hole with a flash-bulb,' I heard her say once, 'but just to be able to ask your eland home to dinner.' The listening elands laughed and swallowed" (35).

Like many of Jarrell's poems, **"Seele im Raum"** addresses interiority with the syntax proper to conversation: it depends on the tension it maintains between the diction and forms of conversation (dinner conversation, say) and the abstract, "higher" language traditionally associated with lyric poems (such as Rilke's "Unicorn"). That tension becomes another way to imagine Jarrell's intersubjective project. Often Jarrell's most lyrical passages ask whether the voices they project can ever be manifest in the real, shared world. Such questions drive several mysterious poems from the 1950s, among them **"The Orient Express"**:

> Outside me there were a few shapes
> Of chairs and tables, things from a primer;
> Outside the window
> There were the chairs and tables of the world . . .
> I saw that the world
> That had seemed to me the plain
> Gray mask of all that was strange
> Behind it—of all that *was*—was all.
>
> (*CP* 65)

Here, as in **"Seele im Raum,"** a desire to present plausible speakers, to create characters who seem like "other people" and show their need to relate—a desire we might call novelistic, or (following Bakhtin) dialogic—exists in tension with lyric's drive to present an inner being separate from social circumstance, an "I" both more specific and more universal than the social types and representatives of the novel. In the terms of **"The Orient Express,"** the novelistic presents the facts, the "gray mask" of the external world, the lyric the "some thing / Behind everything." And in the terms of **"Seele im Raum,"** the novelistic presents only "the skin of being"; pure lyric presents the "raw thing" within. It is when the two versions of persons—the novelistic and the lyric, the exterior and the interior—are given shared ground, shared words, that intersubjective recognitions can take place.

The tangled-up, self-interrupting syntax in **"Seele im Raum"** thus suggests that if the woman—if anyone—has a "naked" being, an interior or imagining self apart from her roles, that interior self has to be understood through hard-to-share speech. Once deprived of her eland, she can "be" only when explaining it to others: "Being is being old / And saying . . . 'To own an eland: that's what I call life!'" Like many repeated terms in Jarrell's poetry ("wish," for example, in **"Next Day"** and **"A Man Meets a Woman . . ."**), "being" becomes what William Empson called a Complex Word and makes a Statement in Words; it includes the noun "human being"; "being" as existence; "being" as the carrier of an adjective (being married, being tall, being American—having the qualities by which others know us); and "being inside" (having a psyche).[35] These versions of being prove hard to reconcile; their incompatibility requires lonely people to invent companions like elands—or like the readers implied by certain poems.

Jarrell has been praised for his mastery of the dramatic monologue, or of forms allied to it.[36] Robert Langbaum argues in a well-known study that dramatic monologue aims "to establish the speaker's existence, not his moral worth but his sheer existence" (*Experience* [*The Poetry of Experience*] 200). Herbert Tucker has shown how modern readers have learned to see all poems *as if they were* dramatic monologues: for Tucker (who disapproves of it) this modern practice satisfies our "thirst for inter-subjective confirmation of the self" (["Dramatic Monologue and the Overhearing of Lyric"] 242).[37] Jarrell's characters seek precisely what Tucker claims modern readers seek. And this is why Jarrell—who in some poems (such as **"A Conversation with the Devil"**) speaks explicitly as a modern author—can make characters in other poems epitomize frustrated modern readers. **"The Woman at the Washington Zoo"** brings this conjunction to its zenith. The woman is an ordinary, sublunary self, excluded from the demesnes of imagination (foreign countries, beast fables, science fiction), which taunt her with unapproachable proximity:

> The saris go by me from the embassies.
>
> Cloth from the moon. Cloth from another planet.
> They look back at the leopard like the leopard.
>
> (*CP* 215)

The Woman sees an exotic world, whose denizens—from leopards to diplomats' wives—seem individuated. But she does not and cannot belong to that world: it won't look at her or return her gaze. She expects to go

> To my bed, so to my grave, with no
> Complaints, no comment: neither from my chief,
> The Deputy Chief Assistant, nor his chief—
> Only I complain . . . this serviceable
> Body that no sunlight dyes, no hand suffuses . . .

Shakespeare's "dyer's hand," "almost subdued / To th'element it works in" is a well-known trope for artistic creation.[38] But when Jarrell reused the allusion in the 1960 essay **"A Sad Heart at the Supermarket,"** he was complaining that conformism, capitalism, consumer culture, subdue our individual natures: he wrote there that "mass culture's"

> values are business values: money, success, celebrity. If we are representative members of our society, [those] values are ours; and even if we are unrepresentative, non-conforming, our hands are—too often—subdued to the element they work in, and our unconscious expectations are all that we consciously reject.
>
> (*SH* 71)

This Washingtonian seems all too "representative," one of the "poor unknown failures" Jarrell's essay later invokes; Jarrell described her elsewhere as "a kind of aging machine part," "a distant relation" to the housewife in **"Seele im Raum"** (*SH* 71; *KA* 320). Both women (in D. W. Winnicott's words) have "become one of the many who do not feel that they exist in their own right as whole human beings" ([*Playing and Reality*] 29).

The woman at the zoo addresses a vulture, with perverse hope, as her "wild brother." Crying out to him, in quintessentially Jarrellian repetitions, "You know what I was, / You see what I am: change me, change me!," she seeks from the vulture-brother-fantasy-companion (as the readers in Jarrell's poems about libraries sought from books) an individuating recognition that both permits, and constitutes, being "changed" (*CP* 216).[39] The colorless woman at the zoo has been taken to complain of sexual loneliness.[40] But as much as she thrills at, and dreads, the sexuality of the vulture image, the Woman also seems here to be complaining that she has no part in imaginative creation. If the woman's invisibility is her problem, a change in who she is will either make possible, or constitute, the solution.

Several of Jarrell's other protagonists also cry out for "change"; the children in **"Children Selecting Books in a Library,"** for example, seek "CHANGE, dear to all things not to themselves endeared" (*CP* 107). These characters want at once to dispose of their familiar selves and to reveal those selves to someone else: for them being changed amounts to being recognized, and the problem the Woman faces is that each seems a prerequisite for the other. She has to be different in order to be noticed and has to be noticed to seem individuated, different. Jessica Benjamin equates the wish for psychic change with the wish for recognition and both with the wish for confirmation of selfhood: for her the self "is reciprocally constituted in relation to the other, dependent on the other's recognition, which it cannot have without being negated, acted on by the other, in a way that changes the self, making it nonidentical" (*Shadow* [*The Shadow of the Other*] 79). Finding no such recognition in life, the Woman at the Washington Zoo seeks it in fantasy, just as readers seek it in literature. *We* therefore recognize *her*; as readers of modern literature, we understand her dilemma as the animals and the diplomats cannot. And it may indicate the Woman's success as a model of reading that Jarrell wrote his own essay about this poem at the request of Cleanth Brooks and Robert Penn Warren, who printed it in the third edition of *Understanding Poetry*.

I have argued that Jarrell's style pivots on his sense of loneliness and on the intersubjectivity he sought as a response. Loneliness, the social psychologist Linda Wood argues, "is failed intersubjectivity"; as such, she continues, it is "paradoxically the most social" of imputed emotions (["Loneliness"] 188-190). To come from the explorer of **"90 North"** to the Woman at the Washington Zoo and the shopper of **"Next Day"** is to see how Jarrell's psychological interests prompt sociological ones. The people in poems such as **"The Woman at the Washington Zoo,"** or **"Next Day,"** or **"The Sick Nought"** risk and fear becoming mere social types: the (or any) new soldier, the (or any) housewife, the (or any) bored student, "anybody." Jarrell's drafts of **"Next Day"** include a prose sketch that summarizes the poem's concerns about personal distinction, bound up as they are with concerns about mortality:

> My friends talk as if I were an exception, and I've always been one, have seemed to myself so truly exceptional, but with age, being old, there are no exceptions, everyone has same commonplace typical representative ending, as if you'd been transformed into woman in street, Everywoman, makes complicated life simple, single, a lonely solitary passive process.
>
> (Berg Collection)

Is she "typical" just because she is aging? Will that process erase her "complicated life," which separates her from "anybody" else? Critics who find the woman unrealistic (because she reads William James) exhibit just the stereotyped reactions she fears, overlooking *her* and seeing only the social group to which she belongs.[41] Jarrell's fictive housewife, looked at askance for her reading, thus resembles the real "upper-middlebrow" housewife in William H. Whyte's *The Organization Man*, who surprised her neighbors by reading Plato and told Whyte, "Now all of them are sure I'm strange" (365).[42]

Just as the poems' speakers feel in danger of fading into indistinguishability, the classes they represent threaten to become the poems' topics, to make them unimaginable as individuals. **"Next Day"**—a representation of one lonely woman, distinguished from others by Jarrell's language—has looked to many readers like a poem about commodity culture, whose typical victim can buy Cheer and Joy but never cheer or joy.[43] The poem, as we have seen, depends on repeated words—"all," "wise," "wish," "see," "flesh," "imagining," "now," "change," "face," "old," "body," "exceptional."

If these words sketch the woman's problems, they also trope the identical commodities at the start of the poem. Lined up on "shelves," these are notionally various but fundamentally indistinguishable—just like the "selves" who buy them, in whose ranks the woman of **"Next Day"** fears she belongs. Jarrell elsewhere encouraged such a reading; he asked in the essay **"A Sad Heart at the Supermarket,"**

> Reader, isn't buying or fantasy-buying an important part of your and my emotional life? . . . It is a standard joke that when a woman is bored or sad she buys something to cheer herself up; but in this respect we are all women together, and can hear complacently the reminder of how feminine this consumer-world of ours has become.
>
> (*SH* 68)

"Next Day" is hardly the only poem whose story of loneliness, selfhood, and failed intersubjectivity also leads to a kind of social criticism. If Jarrell's focus on loneliness led him out toward other, "ordinary," people, his interest in social and cultural threats to individuality, and to its recognition, led him to portray those threats in his works. Jarrell depicts particulars of wartime life; makes poems out of changes in American reading, viewing, and listening habits; and notices changes in the built environment, education, and consumption (from the supermarket to the elementary classroom and the postal service). Later chapters will view more of those social and historical phenomena as they affected Jarrell's verse. The next chapter, however, will show how, and why, they inform his prose.

Notes

1. Sven Birkerts finds "Next Day" "as much as any poem can be, representative" ("Randall Jarrell" 86). Chris Wallace-Crabbe decides that "'Solitary' is an excellent word for ["Next Day"] to end on, for that is what Jarrell's poetry . . . is all about" (58).

2. For more commentary on "Next Day," see Birkerts, "Randall Jarrell" 83-89, Pritchard 301-302, Shapiro, *RJ* 206-210, and Travisano, *Mid-Century* 275-276.

3. Even some of Jarrell's studious defenders have claimed that his poems never found a style of their own: Suzanne Ferguson's 1972 study found his achievement instead in "characters and themes" (5).

4. Suzanne Ferguson calls "90 North" "Jarrell's first fully characteristic poem, and one of his best," while Jarrell's biographer William Pritchard dubs "90 North" the "strongest early intimation of Jarrell's distinctiveness as a poet" (*Poetry* 19: 81).

5. See, for example, Beck *Worlds* 31 ("His speakers . . . never . . . benefit from human interaction"); for other such views, see Kinzie, Mazzaro, and Vendler, "Inconsolable."

6. Jarrell is sometimes credited with having coined the term *postmodernist,* in a 1947 review of Robert Lowell. John Crowe Ransom used the adjective to describe Jarrell's own poems in 1941—according to Thomas Travisano, the first use of *postmodernist* with reference to literature; see Travisano's introduction to "Levels and Opposites" 695. For earlier uses of *postmodern,* see Longenbach 3.

7. For a later diagnosis of solitude as "part of the evolving self-image of modernism," see Bromwich, *Choice* 254-255.

8. The poem presents interesting problems for dating other poems, since on its verso are stanzas from "The Tower," which the *Complete Poems* dates to 1951 (the year it appeared in *Kenyon Review*); either Jarrell did not publish "The Tower" for several years after he wrote it, or he was interested in a tribute to Engels as late as 1950-51.

9. For Altieri's explanation of third-, second- and first-person commitments, see *Canons*: "When the 'I' turns to the singular 'you,' it seeks a relationships defined not by general rules but by specific conditions of adjustment and attunement. . . . The 'you' engages us concretely in what the 'he' or 'she' opens for us" (306).

10. None of the articles appeared; Charlotte Beck suggest that Jarrell never finished an essay on Wordsworth simply because no one had *commissioned* one (*Worlds* 11).

11. Longenbach claims plausibly that "when ['The End of the Line'] was published in the early forties, its argument was unheard of, except by devoted readers of Stevens" (10). David Perkins recalled in 1982 that as late at the 1950s "no powerful body of contemporary criticism . . . presented the romantics favorably" (561).

12. When Jarrell writes, in "A Front," of "bombers banging / Like lost trucks down the levels of the ice," he seems to be remembering the thunder in book 2 of *The Excursion,* "roaring sound, that ceases not to flow, / Like smoke, along the level of the blast" (*CP* 173; *Excursion* 2:699-703). When Jarrell writes, in "The Emancipators," "the apple shone / Like a seashell through your prism, voyager," he invokes Wordsworth's famous lines on a statue at Cambridge "Of Newton with his prism and silent face, / The marble index of a mind for ever / Voyaging through strange seas of Thought, alone" (*CP* 120; *Prelude* 1850 3:61-63). Helen Hagenbuchle finds links between Jarrell's early "The Skaters" and Wordsworth's ice-skating episode in the *Prelude* (104-106). For a detailed discussion of "The Emancipators" see Nemerov 193-197.

13. For more on Wordsworth, sympathy, and acknowledgement, see Bromwich, *Disowned,* esp. 23-25 and 88-91, and Cavell, "Knowing and Acknowledging."

14. Fussell explains that "try as [Jarrell] will to overcome the implications of [the war's] multitudinousness and . . . uniformity and consider this soldier as a unique person, he can't make it" (67). For more on wartime anonymity, see Fussell 59-63, 66-69, and chapter 6; see also my chapter 2.

15. For a longer, later excursus on this theme, along with its derivation from Freud, see "Stories" xii-xiii.

16. For Grossman on "hermeneutic friendship" and "care," see 284-287 and 368-371: "one [friend] seeks to keep the other in being" (370).

17. Spender noted the changes in meter from stanza to stanza in "The Island" in his review of *The Seven League Crutches* (182).

18. For more on "speech" and "The Christmas Roses," see Ferguson, *Poetry* 30, Longenbach 54-55, and Hammer "Who" 403-404.

19. See, for example, Longenbach 55 and Hammer 403.

20. Wallace-Crabbe, for example, diagnoses "Jarrell's indifference to *closure,* his unwillingness to assemble the well-made poem" (49).

21. On Jarrell's use of *War and Children,* see Flynn, *Lost* 46-47.

22. Dickey made "The Truth" a test case—one of his personae calls it "damned poor metrically," while the other exclaims, "if that doesn't move you, you ought to be boiled down for soap" (*RJ* 46).

23. Pritchard has noted the war poems' debt to Pyle: see 122-123. Wallace-Crabbe praises Jarrell's "other voices," Dickey his verisimilitude, both with specific reference to "Transient Barracks," whose "G.I. can of beets" gives Dickey part of his title (53; *Reader* 338-339). For other praise of "Transient Barracks," see Pritchard 124-127.

24. Bromwich comments on the same passage: see *Disowned* 22. For more on Arendt's often invoked distinction between solitude (a necessary condition for original thought) and loneliness (in which thought seems impossible), see *The Life of the Mind,* book 1, chapter 9, esp. 74-75. For more on Jarrell and Arendt, see chapter 2.

25. For other comments on mirrors in Jarrell, see Frances Ferguson, *CE* 170 and Quinn, *CE* 80; see also the discussion of "A Ghost, A Real Ghost" in chapter 4.

26. A considerable secondary literature concerns apostrophe and prosopopoeia (poetic address to an inanimate object), a device Jarrell rarely uses: see Kneale, esp. 141-146.

27. Alfred Kazin remembered that in person "Randall was as full of quotations as a Unitarian minister—they were his theology, too" (*RJ* 91). Keith Monroe has discussed "the submerged or unattributed quotation[s] and the altered cliché[s]" that animate Jarrell's criticism (*CE* 263-264).

28. Another sociolinguist, Jennifer Coates, records a widespread belief that "so" as an adverbial intensifies characterizes women's speech (20). Coates has also described the persistent, and sexist, belief "that women often produce half-finished sentences" (25).

29. Mary Kinzie explains that Jarrell "seemed to many [readers] to have split his imagination in two" (67). Vendler writes that Jarrell put "his passivity into his poetry, his ferocity into his criticism" ("Inconsolable" 36). See Longenbach, chapter 4 ("Randall Jarrell's Semi-Feminine Mind") for an extended, insightful discussion of this split.

30. For another discussion of this poem, "To Be Dead," see Longenbach 55.

31. For Mary's account of the genesis of "The Meteorite," see *Remembering* 9-11; for Randall's letter about the piece of obsidian that prompted it, see *Letters* 258; for the letter in which he enclosed the completed poem, see *Letters* 261-262.

32. Mary Jarrell identified the painting in a December 1977 letter to Sister Bernetta Quinn (cited in Quinn, *Randall Jarrell* 88). For more on "In Galleries," see Quinn, *Randall Jarrell* 86-89.

33. Russell Fowler argues that the woman of "Seele im Raum" is "childlike," therefore "exceptionally fortunate . . . She has not lost her 'soul,' like most of the 'adults' of Jarrell's poetry" (*CE* 183). Charlotte Beck, on the other hand, believes her "psychotic"; Pritchard considers the eland "a symbol for her sickness" (*Worlds* 19; 270). Suzanne Ferguson's nuanced reading explains the eland as a "projection" that seems, after the woman is cured of her illness, to represent the incommunicability of experience: "the outer world inevitably falsifies the inner" (*Poetry* 151-154).

34. For Jarrell's own short note on the German sources, see *CP* 5.

35. On Complex Words and "Statements in Words," see Empson, *Complex,* chapter 2.

36. As early as 1952 Parker Tyler identified Jarrell's chief mode as "dramatic lyrism," though he did not define the term; William Meredith later pronounced Jarrell's "gift . . . essentially dramatic, like Browning's." Kinzie calls him "a great twentieth-century master of the dramatic monologue" (*CE* 140; *RJ* 120; 66).

37. Tucker finds this tendency false to the genre: for him, "dramatic monologue at its best asks us to do without . . . the figuration of inside and outside," of "soul" and "self," or of soul and society (234).

38. The rural people in "A Country Life," too, "are subdued to their own element" (*CP* 20). Jarrell's commentary confirms the allusion (*KA* 321). He spent the summer of 1939 on Shakespeare's sonnets, working alongside—and quarreling with—Ransom: see Robert Lowell's account (*RJ* 101-102). Auden published *The Dyer's Hand* in 1962, two years after *The Woman at the Washington Zoo.*

39. Michel Benamou devotes an entire essay to the repetitions in this poem: see *CE* 241-244. For a skeptical reading of "change" here and elsewhere in Jarrell, see Pritchard 274.

40. Benfey suggests that part of her wants to be raped; Suzanne Ferguson calls her "neurotically hysterical." (130; *Poetry* 188) Jarrell's own explication tells us that "her own life is so terrible to her that, to change, she is willing to accept" even "the obscene sexuality of the flesh-eating death-bird," whose sexual trappings are, "she hopes or pretends or desperately is sure . . . merely external" (*KA* 326).

41. Pritchard, for example, complains that its speaker is "not a real housewife" (300).

42. The Plato reader is actually one of Whyte's examples of well-functioning housewives, with "a rather keen consciousness of self—and the sophistication to realize that while individualistic tastes may raise eyebrows, exercising those tastes" won't necessarily get her ostracized (365). For more on Whyte, see chapter 2.

43. For one such reading, see Karl Shapiro, *CE* 206-207.

Bibliography

Certain titles are cited in the text by abbreviations:

CE: Ferguson, ed., *Critical Essays on Randall Jarrell*

CP: Jarrell, *The Complete Poems*

KA: Jarrell, *Kipling, Auden and Co.*

RJ: Lowell, Taylor, and Penn Warren, eds., *Randall Jarrell 1914-1965*

SH: Jarrell, *A Sad Heart at the Supermarket*

Where other citations require titles, they are given as key words. For example, Jessica Benjamin's *The Bonds of Love* appears as *Bonds*.

Altieri, Charles. *Canons and Consequences: Reflections on the Ethical Force of Imaginative Ideals.* Evanston, Ill.: Northwestern University Press, 1990.

Arendt, Hannah. *The Life of the Mind.* Ed. Mary McCarthy. New York: Harcourt, Brace, 1978.

———. *The Origins of Totalitarianism.* 2d expanded ed. Cleveland: Meridian/World, 1958 (1951).

Auden, W. H. *The English Auden.* Ed. Edward Mendelson. London: Faber and Faber, 1977.

Beck, Charlotte. "Randall Jarrell's Modernism: The Sweet Uses of Personae." *South Atlantic Review* 50, no. 2 (May 1985): 67-73.

———. *Worlds and Lives: The Poetry of Randall Jarrell.* Port Washington, N.Y.: Associated University Presses, 1983.

Benamou, Michel. "The Woman at the Zoo's Fearful Symmetry." *Analects* 1, no. 2 (1961): 2-4. Repr. *CE* 241-245.

Benfey, Christopher. "The Woman in the Mirror: Randall Jarrell and John Berryman." In *Men Writing the Feminine,* edited by Thaïs E. Morgan. Albany: State University of New York Press, 1994. 123-138.

Benjamin, Jessica. *Like Subjects, Love Objects: Essays on Recognition and Sexual Difference.* New Haven: Yale University Press, 1995.

———. *The Shadow of the Other.* New York: Routledge, 1998.

Birkerts, Sven. "Randall Jarrell." *Parnassus* 16, no. 2 (1991): 78-93.

Bromwich, David. *A Choice of Inheritance: Self and Community from Edmund Burke to Robert Frost.* Cambridge: Harvard University Press, 1989.

———. *Disowned by Memory: Wordsworth's Poetry of the 1790s.* Chicago: University of Chicago Press, 1999.

Brooks, Cleanth, and Robert Penn Warren. *Understanding Poetry.* 3d ed. New York: Holt, Rinehart and Winston, 1960.

Cavell, Stanley. *Must We Mean What We Say?* Cambridge: Cambridge University Press, 1981 (1969).

Chodorow, Nancy. *The Reproduction of Mothering: Psychoanalysis and the Sociology of Gender.* Berkeley: University of California Press, 1978.

Coates, Jennifer. *Women, Men, and Language.* 2d ed. Harlow: Longman, 1993.

Dickey, James. *The James Dickey Reader.* Ed. Henry Hart. New York: Simon and Schuster, 1999.

———. "Randall Jarrell." *RJ* 33-48.

Empson, William. *The Structure of Complex Words.* Cambridge: Harvard University Press, 1989. (1951)

Ferguson, Frances C. "Randall Jarrell and the Flotations of Voice." *Georgia Review* 28 (fall 1974): 423-439. Repr. *CE* 163-174.

Ferguson, Suzanne. *The Poetry of Randall Jarrell.* Baton Rouge: Louisiana State University Press, 1971.

———. ed. *Critical Essays on Randall Jarrell.* Boston: G. K. Hall, 1983.

Flynn, Richard. *Randall Jarrell and the Lost World of Childhood.* Athens, Ga.: University of Georgia Press, 1990.

Fowler, Russell. "Randall Jarrell's 'Eland': A Key to Motive and Technique in His Poetry." *Iowa Review* 5, no. 2 (1974): 113-126. Repr. *CE* 176-190.

Fussell, Paul. *Wartime: Understanding and Behavior in the Second World War.* New York: Oxford University Press, 1989.

Grossman, Allen, and Mark Halliday. *The Sighted Singer: Two Works on Poetry for Readers and Writers.* Baltimore: Johns Hopkins University Press, 1992.

Hagenbuchle, Helen. *The Black Goddess: A Study of the Archetypal Feminine in the Poetry of Randall Jarrell.* Zurich: Francke Verlag, 1975.

Hammer, Langdon. "Who Was Randall Jarrell?" *Yale Review* 79, no. 3 (spring 1990): 389-405.

Hartman, Geoffrey. *Wordsworth's Poetry, 1787-1814.* New Haven: Yale University Press, 1971 (1964).

Hernnstein Smith, Barbara. *Poetic Closure: A Study of How Poems End.* Chicago: University of Chicago Press, 1968.

Jarman, Mark. "John and Randall, Randall and John." *Gettysburg Review* 4, no. 4 (autumn 1991): 565-579.

Jarrell, Mary von S. *Remembering Randall.* New York: HarperCollins, 1999.

Jarrell, Randall. *Complete Poems.* New York: Farrar Straus and Giroux, 1969.

———. "Interview." *Analects* 1 (spring 1961): 5-10.

———. *Kipling, Auden, and Co.* New York: Farrar, Straus and Giroux, 1980.

———. *The Letters of Randall Jarrell.* Ed. Mary von S. Jarrell. Boston: Houghton Mifflin, 1985.

———. "Levels and Opposites." Ed. and introd. Thomas Travisano. *Georgia Review* 50, no. 4 (winter 1996): 697-713.

———. *Pictures from an Institution.* Chicago: University of Chicago Press, 1980 (1954).

———. *Poetry and the Age.* Gainesville: University Press of Florida, 2001 (1953).

———. "Previously unpublished poems." *AGNI* 53 (2001): 188-96.

———. *A Sad Heart at the Supermarket: Essays and Fables.* New York: Atheneum, 1962.

———. *The Third Book of Criticism.* New York: Farrar Straus and Giroux, 1969.

———. Manuscripts and papers at the Berg Collection, New York Public Library.

———. Manuscripts and papers at the University of North Carolina-Greensboro.

Kazin, Alfred. "Randall: His Kingdom." *RJ* 86-96.

Kinzie, Mary. *The Cure of Poetry in an Age of Prose.* Chicago: University of Chicago Press, 1993.

Kneale, J. Douglas. "Romantic Aversions: Apostrophe Reconsidered." *ELH* 58, no. 1 (spring 1991): 141-166.

Lakoff, Robin Tolmach. *Talking Power.* New York: Basic Books, 1990.

Langbaum, Robert. *The Poetry of Experience,* New York: Norton, 1957.

Longenbach, James. *Modern Poetry After Modernism.* New York: Oxford University Press, 1998.

Lowell, Robert. "Randall Jarrell." *RJ* 101-112.

Lowell, Robert, Peter Taylor, and Robert Penn Warren, eds. *Randall Jarrell 1914-1965.* New York: Farrar Straus and Giroux, 1967.

Mazzaro, Jerome. "Between Two Worlds: The Post-Modernism of Randall Jarrell." *Salmagundi* 17 (fall 1971): 93-113. Repr. *CE* 82-100.

Meredith, William. "The Lasting Voice." *RJ* 118-124.

Monroe, Keith. "Principle and Practice in the Criticism of Randall Jarrell." *CE* 256-265.

Nemerov, Howard, *Figures of Thought.* Boston: David R. Godine, 1978.

Perkins, David. "How It Was." *Studies in Romanticism* 21, no. 4 (winter 1982): 560-562.

Pritchard, William. *Randall Jarrell: A Literary Life.* New York: Farrar, Straus and Giroux, 1990.

Quinn, Sister Bernetta. *Randall Jarrell.* Boston: Twayne, 1981.

Ransom, John Crowe. *The New Criticism.* Norfolk, Conn.: New Directions, 1941.

Ricoeur, Paul. *Oneself as Another.* Trans. Kathleen Blamey. Chicago: University of Chicago Press, 1992.

Rilke, Rainer Maria. *Selected Poetry of Rainer Maria Rilke.* Ed. and trans. Stephen Mitchell; introd. Robert Hass. Bilingual ed. New York: Vintage, 1984.

Schapiro, Barbara. *Literature and the Relational Self.* New York: New York University Press, 1994.

Schwartz, Delmore. "The Dream From Which No One Wakes." *The Nation.* December 1, 1945. 590. Repr. *CE* 19-21.

Shapiro, Karl. *The Bourgeois Poet.* New York: Random House, 1964.

———. "The Death of Randall Jarrell." *RJ* 195-229.

Spender, Stephen. "Form and Feeling." *The Nation,* February 23, 1952. 182-183.

Stevens, Wallace. *Collected Poetry and Prose.* Ed. Frank Kermode and Joan Richardson. New York: Library of America, 1998.

Taylor, Charles. *Sources of the Self.* Cambridge: Harvard University Press, 1989.

Travisano, Thomas. *Mid-Century Quartet: Bishop, Jarrell, Lowell, Berryman. and the Making of a Postmodern Poetics.* Charlottesville: University of Virginia Press, 1999.

Tucker, Herbert F. "Dramatic Monologue and the Overhearing of Lyric." In *Lyric Poetry: Beyond New Criticism,* edited by Chaviva Hošek and Patrica Parker. Ithaca, N.Y.: Cornell University Press, 1985. 226-246.

Tyler, Parker. "Randall Jarrell's Dramatic Lyrism." *Poetry* 79 (1952): 335-346. Repr. *CE* 140-149.

Vendler, Helen. "The Inconsolable." *The New Republic,* July 23, 1990. 32-36.

Wallace-Crabbe, Chris. *Toil and Spin: Two Directions in Modern Poetry.* Melbourne: Hutchinson, 1980.

Warren, Robert Penn. "Twelve Poets." *American Review* 3, no. 2 (May 1934): 212-228.

Whyte, William H., Jr. *The Organization Man.* New York: Simon and Schuster, 1956.

Williamson, Alan. "Jarrell, the Mother, the Märchen." *Twentieth Century Literature* 40, no. 3 (fall 1994): 283-299.

Winnicott, D. W. *Playing and Reality.* New York: Basic Books, 1971.

Wilson, Edmund. *Axel's Castle.* London: Fontana Library, 1961 (1931).

Wood, Linda. "Loneliness." In *The Social Construction of Emotions,* edited by Rom Harré. Oxford: Basil Blackwell, 1986. 184-208.

Wordsworth, William. *Poetical Works.* Ed. Thomas Hutchinson and E. de Selincourt. New York: Oxford University Press, 1936.

———. *The Prelude: The Four Texts.* Ed. Jonathan Wordsworth. London: Penguin, 1995.

Wordsworth, William, and Samuel Taylor Coleridge. *Lyrical Ballads.* Ed. R. L. Brett and A. R. Jones. London: Routledge, 1991.

Nelson Hathcock (essay date 2003)

SOURCE: Hathcock, Nelson. "'Standardizing Catastrophe': Randall Jarrell and the Bomb." In *Jarrell, Bishop, Lowell, & Co.*, edited by Suzanne Ferguson, pp. 113-25. Knoxville: University of Tennessee Press, 2003.

[*In the following essay, Hathcock addresses the question of why Jarrell, in his post-World War II poetry and criticism, failed to confront the horrifying reality of the atomic bomb, especially America's decision to use the bomb against Japan in 1945. Hathcock avers that Jarrell did not shy away from this issue but chose instead "the shaping of the culture by the bomb as his postwar subject."*]

In 1947 the Manhattan telephone directory listed forty-five companies that had incorporated the magic word "atomic" in their names, among them the Atomic Undergarment Company (Boyer [*By the Bomb's Early Light*] 10). In the commemorative volume of essays on Randall Jarrell, Eleanor Taylor writes of a conversation in Greensboro, also in 1947, among her husband Peter, Randall and Mackie Jarrell, and Clara May and Marc Friedlander. Talk settled on matters of survival and over-refinement. Friedlander said that he didn't like to feel that, if his life depended upon being able to kill and dress an animal, he couldn't do it. The others also felt abashed by their squeamishness, all but Jarrell: "I consider myself the ornament of civilization! When it perishes, let me perish!" (["Greensboro Days"] 235). While it's likely that at the height of his powers Jarrell considered himself much more than mere ornament, it's just as probable that in a civilization spawning the Atomic Undergarment Company he would feel considerably less "ornamental." All the same, this linking his own fate with that of the Western high culture he had always championed was presumably heartfelt. At the time America was flush with the power of a nuclear monopoly, but in a few short years Jarrell's remark would take on an urgency and a somber fatalism with which many would be grappling, consciously and otherwise.

This juxtaposition of historian's fact with friend's recollection introduces an important relationship when we consider Jarrell's post-war work. The connection aids us in explaining why, in a poet justly famed for his imaginative confrontation with modern warfare, we find only a few exceptions to what seems a curious silence about the "unthinkable." It is worthwhile to consider some of the exceptions to that silence as we contemplate Jarrell's postwar, post-Hiroshima state of mind. In September 1945 Jarrell had written to Margaret Marshall of *The Nation*:

> I feel so rotten about the country's response to the bombings at Hiroshima and Nagasaki that I wish I could become a naturalized dog or cat. I believe our culture's chief characteristic, to a being from outside it, would be that we are liars. That all except a few never tell or feel anything near the truth about anything we do. Though even at that we're not bad enough to deserve the end we are going to get.
>
> (*Letters* [*Randall Jarrell's Letters*] 130)

Since Jarrell himself has pinpointed "our culture's chief characteristic," he has also furtively identified himself as "a being from outside it," capable of registering its fraudulence and hypocrisy, and from that perspective would come most of his postwar writing. More than the bombings themselves, the "country's response" offends him, the euphoria not only inappropriate but duplicitous. To a believer in "truth" like Jarrell, the pageantry of fervent nationalism in the wake of Hiroshima and Nagasaki masks a national guilt to which no one can own up without being "un-American." His already long experience as a highly skeptical observer of "the State" permits him to foresee the sanitized prospect for the atomic age being generated by the press, the politicians, and what Eisenhower himself would later dub the "military-industrial complex." This prospect includes justifying the bomb so as to cancel out any moral quandary, even for the "few" who try to "tell or feel" the truth. Being an outsider to the popular American culture of the bomb is, for Jarrell, tantamount to being a defender of Western civilization, yet his witness to world war assures him that this culture is not to be confused with the evil just defeated—we will not deserve our end.

While the letter to Marshall reflects the image of a nation weary of war and willing to rationalize its conclusion by any means possible, it also states unequivocally Jarrell's opposition to that moral compromise. Two months after VJ Day, a *Fortune* poll showed that while many Americans now felt remorse, 53.3 percent still endorsed "without reservation" the use of atomic weapons to end the war. Lewis Mumford noted at the time that "[n]ot the least extraordinary fact about the postwar period is that mass extermination [had] awakened so little moral protest" (qtd. in Winkler [*Life Under a Cloud*] 29). Initially, nationalism and patriotism predominated as most networks, magazines, and newspapers worked to maintain corporate images overtly supportive of the war effort. Thus, even the crew of the Enola Gay could commit its epoch-making moment to verse:

> It was the 6th of August, that much we knew,
> When the boys took off in the morning dew,
> Feeling nervous, sick, and ill at ease
> They flew at the heart of the Japanese,
> With a thunderous blast, a blinding light,
> And the 509th's atomic might.
>
> (qtd. in Boyer 244)

However, within the year, voices of protest had become louder and more numerous as the reality of America's price for victory became more apparent. In 1946 the *New Yorker* would publish John Hersey's *Hiroshima,* a powerful account of the bombing from the perspective of six citizens in that targeted city. Its distribution through the entire spectrum of the media was almost unprecedented—from being broadcast over the ABC radio network to its selection by the Book-of-the-Month Club (Boyer 204, Winkler 31). Admittedly, the scores of commemorations, meditations, editorials, and jeremiads were largely the work of social critics, ministers, journalists, and politicians. In this emerging debate, the voices of established literary figures were few. Probably the most prominent was William Faulkner, using his famed Nobel Prize address of 1950 to reflect upon the situation facing "the young man or woman writing today": "There are no longer problems of the spirit. There is only one question: When will I be blown up?" However, the novelist went on to assert pointedly that the question should be irrelevant for the writer, who must return to "the old verities and truths of the heart." Otherwise, he went on, they are condemned to writing "not of love but of lust, of defeats in which nobody loses anything of value, and victories without hope and worst of all, without pity or compassion." Just before her death, Gertrude Stein might have summarized the situation best for "high culture" when she wrote:

> They asked me what I thought of the atomic bomb. I said I had not been able to take any interest in it. . . . What is the use, if they are really as destructive as all that there is nothing left and if there is nothing there [is] nobody to be interested and nothing to be interested about. . . . So you see the atomic [bomb] is not at all interesting, not any more interesting than any other machine. . . . Sure it will destroy a lot and kill a lot, but it's the living that are interesting not the way of killing them.
>
> (Stein ["Reflections on the Atomic Bomb"] 3-4)

While Stein may have spoken for many who felt cowed or pushed to the margins by the sheer enormity of the subject, the case of Randall Jarrell is somehow different. He had shown himself to be very much interested, not only in the sad fates of the soldiers and citizens who were the fodder of total war, but in the mechanisms of their victimization as well—the economic and ideological structures, the prejudices, and the clanking, grinding machinery. His work had steadfastly refused to commit the dead to silence, summoning them back from the grave to testify repeatedly. In light of Jarrell's record in the war poems, could what Paul Boyer calls arriving at "the appropriate aesthetic for the bomb" (250) have been a sufficiently daunting prospect to cause him to withdraw? Could he have been intimidated by a perceived inadequacy of language in the face of a condition that transcends description? More recently the Japanese writer Ota Yoko formulated the problem in saying, "I live in a nation that has experienced the unprecedented. . . . I am unable to cling to the ordinary sorts of literature that we had before" (qtd. in Schwenger [*Letter Bomb*] 54).

In the case of Jarrell, the answer to all such questions is a qualified "no." Rather than arrive at a particular "aesthetic for the bomb," I propose that he saw the shaping of the culture *by the bomb* as his postwar subject. The "ding dong of doom" he heard was that of a civilization succumbing to its most nihilistic proclivities in the face of imminent threat, a submission that would promote the meager consolations of escapism and would render meaningless the more challenging endeavors of the poet. As in the letter to Marshall, Jarrell's postwar criticism is preoccupied with response, with the consumption of his own work and that of other poets and artists by their putative audiences. Nagged by a growing sensation of his own obsolescence, he could find "the bomb" emblematic of a popular culture that stifles the intellectual and emotional challenge of serious art. During that period of his career when poetic inspiration seemed to have failed him, Jarrell saw evidence of a cultural "death" that was reflected in America's accommodation to the moral and physical ramifications of its nuclear military power.

Patricia Black has suggested that Jarrell's poetry, particularly **The Lost World** (1965), does indeed confront the reality of the bomb, but by means of the "dreamwork" of art. Citing an unnamed source she refers to a conversation in the 1960s between Jarrell and Robert Watson in which Jarrell describes the work-in-progress *Lost World* as "a book of poems about the atom bomb" (["The Atom Bomb"] 31). Black contends that a Freudian reading reveals the volume, particularly the title sequence, as "dream-thoughts" that "concern the threat of atomic annihilation" (32). While this argument deflects the notion that he was mute about the bomb and its attendant issues, Jarrell was facing the reality of that threat long before working on what would be his final book. In poetry and prose alike he addressed himself to the expansive question of art's position in the postwar world because by formulating that problem this poet could feel most acutely the threat of annihilation. Jarrell articulates his conclusion in the mocking poem, **"The Times Worsen,"** included in his essay **"The Obscurity of the Poet"**: "When Art goes, what remains is Life"

(*Poetry and the Age* 20). And, as made clear by his remark on the "end" of civilization recalled by Eleanor Taylor, *that* life is no life for a human being.

Jarrell's famed portrayal of the poet in modern America as "a condemned man for whom the State will not even buy breakfast" draws into epigrammatic concentration both target and threat. The "State" in Jarrell's poetry is always that monolithic, nationalist, corporate entity, regardless of nominal ideology, which inevitably creates a less habitable world through its conversion of the human into soldier, worker, consumer: "thing." We see this effect in the early work produced from Jarrell's scientific education and "radical" youth, but it is also prominent in the poem that most explicitly addresses the dawning of the atomic age. Although prescient in its imagining of a global nuclear scenario, **"1945: The Death of the Gods"** (published in the *Nation* in April 1946) is a somewhat unsatisfying performance, compared with the best of the war poems, and has elicited little comment. Yet, the prophetic mode that in one sense weakens the poem also caustically underscores one of the changes in civilization documented therein.

Wars accelerate various processes, and with blinding speed World War II transformed the very meaning of disproportion. The nineteenth-century sensibility that lurks in Jarrell (how often he would harken back at mid-twentieth century) empowers him to recognize the stark disproportion in modern warfare. He understands what the designation "total war" truly means. But Hiroshima made disproportion itself a force difficult to grasp—the disproportion of the energy yielded by Einsteinian physics versus the energy restricted by a Newtonian system. Always sensitive to the ways in which war tended toward abstraction for everyone but the victims, in **"1945: The Death of the Gods"** Jarrell faces the greatest abstract force yet, and in so doing, succumbs to the allure of rhetoric in his poem. His surrender, however, foregrounds for his audience a tension between the death of a particular ball turret gunner and the death of the gods, between the gunner's sweaty, frozen fur and the "ecumenical realm" of a thousand "human sun[s]," between a powerful image and an oratorical register that will ring tinny and frail, even to Jarrell's ear:

> . . . you eternal States
> Beneath whose shadows men have found the stars
> And graves of men: O warring Deities,
> Tomorrow when the rockets rise like stars
> And earth is blazing with a thousand suns
> That set up there within your realms a realm
> Whose laws are ecumenical, whose life
> Exacts from men a prior obedience—
> Must you learn from your makers how to die?
>
> (***Complete Poems*** 183)

Just as he sees that this new disproportionate world threatens an art that has held the human at its center, Jarrell obviously recognizes "the State" in its technology of modern war as imperiling humanist endeavor in the culture it produces, a world that sees "dread and love, the witnesses of men, / Swallowed up in victory." At this point—in Jarrell's writing and his life—the bomb and the State are one, and the State is one with the culture it both creates and feeds on.

In the essays for a general readership that he began writing in the 1950s, Jarrell reveals himself simultaneously drawn to and repulsed by trends and phenomena in American culture. In some of his diatribes like **"A Sad Heart at the Supermarket"** or **"The Taste of the Age,"** readers detect an uncharacteristic shrillness, but Jarrell's response to America's consumer culture was not knee-jerk derision. He discriminated among products and forms with the same taste and standards he brought to his reading. The four years of his beloved *Road and Track* magazine stacked under his bed were no bar to his attack on the faddish abstract expressionism. When he found the diminishment of the human or the sentimental displacement of intellect with pathos or the willing submission to the manipulations of the State, he condemned heartily.

By the 1950s the bomb had been resolutely absorbed into American mass culture. From the actress who launched her career as "The Anatomic Bomb" to what musicologist Charles Wolfe has called "some of the most bizarre country songs ever written" (Boyer 25) to sci-fi movie after sci-fi movie to advertisements like the one for Mosler's safes that drew Lowell's ire in "For the Union Dead"—America gave Jarrell much to bemoan. This "saturation bombing" affronted him with all the elements of a culture that are imprisoning, alienating, or dehumanizing, so that the weapon of "mass destruction" became almost implicit in "mass culture" in his view. It was a culture that led directly to the widespread construction of shelters and extensive controversies over "shelter ethics": debates over who might ethically be excluded when "the time" came. By 1954 and the H-bomb tests at Bikini, the hoax of civil defense was apparent to most who cared to consider it and confirmed Jarrell's earlier assessment of a culture of "liars." In this context even some of the lightest of Jarrell's popular writing from the period seems like protest. The State wanted its citizens happy in their holes while Jarrell, in **"The Little Cars"** (1954) or **"Go, Man, Go!"** (1957) lauded the sports car and the open road with all the enthusiasm of a Beat poet. By now the "unthinkable" had been appropriated fully by the "unthinking." The Jarrell who quotes Martin Luther in the epigraph of ***A Sad Heart at the Supermarket*** feels himself oppressed equally by both those entities that come at him as one:

> And even if the world should end tomorrow
> I would still plant my little apple-tree.
>
> (vi)

The statement subtly melds resignation and defiance, and that is Jarrell in the face of the mass culture of the fifties and the sixties. In the dynamic of such a culture, the looming extinction that should limn human mortality with even greater importance (death should, after all, *be* the mother of beauty) was instead mocking it into elision.

In his recent book, Thomas Travisano has pointed out that "there is evidence in the polemical essays . . . of the degree to which the burgeoning of a callous and triumphant commercialism in the fifties and sixties disturbed Jarrell" ([*Midcentury Quartet*] 254), and I would also observe how that "callous and triumphant commercialism" is often associated with the image of nuclear weaponry and war. A notable proximity occurs in this passage from **"The Obscurity of the Poet,"** Jarrell's vision of "The World of the Future":

> where, among the related radiances of a kitchen's white-enamelled, electric stove, electric dish-washer, electric refrigerator, electric washing-machine, electric dryer, electric ironer, disposal unit, air conditioner, and Waring Blendor, the home-maker sits in the trim overalls of her profession; where, above the concrete cavern that holds a General Staff, the rockets are invisible in the sky . . . Of this world I often think.
>
> (*P&A* [*Poetry & the Age*] 21)

From the technology of domestic entrapment to the technology of mass destruction the leap is over only a semicolon. The "rockets" preside over a world of creature comforts, making them less a comfort than a desperate attempt at insulation from the life-and-death confrontation above. Because of one, we must have the other. The "concrete caverns" protecting the generals also represent ironically an evolutionary regression in the guise of progress. He explicates the word "media" in **"A Sad Heart . . .":**

> The word has the clear and fatal ring of that new world whose space we occupy so luxuriously and precariously; the world that produces mink stoles, rockabilly records, and tactical weapons by the million; the world Attila, Galileo, Hansel and Gretel never knew.
>
> (["A Sad Heart at the Supermarket"] 65)

Since the luxurious in this world is also precarious, Jarrell suggests a link between our willing indulgence in the immediacy and ease of consumerism and our fear of annihilation. The past to which he alludes is part real, part fairy tale—distinctly invoking brutality, bravery, and helplessness. But it is a Jarrellian world, art sharing the podium with history, safe from "media" which would blandly regard the manufacture of mink stoles as commensurate with the production of tactical weapons.

As an artist and intellectual, Jarrell felt keenly the antagonism of his own society; at base it was the theme of his postwar prose, whether he was decrying a failed educational system or championing a talent that had impressed him. Seeing so much attention and resource lavished upon the products of what Dwight Macdonald would deem in 1960 "masscult," he felt not only ignored, but threatened. Certainly, it would have been difficult for Jarrell to overlook the conjunction of bomb and commerce. Leaving office, even Eisenhower himself warned Congress of the rise of the military-industrial complex. The bomb can be seen simply as the most powerful product of the same corporate, bureaucratic structure that develops FM radio, processed cheese, or Milltown. Of the 125,000 people employed by the Manhattan Project, only a handful at any given time had any grasp of what the final product was to be, a triumph of Max Weber's worst nightmare of bureaucratic efficiency. In 1961 *US News and World Report* brought home the bomb/economy connection in another respect by asking: "If Bombs Do Fall—What Happens to Your Investments?" (Whitfield 223).

In an essay for *Commentary* in 1947, Mary McCarthy saw the connection as one of progressive preparation:

> The movies, the radio, the super-highway have softened us up for the atom bomb; we have lived with them without pleasure, feeling them as a coercion on our natures, a coercion coming seemingly from nowhere and expressing nobody's will. The new coercion finds us without the habit of protest; we are dissident but apart.
>
> (["America the Beautiful"] 205)

Jarrell would remain "dissident but apart" from the Cold War conservatism of, for example, *Reader's Digest,* which created an audience that gave a good joke the same culturally therapeutic power as a good poem, but preferred the joke. To Jarrell, the stymied poet, this process began to seem like a cultural "desertification." Both bomb and debased cultural productions effectively obliterated the urge toward higher standards of human definition, distinction, and achievement. Rather, this culture promoted equalizing and standardizing, "dumbing" everything into rubble.

Later in the decade, perhaps compelled simply by continuing to exist in this shadow, Jarrell's resolve waxes again. His objections to modernist painting reveal his fear that the process of sucking the human out of cultural productions had infected even highbrow art. Jarrell's essay in a 1957 issue of *Art News*—**"Against Abstract Expressionism"**—and a later poem—**"The Old and the New Masters"**—can be examined in tandem to reveal the confluence of the bomb as reality and as cultural metaphor. In the essay Jarrell argues as "devil's advocate" against abstract expressionism, thereby opposing its "canonization." His defense of representational painting is based largely upon its capacity for metaphorical reference beyond the canvas. Conversely he objects to abstract expressionism for its power to reduce and for the manner in which it is promoted as art's ultimate self-referential stage of development. As Jarrell's ironic rehearsal shows, the "defense" of the movement is simply one manifestation of what the movement itself is:

> But ordinarily such painting—a specialized, puritanical reduction of earlier painting—is presented to us as its final evolution, what it always ought to have been and therefore "really" was. When we are told (or, worse still, shown) that painting "really" is "nothing but" this, we are being given one of those definitions which *explain out of existence* [emphasis added] what they appear to define, and put a simpler entity in its place.
>
> (*Kipling, Auden & Co.* 286)

By 1957 to "explain out of existence" has acquired an almost panoramic suggestiveness. The revolution of abstract expressionism, somewhat like the revolution in physics, requires a "specialized, intensive exploitation of one part" and a rejection of the rest. Disregarding its claims to freedom, Jarrell finds in this new art a mass aesthetic—one that boils down difference, distortion, and elaboration into elemental common denominators of shape and color, an act that costs its purveyors relatively little. Abstract expressionism, he says, has "substituted for a heterogeneous, polyphonic process a homogenous, homophonic process" (***KA&C*** [*Kipling, Auden & Co.*] 287), a description that might well fit the treatment of any artistic concept by masscult producers. The overall effect can be likened to a Japanese phrase that many of the survivors of the Hiroshima bomb used to describe their condition in its wake: *muga-muchu*, "without self, without center" (qtd. in Schwenger 49). While Jarrell certainly does not make an overt parallel here, when we turn to **"The Old and the New Masters,"** we can see him explicitly suggesting a similar connection.

As numerous critics have pointed out, the poem begins as response to Auden's "Musée de Beaux Arts" (1938) and constitutes the final blow in a career-long contest with Auden that Jarrell carried on even while praising him. Considered with Jarrell's earlier broadside against abstract expressionism, the text eventually confirms the worst of what he sees in that artistic "revolution." The opening retort to Auden establishes Jarrell's idea of what art should do and has done, in Western civilization, since the Middle Ages:

> About suffering, about adoration, the old masters
> Disagree. When someone suffers, no one else eats
> Or walks or opens the window—no one breathes
> As the sufferers watch the sufferer.
>
> (*CP* [*The Complete Poems*] 332)

By means of example, Jarrell challenges the callous indifference to human calamity that Auden found to be a persistent theme in the work of the Old Masters, primary among them Pieter Brueghel the Elder (1525/30-1569). Jarrell creates a gallery of his own—other paintings elaborately and lovingly described—in which suffering is the single most important fact of human existence. In his rendition of Georges de La Tour's "St. Sebastian Mourned by St. Irene" (1649), Jarrell focuses our attention on the "work of mourning" by Irene and the other figures in the scene. Jarrell connects the image of Sebastian's martyrdom with that of Christ, suggesting that the moment of the painting represents a confluence of both suffering and the recognition of it: "They watch, they are, the one thing in the world." At work here, as we recall Jarrell's essay, is the contrast between the "reduction" in contemporary art and the "concentration" of traditional, representational painting. These figures and their gestures are "the one thing in the world" not because the rest has been eliminated from the visual plane, but because the act of empathetic acknowledgment has been centered and made consequential.

The treatment of Hugo van der Goes's "Nativity" from the Portinari Altarpiece (c. 1475) follows a similar scheme and extends it to include all of time, foregrounding the painter's manipulation of history: "The time of the world concentrates / On this one instant." Jarrell points out the donor's wife and family kneeling in adoration at the scene of the virgin birth, "hundreds / Of years in the future." Ultimately this passage of the poem, as do the paintings, reminds us that "everything / That was or will be in the world is fixed / On its small, helpless, human center."

The third section of the poem brings us to the "new masters" who "paint a subject as they please," offending Jarrell's humanism in the process. The troubles Veronese faced from the Inquisition for his too realistic depiction of Christ at Levi's feast—the dogs playing at his feet—are contrasted with the blithe freedom of the new masters, suggesting that these artists have not only lost the "human center" but have made possible catastrophe on a grand scale:

> Later Christ disappears, the dogs disappear: in abstract
> Understanding, without adoration, the last master puts
> Colors on canvas, a picture of the universe
> In which a bright spot somewhere in the corner
> Is the small radioactive planet men called Earth.
>
> (*CP* 333)

Jarrell's description of the painting-to-come hinges on the "abstract understanding" of the last master. Echoing the nonobjective art that Jarrell has criticized in his essay, the phrase also evokes the cultural amnesia encouraged by the U.S. government at the time. That "understanding," with no "adoration" about it, can be associated with the attempts of Rand Corporation strategists, like Herman Kahn, author of *On Thermonuclear*

War (1960), to calculate scientifically the precise consequences of nuclear war and thereby strategize it. Kahn's comparisons of nuclear scenarios—20 million dead as opposed to 150 million—represented the bloodless considerations that lay behind government myths like civil preparedness and "first strike capability." Reading the poem in a context of cold-war issues teases out Jarrell's suggestion that a culture producing abstract expressionism is also implicated in making winnable nuclear war seem feasible. Both efforts depend upon diminishing the human.

The final image of that "small radioactive planet" was a cultural cliché by the time Jarrell wrote the poem. Robert Payne in his *Report on America* (1949), for example, displaced his readers with an extraterrestrial perspective, pointing out how, when the war has been fought,

> for a few weeks or months or years the clouds of atomic vapor will roll like colored scarves around the body of the earth, and to an inhabitant of Mars looking through a telescope the earth would seem unchanged except for its increasing brightness, for the earth will glow with radioactive vapors.
>
> (qtd. in Boyer 248)

Drawing on what was by then a stock image in this moment of subdued prophecy, Jarrell hints at just how a society that distances itself from human pain—a culture of "distraction"—is entwined with the greatest threat to its own existence. Mass culture encourages a perspective that dissociates self from self. The self-referentiality encouraged by abstract expressionism actually induces a gap between the human and art and between the human and his/her fellow beings. To see the earth as a glowing, insignificant cinder in the corner of the canvas is to capitulate to an "understanding" that is both abstractly pessimistic and escapist at the same time. As the oddly Jarrell-like devil puts it in **"A Conversation with the Devil"** (1951), what use indeed is the devil—"a specialist in personal relations"—in a civilization hell-bent on its own destruction:

> I disliked each life, I assure you, for its own sake.
> —But to deal indifferently in life and death;
> To sell, wholesale, piecemeal, annihilation;
> To—I will not go into particulars—
> This beats me.
>
> (*CP* 32)

Jarrell's commitment both to his "apple tree" and to the canon of Western moral and aesthetic values led him to his jaundiced opinions of American popular culture in the fifties and sixties. Whether this same culture embraced the bomb out of fear, death-wish, or some combination of the two is immaterial. As far as Jarrell is concerned, a common discourse arises from both, for in either case they result in a barren, uninhabitable space for the artist in, to borrow Norman Cousins's phrase, a "standardized catastrophe." Two passages from **"The Obscurity of the Poet"** reiterate just what Jarrell believes is at stake, for himself and all of us. The first draws upon the image in the anecdote with which this essay began: "Art matters not merely because it is the most magnificent ornament and the most nearly unfailing occupation of our lives, but because it is life itself" (22). When Jarrell uses the term "art," he means it to be exclusive, so that in an equation with "life itself," life is dignified, raised above the roiling swarm. That same paragraph closes,

> Goethe said: The only way in which we can come to terms with the great superiority of another person is love. But we can also come to terms with superiority, with true Excellence, by denying that such a thing as Excellence can exist; and, in doing so, we help to destroy it and ourselves.
>
> (*P&A* 23)

The degrading democratization of mass culture, the reinvigorated anti-intellectualism of the period, and the expanding capacity for total destruction are all indicted in this warning. The existential terror of the arms race was indeed a reality for Jarrell, "the bomb" its overarching trope, but his revulsion was just as powerfully triggered by the cultural apocalypse which he believed guaranteed his obscurity in every sense—little seen, little read, and unintelligible when he was. His protest against the self-destructive tendencies of a culture denying the power and value of humanism must be seen in the context of the greater threat to meaning and to life itself. For Jarrell, one certainly made possible the other.

Works Cited

Black, Patricia Rogers. "The Atom Bomb: Jarrell's Dream-Work in 'The Lost World.'" *Mississippi Quarterly* 39:1 (Winter 1985-86): 31-40.

Boyer, Paul. *By the Bomb's Early Light: American Thought and Culture at the Dawn of the Atomic Age.* Chapel Hill: U of North Carolina P, 1985.

Cousins, Norman. "The Standardization of Catastrophe." *Saturday Review of Literature,* 10 August 1946: 18.

Jarrell, Mary, ed. *Randall Jarrell's Letters.* Boston: Houghton, 1985.

Jarrell, Randall. *The Complete Poems.* New York: Noonday, 1969.

———. *Kipling, Auden & Co.: Essays and Reviews 1935-1964.* New York: Farrar, 1980.

———. *Poetry and the Age.* 1953. New York: Noonday, 1972.

———. *A Sad Heart at the Supermarket: Essays and Fables.* New York: Atheneum, 1967.

Macdonald, Dwight. *Against the American Grain: Essays on the Effects of Mass Culture.* New York: Da Capo, 1983.

McCarthy, Mary. "America the Beautiful: Humanist in the Bathtub." *Commentary* 4 (1947): 205.

Stein, Gertrude. "Reflections on the Atomic Bomb." *Yale Poetry Review* 7 (1947): 3-4.

Schwenger, Peter. *Letter Bomb: Nuclear Holocaust and the Exploding World.* Baltimore: Johns Hopkins UP, 1992.

Taylor, Eleanor. "Greensboro Days." *Randall Jarrell: 1914-1965.* Ed. Robert Lowell, Peter Taylor, Robert Penn Warren. New York: Farrar, 1967. 233-40.

Travisano, Thomas. *Midcentury Quartet: Bishop, Lowell, Jarrell, Berryman, and the Making of a Postmodern Aesthetic.* Charlottesville: UP of Virginia, 1999.

Whitfield, Stephen J. *The Culture of the Cold War.* Baltimore: Johns Hopkins UP, 1996.

Winkler, Allan. *Life under a Cloud: American Anxiety about the Atom.* Urbana: U of Illinois P, 1993.

Marc D. Cyr (essay date spring 2004)

SOURCE: Cyr, Marc D. "Randall Jarrell's Answerable Style: Revision of Elegy in 'The Death of the Ball Turret Gunner.'" *Texas Studies in Literature and Language* 46, no. 1 (spring 2004): 92-106.

[*In the following essay, Cyr interprets "The Death of the Ball Turret Gunner" as an example of "anti-elegy" literature. According to the critic, Jarrell rejects the "style and ethic" of the elegy genre in order to address more effectively "the conditions of twentieth-century life in general, and twentieth-century war in particular."*]

This paper is concerned with the position of Randall Jarrell's **"The Death of the Ball Turret Gunner"** in the elegiac tradition, but to define that position I must begin with another genre and another poet: the heroic epic and John Milton. In the preamble to Book IX of *Paradise Lost,* Milton anatomizes and scornfully rejects both the style of traditional epic—"The skill of Artifice or Office mean" ([*John Milton*] 39)—and the heroic ethic of personal courageous acts, proposing instead "the better fortitude / Of Patience and Heroic Martyrdom / Unsung" (31-33). This proposal of a "higher Argument" (42) and prayer for an "answerable style" (20) come after he has demonstrated the inadequacies of epic style and heroic ethic in his account of the war in heaven in Books V and VI, an account many readers find ridiculously funny, with, for example, angels wearing armor and throwing mountains at each other (not to mention Satan inventing the cannon). Arnold Stein calls this episode a "mock heroic" ([*Answerable Style*] 17-20), but William Riggs points out that that mode derides everything to which it is applied, and therefore would tar the loyal angels with the same brush used on the rebels, something Milton wishes to avoid. So Riggs proposes a modification, seeing Milton as writing not mock heroic, but "mock*ed* heroic in which poetic manner is intentionally depreciated by its inability to answer adequately to the demands of a heavenly subject" ([*The Christian Poet in Paradise Lost*] 120).[1]

In **"The Death of the Ball Turret Gunner,"** Jarrell is engaged in a similar project of revising, indeed rejecting the style and ethic of a traditional genre, elegy, to make his poetry more adequately address and render the conditions of twentieth-century life in general, and twentieth-century war in particular. In writing what amounts to an anti-elegy (see below), however, he manages to avoid mocking his elegiac subject, and with this avoidance writes mock*ed* elegiac.

Elegies traditionally have offered to their readers some form of consolation for a particular death and often, by extension, for death itself. If, as Peter M. Sacks puts it, ". . . mourning is an action, a process of work" ([*The English Elegy*] 19), traditional elegies are a part of that process, allowing mourners to find solace in the transcendence or transfiguration and persistence of the elegiac subject. Indeed, the long history of the elegiac tradition is part of that solace; centered on "The vegetation god [who is] the predecessor of almost every elegized subject and provides a fundamental trope by which mortals create their images of immortality" (26-27), ". . . the elegy takes comfort from its self-insertion into a longstanding convention of grief. And . . . an individual elegy may borrow the ritual *context* of consolation. . . . The unique death is absorbed into a natural cycle of repeated occasions" (23-24, Sacks' emphasis).

But Jahan Ramazani argues that the modern era produces a revolution in elegy. He sees most good modern elegies as being "not a guide to 'successful' mourning" ([*Poetry of Mourning*] ix), but "melancholic," "mourning that is unresolved, violent, and ambivalent" (4). They are "anti-consolatory and anti-encomiastic, anti-Romantic and anti-Victorian, anti-conventional and sometimes even anti-literary" (2)—that is, they are anti-elegies and the poets who write them "attack the dead and themselves, their own work and tradition; and they refuse such orthodox consolations as the rebirth of the dead in Nature, in God, or in poetry itself" (4). However, this anti-elegiac movement "does not disprove the existence of the conventions or the genre; 'the transgression requires a law,' as Todorov writes, and the norm becomes visible in being transgressed" (25). Further citing Derrida and others, he argues that in perceiving something as violating a form, we simultaneously perceive the form that is being violated: The new form is embedded in various ways, sometimes by noteworthy absence of traditional elements.

Such transgressive reference is central to **"The Death of the Ball Turret Gunner,"** and Jarrell uses Percy Bysshe Shelley's elegy for John Keats, "Adonais," for this purpose. The connection between these poems was first noted by Leven M. Dawson, and because his arguments are so closely tied to the language of both poems, it is best to quote Jarrell's here in full:

> From my mother's sleep I fell into the State,
> And I hunched in its belly till my wet fur froze.
> Six miles from earth, loosed from its dream of life,
> I woke to black flak and the nightmare fighters.
> When I died they washed me out of the turret with a hose.[2]

Dawson focuses on the first four lines of stanza 39 of "Adonais":

> Peace, peace! he is not dead, he doth not sleep—
> He hath awakened from the dream of life—
> 'Tis we, who lost in stormy visions, keep
> With phantoms an unprofitable strife . . .
>
> ([*Shelley's Poetry and Prose*] 343-46)

Dawson notes that the gunner

> also awakens from the "dream of life." As, paradoxically for Shelley, the death of Keats was birth, birth in the Gunner's new "state" is death; in his condition life is an unnatural, insecure "dream" from which one awakens to "stormy visions" of "strife" with "phantoms" ("black flak and the nightmare fighters") and then dies. . . . Everything in war . . . is reversed: up is down, one ascends to die, life is merely a *dream* of earth, *awakening* or realization is "nightmare." . . . [Man] enters into abnormal states where he must dress unnaturally and regressively and where insensitivity becomes a sustaining virtue.
>
> (Dawson's emphasis ["Jarrell's 'The Death of the Ball Turret Gunner'"])[3]

So far so good, but this sharp focus on **"The Death of the Ball Turret Gunner"** as a war poem distracts Dawson from Jarrell's reversal of the central consolatory movement of traditional elegy: Rather than the vegetation-god figure dying / descending to rise / live again, the gunner rises to die and descends permanently, and the gunner's movement is shorn of even the most rudimentary rites of funerary mourning, the kinds of rites Shelley, following tradition, so voluminously details.

Further, and perhaps more importantly, Dawson's other focus element—stanza 39 of "Adonais"—leads him away from stanza 52. Jarrell's central image, the ball turret itself, is a paradoxical version of Shelley's powerful simile for his conception of the Platonic universe:

> The One remains, the many change and pass;
> Heaven's light forever shines, Earth's shadows fly;
> Life, like a dome of many-coloured glass,
> Stains the white radiance of Eternity,
> Until Death tramples it to fragments.—Die,
> If thou wouldst be with that which thou dost seek!
>
> ([*The Complete Poems*] 460-65)

In a note to the poem, Jarrell explains that "A ball turret was a plexiglass sphere set in the belly of a B-17 or B-24, and inhabited by two .50 caliber machine-guns and one man . . . hunched upside-down in his little sphere, he looked like the foetus in the womb" (**Selected Poems** xiii). The clear plexiglass sphere of the ball turret (only about half of which protruded from the plane's body) is a literally inverted version of Shelley's dome, and the dome is not merely serendipitous: Shelley and Jarrell share not only the use of the dome to represent earthly existence—"Life" or "the State"—but also the philosophy that generates Shelley's original image, a belief in "Necessity" or "Necessarianism," a concept associated with Platonic (or neo-Platonic) philosophy (Notopolous [*Shelley's Poetry and Prose*] 176-77).

Shelley's clearest expressions about this philosophy appear in his notes to *Queen Mab*. In Note 12: 6.198, he declares that

> He who asserts the doctrine of Necessity means that, contemplating the events which compose the moral and material universe, he beholds only an immense and uninterrupted chain of causes and effect, no one of which could occupy any other place than it does occupy, or act in any other place than it does act . . . Motive is to voluntary action in the human mind what cause is to effect in the material universe . . . Every human being is irresistibly impelled to act precisely as he does act . . .
>
> (*Complete Poetical Works,* 1:305-6)[4]

In "Adonais," Shelley's Necessarianism is, besides the apotheosis of Keats, apparent in the poet's attitudes towards the critics he blames for causing Keats' death. For the first two-thirds of the elegy the critics are vilified, but Shelley eventually moves to a recognition (I will not say acceptance) of the fact that they were simply living out their necessary natures, simply being what they had no choice *but* to be (316-33). Similarly, according to Suzanne Ferguson, for Jarrell "Necessity is essentially the working out of Natural Law or Natural process, all that a man in his physical state . . . must acquiesce to" ([*Critical Essays on Randall Jarrell*] 59), to which he adds the effects of man's own impulses and actions, what Jarrell, in **"From the Kingdom of Necessity,"** a postwar review of Robert Lowell's *Lord Weary's Castle,* enumerates as "everything that is closed, turned inward, incestuous, that blinds or binds: the Old Law, imperialism, militarism, capitalism, Calvinism, Authority, the Father, the 'proper Bostonians,' the rich"

(*Poetry and the Age,* 208-9). The forces, natural and human, act through the abstract entities of Trade and the State (S. Ferguson [*The Poetry of Randall Jarrell*] 84) and in Jarrell's war poems these entities perform the same role as Shelley's critics do, as representatives of Necessity.[5] Shelley's Necessarian passage leads into stanza 38 and the final movements of the elegy, the Platonic apotheosis of Keats into a pure white star, "A portion of the Eternal" (340).[6] Unfortunately for the gunner, his dome looks downward and there is no escape. He dies in the State.

Shelley, then, provides the specific foil for Jarrell's anti-elegiac purpose, but besides his own impulses Jarrell also had a forerunner and perhaps model in writing anti-elegiac war poems, Wilfred Owen. Jarrell considered Owen "a poet in the true sense of the word" (*Kipling* [**Kipling, Auden, & Co.**] 169), and William H. Pritchard quotes a letter to Robert Lowell in which Jarrell comments that "a good deal of Owen is the best anybody did with the first world war," and proposes that Jarrell took Owen as his "example" ([*Randall Jarrell*] 112). As well as the poetry, Jarrell also had what might be called an agenda supplied in the Preface that Owen drafted for a volume of his poetry to be published after the war;[7] that Preface reads in part,

> This book is not about heroes. English Poetry is not yet fit to speak of them. Nor is it about deeds or lands or about glory, honour, any might, majesty, dominion or power nor anything except War. Above all I am not concerned with Poetry. My subject is War, and the pity of War. The Poetry is in the pity—Yet these elegies are to this generation in no sense consolatory. They may be to the next. All a poet can do today is warn. That is why the true Poets must be truthful.
>
> ([*Wilfred Owen*] 2:535)

While it is interesting to note that Owen's list of what he excludes is almost a summary of Milton's rejection of epic heroic in *Paradise Lost,* and while the "pity" section has generally drawn most attention,[8] it is the opening and closing statements of what I quote above that I want to look at in the context of this paper.

First, on the issue of "heroes": Like Milton, Owen does not deny their existence, only their traditional depiction and thereby definition. His own depiction has led some readers to see his soldiers as sheer victims, a view most famously held by W. B. Yeats, who excluded Owen (and all other so-called "trench poets") from *The Oxford Book of Modern Verse: 1892-1935* (1936) on the grounds that "passive suffering is not a theme for poetry" (xxxiv). And both Owen and Jarrell can present soldiers as inactive, uninstigating recipients of suffering: For Owen, "The Sentry," "Exposure," and even "Dulce Et Decorum Est" are good examples, and for Jarrell **"The Death of the Ball Turret Gunner"**—the gunner is trapped in the State and we never see him do anything, not even die. Jarrell even offers a defense of this depiction in his attack on Marianne Moore's postwar heroicizing and mythologizing of the war's participants:

> She does not understand that they are heroes in the same sense that the chimney sweeps, the factory children in the blue books, were heroes: routine loss in the routine business of the world . . . she does not remember that most of the people in a war never fight for even a minute—though they bear for years and die forever. They do not fight, but only starve, only suffer, only die: the sum of all this passive misery is that great activity, War.
>
> (*Kipling,* 129)

This sounds very much like Milton's proposed heroic of "Patience and Heroic Martyrdom" and like some form of Necessarian absolution for everyone involved, even combat soldiers: They had no choice.

But Owen and Jarrell do not always leave their soldier-subjects in the diminished position of abject victims; those soldiers often commit old-style heroics, but how those so-called heroics are to be judged is at issue. In "Apologia pro Poemata Meo," for example, Owen presents himself and his companions as "Merry" because "power was on us as we slashed bones bare / Not to feel sickness or remorse of murder" (5-8). In "Insensibility," he calls "Happy" those veterans "who with a thought besmirch / Blood over all our soul" (40-41), who "before they are killed / Can let their veins run cold" (1-2). And in "Spring Offensive," attacking soldiers

> . . . rushed in the body to enter hell,
> . . . there out-fiending all its fiends and flames
> With superhuman inhumanities,
> Long-famous glories, immemorial shames . . .
>
> ([*Wilfred Owen*] 40-43)

Of these, Owen notes that "Some say God caught them even before they fell" (37), but the survivors of the attack "speak not . . . of comrades that went under" (46).

And Jarrell is equally unwilling to derogate his soldier-subjects by turning them into sheer, inactive pawns or depicting them as mere children and not responsible adults. The clearest demonstration of this is **"Eighth Air Force"**: The poem depicts the airmen as a composite of Christ and his executioners, and the speaker as not only one of them but Pilate, Pilate's wife, Lady Macbeth, and perhaps Judas as well.[9] The representation of the airmen as playing like children or sweating in fear is empathetic, even sympathetic, but not exculpatory. The speaker, who is "a man, / [Who] did as these have done" (12-13), responds to an unspoken demand that he "say that man / Is not as men have said: a wolf to man" by calling these men (and hence also himself) "murderers" (4-6). To "content the people" he will "give up these to them" (14-15), but that means of contentment is a lie:

> . . . for this last saviour, man,
> I have lied as I lie now. But what is lying?
> Men wash their hands, in blood, as best they can:
> I find no fault in this just man.
>
> ([*The Complete Poems*] 17-20)

Richard Fein has argued that "just man" means that these are "only man" (["Randall Jarrell's World of War"] 160), and so are only acting as Necessity requires, but these "puppies" (12) are nevertheless also murderers, and the deliberateness of the speaker's lie argues for their participation in war being not just the result of compulsion, but also an act of adult, reasoning will. And while the gunner in **"The Death of the Ball Turret Gunner"** is not seen to act, he is a gunner on a combat mission, as much (at least potentially) murderer as victim, perhaps one of the modern "heroes" for whom Jarrell is searching out, in Owen's words, a "Poetry . . . fit to speak of them."

The other section of Owen's Preface most pertinent here is the last part quoted above, about "these elegies [being] in no sense consolatory." Owen certainly has notable successes in writing non-consolatory elegies—"Insensibility" and "Spring Offensive," for example, and "Exposure" (which Jarrell much admired [see *Kipling* 169])—but regarding **"The Death of the Ball Turret Gunner"** as an anti-elegy, Owen's failures are more instructive. In "Asleep," for example, despite the rest of the poem's pointed mocking of cliched elegiac, he ends with the consolatory note that at least this soldier is out of his suffering: "He sleeps less tremulous, less cold, / Than we who wake, and waking say Alas!" (20-21) Perhaps more enlightening is when Owen is seduced by the traditional form; Sacks argues that there are "numerous moments in which elegists seem to submit, by quotation or translation, to the somehow echoing language of dead poets" (25), this being part of the placement of a particular elegiac subject into "the ritual *context* of consolation" (24, Sacks's emphasis). One poem in which Owen very clearly falls into such a trap is "Elegy in April and September (jabbered among the trees)," which is deliberately modeled on Matthew Arnold's elegies (Stallworthy, n184) and so toothachingly sweet (example: "Still! daffodil! Nay, hail me not so gaily,—/ Your gay gold lily daunts me and deceives . . . ," [4-5]) that a reader can easily be distracted from the point that the young man is dead and gone, period. Another example of this seduction is "Anthem for Doomed Youth": The first seven lines of this sonnet's octave are an angry attack on the "mockeries" (5) of home-front mourning rituals of prayers, bells, and choirs for those killed in battle, but line 8—"And bugles calling for them from sad shires"—seems to toll Owen back into escapist comfort in a sestet that tells us that in the eyes of boys

> . . . Shall shine the holy glimmers of goodbyes.
> The pallor of girls' brows shall be their pall;
> Their flowers the tenderness of patient minds,
> And each slow dusk a drawing-down of blinds.
>
> (11-14)

As Jon Silkin notes, ". . . Owen seems to be caught in the very act of consolatory mourning he condemns . . ." ([*Out of Battle*] 210).[10]

Jarrell was aware of these traps: In a review of Alex Comfort's *The Song of Lazarus,* he notes how the aptly named Comfort massively appropriates his language forms from other poets, such that "In their elegiac, almost pastoral reflection in these poems, death and the War seem hardly more than allegorical emanations of some passive, amoral reality, . . . mak[ing] it hard to take any death seriously" (*Poetry and the Age,* 155). Jarrell himself manages to avoid the traps, though. First, although it echoes the images and the language used for those images in "Adonais," for various reasons **"The Death of the Ball Turret Gunner"** does not come across as in any way Romantic in tone. For one thing, the language is not aureate, either in vocabulary or syntax. This feature could make the poem flat and undramatic (which is how Pritchard characterizes most of Jarrell's other war poems, 111-20) and that seems to be Bruce Weigl's take on the tone, though Weigl does not present it as a negative criticism: "The speaker, a dead man, is alive enough to speak to us of his death but too dead in spirit to evoke anything more than a stripped down version of his brief existence . . ." and therefore ". . . his observations of even his own horrible death read more like reportage than lyric poetry" (["An Autobiography of Nightmare"] 16-17). However, I think this accurately captures only the last line, a line that I think can be described as possessing the same characteristics Jarrell ascribed to the last stanza of Robert Frost's "Neither Out Far Nor In Deep": "a flat ease, [which] takes everything with something harder than contempt, more passive than acceptance" (*Poetry and the Age,* 43). Part of the power of Jarrell's last line is, I believe, that its crudely observational (reportorial?) nature contrasts starkly with the imagistic, often metaphorical (poetic?) nature of the first four. In fact, according to a quantitative acoustic analysis by Linda Bradley Funkhouser, in reading the poem Jarrell (along with a group of professors) shifts tone when reading the fifth line, delivering it "curtly" (["Acoustic Rhythm in Randall Jarrell's 'The Death of the Ball Turret Gunner'"] 391), but of all the readers studied, only Jarrell "consistently observes caesuras" (395), providing a particularly long pause before line 5, thus not only highlighting the last line but also its difference from the preceding four (396). I think Weigl, in his characterization of the entire poem as possessing "literalness" and being an "almost completely unadorned presentation of [the gunner's] death" (16), is reacting to the same quality in Jarrell's poem that has often led readers to describe Owen's war poems as possessing photographic realism, particularly "Dulce et Decorum Est." But, as Ramazani remarks (specifically regarding "Mental Cases"), "What we call the 'realism' of [Owen's] war poetry is a rich intertextual effect. . . . The suffering victims become 'real' precisely because of, not in spite of, the literary intertexts . . ." (78). Owen's poems and **"The Death of the Ball Turret Gunner"** have the quality of making readers *feel* what is being described, and this in turn makes readers feel that they *see* it.

What Pritchard calls the "imagistic brevity" of the first four lines (119) and the affective force of unadorned description in the final line create a constrained tone for the poem, and this serves to help keep it from becoming a particular kind of anti-elegy, a mock-elegy, a form that can not only attack the style but the subject of the poem, something Jarrell clearly wanted to avoid, reviling some poets for being "blinder to the war than they ever were to the peace, who call the war 'this great slapstick' . . ." (**Kipling,** 129). Gavin Ewart's "When a Beau Goes In" offers a useful contrast. Paul Fussell calls Ewart's poem "typical of Second War poetry in its laconic refusal to reach out for any myth" ([*The Great War and Modern Memory*] 57), and that laconic quality of attitude and the language that conveys that attitude—short, choppy lines with a doggerel rhythm; phrasing that is at times so deliberately banal as to seem not childlike, but almost preliterate; the use of slang—seems to bitterly belittle not just the mechanical slaughterhouse of modern war (there is no agency for the Beaufighter's crash; it just happens), but the men themselves:

> When a Beau goes in,
> Into the drink,
> It makes you think,
> Because, you see, they always sink
> But nobody says "Poor lad"
> Or goes about looking sad
> Because, you see, it's war,
> It's the unalterable law.
>
> Although it's perfectly certain
> The pilot's gone for a Burton
> And the observer too
> It's nothing to do with you
> And if they both should go
> To a land where falls no rain nor hail nor driven snow—
> Here, there, or anywhere,
> Do you suppose *they* care?
>
> You shouldn't cry
> Or say a prayer or sigh.
> In the cold sea, in the dark
> It isn't a lark
> But it isn't Original Sin—
> It's just a Beau going in.
>
> (in Fussell, 57-58)

Fussell remarks (his emphasis) that the "flagrantly un-innocent *just* . . . asserts the utter irrelevance of theological or any other connotations" and that "The tone is like that of the opening of Jarrell's **'Losses'**" (58): "It was not dying: everybody died." I find the tone quite different, however: Jarrell's may be hard-eyed and emotionally, even morally enervated, but Ewart's is almost flippant. I am not saying that this is not a realistic or valid response to war, by the way, and I believe "When a Beau Goes In" is a very good poem. But it does convey a sense that these lives being lost are of no value whatsoever to anything—the State?—or anyone—who is "you" in the poem? It can include combatants and non-combatants alike, the speaker, the reader, even (given line 16) the airmen who die. This poem mocks not only traditional views and consolations, but by its tone and inclusivity the casualties who are its (at least putative) subject, turning death into not just a non-event, but almost a joke. It is a mock-elegy.

One of the features that contributes to this effect is the poem's length: Ewart has room to pile up a number of mocked cliches and ironic, even sarcastic remarks. Even were Jarrell so minded, the brevity of **"The Death of the Ball Turret Gunner"** gives no such room. That brevity also keeps him from moving to the other end of the elegiac spectrum and producing a poem of consolation: The longer one goes on in association, even oppositional association with a traditional form deeply grooved by reading and studying into the poem-making mind, the greater the chance that one will fall under its spell. This happens in just eight lines to Owen in "Anthem for Doomed Youth." Jarrell's brevity helps keep him from this trap.

Perhaps more importantly, though, the brevity has thematic implications. First, it opposes the lengthy form of its elegiac foil, "Adonais," eliminating, among other things, all the traditional elements of elegy—the parade of mourners, the mourning by personified elements of nature, etc.—that Shelley so assiduously includes. Also, of course, Shelley addresses his subject's genius and remarkable productivity, while Jarrell's anonymous subject is an apparently ordinary young man, and the very lack of length serves to emphasize the aborting (as David K. Cornelius points out, this is a literal as well as figurative term) of a life so short it is suggested that nothing worth note was done. Indeed, even in the poem itself, the gunner doesn't do anything except fall, wake, hunch, and freeze. We don't even witness his act of dying, and despite the fact that he's a gunner we have no hint of him fighting back against anything, whether the fighters or the State. In this, he closely parallels Keats, whom Shelley notes was not willing, or perhaps able to follow the Pythian example of Byron and fight the forces that attacked him. But then, both Keats and the gunner are ultimately arrayed against Necessity; Jarrell notes that the poems in Lowell's Necessarian *Lord Weary's Castle* "often use cold as a plain and physically correct symbol for what is constricted or static" (**Poetry and the Age,** 210), and the gunner is literally frozen inside the State. Not only did the gunner not do anything of note in his life, but there was no opportunity for doing anything anyway, and this is the common case for soldiers. What the gunner has lost is what Jarrell called "the greatest single subject of the romantics, pure potentiality" (**Poetry and the Age,** 98).

Another effect—although in fact it may be a cause—of the poem's brevity is the telescoping of birth and death. Frances C. Ferguson contrasts this structure with, among other poems, **"Eighth Air Force,"** which she describes as concentrating "the entire poetic effort into the area of the included middle"; **"The Death of the Ball Turret Gunner"**—that is, his life—"consists only of a beginning and an ending" (171), and as Dawson points out, whereas Adonais's death is a transcendent birth, in Jarrell's poem "birth in the Gunner's new 'state' is death" (238). The telescoping also suggests another source for **"The Death of the Ball Turret Gunner"**: T. S. Eliot's "Journey of the Magi." In his copy of Eliot's *The Complete Poems and Plays: 1909-1950* (1952), Jarrell drew three vertical lines next to lines 37-39 and noted in the margin "antithesis oxymoron excl. middle,"[11] and, indeed, in Eliot's dramatic monologue, the Magus's entire focus is on his own Messiah-induced experience. Of the human life of Jesus, there is nothing about the middle, the beginning is a subjective reflection—". . . it was (you may say) satisfactory" (31)—and the end is a brief allusion—"three trees on the low sky" (24). But the significance of those mortal bookends is what occupies the speaker in the conclusion:

> . . . were we led all that way for
> Birth or Death? There was a Birth, certainly,
> We had evidence and no doubt. I had seen birth and death,
> But had thought they were different; this Birth was
> Hard and bitter agony for us, like Death, our death.
> We returned to our places, these Kingdoms,
> But no longer at ease here, in the old dispensation,
> With an alien people clutching their gods.
> I should be glad of another death.
>
> (35-43)

The paradoxical relationship of life and death is at least as old as Christianity itself, but the usual Christian version is the traditional vegetation-god pattern of elegy, having death being birth into a new life; here, as with **"The Death of the Ball Turret Gunner,"** the process is reversed and birth is death. The poems also share elision of the "middle" and a refusal to offer the solace of an assured and glorious afterlife. A reader who expects, even yearns for the consolations of religion or elegy is out of luck with both these poems because the poets are "no longer at ease" with these traditions.

Yet Eliot, while rejecting any easy and comforting sentiment, does not reject religious faith itself—he does not mock Christ or the Magi. Similarly, Jarrell does not mock the gunner, only the elegiac form with its consolatory accretions. In Shelley, Jarrell found a fellow believer in Necessarian philosophy, but in "Adonais," while he discovered serendipitous images, he could not, at least in the face of war, follow all the way to transcendence.[12] In Owen, he found a forerunner in the enterprise of honestly depicting modern war and soldiers, and an ancillary goal to be pursued, an elegiac that is not consolatory. In Eliot, he found the elisive compression that would allow him to capture the essence of war and life, what Owen's Other in "Strange Meeting" calls "The pity of war, the pity war distilled" (25). With **"The Death of the Ball Turret Gunner,"** then, Jarrell is able to formally and thematically apprehend the qualitatively and quantitatively foreshortened nature of modern life, a life distilled in war, and do so without diminishing or devaluing his human subject. That is, he writes a mock*ed*-elegy.

Notes

1. Milton pretty much fails in his efforts to leave the loyal angels unscathed: Even though God and Son direct their "derision" of the "vain designs and tumults vain" (5:736-37) only at the rebel crew, the loyal angels are tumbling in the same tumults and so appear equally ridiculous. Besides Stein and Riggs, see Fish, 190, and Cyr.

2. Unless otherwise noted, all quotations for Jarrell are from *The Complete Poems,* for Shelley *Shelley's Poetry and Prose,* and for Owen *Wilfred Owen: The Complete Poems and Fragments.*

3. In his requiem for Ernie Pyle, Jarrell makes this comment about ordinary GIs "Yet their war's grotesque unnaturalness finally becomes for them a grotesque naturalness, all that they have known or done—except for that endlessly dwelt-on fantasy that was before and may be after the war, their civilian lives and families and home" (*Kipling,* 115).

4. This early conception evolved over the course of Shelley's life, but to what conclusion, if any, is debatable: see Notopolous, 176-203, Pulos, 108, and Reiman, 48.

5. The Necessity/State connection is blatant in other of Jarrell's war poems. For example, in "The Soldier," war is seen in terms of a massive commercial enterprise in which people are "integers" (9) or mathematical "variable[s]" (16) who have been "shadowed past distinction by the deaths / The

States sowed over continents like salt" (10-11). The speaker "faced across the trenches of a continent / The customers whom I was shipped to kill" (3-4) and learned that what "The centuries had dreamed was Chance or Fate" (19) was something else: "We learned—our poor wits sharpened with their blood—/ That last cold center of our wish was Trade" (20-21). Such heavy-handed polemic is also present in "1945: The Death of the Gods," "Siegried," and "Transient Barracks."

6. As Donald Reiman points out, in Shelley's poetry stars "offer the hope to mortals that they, too, can rise above the mutability of this existence into an unchanging fulfillment of the highest human aspirations," and "this existence" is "the terrestrial realm of cyclical necessity" (16). In this context, it is interesting to note that one of Jarrell's jobs in the service was to operate a Link Trainer, a machine that allowed airmen to simulate flying without leaving the ground. In describing the machine, he says, "The navigator (sometimes pilots and bombardiers too) sits in it, and navigates by shooting with his sextant the stars that are in a star dome above his head—we move them pretty much as a planetarium operator does. . . . One trainer in a year certainly saves five or six bombers and five or six crews" (qtd. in Pritchard, 107).

7. In the event, this volume was never published and the Preface is only a draft.

8. Indeed, though he notes that Jarrell "never talked about pity as the war poet's stock-in-trade," Pritchard focuses on this section, as did James Dickey in his review of Jarrell's *Selected Poems* (112).

9. Jarrell calls the airmen "criminals and scapegoats" as Christ was (*Selected,* xiii); Frances Ferguson notes the inclusion of Pilate's wife (173); Richard Flynn, to whose knowledge of Jarrell and Jarrell scholarship I am indebted on several counts, makes the Lady Macbeth connection (36).

10. Ramazani offers an interesting reading of "Anthem": He sees Owen's turn to consolation in the sestet as a deliberate attempt to offer replacements for traditional ceremonies of mourning, but argues that "the earlier stanza more strenuously disrupts elegiac norms than critics have recognized, making this stanza's recuperative effort fall short of consolatory closure" (73). Like Silkin, then, he sees the poem as failing in its purpose, but failing in the opposite direction.

11. After reading a draft of this essay in which I discussed Eliot's poem for comparative purposes but made no argument for it as one of Jarrell's sources, Richard Flynn told me this annotated edition existed and, on a visit to Greensboro, he discovered these marginalia. That the notes were made seven-plus years after the publication of "The Death of the Ball Turret Gunner" creates a chicken-egg conundrum, of course, but Jarrell's thorough acquaintance with Eliot's work argues that the 1927 "Journey of the Magi" influenced Jarrell's poem, rather than that poem influencing Jarrell's notes.

12. Suzanne Ferguson breaks down the themes and stages of Jarrell's career with a focus on Necessity: "in the poems of the thirties, the 'great Necessity' of the natural world and the evils of power politics; in the poems of the early forties, the dehumanizing forces of war and ways to escape or recover from these through dreams, mythologizing, or Christian faith; in the poems of the fifties, and continuing into the sixties, loneliness and fear of aging and death, again opposed by the imagination in dreams and works of art; and in some of the last poems, the defeat of Necessity and time through imaginative recovery of one's own past. The one overriding theme that links and illuminates the others is change, the change that aims toward transcendence" (*Poetry of Randall Jarrell,* 6).

Works Cited

Cornelius, David K. "Jarrell's 'The Death of the Ball Turret Gunner.'" *Explicator* 35.3 (1977): 3.

Cyr, Marc D. "The Archangel Raphael: Narrative Authority in Milton's War in Heaven." *The Journal of Narrative Technique* 17, no. 3 (Fall 1987): 309-16.

Dawson, Leven M. "Jarrell's 'The Death of the Ball Turret Gunner.'" *Explicator* 31 (1972): item 29.

Eliot, T. S. *The Complete Poems and Plays: 1909-1950.* New York: Harcourt, 1952.

Ewart, Gavin. "When a Beau Goes In." *The Poetry of War, 1939-45.* Edited by Ian Hamilton. In Fussell, 57-58.

Fein, Richard. "Randall Jarrell's World of War." *Analects* 1, no. 2 (Spring 1961): 14-23. (Reprinted in S. Ferguson, *Critical,* 149-62.)

Ferguson, Frances C. "Randall Jarrell and the Flotations of Voice." *Georgia Review* 28 (Fall 1974): 423-39. (Reprinted in S. Ferguson, *Critical,* 163-75.)

Ferguson, Suzanne, ed. *Critical Essays on Randall Jarrell.* Boston: G. K. Hall, 1983.

———. *The Poetry of Randall Jarrell.* Baton Rouge: Louisiana State University Press, 1971.

Fish, Stanley. *Surprised by Sin.* New York: St. Martin's, 1967.

Flynn, Richard. *Randall Jarrell and the Lost World of Childhood.* Athens: University of Georgia Press, 1990.

Funkhouser, Linda Bradley. "Acoustic Rhythm in Randall Jarrell's 'The Death of the Ball Turret Gunner.'" *Poetics: International Review for the Theory of Literature* 8 (1979): 381-403.

Fussell, Paul. *The Great War and Modern Memory.* New York: Oxford University Press, 1975.

Jarrell, Randall. *The Complete Poems.* New York: Farrar, Straus, Giroux, 1968.

———. *Kipling, Auden, & Co.: Essays and Reviews 1935-1964.* New York: Farrar, Straus, Giroux, 1980.

———. Marginal notes in Eliot, *The Complete Poems and Plays.* Randall Jarrell Collection, Special Collections & Rare Books, Walter Clinton Jackson Library, UNC Greensboro. By permission of Mary Jarrell.

———. *Poetry and the Age.* New York: Ecco, 1953.

———. *Selected Poems.* New York: Atheneum, 1969.

Milton, John. *John Milton: Complete Poems and Major Prose.* Edited by Merritt Y. Hughes. Indianapolis: Odyssey, 1957.

Notopolous, James A. *The Platonism of Shelley: A Study of Platonism and the Poetic Mind.* New York: Octagon, 1969.

Owen, Wilfred. *Wilfred Owen: The Complete Poems and Fragments.* 2 vols. Edited by Jon Stallworthy. New York: Norton, 1984.

Pritchard, William H. *Randall Jarrell: A Literary Life.* New York: Farrar, Straus, Giroux, 1990.

Pulos, C. E. *The Deep Truth: A Study of Shelley's Scepticism.* Lincoln: University of Nebraska Press, 1962.

Ramazani, Jahan. *Poetry of Mourning: The Modern Elegy from Hardy to Heaney.* Chicago: University of Chicago Press, 1994.

Reiman, Donald H. *Shelley's "The Triumph of Life": A Critical Study.* Urbana: University of Illinois Press, 1965.

Riggs, William G. *The Christian Poet in Paradise Lost.* Berkeley: University of California Press, 1972.

Sacks, Peter M. *The English Elegy: Studies in the Genre from Spenser to Yeats.* Baltimore: Johns Hopkins University Press, 1985.

Shelley, Percy Bysshe. *The Complete Poetical Works of Percy Bysshe Shelley.* Edited by Neville Rogers. 4 vols. Oxford: Clarendon, 1972.

———. *Shelley's Poetry and Prose: Authoritative Texts, Criticism.* Eds. Donald H. Reiman and Sharon B. Powers. New York: Norton, 1977.

Silkin, Jon. *Out of Battle: The Poetry of the Great War.* 2nd ed. New York: St. Martin's, 1998.

Stein, Arnold. *Answerable Style: Essays on Paradise Lost.* Minneapolis: University of Minnesota Press, 1953.

Weigl, Bruce. "An Autobiography of Nightmare." *Field: Contemporary Poetry and Poetics* 35 (1986): 15-18.

Yeats, W. B. Introduction. *The Oxford Book of Modern Verse: 1892-1935.* New York: Oxford University Press, 1936.

R. Clifton Spargo (essay date January 2005)

SOURCE: Spargo, R. Clifton. "The Ethical Uselessness of Grief: Randall Jarrell's 'The Refugees.'" *PMLA* 120, no. 1 (January 2005): 49-65.

[*In the following essay, Spargo situates Jarrell's poem "The Refugees," in both its original version of 1940 and its revision of 1949, within psychological and cultural economies, ultimately questioning any self-satisfaction America has over the death of European refugees.*]

Ever since Theodor Adorno wrote in "On Lyric Poetry and Society" of the marvelous proficiency and simultaneous lack that characterize lyric voice in bourgeois society, the lyric has borne the burden of its necessarily deficient claim of self-expression. In its diminished scope of reference—in other words, as an effect of its narrowing of representational claims and of the field of social significance—the lyric, Adorno suggests, is highly representative of bourgeois voice, perhaps quintessentially representative of all that an individual voice might claim for itself. In seeking a ground for rereading its social significance, we should not, Adorno believes, underestimate the genuine social achievement of the lyric, which has been granted the power "to grasp the universal through immersion in the self." Though our critical response must eventually, even perhaps simultaneously, turn to those other voices who, according to the presumptions of lyrical voice, remain in Adorno's terms only "objects of history" (45), excluded from such full and adequate representation, there is nevertheless an economical efficiency at work in lyrical voice—in the sense that what the lyric calls identity depends always on what it can keep out.

Anyone familiar with the Freudian work of mourning and the recent developments of trauma theory will hear in this a parallel (partly accounted for by Adorno's debt to Freud) to the basic economic premise of the Freudian psychic system. Unpleasure, as the name for those phenomena imposed on the self's integrity when it lacks resources to cope with them, must be kept at a distance. The workings of the psychic system become especially evident under duress, and so in Freud's metapsychological papers, ranging from "Mourning and Melancholia" to *Beyond the Pleasure Principle,* the economic or regulatory principle becomes most overt. According to our cultural narratives for mourning, as Freud saw only too well, the fact of loss promotes participation in symbolic meaning, turning us back on personal narratives derived in cooperation with predominant cultural narratives that have enabled our existence even in the face of adversity. Yet this conflation of an absence that inheres in language with the existential occasion of mourning seems too convenient. It is as if grief, when confronted with adversity and the memory of the adversity another person has suffered, were to treat loss as merely redundant, diminishing the ethical significance of the lost other and deflecting the harsh realities to come because we have always known that every other must eventually be lost to us.

There is in mourning always this quality of redundancy—as a sign of mourning's constitutive excess, its extravagance of expression, its seeming uselessness as ethics. Redundancy is part of the texture of grief's self-referentiality, for grief has happened before, and there are even efficacious models for resolving it. Most of our grief exists in some necessary proportion to identity and to the cultural plot of identification that determines the history of any self as it mourns. Only the wayward expressions of grief, those instances that repeat what has come before yet fail either to occur or to end in their proper moment, make mourning seem self-conscious, awkward, unsuccessful, even ridiculous.

In turning to a lesser-known poem by Randall Jarrell, **"The Refugees"** (1940), I contend that Jarrell's poetics exploits the profuse artifice of grief to suggest grief's futility and to make it a sign of grief's ethical aspirations.[1] Moreover, as Jarrell transposes an implicitly Freudian model of psychic economy onto the political situation of the European refugee crisis triggered by the rise of Nazism, he offers a critique of the cultural economy of identity. And he does so as an admiring reader of Freud, as a poet who—like his most immediate and significant precursor, W. H. Auden, and like many European intellectuals of the era, from Herbert Marcuse to Theodor Adorno, who were exiled to America—blended Freud and Marx in his interpretation of culture. To the extent that we see Freudian terms in a poem that confronts this extraordinary historical situation, we might also discern, through Jarrell's poem, the uncanny specter of a Freud who (having fled Austria in anticipation of the Nazi occupation in 1938) found himself outside the terms of economy in which his own system of identity participates. Such a paradox, though probably not a deliberate irony of Jarrell's, was developed, albeit in slightly different terms, by Auden in an elegy composed on the psychoanalyst's death in 1939, which was part of a series of occasional poems including "Refugee Blues" (1939), one of the clearest antecedents to Jarrell's poem.[2] As Jahan Ramazani has observed, the series of occasional poems in *Another Time* (1940) marked a transitional phase in Auden's career, his fear of world war and his disenchantment with political poetry strangely coinciding with the emergence of a "poetic politics" dialectically inspired by his having wrestled with the legacy of William Butler Yeats in a famous elegy as well as in a number of critical essays on Ireland's great poet. In the essay "Yeats as an Example" (1948), Auden would ultimately credit Yeats with having transformed the occasional poem into a "serious reflective poem of at once personal and public interest" (388), but these words could describe Auden's own efforts in 1939 and perhaps also—despite Jarrell's evidently conflicted response to the Auden poems of this period—Jarrell's own experiment in public, elegiacally connoted poetry.[3]

Jarrell's 1940 poem (and a 1949 revised version of it) are part of a subgenre we might call "refugee poems," of which Auden's 1939 poem is perhaps the best-known example. At least two other Jarrell poems loosely fit the genre—**"For an Emigrant"** (1940) and **"Jews at Haifa"** (1947)—but **"The Refugees"** is of special interest largely because it closely resembles public elegy and thus elucidates the extent to which the crisis that mourning poses to the lyric intimates lyric poetry's ethical meanings. Indeed, explicitly ethical concerns evoked within the formal parameters of the lyric are here treated as though they were also constitutively a matter for politics. Not only does **"The Refugees"** resist much of Adorno's thesis that lyric voice necessarily resides in history even as it manifests the selectively individuated function of bourgeois identity, but, turning always on the thought of those whom the lyric excludes or for whom it has not yet answered, Jarrell's poem challenges an economics of cultural identity the lyric poem typically upholds. By expanding overtly into the province of history to consider those who could not include themselves in social economy and by forging, moreover, an intersection between compassion and grief as though they were conceptually interchangeable, Jarrell suggests that mourning is not just a retrospective concern for a person who can no longer be helped but also potentially an imaginative prolepsis by which one skips over the immediate, public moment in which one might have helped another so as to indulge feelings about what might have been. Since Jarrell thus worries that a generalized account of public responsibility treats the genuine political possibility of refuge as though it were already past, he invokes mourning as a sign of political futility, while suggesting that even as such it traces, if only as rhetorical possibility, the course of another action, an ethical, interventionist response to the refugee.

I

Jarrell's poem seems especially apt for testing the economics of identity as a measure of lyrical form because it is a partial sestina (the poem runs only four, rather than six, stanzas long). With its set allotment of lines and its further restriction of poetic rhyme to the device of repeated words, the sestina is an exercise in the economical constraints of lyrical voice. It is a poet's poem, drawing attention to its artifice to explore the possibilities of expressiveness within stifling formal boundaries. The sestina reminds us of the bounded property of language, of the extent to which all speaking involves newly working from the same material—the limits of a native tongue. Sestina demands a self-consciousness about form not unlike the self-consciousness about economy I suggest as an ethical possibility for the lyric. At the very least, Jarrell's poem charts a course from an explicit, restrictive economics of form toward a set of ethical meanings arising as though in defiance of economy.[4]

Insofar as this competing antieconomic tendency of the lyric is ethically connoted to refer the poem beyond its act of limitation, the poem supposes a larger relation to history, akin to that implicit ethical demand informing Adorno's reading of the historical pressures exerted on lyrical voice. To put this differently, as the lyric gets referred to what is outside the economic system in and by which identity is derived, it must always consider, if only by recollecting a prior neglect, those others who cannot be reconciled to our familiar cultural plots of identity.[5] One of the fundamental questions ethics poses to any economically determined system of thought is whether what occurs in a relation of exteriority has already been anticipated by the system. Several tensions may emerge in the light of exteriority's threat to self-sufficiency: the tension between private and public identity; between pleasure and pain; between resolution and difficulty; indeed, between pleasure and what we call reality. In the lyric, these tensions are internalized and subtly embedded in a figurative logic that suggests the extent to which a poem can never be entirely self-consistent. As a distilled species of lyric, the elegy concentrates the intensity of its figures on the painfulness of a loss posed as the ostensible undoing of lyrical voice.

In the hypothesis of incapability—of silence, deprivation, inconsolable grief—the elegy discovers its voice only by recovering, at least seemingly, a world it had already possessed.[6] If this past were truly binding, there would be an economy even in loss, since Freudian family romance draws much of its persuasive power as a twentieth-century bourgeois narrative from the fact that loss has from the start rendered a paradoxical service to identity, reminding us of an original attachment as well as the crisis of detachment through which we take the fortunate fall into the symbolic workings of language.[7] More than less typical of traditional Western philosophical constructs for identity, what Freud (like Hegel before him) posited as a purportedly natural, albeit bourgeois, fact was that loss eventually proves identity's continued viability by getting appropriated into the realm of the familiar. Every loss we mourn, unoriginal though it may be, harks back as though to an original relationship, and it is thus, paradoxically, because the one who grieves has expected even loss to be familiar, and yet not political, that grief can make no real contribution to culture in the name of the other.

In treating the dialectical habit of mind in which the hypothetical antithesis or alterity presented by any new event refers back to a prior thesis of identity, Hegel turns at a significant point in the *Phenomenology* to the archetypal plot of familial loyalty in *Antigone* to press his case for a natural principle ordering identity even before it enters the public sphere ([*Phenomenology of Spirit,*] esp. 256-78). As George Steiner has demonstrated, Antigone has been frequently appropriated to figure anterior boundaries of political meaning, almost as if she stood originally for the divide between the public and private realms. According to Judith Butler, Antigone signifies those acts of cultural negotiation by which definitions of kinship are normatively fixed. Either by denoting the necessary renunciation (to which the heroine will not yield) of the familial for the political or by representing the limits of kinship's cultural intelligibility, Antigone's moribund loyalty to her brother is a sign of both the antecedent and the simultaneously supervening reign of symbolic meanings. The Hegelian reading of Antigone as standing perversely for kinship rather than for the state must be recast as soon as one acknowledges Antigone's deed to be imbricated with the sovereign will of Creon, as also with the legacy of her cursed father and her quasi-incestuous loyalty to her brother (Butler [*Antigone's Claim*] 27-40). Though it is hardly her main point, Butler treats the question of Antigone's mourning as foregone conclusion: the fate the heroine suffers—to be sealed by Creon's edict alive in a cave—seems continuous with her symbolic marriage to those who are dead. Even though Antigone forces us to view the opposition of public and private through a chiasmus, as though it were finally impossible to discern kinship as an antiquated or transcendent realm of existence prior to or separate from the culturally constructed norms that regulate it, the question of mourning is less contained by than determinative of a crisis in those cultural norms through which our ethical valuation (say, as persistent reverence for a dead brother) takes place.

Though I think it appropriate to investigate mourning as a redundant site of played-out obligations, even as such, mourning elicits a break in the normative possibilities of politics, reconceiving if only by an act of futile dissent the rigorously economic logic by which the sovereign will declares certain losses to be permissibly familiar and, since included in the bounded relationships legitimated by the state, also culturally significant. In this sense, as Butler shows Antigone's adherence to kinship to be inseparable from Creon's sovereign will, she elucidates another feature of the Western construct of the state, which despite its discursive praxis of containing familial or private matters also perpetuates norms of kinship by imagining national preferences as proximate familial relations. As Antigone says, it is Creon who refuses to treat the matter of burial rites as "insignificant" ("παρ' οὐδέν"—literally, as comparable to nothing [Sophocles [*Antigone*], line 35; my trans.]). Often maligned for being loyal and yet apparently affectless, Antigone draws our attention to the paradoxical fact that public grief is always slightly unpersuasive. For Creon's part, even as the king enacts between social and private meanings a division he does not quite believe in (since he will not let the body be buried in private, as a mere familial matter), his ban on mourning rites caricatures the social economy within or against which any practice of mourning operates, insisting on a distinction according to which our valuation of the dead must be continuous with their prior acceptability to the state, their remembered lives only as important as they are politically worthy of memory.

All our remembered dead, but especially those who die by orchestrated violence and thus may provoke unacceptable modes of grief, can upset norms, since grief in its redundancy and spectacle comments on a political division that casts some lives as more worthy than others. Thus, mourning, as an intervention that arrives too late, is also a sign of a prior inconsideration, indifference, or relative callousness. Since the other who dies must hereafter be left out of cultural economy, glimpsed in every death is a possibility of neglect that defines all relationship. The death of the other portends, oddly in retrospect, a radical incapacity in our cultural concepts of identity, an inability to alter the system of identity or amend, under present exigency, the neglect of another who is, or perhaps only seems to be, politically unnecessary or culturally irrelevant. It can be argued, especially through Emmanuel Levinas, that ethics interprets a temporal culpability: one is late to help, approach, or remember the other because every response comes after the constitutive responsibility that demands it.[8] This confession of an inadequacy within ethics is rather like elegiac mourning's confession of its own futility. Mourning's belatedness speaks, even if it is only through the self-accusing griever's melancholic exaggeration, of an irresponsibility within intention as also within identity: one who is late on behalf of another has neglected a set of responsibilities in favor of others.

II

Part of the problem with any public elegy is that readers experience generalized grief as not properly their own. Yeats in "In Memory of Major Robert Gregory" and Auden in elegies for Yeats and Freud infused, perhaps even confused, the public event with a greater sense of personal attachment, interpreting the polis with what Ramazani terms a "small-scale, individualist view," which functions at the same time as a revisioning of politics on the scale of friendship ([*Poetry of Mourning* 182). Any politics of hospitality must always be about this metaphoric intersection, interpreting the public realm as a limited, therefore more readily imagined, sphere of relationship; and any poem trying to wrest unknown victims from an anonymity that seems from afar to be synonymous with their tragic fate must consider, even if it ultimately rejects, such an intersection. If the 1940 version of **"The Refugees"** cannot properly be called a Holocaust poem because it was written before the events became common knowledge and before the final phase of the Nazi genocide was perpetrated, Jarrell speaks specifically as one not yet overwhelmed by the enormity of the Nazi crime, writing from within a moment when it was possible to perceive an international political responsibility for refugees from fascism. At the Evian Conference of 1938, the central nonfascist states convened to discuss the plight of the refugees, but no practical plan for rescue or for providing permanent or temporary asylum emerged. With Evian in the background and with calls proliferating in liberal circles (the prominent journalist Dorothy Thompson's writings perhaps most influential among them) for an American response to the refugee crisis, Americans were often asked to imagine the refugees' situation.

Among noteworthy political journals, the *New Republic*, under the editorship of Malcolm Cowley, took the most active role in criticizing the governmental response to the crisis, indicting the nationalist self-esteem of an America that could barely imagine doing more for the refugees than the fascists had. An essay from July 1938, "Who Wants Refugees?," condemned the countries that assembled at Evian: "If they had proclaimed at once that the unfortunate victims of persecution would be welcomed elsewhere, promptly and with as few obstacles as possible, the humane superiority of democracy over its enemies would have been strikingly demonstrated." "Let the Jews Come In!," from November of the same year, made an urgent practical appeal to modify present immigration restrictions; and one year later an essay by Thomas Mann, citing the experience of refugees in the United States, suggested that although Americans on the whole behaved "magnificently" toward the latest immigrant wave, they were reluctant to admit—because "they don't realize it themselves"—that the received refugees were "not wanted *even here*" (emphasis added). Mann's grateful tone masked a rhetorical irony: the question of how refugees were received (or might still be received) drew his audience into an uncomfortable identification with the fascistic mind, if only by intimating the latent hostility refugees inspired even in America.

Although a number of wartime refugee poems such as Auden's consider the spectacle of grief from within the circumstance of political oppression, Jarrell interpolates an act of mourning into the rhetoric of political compassion as though grief had determined in advance the American public's sense of futility. In this respect, however, the poet was soon to find corroborating examples in the American public sphere, as 1942 gave rise to commemorative ceremonies in which the Jews who had perished and those about to be killed were alike remembered by American Jews and other sympathetic Americans. At a famous Madison Square Garden rally in late July, at which the speakers included Mayor Fiorello La Guardia, Governor Herbert H. Lehman, Senator Henry Cabot Lodge, and Bishop Francis J. McConnell, Rabbi Stephen S. Wise (sometimes faulted by historians of the Holocaust for his failure to solicit more actively American intervention on behalf of the European Jews) spoke with eloquence on the eve of Tishah-b'Ab, the anniversary of the destruction of the Jewish temples in Jerusalem. Casting the present sorrow in the light of an "ancient grief," Wise insisted that the people of New York were not gathered to "mourn the destruction of the Jewish people," almost as though he wished to concede mourning's political futility and overcome it by triumphalist gestures. Invoking from Jews "solemn lamentation and mournful protest" and from the rest of the audience "solemn condemnation of the infamy of the Axis in dooming unarmed and defenseless men," Wise's final demand remained on the scale of sentiment. The rally drew a response from President Franklin D. Roosevelt, who, recognizing the American Jews' willingness to "make every sacrifice for victory," assured Wise that all American citizens "will share in the sorrow of our Jewish fellow citizens" and promised that the Nazi crimes would be subject to "accountability in a day of reckoning which will surely come" ("President" ["President and Prime Minister Speak"]). No proposal for activist policies of rescue or for liberalizing American immigration quotas was forthcoming, and in fact none had ever been directly requested. Though highly public, the demonstration was relatively useless, its organizers seemingly aware of its futility ahead of time. Which is not to say that this public act of mourning stood for nothing; it stood precisely for the sorrow of the people gathered, a symbolic redundancy of grief. Other public acts of mourning followed—a symbolic work stoppage in December 1942 and a pageant in March 1943 held at Madison Square Garden—and all appeared to exhibit not only grief but also the poignant awareness of grief's futility.

Jarrell's public act of mourning was **"The Refugees,"** first published in the winter of 1940 in *Partisan Review* and republished in the *New York Times Book Review* in November 1942, after the first Madison Square Garden demonstration. The poem casts a quasi-journalistic eye on European refugees, forced from their home, traveling by train to an unknown destination associated with their demise. Rather like Wise, who addresses a public whose political indifference he is implicated in, the speaker of Jarrell's poem is at one with his audience, observing the failed similarity of people cast outside political economy. It is as though in their misfortune the refugees were already lapsing from cultural familiarity, in this way imaginatively cast out as they have been politically disfranchised. Though the poem is not properly an elegy—since it addresses a contemporary refugee crisis that Jarrell and his audience should not understand as a fait accompli—Jarrell invokes elegiac idiom to question his American readers' immediate responsibility for refugees who once had lives, and may yet have thoughts, like theirs:

> In the shabby train no seat is vacant.
>   The child in the ripped mask
>   Sprawls undisturbed in the waste
> Of the smashed compartment. Is their calm
>   extravagant?
>   They had faces and lives like you. What was
>   it they possessed,
>   That they were willing to trade for this?
>
> The dried blood sparkles along the mask
>   Of the child who yesterday possessed
>   A country welcomer than this.
> Did he? All night into the waste
>   The train moves silently. The faces are
>   vacant.
>   Have none of them found the cost
>   extravagant?
>
> How could they? They gave what they
>   possessed.
>   Here all the purses are vacant.
>   And what else could satisfy the extravagant
> Tears and wish of the child but this?
>   Impose its cancelling terrible mask
>   On the days and faces and lives they waste?
>
> What else are their lives but a journey to the
>   vacant
>   Satisfaction of death? And the mask
>   They wear tonight through their waste
> Is death's rehearsal. Is it really extravagant
>   To read in their faces: What is there that we
>   possessed
>   That we were unwilling to trade for this?

What distinguishes Jarrell's method of considering persons who are outside a species of thought and imagining how they remain there is his technique of dialectically interrogating both those inside the economy who think slightly or slightingly of the others and those who have been neglected. Jarrell's ironically grudging mode of compassion anticipates the method of a poem such as his **"A Girl in a Library"** (1951), where the speaker initially tries to muster all his tolerance to admit the simple fact of a superficial college girl's humanity ("You are very human" [line 4]), before eventually subjecting himself to her example ("I am a thought of yours: and yet, you do not think . . ." [104]). As that later poem gathers toward an oddly collective thought the speaker has deduced from the girl's thoughtlessness, the poet declares that "the ways we miss our lives are life" (92), a statement that, although here offered in an all-too-ordinary American context, recapitulates the imaginative problem at the heart of **"The Refugees."** Those who should be objects of an immediate compassion are imagined in the earlier political poem through a back-and-forth negotiation that enables an act of imaginative identification, which has been produced from a priorly adverse—even adversarial—identification of the other as a stranger, as someone perhaps barely human.

Indeed, Jarrell's structural use of adversarial identification implicitly recalls a refugee poem by Joy Davidman, which appeared in the *New Republic* in July 1939. In "Jews of No Man's Land," Davidman speaks in the collective voice of Jewish refugees, trapped between Poland and Sudetenland, who after begging to be remembered offer prophetic advice to the witnesses of their misery ("[y]ou who pity us" and "look at us out of the warm rooms"). The fate of these Jews without a land is to serve as a warning to others, who may meet a similar fate "in another country":

> Learn how we were brought to this desolation,
> how we were betrayed by our sleep and our pleasant customs and peace and by the
> > striking hour
> lest it be done to each of you in your nation!

One might read their warning as a veiled curse, as the present victims of Nazism not only express concern for those who are not yet persecuted but also predict future adversity for their audience as though it were the by-product of such concern. But of course the poem is not really spoken by the victims. The poet ventriloquistically speaks for them, imaginatively occupying the perspective of European Jews betrayed by nothing more ominous than "sleep" or "pleasant customs and peace"—all those predictable aspects of the nonmilitarized society—in order to encourage a still largely isolationist American public to embrace the fight against fascism.

Although Jarrell's ironic voice is more softly modulated, his poem's ending approximates Davidman's ventriloquistic device in that Jarrell also depends on an adversarial connotation inspiring identification. If there is hostility in Jarrell's poem, it proceeds implicitly as though from the victims of persecution toward those who will do nothing to spare them—which is to say, generally toward the American public. Instead of deploying the rhetoric of warning, Jarrell evolves a structure of complicity, according to which the acceptance of the very facts of the refugees' fate defines the audience's politically lax conscience. Already in the first stanza the permanence of Jarrell's past tense gives the refugees' story a note of fatalism: by the time the refugees travel toward the "[s]atisfaction of death," their entire journey part of "death's rehearsal," the poet's elegiac fatalism seems fully complicitous with the end he foresees. By glimpsing the refugees just before the finality of fate, still imaginatively close in our and their minds to the moment in which their lives might be altered for the better, Jarrell interprets elegiac voice as though it functioned always under the burden of an impossible simultaneity; he positions us alongside the refugees in their statelessness, calling to mind the question of practical intervention. Split thus between the report of an impossible intervention (it is too late for these refugees) and the remaining possibility of a real political intervention in immigration policy (because it is not too late for others), the speaker's fatalism interrogates contemporary American anti-immigration policies that were actively yielding refugees to suffering and death all across occupied Europe.

Significantly, any practical responsibility for the refugee turns on a question of economy. At the end of the first stanza, Jarrell locates the thought of economy in the minds of those who suffer its restrictions, as if they, rather like his girl in the library, were deciding, if only unconsciously, the ways they are going to miss their own lives. When the poet openly wonders what it was "they possessed, / That they were willing to trade for this . . . ," he alludes possibly to the Nazi policies of extortion, which included not only restricting Jewish finances and eventually seizing Jewish property and money but also charging Jews for the costs of their deportation. Thus, Jarrell points to the ironically narrowed gap between the fate of the Jewish refugees and what they could foresee for themselves as they bargained for their lives from a position of incalculable disadvantage. What they were willing to trade of what they yet possessed is the sign of an occluded hope—a freedom they might have purchased if only they had had any real purchasing or political power. Whatever they hoped for, they did not bargain for "this." The deictic harshness of Jarrell's "this" points to a present reality: *this* is something they undergo, as it were, in the reader's present tense, during the moment of reading. Each time Jarrell closes a line of his roughly hewed and incomplete sestina with "this," it rings with just such a severity—as, for example, when he points in the next stanza to a "country welcomer than this" and so refers not only to the reality of an unwelcoming Germany or Poland but also to the hypothesis of an America that might have been "welcomer" to the refugees were the country not mired in anti-immigrant politics, were it not that, as Thomas Mann suggested, the refugees were not wanted "even here."

III

Like citizens of America or of a larger European democratic tradition, Jarrell's refugees stubbornly conceive of themselves according to the same terms of economy through which an American audience considers their suffering. As people who fall victim to cultural constructs of identity, Jarrell's refugees lack the critical perspective that Edward Said and others have recently attributed to the exile, but nevertheless they partake of an existential condition of being outside economy that promotes critique. At the same time, however, the refugee is someone always close to home—if not in place, at least in the refugee's mind. As Jarrell hesitantly speculates about what the refugees thought they were trading for, his fourfold repetition of "possessed" emphasizes the complex of attachment governing so much of cultural identity. Possessions are the very stuff of cultural affiliation in capitalist economy. There is a hint of Marxist critique in this poem, but it is eminently tinged with compassion. Any false consciousness an audience might attribute to the refugees only reflects our own, as they are implicated in our fate as we in theirs.

Still, Jarrell's focus on the refugees' self-delusion must give us pause, especially in the light of the controversies that were to arise around notions such as the Jews going to their deaths "like sheep to the slaughter" and the collaboration of the Judenrat in the Nazi process of deportation.[9] Blaming the victim takes many forms, and Holocaust historians have worked hard to clarify the real conditions that defined the absence of choice for the Holocaust's victims. The point Jarrell makes about the refugees' limited knowledge, as he generalizes a child's purely pathetic and innocent status as victim to include all refugees, is that the refugees seem ironically familiar to an audience in their inability to imagine how events have become so unwelcome to them. Indeed, the child's voice interprets their persistent hope of home as a willful fantasy. Much as Aristotle tried to exclude from the field of moral decision making everything beyond our voluntary control, Jarrell brings habits of voluntary thought and the exclusions on which such thought is premised into explicit tension with a suffering that comes seemingly from beyond economy. This is the meaning we can give to the spectral voluntariness in the minds of the refugees, a note sounded most strongly at the end of the third stanza when Jarrell wonders about the "days and faces and lives they waste" ([*"The Refugees"*] 18), as if it were the refugees—and not the Nazis deporting them—who wasted their lives. This is astute psychology: the refugees inhabit a state of mind common to victims of violence, preserving the fantasy of subjectively controlling their circumstances—this specter of voluntariness perhaps the only home left to them, a place of psychological refuge. But it is also effective social criticism: the refugees' fantasy of home characterizes the workings of political economy and the fragile, if not altogether illusory, constructs that maintain cultural identity. Still believing in a form of belonging that is no more, the refugees can be called voluntary subjects only in the ironically cruel sense that they cling to the idea that there might have been a choice close to hand through which they could have avoided what now befalls them.

Economy must by definition exclude what it cannot regulate, and it thus inscribes a habit of mind—even in the victims of its restrictions—according to which the safety of that which is internal to the system and therefore under control requires leaving out conspicuous others. Likewise, every welcome of the refugee already puts a strain on cultural economy because the refugee is necessarily an excess. When faced with refugees, political rhetoric turns to considerations of financial economy, asking whether the refugees have anything to contribute and whether they might put too great a strain on the receiving nation. Though these considerations may more or less accurately interpret capitalist economy, they reflect a deep belief that the refugee's exceptionality threatens our cultural economics of identity. During World War II, not only was no effort made to raise the overall number of immigrants allowed into America, but the existing quotas remained drastically underfilled for every year but 1942. This was in part the result of a quota system in place before the war, which allowed for only limited numbers of immigrants from those European nations (especially in eastern Europe) not already well represented as ethnic groups in America. There was a movement afoot in the Senate in 1939 to waive the ratio distribution for the time being and to let immigrants come from regions where persecution was most intense, but the proposal never came to a vote because even liberal politicians feared the negative repercussions of being deemed soft on immigration by the nativist majority (Wyman [*Paper Walls*] 3-26). During this time, the State Department maintained an array of highly restrictive policies around the granting of visas, and potential immigrants had often to prove that they had prospects of supporting themselves in America and were not "likely to become a public charge."[10]

Although Jarrell's poem may seem only remotely cognizant of such specific anti-immigrant measures, his use of the language of economy—words such as *trade, possessed,* and *cost*—echoes the thought process through which many Americans accounted refugees a bad risk. In particular, the special emphasis Jarrell gives to the term *extravagant*—and its intersection with ideas such as *waste* and *satisfaction*—calls for an interrogation of the terms of political economy. *Extra-vagance* is literally a wandering out of bounds, a term that reiterates the fate of the refugee, whose wandering trespasses the ordinary boundaries of economy. Unlike the peripatetic but purposeful Odysseus, however, the refugee can never resolve his or her journey by return, and so his or her wandering remains an extravagant claim on those who must receive the refugee without any assurance that their guest will depart at the proper time.[11] When Jarrell asks of refugees packed into shabby trains, "Is their calm extravagant?" he implies that they have underestimated their situation and failed to recognize their calm as a precarious extravagance. Their calm participates in a thought of economy, as if they might still be returned to a home or welcomer country, when in fact they have become an excess to economy.[12]

With his fourth use of *extravagant,* as also with the third (to which I turn shortly), Jarrell translates his thematic treatment of the tension between economy and the extravagant fate of the refugees into the terms of the ethical—and the poetic—imagination. As the refugees travel to their deaths as though toward a completed transaction in the sphere of political economy, Jarrell pronounces his effort to imagine their fate an extravagance, a wandering of his imagination into the space of the other: "Is it really extravagant / To read in their faces: What is there that we possessed / That we were unwilling to trade for this?" The speaker's extravagance derives from the imaginative presumption whereby he would discern the final thoughts of the refugees, but this presumption epitomizes the entire project of the poem, positioned as it is on the border of an impossible identification. Fearing that to relinquish the possibility of any identification is to surrender the refugee forever to the ostracizing and annihilating fate of being socially constructed as other, the speaker builds on his prior speculations about the ordinary dreams of refugees. He cannot believe his imaginative trespass to be an insult greater than, say, the cultural failure to consider the refugees versions of ourselves. In this sense, the refugees (through the speaker's speculation) ask the question of themselves, as a negative version of their initial economic thought, the colon introducing, as it were, the quoted thought. The refugees seem at last willing to surrender all they possess, which by this point may be nothing more than the ideas belonging to a cultural and political system that now excludes them.

IV

As I have intimated, the historical timing of Jarrell's protoelegy makes it suspect. For even as the 1940 version of **"The Refugees"** protests the unnecessary fate of the European refugees, it imitates the terms of a social economy treating their fate as inevitable and adopts a formal literariness that hardly reflects the urgency of their situation. When Jarrell revised the poem in 1949 to be included in the anthology *Modern American Poetry* (edited by Louis Untermeyer), his alterations perhaps informed by historical consciousness of the Holocaust, he seems to have rebelled in part against the boundedness of his literary form. Whereas in the 1940 version the poet's cooperation with the overly formal poetic exercise of the sestina signals an apparent subscription to social form, which functions as a rationalization emptied of all conviction, in the later poem Jarrell slightly relaxes the sestina form, reconceiving several end words and penning new lines, many of which are pitched with colloquial sentimentality. The effect of his revisions is that the 1949 poem, unlike the conceptually complex original, allows for easy access to the refugees' fate and promotes cooperative identification with them as political victims.

In the original version, the procedure of identification remains at all times precarious. In a 1941 essay on Auden, Jarrell remarked on Auden's rhetorical habit of indulging binary oppositions between "we" and "they," where "we" often designated a form of folkish, mythic belonging of which Auden largely approved (Jarrell, "Changes"). In **"The Refugees,"** Jarrell adopts the Audenesque strategy of opposing "we" to "they" with the ostensible goal of charting the danger of such oppositions. The refugees begin the poem as a "they" of Audenesque proportions, existing impersonally beyond the sphere of imaginative participation and resembling those bourgeois minions in Auden who stand on the periphery of their own humanity, self-condemned to meaninglessness. By importing this rhetorical strategy until he characterizes the refugees as imagining themselves agents of their fate, Jarrell ultimately inverts the antinomy of we/they and holds those of us inside economy—"we" who are welcome in our own countries—responsible for insisting on categorizing an oppositional group of people (the "they" who are not "we"). Once we risk an identification that would extravagantly read the expression on the refugees' faces, we come to the harder question: *what it was we possessed both materially and politically that we were unwilling to trade for this*—which is to say, *what might we do or have done to prevent it from happening?* It is even possible to read the first meaning (as subjective thought of the refugees) and the second (as self-accusation of the reader) as converging, the colon thus marking a movement from the internal thought of the refugees into a designation of collective responsibility aimed, through indirect discourse, at the audience, as though the refugees asked, *What is there that they (the people not in our situation) possessed that they were unwilling to spare us this?*

For the most part, Jarrell describes his refugees from within the hypothesis of a present exigency. Much of the reason it may be extravagant to speculate as to the nature of refugees' thoughts is that their situation seems so desperate as not to permit the luxury of regret. Each time Jarrell uses the term "extravagant," it denotes a speculation in the minds of the refugees—each time, that is, except for in the third stanza: "And what else could satisfy the extravagant / Tears and wish of the child but this?" Although "extravagant" is again part of an interrogative formulation, there is a difference here.

The interrogative emphasis does not fall on the word itself (say, to call attention to the imaginative endeavor); nor is "extravagant" brought into doubt as a descriptor. Rather, it marks the attributed state of the child's teary wishfulness. In its boldness, this is the poem's most extravagantly speculative moment, as the poet's self-conscious anxiety about mourning becomes implicit in the tears and wish of the child, now a figure for the entire project of mourning. Mourning, as such, is pure extravagance. The mourner wanders beyond the boundedness of present exigency in order to contemplate in hindsight the possibilities of relationship, perhaps seeking wishfully to revise the immediate past and imagine what might have been.

It is on this very subject that Jarrell's revised 1949 version of the poem is most interesting. For the changes Jarrell makes turn in large part on his rejection of "extravagant" as the poem's key term in favor of the sentimentally urgent emphasis of the substituted end word "escape." Perhaps Jarrell retrospectively perceived the poem's literariness to be at fault (although he carried over its technique of sophisticated mimetic irony into the overt Holocaust elegy **"A Camp in the Prussian Forest"** [1946], also included in the Untermeyer anthology and thereafter one of Jarrell's most consistently anthologized poems).[13] In at least one instance, the stylized voice of the 1940 version seems to have directly motivated Jarrell's revision: he changes a precious reference to "dried blood" that "sparkles along the mask" into plainer English, "There is blood, dried now, along the mask"—an improvement, even if many other revisions are not. Overall, Jarrell's 1949 revisions serve not only as a commentary on the 1940 version's formal difficulty but also as a gloss on its understated elegiac dimensions. In the first stanza, Jarrell describes the child as before but then strangely interrupts the expected syntactic progression to ventriloquize the child's voice: "But how shall I escape? / They had lives like mine." When Jarrell picks up the stanza's key phrase unchanged ("What was it they possessed / That they were willing to trade for this?"), the sense of the line as formerly relying on the refugees' "extravagant" calm has been altered to make the obvious point that the refugees, as represented by the desperately pleading child, would have wished to escape. In the second stanza, the pitch of sentimentality becomes positively breathless, as Jarrell alters his invasive, potentially insensitive, ironic speculation about the extravagant costs of the refugees' former habits of mind into the tamely urgent phrase "the vacant / Breath rises, vanishes—Escape, Escape!" These changes amount to Jarrell's getting all the way on the side of the refugee child and—in the light of what was to happen to so many European Jews from 1941 to 1944—pleading for the child yet once more, after the fact, as if in the child's own voice.

I wish to emphasize that Jarrell's descent into sentimentality simultaneously realizes and simplifies the elegiac construct of the 1940 version. If the Holocaust intervenes between the 1940 version and the 1949 revision, so also does a poem such as Jarrell's **"Protocols"** (1945), a sentimental elegy deploying the trope of prosopopoeia to speak for two children—one in Odessa, one in Birkenau—who innocently and euphemistically narrate their arrival at mass murder or the gas chambers. In this poem as well as in the 1949 version of **"The Refugees,"** Jarrell proceeds as though the rhetoric of sentimentality might better demonstrate historical consciousness (or dutiful regret) than does a wartime poem that oddly unsettles its audience by espousing a logic neither heroic (in supposing a future of intervention) nor martyrological (in imagining the brave willfulness of the victims). Perhaps the best revision in the 1949 version of **"The Refugees"** is the third stanza. . . .

Only the second line of the stanza remains intact from the original, and what is dropped from the earlier poem includes the line about "the extravagant / Tears and wish of the child," which foregrounded the futility of elegiac sentiment. Even so, there is a carryover of such sentiment into the later version that serves to accent the mournfulness of both the original and the revised poems. When in the 1949 version Jarrell gives the order for the refugees to sleep and then speaks of "emptying hearts" that "escape / Even their own wish," he comments alike on elegiac memory and the fantasy of escape, challenging any form of memory that turns from history. It is not entirely clear from the syntax whether the turning back that follows should be read as the return from sleep or a further fall into sleep's nothingness, but when the victim and audience seem dually commanded to turn to "this / Nothing that hides . . . / The days and faces," what they confront is the force of history's violence enacted as though anonymously on numerous, nameless masses of people. In the original, Jarrell ended the stanza by speaking of the "lives they waste," the vaguely agentive pronominal reference reaching back to the violence of the perpetrators only through the limited perspective of victims who, in their radical passivity, appear to squander their own lives. But the revision settles more firmly on the historical sense of genocide, speaking of "the world they waste," a slightly Audenesque phrase, in such a way that the victims are no longer enfolded as accidental agents into the spectacle of their own ruin. This moment of moral precision interprets both the implicit elegiac outrage of the 1940 version, where the responsibility for wastefulness is attached to the audience's imaginative clinging to a restrictively nationalist economy of identity, and also the later version's sentimental rhetoric, whereby morality means finally inserting oneself into the victim's place. The technique of strident over-identification is fulfilled in the final stanza of the 1949 version, when

Jarrell once more ventriloquizes in the voice of the child—"*For I too shall escape,* We read in their faces"—italicizing the words to locate them as a piece of historical sentiment accurately interpreted by the retrospective audience. The pathos of the refugees' obvious failure to escape draws on the audience's fuller historical knowledge of the Nazi genocide (made public at the Nuremberg trials in 1945 and 1946), but it also forces the poem's final and once paradoxical lines to be read in the clarifying light of history as a species of agentless regret.

V

Of the two versions of this now relatively unknown Jarrell poem, readers will have encountered the earlier one, since it, and not the revision, was included in **The Complete Poems.** In that early form it is not an easy poem, its elliptical, restrictive use of language coinciding with the poem's apparent expression of futility and political resignation. According to the poem's economically contained irony, which imitates the harsh historical consequence of cultural stinginess and reflects the scarcity of political asylum for the refugees, Jarrell has diminished the prospects of political intervention, leaving us to contemplate even the prospect of grief as mere redundancy and excess. So when, in the 1940 version, approximating the perspectives of refugees who grieve for themselves because no one else will, Jarrell asks what could "satisfy" the extravagance of grief, he makes a kind of grim joke. To mourn for oneself is to treat oneself as object or as accomplished event—in other words, much as the democratic, nonfascist nations considered the refugees. Though the 1949 revision may attempt to soften this fiercely fatalistic elegiac logic, Jarrell nevertheless left intact (even in this revised, less severe form) the contrapuntal phrase in the fourth stanza in which he speaks of the "[s]atisfaction of death."

In both the 1940 and the 1949 versions, then, Jarrell plays on the conventions of cathartic grief familiar to us through Aristotelian tragic theory and suggests that the insertion of mourning into this poem requires an awful resolution. If we take for granted that Jarrell disapproves of what he here states as necessity (that the refugees must die), two lines of critique emerge. In the first, the poet addresses himself to a sacrificial economics of mourning, which makes a valuable necessity out of loss. At its most sardonic, such an emphasis supposes that we grieve for others in order to be assured of our better fortune. Jarrell's sense is more likely closer to an expressed reservation about what it takes to motivate our political compassion. Is the child's death somehow necessary to raise the conscience of the American public? As Jarrell conjectures a horizon for political conscience in which we may be willing to trade on the fate of this child and the other refugees for the benefit of others who are similarly vulnerable, he plays on elegiac conventions, asking whether our responsibilities must always be developed from the specter of failure, whether the elegy's hypothesis of belated intervention is in fact a necessary step toward a conscientious regard for the other.

A second, stronger line of critique emerges through Jarrell's implicit charge that such mourning is itself extravagant, having to do with a nonsatisfaction that is peculiarly the ethical motivation of all mourning. A responsibility for the other, I propose, occurs through the other's implicit dissent from premises of satisfaction. Levinas hints at such a meaning in the 1982 essay "Philosophy and Transcendence," in which he figures dissatisfaction as the dislocation and unfulfillment of thought in its persistent quest to return to a conceptual basis; dissatisfaction is the questioning of the teleological nature of thought, of the way in which our thought proceeds toward an end as though toward an intention. If the philosophical history of freedom depends on "the ideal of the satisfied man to whom all the possible is permitted" (15), Levinas suggests that a rereading of philosophy, and thus most forms of cultural knowledge, through ethics must unsettle the conceptual basis of satisfaction.[14] If we elaborate this idea more expansively into the realm of ethics, we might argue—as I believe Jarrell's poem does latently—that insofar as economy always restricts identity to what it already knows and limits responsibility to what culture already articulates, we must always turn from the refugee or foreigner as though in denial of ethics itself. By contrast, if ethics is to continue to inspire responsibility as a new or renewable vocation, it cannot have been decided in advance at the expense of those who never drew up the rules. Conservatism as such is the ruination of ethics. To find the real in what lies beyond the economic schemes of intention and identity and to imagine a mode of receptivity that fails to restrict responsiveness to personal and social satisfactions derived through preconceived systems—this aim would challenge our definition of ethical reality as well our sense of responsibility in history.

If conscience is the negotiation of a cultural boundary, the question about where our world (a world, according to Jarrell's 1949 version, we all might waste) and where our responsibility for it begin and end, then mourning's ethical dimension emerges from the disappointment of economy. The political death of others must trace in us a deeper dissatisfaction with the present order, with all who remain content despite the injustices committed in the name of that order. To speak at all of the "[s]atisfaction of death" is to refer not only to an existential requirement that we must die but also to a view of death embedded harmoniously in the social status quo, as if there were no graver injustice (since we all die eventually) in the socially precipitated harm that befalls others. With Jarrell's ironic use of "we" in the poem's final line—which, while apparently quoting the refugees' thought about what they might have traded to spare themselves, refers to an American audience's collective identity and the patterns of cultural adherence that audience prefers to political intervention—the poem imposes a final urgency interrogating our self-satisfaction. To be satisfied in any sense with the death of the unrescued European refugees—whether we are satisfied as world citizens convinced that we have done all that we reasonably could do on their behalf or as readers of an elegy convinced that we have fulfilled our responsibility through an expression of imaginative compassion—is to have consented to mourning's evident futility as if this were also its only possible meaning.

Notes

1. For readings of elegy sensitive to the question of grief's artifice, see Arnold Stein (esp. 145-49) and Peter Sacks (1-18).

2. Besides Auden's 1939 elegy for Freud, Jarrell might have recalled Kenneth Burke's *The Philosophy of Literary Form,* in which an essay on Hitlerism was juxtaposed to an essay on Freud. Burke (specifically, Burke's *Attitudes toward History*) is credited by Jarrell with providing much of the theoretical background for the earlier of Jarrell's two essays on Auden (Jarrell, "Changes" 326).

3. See Jarrell, "Changes" and "Freud."

4. This is a brief formulation of a central strand of my book *The Ethics of Mourning,* in which I describe mourning's ethical imperatives as based in a paradoxical, impossible defense of the other, as though a lapse from mourning's vigilance might portend some real harm to a still-living person. Thus, typically in mourning—especially in its resistant, melancholic, or antielegiac form—the injustice that might be done to the dead stands for those injustices that bring about, at least potentially, the death of others (esp. 2-6, 27-32). The book also examines what I call "lyrical economy," discerning the ways in which lyric elegy supposes a coincidence of the economies pertaining to mourning, lyrical identity, and broader rubrics for cultural identity. Even while offering a seemingly positive statement of restrictiveness, lyric elegy intimates—through its figurative anxieties about exclusion—the principle of its own critique, as though it were always referred to the lost other who provokes a dissatisfaction with economy (81-127).

5. For, as Adorno suggests, it is through the exertion of social and contradictory forces on individual happiness—a happiness that might coincide with the lyrical statement of economy and a restrictive sphere of identity on which the lyric often concentrates—that the lyric is projected toward a genuine form of the happiness to which it aspires, where it would achieve (at least hypothetically) a dignity it can "attain only along with the happiness of the whole" (49).

6. Peter Sacks offers the most persuasive account of such a Freudian economy of language in the tradition of elegy, arguing that elegiac language refers the occasion of loss back to a primordial condition of language, as though the most recent loss were but a further comment on the original oedipal determination of the psyche (1-18).

7. Without the original loss of the mother, Freud supposes, the ego could never imagine those boundaries, however fictional and provisional, through which identity is established and subsequently maintained (7-64, esp. 14-17).

8. Consult my reading of the properties of belatedness in elegy and the mournful exigencies implicit in Levinas's language (esp. 14-18). For a reading of elegy attuned to a political horizon that is registered by discontinuities in the elegiac tradition and is precipitated by apparent social discontinuities (especially those forcing a reconstruction of gender relations), see Zeiger 11-25.

9. Among the works prominent in controversies over the complicity of victims, Hannah Arendt's book *Eichmann in Jerusalem* (1963), which leaned heavily on Raul Hilberg's severe assessment of the Judenrat, is interesting for at least two reasons: the uproar over it suggests how easily any critical assessment of victims can be misunderstood (Arendt's criticisms of the Judenrat were mistakenly associated with a general accusation she never makes—that the Jews "went like sheep to the slaughter"), and Arendt developed a close relation with Jarrell and was a great admirer of his poetry. One might even hear overtones of the ironic Jarrell (for whom irony is also a mode of compassion) in Arendt's famous book.

10. The "likely to become a public charge" clause is an example of a practical political measure with deep ideological underpinnings. For, as those who lobbied for more liberal immigration policies often emphasized, it was just as plausible to argue from the standpoint of capitalist economics that immigrants, even those without predetermined incomes, provided a boon to the American economy because they contributed to the labor force and put money into the economy (Wyman 3-4, 46-47).

11. The social origins of hospitality, as Julia Kristeva has argued, are based largely in the understanding that the foreigner's visit is provisional and temporary (50-56).

12. When Jarrell ends the second stanza by repeating the theme of extravagance and querying, "Have none of them found the cost extravagant?" the notion of cost refers to visa fees or debates about the financial burden refugees put on the American economy, but it also evokes the political status of the refugees as extravagant beings. Whereas terms such as "extravagant" and "waste" work from the perspective of political frugality, when applied to refugees they render the economic conceit on a suddenly human scale, revaluing a loss that should exceed all crude financial reckonings of fate. Jarrell's implicit objection may be inspired by his enthusiasm for Marx or by a more straightforward humanistic bent, but he asks the reader to reconsider the inhumane terms through which we account (politically) for human life.

13. In a chapter on Jarrell in *The Ethics of Mourning*, I discuss his relation to Auden at greater length and explore the peculiar historical sensibility of "A Camp in the Prussian Forest" (209-40).

14. Initially, Levinas uses "satisfaction" to refer to the manner in which intentionality promises an appropriation of the object to thought and thus a return to the premises of sameness that oriented the striving for the object. As he proceeds to argue against the requirements of satisfaction, he then supposes there might be a form of ethical vigilance independent of philosophy's characteristically retrospective search for an origin of our idea of the infinite or transcendent (esp. 9, 16).

Works Cited

Adorno, Theodor. "On Lyric Poetry and Society." *Notes to Literature*. Ed. Rolf Tiedemann. Trans. Shierry Weber Nicholsen. Vol. 1. New York: Columbia UP, 1991. 37-54.

Arendt, Hannah. *Eichmann in Jerusalem: A Report on the Banality of Evil*. 1963. New York: Penguin, 1964.

Auden, W. H. *Another Time*. New York: Random, 1940.

———. "Yeats as an Example." *Prose, 1939-1948*. Ed. Edward Mendelson. Princeton: Princeton UP, 2002. 384-89. Vol. 2 of *The Complete Works of W. H. Auden*.

Burke, Kenneth. *The Philosophy of Literary Form: Studies in Symbolic Action*. Berkeley: U of California P, 1941.

Butler, Judith. *Antigone's Claim*. New York: Columbia UP, 2000.

Davidman, Joy. "Jews of No Man's Land." *New Republic* 5 July 1939: 248.

Freud, Sigmund. Beyond the Pleasure Principle, *"Group Psychology" and Other Works*. Ed. and trans. James Strachey et al. London: Hogarth, 1955. Vol. 18 of *The Standard Edition of the Complete Psychological Works of Sigmund Freud*.

Hegel, G. W. F. *Phenomenology of Spirit*. Trans. A. V. Miller. Analysis and fwd. by J. N. Findlay. New York: Oxford UP, 1977.

Jarrell, Randall. "Changes of Attitude and Rhetoric in Auden's Poetry." *Southern Review* 7 (1941-42): 326-49.

———. *The Complete Poems*. New York: Farrar, 1969.

———. "Freud to Paul: The Stages of Auden's Ideology." *Partisan Review* 12 (1945): 437-57.

———. "A Girl in the Library." *Poetry* 78.1 (1951): 7-11. Rpt. in *The Seven-League Crutches*. New York: Harcourt, 1951.

———. "Protocols (Birkenau, Odessa)." *Poetry* 66.3 (1945): 121. Rpt. in *Little Friend, Little Friend*. New York: Dial, 1945.

———. "The Refugees." *Partisan Review* 7 (1940): 20-21. Rpt. in *New York Times Book Review* 1 Nov. 1942: 8. Rpt. in *Blood for a Stranger*. New York: Harcourt, 1942. Rev. vers. printed in *Modern American Poetry*. Ed. Louis Untermeyer. New York: Harcourt, 1950.

Kristeva, Julia. *Strangers to Ourselves*. Trans. Leon S. Roudiez. New York: Columbia UP, 1991.

"Let the Jews Come In!" *New Republic* 23 Nov. 1938: 60.

Levinas, Emmanuel. "Philosophy and Transcendence." *Alterity and Transcendence*. Trans. Michael B. Smith. 1995. New York: Columbia UP, 1999.

Mann, Thomas. "America and the Refugee." *New Republic* 11 Nov. 1939: 38-39.

"President and Prime Minister Speak." *Congress Weekly* 14 Aug. 1942: 1-2.

Ramazani, Jahan. *Poetry of Mourning: The Modern Elegy from Hardy to Heaney*. Chicago: U of Chicago P, 1994.

Sacks, Peter. *The English Elegy: Studies in the Genre from Spenser to Yeats*. Baltimore: Johns Hopkins UP, 1985.

Sophocles. *Antigone*. *Antigone, The Women of Trachis, Philoctetes, Oedipus at Colonus*. Ed. and trans. Hugh Lloyd-Jones. Loeb Classical Lib. 21. Cambridge: Harvard UP, 1994. 1-127.

Spargo, R. Clifton. *The Ethics of Mourning: Grief and Responsibility in Elegiac Literature*. Baltimore: Johns Hopkins UP, 2004.

Stein, Arnold. *The House of Death: Messages from the English Renaissance*. Baltimore: Johns Hopkins UP, 1986.

Steiner, George. *Antigones*. New York: Oxford UP, 1984.

Thompson, Dorothy. *Refugees: Anarchy or Organization?* New York: Random, 1938.

"Who Wants Refugees?" *New Republic* 20 July 1938: 291-92.

Wise, Stephen J. "In Sorrow and Protest." *Congress Weekly* 14 Aug. 1942: 4-5.

Wyman, David. *Paper Walls: America and the Refugee Crisis, 1938-1941.* 1968. New York: Pantheon, 1985.

Zeiger, Melissa. *Beyond Consolation: Death, Sexuality, and the Changing Shapes of Elegy.* Ithaca: Cornell UP, 1997.

FURTHER READING

Criticism

Arendt, Hannah. "Randall Jarrell: 1914-1965." In *Men in Dark Times,* pp. 263-67. New York: Harcourt, Brace & World, Inc., 1968.

A eulogy for Jarrell that notes how the German language, traditional folktales, and being part of the German-speaking Arendt household exerted a strong influence on Jarrell's life and work.

Bawer, Bruce. "Jarrell and the Influence of Auden." In *The Middle Generation: The Lives and Poetry of Delmore Schwartz, Randall Jarrell, John Berryman, and Robert Lowell,* pp. 80-9. Hamden, Conn.: Archon Books, 1986.

Traces the influence of W. H. Auden on Jarrell's early poetry.

Beck, Charlotte H. "Randall Jarrell: The Precocious Pupil." In *The Fugitive Legacy: A Critical History,* pp. 73-88. Baton Rouge: Louisiana State University Press, 2001.

Discusses Jarrell's relationship with the four major figures of the Fugitive movement: John Crowe Ransom, Robert Penn Warren, Allen Tate, and Donald Davidson.

Benfey, Christopher. "The Woman in the Mirror: Randall Jarrell and John Berryman." In *Men Writing the Feminine: Literature, Theory, and the Question of Genders,* edited by Thaïs E. Morgan, pp. 123-38. Albany: State University of New York Press, 1994.

Argues that Jarrell's and John Berryman's use of the feminine point of view in many of their poems represents "a probing of repressed and evaded aspects of the poet's own gender identity."

Burt, Stephen. "Randall Jarrell: Time, Verse, and the Sense of the Self." *PN Review* 29, no. 2 (November-December 2002): 40-6.

Studies the manner in which Jarrell represents time in his poetry and the emotions displayed by his characters as they realize they've moved from one time frame to another.

Field: Contemporary Poetry and Politics, no. 35 (fall 1986).

A special issue of the journal that includes reprints of selected poems by Jarrell with analysis and commentary on each poem.

Flynn, Richard. "Happy Families Are All Invented: Randall Jarrell's Fiction for Children." *Children's Literature* 16 (1988): 109-25.

Examines the period during the late 1950s when Jarrell experienced difficulties writing poetry, claiming that the poet was struggling with mortality and the futility of making art that outlives its author.

———. *Randall Jarrell and the Lost World of Childhood,* Athens: University of Georgia Press, 1990, 167 p.

Book-length study of Jarrell's treatment of the themes of childhood and lost innocence in his poetry.

Fowler, Russell T. "Charting the 'Lost World': Rilke's Influence on Randall Jarrell." *Twentieth Century Literature* 30, no. 1 (spring 1984): 100-22.

Focuses on the strong influence on Jarrell's poetry of the German poet Rainer Maria Rilke.

Funkhouser, Linda Bradley. "Acoustic Rhythm in Randall Jarrell's 'The Death of the Ball Turret Gunner.'" *Poetics* 8 (1979): 381-403.

Uses tape recordings of oral readings of "The Death of the Ball Turret Gunner" by Jarrell and by ten different university professors to demonstrate the significance of cadence, rhythmic structure, pause length, and pause position to an analysis of poetic style and critical interpretation.

Kirsch, Adam. "Randall Jarrell." In *The Wounded Surgeon: Confession and Transformation in Six American Poets,* pp. 153-96. New York: W. W. Norton and Company, 2005.

Surveys Jarrell's career as a poet, asserting that the essence of his poetics is "joyful, spontaneous, untutored"—a style of writing that "imitates ordinary ineloquent speech."

Lensing, George S. "The Modernism of Randall Jarrell." *South Carolina Review* 17, no. 1 (fall 1984): 52-60.

Recalls Jarrell's struggle to establish himself as a poet once he rejected modernism and the modernist poets that came before him.

Longenbach, James. "Randall Jarrell's Legacy." *Literary Imagination* 5, no. 2 (spring 2003): 358-68.

    Addresses the criticism by other poets of Jarrell's sentimental tone in his verse, in an age that Jarrell himself described as placing "a tremendous emphasis on the irony and ambiguity of poetry."

Meyers, Jeffrey. "Robert Lowell and Randall Jarrell" and "Randall Jarrell and John Berryman." In *Manic Power: Robert Lowell and His Circle,* pp. 31-58; 59-81. New York: Arbor House, 1987.

    Compares the personal lives, careers, and friendships of Robert Lowell and Jarrell on the one hand, and Jarrell and John Berryman, on the other.

Pritchard, William H. "Randall Jarrell: Poet-Critic." *American Scholar* 52 (1983): 67-77.

    Describes two features of Jarrell's "unique style" of criticism: his use of eviscerating one-liners directed at poets whose work he dislikes, and his ability to convey the majesty of a poet even in the face of glaring errors in his or her work.

Quinn, Mary Bernetta. "Randall Jarrell: His Metamorphoses." In *To Our Lady of Peace,* pp. 168-206. New Brunswick, N.J.: Rutgers University Press, 1955.

    Examines the influence of traditional folktales, such as those by the Brothers Grimm and Hans Christian Andersen, and the role of "the metamorphoses theme" on Jarrell's poetry.

Rosenthal, M. L. "Randall Jarrell." In *Seven American Poets from MacLeish to Nemerov: An Introduction,* edited by Denis Donoghue, pp. 132-70. Minneapolis: University of Minnesota Press, 1975.

    Traces the recurring themes and "poetic personality" of Jarrell in his various books of poetry, from *Blood for a Stranger* to his last original volume of verse, *The Lost World.*

Shapiro, Karl. "Randall Jarrell." In *Randall Jarrell: A Lecture Presented under the Auspices of the Gertrude Clarke Whittall Poetry and Literature Fund, with a Bibliography of Jarrell Materials in the Collections of the Library of Congress,* pp. 1-24. Washington, D.C.: Gertrude Clarke Whittall Poetry and Literature Fund, 1967.

    Analyzes Jarrell within the context of his culture and time, describing him as a poet who tried to reconcile "high culture" with ordinary life.

Travisano, Thomas. *Midcentury Quartet: Bishop, Lowell, Jarrell, Berryman, and the Making of a Postmodern Aesthetic,* Charlottesville: University Press of Virginia, 1999, 325 p.

    Addresses the "complex and ongoing process of artistic interchange, parallel development, and mutual influence" of the leading four confessional poets of twentieth-century American literature.

Voigt, Ellen Bryant. "Lost and Found." *Southern Review* 38, no. 2 (spring 2002): 377-98.

    Describes the development of Jarrell's style as a literary critic during the course of his career.

Additional coverage of Jarrell's life and career is contained in the following sources published by Thomson Gale: *American Writers*; *Beacham's Guide to Literature for Young Adults,* Vol. 5; *Children's Literature Review,* Vol. 6; *Concise Dictionary of American Literary Biography: 1941-1968*; *Contemporary Authors,* Vols. 5-8R, 25-28R; *Contemporary Authors Bibliographical Series,* Vol. 2; *Contemporary Authors New Revision Series,* Vols. 6, 34; *Contemporary Literary Criticism,* Vols. 1, 2, 6, 9, 13, 49; *Dictionary of Literary Biography,* Vols. 48, 52; *DISCovering Authors Modules: Poets*; *Encyclopedia of World Literature in the 20th Century,* Ed. 3; *Exploring Poetry*; *Literature Resource Center*; *Major Authors and Illustrators for Children and Young Adults,* Eds. 1, 2; *Major 20th-Century Writers,* Eds. 1, 2; *Modern American Literature,* Ed. 5; *Poetry Criticism,* Vol. 41; *Poetry for Students,* Vol. 2; *Poets: American and British*; *Reference Guide to American Literature,* Ed. 4; *St. James Guide to Children's Writers,* Vol. 5; and *Something About the Author,* Vol. 7.

Rose Wilder Lane
1887-1968

American novelist, short story writer, biographer, essayist, journalist, travel writer, and historian.

INTRODUCTION

During her lifetime Rose Wilder Lane was considered one of the leading writers of "frontier" fiction in American literature. In such best-selling novels as *Let the Hurricane Roar* (1933) and *Free Land* (1938), she drew vivid fictionalized accounts of her parents' and grandparents' pioneer experiences in the Dakota territories. Even before the publication of these two novels, she was widely read and appreciated as a journalist and feature writer for a number of popular magazines. Lane is also remembered as the daughter of Laura Ingalls Wilder, author of the now-famous *Little House on the Prairie* and similar books for children. Although the extent of Lane's influence on her mother's stories is unclear, since she both typed and edited them, scholars generally agree that she played a major role in shaping the artistic direction of the books. The majority of Lane's own literary efforts were influenced by her political leanings. She penned her most critically acclaimed fiction during the Depression era for an audience struggling with financial hardship. Her pioneer narratives focus on the courage, resilience, and independent spirit of prior generations who had struggled and survived frontier life. Lane's narratives, however, were not idealizations of the American west. As critic Donna Campbell has argued, her fiction "consciously challenged some of the country's favorite myths about itself" by exposing the violence and disappointments that were the reality of the time. Lane abandoned fiction relatively early in her career to promote her political ideology. Her objection to President Franklin D. Roosevelt's New Deal policies, particularly those that affected farmers, prompted her to write manifestos, including *Give Me Liberty* (1936) and *The Discovery of Freedom: Man's Struggle against Authority* (1943), which promoted self-reliance and radical personal freedom. Although Lane's political pieces never achieved the popularity of her fiction, they have since found a new audience among civil libertarians. William Holtz has characterized Lane's later literary career as one marked by unfulfilled potential, stating "after her brief moment of fame with *Free Land*, Lane would live out her life as an obscure prophet of a revolution yet to be completed, when all would embrace 'the terrible effort, the never-lifted burden and risks of individual self-reliance.'"

BIOGRAPHICAL INFORMATION

Lane was born December 5, 1887, in a claim shanty in De Smet, South Dakota. Her parents, Laura Ingalls and Almanzo James Wilder, were struggling pioneer farmers. Lane moved with her parents, first to the Ozark Mountains in Missouri where she attended public school, and later to Crowley, Louisiana, where she continued her high school education. After graduating, she moved to San Francisco and supported herself by working as a telegrapher, office clerk, and newspaper reporter. She married Gillette Lane in 1909, but their marriage was unsuccessful, and they divorced in 1918. Lane continued to support herself by writing romantic serials for the *San Francisco Bulletin*. Her first novel, *Diverging Roads* (1919), appeared initially in serial form and was later published in hardcover with a revised ending. The plot of the novel closely follows Lane's own experience in California as a struggling career woman with a failing marriage. After her divorce, Lane traveled to Europe and wrote for the *Bulletin* and the American Red Cross. She particularly enjoyed visiting Albania, and her book *The Peaks of Shala* (1922) is based on her experiences there.

After extensive traveling, Lane moved back to Missouri in 1928. She supported herself and her parents with earnings from her writing. During the 1920s and 1930s her writing appeared in various magazines, including *Harper's, Ladies Home Journal, Saturday Evening Post,* and *Good Housekeeping.* During this period, Lane also assisted her mother with the publication of her autobiographical series of children's books. At the same time, Lane published her own versions of these stories in the novels *Let the Hurricane Roar* and *Free Land.* As Lane became increasingly interested in politics, her emphasis shifted away from fiction. She published several political essays championing personal freedom and eschewing what she perceived as the growing socialism of American politics. In the 1940s Lane stopped writing highly paid fiction for commercial magazines to avoid paying income taxes. She briefly wrote for *Woman's Day Magazine,* however, as a correspondent during the Vietnam War. Lane died of natural causes on October 30, 1968, in Danbury, Connecticut.

MAJOR WORKS

Although Lane was primarily recognized for her longer works of fiction, she enjoyed some success writing short stories as well. She won second prize in the O. Henry Awards in 1922 for her short story "Innocence," published in *Harper's* that same year. Following in the tradition of such writers as Edgar Lee Masters and Sherwood Anderson, she published a collection of short stories that had been first published in *Saturday Evening Post* and *Ladies Home Journal* between 1932 and 1935. In this volume, *Old Home Town* (1935), the stories, which were drawn from Lane's experiences growing up in Mansfield, Missouri, are set in a small town in the Missouri Ozarks at the beginning of the twentieth century and are linked by their common narrator, an observant young girl named Ernestine. They mainly focus on the restrictions and hypocrisy of small-town culture. Most of the stories in the collection, including "Old Maid," detail in particular the trials that women faced while trying to meet the expectations of respectability placed on them by their family, friends, and community.

In Lane's first critically recognized novel, *Let the Hurricane Roar*, she drew upon the frontier experiences of her maternal grandparents, after whom she named the main characters, Charles and Caroline. The book begins with their wedding and follows their journey to the frontier, where they settle in a "sod shanty" on a homestead claim. Caroline adjusts to the austere lifestyle, remains with her husband throughout the winter, and delivers a healthy baby boy without help from the other women in the community. After planting his first crop, Charles's idealism leads him to make several foolish decisions. He goes deeply into debt buying luxuries they cannot afford. When their crop is ruined by locusts, Caroline stays on the homestead alone to protect their claim, while Charles goes east to work on the railroad. Caroline not only survives the harsh winter but also rescues Charles, who has gotten lost in a blizzard on his way home. The book's major themes of resilience and resourcefulness are exemplified in Caroline, who acts rationally, refuses to give up, and ultimately saves her family from destruction.

Lane's last novel, *Free Land*, first appeared in serial form in the *Saturday Evening Post*. The events of the story were inspired by the life of Lane's father, who is fictionalized in the figure of a young homesteader named David Beaton. *Free Land* chronicles five years of Beaton's struggle in the Dakota plains after he leaves his father's farm to live on a homestead claim. While trying to make his farm successful and provide for his wife and children, Beaton faces devastating weather conditions, substantial debt, and bad luck. Foremost among the novel's motifs, in addition to its themes of self-reliance and perseverance, is the inexhaustible optimism of the protagonist. Despite the hardships he faces, Beaton never loses hope of making his farm successful. Although Beaton's father disapproves of his son's choice to accept government land, he lends him money at the end of the story to settle his debt. Aside from its humanist themes, *Free Land* offers Lane's harsh critique of the Homestead Act as it questions the popular perception of "free land" given by the government by illustrating both the physical and financial burdens placed on pioneering families. In this sense, the novel is highly ironic, a fact noted by a number of critics.

CRITICAL RECEPTION

Lane was a critically acclaimed and popular writer during her lifetime. Her works composed during the Great Depression, especially her novels *Let the Hurricane Roar* and *Free Land*, received favorable reviews and established her reputation as a leading writer of frontier literature. Upon its publication in 1938 *Free Land* quickly achieved best-seller status, and in an article in the *New York Times* Ralph Thompson argued for a Pulitzer Prize nomination for the work. Far from judging her works as merely "regional" stories of sentimental interest, Lane's peers regarded them as serious literature that addressed important themes within the context of pioneer life. But throughout her career, Lane was beset by economic and political pressures that hindered her achievements as an author. Noted scholar William Holtz has posited that her constant need for money to support herself and her parents "led too often to a compromising of the themes her imagination presented her," while her "conservative moral consciousness" and her increasing interest in libertarian politics "began to foreclose the possibilities of exploring the uncharted dimensions of the dilemmas her stories turned on."

Following the Second World War, Lane, along with such other women writers as Edna Ferber, was stigmatized as an author of sentimental fiction and virtually excised from the American literary canon. During this period many of her books went out of print. But since the reissue of *Free Land* in 1984, Lane's work has experienced renewed critical interest. Recent commentators, such as Holtz, Campbell, and Julia C. Ehrhardt, have emphasized Lane's skills as a writer of both fiction and the political essay; in the process, they have argued as well for a reassessment of Lane's place in twentieth-century American literature. Holtz has noted Lane's experimentations with the short story form in her collection *Old Home Town* and has praised her exploration of the American spirit in *Free Land*. Campbell has taken issue with the regionalist label affixed to Lane and her contemporary Edna Ferber, arguing that in their novels both authors critique the "nostalgic pioneer ideology so prevalent in the twenties," even as they capitalize on it. In *Free Land*, Campbell observes, Lane demonstrates "the patent falsehood of the myths of free land and endurance on the Great Plains."

What has emerged is a view of Lane as an author of considerable talent, but one who failed to develop her imagination and art following the success of *Free Land.* As Ehrhardt has concluded, "Lane transformed her pursuit for independence into personal fiction that reflected the struggles of female characters like herself: young women determined to live as independent, self-actualized individuals while confronting the seemingly insurmountable obstacles of poverty, self-doubt, and social disapproval. . . . But though Lane viewed her writing as the vehicle that would bring her the independence she sought, at the height of her career she found herself unable to claim that independence. Irreconcilable contradictions between the political messages of her fiction and the personal realities of her life underwrote this irony, and those contradictions ultimately brought her career as a self-supporting writer to an end."

PRINCIPAL WORKS

Henry Ford's Own Story: How a Farmer Boy Rose to the Power that Goes with Many Millions, Yet Never Lost Touch with Humanity (biography) 1917
Diverging Roads (novel) 1919
The Making of Herbert Hoover (biography) 1920
The Peaks of Shala: Being a Record of Certain Wanderings Among the Hill-Tribes of Albania (travel essay) 1922
He Was a Man (novel) 1925
Hill-Billy (novel) 1926
Cindy: A Romance of the Ozarks (novel) 1928
Let the Hurricane Roar (novel) 1933; also published as *Young Pioneers,* 1976
Old Home Town (short stories) 1935
Give Me Liberty (essay) 1936; revised edition, 1954
Free Land (novel) 1938; also published as *Young Pioneers: The Free Land,* 1980
The Discovery of Freedom: Man's Struggle against Authority (history) 1943
Woman's Day Book of American Needlework (nonfiction) 1963
The Lady and the Tycoon: Letters of Rose Wilder Lane and Jasper Crane (letters) 1973
Rose Wilder Lane: Her Story [with Roger Lea MacBride] (autobiography) 1977
Travels with Zenobia: Paris to Albania by Model T Ford [with Helen Dore Boylston; edited by William Holtz] (travel essay) 1983
A Little House Sampler [with Laura Ingalls Wilder; edited by William T. Anderson] (essays, fiction, journalism, and poetry) 1988
Dorothy Thompson and Rose Wilder Lane, Forty Years of Friendship: Letters, 1921-1960 [edited by Holtz] (letters) 1991
Islam and the Discovery of Freedom (essay) 1997

CRITICISM

William Holtz (essay date fall 1989)

SOURCE: Holtz, William. "Rose Wilder Lane's *Old Home Town.*" *Studies in Short Fiction* 26, no. 4 (fall 1989): 479-87.

[*In the following essay, Holtz critiques Lane's collection of short stories,* Old Home Town, *claiming that a study of the genesis of the work reveals Lane's experimentation with the short story form, while providing "insight into the problems of a writer of slick-paper fiction whose conscience moved her toward more serious efforts."*]

The reissue in 1985 of Rose Wilder Lane's 1935 volume of short stories, **Old Home Town,** by the University of Nebraska Press marked a renewed interest in Lane's fictional chronicling of the American midwest. Her **Let the Hurricane Roar** (1932; continuously in print) and **Free Land** (1938; reissued by Nebraska in 1984) are heroic stories of the settlement of the Dakota prairies, adult versions of the stories her mother, Laura Ingalls Wilder, wrote for children.[1] In **Old Home Town,** however, Lane directed her attention to village life in the Missouri Ozarks at the turn of the century, and the book is promoted today for its quaint picture of times past.[2] The shift paralleled her own removal from the prairies as a child and her growth to maturity in Mansfield, Missouri. It also brought her to deal, first, with the matter of the change from the pioneer experience to the settled life of the small town, and then with the subsequent problem of growth beyond the limits of small-town life—a problem she had faced in her own career, which began with her departure from Mansfield at seventeen and carried her into an adventurous life as a journalist throughout the United States, Europe, and the Middle East in the 1920s and into the common cosmopolitan dalliance with socialism and communism. She was present, she claimed, at the meeting that founded the American Communist Party.[3] Beyond this minimal biographical reading, however, a closer look at the genesis of **Old Home Town** will reveal a formal experiment in rounding a series of short stories toward the larger coherence of the novel. It will also afford an insight into the problems of a writer of slick-paper fiction whose conscience moved her toward more serious efforts. And finally, it will offer us a glimpse into the early stages of a talented fiction-writer's withdrawal from fiction in pursuit of ideological issues.

Old Home Town is composed of a series of short stories, originally published between 1932 and 1935 in the *Saturday Evening Post* and *Ladies' Home Journal*,[4] in which Lane depicted a vanished way of life—the time is 1902-1904—for her readers of the 1930s. Each story satisfies the implicit requirements of slick-paper fiction: a domestic crisis is resolved in a neat twist of plot; the dramatic situation is rendered realistically, but circumspectly in regard to sex; and heart's desire is satisfied after threat and struggle. The general air is of quaint, archaic moral dilemmas before the modern enlightenment. Each story is told by the same narrator, an observant adolescent girl name Ernestine, but the distribution of the stories between two magazines over a period of three years prevents any serial coherence from emerging.

In a financial sense, these stories marked the peak of Lane's career as a writer of short magazine fiction. Much of her previous work had been in a series of "hill-billy" stories, complete with contrived dialect, for the *Country Gentleman,* the Curtis Publishers' organ for rural audiences, while the *Post* was aimed at a more sophisticated urban readership. The prices paid the writers reflected the difference. During the late 1920s, Lane received $600 for her early stories for the *Country Gentleman,* and eventually she worked her prices up to double that. But when she broke into the *Post* with the Ernestine stories, she started at $750 and quickly rose to $1200, even though the *Post* had cut its fees to writers during the Depression, and its top writers commanded much larger fees toward which she could aspire.[5] Such distinctions were of prime concern to Lane: a free-lance writer entirely, she supported herself and several dependents from 1918 to 1968 solely from her typewriter, and she frequently claimed to have no pretensions to be anything more than a good hack.[6]

Yet in her weaker moments she would confess to more serious ambitions, and at times she wrote better than she pretended. She appeared three times in the O. Henry and Edmund O'Brien annual prize collections. Her best story ("Innocence," 1922) won second prize in the O. Henry awards for that year, having appeared in *Harper's* after being rejected by *McCall's,* and at least one reader compared her work favorably with Katherine Mansfield's.[7] She felt a mingled pride and chagrin when her agent failed to place some of her less-formulaic stories in the premium market of the *Post* or *Ladies' Home Journal*—only to place them also with *Harper's,* whose prices were but a third of the *Post's*.[8] And in time she did write her two serious novels, *Let the Hurricane Roar* and *Free Land,* which not only satisfied her literary conscience but also won good prices as serials in the *Post*.

Her gathering of the Ernestine stories from the *Post* and *Ladies' Home Journal* into the anthology she named *Old Home Town* is of a piece with her work in these two novels. Writing in the depths of the Depression, she sought in *Let the Hurricane Roar* and *Free Land* to retrieve from the pioneer past of her forebears exemplary tales of courage and fortitude to inspire the present: implicitly, what would save America would not be the programs of the New Deal but a continuity of spirit with the heroic pioneer past. In gathering the stories that would comprise *Old Home Town,* she sought to retrieve these stories from the triviality of their contrivance and to give them a moral resonance as a whole that they did not manifest singly. Her means to this end was, first, simply to bring together these stories—linked naturally by character, setting, and theme—from their original scattered publication and, second, to preface the collection with a title essay through which the series would be screened. Properly seen, what would emerge would be a portrait of a small town through the growing ethical consciousness of the adolescent narrator, the whole framed in the more comprehensive ethical vision of the preface.

In fact, once the contrivance of plot is set aside, it can be seen that all of the stories turn on the struggles of various victims of a small-town culture in which the second-greatest crime is to be an old maid and the greatest is to yield to a spontaneous impulse from the heart. The victims are mainly women: spinsters, widows, adolescent girls, discontented wives; and their oppressors, representatives of community authority, are in the main parents and husbands, although many women individually work to support the structure of oppression as well: the spirit of Mrs. Grundy reigns over all.

The lead story in the collection may be taken as representative of the whole. **"Old Maid"** appeared first in the *Post* and later was selected for the *O. Henry Memorial Prize Stories of 1933*. It tells of the struggle for respectability and fulfillment of a woman who at age twenty-six has failed to attract a husband; as a consequence, she must suffer the pity and condescension of the townspeople and writhe under the special restrictions of her condition. Without a family, she must live and board with a "respectable" widow and go to church in the company of "respectable" families; while in social gatherings with other women, at church suppers or sewing circles, she must pre-emptively belittle her own worth as merely an old maid. Then a notoriously dissolute bachelor begins to court her; she blossoms into a flushed pride and a new dress and hat. Through young Ernestine's diligent eavesdropping on her parents' conversation, we learn that barbershop gossip reveals the bachelor merely to be toying with her affections to win a bet. A whole bevy of Mrs. Grundys watch expectantly for her downfall; certainly she will lose her job as schoolteacher if she is "talked about." Ernestine's mother feels the injustice keenly but is paralyzed by the town's moral atmosphere. The crisis is precipitated by a violent buggy-accident: while her suitor lies apparently near death, the young woman salvages her respectability by proclaiming their engagement. But the man refuses to die: as he recovers (unable to speak because of a broken jaw), the Grundys speculate avidly on her humiliation when he is able to repudiate her claim. She solves her dilemma with a second-convolution falsehood: she announces that she has changed her mind, that she will break the engagement—thus pre-emptively jilting him before he can jilt her. She later marries the young doctor who has attended her suitor; the suitor, chastened by his brush with death and the blow to his reputation, subsides into querulous defeat.

"Old Maid" displays clearly the moral ambiguity that runs through these stories: the old maid is a victim of the town's hypocrisy, yet she triumphs, not on her own terms but on those of her oppressors, and achieves not moral stature but mere respectability. No one story alone makes the case against the community, but the drift of the series is unmistakable, as is the compromise for the sake of a plot that will solve each dilemma without disturbing the conventional values of the readers of the *Saturday Evening Post* and *Ladies' Home Journal*. The moral revulsion felt by young Ernestine finds no scope in the stories that she witnesses.

Nor does it, finally, in the anthologized version of these stories, in which Lane comes down not on the side of the emotional freedom denied in each of the stories, but rather on the side of the original, powerful Puritan ethos of the nineteenth-century pioneers that had decayed into mere respectability in the town she remembered. Speaking in her own voice in the Preface to *Old Home Town,* and with a force and seriousness that had never appeared in the stories themselves, Lane characterizes the community in broad strokes of reminiscence. She paints a moral geography of the town, framed between the school-house and the cemetery, the right side of the tracks and the wrong; she details the daily, weekly, and yearly cycle of routine and the complex conventions that carry the force of law; she recalls a veneer of petty gentility over the general penury, a mindless respectability that a child questions at her peril, and beneath it all an implicit set of values that, presumably, young Ernestine could formulate only after she has broken away, as she does in the last story, **"Nice Old Lady."** Lane's words in the Preface are:

> It was a hard, narrow, relentless life. It was not comfortable. Nothing was made easy for us. We did not like work and we were not supposed to like it; we were supposed to work, and we did. We did not like discipline, so we suffered until we disciplined ourselves. We saw many things and many opportunities that we ardently wanted and could not pay for, so we did not get them, or got them only after stupendous, heartbreaking effort and self-denial, for debt was much harder to bear than deprivations. We were honest, not because sinful human nature wanted to be, but because the consequences of dishonesty were excessively painful. It was clear that if your word were not as good as your bond, your bond was no good and you were worthless. Not only by precept but by cruel experience we learned that it is impossible to get something for nothing; that he who does not work can not long continue to eat; that the sins of the fathers are visited upon the children even unto the fourth generation; that chickens come home to roost and the way of the transgressor is hard.[9]

The major concerns, then, in *Old Home Town* are formal and thematic. Formally it represents the occasional attempt by short-story writers to round out their efforts by accumulation toward the broader form of the novel. Thematically, it takes its place in the literature of the American small town, specifically in that second wave of fictional representations of small-town life that replaced the nostalgic idealization of the village with a critical realism—as in the work of Edgar Lee Masters, Sherwood Anderson, and Sinclair Lewis.[10] The flight from the village had become a self-defining act for protagonist after protagonist; Ernestine's escape is one of a long succession. If we look for instances, however, in which both the formal experiment and the thematic concern combine, we find few examples: the novel proved to be the better vehicle to develop the theme in a complex analysis of social mores, and for most short-story writers, each story was a fresh start in new circumstances. The single most significant antecedent of *Old Home Town* is probably Sherwood Anderson's *Winesburg, Ohio* (1919), in which Anderson puts together a series of village stories that had appeared singly in different places but are linked by the occasional appearance of George Willard and achieve a thematic unity by virtue of the prefatory fable, "The Book of the Grotesque."[11]

Lane had read *Winesburg,* as well as Anderson's *Many Marriages* (1923) and *Dark Laughter* (1925), some years earlier and had not been impressed. By her standards of realism, the grotesques of Winesburg were like nothing she had known in her home town, and she thought Anderson's preoccupation with sexual themes simply prurient. She had, in fact, met Anderson casually in Paris, and she had so impressed him that he had incorporated her into one of the erotic episodes of *Dark Laughter*—which had redoubled her disgust. But in 1928 she happened to read Anderson's *A Story-Teller's Story* (1924), which so overwhelmed her that she wrote him a long, rambling letter of admiration. Upon sober reflection, she decided not to send it, but she kept it in her files.[12]

What she had found especially striking in that work were Anderson's remarks on the short story, in which he distinguished between stories of plot and stories of form.[13] They were remarks that cut to the heart of her uneasiness about her own work: "You hate plot stories," she wrote to Anderson; "Hurrah! A man who succeeds in really hating, *hating* plot stories without writing 'em!. . . . I don't say *I* do it; no, I write the plot-story cut-to-measure." And although she does not mention the Epilogue to *A Story-Teller's Story,* Lane could hardly have failed to identify herself with Anderson's exemplary tale of the slick-fiction writer who longed to write the truth but could not escape the trammels of his success. Her own work in the 1920s reveals a clear dichotomy between the "plot" stories she wrote for the *Country Gentleman* and her freer efforts in *Harper's,* where she is capable of a subtle and impressionistic prose and delicately muted effects, as an intensely focused foreground consciousness reveals sudden depths. But by the 1930s, she was no longer able to work in both modes, as a moral rather than an aesthetic conscience came to stand over against the "plotting" of the stories in **Old Home Town.** It is likely that by 1935 her respect for Anderson's literary standards brought *Winesburg* into focus not for the form of its stories but as a structural model for **Old Home Town** and as a work of moral seriousness.

Her real material—that is, the destructive morality of her home town—had long been on her mind, but not in a form that she could use with her sensibility or in her marketplace. Only in 1967, and then only in a private letter, could she allude to the stories that were beyond the bounds of her limited realism and the formulas of the *Saturday Evening Post:*

> When I was a "youth"—I mean when I was ceasing to be a girl and becoming a young lady . . . there was an unmarried young lady in our town . . . who gave birth to The Son of God, Jesus Incarnate again, as foretold in the Bible and as she herself testified. Strangely—as I thought, even then—nobody in the town believed her, though all unquestioningly believed that every word of the Bible was the literal word of God dictated by Himself to the scribes.—There was another girl whose father whipped her unmercifully with a blacksnake whip and sent her to her Aunt in Kansas City for an abortion; the aunt sent for the child's father, who went to Kansas City and married the girl. They returned to Mansfield. Five months later her mother and sisters—who in the interim had not spoken to her; nobody in the town did—went away somewhere—St. Louis, Memphis, I don't remember where—and the husband frantically begged neighbor women to come help the girl, the baby being prematurely born. . . . Twenty-five years later this girl, then mother of five, was scornfully refusing to speak to a young girl reputed to be rather "fast," saying virtuously to me that she felt it our duty to maintain morality.—Another girl in town was taken ill in the night, seized with fierce pains; her mother sent for the doctor and was appalled to see a baby born. The girl had laced herself tightly enough to conceal her condition completely. She was not spoken to, by her family or anyone else, so long as I knew. . . .[14]

Such was the *donnée* of Lane's material, the anecdotal terrors of her life in Mansfield; which she could merely reduce to the dimensions of her market. Her only recourse in framing her stories for the magazines was to keep her narratives clear of such abysses, which she could do by plotting her stories as approaches to such crises that are tactfully evaded or as escapes from unspeakable circumstances that antedate the story and the adolescent narrator's observation. Anderson might well have dealt with such explosive material in his own way—by allusion just short of explicitness, and by drawing the grotesques that characters become as result of their descent into the abyss. Both he and Lane participated in and wrote about the twentieth-century revolt against the destructive effects of Puritan morality-become-respectability. But by eschewing the exigencies of "plot," he remained free, in a way that Lane could not, to present a revolutionary theme in a revolutionary form. It is at least possible to speculate that Lane's middle-aged return to the disciplined values of her childhood in Mansfield found its formal equivalent in her yielding to the exigencies of the plotted story: the satisfying closure of plot graphs the satisfying relapse into an orderly and familiar vision of a stable, disciplined society.[15]

As the Depression closed in upon Lane, she found herself on the one hand constrained more and more to produce the formulaic plot-stories favored by the slick-paper magazines and on the other to come to serious terms with her sense of history and the contemporary crisis. The Preface to **Old Home Town** was her attempt to wrench these stories into a significance they did not have singly, much as Anderson had done for his apparently disconnected sketches with his remarks on the grotesque. But as she turned her critical consciousness upon the bygone days in which her stories were set, she discovered a wavering in her conception that the stories themselves did not contain. For although the burden of the stories was that of an oppressive and demeaning social order that the narrator must reject for the sake of her own growth and freedom, Lane upon reflection seemed to doubt the fruits of the rebellion by her generation against that of her parents:

> Now some of us seem to see, in our country's most recent experiences, an unexpected proof that our parents knew what they were talking about. We suspect that, after all, man's life in this hostile universe is not easy and cannot be made so; that facts are seldom pleasant and must be faced; that the only freedom is to be found within the slavery of self-discipline; that everything must be paid for and that putting off the day of reckoning only increases the inexorable bill.
>
> This may be an old-fashioned, middle-class, small-town point of view. All that can be said for it is that it created America.
>
> (24)

So much she had discovered upon returning from her European wanderings to her old home town at the end of the 1920s—to spend the next decade there, tied to the wheel of economic necessity as she worked diligently to support herself and her parents. But as she looked around her, comparing, as she wrote of it, the town she had grown up in with the one she had returned to, it became clear that the small town as she had known it no longer existed; in the homogenization of American culture, it had become, she said, cosmopolitan, while the cities contained many persons who had never shed their small-town point of view. The prefatory essay ends on that dilemma, which became in essence her continuing problem as a social thinker: to cosmopolitanize the strengths of the small-town ethos that she had, like her heroine Ernestine, earlier rejected.

This problem would occupy her the rest of her life, but not as a fiction-writer. She would publish no fiction after *Free Land* in 1938—which, as a best-seller, helped free her from Mansfield and from support of her parents. From this time on, she devoted herself almost entirely to rethinking political philosophy toward a set of principles that have come to be called libertarian—essentially an abstraction of the radical personal freedom and self-reliance of the American frontier into their contemporary equivalents. Obviously this effort required also a formal repudiation of her earlier socialist and communist enthusiasms. Much of her revised thought would find its first appearance in the *Saturday Evening Post* as well, where she found an editorial policy congenial to her opposition to the social policies of the New Deal.[16] A summary of her progress would appear as *The Discovery of Freedom* (1943). Her later years, until her death in 1968, were spent mainly in a voluminous correspondence with a handful of like-minded thinkers that had persisted through the long liberal afterglow of the Roosevelt years. Her mark in thus preserving a political tradition that she had encountered imaginatively in her efforts as a fiction-writer appeared shortly after her death with the establishment of the Libertarian Party, which has fielded a national candidate for president in every election since 1972. The mark in fact became a uniquely personal one, for the candidate in 1976 was Rose Wilder Lane's god-son and heir, Roger Lea McBride—promoter of her works and donor of her papers to the Herbert Hoover Presidential Library, where they have been open to scholars since 1983.

Lane's career, then, must stand as an instructive parable of some of the perils surrounding the literary imagination. A gifted and promising short-story writer at her occasional best, she was beset by economic, moral, and finally political pressures on her literary imagination. The need to command high fees for her stories led too often to a compromising of the themes her imagination presented her, while her increasingly conservative moral consciousness began to foreclose the possibilities of exploring the uncharted dimensions of the dilemmas her stories turned on. As the economic pressures subsided, the moral concern expanded into a political vision that devoured her literary career. *Old Home Town* stands at the earliest verge of this sequence, looking back to Lane's early creative freedom in the 1920s—"Innocence" (1922), aptly named, her best and one of her earliest stories—and forward to the assimilation of her fictional impulse to the exigencies of political theory.

Notes

1. *Old Home Town, Let the Hurricane Roar,* and *Free Land* were first published by Longman, Green. *Let the Hurricane Roar* has been reprinted by Bantam Books since 1976 under the new title of *Young Pioneers.* The "Little House" books by Laura Ingalls Wilder are well-known; less well-know is that Lane had an important hand in her mother's books. For an account, see William T. Anderson, "The Literary Apprenticeship of Laura Ingalls Wilder," *South Dakota History,* 13 (Winter 1983), 285-331.

2. According to the current University of Nebraska Press catalogue, "The automobile was about to arrive, and so was World War I, but life in *Old Home Town* was still pastoral. Rose Wilder Lane has recreated small-town society of that period with a precise feeling for decorum, dress, and kitchen dialogue."

3. Rose Wilder Lane, "Credo," *Saturday Evening Post,* 208 (March 1936), 5-7, 30-31, 34-35.

4. In *Saturday Evening Post:* "Old Maid," 205 (23 July 1932), 10-11, 37, 40, 42; "Country Jake," 206 (26 August 1933), 8-9, 75-76, 78, 80; "Hired Girl," 206 (11 November 1933), 10-11, 57-58, 60-62; "Thankless Child," 207 (2 February 1935), 8-9, 33, 36, 42; "Nice Old Lady," 208 (6 July 1935), 12-13, 56, 59-60, 64. In *Ladies' Home Journal:* "Immoral Woman," 49 (September 1932), 14-15, 62, 64-66; "Long Skirts," 50 (April 1933), 11, 83-84, 86, 88, 89. An eighth story, "Traveling Man," was written contemporaneously with these but was not accepted by either magazine; it appeared for the first time in *Old Home Town* after revision to a first-person narrative to make it consistent with the other stories.

5. Lane's diary entries for February 14 and 25, April 28, 1925; May 12, 1930; April 22, 1932; December 13, 1934; May 5, 1935.

6. Typical are her comments in letters to Guy Moyston. [July] 1924; June 3, 9, and 18, 1925; July 10 and October 20, 1927.

7. "Innocence," in *O. Henry Memorial Award Prize Stories of 1922,* ed. Blanche Colton Williams (Garden City, NY: Doubleday, Page, 1923), pp. 23-35; first published in *Harper's,* 144 (April

1922), 577-84; the comparison with Katherine Mansfield is mentioned in *Harper's,* 149 (January 1924), 291-92. "Yarbwoman," in *The Best Short Stories of 1927,* ed. Edward J. O'Brien (New York: Dodd, Mead, 1928), pp. 180-201; first published in *Harper's,* 153 (July 1928), 210-21. "Old Maid," in *O. Henry Memorial Prize Stories of 1933,* ed. Harry Hansen (Garden City, NY: Doubleday, Doran, 1933), pp. 189-214; first published in *Saturday Evening Post,* 205 (23 July 1932), 10-11, 37, 40, 42.

8. Letters to Guy Moyston, April 7, May 15, August 24, 1925; diary entry September 1, 1924; letters to Guy Moyston, January 3, 1926, September 2, 1927. Lane's best short stories, for which she received the least money, appeared in *Harper's:* in addition to those mentioned, "Autumn," 149 (June 1924), 82-87; "The Blue Bead," 151 (June 1925), 34-46; "Harvest," 158 (January 1929), 226-38. "The Blue Bead" was a finalist in the *Harper's* short-story contest for 1925.

9. Preface, *Old Home Town* (New York: Longman, Green, 1935), p. 23. Subsequent citations are in the text.

10. The theme and its sequence are described by Ima Herron, *The Small Town in American Literature* (Durham, NC: Duke Univ. Press, 1939), especially Chapter X.

11. The stories were published in 1916-17 in *The Little Review* and *The Seven Arts.* Anderson apparently conceived of them as a unified series from the beginning: see William L. Phillips, "How Sherwood Anderson Wrote *Winesburg, Ohio,*" *American Literature,* 23 (March 1951), 7-30.

12. I have described the significance of this episode in "Sherwood Anderson and Rose Wilder Lane: Source and Method in *Dark Laughter,*" *Journal of Modern Literature,* 12 (March 1985), 131-152. The unsent letter is dated May 11, 1928.

13. Sherwood Anderson, *A Story-Teller's Story,* ed. Ray Lewis White (Cleveland, OH: Case Western Reserve Univ. Press, 1968), p. 255.

14. Letter to Norma Lee Browning, 1967. Ellipses mine.

15. The general idea is not new. Certainly it is implicit in Ian Watt's analysis of the "conservative" or "neoclassical" plot of *Tom Jones* in his *The Rise of the Novel* (Berkeley: Univ. of California Press, 1957), Chap. IX. More recently, Frederic Jameson has suggested a similar idea in his "Metacommentary," *PMLA,* 86 (Jan. 1971), 12-13.

16. See her exposition of these values in her "Credo." According to reader response, it was a very popular essay; it was reprinted as a pamphlet under the title of *Give Me Liberty* (Caldwell, ID: Caxton, 1954).

William Holtz (essay date summer 1992)

SOURCE: Holtz, William. "Rose Wilder Lane's *Free Land*: The Political Background." *South Dakota Review* 30, no. 1 (summer 1992): 46-60.

[*In the following essay, Holtz contends that Lane's novel* Free Land *fictionalizes the author's "reaction against the agricultural policies of the New Deal."*]

The 1984 re-issue of Rose Wilder Lane's *Free Land* by the University of Nebraska Press is a sign of the continuing significance this novel has had in the literature of the settlement of the American prairie lands. *Free Land* was a best-seller on its original publication in 1938; and, with Lane's earlier *Let the Hurricane Roar* (1932; continuously in print), it has continued as a minor classic of the Dakota frontier—preserving an adult version of the experience rendered for children in the books by Lane's mother, Laura Ingalls Wilder, particularly in her *The Long Winter.* The writer's connection between mother and daughter is, however, one that can be touched on only marginally here. Rather, I would focus on the genesis of *Free Land* out of the contemporary political circumstances in the 1930s—reading its authorial intent, narrowly, as a reaction against the agricultural policies of the New Deal and, more broadly, as a dramatized alternative to the social philosophy implicit in the whole thrust of government in the Roosevelt administration.

Broadly, I would describe *Free Land* as marking the completion of Rose Wilder Lane's conversion from an early dalliance with socialism and communism to a libertarian ideology that would leave her out of step with the American political mainstream for the remaining thirty years of her life—but that would establish her as a beacon from the past for that remnant committed to the radical individualism implicit in *Free Land.* Her political consciousness emerged early in her childhood, she claimed, as even the white and yellow summer asters along the front-yard fences in her home town of Mansfield, Missouri, carried a populist political symbolism. "To me," she recalled, "a yellow aster still stands for the hated gold standard; the white aster means William Jennings Bryan, whose free coinage of silver would have taken us back to prosperity. But Bryan was defeated by the soulless corporations and our country was forever ruined."[1] This was just a few years after her family had decamped from DeSmet in Dakota Territory, settling in Missouri in 1894 after having been driven from the prairie by years of drought. A few years later, still a high school student, she embraced Christian Socialism and the campaign of Eugene Debs, giving speeches in his behalf and handing out copies of the *Appeal to Reason* while living with her aunt in Crowley, Louisiana.[2]

She came intellectually of age as a newspaperwoman in San Francisco in the years just before World War I, embracing with most of her peers the fashionable socialist opinions of advanced thinkers of the time. And with the Bolshevik Revolution, she advanced to a sentimental identification with the great Russian experiment; although never formally a member of the Communist Party, she consorted readily with Party members and believed, as they did, that "the sun is rising in Russia."[3] Only when she finally traveled to Soviet Georgia in 1923, and encountered Communism at work among the peasant farmers, did she begin to doubt the possibility of a beneficent government arranging lives of suffering people for the better. What she in fact observed was an incompetent bureaucracy attempting to control the production and distribution of food—and effectively condemning whole villages to suffering and starvation that they could have avoided by following their traditional practices. The whole issue was put to her quite succinctly by the Russian peasant who complained to her, "Why doesn't the government go ahead and govern, and let us alone?"[4]

In the next year, Lane returned to the States and settled in on her parents' farm in the Missouri Ozarks. It was, for her, a period of political disengagement and a quest for self-fulfillment, as she developed a modestly prosperous career as a free-lance writer for the national slick-paper magazines. She dreamed of financial success and freedom to lead a life divided between domestic elegance and exotic foreign travel; in fact, she was tied to the needs of her aging parents, the drudgery of farm life and the limited social possibilities of a rural community, and the daily requirement to write something that would sell. Her hope for eventual relief was invested in a small but rapidly growing fund in the 1920s stockmarket. She lost this hope, of course, in the market crash of 1929; and as the nation looked for new hope in Roosevelt's programs after 1932, Lane found herself forced to redouble her efforts at her typewriter just to keep her head above water during a period when editors were buying fewer manuscripts and cutting prices for those they did buy. In this period, she produced a series of unexceptional stories about her childhood years for the *Saturday Evening Post* and *Ladies' Home Journal*; but when they were anthologized as **Old Home Town,** she found herself compelled to attach a preface that set a strong moral screen over these pictures from the past:

> It was a hard, narrow, relentless life. It was not comfortable. Nothing was made easy for us. We did not like work and we were not supposed to like it; we were supposed to work, and we did. We did not like discipline, so we suffered until we disciplined ourselves. We saw many things and many opportunities that we ardently wanted and could not pay for, so we did not get them, or got them only after stupendous, heartbreaking effort and self-denial, for debt was much harder to bear than deprivations. We were honest, not because sinful human nature wanted to be, but because the consequences of dishonesty were excessively painful. It was clear that if your word were not as good as your bond, your bond was no good and you were worthless. Not only by precept but by cruel experience we learned that it is impossible to get something for nothing; that he who does not work can not long continue to eat; that the sins of the fathers are visited upon the children even unto the fourth generation; that chickens come home to roost and the way of the transgressor is hard.
>
> Now some of us seem to see, in our country's most recent experiences, an unexpected proof that our parents knew what they were talking about. We suspect that, after all, man's life in this hostile universe is not easy and cannot be made so; that facts are seldom pleasant and must be faced; that the only freedom is to be found within the slavery of self-discipline; that everything must be paid for and that putting off the day of reckoning only increased the inexorable bill.
>
> This may be an old-fashioned, middle-class, small-town point of view. All that can be said for it is that it created America.[5]

For Lane and for her parents, the Depression was simply another period of hard times, which had always come and always would again. It had been the Panic of 1893, after all, that had shaken them loose from their Dakota home; and years of hard work had retrieved a modest recovery for them. The same principles applied: you tightened your belt, did without, and worked harder. Parents and daughter were equally appalled by the various relief experiments of the New Deal, particularly by the farm programs. For Laura Ingalls and Almanzo Wilder, steeped in Biblical tradition, plowing under crops and killing baby pigs was simply an affront to the Lord's bounty; for their daughter, no traditional Christian, the affront was in the power the government had usurped over individual lives and responsibilities. And although she had once, in her days of prosperity, written to a friend that her pioneer ancestry held no interest for her, Lane's 1933 novella, **Let the Hurricane Roar,** drew on family memories of hardship on the frontier, and the hero and heroine carried the names of her mother's parents, Charles and Caroline Ingalls; the working title for this book as she composed it was simply "Courage." At about this time she also began working with her mother's autobiographical manuscripts, beginning the long process of collaboration that would produce the series of "Little House" books by Laura Ingalls Wilder.[6]

The turning point, however, in Lane's political thinking seems to have been a two-week trip through Iowa, Kansas, Missouri, and Illinois in the summer of 1935. She went as companion to Garet Garrett, who often wrote on economic matters for the *Saturday Evening Post*; he had been commissioned to do a series of articles on the effects of the New Deal programs. Lane had known him since 1923; and she was an ideal companion for such a trip, having an intimate knowledge of farm life and having written extensively on agricultural matters during her years as a journalist in San Francisco during World War I. What they found depressed them both: only a few farmers were committed enough to their own independence to stand apart from the various marketing agreements, crop reductions, and land management programs proffered throughout the land by the army of young field agents from the Department of Agriculture. They both found particularly frightening the element of government coercion, especially in some of the resettlement programs designed to move small farmers off of marginal lands. Garrett returned to the *Post* to write his thoughtful articles;[7] Lane went to the university town of Columbia, Missouri, to research a book on the state's history, but her mind was also occupied with what she had lately seen. Some years later she recalled the worst of it in a letter to a friend:

> In southern Illinois there was a Terror. The Government men went into that county and took no nonsense; they condemned the land—every farm; offered the owners $7 an acre, or nothing; this was a model project, tearing down houses, building new roads, surveying a Community Center all blueprinted. The people were frantic and furious; they hired lawyers, who told them that they could do nothing; they tried to get the facts printed. No newspaper dared do it. The country was listed as rural slums, land as eroded. When I asked to be shown erosion, the answer was, it is sheet erosion. That is, the constant effect of rainfall on all earth. There was not an eroded ditch in the County. Every farm was well cared for, every house in repair, painted, cared for—simple frame houses a few without electricity or plumbing, but many with both. One family had lived there since an ancestor came with George Rogers Clark; another was a depression-refugee from St. Louis, all savings invested in the farm at $25 an acre. None of them wanted to be rehabilitated.[8]

From this experience she dated her conscious determination to oppose the New Deal and, more broadly, the collectivist theory of government generally, which she saw as a relapse from distinctly American traditions into an older and failing European tradition. Stalin's forced collectivization of Soviet agriculture and his extermination of the kulaks struck her as merely an aggravated case of Roosevelt's policies and prophetic of future excesses. In the next year, 1936, she published one of her most popular essays in the *Saturday Evening Post*; entitled simply **"Credo,"** it recounted her early dalliance with Communism and the beginnings of her doubts during her visit to Soviet Georgia. Her encounter with the peasant resentful of the new government was expanded into a prophetic anecdote:

> "It too big," he said. "Too big. And at the top, too small. It will not work. In Moscow there are only men, and man is not God. A man has only a man's head and one hundred heads together do not make one great head. Only God can known Russian."
>
> A westerner among Russians often suddenly feels that they are all slightly mad. At other times, their mysticism seems plain common sense. It is quite true that many heads do not make one great head; in fact, they make a session of Congress. What, then, I asked myself dizzily, is the State? The Communist State—does it exist? Can it exist?
>
> The picture of the economic revolution as the final step to freedom was false as soon as I asked myself that question. For, in practical fact, the State, the Government, cannot exist. . . . What does, in fact, exist, is a man, or a few men, in power over many men.

A philosopher might say simply that Lane had discovered the theory of nominalism, that only particulars are real. But this is not to diminish the force of the discovery that she had really, so to speak, been a nominalist all her life, and that the discovery had profound implications for a theory of government. Implicitly, the present danger was that under the stress of the Depression, Americans would yield up their freedom—and their responsibility—for the promised security of the New Deal, which differed little, she believed, from the state controls of either the Communist or Fascist examples.

> The test of strength comes now, when half of Europe has turned back from democracy to the old stability in which the multitudes, having no authority, have no responsibility, but leave both the power and the burden to a few men in control.

"The question," she put it in its most elementary form, "is whether personal freedom is worth the terrible effort, the never-lifted burden and risks of individual self-reliance."[9]

Out of this frame of mind ***Free Land*** was generated. The direction was marked by a letter to her agent complaining of the changes in her country. "One thing I hate about the New Deal," she wrote, "is that it is killing what, to me, is the American pioneering spirit."[10] ***Let the Hurricane Roar*** had been a simple tale of courage; but she now had an enlarged conception that would let her develop a more complex tale placing that simple courage in a larger context. The material, in sense, was already at hand in the wealth of anecdote from her parents' and grandparents' lives in Dakota. Some impetus as well came from a conversation she had had a few years earlier with Graeme Lorimer of the *Saturday Evening Post,* when she had spoken so strikingly of her family's cheer and courage during a legendary hard winter in Dakota that he could not get it out of his mind. He had written to her agent suggesting that "an article which vividly portrayed these pioneer conditions could be made to speak for itself and it would be very wholesome medicine right now."[11] "I cannot do a first-person pioneer story," Lane wrote back to Bye. "Would they take a third-person fact-story of the HARD WINTER of '73, about my father and mother?" She composed a synopsis that she suggested could be the basis of a series of short stories. Lorimer had not been interested in that project, but he had suggested that a single work be distilled from it.[12]

By the end of 1936, Lane was ready to undertake such a work. Added impetus came from the landslide re-election of Roosevelt, which dispelled any lingering hope Lane had that the country would repudiate the policies that she foresaw as disastrous for her country.

> I think it will be a hundred years, or five hundred, before what America was will begin to stir again in history and to find its voices. . . . I am still au fond so American that I am an optimist believing in life. Anyone who believes in Life must love and have faith in his murderer.[13]

The composition of *Free Land* occupied most of her energies in the year of 1937. She was now squarely within her family's pioneer experience as she attempted to draw together her writing and her ideology. If *Let the Hurricane Roar* had been her mother's parents' story, *Free Land* would become largely her father's story, the one Graeme Lorimer had urged her to write. And although Lane had a wealth of anecdote at hand, much of it was smoothed from years of telling or blurred in childhood memory, and she needed persuasively realistic detail. In the interest of authenticity, she plied her father with letters and a questionnaire about his early life. Her mother went to work on him too, and pried out of the taciturn "oyster," as he called him, details that were new to her after fifty years of married life. After his childhood near Malone, New York, he had moved with his family to a farm near Spring Valley, Minnesota, where he had done a man's work since age thirteen. By eighteen he was independent, a shrewd trader of horses and owner of a fine team. With his sister and brother, he had made a grueling trip in the newly opened Dakota Territory, where all had taken up homesteads, although he was well shy of the legal age of twenty-one. His responses to his daughter's queries, free-form in spelling and innocent of punctuation, provided both the axis and significant detail for her retelling of the family story in *Free Land*.[14]

The title was consciously ironic, an echo of the complaint Lane and her mother bridled against throughout the Depression: "But everything is changed now; there's no more free land." Their response was that there never had been any free land: only hard work conferred ownership. "We often talk of the thing you mention," her mother wrote to Lane, "there being no opportunities now."

> If we had had such opportunities when we were young we would have been rich. If we were only a little younger than we are we would do something about them. Anyone who will half try can make money surprisingly now. How they can keep from it I can't see, nor what they do with the money they can't prevent themselves from making.
>
> . . . Of course, nobodys else business is any of mine. But I find my heart is getting harder. I can have no least sympathy for people any more who can do and will only holler that there is no chance any more.
>
> I wish they *all* might have the opportunities we had when I was young *and no more*. Wouldn't it be fun to watch 'em?

Free Land would pose dramatically just what those opportunities had been.[15]

Free Land was serialized in eight parts in the *Saturday Evening Post* in March and April of 1938; in expanded form, it was published as a book in May, on the eve of the Pulitzer Prize nominations for work of the previous year, an occasion which moved a *New York Times* editorial writer to recommend Lane's book for the prize for next year. It was Lane's most serious and sustained effort as a novelist, and it received uniformly good reviews and rose at once to the best-seller lists, where it remained until August.[16]

Her research for the Missouri book had given her certain insights regarding American character and history, and these had coalesced with family history to make possible a story that she and her admiring readers regarded as representatively American. In five years from age nineteen on, her hero David Beaton pits his courage, skill, and endurance against the Dakota plains in the effort to make a farm for his wife and children. His trial by blizzard, drought, storm, bad luck, Indians, horse-thieves, and assorted minor calamities is met with laconic humor and unshakable optimism—a sustained trial that seems incredible in simple recitation but that is grounded in natural circumstance, firmly conceived character, and the actual history of Lane's own family. Plotting is minimal, confined to the comic relief of David's sister Eliza and her reform of a charming rascal; the real action is episodic, tied to the cycle of the seasons and the human rituals of marriage, birth, and death. By the end of five years, David is still on the land: his substantial capital gone, his substantial debt hanging heavy, but his optimism undampened. "I couldn't sell out today," he tells his father at the end, "every tot and title I own, and pay over half what I owe. But it's a good country. I'll be right here, father, when this farm's worth something."[17]

"This is a false ending," one reviewer complained, ". . . the only false note. . . . It leads one to believe that David conquered. Some did and do conquer. But the odds!" Lane's reply appealed to history: many made good in Dakota, she pointed out, and between the droughts some were actually prosperous. But the real issue was a conception of optimism and the salutary effect of adversity: she quoted a poem from somewhere in her reading, presumably an epitaph from a Greek island tombstone:

> A ship-wrecked sailor, buried on this coast,
>   Bids you set sail.
> Full many a gallant ship, when we were lost,
>   Weathered the gale.[18]

In fact, Lane had gone to some lengths to avoid a facile optimism. Young David's career is framed in that of his father, who watches his son struggle to repeat his own successes as farmer. The older man, first and last, is given to quiet moments watching the stars, when it is clear to him that life, finally, is tragic—when he recalls his own grandfather's summation: "My life has been mostly disappointments." The words were Almanzo Wilder's in a letter to his daughter, and they reach back to his failure as a plains pioneer. In *Free Land*, the rhythm of struggle and setback suggests that, even at the end, nothing is guaranteed for young David Beaton, though Lane does permit herself an ironic *deus ex machina* as David's father resolves to advance his son some much-needed cash—charged to his future inheritance. "I don't know as you noticed it when you was to home," he tells his son, "but ever since you young ones was born to mother and me, I wanted you to have an easier time than we did."[19]

The point, of course, is that David most certainly has not. But he has the character of the ancient Greek sailor or the teen-aged heroine of *Let the Hurricane Roar*: a life-affirming optimism that sustains him against all odds. This understated heroic pathos Lane would ultimately find a basis for in a simple metaphysics, but she had long since found it manifest in human nature: it derived, for her, from that very ground of life she had truly grasped on only rare occasion, the knowledge that human life shared with all creation. It was the essence of this vision that it could be grasped but not held, pursued but not maintained. Thus, eventually, her acceptance of adversity, even her perverse love of failure—for the sake of the vital moment when it is transcended and human nature knows itself.

From such a ground, through a series of implicit major and minor premises, flows a social and political theory that surfaces in Lane's narrative in the thoughts and actions of her characters. David Beaton is a homesteader, but his father has never liked the governmental homestead program:

> He did not believe in giving, or getting, something for nothing. He believed in every man's paying his own way.... The Beatons, men like them, had paid for that public land, had worked and paid taxes to buy it from France and Spain and to settle the war with Mexico. It belonged to the people who had worked to pay for it; it should honestly be sold to lighten their taxes....
>
> "Who supports the Government," he had asked.... We do, don't we? the people? Well then, don't it stand to reason the Government can't support the people?"

But from a corrupt premise corrupt practices flow, as throughout the book the requirements of the Homestead Act are routinely flouted. Even David Beaton lies his age to file a claim, asserting a natural right prior to the legal fiction. "He pushed back his hat and felt fine. Beating a legality was a satisfaction, like paying something on an old grudge. A man knew instinctively that Government was his natural enemy." At such a moment, Lane is but a step from pamphleteering.[20]

Only one reviewer, however, was wholly adequate to Lane's intentions in *Free Land,* and that because he had read her pamphlet **"Give Me Liberty,"** reprinted from her *Saturday Evening Post* essay, **"Credo."** Burton Rascoe, writing in his *Newsweek* book column, said little directly about *Free Land* except to endorse it as "one of the most tonic and engrossing novels that has come along in years." His preamble, however, invoked a kind of populist wisdom embodied in "We, the People" as opposed to the articulate theories of philosophers and intellectuals. Satisfied with the self-evident truths of the American tradition, such a citizen "is largely unaffected by all the vociferous winds of doctrine and does what he feels is his patriotic and social duty without bothering his head about the howling of these winds."

> This sort of American, in cities, villages, and on farms, is the American Rose Wilder Lane understands and sympathizes with so well that her little book **"Give Me Liberty"** might be considered the most eloquent and most revolutionary utterance of the decade in America, if only because it is so completely American in tone and feeling, and so at odds with the theories of the intellectuals who are in such a dither about the hobgoblins of Fascism and Communism that they are challenging us to choose one or the other.
>
> We common people, clothed in our barrels, will just say: "What's the rush? Fascism may be O.K., Communism may be O.K., but we have been experimenting with Americanism for a long time in theory and have given it only a brief trial. Let's see if it will work. If it doesn't the experiment can't be any tougher on the plain man than the experiments in Fascism and Communism."

"Mrs. Lane," Roscoe concluded, "in a dramatic novel, has revealed to us a national soul of which we all partake and which some of us may forget we have."[21]

Lane was deeply gratified to find her ideas re-stated so clearly. When a friend brought her a copy and read it aloud, she was moved to tears. "I do so much want our country to be aware of what it is," she wrote Rascoe at once.

> I try to help that understanding, and it seems to me that I always fail completely because my abilities are so inadequate. But when you see what I try to do, then I haven't wholly failed and perhaps next time I'll do better.[22]

But the next time would not come, at least not as a novel, for **Free Land** effectively ended her career as a fiction writer. "**Free Land** exhausted me," she noted in her diary late in 1939. "I have no ideas for fiction."[23] The occasion for this realization was the rejection by the *Saturday Evening Post* of the opening chapters of another proposed serial. In a trip throughout the west, she had been impressed with the number of itinerant families, more-or-less self-sufficient, riding out the Depression by living in automobiles and trucks and working where they could. In Jackson Hole, Wyoming, she encountered a displaced Missourian named Charles McCrary, who had moved west when a fire destroyed his machine shop. He had for a while taken over a small coalmine near Laramie, where he was able to make a meager living until the taxes required by the National Bituminous Coal Act put him out of business. For a while, he and his family had been self-sufficient vagabonds, traveling and working out of two trucks and a trailer: when Lane met him, he had just managed to build, under contract, a county bridge almost single-handed, using salvaged materials and equipment and heroic ingenuity, for a mere $1500.

Lane saw McCrary as a type of the real American; she began a serial called **"The Forgotten Man,"** fictionalizing his career, and sent the first installment, concerning his coal-mining operations, to the *Saturday Evening Post*. It was refused, however, because the editors thought it was simply anti-New Deal propaganda: what they had hoped for was another **Free Land**. Lane argued that she could not write it otherwise; and editor Adelaide Neall wrote a concerned letter to Lane's agent that marks the shift in Lane's sensibility and mode of conception: "Rose is certainly a sufficiently skilled craftsman to tell a story and let her message or propaganda or what have you develop from that story." The skill remained, of course, but the patience and the faith in her imagination did not; and this failure floats in the wake of her career as a buoy marking a permanent change of direction.[24]

Lane would live another thirty years, but she would write no more fiction—save for shaping hand in the growing list of her mother's books. Her next significant work would be a small book on political theory, which assumed as a metaphysical prime reality the free exercise of human energy in a hostile environment and which traced the emerging concept of human freedom through successive civilizations to its flowering in the United States. **The Discovery of Freedom** (1943) would pass almost unnoticed on its first publication; but it has in the years since been revived by the interest of civil libertarians, for whom Lane remains a seminal figure; it is featured, for example, in the catalog of Laissez Faire Books. After her brief moment of fame with **Free Land**, Lane would live out her life as an obscure prophet of a revolution yet to be completed, when all would embrace "the terrible effort, the never-lifted burden and risks of individual self-reliance." Her stance throughout the Cold War was, of course, militantly anti-communist, as she had a chance to demonstrate in 1965, when at age seventy-eight she went to Vietnam as correspondent for *Woman's Day*.[25] Some measure of her continuing influence appears in the emergence, since her death in 1968, of the Libertarian Party, which has fielded candidates in each election since 1972, and whose presidential candidate in 1976 was Roger MacBride, Lane's adoptive grandson, heir as much to her ideas as to her estate.[26]

Notes

Except where otherwise noted, letters and diary entries cited are from Lane's papers in the Herbert Hoover Presidential Library, West Branch, Iowa.

1. *Old Home Town* (New York: Harper, 1935), p. 9.
2. "Who's Who—And Why," *Saturday Evening Post* 207 (July 6, 1935), 30.
3. Letter to Dorothy Thompson, Aug. 3, 1932.
4. Letter to Guy Moyston, April 1 [1925].
5. *Old Home Town,* pp. 23-24.
6. William T. Anderson, "The Literary Apprenticeship of Laura Ingalls Wilder," *South Dakota History* 13 (Winter 1983), 285-331; and "Laura Ingalls Wilder and Rose Wilder Lane: The Continuing Collaboration," *ibid.* 16 (Summer 1986), 89-143.
7. Garet Garrett, "Saving Agriculture," *Saturday Evening Post* 208 (Oct. 19, 1935), 5-7, 78, 80-82; "Managed Agriculture," *ibid.* (Nov. 2, 1935), 12, 72-74, 76, 79; "Plowing Up Freedom," *ibid.* (Nov. 16, 1935), 16, 68-70, 72.
8. Letter to Jasper Crane, Jan. 30, 1957.
9. "Credo," *Saturday Evening Post* 208 (March 7, 1936), 5-7, 30-31, 34-35.
10. Letter to George Bye, Jan. 22, 1937.
11. Graeme Lorimer to George Bye, April 15, 1932.
12. Letters, Lane to George Bye, April 25, May 8, July 30, 1932. Letters, Bye to Lane, April 28, Aug. 9, 1932. Lane was not accurate in her dating of the hard winter, which was the winter of 1880-81.

13. Letter, Lane to Bye, Nov. 5, 1936.

14. Letters, Laura Ingalls Wilder and Almanzo James Wilder to Lane, March 12, 20, 23, 25, April 14, 1937.

15. Preface to *Free Land.* Letter, Laura Ingalls Wilder to Lane, March 12, 1937.

16. Review by Ralph Thompson, *New York Times,* May 4, 1938, 22.3. Lane followed the book's popularity in the *New York Herald Tribune*'s Sunday Book Section, where it remained on the bestseller list through July 31, 1938. The Pulitzer Prize for 1939 would go to *The Yearling,* by Marjorie Kinnan Rawlings.

17. *Free Land* (New York: Longmans, Green, 1938), p. 331.

18. *New York Times* Book Review by Fred T. Marsh, May 15, 1938; reply by Lane, June 5, 1938.

19. *Free Land,* pp. 6, 330-332.

20. *Free Land,* pp. 7, 29.

21. Burton Rascoe, "We, the People," *Newsweek* 11 (May 9, 1938), 30.

22. Letter, Lane to Rascoe, May 9, 1938 (Univ. of Pennsylvania Library).

23. Diary, Sept. 19, 1939.

24. Letter, Adelaide Neall to George Bye, Sept. 20, 1939. The ms. of "The Forgotten Man" and the notes regarding McCrary's life are in the Hoover Library.

25. "August in Vietnam," *Woman's Day* (Dec. 1965), 33-35, 89-94.

26. Andrew Ward, "The Libertarian Party," *Atlantic* 238 (Sept. 1976), 24-26, 28, 30, 32-33.

Donna Campbell (essay date 2003)

SOURCE: Campbell, Donna. "'Written with a Hard and Ruthless Purpose': Rose Wilder Lane, Edna Ferber, and Middlebrow Regional Fiction." In *Middlebrow Moderns: Popular American Women Writers of the 1920s,* edited by Lisa Botshon and Meredith Goldsmith, pp. 25-44. Boston: Northeastern University Press, 2003.

[*In the following excerpt, taken from a comparative study of the novels of Lane and Edna Ferber, Campbell asserts that Lane and Ferber questioned a number of pioneer myths prevalent during the 1920s and 1930s, such as those of the "Prairie Madonna," of "nativism and racism," and of "the national myth about the acquisition of land and wealth."*]

When Walter Benn Michaels proposed in *Our America* that "the great American modernist texts of the '20s must be understood as deeply committed to the nativist project of racializing the American" (13), his examination left out popular middlebrow novels such as those by Edna Ferber and Rose Wilder Lane, two writers whose novels both complicate and challenge Michaels's assertions. Close contemporaries Lane (1886-1968) and Ferber (1885-1968) carved out careers in journalism and as professional writers of popular fiction before settling on regional fiction. Starting out as a reporter for the *Milwaukee Journal,* Ferber published her first novel, *Dawn O'Hara,* in 1911, and in the following decade she became famous for several story collections—*Roast Beef, Medium* (1913), *Personality Plus* (1914), and *Emma McChesney and Company* (1915)—that examined issues of labor, urban life, and the "New Woman" through the practical eyes of their heroine, middle-aged clothing saleswoman Emma McChesney. Best known today for her collaborative role in writing the "Little House" series of children's books with her mother, Laura Ingalls Wilder, Rose Wilder Lane was far more celebrated than her mother in the 1910s and 1920s, when she worked as a feature writer for the *San Francisco Bulletin* and published serial fiction, travel sketches, and biographies in *Sunset* and other magazines. When Ferber and Lane turned from journalism and short stories to novels in the 1920s, both received not only popular but critical acclaim for their work. Ferber's *So Big* won the Pulitzer Prize in 1925, and a *New York Times* editorial proposed a Pulitzer nomination for Lane's *Free Land* in 1938. In addition, Lane's short fiction had been included in *The Best Short Stories of 1927,* and her **"Innocence"** was an O. Henry Award-winning story in 1922 (Holtz 280).

Despite their popularity and relative critical acclaim in the 1920s, Ferber and Lane were stigmatized in later decades as writers whose popular fiction catered to sentimental tastes. Their regional novels share the trajectory of the pioneer chronicle: the family or individual moves to a new land and attempts to tame it or the surrounding community, with mixed results. In her novels, Lane adopted a persona of the quintessential insider, one whose pioneer roots reached back to the 1630s and included successive waves of western migration, the most recent of which had led to her birth in a Dakota claim shanty in 1886. It was a constructed identity that ignored her world travel, her restlessness, and her belief that farming promised little more than being "a slave" to livestock. No less a pioneer through her background as a member of the few Jewish families in Appleton, Wisconsin, Ferber constructed for herself a position that held in tension an insider's knowledge and an outsider's perspective. Proud of her research and the native knowledge that assured the authenticity of her scenes, Ferber admitted that scenes such as one set in the Chicago produce market were "written purely out of my imagination" (*A Peculiar Treasure* 277). She carefully wrote outsiders as observers into most of her novels, all the while positing a deep complicity and sense of identification between herself and America, which she saw as "the Jew among the nations. It is resourceful, adaptable, maligned, envied, feared, imposed upon" (*A Peculiar Treasure* 10).

From these artificially constructed yet apparently deeply authentic and compelling personae of insider and outsider, both writers inscribed political truths in a nostalgic regionalist context by interrogating the conventions of the genre in which they wrote. First among these is the figure of the "Prairie Madonna," a popular icon of the times pressed into service as an agent of American identity formation. In addition to taking a more realistic look at this figure, Ferber and Lane critique even as they capitalize on the nostalgic pioneer ideology so prevalent in the twenties—Lane by demonstrating the patent falsehood of the myths of free land and endurance on the Great Plains in *Free Land* and Ferber through her misunderstood satiric portrait of "the sunbonnets" and domestic culture in *Cimarron*. Second, they explore 1920s nativism and racism, which Ferber confronts through the theme of miscegenation recast as exogamy or intermarriage, a vision that suggests tolerance rather than nativist sentiment and that challenges Michaels's theories. A third convention that Ferber and Lane discredit is the national myth about the acquisition of land and wealth. Finally, the American penchant for collecting objects of material and social culture is revealed for what it is—a project that supports a unifying narrative of American history but does so through cultural theft and misunderstanding. In these ways, these novelists' representative works, including Ferber's *Cimarron* (1930) and Lane's *Free Land* (1938), reflect on conventional reconstructions of the past through central issues of the twenties and thirties: the complicated legacy of the pioneer myth, the controversy over racism and nativism, the national myth of limitless lands, and the exploitation of objects from other cultures.

First, Ferber and Lane challenged ideas of the conventional Western heroine. Recast as what Sandra L. Myres and others have called the Prairie Madonna, the "sturdy helpmate and civilizer of the frontier" (Myres [*Westering Women and the Frontier Experience*] 2), this figure, often pictured holding a child and framed by the circular opening of the covered wagon, graced such portraits as W. D. H. Koerner's 1921 painting *Madonna of the Prairie*. Writing of these images, Annette Stott has traced a progression from the more passive "True Womanhood" icon of the Prairie Madonna to her more active counterpart of the 1890s and later, the New Woman-inspired "Pioneer Woman." The Pioneer Woman's sunbonnet bespeaks gentility and civilization even as her active poses, frequently holding a gun in one hand and a child in the other, attest to her active participation in the project of westward expansion. According to Stott, representation of these women increased during the 1920s, a period in which cultural awareness of and nostalgia for a usable pioneer past also increased. In writing of this period, Brigitte Georgi-Findlay further contends that women's Western novels and narratives "seem to fall into two categories: those that continue to dramatize the story of an eastern woman, most often a young bride, going west, and those that describe growing up female in the Old West. . . . Many of these texts locate themselves in reference to the popular literature of the 'wild' West, drawing on its romantic and nostalgic elements at the same time that they aim to revise stereotypes" ([*The Frontiers of Women's Writing*] 286-87).

In two of her pioneer novels of the 1930s, **Let the Hurricane Roar** (1933) and **Free Land** (1938), Rose Wilder Lane employs and critiques these figures of the Western heroine as she explores the mythology of homesteading and land settlement that they exemplify. Drawn from tales told by her mother, **Let the Hurricane Roar** is the conventionally celebratory pioneer tale of Charles and Caroline Ingalls. In it, Lane addresses the paradox that both she and her mother avoid confronting in the "Little House" series: that "free land" is an illusion and that the only way to acquire land is to leave it to seek work and money elsewhere. A more complex revision of this essential plot appears in **Free Land,** Lane's last novel before she abandoned writing fiction for books articulating her libertarian philosophy. Based on the experiences of her parents and of her Ingalls grandparents, this novel was Lane's protest against the devaluation of an American tradition of independence that she felt was being undercut by the New Deal. It is a prototypical piece of Great Plains fiction as Diane Quantic defines the genre in *The Nature of the Place:* "the person who attempts to impose his or her will upon the land is overcome by natural disaster, a blizzard, a prairie fire, or a dust storm, and the person who understands the land's potential reaps bountiful harvests" (4). As in **Let the Hurricane Roar** (1933), in **Free Land** Lane transforms the experiences of her father's life—a life that he said had been "mostly disappointments"—into the familiar pioneer surface narrative of persistence and triumph.[1] The protagonist, David Beaton, marries his childhood sweetheart, Mary, and, full of optimism, moves with her out West to take up a claim. Blizzards, droughts, grasshoppers, heat, thunderstorms, horse-thieves, and other natural and man-made disasters plague them, yet at the end of the novel he decides to stay on his land, an ending congruent with the Great Plains myth.

Beneath this surface, however, lies Lane's bleaker, more pessimistic version of the pioneer myth and the Ingalls family story than that shown in the "Little House" books. Written near the time of Wilder's *By the Shores of Silver Lake* (1939) and *The Long Winter* (1940),

Free Land incorporates situations from both works, but it tells the darker stories that Wilder felt were unsuitable for the children's series. Dipping from generalized myth into history, Lane exposes the frontier as the site not of limitless opportunity but of inescapable violence over contested territories. The Beatons meet a claim jumper who has killed a man, and they rescue a woman who is nearly dead after giving birth on the trail; after she recovers, she tells them that her husband has been killed and their sheep clubbed to death by cattlemen. Another episode tells of the settlers' lynching of the Bordens, fictional counterparts to the real-life Benders of Kansas, who murdered travelers for their possessions and buried children alive in their always-plowed and never-planted garden plot.[2] The disputes over land gain special resonance in the subplot involving the Peters family, Lane's thinly disguised fictional counterpart for the Ingalls family in Wilder's work. Like the Ingallses, the fictional Peters family has been forced to leave their farm in Indian Territory, a farm that they settled because they had word from Washington that it would be opened for white settlers. They share with the Ingallses a similar family composition and life history, dialogue and set phrases ("there's plenty more down cellar in a teacup," for example), and a desperate honesty conflicting with the struggle to escape an equally desperate poverty. However, the turned dresses, short rations, and optimistic "making-do" spirit of the "Little House" books become here a narrative of outgrown and worn-out clothes, starvation rations, and a family stretched to the breaking point, as exemplified in a tense near-confrontation when David and Mr. Peters, the Pa Ingalls character, both want to steal lumber from an abandoned claim shanty.

In addition to using the traditional man-against-nature themes of the pioneer novel, Lane contrasts the Peters and Beaton families to demonstrate the hardships of prairie life. *Free Land* pits the figure of the Prairie Madonna represented by Mary, David's conventional and literal-minded wife, against the New Western "Pioneer Woman" heroine represented by the half-wild Peters daughter, Nettie. First seen carrying a rifle, Nettie represents the prototype well, with her keen blue eyes, tanned skin, braids "like an Indian woman's," and ambition to work as a teacher so that she can help support her family. Realizing his wife Mary's limitations, David feels drawn to Nettie but realizes that he can do nothing: "'It's different, with you. Nettie, I—It's—You're so—' 'I know,' she said again. . . . 'It's one of the things that don't happen'" (*Free Land* 156). The Peters family also serves as a point of economic contrast to the Beatons, who are initially better off but sink fast in the inhospitable prairie environment. The more obvious signs of the Beatons' increasing poverty, such as limited food and patched clothing, affect David less than more subtle markers of a loss of status, such as the humiliation of having a sod-thatched roof, burning cow chips for fuel, and driving oxen instead of horses: "Even then, and back in York State, only the French drove oxen" (180). In the end, the Beatons can only survive when David's father offers to give the struggling family $2,000 as a gift against David's eventual inheritance. Having demolished popular conceptions of free land, of happy marriage with a woman who is a soul mate as well as housemate, and of self-sufficiency, Lane paints a picture so realistic that David's decision to stay on the farm brought protests from readers and reviewers, one of whom criticized the "false ending" as "the only false note" in the story (Holtz [*The Ghost in the Little House*] 280).

In addition to debunking regional conventions, both Ferber and Lane substantially rewrote the national myth of limitless lands. In her early autobiographical novel *Diverging Roads,* which she called "the only book I've ever seriously written" (Holtz 77), Lane directly addresses the question of land ownership. After a career as a telegraph operator, her heroine, Helen Davies, marries and is abandoned by her husband, whereupon she takes over his job as a realtor selling undeveloped farmland in northern California. In this work, Lane somewhat romantically suggests that the question of land ownership rests on a partnership that draws together the elemental forces of farmers and land. As a weary Helen confides in her childhood sweetheart, Paul: "A real-estate salesman hasn't any real reason for existing. . . . We aren't needed a bit. The people would simply take the land if they weren't like horses, too stupid to know their own strength. . . . We're just a lot of parasites living off the land without giving anything in return" (*Diverging Roads* 264-65). By the time of *Free Land,* however, Lane's pessimism about the idea of land ownership and the pioneer dream shows in David Beaton's failure despite heroic efforts. Equally skeptical about the rewards of hard work, Ferber uses similar tropes of unearned wealth gained through oil discoveries or gambling to reject American dream ideology. For example, Sabra Cravat's farm, the only fruitful land around the town of Osage, is found to be so only because the soil lacks the oil deposits that enrich the rest of the town. Her careful husbandry, a staple fiction of the homesteading myth, is dwarfed and rendered irrelevant by the unexpected and unearned wealth of the oil fields. Ferber also speaks more directly to the colonization of nature and culture in the West by linking environmental and cultural destruction as she does in her description of the oil lands of Oklahoma and the despoliation of Cherokee land. As Ferber later wrote, "For centuries the Grabbers had gone their way, unchecked. . . . There it all lay in this fabulous virgin continent, and no one to stop them; no one who cared enough or had courage enough or sufficient foresight to sense the inevitable result of this ravaging" (*A Kind of Magic* 114).

Another familiar theme in these regional novels, the creation of an American aesthetic through collecting objects of material culture, raises the possibility of a multicultural revision of "Americana" more inclusive than the conservative definition of American editions and artifacts valued by characters such as Percy Gryce in Edith Wharton's *The House of Mirth,* but it does so at the risk of outright theft of another culture. This collection of objects takes at least two forms, the first being the preservation of one's own cultural past through the preservation of significant objects. In a similar way, the culture of Ferber's *Cimarron* relies heavily on classic books, but Sabra values books as objects rather than as texts. When Sabra begins her literary society, the Philomathea Club, for example, she does not bother to read the books she assigns to others. Like the Thanatopsis Club, Sinclair Lewis's satiric version of a book club in *Main Street,* or Edith Wharton's Lunch Club from "Xingu," for "ladies who pursue Culture in bands, as though it were dangerous to meet alone" (Wharton ["Xingu"] 209), the Philomathea Club values books and reading only as status symbols, and it quickly degenerates into a forum for social competition.

The second form of preservation is the acquisition of objects from another culture, as when Magnolia Ravenal of *Show Boat* signs African-American spirituals to further her career, an appropriation at once tribute and theft.[3] In Ferber's and Lane's work, this acquisition and consumption both of objects and of the collected tales of a romanticized, nostalgic history suggests what Brigitte Georgi-Findlay has described as the 1880s "prehistoric craze and the fascination with antiquity" rooted in ethnology and notions of romantic primitivism (219). In Ferber's work, artifacts such as Selina Peake DeJong's antique Dutch china in *So Big* and Sabra Cravat's handwoven blanket from Mother Bridget exemplify cultural borrowing. Woven by Mother Bridget from strong yarn with an Indian blue dye, the blanket represents a multiply alien culture by evoking the long history of the mission school, its Native-American students, and Roman Catholicism. She gives it to the unheeding Sabra, who carries as a talisman Indian-inspired art into Indian country but fails to see the multiple messages within its beauty.

In Lane's *Free Land,* another act of misguided collection becomes cultural appropriation and outright theft. An educated Easterner and the frontier town's man of science, Dr. Thorne, steals the desiccated, mummified corpse of an Indian baby from an aboveground burial grove. Flushed with excitement at the "sensation" it will cause among scientists, Thorne plans to "send it to the Smithsonian in Washington, D.C." even as David Beaton suggests that "Barnum'd pay you a young fortune for that" (104). In this scene, Lane neatly links two forms of cultural theft; the "scientific" ethnographic observation of the Smithsonian scientists and the tub-thumping commercialism of a P. T. Barnum amount to the same thing: exploitation of the sacred artifacts of Native-American culture for the amusement of the white man. Yet the culture to which such artifacts belong turns out to be neither vanishing nor dead, as Thorne had thought, but very much alive: shortly thereafter, the Indians show up demanding the body, and only the best efforts of the strongest and most respected man in the book can save the situation. Gebbert, a legendary railroad contractor about whom the men compose songs, has all the qualities of a hero: he treats his men fairly, shares their living arrangements, and is not afraid to steal from the institution—the railroad—that steals from him, for "a man that won't steal from a railroad ain't honest" (107).[4] As a hero, he knows enough to respect native culture. A legendary frontiersman, Gebbert speaks with the chiefs respectfully, using "their lingo," and sends David to get the body back within three days, dismissing someone's boast that "any white man can handle six Indians" with "Maybe. Custer's men didn't" (112). The race-to-the-rescue plotting of this episode overshadows but cannot entirely obscure the true tension between the contemporary technological wizardry of telegraph and train used to regain the mummified body and the vanishing but still existent past of confrontations between native peoples and white settlers. Significantly, neither the characters nor the narrative voice mount any kind of defense for this action; indeed, all unite in calling Dr. Thorne a fool.

Despite their status as best-selling regional authors, then, both Ferber and Lane consciously challenged some of the country's favorite myths about itself. As Ferber herself put it when analyzing her books' staying power, "In their very core there lay something more solid, more deeply dimensional than mere entertainment or readability. They had power they had theme they had protest" (*A Kind of Magic* 125). Lane and Ferber wrote popular middlebrow fiction, and both understood the limitations of the forms they had chosen for their writing. Yet in creating middlebrow works that straddle the boundary between high culture and low, in writing novels that both promote and critique regional myths, and in representing race in ways that disrupt the status quo, these two authors change the rules of the genre and, in so doing, reveal their "hard and bitter purpose": to expose and protest the disparity between national promise and regional reality.

Notes

1. See Rose Wilder Lane's interview with Almanzo Wilder prior to writing *Free Land* in A *"Little House" Sampler.*

2. Laura Ingalls Wilder reports the story of the Benders in the *Pioneer Girl* manuscript, the genesis for the "Little House" series. Although John Miller and other Wilder biographers point out that the

dates of the Ingalls family's residence in Kansas would have made contact with the Benders improbable, Wilder remembered the horror she felt as a child upon hearing that a little girl her own age had been buried alive.

3. Magnolia has learned these songs by listening to Julie Dozier, Queenie, and others on the Cotton Blossom. In *Love and Theft,* Lott includes a "self-serving" recollection from the performer Ben Cotton that closely matches Magnolia's experience:

> "I used to sit with them in front of their cabins, and we would start the banjo twanging, and their voices would ring out in the quiet night air in their weird melodies. They did not quite understand me. I was the first white man they had seen who sang as they did; but we were brothers for the time being and were perfectly happy." Despite the harmful effects of such appropriation, Lott suggests, "in addition to the minor disasters bohemia has perpetrated . . . there is in its activities an implicit tribute to, or at the very least a self-marginalizing mimicry of, black culture's male representatives"

(50)

4. In writing *By the Shores of Silver Lake,* Lane questioned the episode in which Uncle Hi in effect steals supplies from the railroad company; Wilder replied that the railroad companies regularly cheated the contractors and that this type of "settling with the company" was common, adding that a common saying was "A man that won't steal from the railroad ain't honest." See Holtz and Romines.

Works Cited

Aldrich, Bess Streeter. *A Lantern in Her Hand.* New York: D. Appleton & Company, 1928.

Altieri, Charles. "Whose America Is Our America: On Walter Benn Michaels's Characterizations of Modernity in America." *Modernism/Modernity* 3, no. 3 (1996): 107-13.

Ferber, Edna. *Cimarron.* New York: Doubleday, 1930.

———. *A Kind of Magic.* Garden City, N.Y.: Doubleday, 1963.

———. Letter to Mary Austin. 17 November 1931. ALS. AU 2372. Mary Austin Collection, Huntington Library, San Marino, Calif.

———. *A Peculiar Treasure.* New York: Doubleday Doran & Co., 1939.

———. *Saratoga Trunk.* Garden City, N.Y.: Doubleday, 1941.

Georgi-Findlay, Brigitte. *The Frontiers of Women's Writing: Women's Narratives and the Rhetoric of Westward Expansion.* Tucson: University of Arizona Press, 1996.

Gilbert, Julie Goldsmith. *Ferber, a Biography.* Garden City, N.Y.: Doubleday, 1978.

Holtz, William V. *The Ghost in the Little House: A Life of Rose Wilder Lane.* Columbia: University of Missouri Press, 1993.

Lane, Rose Wilder. *Diverging Roads.* New York: The Century Company, 1919.

———. *Free Land.* 1938. Lincoln: University of Nebraska Press, 1984.

Lewis, Sinclair. *Main Street.* New York: Harcourt Brace, 1920.

Lott, Eric. *Love and Theft: Blackface Minstrelsy and the American Working Class.* Race and American Culture. New York: Oxford University Press, 1993.

Michaels, Walter Benn. "American Modernism and the Poetics of Identity." *Modernism/Modernity* 1, no. 1 (1994): 38-56.

———. *Our America: Nativism, Modernism, and Pluralism.* Durham, N.C.: Duke University Press, 1995.

———. "Response." *Modernism/Modernity* 3, no. 3 (1996): 121-26.

Myres, Sandra L. *Westering Women and the Frontier Experience, 1800-1915.* Histories of the American Frontier. Albuquerque: University of New Mexico Press, 1982.

Perloff, Marjorie. "Modernism without the Modernists: A Response to Walter Benn Michaels." *Modernism/Modernity* 3, no. 3 (1996): 99-105.

Quantic, Diane Dufva. *The Nature of the Place: A Study of Great Plains Fiction.* Lincoln: University of Nebraska Press, 1995.

Romines, Ann. *Constructing the Little House: Gender, Culture, and Laura Ingalls Wilder.* Amherst: University of Massachusetts Press, 1997.

Shapiro, Laura. *Perfection Salad: Women and Cooking at the Turn of the Century.* 1986; Modern Library Food. New York: Modern Library, 2001.

Stott, Annette. "Prairie Madonnas and Pioneer Women: Images of Emigrant Women in the Art of the Old West." *Prospects: An Annual of American Cultural Studies* 21 (1996): 299-325.

Von Hallberg, Robert. "Literature and History: Neat Fits." *Modernism/Modernity* 3, no. 3 (1996): 115-26.

Wharton, Edith. "Xingu." *The Collected Short Stories of Edith Wharton.* Vol. 2. Ed. R. W. B. Lewis. New York: Scribner, 1968, 209-29.

Wilder, Laura Ingalls, Rose Wilder Lane, and William Anderson. *A Little House Sampler.* New York: Perennial Library, 1989.

Julia C. Ehrhardt (essay date 2004)

SOURCE: Ehrhardt, Julia C. "'Stand Entirely on My Own Feet': Rose Wilder Lane's Literary Declarations of Independence." In *Writers of Conviction: The Personal Politics of Zona Gale, Dorothy Canfield Fisher, Rose Wilder Lane, and Josephine Herbst*, pp. 93-139. Columbia: University of Missouri Press, 2004.

[*In the following essay, Ehrhardt traces the central theme of self-reliance in Lane's fiction and nonfiction writings, arguing that "irreconcilable contradictions between the political messages of her fiction and the personal realities of her life"—specifically, her preoccupation with financial security and care for her mother—undermined her work as a writer.*]

> [T]he joy of freedom . . . comes to one afresh from a thousand little incidents. To go where one wants to go, when one wants to, without consulting any other person's needs or plans; to have no standing appointment, so that one may have companionship or solitude as one's mood dictates; in a word, to have nobody in one's life but one's self—that is both peace and exhilaration.
>
> —Rose Wilder Lane, "If I Could Live My Life Over Again"

> She is a person of unbounded energy, sincere simplicities, of often profound intuitive thought, of insight and understanding. A woman with the rare mixture of good looks, unusual personality and common sense. You also soon discover that she is a person of amazing contradictions, fundamentally the sort of contradictions that make it possible for her to be a globetrotter and still remain a simple, homey woman.
>
> —"At Home in the Ozarks," *Kansas City Star,* June 28, 1925

In 1935, one of the *Saturday Evening Post*'s most popular authors, Rose Wilder Lane, composed an autobiographical sketch for readers curious about her background. Though Lane modestly introduced herself as a "middle-class, middle-aged woman, with white hair and simple tastes," additional details belied this austere description. She told her readers that before devoting herself fully to writing, she had worked in a number of diverse occupations: "I have been office clerk, telegrapher, newspaper reporter, feature writer, advertising writer, farmland salesman." Though born in a "claim shanty" in Dakota Territory, the forty-nine-year-old author reported, she had traveled extensively in the United States, Europe, and the Middle East "as far east as Bagdad," and she identified "California, the Ozarks, and the Balkans" as her home towns. A list of her "favorite things" included buttered popcorn, salted peanuts, Arabic architecture, Tchaikovsky, and "all-American boys about fifteen years old playing basketball." Needless to say, the article provided ample evidence of the "amazing contradictions" a reporter had observed in Lane a decade earlier. The writer was at once both a "born homemaker" and a daring adventurer. She lived in a "demure" Ozark country house, but had plans to build a dream home in Albania. She loved to discuss Balkan politics and to drive recklessly, but also enjoyed sitting in her rocking chair and embroidering designs on old fabric. She devoted herself equally to planning her next visit to Paris and to tending her strawberry beds. As far as writing was concerned, Lane maintained that while the process was difficult, her accomplishments were due to her "overweening curiosity" rather than to any innate talent, claiming, "I think anybody who can write letters can write, if they just relax enough."[1]

Newspaper columnists and readers of the *Saturday Evening Post* may have found it hard to reconcile the oppositional aspects of Lane's identity: the unaffected rural woman and the prize-winning writer who traveled to places "where no American woman has ever been before." Lane herself, though, considered the disparities she embodied as a manifestation of her commitment to the profession she had chosen. A self-made woman in every sense of the word, Lane decided to become a writer so that she could achieve the freedom, the individualism, and the independence that were the essence of her personal politics. From her poverty-stricken girlhood in the Missouri Ozarks through her peripatetic literary career as a newspaper columnist, travel writer for the Red Cross, and one of the most dedicated literary opponents of the New Deal, Lane's foremost personal, professional, and political goal was to stand on her own two feet and to pursue her ambitions free from a variety of social restraints: gender ideologies that urged her to marry rather than pursue a career, the financial and cultural pressures of the "family claim" to place her parents' welfare before her own, and the more subtle societal disapproval of independent women whose curiosity and wanderlust deliberately transgressed the traditional boundaries of female experience. Writing enabled Lane to defy the destiny to which her identity as a poor, uneducated Missouri farmer's daughter ostensibly consigned her: a life of debilitating, backbreaking work that had made her parents old before their time. As she wrote in her 1935 book *Old Home Town*: "We saw many things and many opportunities that we ardently wanted and could not pay for, so we did not get them, or got them only after stupendous, heartbreaking effort and self-denial, for debt was much harder to bear than deprivations."[2] After witnessing firsthand her parents' economic hardships, as well as their personal fantasies that never came to fruition, Lane was determined not to follow in their footsteps, but to strike out on an independent path.

Lane transformed her pursuit for independence into personal political fiction that reflected the struggles of female characters like herself: young women determined to live as independent, self-actualized individuals while confronting the seemingly insurmountable obstacles of poverty, self-doubt, and societal disapproval. Due to a variety of unanticipated complications, however, the freedom and self-reliance she hoped her writing would enable her to achieve remained elusive. She ruefully wrote to a friend in 1925: "There is nothing so good as freedom. I arrived definitively at that conclusion . . . sat down on it, and have steadily sot [sic] ever since."[3] As her dreams for a life dictated solely by the limitations of her own imagination gradually dissipated, her career and her confidence stagnated, but the Great Depression reenergized her. While her trademark themes remained the same, the New Deal prompted Lane to redirect her literary energies. She began to compose critiques of an intrusive government that in her opinion threatened to eradicate the cornerstones of her personal politics: self-reliance, hard work, and perseverance in the face of adversity. Convinced that state-sponsored subsidies intended to rescue the country would have exactly the opposite effect, Lane urged her readers to declare their independence from federally imposed social reforms, insisting that only strict self-reliance could solve the nation's problems.

Lane became a central figure in a 1930s literary movement that has not yet received extensive critical attention: anti-New Deal fiction. The Depression era marked the full emergence of her personal politics; it was during this time that she authored her most well-received fiction and wrote essays that are now regarded as seminal declarations of contemporary libertarian political philosophy.[4] But though Lane viewed her writing as the vehicle that would bring her the independence she sought, at the height of her career she found herself unable to claim that independence. Irreconcilable contradictions between the political messages of her fiction and the personal realities of her life underwrote this irony, and those contradictions ultimately brought her career as a self-supporting writer to an end.

Nothing else in the world is more important to me—to my inner self—as writing is.

> If I can only *strike out*—on *my own line*—not *care* what has been done—or what editors will think of it— Just go right ahead in *my own way*—A little courage, independence, *sure* of myself.
>
> —Rose Wilder Lane, diary entries, June 8, 1932, and September 16, 1931

In 1931, Lane found herself deeply in debt. She owed her parents back rent on her room at Rocky Ridge and back payments of the five-hundred-dollar yearly subsidy she had promised them. Thus, when Laura Wilder completed a memoir of her childhood entitled "Pioneer Girl" and asked her daughter to help her revise it for publication, Lane consented. She calculated that if her parents could live on the income from her mother's writing, she would be free to spend her money and her time as she pleased and perhaps return to Albania. But the energy she devoted to editing what became *Little House in the Big Woods* sidetracked her from pursuing work on a new novel, and she lamented in her diary, "Nothing I have intended has ever been realized!"[5]

By 1932, Lane's writer's block had worsened and her self-confidence had plunged, but Franklin Delano Roosevelt's solution to the nationwide Depression—the New Deal—soon initiated her recovery from melancholia. In Lane's opinion, Roosevelt's relief programs established a dangerous precedent for the country, since they encouraged down-and-out citizens to rely on the government when they should be helping themselves. Convinced that New Deal ideology constituted a no-confidence vote in the ability of Americans to stand on their own feet, Lane feared that the government's lack of faith in its own people would discourage Americans from attempting to solve future national crises on their own. In a letter to her mother's editor, she fiercely lambasted the surfeit of self-pity she saw consuming the country: "Nothing's fundamentally wrong; we're going to pull out of this quite all right. Only we'd do it much sooner if everyone wasn't cringing and crying and yelping like a scared pup." While visiting New York City, Lane shared similar opinions with her friend Graeme Lorimer, son of venerated *Saturday Evening Post* editor George Horace Lorimer. He wrote to George Bye that after recounting stories of her family's "losses and hardships" on the Dakota prairie, Lane had excoriated "yellow" Americans who possessed "plenty to eat and a place to sleep" but who nevertheless complained about the country's prospects. On behalf of his father, Lorimer then asked Bye if Lane would write a *Post* article reminding readers of the pioneer "spirit" that had calmed an earlier generation's anxieties during the Panic of 1893. According to Lorimer, Lane's words would provide a generous dose of "wholesome medicine" to a sick country.[6]

Lane had never considered selling her writing to the *Post*, arguably the nation's most influential middle-class magazine, because she believed it paid writers in nebulous "prestige" rather than offering fair prices for their work. She had also never composed a pioneer story and immediately assumed that the elder Lorimer had confused her with her mother. Nevertheless, the editor's request presented Lane with an ideal literary opportunity, given the *Post*'s endorsement of anti-Roosevelt sentiments and the emergent popularity of farm novels. As best-seller lists of the early 1930s attest, novels about farm life were eagerly perused not only by nostalgic readers who had grown up in pastoral settings but also by audiences nationwide who needed assurance in hard times. The genre, which included works by women writers such as Edna Ferber, Bess Streeter Aldrich, Josephine Johnson, and Ruth Suckow, characteristically presented inspirational accounts of pioneer ingenuity and gumption. Like Grant Wood's idyllic paintings of rural scenes and the 1933 film *State Fair* (based on Phil Stong's 1932 novel), these books romanticized the midwestern farm as the only American institution that was not devastated by the Depression (despite evidence to the contrary). Many of these novels highlighted the determination of indefatigable female protagonists and promulgated the reassuring moral that no matter how difficult the Depression seemed, previous generations of courageous, tight-knit farming families had survived and flourished amid even more dire circumstances. The majority of these texts were politically reactionary, as they endorsed traditional gender roles, romanticized poverty, and discouraged social change.[7]

For George Horace Lorimer to commission a farm story from Lane might initially seem odd considering his magazine's ideological message. In the 1920s, the fiction, editorials, and one-hundred-plus pages of advertising in each weekly issue of the *Saturday Evening Post* constantly reminded the magazine's readers that capitalism and consumerism had made the United States the greatest nation in the world. A stable of writers including F. Scott Fitzgerald wrote stories celebrating the country's prosperity and materialism, while Lorimer's editorial columns echoed the mantra that what was good for business was good for America. But the ideology of the pioneer stories, which Lane herself endorsed, perfectly reflected Lorimer's political convictions. Like Lane, Lorimer adamantly opposed the New Deal and was convinced that the country's economy would improve if Americans continued to work hard, believe in progress, and remain self-reliant. By the early 1930s he was actively seeking fiction that advocated his political stance, and consequently Lane soon became one of the *Post*'s most well-known authors.[8]

Lane transformed her personal politics into a manifesto for American survival in **"Courage,"** a short novel serialized in the *Post* as ***Let the Hurricane Roar.*** Defying literary tradition, Lane imagined the archetypal pioneer hero not as a lone male adventurer, but as a young married mother alone on a homestead. As would Josephine Herbst, Lane used episodes from her own maternal family history as the basis for the novel. She modeled her heroine after her mother's mother, and named the character Caroline after her. The novel opens with the wedding of Charles and Caroline, a teenaged couple eager to "set out to the West." On the eve of the journey, Caroline's in-laws present their son Charles with "a free gift": his independence from the farm plus a team and a wagon. In contrast, the items Caroline receives from her parents are not so much presents as byproducts of her "busy life" as a dutiful farm daughter: patchwork quilts that she has "pieced" herself, pillows that she has made, and foodstuffs that she has helped prepare. The only true gifts she receives are a copy of Tennyson's poems and a brand-new Bible with blank family-record pages "waiting to be written upon."[9]

As a young woman accustomed to hard work and few luxuries, Caroline adapts to the harsh frontier without complaint. When the couple arrive at a forlorn prairie townsite, she immediately rejects the life of relative ease the other women settlers have adopted. When winter comes, instead of boarding in the railroad bunkhouse, the pregnant heroine insists on remaining with her husband in their stark sod shanty in order to protect their land from claim jumpers. Though the townswomen protest Charles's apparent lack of concern for her health, Caroline retorts that she will not need female help when her labor begins: "It's natural to have babies. . . . I do not want anyone else there when the baby is born" (***LHR*** [***Let the Hurricane Roar***] 13). When her water breaks on her seventeenth birthday, Caroline vows that she will not scream or cry, and her stoic determination pays off when she bears a healthy baby boy.

In contrast to his wife's spartan needs, Charles lets his imagination run wild as soon as he finishes planting his first crop. Estimating that the harvest will yield a profit of two thousand dollars, he fantasizes about purchasing a buggy and team, hiring help so he can file on an additional claim, and building a frame house for the family, even though he has not yet earned the title to the homestead: "Here would be the kitchen, the pantry, the dining room, there the two bedrooms—two bedrooms!—and a parlor!" (***LHR*** 31). Initially, Caroline is seduced by the "wider vistas" of the future Charles is constantly "opening" (32):

> At the new house there would be a well, with a pump; she would not carry water up the creek bank any more. The baby would have new clothes—soft flannel petticoats and sheer dresses trimmed with lace. There would be wooden floors, easily swept and mopped. She would do the washing in the big kitchen, where there would be plenty of room . . . suddenly she stopped, Charles' patched, sweat-faded shirt twisted between her hands, and her eyes widened at the thought, "We'll have so many clothes that I'll do the washing only once a week!"
>
> (33-34)

The arduous task of lugging laundry water to the house interrupts Caroline's reverie, and before she gets too carried away she returns to her chores. As she walks to the creek, she happily muses that because of the couple's hard work their baby will never remember his "starved, poor life in a dugout" (37). But when she returns to the sod house, she is chagrined to discover that her husband has gone on a spending spree. Unable to wait for cash at harvest time, Charles has purchased glass windowpanes, a mowing machine, silk dress goods for his wife, and toys for the baby on credit. Though Caroline enjoys the gifts, she cannot believe that her husband has gone into debt without buying what they most desperately need: a milk cow.

Here, Lane reverses the traditional gender dynamics of conspicuous consumption. In the next scene, providence metes out a brutal punishment to Charles because he has not held his impulsive desires in check (just as it has granted Caroline a healthy baby in reward for her hard labor). As if to emphasize that Charles's profligacy has jeopardized his wife and child, the sound of "a woman's frantic screaming" breaks the silence on the prairie while a dark cloud of grasshoppers totally blocks the sun's light (*LHR* 41). The hungry locusts devour every stalk of wheat and then invade the sod house, feasting on the defenseless baby when they can find no more food. After rescuing her infant from the insects' greedy jaws, Caroline begins to weep. "She hated the dugout . . . she hated the broken stove, the heat, the stripped, ugly prairie. She hated the wind that rasped her nerves and covered everything with dust. Her whole life seemed poor and mean. . . . She pitied her defrauded baby. She pitied Charles. . . . They did not deserve this suffering. They had trusted, and been betrayed" (*LHR* 67).

Caroline's frustrations evoke the plight of thousands of Depression-era farm families facing drought and the dust bowl. When Charles begins to cry, though, the heroine's staunch resolve returns: "I guess if there isn't any wheat, we'll get along without it" (*LHR* 56). When Charles announces that the family should "give up the homestead" (76), Caroline insists with uncharacteristic fury that he regain control of what has become the family's most valuable possession: their pride. Stating that she will refuse to accept handouts in town or to board an eastbound train in tacit admission of failure, the hardy woman declares that unlike her peers standing in line for bread, "We aren't going to beg" (75). Refusing to let her husband admit that he has been "licked" (76), Caroline assures him that she can remain on the homestead alone while he travels east to work on the railroad. When Mr. Svenson, her immigrant neighbor, announces that he is abandoning his claim because "ta tam country" is "no tam goot," her grim determination becomes even stronger. "Suddenly she felt that he was a foreigner; no American would talk like that. She said sharply, 'No country's going to feed you with a spoon'" (86). She silently thinks to herself: "It's men that make a country. What's the matter with you?" (87). Only her manners prevent her from expressing a harsher indictment of Svenson's self-pity and his lack of masculine initiative.[10]

With this line, Lane castigates both the men and women in her audience for failing to stand up for themselves. If men are incapable of standing on their own feet (as Lane intimates when Charles breaks his ankle while working on the railroad), women must step up to accept new challenges and responsibilities. When Charles reports that he can no longer work because another man has failed to carry his own weight ("We were moving his feed mill and he could not hold up the heft and let it fall on me" [*LHR* 92]), Caroline vows to find a job in town in order to support herself and her baby. No one hires her, but she refuses to accept handouts. "Charles had made a home for her and she would stay in it. If she had to face loneliness, cold, wolves, outlaws, she'd face them. She'd stay there; she'd be right there when Charles came back" (114-15). Returning home, Caroline composes a letter to Charles but keeps her misfortunes a secret. From her letter, a motivational manifesto for Lane's audience emerges:

> We are having hard times now, but we should not dwell upon them but think of the future. It has never been easy to build up a country, but how much easier it is for us, with such comforts and conveniences . . . than it was for our forefathers. I trust that, like our own parents, we may live to see times more prosperous than they ever have been in the past, and we will then reflect with satisfaction that these hard times were not in vain.
>
> (*LHR* 121-22)

In order to convince her readers that they possess the wherewithal to surmount any disaster, Lane subjects Caroline to a brutal survival test. Snowed in by blizzards, she never has the chance to mail her letter; instead, she tucks it into the family Bible as a prophecy to future generations. Whenever self-pity threatens to overcome her self-confidence, Caroline chides herself as if she were Mr. Svenson: "What is the matter with you? Brace up and show a little decent spunk! It's only a little storm; there'll be lots of them before spring" (*LHR* 127). When fuel runs low during a weeklong blizzard, Caroline smashes and burns all of the furniture, including the baby's cradle, and her determination is rewarded with a serendipitous gift: a cow that she bravely culls from a herd of freezing cattle. Lest we interpret her fortune as an undeserved handout, Caroline reasons that she has earned the cow fair and square by rescuing the rest of the herd from smothering in its own freezing breath. In the climactic scene of the novel, Caroline again risks her life to save a man wandering on the prairie during a blizzard. The man turns out to be none other than Charles, who, by foolishly attempting to beat the snowstorm, has almost lost his life.

Lane thus emphasizes that it is Caroline's courage, resilience, and resourcefulness, as opposed to Charles's impulsive and fool-hardy behavior, that will help the young family to succeed on the frontier. Likewise, Lane intimates that her readers will survive the Depression by following Caroline's example and waiting out the hurricane's roar with patience and perseverance. To accentuate this point, Lane writes the final sentences from the perspective of the baby, Charles Jr.—the fictional equivalent of her readers, themselves children of plucky pioneers: "A light from the future was shining in the baby's face. The big white house was waiting for him, and the acres of wheat fields, the fast driving teams, and the swift buggies. If he remembered at all this life in the dugout, he would think of it only as a brief prelude to more spacious times" (*LHR* 152).

Beginning in 1936, in addition to writing fiction for the *Saturday Evening Post*, Lane also published nonfiction declarations of her own personal politics in the magazine. A decade earlier, she had declared to Guy Moyston that she had no intention of ever writing "political" essays, but the reelection of Franklin Delano Roosevelt prompted her to denounce the country's "dictator" and the threat his policies posed to American liberty. In a March 7, 1936, *Post* article she entitled **"Credo"** (later expanded and published as a pamphlet entitled ***Give Me Liberty***), Lane identified herself as a "fundamentalist American" horrified by the president's program of "national socialism." She warned readers that if they did not respond immediately to this national "emergency," fascism would soon suppress "personal freedom, freedom of movement, of choice of work, freedom of self expression in ways of life, freedom of speech, [and] freedom of conscience." Assuring her readers that they could endure "black nights" of "insecurity" "on their own," she asserted that the "unavoidable risks" of self-reliance were a small price to pay for the individual civil liberties that the citizens of Italy and Russia had lost. Lane also articulated these themes in magazines such as *Cosmopolitan* and *Woman's Day*. When the latter periodical asked Lane to write about whether she would offer financial support to her sons so that they could marry, she responded that she considered it an "insult" to offer a subsidy to any adult human being, including her orphaned charges. She echoed this assertion in another *Woman's Day* piece entitled **"Don't Send Your Son to College."** Explaining why she expected John Turner "to get what he wants by his own efforts," Lane maintained that if her adopted "son" and his peers were never given opportunities to conquer "stupendous obstacles," humankind would be "doomed to stagnation."[11]

In print, Lane discouraged her readers from subsidizing their children for the good of the nation, but there is ample evidence that she did not follow her own advice. Hoping that John would matriculate at a university, she paid his tuition to a military preparatory school in New Mexico. In 1937, Lane sent both John and Al to Europe with a tutor, partly to reward them for earning their diplomas and partly to prepare them for college. (In addition to paying for the Turner brothers' educational pursuits, in the late 1920s Lane helped to finance a Cambridge education for Rexh Meta, a young Albanian man who had saved her life on a harrowing mountain journey in 1921.) For the first time since the 1920s, the writer enjoyed a comfortable income from sales of her books and articles, but after paying off her debts and the cost of the Turners' trip, she had only seven dollars in the bank when she settled at the Grosvenor Hotel in New York City to work on what would be her final novel, *Free Land*. As she wrote to George Bye, she hoped that the morals of this second pioneer book would reach readers like her "own boys . . . whose ideal is Security and whose practice is dependence on government instead of upon one's self."[12]

In that letter, Lane did not explain that it was her own generosity toward the Turners that had encouraged them to adopt these attitudes, nor did she state that she needed to earn money quickly in order to support them. Nor did she acknowledge another disturbing paradox about her Depression-era stories: though they stressed the virtues of independence and self-reliance, Lane had relied heavily on her parents' memories for her pioneer plot lines. *Free Land* was no exception. The writer pledged that her book would correct the popular assumption that the government had given "free land" to its citizens under the auspices of the Homestead Act, which had been repealed in 1935. To document "what free land" had actually "cost" settlers, Lane set out to fictionalize her father's homesteading experiences in Dakota. While researching the book, she sent an extensive questionnaire about his pioneer years to the taciturn man her mother jokingly nicknamed the "oyster." The lack of detail in her father's responses disappointed Lane, as did his bleak assessment of his homesteading experiences. Aside from the satisfaction of harvesting his first wheat crop, Almanzo Wilder informed his daughter, "My life has been mostly disappointments."[13]

Although *Free Land* includes harrowing episodes of hunger, crop failures, and horrific blizzards, Lane transformed her father's failures into a triumphant pioneer epic. Given her motivations for the novel—to correct her audience's assumptions about pioneer history and to again demonstrate her trademark theme of self-reliance—her rose-colored narrative is quite troubling, rife as it is with contradictions that severely compromise the intended message. The story opens as the hero, David Beaton, informs his father that he is leaving the family farm to file on a homestead claim. James Beaton does "not believe in giving, or getting, something for nothing," but rather "in every man's paying his own way," and he bristles at his son's intention to "take" public government land. But the elder Beaton, who started out "at twenty-one, with nothing but his freedom," not only releases the teenager from his farm responsibilities but also presents him with a team of matched horses and a wagon for his journey.[14]

David, heretofore "used to land that gave a man a living" (*FL* [*Free Land*] 80), matures quickly as he proves up on his homestead in Dakota. Unlike Charles in *Let the Hurricane Roar,* David resists the temptation to go into debt and makes do with crude farm tools. While his friends gamble to earn extra money, David works as a teamster, and rather than spending a fortune on trees for his claim, he transplants saplings from a nearby lake. When the Hard Winter of 1880 paralyzes the townsite, David's wife, Mary, and his sister, Eliza, join other townspeople returning to the East. Left alone on the prairie, David must weather the frigid temperatures and record snowfalls that block train traffic, leaving him and the other stranded homesteaders without food or supplies. But by pooling their resources and relying on their ingenuity, they survive the blizzards, and when spring arrives, "every man in town was still on his feet," having "pulled their families through, every one alive" (162).

After the brutal "Hard Winter" that "intended to drive out or kill the settlers" (*FL* 153), David devotes himself to his homestead, adhering to his conviction that "every man's got to lift himself up by his own boot-straps" (231). By the time winter arrives again, he has transformed his barren claim into a bountiful farm. In addition to the money from a successful wheat harvest, a crop of turnips earns David, Mary, and their two children a fortune when root crops fail in the East. With some shrewd trading, David obtains a flock of sheep, and when thieves capture one of his beloved Morgan horses, he deftly rescues it. Unlike some of the other homesteaders—Mr. Peters, who leaves because he cannot feed his family; the Garner brothers, who flee from their creditors; and Eliza, who blackmails a rich neighbor into marriage so she will not have to support herself—David, despite his surname, has not been "beaten" by the land. As in *Let the Hurricane Roar,* Lane intimates that her hardworking, determined, and courageous hero deserves the prosperity he has achieved, but a multitude of other factors also contribute to David's prosperity: an extraordinary amount of good luck coupled with various subsidies that arrive in the nick of time.

In contrast to the straightforward storyline of *Let the Hurricane Roar,* there are a number of perplexing plot turns in *Free Land.* The homesteader standing on his own feet at the end of the story is in fact fortunate to be able to stand at all, due to a life-threatening case of frostbite he suffers soon after arriving in Dakota. When their wagon overturns on the snow-covered prairie, David and Mary are buried in a drift. Luckily, their nearest neighbor, Mr. Peters, finds and rescues them, but not before David's legs have frozen. Over the following month, Mr. Peters and his wife selflessly nurse David back to health, saving his feet from amputation. Other characters in the novel, such as a woman who loses a leg after a blizzard, are not so fortunate. Throughout the book, David also benefits from his father's generosity. When one of his horses suddenly dies, his father replaces it, instructing his son to "take him and pay me when you can" (*FL* 34). Harsh conditions also kill one of Mr. Peters' horses, but no one offers him a new animal. When a tornado threatens to destroy the Beatons' wheat crop, the storm suddenly changes course, missing David's field completely but decimating his neighbors'.

The most telling contradiction in the novel occurs in the final scene, when David's father pays a visit to the homestead. Inspecting the farm, Mr. Beaton is duly impressed with the work David has done:

> He had used the mowing machine to cut the wild grass from a square around the house and stable, and with the scythe he had trimmed down the edges left against the sod walls. . . . The yellow-green corn and starveling garden rows could not be charged to lack of cultivation. The pig was clean in her pen, the hens ruffling in dust-baths were red-combed and bright of eye and feather. . . . Both calves this year were steers and had been vealed. . . . The lately-shorn sheep and their lambs were healthy. . . . No one could say that he had not done his best.
>
> (*FL* 323)

For all his success, however, David confesses that he is nine hundred dollars in debt. After assuring Mr. Beaton that he and Mary will be "on our feet" in two years (329), David receives the most important bailout of his life when his father presents him with two thousand dollars in cash. The elder Beaton explains that the money is merely an advance on David's share of the family estate, but then confesses, "[E]ver since you young ones was born to mother and me, I wanted you to have an easier time than we did" (332). As "the first Beaton ever [to] put his head into the jaws of a new country to open it up" (330), David may be well deserving of this financial boon, but Lane does not explain why, in the terms of this logic, other characters—particularly Mr. Peters and his family—are not equally deserving of such windfalls. At the end of the novel, while David anticipates paying off his mortgages, the Peterses' precarious finances force their daughter to reject a marriage proposal so that she can support the family by teaching school. Thus, the conclusion of the novel imparts precisely the opposite message than Lane intended; in *Free Land,* pioneer self-reliance emerges as a misleading myth rather than an inspirational ideology. Despite his valiant attempts to pull himself up by his bootstraps and stand on his own two feet, David cannot succeed without help from his parents—as well as a surfeit of lucky breaks. Far from illustrating the Beatons' plucky self-reliance, therefore, the novel unintentionally proves Stephanie Coontz's contention that, with the exception of the 1950s suburban family, pioneer homesteaders actually received more government subsidies (in the form of land grants, federally funded transportation initiatives, and military takeovers of Native American lands) than any other class in American history before or since.[15]

The irreconcilable tension between the political theories Lane espoused and the content of her fiction mirrored the growing conflict between theory and practice in her life. The five months of fourteen-to twenty-hour days Lane had invested in *Free Land* paid off in the spring of 1938 when she sold the novel for $25,000. Almost immediately, the book became a best-seller that initiated a *Hurricane*-like deluge of mail from readers convinced that "there was never any such thing." One reader begged Lane to write a sequel: "I am rather anxious to know how David and Mary got along after they received the $2000 and think you should go on with the story."[16] But despite her audience's enthusiasm, Lane did not write a sequel to the novel. The denouement of her relationship with John Turner was forcing her to confront the painful consequences of her personal politics. When the man she called her "adopted son" wrote his declaration of independence from Lane, she lost her impetus—and her ability—to write fiction.

At first glance, the story of Lane's personal politics and the writings that grew out of them is liable to disappoint scholars accustomed to accounts of authorial successes rather than failures, and criticism that resolves contradictions instead of concluding with them. For feminist critics in particular, Lane's political conservatism coupled with her personal struggles renders her a writer easy to overlook, especially given that her era was replete with other women writers whose familiar social agendas and literary successes merit our attention. But I would suggest that Lane's inability to achieve the independence she imagined is precisely the reason we should look at her—and by extension, writers like her—more closely. Her literary accomplishments may fall short of those of the female Modernists that critics traditionally "look at," but her career forces us to acknowledge the incessant personal responsibilities she—and, doubtless, countless other women with literary aspirations—had to fulfill in addition to pursuing her own course. It also reminds us that powerful social strictures delimited the paths that women writers of her generation were free to follow. Finally, Lane's personal politics force us to grapple with a provocative paradox: female literary resistance to social welfare. Looking closely at Rose Wilder Lane—contradictions and all—is not a disappointing scholarly endeavor, but rather one that illustrates the compelling complexities of women's writing and women's personal politics during the Modernist period.

Note

1. Rose Wilder Lane, *An Autobiographical Sketch of Rose Wilder Lane*, 9; "At Home in the Ozarks," *Kansas City Star*, June 28, 1925. Unless otherwise noted, all cited letters, manuscript materials, and articles and reviews from clippings files are archived in the Rose Wilder Lane Collection, Herbert Hoover Presidential Library, West Branch, Iowa.

2. "At Home in the Ozarks"; Rose Wilder Lane, *Old Home Town*, 23.

3. Rose Wilder Lane (hereafter RWL) to Guy Moyston, August 10, 1925.

4. Lane's biographer, William Holtz, contends that "the most important work of her life" was her role as the ghostwriter of her mother's Little House books (*The Ghost in the Little House: A Life of Rose Wilder Lane*, 220). I will not address this topic, in deference to Lane's frequent insistence that Laura Ingalls Wilder wrote the books herself (Ann Romines, *Constructing the Little House: Gender, Culture, and Laura Ingalls Wilder*, 7).

5. Holtz, *Ghost*, 220; Miller, *Becoming*, 163; Lane, diary entry, December 16, 1931.

6. RWL to Marion Fiery [November 1931]; Graeme Lorimer to George Bye, April 15, 1932.

7. RWL to Adelaide Neall, October 4, 1940; Patricia Raub, *Yesterday's Stories: Popular Women's Novels of the Twenties and Thirties*, 57, 59, 68.

8. Jan Cohn, *Creating America: George Horace Lorimer and the* Saturday Evening Post, 218-61 passim.

9. Rose Wilder Lane, *Let the Hurricane Roar*, 6, 5, 6 (hereafter cited parenthetically as *LHR*). In later editions the characters' names are Molly and David. As William Holtz points out, in the 1970s the novel was "dramatized on television as *Young Pioneers*, and the book was reissued under that title with the names of the hero and heroine changed to conform to the television adaptation" (*Ghost*, 373). Though the novel subsequently reappeared under its original title, the characters' original names were not restored.

10. Caroline reacts even more harshly in the draft manuscript, going on to say:

    "Get up and fight it if it isn't what you want it to be! Quit blaming the country, you big cry-baby!"

    ["Courage," 51]

11. RWL to Guy Moyston, July 10, 1927; Lane, diary entry, March 17, 1933; Rose Wilder Lane, *Give Me Liberty*, 73, 72, 23, 65, 35; Rose Wilder Lane, "Should We Help Our Children Marry?" *Woman's Day*, March 1938, 13; Rose Wilder Lane, "Don't Send Your Son to College," *Woman's Day*, August 1938, 5, 4, 44.

12. Holtz, *Ghost*, 268, 269, 184, 109; RWL to George Bye, January 22, 1937.

13. Rose Wilder Lane, MSS outline of *Free Land*; Laura Ingalls Wilder to RWL, March 22, 1937; Almanzo Wilder to RWL [1937].

14. Rose Wilder Lane, *Free Land*, 7, 9 (hereafter cited parenthetically as *FL*).

15. Stephanie Coontz, *The Way We Never Were: American Families and the Nostalgia Trap*, 73.

16. Fred Underwood to RWL, May 1, 1938; illegibly signed letter to RWL, April 26, 1938.

Bibliography

ARCHIVAL COLLECTIONS

Rose Wilder Lane Collection, Herbert Hoover Presidential Library, West Branch, Iowa.

Books and Articles

Cohn, Jan. *Creating America: George Horace Lorimer and the* Saturday Evening Post. Pittsburgh: University of Pittsburgh Press, 1989.

Coontz, Stephanie. *The Way We Never Were: American Families and the Nostalgia Trap.* New York: Basic Books, 1992.

Holtz, William. *The Ghost in the Little House: A Life of Rose Wilder Lane.* Columbia: University of Missouri Press, 1993.

Lane, Rose Wilder. *An Autobiographical Sketch of Rose Wilder Lane.* New York: Longmans, Green, 1935.

———. "Don't Send Your Son to College." *Woman's Day,* August 1938, 4-5, 44.

———. *Free Land.* 1938. Reprint, Lincoln: University of Nebraska Press, 1984.

———. *Give Me Liberty.* Boonton, N.J.: Liberty Library, 1946.

———. "Grandpa's Fiddle I" and "Grandpa's Fiddle II." In *A Little House Sampler: A Collection of Early Stories and Reminiscences,* Laura Ingalls Wilder and Rose Wilder Lane, ed. William Anderson, 60-86. New York: HarperPerennial, 1988.

———. "If I Could Live My Life Over Again." *Cosmopolitan,* March 1925, 32-33, 178.

———. *Let the Hurricane Roar.* New York: Longmans, Green, 1933.

———. *Old Home Town.* 1935. Reprint, Lincoln: University of Nebraska Press, 1985.

———. "Should We Help Our Children Marry?" *Woman's Day,* March 1938, 13.

Miller, John E. *Becoming Laura Ingalls Wilder: The Woman behind the Legend.* Columbia: University of Missouri Press, 1998.

Raub, Patricia. *Yesterday's Stories: Popular Women's Novels of the Twenties and Thirties.* Westport, Conn.: Greenwood Press, 1994.

Romines, Ann. *Constructing the Little House: Gender, Culture, and Laura Ingalls Wilder.* Amherst: University of Massachusetts Press, 1997.

FURTHER READING

Biography

Holtz, William. *The Ghost in the Little House: A Life of Rose Wilder Lane,* Columbia: University of Missouri Press, 1993, 425 p.

Full-length biography of Lane that seeks "to retrieve from obscurity the outlines and then the substance" of the author's life.

Criticism

Fellman, Anita Clair. "Laura Ingalls Wilder and Rose Wilder Lane: The Politics of a Mother-Daughter Relationship." *Signs: Journal of Women in Culture and Society* 15, no. 3 (spring 1990): 535-61.

Discusses Lane's difficult relationship with her mother, applying feminist methods to demonstrate how that relationship affected both writers and informed the way they looked at the world.

Miller, John E. "Rose Wilder Lane and Thomas Hart Benton: A Turn toward History during the 1930s." *American Studies* 37, no. 2 (fall 1996): 83-101.

Examines Lane's failed attempt during the 1930s to write and publish a novel based on the history of Missouri, comparing her efforts to American artist Thomas Hart Benton's 1936 mural "The Social History of Missouri."

Thompson, Ralph. "Books of the Times." *New York Times* (4 May 1938): 21.

Praises *Free Land,* concluding that the novel has "fidelity and charm" and "is a human story told in an honest way."

Additional coverage of Lane's life and career is contained in the following sources published by Thomson Gale: *Contemporary Authors,* Vol. 102; *Contemporary Authors New Revision Series,* Vol. 63; *Literature Resource Center*; *Something About the Author,* Vols. 28, 29; and *Twentieth-Century Western Writers,* Ed. 2.

Jean Shepherd
1921-1999

(Full name Jean Parker Shepherd) American radio performer, novelist, screenwriter, short story writer, essayist, and television scriptwriter.

INTRODUCTION

Jean Shepherd is considered one of the greatest comic voices of commercial radio in post-World War II America. Although he is most widely known for his nightly broadcasts, which aired on WOR-AM in New York City for twenty years, Shepherd also wrote short stories, books, and screenplays for television and film. As a writer, he has been compared to Mark Twain, George Ade, and James Thurber. His broadcasts and writings were mainly comprised of material inspired by his experiences growing up in Hammond, Indiana. With various embellishments and fabrications, Shepherd recreated the details of an Indiana childhood in such books as *In God We Trust: All Others Pay Cash* (1966) and *Wanda Hickey's Night of Golden Memories and Other Disasters* (1971), and later in his hugely popular screenplay, *A Christmas Story* (1983). Like Twain, Shepherd was a writer and a storyteller, and he became adept at shaping his material for both radio and print. By working in different media, he reached a broad audience and influenced the direction of both radio and humor. As James F. Smith has written, "While conforming to several traditions of American humor and fiction, Jean Shepherd adds a new dimension to 20th century American humor and displays an insight into middle class character and culture, making his fiction not only enjoyable but valuable as a tool for discovery."

BIOGRAPHICAL INFORMATION

Shepherd was born in Chicago, Illinois, on July 26, 1921. He grew up in Hammond, an industrial town in northwest Indiana, which Shepherd described as clinging "precariously to the underbody of Chicago like the barnacle clings to the rotten hulk of a tramp steamer." When he was sixteen, Shepherd had his first experience with radio, working as a sportscaster for a local station. After graduating from Hammond High School in 1939, he attended the University of Maryland and Indiana University. During World War II he enlisted and served in the U.S. Army Signal Corps. Following the war Shepherd worked various jobs before he returned to radio broadcasting, first at stations in Cincinnati and Philadelphia, and finally in 1958, at station WOR-AM in New York City. In his program, which filled the overnight time slot, Shepherd read poetry, played records, organized practical jokes, and told stories about growing up in the Midwest. He developed a large following during the twenty years he worked at WOR and also performed at local colleges and universities, as well as the Village Limelight in New York and Carnegie Hall.

Shepherd's first published work, *I, Libertine* (1956), began as a literary hoax. During one of his late-night broadcasts, he decided to play a joke on "people who pretend to know everything," as he later stated in an interview, and made up a story about a best-selling nonexistent book, which he titled *I, Libertine,* written by a British civil servant named Frederick C. Ewing. With the help of Shepherd's late-night listeners, word of the book's popularity spread, and soon bookstores—prompted by requests from customers—began calling *Publisher's Weekly* trying to locate the publisher. The *New York Times Book Review* even included a mention of the book among its list of newly published works, and student listeners of Shepherd continued the hoax by writing papers on *I, Libertine* for their classes. The joke was eventually exposed by the *Wall Street Journal,* which drew international attention. Shortly thereafter, Ballantine Books persuaded Shepherd to write the actual book, which he did with science-fiction author Theodore Sturgeon, who wrote under the pseudonym of Frederick C. Ewing.

With his literary career underway, Shepherd next edited a collection of George Ade's writings about the Midwest, then wrote his first solo novel, *In God We Trust: All Others Pay Cash,* in 1966. His second book, *Wanda Hickey's Night of Golden Memories and Other Disasters,* was published in 1971. In these books, Shepherd balanced comic hyperbole with catalogues of semi-autobiographical detail to create stories that blurred the line between fact and fiction. Shepherd also published two other books during the course of his career, *The Ferrari in the Bedroom* (1972) and *A Fistful of Fig Newtons* (1981). His writings also appeared in various magazines, most notably *Playboy,* but also in *Car and Driver* and *Field and Stream.* Shepherd began writing screenplays for television and film in the 1960s and 1970s. His contributions include several narratives and teleplays for the Public Broadcasting Service (PBS), such as the thirteen-part series *Jean Shepherd's America,* first broadcasted in 1971, and "The Phantom of the Open Hearth" (1977). Shepherd's most popular screenplay was produced and released in 1983. *A Christmas Story,* which Shepherd himself narrated, was drawn from several of the stories previously published in *In God We Trust: All Others Pay Cash* and has remained a widely loved work since its initial release. Shepherd died October 16, 1999, in Sanibel Island, Florida.

MAJOR WORKS

Shepherd's first significant original work, *In God We Trust: All Others Pay Cash,* is a collection of stories inspired by his Midwestern boyhood. The work is often considered a novel due to its frame narrative and its overarching theme—the stories are linked by a common narrator, Ralph, who has returned to his hometown, Hohman, to research changes in the small-town culture of Indiana. When Ralph meets a childhood friend, the two reminisce about the events of their youth, and this frame narrative introduces each of the short stories in the work. The story "Duel in the Snow," in which Ralph wants an "Official Red Ryder Carbine Action Two Hundred Shot Range Model Air Rifle" for Christmas, forms the basis of *A Christmas Story,* and several other stories in the collection also appear in the film. This stories in the collection often focus on the reality and disappointments of Midwestern life.

Shepherd's second book, *Wanda Hickey's Night of Golden Memories and Other Disasters,* shares common features with his first, including its reminiscence of the past and characterization of life in the Midwest. This book, however, has significant differences from the earlier one: the stories are not unified by a fictional narrator or an overarching theme, and New York City figures prominently in the collection, primarily cast in nightmarish contrast to Shepherd's portrait of the Midwest. But like *In God We Trust,* the book blurs the boundary between autobiography and fiction, mixing verisimilitude with hyperbole. Instead of merely recounting his own past, Shepherd intended for the stories of *Wanda Hickey* to have a universal appeal, portraying such familiar situations as the rituals of grooming, the pitfalls of dating, and the inevitably disappointing reality of adolescent life.

Despite Shepherd's critical success as an author, the most significant ongoing project of his career took an oral form. Shepherd's nightly radio broadcasts at WOR are widely regarded as among the funniest, most entertaining, and innovative productions in the medium. *The Jean Shepherd Program* was a collage of poetry, story, music, and commentary, often peppered with tangents and invitations for audience participation. Marshall McLuhan, in an essay from 1964, was the first to recognize Shepherd's project as a new literary form. McLuhan described Shepherd's efforts "as a new medium for a new kind of novel that he writes nightly. The mike is his pen and paper." Although Shepherd's broadcasts and published books may have shared common stories, they were rendered very differently. One of Shepherd's stories in written form might cover a few pages, but when told by Shepherd over the radio it could stretch to an hour, or be repeated with new details over numerous shows. Shepherd's broadcasts, like his books and short stories, blended life and art. Biographer Eugene B. Bergmann has maintained that "as his flow was in part extemporaneous, like a jazzy riff, it appeared that he was merely bringing forth facts out of his past and recent observations. In reality, Shepherd was creating his life—the art, with variations on a theme—in the act of performing it."

CRITICAL RECEPTION

Throughout his career, as both a radio personality and a writer, Shepherd enjoyed a cult status, with an audience of devoted fans. Originally an icon of the late-night American subculture, his popularity increased throughout the 1960s and 1970s, reaching a peak in 1983 with the release of *A Christmas Story,* which has since become a staple of holiday television viewing. Today, critics regard Shepherd as one of the most creative and original radio performers in the history of the medium. Gerald Nachman has declared that Shepherd "reshaped 'talk radio.' . . . There had been radio monologuists before him, but nobody who worked as free-form or as fancifully as he did." Nachman added that "Shepherd may be, with Godfrey Cambridge, the most underrated of all the innovative comic voices of the era." What commentators have praised most about Shepherd is his ability to create comic, poignant, and even painful tales of our adolescent past without becoming nostalgic or sentimental. Shepherd himself summed up his philosophy when he told an interviewer, "Childhood seems good in retrospect because we were not yet aware of the basic truth: that we're all losers, that we're destined to die." Many critics maintain that, as a writer and storyteller, Shepherd is underrated, that his humor embodies his perspective on life. According to Peter A. Scholl, "Shepherd is a 'serious' writer in the sense that he is indeed a chronicler, a keen observer who is reporting what he sees; the trick of his humor is primarily his perspective. The comic effect derives essentially from his attitude toward his subject." Although some critics have faulted Shepherd's work as sounding more embittered than satirical or funny, most agree with James F. Smith, who has asserted that "Shepherd-the-man is not a bitter pessimist or nihilist. While he does not remain in the haze of memory, neither does he become simply another 'American Laocoon' trying to maintain his balance amid the violent crosscurrents of the twentieth century. Though he could be tempted to hide in boyhood memories . . . , Shepherd, like his readers, is fascinated by the adult world and ultimately adjusts to it. So it will always be. We can but grin and bear it—and Shepherd's humor helps us considerably with the grinning."

PRINCIPAL WORKS

I, Libertine [with Theodore Sturgeon as Frederick R. Ewing] (novel) 1956

The America of George Ade, 1866-1944 [editor] (short stories and essays) 1960

In God We Trust: All Others Pay Cash (novel) 1966

*Jean Shepherd's America (television series) 1971, 1985

Wanda Hickey's Night of Golden Memories and Other Disasters (short stories) 1971

The Ferrari in the Bedroom (short stories and essays) 1972

"The Phantom of the Open Hearth" (television script) 1977

A Fistful of Fig Newtons (short stories) 1981

"The Great American Fourth of July and Other Disasters" (television script) 1982

A Christmas Story (screenplay) 1983

"The Star-Crossed Romance of Josephine Cosnowski" (television script) 1985

"Ollie Hopnoodle's Haven of Bliss" (television script) 1989

My Summer Story (screenplay) 1994

†*A Christmas Story* (screenplay and short stories) 2003

*First appeared in 1971; series returned in 1985.

†This work contains a portion of the screenplay *A Christmas Story* and stories previously published in *In God We Trust: All Others Pay Cash* and *Wanda Hickey's Night of Golden Memories and Other Disasters.*

CRITICISM

Joseph F. Trimmer (essay date December 1976)

SOURCE: Trimmer, Joseph F. "Memoryscape: Jean Shepherd's Midwest." *The Old Northwest* 2, no. 4 (December 1976): 357-69.

[*In the following essay, Trimmer aserts that what underlies all of Shepherd's work is "a recognition of the futility of the Midwestern experience" and "a belief that such experiences are somehow more* real *than the romanticism of most fiction or the surrealism of Manhattan."*]

The Midwest is one of our country's most complicated jokes. As with all the gags in the American jokebook, the Midwestern joke plays upon the delightful confusion of appearance and reality. To the outsider, the vast land between the mountains appears as flat and forlorn as the lives of the people who seem content to endure a feckless existence there. To the resident, however, the land that rolls away to the horizon conjures a life of ironic complexity. Loyalty and self-esteem require that the Midwesterner defend his world in public, but in private he admits to a gnawing hunger for an existence of greater substance and significance. In fact, the desire to escape the mocking suspicion of non-being may well be the most distinguishing feature of the Midwestern psyche. Yet once he does escape his environment, the Midwesterner discovers that he is haunted by the desire to return, to relive the rich fulfilling life he once perceived as futile. Ironically, his imagination has transformed a bleak landscape into a blessed memoryscape— the Midwest has become his "heart-land."

No one appreciates the twists and turns of the Midwestern joke better than Jean Shepherd. Born in Chicago in 1929, Shepherd grew up in Hammond, a mill-town in northwest Indiana that "clings precariously to the underbody of Chicago like a barnacle clings to the rotting hulk of a tramp steamer."[1] Confronted by the "icy, detergent-filled waters" of Lake Michigan to the North, the "mile-after-mile monotony" of the Indiana cornfields to the South, and the "thin, drifting coat of blast-furnace dust and refinery waste" everywhere, Shepherd festered into manhood amidst the ennui of the Midwestern depression (**IGWT** [*In God We Trust, All Others Pay Cash*], pp. 16-17). He was briefly a student at the University of Maryland and Indiana University before serving a hitch in the Army Signal Corps. In 1951, following attempts at sportscar racing and a Volkswagen dealership, Shepherd began what would eventually become a very successful career in radio broadcasting with that prominent dispenser of Midwestern culture, radio station WLW in Cincinnati. After several years of "running a hillbilly jamboree and interviewing wild animal acts," Shepherd moved on to a sojourn with station KYW, Philadelphia, before moving finally, in 1958, to station WOR, New York.[2] There, surrounded by the "partly completed and already eroding towers" of Manhattan, Shepherd played records and mused all night about his mythical Indiana boyhood. These nostalgic stories fascinated New York's night people—"cabbies, students cramming on No-Doz, transatlantic pilots flying in on WOR's 50,000 watt signal"—and they soon made Shepherd an "underground" celebrity.[3] And when Marshall McLuhan mentioned him in *Understanding Media* as the creator of a new radio art form, Shepherd seemed destined to escape the vacuity of the Midwest and late night radio and emerge at last into the world of "official people."[4] But he was quick to recognize the joke behind his new fame—his official reality in New

York rested on his ability to recreate the unofficial, unreal kingdom "out there" in Middle America.

When Shepherd began a career as an author in the early sixties, it was evident that he not only understood the Midwestern joke but also intended to exploit its comic complexities. For his first book, he edited a collection of the writings of George Ade, another Indiana humorist who, in the early decades of the century, had escaped the Midwest for momentary fame in New York.[5] In his introduction to the volume, Shepherd reminds his readers that despite the national preference for happy endings, most American writers have been preoccupied with the ideas of impotence and doom. The Midwestern writer has been particularly obsessed with such notions because "the midwest has been swimming in the turgid sea of futility. It is dotted with cities and towns that have never quite made it. Toledos that want to be Detroits, Detroits that want to be Chicagos, and Chicagos that forever want to be New York. And they all know they are running in a fixed race" (*GA* [*The America of George Ade*], p. 10). While some writers weep over this state of affairs, others find the situation humorous. George Ade clearly belongs in the latter category because of his bemused preference for chronicling "the Great Unchronicled. Those who are totally unimportant. So profoundly insignificant that they hardly exist in so far as literature is concerned. Those to whom nothing ever really happens. No tragedy or comedy. No romance or Great Loves. Those who settle for what they get and quietly move on" (*GA*, p. 14).

Ade's great virtue as a humorist was that he obviously loved the Midwestern people he wrote about. He portrayed their frustrations and failures with the "deep compassion of a man who had been there" (*GA*, p. 14). His people were real people, not elaborate fictions. And Shepherd insists that this is the "key to Ade as well as any other true humorist. Ade always maintained that he was not a humorist but a realist. He reported on what he *saw* in life and not what he imagined" (*GA*, p. 15). In fact, Ade finally returned to Indiana to live because he preferred its grim reality to the insubstantial glitter of Gotham.

The qualities Shepherd underlines in Ade's work—a recognition of the futility of the Midwestern experience, a deep affection for those engaged in this fated struggle, and a belief that such experiences are somehow more *real* than the romanticism of most fiction or the surrealism of Manhattan—emerge as dominant characteristics in his own first novel, *In God We Trust, All Others Pay Cash* (1966). This collection of fifteen stories and sixteen bridge chapters concerns **"The Return of the Native to the Indiana Mill Town"** to do a story for an Official magazine. Ralph, the writer-narrator, reveals that his editors expect him to research the changing realities of Indiana's social landscape, but a few minutes amid the terrain of vacant lots, American Legion Halls, high tension wires, and gas stations, convince him that nothing has changed. Thus, rather than research present realities, Ralph stops at a neighborhood tavern, owned and operated by a boyhood crony named Flick, to spend the afternoon engaged in "some really good, solid Whatever-happened-to . . . ?, Did-she-ever-marry . . . ?, When-did-they-put-in-the-bowling-alley-down-at . . . ?" (*IGWT*, p. 19). Such reminiscing prompts Ralph to refashion the rubbish in his memory into stories that alternate careful cataloging of realistic detail with heavy doses of comic hyperbole.

Most of what Ralph remembers takes place in the Depression during the yeasty years of his pre-adolescence. This world is organized by ceremonial events such as Christmas and the Fourth of July or semi-significant events such as trips to the candy store and the neighborhood theater. The cast of characters includes his family, in particular his Old Man, and an assorted collection of boyhood friends and enemies with names such as Junior Kissel, Scut Farkas, and Wilbur Duckworth. The plots usually detail the quest to claim a piece of childhood junk as an official badge of belonging. Most of these quests end in failure, however, thus establishing their common theme as the destruction of romantic expectations.

Ralph's account of his attempt to outwit his fate is the subject of **"Duel in the Snow."** At the age of eleven, he develops an absolute mania for the most impressive item advertised in the seven-pound Christmas issue of *Open Road for Boys*—an Official Red Ryder Carbine Action Two Hundred Shot Range Model Air Rifle. Even though he reports that there are bears loose in the neighborhood, his parents do not seem to acknowledge the practicality of his Christmas gift request. Worse, his mother appears to predict doom for his dream when she says that "you'll shoot out one of your eyes" (*IGWT*, p. 30). This delphic curse follows Ralph everywhere. Atop the snow-frosted throne in Goldblatt's toy department, Santa listens while Ralph begs for his heart's desire, but he only chortles "Ho-Ho-Ho! You'll Shoot Your Eye Out, Kid" (*IGWT*, p. 38). When Ralph feels inspired to write a theme on "What I Want for Christmas," Miss Bodkin returns his blue-lined Indian Chief tablet paper without the usual "Watch margins" or "Check Sp." Instead, she writes, "You'll shoot your eyes out. Merry Christmas" (*IGWT*, p. 40). The drama ends as one might expect. Ralph gets what he wants and then almost gets it in the eye. On Christmas morning, as he practices with his new air rifle and authentic Red Ryder target in the backyard, one of the B-Bs ricochets off the target and slashes across the left side of his face. Although he is able to concoct another explanation of the accident for his parents, Ralph is sure that his wound is a sign from the gods who fix the lives of Midwestern mortals.

A series of similar experiences leads Ralph to ponder what he calls the two streams of life theory. Apparently, we all start out together, but one group of people "goes on to become the official people, peering out at us from television screens; magazine covers. They are forever appearing in newsreels, carrying attaché cases, surrounded by banks of microphones while the world awaits their decisions and statements. And the rest of us go on to become . . . just us . . . , office boy[s] in the Mail Room of Life" (*IGWT*, p. 58). Ralph suggests that the major difference between Them and Us is "how we react to those moments that forever seal our fate. One crowd merely puts on its sunglasses, lights another cigar, and heads for the nearest plush French restaurant in the Jazziest section of town, sits down and orders a drink, and ignores the whole thing. While we, the Doomed, caught in the brilliant glare of illumination, see ourselves inescapably for what we are, and from that day on sulk in the weeds hoping no one will spot us" (*IGWT*, pp. 59-60). In a crazy way, their indifference to reality authenticates them as officially *real*, while our recognition of the way things are guarantees our continued non-existence.

Ralph demonstrates the hypothesis by telling us about a blind date he had with one Junie Jo Prewitt. He prepares for the evening reveling in the "warmth of sweet Human Charity" that prompted him to accept the date. He was doing his friend Swartz a real favor. To his utter amazement, Junie Jo turns out to be "the greatest looking girl I ever saw in my life" (*IGWT*, p. 63). But the evening does not go well. None of Ralph's sure-fire stories works. Not even the one about how "Uncle Carl lost his false teeth down the airshaft" (*IGWT*, pp. 63-64). Then comes the epiphany. As Ralph edges closer to Junie Jo on the streetcar seat, he notices overhead an advertisement that speaks directly to him: "DO YOU OFFEND?" (*IGWT*, p. 64) Ralph suddenly realizes the HE is the Blind Date. "A Blind Date that didn't make it" (*IGWT*, p. 65). His silence for the remainder of the evening suggests that Ralph is no longer blind and that he is looking desperately for a patch of weeds.

In **"Hairy Gertz and the Forty-Seven Crappies"** Ralph remembers one of the few times that he did conquer his sense of insignificance. The occasion is a nighttime fishing excursion with his Old Man and several of his beer-drinking cronies to Cedar Lake, a muddy, mosquito-infested pond fed by some unknown form of seepage. From one side of the lake he hears the hiss of skates from the roller rink; from the other side, he recognizes the whining saxophone of Micky Isley as he and his Moonlight Serenaders play "Red Sails in the Sunset" for the couples at the dance hall. In the middle of the lake are "17,000 fishermen, in wooden rowboats rented at a buck and a half an hour" (*IGWT*, p. 71). As they glide slowly over the submerged mountain of Shell and Sinclair oil cans, the men slurp Atlas Prager and troll for that infamous Midwestern fish, the Crappie. Suddenly, Ralph's bobber goes under and then everyone begins reeling in fish. But Ralph's real victory does not occur with this jackpot catch of forty-seven crappies; that must wait until the crew returns to his mother's kitchen for sandwiches and more beer. When she allows him to stay up with the men and hear Hairy Gertz's legendary story about the Hungarian bartender, his cross-eyed daughter, and the bowlegged dachshund, Ralph knows he has made it.

Unfortunately, success is a fragile thing in the Midwest. In the very next story, Ralph's Old Man, an ardent follower of the Chicago White Sox and trivia contests, is notified that he has actually made it through all the preliminary rounds of Nehi's Great Figures from the World of Sports contest and will soon receive a major award. When the box arrives, the family uncovers a "*life-size* lady's leg, in true blushing-pink flesh tones and wearing a modish black leather pump with a spike heel" (*IGWT*, p. 90). The leg is actually a lamp—"the definitive lamp"—complete with a Lingerie pink shade. The Old Man spends the rest of the evening "in honest, simple Peasant admiration for a thing of transcendent beauty" (*IGWT*, p. 94). But Ralph's mother is visibly upset by the "soft glow of electric Sex" that emanates from the living room window (*IGWT*, p. 94).

The stage is thus set for a real-life drama. According to Ralph, the neurotic battle of the sexes, as portrayed by Edward Albee or Tennessee Williams, is a terrible distortion: "My mother thought 'emasculation' had something to do with woman getting to vote" (*IGWT*, p. 95). *Real* family battles concern "where to go on vacation . . . what kind of car to buy . . . or who is going to take out the garbage" (*IGWT*, p. 94). In this case, the battle begins once Ralph's mother, who was "always jealous of that lamp," inadvertently breaks it one day while dusting. When the Old Man's heroic attempt to restore his symbol of victory fails, the Great Freeze sets in. For three days, the only sound in the house is the "sucking, gargling, choking retch" of the sink (*IGWT*, p. 99). Eventually, the Old Man relents and admits that such dramatic symbols of victory are probably "too jazzy" for his world. Disappointed but undefeated, the perpetually resilient Old Man takes the family to the movies.

And so it goes with all the other people in this world: Ludlow Kissell, the neighborhood drunk, while attempting a spectacular Fourth of July fireworks display, blows up his front porch; Wilbur Duckworth, the high school drum major, while attempting to perform the ultimate trick in the annual Thanksgiving Day parade, throws his baton into the streetcar high-tension line knocking out "generators as far south as Indianapolis" (*IGWT*, p. 195); and the whole community, while attempting to acquire a "magnificent set of Artistic Delux Pearleen

Tableware, the Dinner Service of the Stars," at Leopold Doppler's neighborhood theater, is outraged when it discovers that Leopold has only gravy boats to give away (*IGWT*, pp. 252-53). Euchred beyond human endurance, the theater audience bombards the screen with gravy boats and continues to riot until pacified by a battalion of "blue-jowled policemen" carrying nightsticks (*IGWT*, p. 260). Nobody ever wins. But that is because, Shepherd insists, "futility, and the usual triumph of evil over good . . . is [simply] another name for realism" (*GA*, p. 12).

Shepherd's belief in the unquestionable realism of life in the Midwest emerges as the dominant theme of his second book, *Wanda Hickey's Night of Golden Memories and Other Disasters* (1971).[6] The yoking of "golden memories" and "disasters" in the title suggests the book's thematic similarity to *In God We Trust, All Others Pay Cash*. But there are important differences. For one thing Shepherd makes no attempt to create the illusion of a novel. There is no fictitious Ralph sitting in an Indiana tavern contriving transitions to connect the eight stories in this volume. There is only Shepherd, secluded in his apartment far above the roaring canyon of Manhattan, balancing the nuttiness of New York with the radiance of his Midwestern memories. New York was occasionally a point of departure for some of the stories in *In God We Trust*, but in *Wanda Hickey* it becomes the consistent deviation that measures the more realistic norm of the Midwest. New York may be the dream of many a Midwestern boy, but Shepherd sees it as a nightmare, populated by what he calls the Fellini crowd: "squat females in leather jackets carrying bullwhips, coveys of razor-thin, trilling creatures of indeterminate sex in velvet jackets and elf shoes, . . . [and] scowling, bearded revolutionaries in full Zapata attire, their denim jackets abristle with OFF THE PIGS buttons" (*WH* [*Wanda Hickey's Night of Golden Memories and Other Disasters*], p. 164).

Although Shepherd is baffled by the surrealism of Manhattan, he is equally disturbed by the annoying unreality of television. For example, in response to a sentimental Hollywood film about a trip to the state fair and an insipid commercial about a T.V. family embarking on vacation, Shepherd offers us genuine, accept-no-imitation, authentic journeys. These are not musical comedy affairs, but heroic ordeals of the first order. The family, with its beleaguered champion, the Old Man, must begin early and endure much in its battle with its implacable foe—the traffic. The Old Man, shrieking epic obscenities, is the equal of this ancient enemy, as he is of a host of lesser enemies—flat tire, detours, car sickness, and whining. At the fair, the family must grope its way through the maze of exhibits as it suffers from the sweltering oppression of an Indiana heatwave. Everyone marvels at the grand champion pig named BIG HORACE and the giant forty-seven-pound pumpkin "bearing a striking resemblance to our beloved president Franklin Delano Roosevelt," but as the day wears on, the children become impatient with Mother's microscopic inspection of the quilt exhibit (*WH*, p. 69). Slowly, they begin to consume a compost-heap assortment of hot dogs, candied apples, boiled-buttered corn, and fudge, which is finally vomited in a spectacular testimony to the wonder working powers of the Whirligig Rocket Whip. Up in Michigan, at Ollie Hoopnoodle's Haven of Bliss, the family's summer vacation turns out pretty much the same: the Haven of Bliss has no electricity, the rainy season has begun, and Ollie says the fish stopped biting last week.

Because Shepherd consistently exercises his penchant for comic hyperbole, he can hardly insist on the literal realism of these accounts of his family's disastrous adventures. Nevertheless, his stories do ring true because of his ability to assemble a mass of specific details from his Fibber McGee-closet memory. When he indulges this memory, he produces stories that merely reclaim and catalogue junk. For example, in **"The Return of the Smiling Wimpy Doll,"** Shepherd's mother mails him a package containing seven tons of kid effluvia, including such rare items as a "Gung Ho" cockamamie and a Captain Midnight Three-Way Mystic Dog Whistle. Apparently responding to his mother's note that "you might want to play with it," Shepherd is content to spend the rest of the story fondling, explaining, and re-testing each of these enchanted toys (*WH*, p. 266). When such cataloging is used for its own sake, the drama soon deteriorates.

Shepherd is at his best when he can use his total recall to enrich a coherent and unified plot. The most successful plot in *Wanda Hickey* concerns not the "realistic" journeys of his family but his own romantic excursions into the puzzling world of women. For the adolescent Shepherd, women are mysterious creatures who walk in a kind of "soft haze of approaching dawn" (*WH*, p. 216). Throughout high school, he feels "way down deep among the lower one third of the class, amid that great rabble of faceless mankind who squat among the rancid lunch bags and musky galoshes of academe" (*WH*, p. 216). His three brief romances are deliberate attempts to break out of this isolation and join the pageantry of real life. The intensity of this longing is recaptured in his detailed accounts of the ritual of preparation. What begins as a simple procedure—get haircut, polish car, buy gas, gargle, squeeze blackheads (*WH*, p. 186)—is soon transformed into a hypnotic ode on grooming as he begins to "spread the thick vibrantly aromatic layer of pungent Lifebuoy lather over my Olympian torso" (*WH*, p. 233).

Predictably, Shepherd's elaborate self-anointment is merely the prelude to disaster. His "adventure in alien sensuality" with the neighborhood Polish girl, Josephine Cosnowski, appears to fulfill his most exotic fantasies until he discovers that Josie's old world family is plotting an immediate marriage (**WH,** p. 165). His attempt at "upward mobility" with Daphne Bigalow, the banker's daughter, results in total humiliation when he takes her to see a John Wayne movie at his neighborhood theater (**WH,** p. 227). In the company of the demure goddess from the Northside, Shepherd sees his Southside movie house as he has never seen it before: the ankle-deep piles of candy wrappers and popcorn, the faint odor of mildew and urine deodorant, and the muffled sounds of near copulation punctuated by occasional, molar rattling belches. He is not surprised when he is politely dismissed at the end of the evening. And finally, even Shepherd's attempt to act out the Prom Committee's annual puberty rite with Wanda Hickey, "the only girl who I knew for an absolute fact liked me" (**WH,** p. 303), turns to catastrophe when he tries to down a triple bourbon "the way Gary Cooper used to do in the Silver Dollar Saloon" (**WH,** p. 345). A few minutes later he finds himself on the floor of the men's room—a retching, shuddering wreck. An assessment of Shepherd's career as a Midwestern Lothario recalls George Ade's age advice—**"Don't Try to Account for Anything"** (**GA,** p. 107).

One should try to account for Shepherd's latest book, however, because George Ade's influence is no longer apparent. In his introduction to *The Ferrari in the Bedroom* (1973), Shepherd announces that he has patterned his essays after the "Americana" columns H. L. Mencken wrote for *The American Mercury* in the twenties.[7] This change in comic mentors is accompanied by significant changes in Shepherd's focus, technique, and tone.

Only five of the twenty-one selections in this volume deal with Shepherd's Midwestern memories. Instead, Shepherd focuses on the world he formerly used for a frame, "the High Camp comedy" of contemporary culture (**FB** [*The Ferrari in the Bedroom*], p. viii). The wackiness of daily life in America was, of course, the target of Mencken's comic diatribes. Shepherd's decision to imitate Mencken's model in our time may follow from the fact that "nuttiness is spreading in our land" (**FB,** p. 1). The idiocy Shepherd once equated with New York is now about to engulf us all. Certainly his enthusiasm for what might be termed surrogate Midwests—the primitive cultures in Alaska and Maine—suggests that Shepherd has had to light out for the territories to find the *real* life he once identified with the heartland.

But this change in focus is more than a matter of landscape. Shepherd has also altered the chronological direction and narrative strategy in his stories. Many of the selections begin with excerpts from current newspapers. But rather than using these stories to introduce some personal memory, Shepherd projects them into the future by devising dramas to illustrate some social absurdity. For example, a news item announcing the invention of a special device to prevent drunks from starting their cars stirs Shepherd to concoct a catalogue of zany gadgets to solve the problem of automobile accidents. Since it is finally determined that people cause accidents, Shepherd concludes his essay with news of the invention of a "driverless auto, which excludes humans of all sorts" (**FB,** p. 37).

Shepherd's preoccupation with present realities and future absurdities means that he ceases to be the chief protagonist in his stories and becomes merely an observer offering his dissenting opinion on the craziness that swarms around him. The effect of this change is evident in the first story in the volume, Shepherd's account of his flight to Chicago with a group of folksingers. Appropriately, he is no longer in one place—an Indiana bar or his Manhattan apartment—but high above the "blurred Kodachrome slide" of America in the placeless environment of a 747 (**FB,** p. 2). His solitude is invaded by twanging guitars and quavering voices urging the common man to fight on against the forces of evil. In his earlier writing, such a scene would have prompted Shepherd to reconstruct some calamity from his own feckless youth. Now the scene provokes his outrage. He sympathizes with the disdain of the Old Sarge in the next aisle, and spends the remainder of the essay railing against young people who sing about human misery while traveling on a Champagne Red Carpet flight financed on Dad's Diners Club card.

The most significant modification in Shepherd's new comedy is the matter of tone. When he focuses on the dislocations of the age and ceases to be the foil in his own account of human folly, he no longer seems to care about the people in his stories. Perhaps this is because these people are not *real* people. They have functions—lonesome traveler, shoddy producer, distraught patient—but no substantial identities. These curious aberrations invite invective but not affection. For example, Shepherd can discuss the junk of his childhood with bemused reverence because it helps explain a real world, but contemporary interest in gimcrackery receives his scorn as the latest lunacy in a world of fantasy. He calls it the Abercrombie's Bitch Complex (**FB,** p. 239). He can also luxuriate in the memory of his life as a car worshipper, making annual pilgrimages to the Vatican at the Indianapolis Speedway, but he feels only contempt for the jerk who buys the ultimate masterpiece of SLOB ART, a bed shaped like a Ferrari, and so leaves him "varrooming" on the psychiatrist's couch (**FB,** p. 269).

What we may be witnessing in all this is simply another version of the Midwestern joke. Like Mark Twain before him, Shepherd searched the world beyond the horizon for the bonanza that would authenticate his reality. When he burst the bubble of that illusion, he discovered that his reality was back there on the darkening plain of the republic where he had left it. He assumed, however, as Twain did, that he would always have that vast reservoir of Midwestern memories to "call back and make . . . as real as it ever was, and as blessed."[8] But Shepherd's latest book, like Twain's later writing, is haunted by the madness of dreams rather than the magic of memories. In a sense, both men were snookered by their past, for while they were away, the landscape of their past was also being transformed by the deliriums of the age. When they returned, they discovered that the "life-time guarantee" had run out on the reservoir: the Mississippi Twain once knew was no longer, and the Midwest of Shepherd's boyhood finally became part of franchised, incorporated, deranged America.

These new developments are acknowledged in Shepherd's story about taping a television show on ice fishing at the Playboy Club-Hotel in Geneva, Wisconsin. His appearance on television suggests that he has finally entered the ranks of official people, but he is only semi-official. After all he is not taping the show in the Bahamas. Although disappointed by his "bad draw," Shepherd senses the appropriateness of his return to the heartland, and so invokes the old faith: 'I'll be out of this urban world of phoney values and shallow attitudes and I will be in Wisconsin, where Life is real and Nature beckons" (*FB,* p. 48). But it takes only a few minutes at this Midwestern pleasure dome, amid jiggling Bunnies and jaundiced cameramen, for Shepherd to conclude that he must be "living through an avantgarde film made by a demented Swedish director" (*FB,* p. 57). That night, Shepherd dreams about his new Midwest. One need only set this dream beside the earlier account of **"Hairy Gertz and the Forty-Seven Crappies"** to understand why Shepherd's memoryscape has escaped him:

> I had this dream where I was trying to buy a ticket at the box office that they had set up next to a trout stream in Montana. There were two hundred thousand wildly cheering fans in the stands, watching Elvis Presley and Bob Hope fish for rainbows while Fred McMurray played the saxophone. I couldn't get a ticket. It was sold out, and the next thing I knew I was trying to climb under the fence at this stadium they had built entirely around a North Woods lake, where the cast of *Oh! Calcutta* was fishing from red, white and blue kayaks. They were in costume, and it was being televised by Telstar around the globe, on some show called "Interplanetary Sportsman," choreographed by Gene Kelly, with an original score by Henry Mancini. A giant neon-encrusted blimp sailed overhead, emblazoned:
>
> Roone Arledge Presents
>
> Just at the point when the cast, in costume, was singing a salute to Curt Gowdy to the tune of "Old Black Joe" I woke up in a cold sweat.
>
> (*FB,* p. 71)

Shepherd probably appreciates this latest twist in the Midwestern joke as well as anyone. He may have finally overdrawn at his memorybank or forgotten its combination, but his recent writing suggests that he still finds Midwestern futility amusing. Only, this time around, the futility is a little different. Instead of portraying the comic futility of a real world, Shepherd is perplexed by his inability to find a real world. And there is nothing more futile than trying to locate reality in a fantasy or trying to remember a lost memoryscape.

Notes

1. Jean Shepherd, *In God We Trust, All Others Pay Cash* (New York: Doubleday & Co., Inc., 1966), p. 16. Subsequent quotations from *In God We Trust* will be identified in the text by *IGWT.*

2. Edward Grossman, "Jean Shepherd: Radio's Noble Savage," *Harpers,* 66 (January 1966), 89.

3. Grossman, p. 89.

4. Marshall McLuhan, *Understanding Media: The Extensions of Man* (New York: McGraw-Hill, 1964), pp. 303-04.

5. *The America of George Ade,* ed. Jean Shepherd (New York: G. P. Putnam, 1961). Subsequent quotations from Shepherd's introduction will be identified in the text by *GA.*

6. Jean Shepherd, *Wanda Hickey's Night of Golden Memories and Other Disasters* (New York: Doubleday & Co., Inc., 1971). Subsequent quotations from *Wanda Hickey* will be identified in the text by *WH.*

7. Jean Shepherd, *The Ferrari in the Bedroom* (New York: Dodd, Mead & Co., 1973), p. viii. Subsequent quotations from *The Ferrari in the Bedroom* will be identified in the text by *FB.*

8. Samuel Clemens, *The Autobiography of Mark Twain,* ed. Charles Neider (New York: Harper & Row, 1959), p. 14.

Peter A. Scholl (essay date summer 1978)

SOURCE: Scholl, Peter A. "Jean Shepherd: The Survivor of Hammond." *Great Lakes Review* 5, no. 1 (summer 1978): 7-18.

[*In the following essay, Scholl disagrees with Joseph F. Trimmer's reading of Shepherd's later work, asserting that Shepherd did not adopt a darker, bleaker sense of humor, as Trimmer argues, but merely assumed the pose of "the jaded and unflappable urbanite."*]

Most people who have heard of Jean Shepherd know him as a radio and television performer and are unaware of his credentials as a man of letters. He entered radio work in Cincinnati in 1951 and eventually came to New York's WOR in 1958, where he gained fame for his late-night, free-form talk "about his life and about what he hears, sees and smells as an inhabitant of Manhattan and the world."[1] The show won a loyal following in the Northeast and was syndicated nationally to dozens of stations. In the late 1960s he wrote, directed, and performed in the thirteen-part series **Jean Shepherd's America** for television's Public Broadcasting Service; and more recently, he used material from his books to develop **"The Phantom of the Open Hearth,"** a ninety-minute PBS television special, which was first aired just before Christmas, 1976.

Though he is not as celebrated an author as fellow-Hoosier, Kurt Vonnegut, Jr., Shepherd, too, is on the literary map. I refer to the "Literary Map of Indiana," published by the Indiana Council of Teachers of English: where Hammond and Gary spread a speckled yellow stain across the upper left-hand corner of the *Rand McNally Road Atlas* map of Indiana, there in the same place on the "Literary Map" is a scene from **In God We Trust: All Others Pay Cash**. A small boy in front of his "Crosley Notre-Dame Cathedral model radio" is figuring out Little Orphan Annie's secret message "TO MEMBERS OF THE LITTLE ORPHAN ANNIE SECRET CIRCLE" on his "simulated gold plastic Decoder pin. With Knob."[2] The iris-less orphan girl herself is pictured above him, staring emptily down out of Lake Michigan and across the northern steppes of the Hoosier state. There is no mention of Hammond or Gary on the "Literary Map"; there is only the name of Jean Shepherd. And he deserves to be there, for he is indeed a writer as well as a performer, a writer in the tradition of George Ade, Booth Tarkington, Irwin S. Cobb, and those other Midwestern humorists, James Thurber and Mark Twain.

Thousands of readers of *Playboy* are familiar with his humor pieces and short stories, for which he is the only four-time winner of the *Playboy* humor/satire award. Auto-buffs know him for his regular column in the wide-circulation *Car and Driver* magazine. Many of his stories are finding their ways into high-school and college English anthologies. And though much of his writing is uncollected, he has published four books to date. **The America of George Ade** is a selection of writings by the earlier Hoosier humorist, edited and introduced by Shepherd. Published in 1961, this work reveals a clear indebtedness to Ade, an influence that continues.

His second book, **In God We Trust: All Others Pay Cash** (1966), bears an epigraph from Ade: "There are at least two kinds of education."[3] This work is usually referred to as Shepherd's novel, though it is more accurately described as a series of inter-related short stories, bound together by common characters, a common setting and ambience, and a narrative frame device. The stories (many of them originally published separately in *Playboy*) are prefaced and subsequently joined together by means of a running frame-tale, involving Ralph Wesley Parker, who has come home to Hohman, Indiana—a milltown obviously modeled on Shepherd's hometown, Hammond. Ralph, it is clear, despite disclaimers, is to Jean Shepherd as Mark Twain is to Samuel Clemens—part narrative persona and part personality. "I felt like a spy," says Ralph in the opening sentence. "It was the first time I had ever ridden a cab in my own hometown. When I had left it I was definitely not a cab rider. Now taking cabs was as natural as breathing or putting on shoes" (**IGWT** [*In God We Trust*], p. 15). Ralph feels like a spy because he has exiled himself for years and returns not as a native, dressed in a bowling shirt, but as an urbane sophisticate in a fancy suit and alligator shoes. He is a professional writer out of New York and is on a mission to write a piece for "an Official magazine on The Return Of The Native To The Indiana Mill Town" (*IGWT*, p. 19). The cab ride to Flick's tavern permits Shepherd to, seemingly artlessly and naturally, set the scene for the frame tale and for the linked tales which follow. As he rides to the tavern, Ralph reviews a "thumbnail description of . . . my own despised hometown" that he had written preparatory to his visit:

> Hohman, Indiana, is located in the extreme Northwestern corner of the state, where the state line ends abruptly in the icy, detergent-filled waters of that queen of the Great Lakes, Lake Michigan. It clings to the underbody of Chicago like a barnacle clings to the rotting hulk of the tramp steamer. . . . It is a place people never really come to, but mostly want to leave. And leave they do, to go to the fabled East or to the unbelievable California coast. They rarely talk about where they have come from. There isn't that much to say. At night in Hohman the rabbits still hop through the backyard gardens. The trains thunder though the dark on their way to somewhere else.
>
> (*IGWT,* pp. 16-17)

The tavern he rides to turns out to be run by Flick, his boyhood pal, and thus the frame is established: Ralph and Flick remember the old times together; and the dialogue between the two, set in the tavern, resumes between each tale until the end, when after many beers and many stories, the narrator steps out of the bar (adorned with a sign bearing the line that is the book's title) and "symbolically" declines to look for a cab, but rather becomes a native son once more by heading for the bus stop.

The Hohman of the narrative present is not greatly different from that of Ralph's boyhood: both are industrial wastelands in the tradition of the ash-heaps in Fitzgerald's *The Great Gatsby*. But though the current Hohman is as ugly as ever, and even though in Ralph's youth the community was even worse—the environment perhaps even more polluted, impoverished, and culturally barren—Shepherd manages to communicate a truly genuine fondness for his native region and its inhabitants. And the frame device functions not unlike Twain's frame in "The Notorious Jumping Frog of Calaveras County"; it helps him to adapt the oral tale to the written prose.

Shepherd's third book, **Wanda Hickey's Night of Golden Memories and Other Disasters** (1971), is a collection of related stories, again set in Hohman. The youthful protagonist is no longer called Ralph, but is given the author's name. The title story—about Wanda Hickey's prom night—provided a central theme for the television play **"The Phantom of the Open Hearth."** Most of the material is in keeping with the manner and matter of Shepherd's "novel," except that in most of these tales the main character is somewhat older.

His most recent book, **The Ferrari in the Bedroom** (1972), is a somewhat diffuse collection of essays, stories, and assorted bits of prose on various topics, a number of which were first published elsewhere. Only a few pieces, such as **"The Indy 500"** and **"Harold's Super Service"** (where Shepherd reports he pumped Esso on U.S. 41), deal with his Indiana roots and memories. Noting this book's departure from the subjects and styles of the earlier volumes, Joseph Trimmer concludes that in **Ferrari,** "George Ade's influence is no longer apparent."[4] Trimmer quotes Shepherd's statement in the introduction that in this book, he is trying to preserve the spirit of our time, just as H. L. Mencken preserved the Twenties in his "Americana" columns in *The American Mercury*:

> Re-reading these collections today is like suddenly, magically opening a window offering a clear vision of an earlier age. . . . It is my thesis that our time too should be preserved in like manner. . . . Commencing with this book, I propose to dip at random into my Vast File of Trivia to pass them along to the reader for whatever value they might have.[5]

Trimmer takes this allusion to Mencken too seriously, however, when he infers a "change in comic mentors," which is "accompanied by significant changes in Shepherd's focus, technique, and tone."[6] But the shift is only apparent if one considers his books as a single line of uncomplex development, without regard for material Shepherd has been using on the radio (and in certain magazine articles) over the years while he was working on **In God We Trust** and **Wanda Hickey** and after.[7] It must be kept in mind that one of the persistent poses of Shepherd's radio show and magazine columnist personality is that of the quintessential New Yorker, the jaded and unflappable urbanite, continually amazed, in a manner that is indeed reminiscent of Mencken, at the ways of the booboisie. And if this were the only rhetorical expression Shepherd maintained after the publication of **Ferrari,** Trimmer could possibly be correct in detecting a "change of focus" that "is more than a matter of landscape," and in concluding that "Shepherd has also altered the chronological direction and narrative strategy in his stories," and that the tone of his comedy is darkened, so that "When he focuses on the dislocations of the age and ceases to be the foil in his own account of human folly, he no longer seems to care about people in his stories."[8] But works published subsequent to **Ferrari** do not reveal exclusively the Menckenian or late-Twainian Shepherd, but still seem under the relatively benign influence of George Ade (consider **"Slobbus Americanus in the Cultural Vanguard,"** which appeared in *Car and Driver* in 1974, and the short story **"Lost at C,"** *Playboy,* 1973; both works are discussed below). **Ferrari** has little thematic or formal unity, as it is comprised of various kinds of works, some of which were originally written for at least two different magazines. And so the differences in subject, arrangement, style, and tone that Trimmer perceives when comparing **Ferrari** to the earlier books, possibly tell us more about the way Shepherd shifts his rhetorical stance to meet different subjects, audiences, and occasions, than they tell us about Shepherd's ethos—his mental state and world-view.

Even with hundreds of articles, stories, scripts, and these four books to his credit, Shepherd, when asked to classify himself, does not say that he is first and foremost an author. "I think of myself as a performer," he told an interviewer in 1976, "and I perform in any available media. I'm also a writer. . . ."[9] When classified as a "radio personality," he replied in a similar vein, obviously annoyed at being too easily categorized: "I'm a performer primarily," he said. "I was trained as a actor. I've been in Broadway plays and performed on the stage as a comedian, and I'm really not, or don't think of myself as, a radio talent." Asked if he still had his show on WOR, he answered, "Yes." Asked how often the show comes on, he said, "Five nights a week."[10] And not a radio personality!

"If you think, 'I'm one type of guy, a radio guy,'" he says, "then that's where you stay! But you might as well open yourself up."[11] Clearly he has opened himself up to many experiences, but it is his work as a writer who performs what he has written that I wish to discuss at length.

A writer who performs his work before a live audience on stage—or in a radio booth into a microphone, or in front of a television camera—learns quickly that each medium has its own peculiar demands. The performing humorist learns especially quickly that what works well in print does not necessarily work at all when read or recited verbatim to a live audience. Mark Twain observed from his own long experience as author and entertainer, that

> Written things are not for speech; their form is literary; they are stiff, inflexible, and will not lend themselves to happy and effective delivery with the tongue—where their purpose is to merely entertain, not instruct; they have to be limbered up, broken up, colloquialized, and turned into the common forms of unpremeditated talk—otherwise they will bore the house, not entertain it.[12]
>
> ["Platform Readings"]

Jean Shepherd is a humorist in the tradition of Mark Twain. For not only did both men leave hometowns in the Midwest to become successful and famous, but both returned in their imaginations to their boyhoods. There in the frontier life of Hannibal for Twain and in the depression-blighted life of Hammond for Shepherd, the two found the raw material for their best stories. Like Twain, Shepherd became a seasoned platform entertainer, making thirty or forty college campuses in a given year; he has appeared before sellout crowds in New York's Town Hall and three times in Carnegie Hall. And in recognition of this work, in 1976 he received the International Platform Association's "Mark Twain Award," an honor which highlights the formal and thematic similarities of their work.

On October 7, 1976, Shepherd came to perform at The University of Evansville, in Evansville, Indiana. An account of his performance will be followed by further comment about his affinities with Twain and his work as a humorist generally.

"This is personally a very peculiar and . . . historic evening for me," he began. "I've played Carnegie Hall . . . but this is the first time in all these years that I've played Indiana." His contract stipulated a fifty-minute performance that night, but his monologue flew on for more than two hours. He was clearly thrilled to be "back home again in Indiana." And this was the substance that he used to unify his digressive, floating monologue: his Indiana roots and experiences.

He warmed up the audience by reciting fictionalized facts about his boyhood and hometown, familiar to every Shepherd reader. Hammond is a "carbuncle hanging on the rump of time." It is "a world of belching furnaces, roaring Bessemer Converters, fragrant petroleum distillation plants, and freight yards" (*IGWT,* p. 16). Learning to survive as a kid in Hammond, "I realized . . . you either got hit or you did the hitting—and I did the hitting . . . You notice the shoulders, the mean look . . . I survived Hammond."

"You live in Evansville," he said. The audience, fewer students than old-time Shepherd fans from town, all laughed. "You all laughed," Shepherd responded. "I said you live in Evansville and you all laughed." And this began a pattern that continued throughout the marathon performance. He had a definite outline in mind, but it was open to variation, to response, to audience reaction, or to inspiration. He ad-libbed about what he had learned of the local scene while being driven on a tour of the city that afternoon and he introduced lengthy digressions. But the substance of his main line of discourse was a story published in *Playboy* in 1973, "**Lost at C.**"[13] This is a tale particularly suitable for college audiences as it deals with schools and schooling.

Back in the Warren G. Harding grade school in Hammond, Shepherd first became aware of "a curse that would follow me throughout my life. Along with Martin Perlmutter, Schwartz, Chester Woczniewski, Helen Weathers and poor Francis Xavier Zambarbieri, I was a member of the alphabetical ghetto that sat in the back of the classroom" (**"LAC"** [**"Lost at C"**], p. 143):

> Me and Schwartz and Woczniewski sat so far back in the classroom that the blackboard was only a vague rumor to us. Miss Shields was a shifting figure in the haze on the distant horizon, her voice a faint but ominous drone [here Shepherd imitated the sound] punctuated by squeaking chalk. Within a short time I became adept at reading the inflection, if not the content of those far-off sounds. Danger meant simply being called on.
>
> (**"LAC,"** p. 144)

The published version in *Playboy* goes on to tell how Shepherd evolved his various techniques for avoiding intellectual disgrace:

> I made it a point to wear bland-colored clothes. . . . I learned to weave my body from side to side, dropping a shoulder here, shifting my neck a few degrees to the right there, with the crucial object in mind of always keeping a line of kids between me and the teacher's eagle eye.
>
> (**"LAC,"** p. 144)

But ultimately, in high school algebra, he was called on—to solve an equation on the blackboard "that was well a yard and a half long and was lacerated by mysterious crooked lines and fractions in parentheses, with miniature twos and threes hovering above the whole thing like tiny barnacles . . ." (**"LAC,"** p. 198). In performance, he walked about on the stage, wearing a lapel mike on a long cord and he made use of a blackboard and chalk to illustrate this scene.

Naturally, the young Shepherd solved the equation not through an understanding of algebra, but by sheer luck. His wandering eyes focused on a hulking letterman's "big block number": "Three," I muttered" (**"LAC,"** p. 198). This climax would be reached after about twenty minutes if one were to simply read the story aloud. In the live performance, it came after more than two hours.

This variance gives some indication of the amount of digression, amplification, and adaptation to the audience that Shepherd made on this occasion.

Like the narrator of Twain's "The Story of the Old Ram" from *Roughing It,* which survives in a version written for print and in transcription from oral delivery, Shepherd's memory "persistently threw details in his way that had nothing to do with the tale; these unrelated details would interest him and sidetrack him. . . ."[14] Unlike Jim Blaine's grandfather, however, Shepherd did remember and relate the central events of his story; most of his digressions were pointed and capsulized, with a satiric and self-contained impact: "We're all frauds," he digressed, after telling how he had pretended to be one of the leading intellects at Warren G. Harding. "The Great Myth," he went on, is that each generation of people is smarter than the preceding generation . . . I'm sure a lot of you here subscribe to that theory. It is related to the 'Detroit Idea'—the '76 model is better than the '75 model." But one sustained, digressive sub-plot, a baseball story featuring a Depression-era Chicago White Sox pitcher named "Bullfrog" Bill Dietrich, was never finished. Shepherd spent at least fifteen minutes, intermittently, advancing the story of the famous "portside hurler" in his legendary stand against the Cleveland Indians. But he left the bases loaded at the crucial moment and never finished the tale. Autograph seekers after the show were panting to know the resolution, but Shepherd admitted that it had none.

It needed no ending to be entertaining, for Shepherd, like Twain, is not a joke teller. His stories have no obvious punchline or "snapper." They depend for their success upon the art of the teller.

When Shepherd has been discussed by students of American culture, he has been treated primarily as a "radio personality." Jesse Bier singles him out as "The only full-time practicing humorist really left on the air. . . ."[15] Marshall McLuhan also makes no mention of Shepherd's writing or of his Midwestern roots and material, preferring to discuss his use of the radio—his medium—to his message. In *Understanding Media* McLuhan wrote:

> Jean Shepherd of WOR in New York regards radio as a new medium for a new kind of novel that he writes nightly. The mike is his pen and paper . . . It is his idea that, just as Montaigne was the first to use the page to record his reactions to the new world of printed books, he is the first to use awareness of a totally new world of universal human participation in all human events, private or collective.[16]

It has already been shown that Shepherd resents being categorized simply as a radio performer. I asked him about McLuhan's interesting assertion that his "microphone is his pen." I wanted to know, more specifically, if much of Shepherd's written material existed first in an oral form. I had read much about how Mark Twain's best writings had been shaped, as Walter Blair puts it, by "the stuff and style of fireside storytelling."[17]

I am aware that Twain felt that most oral interviews are "pure twaddle and valueless,"[18] but I think that though the spoken word may be less well-chosen than we might wish, it nevertheless must serve when the speaker has not answered the questions in his writings. So I will offer some of my questions to Shepherd, together with his replies on this matter.

Did his printed stories, I asked, such as **"Lost at C"** or those collected in his books, evolve somehow on the air, as they were spoken aloud, or did he first sit down and write them out? "I wrote them," he replied. "But they do seem very much in keeping with an 'oral' style, or oral tradition," I continued. "They have the flavor of the vernacular."

"Well," he said, "I don't like to write anything down that is totally in the vernacular or in slang, really. Because if you did that . . . in ten years no one would know what you were talking about. I think Tom Wolfe does this and it's a liability. There is a delicate balance that has to be struck here—you have to learn how to write so that it sounds like the way people are talking, but if you look at it carefully, you'll see that's not really the way people talk at all."

Shades of Mark Twain and his dictum, "Spoken speech is one thing, written speech is quite another."[19] Still, I wanted to make it clear that McLuhan's insinuation was thoroughly answered, and I asked a follow-up, saying: "I don't mean to imply that when you wrote down an oral tale that you wrote it down verbatim. . . . But . . . you do tell stories—the same ones that you have written—on the air and in your live performances. What I was asking was a sort of chicken and egg question—which came first?"

To this he responded, "I never just ad-libbed them over the air. I worked very hard to develop a writing style. . . . Discovering a voice that is authentically yours . . . is like athletics—you have to work at it to be any good. You have to work out to make your body strong and flexible so that it can do what you have to do. It's the same thing with writing. . . . You have to practice and build your word power and get to know the language so well that it becomes pliable and expressive of your true self. This is what I mean by developing a style. And naturally there are similarities in the way I write and the sound of my oral style. But they are two separate things."

"If you write," Shepherd told another interviewer, "you have to remember that you're writing for the future." His writing is not a form of instant, intimate communication to the denizens of McLuhan's tribal village: "Don't look for immediate applause [as a writer]," Shepherd cautions. "We live in a society that is immediate everything. . . . TV dinners, multiple choice questions, you never have to write anything out." But he does, and he works hard at it: "Some of those short stories [in *Playboy*]," he says, "may take three or four months to finish. . . . My first novel took six years to finish."[20]

Though Shepherd lives in New York and appeals most to a somewhat sophisticated audience—the people who actually read the humor in *Playboy,* the viewers of public television, people who read non-pornographic, book-length comic tales—he is not a bitter satirist or writer of "coterie comedy," as Bier has characterized him.[21] He is not another Henry Morgan, as Bier also claims. Nor is he another H. L. Mencken, who loathed the species he termed *boobus Americanus*. Indeed, when we find Shepherd echoing Mencken's terminology in a *Car and Driver* column titled **"Slobbus Americanus in the Cultural Vanguard,"** we find that he sympathizes with the *slobbus* at the expense of the critical wit to whom the term might have occurred.[22] The target of his satire is not the unwashed and uncultured average American; on the contrary, it is the so-called cultural elite which criticizes him. He is not a disaffected and alienated spirit who lambastes the Hoosier for comic effect. But he does explore the difference between the Easterner he has become and the kid who "survived Hammond" that he was. He has distanced himself from the "harrassing reality" of his subject matter so that he may write about it; for he is essentially a realist who insists that "the facts of life are funny" (Interview).

He believes in the dignity of man—even in the dignity of the Hoosier. But he also understands that our dignity is an achieved and precarious status, and that men are continually behaving comically. The humorist makes note of these lapses, these imperfections, and presents them in a form that evokes laughter. What Shepherd wrote concerning the characters in the humor of George Ade fits his own characters as well: "There are no heroes or noble figures. . . . All are subject to the same trivial emotions and continual tiny frustrations. . . . [He] has chronicled the Great Unchronicled" (*GA* [*The America of George Ade*], p. 14). Shepherd is a "serious" writer in the sense that he is indeed a chronicler, a keen observer who is reporting what he sees; the trick of his humor is primarily his perspective. The comic effect derives essentially from his attitude toward his subject.

"The American writer," observes Shepherd, "is obsessed with the idea of doom and futility." Our major writers speak of the "essential loneliness of American life," and are "bound by the single theme of the individual trying to find his place in a vast maze with walls forever changing and rules that disappear before they are even understood" (*GA,* p. 9). Shepherd's writing is bound by the same theme, given a comic realization. Yet he knows, as he told me, "You can't go home again. . . . The Kiwanis just isn't enough to fill . . . my life anymore." He performs before audiences at places like Princeton University, where, as he puts it, the audience thinks he's making up the curious Americana that fills his books: "They don't believe that people really go to Kiwanis Clubs." They will laugh at Shepherd's imitation of "a typical Indiana walk. A guy has just come out of Sears and Roebuck in a new suit. . . ." These things are the facts of life, and he is their chronicler. He has survived Hammond and lived to tell the tale; the world laughs at the tale, too, little suspecting that Hammond is the world—that the plight of the Hoosier is the plight of man.

Notes

1. Edward Grossman, "Jean Shepherd: Radio's Nobel Savage," *Harper's,* January 1966, p. 88.

2. Jean Shepherd, *In God We Trust: All Others Pay Cash* (Garden City: Dolphin Books, 1972), pp. 52-55. Subsequent references will be incorporated into the text using the abbreviation *IGWT*.

3. The quotation is the moral at the end of "The Fable of The Bookworm and The Butterfly Who Went into the Law," by George Ade, in Jean Shepherd, *The America of George Ade* (New York: Capricorn Books, 1961), pp. 127-131. Subsequent references will be incorporated into the text using the abbreviation *GA*.

4. Joseph H. Trimmer, "Memoryscape: Jean Shepherd's Midwest," *The Old Northwest*, 2, No. 4 (December 1976), 366.

5. Jean Shepherd, *The Ferrari in the Bedroom* (New York: Dodd, Mead & Company, 1972), p. viii.

6. Trimmer, pp. 366-367.

7. See Grossman and also W. Stewart Pinkerton, Jr., "The Talker: Jean Shepherd Gains Fans, Fortune with Tales of Woe," *The Wall Street Journal,* December 8, 1971, pp. 1, 21, for descriptive accounts of Shepherd's radio material.

8. Trimmer, pp. 366-367.

9. Anonymous interview (I have learned that the interview was conducted over the telephone by Joe Ellsworth), "*Focus 9* Interview with Jean Shepherd," *Focus 9* (November 1976), p. 2. *Focus 9* is a magazine and program guide published for the PBS television affiliate in Evansville, Indiana.

10. Interview with Jean Shepherd, October 7, 1976, Evansville, Indiana. Subsequent references will be incorporated into the text using the abbreviation Interview.

11. "*Focus 9* Interview," p. 2.

12. "Platform Readings," from The Autobiographical Dictation of October 10, 1907, first published in *Mark Twain in Eruption,* edited by Bernard DeVoto (1940), included in Perry Miller, ed., *Major Writers of America: Shorter Edition* (Chicago: Harcourt, Brace & World, 1966), p. 750.

13. Jean Shepherd, "Lost at C," *Playboy* (May 1973), pp. 143-144, 192-198. Subsequent references will be incorporated into the text using the abbreviation "LAC."

14. "Platform Readings," p. 751.

15. Jesse Bier, *The Rise and Fall of American Humor* (Chicago: Holt, Rinehart and Winston, 1968), p. 368.

16. Marshall McLuhan, *Understanding Media: The Extensions of Man* (New York: Signet, 1964), p. 265.

17. Walter Blair, "Mark Twain's Other Masterpiece: 'Jim Baker's Blue-Jay Yarn,'" *Studies in American Humor,* 1, No. 3 (January 1975), 135.

18. *Mark Twain's Letters,* ed. by A. B. Paine (New York: Harper and Brothers, 1917), p. 504.

19. *Ibid.*

20. "*Focus 9* Interview," p. 2.

21. Bier, p. 309.

22. *Car and Driver* (October 1974), pp. 16-18.

Martin A. Jackson (review date 28 February 1982)

SOURCE: Jackson, Martin A. Review of *A Fistful of Fig Newtons. New York Times Book Review* 87 (28 February 1982): 12, 20.

[*In the following assessment, Jackson praises* A Fistful of Fig Newtons, *noting: "What Jean Shepherd does is uncover absurdities and make us look cleanly at our own times."*]

It was 1957, and I was wide awake at 2 A.M., hopelessly trapped, listening to Jean Shepherd's night-long radio show. In the years when Eisenhower was in the White House, Jean Shepherd was a radical in the best sense of the word. He switched on light bulbs in the heads of a whole generation by simply explaining America to us. For five hours at a time, he beamed his erudition and good humor out over the East Coast, and we began to understand this odd nation a bit more. I still think of him as a matchless radio artist, but he's a fine writer, too, maybe one of our major humorists. Please note that a humorist is not a comic: Shepherd doesn't tell jokes; we aren't talking of Don Rickles here. What Jean Shepherd does is uncover absurdities and make us look cleanly at our own times. It's no easy trick.

A Fistful of Fig Newtons, Shepherd's third book, confirms my view. He writes about cars, the Army, summer camps, the sixth grade, his mother's meat loaf and beer-burping college kids in the Holland Tunnel—in short, about our life and times, the ordinary bits and pieces that every American recognizes and that are loaded with meaning for us all. He describes ordering, for example, "a rich slab of the Mother Food of New Jersey. Known to the pizza aficionado as a 'Full-tilt Boogie,' it had everything: anchovies, sausage, green peppers, double cheese, onions, and the greasy thumbprints of Vinnie himself."

Over the years Jean Shepherd has discovered a way of transposing his radio persona into print. All of the pieces in *A Fistful of Fig Newtons* have an aural dimension; they *sound* like Jean Shepherd, in rhythm, vocabulary and structure. It isn't necessary, though, to be a veteran radio listener to appreciate them. The American inner landscape Shepherd depicts will be familiar to anyone born after Herbert Hoover's Administration. His tale of the Great Ice Cream War, for instance, of how Mr. Leggett finally beat out the competition, the upstart Happy Cow, by just for one night giving away ice cream cones, is a story of endurance, bravery and existential choice, written in the juicy vernacular that Jean Shepherd has made his own. So is the epic of Ernie, Shep's G.I. buddy, who gambled for mighty stakes one hot night on a troop train and lost. "Is he out there yet," Shepherd wonders, "a haggard wraith living on berries and dead frogs?"

It is Shepherd's gift and his burden to be addicted to America. He's a piece of flypaper upon which the dust and flotsam of this peculiar civilization have been gathering for years. The sound of his old man's Pontiac revving up in the driveway? Shepherd remembers. The look of a college football hero? Shepherd knows: "Big Al was wedge-shaped; pure sinew, gristle, and covered with a thick, bristly mat of primitive fur. Numerous broken noses had reduced his nostrils to blow-holes."

Shepherd understands the first requirement of the humorist: affection for his subject. He's part of a tradition that includes George Ade, Robert Benchley, James Thurber and even Mark Twain. His wit is a kindly inside needling, a fond reminiscing about the embarrassing moments and quirky habits of people we've all grown up with. He's also kind to New Jersey—surely the mark of a good man.

Jean Shepherd has concentrated on writing for the past few years. It would be nice, though, to have him back on radio, too, to hear that rich Indiana voice on a clear

50,000-watt signal once again. I'd like to listen to him ramble some more about the unforgettable feel of a '39 Chevy on a hot evening. In the meantime, we can read Jean Shepherd, and that is a delight.

James F. Smith (essay date summer 1982)

SOURCE: Smith, James F. "Humor, Cultural History and Jean Shepherd." *Journal of Popular Culture* 16, no. 1 (summer 1982): 1-12.

[*In the following essay, Smith maintains that Shepherd not only offers portrayals of Midwestern American life but analyzes significant points about the "underlying mythology" of the American middle class.*]

As a contemporary humorist, Jean Shepherd has become a recognized commentator on American culture. His work includes a syndicated radio show; a potpourri of stories, sketches and essays appearing in such diverse places as *Playboy, Mademoiselle, Car and Driver* and *Field and Stream*; two television series, **Jean Shepherd's America** and **Shepherd's Pie**; and a feature-length film, **Phantom of the Open Hearth.** Much of Shepherd's popularity rests on his ability to create a vivid portrait of the 1930s and 1940s through the eyes of an Indiana youngster. While Shepherd garrulously weaves "kid stories," seeming to sidestep the bleak side of Depression America, older audiences recall days of radio premiums, family vacations, Ford V8 convertibles, Saturday afternoon serials, and high school formals. Young people hear an account of what it was like "back then" told by a narrator who seems to have total recall of names, places, dates and events. Yet, when Shepherd raises a game of battling tops to the level of epic combat, readers may well suspect that he is doing a good deal more than simply trying to evoke a nostalgic smile or tear. Shepherd insists that his work is not nostalgic at all. It is not recollection but fiction, and with the truth of good fiction his stories provide inroads to the appreciation of American middle class culture. The fact that his work continues to attract new, young audiences (who never played with battling tops or styled D.A. haircuts with Brylcreem) attests to Shepherd's accuracy in spotting the underlying mythology of American life amid the flux of styles and tastes. While conforming to several traditions of American humor and fiction, Jean Shepherd adds a new dimension to 20th century American humor and displays an insight into middle class character and culture, making his fiction not only enjoyable but valuable as a tool for discovery.

Claiming to have been rescued from a life in the steel mills of Hammond, Indiana, by the Korean War and the Army Signal Corps, Shepherd was once considered an "underground phenomenon" or cult hero.[1] When his stories appeared in *Playboy* during the 1960s, Shepherd won the magazine's Humor/Satire Award an unprecedented four times and reached out to an audience larger than his syndicated radio program had allowed. His novel, **In God We Trust, All Others Pay Cash** (1966), and collection of short stories, **Wanda Hickey's Night of Golden Memories and Other Disasters** (1971), thrust him before the mass market and paved the way for his two series broadcast over educational television (something he described in a story as "a great idea but a miserable reality"). Paradoxically Shepherd satirizes American machismo while he appeals to it. In a review of **Jean Shepherd's America,** one critic noted that "Like most American storytellers . . . his material consists of childhood, derring-do, escape, animals, perpetual motion, male camaraderie. Natty Bumppo, Ishmael, Huck Finn, Nick Adams."[2] Arthur Cooper, reviewing the **Wanda Hickey** collection for *Saturday Review,* compared Shepherd to Mark Twain, George Ade and Bill Cosby, concluding that the author's humor "transcends geographical boundaries and touches a nerve common to us all."[3]

One such common nerve might be nostalgia. Confronted with the trials and disappointments of humdrum urban life, the Shepherd-protagonists frequently escape into the relative safety and the occasional small triumphs of childhood memories. But the conclusion he draws is not at all comforting: "Thinking that the old days were good is a terrible sickness. Everything was just as bad then as it is now."[4] Shepherd maintains that one reason his writing is considered nostalgic may be his use of "real things" in his narratives. But to him, passionate attention to the *trivia mundi* is simply his own brand of authenticity:

> In most writing about America, real things that we live with rarely enter the stories. For example, a Norman Mailer character never picks up a bottle of Tab. . . . So my people use things, and I'm very careful always to use stuff in my stories that [is] generic and still being used. . . .[5]
>
> [Author's interview with Jean Shepherd, 22 March 1977]

If nostalgia appeals primarily to those who lived through a certain era, Shepherd's young fans belie the notion that his stories are simply nostalgic. Speaking of **"Wanda Hickey's Night of Golden Memories,"** perhaps his most widely circulated piece, Shepherd notes, "A kid laughing at the prom story is not laughing at an era or a past thing. He's laughing at what happened to him and his friends at the prom."[6]

The swing from present to past combined with the discovery of problems, miseries, as well as triumphs, provides the pattern for many of Shepherd's stories. The protagonist may be disgruntled by present circumstances, but he is ambivalent, at best, toward the past. The world that Shepherd creates is his own imaginary vision of life that his experiences have caused him to see. He invites his readers to join him on trips back to "Hohman," Indiana of the '30s and '40s, and guides them in an adjectival prose style that can only be described as hyperbolic. If we accept this artistic vision, and if we see his fictional world as true, we discover appealing boy-heroes surrounded by a vibrant life full of myth, mystery and magic, offsetting the inadequacy impotence and sense of defeat characteristic of 20th century American humor.

The background against which Shepherd creates his world is a fictionalized Hammond, an industrial town that he remembers as being "tough and mean." In **"The Grandstand Passion Play of Delbert and the Bumpus Hounds,"** the narrator offers both history and geography:

> Ours was not a genteel neighborhood, by any stretch of the imagination. Nestled picturesquely between the looming steel mills and the verminously aromatic oil refineries and encircled by a colorful conglomerate of city dumps and fetid rivers, our northern Indiana town was and is the very essence of the Midwestern industrial heartland of the nation. . . . If Chicago (only a stone's throw away across the polluted lake waters) was Carl Sandburg's "City of the Broad Shoulders," then Hohman had to be that city's broad rear end.[7]

Legend had it that the city's founding father saw no future in the small trading post that was Chicago, so he trudged southward, "set up camp and invested heavily in the land that was destined to become one of the ugliest places of real estate this side of the craters of the moon" (p. 16). Little food for golden memories can be found in the weather which is as miserably cold in winter with gales howling down Lake Michigan as it is miserably hot in the summer under the blazing midwestern sun. This environment seems to be something that the protagonist would try to escape, but with a kind of fierce pride he states:

> My old man, my mother, my kid brother and I slogged along in the great tradition. The old man had his high point every Wednesday at George's Bowling Alley, where he once rolled a historic game in which he got three consecutive strikes. My kid brother's nose ran steadily, winter and summer. My mother made red cabbage, peanut-butter-and-jelly sandwiches, meat loaf and Jell-O in an endless stream. And I studied the principal exports of Peru at the Warren G. Harding School.
>
> ([*Wanda Hickey's Night of Golden Memories and Other Disasters*] p. 16)

Norris Yates, analyzing twentieth century humor, notes the presence of the "little man" hero, a loser or bumbler, usually associated with the white-collar classes and dominated by his environment and the people around him.[8] Shepherd's characters are influenced by their environment, but not dominated by it. Furthermore, the lower-middle-class, blue-collar milieu is a distinct change from the context of James Thurber's successful suburbanites or Robert Benchley's "little" men. And while Hammond undoubtedly provided Shepherd with background locale, his portrait of the town and neighborhood is universal enough that he receives letters from fans convinced that he is actually writing about Newark or Cleveland or Pittsburgh.

A protagonist's retreat into the bygone days of midwestern childhood could be a fit occasion for idyllic images, but Shepherd's full awareness of 20th century complexities makes pastoral images impossible. The fact that much of the action in the stories occurs during the Depression further deflates the notion of nostalgia because Shepherd does not gloss over the grim reality of hard times, though he may occasionally find humor in it. Unlike other critics of industrial America, Shepherd recognizes that there are those who actually like working in the mills and those who can find satisfaction in the lifestyle portrayed in the stories. Where a 19th century naturalistic author would show the oppressive effects of the industrial environment, Shepherd discovers a wealth of experience to be savored there. He manages to draw substance and sustenance from the polluted waste land of Hammond in much the same way that Mark Twain was nourished by pre-industrial Hannibal.

"The Grandstand Passion Play" also draws us into the protagonist's family and reveals two important components of middle class life: a deep seated pride in family traditions and possessions, and the accompanying protective prejudice whenever the family feels threatened. The threat to the Shepherds[9] appears when the Bumpus family moves in next door. "There were thousands of them! The house seemed to age in one week. What had been a nondescript bungalow became a battered, hinge-sprung, sagging hillbilly shack" (p. 19). Though the new family kept to itself, an abrupt contrast to the closely knit Cleveland Street community, ripples of influence radiated throughout the neighborhood. From the moment the Shepherds are awakened by the blasting Bumpus phonograph to the night the Bumpuses mysteriously disappear, there is nothing but bad blood between the two households.

Traditional stereotypes of hill folk are conjured up as the narrator recalls his neighbors. They drive a dilapidated Chevrolet slat-sided truck, perpetually encrusted with bird droppings and Kentucky clay. They throw all their garbage and junk out the windows and doors to be pawed over by their menagerie of hounds, rabbits, goats, pigeons and chickens. Forsaking the "white-porcelain doo-hickey beside their bathtub upstairs," the Bumpuses install an outhouse, complete with moon on the door. The multitude of family members receive predictable treatment: all look ignorant, all have red necks, all chew tobacco and none wear shoes. A touching family portrait is rendered when Cassie, the Bumpus version of "Daisy Mae," returns from reform school:

> Emil grabbed her suitcase and Cassie, the ripest 16-year-old ever to descend on northern Indiana, kissed her father in a way that clouded up windows for blocks around.
>
> "Mah Gawd, Cassie, you sure filled out!" he boomed, slapping her none too paternally on the backside. Maw Bumpus, drying her hands on her apron, yelled from the porch.
>
> "YEW GIT IN HERE, CASSIE, AN' LEAVE YORE PAW ALONE. LEASTWAYS TILL WE'VE ET."
>
> (pp. 31-32)

Shepherd recalls, too, that after this episode, "my father stepped up his spyglass work considerably, since they had no window shades and Cassie liked to dress very casually around the house" (p. 32). In spite of the amusement afforded by the Bumpus clan, the neighbors shun them, noting, "The sea of wreckage spread like a blight onto the surrounding yards" (p. 23). This is quite a deterioration in light of the description of Hohman offered earlier: hillbilly hordes of barbarians assaulting industrial civilization.

But so far only traditional prejudice with accompanying exaggeration and stereotyping is revealed. The Bumpuses really strike the Shepherd family vitals when they ruin Easter Sunday dinner. The importance of the traditional meal is recalled:

> Every three or four months—roughly three times a year—we would make a major food investment. I suppose rich families don't even think about this kind of thing, but ordinary families in those days spent their lives eating canned corn, meat loaf, peanut-butter sandwiches, oatmeal, red cabbage and peas. In such a home, the great meals that came along every few months stuck out like icebergs in the Caribbean. . . . [In] our house, Easter has always meant ham. My father was totally ape over ham.
>
> (p. 36)

While his father could casually suggest that the family go down to the A & P to pick up the food for Easter, Shepherd reminds us that "'a great big ham' meant about half his pay check in those days" (p. 36). The shopping for the meal is surrounded in ceremony, "The old man would go up and down the case, poking, peering, hefting, sniffing, occasionally punching until, eventually, *the* ham was isolated from the common herd" (p. 37). Ritual also prevails in the preparation of the ham:

> Then the old man, the only one who could lift the ham without straining a gut, placed it in the big dark-blue oval pot that was used only for hams. [The ham] just sat there on the stove and bubbled away for maybe two hours, filling the house with a smell that was so luscious, so powerful as to have erotic overtones. The old man paced back and forth, occasionally lifting the lid and prodding the ham with a fork, inhaling deeply. The ham frenzy was upon him.
>
> (p. 38)

After the prescribed boiling time, the ham is placed in the oven, appropriately adorned with brown sugar, butter, cloves, pineapples and cherries. Once baked, the ham is allowed to sit in the oven overnight before being warmed for the Sunday dinner. As the family settles down for a night's rest, all troubles—even the notorious Bumpuses—seem to fade in the comfortable aroma of baked ham coming from the kitchen. Unfortunately, this state dinner is not destined to be, for no sooner is the ham placed on the white enamel kitchen to cool and set than a pack of "blue-ticked Bumpus hounds" roar through the screen door, seize the ham and carry it off to the Bumpus trash heap to be devoured by the moiling pack. To the Shepherds' outrage and consternation, Grandpaw Bumpus sets the tone for the neighbor family's response:

> He whooped wildly, wattles reddening with joy, spraying tobacco juice in all directions, while Cletus, his dimwitted grandson, yelled from the basement door:
>
> "GAHDAM, GRAN'PAW, LOOKA THEM HOUN'S GO! LOOKA THEM OL' BOYS GO! HOT DAMN!"
>
> (p. 43)

Even though the Shepherds wind up eating Easter dinner at "the chop suey joint," they taste nothing but ashes. A piece of their lives has been snatched from them by the slavering jaws of the Bumpus hounds. Though the old man promises revenge, the Bumpuses mysteriously vanish one night before the "crusher" can be inflicted on them.

This story clearly reveals the prejudice of the middle class toward any group that threatens the status quo in the neighborhood. But the most poignant aspect of the tale is the desecration of the family ritual at Easter—appropriately having nothing to do with religion. Shepherd repeatedly emphasizes food in his stories (after all, we are what we consume), and the uniqueness of the special-occasion meal makes the climax more startling. The reality of the Depression that lurks in the background of the narrative adds even more weight.

In spite of such traumas, boyhood is not without its idyllic moments in Shepherd's world. Family outings, county fairs, fishing trips and other events were eagerly awaited by his boy-heroes; and while reality never quite lived up to expectations, it usually proved satisfactory. **"Scut Farkas and the Murderous Mariah"** presents an example of a different kind of idyll having downright supernatural overtones. In this story, Shepherd meets with a force that is almost sinister in its mystery as he finds a small moment of triumph. Childhood ritual and mythology reach their height in the game of battling tops.

During a visit to a museum where he finds a wooden top said to have belonged to young Thomas Jefferson, Shepherd journeys back through his memories to his own finest hour with a "spikesie"—a wooden top equipped with a sharp metal tip. For his crowd, tops are not toys to be spun, but weapons used in battle. A victory is not complete unless the winner's top splits his opponent's. In such a fight, the top becomes "an extension of the will, an instrument of talent and aggression" (p. 96). Technique is an important factor:

> Well did I remember Junior Kissel's economical, slicing sidearm movement, his green top string snapping curtly as he laid his yellow spikesie down right on a dime with a hissing whir. Flick, on the other hand—more erratic, more flamboyant—had a tendency to loft his spikesie, releasing it after a showy, looping overhand motion. . . . His top spun with an exhibitionistic, wobbling playfulness. . . . I myself preferred a sneaky, snakelike, underhand movement, beginning at the hip, swinging down to around the knees, upward slightly, and then the quick release after a fast, whiplike follow-through. Flick was great to watch; Kissel, methodical and clean. I was deadly.
>
> (p. 95)

After perfecting his form through much dedicated practice, Shepherd feels that he is ready to challenge the unconquered Scut Farkas, the most notorious bully of Warren G. Harding School, and his invincible black spikesie, Mariah.

One problem remains, however. Our hero does not have the proper top. Comparing the fighting top to a star hitter's personally selected Louisville Slugger, Shepherd laments that he has not found his ideal weapon. Farkas, on the other hand, sulks around the playground with his top bulging meaningfully in his back pocket, "a continual walking, living, surly challenge." Mariah was indeed unique:

> [It] . . . had at least 50 or more confirmed kills to its credit, as well as half a dozen probables and God knows how many disabling gashes and wounds. Rumor held that this top had been owned by Farkas' father before him. . . . Some said that it was not a top at all, but some kind of foreign knife, and not large as tops go, being of a peculiar squat shape, a kind of small, stunted, pitchblack mushroom, wider above than most and sloping off quickly to a dark-blue, casehardened, glittering saber tip. . . . It spun with a mean, low humming—a truly distinctive, ominous note . . .
>
> (p. 97)

All Shepherd has to face Mariah and Farkas (known by all to have "the evil eye" as well) are the "kid tops" sold at the neighborhood variety stores. He methodically scours all sorts of likely top sources—candy shops, toy stores, dime stores—until on one balmy, spring day when he is at least four miles beyond his usual turf, he happens upon the Total Victory Newsstand and Notions, located in a particularly run-down and disreputable section of town near the roundhouse. Within the dark and dingy shop, he is confronted by "an ancient lady wearing a black shawl over her head" who speaks "with the slightest trace of a European accent" (p. 104). After showing his dismay over the usual assortment of toy tops, he starts to leave when the old lady calls him back. With his Keds ready to spring for his bike, Shepherd nervously waits as she rummages around a back room and returns with a box. From this she pulls a top, saying that she wouldn't sell this one to just *anybody*.

> Great Scott! Cradled in her talons lay a malevolent duplicate of Scut Farkas' evil Mariah. A duplicate in everything—spirit, conformation, size, everything—except color. It was a dull, burnished, scuffed silvery pewter, a color I had never seen on a top before. But then, except for Mariah, I had never seen a black one either.
>
> (pp. 105-106)

The old crone assures him that it will not cost much—the top has been used—but "It's imported. She's a Gypsy top. . . . Good luck, sonny. Careful, she's a mean one" (p. 106). Shepherd is ecstatic: "I had at last come together with the greatest fighting top I had ever seen. It had an oily, heavy, solid feel, a nice comfortable heft like, say, a Colt snub .38 Special feels to the hand. I had already decided to call it Wolf" (p. 106).

After practicing for hours at a time in the murky depths of his basement until he and Wolf are a perfect team, he launches his plan to humble Farkas and Mariah. He baits his trap by luring Kissel into combat on a threatening Friday afternoon. Nature cooperates by providing the appropriate ominous setting.

> It looked like rain as I walked through the alleys, over the fences, through the vacant lots on my way to the playground, kicking sheets of water up from muddy puddles, skipping bottle caps into new lakes as I moved toward the battlefield. . . . The trees dripped warm water under low, gray, ragged clouds. Off to the north, toward Lake Michigan, even though it was full daytime, the steel mills glowed dark red against the low-hanging overcast.
>
> (pp. 110-111)

After demolishing Kissel's top with one of his second string toy tops, Shepherd issues a challenge to all takers. Moments later, Farkas appears and calls our warrior to the fray: "Get up, ya chicken bastard . . . get out ya top" (pp. 112-113).

Shepherd opens with his doomed toy top. Even though he scores a direct hit on Mariah, the black top again proves to be deadly as it neatly splits Shepherd's second string top in two. As Farkas casually picks up Mariah and begins to leave,

[my] hand slipped down into my back pocket, quickly snaked Wolf out into the open, and in the twinkling of a moment, I had him wound and instantly laid Wolf down hard and solid. Its high, thin note, steady as a dentist's drill and twice as nasty, cut through the falling rain and stopped Farkas in his tracks.

(p. 115)

Now both boys are out for the kill. Try as they might, neither can score a hit on the other. "The two insane tops, grimy, covered with mud, leaped like live things.... They hated each other; yet they seemed to be in league" (p. 117). With no victory forthcoming from strike and split fighting, Farkas decides that they will play "keepers." A circle is drawn, and the two tops spun inside—the winner, whose top bumps the other out of the circle first, keeps both tops. Neither top gives an inch until both dart out together, topple over the curb, and continue spinning amid the rush of water down the gutter. Both disappear down a sewer.

> Farkas, his face white, his eyes glazed, stared down into the raging flood through the grille of the drain. Then, without a word, he arose and ... walked off down the street in the rain. I knew I would never see Wolf again. But somehow I knew that neither Wolf nor Mariah were [sic] finished. They would go on.
>
> (p. 119)

And if this unconventional finish were not enough to shroud the battle in mystery, Shepherd claims to have never been able to find the Total Victory Newsstand again.

Shepherd claims that this is one of his favorite stories. Using the ritual of a childhood game, he creates invincible weapons. Perhaps this is a crude but plausible reflection of any conflict, even between world powers. The "bully" remains invincible until his weapon is evenly matched. Given equal weapons, the result of the conflict is inconclusive—everything goes down to the drain, so to speak. Somehow, two tops washed into the sewer provide a less threatening tableau than the doomsday of *Dr. Strangelove*.

Equally mysterious and at least as threatening is Shepherd's introduction to another kind of battle: the relationship between the sexes. His problems multiply rapidly as he leaves the safe harbor of boyhood for the uncharted seas of adolescence. In **"The Star-Crossed Romance of Josephine Cosnowski,"** Shepherd learns that the erotic folklore surrounding Polish girls from East Chicago is only a mask for Roman Catholicism and the trap of early marriage. On a date with his dream girl, Daphne Bigelow, he discovers that the gulf between his world of Cleveland Street and the Orpheum Theater and Daphne's world of Waverly Street and the chauffeur-driven Cadillac is too great to traverse on a cross-town bus. But **"Wanda Hickey's Night of Golden Memories"** provides us with Shepherd's most memorable initiation into the "civilized" adult world.

Television proves to be the springboard for Shepherd's memories. Watching an educational TV special about puberty rites, the narrator is reminded of his experience at a junior prom. For weeks the preparations for this rite of passage fill his waking hours. He arranges for the rental of his traditional costume, a white-jacketed summer formal. His precious Ford V8 convertible is polished, and everything seems set. His only problem is that he cannot steel himself to ask Daphne Bigelow to be his date.

> Time and again, I spotted her in the halls, drifting by on gossamer wings, her radiant complexion casting a glow on all those around her, her brilliant smile lighting up the corners of her 202 homeroom. But each time, I broke out into a fevered sweat and chickened out at the last instant.
>
> (p. 312)

The days pass; all his pals are lined up with dates. Then one evening, while he moodily waters the lawn, he accidentally squirts Wanda Hickey, the only girl he knows "for an absolute fact" ever liked him. As they pass the time with adolescent small talk, the subject of the prom is raised.

> It was then I realized that there was no sense fighting it. Some guys are born to dance forever with the Daphne Bigelows on shining ballroom floors under endless starry skies. Others—well, they do the best they can. I didn't know that yet, but I was beginning to suspect something.
>
> (p. 318)

He finally asks Wanda to the prom and makes arrangements to double date with his friend Schwartz. Excitement reigns until his limited finances begin to disturb him the day before the dance. However, his old man saves the day quite unexpectedly. After remarking that he always wished he had gone to a prom—he had barely finished the eighth grade when he had to quit school and go to work—the old man gives Shepherd a twenty dollar bill he had won at the bowling alley that night, cautioning him, "Don't tell Ma."

> I took the $20, glommed on to it the way the proverbial drowning man grabs at a straw. I was so astounded at this unprecedented gesture that it never occurred to me to say thanks. He would have been embarrassed if I had. A miracle had come to pass. There was no doubt about it—the prom was going to be an unqualified gas.
>
> (p. 326)

On the day of the prom, events click by according to custom. Shepherd is out early, dusting off his car and yelling at his runny-nosed brother for dripping on the fender. His own preening begins with *two* showers (wearing out a new bar of Lifebuoy) and his second shave of the week. He squeezes blackheads, splashes on Aqua Valva, and combs his D.A. into just the right "insouciant pitch." Getting clad in the summer formal and patent leather dancing pumps proves to be an epic struggle, but the result seems worth the trouble:

> Posing before the full-length mirror on the bathroom door, I noted the rich accent of my velvet stripes, the gleam of my pumps, the magnificent dash and sparkle of my high-fashion cummerbund. What a sight! What a feeling! This is the way life should be. This is what it's all about.
>
> (p. 333)

He drives to Wanda's, presents his date, who looks unusually attractive herself, with her orchid corsage, and they tool off to the Cherrywood Country Club to dance to Mickey Isley and his Magic Music Makers.

Shepherd encounters a number of discouraging pitfalls in the process of becoming civilized, no matter how hard he tries to be as suave as Cary Grant. As he and Wanda move in a mechanical, Arthur-Murray-ad box-step, Schwartz (doing precisely the same behind him) continually digs his elbow into Shepherd's ribs. As sweat begins to soak his shirt, jacket and jockey shorts, Shepherd begins to develop itches and rashes. His "dashing" wing collar chafes his neck badly, and his patent leather shoes clamp his feet mercilessly. Meanwhile, Wanda looks at him adoringly, "her great liquid myopic eyes catching the reflection of the red and green lanterns overhead" (p. 339). When the dance is over, they leave the club to find that the balmy June night has been punctuated by a violent thunderstorm, and that Shepherd had left the Ford out with the top down. He bails out the car, hoists the top at the expense of running down his battery, gets a push-start. Finally, all pile in the soggy car, somewhat the worse for wear.

> Do you know what happens to a maroon-wool carnation on a white-serge lapel in a heavy June downpour in the Midwest, where it rains not water but carbolic acid from the steel-mill fallout? I had a dark, wide, spreading maroon stripe that went all the way down to the bottom of my white coat. My French cuffs were covered with grease from fighting the top, and I had cracked a thumbnail, which was beginning to throb.
>
> (p. 341)

But the worst is yet to come.

Shepherd, Wanda, Schwartz and Clara proceed to the Red Rooster, a notorious road house which was considered the only place to cap the evening of the junior prom. "An aura of undefined sin was always connected with the name. . . . But the only thing we knew for sure . . . was that anybody on the far side of seven years old could procure any known drink without question" (p. 342). Knowing that better things are expected of him on prom night, Shepherd passes up his usual Kayo the Wonder Drink in favor of bourbon on the rocks. Not to be outdone by the merrymaking throng at the Rooster, he adds a phrase that he heard his old man use often down at the Bluebird Tavern, "And make it a triple." Schwartz follows suit, and they order pink ladies for the girls. Triple bourbon on the rocks proves lethal, especially on an empty stomach: "Down it went—a screaming 90 proof rocket searing savagely down my gullet. For an instant, I sat stunned, unable to comprehend what had happened. Eyes watering copiously, I had the brief urge to sneeze, but my throat seemed to be paralyzed" (p. 345). Barely capable of responding to Wanda's ecstatic cooing, "Isn't this romantic? Isn't this the most wonderful night in all our lives?" (p. 345), Shepherd is served another drink because he is afraid to move enough to say no. After downing this glass to the girls' toast, "Let's drink to the happiest night of our lives," he tries to calm the tempest in his stomach by wolfing down the meal he had ordered—lamb chops, turnips, mashed potatoes, cole slaw and strawberry shortcake. The inevitable happens, and he runs for the men's room.

> Twenty seconds later, I was on my knees, gripping the bowl of the john like a life preserver in pitching seas. Schwartz, imitating me as usual, lay almost prostrate on the tiles beside me, his body racked with heaving sobs. . . . All of it came rushing out of me in a great roaring torrent. . . . For long minutes, we lay there limp and quivering, smelling to high heaven, too weak to get up. It was the absolute high point of the junior prom; the rest was anticlimax.
>
> (pp. 347-384)

He recovers his faculties enough to pay the check with his old man's twenty, and they drive home. Even though the undaunted Wanda waits expectantly for her good night kiss, Shepherd is too queasy to complete the final ritual encounter when he smells sauerkraut on her breath. He dashes from her front porch and speeds toward home. Wanda has survived the evening with considerably less trauma, perhaps confirming the traditional belief that the female is more in tune with the demands of civilization than the male. Shepherd's knowing father, up early for a fishing trip, sardonically offers the boy some food, then assures him that his head will "stop banging" in a couple of days. In the meantime, all he could do is tumble into bed, totally exhausted by this stage of his puberty rites.

Finally, Shepherd offers a tale of adult experience, **"The Return of the Smiling Wimpy Doll,"** which in many ways functions as a frame-tale for his fiction. For it is in this story that we find Shepherd's most explicit statement of his feeling toward the past.

During the Christmas season, Shepherd finds himself in Manhattan, surrounded by icons of modern life—typified by his "Deluxe Yule A-Go-Go Tuneful Musical Revolving Puncture Proof Table-Model Aluminum Xmas

Tree" (which he cannot make work). He receives a package from his mother: a box labeled "Life—the complete cereal" containing relics of his boyhood. At first he is simply nonplussed by this array of junk thrown out in a flurry of holiday housecleaning. Then temptation and curiosity prove too great, and he opens the box to find a host of items: Brownie, his teddy bear; his Wimpy doll; a Buck Rogers leather flight helmet; a Flash Gordon Zap Gun; an official Jack Armstrong Wheaties pedometer; an Ed Wynn Fire Chief hat; and "seven tons of kid effluvia." Each gives rise to a memory, and fortified with several healthy belts of scotch, he endures a nostalgia binge to end them all. But, as always, he is jolted to reality.

> An angry wind laden with sooty ice crystals banged briefly at the windows of my apartment. It was getting colder. Sadly, I returned to the dusty magic mountain of illusion—lost and gone, grieved only by the wind. I had had enough. Back into the box I stuffed . . . the whole teeming throng . . . from out of the past. . . . For a fleeting moment, I considered shoving the whole sorry mess out onto the garbage landing. But I chickened out. Staggering under the load, I dragged my childhood to the hall closet.
>
> (pp. 294-295)

The load is heavy, but it is his life (he wonders for a moment just how diabolical his mother had been in packing the whole works in a Life cereal carton), and though he can try, he cannot relegate these memories to the trash heap. He knows that he must carry these memories with him. Times were no better then, but they cannot be denied.

Shepherd's tales, then, may seen nostalgic, but they are also much more. In his ambivalence toward the past, we can find traces of the ironic voice that R. W. B. Lewis identifies as part of the "American Adam" tradition,[10] and so the comparison between Shepherd and authors such as Cooper, Melville, Mark Twain and Hemingway does not seem totally inappropriate. Furthermore, Robert Morseberger has suggested that unlike the characters of 19th century humorists, modern protagonists "dramatize a sense of inadequacy, impotence, and defeat before the complexities and destructive potential of the century."[11] Often they are characterized as "hypersensitive." Shepherd's protagonists possess a heightened sensitivity to the possibilities of life and the complex of humanity as a result of the collision of their innocence with reality. We can see this clearly in the tale of **"The Smiling Wimpy Doll."** James Thurber said "The things that we laugh at are awful while they are going on, but get funny when we look back. And other people laugh because they've been through it too. The closest thing to humor is tragedy."[12] But the tragedy in Shepherd's stories is softened by small triumphs.

In the tradition of the American romance, Shepherd focuses on depicting his *persona*'s discovery of his own identity in terms of his world. Also, we can find a modernized American folklore in Shepherd's work: the tall tale in his imaginative and exaggerated response to native conditions and survival in Hammond's ghastly ecology; the "wonder" in incidents such as his father's unprecedented generosity before the prom; and even supernatural motifs in the story of the battling tops. We can hear echoes of fellow Hoosier George Ade and his *Fables* in the types and caricatures that Shepherd presents, and echoes of Bill Cosby's monologues in the vivid recollection of boyhood amusements in their mock-epic grandeur. Though the pastoral setting of Mark Twain's middle west was metamorphosed into the industrial landscape of today, even refinery aromas and blast furnace dust can be a matrix against which Shepherd sketches moments of promise.

No Davy Crockett, Buffalo Bill Cody, or George Custer, Shepherd's *persona* becomes a kind of everyman hero. Like most of us, he can aspire to greatness and distinction, start out even with everyone else, and still end up short of his dreams:

> Mewling, puking babes. That's the way we all start. . . . Then gradually, surely, we begin to divide into two streams, all marching together up that long yellow brick road of life, but on opposite sides of the street. One crowd goes on to become the Official people, peering out at us from television screens; magazine covers. . . . And the rest of us go on to become . . . just us.[13]
>
> [*In God We Trust, All Others Pay Cash*]

This phenomenon may be particularly American, for the democratic tradition leads us to believe that all people really do start out alike. Whatever sense of betrayal might be present in the stories, Shepherd-the-man is not a bitter pessimist or nihilist. While he does not remain in the haze of memory, neither does he become simply another "American Laocoon" trying to maintain his balance amid the violent crosscurrents of the 20th century. Though he could be tempted to hide in boyhood memories, to "light out" with Huck Finn for the "territory," fleeing women, social responsibility, and all other attempts at civilization, Shepherd, like his readers, is fascinated by the adult world and ultimately adjusts to it. So it will always be. We can but grin and bear it—and Shepherd's humor helps us considerably with the grinning.

Notes

1. Edward Crossman, "Jean Shepherd: Radio's Noble Savage," *Harper's*, Jan. 1966, pp. 88-89.
2. Cyclops TV Review, "The Swish of Windshield Wipers: Jean Shepherd's 'America'." *Life* 73 (1 Sept. 1972), p. 14.
3. Arthur Cooper, Rev. of *Wanda Hickey's Night of Golden Memories and Other Disasters* by Jean Shepherd, *Saturday Review*, 54 (13 Nov. 1971), pp. 68-69.

4. Cooper, p. 68.

5. Author's interview with Jean Shepherd, 22 March 1977.

6. Author's interview with Jean Shepherd, 22 March 1977.

7. Jean Shepherd, *Wanda Hickey's Night of Golden Memories and Other Disasters* (Garden City, N.Y.: Doubleday, 1971), p. 15. Subsequent references will appear as page numbers in the text.

8. Norris Yates, *The American Humorist: Conscience of the Twentieth Century* (Ames, Ia.: Iowa State Univ. Press, 1964), pp. 353-355.

9. Even though Shepherd flatly denies that these stories are autobiographical, he does refer to the family in his story as the "Shepherd" family. For the sake of convenience, I will refer to the hero as "Shepherd" since the stories in *Wanda Hickey's Night* do not use any other name. In some other stories, the protagonist is called "Ralph," but none of these is included here.

10. R. W. B. Lewis, *The American Adam: Innocence, Tragedy, and Tradition in the Nineteenth Century* (Chicago: Univ. of Chicago Press, 1955), pp. 7, 195-196.

11. Robert E. Morseberger, *James Thurber* (New York: Twayne Publishers, 1964), p. 18.

12. Quoted in Morseberger, p. 21.

13. Jean Shepherd, *In God We Trust, All Others Pay Cash* (Garden City, N.Y.: Doubleday, 1966), p. 58.

Gerald Nachman (essay date 2003)

SOURCE: Nachman, Gerald. "Out of Thin Air: Jean Shepherd; Bob Elliott and Ray Goulding." In *Seriously Funny: The Rebel Comedians of the 1950s and 1960s*, pp. 265-93. New York: Pantheon Books, 2003.

[*In the following essay, Nachman considers Shepherd's reputation as a "purveyor of nostalgia," noting that interviews with the author reveal a less idealized vision of the past.*]

> There's a nostalgia for an unlived past.
> —Jean Shepherd

> We were sort of one of a kind.
> —Bob Elliott

"Okay, Gang, are you ready to play radio? Are you ready to shuffle off the mortal coil of mediocrity? I am if you are. Yes, you fatheads out there in the darkness, you losers in the Sargasso Sea of existence, take heart, because WOR, in its never-ending crusade of public service, is once again proud to bring you . . . The Jean Shepherd Program!"

Shepherd was no routine comedian. He was a witty radio raconteur who came of age in the fifties and sixties spinning nocturnal satirical monologues that became their own comic form. Just when network-radio comedy was having its bones picked clean by television, a few comics jumped into the void. None landed more resonantly than the bemused and crackling voice belonging to Jean Shepherd.

With his meandering, real-life fables shot through with sardonic undertones, he reshaped "talk radio." He became a dominant presence in New York before radio was set on today's news/music/sports/call-in autopilot. There had been radio monologuists before him, but nobody who worked as free-form or as fancifully as he did. No satirist covered as many life situations and (except for Bob & Ray) none held forth on the air for as long. He had a brief parallel stand-up comedy career in clubs—mostly at the Limelight Café in Greenwich Village (from 1962 to '67), from which his Saturday-night shows were broadcast. He also spun off his soliloquies into record albums, TV series, magazine pieces, and a shelf of short stories. "I'm a storyteller," he said. "A storyteller can work in any medium."

In his heyday, he became a comic keynote at colleges and concert halls. He gave readings, narrated video documentaries on Babe Ruth, Christmas, Norman Rockwell, Thanksgiving, and the Chicago White Sox, his raging passion. He turned up in a variety of magazines, from *Car and Driver* to *Mademoiselle*; his primary outlet for prose, however, was *Playboy*, where he had a fixed pulpit. He devised, produced, wrote, and narrated two TV series for PBS, ***Jean Shepherd's America*** and ***Shepherd's Pie*** (the latter spun off from *The Great American Dream Machine*), and appeared in and cowrote ***New Faces of 1962.*** He was seriously considered as a host for *The Tonight Show*—Steve Allen suggested him—but was felt to be too eccentric.

Most of his writing and TV gigs were versions of his bittersweet radio tales of growing up in Hammond, Indiana, which he brought alive as a community of eccentrics. He could seize upon relics and minutiae from his past—the dismayingly chintzy prize in a box of Cracker Jack, say—and subtly, slowly tease them out into rich cautionary tales with warnings about beguiling come-ons, flimsy promises, childhood naïveté, and life's disappointments in general.

Shepherd may be, with Godfrey Cambridge, the most underrated of all the innovative comic voices of the era; certainly he had the most rabid cult, verging on a fundamentalist religion. For his acolytes, his *Voice in the Night* program was not just a cult, it was a cause, and it remains alive and kicking on the Internet, where his tapes are available and where his memory is still lovingly tended since his death in 1999, at age seventy-eight. His friend and radio colleague Ron Della Chiesa says, "He had probably the largest cult following of any radio personality in America. Of course, Jean would be the first to say, 'What do you mean by *cult*, Ron?'"

Shepherd was mainly a New York/East Coast on-air phenomenon but was heard in a few select syndicate markets, at one point close to twenty. WOR's AM signal carried his voice far afield at night to many surrounding cities. He broke through during the 1960s as an urban folklorist, spinning compelling yarns of growing up in Indiana in the thirties and forties, and saw the American dream reflected in the fun-house mirror of his mind. One grateful listener recalls: "Jean Shepherd had a positive, warm humanity that I didn't experience in my life. It gave me a genuine sense of comfort and peace. For many people who lie in bed alone at night, and feel cut off, he was like a bridge to a hope of some kind, to a connection with other human beings. He created a world that most of us did not inhabit but would like to have inhabited."

Other sixties stand-up comics have been compared to Mark Twain—Bill Cosby, Jonathan Winters, Richard Pryor—but Shepherd perhaps came the closest. He re-created the lay of the land—its sounds, music, smells, and characters, miming the very scenes and scents of his, of everybody's, boyhood; he called them "sensual essays." Invariably, he was likened to midwesterners James Thurber and George Ade, his idol, a fellow Indiana humorist whose ironic voice matched Shepherd's on-air voice, but Shepherd dug much deeper.

The Midwest has long harbored acerbic folk humorists. His closest radio heir is Garrison Keillor, whose whimsy-laden Minnesota memoirs of life in the mythical town of Lake Wobegon are funny and poignant, if much less freewheeling than Shepherd's, whose imagination floated far beyond the Midwest. Shepherd was a more blue-collar, urban comic than Keillor. More in the Shepherd vein was Paul Rhymer, whose thirties and forties radio program *Vic and Sade,* set in a small Illinois town, was a major influence on Shepherd, who, like Rhymer, had a weakness for goofy names—Wanda Hickey, Ollie Hopnoodle, the Bumpus family.

Shepherd recoiled from being tagged a purveyor of nostalgia; he preferred to call himself a "commentator." He ventured farther than nostalgia; he was almost antinostalgia. His every recollection was heavily laced with cynicism. Just because his tales took place in the past didn't make them nostalgic, any more than American history is nostalgia. His relics and references—his use of pop songs, ads, toys, comic books—were evocative, but the scenes were not bathed in amber. For Shepherd, the past was just his jumping-off place. As he once said, "The great American myth is that things used to be wonderful, and the future will be wonderful, too. It's just the present that happens to stink."

His people, noted a *Wall Street Journal* writer, "flirt valiantly but briefly with victory, only to go down in the end to crushing defeat. If there is a constant theme, it is the absolute certainty of daily humiliation in life"—as when his high school coach gave an inspirational pep talk and the fired-up team ran out and lost by a score of 56 to 5. He told one interviewer, "Childhood seems good in retrospect because we were not yet aware of the basic truth: that we're all losers, that we're destined to die."

Della Chiesa says, "He hated that word *nostalgia*. He didn't even like to be pigeonholed as a 'radio personality.' He felt his real genius was in his writing, and yet people constantly brought up radio because they grew up with it. He was a part of their adolescent years." Ironically, Shepherd himself is now a nostalgic memory for his former avid listeners—and there was no such thing as a non-avid Jean Shepherd listener. His audience, says public radio producer Larry Josephson, "were mostly geeks and loners—like me, the smartest kid in high school who had no friends. All of Shepherd's fans are alienated in some way. Mainstream people don't get Jean Shepherd." As Jerry Tallmer wrote in a *New York Post* profile: "His show from the mud-flats of New Jersey brought him to the attention of Manhattan's sleepless disciples of deep thought and nonconformity"—four hundred thousand of them on a good night.

Like a lot of people, Kenneth Turan, the film critic for the *Los Angeles Times,* discovered Shepherd while idly twisting the dial late one night. "When you heard this voice it stopped you. It was such a hypnotic voice. He'd go off on these tangents and he'd somehow bring you back. It was intoxicating. I never talked to anyone about listening to Shepherd because I didn't have any friends who I thought would understand it." Shepherd provided the same sense of private discovery that many of the era's satirists did. "It almost seemed like if I mentioned it, it would go away—like a dream," observed Turan.

Jules Feiffer remembers hearing Shepherd while hunched over his drawing board in his apartment: "I stumbled on this soothing voice of Jean Shepherd, who was remembering all the things from his past." His Indiana boyhood was a universe away from Feiffer's New York, "and yet it seemed to be everything that I knew and recognized. He was the book you picked up in the middle of the night when you felt so lonely, and suddenly you found the page that relates directly to you. Shepherd was that page."

He was very much of his own time, often playing off the day's headlines, but the monologues that held listeners most rapt, and for which he was best known, were the wry misadventures of his youth. He claimed, in a 1972 interview with yet another great midwestern radio raconteur, Studs Terkel, that his real interest was in "American rituals," often rooted in the past, but not always. Shepherd could discuss a contemporary Thanksgiving as easily as he could one from his boyhood—or just vamp for an hour on the first Thanksgiving. Or, for that matter, on Mail Pouch Chewing Tobacco, political second bananas, Boy Scout camp, firemen, working in a piano factory, Jack Paar interviewing Zsa Zsa Gabor, druids, the March on Washington, or whoopee parties. Mort Sahl-like, Shepherd could weave a winding tale that, in its final seconds, would somehow circle back to his opening premise and, in the peroration, build to a climactic moment embedded with a rueful moral.

One typical Jean Shepherd story revealed the kind of Joycean epiphanies he regularly explored: it began with a seemingly idle remark about realizing, as an adolescent, what a "slob" he was. He discusses all the meatloaf dinners he ate at home as opposed to the fancy foods he only read about, like raw clams. This early memory of home life segues neatly into a story about a time at college when a girl invited him to dinner with her family. He remembers, among a million other things, her remark to him: "Don't bother to dress." Nevertheless, he dons his Penney's sport coat and Ward's slacks with great care, and as he approaches the girl's address, he sees that the houses are getting bigger and bigger, until he arrives at a large home with pillars and a brass knocker. A butler greets him and he enters to find twenty people present, as Nancy, the girl, runs over and kisses him; nobody ever kissed quite so casually in *his* circles, he notes. Shep takes a drink from a long-stemmed glass, a drink that even has a name—martini. *"My old man would only say, 'How 'bout some booze?' We didn't have any actual names for it—it was just called 'booze.'"*

As they move on to dinner at a table decked with linen and crystal, Nancy asks him, "Have you had any fresh escargot this season yet?" Shepherd: *"Suddenly, in front of me, was this plate of something which had always been rumored in our house—that people somewhere, someplace, ate—and we'd never really believed it—snails. And whenever it was mentioned, it was always, 'Oh, ugh!' And my meat-loaf insides are churning. What am I gonna do? I can't chicken out. And with this little fork, I fished it out and put it in my mouth and, Oh, my God! Oh, my God! It was fantastic! Then I made a total pig of myself and went slurp, slurp, slurp. And then the lesson hit me. I looked around and I saw all these other people who'd been doing this all their lives. They weren't surprised at snails. And then it began to sneak in on me—what other terrible stuff did I learn at home, what other things do I think are awful? I ate the snails, and late that night, when I got home, I'm laying in the dormitory room and I can feel them snails, there's an aftertaste, and I begin to suspect that night that there was a fantastic unbelievable world out there. And I was just beginning to taste it, and God knows where it would lead!"* Classic, definitive, sumptuous Jean Shepherd.

While Shepherd spoke, his voice would rise and crack with intensity and merriment as he approached a crescendo, then fade to a whisper before gathering steam again, plunging forward toward the climax. As you listened in bed, eyes closed, it was like taking a lulling train ride across country. He told Terkel: "I've tried in my writing to do something very few writers have tried to do, and that is to write about American traditions—rather than American sex, or problems, or traumas. We all live a life apart from these problems—we have a race problem, we have this problem, that problem—but we all have a daily life: standing for ice cream at the Carvel's, going into the drive-in at McDonald's, being in the library and seeing that the book you've been waiting for has been stolen."

When Terkel said to him, "You cover an aspect of American life that nobody else ever covers" (meaning the past), Shepherd bristled and said: "You think it's the *past*. Most people who become writers think that everything they used to do no longer happens. I evoke a time past for all people, including a seventeen-year-old's time past, because I'm writing about American rituals. The one thing about a ritual is, it *does* continue."

He went on: "We don't recognize our own rituals—the two-week vacation, the graduation, the Sunday-afternoon dinner. When I say the word *prom*, for people of all ages, from ninety to a guy who's twelve, it evokes a whole series of images. I try to telescope an experience, so I have 'em do everything in absolute detail." At his mention that "county fairs never change," he reels off a catalogue of homemade cakes, pies, and candies at the fair, with every goody's specific name. He continued: "The coffee break is as ritualistic from one end of the country to the other. You go into an office in Tacoma and they're sitting around with the paper cups and the looks on the faces are the same. It's as much a ritual as the English teatime rituals. We're getting old enough now as a country so that we have recognized national rituals."

Shepherd's response to the persistent nostalgia charge: "I don't think there's any one of us, no matter where we live, who doesn't have a secret place, whatever it is. It's like Oz. It's why Americans are so hung up on western movies—it's a dream world. There's a nostalgia for an unlived past." He added: "There's also a small-town myth in America—where people are simply more honest. But most of the people who saw *Our Town* were urban people; it was a Broadway play." He loved upsetting as well as celebrating myths. New York itself was one of his favorite myths, and he could nail it in three lines: "*It's the capital of the world for the disenchanted. It's a goal, Nirvana, for thousands of guys, but they get here and they discovery they still have trouble with their chicks. It's like getting to heaven only to find out that heaven is just like the office.*"

Shepherd was emphatically American, and only secondarily a mid-westerner or a New Yorker. That unlived past he spoke of he relived and rhapsodized about with a cutting honesty unlike anything Norman Rockwell ever painted. But it was a past that was, for the most part, imaginary, even for those who lived it and who, he joked, longed for an even *earlier* past. His rule of thumb, he said, speaking of his TV series ***Jean Shepherd's America***: "I want people twenty years from now to look at my show and feel as if it had been filmed that afternoon."

When fixated, he could drone on (a long-winded monologue on, say, gliding, one of his joys, drifts past the point of interest) or grow too frantic, revving himself up to an overblown climax. He knew how to create in listeners the feeling that he was headed *somewhere*, so he whipped himself into a frenzy to grab ears he might have lost otherwise; when he was all finished, you might wonder, Now what was *that* all about? Edward Grossman wrote a valentine to Shepherd in *Harper's* in 1966, but also noted: "Shepherd's fund of stories is not inexhaustible. He repeats himself and sometimes he serves up just plain cold turkey." Shepherd's amusing personality and persuasive delivery could mesmerize you even when the subject did not. He said, "I believe that the spoken word, the voice itself, is a far more expressive instrument than a typewriter. A typewriter, no matter who the person is behind it, is still a substitute for the human voice."

His radio show's merrily galloping theme song, "The Bahnfrei Overture," by Eduard Strauss, begins with a bugle fanfare calling horses to the gate. It was the perfect blast to bring him trotting out in a burst of excitement. Each show would end with his concluding words, often barely audible under the prancing theme, as you imagined him riding off into the gathering dusk—or into the night, when the show aired at eleven P.M. or one A.M. He was a seductive campfire storyteller, the perfect radio bedtime companion. To build bridges between segments, to augment the narrative, or just to amuse himself, he liked to twang his Jew's harp and hum or sing a favorite song ("Just a Gigolo," "The Sheik of Araby," "Margie," "Ragtime Cowboy Joe," "You Are My Sunshine," "Yellow Dog Blues," "After You've Gone").

There was a primal secret chuckle lurking behind every line, a kind of audible twinkle, and although he wove yarns about his hometown, he manned a postmodern cracker barrel. The bemused voice, whether chortling slyly or in full maniacal cry, was by turns self-mocking, seductive, manic, querulous, and reflective. For all those nostalgia trips back home to Indiana, however, his voice was tinged with quizzical suspicion. Shepherd might wax philosophical, or poetical, but never sentimental—especially when talking about "my old man," a favorite topic.

Shepherd called his "night people" "slobs" and "fat heads," regarded as terms of endearment by the invisible congregation who excused all his affectionate slurs. He was once fired from WOR for writing a piece in *MAD* that the station took to be an attack on advertisers and sheep-like consumers, entitled **"The Night People vs. Creeping Meatballism"** (the day people). He was quickly rehired when listeners threatened an uprising.

One such night person, Paul Krassner, the editor of *The Realist,* to which Shepherd contributed, recalled: "My idea of a hot date then was to find a girl who also liked Shepherd and lie in bed with her all night listening to him. It ruined my schooling. I'd wake up and he'd be talking about how to explain an amusement park to Venusians." Krassner remembers how, in a moment worthy of *Network,* Shepherd would ask listeners to turn their radios way down, and then, when he signaled, they were to turn the volume all the way up as he screamed some epithet like, "*You filthy pragmatists, I'm going to get you!*" He was convinced that the angry Howard Beale character in *Network* was based on him; yet the film's famous line, "*I'm mad as hell and I'm not going to take it anymore,*" lacks Shepherd's ironic tone. Much closer is the wry Murray Burns character in *A Thousand Clowns,* who also had a penchant for shouting at neighbors out the window and putting on the straight world while sidling through life making grim wisecracks.

Shepherd might slide into the evening's subject with a news item ("Listen to this one! Dateline Hong Kong . . .") and proceed to discuss, in a silly, tasteless Charlie Chan accent, the fact that the Chinese Communists had decreed what shall be the party's official sense of humor. Or he would refer to some phrase he had overheard, before constructing an elaborate sand-castle reverie. There were digressions, footnotes, parenthetical jokes, random observations, and stories within stories, augmented by an occasional sound effect or snatch of music.

Della Chiesa watched him do the show a few times. "He had notes, handwritten, how he would open and where he was gonna end, but there was no script whatsoever. He had the story framed in his mind and a sketchy outline to remind him where he was going—and he'd always end the story *exactly* on time, timed out to perfection. He didn't like anyone in the studio with him, and he didn't want anyone to talk or say anything when he was on the air."

Herb Squire, Shepherd's longtime engineer at WOR, recalled: "You had to pay attention. You learned very quickly it was a one-on-one situation. The engineer was the audience. You had to react and become very animated in your reactions to his material, because if he didn't get a response, it's like any performer—he would feel up the creek without a paddle. Most of the shows were live. No substitute hosts, no reruns. Jean's material was so far ahead of its time. It wasn't the normal radio for the fifties or sixties."

Every night, of course, was different ("I'm antiformat," said Shepherd) and sounded as if he'd decided what he might discuss in the elevator on his way up to the studio. Some nights he would stay on one theme; other nights he zigzagged from topic to topic, at the mercy of demon whims. He dipped at will into his bottomless memory vault of growing up, being in the service, toiling in the steel mills of Gary, Indiana, and working as a pin boy. It was one-third autobiographical, one-third embellished reality, and one-third total make-believe. He had the zeal of a great storyteller and an eye for detail that made everything ring true. And since it all sounded authentic, it really didn't matter what part was fiction. Many of his sagas would begin simply, *"I'm a kid, see . . ."*

The filmmaker Ben Thum remembers sitting transfixed in his car one cold winter night in the late fifties: "Shep was reminiscing about working in a bicycle factory in Hammond, and it was so fascinating that I barely noticed the chill inside my 1957 Ford Fairlane convertible with the broken heater. With maybe fifteen minutes left before sign-off, I chose to shiver in the car rather than enter the warm house, just so I would not miss a second of what had evolved into a highly compelling story."

Shepherd's tales first appeared in revised print form as the story collection **In God We Trust, All Others Pay Cash** (1966), the basis for the now classic 1983 holiday film *A Christmas Story,* narrated by Shepherd—about a kid named Ralphie who yearns for a Red Ryder BB air rifle for Christmas. The movie has achieved *It's a Wonderful Life* holiday cult status on television and later inspired TV's hit *The Wonder Years.* Subsequent story collections emerged, beginning with **Wanda Hickey's Night of Golden Memories, and Other Disasters** (1971), followed by **A Fistful of Fig Newtons** (1981) and **The Ferrari in the Bedroom** (1972), which a Boston TV cable station aired in a nonstop reading for twenty-four hours in 2000 in tribute to the recently departed Shepherd.

Wanda Hickey, a best-seller, plugged into more people than made up his broadcasting base. Wanda, says Shepherd, is the girl that every guy settles for, as opposed to his female fantasy, the cool patrician Diane Bigelow. "Wanda Hickey," he explained, *"is the girl who, at the age of fourteen, is already middle-age and mentally the mother of four kids—the one we all took to the prom. Diane Bigelow is the girl who is always seen from a distance with a guy who looks like John Lindsay."* His hero takes Wanda Hickey to what is "his first social—not sexual—situation" in a story full of richly observed details.

Harry Shearer, who hosts his own ruminative (weekly) program, *Le Show,* on National Public Radio, narrated NPR's tribute to Shepherd, saying: "Shepherd told supercilious easterners stories about the Midwest—not a romanticized Midwest of small-town life, but the Midwest that we never really knew existed—the Midwest of steel mills and tornadoes." As Shearer noted, "Shepherd's home base was not a free forum or even a public radio station; it was about as mainstream a talk station as you could get—friendly, chatty, celebrity-filled talk. Shepherd was the odd man out. That's probably why he appealed to generations of alienated teenagers. His stories evoked the pain and fear of childhood, not 'My favorite toy' or 'My favorite candy.'"

Shepherd's steel-mill days at Inland Steel evoked a Dantean vision of hell, full of roaring furnaces, open "soaking pits," and gruff, beetle-browed coworkers. As *Time*'s Ed Grant noted in 2000: "Despite the infectious exuberance and sharply honed sense of absurdity that always symbolized Shepherd's narration, there is a subtle undercurrent of sadness for the innocent past that can never be recaptured."

He recaptured its wispy memory on the air, but off the air he insisted that none of the stories were from his life, maybe to give them more literary status. Shep's childhood chums claim otherwise. He left Hammond at seventeen and never returned, and his bitterness toward the town increased when he heard that his version of the place wounded its citizens, though few there had ever heard his shows. "My work is not autobiographical. You draw upon all the things that you knew from that period, but more from that *place* than that period." Those who said that he wrote of what Terkel called "the aches and pains of growing up" made Shepherd wince. He claimed, rather, that he wrote of the "cosmic human comedy" and called himself a modern-day Candide.

Marshall McLuhan said that Shepherd had reinvented radio as "a new medium for a new kind of novel that he writes nightly. The mike is his pen and pencil." He compared him to Montaigne. Shepherd readily agreed: "What throws people about me is that they think of me as talking. They don't recognize the fact that what I'm doing is extraordinary. I have a very idiomatic style, which makes every guy who listens to me seriously believe that if he had a microphone that he could do what I do. If you're a writer, people recognize writing as something they can't do. Yet what I'm doing is oral writing. It's taken years for me to learn how to edit, to phrase, to give pause, beat, momentum, and to keep a theme running through the whole thing."

As with any print columnist, the word was Shepherd's oyster. He was as likely to discuss the flying magazines of the 1930s as to salute Jack Benny on his death. He was a nut on the poetry of Robert Service and Lawrence Ferlinghetti, and of Saxe Rohmer, the author of the Fu Manchu stories. Like any great monologuist/writer, he took you into his world, which was eccentric, egocentric, and idiosyncratic. The titles of his individual broadcasts (now available on tape via his Web site, www.flicklives.com) give a flavor of Shepherd's eclectic world: "Tennis Date with First Love," "Americans and Their Cars," "Rude Noises in Company K," "Midwestern Drugstores and Drive-Ins," "Why I'm Such a Sorehead," "The Smell of Homes," "Love at the USO," "Hamburger Binge," "First New Suit Out of the Army," "A&W Root Beer Stand," "Shoplifting," "First Shaves," "Junk in the Basement." When he struck a rich vein, like high school halftime shows, he strip-mined it.

As he explained, "I think that there is a whole area of the wild, swinging anthill that we're all a part of that goes almost completely unreported and unnoticed by the vast body of the press and literature. It's a kind of recording of the daily frustration and the momentary exaltation of the fact of living itself."

Little was beyond his interests—he was also a serious photographer, illustrated his own books, and collected antiques—and it is that wide-ranging unpredictability, curiosity, and passion that grabbed listeners for decades. Somebody called him a "comic anthropologist," sifting through the cultural remains for any jawbone or cracked urn from which he could reconstruct a nation's folkways—a Wimpy doll, a pack of Walnettos, an old vaudeville song.

He evoked the past with precision but never gilded it. Even the stories that sounded merely nostalgic were implanted with a life lesson—"and no lesson ever came cheap," noted Shearer. The stories were studded with epigrams, curbstone philosophy, wistful footnotes, and wisecracks. In one unforgettable Shepherd radio piece, he exhumed an ad in the back of a comic book, **"See Through X-Ray Eyes"**—"I had a lot of ideas of what I would like to see through. I had all *kinds* of plans." He sent away for the "X-ray eyes" for ten cents and got back a tiny tube that allowed him to see the bones in his hand by holding it up to a bright light. He quickly spies on a girl in the front row of his class but learns, to his dismay, "It does not look through flowered print dresses." Another classic Shepherd shaggy-dog story was of being duped by a commercial on *Little Orphan Annie* when he sent in his money for a decoder trinket, only to learn that the secret message was: "Buy Ovaltine."

He was equally a master at skewering trends and contemporary clichés, as in this profile of a Bennington College girl in 1956 that's as exacting as anything from Mort Sahl, Woody Allen, or Nichols & May: "*She thinks Harry Belafonte is* authentic. *Mabel Mercer is a great actress and does such wonderful things with Cole Porter. Anna Magnani is the only film actress our girl cares to discuss. However, she saw* Marty *twice because it was about* real *people.*"

Eugene B. Bergmann (essay date 2005)

SOURCE: Bergmann, Eugene B. "Foibles: The Real Jean Shepherd." In *Excelsior, You Fathead! The Art and Enigma of Jean Shepherd,* pp. 23-38. New York: Applause Theatre & Cinema Books, 2005.

[*In the following essay Bergmann discusses the persona Shepherd used, concluding that "it will never be fully possible to separate Shepherd's reality from his performance—or indeed, from his everyday talk."*]

> [*Spoken over the opening theme, in a mock-dramatic imitation of the 1950s The Shadow radio adventure.*] *Yes, the secret powers which I have been given by a visitor from another planet have enabled me to hold you hypnotically night after night, to cloud your reason, to befog—to continually becloud your mind so you don't know which end is up.*[1]
>
> [September 29, 1965]

According to Dan Beach, who knew Shepherd professionally and as a friend for decades, "Trying to make a point with Shep was useless; he entertained no ideas other than his own."[2] From this report and similar comments from others who knew him, it appears that Jean Shepherd, in his life as in his art, was a dedicated monologist. How fortunate for him and for his radio audience that his life in art found outlet in the one-way communication tool of a microphone. (In his live broadcast performances in the 1960s from the Limelight café, any unasked-for attempt at interaction from the audience was met with a harsh rebuke.) With his microphone, Shepherd shut off all but the input he chose to allow. With it, he controlled the expression of his inner life and the materials of his real and invented biography—his feelings, prejudices, beliefs, and his view of the world.

Jean was probably born some time in July, between 1921 and maybe 1926—the reality was private. According to his death certificate, he was born in Chicago on July 26, 1921.[3] He grew up on "the South Side of Chicago" and on Cleveland Street in Hammond, Indiana. Maybe as a kid, he had friends named Flick, Bruner, Schwartz, and so on.[4] Although he told hundreds of stories about his kidhood, the extent to which the tales were true to the "real" Jean Shepherd is difficult to discern. His adolescence is almost a blank record. He spent time in the Army Signal Corps during World War II, and a few semesters in college.

He got out of the small-town, small-minded, intellectually limited world of the midwestern mill town. He found (nearly) free rein in radio in smaller cities; jobs that eventually led to the big time—New York City—where he did a night-long radio program. He wrote articles and books, made records, did live performances, created several television series and movies, and acted in plays. He was an acknowledged master of the arcane art of *Kopfspielen*.

He lived in various locations in and around the New York City area and was married several times, once to an actress and, finally and most enduringly, to his producer. He was a man of the world—with a taste for exotic cars, fine food, travel, and friends in the arts.

He retired to a small island off the coast of Florida. On October 16, 1999, at 78, he died.[5] He kept his private life as private as he could. The *New York Times* obit referred to him as a raconteur and wit and quoted his closest friend of his final years as saying he had no survivors. His two children subsequently indicated that they were survivors.[6]

Jean Shepherd had a persona that listeners felt they knew very well indeed, but they were wrong: "The factual record shows that Shep . . ." "But his kid brother in later years said . . ." "People who knew him said that . . ." "Shep tells us on the radio that . . . and he also tells us that . . ." The real Jean Shepherd? Occasionally he took on (only for a few moments) the persona of one of his created characters, with appropriate voice, such as the effeminate Mr. Chucky, and the "little old lady" who frequently wrote in complaining about his broadcasts. When reading little strange-but-true news items, he became a self-important Walter Winchell-type character named Grubbage. Sometimes he just introduced himself with a fictitious name and then went on as himself:

> Grubbage here.
>
> I'm friendly Fred.
>
> This is Uncle Fred.
>
> This is Skeezix.
>
> This is Clark Smathers.
>
> This is Uncle Wiggly.
>
> My name is Harold Everyman.
>
> Harold Monolith here, rising like a single block of granite.
>
> Hello gang, this is King Kong here.
>
> This is old Ben Watanabee here, yowsa, yowsa, yowsa.
>
> This is Allie Khan, and we'll be back again immediately after 14,022 hours have passed. And we'll be back tomorrow at five minutes past nine for the insignificant hour. For those of you who love impedimenta and effluvia, stay tuned for—speaking of effluvia—for Ed Pedit who follows in just a moment. He speaks very fluent effluvia.

In a program titled **"Fake Shepherds,"** Shepherd read from a Rutgers University article about someone who impersonated him at a personal appearance:

> *I might as well tell you the truth about this thing. There is no Jean Shepherd. Jean Shepherd is a composite name. It's an entertainment concept, and there's actually a stable of Jean Shepherds. I am the fourth one. I work Mondays and Wednesdays and the other Shepherds work Tuesday. There's one who works—I never met the one who works on Thursdays. Tall skinny guy. And there are six Jean Shepherds that have been beating out there in the bushes and playing colleges.*
>
> *Now you see what I'm telling you? [Talking to someone in the control room.] I just tell you the truth—and do you buy it? No. Okay, that's all I can say. I mean, the truth hurts.[7]*
>
> [Date unknown]
>
> *I suppose a lot of you people are wondering why I'm talking like this. [Talking about people who do good, skillful jobs substituting for others.] Well, I'm not actually Jean Shepherd. I'm a guy who wrote him a letter. I told him I did a great Jean Shepherd imitation. And I've been doing the show for the last three nights. He's coming back tomorrow night. It's the first time I've been on radio. There's nothing to it.[8]*
>
> [February 3, 1975]

Jean Shepherd told the story of his life and mind on radio, in writing, television, and movies. Only part of it was true to fact—all of it was true to the artistic construct he wanted listeners to perceive as the persona "Jean Shepherd." There was a rock bed of verisimilitude consisting of incidents and events from his real life—he gave what could be simply and easily believed, always with a profuse richness of minute, idiosyncratic detail that drew listeners in and convinced them that his tales were nothing less than the truth. One always believed Shep. He told it so believably, so intimately, that he seemed to bare his life, soul, and beliefs to each of us alone. Shep was our best friend and confidant in the quarter-to-three AM openness and intimacy of a bar or a dorm.

His stories contained stuff we knew was true, or easily verified, that melded seamlessly into each increment toward the unlikely and unbelievable. We did not know where to draw the line. We did not know there was a place for a line. We did not know that a line had any need to be thought about. Worst of all—no, best of all—there was no identifiable borderland where a theoretical line might accurately have been drawn. A "line" was too rigid a metaphor for trying to separate the meat from the bread in Shepherd's *chef-d'oeuvre* meatloaf.

What about his "autobiography"? As Henry Miller once told a friend, "I had a thousand faces, all of them genuine."[9] In *Lying: A Metaphorical Memoir*, Lauren Slater wrote, "This is my tale, and I have written it over and over again, and, depending on my mood and my auras, the story always seems to change, and yet it always seems true."[10] Will the real Jean Shepherd please stand up? The true story of Jean Shepherd, creator, is not the chronology of his life, but consists of what he said in more or less spontaneous flight—a sound collage constructed across decades—which is to say, the life of his mind as artist. In *Design and Truth in Autobiography*, Roy Pascal says: "In the novel, everything is tightly bound, everything is closely related to the theme. Now this is true in part in autobiography. Henry James repeatedly speaks of everything in his life 'signifying,' bringing some accretion of understanding and insight, a continuous, almost imperceptible assimilation."[11]

Jean Shepherd's stories of his childhood always signified, but as "truth" they were especially suspect. How truthful were the details of his anecdotes and philosophical homilies? Did he make most of it up just to illustrate some life lesson—just to tell a story? Was *Field and Stream* really a great literary influence on him, as he once claimed? Or had he transformed and amplified some hint from his past into a parable to illustrate that any vicarious tale that takes one away from one's drab everyday life, providing much-needed fantasy, becomes indeed, an important part of dealing with one's world?

Shepherd told fables for our time. He was a weaver of tales and parables, ones that may or may not have been partly true to fact. Was his radio material more likely to be true than his written work? Were his earlier short anecdotes more likely to have been true than the later material, when maybe he'd used up so much of his biography that he *had* to make up more? Given that his observations and commentaries gave so many clues for ferreting out the bogus in all of life, it is indeed an irony that he manipulated the facts of his *own* artist's life. His real life was none of our business—our business, and his, was his *art*.

Although one might presume that he never articulated a belief he did not actually hold, one might take cognizance of some contradictions—maybe the belief he articulated at any one time more suited his current monologue; maybe he forgot what he had earlier believed; or, over time, maybe he changed his mind. One example is his comment from a broadcast that he did not much follow the funnies; at another time (a *Village Voice* article) he said that his moral outlook was significantly influenced by such funnies as *Little Orphan Annie*.

"I'll Never Forget . . ."

I'll never forget one time, I'm a kid about—oh, I must have been in about in the eighth grade. [Pause.] In fact, I know it was eighth grade because I remember the teacher who read this story to us.[12]

[December 30, 1965]

That "I'll never forget" was a favorite ploy of Shepherd's to convince us it's true, combined here with another technique for convincing us of the truth—he would often hesitate as though unsure of a detail, and then suddenly "remember"—thus in his narration confirming the detail for himself, and so very artfully confirming for us its veracity.

What was the nature of Jean Shepherd's memory? He conjured up a profusion of details into such a reality—he "remembered" so much—that listeners should logically ask how so much could happen to one person. Likely, much of the remembering was not of specific incidents, but of the ways life happens to all of us—the truly seeing and being able to report back perceptively and inventively, the being alive to experience—the "signifying" that Henry James spoke of and Ernest Hemingway worked so hard to put in his work.

When one speaks of the "truth" in Shepherd, one deals with at least three kinds of lies.[13] Type A was fictional art told as truth. Type B was Shep denying a truth or creating a lie to confound those who would confuse his art with his biography. These first two were the province of Jean Shepherd as artist. Type C was the bald-faced lie Shepherd told about himself for no apparent reason other than that it might better fit the image that he wanted to project, such as whether he graduated from college, when he was in the army, and whether he ever had children. This type-C bald-faced lie is the province of a psycho-biographer, who might discover to what extent type-C lies might become an inseparable component with types A and B. It's one of those conundrums that some biographers thrive on and give the rest of us migraines.

What was "truth," what was hyperbole, what was downright fabrication? Kid brother Randy—yes, he had a kid brother, Randy. Friend Flick—yes, there is a photo of Flick's Tap and a photo of Flick in Shepherd's high school yearbook. Hohman, Indiana—we know he lived in Hammond, not too far from Hohman Avenue. Yes, he really lived on Cleveland Street.[14] And what more perfect concoction for the ironic workings of his mind than his claim that his primary education had been at a school named for Warren G. Harding, someone regarded by historians as one of the more inconsequential of our presidents? As he put it in his 1985 talk to a ham radio convention, "We did not realize this, at the age of twelve—we were going to a school named after the worst president in history." Surely the name of this school was one more dry, fictional joke on the theme of the apparently powerful/actually ineffective—until one sees the photo of the sign in front of an otherwise undistinguished two-story building in Hammond: "Harding Elementary School." We have been confounded by fact.

He told it as though it were true. We believed it, yet in his book disclaimers, and in later years, he said it was all made up. Reports say that he hid many important facts of his life even from his wife. Did he dislike having people delve into his personal life? Was he just being ornery in denying the *truth*? Did he feel it was more of an art if it were all made up? Was it a mix that can only be evaluated as *creative*?

In a talk at Fairleigh Dickinson University in 1967, Shepherd said that "Flick, Schwartz, and Brunner were real people . . . there are three characters that run through—you see I work on the air as a short story writer—literally. I take people out of my past or I put them and use them as composite characters just as any good writer would. You don't write out of a vacuum. And Flick, Schwartz, and Brunner are real people. I used real names, but they're not really *exactly* like they are in the stories. I've taken other—naturally, I've taken other characteristics." This seems to be a straightforward and reasonable description of the creative process—one contradicted by Shepherd in other interviews, when he claimed that those same people never existed.

Barry Farber, who shared an office at WOR with Shepherd and became his friend, interviewed him on the air on June 26, 1975. Describing his stories as allegories, Shepherd said, "In America they think they're memories about boyhood and they never are. None of these stories, by the way, are based on any of my own memories. None of them are based on any—the families are all—I've created a mythical family—like—like Faulkner created a mythical county."

The story has it that when **In God We Trust: All Others Pay Cash,** Shepherd's strung-together compilation of seemingly true childhood stories,[15] appeared on the *New York Times* bestseller list, he called the *Times* and insisted that they switch it from the nonfiction to the fiction category. The listing in either category remains elusive, but the easy confusion between truth and fiction remains the issue.

Often, in the middle of some apparent hyperbole, Shepherd exclaimed, "This is the truth, I'm not exaggerating." Often his listeners had good reason to question the literal veracity of his word—especially within the context of fantastic or hard-to-believe details. At other times he knew nobody was going to believe the details—for instance, when he described his Warren G. Harding grammar school as being made out of balsa wood and silly putty. Ah, yes, what is "truth"? Did we settle that one in our freshman or sophomore year?

What can we know about someone who constantly, in public, invented his past and present life, who constantly told stories—fictions about his life? Shepherd's disclaimer in his 1972 book, **The Ferrari in the Bedroom,** possibly giving us the answer as forthrightly as he cared to at the time, says that "Large parts of the following are fiction; other parts based on fact. Still others are pure mythology. Some characters are real; others are figments of a harassed imagination. To the real, I apologize. To the others, the back of my hand."[16]

Shepherd was not the only monologist ever to sit at a table and talk about himself—and make a living at it. Others followed this public journey into self-absorption and analysis. For example, Spalding Gray, twenty years younger, sat before audiences performing his theater pieces. His performances, according to an obituary, were "closely observed autobiography, performed in a style that alternated between conspiratorial whispers and antic screams as he roamed through topics large and small."[17] An appreciation of him comments, "He was not above bending the sequences of events so that his life would, in the retelling, conform to the narrative structure he was building."[18] Spalding Gray's refashioning of his autobiography certainly bears resemblance to what Shepherd began doing on the radio several decades before. Both of them shared a pattern used by other artists in their own ways: refashioning of their autobiographies to suit artistic purposes.

The following reference in *The American Humorist: Conscience of the 20th Century,* by Norris W. Yates (1964), suggests a close-to-home precedent for Shepherd, someone who combined fact with large portions of fiction. It refers to Kin Hubbard of Brown County, Indiana (active 1904-1930). Every year from 1906 until 1930, Hubbard published volumes about a character he had created named Abe: "Hubbard's version of Brown County was actually a composite of the real Brown County, which lies in south central Indiana, and of Bellefontaine, Ohio. Certain names of buildings, such as Melodeon Hall, and many of the names of Abe's acquaintances, usually altered in part, were based on actual buildings and names in Bellefontaine."

Of course, this is common. Literature is filled with novels using parts of the author's real life more or less transformed into the fiction. Ernest Hemingway and Henry Miller are two prominent American examples.

Far less frequently encountered was Shepherd's mode of action—he fabricated a fiction with such illusions of verisimilitude that he convinced us of its autobiographical truth. Some autobiography! Like Escher's drawing of an artist's hand in the act of drawing itself.[19] He invented it. The Jean Shepherd persona became what he invented.

In the following, he explained why he told his stories as if they had all really happened to him.

> Never grab a guy's elbow and say, "Hey, boy did I hear a great joke—Hey, did you hear the joke about . . ." You've already lost him.[20]
>
> [January 14, 1971]

On Alan Colmes' 1998 call-in show more than twenty-five years later, Shepherd gave what was very likely his "final" interview, and probably told the truth about his fictions:

> I'm an actor, you know, and I want my stuff to sound *real*. And so when I tell a story, I tell it in the first person—so it sounds like—by the way, to tell a good story—in the first person—that it sounds like it actually happened to me. It didn't. It's a story I invented but I put it in the first person so it would sound like—you know—a narrative—the guy telling the story. And, when I did this stuff people took me literally. They thought these things happened to me.[21]
>
> [December 16, 1998, radio interview, WEVD]

Decades after his radio broadcast had ended, Shepherd, while apparently admitting his subterfuge, seems to be putting the onus on his listeners for believing it was true: "They thought these things happened to me." The real cause of the misunderstanding is the skill with which Shepherd had plied his art.

In *Understanding Media,* Marshall McLuhan writes:

> Jean Shepherd of WOR in New York regards radio as a new medium for a new kind of novel that he writes nightly. The mike is his pen and paper. His audience and their knowledge of the daily events of the world provide his characters, his scenes, and moods. It is his idea that, just as Montaigne was the first to use the page to record his reactions to the new world of printed books, he is the first to use radio as an essay and novel form for recording our common awareness of a totally new world of universal participation in all human events, private or collective.[22]
>
> *Hey, why do I enjoy doing this show so much? What's the matter with me? I can't figure it out. You know? You know, it bothers me sometimes because—you're supposed to, you know, you're supposed to look at your work as work. No, I'll tell you this is, uh—you know, the Protestant ethic—causes me a little problem at this point and—really. The other day this guy interviewed me. He says, "You must get very tired. Always thinking of new things or trying to do stuff every night on your show and all that."*
>
> *And I said, [Shep speaking in mock solemn voice] "Yes, that is true. I get extremely tired." And he said, "Uh—yes, it must drain everything out of you. I just don't know how you can continue to do this—you know, producing forty-five minutes of stuff every night. Most nightclub comics, they got twenty minutes of material which they work—you know—milk like a cow—around the country for years on end. You must really—it must be a terrible strain—it must be an awful lot of work." [Shep, mock solemn.] "Yes, yes, as a matter of fact." And of course there I am having trouble with the Protestant ethic, see—I have to pretend.*[23]
>
> [Undated excerpt from NPR tribute]

Although Shepherd felt he had to pretend to the interviewer, his listeners knew he enjoyed his broadcasts. He had such a laid-back conversational style, and it did seem so easy for him to just sit down at the mike and talk. However, in planning at least the outlines of his programs, Shepherd worked hard to create the illusion of ease. Shepherd the artist was a deceiver.

He told at least three versions of his father's frustrated attempts to undo a pair of apparently inextricably linked nails. The familiar Chinese nail puzzle. Once, he said his old man unbent them with pliers, in another version, his father flattened them out with a hammer, and still another time he sawed them apart. All *three* can't be true. Did his father have a set of nail puzzles, or two sets, or three—or none at all? If he had a set, did he unbend it, saw it, hammer it—does it matter? Shepherd's point was not how his old man "solved" the puzzle. Maybe it was another invented Shep-tale, dramatizing his attitude toward his old man while commenting on his inevitable failures. Using his old man, he applied a new metaphor: undoing Chinese nail puzzles as the American Everyman's false triumph over inevitable defeat in his ceaseless battle with reality.

As books sometimes make use of an ancient tale, updating it to give a sense of a universal human situation (such as James Joyce did by having Leopold Bloom recapitulate the adventures of Ulysses through an ordinary day in Dublin), Shepherd's old man three times unknowingly reenacted Alexander the Great's solution: Alexander did not untie the baffling Gordian knot, but sliced it with a sword. If Shepherd's listeners didn't get the historical metaphor, or didn't think Shep had the reference in mind, to make it clear, at the end of one broadcast featuring the nail puzzle story, he referred to Gordian knots. Shepherd used metaphor and he used memory:

> *But why I happen to be able to pull it out of my vast Kodachrome file—busted-up slides of memory, is because, one, it happens to be my profession. You know, my job, the work that I've chosen in life, is mostly, totally, introspection—and then transmitting it out. That's what an artist does, really. He pulls things out of his memory and his—and his perceptive nerve endings,*

and he tries to pour it into some form where he can tell the other people—"see what it is." It's what Norman Mailer does, it's what all people who attempt to interpret life do—whether they're doing it on the radio, or television, movies, newsreels, sculpture, or scratching it in the sand, or writing dirty words on the subway. They're all trying to say—it. Whatever it is. Nobody can quite grab ahold of it and say why they say it, but they do—and that's it. Squirrels do not write short stories. They do not. There has been no recorded instance of a bear sitting down, taking his felt tip pen in hand and starting out—"Call me Ishmael." Never. [Laughs.] Man yes, bears no. It's one of the great differences between man and beast.[24]

[September 21, 1969]

Yet, Jean Shepherd worked at *really* making it seem to be truth—his was not a one-time skit. It was a continuous, one-on-one con game (other than when he admitted the fiction in the almost never read disclaimers in the front of his books). And although he did not tell his tale in chronological fashion as in a straightforward autobiography, the most powerful case for the seeming verisimilitude of what Shepherd said was that to such a large extent he maintained a coherent story of his life and thoughts throughout his long career. What was considered his incredible memory was in large part an act of remembering details, feelings, and situations—close observation—and using them all in his fictional invention. Jean Shepherd had it both ways: he had us believing it was all true, so we were more personally involved in it—and he could make up whatever he wanted, because after all, it was all fiction. He combined invention with introspection into some kind of exquisite Gordian knot. In the *Realist* magazine interview of October 1960, Shepherd said:

I got a call here a couple of weeks ago from a doctor who is a well-known psychiatrist in town and is a lecturer at one of the universities here. And he said, "You know, I've been listening to you for three years, Shepherd, and it might be of some interest to you to know that I feel you're the most completely analyzed man I've ever met." Apparently, this is a great compliment from an analysis man.

And then I got to thinking about it, and I thought—well, you see, what I do on the show, I guess, makes people wonder about me—the psychological problems involved. I am always looking for my own motives within me, trying to *extend* those motives to find out why other things happen, why *other* people do things. Freud, for example, when he came up with his most important work in the late 19th century, it was by looking at himself—not other people, but himself—and *then* looking at other people.

I don't think it's pertinent to my work as to whether I've been analyzed or not, but I will say this in all truthfulness: that my work is probably as great a purgative as any analysis could ever be, and more, because you can really be truthful when you're talking into a faceless microphone instead of to a living individual, an analyst.

Most who are familiar with Shepherd's work admire his ability to remember. They think he remembered the details of what happened in all the stories he told. But what was truly extraordinary was his ability to remember so many bits and pieces from the past and present, which made his monologues seem real through their detail. Actual remembering was not a simple act with Jean Shepherd; it was a major tool of his creativity.

Do you ever have the feeling that half the stuff you remember just didn't exist at all? That you sort of made it up? [Here, more than in most cases, he is obviously talking to personnel in the control room.] Or in some nutty way? You mean you don't have that problem ever, Herb [Squire, his engineer]? You mean you—you really believe that everything you remember actually happened?[25]

[November 1971]

In the above excerpt, he seems to be musing aloud directly to people in the control room (knowing, of course, that his words are also going out over the air), rather than just stimulating the minds of anonymous listeners. It just might be that this idea was not quite a production of the Shepherd-constructed persona, but rather an oblique projection of a real Jean exploring the issue. Whatever the case, Shepherd here contemplates the truth and falsity of memory (and, by implication, his own "remembering" as a storytelling device). Maybe Shepherd was not always sure how much he was making up and was suggesting that to some extent we all create our memories. Certainly, it seemed for Shepherd that memory is a baffling mix of conscious and unconscious fabrication. Thus it will never be fully possible to separate Shepherd's reality from his performance—or indeed, from his everyday talk. As Shepherd's friend Bob Brown puts it, "He had the ability to weave things that really couldn't possibly be true—in conversation. He was a difficult guy to know where reality stopped and fiction began. What he saw—or whether he saw it literally or whether he saw it in his mind—became reality for everybody around him."

Just as Shepherd often told stories about himself and others on his show and in interviews as though they were factual, several times he used television to storytell rather than act as historian, the role that the situation would seem to have required. Two such projects stand out.

The first, a video history of the Chicago White Sox, which Shepherd narrates, consists of two rather distinct formats. He is onscreen from time to time describing his personal interests in baseball, and especially in the White Sox. During the documentary footage sections, he narrates what sounds like a script written to reflect the straightforward history of the team. When history reaches the first All-Star Game in the major leagues (at the White Sox's Comiskey Park), with Babe Ruth hitting the first home run in an All-Star Game, one sees the Babe hit it as Shepherd tells us that his father and Uncle Carl were at the game and his father just missed catching that ball, lunging, and then landing empty handed in a woman's lap.[26]

One imagines that most innocent viewers of the documentary think this really happened, but one should think again. Shepherd aficionados may recall the similarity to his radio story told in 1966, of his father booing Yankee pitcher Marius Russo from the upper deck in left field. Of course, in retaliation to the old man's raspberries, "Marius Russo hit a home run that almost decapitated the old man!" Shepherd continued, emphasizing the story's veracity, "So help me, I swear . . . but I am here as a witness to tell you that my old man lost a ballgame—against the New York Yankees." Another and better-known "true" story was that of the old man taunting that other Yankee great, Lou Gehrig, who responded by aiming a home run ball into the right field stands, just missing Shepherd's father. Reflecting on all these stories, some will recall the interview after Shepherd's radio days in which, asked to tell about his father and Lou Gehrig, he responded in a moment of truth, "Don't forget, I'm a storyteller, not a historian."[27] One wonders if, when producing the television documentary about the Chicago White Sox, Major League Baseball and the Sox organization were sufficiently aware of that.

The second project was the television show *Home for the Holidays: A History of Thanksgiving*. First aired on the History Channel in 1994, Shepherd appears for only a minute, right after a narrator discusses Norman Rockwell's *Freedom from Want* (the artist's famous 1943 *Saturday Evening Post* illustration depicting a family Thanksgiving dinner). Shepherd begins speaking: "As a kid I got a job selling the *Saturday Evening Post* [with the *Freedom from Want* picture in it]. And I remember one day—as clear as a bell . . ." In 1943 Shepherd was a twenty-two-year-old "kid" whose 24/7 job (according to official records[28]) was not selling magazines door to door but tapping out code in the Army Signal Corps.

So Shepherd consciously presented his fabrications as truth, while on the other hand he would complain that supposed historical records did not adequately convey life's little realities:

> . . . this show about George Washington. All these people wrote me [long letters] about how I could read a book—it says read this book and it'll tell you how Jefferson was, and I say booj-whaa, booj-whaa! I have never known—I have known many a person that has been written about in contemporary accounts. In fact, it's funny, I knew Malcolm X, and I might as well tell you that, I knew Malcolm X, but he does not come out, in any of the interviews or the paper accounts that I have read about him. He just isn't the way he is described. The way the newspapers describe him. That is, in person. When you're sitting down having a cup of coffee with Malcolm X.
>
> I've known other people who've been written up in newspapers, and they never are—and even in very serious books—in short, I don't believe the written account of the person can ever quite capture that person.
>
> I still wonder how George Washington really was—when he was putting his teeth in in the morning. You know—putting on his socks. He's got to go off to another hard day in the Revolution. He's sitting in his tent. Well, of course he has had hard days in the Revolution. He's sitting in his tent, you know. It's about the second or third year of the Revolution and he's sitting in his tent.
>
> They've been chased all over New Jersey, you know. And it looks like things are going from bad to worse, and now they're going even from worse to worser. And he's sitting in his tent, and he's pulling on his socks, and the wind is blowing in underneath the cot and he hears a couple of guys griping out there and another guy—fistfights breaking out there among the riflemen, and he puts his head in his hands and he just sort of rubs his temples for a minute, you know, before he puts his wig on, says, "Oh boy, what a can of peas we've opened up! What a can of peas! Oh jeez, oh man!" And these things are never brought out—not in the contemporary accounts of him.[29]
>
> [February 26, 1965]

The biography, whether of someone like Washington, or the autobiography—what in Shepherd and some others could be termed the "created self" and the "performing self"—is a tricky and subtle business of simulation.

> . . . the human urge to recreate the world, be it through the imaginative transactions of art . . . or the grinding gears of memory. This rage to simulate reality . . .[30]
>
> —Michiko Kakutani [*New York Times*]

Why did Jean Shepherd take for his subject his own life, feelings, and observations? Why did Shepherd simulate reality through embellishment and lies? Certainly part of the reason was his enormous ego. In addition, as his work was to be incessant talk, perhaps he had to have the broadest possible field to work in—the world outside plus his world within. It would be nice to put all Shepherd's stories and comments together in a seamless web. But the pieces inconveniently overlap at different angles. The same threads produce different webs (and, crucially, these inconsistencies—minor though they are—cannot be accounted for by the vicissitudes of memory). With Jean Shepherd, how can one tell the portraitist from the artistically constructed self-portrait? Were there times when Shepherd could not tell them apart? For his audience, they were almost always the same.

As his flow was in part extemporaneous, like a jazzy riff, it appeared that he was merely bringing forth facts out of his past and recent observations. In reality, Shepherd was creating his life—the art, with variations on a theme—in the act of performing it. In his 1971 book,

The Performing Self, Richard Poirier discusses how certain artists—especially writers—contemplate themselves in the act of creation. Their art is a performance—a "self-discovering, self-watching" act. Poirier quotes Norman Mailer's thoughts on Hemingway: "The first art work in an artist is the shaping of his own personality."[31] Many writers have worked a near-mythic transformation—among poets, Walt Whitman did it, as did Robert Frost, and James Dickey reveled in it, writing, "One finds that the mode, the manner in which a man lies, and what he lies about—these things and the *form* of his lies—are the main things to investigate in a poet's life and work."[32] The massive Dickey biography is subtitled *The World as a Lie.* Jean Shepherd was just such a creative liar and a performing self—primarily in the ephemeral art of radio.

Shepherd's creative lying is never more delightfully developed than in stories of his childhood. Although in his early days in front of a microphone Shepherd speaks less of these days than he would from the mid-1960s on, in many of his most captivating extended stories he portrayed himself as a kid on the South Side of Chicago and in the contiguous Hammond, Indiana. We are about to enter the wonderful world of childhood, full of the trappings of nostalgia. But it is a Jean Shepherd kidhood of shattered illusions and nearly shooting your eye out. A kidhood where the stink of steel mills and being hoodwinked by Little Orphan Annie are not at all the nostalgia one might expect.

Notes

1. September 29, 1965.
2. In a letter to E. Bergmann, September 27, 2001.
3. The death certificate accurately establishes Shepherd's birth date—many secondary sources, such as articles and interviews with him, give varied years, all of which contribute to the illusion that Shepherd often sought to give—that he was a number of years younger than the facts prove. Ronald Lande Smith, author of *The Stars of Stand-Up Comedy: A Biographical Encyclopedia* (New York: Garland Publishing, 1986) in the book's preface, comments on the unreliability of information from many of his informants. He says that they "were either wary of revealing biographical material or didn't give a damn about posterity." He goes on to say, "In fact, the ultimate source was often unreliable. Performers are notorious for changing birth dates, forgetting career details, and embellishing anecdotes." Writing that he did his best to ferret out the truth, in the article about Shepherd he gives the birth date as two years later than do official records, probably having taken Shepherd's word for it.
4. The uncertainty and confusion fostered by Shepherd regarding what was true and fictitious in his life stories are difficult to dispel. A number of those who appear in his stories are indeed based on real people (at least as far as their names). The details in the stories are far more likely to have been, at least in part, fabricated.
5. Death certificate, Lee County, Florida.
6. *New York Times* obituary, October 18, 1999, and petition by Shepherd's son and daughter in the probate division of the Circuit Court of Lee County, Florida, January 21, 2000.
7. Date unknown.
8. February 3, 1975.
9. From the dust jacket of the biography of Miller: Jay Martin, *Always Merry and Bright,* Santa Barbara: Capa Press, 1978.
10. New York: Random House, 2000.
11. Cambridge, MA: Harvard University Press, 1960, 175.
12. December 30, 1965.
13. Beyond the artistic trickery used to give the illusion of truth, there are other problems in determining accuracy regarding Shepherd. He often falsified his age and other personal and professional information in interviews. Despite his reputation for remembering, he also seemed to forget details of his past activities. There are also numerous reporting errors, such as a *New York Times* article of October 31, 1970, stating that Shepherd's theme song was "The Sheik of Araby." Though this was a favorite song of Shepherd's, his theme song (which sounded a lot like "The William Tell Overture"), played at the beginning and end of virtually every Shepherd program for twenty-one years, was the Eduard Strauss polka, "Bahn Frei."
14. Death certificate, Lee County, Florida.
15. New York: Doubleday, 1966.
16. New York: Dodd, Mead and Company, 1972.
17. Shaila K. Dewan and Jesse McKinley, *New York Times,* March 9, 2004.
18. Bruce Weber, *New York Times,* March 9, 2004.
19. See *Drawing Hands* lithograph, 1948, by M. C. Escher, reproduced in Bruno Ernst's *The Magic Mirror of M. C. Escher,* Ballantine Books, 1976, 26.
20. January 14, 1971.
21. December 16, 1998, radio interview, WEVD.
22. Cambridge, MA: MIT Press, 1964; Reprint edition, 1994, 303-304.

23. Undated excerpt from NPR tribute.
24. September 21, 1969.
25. November 1971.
26. *Chicago White Sox: A Visual History,* Sports Collectors Edition, 1987.
27. Interview with Anne Ligouri on WFAN, December 20, 1997.
28. Information releasable under the Freedom of Information Act; Shepherd's army record shows "Dates of Service: July 20, 1942, to December 16, 1944."
29. February 26, 1965.
30. *New York Times* book review, June 20, 2000.
31. New York: Oxford University Press, 1971.
32. Quoted in Henry Hart, *James Dickey: The World as a Lie,* New York: Picador USA, 2000, xii.

FURTHER READING

Criticism

Cooper, Arthur. Review of *Wanda Hickey's Night of Golden Memories and Other Disasters. Saturday Review* 54, no. 46 (13 November 1971): 68-9.

    Responds favorably to Shepherd's brand of humor.

Grossman, Edward. Review of *The Ferrari in the Bedroom. Commentary* 56, no. 6 (December 1973): 84-8.

    Contends that the stories in *The Ferrari in the Bedroom* are "not so much satirical or funny as embittered."

Martin, James. "'Of Many Things.'" *America* (6 November 1999): 2.

    Recalls reading Shepherd's stories as a child, especially the collection *Wanda Hickey's Night of Golden Memories.*

McLuhan, Marshall. "Radio: The Tribal Drum." In *Understanding Media: The Extensions of Man,* pp. 297-307. New York: McGraw-Hill Book Company, 1964.

    Notes Shepherd's innovative use of the medium of radio, claiming that he is "the first to use radio as an essay and novel form for recording our common awareness of a totally new world of universal human participation in all human events, private or collective."

Pinkwater, Daniel. "Voice in the Dark." *New York Times Magazine* (2 January 2000): 21.

    Refers to Shepherd as "the inventor of free-form radio" and asserts that he "was an artist and an innovator, and one of the tiny handful of radio geniuses ever to exist."

Whalen, John M. "Jean Shepherd, Looking Life in the Eye and Laughing." *Washington Post* (21 October 1999): C1-C2.

    Offers an appreciation of Shepherd, saying that he "told about life the way it really is. Not the way it is portrayed in movies or advertising or in most fiction."

Additional coverage of Shepherd's life and career is contained in the following sources published by Thomson Gale: *Authors in the News,* Vol. 2; *Contemporary Authors,* Vols. 77-80, 187; and *Literature Resource Center.*

How to Use This Index

The main references

> **Calvino, Italo**
> 1923-1985 .... CLC 5, 8, 11, 22, 33, 39, 73; SSC 3, 48

list all author entries in the following Thomson Gale Literary Criticism series:

AAL = Asian American Literature
BG = The Beat Generation: A Gale Critical Companion
BLC = Black Literature Criticism
BLCS = Black Literature Criticism Supplement
CLC = Contemporary Literary Criticism
CLR = Children's Literature Review
CMLC = Classical and Medieval Literature Criticism
DC = Drama Criticism
FL = Feminism in Literature: A Gale Critical Companion
GL = Gothic Literature: A Gale Critical Companion
HLC = Hispanic Literature Criticism
HLCS = Hispanic Literature Criticism Supplement
HR = Harlem Renaissance: A Gale Critical Companion
LC = Literature Criticism from 1400 to 1800
NCLC = Nineteenth-Century Literature Criticism
NNAL = Native North American Literature
PC = Poetry Criticism
SSC = Short Story Criticism
TCLC = Twentieth-Century Literary Criticism
WLC = World Literature Criticism, 1500 to the Present
WLCS = World Literature Criticism Supplement

The cross-references

> See also CA 85-88, 116; CANR 23, 61;
> DAM NOV; DLB 196; EW 13; MTCW 1, 2;
> RGSF 2; RGWL 2; SFW 4; SSFS 12

list all author entries in the following Thomson Gale biographical and literary sources:

AAYA = Authors & Artists for Young Adults
AFAW = African American Writers
AFW = African Writers
AITN = Authors in the News
AMW = American Writers
AMWR = American Writers Retrospective Supplement
AMWS = American Writers Supplement
ANW = American Nature Writers
AW = Ancient Writers
BEST = Bestsellers
BPFB = Beacham's Encyclopedia of Popular Fiction: Biography and Resources
BRW = British Writers
BRWS = British Writers Supplement
BW = Black Writers
BYA = Beacham's Guide to Literature for Young Adults
CA = Contemporary Authors
CAAS = Contemporary Authors Autobiography Series
CABS = Contemporary Authors Bibliographical Series
CAD = Contemporary American Dramatists
CANR = Contemporary Authors New Revision Series
CAP = Contemporary Authors Permanent Series
CBD = Contemporary British Dramatists
CCA = Contemporary Canadian Authors
CD = Contemporary Dramatists
CDALB = Concise Dictionary of American Literary Biography

CDALBS = *Concise Dictionary of American Literary Biography Supplement*
CDBLB = *Concise Dictionary of British Literary Biography*
CMW = *St. James Guide to Crime & Mystery Writers*
CN = *Contemporary Novelists*
CP = *Contemporary Poets*
CPW = *Contemporary Popular Writers*
CSW = *Contemporary Southern Writers*
CWD = *Contemporary Women Dramatists*
CWP = *Contemporary Women Poets*
CWRI = *St. James Guide to Children's Writers*
CWW = *Contemporary World Writers*
DA = *DISCovering Authors*
DA3 = *DISCovering Authors 3.0*
DAB = *DISCovering Authors: British Edition*
DAC = *DISCovering Authors: Canadian Edition*
DAM = *DISCovering Authors: Modules*
   DRAM: *Dramatists Module;* ***MST:*** *Most-studied Authors Module;*
   MULT: *Multicultural Authors Module;* ***NOV:*** *Novelists Module;*
   POET: *Poets Module;* ***POP:*** *Popular Fiction and Genre Authors Module*
DFS = *Drama for Students*
DLB = *Dictionary of Literary Biography*
DLBD = *Dictionary of Literary Biography Documentary Series*
DLBY = *Dictionary of Literary Biography Yearbook*
DNFS = *Literature of Developing Nations for Students*
EFS = *Epics for Students*
EXPN = *Exploring Novels*
EXPP = *Exploring Poetry*
EXPS = *Exploring Short Stories*
EW = *European Writers*
FANT = *St. James Guide to Fantasy Writers*
FW = *Feminist Writers*
GFL = *Guide to French Literature,* Beginnings to 1789, 1798 to the Present
GLL = *Gay and Lesbian Literature*
HGG = *St. James Guide to Horror, Ghost & Gothic Writers*
HW = *Hispanic Writers*
IDFW = *International Dictionary of Films and Filmmakers: Writers and Production Artists*
IDTP = *International Dictionary of Theatre: Playwrights*
LAIT = *Literature and Its Times*
LAW = *Latin American Writers*
JRDA = *Junior DISCovering Authors*
MAICYA = *Major Authors and Illustrators for Children and Young Adults*
MAICYAS = *Major Authors and Illustrators for Children and Young Adults Supplement*
MAWW = *Modern American Women Writers*
MJW = *Modern Japanese Writers*
MTCW = *Major 20th-Century Writers*
NCFS = *Nonfiction Classics for Students*
NFS = *Novels for Students*
PAB = *Poets: American and British*
PFS = *Poetry for Students*
RGAL = *Reference Guide to American Literature*
RGEL = *Reference Guide to English Literature*
RGSF = *Reference Guide to Short Fiction*
RGWL = *Reference Guide to World Literature*
RHW = *Twentieth-Century Romance and Historical Writers*
SAAS = *Something about the Author Autobiography Series*
SATA = *Something about the Author*
SFW = *St. James Guide to Science Fiction Writers*
SSFS = *Short Stories for Students*
TCWW = *Twentieth-Century Western Writers*
WLIT = *World Literature and Its Times*
WP = *World Poets*
YABC = *Yesterday's Authors of Books for Children*
YAW = *St. James Guide to Young Adult Writers*

Literary Criticism Series Cumulative Author Index

20/1631
See Upward, Allen

A/C Cross
See Lawrence, T(homas) E(dward)

A. M.
See Megged, Aharon

Abasiyanik, Sait Faik 1906-1954
See Sait Faik
See also CA 123; 231

Abbey, Edward 1927-1989 .... **CLC 36, 59; TCLC 160**
See also AMWS 13; ANW; CA 45-48; 128; CANR 2, 41, 131; DA3; DLB 256, 275; LATS 1:2; MTCW 2; MTFW 2005; TCWW 1, 2

Abbott, Edwin A. 1838-1926 .... **TCLC 139**
See also DLB 178

Abbott, Lee K(ittredge) 1947- .... **CLC 48**
See also CA 124; CANR 51, 101; DLB 130

Abe, Kobo 1924-1993 ...... **CLC 8, 22, 53, 81; SSC 61; TCLC 131**
See also CA 65-68; 140; CANR 24, 60; DAM NOV; DFS 14; DLB 182; EWL 3; MJW; MTCW 1, 2; MTFW 2005; NFS 22; RGWL 3; SFW 4

Abe Kobo
See Abe, Kobo

Abelard, Peter c. 1079-c. 1142 ..... **CMLC 11, 77**
See also DLB 115, 208

Abell, Kjeld 1901-1961 .... **CLC 15**
See also CA 191; 111; DLB 214; EWL 3

Abercrombie, Lascelles 1881-1938 .... **TCLC 141**
See also CA 112; DLB 19; RGEL 2

Abish, Walter 1931- .... **CLC 22; SSC 44**
See also CA 101; CANR 37, 114; CN 3, 4, 5, 6; DLB 130, 227; MAL 5

Abrahams, Peter (Henry) 1919- .... **CLC 4**
See also AFW; BW 1; CA 57-60; CANR 26, 125; CDWLB 3; CN 1, 2, 3, 4, 5, 6; DLB 117, 225; EWL 3; MTCW 1, 2; RGEL 2; WLIT 2

Abrams, M(eyer) H(oward) 1912- ... **CLC 24**
See also CA 57-60; CANR 13, 33; DLB 67

Abse, Dannie 1923- .... **CLC 7, 29; PC 41**
See also CA 53-56; CAAS 1; CANR 4, 46, 74, 124; CBD; CN 1, 2, 3; CP 1, 2, 3, 4, 5, 6, 7; DAB; DAM POET; DLB 27, 245; MTCW 2

Abutsu 1222(?)-1283 .... **CMLC 46**
See Abutsu-ni

Abutsu-ni
See Abutsu
See also DLB 203

Achebe, (Albert) Chinua(lumogu) 1930- ..... **BLC 1; CLC 1, 3, 5, 7, 11, 26, 51, 75, 127, 152; WLC**
See also AAYA 15; AFW; BPFB 1; BRWC 2; BW 2, 3; CA 1-4R; CANR 6, 26, 47, 124; CDWLB 3; CLR 20; CN 1, 2, 3, 4, 5, 6, 7; CP 2, 3, 4, 5, 6, 7; CWRI 5; DA; DA3; DAB; DAC; DAM MST, MULT, NOV; DLB 117; DNFS 1; EWL 3; EXPN; EXPS; LAIT 2; LATS 1:2; MAICYA 1, 2; MTCW 1, 2; MTFW 2005; NFS 2; RGEL 2; RGSF 2; SATA 38, 40; SATA-Brief 38; SSFS 3, 13; TWA; WLIT 2; WWE 1

Acker, Kathy 1948-1997 .... **CLC 45, 111**
See also AMWS 12; CA 117; 122; 162; CANR 55; CN 5, 6; MAL 5

Ackroyd, Peter 1949- .... **CLC 34, 52, 140**
See also BRWS 6; CA 123; 127; CANR 51, 74, 99, 132; CN 4, 5, 6, 7; DLB 155, 231; HGG; INT CA-127; MTCW 2; MTFW 2005; RHW; SATA 153; SUFW 2

Acorn, Milton 1923-1986 .... **CLC 15**
See also CA 103; CCA 1; CP 1, 2, 3, 4; DAC; DLB 53; INT CA-103

Adam de la Halle c. 1250-c. 1285 .... **CMLC 80**

Adamov, Arthur 1908-1970 .... **CLC 4, 25**
See also CA 17-18; 25-28R; CAP 2; DAM DRAM; DLB 321; EWL 3; GFL 1789 to the Present; MTCW 1; RGWL 2, 3

Adams, Alice (Boyd) 1926-1999 .. **CLC 6, 13, 46; SSC 24**
See also CA 81-84; 179; CANR 26, 53, 75, 88, 136; CN 4, 5, 6; CSW; DLB 234; DLBY 1986; INT CANR-26; MTCW 1, 2; MTFW 2005; SSFS 14, 21

Adams, Andy 1859-1935 .... **TCLC 56**
See also TCWW 1, 2; YABC 1

Adams, (Henry) Brooks 1848-1927 .... **TCLC 80**
See also CA 123; 193; DLB 47

Adams, Douglas (Noel) 1952-2001 .. **CLC 27, 60**
See also AAYA 4, 33; BEST 89:3; BYA 14; CA 106; 197; CANR 34, 64, 124; CPW; DA3; DAM POP; DLB 261; DLBY 1983; JRDA; MTCW 2; MTFW 2005; NFS 7; SATA 116; SATA-Obit 128; SFW 4

Adams, Francis 1862-1893 .... **NCLC 33**

Adams, Henry (Brooks) 1838-1918 .... **TCLC 4, 52**
See also AMW; CA 104; 133; CANR 77; DA; DAB; DAC; DAM MST; DLB 12, 47, 189, 284; EWL 3; MAL 5; MTCW 2; NCFS 1; RGAL 4; TUS

Adams, John 1735-1826 .... **NCLC 106**
See also DLB 31, 183

Adams, Richard (George) 1920- ... **CLC 4, 5, 18**
See also AAYA 16; AITN 1, 2; BPFB 1; BYA 5; CA 49-52; CANR 3, 35, 128; CLR 20; CN 4, 5, 6, 7; DAM NOV; DLB 261; FANT; JRDA; LAIT 5; MAICYA 1, 2; MTCW 1, 2; NFS 11; SATA 7, 69; YAW

Adamson, Joy(-Friederike Victoria) 1910-1980 .... **CLC 17**
See also CA 69-72; 93-96; CANR 22; MTCW 1; SATA 11; SATA-Obit 22

Adcock, Fleur 1934- .... **CLC 41**
See also CA 25-28R, 182; CAAE 182; CAAS 23; CANR 11, 34, 69, 101; CP 1, 2, 3, 4, 5, 6, 7; CWP; DLB 40; FW; WWE 1

Addams, Charles (Samuel) 1912-1988 .... **CLC 30**
See also CA 61-64; 126; CANR 12, 79

Addams, (Laura) Jane 1860-1935 . **TCLC 76**
See also AMWS 1; CA 194; DLB 303; FW

Addison, Joseph 1672-1719 .... **LC 18**
See also BRW 3; CDBLB 1660-1789; DLB 101; RGEL 2; WLIT 3

Adler, Alfred (F.) 1870-1937 .... **TCLC 61**
See also CA 119; 159

Adler, C(arole) S(chwerdtfeger) 1932- .... **CLC 35**
See also AAYA 4, 41; CA 89-92; CANR 19, 40, 101; CLR 78; JRDA; MAICYA 1, 2; SAAS 15; SATA 26, 63, 102, 126; YAW

Adler, Renata 1938- .... **CLC 8, 31**
See also CA 49-52; CANR 95; CN 4, 5, 6; MTCW 1

Adorno, Theodor W(iesengrund) 1903-1969 .... **TCLC 111**
See also CA 89-92; 25-28R; CANR 89; DLB 242; EWL 3

Ady, Endre 1877-1919 .... **TCLC 11**
See also CA 107; CDWLB 4; DLB 215; EW 9; EWL 3

A.E. .... **TCLC 3, 10**
See Russell, George William
See also DLB 19

Aelfric c. 955-c. 1010 .... **CMLC 46**
See also DLB 146

Aeschines c. 390B.C.-c. 320B.C. ..... **CMLC 47**
See also DLB 176

Aeschylus 525(?)B.C.-456(?)B.C. .. **CMLC 11, 51; DC 8; WLCS**
See also AW 1; CDWLB 1; DA; DAB; DAC; DAM DRAM, MST; DFS 5, 10; DLB 176; LMFS 1; RGWL 2, 3; TWA

Aesop 620(?)B.C.-560(?)B.C. .... **CMLC 24**
See also CLR 14; MAICYA 1, 2; SATA 64

Affable Hawk
See MacCarthy, Sir (Charles Otto) Desmond

Africa, Ben
See Bosman, Herman Charles
Afton, Effie
See Harper, Frances Ellen Watkins
Agapida, Fray Antonio
See Irving, Washington
Agee, James (Rufus) 1909-1955 ...... **TCLC 1, 19**
See also AAYA 44; AITN 1; AMW; CA 108; 148; CANR 131; CDALB 1941-1968; DAM NOV; DLB 2, 26, 152; DLBY 1989; EWL 3; LAIT 3; LATS 1:2; MAL 5; MTCW 2; MTFW 2005; NFS 22; RGAL 4; TUS
Aghill, Gordon
See Silverberg, Robert
Agnon, S(hmuel) Y(osef Halevi) 1888-1970 .... **CLC 4, 8, 14; SSC 30; TCLC 151**
See also CA 17-18; 25-28R; CANR 60, 102; CAP 2; EWL 3; MTCW 1, 2; RGSF 2; RGWL 2, 3; WLIT 6
Agrippa von Nettesheim, Henry Cornelius 1486-1535 .... **LC 27**
Aguilera Malta, Demetrio 1909-1981 .... **HLCS 1**
See also CA 111; 124; CANR 87; DAM MULT, NOV; DLB 145; EWL 3; HW 1; RGWL 3
Agustini, Delmira 1886-1914 .... **HLCS 1**
See also CA 166; DLB 290; HW 1, 2; LAW
Aherne, Owen
See Cassill, R(onald) V(erlin)
Ai 1947- .... **CLC 4, 14, 69**
See also CA 85-88; CAAS 13; CANR 70; DLB 120; PFS 16
Aickman, Robert (Fordyce) 1914-1981 .... **CLC 57**
See also CA 5-8R; CANR 3, 72, 100; DLB 261; HGG; SUFW 1, 2
Aidoo, (Christina) Ama Ata 1942- .... **BLCS; CLC 177**
See also AFW; BW 1; CA 101; CANR 62, 144; CD 5, 6; CDWLB 3; CN 6, 7; CWD; CWP; DLB 117; DNFS 1, 2; EWL 3; FW; WLIT 2
Aiken, Conrad (Potter) 1889-1973 .... **CLC 1, 3, 5, 10, 52; PC 26; SSC 9**
See also AMW; CA 5-8R; 45-48; CANR 4, 60; CDALB 1929-1941; CN 1; CP 1; DAM NOV, POET; DLB 9, 45, 102; EWL 3; EXPS; HGG; MAL 5; MTCW 1, 2; MTFW 2005; RGAL 4; RGSF 2; SATA 3, 30; SSFS 8; TUS
Aiken, Joan (Delano) 1924-2004 ...... **CLC 35**
See also AAYA 1, 25; CA 9-12R; 182; 223; CAAE 182; CANR 4, 23, 34, 64, 121; CLR 1, 19, 90; DLB 161; FANT; HGG; JRDA; MAICYA 1, 2; MTCW 1; RHW; SAAS 1; SATA 2, 30, 73; SATA-Essay 109; SATA-Obit 152; SUFW 1; WYA; YAW
Ainsworth, William Harrison 1805-1882 .... **NCLC 13**
See also DLB 21; HGG; RGEL 2; SATA 24; SUFW 1
Aitmatov, Chingiz (Torekulovich) 1928- .... **CLC 71**
See Aytmatov, Chingiz
See also CA 103; CANR 38; CWW 2; DLB 302; MTCW 1; RGSF 2; SATA 56
Akers, Floyd
See Baum, L(yman) Frank
Akhmadulina, Bella Akhatovna 1937- .... **CLC 53; PC 43**
See also CA 65-68; CWP; CWW 2; DAM POET; EWL 3

Akhmatova, Anna 1888-1966 ..... **CLC 11, 25, 64, 126; PC 2, 55**
See also CA 19-20; 25-28R; CANR 35; CAP 1; DA3; DAM POET; DLB 295; EW 10; EWL 3; FL 1:5; MTCW 1, 2; PFS 18; RGWL 2, 3
Aksakov, Sergei Timofeyvich 1791-1859 .... **NCLC 2**
See also DLB 198
Aksenov, Vasilii (Pavlovich)
See Aksyonov, Vassily (Pavlovich)
See also CWW 2
Aksenov, Vassily
See Aksyonov, Vassily (Pavlovich)
Akst, Daniel 1956- .... **CLC 109**
See also CA 161; CANR 110
Aksyonov, Vassily (Pavlovich) 1932- .... **CLC 22, 37, 101**
See Aksenov, Vasilii (Pavlovich)
See also CA 53-56; CANR 12, 48, 77; DLB 302; EWL 3
Akutagawa Ryunosuke 1892-1927 ... **SSC 44; TCLC 16**
See also CA 117; 154; DLB 180; EWL 3; MJW; RGSF 2; RGWL 2, 3
Alabaster, William 1568-1640 .... **LC 90**
See also DLB 132; RGEL 2
Alain 1868-1951 .... **TCLC 41**
See also CA 163; EWL 3; GFL 1789 to the Present
Alain de Lille c. 1116-c. 1203 .... **CMLC 53**
See also DLB 208
Alain-Fournier .... **TCLC 6**
See Fournier, Henri-Alban
See also DLB 65; EWL 3; GFL 1789 to the Present; RGWL 2, 3
Al-Amin, Jamil Abdullah 1943- .... **BLC 1**
See also BW 1, 3; CA 112; 125; CANR 82; DAM MULT
Alanus de Insluis
See Alain de Lille
Alarcon, Pedro Antonio de 1833-1891 .... **NCLC 1; SSC 64**
Alas (y Urena), Leopoldo (Enrique Garcia) 1852-1901 .... **TCLC 29**
See also CA 113; 131; HW 1; RGSF 2
Albee, Edward (Franklin) (III) 1928- .. **CLC 1, 2, 3, 5, 9, 11, 13, 25, 53, 86, 113; DC 11; WLC**
See also AAYA 51; AITN 1; AMW; CA 5-8R; CABS 3; CAD; CANR 8, 54, 74, 124; CD 5, 6; CDALB 1941-1968; DA; DA3; DAB; DAC; DAM DRAM, MST; DFS 2, 3, 8, 10, 13, 14; DLB 7, 266; EWL 3; INT CANR-8; LAIT 4; LMFS 2; MAL 5; MTCW 1, 2; MTFW 2005; RGAL 4; TUS
Alberti (Merello), Rafael
See Alberti, Rafael
See also CWW 2
Alberti, Rafael 1902-1999 .... **CLC 7**
See Alberti (Merello), Rafael
See also CA 85-88; 185; CANR 81; DLB 108; EWL 3; HW 2; RGWL 2, 3
Albert the Great 1193(?)-1280 ...... **CMLC 16**
See also DLB 115
Alcaeus c. 620B.C.- .... **CMLC 65**
See also DLB 176
Alcala-Galiano, Juan Valera y
See Valera y Alcala-Galiano, Juan
Alcayaga, Lucila Godoy
See Godoy Alcayaga, Lucila
Alciato, Andrea 1492-1550 .... **LC 116**
Alcott, Amos Bronson 1799-1888 ... **NCLC 1, 167**
See also DLB 1, 223

Alcott, Louisa May 1832-1888 . **NCLC 6, 58, 83; SSC 27; WLC**
See also AAYA 20; AMWS 1; BPFB 1; BYA 2; CDALB 1865-1917; CLR 1, 38; DA; DA3; DAB; DAC; DAM MST, NOV; DLB 1, 42, 79, 223, 239, 242; DLBD 14; FL 1:2; FW; JRDA; LAIT 2; MAICYA 1, 2; NFS 12; RGAL 4; SATA 100; TUS; WCH; WYA; YABC 1; YAW
Alcuin c. 730-804 .... **CMLC 69**
See also DLB 148
Aldanov, M. A.
See Aldanov, Mark (Alexandrovich)
Aldanov, Mark (Alexandrovich) 1886-1957 .... **TCLC 23**
See also CA 118; 181; DLB 317
Aldington, Richard 1892-1962 .... **CLC 49**
See also CA 85-88; CANR 45; DLB 20, 36, 100, 149; LMFS 2; RGEL 2
Aldiss, Brian W(ilson) 1925- . **CLC 5, 14, 40; SSC 36**
See also AAYA 42; CA 5-8R, 190; CAAE 190; CAAS 2; CANR 5, 28, 64, 121; CN 1, 2, 3, 4, 5, 6, 7; DAM NOV; DLB 14, 261, 271; MTCW 1, 2; MTFW 2005; SATA 34; SCFW 1, 2; SFW 4
Aldrich, Bess Streeter 1881-1954 .... **TCLC 125**
See also CLR 70; TCWW 2
Alegria, Claribel
See Alegria, Claribel (Joy)
See also CWW 2; DLB 145, 283
Alegria, Claribel (Joy) 1924- .... **CLC 75; HLCS 1; PC 26**
See Alegria, Claribel
See also CA 131; CAAS 15; CANR 66, 94, 134; DAM MULT; EWL 3; HW 1; MTCW 2; MTFW 2005; PFS 21
Alegria, Fernando 1918- .... **CLC 57**
See also CA 9-12R; CANR 5, 32, 72; EWL 3; HW 1, 2
Aleichem, Sholom .... **SSC 33; TCLC 1, 35**
See Rabinovitch, Sholem
See also TWA
Aleixandre, Vicente 1898-1984 .... **HLCS 1; TCLC 113**
See also CANR 81; DLB 108; EWL 3; HW 2; MTCW 1, 2; RGWL 2, 3
Aleman, Mateo 1547-1615(?) .... **LC 81**
Alencar, Jose de 1829-1877 .... **NCLC 157**
See also DLB 307; LAW; WLIT 1
Alencon, Marguerite d'
See de Navarre, Marguerite
Alepoudelis, Odysseus
See Elytis, Odysseus
See also CWW 2
Aleshkovsky, Joseph 1929-
See Aleshkovsky, Yuz
See also CA 121; 128
Aleshkovsky, Yuz .... **CLC 44**
See Aleshkovsky, Joseph
See also DLB 317
Alexander, Lloyd (Chudley) 1924- ... **CLC 35**
See also AAYA 1, 27; BPFB 1; BYA 5, 6, 7, 9, 10, 11; CA 1-4R; CANR 1, 24, 38, 55, 113; CLR 1, 5, 48; CWRI 5; DLB 52; FANT; JRDA; MAICYA 1, 2; MAICYAS 1; MTCW 1; SAAS 19; SATA 3, 49, 81, 129, 135; SUFW; TUS; WYA; YAW
Alexander, Meena 1951- .... **CLC 121**
See also CA 115; CANR 38, 70, 146; CP 7; CWP; FW
Alexander, Samuel 1859-1938 .... **TCLC 77**
Alexeyev, Constantin (Sergeivich)
See Stanislavsky, Konstantin (Sergeivich)

Alexie, Sherman (Joseph, Jr.)
1966- .... **CLC 96, 154; NNAL; PC 53**
See also AAYA 28; BYA 15; CA 138; CANR 65, 95, 133; CN 7; DA3; DAM MULT; DLB 175, 206, 278; LATS 1:2; MTCW 2; MTFW 2005; NFS 17; SSFS 18

al-Farabi 870(?)-950 .... **CMLC 58**
See also DLB 115

Alfau, Felipe 1902-1999 .... **CLC 66**
See also CA 137

Alfieri, Vittorio 1749-1803 .... **NCLC 101**
See also EW 4; RGWL 2, 3; WLIT 7

Alfonso X 1221-1284 .... **CMLC 78**

Alfred, Jean Gaston
See Ponge, Francis

Alger, Horatio, Jr. 1832-1899 .... **NCLC 8, 83**
See also CLR 87; DLB 42; LAIT 2; RGAL 4; SATA 16; TUS

Al-Ghazali, Muhammad ibn Muhammad
1058-1111 .... **CMLC 50**
See also DLB 115

Algren, Nelson 1909-1981 ..... **CLC 4, 10, 33; SSC 33**
See also AMWS 9; BPFB 1; CA 13-16R; 103; CANR 20, 61; CDALB 1941-1968; CN 1, 2; DLB 9; DLBY 1981, 1982, 2000; EWL 3; MAL 5; MTCW 1, 2; MTFW 2005; RGAL 4; RGSF 2

al-Hariri, al-Qasim ibn 'Ali Abu Muhammad al-Basri
1054-1122 .... **CMLC 63**
See also RGWL 3

Ali, Ahmed 1908-1998 .... **CLC 69**
See also CA 25-28R; CANR 15, 34; CN 1, 2, 3, 4, 5; EWL 3

Ali, Tariq 1943- .... **CLC 173**
See also CA 25-28R; CANR 10, 99

Alighieri, Dante
See Dante
See also WLIT 7

al-Kindi, Abu Yusuf Ya'qub ibn Ishaq c. 801-c. 873 .... **CMLC 80**

Allan, John B.
See Westlake, Donald E(dwin)

Allan, Sidney
See Hartmann, Sadakichi

Allan, Sydney
See Hartmann, Sadakichi

Allard, Janet .... **CLC 59**

Allen, Edward 1948- .... **CLC 59**

Allen, Fred 1894-1956 .... **TCLC 87**

Allen, Paula Gunn 1939- .... **CLC 84, 202; NNAL**
See also AMWS 4; CA 112; 143; CANR 63, 130; CWP; DA3; DAM MULT; DLB 175; FW; MTCW 2; MTFW 2005; RGAL 4; TCWW 2

Allen, Roland
See Ayckbourn, Alan

Allen, Sarah A.
See Hopkins, Pauline Elizabeth

Allen, Sidney H.
See Hartmann, Sadakichi

Allen, Woody 1935- .... **CLC 16, 52, 195**
See also AAYA 10, 51; AMWS 15; CA 33-36R; CANR 27, 38, 63, 128; DAM POP; DLB 44; MTCW 1; SSFS 21

Allende, Isabel 1942- ... **CLC 39, 57, 97, 170; HLC 1; SSC 65; WLCS**
See also AAYA 18; CA 125; 130; CANR 51, 74, 129; CDWLB 3; CLR 99; CWW 2; DA3; DAM MULT, NOV; DLB 145; DNFS 1; EWL 3; FL 1:5; FW; HW 1, 2; INT CA-130; LAIT 5; LAWS 1; LMFS 2; MTCW 1, 2; MTFW 2005; NCFS 1; NFS 6, 18; RGSF 2; RGWL 3; SATA 163; SSFS 11, 16; WLIT 1

Alleyn, Ellen
See Rossetti, Christina

Alleyne, Carla D. .... **CLC 65**

Allingham, Margery (Louise)
1904-1966 .... **CLC 19**
See also CA 5-8R; 25-28R; CANR 4, 58; CMW 4; DLB 77; MSW; MTCW 1, 2

Allingham, William 1824-1889 ...... **NCLC 25**
See also DLB 35; RGEL 2

Allison, Dorothy E. 1949- .... **CLC 78, 153**
See also AAYA 53; CA 140; CANR 66, 107; CN 7; CSW; DA3; FW; MTCW 2; MTFW 2005; NFS 11; RGAL 4

Alloula, Malek .... **CLC 65**

Allston, Washington 1779-1843 .... **NCLC 2**
See also DLB 1, 235

Almedingen, E. M. .... **CLC 12**
See Almedingen, Martha Edith von
See also SATA 3

Almedingen, Martha Edith von 1898-1971
See Almedingen, E. M.
See also CA 1-4R; CANR 1

Almodovar, Pedro 1949(?)- .... **CLC 114; HLCS 1**
See also CA 133; CANR 72; HW 2

Almqvist, Carl Jonas Love
1793-1866 .... **NCLC 42**

al-Mutanabbi, Ahmad ibn al-Husayn Abu al-Tayyib al-Jufi al-Kindi
915-965 .... **CMLC 66**
See Mutanabbi, Al-
See also RGWL 3

Alonso, Damaso 1898-1990 .... **CLC 14**
See also CA 110; 131; 130; CANR 72; DLB 108; EWL 3; HW 1, 2

Alov
See Gogol, Nikolai (Vasilyevich)

al'Sadaawi, Nawal
See El Saadawi, Nawal
See also FW

al-Shaykh, Hanan 1945- .... **CLC 218**
See also CA 135; CANR 111; WLIT 6

Al Siddik
See Rolfe, Frederick (William Serafino Austin Lewis Mary)
See also GLL 1; RGEL 2

Alta 1942- .... **CLC 19**
See also CA 57-60

Alter, Robert B(ernard) 1935- .... **CLC 34**
See also CA 49-52; CANR 1, 47, 100

Alther, Lisa 1944- .... **CLC 7, 41**
See also BPFB 1; CA 65-68; CAAS 30; CANR 12, 30, 51; CN 4, 5, 6, 7; CSW; GLL 2; MTCW 1

Althusser, L.
See Althusser, Louis

Althusser, Louis 1918-1990 .... **CLC 106**
See also CA 131; 132; CANR 102; DLB 242

Altman, Robert 1925- .... **CLC 16, 116**
See also CA 73-76; CANR 43

Alurista .... **HLCS 1; PC 34**
See Urista (Heredia), Alberto (Baltazar)
See also CA 45-48R; DLB 82; LLW

Alvarez, A(lfred) 1929- .... **CLC 5, 13**
See also CA 1-4R; CANR 3, 33, 63, 101, 134; CN 3, 4, 5, 6; CP 1, 2, 3, 4, 5, 6, 7; DLB 14, 40; MTFW 2005

Alvarez, Alejandro Rodriguez 1903-1965
See Casona, Alejandro
See also CA 131; 93-96; HW 1

Alvarez, Julia 1950- .... **CLC 93; HLCS 1**
See also AAYA 25; AMWS 7; CA 147; CANR 69, 101, 133; DA3; DLB 282; LATS 1:2; LLW; MTCW 2; MTFW 2005; NFS 5, 9; SATA 129; WLIT 1

Alvaro, Corrado 1896-1956 .... **TCLC 60**
See also CA 163; DLB 264; EWL 3

Amado, Jorge 1912-2001 ... **CLC 13, 40, 106; HLC 1**
See also CA 77-80; 201; CANR 35, 74, 135; CWW 2; DAM MULT, NOV; DLB 113, 307; EWL 3; HW 2; LAW; LAWS 1; MTCW 1, 2; MTFW 2005; RGWL 2, 3; TWA; WLIT 1

Ambler, Eric 1909-1998 .... **CLC 4, 6, 9**
See also BRWS 4; CA 9-12R; 171; CANR 7, 38, 74; CMW 4; CN 1, 2, 3, 4, 5, 6; DLB 77; MSW; MTCW 1, 2; TEA

Ambrose, Stephen E(dward)
1936-2002 .... **CLC 145**
See also AAYA 44; CA 1-4R; 209; CANR 3, 43, 57, 83, 105; MTFW 2005; NCFS 2; SATA 40, 138

Amichai, Yehuda 1924-2000 .. **CLC 9, 22, 57, 116; PC 38**
See also CA 85-88; 189; CANR 46, 60, 99, 132; CWW 2; EWL 3; MTCW 1, 2; MTFW 2005; WLIT 6

Amichai, Yehudah
See Amichai, Yehuda

Amiel, Henri Frederic 1821-1881 .... **NCLC 4**
See also DLB 217

Amis, Kingsley (William)
1922-1995 ...... **CLC 1, 2, 3, 5, 8, 13, 40, 44, 129**
See also AITN 2; BPFB 1; BRWS 2; CA 9-12R; 150; CANR 8, 28, 54; CDBLB 1945-1960; CN 1, 2, 3, 4, 5, 6; CP 1, 2, 3, 4; DA; DA3; DAB; DAC; DAM MST, NOV; DLB 15, 27, 100, 139; DLBY 1996; EWL 3; HGG; INT CANR-8; MTCW 1, 2; MTFW 2005; RGEL 2; RGSF 2; SFW 4

Amis, Martin (Louis) 1949- .... **CLC 4, 9, 38, 62, 101, 213**
See also BEST 90:3; BRWS 4; CA 65-68; CANR 8, 27, 54, 73, 95, 132; CN 5, 6, 7; DA3; DLB 14, 194; EWL 3; INT CANR-27; MTCW 2; MTFW 2005

Ammianus Marcellinus c. 330-c. 395 .... **CMLC 60**
See also AW 2; DLB 211

Ammons, A(rchie) R(andolph)
1926-2001 ...... **CLC 2, 3, 5, 8, 9, 25, 57, 108; PC 16**
See also AITN 1; AMWS 7; CA 9-12R; 193; CANR 6, 36, 51, 73, 107; CP 1, 2, 3, 4, 5, 6, 7; CSW; DAM POET; DLB 5, 165; EWL 3; MAL 5; MTCW 1, 2; PFS 19; RGAL 4; TCLE 1:1

Amo, Tauraatua i
See Adams, Henry (Brooks)

Amory, Thomas 1691(?)-1788 .... **LC 48**
See also DLB 39

Anand, Mulk Raj 1905-2004 ...... **CLC 23, 93**
See also CA 65-68; 231; CANR 32, 64; CN 1, 2, 3, 4, 5, 6, 7; DAM NOV; EWL 3; MTCW 1, 2; MTFW 2005; RGSF 2

Anatol
See Schnitzler, Arthur

Anaximander c. 611B.C.-c. 546B.C. .... **CMLC 22**

Anaya, Rudolfo A(lfonso) 1937- ...... **CLC 23, 148; HLC 1**
See also AAYA 20; BYA 13; CA 45-48; CAAS 4; CANR 1, 32, 51, 124; CN 4, 5, 6, 7; DAM MULT, NOV; DLB 82, 206, 278; HW 1; LAIT 4; LLW; MAL 5; MTCW 1, 2; MTFW 2005; NFS 12; RGAL 4; RGSF 2; TCWW 2; WLIT 1

Andersen, Hans Christian
1805-1875 .... **NCLC 7, 79; SSC 6, 56; WLC**
See also AAYA 57; CLR 6; DA; DA3; DAB; DAC; DAM MST, POP; EW 6; MAICYA 1, 2; RGSF 2; RGWL 2, 3; SATA 100; TWA; WCH; YABC 1

Anderson, C. Farley
See Mencken, H(enry) L(ouis); Nathan, George Jean

Anderson, Jessica (Margaret) Queale 1916- .... **CLC 37**
See also CA 9-12R; CANR 4, 62; CN 4, 5, 6, 7

Anderson, Jon (Victor) 1940- .... **CLC 9**
See also CA 25-28R; CANR 20; CP 1, 3, 4; DAM POET

Anderson, Lindsay (Gordon) 1923-1994 .... **CLC 20**
See also CA 125; 128; 146; CANR 77

Anderson, Maxwell 1888-1959 .... **TCLC 2, 144**
See also CA 105; 152; DAM DRAM; DFS 16, 20; DLB 7, 228; MAL 5; MTCW 2; MTFW 2005; RGAL 4

Anderson, Poul (William) 1926-2001 .... **CLC 15**
See also AAYA 5, 34; BPFB 1; BYA 6, 8, 9; CA 1-4R, 181; 199; CAAE 181; CAAS 2; CANR 2, 15, 34, 64, 110; CLR 58; DLB 8; FANT; INT CANR-15; MTCW 1, 2; MTFW 2005; SATA 90; SATA-Brief 39; SATA-Essay 106; SCFW 1, 2; SFW 4; SUFW 1, 2

Anderson, Robert (Woodruff) 1917- .... **CLC 23**
See also AITN 1; CA 21-24R; CANR 32; CD 6; DAM DRAM; DLB 7; LAIT 5

Anderson, Roberta Joan
See Mitchell, Joni

Anderson, Sherwood 1876-1941 .. **SSC 1, 46; TCLC 1, 10, 24, 123; WLC**
See also AAYA 30; AMW; AMWC 2; BPFB 1; CA 104; 121; CANR 61; CDALB 1917-1929; DA; DA3; DAB; DAC; DAM MST, NOV; DLB 4, 9, 86; DLBD 1; EWL 3; EXPS; GLL 2; MAL 5; MTCW 1, 2; MTFW 2005; NFS 4; RGAL 4; RGSF 2; SSFS 4, 10, 11; TUS

Andier, Pierre
See Desnos, Robert

Andouard
See Giraudoux, Jean(-Hippolyte)

Andrade, Carlos Drummond de ...... **CLC 18**
See Drummond de Andrade, Carlos
See also EWL 3; RGWL 2, 3

Andrade, Mario de .... **TCLC 43**
See de Andrade, Mario
See also DLB 307; EWL 3; LAW; RGWL 2, 3; WLIT 1

Andreae, Johann V(alentin) 1586-1654 .... **LC 32**
See also DLB 164

Andreas Capellanus fl. c. 1185- .... **CMLC 45**
See also DLB 208

Andreas-Salome, Lou 1861-1937 ... **TCLC 56**
See also CA 178; DLB 66

Andreev, Leonid
See Andreyev, Leonid (Nikolaevich)
See also DLB 295; EWL 3

Andress, Lesley
See Sanders, Lawrence

Andrewes, Lancelot 1555-1626 .... **LC 5**
See also DLB 151, 172

Andrews, Cicily Fairfield
See West, Rebecca

Andrews, Elton V.
See Pohl, Frederik

Andreyev, Leonid (Nikolaevich) 1871-1919 .... **TCLC 3**
See Andreev, Leonid
See also CA 104; 185

Andric, Ivo 1892-1975 .... **CLC 8; SSC 36; TCLC 135**
See also CA 81-84; 57-60; CANR 43, 60; CDWLB 4; DLB 147; EW 11; EWL 3; MTCW 1; RGSF 2; RGWL 2, 3

Androvar
See Prado (Calvo), Pedro

Angela of Foligno 1248(?)-1309 .... **CMLC 76**

Angelique, Pierre
See Bataille, Georges

Angell, Roger 1920- .... **CLC 26**
See also CA 57-60; CANR 13, 44, 70, 144; DLB 171, 185

Angelou, Maya 1928- ... **BLC 1; CLC 12, 35, 64, 77, 155; PC 32; WLCS**
See also AAYA 7, 20; AMWS 4; BPFB 1; BW 2, 3; BYA 2; CA 65-68; CANR 19, 42, 65, 111, 133; CDALBS; CLR 53; CP 4, 5, 6, 7; CPW; CSW; CWP; DA; DA3; DAB; DAC; DAM MST, MULT, POET, POP; DLB 38; EWL 3; EXPN; EXPP; FL 1:5; LAIT 4; MAICYA 1; MAICYAS 1; MAL 5; MAWW; MTCW 1, 2; MTFW 2005; NCFS 2; NFS 2; PFS 2, 3; RGAL 4; SATA 49, 136; TCLE 1:1; WYA; YAW

Angouleme, Marguerite d'
See de Navarre, Marguerite

Anna Comnena 1083-1153 .... **CMLC 25**

Annensky, Innokentii Fedorovich
See Annensky, Innokenty (Fyodorovich)
See also DLB 295

Annensky, Innokenty (Fyodorovich) 1856-1909 .... **TCLC 14**
See also CA 110; 155; EWL 3

Annunzio, Gabriele d'
See D'Annunzio, Gabriele

Anodos
See Coleridge, Mary E(lizabeth)

Anon, Charles Robert
See Pessoa, Fernando (Antonio Nogueira)

Anouilh, Jean (Marie Lucien Pierre) 1910-1987 . **CLC 1, 3, 8, 13, 40, 50; DC 8, 21**
See also AAYA 67; CA 17-20R; 123; CANR 32; DAM DRAM; DFS 9, 10, 19; DLB 321; EW 13; EWL 3; GFL 1789 to the Present; MTCW 1, 2; MTFW 2005; RGWL 2, 3; TWA

Anselm of Canterbury 1033(?)-1109 .... **CMLC 67**
See also DLB 115

Anthony, Florence
See Ai

Anthony, John
See Ciardi, John (Anthony)

Anthony, Peter
See Shaffer, Anthony (Joshua); Shaffer, Peter (Levin)

Anthony, Piers 1934- .... **CLC 35**
See also AAYA 11, 48; BYA 7; CA 200; CAAE 200; CANR 28, 56, 73, 102, 133; CPW; DAM POP; DLB 8; FANT; MAICYA 2; MAICYAS 1; MTCW 1, 2; MTFW 2005; SAAS 22; SATA 84, 129; SATA-Essay 129; SFW 4; SUFW 1, 2; YAW

Anthony, Susan B(rownell) 1820-1906 .... **TCLC 84**
See also CA 211; FW

Antiphon c. 480B.C.-c. 411B.C. .... **CMLC 55**

Antoine, Marc
See Proust, (Valentin-Louis-George-Eugene) Marcel

Antoninus, Brother
See Everson, William (Oliver)
See also CP 1

Antonioni, Michelangelo 1912- .... **CLC 20, 144**
See also CA 73-76; CANR 45, 77

Antschel, Paul 1920-1970
See Celan, Paul
See also CA 85-88; CANR 33, 61; MTCW 1; PFS 21

Anwar, Chairil 1922-1949 .... **TCLC 22**
See Chairil Anwar
See also CA 121; 219; RGWL 3

Anzaldua, Gloria (Evanjelina) 1942-2004 .... **CLC 200; HLCS 1**
See also CA 175; 227; CSW; CWP; DLB 122; FW; LLW; RGAL 4; SATA-Obit 154

Apess, William 1798-1839(?) .... **NCLC 73; NNAL**
See also DAM MULT; DLB 175, 243

Apollinaire, Guillaume 1880-1918 .... **PC 7; TCLC 3, 8, 51**
See Kostrowitzki, Wilhelm Apollinaris de
See also CA 152; DAM POET; DLB 258, 321; EW 9; EWL 3; GFL 1789 to the Present; MTCW 2; RGWL 2, 3; TWA; WP

Apollonius of Rhodes
See Apollonius Rhodius
See also AW 1; RGWL 2, 3

Apollonius Rhodius c. 300B.C.-c. 220B.C. .... **CMLC 28**
See Apollonius of Rhodes
See also DLB 176

Appelfeld, Aharon 1932- ... **CLC 23, 47; SSC 42**
See also CA 112; 133; CANR 86; CWW 2; DLB 299; EWL 3; RGSF 2; WLIT 6

Apple, Max (Isaac) 1941- .... **CLC 9, 33; SSC 50**
See also CA 81-84; CANR 19, 54; DLB 130

Appleman, Philip (Dean) 1926- .... **CLC 51**
See also CA 13-16R; CAAS 18; CANR 6, 29, 56

Appleton, Lawrence
See Lovecraft, H(oward) P(hillips)

Apteryx
See Eliot, T(homas) S(tearns)

Apuleius, (Lucius Madaurensis) 125(?)-175(?) .... **CMLC 1**
See also AW 2; CDWLB 1; DLB 211; RGWL 2, 3; SUFW

Aquin, Hubert 1929-1977 .... **CLC 15**
See also CA 105; DLB 53; EWL 3

Aquinas, Thomas 1224(?)-1274 ...... **CMLC 33**
See also DLB 115; EW 1; TWA

Aragon, Louis 1897-1982 .... **CLC 3, 22; TCLC 123**
See also CA 69-72; 108; CANR 28, 71; DAM NOV, POET; DLB 72, 258; EW 11; EWL 3; GFL 1789 to the Present; GLL 2; LMFS 2; MTCW 1, 2; RGWL 2, 3

Arany, Janos 1817-1882 .... **NCLC 34**

Aranyos, Kakay 1847-1910
See Mikszath, Kalman

Aratus of Soli c. 315B.C.-c. 240B.C. .... **CMLC 64**
See also DLB 176

Arbuthnot, John 1667-1735 .... **LC 1**
See also DLB 101

Archer, Herbert Winslow
See Mencken, H(enry) L(ouis)

Archer, Jeffrey (Howard) 1940- .... **CLC 28**
See also AAYA 16; BEST 89:3; BPFB 1; CA 77-80; CANR 22, 52, 95, 136; CPW; DA3; DAM POP; INT CANR-22; MTFW 2005

Archer, Jules 1915- .... **CLC 12**
See also CA 9-12R; CANR 6, 69; SAAS 5; SATA 4, 85

Archer, Lee
See Ellison, Harlan (Jay)

Archilochus c. 7th cent. B.C.- .... **CMLC 44**
See also DLB 176

Arden, John 1930- .... **CLC 6, 13, 15**
See also BRWS 2; CA 13-16R; CAAS 4; CANR 31, 65, 67, 124; CBD; CD 5, 6; DAM DRAM; DFS 9; DLB 13, 245; EWL 3; MTCW 1

Arenas, Reinaldo 1943-1990 .. **CLC 41; HLC 1**
See also CA 124; 128; 133; CANR 73, 106; DAM MULT; DLB 145; EWL 3; GLL 2; HW 1; LAW; LAWS 1; MTCW 2; MTFW 2005; RGSF 2; RGWL 3; WLIT 1

Arendt, Hannah 1906-1975 .... **CLC 66, 98**
See also CA 17-20R; 61-64; CANR 26, 60; DLB 242; MTCW 1, 2

Aretino, Pietro 1492-1556 .... **LC 12**
See also RGWL 2, 3

Arghezi, Tudor .... **CLC 80**
See Theodorescu, Ion N.
See also CA 167; CDWLB 4; DLB 220; EWL 3

Arguedas, Jose Maria 1911-1969 .... **CLC 10, 18; HLCS 1; TCLC 147**
See also CA 89-92; CANR 73; DLB 113; EWL 3; HW 1; LAW; RGWL 2, 3; WLIT 1

Argueta, Manlio 1936- .... **CLC 31**
See also CA 131; CANR 73; CWW 2; DLB 145; EWL 3; HW 1; RGWL 3

Arias, Ron(ald Francis) 1941- .... **HLC 1**
See also CA 131; CANR 81, 136; DAM MULT; DLB 82; HW 1, 2; MTCW 2; MTFW 2005

Ariosto, Lodovico
See Ariosto, Ludovico
See also WLIT 7

Ariosto, Ludovico 1474-1533 ... **LC 6, 87; PC 42**
See Ariosto, Lodovico
See also EW 2; RGWL 2, 3

Aristides
See Epstein, Joseph

Aristophanes 450B.C.-385B.C. .... **CMLC 4, 51; DC 2; WLCS**
See also AW 1; CDWLB 1; DA; DA3; DAB; DAC; DAM DRAM, MST; DFS 10; DLB 176; LMFS 1; RGWL 2, 3; TWA

Aristotle 384B.C.-322B.C. .... **CMLC 31; WLCS**
See also AW 1; CDWLB 1; DA; DA3; DAB; DAC; DAM MST; DLB 176; RGWL 2, 3; TWA

Arlt, Roberto (Godofredo Christophersen) 1900-1942 .... **HLC 1; TCLC 29**
See also CA 123; 131; CANR 67; DAM MULT; DLB 305; EWL 3; HW 1, 2; IDTP; LAW

Armah, Ayi Kwei 1939- . **BLC 1; CLC 5, 33, 136**
See also AFW; BRWS 10; BW 1; CA 61-64; CANR 21, 64; CDWLB 3; CN 1, 2, 3, 4, 5, 6, 7; DAM MULT, POET; DLB 117; EWL 3; MTCW 1; WLIT 1

Armatrading, Joan 1950- .... **CLC 17**
See also CA 114; 186

Armitage, Frank
See Carpenter, John (Howard)

Armstrong, Jeannette (C.) 1948- .... **NNAL**
See also CA 149; CCA 1; CN 6, 7; DAC; SATA 102

Arnette, Robert
See Silverberg, Robert

Arnim, Achim von (Ludwig Joachim von Arnim) 1781-1831 .. **NCLC 5, 159; SSC 29**
See also DLB 90

Arnim, Bettina von 1785-1859 ...... **NCLC 38, 123**
See also DLB 90; RGWL 2, 3

Arnold, Matthew 1822-1888 ..... **NCLC 6, 29, 89, 126; PC 5; WLC**
See also BRW 5; CDBLB 1832-1890; DA; DAB; DAC; DAM MST, POET; DLB 32, 57; EXPP; PAB; PFS 2; TEA; WP

Arnold, Thomas 1795-1842 .... **NCLC 18**
See also DLB 55

Arnow, Harriette (Louisa) Simpson 1908-1986 .... **CLC 2, 7, 18**
See also BPFB 1; CA 9-12R; 118; CANR 14; CN 2, 3, 4; DLB 6; FW; MTCW 1, 2; RHW; SATA 42; SATA-Obit 47

Arouet, Francois-Marie
See Voltaire

Arp, Hans
See Arp, Jean

Arp, Jean 1887-1966 .... **CLC 5; TCLC 115**
See also CA 81-84; 25-28R; CANR 42, 77; EW 10

Arrabal
See Arrabal, Fernando

Arrabal (Teran), Fernando
See Arrabal, Fernando
See also CWW 2

Arrabal, Fernando 1932- ... **CLC 2, 9, 18, 58**
See Arrabal (Teran), Fernando
See also CA 9-12R; CANR 15; DLB 321; EWL 3; LMFS 2

Arreola, Juan Jose 1918-2001 .... **CLC 147; HLC 1; SSC 38**
See also CA 113; 131; 200; CANR 81; CWW 2; DAM MULT; DLB 113; DNFS 2; EWL 3; HW 1, 2; LAW; RGSF 2

Arrian c. 89(?)-c. 155(?) .... **CMLC 43**
See also DLB 176

Arrick, Fran .... **CLC 30**
See Gaberman, Judie Angell
See also BYA 6

Arrley, Richmond
See Delany, Samuel R(ay), Jr.

Artaud, Antonin (Marie Joseph) 1896-1948 .... **DC 14; TCLC 3, 36**
See also CA 104; 149; DA3; DAM DRAM; DFS 22; DLB 258, 321; EW 11; EWL 3; GFL 1789 to the Present; MTCW 2; MTFW 2005; RGWL 2, 3

Arthur, Ruth M(abel) 1905-1979 ..... **CLC 12**
See also CA 9-12R; 85-88; CANR 4; CWRI 5; SATA 7, 26

Artsybashev, Mikhail (Petrovich) 1878-1927 .... **TCLC 31**
See also CA 170; DLB 295

Arundel, Honor (Morfydd) 1919-1973 .... **CLC 17**
See also CA 21-22; 41-44R; CAP 2; CLR 35; CWRI 5; SATA 4; SATA-Obit 24

Arzner, Dorothy 1900-1979 .... **CLC 98**

Asch, Sholem 1880-1957 .... **TCLC 3**
See also CA 105; EWL 3; GLL 2

Ascham, Roger 1516(?)-1568 .... **LC 101**
See also DLB 236

Ash, Shalom
See Asch, Sholem

Ashbery, John (Lawrence) 1927- .. **CLC 2, 3, 4, 6, 9, 13, 15, 25, 41, 77, 125, 221; PC 26**
See Berry, Jonas
See also AMWS 3; CA 5-8R; CANR 9, 37, 66, 102, 132; CP 1, 2, 3, 4, 5, 6, 7; DA3; DAM POET; DLB 5, 165; DLBY 1981; EWL 3; INT CANR-9; MAL 5; MTCW 1, 2; MTFW 2005; PAB; PFS 11; RGAL 4; TCLE 1:1; WP

Ashdown, Clifford
See Freeman, R(ichard) Austin

Ashe, Gordon
See Creasey, John

Ashton-Warner, Sylvia (Constance) 1908-1984 .... **CLC 19**
See also CA 69-72; 112; CANR 29; CN 1, 2, 3; MTCW 1, 2

Asimov, Isaac 1920-1992 ..... **CLC 1, 3, 9, 19, 26, 76, 92**
See also AAYA 13; BEST 90:2; BPFB 1; BYA 4, 6, 7, 9; CA 1-4R; 137; CANR 2, 19, 36, 60, 125; CLR 12, 79; CMW 4; CN 1, 2, 3, 4, 5; CPW; DA3; DAM POP; DLB 8; DLBY 1992; INT CANR-19; JRDA; LAIT 5; LMFS 2; MAICYA 1, 2; MAL 5; MTCW 1, 2; MTFW 2005; RGAL 4; SATA 1, 26, 74; SCFW 1, 2; SFW 4; SSFS 17; TUS; YAW

Askew, Anne 1521(?)-1546 .... **LC 81**
See also DLB 136

Assis, Joaquim Maria Machado de
See Machado de Assis, Joaquim Maria

Astell, Mary 1666-1731 .... **LC 68**
See also DLB 252; FW

Astley, Thea (Beatrice May) 1925-2004 .... **CLC 41**
See also CA 65-68; 229; CANR 11, 43, 78; CN 1, 2, 3, 4, 5, 6, 7; DLB 289; EWL 3

Astley, William 1855-1911
See Warung, Price

Aston, James
See White, T(erence) H(anbury)

Asturias, Miguel Angel 1899-1974 .... **CLC 3, 8, 13; HLC 1**
See also CA 25-28; 49-52; CANR 32; CAP 2; CDWLB 3; DA3; DAM MULT, NOV; DLB 113, 290; EWL 3; HW 1; LAW; LMFS 2; MTCW 1, 2; RGWL 2, 3; WLIT 1

Atares, Carlos Saura
See Saura (Atares), Carlos

Athanasius c. 295-c. 373 .... **CMLC 48**

Atheling, William
See Pound, Ezra (Weston Loomis)

Atheling, William, Jr.
See Blish, James (Benjamin)

Atherton, Gertrude (Franklin Horn) 1857-1948 .... **TCLC 2**
See also CA 104; 155; DLB 9, 78, 186; HGG; RGAL 4; SUFW 1; TCWW 1, 2

Atherton, Lucius
See Masters, Edgar Lee

Atkins, Jack
See Harris, Mark

Atkinson, Kate 1951- .... **CLC 99**
See also CA 166; CANR 101; DLB 267

Attaway, William (Alexander) 1911-1986 .... **BLC 1; CLC 92**
See also BW 2, 3; CA 143; CANR 82; DAM MULT; DLB 76; MAL 5

Atticus
See Fleming, Ian (Lancaster); Wilson, (Thomas) Woodrow

Atwood, Margaret (Eleanor) 1939- ... **CLC 2, 3, 4, 8, 13, 15, 25, 44, 84, 135; PC 8; SSC 2, 46; WLC**
See also AAYA 12, 47; AMWS 13; BEST 89:2; BPFB 1; CA 49-52; CANR 3, 24, 33, 59, 95, 133; CN 2, 3, 4, 5, 6, 7; CP 1, 2, 3, 4, 5, 6, 7; CPW; CWP; DA; DA3; DAB; DAC; DAM MST, NOV, POET; DLB 53, 251; EWL 3; EXPN; FL 1:5; FW; GL 2; INT CANR-24; LAIT 5; MTCW 1, 2; MTFW 2005; NFS 4, 12, 13, 14, 19; PFS 7; RGSF 2; SATA 50; SSFS 3, 13; TCLE 1:1; TWA; WWE 1; YAW

Aubigny, Pierre d'
See Mencken, H(enry) L(ouis)

Aubin, Penelope 1685-1731(?) .... **LC 9**
See also DLB 39

Auchincloss, Louis (Stanton) 1917- .. **CLC 4, 6, 9, 18, 45; SSC 22**
See also AMWS 4; CA 1-4R; CANR 6, 29, 55, 87, 130; CN 1, 2, 3, 4, 5, 6, 7; DAM NOV; DLB 2, 244; DLBY 1980; EWL 3; INT CANR-29; MAL 5; MTCW 1; RGAL 4

Auden, W(ystan) H(ugh) 1907-1973 . **CLC 1, 2, 3, 4, 6, 9, 11, 14, 43, 123; PC 1; WLC**
See also AAYA 18; AMWS 2; BRW 7; BRWR 1; CA 9-12R; 45-48; CANR 5, 61, 105; CDBLB 1914-1945; CP 1, 2; DA; DA3; DAB; DAC; DAM DRAM, MST, POET; DLB 10, 20; EWL 3; EXPP; MAL 5; MTCW 1, 2; MTFW 2005; PAB; PFS 1, 3, 4, 10; TUS; WP

Audiberti, Jacques 1899-1965 .... **CLC 38**
See also CA 25-28R; DAM DRAM; DLB 321; EWL 3

Audubon, John James 1785-1851 . **NCLC 47**
See also ANW; DLB 248

Auel, Jean M(arie) 1936- .... **CLC 31, 107**
See also AAYA 7, 51; BEST 90:4; BPFB 1; CA 103; CANR 21, 64, 115; CPW; DA3; DAM POP; INT CANR-21; NFS 11; RHW; SATA 91

Auerbach, Erich 1892-1957 .... **TCLC 43**
See also CA 118; 155; EWL 3

Augier, Emile 1820-1889 .... **NCLC 31**
See also DLB 192; GFL 1789 to the Present

August, John
See De Voto, Bernard (Augustine)

Augustine, St. 354-430 .... **CMLC 6; WLCS**
See also DA; DA3; DAB; DAC; DAM MST; DLB 115; EW 1; RGWL 2, 3

Aunt Belinda
See Braddon, Mary Elizabeth

Aunt Weedy
See Alcott, Louisa May

Aurelius
See Bourne, Randolph S(illiman)

Aurelius, Marcus 121-180 .... **CMLC 45**
See Marcus Aurelius
See also RGWL 2, 3

Aurobindo, Sri
See Ghose, Aurabinda

Aurobindo Ghose
See Ghose, Aurabinda

Austen, Jane 1775-1817 .... **NCLC 1, 13, 19, 33, 51, 81, 95, 119, 150; WLC**
See also AAYA 19; BRW 4; BRWC 1; BRWR 2; BYA 3; CDBLB 1789-1832; DA; DA3; DAB; DAC; DAM MST, NOV; DLB 116; EXPN; FL 1:2; GL 2; LAIT 2; LATS 1:1; LMFS 1; NFS 1, 14, 18, 20, 21; TEA; WLIT 3; WYAS 1

Auster, Paul 1947- .... **CLC 47, 131**
See also AMWS 12; CA 69-72; CANR 23, 52, 75, 129; CMW 4; CN 5, 6, 7; DA3; DLB 227; MAL 5; MTCW 2; MTFW 2005; SUFW 2; TCLE 1:1

Austin, Frank
See Faust, Frederick (Schiller)

Austin, Mary (Hunter) 1868-1934 . **TCLC 25**
See also ANW; CA 109; 178; DLB 9, 78, 206, 221, 275; FW; TCWW 1, 2

Averroes 1126-1198 .... **CMLC 7**
See also DLB 115

Avicenna 980-1037 .... **CMLC 16**
See also DLB 115

Avison, Margaret (Kirkland) 1918- .. **CLC 2, 4, 97**
See also CA 17-20R; CANR 134; CP 1, 2, 3, 4, 5, 6, 7; DAC; DAM POET; DLB 53; MTCW 1

Axton, David
See Koontz, Dean R.

Ayckbourn, Alan 1939- ...... **CLC 5, 8, 18, 33, 74; DC 13**
See also BRWS 5; CA 21-24R; CANR 31, 59, 118; CBD; CD 5, 6; DAB; DAM DRAM; DFS 7; DLB 13, 245; EWL 3; MTCW 1, 2; MTFW 2005

Aydy, Catherine
See Tennant, Emma (Christina)

Ayme, Marcel (Andre) 1902-1967 ... **CLC 11; SSC 41**
See also CA 89-92; CANR 67, 137; CLR 25; DLB 72; EW 12; EWL 3; GFL 1789 to the Present; RGSF 2; RGWL 2, 3; SATA 91

Ayrton, Michael 1921-1975 .... **CLC 7**
See also CA 5-8R; 61-64; CANR 9, 21

Aytmatov, Chingiz
See Aitmatov, Chingiz (Torekulovich)
See also EWL 3

Azorin .... **CLC 11**
See Martinez Ruiz, Jose
See also DLB 322; EW 9; EWL 3

Azuela, Mariano 1873-1952 .. **HLC 1; TCLC 3, 145**
See also CA 104; 131; CANR 81; DAM MULT; EWL 3; HW 1, 2; LAW; MTCW 1, 2; MTFW 2005

Ba, Mariama 1929-1981 .... **BLCS**
See also AFW; BW 2; CA 141; CANR 87; DNFS 2; WLIT 2

Baastad, Babbis Friis
See Friis-Baastad, Babbis Ellinor

Bab
See Gilbert, W(illiam) S(chwenck)

Babbis, Eleanor
See Friis-Baastad, Babbis Ellinor

Babel, Isaac
See Babel, Isaak (Emmanuilovich)
See also EW 11; SSFS 10

Babel, Isaak (Emmanuilovich) 1894-1941(?) . **SSC 16, 78; TCLC 2, 13, 171**
See Babel, Isaac
See also CA 104; 155; CANR 113; DLB 272; EWL 3; MTCW 2; MTFW 2005; RGSF 2; RGWL 2, 3; TWA

Babits, Mihaly 1883-1941 .... **TCLC 14**
See also CA 114; CDWLB 4; DLB 215; EWL 3

Babur 1483-1530 .... **LC 18**

Babylas 1898-1962
See Ghelderode, Michel de

Baca, Jimmy Santiago 1952- . **HLC 1; PC 41**
See also CA 131; CANR 81, 90, 146; CP 7; DAM MULT; DLB 122; HW 1, 2; LLW; MAL 5

Baca, Jose Santiago
See Baca, Jimmy Santiago

Bacchelli, Riccardo 1891-1985 .... **CLC 19**
See also CA 29-32R; 117; DLB 264; EWL 3

Bach, Richard (David) 1936- .... **CLC 14**
See also AITN 1; BEST 89:2; BPFB 1; BYA 5; CA 9-12R; CANR 18, 93; CPW; DAM NOV, POP; FANT; MTCW 1; SATA 13

Bache, Benjamin Franklin 1769-1798 .... **LC 74**
See also DLB 43

Bachelard, Gaston 1884-1962 ...... **TCLC 128**
See also CA 97-100; 89-92; DLB 296; GFL 1789 to the Present

Bachman, Richard
See King, Stephen

Bachmann, Ingeborg 1926-1973 .... **CLC 69**
See also CA 93-96; 45-48; CANR 69; DLB 85; EWL 3; RGWL 2, 3

Bacon, Francis 1561-1626 .... **LC 18, 32**
See also BRW 1; CDBLB Before 1660; DLB 151, 236, 252; RGEL 2; TEA

Bacon, Roger 1214(?)-1294 .... **CMLC 14**
See also DLB 115

Bacovia, George 1881-1957 .... **TCLC 24**
See Vasiliu, Gheorghe
See also CDWLB 4; DLB 220; EWL 3

Badanes, Jerome 1937-1995 .... **CLC 59**
See also CA 234

Bagehot, Walter 1826-1877 .... **NCLC 10**
See also DLB 55

Bagnold, Enid 1889-1981 .... **CLC 25**
See also BYA 2; CA 5-8R; 103; CANR 5, 40; CBD; CN 2; CWD; CWRI 5; DAM DRAM; DLB 13, 160, 191, 245; FW; MAICYA 1, 2; RGEL 2; SATA 1, 25

Bagritsky, Eduard .... **TCLC 60**
See Dzyubin, Eduard Georgievich

Bagrjana, Elisaveta
See Belcheva, Elisaveta Lyubomirova

Bagryana, Elisaveta .... **CLC 10**
See Belcheva, Elisaveta Lyubomirova
See also CA 178; CDWLB 4; DLB 147; EWL 3

Bailey, Paul 1937- .... **CLC 45**
See also CA 21-24R; CANR 16, 62, 124; CN 1, 2, 3, 4, 5, 6, 7; DLB 14, 271; GLL 2

Baillie, Joanna 1762-1851 .... **NCLC 71, 151**
See also DLB 93; GL 2; RGEL 2

Bainbridge, Beryl (Margaret) 1934- . **CLC 4, 5, 8, 10, 14, 18, 22, 62, 130**
See also BRWS 6; CA 21-24R; CANR 24, 55, 75, 88, 128; CN 2, 3, 4, 5, 6, 7; DAM NOV; DLB 14, 231; EWL 3; MTCW 1, 2; MTFW 2005

Baker, Carlos (Heard) 1909-1987 .... **TCLC 119**
See also CA 5-8R; 122; CANR 3, 63; DLB 103

Baker, Elliott 1922- .... **CLC 8**
See also CA 45-48; CANR 2, 63; CN 1, 2, 3, 4, 5, 6, 7

Baker, Jean H. .... **TCLC 3, 10**
See Russell, George William

Baker, Nicholson 1957- .... **CLC 61, 165**
See also AMWS 13; CA 135; CANR 63, 120, 138; CN 6; CPW; DA3; DAM POP; DLB 227; MTFW 2005

Baker, Ray Stannard 1870-1946 .... **TCLC 47**
See also CA 118

Baker, Russell (Wayne) 1925- .... **CLC 31**
See also BEST 89:4; CA 57-60; CANR 11, 41, 59, 137; MTCW 1, 2; MTFW 2005

Bakhtin, M.
See Bakhtin, Mikhail Mikhailovich

Bakhtin, M. M.
See Bakhtin, Mikhail Mikhailovich

Bakhtin, Mikhail
See Bakhtin, Mikhail Mikhailovich

Bakhtin, Mikhail Mikhailovich 1895-1975 .... **CLC 83; TCLC 160**
See also CA 128; 113; DLB 242; EWL 3

Bakshi, Ralph 1938(?)- .... **CLC 26**
See also CA 112; 138; IDFW 3

Bakunin, Mikhail (Alexandrovich) 1814-1876 .... **NCLC 25, 58**
See also DLB 277

Baldwin, James (Arthur) 1924-1987 . **BLC 1; CLC 1, 2, 3, 4, 5, 8, 13, 15, 17, 42, 50, 67, 90, 127; DC 1; SSC 10, 33; WLC**
See also AAYA 4, 34; AFAW 1, 2; AMWR 2; AMWS 1; BPFB 1; BW 1; CA 1-4R; 124; CABS 1; CAD; CANR 3, 24; CDALB 1941-1968; CN 1, 2, 3, 4; CPW; DA; DA3; DAB; DAC; DAM MST, MULT, NOV, POP; DFS 11, 15; DLB 2, 7, 33, 249, 278; DLBY 1987; EWL 3;

EXPS; LAIT 5; MAL 5; MTCW 1, 2; MTFW 2005; NCFS 4; NFS 4; RGAL 4; RGSF 2; SATA 9; SATA-Obit 54; SSFS 2, 18; TUS

Baldwin, William c. 1515-1563 .... **LC 113**
See also DLB 132

Bale, John 1495-1563 .... **LC 62**
See also DLB 132; RGEL 2; TEA

Ball, Hugo 1886-1927 .... **TCLC 104**

Ballard, J(ames) G(raham) 1930- . **CLC 3, 6, 14, 36, 137; SSC 1, 53**
See also AAYA 3, 52; BRWS 5; CA 5-8R; CANR 15, 39, 65, 107, 133; CN 1, 2, 3, 4, 5, 6, 7; DA3; DAM NOV, POP; DLB 14, 207, 261, 319; EWL 3; HGG; MTCW 1, 2; MTFW 2005; NFS 8; RGEL 2; RGSF 2; SATA 93; SCFW 1, 2; SFW 4

Balmont, Konstantin (Dmitriyevich)
1867-1943 .... **TCLC 11**
See also CA 109; 155; DLB 295; EWL 3

Baltausis, Vincas 1847-1910
See Mikszath, Kalman

Balzac, Honore de 1799-1850 ... **NCLC 5, 35, 53, 153; SSC 5, 59; WLC**
See also DA; DA3; DAB; DAC; DAM MST, NOV; DLB 119; EW 5; GFL 1789 to the Present; LMFS 1; RGSF 2; RGWL 2, 3; SSFS 10; SUFW; TWA

Bambara, Toni Cade 1939-1995 .... **BLC 1; CLC 19, 88; SSC 35; TCLC 116; WLCS**
See also AAYA 5, 49; AFAW 2; AMWS 11; BW 2, 3; BYA 12, 14; CA 29-32R; 150; CANR 24, 49, 81; CDALBS; DA; DA3; DAC; DAM MST, MULT; DLB 38, 218; EXPS; MAL 5; MTCW 1, 2; MTFW 2005; RGAL 4; RGSF 2; SATA 112; SSFS 4, 7, 12, 21

Bamdad, A.
See Shamlu, Ahmad

Bamdad, Alef
See Shamlu, Ahmad

Banat, D. R.
See Bradbury, Ray (Douglas)

Bancroft, Laura
See Baum, L(yman) Frank

Banim, John 1798-1842 .... **NCLC 13**
See also DLB 116, 158, 159; RGEL 2

Banim, Michael 1796-1874 .... **NCLC 13**
See also DLB 158, 159

Banjo, The
See Paterson, A(ndrew) B(arton)

Banks, Iain
See Banks, Iain M(enzies)
See also BRWS 11

Banks, Iain M(enzies) 1954- .... **CLC 34**
See Banks, Iain
See also CA 123; 128; CANR 61, 106; DLB 194, 261; EWL 3; HGG; INT CA-128; MTFW 2005; SFW 4

Banks, Lynne Reid .... **CLC 23**
See Reid Banks, Lynne
See also AAYA 6; BYA 7; CLR 86; CN 4, 5, 6

Banks, Russell (Earl) 1940- .... **CLC 37, 72, 187; SSC 42**
See also AAYA 45; AMWS 5; CA 65-68; CAAS 15; CANR 19, 52, 73, 118; CN 4, 5, 6, 7; DLB 130, 278; EWL 3; MAL 5; MTCW 2; MTFW 2005; NFS 13

Banville, John 1945- .... **CLC 46, 118**
See also CA 117; 128; CANR 104; CN 4, 5, 6, 7; DLB 14, 271; INT CA-128

Banville, Theodore (Faullain) de
1832-1891 .... **NCLC 9**
See also DLB 217; GFL 1789 to the Present

Baraka, Amiri 1934- .... **BLC 1; CLC 1, 2, 3, 5, 10, 14, 33, 115, 213; DC 6; PC 4; WLCS**
See Jones, LeRoi
See also AAYA 63; AFAW 1, 2; AMWS 2; BW 2, 3; CA 21-24R; CABS 3; CAD; CANR 27, 38, 61, 133; CD 3, 5, 6; CDALB 1941-1968; CP 4, 5, 6, 7; CPW; DA; DA3; DAC; DAM MST, MULT, POET, POP; DFS 3, 11, 16; DLB 5, 7, 16, 38; DLBD 8; EWL 3; MAL 5; MTCW 1, 2; MTFW 2005; PFS 9; RGAL 4; TCLE 1:1; TUS; WP

Baratynsky, Evgenii Abramovich
1800-1844 .... **NCLC 103**
See also DLB 205

Barbauld, Anna Laetitia
1743-1825 .... **NCLC 50**
See also DLB 107, 109, 142, 158; RGEL 2

Barbellion, W. N. P. .... **TCLC 24**
See Cummings, Bruce F(rederick)

Barber, Benjamin R. 1939- .... **CLC 141**
See also CA 29-32R; CANR 12, 32, 64, 119

Barbera, Jack (Vincent) 1945- .... **CLC 44**
See also CA 110; CANR 45

Barbey d'Aurevilly, Jules-Amedee
1808-1889 .... **NCLC 1; SSC 17**
See also DLB 119; GFL 1789 to the Present

Barbour, John c. 1316-1395 .... **CMLC 33**
See also DLB 146

Barbusse, Henri 1873-1935 .... **TCLC 5**
See also CA 105; 154; DLB 65; EWL 3; RGWL 2, 3

Barclay, Alexander c. 1475-1552 .... **LC 109**
See also DLB 132

Barclay, Bill
See Moorcock, Michael (John)

Barclay, William Ewert
See Moorcock, Michael (John)

Barea, Arturo 1897-1957 .... **TCLC 14**
See also CA 111; 201

Barfoot, Joan 1946- .... **CLC 18**
See also CA 105; CANR 141

Barham, Richard Harris
1788-1845 .... **NCLC 77**
See also DLB 159

Baring, Maurice 1874-1945 .... **TCLC 8**
See also CA 105; 168; DLB 34; HGG

Baring-Gould, Sabine 1834-1924 ... **TCLC 88**
See also DLB 156, 190

Barker, Clive 1952- .... **CLC 52, 205; SSC 53**
See also AAYA 10, 54; BEST 90:3; BPFB 1; CA 121; 129; CANR 71, 111, 133; CPW; DA3; DAM POP; DLB 261; HGG; INT CA-129; MTCW 1, 2; MTFW 2005; SUFW 2

Barker, George Granville
1913-1991 .... **CLC 8, 48**
See also CA 9-12R; 135; CANR 7, 38; CP 1, 2, 3, 4; DAM POET; DLB 20; EWL 3; MTCW 1

Barker, Harley Granville
See Granville-Barker, Harley
See also DLB 10

Barker, Howard 1946- .... **CLC 37**
See also CA 102; CBD; CD 5, 6; DLB 13, 233

Barker, Jane 1652-1732 .... **LC 42, 82**
See also DLB 39, 131

Barker, Pat(ricia) 1943- ...... **CLC 32, 94, 146**
See also BRWS 4; CA 117; 122; CANR 50, 101; CN 6, 7; DLB 271; INT CA-122

Barlach, Ernst (Heinrich)
1870-1938 .... **TCLC 84**
See also CA 178; DLB 56, 118; EWL 3

Barlow, Joel 1754-1812 .... **NCLC 23**
See also AMWS 2; DLB 37; RGAL 4

Barnard, Mary (Ethel) 1909- .... **CLC 48**
See also CA 21-22; CAP 2; CP 1

Barnes, Djuna 1892-1982 .... **CLC 3, 4, 8, 11, 29, 127; SSC 3**
See Steptoe, Lydia
See also AMWS 3; CA 9-12R; 107; CAD; CANR 16, 55; CN 1, 2, 3; CWD; DLB 4, 9, 45; EWL 3; GLL 1; MAL 5; MTCW 1, 2; MTFW 2005; RGAL 4; TCLE 1:1; TUS

Barnes, Jim 1933- .... **NNAL**
See also CA 108, 175; CAAE 175; CAAS 28; DLB 175

Barnes, Julian (Patrick) 1946- . **CLC 42, 141**
See also BRWS 4; CA 102; CANR 19, 54, 115, 137; CN 4, 5, 6, 7; DAB; DLB 194; DLBY 1993; EWL 3; MTCW 2; MTFW 2005

Barnes, Peter 1931-2004 .... **CLC 5, 56**
See also CA 65-68; 230; CAAS 12; CANR 33, 34, 64, 113; CBD; CD 5, 6; DFS 6; DLB 13, 233; MTCW 1

Barnes, William 1801-1886 .... **NCLC 75**
See also DLB 32

Baroja (y Nessi), Pio 1872-1956 .... **HLC 1; TCLC 8**
See also CA 104; EW 9

Baron, David
See Pinter, Harold

Baron Corvo
See Rolfe, Frederick (William Serafino Austin Lewis Mary)

Barondess, Sue K(aufman)
1926-1977 .... **CLC 8**
See Kaufman, Sue
See also CA 1-4R; 69-72; CANR 1

Baron de Teive
See Pessoa, Fernando (Antonio Nogueira)

Baroness Von S.
See Zangwill, Israel

Barres, (Auguste-)Maurice
1862-1923 .... **TCLC 47**
See also CA 164; DLB 123; GFL 1789 to the Present

Barreto, Afonso Henrique de Lima
See Lima Barreto, Afonso Henrique de

Barrett, Andrea 1954- .... **CLC 150**
See also CA 156; CANR 92; CN 7

Barrett, Michele .... **CLC 65**

Barrett, (Roger) Syd 1946- .... **CLC 35**

Barrett, William (Christopher)
1913-1992 .... **CLC 27**
See also CA 13-16R; 139; CANR 11, 67; INT CANR-11

Barrett Browning, Elizabeth
1806-1861 ... **NCLC 1, 16, 61, 66; PC 6, 62; WLC**
See also AAYA 63; BRW 4; CDBLB 1832-1890; DA; DA3; DAB; DAC; DAM MST, POET; DLB 32, 199; EXPP; FL 1:2; PAB; PFS 2, 16, 23; TEA; WLIT 4; WP

Barrie, J(ames) M(atthew)
1860-1937 .... **TCLC 2, 164**
See also BRWS 3; BYA 5; CA 104; 136; CANR 77; CDBLB 1890-1914; CLR 16; CWRI 5; DA3; DAB; DAM DRAM; DFS 7; DLB 10, 141, 156; EWL 3; FANT; MAICYA 1, 2; MTCW 2; MTFW 2005; SATA 100; SUFW; WCH; WLIT 4; YABC 1

Barrington, Michael
See Moorcock, Michael (John)

Barrol, Grady
See Bograd, Larry

Barry, Mike
See Malzberg, Barry N(athaniel)

Barry, Philip 1896-1949 .... **TCLC 11**
See also CA 109; 199; DFS 9; DLB 7, 228; MAL 5; RGAL 4

Bart, Andre Schwarz
See Schwarz-Bart, Andre

Barth, John (Simmons) 1930- ... **CLC 1, 2, 3, 5, 7, 9, 10, 14, 27, 51, 89, 214; SSC 10, 89**
See also AITN 1, 2; AMW; BPFB 1; CA 1-4R; CABS 1; CANR 5, 23, 49, 64, 113; CN 1, 2, 3, 4, 5, 6, 7; DAM NOV; DLB 2, 227; EWL 3; FANT; MAL 5; MTCW 1; RGAL 4; RGSF 2; RHW; SSFS 6; TUS

Barthelme, Donald 1931-1989 ... **CLC 1, 2, 3, 5, 6, 8, 13, 23, 46, 59, 115; SSC 2, 55**
See also AMWS 4; BPFB 1; CA 21-24R; 129; CANR 20, 58; CN 1, 2, 3, 4; DA3; DAM NOV; DLB 2, 234; DLBY 1980, 1989; EWL 3; FANT; LMFS 2; MAL 5; MTCW 1, 2; MTFW 2005; RGAL 4; RGSF 2; SATA 7; SATA-Obit 62; SSFS 17

Barthelme, Frederick 1943- ...... **CLC 36, 117**
See also AMWS 11; CA 114; 122; CANR 77; CN 4, 5, 6, 7; CSW; DLB 244; DLBY 1985; EWL 3; INT CA-122

Barthes, Roland (Gerard) 1915-1980 .... **CLC 24, 83; TCLC 135**
See also CA 130; 97-100; CANR 66; DLB 296; EW 13; EWL 3; GFL 1789 to the Present; MTCW 1, 2; TWA

Bartram, William 1739-1823 .... **NCLC 145**
See also ANW; DLB 37

Barzun, Jacques (Martin) 1907- ..... **CLC 51, 145**
See also CA 61-64; CANR 22, 95

Bashevis, Isaac
See Singer, Isaac Bashevis

Bashkirtseff, Marie 1859-1884 .... **NCLC 27**

Basho, Matsuo
See Matsuo Basho
See also RGWL 2, 3; WP

Basil of Caesaria c. 330-379 .... **CMLC 35**

Basket, Raney
See Edgerton, Clyde (Carlyle)

Bass, Kingsley B., Jr.
See Bullins, Ed

Bass, Rick 1958- .... **CLC 79, 143; SSC 60**
See also ANW; CA 126; CANR 53, 93, 145; CSW; DLB 212, 275

Bassani, Giorgio 1916-2000 .... **CLC 9**
See also CA 65-68; 190; CANR 33; CWW 2; DLB 128, 177, 299; EWL 3; MTCW 1; RGWL 2, 3

Bastian, Ann .... **CLC 70**

Bastos, Augusto (Antonio) Roa
See Roa Bastos, Augusto (Jose Antonio)

Bataille, Georges 1897-1962 .... **CLC 29; TCLC 155**
See also CA 101; 89-92; EWL 3

Bates, H(erbert) E(rnest) 1905-1974 .... **CLC 46; SSC 10**
See also CA 93-96; 45-48; CANR 34; CN 1; DA3; DAB; DAM POP; DLB 162, 191; EWL 3; EXPS; MTCW 1, 2; RGSF 2; SSFS 7

Bauchart
See Camus, Albert

Baudelaire, Charles 1821-1867 . **NCLC 6, 29, 55, 155; PC 1; SSC 18; WLC**
See also DA; DA3; DAB; DAC; DAM MST, POET; DLB 217; EW 7; GFL 1789 to the Present; LMFS 2; PFS 21; RGWL 2, 3; TWA

Baudouin, Marcel
See Peguy, Charles (Pierre)

Baudouin, Pierre
See Peguy, Charles (Pierre)

Baudrillard, Jean 1929- .... **CLC 60**
See also DLB 296

Baum, L(yman) Frank 1856-1919 .. **TCLC 7, 132**
See also AAYA 46; BYA 16; CA 108; 133; CLR 15; CWRI 5; DLB 22; FANT; JRDA; MAICYA 1, 2; MTCW 1, 2; NFS 13; RGAL 4; SATA 18, 100; WCH

Baum, Louis F.
See Baum, L(yman) Frank

Baumbach, Jonathan 1933- .... **CLC 6, 23**
See also CA 13-16R; CAAS 5; CANR 12, 66, 140; CN 3, 4, 5, 6, 7; DLBY 1980; INT CANR-12; MTCW 1

Bausch, Richard (Carl) 1945- .... **CLC 51**
See also AMWS 7; CA 101; CAAS 14; CANR 43, 61, 87; CN 7; CSW; DLB 130; MAL 5

Baxter, Charles (Morley) 1947- . **CLC 45, 78**
See also CA 57-60; CANR 40, 64, 104, 133; CPW; DAM POP; DLB 130; MAL 5; MTCW 2; MTFW 2005; TCLE 1:1

Baxter, George Owen
See Faust, Frederick (Schiller)

Baxter, James K(eir) 1926-1972 .... **CLC 14**
See also CA 77-80; CP 1; EWL 3

Baxter, John
See Hunt, E(verette) Howard, (Jr.)

Bayer, Sylvia
See Glassco, John

Bayle, Pierre 1647-1706 .... **LC 126**
See also DLB 268, 313; GFL Beginnings to 1789

Baynton, Barbara 1857-1929 .... **TCLC 57**
See also DLB 230; RGSF 2

Beagle, Peter S(oyer) 1939- .... **CLC 7, 104**
See also AAYA 47; BPFB 1; BYA 9, 10, 16; CA 9-12R; CANR 4, 51, 73, 110; DA3; DLBY 1980; FANT; INT CANR-4; MTCW 2; MTFW 2005; SATA 60, 130; SUFW 1, 2; YAW

Bean, Normal
See Burroughs, Edgar Rice

Beard, Charles A(ustin) 1874-1948 .... **TCLC 15**
See also CA 115; 189; DLB 17; SATA 18

Beardsley, Aubrey 1872-1898 .... **NCLC 6**

Beattie, Ann 1947- ..... **CLC 8, 13, 18, 40, 63, 146; SSC 11**
See also AMWS 5; BEST 90:2; BPFB 1; CA 81-84; CANR 53, 73, 128; CN 4, 5, 6, 7; CPW; DA3; DAM NOV, POP; DLB 218, 278; DLBY 1982; EWL 3; MAL 5; MTCW 1, 2; MTFW 2005; RGAL 4; RGSF 2; SSFS 9; TUS

Beattie, James 1735-1803 .... **NCLC 25**
See also DLB 109

Beauchamp, Kathleen Mansfield 1888-1923
See Mansfield, Katherine
See also CA 104; 134; DA; DA3; DAC; DAM MST, MTCW 2; TEA

Beaumarchais, Pierre-Augustin Caron de 1732-1799 .... **DC 4; LC 61**
See also DAM DRAM; DFS 14, 16; DLB 313; EW 4; GFL Beginnings to 1789; RGWL 2, 3

Beaumont, Francis 1584(?)-1616 .. **DC 6; LC 33**
See also BRW 2; CDBLB Before 1660; DLB 58; TEA

Beauvoir, Simone (Lucie Ernestine Marie Bertrand) de 1908-1986 .... **CLC 1, 2, 4, 8, 14, 31, 44, 50, 71, 124; SSC 35; WLC**
See also BPFB 1; CA 9-12R; 118; CANR 28, 61; DA; DA3; DAB; DAC; DAM MST, NOV; DLB 72; DLBY 1986; EW 12; EWL 3; FL 1:5; FW; GFL 1789 to the Present; LMFS 2; MTCW 1, 2; MTFW 2005; RGSF 2; RGWL 2, 3; TWA

Becker, Carl (Lotus) 1873-1945 ..... **TCLC 63**
See also CA 157; DLB 17

Becker, Jurek 1937-1997 .... **CLC 7, 19**
See also CA 85-88; 157; CANR 60, 117; CWW 2; DLB 75, 299; EWL 3

Becker, Walter 1950- .... **CLC 26**

Beckett, Samuel (Barclay) 1906-1989 .. **CLC 1, 2, 3, 4, 6, 9, 10, 11, 14, 18, 29, 57, 59, 83; DC 22; SSC 16, 74; TCLC 145; WLC**
See also BRWC 2; BRWR 1; BRWS 1; CA 5-8R; 130; CANR 33, 61; CBD; CDBLB 1945-1960; CN 1, 2, 3, 4; CP 1, 2, 3, 4; DA; DA3; DAB; DAC; DAM DRAM, MST, NOV; DFS 2, 7, 18; DLB 13, 15, 233, 319, 321; DLBY 1990; EWL 3; GFL 1789 to the Present; LATS 1:2; LMFS 2; MTCW 1, 2; MTFW 2005; RGSF 2; RGWL 2, 3; SSFS 15; TEA; WLIT 4

Beckford, William 1760-1844 .... **NCLC 16**
See also BRW 3; DLB 39, 213; GL 2; HGG; LMFS 1; SUFW

Beckham, Barry (Earl) 1944- .... **BLC 1**
See also BW 1; CA 29-32R; CANR 26, 62; CN 1, 2, 3, 4, 5, 6; DAM MULT; DLB 33

Beckman, Gunnel 1910- .... **CLC 26**
See also CA 33-36R; CANR 15, 114; CLR 25; MAICYA 1, 2; SAAS 9; SATA 6

Becque, Henri 1837-1899 .... **DC 21; NCLC 3**
See also DLB 192; GFL 1789 to the Present

Becquer, Gustavo Adolfo 1836-1870 .... **HLCS 1; NCLC 106**
See also DAM MULT

Beddoes, Thomas Lovell 1803-1849 .. **DC 15; NCLC 3, 154**
See also BRWS 11; DLB 96

Bede c. 673-735 .... **CMLC 20**
See also DLB 146; TEA

Bedford, Denton R. 1907-(?) .... **NNAL**

Bedford, Donald F.
See Fearing, Kenneth (Flexner)

Beecher, Catharine Esther 1800-1878 .... **NCLC 30**
See also DLB 1, 243

Beecher, John 1904-1980 .... **CLC 6**
See also AITN 1; CA 5-8R; 105; CANR 8; CP 1, 2, 3

Beer, Johann 1655-1700 .... **LC 5**
See also DLB 168

Beer, Patricia 1924- .... **CLC 58**
See also CA 61-64; 183; CANR 13, 46; CP 1, 2, 3, 4; CWP; DLB 40; FW

Beerbohm, Max
See Beerbohm, (Henry) Max(imilian)

Beerbohm, (Henry) Max(imilian) 1872-1956 .... **TCLC 1, 24**
See also BRWS 2; CA 104; 154; CANR 79; DLB 34, 100; FANT; MTCW 2

Beer-Hofmann, Richard 1866-1945 .... **TCLC 60**
See also CA 160; DLB 81

Beg, Shemus
See Stephens, James

Begiebing, Robert J(ohn) 1946- .... **CLC 70**
See also CA 122; CANR 40, 88

Begley, Louis 1933- .... **CLC 197**
See also CA 140; CANR 98; DLB 299; TCLE 1:1

Behan, Brendan (Francis) 1923-1964 .... **CLC 1, 8, 11, 15, 79**
See also BRWS 2; CA 73-76; CANR 33, 121; CBD; CDBLB 1945-1960; DAM DRAM; DFS 7; DLB 13, 233; EWL 3; MTCW 1, 2

Behn, Aphra 1640(?)-1689 .. **DC 4; LC 1, 30, 42; PC 13; WLC**
See also BRWS 3; DA; DA3; DAB; DAC; DAM DRAM, MST, NOV, POET; DFS 16; DLB 39, 80, 131; FW; TEA; WLIT 3

Behrman, S(amuel) N(athaniel)
1893-1973 .... **CLC 40**
See also CA 13-16; 45-48; CAD; CAP 1;
DLB 7, 44; IDFW 3; MAL 5; RGAL 4

Bekederemo, J. P. Clark
See Clark Bekederemo, J(ohnson) P(epper)
See also CD 6

Belasco, David 1853-1931 .... **TCLC 3**
See also CA 104; 168; DLB 7; MAL 5;
RGAL 4

Belcheva, Elisaveta Lyubomirova
1893-1991 .... **CLC 10**
See Bagryana, Elisaveta

Beldone, Phil "Cheech"
See Ellison, Harlan (Jay)

Beleno
See Azuela, Mariano

Belinski, Vissarion Grigoryevich
1811-1848 .... **NCLC 5**
See also DLB 198

Belitt, Ben 1911- .... **CLC 22**
See also CA 13-16R; CAAS 4; CANR 7,
77; CP 1, 2, 3, 4; DLB 5

Belknap, Jeremy 1744-1798 .... **LC 115**
See also DLB 30, 37

Bell, Gertrude (Margaret Lowthian)
1868-1926 .... **TCLC 67**
See also CA 167; CANR 110; DLB 174

Bell, J. Freeman
See Zangwill, Israel

Bell, James Madison 1826-1902 .... **BLC 1;
TCLC 43**
See also BW 1; CA 122; 124; DAM MULT;
DLB 50

Bell, Madison Smartt 1957- ...... **CLC 41, 102**
See also AMWS 10; BPFB 1; CA 111, 183;
CAAE 183; CANR 28, 54, 73, 134; CN
5, 6, 7; CSW; DLB 218, 278; MTCW 2;
MTFW 2005

Bell, Marvin (Hartley) 1937- .... **CLC 8, 31**
See also CA 21-24R; CAAS 14; CANR 59,
102; CP 1, 2, 3, 4, 5, 6, 7; DAM POET;
DLB 5; MAL 5; MTCW 1

Bell, W. L. D.
See Mencken, H(enry) L(ouis)

Bellamy, Atwood C.
See Mencken, H(enry) L(ouis)

Bellamy, Edward 1850-1898 ..... **NCLC 4, 86,
147**
See also DLB 12; NFS 15; RGAL 4; SFW 4

Belli, Gioconda 1948- .... **HLCS 1**
See also CA 152; CANR 143; CWW 2;
DLB 290; EWL 3; RGWL 3

Bellin, Edward J.
See Kuttner, Henry

Bello, Andres 1781-1865 .... **NCLC 131**
See also LAW

**Belloc, (Joseph) Hilaire (Pierre Sebastien
Rene Swanton)** 1870-1953 .... **PC 24;
TCLC 7, 18**
See also CA 106; 152; CLR 102; CWRI 5;
DAM POET; DLB 19, 100, 141, 174;
EWL 3; MTCW 2; MTFW 2005; SATA
112; WCH; YABC 1

Belloc, Joseph Peter Rene Hilaire
See Belloc, (Joseph) Hilaire (Pierre Sebastien Rene Swanton)

Belloc, Joseph Pierre Hilaire
See Belloc, (Joseph) Hilaire (Pierre Sebastien Rene Swanton)

Belloc, M. A.
See Lowndes, Marie Adelaide (Belloc)

Belloc-Lowndes, Mrs.
See Lowndes, Marie Adelaide (Belloc)

Bellow, Saul 1915-2005 ...... **CLC 1, 2, 3, 6, 8,
10, 13, 15, 25, 33, 34, 63, 79, 190, 200;
SSC 14; WLC**
See also AITN 2; AMW; AMWC 2; AMWR
2; BEST 89:3; BPFB 1; CA 5-8R; 238;
CABS 1; CANR 29, 53, 95, 132; CDALB
1941-1968; CN 1, 2, 3, 4, 5, 6, 7; DA;
DA3; DAB; DAC; DAM MST, NOV,
POP; DLB 2, 28, 299; DLBD 3; DLBY
1982; EWL 3; MAL 5; MTCW 1, 2;
MTFW 2005; NFS 4, 14; RGAL 4; RGSF
2; SSFS 12; TUS

Belser, Reimond Karel Maria de 1929-
See Ruyslinck, Ward
See also CA 152

Bely, Andrey .... **PC 11; TCLC 7**
See Bugayev, Boris Nikolayevich
See also DLB 295; EW 9; EWL 3

Belyi, Andrei
See Bugayev, Boris Nikolayevich
See also RGWL 2, 3

Bembo, Pietro 1470-1547 .... **LC 79**
See also RGWL 2, 3

Benary, Margot
See Benary-Isbert, Margot

Benary-Isbert, Margot 1889-1979 .... **CLC 12**
See also CA 5-8R; 89-92; CANR 4, 72;
CLR 12; MAICYA 1, 2; SATA 2; SATA-
Obit 21

Benavente (y Martinez), Jacinto
1866-1954 .... **DC 26; HLCS 1; TCLC 3**
See also CA 106; 131; CANR 81; DAM
DRAM, MULT; EWL 3; GLL 2; HW 1,
2; MTCW 1, 2

Benchley, Peter 1940- .... **CLC 4, 8**
See also AAYA 14; AITN 2; BPFB 1; CA
17-20R; CANR 12, 35, 66, 115; CPW;
DAM NOV, POP; HGG; MTCW 1, 2;
MTFW 2005; SATA 3, 89, 164

Benchley, Peter Bradford
See Benchley, Peter

Benchley, Robert (Charles)
1889-1945 .... **TCLC 1, 55**
See also CA 105; 153; DLB 11; MAL 5;
RGAL 4

Benda, Julien 1867-1956 .... **TCLC 60**
See also CA 120; 154; GFL 1789 to the Present

Benedict, Ruth (Fulton)
1887-1948 .... **TCLC 60**
See also CA 158; DLB 246

Benedikt, Michael 1935- .... **CLC 4, 14**
See also CA 13-16R; CANR 7; CP 1, 2, 3,
4, 5, 6, 7; DLB 5

Benet, Juan 1927-1993 .... **CLC 28**
See also CA 143; EWL 3

Benet, Stephen Vincent 1898-1943 ..... **PC 64;
SSC 10, 86; TCLC 7**
See also AMWS 11; CA 104; 152; DA3;
DAM POET; DLB 4, 48, 102, 249, 284;
DLBY 1997; EWL 3; HGG; MAL 5;
MTCW 2; MTFW 2005; RGAL 4; RGSF
2; SUFW; WP; YABC 1

Benet, William Rose 1886-1950 ..... **TCLC 28**
See also CA 118; 152; DAM POET; DLB
45; RGAL 4

Benford, Gregory (Albert) 1941- ...... **CLC 52**
See also BPFB 1; CA 69-72, 175; CAAE
175; CAAS 27; CANR 12, 24, 49, 95,
134; CN 7; CSW; DLBY 1982; MTFW
2005; SCFW 2; SFW 4

Bengtsson, Frans (Gunnar)
1894-1954 .... **TCLC 48**
See also CA 170; EWL 3

Benjamin, David
See Slavitt, David R(ytman)

Benjamin, Lois
See Gould, Lois

Benjamin, Walter 1892-1940 .... **TCLC 39**
See also CA 164; DLB 242; EW 11; EWL 3

Ben Jelloun, Tahar 1944-
See Jelloun, Tahar ben
See also CA 135; CWW 2; EWL 3; RGWL
3; WLIT 2

Benn, Gottfried 1886-1956 .. **PC 35; TCLC 3**
See also CA 106; 153; DLB 56; EWL 3;
RGWL 2, 3

Bennett, Alan 1934- .... **CLC 45, 77**
See also BRWS 8; CA 103; CANR 35, 55,
106; CBD; CD 5, 6; DAB; DAM MST;
DLB 310; MTCW 1, 2; MTFW 2005

Bennett, (Enoch) Arnold
1867-1931 .... **TCLC 5, 20**
See also BRW 6; CA 106; 155; CDBLB
1890-1914; DLB 10, 34, 98, 135; EWL 3;
MTCW 2

Bennett, Elizabeth
See Mitchell, Margaret (Munnerlyn)

Bennett, George Harold 1930-
See Bennett, Hal
See also BW 1; CA 97-100; CANR 87

Bennett, Gwendolyn B. 1902-1981 .... **HR 1:2**
See also BW 1; CA 125; DLB 51; WP

Bennett, Hal .... **CLC 5**
See Bennett, George Harold
See also DLB 33

Bennett, Jay 1912- .... **CLC 35**
See also AAYA 10; CA 69-72; CANR 11,
42, 79; JRDA; SAAS 4; SATA 41, 87;
SATA-Brief 27; WYA; YAW

Bennett, Louise (Simone) 1919- .... **BLC 1;
CLC 28**
See also BW 2, 3; CA 151; CDWLB 3; CP
1, 2, 3, 4, 5, 6, 7; DAM MULT; DLB 117;
EWL 3

Benson, A. C. 1862-1925 .... **TCLC 123**
See also DLB 98

Benson, E(dward) F(rederic)
1867-1940 .... **TCLC 27**
See also CA 114; 157; DLB 135, 153;
HGG; SUFW 1

Benson, Jackson J. 1930- .... **CLC 34**
See also CA 25-28R; DLB 111

Benson, Sally 1900-1972 .... **CLC 17**
See also CA 19-20; 37-40R; CAP 1; SATA
1, 35; SATA-Obit 27

Benson, Stella 1892-1933 .... **TCLC 17**
See also CA 117; 154, 155; DLB 36, 162;
FANT; TEA

Bentham, Jeremy 1748-1832 .... **NCLC 38**
See also DLB 107, 158, 252

Bentley, E(dmund) C(lerihew)
1875-1956 .... **TCLC 12**
See also CA 108; 232; DLB 70; MSW

Bentley, Eric (Russell) 1916- .... **CLC 24**
See also CA 5-8R; CAD; CANR 6, 67;
CBD; CD 5, 6; INT CANR-6

ben Uzair, Salem
See Horne, Richard Henry Hengist

Beranger, Pierre Jean de
1780-1857 .... **NCLC 34**

Berdyaev, Nicolas
See Berdyaev, Nikolai (Aleksandrovich)

Berdyaev, Nikolai (Aleksandrovich)
1874-1948 .... **TCLC 67**
See also CA 120; 157

Berdyayev, Nikolai (Aleksandrovich)
See Berdyaev, Nikolai (Aleksandrovich)

Berendt, John (Lawrence) 1939- ...... **CLC 86**
See also CA 146; CANR 75, 93; DA3;
MTCW 2; MTFW 2005

Beresford, J(ohn) D(avys)
1873-1947 .... **TCLC 81**
See also CA 112; 155; DLB 162, 178, 197;
SFW 4; SUFW 1

Bergelson, David (Rafailovich)
1884-1952 .... **TCLC 81**
See Bergelson, Dovid
See also CA 220

Bergelson, Dovid
See Bergelson, David (Rafailovich)
See also EWL 3

Berger, Colonel
See Malraux, (Georges-)Andre

Berger, John (Peter) 1926- .... **CLC 2, 19**
See also BRWS 4; CA 81-84; CANR 51, 78, 117; CN 1, 2, 3, 4, 5, 6, 7; DLB 14, 207, 319

Berger, Melvin H. 1927- .... **CLC 12**
See also CA 5-8R; CANR 4, 142; CLR 32; SAAS 2; SATA 5, 88, 158; SATA-Essay 124

Berger, Thomas (Louis) 1924- .. **CLC 3, 5, 8, 11, 18, 38**
See also BPFB 1; CA 1-4R; CANR 5, 28, 51, 128; CN 1, 2, 3, 4, 5, 6, 7; DAM NOV; DLB 2; DLBY 1980; EWL 3; FANT; INT CANR-28; MAL 5; MTCW 1, 2; MTFW 2005; RHW; TCLE 1:1; TCWW 1, 2

Bergman, (Ernst) Ingmar 1918- ...... **CLC 16, 72, 210**
See also AAYA 61; CA 81-84; CANR 33, 70; CWW 2; DLB 257; MTCW 2; MTFW 2005

Bergson, Henri(-Louis) 1859-1941 . **TCLC 32**
See also CA 164; EW 8; EWL 3; GFL 1789 to the Present

Bergstein, Eleanor 1938- .... **CLC 4**
See also CA 53-56; CANR 5

Berkeley, George 1685-1753 .... **LC 65**
See also DLB 31, 101, 252

Berkoff, Steven 1937- .... **CLC 56**
See also CA 104; CANR 72; CBD; CD 5, 6

Berlin, Isaiah 1909-1997 .... **TCLC 105**
See also CA 85-88; 162

Bermant, Chaim (Icyk) 1929-1998 ... **CLC 40**
See also CA 57-60; CANR 6, 31, 57, 105; CN 2, 3, 4, 5, 6

Bern, Victoria
See Fisher, M(ary) F(rances) K(ennedy)

Bernanos, (Paul Louis) Georges
1888-1948 .... **TCLC 3**
See also CA 104; 130; CANR 94; DLB 72; EWL 3; GFL 1789 to the Present; RGWL 2, 3

Bernard, April 1956- .... **CLC 59**
See also CA 131; CANR 144

Bernard of Clairvaux 1090-1153 .. **CMLC 71**
See also DLB 208

Berne, Victoria
See Fisher, M(ary) F(rances) K(ennedy)

Bernhard, Thomas 1931-1989 ...... **CLC 3, 32, 61; DC 14; TCLC 165**
See also CA 85-88; 127; CANR 32, 57; CDWLB 2; DLB 85, 124; EWL 3; MTCW 1; RGWL 2, 3

Bernhardt, Sarah (Henriette Rosine)
1844-1923 .... **TCLC 75**
See also CA 157

Bernstein, Charles 1950- .... **CLC 142**
See also CA 129; CAAS 24; CANR 90; CP 4, 5, 6, 7; DLB 169

Bernstein, Ingrid
See Kirsch, Sarah

Beroul fl. c. 12th cent. - .... **CMLC 75**

Berriault, Gina 1926-1999 .... **CLC 54, 109; SSC 30**
See also CA 116; 129; 185; CANR 66; DLB 130; SSFS 7,11

Berrigan, Daniel 1921- .... **CLC 4**
See also CA 33-36R; 187; CAAE 187; CAAS 1; CANR 11, 43, 78; CP 1, 2, 3, 4, 5, 6, 7; DLB 5

Berrigan, Edmund Joseph Michael, Jr.
1934-1983
See Berrigan, Ted
See also CA 61-64; 110; CANR 14, 102

Berrigan, Ted .... **CLC 37**
See Berrigan, Edmund Joseph Michael, Jr.
See also CP 1, 2, 3; DLB 5, 169; WP

Berry, Charles Edward Anderson 1931-
See Berry, Chuck
See also CA 115

Berry, Chuck .... **CLC 17**
See Berry, Charles Edward Anderson

Berry, Jonas
See Ashbery, John (Lawrence)
See also GLL 1

Berry, Wendell (Erdman) 1934- ... **CLC 4, 6, 8, 27, 46; PC 28**
See also AITN 1; AMWS 10; ANW; CA 73-76; CANR 50, 73, 101, 132; CP 1, 2, 3, 4, 5, 6, 7; CSW; DAM POET; DLB 5, 6, 234, 275; MTCW 2; MTFW 2005; TCLE 1:1

Berryman, John 1914-1972 ... **CLC 1, 2, 3, 4, 6, 8, 10, 13, 25, 62; PC 64**
See also AMW; CA 13-16; 33-36R; CABS 2; CANR 35; CAP 1; CDALB 1941-1968; CP 1; DAM POET; DLB 48; EWL 3; MAL 5; MTCW 1, 2; MTFW 2005; PAB; RGAL 4; WP

Bertolucci, Bernardo 1940- .... **CLC 16, 157**
See also CA 106; CANR 125

Berton, Pierre (Francis de Marigny)
1920-2004 .... **CLC 104**
See also CA 1-4R; 233; CANR 2, 56, 144; CPW; DLB 68; SATA 99; SATA-Obit 158

Bertrand, Aloysius 1807-1841 .... **NCLC 31**
See Bertrand, Louis oAloysiusc

Bertrand, Louis oAloysiusc
See Bertrand, Aloysius
See also DLB 217

Bertran de Born c. 1140-1215 .... **CMLC 5**

Besant, Annie (Wood) 1847-1933 ..... **TCLC 9**
See also CA 105; 185

Bessie, Alvah 1904-1985 .... **CLC 23**
See also CA 5-8R; 116; CANR 2, 80; DLB 26

Bestuzhev, Aleksandr Aleksandrovich
1797-1837 .... **NCLC 131**
See also DLB 198

Bethlen, T. D.
See Silverberg, Robert

Beti, Mongo .... **BLC 1; CLC 27**
See Biyidi, Alexandre
See also AFW; CANR 79; DAM MULT; EWL 3; WLIT 2

Betjeman, John 1906-1984 ...... **CLC 2, 6, 10, 34, 43**
See also BRW 7; CA 9-12R; 112; CANR 33, 56; CDBLB 1945-1960; CP 1, 2, 3; DA3; DAB; DAM MST, POET; DLB 20; DLBY 1984; EWL 3; MTCW 1, 2

Bettelheim, Bruno 1903-1990 .... **CLC 79; TCLC 143**
See also CA 81-84; 131; CANR 23, 61; DA3; MTCW 1, 2

Betti, Ugo 1892-1953 .... **TCLC 5**
See also CA 104; 155; EWL 3; RGWL 2, 3

Betts, Doris (Waugh) 1932- ...... **CLC 3, 6, 28; SSC 45**
See also CA 13-16R; CANR 9, 66, 77; CN 6, 7; CSW; DLB 218; DLBY 1982; INT CANR-9; RGAL 4

Bevan, Alistair
See Roberts, Keith (John Kingston)

Bey, Pilaff
See Douglas, (George) Norman

Bialik, Chaim Nachman
1873-1934 .... **TCLC 25**
See Bialik, Hayyim Nahman
See also CA 170; EWL 3

Bialik, Hayyim Nahman
See Bialik, Chaim Nachman
See also WLIT 6

Bickerstaff, Isaac
See Swift, Jonathan

Bidart, Frank 1939- .... **CLC 33**
See also AMWS 15; CA 140; CANR 106; CP 7

Bienek, Horst 1930- .... **CLC 7, 11**
See also CA 73-76; DLB 75

Bierce, Ambrose (Gwinett)
1842-1914(?) ..... **SSC 9, 72; TCLC 1, 7, 44; WLC**
See also AAYA 55; AMW; BYA 11; CA 104; 139; CANR 78; CDALB 1865-1917; DA; DA3; DAC; DAM MST; DLB 11, 12, 23, 71, 74, 186; EWL 3; EXPS; HGG; LAIT 2; MAL 5; RGAL 4; RGSF 2; SSFS 9; SUFW 1

Biggers, Earl Derr 1884-1933 .... **TCLC 65**
See also CA 108; 153; DLB 306

Billiken, Bud
See Motley, Willard (Francis)

Billings, Josh
See Shaw, Henry Wheeler

Billington, (Lady) Rachel (Mary)
1942- .... **CLC 43**
See also AITN 2; CA 33-36R; CANR 44; CN 4, 5, 6, 7

Binchy, Maeve 1940- .... **CLC 153**
See also BEST 90:1; BPFB 1; CA 127; 134; CANR 50, 96, 134; CN 5, 6, 7; CPW; DA3; DAM POP; DLB 319; INT CA-134; MTCW 2; MTFW 2005; RHW

Binyon, T(imothy) J(ohn)
1936-2004 .... **CLC 34**
See also CA 111; 232; CANR 28, 140

Bion 335B.C.-245B.C. .... **CMLC 39**

Bioy Casares, Adolfo 1914-1999 ... **CLC 4, 8, 13, 88; HLC 1; SSC 17**
See Casares, Adolfo Bioy; Miranda, Javier; Sacastru, Martin
See also CA 29-32R; 177; CANR 19, 43, 66; CWW 2; DAM MULT; DLB 113; EWL 3; HW 1, 2; LAW; MTCW 1, 2; MTFW 2005

Birch, Allison .... **CLC 65**

Bird, Cordwainer
See Ellison, Harlan (Jay)

Bird, Robert Montgomery
1806-1854 .... **NCLC 1**
See also DLB 202; RGAL 4

Birkerts, Sven 1951- .... **CLC 116**
See also CA 128; 133, 176; CAAE 176; CAAS 29; INT CA-133

Birney, (Alfred) Earle 1904-1995 .. **CLC 1, 4, 6, 11; PC 52**
See also CA 1-4R; CANR 5, 20; CN 1, 2, 3, 4; CP 1, 2, 3, 4; DAC; DAM MST, POET; DLB 88; MTCW 1; PFS 8; RGEL 2

Biruni, al 973-1048(?) .... **CMLC 28**

Bishop, Elizabeth 1911-1979 .... **CLC 1, 4, 9, 13, 15, 32; PC 3, 34; TCLC 121**
See also AMWR 2; AMWS 1; CA 5-8R; 89-92; CABS 2; CANR 26, 61, 108; CDALB 1968-1988; CP 1, 2, 3; DA; DA3; DAC; DAM MST, POET; DLB 5, 169; EWL 3; GLL 2; MAL 5; MAWW; MTCW 1, 2; PAB; PFS 6, 12; RGAL 4; SATA-Obit 24; TUS; WP

Bishop, John 1935- .... **CLC 10**
See also CA 105

Bishop, John Peale 1892-1944 ..... **TCLC 103**
See also CA 107; 155; DLB 4, 9, 45; MAL 5; RGAL 4

Bissett, Bill 1939- .... **CLC 18; PC 14**
See also CA 69-72; CAAS 19; CANR 15; CCA 1; CP 1, 2, 3, 4, 5, 6, 7; DLB 53; MTCW 1

Bissoondath, Neil (Devindra) 1955- .... **CLC 120**
See also CA 136; CANR 123; CN 6, 7; DAC

Bitov, Andrei (Georgievich) 1937- ... **CLC 57**
See also CA 142; DLB 302

Biyidi, Alexandre 1932-
See Beti, Mongo
See also BW 1, 3; CA 114; 124; CANR 81; DA3; MTCW 1, 2

Bjarme, Brynjolf
See Ibsen, Henrik (Johan)

Bjoernson, Bjoernstjerne (Martinius) 1832-1910 .... **TCLC 7, 37**
See also CA 104

Black, Robert
See Holdstock, Robert P.

Blackburn, Paul 1926-1971 .... **CLC 9, 43**
See also BG 1:2; CA 81-84; 33-36R; CANR 34; CP 1; DLB 16; DLBY 1981

Black Elk 1863-1950 .... **NNAL; TCLC 33**
See also CA 144; DAM MULT; MTCW 2; MTFW 2005; WP

Black Hawk 1767-1838 .... **NNAL**

Black Hobart
See Sanders, (James) Ed(ward)

Blacklin, Malcolm
See Chambers, Aidan

Blackmore, R(ichard) D(oddridge) 1825-1900 .... **TCLC 27**
See also CA 120; DLB 18; RGEL 2

Blackmur, R(ichard) P(almer) 1904-1965 .... **CLC 2, 24**
See also AMWS 2; CA 11-12; 25-28R; CANR 71; CAP 1; DLB 63; EWL 3; MAL 5

Black Tarantula
See Acker, Kathy

Blackwood, Algernon (Henry) 1869-1951 .... **TCLC 5**
See also CA 105; 150; DLB 153, 156, 178; HGG; SUFW 1

Blackwood, Caroline (Maureen) 1931-1996 .... **CLC 6, 9, 100**
See also BRWS 9; CA 85-88; 151; CANR 32, 61, 65; CN 3, 4, 5, 6; DLB 14, 207; HGG; MTCW 1

Blade, Alexander
See Hamilton, Edmond; Silverberg, Robert

Blaga, Lucian 1895-1961 .... **CLC 75**
See also CA 157; DLB 220; EWL 3

Blair, Eric (Arthur) 1903-1950 .... **TCLC 123**
See Orwell, George
See also CA 104; 132; DA; DA3; DAB; DAC; DAM MST, NOV; MTCW 1, 2; MTFW 2005; SATA 29

Blair, Hugh 1718-1800 .... **NCLC 75**

Blais, Marie-Claire 1939- .... **CLC 2, 4, 6, 13, 22**
See also CA 21-24R; CAAS 4; CANR 38, 75, 93; CWW 2; DAC; DAM MST; DLB 53; EWL 3; FW; MTCW 1, 2; MTFW 2005; TWA

Blaise, Clark 1940- .... **CLC 29**
See also AITN 2; CA 53-56; 231; CAAE 231; CAAS 3; CANR 5, 66, 106; CN 4, 5, 6, 7; DLB 53; RGSF 2

Blake, Fairley
See De Voto, Bernard (Augustine)

Blake, Nicholas
See Day Lewis, C(ecil)
See also DLB 77; MSW

Blake, Sterling
See Benford, Gregory (Albert)

Blake, William 1757-1827 . **NCLC 13, 37, 57, 127; PC 12, 63; WLC**
See also AAYA 47; BRW 3; BRWR 1; CD-BLB 1789-1832; CLR 52; DA; DA3; DAB; DAC; DAM MST, POET; DLB 93, 163; EXPP; LATS 1:1; LMFS 1; MAICYA 1, 2; PAB; PFS 2, 12; SATA 30; TEA; WCH; WLIT 3; WP

Blanchot, Maurice 1907-2003 .... **CLC 135**
See also CA 117; 144; 213; CANR 138; DLB 72, 296; EWL 3

Blasco Ibanez, Vicente 1867-1928 . **TCLC 12**
See Ibanez, Vicente Blasco
See also BPFB 1; CA 110; 131; CANR 81; DA3; DAM NOV; EW 8; EWL 3; HW 1, 2; MTCW 1

Blatty, William Peter 1928- .... **CLC 2**
See also CA 5-8R; CANR 9, 124; DAM POP; HGG

Bleeck, Oliver
See Thomas, Ross (Elmore)

Blessing, Lee (Knowlton) 1949- .... **CLC 54**
See also CA 236; CAD; CD 5, 6

Blight, Rose
See Greer, Germaine

Blish, James (Benjamin) 1921-1975 . **CLC 14**
See also BPFB 1; CA 1-4R; 57-60; CANR 3; CN 2; DLB 8; MTCW 1; SATA 66; SCFW 1, 2; SFW 4

Bliss, Frederick
See Card, Orson Scott

Bliss, Reginald
See Wells, H(erbert) G(eorge)

Blixen, Karen (Christentze Dinesen) 1885-1962
See Dinesen, Isak
See also CA 25-28; CANR 22, 50; CAP 2; DA3; DLB 214; LMFS 1; MTCW 1, 2; SATA 44; SSFS 20

Bloch, Robert (Albert) 1917-1994 .... **CLC 33**
See also AAYA 29; CA 5-8R, 179; 146; CAAE 179; CAAS 20; CANR 5, 78; DA3; DLB 44; HGG; INT CANR-5; MTCW 2; SATA 12; SATA-Obit 82; SFW 4; SUFW 1, 2

Blok, Alexander (Alexandrovich) 1880-1921 .... **PC 21; TCLC 5**
See also CA 104; 183; DLB 295; EW 9; EWL 3; LMFS 2; RGWL 2, 3

Blom, Jan
See Breytenbach, Breyten

Bloom, Harold 1930- .... **CLC 24, 103, 221**
See also CA 13-16R; CANR 39, 75, 92, 133; DLB 67; EWL 3; MTCW 2; MTFW 2005; RGAL 4

Bloomfield, Aurelius
See Bourne, Randolph S(illiman)

Bloomfield, Robert 1766-1823 ..... **NCLC 145**
See also DLB 93

Blount, Roy (Alton), Jr. 1941- .... **CLC 38**
See also CA 53-56; CANR 10, 28, 61, 125; CSW; INT CANR-28; MTCW 1, 2; MTFW 2005

Blowsnake, Sam 1875-(?) .... **NNAL**

Bloy, Leon 1846-1917 .... **TCLC 22**
See also CA 121; 183; DLB 123; GFL 1789 to the Present

Blue Cloud, Peter (Aroniawenrate) 1933- .... **NNAL**
See also CA 117; CANR 40; DAM MULT

Bluggage, Oranthy
See Alcott, Louisa May

Blume, Judy (Sussman) 1938- .... **CLC 12, 30**
See also AAYA 3, 26; BYA 1, 8, 12; CA 29-32R; CANR 13, 37, 66, 124; CLR 2, 15, 69; CPW; DA3; DAM NOV, POP; DLB 52; JRDA; MAICYA 1, 2; MAICYAS 1; MTCW 1, 2; MTFW 2005; SATA 2, 31, 79, 142; WYA; YAW

Blunden, Edmund (Charles) 1896-1974 .... **CLC 2, 56; PC 66**
See also BRW 6; BRWS 11; CA 17-18; 45-48; CANR 54; CAP 2; CP 1, 2; DLB 20, 100, 155; MTCW 1; PAB

Bly, Robert (Elwood) 1926- .... **CLC 1, 2, 5, 10, 15, 38, 128; PC 39**
See also AMWS 4; CA 5-8R; CANR 41, 73, 125; CP 1, 2, 3, 4, 5, 6, 7; DA3; DAM POET; DLB 5; EWL 3; MAL 5; MTCW 1, 2; MTFW 2005; PFS 6, 17; RGAL 4

Boas, Franz 1858-1942 .... **TCLC 56**
See also CA 115; 181

Bobette
See Simenon, Georges (Jacques Christian)

Boccaccio, Giovanni 1313-1375 ... **CMLC 13, 57; SSC 10, 87**
See also EW 2; RGSF 2; RGWL 2, 3; TWA; WLIT 7

Bochco, Steven 1943- .... **CLC 35**
See also AAYA 11; CA 124; 138

Bode, Sigmund
See O'Doherty, Brian

Bodel, Jean 1167(?)-1210 .... **CMLC 28**

Bodenheim, Maxwell 1892-1954 .... **TCLC 44**
See also CA 110; 187; DLB 9, 45; MAL 5; RGAL 4

Bodenheimer, Maxwell
See Bodenheim, Maxwell

Bodker, Cecil 1927-
See Bodker, Cecil

Bodker, Cecil 1927- .... **CLC 21**
See also CA 73-76; CANR 13, 44, 111; CLR 23; MAICYA 1, 2; SATA 14, 133

Boell, Heinrich (Theodor) 1917-1985 ..... **CLC 2, 3, 6, 9, 11, 15, 27, 32, 72; SSC 23; WLC**
See Boll, Heinrich (Theodor)
See also CA 21-24R; 116; CANR 24; DA; DA3; DAB; DAC; DAM MST, NOV; DLB 69; DLBY 1985; MTCW 1, 2; MTFW 2005; SSFS 20; TWA

Boerne, Alfred
See Doeblin, Alfred

Boethius c. 480-c. 524 .... **CMLC 15**
See also DLB 115; RGWL 2, 3

Boff, Leonardo (Genezio Darci) 1938- .... **CLC 70; HLC 1**
See also CA 150; DAM MULT; HW 2

Bogan, Louise 1897-1970 .... **CLC 4, 39, 46, 93; PC 12**
See also AMWS 3; CA 73-76; 25-28R; CANR 33, 82; CP 1; DAM POET; DLB 45, 169; EWL 3; MAL 5; MAWW; MTCW 1, 2; PFS 21; RGAL 4

Bogarde, Dirk
See Van Den Bogarde, Derek Jules Gaspard Ulric Niven
See also DLB 14

Bogosian, Eric 1953- .... **CLC 45, 141**
See also CA 138; CAD; CANR 102; CD 5, 6

Bograd, Larry 1953- .... **CLC 35**
See also CA 93-96; CANR 57; SAAS 21; SATA 33, 89; WYA

Boiardo, Matteo Maria 1441-1494 .... **LC 6**

Boileau-Despreaux, Nicolas 1636-1711 . **LC 3**
See also DLB 268; EW 3; GFL Beginnings to 1789; RGWL 2, 3

Boissard, Maurice
See Leautaud, Paul

Bojer, Johan 1872-1959 .... **TCLC 64**
See also CA 189; EWL 3

Bok, Edward W(illiam) 1863-1930 .... **TCLC 101**
See also CA 217; DLB 91; DLBD 16

Boker, George Henry 1823-1890 . **NCLC 125**
See also RGAL 4
Boland, Eavan (Aisling) 1944- .. **CLC 40, 67, 113; PC 58**
See also BRWS 5; CA 143, 207; CAAE 207; CANR 61; CP 1, 7; CWP; DAM POET; DLB 40; FW; MTCW 2; MTFW 2005; PFS 12, 22
Boll, Heinrich (Theodor)
See Boell, Heinrich (Theodor)
See also BPFB 1; CDWLB 2; EW 13; EWL 3; RGSF 2; RGWL 2, 3
Bolt, Lee
See Faust, Frederick (Schiller)
Bolt, Robert (Oxton) 1924-1995 ...... **CLC 14; TCLC 175**
See also CA 17-20R; 147; CANR 35, 67; CBD; DAM DRAM; DFS 2; DLB 13, 233; EWL 3; LAIT 1; MTCW 1
Bombal, Maria Luisa 1910-1980 .... **HLCS 1; SSC 37**
See also CA 127; CANR 72; EWL 3; HW 1; LAW; RGSF 2
Bombet, Louis-Alexandre-Cesar
See Stendhal
Bomkauf
See Kaufman, Bob (Garnell)
Bonaventura .... **NCLC 35**
See also DLB 90
Bonaventure 1217(?)-1274 .... **CMLC 79**
See also DLB 115; LMFS 1
Bond, Edward 1934- .... **CLC 4, 6, 13, 23**
See also AAYA 50; BRWS 1; CA 25-28R; CANR 38, 67, 106; CBD; CD 5, 6; DAM DRAM; DFS 3, 8; DLB 13, 310; EWL 3; MTCW 1
Bonham, Frank 1914-1989 .... **CLC 12**
See also AAYA 1; BYA 1, 3; CA 9-12R; CANR 4, 36; JRDA; MAICYA 1, 2; SAAS 3; SATA 1, 49; SATA-Obit 62; TCWW 1, 2; YAW
Bonnefoy, Yves 1923- . **CLC 9, 15, 58; PC 58**
See also CA 85-88; CANR 33, 75, 97, 136; CWW 2; DAM MST, POET; DLB 258; EWL 3; GFL 1789 to the Present; MTCW 1, 2; MTFW 2005
Bonner, Marita .... **HR 1:2**
See Occomy, Marita (Odette) Bonner
Bonnin, Gertrude 1876-1938 .... **NNAL**
See Zitkala-Sa
See also CA 150; DAM MULT
Bontemps, Arna(ud Wendell) 1902-1973 .. **BLC 1; CLC 1, 18; HR 1:2**
See also BW 1; CA 1-4R; 41-44R; CANR 4, 35; CLR 6; CP 1; CWRI 5; DA3; DAM MULT, NOV, POET; DLB 48, 51; JRDA; MAICYA 1, 2; MAL 5; MTCW 1, 2; SATA 2, 44; SATA-Obit 24; WCH; WP
Boot, William
See Stoppard, Tom
Booth, Martin 1944-2004 .... **CLC 13**
See also CA 93-96, 188; 223; CAAE 188; CAAS 2; CANR 92; CP 1, 2, 3, 4
Booth, Philip 1925- .... **CLC 23**
See also CA 5-8R; CANR 5, 88; CP 1, 2, 3, 4, 5, 6, 7; DLBY 1982
Booth, Wayne C(layson) 1921-2005 . **CLC 24**
See also CA 1-4R; CAAS 5; CANR 3, 43, 117; DLB 67
Borchert, Wolfgang 1921-1947 .... **TCLC 5**
See also CA 104; 188; DLB 69, 124; EWL 3
Borel, Petrus 1809-1859 .... **NCLC 41**
See also DLB 119; GFL 1789 to the Present
Borges, Jorge Luis 1899-1986 ... **CLC 1, 2, 3, 4, 6, 8, 9, 10, 13, 19, 44, 48, 83; HLC 1; PC 22, 32; SSC 4, 41; TCLC 109; WLC**
See also AAYA 26; BPFB 1; CA 21-24R; CANR 19, 33, 75, 105, 133; CDWLB 3; DA; DA3; DAB; DAC; DAM MST, MULT; DLB 113, 283; DLBY 1986; DNFS 1, 2; EWL 3; HW 1, 2; LAW; LMFS 2; MSW; MTCW 1, 2; MTFW 2005; RGSF 2; RGWL 2, 3; SFW 4; SSFS 17; TWA; WLIT 1
Borowski, Tadeusz 1922-1951 .... **SSC 48; TCLC 9**
See also CA 106; 154; CDWLB 4; DLB 215; EWL 3; RGSF 2; RGWL 3; SSFS 13
Borrow, George (Henry) 1803-1881 .... **NCLC 9**
See also DLB 21, 55, 166
Bosch (Gavino), Juan 1909-2001 ..... **HLCS 1**
See also CA 151; 204; DAM MST, MULT; DLB 145; HW 1, 2
Bosman, Herman Charles 1905-1951 .... **TCLC 49**
See Malan, Herman
See also CA 160; DLB 225; RGSF 2
Bosschere, Jean de 1878(?)-1953 ... **TCLC 19**
See also CA 115; 186
Boswell, James 1740-1795 ... **LC 4, 50; WLC**
See also BRW 3; CDBLB 1660-1789; DA; DAB; DAC; DAM MST; DLB 104, 142; TEA; WLIT 3
Bottomley, Gordon 1874-1948 ..... **TCLC 107**
See also CA 120; 192; DLB 10
Bottoms, David 1949- .... **CLC 53**
See also CA 105; CANR 22; CSW; DLB 120; DLBY 1983
Boucicault, Dion 1820-1890 .... **NCLC 41**
Boucolon, Maryse
See Conde, Maryse
Bourdieu, Pierre 1930-2002 .... **CLC 198**
See also CA 130; 204
Bourget, Paul (Charles Joseph) 1852-1935 .... **TCLC 12**
See also CA 107; 196; DLB 123; GFL 1789 to the Present
Bourjaily, Vance (Nye) 1922- .... **CLC 8, 62**
See also CA 1-4R; CAAS 1; CANR 2, 72; CN 1, 2, 3, 4, 5, 6, 7; DLB 2, 143; MAL 5
Bourne, Randolph S(illiman) 1886-1918 .... **TCLC 16**
See also AMW; CA 117; 155; DLB 63; MAL 5
Bova, Ben(jamin William) 1932- .... **CLC 45**
See also AAYA 16; CA 5-8R; CAAS 18; CANR 11, 56, 94, 111; CLR 3, 96; DLBY 1981; INT CANR-11; MAICYA 1, 2; MTCW 1; SATA 6, 68, 133; SFW 4
Bowen, Elizabeth (Dorothea Cole) 1899-1973 . **CLC 1, 3, 6, 11, 15, 22, 118; SSC 3, 28, 66; TCLC 148**
See also BRWS 2; CA 17-18; 41-44R; CANR 35, 105; CAP 2; CDBLB 1945-1960; CN 1; DA3; DAM NOV; DLB 15, 162; EWL 3; EXPS; FW; HGG; MTCW 1, 2; MTFW 2005; NFS 13; RGSF 2; SSFS 5; SUFW 1; TEA; WLIT 4
Bowering, George 1935- .... **CLC 15, 47**
See also CA 21-24R; CAAS 16; CANR 10; CN 7; CP 1, 2, 3, 4, 5, 6, 7; DLB 53
Bowering, Marilyn R(uthe) 1949- .... **CLC 32**
See also CA 101; CANR 49; CP 4, 5, 6, 7; CWP
Bowers, Edgar 1924-2000 .... **CLC 9**
See also CA 5-8R; 188; CANR 24; CP 1, 2, 3, 4, 5, 6, 7; CSW; DLB 5
Bowers, Mrs. J. Milton 1842-1914
See Bierce, Ambrose (Gwinett)
Bowie, David .... **CLC 17**
See Jones, David Robert

Bowles, Jane (Sydney) 1917-1973 ..... **CLC 3, 68**
See Bowles, Jane Auer
See also CA 19-20; 41-44R; CAP 2; CN 1; MAL 5
Bowles, Jane Auer
See Bowles, Jane (Sydney)
See also EWL 3
Bowles, Paul (Frederick) 1910-1999 . **CLC 1, 2, 19, 53; SSC 3**
See also AMWS 4; CA 1-4R; 186; CAAS 1; CANR 1, 19, 50, 75; CN 1, 2, 3, 4, 5, 6; DA3; DLB 5, 6, 218; EWL 3; MAL 5; MTCW 1, 2; MTFW 2005; RGAL 4; SSFS 17
Bowles, William Lisle 1762-1850 . **NCLC 103**
See also DLB 93
Box, Edgar
See Vidal, (Eugene Luther) Gore
See also GLL 1
Boyd, James 1888-1944 .... **TCLC 115**
See also CA 186; DLB 9; DLBD 16; RGAL 4; RHW
Boyd, Nancy
See Millay, Edna St. Vincent
See also GLL 1
Boyd, Thomas (Alexander) 1898-1935 .... **TCLC 111**
See also CA 111; 183; DLB 9; DLBD 16, 316
Boyd, William (Andrew Murray) 1952- .... **CLC 28, 53, 70**
See also CA 114; 120; CANR 51, 71, 131; CN 4, 5, 6, 7; DLB 231
Boyesen, Hjalmar Hjorth 1848-1895 .... **NCLC 135**
See also DLB 12, 71; DLBD 13; RGAL 4
Boyle, Kay 1902-1992 .... **CLC 1, 5, 19, 58, 121; SSC 5**
See also CA 13-16R; 140; CAAS 1; CANR 29, 61, 110; CN 1, 2, 3, 4, 5; CP 1, 2, 3, 4; DLB 4, 9, 48, 86; DLBY 1993; EWL 3; MAL 5; MTCW 1, 2; MTFW 2005; RGAL 4; RGSF 2; SSFS 10, 13, 14
Boyle, Mark
See Kienzle, William X(avier)
Boyle, Patrick 1905-1982 .... **CLC 19**
See also CA 127
Boyle, T. C.
See Boyle, T(homas) Coraghessan
See also AMWS 8
Boyle, T(homas) Coraghessan 1948- .... **CLC 36, 55, 90; SSC 16**
See Boyle, T. C.
See also AAYA 47; BEST 90:4; BPFB 1; CA 120; CANR 44, 76, 89, 132; CN 6, 7; CPW; DA3; DAM POP; DLB 218, 278; DLBY 1986; EWL 3; MAL 5; MTCW 2; MTFW 2005; SSFS 13, 19
Boz
See Dickens, Charles (John Huffam)
Brackenridge, Hugh Henry 1748-1816 .... **NCLC 7**
See also DLB 11, 37; RGAL 4
Bradbury, Edward P.
See Moorcock, Michael (John)
See also MTCW 2
Bradbury, Malcolm (Stanley) 1932-2000 .... **CLC 32, 61**
See also CA 1-4R; CANR 1, 33, 91, 98, 137; CN 1, 2, 3, 4, 5, 6, 7; CP 1; DA3; DAM NOV; DLB 14, 207; EWL 3; MTCW 1, 2; MTFW 2005
Bradbury, Ray (Douglas) 1920- ..... **CLC 1, 3, 10, 15, 42, 98; SSC 29, 53; WLC**
See also AAYA 15; AITN 1, 2; AMWS 4; BPFB 1; BYA 4, 5, 11; CA 1-4R; CANR 2, 30, 75, 125; CDALB 1968-1988; CN 1, 2, 3, 4, 5, 6, 7; CPW; DA; DA3; DAB; DAC; DAM MST, NOV, POP; DLB 2, 8;

EXPN; EXPS; HGG; LAIT 3, 5; LATS 1:2; LMFS 2; MAL 5; MTCW 1, 2; MTFW 2005; NFS 1, 22; RGAL 4; RGSF 2; SATA 11, 64, 123; SCFW 1, 2; SFW 4; SSFS 1, 20; SUFW 1, 2; TUS; YAW

Braddon, Mary Elizabeth
1837-1915 .... **TCLC 111**
See also BRWS 8; CA 108; 179; CMW 4; DLB 18, 70, 156; HGG

Bradfield, Scott (Michael) 1955- .... **SSC 65**
See also CA 147; CANR 90; HGG; SUFW 2

Bradford, Gamaliel 1863-1932 .... **TCLC 36**
See also CA 160; DLB 17

Bradford, William 1590-1657 .... **LC 64**
See also DLB 24, 30; RGAL 4

Bradley, David (Henry), Jr. 1950- .... **BLC 1; CLC 23, 118**
See also BW 1, 3; CA 104; CANR 26, 81; CN 4, 5, 6, 7; DAM MULT; DLB 33

Bradley, John Ed(mund, Jr.) 1958- . **CLC 55**
See also CA 139; CANR 99; CN 6, 7; CSW

Bradley, Marion Zimmer
1930-1999 .... **CLC 30**
See Chapman, Lee; Dexter, John; Gardner, Miriam; Ives, Morgan; Rivers, Elfrida
See also AAYA 40; BPFB 1; CA 57-60; 185; CAAS 10; CANR 7, 31, 51, 75, 107; CPW; DA3; DAM POP; DLB 8; FANT; FW; MTCW 1, 2; MTFW 2005; SATA 90, 139; SATA-Obit 116; SFW 4; SUFW 2; YAW

Bradshaw, John 1933- .... **CLC 70**
See also CA 138; CANR 61

Bradstreet, Anne 1612(?)-1672 .... **LC 4, 30; PC 10**
See also AMWS 1; CDALB 1640-1865; DA; DA3; DAC; DAM MST, POET; DLB 24; EXPP; FW; PFS 6; RGAL 4; TUS; WP

Brady, Joan 1939- .... **CLC 86**
See also CA 141

Bragg, Melvyn 1939- .... **CLC 10**
See also BEST 89:3; CA 57-60; CANR 10, 48, 89; CN 1, 2, 3, 4, 5, 6, 7; DLB 14, 271; RHW

Brahe, Tycho 1546-1601 .... **LC 45**
See also DLB 300

Braine, John (Gerard) 1922-1986 . **CLC 1, 3, 41**
See also CA 1-4R; 120; CANR 1, 33; CDBLB 1945-1960; CN 1, 2, 3, 4; DLB 15; DLBY 1986; EWL 3; MTCW 1

Braithwaite, William Stanley (Beaumont)
1878-1962 .... **BLC 1; HR 1:2; PC 52**
See also BW 1; CA 125; DAM MULT; DLB 50, 54; MAL 5

Bramah, Ernest 1868-1942 .... **TCLC 72**
See also CA 156; CMW 4; DLB 70; FANT

Brammer, Billy Lee
See Brammer, William

Brammer, William 1929-1978 .... **CLC 31**
See also CA 235; 77-80

Brancati, Vitaliano 1907-1954 .... **TCLC 12**
See also CA 109; DLB 264; EWL 3

Brancato, Robin F(idler) 1936- .... **CLC 35**
See also AAYA 9, 68; BYA 6; CA 69-72; CANR 11, 45; CLR 32; JRDA; MAICYA 2; MAICYAS 1; SAAS 9; SATA 97; WYA; YAW

Brand, Dionne 1953- .... **CLC 192**
See also BW 2; CA 143; CANR 143; CWP

Brand, Max
See Faust, Frederick (Schiller)
See also BPFB 1; TCWW 1, 2

Brand, Millen 1906-1980 .... **CLC 7**
See also CA 21-24R; 97-100; CANR 72

Branden, Barbara .... **CLC 44**
See also CA 148

Brandes, Georg (Morris Cohen)
1842-1927 .... **TCLC 10**
See also CA 105; 189; DLB 300

Brandys, Kazimierz 1916-2000 .... **CLC 62**
See also CA 239; EWL 3

Branley, Franklyn M(ansfield)
1915-2002 .... **CLC 21**
See also CA 33-36R; 207; CANR 14, 39; CLR 13; MAICYA 1, 2; SAAS 16; SATA 4, 68, 136

Brant, Beth (E.) 1941- .... **NNAL**
See also CA 144; FW

Brant, Sebastian 1457-1521 .... **LC 112**
See also DLB 179; RGWL 2, 3

Brathwaite, Edward Kamau
1930- .... **BLCS; CLC 11; PC 56**
See also BW 2, 3; CA 25-28R; CANR 11, 26, 47, 107; CDWLB 3; CP 1, 2, 3, 4, 5, 6, 7; DAM POET; DLB 125; EWL 3

Brathwaite, Kamau
See Brathwaite, Edward Kamau

Brautigan, Richard (Gary)
1935-1984 .... **CLC 1, 3, 5, 9, 12, 34, 42; TCLC 133**
See also BPFB 1; CA 53-56; 113; CANR 34; CN 1, 2, 3; CP 1, 2, 3, 4; DA3; DAM NOV; DLB 2, 5, 206; DLBY 1980, 1984; FANT; MAL 5; MTCW 1; RGAL 4; SATA 56

Brave Bird, Mary .... **NNAL**
See Crow Dog, Mary (Ellen)

Braverman, Kate 1950- .... **CLC 67**
See also CA 89-92; CANR 141

Brecht, (Eugen) Bertolt (Friedrich)
1898-1956 ..... **DC 3; TCLC 1, 6, 13, 35, 169; WLC**
See also CA 104; 133; CANR 62; CDWLB 2; DA; DA3; DAB; DAC; DAM DRAM, MST; DFS 4, 5, 9; DLB 56, 124; EW 11; EWL 3; IDTP; MTCW 1, 2; MTFW 2005; RGWL 2, 3; TWA

Brecht, Eugen Berthold Friedrich
See Brecht, (Eugen) Bertolt (Friedrich)

Bremer, Fredrika 1801-1865 .... **NCLC 11**
See also DLB 254

Brennan, Christopher John
1870-1932 .... **TCLC 17**
See also CA 117; 188; DLB 230; EWL 3

Brennan, Maeve 1917-1993 ... **CLC 5; TCLC 124**
See also CA 81-84; CANR 72, 100

Brenner, Jozef 1887-1919
See Csath, Geza
See also CA 240

Brent, Linda
See Jacobs, Harriet A(nn)

Brentano, Clemens (Maria)
1778-1842 .... **NCLC 1**
See also DLB 90; RGWL 2, 3

Brent of Bin Bin
See Franklin, (Stella Maria Sarah) Miles (Lampe)

Brenton, Howard 1942- .... **CLC 31**
See also CA 69-72; CANR 33, 67; CBD; CD 5, 6; DLB 13; MTCW 1

Breslin, James 1930-
See Breslin, Jimmy
See also CA 73-76; CANR 31, 75, 139; DAM NOV; MTCW 1, 2; MTFW 2005

Breslin, Jimmy .... **CLC 4, 43**
See Breslin, James
See also AITN 1; DLB 185; MTCW 2

Bresson, Robert 1901(?)-1999 .... **CLC 16**
See also CA 110; 187; CANR 49

Breton, Andre 1896-1966 .. **CLC 2, 9, 15, 54; PC 15**
See also CA 19-20; 25-28R; CANR 40, 60; CAP 2; DLB 65, 258; EW 11; EWL 3; GFL 1789 to the Present; LMFS 2; MTCW 1, 2; MTFW 2005; RGWL 2, 3; TWA; WP

Breytenbach, Breyten 1939(?)- .. **CLC 23, 37, 126**
See also CA 113; 129; CANR 61, 122; CWW 2; DAM POET; DLB 225; EWL 3

Bridgers, Sue Ellen 1942- .... **CLC 26**
See also AAYA 8, 49; BYA 7, 8; CA 65-68; CANR 11, 36; CLR 18; DLB 52; JRDA; MAICYA 1, 2; SAAS 1; SATA 22, 90; SATA-Essay 109; WYA; YAW

Bridges, Robert (Seymour)
1844-1930 .... **PC 28; TCLC 1**
See also BRW 6; CA 104; 152; CDBLB 1890-1914; DAM POET; DLB 19, 98

Bridie, James .... **TCLC 3**
See Mavor, Osborne Henry
See also DLB 10; EWL 3

Brin, David 1950- .... **CLC 34**
See also AAYA 21; CA 102; CANR 24, 70, 125, 127; INT CANR-24; SATA 65; SCFW 2; SFW 4

Brink, Andre (Philippus) 1935- . **CLC 18, 36, 106**
See also AFW; BRWS 6; CA 104; CANR 39, 62, 109, 133; CN 4, 5, 6, 7; DLB 225; EWL 3; INT CA-103; LATS 1:2; MTCW 1, 2; MTFW 2005; WLIT 2

Brinsmead, H. F(ay)
See Brinsmead, H(esba) F(ay)

Brinsmead, H. F.
See Brinsmead, H(esba) F(ay)

Brinsmead, H(esba) F(ay) 1922- ...... **CLC 21**
See also CA 21-24R; CANR 10; CLR 47; CWRI 5; MAICYA 1, 2; SAAS 5; SATA 18, 78

Brittain, Vera (Mary) 1893(?)-1970 . **CLC 23**
See also BRWS 10; CA 13-16; 25-28R; CANR 58; CAP 1; DLB 191; FW; MTCW 1, 2

Broch, Hermann 1886-1951 .... **TCLC 20**
See also CA 117; 211; CDWLB 2; DLB 85, 124; EW 10; EWL 3; RGWL 2, 3

Brock, Rose
See Hansen, Joseph
See also GLL 1

Brod, Max 1884-1968 .... **TCLC 115**
See also CA 5-8R; 25-28R; CANR 7; DLB 81; EWL 3

Brodkey, Harold (Roy) 1930-1996 .. **CLC 56; TCLC 123**
See also CA 111; 151; CANR 71; CN 4, 5, 6; DLB 130

Brodsky, Iosif Alexandrovich 1940-1996
See Brodsky, Joseph
See also AITN 1; CA 41-44R; 151; CANR 37, 106; DA3; DAM POET; MTCW 1, 2; MTFW 2005; RGWL 2, 3

Brodsky, Joseph . **CLC 4, 6, 13, 36, 100; PC 9**
See Brodsky, Iosif Alexandrovich
See also AMWS 8; CWW 2; DLB 285; EWL 3; MTCW 1

Brodsky, Michael (Mark) 1948- .... **CLC 19**
See also CA 102; CANR 18, 41, 58; DLB 244

Brodzki, Bella ed. .... **CLC 65**

Brome, Richard 1590(?)-1652 .... **LC 61**
See also BRWS 10; DLB 58

Bromell, Henry 1947- .... **CLC 5**
See also CA 53-56; CANR 9, 115, 116

Bromfield, Louis (Brucker)
1896-1956 .... **TCLC 11**
See also CA 107; 155; DLB 4, 9, 86; RGAL 4; RHW

Broner, E(sther) M(asserman)
1930- .... **CLC 19**
See also CA 17-20R; CANR 8, 25, 72; CN 4, 5, 6; DLB 28

Bronk, William (M.) 1918-1999 .... **CLC 10**
See also CA 89-92; 177; CANR 23; CP 3, 4, 5, 6, 7; DLB 165

Bronstein, Lev Davidovich
See Trotsky, Leon

Bronte, Anne 1820-1849 ..... **NCLC 4, 71, 102**
See also BRW 5; BRWR 1; DA3; DLB 21, 199; TEA

Bronte, (Patrick) Branwell
1817-1848 .... **NCLC 109**

Bronte, Charlotte 1816-1855 ...... **NCLC 3, 8, 33, 58, 105, 155; WLC**
See also AAYA 17; BRW 5; BRWC 2; BRWR 1; BYA 2; CDBLB 1832-1890; DA; DA3; DAB; DAC; DAM MST, NOV; DLB 21, 159, 199; EXPN; FL 1:2; GL 2; LAIT 2; NFS 4; TEA; WLIT 4

Bronte, Emily (Jane) 1818-1848 ... **NCLC 16, 35, 165; PC 8; WLC**
See also AAYA 17; BPFB 1; BRW 5; BRWC 1; BRWR 1; BYA 3; CDBLB 1832-1890; DA; DA3; DAB; DAC; DAM MST, NOV, POET; DLB 21, 32, 199; EXPN; FL 1:2; GL 2; LAIT 1; TEA; WLIT 3

Brontes
See Bronte, Anne; Bronte, Charlotte; Bronte, Emily (Jane)

Brooke, Frances 1724-1789 .... **LC 6, 48**
See also DLB 39, 99

Brooke, Henry 1703(?)-1783 .... **LC 1**
See also DLB 39

Brooke, Rupert (Chawner)
1887-1915 ...... **PC 24; TCLC 2, 7; WLC**
See also BRWS 3; CA 104; 132; CANR 61; CDBLB 1914-1945; DA; DAB; DAC; DAM MST, POET; DLB 19, 216; EXPP; GLL 2; MTCW 1, 2; MTFW 2005; PFS 7; TEA

Brooke-Haven, P.
See Wodehouse, P(elham) G(renville)

Brooke-Rose, Christine 1926(?)- ..... **CLC 40, 184**
See also BRWS 4; CA 13-16R; CANR 58, 118; CN 1, 2, 3, 4, 5, 6, 7; DLB 14, 231; EWL 3; SFW 4

Brookner, Anita 1928- .. **CLC 32, 34, 51, 136**
See also BRWS 4; CA 114; 120; CANR 37, 56, 87, 130; CN 4, 5, 6, 7; CPW; DA3; DAB; DAM POP; DLB 194; DLBY 1987; EWL 3; MTCW 1, 2; MTFW 2005; TEA

Brooks, Cleanth 1906-1994 . **CLC 24, 86, 110**
See also AMWS 14; CA 17-20R; 145; CANR 33, 35; CSW; DLB 63; DLBY 1994; EWL 3; INT CANR-35; MAL 5; MTCW 1, 2; MTFW 2005

Brooks, George
See Baum, L(yman) Frank

Brooks, Gwendolyn (Elizabeth)
1917-2000 ... **BLC 1; CLC 1, 2, 4, 5, 15, 49, 125; PC 7; WLC**
See also AAYA 20; AFAW 1, 2; AITN 1; AMWS 3; BW 2, 3; CA 1-4R; 190; CANR 1, 27, 52, 75, 132; CDALB 1941-1968; CLR 27; CP 1, 2, 3, 4, 5, 6, 7; CWP; DA; DA3; DAC; DAM MST, MULT, POET; DLB 5, 76, 165; EWL 3; EXPP; FL 1:5; MAL 5; MAWW; MTCW 1, 2; MTFW 2005; PFS 1, 2, 4, 6; RGAL 4; SATA 6; SATA-Obit 123; TUS; WP

Brooks, Mel .... **CLC 12, 217**
See Kaminsky, Melvin
See also AAYA 13, 48; DLB 26

Brooks, Peter (Preston) 1938- .... **CLC 34**
See also CA 45-48; CANR 1, 107

Brooks, Van Wyck 1886-1963 .... **CLC 29**
See also AMW; CA 1-4R; CANR 6; DLB 45, 63, 103; MAL 5; TUS

Brophy, Brigid (Antonia)
1929-1995 .... **CLC 6, 11, 29, 105**
See also CA 5-8R; 149; CAAS 4; CANR 25, 53; CBD; CN 1, 2, 3, 4, 5, 6; CWD; DA3; DLB 14, 271; EWL 3; MTCW 1, 2

Brosman, Catharine Savage 1934- ..... **CLC 9**
See also CA 61-64; CANR 21, 46

Brossard, Nicole 1943- .... **CLC 115, 169**
See also CA 122; CAAS 16; CANR 140; CCA 1; CWP; CWW 2; DLB 53; EWL 3; FW; GLL 2; RGWL 3

Brother Antoninus
See Everson, William (Oliver)

The Brothers Quay
See Quay, Stephen; Quay, Timothy

Broughton, T(homas) Alan 1936- ..... **CLC 19**
See also CA 45-48; CANR 2, 23, 48, 111

Broumas, Olga 1949- .... **CLC 10, 73**
See also CA 85-88; CANR 20, 69, 110; CP 7; CWP; GLL 2

Broun, Heywood 1888-1939 .... **TCLC 104**
See also DLB 29, 171

Brown, Alan 1950- .... **CLC 99**
See also CA 156

Brown, Charles Brockden
1771-1810 ....**NCLC 22, 74, 122**
See also AMWS 1; CDALB 1640-1865; DLB 37, 59, 73; FW; GL 2; HGG; LMFS 1; RGAL 4; TUS

Brown, Christy 1932-1981 .... **CLC 63**
See also BYA 13; CA 105; 104; CANR 72; DLB 14

Brown, Claude 1937-2002 ... **BLC 1; CLC 30**
See also AAYA 7; BW 1, 3; CA 73-76; 205; CANR 81; DAM MULT

Brown, Dan 1964- .... **CLC 209**
See also AAYA 55; CA 217; MTFW 2005

Brown, Dee (Alexander)
1908-2002 .... **CLC 18, 47**
See also AAYA 30; CA 13-16R; 212; CAAS 6; CANR 11, 45, 60; CPW; CSW; DA3; DAM POP; DLBY 1980; LAIT 2; MTCW 1, 2; MTFW 2005; NCFS 5; SATA 5, 110; SATA-Obit 141; TCWW 1, 2

Brown, George
See Wertmueller, Lina

Brown, George Douglas
1869-1902 .... **TCLC 28**
See Douglas, George
See also CA 162

Brown, George Mackay 1921-1996 ... **CLC 5, 48, 100**
See also BRWS 6; CA 21-24R; 151; CAAS 6; CANR 12, 37, 67; CN 1, 2, 3, 4, 5, 6; CP 1, 2, 3, 4; DLB 14, 27, 139, 271; MTCW 1; RGSF 2; SATA 35

Brown, (William) Larry 1951-2004 . **CLC 73**
See also CA 130; 134; 233; CANR 117, 145; CSW; DLB 234; INT CA-134

Brown, Moses
See Barrett, William (Christopher)

Brown, Rita Mae 1944- .... **CLC 18, 43, 79**
See also BPFB 1; CA 45-48; CANR 2, 11, 35, 62, 95, 138; CN 5, 6, 7; CPW; CSW; DA3; DAM NOV, POP; FW; INT CANR-11; MAL 5; MTCW 1, 2; MTFW 2005; NFS 9; RGAL 4; TUS

Brown, Roderick (Langmere) Haig-
See Haig-Brown, Roderick (Langmere)

Brown, Rosellen 1939- .... **CLC 32, 170**
See also CA 77-80; CAAS 10; CANR 14, 44, 98; CN 6, 7

Brown, Sterling Allen 1901-1989 ...... **BLC 1; CLC 1, 23, 59; HR 1:2; PC 55**
See also AFAW 1, 2; BW 1, 3; CA 85-88; 127; CANR 26; CP 3, 4; DA3; DAM MULT, POET; DLB 48, 51, 63; MAL 5; MTCW 1, 2; MTFW 2005; RGAL 4; WP

Brown, Will
See Ainsworth, William Harrison

Brown, William Hill 1765-1793 .... **LC 93**
See also DLB 37

Brown, William Wells 1815-1884 ...... **BLC 1; DC 1; NCLC 2, 89**
See also DAM MULT; DLB 3, 50, 183, 248; RGAL 4

Browne, (Clyde) Jackson 1948(?)- ... **CLC 21**
See also CA 120

Browne, Sir Thomas 1605-1682 .... **LC 111**
See also BRW 2; DLB 151

Browning, Robert 1812-1889 . **NCLC 19, 79; PC 2, 61; WLCS**
See also BRW 4; BRWC 2; BRWR 2; CDBLB 1832-1890; CLR 97; DA; DA3; DAB; DAC; DAM MST, POET; DLB 32, 163; EXPP; LATS 1:1; PAB; PFS 1, 15; RGEL 2; TEA; WLIT 4; WP; YABC 1

Browning, Tod 1882-1962 .... **CLC 16**
See also CA 141; 117

Brownmiller, Susan 1935- .... **CLC 159**
See also CA 103; CANR 35, 75, 137; DAM NOV; FW; MTCW 1, 2; MTFW 2005

Brownson, Orestes Augustus
1803-1876 .... **NCLC 50**
See also DLB 1, 59, 73, 243

Bruccoli, Matthew J(oseph) 1931- ... **CLC 34**
See also CA 9-12R; CANR 7, 87; DLB 103

Bruce, Lenny .... **CLC 21**
See Schneider, Leonard Alfred

Bruchac, Joseph III 1942- .... **NNAL**
See also AAYA 19; CA 33-36R; CANR 13, 47, 75, 94, 137; CLR 46; CWRI 5; DAM MULT; JRDA; MAICYA 2; MAICYAS 1; MTCW 2; MTFW 2005; SATA 42, 89, 131

Bruin, John
See Brutus, Dennis

Brulard, Henri
See Stendhal

Brulls, Christian
See Simenon, Georges (Jacques Christian)

Brunetto Latini c. 1220-1294 .... **CMLC 73**

Brunner, John (Kilian Houston)
1934-1995 .... **CLC 8, 10**
See also CA 1-4R; 149; CAAS 8; CANR 2, 37; CPW; DAM POP; DLB 261; MTCW 1, 2; SCFW 1, 2; SFW 4

Bruno, Giordano 1548-1600 .... **LC 27**
See also RGWL 2, 3

Brutus, Dennis 1924- ... **BLC 1; CLC 43; PC 24**
See also AFW; BW 2, 3; CA 49-52; CAAS 14; CANR 2, 27, 42, 81; CDWLB 3; CP 1, 2, 3, 4, 5, 6, 7; DAM MULT, POET; DLB 117, 225; EWL 3

Bryan, C(ourtlandt) D(ixon) B(arnes)
1936- .... **CLC 29**
See also CA 73-76; CANR 13, 68; DLB 185; INT CANR-13

Bryan, Michael
See Moore, Brian
See also CCA 1

Bryan, William Jennings
1860-1925 .... **TCLC 99**
See also DLB 303

Bryant, William Cullen 1794-1878 . **NCLC 6, 46; PC 20**
See also AMWS 1; CDALB 1640-1865; DA; DAB; DAC; DAM MST, POET; DLB 3, 43, 59, 189, 250; EXPP; PAB; RGAL 4; TUS

Bryusov, Valery Yakovlevich 1873-1924 .... **TCLC 10**
See also CA 107; 155; EWL 3; SFW 4

Buchan, John 1875-1940 .... **TCLC 41**
See also CA 108; 145; CMW 4; DAB; DAM POP; DLB 34, 70, 156; HGG; MSW; MTCW 2; RGEL 2; RHW; YABC 2

Buchanan, George 1506-1582 .... **LC 4**
See also DLB 132

Buchanan, Robert 1841-1901 .... **TCLC 107**
See also CA 179; DLB 18, 35

Buchheim, Lothar-Guenther 1918- .... **CLC 6**
See also CA 85-88

Buchner, (Karl) Georg 1813-1837 .... **NCLC 26, 146**
See also CDWLB 2; DLB 133; EW 6; RGSF 2; RGWL 2, 3; TWA

Buchwald, Art(hur) 1925- .... **CLC 33**
See also AITN 1; CA 5-8R; CANR 21, 67, 107; MTCW 1, 2; SATA 10

Buck, Pearl S(ydenstricker) 1892-1973 ..... **CLC 7, 11, 18, 127**
See also AAYA 42; AITN 1; AMWS 2; BPFB 1; CA 1-4R; 41-44R; CANR 1, 34; CDALBS; CN 1; DA; DA3; DAB; DAC; DAM MST, NOV, POP; DLB 9, 102; EWL 3; LAIT 3; MAL 5; MTCW 1, 2; MTFW 2005; RGAL 4; RHW; SATA 1, 25; TUS

Buckler, Ernest 1908-1984 .... **CLC 13**
See also CA 11-12; 114; CAP 1; CCA 1; CN 1, 2, 3; DAC; DAM MST; DLB 68; SATA 47

Buckley, Christopher (Taylor) 1952- .... **CLC 165**
See also CA 139; CANR 119

Buckley, Vincent (Thomas) 1925-1988 .... **CLC 57**
See also CA 101; CP 1, 2, 3, 4; DLB 289

Buckley, William F(rank), Jr. 1925- . **CLC 7, 18, 37**
See also AITN 1; BPFB 1; CA 1-4R; CANR 1, 24, 53, 93, 133; CMW 4; CPW; DA3; DAM POP; DLB 137; DLBY 1980; INT CANR-24; MTCW 1, 2; MTFW 2005; TUS

Buechner, (Carl) Frederick 1926- . **CLC 2, 4, 6, 9**
See also AMWS 12; BPFB 1; CA 13-16R; CANR 11, 39, 64, 114, 138; CN 1, 2, 3, 4, 5, 6, 7; DAM NOV; DLBY 1980; INT CANR-11; MAL 5; MTCW 1, 2; MTFW 2005; TCLE 1:1

Buell, John (Edward) 1927- .... **CLC 10**
See also CA 1-4R; CANR 71; DLB 53

Buero Vallejo, Antonio 1916-2000 ... **CLC 15, 46, 139; DC 18**
See also CA 106; 189; CANR 24, 49, 75; CWW 2; DFS 11; EWL 3; HW 1; MTCW 1, 2

Bufalino, Gesualdo 1920-1996 .... **CLC 74**
See also CA 209; CWW 2; DLB 196

Bugayev, Boris Nikolayevich 1880-1934 .... **PC 11; TCLC 7**
See Bely, Andrey; Belyi, Andrei
See also CA 104; 165; MTCW 2; MTFW 2005

Bukowski, Charles 1920-1994 ... **CLC 2, 5, 9, 41, 82, 108; SSC 45**
See also CA 17-20R; 144; CANR 40, 62, 105; CN 4, 5; CP 1, 2, 3, 4; CPW; DA3; DAM NOV, POET; DLB 5, 130, 169; EWL 3; MAL 5; MTCW 1, 2; MTFW 2005

Bulgakov, Mikhail (Afanas'evich) 1891-1940 ..... **SSC 18; TCLC 2, 16, 159**
See also BPFB 1; CA 105; 152; DAM DRAM, NOV; DLB 272; EWL 3; MTCW 2; MTFW 2005; NFS 8; RGSF 2; RGWL 2, 3; SFW 4; TWA

Bulgya, Alexander Alexandrovich 1901-1956 .... **TCLC 53**
See Fadeev, Aleksandr Aleksandrovich; Fadeev, Alexandr Alexandrovich; Fadeyev, Alexander
See also CA 117; 181

Bullins, Ed 1935- ... **BLC 1; CLC 1, 5, 7; DC 6**
See also BW 2, 3; CA 49-52; CAAS 16; CAD; CANR 24, 46, 73, 134; CD 5, 6; DAM DRAM, MULT; DLB 7, 38, 249; EWL 3; MAL 5; MTCW 1, 2; MTFW 2005; RGAL 4

Bulosan, Carlos 1911-1956 .... **AAL**
See also CA 216; DLB 312; RGAL 4

Bulwer-Lytton, Edward (George Earle Lytton) 1803-1873 .... **NCLC 1, 45**
See also DLB 21; RGEL 2; SFW 4; SUFW 1; TEA

Bunin, Ivan Alexeyevich 1870-1953 ... **SSC 5; TCLC 6**
See also CA 104; DLB 317; EWL 3; RGSF 2; RGWL 2, 3; TWA

Bunting, Basil 1900-1985 ...... **CLC 10, 39, 47**
See also BRWS 7; CA 53-56; 115; CANR 7; CP 1, 2, 3, 4; DAM POET; DLB 20; EWL 3; RGEL 2

Bunuel, Luis 1900-1983 ... **CLC 16, 80; HLC 1**
See also CA 101; 110; CANR 32, 77; DAM MULT; HW 1

Bunyan, John 1628-1688 ..... **LC 4, 69; WLC**
See also BRW 2; BYA 5; CDBLB 1660-1789; DA; DAB; DAC; DAM MST; DLB 39; RGEL 2; TEA; WCH; WLIT 3

Buravsky, Alexandr .... **CLC 59**

Burckhardt, Jacob (Christoph) 1818-1897 .... **NCLC 49**
See also EW 6

Burford, Eleanor
See Hibbert, Eleanor Alice Burford

Burgess, Anthony . **CLC 1, 2, 4, 5, 8, 10, 13, 15, 22, 40, 62, 81, 94**
See Wilson, John (Anthony) Burgess
See also AAYA 25; AITN 1; BRWS 1; CDBLB 1960 to Present; CN 1, 2, 3, 4, 5; DAB; DLB 14, 194, 261; DLBY 1998; EWL 3; RGEL 2; RHW; SFW 4; YAW

Burke, Edmund 1729(?)-1797 .... **LC 7, 36; WLC**
See also BRW 3; DA; DA3; DAB; DAC; DAM MST; DLB 104, 252; RGEL 2; TEA

Burke, Kenneth (Duva) 1897-1993 ... **CLC 2, 24**
See also AMW; CA 5-8R; 143; CANR 39, 74, 136; CN 1, 2; CP 1, 2, 3, 4; DLB 45, 63; EWL 3; MAL 5; MTCW 1, 2; MTFW 2005; RGAL 4

Burke, Leda
See Garnett, David

Burke, Ralph
See Silverberg, Robert

Burke, Thomas 1886-1945 .... **TCLC 63**
See also CA 113; 155; CMW 4; DLB 197

Burney, Fanny 1752-1840 .... **NCLC 12, 54, 107**
See also BRWS 3; DLB 39; FL 1:2; NFS 16; RGEL 2; TEA

Burney, Frances
See Burney, Fanny

Burns, Robert 1759-1796 ... **LC 3, 29, 40; PC 6; WLC**
See also AAYA 51; BRW 3; CDBLB 1789-1832; DA; DA3; DAB; DAC; DAM MST, POET; DLB 109; EXPP; PAB; RGEL 2; TEA; WP

Burns, Tex
See L'Amour, Louis (Dearborn)

Burnshaw, Stanley 1906- .... **CLC 3, 13, 44**
See also CA 9-12R; CP 1, 2, 3, 4, 5, 6, 7; DLB 48; DLBY 1997

Burr, Anne 1937- .... **CLC 6**
See also CA 25-28R

Burroughs, Edgar Rice 1875-1950 . **TCLC 2, 32**
See also AAYA 11; BPFB 1; BYA 4, 9; CA 104; 132; CANR 131; DA3; DAM NOV; DLB 8; FANT; MTCW 1, 2; MTFW 2005; RGAL 4; SATA 41; SCFW 1, 2; SFW 4; TCWW 1, 2; TUS; YAW

Burroughs, William S(eward) 1914-1997 .. **CLC 1, 2, 5, 15, 22, 42, 75, 109; TCLC 121; WLC**
See Lee, William; Lee, Willy
See also AAYA 60; AITN 2; AMWS 3; BG 1:2; BPFB 1; CA 9-12R; 160; CANR 20, 52, 104; CN 1, 2, 3, 4, 5, 6; CPW; DA; DA3; DAB; DAC; DAM MST, NOV, POP; DLB 2, 8, 16, 152, 237; DLBY 1981, 1997; EWL 3; HGG; LMFS 2; MAL 5; MTCW 1, 2; MTFW 2005; RGAL 4; SFW 4

Burton, Sir Richard F(rancis) 1821-1890 .... **NCLC 42**
See also DLB 55, 166, 184; SSFS 21

Burton, Robert 1577-1640 .... **LC 74**
See also DLB 151; RGEL 2

Buruma, Ian 1951- .... **CLC 163**
See also CA 128; CANR 65, 141

Busch, Frederick 1941- ... **CLC 7, 10, 18, 47, 166**
See also CA 33-36R; CAAS 1; CANR 45, 73, 92; CN 1, 2, 3, 4, 5, 6, 7; DLB 6, 218

Bush, Barney (Furman) 1946- .... **NNAL**
See also CA 145

Bush, Ronald 1946- .... **CLC 34**
See also CA 136

Bustos, F(rancisco)
See Borges, Jorge Luis

Bustos Domecq, H(onorio)
See Bioy Casares, Adolfo; Borges, Jorge Luis

Butler, Octavia E(stelle) 1947- .. **BLCS; CLC 38, 121**
See also AAYA 18, 48; AFAW 2; AMWS 13; BPFB 1; BW 2, 3; CA 73-76; CANR 12, 24, 38, 73, 145; CLR 65; CN 7; CPW; DA3; DAM MULT, POP; DLB 33; LATS 1:2; MTCW 1, 2; MTFW 2005; NFS 8, 21; SATA 84; SCFW 2; SFW 4; SSFS 6; TCLE 1:1; YAW

Butler, Robert Olen, (Jr.) 1945- .... **CLC 81, 162**
See also AMWS 12; BPFB 1; CA 112; CANR 66, 138; CN 7; CSW; DAM POP; DLB 173; INT CA-112; MAL 5; MTCW 2; MTFW 2005; SSFS 11

Butler, Samuel 1612-1680 .... **LC 16, 43**
See also DLB 101, 126; RGEL 2

Butler, Samuel 1835-1902 .... **TCLC 1, 33; WLC**
See also BRWS 2; CA 143; CDBLB 1890-1914; DA; DA3; DAB; DAC; DAM MST, NOV; DLB 18, 57, 174; RGEL 2; SFW 4; TEA

Butler, Walter C.
See Faust, Frederick (Schiller)

Butor, Michel (Marie Francois)
1926- .... **CLC 1, 3, 8, 11, 15, 161**
See also CA 9-12R; CANR 33, 66; CWW 2; DLB 83; EW 13; EWL 3; GFL 1789 to the Present; MTCW 1, 2; MTFW 2005

Butts, Mary 1890(?)-1937 .... **TCLC 77**
See also CA 148; DLB 240

Buxton, Ralph
See Silverstein, Alvin; Silverstein, Virginia B(arbara Opshelor)

Buzo, Alex
See Buzo, Alexander (John)
See also DLB 289

Buzo, Alexander (John) 1944- .... **CLC 61**
See also CA 97-100; CANR 17, 39, 69; CD 5, 6

Buzzati, Dino 1906-1972 .... **CLC 36**
See also CA 160; 33-36R; DLB 177; RGWL 2, 3; SFW 4

Byars, Betsy (Cromer) 1928- .... **CLC 35**
See also AAYA 19; BYA 3; CA 33-36R, 183; CAAE 183; CANR 18, 36, 57, 102; CLR 1, 16, 72; DLB 52; INT CANR-18; JRDA; MAICYA 1, 2; MAICYAS 1; MTCW 1; SAAS 1; SATA 4, 46, 80, 163; SATA-Essay 108; WYA; YAW

Byatt, A(ntonia) S(usan Drabble)
1936- .... **CLC 19, 65, 136**
See also BPFB 1; BRWC 2; BRWS 4; CA 13-16R; CANR 13, 33, 50, 75, 96, 133; CN 1, 2, 3, 4, 5, 6; DA3; DAM NOV, POP; DLB 14, 194; EWL 3; MTCW 1, 2; MTFW 2005; RGSF 2; RHW; TEA

Byrd, William II 1674-1744 .... **LC 112**
See also DLB 24, 140; RGAL 4

Byrne, David 1952- .... **CLC 26**
See also CA 127

Byrne, John Keyes 1926-
See Leonard, Hugh
See also CA 102; CANR 78, 140; INT CA-102

Byron, George Gordon (Noel)
1788-1824 ..... **DC 24; NCLC 2, 12, 109, 149; PC 16; WLC**
See also AAYA 64; BRW 4; BRWC 2; CDBLB 1789-1832; DA; DA3; DAB; DAC; DAM MST, POET; DLB 96, 110; EXPP; LMFS 1; PAB; PFS 1, 14; RGEL 2; TEA; WLIT 3; WP

Byron, Robert 1905-1941 .... **TCLC 67**
See also CA 160; DLB 195

C. 3. 3.
See Wilde, Oscar (Fingal O'Flahertie Wills)

Caballero, Fernan 1796-1877 .... **NCLC 10**

Cabell, Branch
See Cabell, James Branch

Cabell, James Branch 1879-1958 .... **TCLC 6**
See also CA 105; 152; DLB 9, 78; FANT; MAL 5; MTCW 2; RGAL 4; SUFW 1

Cabeza de Vaca, Alvar Nunez
1490-1557(?) .... **LC 61**

Cable, George Washington
1844-1925 .... **SSC 4; TCLC 4**
See also CA 104; 155; DLB 12, 74; DLBD 13; RGAL 4; TUS

Cabral de Melo Neto, Joao
1920-1999 .... **CLC 76**
See Melo Neto, Joao Cabral de
See also CA 151; DAM MULT; DLB 307; LAW; LAWS 1

Cabrera Infante, G(uillermo)
1929-2005 ..... **CLC 5, 25, 45, 120; HLC 1; SSC 39**
See also CA 85-88; 236; CANR 29, 65, 110; CDWLB 3; CWW 2; DA3; DAM MULT; DLB 113; EWL 3; HW 1, 2; LAW; LAWS 1; MTCW 1, 2; MTFW 2005; RGSF 2; WLIT 1

Cade, Toni
See Bambara, Toni Cade

Cadmus and Harmonia
See Buchan, John

Caedmon fl. 658-680 .... **CMLC 7**
See also DLB 146

Caeiro, Alberto
See Pessoa, Fernando (Antonio Nogueira)

Caesar, Julius .... **CMLC 47**
See Julius Caesar
See also AW 1; RGWL 2, 3

Cage, John (Milton), (Jr.)
1912-1992 .... **CLC 41; PC 58**
See also CA 13-16R; 169; CANR 9, 78; DLB 193; INT CANR-9; TCLE 1:1

Cahan, Abraham 1860-1951 .... **TCLC 71**
See also CA 108; 154; DLB 9, 25, 28; MAL 5; RGAL 4

Cain, G.
See Cabrera Infante, G(uillermo)

Cain, Guillermo
See Cabrera Infante, G(uillermo)

Cain, James M(allahan) 1892-1977 .. **CLC 3, 11, 28**
See also AITN 1; BPFB 1; CA 17-20R; 73-76; CANR 8, 34, 61; CMW 4; CN 1, 2; DLB 226; EWL 3; MAL 5; MSW; MTCW 1; RGAL 4

Caine, Hall 1853-1931 .... **TCLC 97**
See also RHW

Caine, Mark
See Raphael, Frederic (Michael)

Calasso, Roberto 1941- .... **CLC 81**
See also CA 143; CANR 89

Calderon de la Barca, Pedro
1600-1681 .... **DC 3; HLCS 1; LC 23**
See also EW 2; RGWL 2, 3; TWA

Caldwell, Erskine (Preston)
1903-1987 .... **CLC 1, 8, 14, 50, 60; SSC 19; TCLC 117**
See also AITN 1; AMW; BPFB 1; CA 1-4R; 121; CAAS 1; CANR 2, 33; CN 1, 2, 3, 4; DA3; DAM NOV; DLB 9, 86; EWL 3; MAL 5; MTCW 1, 2; MTFW 2005; RGAL 4; RGSF 2; TUS

Caldwell, (Janet Miriam) Taylor (Holland)
1900-1985 .... **CLC 2, 28, 39**
See also BPFB 1; CA 5-8R; 116; CANR 5; DA3; DAM NOV, POP; DLBD 17; MTCW 1; RHW

Calhoun, John Caldwell
1782-1850 .... **NCLC 15**
See also DLB 3, 248

Calisher, Hortense 1911- ..... **CLC 2, 4, 8, 38, 134; SSC 15**
See also CA 1-4R; CANR 1, 22, 117; CN 1, 2, 3, 4, 5, 6, 7; DA3; DAM NOV; DLB 2, 218; INT CANR-22; MAL 5; MTCW 1, 2; MTFW 2005; RGAL 4; RGSF 2

Callaghan, Morley Edward
1903-1990 ..... **CLC 3, 14, 41, 65; TCLC 145**
See also CA 9-12R; 132; CANR 33, 73; CN 1, 2, 3, 4; DAC; DAM MST; DLB 68; EWL 3; MTCW 1, 2; MTFW 2005; RGEL 2; RGSF 2; SSFS 19

Callimachus c. 305B.C.-c. 240B.C. .... **CMLC 18**
See also AW 1; DLB 176; RGWL 2, 3

Calvin, Jean
See Calvin, John
See also GFL Beginnings to 1789

Calvin, John 1509-1564 .... **LC 37**
See Calvin, Jean

Calvino, Italo 1923-1985 .... **CLC 5, 8, 11, 22, 33, 39, 73; SSC 3, 48**
See also AAYA 58; CA 85-88; 116; CANR 23, 61, 132; DAM NOV; DLB 196; EW 13; EWL 3; MTCW 1, 2; MTFW 2005; RGSF 2; RGWL 2, 3; SFW 4; SSFS 12; WLIT 7

Camara Laye
See Laye, Camara
See also EWL 3

Camden, William 1551-1623 .... **LC 77**
See also DLB 172

Cameron, Carey 1952- .... **CLC 59**
See also CA 135

Cameron, Peter 1959- .... **CLC 44**
See also AMWS 12; CA 125; CANR 50, 117; DLB 234; GLL 2

Camoens, Luis Vaz de 1524(?)-1580
See Camoes, Luis de
See also EW 2

Camoes, Luis de 1524(?)-1580 . **HLCS 1; LC 62; PC 31**
See Camoens, Luis Vaz de
See also DLB 287; RGWL 2, 3

Campana, Dino 1885-1932 .... **TCLC 20**
See also CA 117; DLB 114; EWL 3

Campanella, Tommaso 1568-1639 .... **LC 32**
See also RGWL 2, 3

Campbell, John W(ood, Jr.)
1910-1971 .... **CLC 32**
See also CA 21-22; 29-32R; CANR 34; CAP 2; DLB 8; MTCW 1; SCFW 1, 2; SFW 4

Campbell, Joseph 1904-1987 .... **CLC 69; TCLC 140**
See also AAYA 3, 66; BEST 89:2; CA 1-4R; 124; CANR 3, 28, 61, 107; DA3; MTCW 1, 2

Campbell, Maria 1940- .... **CLC 85; NNAL**
See also CA 102; CANR 54; CCA 1; DAC

Campbell, (John) Ramsey 1946- ..... **CLC 42; SSC 19**
See also AAYA 51; CA 57-60, 228; CAAE 228; CANR 7, 102; DLB 261; HGG; INT CANR-7; SUFW 1, 2

Campbell, (Ignatius) Roy (Dunnachie)
1901-1957 .... **TCLC 5**
See also AFW; CA 104; 155; DLB 20, 225; EWL 3; MTCW 2; RGEL 2

Campbell, Thomas 1777-1844 .... **NCLC 19**
See also DLB 93, 144; RGEL 2

Campbell, Wilfred .... **TCLC 9**
See Campbell, William

Campbell, William 1858(?)-1918
See Campbell, Wilfred
See also CA 106; DLB 92

Campbell, William Edward March
1893-1954
See March, William
See also CA 108

Campion, Jane 1954- .... **CLC 95**
See also AAYA 33; CA 138; CANR 87

Campion, Thomas 1567-1620 .... **LC 78**
See also CDBLB Before 1660; DAM POET; DLB 58, 172; RGEL 2

Camus, Albert 1913-1960 ..... **CLC 1, 2, 4, 9, 11, 14, 32, 63, 69, 124; DC 2; SSC 9, 76; WLC**
See also AAYA 36; AFW; BPFB 1; CA 89-92; CANR 131; DA; DA3; DAB; DAC; DAM DRAM, MST, NOV; DLB 72, 321; EW 13; EWL 3; EXPN; EXPS; GFL 1789 to the Present; LATS 1:2; LMFS 2; MTCW 1, 2; MTFW 2005; NFS 6, 16; RGSF 2; RGWL 2, 3; SSFS 4; TWA

Canby, Vincent 1924-2000 .... **CLC 13**
See also CA 81-84; 191

Cancale
See Desnos, Robert

Canetti, Elias 1905-1994 .. **CLC 3, 14, 25, 75, 86; TCLC 157**
See also CA 21-24R; 146; CANR 23, 61, 79; CDWLB 2; CWW 2; DA3; DLB 85, 124; EW 12; EWL 3; MTCW 1, 2; MTFW 2005; RGWL 2, 3; TWA

Canfield, Dorothea F.
See Fisher, Dorothy (Frances) Canfield

Canfield, Dorothea Frances
See Fisher, Dorothy (Frances) Canfield

Canfield, Dorothy
See Fisher, Dorothy (Frances) Canfield

Canin, Ethan 1960- .... **CLC 55; SSC 70**
See also CA 131; 135; MAL 5

Cankar, Ivan 1876-1918 .... **TCLC 105**
See also CDWLB 4; DLB 147; EWL 3

Cannon, Curt
See Hunter, Evan

Cao, Lan 1961- .... **CLC 109**
See also CA 165

Cape, Judith
See Page, P(atricia) K(athleen)
See also CCA 1

Capek, Karel 1890-1938 .... **DC 1; SSC 36; TCLC 6, 37; WLC**
See also CA 104; 140; CDWLB 4; DA; DA3; DAB; DAC; DAM DRAM, MST, NOV; DFS 7, 11; DLB 215; EW 10; EWL 3; MTCW 2; MTFW 2005; RGSF 2; RGWL 2, 3; SCFW 1, 2; SFW 4

Capote, Truman 1924-1984 . **CLC 1, 3, 8, 13, 19, 34, 38, 58; SSC 2, 47; TCLC 164; WLC**
See also AAYA 61; AMWS 3; BPFB 1; CA 5-8R; 113; CANR 18, 62; CDALB 1941-1968; CN 1, 2, 3; CPW; DA; DA3; DAB; DAC; DAM MST, NOV, POP; DLB 2, 185, 227; DLBY 1980, 1984; EWL 3; EXPS; GLL 1; LAIT 3; MAL 5; MTCW 1, 2; MTFW 2005; NCFS 1; RGAL 4; RGSF 2; SATA 91; SSFS 2; TUS

Capra, Frank 1897-1991 .... **CLC 16**
See also AAYA 52; CA 61-64; 135

Caputo, Philip 1941- .... **CLC 32**
See also AAYA 60; CA 73-76; CANR 40, 135; YAW

Caragiale, Ion Luca 1852-1912 ...... **TCLC 76**
See also CA 157

Card, Orson Scott 1951- .... **CLC 44, 47, 50**
See also AAYA 11, 42; BPFB 1; BYA 5, 8; CA 102; CANR 27, 47, 73, 102, 106, 133; CPW; DA3; DAM POP; FANT; INT CANR-27; MTCW 1, 2; MTFW 2005; NFS 5; SATA 83, 127; SCFW 2; SFW 4; SUFW 2; YAW

Cardenal, Ernesto 1925- .... **CLC 31, 161; HLC 1; PC 22**
See also CA 49-52; CANR 2, 32, 66, 138; CWW 2; DAM MULT, POET; DLB 290; EWL 3; HW 1, 2; LAWS 1; MTCW 1, 2; MTFW 2005; RGWL 2, 3

Cardinal, Marie 1929-2001 .... **CLC 189**
See also CA 177; CWW 2; DLB 83; FW

Cardozo, Benjamin N(athan)
1870-1938 .... **TCLC 65**
See also CA 117; 164

Carducci, Giosue (Alessandro Giuseppe)
1835-1907 .... **PC 46; TCLC 32**
See also CA 163; EW 7; RGWL 2, 3

Carew, Thomas 1595(?)-1640 . **LC 13; PC 29**
See also BRW 2; DLB 126; PAB; RGEL 2

Carey, Ernestine Gilbreth 1908- ...... **CLC 17**
See also CA 5-8R; CANR 71; SATA 2

Carey, Peter 1943- .... **CLC 40, 55, 96, 183**
See also CA 123; 127; CANR 53, 76, 117; CN 4, 5, 6, 7; DLB 289; EWL 3; INT CA-127; MTCW 1, 2; MTFW 2005; RGSF 2; SATA 94

Carleton, William 1794-1869 .... **NCLC 3**
See also DLB 159; RGEL 2; RGSF 2

Carlisle, Henry (Coffin) 1926- .... **CLC 33**
See also CA 13-16R; CANR 15, 85

Carlsen, Chris
See Holdstock, Robert P.

Carlson, Ron(ald F.) 1947- .... **CLC 54**
See also CA 105, 189; CAAE 189; CANR 27; DLB 244

Carlyle, Thomas 1795-1881 ..... **NCLC 22, 70**
See also BRW 4; CDBLB 1789-1832; DA; DAB; DAC; DAM MST; DLB 55, 144, 254; RGEL 2; TEA

Carman, (William) Bliss 1861-1929 ... **PC 34; TCLC 7**
See also CA 104; 152; DAC; DLB 92; RGEL 2

Carnegie, Dale 1888-1955 .... **TCLC 53**
See also CA 218

Carossa, Hans 1878-1956 .... **TCLC 48**
See also CA 170; DLB 66; EWL 3

Carpenter, Don(ald Richard)
1931-1995 .... **CLC 41**
See also CA 45-48; 149; CANR 1, 71

Carpenter, Edward 1844-1929 .... **TCLC 88**
See also CA 163; GLL 1

Carpenter, John (Howard) 1948- ... **CLC 161**
See also AAYA 2; CA 134; SATA 58

Carpenter, Johnny
See Carpenter, John (Howard)

Carpentier (y Valmont), Alejo
1904-1980 . **CLC 8, 11, 38, 110; HLC 1; SSC 35**
See also CA 65-68; 97-100; CANR 11, 70; CDWLB 3; DAM MULT; DLB 113; EWL 3; HW 1; LAW; LMFS 2; RGSF 2; RGWL 2, 3; WLIT 1

Carr, Caleb 1955- .... **CLC 86**
See also CA 147; CANR 73, 134; DA3

Carr, Emily 1871-1945 .... **TCLC 32**
See also CA 159; DLB 68; FW; GLL 2

Carr, John Dickson 1906-1977 .... **CLC 3**
See Fairbairn, Roger
See also CA 49-52; 69-72; CANR 3, 33, 60; CMW 4; DLB 306; MSW; MTCW 1, 2

Carr, Philippa
See Hibbert, Eleanor Alice Burford

Carr, Virginia Spencer 1929- .... **CLC 34**
See also CA 61-64; DLB 111

Carrere, Emmanuel 1957- .... **CLC 89**
See also CA 200

Carrier, Roch 1937- .... **CLC 13, 78**
See also CA 130; CANR 61; CCA 1; DAC; DAM MST; DLB 53; SATA 105

Carroll, James Dennis
See Carroll, Jim

Carroll, James P. 1943(?)- .... **CLC 38**
See also CA 81-84; CANR 73, 139; MTCW 2; MTFW 2005

Carroll, Jim 1951- .... **CLC 35, 143**
See also AAYA 17; CA 45-48; CANR 42, 115; NCFS 5

Carroll, Lewis ..... **NCLC 2, 53, 139; PC 18; WLC**
See Dodgson, Charles L(utwidge)
See also AAYA 39; BRW 5; BYA 5, 13; CDBLB 1832-1890; CLR 2, 18; DLB 18, 163, 178; DLBY 1998; EXPN; EXPP; FANT; JRDA; LAIT 1; NFS 7; PFS 11; RGEL 2; SUFW 1; TEA; WCH

Carroll, Paul Vincent 1900-1968 ...... **CLC 10**
See also CA 9-12R; 25-28R; DLB 10; EWL 3; RGEL 2

Carruth, Hayden 1921- ..... **CLC 4, 7, 10, 18, 84; PC 10**
See also CA 9-12R; CANR 4, 38, 59, 110; CP 1, 2, 3, 4, 5, 6, 7; DLB 5, 165; INT CANR-4; MTCW 1, 2; MTFW 2005; SATA 47

Carson, Anne 1950- .... **CLC 185; PC 64**
See also AMWS 12; CA 203; DLB 193; PFS 18; TCLE 1:1

Carson, Ciaran 1948- .... **CLC 201**
See also CA 112; 153; CANR 113; CP 7

Carson, Rachel
See Carson, Rachel Louise
See also AAYA 49; DLB 275

Carson, Rachel Louise 1907-1964 .... **CLC 71**
See Carson, Rachel
See also AMWS 9; ANW; CA 77-80; CANR 35; DA3; DAM POP; FW; LAIT 4; MAL 5; MTCW 1, 2; MTFW 2005; NCFS 1; SATA 23

Carter, Angela (Olive) 1940-1992 ...... **CLC 5, 41, 76; SSC 13, 85; TCLC 139**
See also BRWS 3; CA 53-56; 136; CANR 12, 36, 61, 106; CN 3, 4, 5; DA3; DLB 14, 207, 261, 319; EXPS; FANT; FW; GL 2; MTCW 1, 2; MTFW 2005; RGSF 2; SATA 66; SATA-Obit 70; SFW 4; SSFS 4, 12; SUFW 2; WLIT 4

Carter, Nick
See Smith, Martin Cruz

Carver, Raymond 1938-1988 ..... **CLC 22, 36, 53, 55, 126; PC 54; SSC 8, 51**
See also AAYA 44; AMWS 3; BPFB 1; CA 33-36R; 126; CANR 17, 34, 61, 103; CN 4; CPW; DA3; DAM NOV; DLB 130; DLBY 1984, 1988; EWL 3; MAL 5; MTCW 1, 2; MTFW 2005; PFS 17; RGAL 4; RGSF 2; SSFS 3, 6, 12, 13; TCLE 1:1; TCWW 2; TUS

Cary, Elizabeth, Lady Falkland
1585-1639 .... **LC 30**

Cary, (Arthur) Joyce (Lunel)
1888-1957 .... **TCLC 1, 29**
See also BRW 7; CA 104; 164; CDBLB 1914-1945; DLB 15, 100; EWL 3; MTCW 2; RGEL 2; TEA

Casal, Julian del 1863-1893 .... **NCLC 131**
See also DLB 283; LAW

Casanova, Giacomo
See Casanova de Seingalt, Giovanni Jacopo
See also WLIT 7

Casanova de Seingalt, Giovanni Jacopo
1725-1798 .... **LC 13**
See Casanova, Giacomo

Casares, Adolfo Bioy
See Bioy Casares, Adolfo
See also RGSF 2

Casas, Bartolome de las 1474-1566
See Las Casas, Bartolome de
See also WLIT 1

Casely-Hayford, J(oseph) E(phraim)
1866-1903 .... **BLC 1; TCLC 24**
See also BW 2; CA 123; 152; DAM MULT

Casey, John (Dudley) 1939- .... **CLC 59**
See also BEST 90:2; CA 69-72; CANR 23, 100

Casey, Michael 1947- .... **CLC 2**
See also CA 65-68; CANR 109; CP 2, 3; DLB 5

Casey, Patrick
See Thurman, Wallace (Henry)

Casey, Warren (Peter) 1935-1988 ..... **CLC 12**
See also CA 101; 127; INT CA-101

Casona, Alejandro .... **CLC 49**
See Alvarez, Alejandro Rodriguez
See also EWL 3

Cassavetes, John 1929-1989 .... **CLC 20**
See also CA 85-88; 127; CANR 82

Cassian, Nina 1924- .... **PC 17**
See also CWP; CWW 2

Cassill, R(onald) V(erlin)
1919-2002 .... **CLC 4, 23**
See also CA 9-12R; 208; CAAS 1; CANR 7, 45; CN 1, 2, 3, 4, 5, 6, 7; DLB 6, 218; DLBY 2002

Cassiodorus, Flavius Magnus c. 490(?)-c.
583(?) .... **CMLC 43**

Cassirer, Ernst 1874-1945 .... **TCLC 61**
See also CA 157

Cassity, (Allen) Turner 1929- .... **CLC 6, 42**
See also CA 17-20R, 223; CAAE 223; CAAS 8; CANR 11; CSW; DLB 105

Castaneda, Carlos (Cesar Aranha)
1931(?)-1998 .... **CLC 12, 119**
See also CA 25-28R; CANR 32, 66, 105; DNFS 1; HW 1; MTCW 1

Castedo, Elena 1937- .... **CLC 65**
See also CA 132

Castedo-Ellerman, Elena
See Castedo, Elena

Castellanos, Rosario 1925-1974 .... **CLC 66; HLC 1; SSC 39, 68**
See also CA 131; 53-56; CANR 58; CDWLB 3; DAM MULT; DLB 113, 290; EWL 3; FW; HW 1; LAW; MTCW 2; MTFW 2005; RGSF 2; RGWL 2, 3

Castelvetro, Lodovico 1505-1571 .... **LC 12**

Castiglione, Baldassare 1478-1529 ...... **LC 12**
See Castiglione, Baldesar
See also LMFS 1; RGWL 2, 3

Castiglione, Baldesar
See Castiglione, Baldassare
See also EW 2; WLIT 7

Castillo, Ana (Hernandez Del)
1953- .... **CLC 151**
See also AAYA 42; CA 131; CANR 51, 86, 128; CWP; DLB 122, 227; DNFS 2; FW; HW 1; LLW; PFS 21

Castle, Robert
See Hamilton, Edmond

Castro (Ruz), Fidel 1926(?)- .... **HLC 1**
See also CA 110; 129; CANR 81; DAM MULT; HW 2

Castro, Guillen de 1569-1631 .... **LC 19**

Castro, Rosalia de 1837-1885 ... **NCLC 3, 78; PC 41**
See also DAM MULT

Cather, Willa (Sibert) 1873-1947 . **SSC 2, 50; TCLC 1, 11, 31, 99, 132, 152; WLC**
See also AAYA 24; AMW; AMWC 1; AMWR 1; BPFB 1; CA 104; 128; CDALB 1865-1917; CLR 98; DA; DA3; DAB; DAC; DAM MST, NOV; DLB 9, 54, 78, 256; DLBD 1; EWL 3; EXPN; EXPS; FL 1:5; LAIT 3; LATS 1:1; MAL 5; MAWW; MTCW 1, 2; MTFW 2005; NFS 2, 19; RGAL 4; RGSF 2; RHW; SATA 30; SSFS 2, 7, 16; TCWW 1, 2; TUS

Catherine II
See Catherine the Great
See also DLB 150

Catherine the Great 1729-1796 .... **LC 69**
See Catherine II

Cato, Marcus Porcius
234B.C.-149B.C. .... **CMLC 21**
See Cato the Elder

Cato, Marcus Porcius, the Elder
See Cato, Marcus Porcius

Cato the Elder
See Cato, Marcus Porcius
See also DLB 211

Catton, (Charles) Bruce 1899-1978 . **CLC 35**
See also AITN 1; CA 5-8R; 81-84; CANR 7, 74; DLB 17; MTCW 2; MTFW 2005; SATA 2; SATA-Obit 24

Catullus c. 84B.C.-54B.C. .... **CMLC 18**
See also AW 2; CDWLB 1; DLB 211; RGWL 2, 3

Cauldwell, Frank
See King, Francis (Henry)

Caunitz, William J. 1933-1996 .... **CLC 34**
See also BEST 89:3; CA 125; 130; 152; CANR 73; INT CA-130

Causley, Charles (Stanley)
1917-2003 .... **CLC 7**
See also CA 9-12R; 223; CANR 5, 35, 94; CLR 30; CP 1, 2, 3, 4; CWRI 5; DLB 27; MTCW 1; SATA 3, 66; SATA-Obit 149

Caute, (John) David 1936- .... **CLC 29**
See also CA 1-4R; CAAS 4; CANR 1, 33, 64, 120; CBD; CD 5, 6; CN 1, 2, 3, 4, 5, 6, 7; DAM NOV; DLB 14, 231

Cavafy, C(onstantine) P(eter) .... **PC 36; TCLC 2, 7**
See Kavafis, Konstantinos Petrou
See also CA 148; DA3; DAM POET; EW 8; EWL 3; MTCW 2; PFS 19; RGWL 2, 3; WP

Cavalcanti, Guido c. 1250-c.
1300 .... **CMLC 54**
See also RGWL 2, 3; WLIT 7

Cavallo, Evelyn
See Spark, Muriel (Sarah)

Cavanna, Betty .... **CLC 12**
See Harrison, Elizabeth (Allen) Cavanna
See also JRDA; MAICYA 1; SAAS 4; SATA 1, 30

Cavendish, Margaret Lucas
1623-1673 .... **LC 30**
See also DLB 131, 252, 281; RGEL 2

Caxton, William 1421(?)-1491(?) .... **LC 17**
See also DLB 170

Cayer, D. M.
See Duffy, Maureen (Patricia)

Cayrol, Jean 1911-2005 .... **CLC 11**
See also CA 89-92; 236; DLB 83; EWL 3

Cela (y Trulock), Camilo Jose
See Cela, Camilo Jose
See also CWW 2

Cela, Camilo Jose 1916-2002 .... **CLC 4, 13, 59, 122; HLC 1; SSC 71**
See Cela (y Trulock), Camilo Jose
See also BEST 90:2; CA 21-24R; 206; CAAS 10; CANR 21, 32, 76, 139; DAM MULT; DLB 322; DLBY 1989; EW 13; EWL 3; HW 1; MTCW 1, 2; MTFW 2005; RGSF 2; RGWL 2, 3

Celan, Paul .... **CLC 10, 19, 53, 82; PC 10**
See Antschel, Paul
See also CDWLB 2; DLB 69; EWL 3; RGWL 2, 3

Celine, Louis-Ferdinand .. **CLC 1, 3, 4, 7, 9, 15, 47, 124**
See Destouches, Louis-Ferdinand
See also DLB 72; EW 11; EWL 3; GFL 1789 to the Present; RGWL 2, 3

Cellini, Benvenuto 1500-1571 .... **LC 7**
See also WLIT 7

Cendrars, Blaise .... **CLC 18, 106**
See Sauser-Hall, Frederic
See also DLB 258; EWL 3; GFL 1789 to the Present; RGWL 2, 3; WP

Centlivre, Susanna 1669(?)-1723 .... **DC 25; LC 65**
See also DLB 84; RGEL 2

Cernuda (y Bidon), Luis
1902-1963 .... **CLC 54; PC 62**
See also CA 131; 89-92; DAM POET; DLB 134; EWL 3; GLL 1; HW 1; RGWL 2, 3

Cervantes, Lorna Dee 1954- ...... **HLCS 1; PC 35**
See also CA 131; CANR 80; CWP; DLB 82; EXPP; HW 1; LLW

Cervantes (Saavedra), Miguel de
1547-1616 .... **HLCS; LC 6, 23, 93; SSC 12; WLC**
See also AAYA 56; BYA 1, 14; DA; DAB; DAC; DAM MST, NOV; EW 2; LAIT 1; LATS 1:1; LMFS 1; NFS 8; RGSF 2; RGWL 2, 3; TWA

Cesaire, Aime (Fernand) 1913- .... **BLC 1; CLC 19, 32, 112; DC 22; PC 25**
See also BW 2, 3; CA 65-68; CANR 24, 43, 81; CWW 2; DA3; DAM MULT, POET; DLB 321; EWL 3; GFL 1789 to the Present; MTCW 1, 2; MTFW 2005; WP

Chabon, Michael 1963- ... **CLC 55, 149; SSC 59**
See also AAYA 45; AMWS 11; CA 139; CANR 57, 96, 127, 138; DLB 278; MAL 5; MTFW 2005; SATA 145

Chabrol, Claude 1930- .... **CLC 16**
See also CA 110

Chairil Anwar
See Anwar, Chairil
See also EWL 3

Challans, Mary 1905-1983
See Renault, Mary
See also CA 81-84; 111; CANR 74; DA3; MTCW 2; MTFW 2005; SATA 23; SATA-Obit 36; TEA

Challis, George
See Faust, Frederick (Schiller)

Chambers, Aidan 1934- .... **CLC 35**
See also AAYA 27; CA 25-28R; CANR 12, 31, 58, 116; JRDA; MAICYA 1, 2; SAAS 12; SATA 1, 69, 108; WYA; YAW

Chambers, James 1948-
See Cliff, Jimmy
See also CA 124

Chambers, Jessie
See Lawrence, D(avid) H(erbert Richards)
See also GLL 1

Chambers, Robert W(illiam)
1865-1933 .... **TCLC 41**
See also CA 165; DLB 202; HGG; SATA 107; SUFW 1

Chambers, (David) Whittaker
1901-1961 .... **TCLC 129**
See also CA 89-92; DLB 303

Chamisso, Adelbert von
1781-1838 .... **NCLC 82**
See also DLB 90; RGWL 2, 3; SUFW 1

Chance, James T.
See Carpenter, John (Howard)

Chance, John T.
See Carpenter, John (Howard)

Chandler, Raymond (Thornton)
1888-1959 .... **SSC 23; TCLC 1, 7**
See also AAYA 25; AMWC 2; AMWS 4; BPFB 1; CA 104; 129; CANR 60, 107; CDALB 1929-1941; CMW 4; DA3; DLB 226, 253; DLBD 6; EWL 3; MAL 5; MSW; MTCW 1, 2; MTFW 2005; NFS 17; RGAL 4; TUS

Chang, Diana 1934- .... **AAL**
See also CA 228; CWP; DLB 312; EXPP

Chang, Eileen 1921-1995 .... **AAL; SSC 28**
See Chang Ai-Ling; Zhang Ailing
See also CA 166

Chang, Jung 1952- .... **CLC 71**
See also CA 142

Chang Ai-Ling
See Chang, Eileen
See also EWL 3

Channing, William Ellery
1780-1842 .... **NCLC 17**
See also DLB 1, 59, 235; RGAL 4

Chao, Patricia 1955- .... **CLC 119**
See also CA 163

Chaplin, Charles Spencer
1889-1977 .... **CLC 16**
See Chaplin, Charlie
See also CA 81-84; 73-76

Chaplin, Charlie
See Chaplin, Charles Spencer
See also AAYA 61; DLB 44

Chapman, George 1559(?)-1634 . **DC 19; LC 22, 116**
See also BRW 1; DAM DRAM; DLB 62, 121; LMFS 1; RGEL 2

Chapman, Graham 1941-1989 .... **CLC 21**
See Monty Python
See also CA 116; 129; CANR 35, 95

Chapman, John Jay 1862-1933 .... **TCLC 7**
See also AMWS 14; CA 104; 191

Chapman, Lee
See Bradley, Marion Zimmer
See also GLL 1

Chapman, Walker
See Silverberg, Robert

Chappell, Fred (Davis) 1936- .... **CLC 40, 78, 162**
See also CA 5-8R, 198; CAAE 198; CAAS 4; CANR 8, 33, 67, 110; CN 6; CP 7; CSW; DLB 6, 105; HGG

Char, Rene(-Emile) 1907-1988 .... **CLC 9, 11, 14, 55; PC 56**
See also CA 13-16R; 124; CANR 32; DAM POET; DLB 258; EWL 3; GFL 1789 to the Present; MTCW 1, 2; RGWL 2, 3

Charby, Jay
See Ellison, Harlan (Jay)

Chardin, Pierre Teilhard de
See Teilhard de Chardin, (Marie Joseph) Pierre

Chariton fl. 1st cent. (?)- .... **CMLC 49**

Charlemagne 742-814 .... **CMLC 37**

Charles I 1600-1649 .... **LC 13**

Charriere, Isabelle de 1740-1805 .. **NCLC 66**
See also DLB 313

Chartier, Alain c. 1392-1430 .... **LC 94**
See also DLB 208

Chartier, Emile-Auguste
See Alain

Charyn, Jerome 1937- .... **CLC 5, 8, 18**
See also CA 5-8R; CAAS 1; CANR 7, 61, 101; CMW 4; CN 1, 2, 3, 4, 5, 6, 7; DLBY 1983; MTCW 1

Chase, Adam
See Marlowe, Stephen

Chase, Mary (Coyle) 1907-1981 .... **DC 1**
See also CA 77-80; 105; CAD; CWD; DFS 11; DLB 228; SATA 17; SATA-Obit 29

Chase, Mary Ellen 1887-1973 .... **CLC 2; TCLC 124**
See also CA 13-16; 41-44R; CAP 1; SATA 10

Chase, Nicholas
See Hyde, Anthony
See also CCA 1

Chateaubriand, Francois Rene de 1768-1848 .... **NCLC 3, 134**
See also DLB 119; EW 5; GFL 1789 to the Present; RGWL 2, 3; TWA

Chatelet, Gabrielle-Emilie Du
See du Chatelet, Emilie
See also DLB 313

Chatterje, Sarat Chandra 1876-1936(?)
See Chatterji, Saratchandra
See also CA 109

Chatterji, Bankim Chandra 1838-1894 .... **NCLC 19**

Chatterji, Saratchandra .... **TCLC 13**
See Chatterje, Sarat Chandra
See also CA 186; EWL 3

Chatterton, Thomas 1752-1770 .... **LC 3, 54**
See also DAM POET; DLB 109; RGEL 2

Chatwin, (Charles) Bruce 1940-1989 .... **CLC 28, 57, 59**
See also AAYA 4; BEST 90:1; BRWS 4; CA 85-88; 127; CPW; DAM POP; DLB 194, 204; EWL 3; MTFW 2005

Chaucer, Daniel
See Ford, Ford Madox
See also RHW

Chaucer, Geoffrey 1340(?)-1400 .. **LC 17, 56; PC 19, 58; WLCS**
See also BRW 1; BRWC 1; BRWR 2; CD-BLB Before 1660; DA; DA3; DAB; DAC; DAM MST, POET; DLB 146; LAIT 1; PAB; PFS 14; RGEL 2; TEA; WLIT 3; WP

Chavez, Denise (Elia) 1948- .... **HLC 1**
See also CA 131; CANR 56, 81, 137; DAM MULT; DLB 122; FW; HW 1, 2; LLW; MAL 5; MTCW 2; MTFW 2005

Chaviaras, Strates 1935-
See Haviaras, Stratis
See also CA 105

Chayefsky, Paddy .... **CLC 23**
See Chayefsky, Sidney
See also CAD; DLB 7, 44; DLBY 1981; RGAL 4

Chayefsky, Sidney 1923-1981
See Chayefsky, Paddy
See also CA 9-12R; 104; CANR 18; DAM DRAM

Chedid, Andree 1920- .... **CLC 47**
See also CA 145; CANR 95; EWL 3

Cheever, John 1912-1982 ..... **CLC 3, 7, 8, 11, 15, 25, 64; SSC 1, 38, 57; WLC**
See also AAYA 65; AMWS 1; BPFB 1; CA 5-8R; 106; CABS 1; CANR 5, 27, 76; CDALB 1941-1968; CN 1, 2, 3; CPW; DA; DA3; DAB; DAC; DAM MST, NOV, POP; DLB 2, 102, 227; DLBY 1980, 1982; EWL 3; EXPS; INT CANR-5; MAL 5; MTCW 1, 2; MTFW 2005; RGAL 4; RGSF 2; SSFS 2, 14; TUS

Cheever, Susan 1943- .... **CLC 18, 48**
See also CA 103; CANR 27, 51, 92; DLBY 1982; INT CANR-27

Chekhonte, Antosha
See Chekhov, Anton (Pavlovich)

Chekhov, Anton (Pavlovich) 1860-1904 .... **DC 9; SSC 2, 28, 41, 51, 85; TCLC 3, 10, 31, 55, 96, 163; WLC**
See also AAYA 68; BYA 14; CA 104; 124; DA; DA3; DAB; DAC; DAM DRAM, MST; DFS 1, 5, 10, 12; DLB 277; EW 7; EWL 3; EXPS; LAIT 3; LATS 1:1; RGSF 2; RGWL 2, 3; SATA 90; SSFS 5, 13, 14; TWA

Cheney, Lynne V. 1941- .... **CLC 70**
See also CA 89-92; CANR 58, 117; SATA 152

Chernyshevsky, Nikolai Gavrilovich
See Chernyshevsky, Nikolay Gavrilovich
See also DLB 238

Chernyshevsky, Nikolay Gavrilovich 1828-1889 .... **NCLC 1**
See Chernyshevsky, Nikolai Gavrilovich

Cherry, Carolyn Janice 1942-
See Cherryh, C. J.
See also CA 65-68; CANR 10

Cherryh, C. J. .... **CLC 35**
See Cherry, Carolyn Janice
See also AAYA 24; BPFB 1; DLBY 1980; FANT; SATA 93; SCFW 2; SFW 4; YAW

Chesnutt, Charles W(addell) 1858-1932 .... **BLC 1; SSC 7, 54; TCLC 5, 39**
See also AFAW 1, 2; AMWS 14; BW 1, 3; CA 106; 125; CANR 76; DAM MULT; DLB 12, 50, 78; EWL 3; MAL 5; MTCW 1, 2; MTFW 2005; RGAL 4; RGSF 2; SSFS 11

Chester, Alfred 1929(?)-1971 .... **CLC 49**
See also CA 196; 33-36R; DLB 130; MAL 5

Chesterton, G(ilbert) K(eith) 1874-1936 . **PC 28; SSC 1, 46; TCLC 1, 6, 64**
See also AAYA 57; BRW 6; CA 104; 132; CANR 73, 131; CDBLB 1914-1945; CMW 4; DAM NOV, POET; DLB 10, 19, 34, 70, 98, 149, 178; EWL 3; FANT; MSW; MTCW 1, 2; MTFW 2005; RGEL 2; RGSF 2; SATA 27; SUFW 1

Chettle, Henry 1560-1607(?) .... **LC 112**
See also DLB 136; RGEL 2

Chiang, Pin-chin 1904-1986
See Ding Ling
See also CA 118

Chief Joseph 1840-1904 .... **NNAL**
See also CA 152; DA3; DAM MULT

Chief Seattle 1786(?)-1866 .... **NNAL**
See also DA3; DAM MULT

Ch'ien, Chung-shu 1910-1998 .... **CLC 22**
See Qian Zhongshu
See also CA 130; CANR 73; MTCW 1, 2

Chikamatsu Monzaemon 1653-1724 ... **LC 66**
See also RGWL 2, 3

Child, L. Maria
See Child, Lydia Maria

Child, Lydia Maria 1802-1880 .. **NCLC 6, 73**
See also DLB 1, 74, 243; RGAL 4; SATA 67

Child, Mrs.
See Child, Lydia Maria

Child, Philip 1898-1978 .... **CLC 19, 68**
See also CA 13-14; CAP 1; CP 1; DLB 68; RHW; SATA 47

Childers, (Robert) Erskine 1870-1922 .... **TCLC 65**
See also CA 113; 153; DLB 70

Childress, Alice 1920-1994 . **BLC 1; CLC 12, 15, 86, 96; DC 4; TCLC 116**
See also AAYA 8; BW 2, 3; BYA 2; CA 45-48; 146; CAD; CANR 3, 27, 50, 74; CLR 14; CWD; DA3; DAM DRAM, MULT, NOV; DFS 2, 8, 14; DLB 7, 38, 249; JRDA; LAIT 5; MAICYA 1, 2; MAICYAS 1; MAL 5; MTCW 1, 2; MTFW 2005; RGAL 4; SATA 7, 48, 81; TUS; WYA; YAW

Chin, Frank (Chew, Jr.) 1940- .... **AAL; CLC 135; DC 7**
See also CA 33-36R; CAD; CANR 71; CD 5, 6; DAM MULT; DLB 206, 312; LAIT 5; RGAL 4

Chin, Marilyn (Mei Ling) 1955- .... **PC 40**
See also CA 129; CANR 70, 113; CWP; DLB 312

Chislett, (Margaret) Anne 1943- ...... **CLC 34**
See also CA 151

Chitty, Thomas Willes 1926- .... **CLC 11**
See Hinde, Thomas
See also CA 5-8R; CN 7

Chivers, Thomas Holley 1809-1858 .... **NCLC 49**
See also DLB 3, 248; RGAL 4

Choi, Susan 1969- .... **CLC 119**
See also CA 223

Chomette, Rene Lucien 1898-1981
See Clair, Rene
See also CA 103

Chomsky, (Avram) Noam 1928- ...... **CLC 132**
See also CA 17-20R; CANR 28, 62, 110, 132; DA3; DLB 246; MTCW 1, 2; MTFW 2005

Chona, Maria 1845(?)-1936 .... **NNAL**
See also CA 144

Chopin, Kate ...... **SSC 8, 68; TCLC 127; WLCS**
See Chopin, Katherine
See also AAYA 33; AMWR 2; AMWS 1; BYA 11, 15; CDALB 1865-1917; DA; DAB; DLB 12, 78; EXPN; EXPS; FL 1:3; FW; LAIT 3; MAL 5; MAWW; NFS 3; RGAL 4; RGSF 2; SSFS 2, 13, 17; TUS

Chopin, Katherine 1851-1904
See Chopin, Kate
See also CA 104; 122; DA3; DAC; DAM MST, NOV

Chretien de Troyes c. 12th cent. - . **CMLC 10**
See also DLB 208; EW 1; RGWL 2, 3; TWA

Christie
See Ichikawa, Kon

Christie, Agatha (Mary Clarissa)
1890-1976 .. **CLC 1, 6, 8, 12, 39, 48, 110**
See also AAYA 9; AITN 1, 2; BPFB 1; BRWS 2; CA 17-20R; 61-64; CANR 10, 37, 108; CBD; CDBLB 1914-1945; CMW 4; CN 1, 2; CPW; CWD; DA3; DAB; DAC; DAM NOV; DFS 2; DLB 13, 77, 245; MSW; MTCW 1, 2; MTFW 2005; NFS 8; RGEL 2; RHW; SATA 36; TEA; YAW

Christie, Philippa .... **CLC 21**
See Pearce, Philippa
See also BYA 5; CANR 109; CLR 9; DLB 161; MAICYA 1; SATA 1, 67, 129

Christina of Sweden 1626-1689 .... **LC 124**

Christine de Pizan 1365(?)-1431(?) ...... **LC 9; PC 68**
See also DLB 208; RGWL 2, 3

Chuang Tzu c. 369B.C.-c.
286B.C. .... **CMLC 57**

Chubb, Elmer
See Masters, Edgar Lee

Chulkov, Mikhail Dmitrievich
1743-1792 .... **LC 2**
See also DLB 150

Churchill, Caryl 1938- .... **CLC 31, 55, 157; DC 5**
See Churchill, Chick
See also BRWS 4; CA 102; CANR 22, 46, 108; CBD; CD 6; CWD; DFS 12, 16; DLB 13, 310; EWL 3; FW; MTCW 1; RGEL 2

Churchill, Charles 1731-1764 .... **LC 3**
See also DLB 109; RGEL 2

Churchill, Chick
See Churchill, Caryl
See also CD 5

Churchill, Sir Winston (Leonard Spencer)
1874-1965 .... **TCLC 113**
See also BRW 6; CA 97-100; CDBLB 1890-1914; DA3; DLB 100; DLBD 16; LAIT 4; MTCW 1, 2

Chute, Carolyn 1947- .... **CLC 39**
See also CA 123; CANR 135; CN 7

Ciardi, John (Anthony) 1916-1986 . **CLC 10, 40, 44, 129; PC 69**
See also CA 5-8R; 118; CAAS 2; CANR 5, 33; CLR 19; CP 1, 2, 3, 4; CWRI 5; DAM POET; DLB 5; DLBY 1986; INT CANR-5; MAICYA 1, 2; MAL 5; MTCW 1, 2; MTFW 2005; RGAL 4; SAAS 26; SATA 1, 65; SATA-Obit 46

Cibber, Colley 1671-1757 .... **LC 66**
See also DLB 84; RGEL 2

Cicero, Marcus Tullius
106B.C.-43B.C. .... **CMLC 3, 81**
See also AW 1; CDWLB 1; DLB 211; RGWL 2, 3

Cimino, Michael 1943- .... **CLC 16**
See also CA 105

Cioran, E(mil) M. 1911-1995 .... **CLC 64**
See also CA 25-28R; 149; CANR 91; DLB 220; EWL 3

Cisneros, Sandra 1954- .... **CLC 69, 118, 193; HLC 1; PC 52; SSC 32, 72**
See also AAYA 9, 53; AMWS 7; CA 131; CANR 64, 118; CN 7; CWP; DA3; DAM MULT; DLB 122, 152; EWL 3; EXPN; FL 1:5; FW; HW 1, 2; LAIT 5; LATS 1:2; LLW; MAICYA 2; MAL 5; MTCW 2; MTFW 2005; NFS 2; PFS 19; RGAL 4; RGSF 2; SSFS 3, 13; WLIT 1; YAW

Cixous, Helene 1937- .... **CLC 92**
See also CA 126; CANR 55, 123; CWW 2; DLB 83, 242; EWL 3; FL 1:5; FW; GLL 2; MTCW 1, 2; MTFW 2005; TWA

Clair, Rene .... **CLC 20**
See Chomette, Rene Lucien

Clampitt, Amy 1920-1994 .... **CLC 32; PC 19**
See also AMWS 9; CA 110; 146; CANR 29, 79; CP 4; DLB 105; MAL 5

Clancy, Thomas L., Jr. 1947-
See Clancy, Tom
See also CA 125; 131; CANR 62, 105; DA3; INT CA-131; MTCW 1, 2; MTFW 2005

Clancy, Tom .... **CLC 45, 112**
See Clancy, Thomas L., Jr.
See also AAYA 9, 51; BEST 89:1, 90:1; BPFB 1; BYA 10, 11; CANR 132; CMW 4; CPW; DAM NOV, POP; DLB 227

Clare, John 1793-1864 .. **NCLC 9, 86; PC 23**
See also BRWS 11; DAB; DAM POET; DLB 55, 96; RGEL 2

Clarin
See Alas (y Urena), Leopoldo (Enrique Garcia)

Clark, Al C.
See Goines, Donald

Clark, Brian (Robert)
See Clark, (Robert) Brian
See also CD 6

Clark, (Robert) Brian 1932- .... **CLC 29**
See Clark, Brian (Robert)
See also CA 41-44R; CANR 67; CBD; CD 5

Clark, Curt
See Westlake, Donald E(dwin)

Clark, Eleanor 1913-1996 .... **CLC 5, 19**
See also CA 9-12R; 151; CANR 41; CN 1, 2, 3, 4, 5, 6; DLB 6

Clark, J. P.
See Clark Bekederemo, J(ohnson) P(epper)
See also CDWLB 3; DLB 117

Clark, John Pepper
See Clark Bekederemo, J(ohnson) P(epper)
See also AFW; CD 5; CP 1, 2, 3, 4, 5, 6, 7; RGEL 2

Clark, Kenneth (Mackenzie)
1903-1983 .... **TCLC 147**
See also CA 93-96; 109; CANR 36; MTCW 1, 2; MTFW 2005

Clark, M. R.
See Clark, Mavis Thorpe

Clark, Mavis Thorpe 1909-1999 ...... **CLC 12**
See also CA 57-60; CANR 8, 37, 107; CLR 30; CWRI 5; MAICYA 1, 2; SAAS 5; SATA 8, 74

Clark, Walter Van Tilburg
1909-1971 .... **CLC 28**
See also CA 9-12R; 33-36R; CANR 63, 113; CN 1; DLB 9, 206; LAIT 2; MAL 5; RGAL 4; SATA 8; TCWW 1, 2

Clark Bekederemo, J(ohnson) P(epper)
1935- .... **BLC 1; CLC 38; DC 5**
See Bekederemo, J. P. Clark; Clark, J. P.; Clark, John Pepper
See also BW 1; CA 65-68; CANR 16, 72; DAM DRAM, MULT; DFS 13; EWL 3; MTCW 2; MTFW 2005

Clarke, Arthur C(harles) 1917- .... **CLC 1, 4, 13, 18, 35, 136; SSC 3**
See also AAYA 4, 33; BPFB 1; BYA 13; CA 1-4R; CANR 2, 28, 55, 74, 130; CN 1, 2, 3, 4, 5, 6, 7; CPW; DA3; DAM POP; DLB 261; JRDA; LAIT 5; MAICYA 1, 2; MTCW 1, 2; MTFW 2005; SATA 13, 70, 115; SCFW 1, 2; SFW 4; SSFS 4, 18; TCLE 1:1; YAW

Clarke, Austin 1896-1974 .... **CLC 6, 9**
See also CA 29-32; 49-52; CAP 2; CP 1, 2; DAM POET; DLB 10, 20; EWL 3; RGEL 2

Clarke, Austin C(hesterfield) 1934- .. **BLC 1; CLC 8, 53; SSC 45**
See also BW 1; CA 25-28R; CAAS 16; CANR 14, 32, 68, 140; CN 1, 2, 3, 4, 5, 6, 7; DAC; DAM MULT; DLB 53, 125; DNFS 2; MTCW 2; MTFW 2005; RGSF 2

Clarke, Gillian 1937- .... **CLC 61**
See also CA 106; CP 3, 4, 5, 6, 7; CWP; DLB 40

Clarke, Marcus (Andrew Hislop)
1846-1881 .... **NCLC 19**
See also DLB 230; RGEL 2; RGSF 2

Clarke, Shirley 1925-1997 .... **CLC 16**
See also CA 189

Clash, The
See Headon, (Nicky) Topper; Jones, Mick; Simonon, Paul; Strummer, Joe

Claudel, Paul (Louis Charles Marie)
1868-1955 .... **TCLC 2, 10**
See also CA 104; 165; DLB 192, 258, 321; EW 8; EWL 3; GFL 1789 to the Present; RGWL 2, 3; TWA

Claudian 370(?)-404(?) .... **CMLC 46**
See also RGWL 2, 3

Claudius, Matthias 1740-1815 .... **NCLC 75**
See also DLB 97

Clavell, James (duMaresq)
1925-1994 .... **CLC 6, 25, 87**
See also BPFB 1; CA 25-28R; 146; CANR 26, 48; CN 5; CPW; DA3; DAM NOV, POP; MTCW 1, 2; MTFW 2005; NFS 10; RHW

Clayman, Gregory .... **CLC 65**

Cleaver, (Leroy) Eldridge
1935-1998 .... **BLC 1; CLC 30, 119**
See also BW 1, 3; CA 21-24R; 167; CANR 16, 75; DA3; DAM MULT; MTCW 2; YAW

Cleese, John (Marwood) 1939- .... **CLC 21**
See Monty Python
See also CA 112; 116; CANR 35; MTCW 1

Cleishbotham, Jebediah
See Scott, Sir Walter

Cleland, John 1710-1789 .... **LC 2, 48**
See also DLB 39; RGEL 2

Clemens, Samuel Langhorne 1835-1910
See Twain, Mark
See also CA 104; 135; CDALB 1865-1917; DA; DA3; DAB; DAC; DAM MST, NOV; DLB 12, 23, 64, 74, 186, 189; JRDA; LMFS 1; MAICYA 1, 2; NCFS 4; NFS 20; SATA 100; YABC 2

Clement of Alexandria
150(?)-215(?) .... **CMLC 41**

Cleophil
See Congreve, William

Clerihew, E.
See Bentley, E(dmund) C(lerihew)

Clerk, N. W.
See Lewis, C(live) S(taples)

Cleveland, John 1613-1658 .... **LC 106**
See also DLB 126; RGEL 2

Cliff, Jimmy .... **CLC 21**
See Chambers, James
See also CA 193

Cliff, Michelle 1946- .... **BLCS; CLC 120**
See also BW 2; CA 116; CANR 39, 72; CDWLB 3; DLB 157; FW; GLL 2

Clifford, Lady Anne 1590-1676 .... **LC 76**
See also DLB 151

Clifton, (Thelma) Lucille 1936- .... **BLC 1; CLC 19, 66, 162; PC 17**
See also AFAW 2; BW 2, 3; CA 49-52; CANR 2, 24, 42, 76, 97, 138; CLR 5; CP 2, 3, 4, 5, 6, 7; CSW; CWP; CWRI 5;

DA3; DAM MULT, POET; DLB 5, 41; EXPP; MAICYA 1, 2; MTCW 1, 2; MTFW 2005; PFS 1, 14; SATA 20, 69, 128; WP

Clinton, Dirk
See Silverberg, Robert

Clough, Arthur Hugh 1819-1861 .. **NCLC 27, 163**
See also BRW 5; DLB 32; RGEL 2

Clutha, Janet Paterson Frame 1924-2004
See Frame, Janet
See also CA 1-4R; 224; CANR 2, 36, 76, 135; MTCW 1, 2; SATA 119

Clyne, Terence
See Blatty, William Peter

Cobalt, Martin
See Mayne, William (James Carter)

Cobb, Irvin S(hrewsbury) 1876-1944 .... **TCLC 77**
See also CA 175; DLB 11, 25, 86

Cobbett, William 1763-1835 .... **NCLC 49**
See also DLB 43, 107, 158; RGEL 2

Coburn, D(onald) L(ee) 1938- .... **CLC 10**
See also CA 89-92

Cocteau, Jean (Maurice Eugene Clement) 1889-1963 ...... **CLC 1, 8, 15, 16, 43; DC 17; TCLC 119; WLC**
See also CA 25-28; CANR 40; CAP 2; DA; DA3; DAB; DAC; DAM DRAM, MST, NOV; DLB 65, 258, 321; EW 10; EWL 3; GFL 1789 to the Present; MTCW 1, 2; RGWL 2, 3; TWA

Codrescu, Andrei 1946- .... **CLC 46, 121**
See also CA 33-36R; CAAS 19; CANR 13, 34, 53, 76, 125; CN 7; DA3; DAM POET; MAL 5; MTCW 2; MTFW 2005

Coe, Max
See Bourne, Randolph S(illiman)

Coe, Tucker
See Westlake, Donald E(dwin)

Coen, Ethan 1958- .... **CLC 108**
See also AAYA 54; CA 126; CANR 85

Coen, Joel 1955- .... **CLC 108**
See also AAYA 54; CA 126; CANR 119

The Coen Brothers
See Coen, Ethan; Coen, Joel

Coetzee, J(ohn) M(axwell) 1940- ..... **CLC 23, 33, 66, 117, 161, 162**
See also AAYA 37; AFW; BRWS 6; CA 77-80; CANR 41, 54, 74, 114, 133; CN 4, 5, 6, 7; DA3; DAM NOV; DLB 225; EWL 3; LMFS 2; MTCW 1, 2; MTFW 2005; NFS 21; WLIT 2; WWE 1

Coffey, Brian
See Koontz, Dean R.

Coffin, Robert P(eter) Tristram 1892-1955 .... **TCLC 95**
See also CA 123; 169; DLB 45

Cohan, George M(ichael) 1878-1942 .... **TCLC 60**
See also CA 157; DLB 249; RGAL 4

Cohen, Arthur A(llen) 1928-1986 ...... **CLC 7, 31**
See also CA 1-4R; 120; CANR 1, 17, 42; DLB 28

Cohen, Leonard (Norman) 1934- .... **CLC 3, 38**
See also CA 21-24R; CANR 14, 69; CN 1, 2, 3, 4, 5, 6; CP 1, 2, 3, 4, 5, 6, 7; DAC; DAM MST; DLB 53; EWL 3; MTCW 1

Cohen, Matt(hew) 1942-1999 .... **CLC 19**
See also CA 61-64; 187; CAAS 18; CANR 40; CN 1, 2, 3, 4, 5, 6; DAC; DLB 53

Cohen-Solal, Annie 1948- .... **CLC 50**
See also CA 239

Colegate, Isabel 1931- .... **CLC 36**
See also CA 17-20R; CANR 8, 22, 74; CN 4, 5, 6, 7; DLB 14, 231; INT CANR-22; MTCW 1

Coleman, Emmett
See Reed, Ishmael (Scott)

Coleridge, Hartley 1796-1849 .... **NCLC 90**
See also DLB 96

Coleridge, M. E.
See Coleridge, Mary E(lizabeth)

Coleridge, Mary E(lizabeth) 1861-1907 .... **TCLC 73**
See also CA 116; 166; DLB 19, 98

Coleridge, Samuel Taylor 1772-1834 ...... **NCLC 9, 54, 99, 111; PC 11, 39, 67; WLC**
See also AAYA 66; BRW 4; BRWR 2; BYA 4; CDBLB 1789-1832; DA; DA3; DAB; DAC; DAM MST, POET; DLB 93, 107; EXPP; LATS 1:1; LMFS 1; PAB; PFS 4, 5; RGEL 2; TEA; WLIT 3; WP

Coleridge, Sara 1802-1852 .... **NCLC 31**
See also DLB 199

Coles, Don 1928- .... **CLC 46**
See also CA 115; CANR 38; CP 7

Coles, Robert (Martin) 1929- .... **CLC 108**
See also CA 45-48; CANR 3, 32, 66, 70, 135; INT CANR-32; SATA 23

Colette, (Sidonie-Gabrielle) 1873-1954 .... **SSC 10; TCLC 1, 5, 16**
See Willy, Colette
See also CA 104; 131; DA3; DAM NOV; DLB 65; EW 9; EWL 3; GFL 1789 to the Present; MTCW 1, 2; MTFW 2005; RGWL 2, 3; TWA

Collett, (Jacobine) Camilla (Wergeland) 1813-1895 .... **NCLC 22**

Collier, Christopher 1930- .... **CLC 30**
See also AAYA 13; BYA 2; CA 33-36R; CANR 13, 33, 102; JRDA; MAICYA 1, 2; SATA 16, 70; WYA; YAW 1

Collier, James Lincoln 1928- .... **CLC 30**
See also AAYA 13; BYA 2; CA 9-12R; CANR 4, 33, 60, 102; CLR 3; DAM POP; JRDA; MAICYA 1, 2; SAAS 21; SATA 8, 70; WYA; YAW 1

Collier, Jeremy 1650-1726 .... **LC 6**

Collier, John 1901-1980 . **SSC 19; TCLC 127**
See also CA 65-68; 97-100; CANR 10; CN 1, 2; DLB 77, 255; FANT; SUFW 1

Collier, Mary 1690-1762 .... **LC 86**
See also DLB 95

Collingwood, R(obin) G(eorge) 1889(?)-1943 .... **TCLC 67**
See also CA 117; 155; DLB 262

Collins, Billy 1941- .... **PC 68**
See also AAYA 64; CA 151; CANR 92; MTFW 2005; PFS 18

Collins, Hunt
See Hunter, Evan

Collins, Linda 1931- .... **CLC 44**
See also CA 125

Collins, Tom
See Furphy, Joseph
See also RGEL 2

Collins, (William) Wilkie 1824-1889 .... **NCLC 1, 18, 93**
See also BRWS 6; CDBLB 1832-1890; CMW 4; DLB 18, 70, 159; GL 2; MSW; RGEL 2; RGSF 2; SUFW 1; WLIT 4

Collins, William 1721-1759 .... **LC 4, 40**
See also BRW 3; DAM POET; DLB 109; RGEL 2

Collodi, Carlo .... **NCLC 54**
See Lorenzini, Carlo
See also CLR 5; WCH; WLIT 7

Colman, George
See Glassco, John

Colman, George, the Elder 1732-1794 .... **LC 98**
See also RGEL 2

Colonna, Vittoria 1492-1547 .... **LC 71**
See also RGWL 2, 3

Colt, Winchester Remington
See Hubbard, L(afayette) Ron(ald)

Colter, Cyrus J. 1910-2002 .... **CLC 58**
See also BW 1; CA 65-68; 205; CANR 10, 66; CN 2, 3, 4, 5, 6; DLB 33

Colton, James
See Hansen, Joseph
See also GLL 1

Colum, Padraic 1881-1972 .... **CLC 28**
See also BYA 4; CA 73-76; 33-36R; CANR 35; CLR 36; CP 1; CWRI 5; DLB 19; MAICYA 1, 2; MTCW 1; RGEL 2; SATA 15; WCH

Colvin, James
See Moorcock, Michael (John)

Colwin, Laurie (E.) 1944-1992 .... **CLC 5, 13, 23, 84**
See also CA 89-92; 139; CANR 20, 46; DLB 218; DLBY 1980; MTCW 1

Comfort, Alex(ander) 1920-2000 .... **CLC 7**
See also CA 1-4R; 190; CANR 1, 45; CN 1, 2, 3, 4; CP 1, 2, 3, 4, 5, 6, 7; DAM POP; MTCW 2

Comfort, Montgomery
See Campbell, (John) Ramsey

Compton-Burnett, I(vy) 1892(?)-1969 .... **CLC 1, 3, 10, 15, 34**
See also BRW 7; CA 1-4R; 25-28R; CANR 4; DAM NOV; DLB 36; EWL 3; MTCW 1, 2; RGEL 2

Comstock, Anthony 1844-1915 ...... **TCLC 13**
See also CA 110; 169

Comte, Auguste 1798-1857 .... **NCLC 54**

Conan Doyle, Arthur
See Doyle, Sir Arthur Conan
See also BPFB 1; BYA 4, 5, 11

Conde (Abellan), Carmen 1901-1996 .... **HLCS 1**
See also CA 177; CWW 2; DLB 108; EWL 3; HW 2

Conde, Maryse 1937- ...... **BLCS; CLC 52, 92**
See also BW 2, 3; CA 110, 190; CAAE 190; CANR 30, 53, 76; DAM MULT; EWL 3; MTCW 2; MTFW 2005

Condillac, Etienne Bonnot de 1714-1780 .... **LC 26**
See also DLB 313

Condon, Richard (Thomas) 1915-1996 .... **CLC 4, 6, 8, 10, 45, 100**
See also BEST 90:3; BPFB 1; CA 1-4R; 151; CAAS 1; CANR 2, 23; CMW 4; CN 1, 2, 3, 4, 5, 6; DAM NOV; INT CANR-23; MAL 5; MTCW 1, 2

Condorcet .... **LC 104**
See Condorcet, marquis de Marie-Jean-Antoine-Nicolas Caritat
See also GFL Beginnings to 1789

Condorcet, marquis de Marie-Jean-Antoine-Nicolas Caritat 1743-1794
See Condorcet
See also DLB 313

Confucius 551B.C.-479B.C. ..... **CMLC 19, 65; WLCS**
See also DA; DA3; DAB; DAC; DAM MST

Congreve, William 1670-1729 ... **DC 2; LC 5, 21; WLC**
See also BRW 2; CDBLB 1660-1789; DA; DAB; DAC; DAM DRAM, MST, POET; DFS 15; DLB 39, 84; RGEL 2; WLIT 3

Conley, Robert J(ackson) 1940- .... **NNAL**
See also CA 41-44R; CANR 15, 34, 45, 96; DAM MULT; TCWW 2

Connell, Evan S(helby), Jr. 1924- . **CLC 4, 6, 45**
See also AAYA 7; AMWS 14; CA 1-4R; CAAS 2; CANR 2, 39, 76, 97, 140; CN 1, 2, 3, 4, 5, 6; DAM NOV; DLB 2; DLBY 1981; MAL 5; MTCW 1, 2; MTFW 2005

Connelly, Marc(us Cook) 1890-1980 . **CLC 7**
See also CA 85-88; 102; CAD; CANR 30; DFS 12; DLB 7; DLBY 1980; MAL 5; RGAL 4; SATA-Obit 25

Connor, Ralph .... **TCLC 31**
See Gordon, Charles William
See also DLB 92; TCWW 1, 2

Conrad, Joseph 1857-1924 ..... **SSC 9, 67, 69, 71; TCLC 1, 6, 13, 25, 43, 57; WLC**
See also AAYA 26; BPFB 1; BRW 6; BRWC 1; BRWR 2; BYA 2; CA 104; 131; CANR 60; CDBLB 1890-1914; DA; DA3; DAB; DAC; DAM MST, NOV; DLB 10, 34, 98, 156; EWL 3; EXPN; EXPS; LAIT 2; LATS 1:1; LMFS 1; MTCW 1, 2; MTFW 2005; NFS 2, 16; RGEL 2; RGSF 2; SATA 27; SSFS 1, 12; TEA; WLIT 4

Conrad, Robert Arnold
See Hart, Moss

Conroy, (Donald) Pat(rick) 1945- ... **CLC 30, 74**
See also AAYA 8, 52; AITN 1; BPFB 1; CA 85-88; CANR 24, 53, 129; CN 7; CPW; CSW; DA3; DAM NOV, POP; DLB 6; LAIT 5; MAL 5; MTCW 1, 2; MTFW 2005

Constant (de Rebecque), (Henri) Benjamin 1767-1830 .... **NCLC 6**
See also DLB 119; EW 4; GFL 1789 to the Present

Conway, Jill K(er) 1934- .... **CLC 152**
See also CA 130; CANR 94

Conybeare, Charles Augustus
See Eliot, T(homas) S(tearns)

Cook, Michael 1933-1994 .... **CLC 58**
See also CA 93-96; CANR 68; DLB 53

Cook, Robin 1940- .... **CLC 14**
See also AAYA 32; BEST 90:2; BPFB 1; CA 108; 111; CANR 41, 90, 109; CPW; DA3; DAM POP; HGG; INT CA-111

Cook, Roy
See Silverberg, Robert

Cooke, Elizabeth 1948- .... **CLC 55**
See also CA 129

Cooke, John Esten 1830-1886 .... **NCLC 5**
See also DLB 3, 248; RGAL 4

Cooke, John Estes
See Baum, L(yman) Frank

Cooke, M. E.
See Creasey, John

Cooke, Margaret
See Creasey, John

Cooke, Rose Terry 1827-1892 ...... **NCLC 110**
See also DLB 12, 74

Cook-Lynn, Elizabeth 1930- .... **CLC 93; NNAL**
See also CA 133; DAM MULT; DLB 175

Cooney, Ray .... **CLC 62**
See also CBD

Cooper, Anthony Ashley 1671-1713 .. **LC 107**
See also DLB 101

Cooper, Dennis 1953- .... **CLC 203**
See also CA 133; CANR 72, 86; GLL 1; HGG

Cooper, Douglas 1960- .... **CLC 86**

Cooper, Henry St. John
See Creasey, John

Cooper, J(oan) California (?)- .... **CLC 56**
See also AAYA 12; BW 1; CA 125; CANR 55; DAM MULT; DLB 212

Cooper, James Fenimore 1789-1851 .... **NCLC 1, 27, 54**
See also AAYA 22; AMW; BPFB 1; CDALB 1640-1865; DA3; DLB 3, 183, 250, 254; LAIT 1; NFS 9; RGAL 4; SATA 19; TUS; WCH

Cooper, Susan Fenimore 1813-1894 .... **NCLC 129**
See also ANW; DLB 239, 254

Coover, Robert (Lowell) 1932- ...... **CLC 3, 7, 15, 32, 46, 87, 161; SSC 15**
See also AMWS 5; BPFB 1; CA 45-48; CANR 3, 37, 58, 115; CN 1, 2, 3, 4, 5, 6, 7; DAM NOV; DLB 2, 227; DLBY 1981; EWL 3; MAL 5; MTCW 1, 2; MTFW 2005; RGAL 4; RGSF 2

Copeland, Stewart (Armstrong) 1952- .... **CLC 26**

Copernicus, Nicolaus 1473-1543 .... **LC 45**

Coppard, A(lfred) E(dgar) 1878-1957 .... **SSC 21; TCLC 5**
See also BRWS 8; CA 114; 167; DLB 162; EWL 3; HGG; RGEL 2; RGSF 2; SUFW 1; YABC 1

Coppee, Francois 1842-1908 .... **TCLC 25**
See also CA 170; DLB 217

Coppola, Francis Ford 1939- ... **CLC 16, 126**
See also AAYA 39; CA 77-80; CANR 40, 78; DLB 44

Copway, George 1818-1869 .... **NNAL**
See also DAM MULT; DLB 175, 183

Corbiere, Tristan 1845-1875 .... **NCLC 43**
See also DLB 217; GFL 1789 to the Present

Corcoran, Barbara (Asenath) 1911- .... **CLC 17**
See also AAYA 14; CA 21-24R; 191; CAAE 191; CAAS 2; CANR 11, 28, 48; CLR 50; DLB 52; JRDA; MAICYA 2; MAIC-YAS 1; RHW; SAAS 20; SATA 3, 77; SATA-Essay 125

Cordelier, Maurice
See Giraudoux, Jean(-Hippolyte)

Corelli, Marie .... **TCLC 51**
See Mackay, Mary
See also DLB 34, 156; RGEL 2; SUFW 1

Corinna c. 225B.C.-c. 305B.C. ...... **CMLC 72**

Corman, Cid .... **CLC 9**
See Corman, Sidney
See also CAAS 2; CP 1, 2, 3, 4, 5, 6, 7; DLB 5, 193

Corman, Sidney 1924-2004
See Corman, Cid
See also CA 85-88; 225; CANR 44; DAM POET

Cormier, Robert (Edmund) 1925-2000 .... **CLC 12, 30**
See also AAYA 3, 19; BYA 1, 2, 6, 8, 9; CA 1-4R; CANR 5, 23, 76, 93; CDALB 1968-1988; CLR 12, 55; DA; DAB; DAC; DAM MST, NOV; DLB 52; EXPN; INT CANR-23; JRDA; LAIT 5; MAICYA 1, 2; MTCW 1, 2; MTFW 2005; NFS 2, 18; SATA 10, 45, 83; SATA-Obit 122; WYA; YAW

Corn, Alfred (DeWitt III) 1943- .... **CLC 33**
See also CA 179; CAAE 179; CAAS 25; CANR 44; CP 3, 4, 5, 6, 7; CSW; DLB 120, 282; DLBY 1980

Corneille, Pierre 1606-1684 ... **DC 21; LC 28**
See also DAB; DAM MST; DFS 21; DLB 268; EW 3; GFL Beginnings to 1789; RGWL 2, 3; TWA

Cornwell, David John Moore 1931- . **CLC 9, 15**
See le Carré, John
See also CA 5-8R; CANR 13, 33, 59, 107, 132; DA3; DAM POP; MTCW 1, 2; MTFW 2005

Cornwell, Patricia (Daniels) 1956- . **CLC 155**
See also AAYA 16, 56; BPFB 1; CA 134; CANR 53, 131; CMW 4; CPW; CSW; DAM POP; DLB 306; MSW; MTCW 2; MTFW 2005

Corso, (Nunzio) Gregory 1930-2001 . **CLC 1, 11; PC 33**
See also AMWS 12; BG 1:2; CA 5-8R; 193; CANR 41, 76, 132; CP 1, 2, 3, 4, 5, 6, 7; DA3; DLB 5, 16, 237; LMFS 2; MAL 5; MTCW 1, 2; MTFW 2005; WP

Cortazar, Julio 1914-1984 ... **CLC 2, 3, 5, 10, 13, 15, 33, 34, 92; HLC 1; SSC 7, 76**
See also BPFB 1; CA 21-24R; CANR 12, 32, 81; CDWLB 3; DA3; DAM MULT, NOV; DLB 113; EWL 3; EXPS; HW 1, 2; LAW; MTCW 1, 2; MTFW 2005; RGSF 2; RGWL 2, 3; SSFS 3, 20; TWA; WLIT 1

Cortes, Hernan 1485-1547 .... **LC 31**

Corvinus, Jakob
See Raabe, Wilhelm (Karl)

Corwin, Cecil
See Kornbluth, C(yril) M.

Cosic, Dobrica 1921- .... **CLC 14**
See also CA 122; 138; CDWLB 4; CWW 2; DLB 181; EWL 3

Costain, Thomas B(ertram) 1885-1965 .... **CLC 30**
See also BYA 3; CA 5-8R; 25-28R; DLB 9; RHW

Costantini, Humberto 1924(?)-1987 . **CLC 49**
See also CA 131; 122; EWL 3; HW 1

Costello, Elvis 1954- .... **CLC 21**
See also CA 204

Costenoble, Philostene
See Ghelderode, Michel de

Cotes, Cecil V.
See Duncan, Sara Jeannette

Cotter, Joseph Seamon Sr. 1861-1949 .... **BLC 1; TCLC 28**
See also BW 1; CA 124; DAM MULT; DLB 50

Couch, Arthur Thomas Quiller
See Quiller-Couch, Sir Arthur (Thomas)

Coulton, James
See Hansen, Joseph

Couperus, Louis (Marie Anne) 1863-1923 .... **TCLC 15**
See also CA 115; EWL 3; RGWL 2, 3

Coupland, Douglas 1961- .... **CLC 85, 133**
See also AAYA 34; CA 142; CANR 57, 90, 130; CCA 1; CN 7; CPW; DAC; DAM POP

Court, Wesli
See Turco, Lewis (Putnam)

Courtenay, Bryce 1933- .... **CLC 59**
See also CA 138; CPW

Courtney, Robert
See Ellison, Harlan (Jay)

Cousteau, Jacques-Yves 1910-1997 .. **CLC 30**
See also CA 65-68; 159; CANR 15, 67; MTCW 1; SATA 38, 98

Coventry, Francis 1725-1754 .... **LC 46**

Coverdale, Miles c. 1487-1569 .... **LC 77**
See also DLB 167

Cowan, Peter (Walkinshaw) 1914-2002 .... **SSC 28**
See also CA 21-24R; CANR 9, 25, 50, 83; CN 1, 2, 3, 4, 5, 6, 7; DLB 260; RGSF 2

Coward, Noel (Peirce) 1899-1973 . **CLC 1, 9, 29, 51**
See also AITN 1; BRWS 2; CA 17-18; 41-44R; CANR 35, 132; CAP 2; CBD; CD-BLB 1914-1945; DA3; DAM DRAM; DFS 3, 6; DLB 10, 245; EWL 3; IDFW 3, 4; MTCW 1, 2; MTFW 2005; RGEL 2; TEA

Cowley, Abraham 1618-1667 .... **LC 43**
See also BRW 2; DLB 131, 151; PAB; RGEL 2

Cowley, Malcolm 1898-1989 .... **CLC 39**
See also AMWS 2; CA 5-8R; 128; CANR 3, 55; CP 1, 2, 3, 4; DLB 4, 48; DLBY 1981, 1989; EWL 3; MAL 5; MTCW 1, 2; MTFW 2005

Cowper, William 1731-1800 ...... **NCLC 8, 94; PC 40**
See also BRW 3; DA3; DAM POET; DLB 104, 109; RGEL 2

Cox, William Trevor 1928-
See Trevor, William
See also CA 9-12R; CANR 4, 37, 55, 76, 102, 139; DAM NOV; INT CANR-37; MTCW 1, 2; MTFW 2005; TEA

Coyne, P. J.
See Masters, Hilary

Cozzens, James Gould 1903-1978 . **CLC 1, 4, 11, 92**
See also AMW; BPFB 1; CA 9-12R; 81-84; CANR 19; CDALB 1941-1968; CN 1, 2; DLB 9, 294; DLBD 2; DLBY 1984, 1997; EWL 5; MAL 5; MTCW 1, 2; MTFW 2005; RGAL 4

Crabbe, George 1754-1832 .... **NCLC 26, 121**
See also BRW 3; DLB 93; RGEL 2

Crace, Jim 1946- .... **CLC 157; SSC 61**
See also CA 128; 135; CANR 55, 70, 123; CN 5, 6, 7; DLB 231; INT CA-135

Craddock, Charles Egbert
See Murfree, Mary Noailles

Craig, A. A.
See Anderson, Poul (William)

Craik, Mrs.
See Craik, Dinah Maria (Mulock)
See also RGEL 2

Craik, Dinah Maria (Mulock)
1826-1887 .... **NCLC 38**
See Craik, Mrs.; Mulock, Dinah Maria
See also DLB 35, 163; MAICYA 1, 2; SATA 34

Cram, Ralph Adams 1863-1942 ..... **TCLC 45**
See also CA 160

Cranch, Christopher Pearse
1813-1892 .... **NCLC 115**
See also DLB 1, 42, 243

Crane, (Harold) Hart 1899-1932 .... **PC 3; TCLC 2, 5, 80; WLC**
See also AMW; AMWR 2; CA 104; 127; CDALB 1917-1929; DA; DA3; DAB; DAC; DAM MST, POET; DLB 4, 48; EWL 5; MAL 5; MTCW 1, 2; MTFW 2005; RGAL 4; TUS

Crane, R(onald) S(almon)
1886-1967 .... **CLC 27**
See also CA 85-88; DLB 63

Crane, Stephen (Townley)
1871-1900 ...... **SSC 7, 56, 70; TCLC 11, 17, 32; WLC**
See also AAYA 21; AMW; AMWC 1; BPFB 1; BYA 3; CA 109; 140; CANR 84; CDALB 1865-1917; DA; DA3; DAB; DAC; DAM MST, NOV, POET; DLB 12, 54, 78; EXPN; EXPS; LAIT 2; LMFS 2; MAL 5; NFS 4, 20; PFS 9; RGAL 4; RGSF 2; SSFS 4; TUS; WYA; YABC 2

Cranmer, Thomas 1489-1556 .... **LC 95**
See also DLB 132, 213

Cranshaw, Stanley
See Fisher, Dorothy (Frances) Canfield

Crase, Douglas 1944- .... **CLC 58**
See also CA 106

Crashaw, Richard 1612(?)-1649 .... **LC 24**
See also BRW 2; DLB 126; PAB; RGEL 2

Cratinus c. 519B.C.-c. 422B.C. ...... **CMLC 54**
See also LMFS 1

Craven, Margaret 1901-1980 .... **CLC 17**
See also BYA 2; CA 103; CCA 1; DAC; LAIT 5

Crawford, F(rancis) Marion
1854-1909 .... **TCLC 10**
See also CA 107; 168; DLB 71; HGG; RGAL 4; SUFW 1

Crawford, Isabella Valancy
1850-1887 .... **NCLC 12, 127**
See also DLB 92; RGEL 2

Crayon, Geoffrey
See Irving, Washington

Creasey, John 1908-1973 .... **CLC 11**
See Marric, J. J.
See also CA 5-8R; 41-44R; CANR 8, 59; CMW 4; DLB 77; MTCW 1

Crebillon, Claude Prosper Jolyot de (fils)
1707-1777 .... **LC 1, 28**
See also DLB 313; GFL Beginnings to 1789

Credo
See Creasey, John

Credo, Alvaro J. de
See Prado (Calvo), Pedro

Creeley, Robert (White) 1926-2005 .. **CLC 1, 2, 4, 8, 11, 15, 36, 78**
See also AMWS 4; CA 1-4R; 237; CAAS 10; CANR 23, 43, 89, 137; CP 1, 2, 3, 4, 5, 6, 7; DA3; DAM POET; DLB 5, 16, 169; DLBD 17; EWL 3; MAL 5; MTCW 1, 2; MTFW 2005; PFS 21; RGAL 4; WP

Crenne, Helisenne de 1510-1560 .... **LC 113**

Crevecoeur, Hector St. John de
See Crevecoeur, Michel Guillaume Jean de
See also ANW

Crevecoeur, Michel Guillaume Jean de
1735-1813 .... **NCLC 105**
See Crevecoeur, Hector St. John de
See also AMWS 1; DLB 37

Crevel, Rene 1900-1935 .... **TCLC 112**
See also GLL 2

Crews, Harry (Eugene) 1935- ..... **CLC 6, 23, 49**
See also AITN 1; AMWS 11; BPFB 1; CA 25-28R; CANR 20, 57; CN 3, 4, 5, 6, 7; CSW; DA3; DLB 6, 143, 185; MTCW 1, 2; MTFW 2005; RGAL 4

Crichton, (John) Michael 1942- .... **CLC 2, 6, 54, 90**
See also AAYA 10, 49; AITN 2; BPFB 1; CA 25-28R; CANR 13, 40, 54, 76, 127; CMW 4; CN 2, 3, 6, 7; CPW; DA3; DAM NOV, POP; DLB 292; DLBY 1981; INT CANR-13; JRDA; MTCW 1, 2; MTFW 2005; SATA 9, 88; SFW 4; YAW

Crispin, Edmund .... **CLC 22**
See Montgomery, (Robert) Bruce
See also DLB 87; MSW

Cristofer, Michael 1945- .... **CLC 28**
See also CA 110; 152; CAD; CD 5, 6; DAM DRAM; DFS 15; DLB 7

Criton
See Alain

Croce, Benedetto 1866-1952 .... **TCLC 37**
See also CA 120; 155; EW 8; EWL 3; WLIT 7

Crockett, David 1786-1836 .... **NCLC 8**
See also DLB 3, 11, 183, 248

Crockett, Davy
See Crockett, David

Crofts, Freeman Wills 1879-1957 .. **TCLC 55**
See also CA 115; 195; CMW 4; DLB 77; MSW

Croker, John Wilson 1780-1857 .... **NCLC 10**
See also DLB 110

Crommelynck, Fernand 1885-1970 .. **CLC 75**
See also CA 189; 89-92; EWL 3

Cromwell, Oliver 1599-1658 .... **LC 43**

Cronenberg, David 1943- .... **CLC 143**
See also CA 138; CCA 1

Cronin, A(rchibald) J(oseph)
1896-1981 .... **CLC 32**
See also BPFB 1; CA 1-4R; 102; CANR 5; CN 2; DLB 191; SATA 47; SATA-Obit 25

Cross, Amanda
See Heilbrun, Carolyn G(old)
See also BPFB 1; CMW; CPW; DLB 306; MSW

Crothers, Rachel 1878-1958 .... **TCLC 19**
See also CA 113; 194; CAD; CWD; DLB 7, 266; RGAL 4

Croves, Hal
See Traven, B.

Crow Dog, Mary (Ellen) (?)- .... **CLC 93**
See Brave Bird, Mary
See also CA 154

Crowfield, Christopher
See Stowe, Harriet (Elizabeth) Beecher

Crowley, Aleister .... **TCLC 7**
See Crowley, Edward Alexander
See also GLL 1

Crowley, Edward Alexander 1875-1947
See Crowley, Aleister
See also CA 104; HGG

Crowley, John 1942- .... **CLC 57**
See also AAYA 57; BPFB 1; CA 61-64; CANR 43, 98, 138; DLBY 1982; FANT; MTFW 2005; SATA 65, 140; SFW 4; SUFW 2

Crowne, John 1641-1712 .... **LC 104**
See also DLB 80; RGEL 2

Crud
See Crumb, R(obert)

Crumarums
See Crumb, R(obert)

Crumb, R(obert) 1943- .... **CLC 17**
See also CA 106; CANR 107

Crumbum
See Crumb, R(obert)

Crumski
See Crumb, R(obert)

Crum the Bum
See Crumb, R(obert)

Crunk
See Crumb, R(obert)

Crustt
See Crumb, R(obert)

Crutchfield, Les
See Trumbo, Dalton

Cruz, Victor Hernandez 1949- ... **HLC 1; PC 37**
See also BW 2; CA 65-68; CAAS 17; CANR 14, 32, 74, 132; CP 1, 2, 3, 4, 5, 6, 7; DAM MULT, POET; DLB 41; DNFS 1; EXPP; HW 1, 2; LLW; MTCW 2; MTFW 2005; PFS 16; WP

Cryer, Gretchen (Kiger) 1935- .... **CLC 21**
See also CA 114; 123

Csath, Geza .... **TCLC 13**
See Brenner, Jozef
See also CA 111

Cudlip, David R(ockwell) 1933- .... **CLC 34**
See also CA 177

Cullen, Countee 1903-1946 . **BLC 1; HR 1:2; PC 20; TCLC 4, 37; WLCS**
See also AFAW 2; AMWS 4; BW 1; CA 108; 124; CDALB 1917-1929; DA; DA3; DAC; DAM MST, MULT, POET; DLB 4, 48, 51; EWL 3; EXPP; LMFS 2; MAL 5; MTCW 1, 2; MTFW 2005; PFS 3; RGAL 4; SATA 18; WP

Culleton, Beatrice 1949- .... **NNAL**
See also CA 120; CANR 83; DAC

Cum, R.
See Crumb, R(obert)

Cumberland, Richard
1732-1811 .... **NCLC 167**
See also DLB 89; RGEL 2

Cummings, Bruce F(rederick) 1889-1919
See Barbellion, W. N. P.
See also CA 123

Cummings, E(dward) E(stlin)
1894-1962 .. **CLC 1, 3, 8, 12, 15, 68; PC 5; TCLC 137; WLC**
See also AAYA 41; AMW; CA 73-76; CANR 31; CDALB 1929-1941; DA; DA3; DAB; DAC; DAM MST, POET; DLB 4, 48; EWL 3; EXPP; MAL 5; MTCW 1, 2; MTFW 2005; PAB; PFS 1, 3, 12, 13, 19; RGAL 4; TUS; WP

Cummins, Maria Susanna
1827-1866 .... **NCLC 139**
See also DLB 42; YABC 1

Cunha, Euclides (Rodrigues Pimenta) da
1866-1909 .... **TCLC 24**
See also CA 123; 219; DLB 307; LAW; WLIT 1

Cunningham, E. V.
See Fast, Howard (Melvin)

Cunningham, J(ames) V(incent)
1911-1985 .... **CLC 3, 31**
See also CA 1-4R; 115; CANR 1, 72; CP 1, 2, 3, 4; DLB 5

Cunningham, Julia (Woolfolk)
1916- .... **CLC 12**
See also CA 9-12R; CANR 4, 19, 36; CWRI 5; JRDA; MAICYA 1, 2; SAAS 2; SATA 1, 26, 132

Cunningham, Michael 1952- .... **CLC 34**
See also AMWS 15; CA 136; CANR 96; CN 7; DLB 292; GLL 2; MTFW 2005

Cunninghame Graham, R. B.
See Cunninghame Graham, Robert (Gallnigad) Bontine

Cunninghame Graham, Robert (Gallnigad) Bontine 1852-1936 .... **TCLC 19**
See Graham, R(obert) B(ontine) Cunninghame
See also CA 119; 184

Curnow, (Thomas) Allen (Monro)
1911-2001 .... **PC 48**
See also CA 69-72; 202; CANR 48, 99; CP 1, 2, 3, 4, 5, 6, 7; EWL 3; RGEL 2

Currie, Ellen 19(?)- .... **CLC 44**

Curtin, Philip
See Lowndes, Marie Adelaide (Belloc)

Curtin, Phillip
See Lowndes, Marie Adelaide (Belloc)

Curtis, Price
See Ellison, Harlan (Jay)

Cusanus, Nicolaus 1401-1464 .... **LC 80**
See Nicholas of Cusa

Cutrate, Joe
See Spiegelman, Art

Cynewulf c. 770- .... **CMLC 23**
See also DLB 146; RGEL 2

Cyrano de Bergerac, Savinien de
1619-1655 .... **LC 65**
See also DLB 268; GFL Beginnings to 1789; RGWL 2, 3

Cyril of Alexandria c. 375-c. 430 . **CMLC 59**

Czaczkes, Shmuel Yosef Halevi
See Agnon, S(hmuel) Y(osef Halevi)

Dabrowska, Maria (Szumska)
1889-1965 .... **CLC 15**
See also CA 106; CDWLB 4; DLB 215; EWL 3

Dabydeen, David 1955- .... **CLC 34**
See also BW 1; CA 125; CANR 56, 92; CN 6, 7; CP 7

Dacey, Philip 1939- .... **CLC 51**
See also CA 37-40R, 231; CAAE 231; CAAS 17; CANR 14, 32, 64; CP 4, 5, 6, 7; DLB 105

Dacre, Charlotte c. 1772-1825(?) . **NCLC 151**

Dafydd ap Gwilym c. 1320-c. 1380 ..... **PC 56**

Dagerman, Stig (Halvard)
1923-1954 .... **TCLC 17**
See also CA 117; 155; DLB 259; EWL 3

D'Aguiar, Fred 1960- .... **CLC 145**
See also CA 148; CANR 83, 101; CN 7; CP 7; DLB 157; EWL 3

Dahl, Roald 1916-1990 ...... **CLC 1, 6, 18, 79; TCLC 173**
See also AAYA 15; BPFB 1; BRWS 4; BYA 5; CA 1-4R; 133; CANR 6, 32, 37, 62; CLR 1, 7, 41; CN 1, 2, 3, 4; CPW; DA3; DAB; DAC; DAM MST, NOV, POP; DLB 139, 255; HGG; JRDA; MAICYA 1, 2; MTCW 1, 2; MTFW 2005; RGSF 2; SATA 1, 26, 73; SATA-Obit 65; SSFS 4; TEA; YAW

Dahlberg, Edward 1900-1977 .. **CLC 1, 7, 14**
See also CA 9-12R; 69-72; CANR 31, 62; CN 1, 2; DLB 48; MAL 5; MTCW 1; RGAL 4

Daitch, Susan 1954- .... **CLC 103**
See also CA 161

Dale, Colin .... **TCLC 18**
See Lawrence, T(homas) E(dward)

Dale, George E.
See Asimov, Isaac

D'Alembert, Jean Le Rond
1717-1783 .... **LC 126**
DLB 313; GFL Beginnings to 1789

Dalton, Roque 1935-1975(?) ..... **HLCS 1; PC 36**
See also CA 176; DLB 283; HW 2

Daly, Elizabeth 1878-1967 .... **CLC 52**
See also CA 23-24; 25-28R; CANR 60; CAP 2; CMW 4

Daly, Mary 1928- .... **CLC 173**
See also CA 25-28R; CANR 30, 62; FW; GLL 1; MTCW 1

Daly, Maureen 1921- .... **CLC 17**
See also AAYA 5, 58; BYA 6; CANR 37, 83, 108; CLR 96; JRDA; MAICYA 1, 2; SAAS 1; SATA 2, 129; WYA; YAW

Damas, Leon-Gontran 1912-1978 .... **CLC 84**
See also BW 1; CA 125; 73-76; EWL 3

Dana, Richard Henry Sr.
1787-1879 .... **NCLC 53**

Daniel, Samuel 1562(?)-1619 .... **LC 24**
See also DLB 62; RGEL 2

Daniels, Brett
See Adler, Renata

Dannay, Frederic 1905-1982 .... **CLC 11**
See Queen, Ellery
See also CA 1-4R; 107; CANR 1, 39; CMW 4; DAM POP; DLB 137; MTCW 1

D'Annunzio, Gabriele 1863-1938 ... **TCLC 6, 40**
See also CA 104; 155; EW 8; EWL 3; RGWL 2, 3; TWA; WLIT 7

Danois, N. le
See Gourmont, Remy(-Marie-Charles) de

Dante 1265-1321 .... **CMLC 3, 18, 39, 70; PC 21; WLCS**
See Alighieri, Dante
See also DA; DA3; DAB; DAC; DAM MST, POET; EFS 1; EW 1; LAIT 1; RGWL 2, 3; TWA; WP

d'Antibes, Germain
See Simenon, Georges (Jacques Christian)

Danticat, Edwidge 1969- .... **CLC 94, 139**
See also AAYA 29; CA 152, 192; CAAE 192; CANR 73, 129; CN 7; DNFS 1; EXPS; LATS 1:2; MTCW 2; MTFW 2005; SSFS 1; YAW

Danvers, Dennis 1947- .... **CLC 70**

Danziger, Paula 1944-2004 .... **CLC 21**
See also AAYA 4, 36; BYA 6, 7, 14; CA 112; 115; 229; CANR 37, 132; CLR 20; JRDA; MAICYA 1, 2; MTFW 2005; SATA 36, 63, 102, 149; SATA-Brief 30; SATA-Obit 155; WYA; YAW

Da Ponte, Lorenzo 1749-1838 .... **NCLC 50**

d'Aragona, Tullia 1510(?)-1556 .... **LC 121**

Dario, Ruben 1867-1916 .... **HLC 1; PC 15; TCLC 4**
See also CA 131; CANR 81; DAM MULT; DLB 290; EWL 3; HW 1, 2; LAW; MTCW 1, 2; MTFW 2005; RGWL 2, 3

Darley, George 1795-1846 .... **NCLC 2**
See also DLB 96; RGEL 2

Darrow, Clarence (Seward)
1857-1938 .... **TCLC 81**
See also CA 164; DLB 303

Darwin, Charles 1809-1882 .... **NCLC 57**
See also BRWS 7; DLB 57, 166; LATS 1:1; RGEL 2; TEA; WLIT 4

Darwin, Erasmus 1731-1802 .... **NCLC 106**
See also DLB 93; RGEL 2

Daryush, Elizabeth 1887-1977 ...... **CLC 6, 19**
See also CA 49-52; CANR 3, 81; DLB 20

Das, Kamala 1934- .... **CLC 191; PC 43**
See also CA 101; CANR 27, 59; CP 1, 2, 3, 4, 5, 6, 7; CWP; FW

Dasgupta, Surendranath
1887-1952 .... **TCLC 81**
See also CA 157

Dashwood, Edmee Elizabeth Monica de la Pasture 1890-1943
See Delafield, E. M.
See also CA 119; 154

da Silva, Antonio Jose
1705-1739 .... **NCLC 114**

Daudet, (Louis Marie) Alphonse
1840-1897 .... **NCLC 1**
See also DLB 123; GFL 1789 to the Present; RGSF 2

d'Aulnoy, Marie-Catherine c.
1650-1705 .... **LC 100**

Daumal, Rene 1908-1944 .... **TCLC 14**
See also CA 114; EWL 3

Davenant, William 1606-1668 .... **LC 13**
See also DLB 58, 126; RGEL 2

Davenport, Guy (Mattison, Jr.)
1927-2005 .... **CLC 6, 14, 38; SSC 16**
See also CA 33-36R; 235; CANR 23, 73; CN 3, 4, 5, 6; CSW; DLB 130

David, Robert
See Nezval, Vitezslav

Davidson, Avram (James) 1923-1993
See Queen, Ellery
See also CA 101; 171; CANR 26; DLB 8; FANT; SFW 4; SUFW 1, 2

Davidson, Donald (Grady)
1893-1968 .... **CLC 2, 13, 19**
See also CA 5-8R; 25-28R; CANR 4, 84; DLB 45

Davidson, Hugh
See Hamilton, Edmond

Davidson, John 1857-1909 .... **TCLC 24**
See also CA 118; 217; DLB 19; RGEL 2

Davidson, Sara 1943- .... **CLC 9**
See also CA 81-84; CANR 44, 68; DLB 185

Davie, Donald (Alfred) 1922-1995 .... **CLC 5, 8, 10, 31; PC 29**
See also BRWS 6; CA 1-4R; 149; CAAS 3; CANR 1, 44; CP 1, 2, 3, 4; DLB 27; MTCW 1; RGEL 2

Davie, Elspeth 1918-1995 .... **SSC 52**
See also CA 120; 126; 150; CANR 141; DLB 139

Davies, Ray(mond Douglas) 1944- ... **CLC 21**
See also CA 116; 146; CANR 92

Davies, Rhys 1901-1978 .... **CLC 23**
See also CA 9-12R; 81-84; CANR 4; CN 1, 2; DLB 139, 191

Davies, (William) Robertson
1913-1995 .... **CLC 2, 7, 13, 25, 42, 75, 91; WLC**
See Marchbanks, Samuel
See also BEST 89:2; BPFB 1; CA 33-36R; 150; CANR 17, 42, 103; CN 1, 2, 3, 4, 5, 6; CPW; DA; DA3; DAB; DAC; DAM MST, NOV, POP; DLB 68; EWL 3; HGG; INT CANR-17; LAIT 5; MTCW 1, 2; MTFW 2005; RGEL 2; TWA

Davies, Sir John 1569-1626 .... **LC 85**
See also DLB 172

Davies, Walter C.
See Kornbluth, C(yril) M.

Davies, William Henry 1871-1940 ... **TCLC 5**
See also BRWS 11; CA 104; 179; DLB 19, 174; EWL 3; RGEL 2

Da Vinci, Leonardo 1452-1519 ..... **LC 12, 57, 60**
See also AAYA 40

Davis, Angela (Yvonne) 1944- .... **CLC 77**
See also BW 2, 3; CA 57-60; CANR 10, 81; CSW; DA3; DAM MULT; FW

Davis, B. Lynch
See Bioy Casares, Adolfo; Borges, Jorge Luis

Davis, Frank Marshall 1905-1987 ...... **BLC 1**
See also BW 2, 3; CA 125; 123; CANR 42, 80; DAM MULT; DLB 51

Davis, Gordon
See Hunt, E(verette) Howard, (Jr.)

Davis, H(arold) L(enoir) 1896-1960 . **CLC 49**
See also ANW; CA 178; 89-92; DLB 9, 206; SATA 114; TCWW 1, 2

Davis, Natalie Zemon 1928- .... **CLC 204**
See also CA 53-56; CANR 58, 100

Davis, Rebecca (Blaine) Harding
1831-1910 .... **SSC 38; TCLC 6**
See also CA 104; 179; DLB 74, 239; FW; NFS 14; RGAL 4; TUS

Davis, Richard Harding
1864-1916 .... **TCLC 24**
See also CA 114; 179; DLB 12, 23, 78, 79, 189; DLBD 13; RGAL 4

Davison, Frank Dalby 1893-1970 ..... **CLC 15**
See also CA 217; 116; DLB 260

Davison, Lawrence H.
See Lawrence, D(avid) H(erbert Richards)

Davison, Peter (Hubert) 1928-2004 . **CLC 28**
See also CA 9-12R; 234; CAAS 4; CANR 3, 43, 84; CP 1, 2, 3, 4, 5, 6, 7; DLB 5

Davys, Mary 1674-1732 .... **LC 1, 46**
See also DLB 39

Dawson, (Guy) Fielding (Lewis)
1930-2002 .... **CLC 6**
See also CA 85-88; 202; CANR 108; DLB 130; DLBY 2002

Dawson, Peter
See Faust, Frederick (Schiller)
See also TCWW 1, 2

Day, Clarence (Shepard, Jr.)
1874-1935 .... **TCLC 25**
See also CA 108; 199; DLB 11

Day, John 1574(?)-1640(?) .... **LC 70**
See also DLB 62, 170; RGEL 2

Day, Thomas 1748-1789 .... **LC 1**
See also DLB 39; YABC 1

Day Lewis, C(ecil) 1904-1972 . **CLC 1, 6, 10; PC 11**
See Blake, Nicholas; Lewis, C. Day
See also BRWS 3; CA 13-16; 33-36R; CANR 34; CAP 1; CP 1; CWRI 5; DAM POET; DLB 15, 20; EWL 3; MTCW 1, 2; RGEL 2

Dazai Osamu .... **SSC 41; TCLC 11**
See Tsushima, Shuji
See also CA 164; DLB 182; EWL 3; MJW; RGSF 2; RGWL 2, 3; TWA

de Andrade, Carlos Drummond
See Drummond de Andrade, Carlos

de Andrade, Mario 1892(?)-1945
See Andrade, Mario de
See also CA 178; HW 2

Deane, Norman
See Creasey, John

Deane, Seamus (Francis) 1940- .... **CLC 122**
See also CA 118; CANR 42

de Beauvoir, Simone (Lucie Ernestine Marie Bertrand)
See Beauvoir, Simone (Lucie Ernestine Marie Bertrand) de

de Beer, P.
See Bosman, Herman Charles

De Botton, Alain 1969- .... **CLC 203**
See also CA 159; CANR 96

de Brissac, Malcolm
See Dickinson, Peter (Malcolm de Brissac)

de Campos, Alvaro
See Pessoa, Fernando (Antonio Nogueira)

de Chardin, Pierre Teilhard
See Teilhard de Chardin, (Marie Joseph) Pierre

de Crenne, Helisenne c. 1510-c. 1560 .... **LC 113**

Dee, John 1527-1608 .... **LC 20**
See also DLB 136, 213

Deer, Sandra 1940- .... **CLC 45**
See also CA 186

De Ferrari, Gabriella 1941- .... **CLC 65**
See also CA 146

de Filippo, Eduardo 1900-1984 ... **TCLC 127**
See also CA 132; 114; EWL 3; MTCW 1; RGWL 2, 3

Defoe, Daniel 1660(?)-1731 .... **LC 1, 42, 108; WLC**
See also AAYA 27; BRW 3; BRWR 1; BYA 4; CDBLB 1660-1789; CLR 61; DA; DA3; DAB; DAC; DAM MST, NOV; DLB 39, 95, 101; JRDA; LAIT 1; LMFS 1; MAICYA 1, 2; NFS 9, 13; RGEL 2; SATA 22; TEA; WCH; WLIT 3

de Gourmont, Remy(-Marie-Charles)
See Gourmont, Remy(-Marie-Charles) de

de Gournay, Marie le Jars
1566-1645 .... **LC 98**
See also FW

de Hartog, Jan 1914-2002 .... **CLC 19**
See also CA 1-4R; 210; CANR 1; DFS 12

de Hostos, E. M.
See Hostos (y Bonilla), Eugenio Maria de

de Hostos, Eugenio M.
See Hostos (y Bonilla), Eugenio Maria de

Deighton, Len .... **CLC 4, 7, 22, 46**
See Deighton, Leonard Cyril
See also AAYA 6; BEST 89:2; BPFB 1; CDBLB 1960 to Present; CMW 4; CN 1, 2, 3, 4, 5, 6, 7; CPW; DLB 87

Deighton, Leonard Cyril 1929-
See Deighton, Len
See also AAYA 57; CA 9-12R; CANR 19, 33, 68; DA3; DAM NOV, POP; MTCW 1, 2; MTFW 2005

Dekker, Thomas 1572(?)-1632 ..... **DC 12; LC 22**
See also CDBLB Before 1660; DAM DRAM; DLB 62, 172; LMFS 1; RGEL 2

de Laclos, Pierre Ambroise Franois
See Laclos, Pierre-Ambroise Francois

Delacroix, (Ferdinand-Victor-)Eugene
1798-1863 .... **NCLC 133**
See also EW 5

Delafield, E. M. .... **TCLC 61**
See Dashwood, Edmee Elizabeth Monica de la Pasture
See also DLB 34; RHW

de la Mare, Walter (John)
1873-1956 . **SSC 14; TCLC 4, 53; WLC**
See also CA 163; CDBLB 1914-1945; CLR 23; CWRI 5; DA3; DAB; DAC; DAM MST, POET; DLB 19, 153, 162, 255, 284; EWL 3; EXPP; HGG; MAICYA 1, 2; MTCW 2; MTFW 2005; RGEL 2; RGSF 2; SATA 16; SUFW 1; TEA; WCH

de Lamartine, Alphonse (Marie Louis Prat)
See Lamartine, Alphonse (Marie Louis Prat) de

Delaney, Franey
See O'Hara, John (Henry)

Delaney, Shelagh 1939- .... **CLC 29**
See also CA 17-20R; CANR 30, 67; CBD; CD 5, 6; CDBLB 1960 to Present; CWD; DAM DRAM; DFS 7; DLB 13; MTCW 1

Delany, Martin Robison
1812-1885 .... **NCLC 93**
See also DLB 50; RGAL 4

Delany, Mary (Granville Pendarves)
1700-1788 .... **LC 12**

Delany, Samuel R(ay), Jr. 1942- ..... **BLC 1; CLC 8, 14, 38, 141**
See also AAYA 24; AFAW 2; BPFB 1; BW 2, 3; CA 81-84; CANR 27, 43, 116; CN 2, 3, 4, 5, 6, 7; DAM MULT; DLB 8, 33; FANT; MAL 5; MTCW 1, 2; RGAL 4; SATA 92; SCFW 1, 2; SFW 4; SUFW 2

De la Ramee, Marie Louise (Ouida)
1839-1908
See Ouida
See also CA 204; SATA 20

de la Roche, Mazo 1879-1961 .... **CLC 14**
See also CA 85-88; CANR 30; DLB 68; RGEL 2; RHW; SATA 64

De La Salle, Innocent
See Hartmann, Sadakichi

de Laureamont, Comte
See Lautreamont

Delbanco, Nicholas (Franklin)
1942- .... **CLC 6, 13, 167**
See also CA 17-20R; 189; CAAE 189; CAAS 2; CANR 29, 55, 116; CN 7; DLB 6, 234

del Castillo, Michel 1933- .... **CLC 38**
See also CA 109; CANR 77

Deledda, Grazia (Cosima)
1875(?)-1936 .... **TCLC 23**
See also CA 123; 205; DLB 264; EWL 3; RGWL 2, 3; WLIT 7

Deleuze, Gilles 1925-1995 .... **TCLC 116**
See also DLB 296

Delgado, Abelardo (Lalo) B(arrientos)
1930-2004 .... **HLC 1**
See also CA 131; 230; CAAS 15; CANR 90; DAM MST, MULT; DLB 82; HW 1, 2

Delibes, Miguel .... **CLC 8, 18**
See Delibes Setien, Miguel
See also DLB 322; EWL 3

Delibes Setien, Miguel 1920-
See Delibes, Miguel
See also CA 45-48; CANR 1, 32; CWW 2; HW 1; MTCW 1

DeLillo, Don 1936- ...... **CLC 8, 10, 13, 27, 39, 54, 76, 143, 210, 213**
See also AMWC 2; AMWS 6; BEST 89:1; BPFB 1; CA 81-84; CANR 21, 76, 92, 133; CN 3, 4, 5, 6, 7; CPW; DA3; DAM NOV, POP; DLB 6, 173; EWL 3; MAL 5; MTCW 1, 2; MTFW 2005; RGAL 4; TUS

de Lisser, H. G.
See De Lisser, H(erbert) G(eorge)
See also DLB 117

De Lisser, H(erbert) G(eorge)
1878-1944 .... **TCLC 12**
See de Lisser, H. G.
See also BW 2; CA 109; 152

Deloire, Pierre
See Peguy, Charles (Pierre)

Deloney, Thomas 1543(?)-1600 .... **LC 41**
See also DLB 167; RGEL 2

Deloria, Ella (Cara) 1889-1971(?) ..... **NNAL**
See also CA 152; DAM MULT; DLB 175

Deloria, Vine (Victor), Jr.
1933-2005 .... **CLC 21, 122; NNAL**
See also CA 53-56; CANR 5, 20, 48, 98; DAM MULT; DLB 175; MTCW 1; SATA 21

del Valle-Inclan, Ramon (Maria)
See Valle-Inclan, Ramon (Maria) del
See also DLB 322

Del Vecchio, John M(ichael) 1947- .. **CLC 29**
See also CA 110; DLBD 9

de Man, Paul (Adolph Michel)
1919-1983 .... **CLC 55**
See also CA 128; 111; CANR 61; DLB 67; MTCW 1, 2

DeMarinis, Rick 1934- .... **CLC 54**
See also CA 57-60, 184; CAAE 184; CAAS 24; CANR 9, 25, 50; DLB 218; TCWW 2

de Maupassant, (Henri Rene Albert) Guy
See Maupassant, (Henri Rene Albert) Guy de

Dembry, R. Emmet
See Murfree, Mary Noailles

Demby, William 1922- .... **BLC 1; CLC 53**
See also BW 1, 3; CA 81-84; CANR 81; DAM MULT; DLB 33

de Menton, Francisco
See Chin, Frank (Chew, Jr.)

Demetrius of Phalerum c.
307B.C.- .... **CMLC 34**

Demijohn, Thom
See Disch, Thomas M(ichael)

De Mille, James 1833-1880 .... **NCLC 123**
See also DLB 99, 251

Deming, Richard 1915-1983
See Queen, Ellery
See also CA 9-12R; CANR 3, 94; SATA 24

Democritus c. 460B.C.-c. 370B.C. . . **CMLC 47**

de Montaigne, Michel (Eyquem)
See Montaigne, Michel (Eyquem) de

de Montherlant, Henry (Milon)
See Montherlant, Henry (Milon) de

Demosthenes 384B.C.-322B.C. ...... **CMLC 13**
See also AW 1; DLB 176; RGWL 2, 3

de Musset, (Louis Charles) Alfred
See Musset, (Louis Charles) Alfred de

de Natale, Francine
See Malzberg, Barry N(athaniel)

de Navarre, Marguerite 1492-1549 ... **LC 61; SSC 85**
See Marguerite d'Angouleme; Marguerite de Navarre

Denby, Edwin (Orr) 1903-1983 .... **CLC 48**
See also CA 138; 110; CP 1

de Nerval, Gerard
See Nerval, Gerard de

Denham, John 1615-1669 .... **LC 73**
See also DLB 58, 126; RGEL 2

Denis, Julio
See Cortazar, Julio

Denmark, Harrison
See Zelazny, Roger (Joseph)

Dennis, John 1658-1734 .... **LC 11**
See also DLB 101; RGEL 2

Dennis, Nigel (Forbes) 1912-1989 .... **CLC 8**
See also CA 25-28R; 129; CN 1, 2, 3, 4; DLB 13, 15, 233; EWL 3; MTCW 1

Dent, Lester 1904-1959 .... **TCLC 72**
See also CA 112; 161; CMW 4; DLB 306; SFW 4

De Palma, Brian (Russell) 1940- .... **CLC 20**
See also CA 109

De Quincey, Thomas 1785-1859 ..... **NCLC 4, 87**
See also BRW 4; CDBLB 1789-1832; DLB 110, 144; RGEL 2

Deren, Eleanora 1908(?)-1961
See Deren, Maya
See also CA 192; 111

Deren, Maya .... **CLC 16, 102**
See Deren, Eleanora

Derleth, August (William)
1909-1971 .... **CLC 31**
See also BPFB 1; BYA 9, 10; CA 1-4R; 29-32R; CANR 4; CMW 4; CN 1; DLB 9; DLBD 17; HGG; SATA 5; SUFW 1

Der Nister 1884-1950 .... **TCLC 56**
See Nister, Der

de Routisie, Albert
See Aragon, Louis

Derrida, Jacques 1930-2004 .... **CLC 24, 87**
See also CA 124; 127; 232; CANR 76, 98, 133; DLB 242; EWL 3; LMFS 2; MTCW 2; TWA

Derry Down Derry
See Lear, Edward

Dersonnes, Jacques
See Simenon, Georges (Jacques Christian)

Der Stricker c. 1190-c. 1250 .... **CMLC 75**
See also DLB 138

Desai, Anita 1937- .... **CLC 19, 37, 97, 175**
See also BRWS 5; CA 81-84; CANR 33, 53, 95, 133; CN 1, 2, 3, 4, 5, 6, 7; CWRI 5; DA3; DAB; DAM NOV; DLB 271; DNFS 2; EWL 3; FW; MTCW 1, 2; MTFW 2005; SATA 63, 126

Desai, Kiran 1971- .... **CLC 119**
See also BYA 16; CA 171; CANR 127

de Saint-Luc, Jean
See Glassco, John

de Saint Roman, Arnaud
See Aragon, Louis

Desbordes-Valmore, Marceline
1786-1859 .... **NCLC 97**
See also DLB 217

Descartes, Rene 1596-1650 .... **LC 20, 35**
See also DLB 268; EW 3; GFL Beginnings to 1789

Deschamps, Eustache 1340(?)-1404 .. **LC 103**
See also DLB 208

De Sica, Vittorio 1901(?)-1974 .... **CLC 20**
See also CA 117

Desnos, Robert 1900-1945 .... **TCLC 22**
See also CA 121; 151; CANR 107; DLB 258; EWL 3; LMFS 2

Destouches, Louis-Ferdinand
1894-1961 .... **CLC 9, 15**
See Celine, Louis-Ferdinand
See also CA 85-88; CANR 28; MTCW 1

de Tolignac, Gaston
See Griffith, D(avid Lewelyn) W(ark)

Deutsch, Babette 1895-1982 .... **CLC 18**
See also BYA 3; CA 1-4R; 108; CANR 4, 79; CP 1, 2, 3; DLB 45; SATA 1; SATA-Obit 33

Devenant, William 1606-1649 .... **LC 13**

Devkota, Laxmiprasad 1909-1959 . **TCLC 23**
See also CA 123

De Voto, Bernard (Augustine)
1897-1955 .... **TCLC 29**
See also CA 113; 160; DLB 9, 256; MAL 5; TCWW 1, 2

De Vries, Peter 1910-1993 ..... **CLC 1, 2, 3, 7, 10, 28, 46**
See also CA 17-20R; 142; CANR 41; CN 1, 2, 3, 4, 5; DAM NOV; DLB 6; DLBY 1982; MAL 5; MTCW 1, 2; MTFW 2005

Dewey, John 1859-1952 .... **TCLC 95**
See also CA 114; 170; CANR 144; DLB 246, 270; RGAL 4

Dexter, John
See Bradley, Marion Zimmer
See also GLL 1

Dexter, Martin
See Faust, Frederick (Schiller)

Dexter, Pete 1943- .... **CLC 34, 55**
See also BEST 89:2; CA 127; 131; CANR 129; CPW; DAM POP; INT CA-131; MAL 5; MTCW 1; MTFW 2005

Diamano, Silmang
See Senghor, Leopold Sedar

Diamond, Neil 1941- .... **CLC 30**
See also CA 108

Diaz del Castillo, Bernal c.
1496-1584 .... **HLCS 1; LC 31**
See also DLB 318; LAW

di Bassetto, Corno
See Shaw, George Bernard

Dick, Philip K(indred) 1928-1982 ... **CLC 10, 30, 72; SSC 57**
See also AAYA 24; BPFB 1; BYA 11; CA 49-52; 106; CANR 2, 16, 132; CN 2, 3; CPW; DA3; DAM NOV, POP; DLB 8; MTCW 1, 2; MTFW 2005; NFS 5; SCFW 1, 2; SFW 4

Dickens, Charles (John Huffam)
1812-1870 .... **NCLC 3, 8, 18, 26, 37, 50, 86, 105, 113, 161; SSC 17, 49, 88; WLC**
See also AAYA 23; BRW 5; BRWC 1, 2; BYA 1, 2, 3, 13, 14; CDBLB 1832-1890; CLR 95; CMW 4; DA; DA3; DAB; DAC; DAM MST, NOV; DLB 21, 55, 70, 159, 166; EXPN; GL 2; HGG; JRDA; LAIT 1, 2; LATS 1:1; LMFS 1; MAICYA 1, 2; NFS 4, 5, 10, 14, 20; RGEL 2; RGSF 2; SATA 15; SUFW 1; TEA; WCH; WLIT 4; WYA

Dickey, James (Lafayette)
1923-1997 .... **CLC 1, 2, 4, 7, 10, 15, 47, 109; PC 40; TCLC 151**
See also AAYA 50; AITN 1, 2; AMWS 4; BPFB 1; CA 9-12R; 156; CABS 2; CANR 10, 48, 61, 105; CDALB 1968-1988; CP 1, 2, 3, 4; CPW; CSW; DA3; DAM NOV, POET, POP; DLB 5, 193; DLBD 7; DLBY 1982, 1993, 1996, 1997, 1998; EWL 3; INT CANR-10; MAL 5; MTCW 1, 2; NFS 9; PFS 6, 11; RGAL 4; TUS

Dickey, William 1928-1994 .... **CLC 3, 28**
See also CA 9-12R; 145; CANR 24, 79; CP 1, 2, 3, 4; DLB 5

Dickinson, Charles 1951- .... **CLC 49**
See also CA 128; CANR 141

Dickinson, Emily (Elizabeth)
1830-1886 ... **NCLC 21, 77; PC 1; WLC**
See also AAYA 22; AMW; AMWR 1; CDALB 1865-1917; DA; DA3; DAB; DAC; DAM MST, POET; DLB 1, 243; EXPP; FL 1:3; MAWW; PAB; PFS 1, 2, 3, 4, 5, 6, 8, 10, 11, 13, 16; RGAL 4; SATA 29; TUS; WP; WYA

Dickinson, Mrs. Herbert Ward
See Phelps, Elizabeth Stuart

Dickinson, Peter (Malcolm de Brissac)
1927- .... **CLC 12, 35**
See also AAYA 9, 49; BYA 5; CA 41-44R; CANR 31, 58, 88, 134; CLR 29; CMW 4; DLB 87, 161, 276; JRDA; MAICYA 1, 2; SATA 5, 62, 95, 150; SFW 4; WYA; YAW

Dickson, Carr
See Carr, John Dickson

Dickson, Carter
See Carr, John Dickson

Diderot, Denis 1713-1784 .... **LC 26, 126**
See also DLB 313; EW 4; GFL Beginnings to 1789; LMFS 1; RGWL 2, 3

Didion, Joan 1934- . **CLC 1, 3, 8, 14, 32, 129**
See also AITN 1; AMWS 4; CA 5-8R; CANR 14, 52, 76, 125; CDALB 1968-1988; CN 2, 3, 4, 5, 6, 7; DA3; DAM NOV; DLB 2, 173, 185; DLBY 1981, 1986; EWL 3; MAL 5; MAWW; MTCW 1, 2; MTFW 2005; NFS 3; RGAL 4; TCLE 1:1; TCWW 2; TUS

di Donato, Pietro 1911-1992 .... **TCLC 159**
See also CA 101; 136; DLB 9

Dietrich, Robert
See Hunt, E(verette) Howard, (Jr.)

Difusa, Pati
See Almodovar, Pedro

Dillard, Annie 1945- ...... **CLC 9, 60, 115, 216**
See also AAYA 6, 43; AMWS 6; ANW; CA 49-52; CANR 3, 43, 62, 90, 125; DA3; DAM NOV; DLB 275, 278; DLBY 1980; LAIT 4, 5; MAL 5; MTCW 1, 2; MTFW 2005; NCFS 1; RGAL 4; SATA 10, 140; TCLE 1:1; TUS

Dillard, R(ichard) H(enry) W(ilde)
1937- .... **CLC 5**
See also CA 21-24R; CAAS 7; CANR 10; CP 2, 3, 4, 5, 6, 7; CSW; DLB 5, 244

Dillon, Eilis 1920-1994 .... **CLC 17**
See also CA 9-12R, 182; 147; CAAE 182; CAAS 3; CANR 4, 38, 78; CLR 26; MAICYA 1, 2; MAICYAS 1; SATA 2, 74; SATA-Essay 105; SATA-Obit 83; YAW

Dimont, Penelope
See Mortimer, Penelope (Ruth)

Dinesen, Isak ...... **CLC 10, 29, 95; SSC 7, 75**
See Blixen, Karen (Christentze Dinesen)
See also EW 10; EWL 3; EXPS; FW; GL 2; HGG; LAIT 3; MTCW 1; NCFS 2; NFS 9; RGSF 2; RGWL 2, 3; SSFS 3, 6, 13; WLIT 2

Ding Ling .... **CLC 68**
See Chiang, Pin-chin
See also RGWL 3

Diphusa, Patty
See Almodovar, Pedro

Disch, Thomas M(ichael) 1940- ... **CLC 7, 36**
See Disch, Tom
See also AAYA 17; BPFB 1; CA 21-24R; CAAS 4; CANR 17, 36, 54, 89; CLR 18; CP 7; DA3; DLB 8; HGG; MAICYA 1, 2; MTCW 1, 2; MTFW 2005; SAAS 15; SATA 92; SCFW 1, 2; SFW 4; SUFW 2

Disch, Tom
See Disch, Thomas M(ichael)
See also DLB 282

d'Isly, Georges
See Simenon, Georges (Jacques Christian)

Disraeli, Benjamin 1804-1881 ... **NCLC 2, 39, 79**
See also BRW 4; DLB 21, 55; RGEL 2

Ditcum, Steve
See Crumb, R(obert)

Dixon, Paige
See Corcoran, Barbara (Asenath)

Dixon, Stephen 1936- .... **CLC 52; SSC 16**
See also AMWS 12; CA 89-92; CANR 17, 40, 54, 91; CN 4, 5, 6, 7; DLB 130; MAL 5

Dixon, Thomas, Jr. 1864-1946 ..... **TCLC 163**
See also RHW

Djebar, Assia 1936- .... **CLC 182**
See also CA 188; EWL 3; RGWL 3; WLIT 2

Doak, Annie
See Dillard, Annie

Dobell, Sydney Thompson
1824-1874 .... **NCLC 43**
See also DLB 32; RGEL 2

Doblin, Alfred .... **TCLC 13**
See Doeblin, Alfred
See also CDWLB 2; EWL 3; RGWL 2, 3

Dobroliubov, Nikolai Aleksandrovich
See Dobrolyubov, Nikolai Alexandrovich
See also DLB 277

Dobrolyubov, Nikolai Alexandrovich
1836-1861 .... **NCLC 5**
See Dobroliubov, Nikolai Aleksandrovich

Dobson, Austin 1840-1921 .... **TCLC 79**
See also DLB 35, 144

Dobyns, Stephen 1941- .... **CLC 37**
See also AMWS 13; CA 45-48; CANR 2, 18, 99; CMW 4; CP 4, 5, 6, 7; PFS 23

Doctorow, E(dgar) L(aurence)
1931- .... **CLC 6, 11, 15, 18, 37, 44, 65, 113, 214**
See also AAYA 22; AITN 2; AMWS 4; BEST 89:3; BPFB 1; CA 45-48; CANR 2, 33, 51, 76, 97, 133; CDALB 1968-1988; CN 3, 4, 5, 6, 7; CPW; DA3; DAM NOV, POP; DLB 2, 28, 173; DLBY 1980; EWL 3; LAIT 3; MAL 5; MTCW 1, 2; MTFW 2005; NFS 6; RGAL 4; RHW; TCLE 1:1; TCWW 1, 2; TUS

Dodgson, Charles L(utwidge) 1832-1898
See Carroll, Lewis
See also CLR 2; DA; DA3; DAB; DAC; DAM MST, NOV, POET; MAICYA 1, 2; SATA 100; YABC 2

Dodsley, Robert 1703-1764 .... **LC 97**
See also DLB 95; RGEL 2

Dodson, Owen (Vincent) 1914-1983 .. **BLC 1; CLC 79**
See also BW 1; CA 65-68; 110; CANR 24; DAM MULT; DLB 76

Doeblin, Alfred 1878-1957 .... **TCLC 13**
See Doblin, Alfred
See also CA 110; 141; DLB 66

Doerr, Harriet 1910-2002 .... **CLC 34**
See also CA 117; 122; 213; CANR 47; INT CA-122; LATS 1:2

Domecq, H(onorio Bustos)
See Bioy Casares, Adolfo

Domecq, H(onorio) Bustos
See Bioy Casares, Adolfo; Borges, Jorge Luis

Domini, Rey
See Lorde, Audre (Geraldine)
See also GLL 1

Dominique
See Proust, (Valentin-Louis-George-Eugene) Marcel

Don, A
See Stephen, Sir Leslie

Donaldson, Stephen R(eeder)
1947- .... **CLC 46, 138**
See also AAYA 36; BPFB 1; CA 89-92; CANR 13, 55, 99; CPW; DAM POP; FANT; INT CANR-13; SATA 121; SFW 4; SUFW 1, 2

Donleavy, J(ames) P(atrick) 1926- ..... **CLC 1, 4, 6, 10, 45**
See also AITN 2; BPFB 1; CA 9-12R; CANR 24, 49, 62, 80, 124; CBD; CD 5, 6; CN 1, 2, 3, 4, 5, 6, 7; DLB 6, 173; INT CANR-24; MAL 5; MTCW 1, 2; MTFW 2005; RGAL 4

Donnadieu, Marguerite
See Duras, Marguerite

Donne, John 1572-1631 ... **LC 10, 24, 91; PC 1, 43; WLC**
See also AAYA 67; BRW 1; BRWC 1; BRWR 2; CDBLB Before 1660; DA; DAB; DAC; DAM MST, POET; DLB 121, 151; EXPP; PAB; PFS 2, 11; RGEL 3; TEA; WLIT 3; WP

Donnell, David 1939(?)- .... **CLC 34**
See also CA 197

Donoghue, Denis 1928- .... **CLC 209**
See also CA 17-20R; CANR 16, 102

Donoghue, P. S.
See Hunt, E(verette) Howard, (Jr.)

Donoso (Yanez), Jose 1924-1996 ... **CLC 4, 8, 11, 32, 99; HLC 1; SSC 34; TCLC 133**
See also CA 81-84; 155; CANR 32, 73; CDWLB 3; CWW 2; DAM MULT; DLB 113; EWL 3; HW 1, 2; LAW; LAWS 1; MTCW 1, 2; MTFW 2005; RGSF 2; WLIT 1

Donovan, John 1928-1992 .... **CLC 35**
See also AAYA 20; CA 97-100; 137; CLR 3; MAICYA 1, 2; SATA 72; SATA-Brief 29; YAW

Don Roberto
See Cunninghame Graham, Robert (Gallnigad) Bontine

Doolittle, Hilda 1886-1961 . **CLC 3, 8, 14, 31, 34, 73; PC 5; WLC**
See H. D.
See also AAYA 66; AMWS 1; CA 97-100; CANR 35, 131; DA; DAC; DAM MST, POET; DLB 4, 45; EWL 3; FW; GLL 1; LMFS 2; MAL 5; MAWW; MTCW 1, 2; MTFW 2005; PFS 6; RGAL 4

Doppo, Kunikida .... **TCLC 99**
See Kunikida Doppo

Dorfman, Ariel 1942- .... **CLC 48, 77, 189; HLC 1**
See also CA 124; 130; CANR 67, 70, 135; CWW 2; DAM MULT; DFS 4; EWL 3; HW 1, 2; INT CA-130; WLIT 1

Dorn, Edward (Merton)
1929-1999 .... **CLC 10, 18**
See also CA 93-96; 187; CANR 42, 79; CP 1, 2, 3, 4, 5, 6, 7; DLB 5; INT CA-93-96; WP

Dor-Ner, Zvi .... **CLC 70**

Dorris, Michael (Anthony)
1945-1997 .... **CLC 109; NNAL**
See also AAYA 20; BEST 90:1; BYA 12; CA 102; 157; CANR 19, 46, 75; CLR 58; DA3; DAM MULT, NOV; DLB 175; LAIT 5; MTCW 2; MTFW 2005; NFS 3; RGAL 4; SATA 75; SATA-Obit 94; TCWW 2; YAW

Dorris, Michael A.
See Dorris, Michael (Anthony)

Dorsan, Luc
See Simenon, Georges (Jacques Christian)

Dorsange, Jean
See Simenon, Georges (Jacques Christian)

Dorset
See Sackville, Thomas

Dos Passos, John (Roderigo)
1896-1970 ... **CLC 1, 4, 8, 11, 15, 25, 34, 82; WLC**
See also AMW; BPFB 1; CA 1-4R; 29-32R; CANR 3; CDALB 1929-1941; DA; DA3; DAB; DAC; DAM MST, NOV; DLB 4, 9, 274, 316; DLBD 1, 15; DLBY 1996; EWL 3; MAL 5; MTCW 1, 2; MTFW 2005; NFS 14; RGAL 4; TUS

Dossage, Jean
See Simenon, Georges (Jacques Christian)

Dostoevsky, Fedor Mikhailovich
1821-1881 .. **NCLC 2, 7, 21, 33, 43, 119, 167; SSC 2, 33, 44; WLC**
See Dostoevsky, Fyodor
See also AAYA 40; DA; DA3; DAB; DAC; DAM MST, NOV; EW 7; EXPN; NFS 3, 8; RGSF 2; RGWL 2, 3; SSFS 8; TWA

Dostoevsky, Fyodor
See Dostoevsky, Fedor Mikhailovich
See also DLB 238; LATS 1:1; LMFS 1, 2

Doty, M. R.
See Doty, Mark (Alan)

Doty, Mark
See Doty, Mark (Alan)

Doty, Mark (Alan) 1953(?)- ..... **CLC 176; PC 53**
See also AMWS 11; CA 161, 183; CAAE 183; CANR 110

Doty, Mark A.
See Doty, Mark (Alan)

Doughty, Charles M(ontagu)
1843-1926 .... **TCLC 27**
See also CA 115; 178; DLB 19, 57, 174

Douglas, Ellen .... **CLC 73**
See Haxton, Josephine Ayres; Williamson, Ellen Douglas
See also CN 5, 6, 7; CSW; DLB 292

Douglas, Gavin 1475(?)-1522 .... **LC 20**
See also DLB 132; RGEL 2
Douglas, George
See Brown, George Douglas
See also RGEL 2
Douglas, Keith (Castellain)
1920-1944 .... **TCLC 40**
See also BRW 7; CA 160; DLB 27; EWL 3; PAB; RGEL 2
Douglas, Leonard
See Bradbury, Ray (Douglas)
Douglas, Michael
See Crichton, (John) Michael
Douglas, (George) Norman
1868-1952 .... **TCLC 68**
See also BRW 6; CA 119; 157; DLB 34, 195; RGEL 2
Douglas, William
See Brown, George Douglas
Douglass, Frederick 1817(?)-1895 ..... **BLC 1; NCLC 7, 55, 141; WLC**
See also AAYA 48; AFAW 1, 2; AMWC 1; AMWS 3; CDALB 1640-1865; DA; DA3; DAC; DAM MST, MULT; DLB 1, 43, 50, 79, 243; FW; LAIT 2; NCFS 2; RGAL 4; SATA 29
Dourado, (Waldomiro Freitas) Autran
1926- .... **CLC 23, 60**
See also CA 25-28R; 179; CANR 34, 81; DLB 145, 307; HW 2
Dourado, Waldomiro Freitas Autran
See Dourado, (Waldomiro Freitas) Autran
Dove, Rita (Frances) 1952- . **BLCS; CLC 50, 81; PC 6**
See also AAYA 46; AMWS 4; BW 2; CA 109; CAAS 19; CANR 27, 42, 68, 76, 97, 132; CDALBS; CP 7; CSW; CWP; DA3; DAM MULT, POET; DLB 120; EWL 3; EXPP; MAL 5; MTCW 2; MTFW 2005; PFS 1, 15; RGAL 4
Doveglion
See Villa, Jose Garcia
Dowell, Coleman 1925-1985 .... **CLC 60**
See also CA 25-28R; 117; CANR 10; DLB 130; GLL 2
Dowson, Ernest (Christopher)
1867-1900 .... **TCLC 4**
See also CA 105; 150; DLB 19, 135; RGEL 2
Doyle, A. Conan
See Doyle, Sir Arthur Conan
Doyle, Sir Arthur Conan
1859-1930 . **SSC 12, 83; TCLC 7; WLC**
See Conan Doyle, Arthur
See also AAYA 14; BRWS 2; CA 104; 122; CANR 131; CDBLB 1890-1914; CMW 4; DA; DA3; DAB; DAC; DAM MST, NOV; DLB 18, 70, 156, 178; EXPS; HGG; LAIT 2; MSW; MTCW 1, 2; MTFW 2005; RGEL 2; RGSF 2; RHW; SATA 24; SCFW 1, 2; SFW 4; SSFS 2; TEA; WCH; WLIT 4; WYA; YAW
Doyle, Conan
See Doyle, Sir Arthur Conan
Doyle, John
See Graves, Robert (von Ranke)
Doyle, Roddy 1958- .... **CLC 81, 178**
See also AAYA 14; BRWS 5; CA 143; CANR 73, 128; CN 6, 7; DA3; DLB 194; MTCW 2; MTFW 2005
Doyle, Sir A. Conan
See Doyle, Sir Arthur Conan
Dr. A
See Asimov, Isaac; Silverstein, Alvin; Silverstein, Virginia B(arbara Opshelor)

Drabble, Margaret 1939- ...... **CLC 2, 3, 5, 8, 10, 22, 53, 129**
See also BRWS 4; CA 13-16R; CANR 18, 35, 63, 112, 131; CDBLB 1960 to Present; CN 1, 2, 3, 4, 5, 6, 7; CPW; DA3; DAB; DAC; DAM MST, NOV, POP; DLB 14, 155, 231; EWL 3; FW; MTCW 1, 2; MTFW 2005; RGEL 2; SATA 48; TEA
Drakulic, Slavenka 1949- .... **CLC 173**
See also CA 144; CANR 92
Drakulic-Ilic, Slavenka
See Drakulic, Slavenka
Drapier, M. B.
See Swift, Jonathan
Drayham, James
See Mencken, H(enry) L(ouis)
Drayton, Michael 1563-1631 .... **LC 8**
See also DAM POET; DLB 121; RGEL 2
Dreadstone, Carl
See Campbell, (John) Ramsey
Dreiser, Theodore (Herman Albert)
1871-1945 .... **SSC 30; TCLC 10, 18, 35, 83; WLC**
See also AMW; AMWC 2; AMWR 2; BYA 15, 16; CA 106; 132; CDALB 1865-1917; DA; DA3; DAC; DAM MST, NOV; DLB 9, 12, 102, 137; DLBD 1; EWL 3; LAIT 2; LMFS 2; MAL 5; MTCW 1, 2; MTFW 2005; NFS 8, 17; RGAL 4; TUS
Drexler, Rosalyn 1926- .... **CLC 2, 6**
See also CA 81-84; CAD; CANR 68, 124; CD 5, 6; CWD; MAL 5
Dreyer, Carl Theodor 1889-1968 ...... **CLC 16**
See also CA 116
Drieu la Rochelle, Pierre(-Eugene)
1893-1945 .... **TCLC 21**
See also CA 117; DLB 72; EWL 3; GFL 1789 to the Present
Drinkwater, John 1882-1937 .... **TCLC 57**
See also CA 109; 149; DLB 10, 19, 149; RGEL 2
Drop Shot
See Cable, George Washington
Droste-Hulshoff, Annette Freiin von
1797-1848 .... **NCLC 3, 133**
See also CDWLB 2; DLB 133; RGSF 2; RGWL 2, 3
Drummond, Walter
See Silverberg, Robert
Drummond, William Henry
1854-1907 .... **TCLC 25**
See also CA 160; DLB 92
Drummond de Andrade, Carlos
1902-1987 .... **CLC 18; TCLC 139**
See Andrade, Carlos Drummond de
See also CA 132; 123; DLB 307; LAW
Drummond of Hawthornden, William
1585-1649 .... **LC 83**
See also DLB 121, 213; RGEL 2
Drury, Allen (Stuart) 1918-1998 .... **CLC 37**
See also CA 57-60; 170; CANR 18, 52; CN 1, 2, 3, 4, 5, 6; INT CANR-18
Druse, Eleanor
See King, Stephen
Dryden, John 1631-1700 ..... **DC 3; LC 3, 21, 115; PC 25; WLC**
See also BRW 2; CDBLB 1660-1789; DA; DAB; DAC; DAM DRAM, MST, POET; DLB 80, 101, 131; EXPP; IDTP; LMFS 1; RGEL 2; TEA; WLIT 3
du Bellay, Joachim 1524-1560 .... **LC 92**
See also GFL Beginnings to 1789; RGWL 2, 3
Duberman, Martin (Bauml) 1930- ..... **CLC 8**
See also CA 1-4R; CAD; CANR 2, 63, 137; CD 5, 6
Dubie, Norman (Evans) 1945- .... **CLC 36**
See also CA 69-72; CANR 12, 115; CP 3, 4, 5, 6, 7; DLB 120; PFS 12

Du Bois, W(illiam) E(dward) B(urghardt)
1868-1963 ...... **BLC 1; CLC 1, 2, 13, 64, 96; HR 1:2; TCLC 169; WLC**
See also AAYA 40; AFAW 1, 2; AMWC 1; AMWS 2; BW 1, 3; CA 85-88; CANR 34, 82, 132; CDALB 1865-1917; DA; DA3; DAC; DAM MST, MULT, NOV; DLB 47, 50, 91, 246, 284; EWL 3; EXPP; LAIT 2; LMFS 2; MAL 5; MTCW 1, 2; MTFW 2005; NCFS 1; PFS 13; RGAL 4; SATA 42
Dubus, Andre 1936-1999 ..... **CLC 13, 36, 97; SSC 15**
See also AMWS 7; CA 21-24R; 177; CANR 17; CN 5, 6; CSW; DLB 130; INT CANR-17; RGAL 4; SSFS 10; TCLE 1:1
Duca Minimo
See D'Annunzio, Gabriele
Ducharme, Rejean 1941- .... **CLC 74**
See also CA 165; DLB 60
du Chatelet, Emilie 1706-1749 .... **LC 96**
See Chatelet, Gabrielle-Emilie Du
Duchen, Claire .... **CLC 65**
Duclos, Charles Pinot- 1704-1772 .... **LC 1**
See also GFL Beginnings to 1789
Dudek, Louis 1918-2001 .... **CLC 11, 19**
See also CA 45-48; 215; CAAS 14; CANR 1; CP 1, 2, 3, 4, 5, 6, 7; DLB 88
Duerrenmatt, Friedrich 1921-1990 ... **CLC 1, 4, 8, 11, 15, 43, 102**
See Durrenmatt, Friedrich
See also CA 17-20R; CANR 33; CMW 4; DAM DRAM; DLB 69, 124; MTCW 1, 2
Duffy, Bruce 1953(?)- .... **CLC 50**
See also CA 172
Duffy, Maureen (Patricia) 1933- .... **CLC 37**
See also CA 25-28R; CANR 33, 68; CBD; CN 1, 2, 3, 4, 5, 6, 7; CP 7; CWD; CWP; DFS 15; DLB 14, 310; FW; MTCW 1
Du Fu
See Tu Fu
See also RGWL 2, 3
Dugan, Alan 1923-2003 .... **CLC 2, 6**
See also CA 81-84; 220; CANR 119; CP 1, 2, 3, 4, 5, 6, 7; DLB 5; MAL 5; PFS 10
du Gard, Roger Martin
See Martin du Gard, Roger
Duhamel, Georges 1884-1966 .... **CLC 8**
See also CA 81-84; 25-28R; CANR 35; DLB 65; EWL 3; GFL 1789 to the Present; MTCW 1
Dujardin, Edouard (Emile Louis)
1861-1949 .... **TCLC 13**
See also CA 109; DLB 123
Duke, Raoul
See Thompson, Hunter S(tockton)
Dulles, John Foster 1888-1959 .... **TCLC 72**
See also CA 115; 149
Dumas, Alexandre (pere)
1802-1870 .... **NCLC 11, 71; WLC**
See also AAYA 22; BYA 3; DA; DA3; DAB; DAC; DAM MST, NOV; DLB 119, 192; EW 6; GFL 1789 to the Present; LAIT 1, 2; NFS 14, 19; RGWL 2, 3; SATA 18; TWA; WCH
Dumas, Alexandre (fils) 1824-1895 .... **DC 1; NCLC 9**
See also DLB 192; GFL 1789 to the Present; RGWL 2, 3
Dumas, Claudine
See Malzberg, Barry N(athaniel)
Dumas, Henry L. 1934-1968 .... **CLC 6, 62**
See also BW 1; CA 85-88; DLB 41; RGAL 4
du Maurier, Daphne 1907-1989 .. **CLC 6, 11, 59; SSC 18**
See also AAYA 37; BPFB 1; BRWS 3; CA 5-8R; 128; CANR 6, 55; CMW 4; CN 1, 2, 3, 4; CPW; DA3; DAB; DAC; DAM

MST, POP; DLB 191; GL 2; HGG; LAIT 3; MSW; MTCW 1, 2; NFS 12; RGEL 2; RGSF 2; RHW; SATA 27; SATA-Obit 60; SSFS 14, 16; TEA

Du Maurier, George 1834-1896 ..... **NCLC 86**
See also DLB 153, 178; RGEL 2

Dunbar, Paul Laurence 1872-1906 ... **BLC 1; PC 5; SSC 8; TCLC 2, 12; WLC**
See also AFAW 1, 2; AMWS 2; BW 1, 3; CA 104; 124; CANR 79; CDALB 1865-1917; DA; DA3; DAC; DAM MST, MULT, POET; DLB 50, 54, 78; EXPP; MAL 5; RGAL 4; SATA 34

Dunbar, William 1460(?)-1520(?) .... **LC 20; PC 67**
See also BRWS 8; DLB 132, 146; RGEL 2

Dunbar-Nelson, Alice .... **HR 1:2**
See Nelson, Alice Ruth Moore Dunbar

Duncan, Dora Angela
See Duncan, Isadora

Duncan, Isadora 1877(?)-1927 .... **TCLC 68**
See also CA 118; 149

Duncan, Lois 1934- .... **CLC 26**
See also AAYA 4, 34; BYA 6, 8; CA 1-4R; CANR 2, 23, 36, 111; CLR 29; JRDA; MAICYA 1, 2; MAICYAS 1; MTFW 2005; SAAS 2; SATA 1, 36, 75, 133, 141; SATA-Essay 141; WYA; YAW

Duncan, Robert (Edward)
1919-1988 .... **CLC 1, 2, 4, 7, 15, 41, 55; PC 2**
See also BG 1:2; CA 9-12R; 124; CANR 28, 62; CP 1, 2, 3, 4; DAM POET; DLB 5, 16, 193; EWL 3; MAL 5; MTCW 1, 2; MTFW 2005; PFS 13; RGAL 4; WP

Duncan, Sara Jeannette
1861-1922 .... **TCLC 60**
See also CA 157; DLB 92

Dunlap, William 1766-1839 .... **NCLC 2**
See also DLB 30, 37, 59; RGAL 4

Dunn, Douglas (Eaglesham) 1942- .... **CLC 6, 40**
See also BRWS 10; CA 45-48; CANR 2, 33, 126; CP 1, 2, 3, 4, 5, 6, 7; DLB 40; MTCW 1

Dunn, Katherine (Karen) 1945- .... **CLC 71**
See also CA 33-36R; CANR 72; HGG; MTCW 2; MTFW 2005

Dunn, Stephen (Elliott) 1939- .. **CLC 36, 206**
See also AMWS 11; CA 33-36R; CANR 12, 48, 53, 105; CP 3, 4, 5, 6, 7; DLB 105; PFS 21

Dunne, Finley Peter 1867-1936 .... **TCLC 28**
See also CA 108; 178; DLB 11, 23; RGAL 4

Dunne, John Gregory 1932-2003 ..... **CLC 28**
See also CA 25-28R; 222; CANR 14, 50; CN 5, 6, 7; DLBY 1980

Dunsany, Lord .... **TCLC 2, 59**
See Dunsany, Edward John Moreton Drax Plunkett
See also DLB 77, 153, 156, 255; FANT; IDTP; RGEL 2; SFW 4; SUFW 1

Dunsany, Edward John Moreton Drax Plunkett 1878-1957
See Dunsany, Lord
See also CA 104; 148; DLB 10; MTCW 2

Duns Scotus, John 1266(?)-1308 ... **CMLC 59**
See also DLB 115

du Perry, Jean
See Simenon, Georges (Jacques Christian)

Durang, Christopher (Ferdinand)
1949- .... **CLC 27, 38**
See also CA 105; CAD; CANR 50, 76, 130; CD 5, 6; MTCW 2; MTFW 2005

Duras, Claire de 1777-1832 .... **NCLC 154**

Duras, Marguerite 1914-1996 . **CLC 3, 6, 11, 20, 34, 40, 68, 100; SSC 40**
See also BPFB 1; CA 25-28R; 151; CANR 50; CWW 2; DFS 21; DLB 83, 321; EWL 3; FL 1:5; GFL 1789 to the Present; IDFW 4; MTCW 1, 2; RGWL 2, 3; TWA

Durban, (Rosa) Pam 1947- .... **CLC 39**
See also CA 123; CANR 98; CSW

Durcan, Paul 1944- .... **CLC 43, 70**
See also CA 134; CANR 123; CP 1, 7; DAM POET; EWL 3

Durfey, Thomas 1653-1723 .... **LC 94**
See also DLB 80; RGEL 2

Durkheim, Emile 1858-1917 .... **TCLC 55**

Durrell, Lawrence (George)
1912-1990 ..... **CLC 1, 4, 6, 8, 13, 27, 41**
See also BPFB 1; BRWS 1; CA 9-12R; 132; CANR 40, 77; CDBLB 1945-1960; CN 1, 2, 3, 4; CP 1, 2, 3, 4; DAM NOV; DLB 15, 27, 204; DLBY 1990; EWL 3; MTCW 1, 2; RGEL 2; SFW 4; TEA

Durrenmatt, Friedrich
See Duerrenmatt, Friedrich
See also CDWLB 2; EW 13; EWL 3; RGWL 2, 3

Dutt, Michael Madhusudan
1824-1873 .... **NCLC 118**

Dutt, Toru 1856-1877 .... **NCLC 29**
See also DLB 240

Dwight, Timothy 1752-1817 .... **NCLC 13**
See also DLB 37; RGAL 4

Dworkin, Andrea 1946-2005 ..... **CLC 43, 123**
See also CA 77-80; 238; CAAS 21; CANR 16, 39, 76, 96; FL 1:5; FW; GLL 1; INT CANR-16; MTCW 1, 2; MTFW 2005

Dwyer, Deanna
See Koontz, Dean R.

Dwyer, K. R.
See Koontz, Dean R.

Dybek, Stuart 1942- .... **CLC 114; SSC 55**
See also CA 97-100; CANR 39; DLB 130

Dye, Richard
See De Voto, Bernard (Augustine)

Dyer, Geoff 1958- .... **CLC 149**
See also CA 125; CANR 88

Dyer, George 1755-1841 .... **NCLC 129**
See also DLB 93

Dylan, Bob 1941- .... **CLC 3, 4, 6, 12, 77; PC 37**
See also CA 41-44R; CANR 108; CP 1, 2, 3, 4, 5, 6, 7; DLB 16

Dyson, John 1943- .... **CLC 70**
See also CA 144

Dzyubin, Eduard Georgievich 1895-1934
See Bagritsky, Eduard
See also CA 170

E. V. L.
See Lucas, E(dward) V(errall)

Eagleton, Terence (Francis) 1943- .. **CLC 63, 132**
See also CA 57-60; CANR 7, 23, 68, 115; DLB 242; LMFS 2; MTCW 1, 2; MTFW 2005

Eagleton, Terry
See Eagleton, Terence (Francis)

Early, Jack
See Scoppettone, Sandra
See also GLL 1

East, Michael
See West, Morris L(anglo)

Eastaway, Edward
See Thomas, (Philip) Edward

Eastlake, William (Derry)
1917-1997 .... **CLC 8**
See also CA 5-8R; 158; CAAS 1; CANR 5, 63; CN 1, 2, 3, 4, 5, 6; DLB 6, 206; INT CANR-5; MAL 5; TCWW 1, 2

Eastman, Charles A(lexander)
1858-1939 .... **NNAL; TCLC 55**
See also CA 179; CANR 91; DAM MULT; DLB 175; YABC 1

Eaton, Edith Maude 1865-1914 .... **AAL**
See Far, Sui Sin
See also CA 154; DLB 221, 312; FW

Eaton, (Lillie) Winnifred 1875-1954 .... **AAL**
See also CA 217; DLB 221, 312; RGAL 4

Eberhart, Richard 1904-2005 ...... **CLC 3, 11, 19, 56**
See also AMW; CA 1-4R; 240; CANR 2, 125; CDALB 1941-1968; CP 1, 2, 3, 4, 5, 6, 7; DAM POET; DLB 48; MAL 5; MTCW 1; RGAL 4

Eberhart, Richard Ghormley
See Eberhart, Richard

Eberstadt, Fernanda 1960- .... **CLC 39**
See also CA 136; CANR 69, 128

Echegaray (y Eizaguirre), Jose (Maria Waldo) 1832-1916 .... **HLCS 1; TCLC 4**
See also CA 104; CANR 32; EWL 3; HW 1; MTCW 1

Echeverria, (Jose) Esteban (Antonino)
1805-1851 .... **NCLC 18**
See also LAW

Echo
See Proust, (Valentin-Louis-George-Eugene) Marcel

Eckert, Allan W. 1931- .... **CLC 17**
See also AAYA 18; BYA 2; CA 13-16R; CANR 14, 45; INT CANR-14; MAICYA 2; MAICYAS 1; SAAS 21; SATA 29, 91; SATA-Brief 27

Eckhart, Meister 1260(?)-1327(?) .. **CMLC 9, 80**
See also DLB 115; LMFS 1

Eckmar, F. R.
See de Hartog, Jan

Eco, Umberto 1932- .... **CLC 28, 60, 142**
See also BEST 90:1; BPFB 1; CA 77-80; CANR 12, 33, 55, 110, 131; CPW; CWW 2; DA3; DAM NOV, POP; DLB 196, 242; EWL 3; MSW; MTCW 1, 2; MTFW 2005; NFS 22; RGWL 3; WLIT 7

Eddison, E(ric) R(ucker)
1882-1945 .... **TCLC 15**
See also CA 109; 156; DLB 255; FANT; SFW 4; SUFW 1

Eddy, Mary (Ann Morse) Baker
1821-1910 .... **TCLC 71**
See also CA 113; 174

Edel, (Joseph) Leon 1907-1997 .. **CLC 29, 34**
See also CA 1-4R; 161; CANR 1, 22, 112; DLB 103; INT CANR-22

Eden, Emily 1797-1869 .... **NCLC 10**

Edgar, David 1948- .... **CLC 42**
See also CA 57-60; CANR 12, 61, 112; CBD; CD 5, 6; DAM DRAM; DFS 15; DLB 13, 233; MTCW 1

Edgerton, Clyde (Carlyle) 1944- .... **CLC 39**
See also AAYA 17; CA 118; 134; CANR 64, 125; CN 7; CSW; DLB 278; INT CA-134; TCLE 1:1; YAW

Edgeworth, Maria 1768-1849 ... **NCLC 1, 51, 158; SSC 86**
See also BRWS 3; DLB 116, 159, 163; FL 1:3; FW; RGEL 2; SATA 21; TEA; WLIT 3

Edmonds, Paul
See Kuttner, Henry

Edmonds, Walter D(umaux)
1903-1998 .... **CLC 35**
See also BYA 2; CA 5-8R; CANR 2; CWRI 5; DLB 9; LAIT 1; MAICYA 1, 2; MAL 5; RHW; SAAS 4; SATA 1, 27; SATA-Obit 99

Edmondson, Wallace
See Ellison, Harlan (Jay)

Edson, Margaret 1961- ...... **CLC 199; DC 24**
See also CA 190; DFS 13; DLB 266
Edson, Russell 1935- .... **CLC 13**
See also CA 33-36R; CANR 115; CP 2, 3, 4, 5, 6, 7; DLB 244; WP
Edwards, Bronwen Elizabeth
See Rose, Wendy
Edwards, G(erald) B(asil)
1899-1976 .... **CLC 25**
See also CA 201; 110
Edwards, Gus 1939- .... **CLC 43**
See also CA 108; INT CA-108
Edwards, Jonathan 1703-1758 .... **LC 7, 54**
See also AMW; DA; DAC; DAM MST; DLB 24, 270; RGAL 4; TUS
Edwards, Sarah Pierpont 1710-1758 .. **LC 87**
See also DLB 200
Efron, Marina Ivanovna Tsvetaeva
See Tsvetaeva (Efron), Marina (Ivanovna)
Egeria fl. 4th cent. - .... **CMLC 70**
Egoyan, Atom 1960- .... **CLC 151**
See also AAYA 63; CA 157
Ehle, John (Marsden, Jr.) 1925- ...... **CLC 27**
See also CA 9-12R; CSW
Ehrenbourg, Ilya (Grigoryevich)
See Ehrenburg, Ilya (Grigoryevich)
Ehrenburg, Ilya (Grigoryevich)
1891-1967 .... **CLC 18, 34, 62**
See Erenburg, Il'ia Grigor'evich
See also CA 102; 25-28R; EWL 3
Ehrenburg, Ilyo (Grigoryevich)
See Ehrenburg, Ilya (Grigoryevich)
Ehrenreich, Barbara 1941- .... **CLC 110**
See also BEST 90:4; CA 73-76; CANR 16, 37, 62, 117; DLB 246; FW; MTCW 1, 2; MTFW 2005
Eich, Gunter
See Eich, Gunter
See also RGWL 2, 3
Eich, Gunter 1907-1972 .... **CLC 15**
See Eich, Gunter
See also CA 111; 93-96; DLB 69, 124; EWL 3
Eichendorff, Joseph 1788-1857 .... **NCLC 8**
See also DLB 90; RGWL 2, 3
Eigner, Larry .... **CLC 9**
See Eigner, Laurence (Joel)
See also CAAS 23; CP 1, 2, 3, 4; DLB 5; WP
Eigner, Laurence (Joel) 1927-1996
See Eigner, Larry
See also CA 9-12R; 151; CANR 6, 84; CP 7; DLB 193
Eilhart von Oberge c. 1140-c.
1195 .... **CMLC 67**
See also DLB 148
Einhard c. 770-840 .... **CMLC 50**
See also DLB 148
Einstein, Albert 1879-1955 .... **TCLC 65**
See also CA 121; 133; MTCW 1, 2
Eiseley, Loren
See Eiseley, Loren Corey
See also DLB 275
Eiseley, Loren Corey 1907-1977 .... **CLC 7**
See Eiseley, Loren
See also AAYA 5; ANW; CA 1-4R; 73-76; CANR 6; DLBD 17
Eisenstadt, Jill 1963- .... **CLC 50**
See also CA 140
Eisenstein, Sergei (Mikhailovich)
1898-1948 .... **TCLC 57**
See also CA 114; 149
Eisner, Simon
See Kornbluth, C(yril) M.
Ekeloef, (Bengt) Gunnar
1907-1968 .... **CLC 27; PC 23**
See Ekelof, (Bengt) Gunnar
See also CA 123; 25-28R; DAM POET

Ekelof, (Bengt) Gunnar 1907-1968
See Ekeloef, (Bengt) Gunnar
See also DLB 259; EW 12; EWL 3
Ekelund, Vilhelm 1880-1949 .... **TCLC 75**
See also CA 189; EWL 3
Ekwensi, C. O. D.
See Ekwensi, Cyprian (Odiatu Duaka)
Ekwensi, Cyprian (Odiatu Duaka)
1921- .... **BLC 1; CLC 4**
See also AFW; BW 2, 3; CA 29-32R; CANR 18, 42, 74, 125; CDWLB 3; CN 1, 2, 3, 4, 5, 6; CWRI 5; DAM MULT; DLB 117; EWL 3; MTCW 1, 2; RGEL 2; SATA 66; WLIT 2
Elaine .... **TCLC 18**
See Leverson, Ada Esther
El Crummo
See Crumb, R(obert)
Elder, Lonne III 1931-1996 ..... **BLC 1; DC 8**
See also BW 1, 3; CA 81-84; 152; CAD; CANR 25; DAM MULT; DLB 7, 38, 44; MAL 5
Eleanor of Aquitaine 1122-1204 ... **CMLC 39**
Elia
See Lamb, Charles
Eliade, Mircea 1907-1986 .... **CLC 19**
See also CA 65-68; 119; CANR 30, 62; CDWLB 4; DLB 220; EWL 3; MTCW 1; RGWL 3; SFW 4
Eliot, A. D.
See Jewett, (Theodora) Sarah Orne
Eliot, Alice
See Jewett, (Theodora) Sarah Orne
Eliot, Dan
See Silverberg, Robert
Eliot, George 1819-1880 ...... **NCLC 4, 13, 23, 41, 49, 89, 118; PC 20; SSC 72; WLC**
See Evans, Mary Ann
See also BRW 5; BRWC 1, 2; BRWR 2; CDBLB 1832-1890; CN 7; CPW; DA; DA3; DAB; DAC; DAM MST, NOV; DLB 21, 35, 55; FL 1:3; LATS 1:1; LMFS 1; NFS 17, 20; RGEL 2; RGSF 2; SSFS 8; TEA; WLIT 3
Eliot, John 1604-1690 .... **LC 5**
See also DLB 24
Eliot, T(homas) S(tearns)
1888-1965 ...... **CLC 1, 2, 3, 6, 9, 10, 13, 15, 24, 34, 41, 55, 57, 113; PC 5, 31; WLC**
See also AAYA 28; AMW; AMWC 1; AMWR 1; BRW 7; BRWR 2; CA 5-8R; 25-28R; CANR 41; CBD; CDALB 1929-1941; DA; DA3; DAB; DAC; DAM DRAM, MST, POET; DFS 4, 13; DLB 7, 10, 45, 63, 245; DLBY 1988; EWL 3; EXPP; LAIT 3; LATS 1:1; LMFS 2; MAL 5; MTCW 1, 2; MTFW 2005; NCFS 5; PAB; PFS 1, 7, 20; RGAL 4; RGEL 2; TUS; WLIT 4; WP
Elisabeth of Schönau c.
1129-1165 .... **CMLC 82**
Elizabeth 1866-1941 .... **TCLC 41**
Elizabeth I 1533-1603 .... **LC 118**
See also DLB 136
Elkin, Stanley L(awrence)
1930-1995 .. **CLC 4, 6, 9, 14, 27, 51, 91; SSC 12**
See also AMWS 6; BPFB 1; CA 9-12R; 148; CANR 8, 46; CN 1, 2, 3, 4, 5, 6; CPW; DAM NOV, POP; DLB 2, 28, 218, 278; DLBY 1980; EWL 3; INT CANR-8; MAL 5; MTCW 1, 2; MTFW 2005; RGAL 4; TCLE 1:1
Elledge, Scott .... **CLC 34**
Eller, Scott
See Shepard, James R.
Elliott, Don
See Silverberg, Robert

Elliott, George P(aul) 1918-1980 .... **CLC 2**
See also CA 1-4R; 97-100; CANR 2; CN 1, 2; CP 3; DLB 244; MAL 5
Elliott, Janice 1931-1995 .... **CLC 47**
See also CA 13-16R; CANR 8, 29, 84; CN 5, 6, 7; DLB 14; SATA 119
Elliott, Sumner Locke 1917-1991 ..... **CLC 38**
See also CA 5-8R; 134; CANR 2, 21; DLB 289
Elliott, William
See Bradbury, Ray (Douglas)
Ellis, A. E. .... **CLC 7**
Ellis, Alice Thomas .... **CLC 40**
See Haycraft, Anna (Margaret)
See also CN 4, 5, 6; DLB 194
Ellis, Bret Easton 1964- ...... **CLC 39, 71, 117**
See also AAYA 2, 43; CA 118; 123; CANR 51, 74, 126; CN 6, 7; CPW; DA3; DAM POP; DLB 292; HGG; INT CA-123; MTCW 2; MTFW 2005; NFS 11
Ellis, (Henry) Havelock
1859-1939 .... **TCLC 14**
See also CA 109; 169; DLB 190
Ellis, Landon
See Ellison, Harlan (Jay)
Ellis, Trey 1962- .... **CLC 55**
See also CA 146; CANR 92; CN 7
Ellison, Harlan (Jay) 1934- ... **CLC 1, 13, 42, 139; SSC 14**
See also AAYA 29; BPFB 1; BYA 14; CA 5-8R; CANR 5, 46, 115; CPW; DAM POP; DLB 8; HGG; INT CANR-5; MTCW 1, 2; MTFW 2005; SCFW 2; SFW 4; SSFS 13, 14, 15, 21; SUFW 1, 2
Ellison, Ralph (Waldo) 1914-1994 .... **BLC 1; CLC 1, 3, 11, 54, 86, 114; SSC 26, 79; WLC**
See also AAYA 19; AFAW 1, 2; AMWC 2; AMWR 2; AMWS 2; BPFB 1; BW 1, 3; BYA 2; CA 9-12R; 145; CANR 24, 53; CDALB 1941-1968; CN 1, 2, 3, 4, 5; CSW; DA; DA3; DAB; DAC; DAM MST, MULT, NOV; DLB 2, 76, 227; DLBY 1994; EWL 3; EXPN; EXPS; LAIT 4; MAL 5; MTCW 1, 2; MTFW 2005; NCFS 3; NFS 2, 21; RGAL 4; RGSF 2; SSFS 1, 11; YAW
Ellmann, Lucy (Elizabeth) 1956- ..... **CLC 61**
See also CA 128
Ellmann, Richard (David)
1918-1987 .... **CLC 50**
See also BEST 89:2; CA 1-4R; 122; CANR 2, 28, 61; DLB 103; DLBY 1987; MTCW 1, 2; MTFW 2005
Elman, Richard (Martin)
1934-1997 .... **CLC 19**
See also CA 17-20R; 163; CAAS 3; CANR 47; TCLE 1:1
Elron
See Hubbard, L(afayette) Ron(ald)
El Saadawi, Nawal 1931- .... **CLC 196**
See al'Sadaawi, Nawal; Sa'adawi, al-Nawal; Saadawi, Nawal El; Sa'dawi, Nawal al-
See also CA 118; CAAS 11; CANR 44, 92
Eluard, Paul .... **PC 38; TCLC 7, 41**
See Grindel, Eugene
See also EWL 3; GFL 1789 to the Present; RGWL 2, 3
Elyot, Thomas 1490(?)-1546 .... **LC 11**
See also DLB 136; RGEL 2
Elytis, Odysseus 1911-1996 .... **CLC 15, 49, 100; PC 21**
See Alepoudelis, Odysseus
See also CA 102; 151; CANR 94; CWW 2; DAM POET; EW 13; EWL 3; MTCW 1, 2; RGWL 2, 3

Emecheta, (Florence Onye) Buchi
1944- ...... **BLC 2; CLC 14, 48, 128, 214**
See also AAYA 67; AFW; BW 2, 3; CA 81-84; CANR 27, 81, 126; CDWLB 3; CN 4, 5, 6, 7; CWRI 5; DA3; DAM MULT; DLB 117; EWL 3; FL 1:5; FW; MTCW 1, 2; MTFW 2005; NFS 12, 14; SATA 66; WLIT 2

Emerson, Mary Moody
1774-1863 .... **NCLC 66**

Emerson, Ralph Waldo 1803-1882 . **NCLC 1, 38, 98; PC 18; WLC**
See also AAYA 60; AMW; ANW; CDALB 1640-1865; DA; DA3; DAB; DAC; DAM MST, POET; DLB 1, 59, 73, 183, 223, 270; EXPP; LAIT 2; LMFS 1; NCFS 3; PFS 4, 17; RGAL 4; TUS; WP

Eminescu, Mihail 1850-1889 .. **NCLC 33, 131**

Empedocles 5th cent. B.C.- .... **CMLC 50**
See also DLB 176

Empson, William 1906-1984 ... **CLC 3, 8, 19, 33, 34**
See also BRWS 2; CA 17-20R; 112; CANR 31, 61; CP 1, 2, 3; DLB 20; EWL 3; MTCW 1, 2; RGEL 2

Enchi, Fumiko (Ueda) 1905-1986 ..... **CLC 31**
See Enchi Fumiko
See also CA 129; 121; FW; MJW

Enchi Fumiko
See Enchi, Fumiko (Ueda)
See also DLB 182; EWL 3

Ende, Michael (Andreas Helmuth)
1929-1995 .... **CLC 31**
See also BYA 5; CA 118; 124; 149; CANR 36, 110; CLR 14; DLB 75; MAICYA 1, 2; MAICYAS 1; SATA 61, 130; SATA-Brief 42; SATA-Obit 86

Endo, Shusaku 1923-1996 ..... **CLC 7, 14, 19, 54, 99; SSC 48; TCLC 152**
See Endo Shusaku
See also CA 29-32R; 153; CANR 21, 54, 131; DA3; DAM NOV; MTCW 1, 2; MTFW 2005; RGSF 2; RGWL 2, 3

Endo Shusaku
See Endo, Shusaku
See also CWW 2; DLB 182; EWL 3

Engel, Marian 1933-1985 .... **CLC 36; TCLC 137**
See also CA 25-28R; CANR 12; CN 2, 3; DLB 53; FW; INT CANR-12

Engelhardt, Frederick
See Hubbard, L(afayette) Ron(ald)

Engels, Friedrich 1820-1895 .. **NCLC 85, 114**
See also DLB 129; LATS 1:1

Enright, D(ennis) J(oseph)
1920-2002 .... **CLC 4, 8, 31**
See also CA 1-4R; 211; CANR 1, 42, 83; CN 1, 2; CP 1, 2, 3, 4, 5, 6, 7; DLB 27; EWL 3; SATA 25; SATA-Obit 140

Ensler, Eve 1953- .... **CLC 212**
See also CA 172; CANR 126

Enzensberger, Hans Magnus
1929- .... **CLC 43; PC 28**
See also CA 116; 119; CANR 103; CWW 2; EWL 3

Ephron, Nora 1941- .... **CLC 17, 31**
See also AAYA 35; AITN 2; CA 65-68; CANR 12, 39, 83; DFS 22

Epicurus 341B.C.-270B.C. .... **CMLC 21**
See also DLB 176

Epsilon
See Betjeman, John

Epstein, Daniel Mark 1948- .... **CLC 7**
See also CA 49-52; CANR 2, 53, 90

Epstein, Jacob 1956- .... **CLC 19**
See also CA 114

Epstein, Jean 1897-1953 .... **TCLC 92**

Epstein, Joseph 1937- .... **CLC 39, 204**
See also AMWS 14; CA 112; 119; CANR 50, 65, 117

Epstein, Leslie 1938- .... **CLC 27**
See also AMWS 12; CA 73-76, 215; CAAE 215; CAAS 12; CANR 23, 69; DLB 299

Equiano, Olaudah 1745(?)-1797 . **BLC 2; LC 16**
See also AFAW 1, 2; CDWLB 3; DAM MULT; DLB 37, 50; WLIT 2

Erasmus, Desiderius 1469(?)-1536 ..... **LC 16, 93**
See also DLB 136; EW 2; LMFS 1; RGWL 2, 3; TWA

Erdman, Paul E(mil) 1932- .... **CLC 25**
See also AITN 1; CA 61-64; CANR 13, 43, 84

Erdrich, (Karen) Louise 1954- .. **CLC 39, 54, 120, 176; NNAL; PC 52**
See also AAYA 10, 47; AMWS 4; BEST 89:1; BPFB 1; CA 114; CANR 41, 62, 118, 138; CDALBS; CN 5, 6, 7; CP 7; CPW; CWP; DA3; DAM MULT, NOV, POP; DLB 152, 175, 206; EWL 3; EXPP; FL 1:5; LAIT 5; LATS 1:2; MAL 5; MTCW 1, 2; MTFW 2005; NFS 5; PFS 14; RGAL 4; SATA 94, 141; SSFS 14; TCWW 2

Erenburg, Ilya (Grigoryevich)
See Ehrenburg, Ilya (Grigoryevich)

Erickson, Stephen Michael 1950-
See Erickson, Steve
See also CA 129; SFW 4

Erickson, Steve .... **CLC 64**
See Erickson, Stephen Michael
See also CANR 60, 68, 136; MTFW 2005; SUFW 2

Erickson, Walter
See Fast, Howard (Melvin)

Ericson, Walter
See Fast, Howard (Melvin)

Eriksson, Buntel
See Bergman, (Ernst) Ingmar

Eriugena, John Scottus c.
810-877 .... **CMLC 65**
See also DLB 115

Ernaux, Annie 1940- .... **CLC 88, 184**
See also CA 147; CANR 93; MTFW 2005; NCFS 3, 5

Erskine, John 1879-1951 .... **TCLC 84**
See also CA 112; 159; DLB 9, 102; FANT

Eschenbach, Wolfram von
See Wolfram von Eschenbach
See also RGWL 3

Eseki, Bruno
See Mphahlele, Ezekiel

Esenin, Sergei (Alexandrovich)
1895-1925 .... **TCLC 4**
See Yesenin, Sergey
See also CA 104; RGWL 2, 3

Eshleman, Clayton 1935- .... **CLC 7**
See also CA 33-36R, 212; CAAE 212; CAAS 6; CANR 93; CP 1, 2, 3, 4, 5, 6, 7; DLB 5

Espriella, Don Manuel Alvarez
See Southey, Robert

Espriu, Salvador 1913-1985 .... **CLC 9**
See also CA 154; 115; DLB 134; EWL 3

Espronceda, Jose de 1808-1842 ..... **NCLC 39**

Esquivel, Laura 1951(?)- ... **CLC 141; HLCS 1**
See also AAYA 29; CA 143; CANR 68, 113; DA3; DNFS 2; LAIT 3; LMFS 2; MTCW 2; MTFW 2005; NFS 5; WLIT 1

Esse, James
See Stephens, James

Esterbrook, Tom
See Hubbard, L(afayette) Ron(ald)

Estleman, Loren D. 1952- .... **CLC 48**
See also AAYA 27; CA 85-88; CANR 27, 74, 139; CMW 4; CPW; DA3; DAM NOV, POP; DLB 226; INT CANR-27; MTCW 1, 2; MTFW 2005; TCWW 1, 2

Etherege, Sir George 1636-1692 . **DC 23; LC 78**
See also BRW 2; DAM DRAM; DLB 80; PAB; RGEL 2

Euclid 306B.C.-283B.C. .... **CMLC 25**

Eugenides, Jeffrey 1960(?)- .... **CLC 81, 212**
See also AAYA 51; CA 144; CANR 120; MTFW 2005

Euripides c. 484B.C.-406B.C. .... **CMLC 23, 51; DC 4; WLCS**
See also AW 1; CDWLB 1; DA; DA3; DAB; DAC; DAM DRAM, MST; DFS 1, 4, 6; DLB 176; LAIT 1; LMFS 1; RGWL 2, 3

Evan, Evin
See Faust, Frederick (Schiller)

Evans, Caradoc 1878-1945 ... **SSC 43; TCLC 85**
See also DLB 162

Evans, Evan
See Faust, Frederick (Schiller)

Evans, Marian
See Eliot, George

Evans, Mary Ann
See Eliot, George
See also NFS 20

Evarts, Esther
See Benson, Sally

Everett, Percival
See Everett, Percival L.
See also CSW

Everett, Percival L. 1956- .... **CLC 57**
See Everett, Percival
See also BW 2; CA 129; CANR 94, 134; CN 7; MTFW 2005

Everson, R(onald) G(ilmour)
1903-1992 .... **CLC 27**
See also CA 17-20R; CP 1, 2, 3, 4; DLB 88

Everson, William (Oliver)
1912-1994 .... **CLC 1, 5, 14**
See Antoninus, Brother
See also BG 1:2; CA 9-12R; 145; CANR 20; CP 2, 3, 4; DLB 5, 16, 212; MTCW 1

Evtushenko, Evgenii Aleksandrovich
See Yevtushenko, Yevgeny (Alexandrovich)
See also CWW 2; RGWL 2, 3

Ewart, Gavin (Buchanan)
1916-1995 .... **CLC 13, 46**
See also BRWS 7; CA 89-92; 150; CANR 17, 46; CP 1, 2, 3, 4; DLB 40; MTCW 1

Ewers, Hanns Heinz 1871-1943 ..... **TCLC 12**
See also CA 109; 149

Ewing, Frederick R.
See Sturgeon, Theodore (Hamilton)

Exley, Frederick (Earl) 1929-1992 .... **CLC 6, 11**
See also AITN 2; BPFB 1; CA 81-84; 138; CANR 117; DLB 143; DLBY 1981

Eynhardt, Guillermo
See Quiroga, Horacio (Sylvestre)

Ezekiel, Nissim (Moses) 1924-2004 .. **CLC 61**
See also CA 61-64; 223; CP 1, 2, 3, 4, 5, 6, 7; EWL 3

Ezekiel, Tish O'Dowd 1943- .... **CLC 34**
See also CA 129

Fadeev, Aleksandr Aleksandrovich
See Bulgya, Alexander Alexandrovich
See also DLB 272

Fadeev, Alexandr Alexandrovich
See Bulgya, Alexander Alexandrovich
See also EWL 3

Fadeyev, A.
See Bulgya, Alexander Alexandrovich

Fadeyev, Alexander .... **TCLC 53**
See Bulgya, Alexander Alexandrovich
Fagen, Donald 1948- .... **CLC 26**
Fainzilberg, Ilya Arnoldovich 1897-1937
See Ilf, Ilya
See also CA 120; 165
Fair, Ronald L. 1932- .... **CLC 18**
See also BW 1; CA 69-72; CANR 25; DLB 33
Fairbairn, Roger
See Carr, John Dickson
Fairbairns, Zoe (Ann) 1948- .... **CLC 32**
See also CA 103; CANR 21, 85; CN 4, 5, 6, 7
Fairfield, Flora
See Alcott, Louisa May
Fairman, Paul W. 1916-1977
See Queen, Ellery
See also CA 114; SFW 4
Falco, Gian
See Papini, Giovanni
Falconer, James
See Kirkup, James
Falconer, Kenneth
See Kornbluth, C(yril) M.
Falkland, Samuel
See Heijermans, Herman
Fallaci, Oriana 1930- .... **CLC 11, 110**
See also CA 77-80; CANR 15, 58, 134; FW; MTCW 1
Faludi, Susan 1959- .... **CLC 140**
See also CA 138; CANR 126; FW; MTCW 2; MTFW 2005; NCFS 3
Faludy, George 1913- .... **CLC 42**
See also CA 21-24R
Faludy, Gyoergy
See Faludy, George
Fanon, Frantz 1925-1961 .... **BLC 2; CLC 74**
See also BW 1; CA 116; 89-92; DAM MULT; DLB 296; LMFS 2; WLIT 2
Fanshawe, Ann 1625-1680 .... **LC 11**
Fante, John (Thomas) 1911-1983 .... **CLC 60; SSC 65**
See also AMWS 11; CA 69-72; 109; CANR 23, 104; DLB 130; DLBY 1983
Far, Sui Sin .... **SSC 62**
See Eaton, Edith Maude
See also SSFS 4
Farah, Nuruddin 1945- ...... **BLC 2; CLC 53, 137**
See also AFW; BW 2, 3; CA 106; CANR 81; CDWLB 3; CN 4, 5, 6, 7; DAM MULT; DLB 125; EWL 3; WLIT 2
Fargue, Leon-Paul 1876(?)-1947 .... **TCLC 11**
See also CA 109; CANR 107; DLB 258; EWL 3
Farigoule, Louis
See Romains, Jules
Farina, Richard 1936(?)-1966 .... **CLC 9**
See also CA 81-84; 25-28R
Farley, Walter (Lorimer) 1915-1989 .... **CLC 17**
See also AAYA 58; BYA 14; CA 17-20R; CANR 8, 29, 84; DLB 22; JRDA; MAI-CYA 1, 2; SATA 2, 43, 132; YAW
Farmer, Philip Jose 1918- .... **CLC 1, 19**
See also AAYA 28; BPFB 1; CA 1-4R; CANR 4, 35, 111; DLB 8; MTCW 1; SATA 93; SCFW 1, 2; SFW 4
Farquhar, George 1677-1707 .... **LC 21**
See also BRW 2; DAM DRAM; DLB 84; RGEL 2
Farrell, J(ames) G(ordon) 1935-1979 .... **CLC 6**
See also CA 73-76; 89-92; CANR 36; CN 1, 2; DLB 14, 271; MTCW 1; RGEL 2; RHW; WLIT 4

Farrell, James T(homas) 1904-1979 . **CLC 1, 4, 8, 11, 66; SSC 28**
See also AMW; BPFB 1; CA 5-8R; 89-92; CANR 9, 61; CN 1, 2; DLB 4, 9, 86; DLBD 2; EWL 3; MAL 5; MTCW 1, 2; MTFW 2005; RGAL 4
Farrell, Warren (Thomas) 1943- ...... **CLC 70**
See also CA 146; CANR 120
Farren, Richard J.
See Betjeman, John
Farren, Richard M.
See Betjeman, John
Fassbinder, Rainer Werner 1946-1982 .... **CLC 20**
See also CA 93-96; 106; CANR 31
Fast, Howard (Melvin) 1914-2003 .. **CLC 23, 131**
See also AAYA 16; BPFB 1; CA 1-4R, 181; 214; CAAE 181; CAAS 18; CANR 1, 33, 54, 75, 98, 140; CMW 4; CN 1, 2, 3, 4, 5, 6, 7; CPW; DAM NOV; DLB 9; INT CANR-33; LATS 1:1; MAL 5; MTCW 2; MTFW 2005; RHW; SATA 7; SATA-Essay 107; TCWW 1, 2; YAW
Faulcon, Robert
See Holdstock, Robert P.
Faulkner, William (Cuthbert) 1897-1962 .... **CLC 1, 3, 6, 8, 9, 11, 14, 18, 28, 52, 68; SSC 1, 35, 42; TCLC 141; WLC**
See also AAYA 7; AMW; AMWR 1; BPFB 1; BYA 5, 15; CA 81-84; CANR 33; CDALB 1929-1941; DA; DA3; DAB; DAC; DAM MST, NOV; DB 9, 11, 44, 102, 316; DLBD 2; DLBY 1986, 1997; EWL 3; EXPN; EXPS; GL 2; LAIT 2; LATS 1:1; LMFS 2; MAL 5; MTCW 1, 2; MTFW 2005; NFS 4, 8, 13; RGAL 4; RGSF; SSFS 2, 5, 6, 12; TUS
Fauset, Jessie Redmon 1882(?)-1961 .. **BLC 2; CLC 19, 54; HR 1:2**
See also AFAW 2; BW 1; CA 109; CANR 83; DAM MULT; DLB 51; FW; LMFS 2; MAL 5; MAWW
Faust, Frederick (Schiller) 1892-1944 .... **TCLC 49**
See Brand, Max; Dawson, Peter; Frederick, John
See also CA 108; 152; CANR 143; DAM POP; DLB 256; TUS
Faust, Irvin 1924- .... **CLC 8**
See also CA 33-36R; CANR 28, 67; CN 1, 2, 3, 4, 5, 6, 7; DLB 2, 28, 218, 278; DLBY 1980
Faustino, Domingo 1811-1888 ...... **NCLC 123**
Fawkes, Guy
See Benchley, Robert (Charles)
Fearing, Kenneth (Flexner) 1902-1961 .... **CLC 51**
See also CA 93-96; CANR 59; CMW 4; DLB 9; MAL 5; RGAL 4
Fecamps, Elise
See Creasey, John
Federman, Raymond 1928- .... **CLC 6, 47**
See also CA 17-20R, 208; CAAE 208; CAAS 8; CANR 10, 43, 83, 108; CN 3, 4, 5, 6; DLBY 1980
Federspiel, J(uerg) F. 1931- .... **CLC 42**
See also CA 146
Feiffer, Jules (Ralph) 1929- ...... **CLC 2, 8, 64**
See also AAYA 3, 62; CA 17-20R; CAD; CANR 30, 59, 129; CD 5, 6; DAM DRAM; DLB 7, 44; INT CANR-30; MTCW 1; SATA 8, 61, 111, 157
Feige, Hermann Albert Otto Maximilian
See Traven, B.
Feinberg, David B. 1956-1994 .... **CLC 59**
See also CA 135; 147

Feinstein, Elaine 1930- .... **CLC 36**
See also CA 69-72; CAAS 1; CANR 31, 68, 121; CN 3, 4, 5, 6, 7; CP 2, 3, 4, 5, 6, 7; CWP; DLB 14, 40; MTCW 1
Feke, Gilbert David .... **CLC 65**
Feldman, Irving (Mordecai) 1928- ..... **CLC 7**
See also CA 1-4R; CANR 1; CP 1, 2, 3, 4, 5, 6, 7; DLB 169; TCLE 1:1
Felix-Tchicaya, Gerald
See Tchicaya, Gerald Felix
Fellini, Federico 1920-1993 .... **CLC 16, 85**
See also CA 65-68; 143; CANR 33
Felltham, Owen 1602(?)-1668 .... **LC 92**
See also DLB 126, 151
Felsen, Henry Gregor 1916-1995 ...... **CLC 17**
See also CA 1-4R; 180; CANR 1; SAAS 2; SATA 1
Felski, Rita .... **CLC 65**
Fenno, Jack
See Calisher, Hortense
Fenollosa, Ernest (Francisco) 1853-1908 .... **TCLC 91**
Fenton, James Martin 1949- .... **CLC 32, 209**
See also CA 102; CANR 108; CP 2, 3, 4, 5, 6, 7; DLB 40; PFS 11
Ferber, Edna 1887-1968 .... **CLC 18, 93**
See also AITN 1; CA 5-8R; 25-28R; CANR 68, 105; DLB 9, 28, 86, 266; MAL 5; MTCW 1, 2; MTFW 2005; RGAL 4; RHW; SATA 7; TCWW 1, 2
Ferdowsi, Abu'l Qasem 940-1020(?) .... **CMLC 43**
See Firdawsi, Abu al-Qasim
See also RGWL 2, 3
Ferguson, Helen
See Kavan, Anna
Ferguson, Niall 1964- .... **CLC 134**
See also CA 190
Ferguson, Samuel 1810-1886 .... **NCLC 33**
See also DLB 32; RGEL 2
Fergusson, Robert 1750-1774 .... **LC 29**
See also DLB 109; RGEL 2
Ferling, Lawrence
See Ferlinghetti, Lawrence (Monsanto)
Ferlinghetti, Lawrence (Monsanto) 1919(?)- ...... **CLC 2, 6, 10, 27, 111; PC 1**
See also BG 1:2; CA 5-8R; CAD; CANR 3, 41, 73, 125; CDALB 1941-1968; CP 1, 2, 3, 4, 5, 6, 7; DA3; DAM POET; DLB 5, 16; MAL 5; MTCW 1, 2; MTFW 2005; RGAL 4; WP
Fern, Fanny
See Parton, Sara Payson Willis
Fernandez, Vicente Garcia Huidobro
See Huidobro Fernandez, Vicente Garcia
Fernandez-Armesto, Felipe .... **CLC 70**
Fernandez de Lizardi, Jose Joaquin
See Lizardi, Jose Joaquin Fernandez de
Ferre, Rosario 1938- ...... **CLC 139; HLCS 1; SSC 36**
See also CA 131; CANR 55, 81, 134; CWW 2; DLB 145; EWL 3; HW 1; LAWS 1; MTCW 2; MTFW 2005; WLIT 1
Ferrer, Gabriel (Francisco Victor) Miro
See Miro (Ferrer), Gabriel (Francisco Victor)
Ferrier, Susan (Edmonstone) 1782-1854 .... **NCLC 8**
See also DLB 116; RGEL 2
Ferrigno, Robert 1948(?)- .... **CLC 65**
See also CA 140; CANR 125
Ferron, Jacques 1921-1985 .... **CLC 94**
See also CA 117; 129; CCA 1; DAC; DLB 60; EWL 3
Feuchtwanger, Lion 1884-1958 .... **TCLC 3**
See also CA 104; 187; DLB 66; EWL 3
Feuerbach, Ludwig 1804-1872 ..... **NCLC 139**
See also DLB 133

Feuillet, Octave 1821-1890 .... **NCLC 45**
See also DLB 192
Feydeau, Georges (Leon Jules Marie)
1862-1921 .... **TCLC 22**
See also CA 113; 152; CANR 84; DAM DRAM; DLB 192; EWL 3; GFL 1789 to the Present; RGWL 2, 3
Fichte, Johann Gottlieb
1762-1814 .... **NCLC 62**
See also DLB 90
Ficino, Marsilio 1433-1499 .... **LC 12**
See also LMFS 1
Fiedeler, Hans
See Doeblin, Alfred
Fiedler, Leslie A(aron) 1917-2003 ..... **CLC 4, 13, 24**
See also AMWS 13; CA 9-12R; 212; CANR 7, 63; CN 1, 2, 3, 4, 5, 6; DLB 28, 67; EWL 3; MAL 5; MTCW 1, 2; RGAL 4; TUS
Field, Andrew 1938- .... **CLC 44**
See also CA 97-100; CANR 25
Field, Eugene 1850-1895 .... **NCLC 3**
See also DLB 23, 42, 140; DLBD 13; MAICYA 1, 2; RGAL 4; SATA 16
Field, Gans T.
See Wellman, Manly Wade
Field, Michael 1915-1971 .... **TCLC 43**
See also CA 29-32R
Fielding, Helen 1958- .... **CLC 146, 217**
See also AAYA 65; CA 172; CANR 127; DLB 231; MTFW 2005
Fielding, Henry 1707-1754 .... **LC 1, 46, 85; WLC**
See also BRW 3; BRWR 1; CDBLB 1660-1789; DA; DA3; DAB; DAC; DAM DRAM, MST, NOV; DLB 39, 84, 101; NFS 18; RGEL 2; TEA; WLIT 3
Fielding, Sarah 1710-1768 .... **LC 1, 44**
See also DLB 39; RGEL 2; TEA
Fields, W. C. 1880-1946 .... **TCLC 80**
See also DLB 44
Fierstein, Harvey (Forbes) 1954- ..... **CLC 33**
See also CA 123; 129; CAD; CD 5, 6; CPW; DA3; DAM DRAM, POP; DFS 6; DLB 266; GLL; MAL 5
Figes, Eva 1932- .... **CLC 31**
See also CA 53-56; CANR 4, 44, 83; CN 2, 3, 4, 5, 6, 7; DLB 14, 271; FW
Filippo, Eduardo de
See de Filippo, Eduardo
Finch, Anne 1661-1720 .... **LC 3; PC 21**
See also BRWS 9; DLB 95
Finch, Robert (Duer Claydon)
1900-1995 .... **CLC 18**
See also CA 57-60; CANR 9, 24, 49; CP 1, 2, 3, 4; DLB 88
Findley, Timothy (Irving Frederick)
1930-2002 .... **CLC 27, 102**
See also CA 25-28R; 206; CANR 12, 42, 69, 109; CCA 1; CN 4, 5, 6, 7; DAC; DAM MST; DLB 53; FANT; RHW
Fink, William
See Mencken, H(enry) L(ouis)
Firbank, Louis 1942-
See Reed, Lou
See also CA 117
Firbank, (Arthur Annesley) Ronald
1886-1926 .... **TCLC 1**
See also BRWS 2; CA 104; 177; DLB 36; EWL 3; RGEL 2
Firdawsi, Abu al-Qasim
See Ferdowsi, Abu'l Qasem
See also WLIT 6
Fish, Stanley
See Fish, Stanley Eugene
Fish, Stanley E.
See Fish, Stanley Eugene

Fish, Stanley Eugene 1938- .... **CLC 142**
See also CA 112; 132; CANR 90; DLB 67
Fisher, Dorothy (Frances) Canfield
1879-1958 .... **TCLC 87**
See also CA 114; 136; CANR 80; CLR 71; CWRI 5; DLB 9, 102, 284; MAICYA 1, 2; MAL 5; YABC 1
Fisher, M(ary) F(rances) K(ennedy)
1908-1992 .... **CLC 76, 87**
See also CA 77-80; 138; CANR 44; MTCW 2
Fisher, Roy 1930- .... **CLC 25**
See also CA 81-84; CAAS 10; CANR 16; CP 1, 2, 3, 4, 5, 6, 7; DLB 40
Fisher, Rudolph 1897-1934 . **BLC 2; HR 1:2; SSC 25; TCLC 11**
See also BW 1, 3; CA 107; 124; CANR 80; DAM MULT; DLB 51, 102
Fisher, Vardis (Alvero) 1895-1968 ..... **CLC 7; TCLC 140**
See also CA 5-8R; 25-28R; CANR 68; DLB 9, 206; MAL 5; RGAL 4; TCWW 1, 2
Fiske, Tarleton
See Bloch, Robert (Albert)
Fitch, Clarke
See Sinclair, Upton (Beall)
Fitch, John IV
See Cormier, Robert (Edmund)
Fitzgerald, Captain Hugh
See Baum, L(yman) Frank
FitzGerald, Edward 1809-1883 .... **NCLC 9, 153**
See also BRW 4; DLB 32; RGEL 2
Fitzgerald, F(rancis) Scott (Key)
1896-1940 ... **SSC 6, 31, 75; TCLC 1, 6, 14, 28, 55, 157; WLC**
See also AAYA 24; AITN 1; AMW; AMWC 2; AMWR 1; BPFB 1; CA 110; 123; CDALB 1917-1929; DA; DA3; DAB; DAC; DAM MST, NOV; DLB 4, 9, 86, 219, 273; DLBD 1, 15, 16; DLBY 1981, 1996; EWL 3; EXPN; EXPS; LAIT 3; MAL 5; MTCW 1, 2; MTFW 2005; NFS 2, 19, 20; RGAL 4; RGSF 2; SSFS 4, 15, 21; TUS
Fitzgerald, Penelope 1916-2000 . **CLC 19, 51, 61, 143**
See also BRWS 5; CA 85-88; 190; CAAS 10; CANR 56, 86, 131; CN 3, 4, 5, 6, 7; DLB 14, 194; EWL 3; MTCW 2; MTFW 2005
Fitzgerald, Robert (Stuart)
1910-1985 .... **CLC 39**
See also CA 1-4R; 114; CANR 1; CP 1, 2, 3, 4; DLBY 1980; MAL 5
FitzGerald, Robert D(avid)
1902-1987 .... **CLC 19**
See also CA 17-20R; CP 1, 2, 3, 4; DLB 260; RGEL 2
Fitzgerald, Zelda (Sayre)
1900-1948 .... **TCLC 52**
See also AMWS 9; CA 117; 126; DLBY 1984
Flanagan, Thomas (James Bonner)
1923-2002 .... **CLC 25, 52**
See also CA 108; 206; CANR 55; CN 3, 4, 5, 6, 7; DLBY 1980; INT CA-108; MTCW 1; RHW; TCLE 1:1
Flaubert, Gustave 1821-1880 .... **NCLC 2, 10, 19, 62, 66, 135; SSC 11, 60; WLC**
See also DA; DA3; DAB; DAC; DAM MST, NOV; DLB 119, 301; EW 7; EXPS; GFL 1789 to the Present; LAIT 2; LMFS 1; NFS 14; RGSF 2; RGWL 2, 3; SSFS 6; TWA
Flavius Josephus
See Josephus, Flavius
Flecker, Herman Elroy
See Flecker, (Herman) James Elroy

Flecker, (Herman) James Elroy
1884-1915 .... **TCLC 43**
See also CA 109; 150; DLB 10, 19; RGEL 2
Fleming, Ian (Lancaster) 1908-1964 . **CLC 3, 30**
See also AAYA 26; BPFB 1; CA 5-8R; CANR 59; CDBLB 1945-1960; CMW 4; CPW; DA3; DAM POP; DLB 87, 201; MSW; MTCW 1, 2; MTFW 2005; RGEL 2; SATA 9; TEA; YAW
Fleming, Thomas (James) 1927- ...... **CLC 37**
See also CA 5-8R; CANR 10, 102; INT CANR-10; SATA 8
Fletcher, John 1579-1625 .... **DC 6; LC 33**
See also BRW 2; CDBLB Before 1660; DLB 58; RGEL 2; TEA
Fletcher, John Gould 1886-1950 .... **TCLC 35**
See also CA 107; 167; DLB 4, 45; LMFS 2; MAL 5; RGAL 4
Fleur, Paul
See Pohl, Frederik
Flieg, Helmut
See Heym, Stefan
Flooglebuckle, Al
See Spiegelman, Art
Flora, Fletcher 1914-1969
See Queen, Ellery
See also CA 1-4R; CANR 3, 85
Flying Officer X
See Bates, H(erbert) E(rnest)
Fo, Dario 1926- .... **CLC 32, 109; DC 10**
See also CA 116; 128; CANR 68, 114, 134; CWW 2; DA3; DAM DRAM; DLBY 1997; EWL 3; MTCW 1, 2; MTFW 2005; WLIT 7
Fogarty, Jonathan Titulescu Esq.
See Farrell, James T(homas)
Follett, Ken(neth Martin) 1949- .... **CLC 18**
See also AAYA 6, 50; BEST 89:4; BPFB 1; CA 81-84; CANR 13, 33, 54, 102; CMW 4; CPW; DA3; DAM NOV, POP; DLB 87; DLBY 1981; INT CANR-33; MTCW 1
Fondane, Benjamin 1898-1944 ..... **TCLC 159**
Fontane, Theodor 1819-1898 . **NCLC 26, 163**
See also CDWLB 2; DLB 129; EW 6; RGWL 2, 3; TWA
Fonte, Moderata 1555-1592 .... **LC 118**
Fontenot, Chester .... **CLC 65**
Fonvizin, Denis Ivanovich
1744(?)-1792 .... **LC 81**
See also DLB 150; RGWL 2, 3
Foote, Horton 1916- .... **CLC 51, 91**
See also CA 73-76; CAD; CANR 34, 51, 110; CD 5, 6; CSW; DA3; DAM DRAM; DFS 20; DLB 26, 266; EWL 3; INT CANR-34; MTFW 2005
Foote, Mary Hallock 1847-1938 .. **TCLC 108**
See also DLB 186, 188, 202, 221; TCWW 2
Foote, Samuel 1721-1777 .... **LC 106**
See also DLB 89; RGEL 2
Foote, Shelby 1916-2005 .... **CLC 75**
See also AAYA 40; CA 5-8R; 240; CANR 3, 45, 74, 131; CN 1, 2, 3, 4, 5, 6, 7; CPW; CSW; DA3; DAM NOV, POP; DLB 2, 17; MAL 5; MTCW 2; MTFW 2005; RHW
Forbes, Cosmo
See Lewton, Val
Forbes, Esther 1891-1967 .... **CLC 12**
See also AAYA 17; BYA 2; CA 13-14; 25-28R; CAP 1; CLR 27; DLB 22; JRDA; MAICYA 1, 2; RHW; SATA 2, 100; YAW

Forche, Carolyn (Louise) 1950- .... **CLC 25, 83, 86; PC 10**
See also CA 109; 117; CANR 50, 74, 138; CP 4, 5, 6, 7; CWP; DA3; DAM POET; DLB 5, 193; INT CA-117; MAL 5; MTCW 2; MTFW 2005; PFS 18; RGAL 4

Ford, Elbur
See Hibbert, Eleanor Alice Burford

Ford, Ford Madox 1873-1939 ... **TCLC 1, 15, 39, 57, 172**
See Chaucer, Daniel
See also BRW 6; CA 104; 132; CANR 74; CDBLB 1914-1945; DA3; DAM NOV; DLB 34, 98, 162; EWL 3; MTCW 1, 2; RGEL 2; TEA

Ford, Henry 1863-1947 .... **TCLC 73**
See also CA 115; 148

Ford, Jack
See Ford, John

Ford, John 1586-1639 .... **DC 8; LC 68**
See also BRW 2; CDBLB Before 1660; DA3; DAM DRAM; DFS 7; DLB 58; IDTP; RGEL 2

Ford, John 1895-1973 .... **CLC 16**
See also CA 187; 45-48

Ford, Richard 1944- .... **CLC 46, 99, 205**
See also AMWS 5; CA 69-72; CANR 11, 47, 86, 128; CN 5, 6, 7; CSW; DLB 227; EWL 3; MAL 5; MTCW 2; MTFW 2005; RGAL 4; RGSF 2

Ford, Webster
See Masters, Edgar Lee

Foreman, Richard 1937- .... **CLC 50**
See also CA 65-68; CAD; CANR 32, 63, 143; CD 5, 6

Forester, C(ecil) S(cott) 1899-1966 . **CLC 35; TCLC 152**
See also CA 73-76; 25-28R; CANR 83; DLB 191; RGEL 2; RHW; SATA 13

Forez
See Mauriac, Francois (Charles)

Forman, James
See Forman, James D(ouglas)

Forman, James D(ouglas) 1932- .... **CLC 21**
See also AAYA 17; CA 9-12R; CANR 4, 19, 42; JRDA; MAICYA 1, 2; SATA 8, 70; YAW

Forman, Milos 1932- .... **CLC 164**
See also AAYA 63; CA 109

Fornes, Maria Irene 1930- .... **CLC 39, 61, 187; DC 10; HLCS 1**
See also CA 25-28R; CAD; CANR 28, 81; CD 5, 6; CWD; DLB 7; HW 1, 2; INT CANR-28; LLW; MAL 5; MTCW 1; RGAL 4

Forrest, Leon (Richard) 1937-1997 .... **BLCS; CLC 4**
See also AFAW 2; BW 2; CA 89-92; 162; CAAS 7; CANR 25, 52, 87; CN 4, 5, 6; DLB 33

Forster, E(dward) M(organ) 1879-1970 ...... **CLC 1, 2, 3, 4, 9, 10, 13, 15, 22, 45, 77; SSC 27; TCLC 125; WLC**
See also AAYA 2, 37; BRW 6; BRWR 2; BYA 12; CA 13-14; 25-28R; CANR 45; CAP 1; CDBLB 1914-1945; DA; DA3; DAB; DAC; DAM MST, NOV; DLB 34, 98, 162, 178, 195; DLBD 10; EWL 3; EXPN; LAIT 3; LMFS 1; MTCW 1, 2; MTFW 2005; NCFS 1; NFS 3, 10, 11; RGEL 2; RGSF 2; SATA 57; SUFW 1; TEA; WLIT 4

Forster, John 1812-1876 .... **NCLC 11**
See also DLB 144, 184

Forster, Margaret 1938- .... **CLC 149**
See also CA 133; CANR 62, 115; CN 4, 5, 6, 7; DLB 155, 271

Forsyth, Frederick 1938- .... **CLC 2, 5, 36**
See also BEST 89:4; CA 85-88; CANR 38, 62, 115, 137; CMW; CN 3, 4, 5, 6, 7; CPW; DAM NOV, POP; DLB 87; MTCW 1, 2; MTFW 2005

Forten, Charlotte L. 1837-1914 .... **BLC 2; TCLC 16**
See Grimke, Charlotte L(ottie) Forten
See also DLB 50, 239

Fortinbras
See Grieg, (Johan) Nordahl (Brun)

Foscolo, Ugo 1778-1827 .... **NCLC 8, 97**
See also EW 5; WLIT 7

Fosse, Bob .... **CLC 20**
See Fosse, Robert Louis

Fosse, Robert Louis 1927-1987
See Fosse, Bob
See also CA 110; 123

Foster, Hannah Webster 1758-1840 .... **NCLC 99**
See also DLB 37, 200; RGAL 4

Foster, Stephen Collins 1826-1864 .... **NCLC 26**
See also RGAL 4

Foucault, Michel 1926-1984 . **CLC 31, 34, 69**
See also CA 105; 113; CANR 34; DLB 242; EW 13; EWL 3; GFL 1789 to the Present; GLL 1; LMFS 2; MTCW 1, 2; TWA

Fouque, Friedrich (Heinrich Karl) de la Motte 1777-1843 .... **NCLC 2**
See also DLB 90; RGWL 2, 3; SUFW 1

Fourier, Charles 1772-1837 .... **NCLC 51**

Fournier, Henri-Alban 1886-1914
See Alain-Fournier
See also CA 104; 179

Fournier, Pierre 1916-1997 .... **CLC 11**
See Gascar, Pierre
See also CA 89-92; CANR 16, 40

Fowles, John (Robert) 1926- . **CLC 1, 2, 3, 4, 6, 9, 10, 15, 33, 87; SSC 33**
See also BPFB 1; BRWS 1; CA 5-8R; CANR 25, 71, 103; CDBLB 1960 to Present; CN 1, 2, 3, 4, 5, 6, 7; DA3; DAB; DAC; DAM MST; DLB 14, 139, 207; EWL 3; HGG; MTCW 1, 2; MTFW 2005; NFS 21; RGEL 2; RHW; SATA 22; TEA; WLIT 4

Fox, Paula 1923- .... **CLC 2, 8, 121**
See also AAYA 3, 37; BYA 3, 8; CA 73-76; CANR 20, 36, 62, 105; CLR 1, 44, 96; DLB 52; JRDA; MAICYA 1, 2; MTCW 1; NFS 12; SATA 17, 60, 120; WYA; YAW

Fox, William Price (Jr.) 1926- .... **CLC 22**
See also CA 17-20R; CAAS 19; CANR 11, 142; CSW; DLB 2; DLBY 1981

Foxe, John 1517(?)-1587 .... **LC 14**
See also DLB 132

Frame, Janet .. **CLC 2, 3, 6, 22, 66, 96; SSC 29**
See Clutha, Janet Paterson Frame
See also CN 1, 2, 3, 4, 5, 6, 7; CP 2, 3, 4; CWP; EWL 3; RGEL 2; RGSF 2; TWA

France, Anatole .... **TCLC 9**
See Thibault, Jacques Anatole Francois
See also DLB 123; EWL 3; GFL 1789 to the Present; RGWL 2, 3; SUFW 1

Francis, Claude .... **CLC 50**
See also CA 192

Francis, Dick
See Francis, Richard Stanley
See also CN 2, 3, 4, 5, 6

Francis, Richard Stanley 1920- ... **CLC 2, 22, 42, 102**
See Francis, Dick
See also AAYA 5, 21; BEST 89:3; BPFB 1; CA 5-8R; CANR 9, 42, 68, 100, 141; CDBLB 1960 to Present; CMW 4; CN 7; DA3; DAM POP; DLB 87; INT CANR-9; MSW; MTCW 1, 2; MTFW 2005

Francis, Robert (Churchill) 1901-1987 .... **CLC 15; PC 34**
See also AMWS 9; CA 1-4R; 123; CANR 1; CP 1, 2, 3, 4; EXPP; PFS 12; TCLE 1:1

Francis, Lord Jeffrey
See Jeffrey, Francis
See also DLB 107

Frank, Anne(lies Marie) 1929-1945 .... **TCLC 17; WLC**
See also AAYA 12; BYA 1; CA 113; 133; CANR 68; CLR 101; DA; DA3; DAB; DAC; DAM MST; LAIT 4; MAICYA 2; MAICYAS 1; MTCW 1, 2; MTFW 2005; NCFS 2; SATA 87; SATA-Brief 42; WYA; YAW

Frank, Bruno 1887-1945 .... **TCLC 81**
See also CA 189; DLB 118; EWL 3

Frank, Elizabeth 1945- .... **CLC 39**
See also CA 121; 126; CANR 78; INT CA-126

Frankl, Viktor E(mil) 1905-1997 ...... **CLC 93**
See also CA 65-68; 161

Franklin, Benjamin
See Hasek, Jaroslav (Matej Frantisek)

Franklin, Benjamin 1706-1790 .... **LC 25; WLCS**
See also AMW; CDALB 1640-1865; DA; DA3; DAB; DAC; DLB 24, 43, 73, 183; LAIT 1; RGAL 4; TUS

Franklin, (Stella Maria Sarah) Miles (Lampe) 1879-1954 .... **TCLC 7**
See also CA 104; 164; DLB 230; FW; MTCW 2; RGEL 2; TWA

Franzen, Jonathan 1959- .... **CLC 202**
See also AAYA 65; CA 129; CANR 105

Fraser, Antonia (Pakenham) 1932- . **CLC 32, 107**
See also AAYA 57; CA 85-88; CANR 44, 65, 119; CMW; DLB 276; MTCW 1, 2; MTFW 2005; SATA-Brief 32

Fraser, George MacDonald 1925- ...... **CLC 7**
See also AAYA 48; CA 45-48, 180; CAAE 180; CANR 2, 48, 74; MTCW 2; RHW

Fraser, Sylvia 1935- .... **CLC 64**
See also CA 45-48; CANR 1, 16, 60; CCA 1

Frayn, Michael 1933- .... **CLC 3, 7, 31, 47, 176; DC 27**
See also BRWC 2; BRWS 7; CA 5-8R; CANR 30, 69, 114, 133; CBD; CD 5, 6; CN 1, 2, 3, 4, 5, 6, 7; DAM DRAM, NOV; DFS 22; DLB 13, 14, 194, 245; FANT; MTCW 1, 2; MTFW 2005; SFW 4

Fraze, Candida (Merrill) 1945- .... **CLC 50**
See also CA 126

Frazer, Andrew
See Marlowe, Stephen

Frazer, J(ames) G(eorge) 1854-1941 .... **TCLC 32**
See also BRWS 3; CA 118; NCFS 5

Frazer, Robert Caine
See Creasey, John

Frazer, Sir James George
See Frazer, J(ames) G(eorge)

Frazier, Charles 1950- .... **CLC 109**
See also AAYA 34; CA 161; CANR 126; CSW; DLB 292; MTFW 2005

Frazier, Ian 1951- .... **CLC 46**
See also CA 130; CANR 54, 93

Frederic, Harold 1856-1898 .... **NCLC 10**
See also AMW; DLB 12, 23; DLBD 13; MAL 5; NFS 22; RGAL 4

Frederick, John
See Faust, Frederick (Schiller)
See also TCWW 2

Frederick the Great 1712-1786 .... **LC 14**
Fredro, Aleksander 1793-1876 .... **NCLC 8**
Freeling, Nicolas 1927-2003 .... **CLC 38**
See also CA 49-52; 218; CAAS 12; CANR 1, 17, 50, 84; CMW 4; CN 1, 2, 3, 4, 5, 6; DLB 87
Freeman, Douglas Southall
1886-1953 .... **TCLC 11**
See also CA 109; 195; DLB 17; DLBD 17
Freeman, Judith 1946- .... **CLC 55**
See also CA 148; CANR 120; DLB 256
Freeman, Mary E(leanor) Wilkins
1852-1930 .... **SSC 1, 47; TCLC 9**
See also CA 106; 177; DLB 12, 78, 221; EXPS; FW; HGG; MAWW; RGAL 4; RGSF 2; SSFS 4, 8; SUFW 1; TUS
Freeman, R(ichard) Austin
1862-1943 .... **TCLC 21**
See also CA 113; CANR 84; CMW 4; DLB 70
French, Albert 1943- .... **CLC 86**
See also BW 3; CA 167
French, Antonia
See Kureishi, Hanif
French, Marilyn 1929- .. **CLC 10, 18, 60, 177**
See also BPFB 1; CA 69-72; CANR 3, 31, 134; CN 5, 6, 7; CPW; DAM DRAM, NOV, POP; FL 1:5; FW; INT CANR-31; MTCW 1, 2; MTFW 2005
French, Paul
See Asimov, Isaac
Freneau, Philip Morin 1752-1832 .. **NCLC 1, 111**
See also AMWS 2; DLB 37, 43; RGAL 4
Freud, Sigmund 1856-1939 .... **TCLC 52**
See also CA 115; 133; CANR 69; DLB 296; EW 8; EWL 3; LATS 1:1; MTCW 1, 2; MTFW 2005; NCFS 3; TWA
Freytag, Gustav 1816-1895 .... **NCLC 109**
See also DLB 129
Friedan, Betty (Naomi) 1921- .... **CLC 74**
See also CA 65-68; CANR 18, 45, 74; DLB 246; FW; MTCW 1, 2; MTFW 2005; NCFS 5
Friedlander, Saul 1932- .... **CLC 90**
See also CA 117; 130; CANR 72
Friedman, B(ernard) H(arper)
1926- .... **CLC 7**
See also CA 1-4R; CANR 3, 48
Friedman, Bruce Jay 1930- ...... **CLC 3, 5, 56**
See also CA 9-12R; CAD; CANR 25, 52, 101; CD 5, 6; CN 1, 2, 3, 4, 5, 6, 7; DLB 2, 28, 244; INT CANR-25; MAL 5; SSFS 18
Friel, Brian 1929- .... **CLC 5, 42, 59, 115; DC 8; SSC 76**
See also BRWS 5; CA 21-24R; CANR 33, 69, 131; CBD; CD 5, 6; DFS 11; DLB 13, 319; EWL 3; MTCW 1; RGEL 2; TEA
Friis-Baastad, Babbis Ellinor
1921-1970 .... **CLC 12**
See also CA 17-20R; 134; SATA 7
Frisch, Max (Rudolf) 1911-1991 ... **CLC 3, 9, 14, 18, 32, 44; TCLC 121**
See also CA 85-88; 134; CANR 32, 74; CDWLB 2; DAM DRAM, NOV; DLB 69, 124; EW 13; EWL 3; MTCW 1, 2; MTFW 2005; RGWL 2, 3
Fromentin, Eugene (Samuel Auguste)
1820-1876 .... **NCLC 10, 125**
See also DLB 123; GFL 1789 to the Present
Frost, Frederick
See Faust, Frederick (Schiller)
Frost, Robert (Lee) 1874-1963 .. **CLC 1, 3, 4, 9, 10, 13, 15, 26, 34, 44; PC 1, 39, 71; WLC**
See also AAYA 21; AMW; AMWR 1; CA 89-92; CANR 33; CDALB 1917-1929; CLR 67; DA; DA3; DAB; DAC; DAM MST, POET; DLB 54, 284; DLBD 7; EWL 3; EXPP; MAL 5; MTCW 1, 2; MTFW 2005; PAB; PFS 1, 2, 3, 4, 5, 6, 7, 10, 13; RGAL 4; SATA 14; TUS; WP; WYA
Froude, James Anthony
1818-1894 .... **NCLC 43**
See also DLB 18, 57, 144
Froy, Herald
See Waterhouse, Keith (Spencer)
Fry, Christopher 1907-2005 ... **CLC 2, 10, 14**
See also BRWS 3; CA 17-20R; 240; CAAS 23; CANR 9, 30, 74, 132; CBD; CD 5, 6; CP 1, 2, 3, 4, 5, 6, 7; DAM DRAM; DLB 13; EWL 3; MTCW 1, 2; MTFW 2005; RGEL 2; SATA 66; TEA
Frye, (Herman) Northrop
1912-1991 .... **CLC 24, 70; TCLC 165**
See also CA 5-8R; 133; CANR 8, 37; DLB 67, 68, 246; EWL 3; MTCW 1, 2; MTFW 2005; RGAL 4; TWA
Fuchs, Daniel 1909-1993 .... **CLC 8, 22**
See also CA 81-84; 142; CAAS 5; CANR 40; CN 1, 2, 3, 4, 5; DLB 9, 26, 28; DLBY 1993; MAL 5
Fuchs, Daniel 1934- .... **CLC 34**
See also CA 37-40R; CANR 14, 48
Fuentes, Carlos 1928- .. **CLC 3, 8, 10, 13, 22, 41, 60, 113; HLC 1; SSC 24; WLC**
See also AAYA 4, 45; AITN 2; BPFB 1; CA 69-72; CANR 10, 32, 68, 104, 138; CDWLB 3; CWW 2; DA; DA3; DAB; DAC; DAM MST, MULT, NOV; DLB 113; DNFS 2; EWL 3; HW 1, 2; LAIT 3; LATS 1:2; LAW; LAWS 1; LMFS 2; MTCW 1, 2; MTFW 2005; NFS 8; RGSF 2; RGWL 2, 3; TWA; WLIT 1
Fuentes, Gregorio Lopez y
See Lopez y Fuentes, Gregorio
Fuertes, Gloria 1918-1998 .... **PC 27**
See also CA 178, 180; DLB 108; HW 2; SATA 115
Fugard, (Harold) Athol 1932- . **CLC 5, 9, 14, 25, 40, 80, 211; DC 3**
See also AAYA 17; AFW; CA 85-88; CANR 32, 54, 118; CD 5, 6; DAM DRAM; DFS 3, 6, 10; DLB 225; DNFS 1, 2; EWL 3; LATS 1:2; MTCW 1; MTFW 2005; RGEL 2; WLIT 2
Fugard, Sheila 1932- .... **CLC 48**
See also CA 125
Fujiwara no Teika 1162-1241 .... **CMLC 73**
See also DLB 203
Fukuyama, Francis 1952- .... **CLC 131**
See also CA 140; CANR 72, 125
Fuller, Charles (H.), (Jr.) 1939- .... **BLC 2; CLC 25; DC 1**
See also BW 2; CA 108; 112; CAD; CANR 87; CD 5, 6; DAM MULT; DFS 8; DLB 38, 266; EWL 3; INT CA-112; MAL 5; MTCW 1
Fuller, Henry Blake 1857-1929 .... **TCLC 103**
See also CA 108; 177; DLB 12; RGAL 4
Fuller, John (Leopold) 1937- .... **CLC 62**
See also CA 21-24R; CANR 9, 44; CP 1, 2, 3, 4, 5, 6, 7; DLB 40
Fuller, Margaret
See Ossoli, Sarah Margaret (Fuller)
See also AMWS 2; DLB 183, 223, 239; FL 1:3
Fuller, Roy (Broadbent) 1912-1991 ... **CLC 4, 28**
See also BRWS 7; CA 5-8R; 135; CAAS 10; CANR 53, 83; CN 1, 2, 3, 4, 5; CP 1, 2, 3, 4; CWRI 5; DLB 15, 20; EWL 3; RGEL 2; SATA 87
Fuller, Sarah Margaret
See Ossoli, Sarah Margaret (Fuller)
Fuller, Sarah Margaret
See Ossoli, Sarah Margaret (Fuller)
See also DLB 1, 59, 73
Fuller, Thomas 1608-1661 .... **LC 111**
See also DLB 151
Fulton, Alice 1952- .... **CLC 52**
See also CA 116; CANR 57, 88; CP 7; CWP; DLB 193
Furphy, Joseph 1843-1912 .... **TCLC 25**
See Collins, Tom
See also CA 163; DLB 230; EWL 3; RGEL 2
Fuson, Robert H(enderson) 1927- .... **CLC 70**
See also CA 89-92; CANR 103
Fussell, Paul 1924- .... **CLC 74**
See also BEST 90:1; CA 17-20R; CANR 8, 21, 35, 69, 135; INT CANR-21; MTCW 1, 2; MTFW 2005
Futabatei, Shimei 1864-1909 .... **TCLC 44**
See Futabatei Shimei
See also CA 162; MJW
Futabatei Shimei
See Futabatei, Shimei
See also DLB 180; EWL 3
Futrelle, Jacques 1875-1912 .... **TCLC 19**
See also CA 113; 155; CMW 4
Gaboriau, Emile 1835-1873 .... **NCLC 14**
See also CMW 4; MSW
Gadda, Carlo Emilio 1893-1973 ...... **CLC 11; TCLC 144**
See also CA 89-92; DLB 177; EWL 3; WLIT 7
Gaddis, William 1922-1998 ... **CLC 1, 3, 6, 8, 10, 19, 43, 86**
See also AMWS 4; BPFB 1; CA 17-20R; 172; CANR 21, 48; CN 1, 2, 3, 4, 5, 6; DLB 2, 278; EWL 3; MAL 5; MTCW 1, 2; MTFW 2005; RGAL 4
Gaelique, Moruen le
See Jacob, (Cyprien-)Max
Gage, Walter
See Inge, William (Motter)
Gaiman, Neil (Richard) 1960- .... **CLC 195**
See also AAYA 19, 42; CA 133; CANR 81, 129; DLB 261; HGG; MTFW 2005; SATA 85, 146; SFW 4; SUFW 2
Gaines, Ernest J(ames) 1933- .. **BLC 2; CLC 3, 11, 18, 86, 181; SSC 68**
See also AAYA 18; AFAW 1, 2; AITN 1; BPFB 2; BW 2, 3; BYA 6; CA 9-12R; CANR 6, 24, 42, 75, 126; CDALB 1968-1988; CLR 62; CN 1, 2, 3, 4, 5, 6, 7; CSW; DA3; DAM MULT; DLB 2, 33, 152; DLBY 1980; EWL 3; EXPN; LAIT 5; LATS 1:2; MAL 5; MTCW 1, 2; MTFW 2005; NFS 5, 7, 16; RGAL 4; RGSF 2; RHW; SATA 86; SSFS 5; YAW
Gaitskill, Mary (Lawrence) 1954- .... **CLC 69**
See also CA 128; CANR 61; DLB 244; TCLE 1:1
Gaius Suetonius Tranquillus
See Suetonius
Galdos, Benito Perez
See Perez Galdos, Benito
See also EW 7
Gale, Zona 1874-1938 .... **TCLC 7**
See also CA 105; 153; CANR 84; DAM DRAM; DFS 17; DLB 9, 78, 228; RGAL 4
Galeano, Eduardo (Hughes) 1940- . **CLC 72; HLCS 1**
See also CA 29-32R; CANR 13, 32, 100; HW 1
Galiano, Juan Valera y Alcala
See Valera y Alcala-Galiano, Juan
Galilei, Galileo 1564-1642 .... **LC 45**
Gallagher, Tess 1943- .... **CLC 18, 63; PC 9**
See also CA 106; CP 3, 4, 5, 6, 7; CWP; DAM POET; DLB 120, 212, 244; PFS 16

Gallant, Mavis 1922- ..... **CLC 7, 18, 38, 172; SSC 5, 78**
See also CA 69-72; CANR 29, 69, 117; CCA 1; CN 1, 2, 3, 4, 5, 6, 7; DAC; DAM MST; DLB 53; EWL 3; MTCW 1, 2; MTFW 2005; RGEL 2; RGSF 2

Gallant, Roy A(rthur) 1924- .... **CLC 17**
See also CA 5-8R; CANR 4, 29, 54, 117; CLR 30; MAICYA 1, 2; SATA 4, 68, 110

Gallico, Paul (William) 1897-1976 ..... **CLC 2**
See also AITN 1; CA 5-8R; 69-72; CANR 23; CN 1, 2; DLB 9, 171; FANT; MAICYA 1, 2; SATA 13

Gallo, Max Louis 1932- .... **CLC 95**
See also CA 85-88

Gallois, Lucien
See Desnos, Robert

Gallup, Ralph
See Whitemore, Hugh (John)

Galsworthy, John 1867-1933 .... **SSC 22; TCLC 1, 45; WLC**
See also BRW 6; CA 104; 141; CANR 75; CDBLB 1890-1914; DA; DA3; DAB; DAC; DAM DRAM, MST, NOV; DLB 10, 34, 98, 162; DLBD 16; EWL 3; MTCW 2; RGEL 2; SSFS 3; TEA

Galt, John 1779-1839 .... **NCLC 1, 110**
See also DLB 99, 116, 159; RGEL 2; RGSF 2

Galvin, James 1951- .... **CLC 38**
See also CA 108; CANR 26

Gamboa, Federico 1864-1939 .... **TCLC 36**
See also CA 167; HW 2; LAW

Gandhi, M. K.
See Gandhi, Mohandas Karamchand

Gandhi, Mahatma
See Gandhi, Mohandas Karamchand

Gandhi, Mohandas Karamchand 1869-1948 .... **TCLC 59**
See also CA 121; 132; DA3; DAM MULT; MTCW 1, 2

Gann, Ernest Kellogg 1910-1991 ..... **CLC 23**
See also AITN 1; BPFB 2; CA 1-4R; 136; CANR 1, 83; RHW

Gao Xingjian 1940- .... **CLC 167**
See Xingjian, Gao
See also MTFW 2005

Garber, Eric 1943(?)-
See Holleran, Andrew
See also CANR 89

Garcia, Cristina 1958- .... **CLC 76**
See also AMWS 11; CA 141; CANR 73, 130; CN 7; DLB 292; DNFS 1; EWL 3; HW 2; LLW; MTFW 2005

Garcia Lorca, Federico 1898-1936 .... **DC 2; HLC 2; PC 3; TCLC 1, 7, 49; WLC**
See Lorca, Federico Garcia
See also AAYA 46; CA 104; 131; CANR 81; DA; DA3; DAB; DAC; DAM DRAM, MST, MULT, POET; DFS 4, 10; DLB 108; EWL 3; HW 1, 2; LATS 1:2; MTCW 1, 2; MTFW 2005; TWA

Garcia Marquez, Gabriel (Jose) 1928- .... **CLC 2, 3, 8, 10, 15, 27, 47, 55, 68, 170; HLC 1; SSC 8, 83; WLC**
See also AAYA 3, 33; BEST 89:1, 90:4; BPFB 2; BYA 12, 16; CA 33-36R; CANR 10, 28, 50, 75, 82, 128; CDWLB 3; CPW; CWW 2; DA; DA3; DAB; DAC; DAM MST, MULT, NOV, POP; DLB 113; DNFS 1, 2; EWL 3; EXPN; EXPS; HW 1, 2; LAIT 2; LATS 1:2; LAW; LAWS 1; LMFS 2; MTCW 1, 2; MTFW 2005; NCFS 3; NFS 1, 5, 10; RGSF 2; RGWL 2, 3; SSFS 1, 6, 16, 21; TWA; WLIT 1

Garcilaso de la Vega, El Inca 1539-1616 .... **HLCS 1**
See also DLB 318; LAW

Gard, Janice
See Latham, Jean Lee

Gard, Roger Martin du
See Martin du Gard, Roger

Gardam, Jane (Mary) 1928- .... **CLC 43**
See also CA 49-52; CANR 2, 18, 33, 54, 106; CLR 12; DLB 14, 161, 231; MAICYA 1, 2; MTCW 1; SAAS 9; SATA 39, 76, 130; SATA-Brief 28; YAW

Gardner, Herb(ert George) 1934-2003 .... **CLC 44**
See also CA 149; 220; CAD; CANR 119; CD 5, 6; DFS 18, 20

Gardner, John (Champlin), Jr. 1933-1982 ...... **CLC 2, 3, 5, 7, 8, 10, 18, 28, 34; SSC 7**
See also AAYA 45; AITN 1; AMWS 6; BPFB 2; CA 65-68; 107; CANR 33, 73; CDALBS; CN 2, 3; CPW; DA3; DAM NOV, POP; DLB 2; DLBY 1982; EWL 3; FANT; LATS 1:2; MAL 5; MTCW 1, 2; MTFW 2005; NFS 3; RGAL 4; RGSF 2; SATA 40; SATA-Obit 31; SSFS 8

Gardner, John (Edmund) 1926- .... **CLC 30**
See also CA 103; CANR 15, 69, 127; CMW 4; CPW; DAM POP; MTCW 1

Gardner, Miriam
See Bradley, Marion Zimmer
See also GLL 1

Gardner, Noel
See Kuttner, Henry

Gardons, S. S.
See Snodgrass, W(illiam) D(e Witt)

Garfield, Leon 1921-1996 .... **CLC 12**
See also AAYA 8; BYA 1, 3; CA 17-20R; 152; CANR 38, 41, 78; CLR 21; DLB 161; JRDA; MAICYA 1, 2; MAICYAS 1; SATA 1, 32, 76; SATA-Obit 90; TEA; WYA; YAW

Garland, (Hannibal) Hamlin 1860-1940 .... **SSC 18; TCLC 3**
See also CA 104; DLB 12, 71, 78, 186; MAL 5; RGAL 4; RGSF 2; TCWW 1, 2

Garneau, (Hector de) Saint-Denys 1912-1943 .... **TCLC 13**
See also CA 111; DLB 88

Garner, Alan 1934- .... **CLC 17**
See also AAYA 18; BYA 3, 5; CA 73-76, 178; CAAE 178; CANR 15, 64, 134; CLR 20; CPW; DAB; DAM POP; DLB 161, 261; FANT; MAICYA 1, 2; MTCW 1, 2; MTFW 2005; SATA 18, 69; SATA-Essay 108; SUFW 1, 2; YAW

Garner, Hugh 1913-1979 .... **CLC 13**
See Warwick, Jarvis
See also CA 69-72; CANR 31; CCA 1; CN 1, 2; DLB 68

Garnett, David 1892-1981 .... **CLC 3**
See also CA 5-8R; 103; CANR 17, 79; CN 1, 2; DLB 34; FANT; MTCW 2; RGEL 2; SFW 4; SUFW 1

Garnier, Robert c. 1545-1590 .... **LC 119**
See also GFL Beginnings to 1789

Garos, Stephanie
See Katz, Steve

Garrett, George (Palmer, Jr.) 1929- . **CLC 3, 11, 51; SSC 30**
See also AMWS 7; BPFB 2; CA 1-4R, 202; CAAE 202; CAAS 5; CANR 1, 42, 67, 109; CN 1, 2, 3, 4, 5, 6, 7; CP 1, 2, 3, 4, 5, 6, 7; CSW; DLB 2, 5, 130, 152; DLBY 1983

Garrick, David 1717-1779 .... **LC 15**
See also DAM DRAM; DLB 84, 213; RGEL 2

Garrigue, Jean 1914-1972 .... **CLC 2, 8**
See also CA 5-8R; 37-40R; CANR 20; CP 1; MAL 5

Garrison, Frederick
See Sinclair, Upton (Beall)

Garrison, William Lloyd 1805-1879 .... **NCLC 149**
See also CDALB 1640-1865; DLB 1, 43, 235

Garro, Elena 1920(?)-1998 .. **HLCS 1; TCLC 153**
See also CA 131; 169; CWW 2; DLB 145; EWL 3; HW 1; LAWS 1; WLIT 1

Garth, Will
See Hamilton, Edmond; Kuttner, Henry

Garvey, Marcus (Moziah, Jr.) 1887-1940 ... **BLC 2; HR 1:2; TCLC 41**
See also BW 1; CA 120; 124; CANR 79; DAM MULT

Gary, Romain .... **CLC 25**
See Kacew, Romain
See also DLB 83, 299

Gascar, Pierre .... **CLC 11**
See Fournier, Pierre
See also EWL 3

Gascoigne, George 1539-1577 .... **LC 108**
See also DLB 136; RGEL 2

Gascoyne, David (Emery) 1916-2001 .... **CLC 45**
See also CA 65-68; 200; CANR 10, 28, 54; CP 1, 2, 3, 4, 5, 6, 7; DLB 20; MTCW 1; RGEL 2

Gaskell, Elizabeth Cleghorn 1810-1865 .... **NCLC 5, 70, 97, 137; SSC 25**
See also BRW 5; CDBLB 1832-1890; DAB; DAM MST; DLB 21, 144, 159; RGEL 2; RGSF 2; TEA

Gass, William H(oward) 1924- . **CLC 1, 2, 8, 11, 15, 39, 132; SSC 12**
See also AMWS 6; CA 17-20R; CANR 30, 71, 100; CN 1, 2, 3, 4, 5, 6, 7; DLB 2, 227; EWL 3; MAL 5; MTCW 1, 2; MTFW 2005; RGAL 4

Gassendi, Pierre 1592-1655 .... **LC 54**
See also GFL Beginnings to 1789

Gasset, Jose Ortega y
See Ortega y Gasset, Jose

Gates, Henry Louis, Jr. 1950- ... **BLCS; CLC 65**
See also BW 2, 3; CA 109; CANR 25, 53, 75, 125; CSW; DA3; DAM MULT; DLB 67; EWL 3; MAL 5; MTCW 2; MTFW 2005; RGAL 4

Gautier, Theophile 1811-1872 .. **NCLC 1, 59; PC 18; SSC 20**
See also DAM POET; DLB 119; EW 6; GFL 1789 to the Present; RGWL 2, 3; SUFW; TWA

Gay, John 1685-1732 .... **LC 49**
See also BRW 3; DAM DRAM; DLB 84, 95; RGEL 2; WLIT 3

Gay, Oliver
See Gogarty, Oliver St. John

Gay, Peter (Jack) 1923- .... **CLC 158**
See also CA 13-16R; CANR 18, 41, 77; INT CANR-18

Gaye, Marvin (Pentz, Jr.) 1939-1984 .... **CLC 26**
See also CA 195; 112

Gebler, Carlo (Ernest) 1954- .... **CLC 39**
See also CA 119; 133; CANR 96; DLB 271

Gee, Maggie (Mary) 1948- .... **CLC 57**
See also CA 130; CANR 125; CN 4, 5, 6, 7; DLB 207; MTFW 2005

Gee, Maurice (Gough) 1931- .... **CLC 29**
See also AAYA 42; CA 97-100; CANR 67, 123; CLR 56; CN 2, 3, 4, 5, 6, 7; CWRI 5; EWL 3; MAICYA 2; RGSF 2; SATA 46, 101

Geiogamah, Hanay 1945- .... **NNAL**
See also CA 153; DAM MULT; DLB 175

Gelbart, Larry
See Gelbart, Larry (Simon)
See also CAD; CD 5, 6

Gelbart, Larry (Simon) 1928- .... **CLC 21, 61**
See Gelbart, Larry
See also CA 73-76; CANR 45, 94

Gelber, Jack 1932-2003 ...... **CLC 1, 6, 14, 79**
See also CA 1-4R; 216; CAD; CANR 2; DLB 7, 228; MAL 5

Gellhorn, Martha (Ellis)
1908-1998 .... **CLC 14, 60**
See also CA 77-80; 164; CANR 44; CN 1, 2, 3, 4, 5, 6 7; DLBY 1982, 1998

Genet, Jean 1910-1986 .. **CLC 1, 2, 5, 10, 14, 44, 46; DC 25; TCLC 128**
See also CA 13-16R; CANR 18; DA3; DAM DRAM; DFS 10; DLB 72, 321; DLBY 1986; EW 13; EWL 3; GFL 1789 to the Present; GLL 1; LMFS 2; MTCW 1, 2; MTFW 2005; RGWL 2, 3; TWA

Gent, Peter 1942- .... **CLC 29**
See also AITN 1; CA 89-92; DLBY 1982

Gentile, Giovanni 1875-1944 .... **TCLC 96**
See also CA 119

Gentlewoman in New England, A
See Bradstreet, Anne

Gentlewoman in Those Parts, A
See Bradstreet, Anne

Geoffrey of Monmouth c.
1100-1155 .... **CMLC 44**
See also DLB 146; TEA

George, Jean
See George, Jean Craighead

George, Jean Craighead 1919- .... **CLC 35**
See also AAYA 8; BYA 2, 4; CA 5-8R; CANR 25; CLR 1; 80; DLB 52; JRDA; MAICYA 1, 2; SATA 2, 68, 124; WYA; YAW

George, Stefan (Anton) 1868-1933 . **TCLC 2, 14**
See also CA 104; 193; EW 8; EWL 3

Georges, Georges Martin
See Simenon, Georges (Jacques Christian)

Gerald of Wales c. 1146-c. 1223 ... **CMLC 60**

Gerhardi, William Alexander
See Gerhardie, William Alexander

Gerhardie, William Alexander
1895-1977 .... **CLC 5**
See also CA 25-28R; 73-76; CANR 18; CN 1, 2; DLB 36; RGEL 2

Gerson, Jean 1363-1429 .... **LC 77**
See also DLB 208

Gersonides 1288-1344 .... **CMLC 49**
See also DLB 115

Gerstler, Amy 1956- .... **CLC 70**
See also CA 146; CANR 99

Gertler, T. .... **CLC 34**
See also CA 116; 121

Gertsen, Aleksandr Ivanovich
See Herzen, Aleksandr Ivanovich

Ghalib .... **NCLC 39, 78**
See Ghalib, Asadullah Khan

Ghalib, Asadullah Khan 1797-1869
See Ghalib
See also DAM POET; RGWL 2, 3

Ghelderode, Michel de 1898-1962 ..... **CLC 6, 11; DC 15**
See also CA 85-88; CANR 40, 77; DAM DRAM; DLB 321; EW 11; EWL 3; TWA

Ghiselin, Brewster 1903-2001 .... **CLC 23**
See also CA 13-16R; CAAS 10; CANR 13; CP 1, 2, 3, 4, 5, 6, 7

Ghose, Aurobindo 1872-1950 .... **TCLC 63**
See Ghose, Aurobindo
See also CA 163

Ghose, Aurobindo
See Ghose, Aurobinda
See also EWL 3

Ghose, Zulfikar 1935- .... **CLC 42, 200**
See also CA 65-68; CANR 67; CN 1, 2, 3, 4, 5, 6, 7; CP 1, 2, 3, 4, 5, 6, 7; EWL 3

Ghosh, Amitav 1956- .... **CLC 44, 153**
See also CA 147; CANR 80; CN 6, 7; WWE 1

Giacosa, Giuseppe 1847-1906 .... **TCLC 7**
See also CA 104

Gibb, Lee
See Waterhouse, Keith (Spencer)

Gibbon, Edward 1737-1794 .... **LC 97**
See also BRW 3; DLB 104; RGEL 2

Gibbon, Lewis Grassic .... **TCLC 4**
See Mitchell, James Leslie
See also RGEL 2

Gibbons, Kaye 1960- .... **CLC 50, 88, 145**
See also AAYA 34; AMWS 10; CA 151; CANR 75, 127; CN 7; CSW; DA3; DAM POP; DLB 292; MTCW 2; MTFW 2005; NFS 3; RGAL 4; SATA 117

Gibran, Kahlil 1883-1931 . **PC 9; TCLC 1, 9**
See also CA 104; 150; DA3; DAM POET, POP; EWL 3; MTCW 2; WLIT 6

Gibran, Khalil
See Gibran, Kahlil

Gibson, Mel 1956- .... **CLC 215**

Gibson, William 1914- .... **CLC 23**
See also CA 9-12R; CAD; CANR 9, 42, 75, 125; CD 5, 6; DA; DAB; DAC; DAM DRAM, MST; DFS 2; DLB 7; LAIT 2; MAL 5; MTCW 2; MTFW 2005; SATA 66; YAW

Gibson, William (Ford) 1948- ... **CLC 39, 63, 186, 192; SSC 52**
See also AAYA 12, 59; BPFB 2; CA 126; 133; CANR 52, 90, 106; CN 6, 7; CPW; DA3; DAM POP; DLB 251; MTCW 2; MTFW 2005; SCFW 2; SFW 4

Gide, Andre (Paul Guillaume)
1869-1951 ...... **SSC 13; TCLC 5, 12, 36, 177; WLC**
See also CA 104; 124; DA; DA3; DAB; DAC; DAM MST, NOV; DLB 65, 321; EW 8; EWL 3; GFL 1789 to the Present; MTCW 1, 2; MTFW 2005; NFS 21; RGSF 2; RGWL 2, 3; TWA

Gifford, Barry (Colby) 1946- .... **CLC 34**
See also CA 65-68; CANR 9, 30, 40, 90

Gilbert, Frank
See De Voto, Bernard (Augustine)

Gilbert, W(illiam) S(chwenck)
1836-1911 .... **TCLC 3**
See also CA 104; 173; DAM DRAM, POET; RGEL 2; SATA 36

Gilbreth, Frank B(unker), Jr.
1911-2001 .... **CLC 17**
See also CA 9-12R; SATA 2

Gilchrist, Ellen (Louise) 1935- .. **CLC 34, 48, 143; SSC 14, 63**
See also BPFB 2; CA 113; 116; CANR 41, 61, 104; CN 4, 5, 6, 7; CPW; CSW; DAM POP; DLB 130; EWL 3; EXPS; MTCW 1, 2; MTFW 2005; RGAL 4; RGSF 2; SSFS 9

Giles, Molly 1942- .... **CLC 39**
See also CA 126; CANR 98

Gill, Eric .... **TCLC 85**
See Gill, (Arthur) Eric (Rowton Peter Joseph)

Gill, (Arthur) Eric (Rowton Peter Joseph)
1882-1940
See Gill, Eric
See also CA 120; DLB 98

Gill, Patrick
See Creasey, John

Gillette, Douglas .... **CLC 70**

Gilliam, Terry (Vance) 1940- .... **CLC 21, 141**
See Monty Python
See also AAYA 19, 59; CA 108; 113; CANR 35; INT CA-113

Gillian, Jerry
See Gilliam, Terry (Vance)

Gilliatt, Penelope (Ann Douglass)
1932-1993 .... **CLC 2, 10, 13, 53**
See also AITN 2; CA 13-16R; 141; CANR 49; CN 1, 2, 3, 4, 5; DLB 14

Gilligan, Carol 1936- .... **CLC 208**
See also CA 142; CANR 121; FW

Gilman, Charlotte (Anna) Perkins (Stetson)
1860-1935 ...... **SSC 13, 62; TCLC 9, 37, 117**
See also AMWS 11; BYA 11; CA 106; 150; DLB 221; EXPS; FL 1:5; FW; HGG; LAIT 2; MAWW; MTCW 2; MTFW 2005; RGAL 4; RGSF 2; SFW 4; SSFS 1, 18

Gilmour, David 1946- .... **CLC 35**

Gilpin, William 1724-1804 .... **NCLC 30**

Gilray, J. D.
See Mencken, H(enry) L(ouis)

Gilroy, Frank D(aniel) 1925- .... **CLC 2**
See also CA 81-84; CAD; CANR 32, 64, 86; CD 5, 6; DFS 17; DLB 7

Gilstrap, John 1957(?)- .... **CLC 99**
See also AAYA 67; CA 160; CANR 101

Ginsberg, Allen 1926-1997 .... **CLC 1, 2, 3, 4, 6, 13, 36, 69, 109; PC 4, 47; TCLC 120; WLC**
See also AAYA 33; AITN 1; AMWC 1; AMWS 2; BG 1:2; CA 1-4R; 157; CANR 2, 41, 63, 95; CDALB 1941-1968; CP 1, 2, 3, 4, 5, 6; DA; DA3; DAB; DAC; DAM MST, POET; DLB 5, 16, 169, 237; EWL 3; GLL 1; LMFS 2; MAL 5; MTCW 1, 2; MTFW 2005; PAB; PFS 5; RGAL 4; TUS; WP

Ginzburg, Eugenia .... **CLC 59**
See Ginzburg, Evgeniia

Ginzburg, Evgeniia 1904-1977
See Ginzburg, Eugenia
See also DLB 302

Ginzburg, Natalia 1916-1991 .... **CLC 5, 11, 54, 70; SSC 65; TCLC 156**
See also CA 85-88; 135; CANR 33; DFS 14; DLB 177; EW 13; EWL 3; MTCW 1, 2; MTFW 2005; RGWL 2, 3

Giono, Jean 1895-1970 .... **CLC 4, 11; TCLC 124**
See also CA 45-48; 29-32R; CANR 2, 35; DLB 72, 321; EWL 3; GFL 1789 to the Present; MTCW 1; RGWL 2, 3

Giovanni, Nikki 1943- ..... **BLC 2; CLC 2, 4, 19, 64, 117; PC 19; WLCS**
See also AAYA 22; AITN 1; BW 2, 3; CA 29-32R; CAAS 6; CANR 18, 41, 60, 91, 130; CDALBS; CLR 6, 73; CP 2, 3, 4, 5, 6, 7; CSW; CWP; CWRI 5; DA; DA3; DAB; DAC; DAM MST, MULT, POET; DLB 5, 41; EWL 3; EXPP; INT CANR-18; MAICYA 1, 2; MAL 5; MTCW 1, 2; MTFW 2005; PFS 17; RGAL 4; SATA 24, 107; TUS; YAW

Giovene, Andrea 1904-1998 .... **CLC 7**
See also CA 85-88

Gippius, Zinaida (Nikolaevna) 1869-1945
See Hippius, Zinaida (Nikolaevna)
See also CA 106; 212

Giraudoux, Jean(-Hippolyte)
1882-1944 .... **TCLC 2, 7**
See also CA 104; 196; DAM DRAM; DLB 65, 321; EW 9; EWL 3; GFL 1789 to the Present; RGWL 2, 3; TWA

Gironella, Jose Maria (Pous)
1917-2003 .... **CLC 11**
See also CA 101; 212; EWL 3; RGWL 2, 3

Gissing, George (Robert)
1857-1903 .... **SSC 37; TCLC 3, 24, 47**
See also BRW 5; CA 105; 167; DLB 18, 135, 184; RGEL 2; TEA

Gitlin, Todd 1943- .... **CLC 201**
See also CA 29-32R; CANR 25, 50, 88

Giurlani, Aldo
See Palazzeschi, Aldo

Gladkov, Fedor Vasil'evich
See Gladkov, Fyodor (Vasilyevich)
See also DLB 272

Gladkov, Fyodor (Vasilyevich)
1883-1958 .... **TCLC 27**
See Gladkov, Fedor Vasil'evich
See also CA 170; EWL 3

Glancy, Diane 1941- .... **CLC 210; NNAL**
See also CA 136, 225; CAAE 225; CAAS 24; CANR 87; DLB 175

Glanville, Brian (Lester) 1931- .... **CLC 6**
See also CA 5-8R; CAAS 9; CANR 3, 70; CN 1, 2, 3, 4, 5, 6, 7; DLB 15, 139; SATA 42

Glasgow, Ellen (Anderson Gholson)
1873-1945 .... **SSC 34; TCLC 2, 7**
See also AMW; CA 104; 164; DLB 9, 12; MAL 5; MAWW; MTCW 2; MTFW 2005; RGEL 4; RHW; SSFS 9; TUS

Glaspell, Susan 1882(?)-1948 ..... **DC 10; SSC 41; TCLC 55, 175**
See also AMWS 3; CA 110; 154; DFS 8, 18; DLB 7, 9, 78, 228; MAWW; RGAL 4; SSFS 3; TCWW 2; TUS; YABC 2

Glassco, John 1909-1981 .... **CLC 9**
See also CA 13-16R; 102; CANR 15; CN 1, 2; CP 1, 2, 3; DLB 68

Glasscock, Amnesia
See Steinbeck, John (Ernst)

Glasser, Ronald J. 1940(?)- .... **CLC 37**
See also CA 209

Glassman, Joyce
See Johnson, Joyce

Gleick, James (W.) 1954- .... **CLC 147**
See also CA 131; 137; CANR 97; INT CA-137

Glendinning, Victoria 1937- .... **CLC 50**
See also CA 120; 127; CANR 59, 89; DLB 155

Glissant, Edouard (Mathieu)
1928- .... **CLC 10, 68**
See also CA 153; CANR 111; CWW 2; DAM MULT; EWL 3; RGWL 3

Gloag, Julian 1930- .... **CLC 40**
See also AITN 1; CA 65-68; CANR 10, 70; CN 1, 2, 3, 4, 5, 6

Glowacki, Aleksander
See Prus, Boleslaw

Gluck, Louise (Elisabeth) 1943- .. **CLC 7, 22, 44, 81, 160; PC 16**
See also AMWS 5; CA 33-36R; CANR 40, 69, 108, 133; CP 1, 2, 3, 4, 5, 6, 7; CWP; DA3; DAM POET; DLB 5; MAL 5; MTCW 2; MTFW 2005; PFS 5, 15; RGAL 4; TCLE 1:1

Glyn, Elinor 1864-1943 .... **TCLC 72**
See also DLB 153; RHW

Gobineau, Joseph-Arthur
1816-1882 .... **NCLC 17**
See also DLB 123; GFL 1789 to the Present

Godard, Jean-Luc 1930- .... **CLC 20**
See also CA 93-96

Godden, (Margaret) Rumer
1907-1998 .... **CLC 53**
See also AAYA 6; BPFB 2; BYA 2, 5; CA 5-8R; 172; CANR 4, 27, 36, 55, 80; CLR 20; CN 1, 2, 3, 4, 5, 6; CWRI 5; DLB 161; MAICYA 1, 2; RHW; SAAS 12; SATA 3, 36; SATA-Obit 109; TEA

Godoy Alcayaga, Lucila 1899-1957 .. **HLC 2; PC 32; TCLC 2**
See Mistral, Gabriela
See also BW 2; CA 104; 131; CANR 81; DAM MULT; DNFS 1; HW 1, 2; MTCW 1, 2; MTFW 2005

Godwin, Gail 1937- .... **CLC 5, 8, 22, 31, 69, 125**
See also BPFB 2; CA 29-32R; CANR 15, 43, 69, 132; CN 3, 4, 5, 6, 7; CPW; CSW; DA3; DAM POP; DLB 6, 234; INT CANR-15; MAL 5; MTCW 1, 2; MTFW 2005

Godwin, Gail Kathleen
See Godwin, Gail

Godwin, William 1756-1836 .. **NCLC 14, 130**
See also CDBLB 1789-1832; CMW 4; DLB 39, 104, 142, 158, 163, 262; GL 2; HGG; RGEL 2

Goebbels, Josef
See Goebbels, (Paul) Joseph

Goebbels, (Paul) Joseph
1897-1945 .... **TCLC 68**
See also CA 115; 148

Goebbels, Joseph Paul
See Goebbels, (Paul) Joseph

Goethe, Johann Wolfgang von
1749-1832 . **DC 20; NCLC 4, 22, 34, 90, 154; PC 5; SSC 38; WLC**
See also CDWLB 2; DA; DA3; DAB; DAC; DAM DRAM, MST, POET; DLB 94; EW 5; GL 2; LATS 1; LMFS 1:1; RGWL 2, 3; TWA

Gogarty, Oliver St. John
1878-1957 .... **TCLC 15**
See also CA 109; 150; DLB 15, 19; RGEL 2

Gogol, Nikolai (Vasilyevich)
1809-1852 .... **DC 1; NCLC 5, 15, 31, 162; SSC 4, 29, 52; WLC**
See also DA; DAB; DAC; DAM DRAM, MST; DFS 12; DLB 198; EW 6; EXPS; RGSF 2; RGWL 2, 3; SSFS 7; TWA

Goines, Donald 1937(?)-1974 ... **BLC 2; CLC 80**
See also AITN 1; BW 1, 3; CA 124; 114; CANR 82; CMW 4; DA3; DAM MULT, POP; DLB 33

Gold, Herbert 1924- ... **CLC 4, 7, 14, 42, 152**
See also CA 9-12R; CANR 17, 45, 125; CN 1, 2, 3, 4, 5, 6, 7; DLB 2; DLBY 1981; MAL 5

Goldbarth, Albert 1948- .... **CLC 5, 38**
See also AMWS 12; CA 53-56; CANR 6, 40; CP 3, 4, 5, 6, 7; DLB 120

Goldberg, Anatol 1910-1982 .... **CLC 34**
See also CA 131; 117

Goldemberg, Isaac 1945- .... **CLC 52**
See also CA 69-72; CAAS 12; CANR 11, 32; EWL 3; HW 1; WLIT 1

Golding, Arthur 1536-1606 .... **LC 101**
See also DLB 136

Golding, William (Gerald)
1911-1993 ..... **CLC 1, 2, 3, 8, 10, 17, 27, 58, 81; WLC**
See also AAYA 5, 44; BPFB 2; BRWR 1; BRWS 1; BYA 2; CA 5-8R; 141; CANR 13, 33, 54; CD 5; CDBLB 1945-1960; CLR 94; CN 1, 2, 3, 4; DA; DA3; DAB; DAC; DAM MST, NOV; DLB 15, 100, 255; EWL 3; EXPN; HGG; LAIT 4; MTCW 1, 2; MTFW 2005; NFS 2; RGEL 2; RHW; SFW 4; TEA; WLIT 4; YAW

Goldman, Emma 1869-1940 .... **TCLC 13**
See also CA 110; 150; DLB 221; FW; RGAL 4; TUS

Goldman, Francisco 1954- .... **CLC 76**
See also CA 162

Goldman, William (W.) 1931- ...... **CLC 1, 48**
See also BPFB 2; CA 9-12R; CANR 29, 69, 106; CN 1, 2, 3, 4, 5, 6, 7; DLB 44; FANT; IDFW 3, 4

Goldmann, Lucien 1913-1970 .... **CLC 24**
See also CA 25-28; CAP 2

Goldoni, Carlo 1707-1793 .... **LC 4**
See also DAM DRAM; EW 4; RGWL 2, 3; WLIT 7

Goldsberry, Steven 1949- .... **CLC 34**
See also CA 131

Goldsmith, Oliver 1730-1774 .... **DC 8; LC 2, 48, 122; WLC**
See also BRW 3; CDBLB 1660-1789; DA; DAB; DAC; DAM DRAM, MST, NOV, POET; DFS 1; DLB 39, 89, 104, 109, 142; IDTP; RGEL 2; SATA 26; TEA; WLIT 3

Goldsmith, Peter
See Priestley, J(ohn) B(oynton)

Gombrowicz, Witold 1904-1969 .... **CLC 4, 7, 11, 49**
See also CA 19-20; 25-28R; CANR 105; CAP 2; CDWLB 4; DAM DRAM; DLB 215; EW 12; EWL 3; RGWL 2, 3; TWA

Gomez de Avellaneda, Gertrudis
1814-1873 .... **NCLC 111**
See also LAW

Gomez de la Serna, Ramon
1888-1963 .... **CLC 9**
See also CA 153; 116; CANR 79; EWL 3; HW 1, 2

Goncharov, Ivan Alexandrovich
1812-1891 .... **NCLC 1, 63**
See also DLB 238; EW 6; RGWL 2, 3

Goncourt, Edmond (Louis Antoine Huot) de
1822-1896 .... **NCLC 7**
See also DLB 123; EW 7; GFL 1789 to the Present; RGWL 2, 3

Goncourt, Jules (Alfred Huot) de
1830-1870 .... **NCLC 7**
See also DLB 123; EW 7; GFL 1789 to the Present; RGWL 2, 3

Gongora (y Argote), Luis de
1561-1627 .... **LC 72**
See also RGWL 2, 3

Gontier, Fernande 19(?)- .... **CLC 50**

Gonzalez Martinez, Enrique
See Gonzalez Martinez, Enrique
See also DLB 290

Gonzalez Martinez, Enrique
1871-1952 .... **TCLC 72**
See Gonzalez Martinez, Enrique
See also CA 166; CANR 81; EWL 3; HW 1, 2

Goodison, Lorna 1947- .... **PC 36**
See also CA 142; CANR 88; CP 7; CWP; DLB 157; EWL 3

Goodman, Paul 1911-1972 ...... **CLC 1, 2, 4, 7**
See also CA 19-20; 37-40R; CAD; CANR 34; CAP 2; CN 1; DLB 130, 246; MAL 5; MTCW 1; RGAL 4

GoodWeather, Harley
See King, Thomas

Googe, Barnabe 1540-1594 .... **LC 94**
See also DLB 132; RGEL 2

Gordimer, Nadine 1923- ...... **CLC 3, 5, 7, 10, 18, 33, 51, 70, 123, 160, 161; SSC 17, 80; WLCS**
See also AAYA 39; AFW; BRWS 2; CA 5-8R; CANR 3, 28, 56, 88, 131; CN 1, 2, 3, 4, 5, 6, 7; DA; DA3; DAB; DAC; DAM MST, NOV; DLB 225; EWL 3; EXPS; INT CANR-28; LATS 1:2; MTCW 1, 2; MTFW 2005; NFS 4; RGEL 2; RGSF 2; SSFS 2, 14, 19; TWA; WLIT 2; YAW

Gordon, Adam Lindsay
1833-1870 .... **NCLC 21**
See also DLB 230

Gordon, Caroline 1895-1981 . **CLC 6, 13, 29, 83; SSC 15**
See also AMW; CA 11-12; 103; CANR 36; CAP 1; CN 1, 2; DLB 4, 9, 102; DLBD 17; DLBY 1981; EWL 3; MAL 5; MTCW 1, 2; MTFW 2005; RGAL 4; RGSF 2

Gordon, Charles William 1860-1937
See Connor, Ralph
See also CA 109

Gordon, Mary (Catherine) 1949- .... **CLC 13, 22, 128, 216; SSC 59**
See also AMWS 4; BPFB 2; CA 102; CANR 44, 92; CN 4, 5, 6, 7; DLB 6; DLBY 1981; FW; INT CA-102; MAL 5; MTCW 1

Gordon, N. J.
See Bosman, Herman Charles

Gordon, Sol 1923- .... **CLC 26**
See also CA 53-56; CANR 4; SATA 11

Gordone, Charles 1925-1995 .. **CLC 1, 4; DC 8**
See also BW 1, 3; CA 93-96, 180; 150; CAAE 180; CAD; CANR 55; DAM DRAM; DLB 7; INT CA-93-96; MTCW 1

Gore, Catherine 1800-1861 .... **NCLC 65**
See also DLB 116; RGEL 2

Gorenko, Anna Andreevna
See Akhmatova, Anna

Gorky, Maxim .... **SSC 28; TCLC 8; WLC**
See Peshkov, Alexei Maximovich
See also DAB; DFS 9; DLB 295; EW 8; EWL 3; TWA

Goryan, Sirak
See Saroyan, William

Gosse, Edmund (William)
1849-1928 .... **TCLC 28**
See also CA 117; DLB 57, 144, 184; RGEL 2

Gotlieb, Phyllis (Fay Bloom) 1926- .. **CLC 18**
See also CA 13-16R; CANR 7, 135; CN 7; CP 1, 2, 3, 4; DLB 88, 251; SFW 4

Gottesman, S. D.
See Kornbluth, C(yril) M.; Pohl, Frederik

Gottfried von Strassburg fl. c.
1170-1215 .... **CMLC 10**
See also CDWLB 2; DLB 138; EW 1; RGWL 2, 3

Gotthelf, Jeremias 1797-1854 .... **NCLC 117**
See also DLB 133; RGWL 2, 3

Gottschalk, Laura Riding
See Jackson, Laura (Riding)

Gould, Lois 1932(?)-2002 .... **CLC 4, 10**
See also CA 77-80; 208; CANR 29; MTCW 1

Gould, Stephen Jay 1941-2002 .... **CLC 163**
See also AAYA 26; BEST 90:2; CA 77-80; 205; CANR 10, 27, 56, 75, 125; CPW; INT CANR-27; MTCW 1, 2; MTFW 2005

Gourmont, Remy(-Marie-Charles) de
1858-1915 .... **TCLC 17**
See also CA 109; 150; GFL 1789 to the Present; MTCW 2

Gournay, Marie le Jars de
See de Gournay, Marie le Jars

Govier, Katherine 1948- .... **CLC 51**
See also CA 101; CANR 18, 40, 128; CCA 1

Gower, John c. 1330-1408 .... **LC 76; PC 59**
See also BRW 1; DLB 146; RGEL 2

Goyen, (Charles) William
1915-1983 .... **CLC 5, 8, 14, 40**
See also AITN 2; CA 5-8R; 110; CANR 6, 71; CN 1, 2, 3; DLB 2, 218; DLBY 1983; EWL 3; INT CANR-6; MAL 5

Goytisolo, Juan 1931- .... **CLC 5, 10, 23, 133; HLC 1**
See also CA 85-88; CANR 32, 61, 131; CWW 2; DAM MULT; DLB 322; EWL 3; GLL 2; HW 1, 2; MTCW 1, 2; MTFW 2005

Gozzano, Guido 1883-1916 .... **PC 10**
See also CA 154; DLB 114; EWL 3

Gozzi, (Conte) Carlo 1720-1806 .... **NCLC 23**

Grabbe, Christian Dietrich
1801-1836 .... **NCLC 2**
See also DLB 133; RGWL 2, 3

Grace, Patricia Frances 1937- .... **CLC 56**
See also CA 176; CANR 118; CN 4, 5, 6, 7; EWL 3; RGSF 2

Gracian y Morales, Baltasar
1601-1658 .... **LC 15**

Gracq, Julien .... **CLC 11, 48**
See Poirier, Louis
See also CWW 2; DLB 83; GFL 1789 to the Present

Grade, Chaim 1910-1982 .... **CLC 10**
See also CA 93-96; 107; EWL 3

Graduate of Oxford, A
See Ruskin, John

Grafton, Garth
See Duncan, Sara Jeannette

Grafton, Sue 1940- .... **CLC 163**
See also AAYA 11, 49; BEST 90:3; CA 108; CANR 31, 55, 111, 134; CMW 4; CPW; CSW; DA3; DAM POP; DLB 226; FW; MSW; MTFW 2005

Graham, John
See Phillips, David Graham

Graham, Jorie 1950- .... **CLC 48, 118; PC 59**
See also AAYA 67; CA 111; CANR 63, 118; CP 4, 5, 6, 7; CWP; DLB 120; EWL 3; MTFW 2005; PFS 10, 17; TCLE 1:1

Graham, R(obert) B(ontine) Cunninghame
See Cunninghame Graham, Robert (Gallnigad) Bontine
See also DLB 98, 135, 174; RGEL 2; RGSF 2

Graham, Robert
See Haldeman, Joe (William)

Graham, Tom
See Lewis, (Harry) Sinclair

Graham, W(illiam) S(idney)
1918-1986 .... **CLC 29**
See also BRWS 7; CA 73-76; 118; CP 1, 2, 3, 4; DLB 20; RGEL 2

Graham, Winston (Mawdsley)
1910-2003 .... **CLC 23**
See also CA 49-52; 218; CANR 2, 22, 45, 66; CMW 4; CN 1, 2, 3, 4, 5, 6, 7; DLB 77; RHW

Grahame, Kenneth 1859-1932 ...... **TCLC 64, 136**
See also BYA 5; CA 108; 136; CANR 80; CLR 5; CWRI 5; DA3; DAB; DLB 34, 141, 178; FANT; MAICYA 1, 2; MTCW 2; NFS 20; RGEL 2; SATA 100; TEA; WCH; YABC 1

Granger, Darius John
See Marlowe, Stephen

Granin, Daniil 1918- .... **CLC 59**
See also DLB 302

Granovsky, Timofei Nikolaevich
1813-1855 .... **NCLC 75**
See also DLB 198

Grant, Skeeter
See Spiegelman, Art

Granville-Barker, Harley
1877-1946 .... **TCLC 2**
See Barker, Harley Granville
See also CA 104; 204; DAM DRAM; RGEL 2

Granzotto, Gianni
See Granzotto, Giovanni Battista

Granzotto, Giovanni Battista
1914-1985 .... **CLC 70**
See also CA 166

Grass, Guenter (Wilhelm) 1927- ... **CLC 1, 2, 4, 6, 11, 15, 22, 32, 49, 88, 207; WLC**
See Grass, Gunter
See also BPFB 2; CA 13-16R; CANR 20, 75, 93, 133; CDWLB 2; DA; DA3; DAB; DAC; DAM MST, NOV; DLB 75, 124; EW 13; EWL 3; MTCW 1, 2; MTFW 2005; RGWL 2, 3; TWA

Grass, Gunter (Wilhelm)
See Grass, Guenter (Wilhelm)
See also CWW 2

Gratton, Thomas
See Hulme, T(homas) E(rnest)

Grau, Shirley Ann 1929- .... **CLC 4, 9, 146; SSC 15**
See also CA 89-92; CANR 22, 69; CN 1, 2, 3, 4, 5, 6, 7; CSW; DLB 2, 218; INT CA-89-92; CANR-22; MTCW 1

Gravel, Fern
See Hall, James Norman

Graver, Elizabeth 1964- .... **CLC 70**
See also CA 135; CANR 71, 129

Graves, Richard Perceval
1895-1985 .... **CLC 44**
See also CA 65-68; CANR 9, 26, 51

Graves, Robert (von Ranke)
1895-1985 .. **CLC 1, 2, 6, 11, 39, 44, 45; PC 6**
See also BPFB 2; BRW 7; BYA 4; CA 5-8R; 117; CANR 5, 36; CDBLB 1914-1945; CN 1, 2, 3; CP 1, 2, 3, 4; DA3; DAB; DAC; DAM MST, POET; DLB 20, 100, 191; DLBD 18; DLBY 1985; EWL 3; LATS 1:1; MTCW 1, 2; MTFW 2005; NCFS 2; NFS 21; RGEL 2; RHW; SATA 45; TEA

Graves, Valerie
See Bradley, Marion Zimmer

Gray, Alasdair (James) 1934- .... **CLC 41**
See also BRWS 9; CA 126; CANR 47, 69, 106, 140; CN 4, 5, 6, 7; DLB 194, 261, 319; HGG; INT CA-126; MTCW 1, 2; MTFW 2005; RGSF 2; SUFW 2

Gray, Amlin 1946- .... **CLC 29**
See also CA 138

Gray, Francine du Plessix 1930- ..... **CLC 22, 153**
See also BEST 90:3; CA 61-64; CAAS 2; CANR 11, 33, 75, 81; DAM NOV; INT CANR-11; MTCW 1, 2; MTFW 2005

Gray, John (Henry) 1866-1934 ...... **TCLC 19**
See also CA 119; 162; RGEL 2

Gray, John Lee
See Jakes, John (William)

Gray, Simon (James Holliday)
1936- .... **CLC 9, 14, 36**
See also AITN 1; CA 21-24R; CAAS 3; CANR 32, 69; CBD; CD 5, 6; CN 1, 2, 3; DLB 13; EWL 3; MTCW 1; RGEL 2

Gray, Spalding 1941-2004 .... **CLC 49, 112; DC 7**
See also AAYA 62; CA 128; 225; CAD; CANR 74, 138; CD 5, 6; CPW; DAM POP; MTCW 2; MTFW 2005

Gray, Thomas 1716-1771 .... **LC 4, 40; PC 2; WLC**
See also BRW 3; CDBLB 1660-1789; DA; DA3; DAB; DAC; DAM MST; DLB 109; EXPP; PAB; PFS 9; RGEL 2; TEA; WP

Grayson, David
See Baker, Ray Stannard

Grayson, Richard (A.) 1951- .... **CLC 38**
See also CA 85-88, 210; CAAE 210; CANR 14, 31, 57; DLB 234

Greeley, Andrew M(oran) 1928- ...... **CLC 28**
See also BPFB 2; CA 5-8R; CAAS 7; CANR 7, 43, 69, 104, 136; CMW 4; CPW; DA3; DAM POP; MTCW 1, 2; MTFW 2005

Green, Anna Katharine
1846-1935 .... **TCLC 63**
See also CA 112; 159; CMW 4; DLB 202, 221; MSW

Green, Brian
See Card, Orson Scott

Green, Hannah
See Greenberg, Joanne (Goldenberg)

Green, Hannah 1927(?)-1996 .... **CLC 3**
See also CA 73-76; CANR 59, 93; NFS 10

Green, Henry .... **CLC 2, 13, 97**
See Yorke, Henry Vincent
See also BRWS 2; CA 175; DLB 15; EWL 3; RGEL 2

Green, Julian .... **CLC 3, 11, 77**
See Green, Julien (Hartridge)
See also EWL 3; GFL 1789 to the Present; MTCW 2

Green, Julien (Hartridge) 1900-1998
See Green, Julian
See also CA 21-24R; 169; CANR 33, 87; CWW 2; DLB 4, 72; MTCW 1, 2; MTFW 2005

Green, Paul (Eliot) 1894-1981 .... **CLC 25**
See also AITN 1; CA 5-8R; 103; CAD; CANR 3; DAM DRAM; DLB 7, 9, 249; DLBY 1981; MAL 5; RGAL 4

Greenaway, Peter 1942- .... **CLC 159**
See also CA 127

Greenberg, Ivan 1908-1973
See Rahv, Philip
See also CA 85-88

Greenberg, Joanne (Goldenberg)
1932- .... **CLC 7, 30**
See also AAYA 12, 67; CA 5-8R; CANR 14, 32, 69; CN 6, 7; SATA 25; YAW

Greenberg, Richard 1959(?)- .... **CLC 57**
See also CA 138; CAD; CD 5, 6

Greenblatt, Stephen J(ay) 1943- .... **CLC 70**
See also CA 49-52; CANR 115

Greene, Bette 1934- .... **CLC 30**
See also AAYA 7; BYA 3; CA 53-56; CANR 4, 146; CLR 2; CWRI 5; JRDA; LAIT 4; MAICYA 1, 2; NFS 10; SAAS 16; SATA 8, 102, 161; WYA; YAW

Greene, Gael .... **CLC 8**
See also CA 13-16R; CANR 10

Greene, Graham (Henry)
1904-1991 .... **CLC 1, 3, 6, 9, 14, 18, 27, 37, 70, 72, 125; SSC 29; WLC**
See also AAYA 61; AITN 2; BPFB 2; BRWR 2; BRWS 1; BYA 3; CA 13-16R; 133; CANR 35, 61, 131; CBD; CDBLB 1945-1960; CMW 4; CN 1, 2, 3, 4; DA; DA3; DAB; DAC; DAM MST, NOV; DLB 13, 15, 77, 100, 162, 201, 204; DLBY 1991; EWL 3; MSW; MTCW 1, 2; MTFW 2005; NFS 16; RGEL 2; SATA 20; SSFS 14; TEA; WLIT 4

Greene, Robert 1558-1592 .... **LC 41**
See also BRWS 8; DLB 62, 167; IDTP; RGEL 2; TEA

Greer, Germaine 1939- .... **CLC 131**
See also AITN 1; CA 81-84; CANR 33, 70, 115, 133; FW; MTCW 1, 2; MTFW 2005

Greer, Richard
See Silverberg, Robert

Gregor, Arthur 1923- .... **CLC 9**
See also CA 25-28R; CAAS 10; CANR 11; CP 1, 2, 3, 4, 5, 6, 7; SATA 36

Gregor, Lee
See Pohl, Frederik

Gregory, Lady Isabella Augusta (Persse)
1852-1932 .... **TCLC 1, 176**
See also BRW 6; CA 104; 184; DLB 10; IDTP; RGEL 2

Gregory, J. Dennis
See Williams, John A(lfred)

Grekova, I. .... **CLC 59**
See Ventsel, Elena Sergeevna
See also CWW 2

Grendon, Stephen
See Derleth, August (William)

Grenville, Kate 1950- .... **CLC 61**
See also CA 118; CANR 53, 93; CN 7

Grenville, Pelham
See Wodehouse, P(elham) G(renville)

Greve, Felix Paul (Berthold Friedrich)
1879-1948
See Grove, Frederick Philip
See also CA 104; 141, 175; CANR 79; DAC; DAM MST

Greville, Fulke 1554-1628 .... **LC 79**
See also BRWS 11; DLB 62, 172; RGEL 2

Grey, Lady Jane 1537-1554 .... **LC 93**
See also DLB 132

Grey, Zane 1872-1939 .... **TCLC 6**
See also BPFB 2; CA 104; 132; DA3; DAM POP; DLB 9, 212; MTCW 1, 2; MTFW 2005; RGAL 4; TCWW 1, 2; TUS

Griboedov, Aleksandr Sergeevich
1795(?)-1829 .... **NCLC 129**
See also DLB 205; RGWL 2, 3

Grieg, (Johan) Nordahl (Brun)
1902-1943 .... **TCLC 10**
See also CA 107; 189; EWL 3

Grieve, C(hristopher) M(urray)
1892-1978 .... **CLC 11, 19**
See MacDiarmid, Hugh; Pteleon
See also CA 5-8R; 85-88; CANR 33, 107; DAM POET; MTCW 1; RGEL 2

Griffin, Gerald 1803-1840 .... **NCLC 7**
See also DLB 159; RGEL 2

Griffin, John Howard 1920-1980 ..... **CLC 68**
See also AITN 1; CA 1-4R; 101; CANR 2

Griffin, Peter 1942- .... **CLC 39**
See also CA 136

Griffith, D(avid) W(ark)
1875(?)-1948 .... **TCLC 68**
See also CA 119; 150; CANR 80

Griffith, Lawrence
See Griffith, D(avid) Lewelyn) W(ark)

Griffiths, Trevor 1935- .... **CLC 13, 52**
See also CA 97-100; CANR 45; CBD; CD 5, 6; DLB 13, 245

Griggs, Sutton (Elbert)
1872-1930 .... **TCLC 77**
See also CA 123; 186; DLB 50

Grigson, Geoffrey (Edward Harvey)
1905-1985 .... **CLC 7, 39**
See also CA 25-28R; 118; CANR 20, 33; CP 1, 2, 3, 4; DLB 27; MTCW 1, 2

Grile, Dod
See Bierce, Ambrose (Gwinett)

Grillparzer, Franz 1791-1872 .... **DC 14; NCLC 1, 102; SSC 37**
See also CDWLB 2; DLB 133; EW 5; RGWL 2, 3; TWA

Grimble, Reverend Charles James
See Eliot, T(homas) S(tearns)

Grimke, Angelina (Emily) Weld
1880-1958 .... **HR 1:2**
See Weld, Angelina (Emily) Grimke
See also BW 1; CA 124; DAM POET; DLB 50, 54

Grimke, Charlotte L(ottie) Forten
1837(?)-1914
See Forten, Charlotte L.
See also BW 1; CA 117; 124; DAM MULT, POET

Grimm, Jacob Ludwig Karl
1785-1863 .... **NCLC 3, 77; SSC 36, 88**
See also DLB 90; MAICYA 1, 2; RGSF 2; RGWL 2, 3; SATA 22; WCH

Grimm, Wilhelm Karl 1786-1859 .. **NCLC 3, 77; SSC 36, 88**
See also CDWLB 2; DLB 90; MAICYA 1, 2; RGSF 2; RGWL 2, 3; SATA 22; WCH

Grimmelshausen, Hans Jakob Christoffel von
See Grimmelshausen, Johann Jakob Christoffel von
See also RGWL 2, 3

Grimmelshausen, Johann Jakob Christoffel von 1621-1676 .... **LC 6**
See Grimmelshausen, Hans Jakob Christoffel von
See also CDWLB 2; DLB 168

Grindel, Eugene 1895-1952
See Eluard, Paul
See also CA 104; 193; LMFS 2

Grisham, John 1955- .... **CLC 84**
See also AAYA 14, 47; BPFB 2; CA 138; CANR 47, 69, 114, 133; CMW 4; CN 6, 7; CPW; CSW; DA3; DAM POP; MSW; MTCW 2; MTFW 2005

Grosseteste, Robert 1175(?)-1253 . **CMLC 62**
See also DLB 115

Grossman, David 1954- .... **CLC 67**
See also CA 138; CANR 114; CWW 2; DLB 299; EWL 3; WLIT 6

Grossman, Vasilii Semenovich
See Grossman, Vasily (Semenovich)
See also DLB 272

Grossman, Vasily (Semenovich)
1905-1964 .... **CLC 41**
See Grossman, Vasilii Semenovich
See also CA 124; 130; MTCW 1

Grove, Frederick Philip .... **TCLC 4**
See Greve, Felix Paul (Berthold Friedrich)
See also DLB 92; RGEL 2; TCWW 1, 2

Grubb
See Crumb, R(obert)

Grumbach, Doris (Isaac) 1918- . **CLC 13, 22, 64**
See also CA 5-8R; CAAS 2; CANR 9, 42, 70, 127; CN 6, 7; INT CANR-9; MTCW 2; MTFW 2005

Grundtvig, Nikolai Frederik Severin
1783-1872 .... **NCLC 1, 158**
See also DLB 300

Grunge
See Crumb, R(obert)

Grunwald, Lisa 1959- .... **CLC 44**
See also CA 120

Gryphius, Andreas 1616-1664 .... **LC 89**
See also CDWLB 2; DLB 164; RGWL 2, 3

Guare, John 1938- .... **CLC 8, 14, 29, 67; DC 20**
See also CA 73-76; CAD; CANR 21, 69, 118; CD 5, 6; DAM DRAM; DFS 8, 13; DLB 7, 249; EWL 3; MAL 5; MTCW 1, 2; RGAL 4

Guarini, Battista 1537-1612 .... **LC 102**

Gubar, Susan (David) 1944- .... **CLC 145**
See also CA 108; CANR 45, 70, 139; FW; MTCW 1; RGAL 4

Gudjonsson, Halldor Kiljan 1902-1998
See Halldor Laxness
See also CA 103; 164

Guenter, Erich
See Eich, Gunter

Guest, Barbara 1920- .... **CLC 34; PC 55**
See also BG 1:2; CA 25-28R; CANR 11, 44, 84; CP 1, 2, 3, 4, 5, 6, 7; CWP; DLB 5, 193

Guest, Edgar A(lbert) 1881-1959 ... **TCLC 95**
See also CA 112; 168

Guest, Judith (Ann) 1936- .... **CLC 8, 30**
See also AAYA 7, 66; CA 77-80; CANR 15, 75, 138; DA3; DAM NOV, POP; EXPN; INT CANR-15; LAIT 5; MTCW 1, 2; MTFW 2005; NFS 1

Guevara, Che .... **CLC 87; HLC 1**
See Guevara (Serna), Ernesto

Guevara (Serna), Ernesto
1928-1967 .... **CLC 87; HLC 1**
See Guevara, Che
See also CA 127; 111; CANR 56; DAM MULT; HW 1

Guicciardini, Francesco 1483-1540 ..... **LC 49**

Guild, Nicholas M. 1944- .... **CLC 33**
See also CA 93-96

Guillemin, Jacques
See Sartre, Jean-Paul

Guillen, Jorge 1893-1984 . **CLC 11; HLCS 1; PC 35**
See also CA 89-92; 112; DAM MULT, POET; DLB 108; EWL 3; HW 1; RGWL 2, 3

Guillen, Nicolas (Cristobal)
1902-1989 .... **BLC 2; CLC 48, 79; HLC 1; PC 23**
See also BW 2; CA 116; 125; 129; CANR 84; DAM MST, MULT, POET; DLB 283; EWL 3; HW 1; LAW; RGWL 2, 3; WP

Guillen y Alvarez, Jorge
See Guillen, Jorge

Guillevic, (Eugene) 1907-1997 .... **CLC 33**
See also CA 93-96; CWW 2

Guillois
See Desnos, Robert

Guillois, Valentin
See Desnos, Robert

Guimaraes Rosa, Joao 1908-1967 .... **HLCS 2**
See Rosa, Joao Guimaraes
See also CA 175; LAW; RGSF 2; RGWL 2, 3

Guiney, Louise Imogen
1861-1920 .... **TCLC 41**
See also CA 160; DLB 54; RGAL 4

Guinizelli, Guido c. 1230-1276 ...... **CMLC 49**
See Guinizzelli, Guido

Guinizzelli, Guido
See Guinizelli, Guido
See also WLIT 7

Guiraldes, Ricardo (Guillermo)
1886-1927 .... **TCLC 39**
See also CA 131; EWL 3; HW 1; LAW; MTCW 1

Gumilev, Nikolai (Stepanovich)
1886-1921 .... **TCLC 60**
See Gumilyov, Nikolay Stepanovich
See also CA 165; DLB 295

Gumilyov, Nikolay Stepanovich
See Gumilev, Nikolai (Stepanovich)
See also EWL 3

Gump, P. Q.
See Card, Orson Scott

Gunesekera, Romesh 1954- .... **CLC 91**
See also BRWS 10; CA 159; CANR 140; CN 6, 7; DLB 267

Gunn, Bill .... **CLC 5**
See Gunn, William Harrison
See also DLB 38

Gunn, Thom(son William)
1929-2004 . **CLC 3, 6, 18, 32, 81; PC 26**
See also BRWS 4; CA 17-20R; 227; CANR 9, 33, 116; CDBLB 1960 to Present; CP 1, 2, 3, 4, 5, 6, 7; DAM POET; DLB 27; INT CANR-33; MTCW 1; PFS 9; RGEL 2

Gunn, William Harrison 1934(?)-1989
See Gunn, Bill
See also AITN 1; BW 1, 3; CA 13-16R; 128; CANR 12, 25, 76

Gunn Allen, Paula
See Allen, Paula Gunn

Gunnars, Kristjana 1948- .... **CLC 69**
See also CA 113; CCA 1; CP 7; CWP; DLB 60

Gunter, Erich
See Eich, Gunter

Gurdjieff, G(eorgei) I(vanovich)
1877(?)-1949 .... **TCLC 71**
See also CA 157

Gurganus, Allan 1947- .... **CLC 70**
See also BEST 90:1; CA 135; CANR 114; CN 6, 7; CPW; CSW; DAM POP; GLL 1

Gurney, A. R.
See Gurney, A(lbert) R(amsdell), Jr.
See also DLB 266

Gurney, A(lbert) R(amsdell), Jr.
1930- .... **CLC 32, 50, 54**
See Gurney, A. R.
See also AMWS 5; CA 77-80; CAD; CANR 32, 64, 121; CD 5, 6; DAM DRAM; EWL 3

Gurney, Ivor (Bertie) 1890-1937 ... **TCLC 33**
See also BRW 6; CA 167; DLBY 2002; PAB; RGEL 2

Gurney, Peter
See Gurney, A(lbert) R(amsdell), Jr.

Guro, Elena (Genrikhovna)
1877-1913 .... **TCLC 56**
See also DLB 295

Gustafson, James M(oody) 1925- ... **CLC 100**
See also CA 25-28R; CANR 37

Gustafson, Ralph (Barker)
1909-1995 .... **CLC 36**
See also CA 21-24R; CANR 8, 45, 84; CP 1, 2, 3, 4; DLB 88; RGEL 2

Gut, Gom
See Simenon, Georges (Jacques Christian)

Guterson, David 1956- .... **CLC 91**
See also CA 132; CANR 73, 126; CN 7; DLB 292; MTCW 2; MTFW 2005; NFS 13

Guthrie, A(lfred) B(ertram), Jr.
1901-1991 .... **CLC 23**
See also CA 57-60; 134; CANR 24; CN 1, 2, 3; DLB 6, 212; MAL 5; SATA 62; SATA-Obit 67; TCWW 1, 2

Guthrie, Isobel
See Grieve, C(hristopher) M(urray)

Guthrie, Woodrow Wilson 1912-1967
See Guthrie, Woody
See also CA 113; 93-96

Guthrie, Woody .... **CLC 35**
See Guthrie, Woodrow Wilson
See also DLB 303; LAIT 3

Gutierrez Najera, Manuel
1859-1895 .... **HLCS 2; NCLC 133**
See also DLB 290; LAW

Guy, Rosa (Cuthbert) 1925- .... **CLC 26**
See also AAYA 4, 37; BW 2; CA 17-20R; CANR 14, 34, 83; CLR 13; DLB 33; DNFS 1; JRDA; MAICYA 1, 2; SATA 14, 62, 122; YAW

Gwendolyn
See Bennett, (Enoch) Arnold

H. D. .... **CLC 3, 8, 14, 31, 34, 73; PC 5**
See Doolittle, Hilda
See also FL 1:5

H. de V.
See Buchan, John

Haavikko, Paavo Juhani 1931- .. **CLC 18, 34**
See also CA 106; CWW 2; EWL 3

Habbema, Koos
See Heijermans, Herman

Habermas, Juergen 1929- .... **CLC 104**
See also CA 109; CANR 85; DLB 242

Habermas, Jurgen
See Habermas, Juergen

Hacker, Marilyn 1942- ...... **CLC 5, 9, 23, 72, 91; PC 47**
See also CA 77-80; CANR 68, 129; CP 3, 4, 5, 6, 7; CWP; DAM POET; DLB 120, 282; FW; GLL 2; MAL 5; PFS 19

Hadewijch of Antwerp fl. 1250- ... **CMLC 61**
See also RGWL 3

Hadrian 76-138 .... **CMLC 52**

Haeckel, Ernst Heinrich (Philipp August)
1834-1919 .... **TCLC 83**
See also CA 157

Hafiz c. 1326-1389(?) .... **CMLC 34**
See also RGWL 2, 3; WLIT 6

Hagedorn, Jessica T(arahata)
1949- .... **CLC 185**
See also CA 139; CANR 69; CWP; DLB 312; RGAL 4

Haggard, H(enry) Rider
1856-1925 .... **TCLC 11**
See also BRWS 3; BYA 4, 5; CA 108; 148; CANR 112; DLB 70, 156, 174, 178; FANT; LMFS 1; MTCW 2; RGEL 2; RHW; SATA 16; SCFW 1, 2; SFW 4; SUFW 1; WLIT 4

Hagiosy, L.
See Larbaud, Valery (Nicolas)

Hagiwara, Sakutaro 1886-1942 .... **PC 18; TCLC 60**
See Hagiwara Sakutaro
See also CA 154; RGWL 3

Hagiwara Sakutaro
See Hagiwara, Sakutaro
See also EWL 3

Haig, Fenil
See Ford, Ford Madox

Haig-Brown, Roderick (Langmere)
1908-1976 .... **CLC 21**
See also CA 5-8R; 69-72; CANR 4, 38, 83; CLR 31; CWRI 5; DLB 88; MAICYA 1, 2; SATA 12; TCWW 2

Haight, Rip
See Carpenter, John (Howard)

Hailey, Arthur 1920-2004 .... **CLC 5**
See also AITN 2; BEST 90:3; BPFB 2; CA 1-4R; 233; CANR 2, 36, 75; CCA 1; CN 1, 2, 3, 4, 5, 6, 7; CPW; DAM NOV, POP; DLB 88; DLBY 1982; MTCW 1, 2; MTFW 2005

Hailey, Elizabeth Forsythe 1938- ..... **CLC 40**
See also CA 93-96, 188; CAAE 188; CAAS 1; CANR 15, 48; INT CANR-15

Haines, John (Meade) 1924- .... **CLC 58**
See also AMWS 12; CA 17-20R; CANR 13, 34; CP 1, 2, 3, 4; CSW; DLB 5, 212; TCLE 1:1

Hakluyt, Richard 1552-1616 .... **LC 31**
See also DLB 136; RGEL 2

Haldeman, Joe (William) 1943- .... **CLC 61**
See Graham, Robert
See also AAYA 38; CA 53-56, 179; CAAE 179; CAAS 25; CANR 6, 70, 72, 130; DLB 8; INT CANR-6; SCFW 2; SFW 4

Hale, Janet Campbell 1947- .... **NNAL**
See also CA 49-52; CANR 45, 75; DAM MULT; DLB 175; MTCW 2; MTFW 2005

Hale, Sarah Josepha (Buell)
1788-1879 .... **NCLC 75**
See also DLB 1, 42, 73, 243

Halevy, Elie 1870-1937 .... **TCLC 104**

Haley, Alex(ander Murray Palmer)
1921-1992 .... **BLC 2; CLC 8, 12, 76; TCLC 147**
See also AAYA 26; BPFB 2; BW 2, 3; CA 77-80; 136; CANR 61; CDALBS; CPW; CSW; DA; DA3; DAB; DAC; DAM MST, MULT, POP; DLB 38; LAIT 5; MTCW 1, 2; NFS 9

Haliburton, Thomas Chandler
1796-1865 .... **NCLC 15, 149**
See also DLB 11, 99; RGEL 2; RGSF 2

Hall, Donald (Andrew, Jr.) 1928- ...... **CLC 1, 13, 37, 59, 151; PC 70**
See also AAYA 63; CA 5-8R; CAAS 7; CANR 2, 44, 64, 106, 133; CP 1, 2, 3, 4, 5, 6, 7; DAM POET; DLB 5; MAL 5; MTCW 2; MTFW 2005; RGAL 4; SATA 23, 97

Hall, Frederic Sauser
See Sauser-Hall, Frederic

Hall, James
See Kuttner, Henry

Hall, James Norman 1887-1951 ..... **TCLC 23**
See also CA 123; 173; LAIT 1; RHW 1; SATA 21

Hall, Joseph 1574-1656 .... **LC 91**
See also DLB 121, 151; RGEL 2

Hall, (Marguerite) Radclyffe
1880-1943 .... **TCLC 12**
See also BRWS 6; CA 110; 150; CANR 83; DLB 191; MTCW 2; MTFW 2005; RGEL 2; RHW

Hall, Rodney 1935- .... **CLC 51**
See also CA 109; CANR 69; CN 6, 7; CP 1, 2, 3, 4, 5, 6, 7; DLB 289

Hallam, Arthur Henry
1811-1833 .... **NCLC 110**
See also DLB 32

Halldor Laxness .... **CLC 25**
See Gudjonsson, Halldor Kiljan
See also DLB 293; EW 12; EWL 3; RGWL 2, 3

Halleck, Fitz-Greene 1790-1867 .... **NCLC 47**
See also DLB 3, 250; RGAL 4

Halliday, Michael
See Creasey, John

Halpern, Daniel 1945- .... **CLC 14**
See also CA 33-36R; CANR 93; CP 3, 4, 5, 6, 7

Hamburger, Michael (Peter Leopold)
1924- .... **CLC 5, 14**
See also CA 5-8R, 196; CAAE 196; CAAS 4; CANR 2, 47; CP 1, 2, 3, 4, 5, 6, 7; DLB 27

Hamill, Pete 1935- .... **CLC 10**
See also CA 25-28R; CANR 18, 71, 127

Hamilton, Alexander
1755(?)-1804 .... **NCLC 49**
See also DLB 37

Hamilton, Clive
See Lewis, C(live) S(taples)

Hamilton, Edmond 1904-1977 .... **CLC 1**
See also CA 1-4R; CANR 3, 84; DLB 8; SATA 118; SFW 4

Hamilton, Elizabeth 1758-1816 ... **NCLC 153**
See also DLB 116, 158

Hamilton, Eugene (Jacob) Lee
See Lee-Hamilton, Eugene (Jacob)

Hamilton, Franklin
See Silverberg, Robert

Hamilton, Gail
See Corcoran, Barbara (Asenath)

Hamilton, (Robert) Ian 1938-2001 . **CLC 191**
See also CA 106; 203; CANR 41, 67; CP 1, 2, 3, 4, 5, 6, 7; DLB 40, 155

Hamilton, Jane 1957- .... **CLC 179**
See also CA 147; CANR 85, 128; CN 7; MTFW 2005

Hamilton, Mollie
See Kaye, M(ary) M(argaret)

Hamilton, (Anthony Walter) Patrick
1904-1962 .... **CLC 51**
See also CA 176; 113; DLB 10, 191

Hamilton, Virginia (Esther)
1936-2002 .... **CLC 26**
See also AAYA 2, 21; BW 2, 3; BYA 1, 2, 8; CA 25-28R; 206; CANR 20, 37, 73, 126; CLR 1, 11, 40; DAM MULT; DLB 33, 52; DLBY 2001; INT CANR-20; JRDA; LAIT 5; MAICYA 1, 2; MAICYAS 1; MTCW 1, 2; MTFW 2005; SATA 4, 56, 79, 123; SATA-Obit 132; WYA; YAW

Hammett, (Samuel) Dashiell
1894-1961 .... **CLC 3, 5, 10, 19, 47; SSC 17**
See also AAYA 59; AITN 1; AMWS 4; BPFB 2; CA 81-84; CANR 42; CDALB 1929-1941; CMW 4; DA3; DLB 226, 280; DLBD 6; DLBY 1996; EWL 3; LAIT 3; MAL 5; MSW; MTCW 1, 2; MTFW 2005; NFS 21; RGAL 4; RGSF 2; TUS

Hammon, Jupiter 1720(?)-1800(?) .... **BLC 2; NCLC 5; PC 16**
See also DAM MULT, POET; DLB 31, 50

Hammond, Keith
See Kuttner, Henry

Hamner, Earl (Henry), Jr. 1923- .... **CLC 12**
See also AITN 1; CA 73-76; DLB 6

Hampton, Christopher (James)
1946- .... **CLC 4**
See also CA 25-28R; CD 5, 6; DLB 13; MTCW 1

Hamsun, Knut .... **TCLC 2, 14, 49, 151**
See Pedersen, Knut
See also DLB 297; EW 8; EWL 3; RGWL 2, 3

Handke, Peter 1942- .... **CLC 5, 8, 10, 15, 38, 134; DC 17**
See also CA 77-80; CANR 33, 75, 104, 133; CWW 2; DAM DRAM, NOV; DLB 85, 124; EWL 3; MTCW 1, 2; MTFW 2005; TWA

Handy, W(illiam) C(hristopher)
1873-1958 .... **TCLC 97**
See also BW 3; CA 121; 167

Hanley, James 1901-1985 ..... **CLC 3, 5, 8, 13**
See also CA 73-76; 117; CANR 36; CBD; CN 1, 2, 3; DLB 191; EWL 3; MTCW 1; RGEL 2

Hannah, Barry 1942- .... **CLC 23, 38, 90**
See also BPFB 2; CA 108; 110; CANR 43, 68, 113; CN 4, 5, 6, 7; CSW; DLB 6, 234; INT CA-110; MTCW 1; RGSF 2

Hannon, Ezra
See Hunter, Evan

Hansberry, Lorraine (Vivian)
1930-1965 ... **BLC 2; CLC 17, 62; DC 2**
See also AAYA 25; AFAW 1, 2; AMWS 4; BW 1, 3; CA 109; 25-28R; CABS 3; CAD; CANR 58; CDALB 1941-1968; CWD; DA; DA3; DAB; DAC; DAM DRAM, MST, MULT; DFS 2; DLB 7, 38; EWL 3; FL 1:6; FW; LAIT 4; MAL 5; MTCW 1, 2; MTFW 2005; RGAL 4; TUS

Hansen, Joseph 1923-2004 .... **CLC 38**
See Brock, Rose; Colton, James
See also BPFB 2; CA 29-32R; 233; CAAS 17; CANR 16, 44, 66, 125; CMW 4; DLB 226; GLL 1; INT CANR-16

Hansen, Martin A(lfred)
1909-1955 .... **TCLC 32**
See also CA 167; DLB 214; EWL 3

Hansen and Philipson eds. .... **CLC 65**

Hanson, Kenneth O(stlin) 1922- .... **CLC 13**
See also CA 53-56; CANR 7; CP 1, 2, 3, 4

Hardwick, Elizabeth (Bruce) 1916- . **CLC 13**
See also AMWS 3; CA 5-8R; CANR 3, 32, 70, 100, 139; CN 4, 5, 6; CSW; DA3; DAM NOV; DLB 6; MAWW; MTCW 1, 2; MTFW 2005; TCLE 1:1

Hardy, Thomas 1840-1928 .... **PC 8; SSC 2, 60; TCLC 4, 10, 18, 32, 48, 53, 72, 143, 153; WLC**
See also BRW 6; BRWC 1, 2; BRWR 1; CA 104; 123; CDBLB 1890-1914; DA; DA3; DAB; DAC; DAM MST, NOV, POET; DLB 18, 19, 135, 284; EWL 3; EXPN; EXPP; LAIT 2; MTCW 1, 2; MTFW 2005; NFS 3, 11, 15, 19; PFS 3, 4, 18; RGEL 2; RGSF 2; TEA; WLIT 4

Hare, David 1947- . **CLC 29, 58, 136; DC 26**
See also BRWS 4; CA 97-100; CANR 39, 91; CBD; CD 5, 6; DFS 4, 7, 16; DLB 13, 310; MTCW 1; TEA

Harewood, John
See Van Druten, John (William)

Harford, Henry
See Hudson, W(illiam) H(enry)

Hargrave, Leonie
See Disch, Thomas M(ichael)

Hariri, Al- al-Qasim ibn 'Ali Abu Muhammad al-Basri
See al-Hariri, al-Qasim ibn 'Ali Abu Muhammad al-Basri

Harjo, Joy 1951- ..... **CLC 83; NNAL; PC 27**
See also AMWS 12; CA 114; CANR 35, 67, 91, 129; CP 7; DAM MULT; DLB 120, 175; EWL 3; MTCW 2; MTFW 2005; PFS 15; RGAL 4

Harlan, Louis R(udolph) 1922- .... **CLC 34**
See also CA 21-24R; CANR 25, 55, 80

Harling, Robert 1951(?)- .... **CLC 53**
See also CA 147

Harmon, William (Ruth) 1938- .... **CLC 38**
See also CA 33-36R; CANR 14, 32, 35; SATA 65

Harper, F. E. W.
See Harper, Frances Ellen Watkins

Harper, Frances E. W.
See Harper, Frances Ellen Watkins

Harper, Frances E. Watkins
See Harper, Frances Ellen Watkins

Harper, Frances Ellen
See Harper, Frances Ellen Watkins

Harper, Frances Ellen Watkins
1825-1911 ..... **BLC 2; PC 21; TCLC 14**
See also AFAW 1, 2; BW 1, 3; CA 111; 125; CANR 79; DAM MULT, POET; DLB 50, 221; MAWW; RGAL 4

Harper, Michael S(teven) 1938- ... **CLC 7, 22**
See also AFAW 2; BW 1; CA 33-36R, 224; CAAE 224; CANR 24, 108; CP 2, 3, 4, 5, 6, 7; DLB 41; RGAL 4; TCLE 1:1

Harper, Mrs. F. E. W.
See Harper, Frances Ellen Watkins

Harpur, Charles 1813-1868 .... **NCLC 114**
See also DLB 230; RGEL 2

Harris, Christie
See Harris, Christie (Lucy) Irwin

Harris, Christie (Lucy) Irwin
1907-2002 .... **CLC 12**
See also CA 5-8R; CANR 6, 83; CLR 47; DLB 88; JRDA; MAICYA 1, 2; SAAS 10; SATA 6, 74; SATA-Essay 116

Harris, Frank 1856-1931 .... **TCLC 24**
See also CA 109; 150; CANR 80; DLB 156, 197; RGEL 2

Harris, George Washington
1814-1869 .... **NCLC 23, 165**
See also DLB 3, 11, 248; RGAL 4

Harris, Joel Chandler 1848-1908 ..... **SSC 19; TCLC 2**
See also CA 104; 137; CANR 80; CLR 49; DLB 11, 23, 42, 78, 91; LAIT 2; MAICYA 1, 2; RGSF 2; SATA 100; WCH; YABC 1

Harris, John (Wyndham Parkes Lucas) Beynon 1903-1969
See Wyndham, John
See also CA 102; 89-92; CANR 84; SATA 118; SFW 4

Harris, MacDonald .... CLC 9
See Heiney, Donald (William)

Harris, Mark 1922- .... CLC 19
See also CA 5-8R; CAAS 3; CANR 2, 55, 83; CN 1, 2, 3, 4, 5, 6, 7; DLB 2; DLBY 1980

Harris, Norman .... CLC 65

Harris, (Theodore) Wilson 1921- .... CLC 25, 159
See also BRWS 5; BW 2, 3; CA 65-68; CAAS 16; CANR 11, 27, 69, 114; CDWLB 3; CN 1, 2, 3, 4, 5, 6, 7; CP 1, 2, 3, 4, 5, 6, 7; DLB 117; EWL 3; MTCW 1; RGEL 2

Harrison, Barbara Grizzuti 1934-2002 .... CLC 144
See also CA 77-80; 205; CANR 15, 48; INT CANR-15

Harrison, Elizabeth (Allen) Cavanna 1909-2001
See Cavanna, Betty
See also CA 9-12R; 200; CANR 6, 27, 85, 104, 121; MAICYA 2; SATA 142; YAW

Harrison, Harry (Max) 1925- .... CLC 42
See also CA 1-4R; CANR 5, 21, 84; DLB 8; SATA 4; SCFW 2; SFW 4

Harrison, James (Thomas) 1937- ...... CLC 6, 14, 33, 66, 143; SSC 19
See Harrison, Jim
See also CA 13-16R; CANR 8, 51, 79, 142; DLBY 1982; INT CANR-8

Harrison, Jim
See Harrison, James (Thomas)
See also AMWS 8; CN 5, 6; CP 1, 2, 3, 4, 5, 6, 7; RGAL 4; TCWW 2; TUS

Harrison, Kathryn 1961- .... CLC 70, 151
See also CA 144; CANR 68, 122

Harrison, Tony 1937- .... CLC 43, 129
See also BRWS 5; CA 65-68; CANR 44, 98; CBD; CD 5, 6; CP 2, 3, 4, 5, 6, 7; DLB 40, 245; MTCW 1; RGEL 2

Harriss, Will(ard Irvin) 1922- .... CLC 34
See also CA 111

Hart, Ellis
See Ellison, Harlan (Jay)

Hart, Josephine 1942(?)- .... CLC 70
See also CA 138; CANR 70; CPW; DAM POP

Hart, Moss 1904-1961 .... CLC 66
See also CA 109; 89-92; CANR 84; DAM DRAM; DFS 1; DLB 7, 266; RGAL 4

Harte, (Francis) Bret(t) 1836(?)-1902 ... SSC 8, 59; TCLC 1, 25; WLC
See also AMWS 2; CA 104; 140; CANR 80; CDALB 1865-1917; DA; DA3; DAC; DAM MST; DLB 12, 64, 74, 79, 186; EXPS; LAIT 2; RGAL 4; RGSF 2; SATA 26; SSFS 3; TUS

Hartley, L(eslie) P(oles) 1895-1972 ... CLC 2, 22
See also BRWS 7; CA 45-48; 37-40R; CANR 33; CN 1; DLB 15, 139; EWL 3; HGG; MTCW 1, 2; MTFW 2005; RGEL 2; RGSF 2; SUFW 1

Hartman, Geoffrey H. 1929- .... CLC 27
See also CA 117; 125; CANR 79; DLB 67

Hartmann, Sadakichi 1869-1944 ... TCLC 73
See also CA 157; DLB 54

Hartmann von Aue c. 1170-c. 1210 .... CMLC 15
See also CDWLB 2; DLB 138; RGWL 2, 3

Hartog, Jan de
See de Hartog, Jan

Haruf, Kent 1943- .... CLC 34
See also AAYA 44; CA 149; CANR 91, 131

Harvey, Caroline
See Trollope, Joanna

Harvey, Gabriel 1550(?)-1631 .... LC 88
See also DLB 167, 213, 281

Harwood, Ronald 1934- .... CLC 32
See also CA 1-4R; CANR 4, 55; CBD; CD 5, 6; DAM DRAM, MST; DLB 13

Hasegawa Tatsunosuke
See Futabatei, Shimei

Hasek, Jaroslav (Matej Frantisek) 1883-1923 .... SSC 69; TCLC 4
See also CA 104; 129; CDWLB 4; DLB 215; EW 9; EWL 3; MTCW 1, 2; RGSF 2; RGWL 2, 3

Hass, Robert 1941- ... CLC 18, 39, 99; PC 16
See also AMWS 6; CA 111; CANR 30, 50, 71; CP 3, 4, 5, 6, 7; DLB 105, 206; EWL 3; MAL 5; MTFW 2005; RGAL 4; SATA 94; TCLE 1:1

Hastings, Hudson
See Kuttner, Henry

Hastings, Selina .... CLC 44

Hathorne, John 1641-1717 .... LC 38

Hatteras, Amelia
See Mencken, H(enry) L(ouis)

Hatteras, Owen .... TCLC 18
See Mencken, H(enry) L(ouis); Nathan, George Jean

Hauptmann, Gerhart (Johann Robert) 1862-1946 .... SSC 37; TCLC 4
See also CA 104; 153; CDWLB 2; DAM DRAM; DLB 66, 118; EW 8; EWL 3; RGSF 2; RGWL 2, 3; TWA

Havel, Vaclav 1936- ..... CLC 25, 58, 65, 123; DC 6
See also CA 104; CANR 36, 63, 124; CDWLB 4; CWW 2; DA3; DAM DRAM; DFS 10; DLB 232; EWL 3; LMFS 2; MTCW 1, 2; MTFW 2005; RGWL 3

Haviaras, Stratis .... CLC 33
See Chaviaras, Strates

Hawes, Stephen 1475(?)-1529(?) .... LC 17
See also DLB 132; RGEL 2

Hawkes, John (Clendennin Burne, Jr.) 1925-1998 .. CLC 1, 2, 3, 4, 7, 9, 14, 15, 27, 49
See also BPFB 2; CA 1-4R; 167; CANR 2, 47, 64; CN 1, 2, 3, 4, 5, 6; DLB 2, 7, 227; DLBY 1980, 1998; EWL 3; MAL 5; MTCW 1, 2; MTFW 2005; RGAL 4

Hawking, S. W.
See Hawking, Stephen W(illiam)

Hawking, Stephen W(illiam) 1942- . CLC 63, 105
See also AAYA 13; BEST 89:1; CA 126; 129; CANR 48, 115; CPW; DA3; MTCW 2; MTFW 2005

Hawkins, Anthony Hope
See Hope, Anthony

Hawthorne, Julian 1846-1934 .... TCLC 25
See also CA 165; HGG

Hawthorne, Nathaniel 1804-1864 ... NCLC 2, 10, 17, 23, 39, 79, 95, 158; SSC 3, 29, 39, 89; WLC
See also AAYA 18; AMW; AMWC 1; AMWR 1; BPFB 2; BYA 3; CDALB 1640-1865; CLR 103; DA; DA3; DAB; DAC; DAM MST, NOV; DLB 1, 74, 183, 223, 269; EXPN; EXPS; GL 2; HGG; LAIT 1; NFS 1, 20; RGAL 4; RGSF 2; SSFS 1, 7, 11, 15; SUFW 1; TUS; WCH; YABC 2

Hawthorne, Sophia Peabody 1809-1871 .... NCLC 150
See also DLB 183, 239

Haxton, Josephine Ayres 1921-
See Douglas, Ellen
See also CA 115; CANR 41, 83

Hayaseca y Eizaguirre, Jorge
See Echegaray (y Eizaguirre), Jose (Maria Waldo)

Hayashi, Fumiko 1904-1951 .... TCLC 27
See Hayashi Fumiko
See also CA 161

Hayashi Fumiko
See Hayashi, Fumiko
See also DLB 180; EWL 3

Haycraft, Anna (Margaret) 1932-2005
See Ellis, Alice Thomas
See also CA 122; 237; CANR 90, 141; MTCW 2; MTFW 2005

Hayden, Robert E(arl) 1913-1980 ..... BLC 2; CLC 5, 9, 14, 37; PC 6
See also AFAW 1, 2; AMWS 2; BW 1, 3; CA 69-72; 97-100; CABS 2; CANR 24, 75, 82; CDALB 1941-1968; CP 1, 2, 3; DA; DAC; DAM MST, MULT, POET; DLB 5, 76; EWL 3; EXPP; MAL 5; MTCW 1, 2; PFS 1; RGAL 4; SATA 19; SATA-Obit 26; WP

Haydon, Benjamin Robert 1786-1846 .... NCLC 146
See also DLB 110

Hayek, F(riedrich) A(ugust von) 1899-1992 .... TCLC 109
See also CA 93-96; 137; CANR 20; MTCW 1, 2

Hayford, J(oseph) E(phraim) Casely
See Casely-Hayford, J(oseph) E(phraim)

Hayman, Ronald 1932- .... CLC 44
See also CA 25-28R; CANR 18, 50, 88; CD 5, 6; DLB 155

Hayne, Paul Hamilton 1830-1886 . NCLC 94
See also DLB 3, 64, 79, 248; RGAL 4

Hays, Mary 1760-1843 .... NCLC 114
See also DLB 142, 158; RGEL 2

Haywood, Eliza (Fowler) 1693(?)-1756 .... LC 1, 44
See also DLB 39; RGEL 2

Hazlitt, William 1778-1830 ...... NCLC 29, 82
See also BRW 4; DLB 110, 158; RGEL 2; TEA

Hazzard, Shirley 1931- .... CLC 18, 218
See also CA 9-12R; CANR 4, 70, 127; CN 1, 2, 3, 4, 5, 6, 7; DLB 289; DLBY 1982; MTCW 1

Head, Bessie 1937-1986 ...... BLC 2; CLC 25, 67; SSC 52
See also AFW; BW 2, 3; CA 29-32R; 119; CANR 25, 82; CDWLB 3; CN 1, 2, 3, 4; DA3; DAM MULT; DLB 117, 225; EWL 3; EXPS; FL 1:6; FW; MTCW 1, 2; MTFW 2005; RGSF 2; SSFS 5, 13; WLIT 2; WWE 1

Headon, (Nicky) Topper 1956(?)- ..... CLC 30

Heaney, Seamus (Justin) 1939- ..... CLC 5, 7, 14, 25, 37, 74, 91, 171; PC 18; WLCS
See also AAYA 61; BRWR 1; BRWS 2; CA 85-88; CANR 25, 48, 75, 91, 128; CDBLB 1960 to Present; CP 1, 2, 3, 4, 5, 6, 7; DA3; DAB; DAM POET; DLB 40; DLBY 1995; EWL 3; EXPP; MTCW 1, 2; MTFW 2005; PAB; PFS 2, 5, 8, 17; RGEL 2; TEA; WLIT 4

Hearn, (Patricio) Lafcadio (Tessima Carlos) 1850-1904 .... TCLC 9
See also CA 105; 166; DLB 12, 78, 189; HGG; MAL 5; RGAL 4

Hearne, Samuel 1745-1792 .... LC 95
See also DLB 99

Hearne, Vicki 1946-2001 .... CLC 56
See also CA 139; 201

Hearon, Shelby 1931- .... **CLC 63**
See also AITN 2; AMWS 8; CA 25-28R; CANR 18, 48, 103, 146; CSW

Heat-Moon, William Least .... **CLC 29**
See Trogdon, William (Lewis)
See also AAYA 9

Hebbel, Friedrich 1813-1863 . **DC 21; NCLC 43**
See also CDWLB 2; DAM DRAM; DLB 129; EW 6; RGWL 2, 3

Hebert, Anne 1916-2000 .... **CLC 4, 13, 29**
See also CA 85-88; 187; CANR 69, 126; CCA 1; CWP; CWW 2; DA3; DAC; DAM MST, POET; DLB 68; EWL 3; GFL 1789 to the Present; MTCW 1, 2; MTFW 2005; PFS 20

Hecht, Anthony (Evan) 1923-2004 .... **CLC 8, 13, 19; PC 70**
See also AMWS 10; CA 9-12R; 232; CANR 6, 108; CP 1, 2, 3, 4, 5, 6, 7; DAM POET; DLB 5, 169; EWL 3; PFS 6; WP

Hecht, Ben 1894-1964 ..... **CLC 8; TCLC 101**
See also CA 85-88; DFS 9; DLB 7, 9, 25, 26, 28, 86; FANT; IDFW 3, 4; RGAL 4

Hedayat, Sadeq 1903-1951 .... **TCLC 21**
See also CA 120; EWL 3; RGSF 2

Hegel, Georg Wilhelm Friedrich 1770-1831 .... **NCLC 46, 151**
See also DLB 90; TWA

Heidegger, Martin 1889-1976 .... **CLC 24**
See also CA 81-84; 65-68; CANR 34; DLB 296; MTCW 1, 2; MTFW 2005

Heidenstam, (Carl Gustaf) Verner von 1859-1940 .... **TCLC 5**
See also CA 104

Heidi Louise
See Erdrich, (Karen) Louise

Heifner, Jack 1946- .... **CLC 11**
See also CA 105; CANR 47

Heijermans, Herman 1864-1924 .... **TCLC 24**
See also CA 123; EWL 3

Heilbrun, Carolyn G(old) 1926-2003 .... **CLC 25, 173**
See Cross, Amanda
See also CA 45-48; 220; CANR 1, 28, 58, 94; FW

Hein, Christoph 1944- .... **CLC 154**
See also CA 158; CANR 108; CDWLB 2; CWW 2; DLB 124

Heine, Heinrich 1797-1856 .... **NCLC 4, 54, 147; PC 25**
See also CDWLB 2; DLB 90; EW 5; RGWL 2, 3; TWA

Heinemann, Larry (Curtiss) 1944- .. **CLC 50**
See also CA 110; CAAS 21; CANR 31, 81; DLBD 9; INT CANR-31

Heiney, Donald (William) 1921-1993
See Harris, MacDonald
See also CA 1-4R; 142; CANR 3, 58; FANT

Heinlein, Robert A(nson) 1907-1988 . **CLC 1, 3, 8, 14, 26, 55; SSC 55**
See also AAYA 17; BPFB 2; BYA 4, 13; CA 1-4R; 125; CANR 1, 20, 53; CLR 75; CN 1, 2, 3, 4; CPW; DA3; DAM POP; DLB 8; EXPS; JRDA; LAIT 5; LMFS 2; MAICYA 1, 2; MTCW 1, 2; MTFW 2005; RGAL 4; SATA 9, 69; SATA-Obit 56; SCFW 1, 2; SFW 4; SSFS 7; YAW

Helforth, John
See Doolittle, Hilda

Heliodorus fl. 3rd cent. - .... **CMLC 52**

Hellenhofferu, Vojtech Kapristian z
See Hasek, Jaroslav (Matej Frantisek)

Heller, Joseph 1923-1999 . **CLC 1, 3, 5, 8, 11, 36, 63; TCLC 131, 151; WLC**
See also AAYA 24; AITN 1; AMWS 4; BPFB 2; BYA 1; CA 5-8R; 187; CABS 1; CANR 8, 42, 66, 126; CN 1, 2, 3, 4, 5, 6; CPW; DA; DA3; DAB; DAC; DAM MST, NOV, POP; DLB 2, 28, 227; DLBY 1980, 2002; EWL 3; EXPN; INT CANR-8; LAIT 4; MAL 5; MTCW 1, 2; MTFW 2005; NFS 1; RGAL 4; TUS; YAW

Hellman, Lillian (Florence) 1906-1984 .. **CLC 2, 4, 8, 14, 18, 34, 44, 52; DC 1; TCLC 119**
See also AAYA 47; AITN 1, 2; AMWS 1; CA 13-16R; 112; CAD; CANR 33; CWD; DA3; DAM DRAM; DFS 1, 3, 14; DLB 7, 228; DLBY 1984; EWL 3; FL 1:6; FW; LAIT 3; MAL 5; MAWW; MTCW 1, 2; MTFW 2005; RGAL 4; TUS

Helprin, Mark 1947- .... **CLC 7, 10, 22, 32**
See also CA 81-84; CANR 47, 64, 124; CDALBS; CN 7; CPW; DA3; DAM NOV, POP; DLBY 1985; FANT; MAL 5; MTCW 1, 2; MTFW 2005; SUFW 2

Helvetius, Claude-Adrien 1715-1771 .. **LC 26**
See also DLB 313

Helyar, Jane Penelope Josephine 1933-
See Poole, Josephine
See also CA 21-24R; CANR 10, 26; CWRI 5; SATA 82, 138; SATA-Essay 138

Hemans, Felicia 1793-1835 .... **NCLC 29, 71**
See also DLB 96; RGEL 2

Hemingway, Ernest (Miller) 1899-1961 .... **CLC 1, 3, 6, 8, 10, 13, 19, 30, 34, 39, 41, 44, 50, 61, 80; SSC 1, 25, 36, 40, 63; TCLC 115; WLC**
See also AAYA 19; AMW; AMWC 1; AMWR 1; BPFB 2; BYA 2, 3, 13, 15; CA 77-80; CANR 34; CDALB 1917-1929; DA; DA3; DAB; DAC; DAM MST, NOV; DLB 4, 9, 102, 210, 308, 316; DLBD 1, 15, 16; DLBY 1981, 1987, 1996, 1998; EWL 3; EXPN; EXPS; LAIT 3, 4; LATS 1:1; MAL 5; MTCW 1, 2; MTFW 2005; NFS 1, 5, 6, 14; RGAL 4; RGSF 2; SSFS 17; TUS; WYA

Hempel, Amy 1951- .... **CLC 39**
See also CA 118; 137; CANR 70; DA3; DLB 218; EXPS; MTCW 2; MTFW 2005; SSFS 2

Henderson, F. C.
See Mencken, H(enry) L(ouis)

Henderson, Sylvia
See Ashton-Warner, Sylvia (Constance)

Henderson, Zenna (Chlarson) 1917-1983 .... **SSC 29**
See also CA 1-4R; 133; CANR 1, 84; DLB 8; SATA 5; SFW 4

Henkin, Joshua .... **CLC 119**
See also CA 161

Henley, Beth .... **CLC 23; DC 6, 14**
See Henley, Elizabeth Becker
See also CABS 3; CAD; CD 5, 6; CSW; CWD; DFS 2; DLBY 1986; FW

Henley, Elizabeth Becker 1952-
See Henley, Beth
See also CA 107; CANR 32, 73, 140; DA3; DAM DRAM, MST; DFS 21; MTCW 1, 2; MTFW 2005

Henley, William Ernest 1849-1903 .. **TCLC 8**
See also CA 105; 234; DLB 19; RGEL 2

Hennissart, Martha 1929-
See Lathen, Emma
See also CA 85-88; CANR 64

Henry VIII 1491-1547 .... **LC 10**
See also DLB 132

Henry, O. ..... **SSC 5, 49; TCLC 1, 19; WLC**
See Porter, William Sydney
See also AAYA 41; AMWS 2; EXPS; RGAL 4; RGSF 2; SSFS 2, 18; TCWW 1, 2

Henry, Patrick 1736-1799 .... **LC 25**
See also LAIT 1

Henryson, Robert 1430(?)-1506(?) ...... **LC 20, 110; PC 65**
See also BRWS 7; DLB 146; RGEL 2

Henschke, Alfred
See Klabund

Henson, Lance 1944- .... **NNAL**
See also CA 146; DLB 175

Hentoff, Nat(han Irving) 1925- .... **CLC 26**
See also AAYA 4, 42; BYA 6; CA 1-4R; CAAS 6; CANR 5, 25, 77, 114; CLR 1, 52; INT CANR-25; JRDA; MAICYA 1, 2; SATA 42, 69, 133; SATA-Brief 27; WYA; YAW

Heppenstall, (John) Rayner 1911-1981 .... **CLC 10**
See also CA 1-4R; 103; CANR 29; CN 1, 2; CP 1, 2, 3; EWL 3

Heraclitus c. 540B.C.-c. 450B.C. ... **CMLC 22**
See also DLB 176

Herbert, Frank (Patrick) 1920-1986 .... **CLC 12, 23, 35, 44, 85**
See also AAYA 21; BPFB 2; BYA 5, 14; CA 53-56; 118; CANR 5, 43; CDALBS; CPW; DAM POP; DLB 8; INT CANR-5; LAIT 5; MTCW 1, 2; MTFW 2005; NFS 17; SATA 9, 37; SATA-Obit 47; SCFW 1, 2; SFW 4; YAW

Herbert, George 1593-1633 . **LC 24, 121; PC 4**
See also BRW 2; BRWR 2; CDBLB Before 1660; DAB; DAM POET; DLB 126; EXPP; RGEL 2; TEA; WP

Herbert, Zbigniew 1924-1998 ..... **CLC 9, 43; PC 50; TCLC 168**
See also CA 89-92; 169; CANR 36, 74; CDWLB 4; CWW 2; DAM POET; DLB 232; EWL 3; MTCW 1; PFS 22

Herbst, Josephine (Frey) 1897-1969 .... **CLC 34**
See also CA 5-8R; 25-28R; DLB 9

Herder, Johann Gottfried von 1744-1803 .... **NCLC 8**
See also DLB 97; EW 4; TWA

Heredia, Jose Maria 1803-1839 .... **HLCS 2**
See also LAW

Hergesheimer, Joseph 1880-1954 ... **TCLC 11**
See also CA 109; 194; DLB 102, 9; RGAL 4

Herlihy, James Leo 1927-1993 .... **CLC 6**
See also CA 1-4R; 143; CAD; CANR 2; CN 1, 2, 3, 4, 5

Herman, William
See Bierce, Ambrose (Gwinett)

Hermogenes fl. c. 175- .... **CMLC 6**

Hernandez, Jose 1834-1886 .... **NCLC 17**
See also LAW; RGWL 2, 3; WLIT 1

Herodotus c. 484B.C.-c. 420B.C. .. **CMLC 17**
See also AW 1; CDWLB 1; DLB 176; RGWL 2, 3; TWA

Herrick, Robert 1591-1674 .... **LC 13; PC 9**
See also BRW 2; BRWC 2; DA; DAB; DAC; DAM MST, POP; DLB 126; EXPP; PFS 13; RGAL 4; RGEL 2; TEA; WP

Herring, Guilles
See Somerville, Edith Oenone

Herriot, James 1916-1995 .... **CLC 12**
See Wight, James Alfred
See also AAYA 1, 54; BPFB 2; CA 148; CANR 40; CLR 80; CPW; DAM POP; LAIT 3; MAICYA 2; MAICYAS 1; MTCW 2; SATA 86, 135; TEA; YAW

Herris, Violet
See Hunt, Violet

Herrmann, Dorothy 1941- .... **CLC 44**
See also CA 107

Herrmann, Taffy
See Herrmann, Dorothy

Hersey, John (Richard) 1914-1993 .... **CLC 1, 2, 7, 9, 40, 81, 97**
See also AAYA 29; BPFB 2; CA 17-20R; 140; CANR 33; CDALBS; CN 1, 2, 3, 4, 5; CPW; DAM POP; DLB 6, 185, 278, 299; MAL 5; MTCW 1, 2; MTFW 2005; SATA 25; SATA-Obit 76; TUS

Herzen, Aleksandr Ivanovich
1812-1870 .... **NCLC 10, 61**
See Herzen, Alexander

Herzen, Alexander
See Herzen, Aleksandr Ivanovich
See also DLB 277

Herzl, Theodor 1860-1904 .... **TCLC 36**
See also CA 168

Herzog, Werner 1942- .... **CLC 16**
See also CA 89-92

Hesiod c. 8th cent. B.C.- .... **CMLC 5**
See also AW 1; DLB 176; RGWL 2, 3

Hesse, Hermann 1877-1962 ... **CLC 1, 2, 3, 6, 11, 17, 25, 69; SSC 9, 49; TCLC 148; WLC**
See also AAYA 43; BPFB 2; CA 17-18; CAP 2; CDWLB 2; DA; DA3; DAB; DAC; DAM MST, NOV; DLB 66; EW 9; EWL 3; EXPN; LAIT 1; MTCW 1, 2; MTFW 2005; NFS 6, 15; RGWL 2, 3; SATA 50; TWA

Hewes, Cady
See De Voto, Bernard (Augustine)

Heyen, William 1940- .... **CLC 13, 18**
See also CA 33-36R, 220; CAAE 220; CAAS 9; CANR 98; CP 3, 4, 5, 6, 7; DLB 5

Heyerdahl, Thor 1914-2002 .... **CLC 26**
See also CA 5-8R; 207; CANR 5, 22, 66, 73; LAIT 4; MTCW 1, 2; MTFW 2005; SATA 2, 52

Heym, Georg (Theodor Franz Arthur)
1887-1912 .... **TCLC 9**
See also CA 106; 181

Heym, Stefan 1913-2001 .... **CLC 41**
See also CA 9-12R; 203; CANR 4; CWW 2; DLB 69; EWL 3

Heyse, Paul (Johann Ludwig von)
1830-1914 .... **TCLC 8**
See also CA 104; 209; DLB 129

Heyward, (Edwin) DuBose
1885-1940 .... **HR 1:2; TCLC 59**
See also CA 108; 157; DLB 7, 9, 45, 249; MAL 5; SATA 21

Heywood, John 1497(?)-1580(?) .... **LC 65**
See also DLB 136; RGEL 2

Heywood, Thomas 1573(?)-1641 .... **LC 111**
See also DAM DRAM; DLB 62; LMFS 1; RGEL 2; TEA

Hibbert, Eleanor Alice Burford
1906-1993 .... **CLC 7**
See Holt, Victoria
See also BEST 90:4; CA 17-20R; 140; CANR 9, 28, 59; CMW 4; CPW; DAM POP; MTCW 2; MTFW 2005; RHW; SATA 2; SATA-Obit 74

Hichens, Robert (Smythe)
1864-1950 .... **TCLC 64**
See also CA 162; DLB 153; HGG; RHW; SUFW

Higgins, Aidan 1927- .... **SSC 68**
See also CA 9-12R; CANR 70, 115; CN 1, 2, 3, 4, 5, 6, 7; DLB 14

Higgins, George V(incent)
1939-1999 .... **CLC 4, 7, 10, 18**
See also BPFB 2; CA 77-80; 186; CAAS 5; CANR 17, 51, 89, 96; CMW 4; CN 2, 3, 4, 5, 6; DLB 2; DLBY 1981, 1998; INT CANR-17; MSW; MTCW 1

Higginson, Thomas Wentworth
1823-1911 .... **TCLC 36**
See also CA 162; DLB 1, 64, 243

Higgonet, Margaret ed. .... **CLC 65**

Highet, Helen
See MacInnes, Helen (Clark)

Highsmith, (Mary) Patricia
1921-1995 .... **CLC 2, 4, 14, 42, 102**
See Morgan, Claire
See also AAYA 48; BRWS 5; CA 1-4R; 147; CANR 1, 20, 48, 62, 108; CMW 4; CN 1, 2, 3, 4, 5; CPW; DA3; DAM NOV, POP; DLB 306; MSW; MTCW 1, 2; MTFW 2005

Highwater, Jamake (Mamake)
1942(?)-2001 .... **CLC 12**
See also AAYA 7; BPFB 2; BYA 4; CA 65-68; 199; CAAS 7; CANR 10, 34, 84; CLR 17; CWRI 5; DLB 52; DLBY 1985; JRDA; MAICYA 1, 2; SATA 32, 69; SATA-Brief 30

Highway, Tomson 1951- ...... **CLC 92; NNAL**
See also CA 151; CANR 75; CCA 1; CD 5, 6; CN 7; DAC; DAM MULT; DFS 2; MTCW 2

Hijuelos, Oscar 1951- .... **CLC 65; HLC 1**
See also AAYA 25; AMWS 8; BEST 90:1; CA 123; CANR 50, 75, 125; CPW; DA3; DAM MULT, POP; DLB 145; HW 1, 2; LLW; MAL 5; MTCW 2; MTFW 2005; NFS 17; RGAL 4; WLIT 1

Hikmet, Nazim 1902-1963 .... **CLC 40**
See Nizami of Ganja
See also CA 141; 93-96; EWL 3; WLIT 6

Hildegard von Bingen 1098-1179 . **CMLC 20**
See also DLB 148

Hildesheimer, Wolfgang 1916-1991 .. **CLC 49**
See also CA 101; 135; DLB 69, 124; EWL 3

Hill, Geoffrey (William) 1932- .... **CLC 5, 8, 18, 45**
See also BRWS 5; CA 81-84; CANR 21, 89; CDBLB 1960 to Present; CP 1, 2, 3, 4, 5, 6, 7; DAM POET; DLB 40; EWL 3; MTCW 1; RGEL 2

Hill, George Roy 1921-2002 .... **CLC 26**
See also CA 110; 122; 213

Hill, John
See Koontz, Dean R.

Hill, Susan (Elizabeth) 1942- .... **CLC 4, 113**
See also CA 33-36R; CANR 29, 69, 129; CN 2, 3, 4, 5, 6, 7; DAB; DAM MST, NOV; DLB 14, 139; HGG; MTCW 1; RHW

Hillard, Asa G. III .... **CLC 70**

Hillerman, Tony 1925- .... **CLC 62, 170**
See also AAYA 40; BEST 89:1; BPFB 2; CA 29-32R; CANR 21, 42, 65, 97, 134; CMW 4; CPW; DA3; DAM POP; DLB 206, 306; MAL 5; MSW; MTCW 2; MTFW 2005; RGAL 4; SATA 6; TCWW 2; YAW

Hillesum, Etty 1914-1943 .... **TCLC 49**
See also CA 137

Hilliard, Noel (Harvey) 1929-1996 ... **CLC 15**
See also CA 9-12R; CANR 7, 69; CN 1, 2, 3, 4, 5, 6

Hillis, Rick 1956- .... **CLC 66**
See also CA 134

Hilton, James 1900-1954 .... **TCLC 21**
See also CA 108; 169; DLB 34, 77; FANT; SATA 34

Hilton, Walter (?)-1396 .... **CMLC 58**
See also DLB 146; RGEL 2

Himes, Chester (Bomar) 1909-1984 .. **BLC 2; CLC 2, 4, 7, 18, 58, 108; TCLC 139**
See also AFAW 2; BPFB 2; BW 2; CA 25-28R; 114; CANR 22, 89; CMW 4; CN 1, 2, 3; DAM MULT; DLB 2, 76, 143, 226; EWL 3; MAL 5; MSW; MTCW 1, 2; MTFW 2005; RGAL 4

Himmelfarb, Gertrude 1922- .... **CLC 202**
See also CA 49-52; CANR 28, 66, 102

Hinde, Thomas .... **CLC 6, 11**
See Chitty, Thomas Willes
See also CN 1, 2, 3, 4, 5, 6; EWL 3

Hine, (William) Daryl 1936- .... **CLC 15**
See also CA 1-4R; CAAS 15; CANR 1, 20; CP 1, 2, 3, 4, 5, 6, 7; DLB 60

Hinkson, Katharine Tynan
See Tynan, Katharine

Hinojosa(-Smith), Rolando (R.)
1929- .... **HLC 1**
See Hinojosa-Smith, Rolando
See also CA 131; CAAS 16; CANR 62; DAM MULT; DLB 82; HW 1, 2; LLW; MTCW 2; MTFW 2005; RGAL 4

Hinton, S(usan) E(loise) 1950- ... **CLC 30, 111**
See also AAYA 2, 33; BPFB 2; BYA 2, 3; CA 81-84; CANR 32, 62, 92, 133; CDALBS; CLR 3, 23; CPW; DA; DA3; DAB; DAC; DAM MST, NOV; JRDA; LAIT 5; MAICYA 1, 2; MTCW 1, 2; MTFW 2005 !**; NFS 5, 9, 15, 16; SATA 19, 58, 115, 160; WYA; YAW

Hippius, Zinaida (Nikolaevna) .... **TCLC 9**
See Gippius, Zinaida (Nikolaevna)
See also DLB 295; EWL 3

Hiraoka, Kimitake 1925-1970
See Mishima, Yukio
See also CA 97-100; 29-32R; DA3; DAM DRAM; GLL 1; MTCW 1, 2

Hirsch, E(ric) D(onald), Jr. 1928- .... **CLC 79**
See also CA 25-28R; CANR 27, 51; DLB 67; INT CANR-27; MTCW 1

Hirsch, Edward 1950- .... **CLC 31, 50**
See also CA 104; CANR 20, 42, 102; CP 7; DLB 120; PFS 22

Hitchcock, Alfred (Joseph)
1899-1980 .... **CLC 16**
See also AAYA 22; CA 159; 97-100; SATA 27; SATA-Obit 24

Hitchens, Christopher (Eric)
1949- .... **CLC 157**
See also CA 152; CANR 89

Hitler, Adolf 1889-1945 .... **TCLC 53**
See also CA 117; 147

Hoagland, Edward (Morley) 1932- .. **CLC 28**
See also ANW; CA 1-4R; CANR 2, 31, 57, 107; CN 1, 2, 3, 4, 5, 6, 7; DLB 6; SATA 51; TCWW 2

Hoban, Russell (Conwell) 1925- ... **CLC 7, 25**
See also BPFB 2; CA 5-8R; CANR 23, 37, 66, 114, 138; CLR 3, 69; CN 4, 5, 6, 7; CWRI 5; DAM NOV; DLB 52; FANT; MAICYA 1, 2; MTCW 1, 2; MTFW 2005; SATA 1, 40, 78, 136; SFW 4; SUFW 2; TCLE 1:1

Hobbes, Thomas 1588-1679 .... **LC 36**
See also DLB 151, 252, 281; RGEL 2

Hobbs, Perry
See Blackmur, R(ichard) P(almer)

Hobson, Laura Z(ametkin)
1900-1986 .... **CLC 7, 25**
See also BPFB 2; CA 17-20R; 118; CANR 55; CN 1, 2, 3, 4; DLB 28; SATA 52

Hoccleve, Thomas c. 1368-c. 1437 ...... **LC 75**
See also DLB 146; RGEL 2

Hoch, Edward D(entinger) 1930-
See Queen, Ellery
See also CA 29-32R; CANR 11, 27, 51, 97; CMW 4; DLB 306; SFW 4

Hochhuth, Rolf 1931- .... **CLC 4, 11, 18**
See also CA 5-8R; CANR 33, 75, 136; CWW 2; DAM DRAM; DLB 124; EWL 3; MTCW 1, 2; MTFW 2005

Hochman, Sandra 1936- .... **CLC 3, 8**
See also CA 5-8R; CP 1, 2, 3, 4; DLB 5

Hochwaelder, Fritz 1911-1986 .... **CLC 36**
See Hochwalder, Fritz
See also CA 29-32R; 120; CANR 42; DAM DRAM; MTCW 1; RGWL 3

Hochwalder, Fritz
See Hochwaelder, Fritz
See also EWL 3; RGWL 2

Hocking, Mary (Eunice) 1921- .... **CLC 13**
See also CA 101; CANR 18, 40
Hodgins, Jack 1938- .... **CLC 23**
See also CA 93-96; CN 4, 5, 6, 7; DLB 60
Hodgson, William Hope
1877(?)-1918 .... **TCLC 13**
See also CA 111; 164; CMW 4; DLB 70, 153, 156, 178; HGG; MTCW 2; SFW 4; SUFW 1
Hoeg, Peter 1957- .... **CLC 95, 156**
See also CA 151; CANR 75; CMW 4; DA3; DLB 214; EWL 3; MTCW 2; MTFW 2005; NFS 17; RGWL 3; SSFS 18
Hoffman, Alice 1952- .... **CLC 51**
See also AAYA 37; AMWS 10; CA 77-80; CANR 34, 66, 100, 138; CN 4, 5, 6, 7; CPW; DAM NOV; DLB 292; MAL 5; MTCW 1, 2; MTFW 2005; TCLE 1:1
Hoffman, Daniel (Gerard) 1923- . **CLC 6, 13, 23**
See also CA 1-4R; CANR 4, 142; CP 1, 2, 3, 4, 5, 6, 7; DLB 5; TCLE 1:1
Hoffman, Eva 1945- .... **CLC 182**
See also CA 132; CANR 146
Hoffman, Stanley 1944- .... **CLC 5**
See also CA 77-80
Hoffman, William 1925- .... **CLC 141**
See also CA 21-24R; CANR 9, 103; CSW; DLB 234; TCLE 1:1
Hoffman, William M.
See Hoffman, William M(oses)
See also CAD; CD 5, 6
Hoffman, William M(oses) 1939- ..... **CLC 40**
See Hoffman, William M.
See also CA 57-60; CANR 11, 71
Hoffmann, E(rnst) T(heodor) A(madeus)
1776-1822 .... **NCLC 2; SSC 13**
See also CDWLB 2; DLB 90; EW 5; GL 2; RGSF 2; RGWL 2, 3; SATA 27; SUFW 1; WCH
Hofmann, Gert 1931-1993 .... **CLC 54**
See also CA 128; CANR 145; EWL 3
Hofmannsthal, Hugo von 1874-1929 ... **DC 4; TCLC 11**
See also CA 106; 153; CDWLB 2; DAM DRAM; DFS 17; DLB 81, 118; EW 9; EWL 3; RGWL 2, 3
Hogan, Linda 1947- ..... **CLC 73; NNAL; PC 35**
See also AMWS 4; ANW; BYA 12; CA 120, 226; CAAE 226; CANR 45, 73, 129; CWP; DAM MULT; DLB 175; SATA 132; TCWW 2
Hogarth, Charles
See Creasey, John
Hogarth, Emmett
See Polonsky, Abraham (Lincoln)
Hogarth, William 1697-1764 .... **LC 112**
See also AAYA 56
Hogg, James 1770-1835 .... **NCLC 4, 109**
See also BRWS 10; DLB 93, 116, 159; GL 2; HGG; RGEL 2; SUFW 1
Holbach, Paul-Henri Thiry
1723-1789 .... **LC 14**
See also DLB 313
Holberg, Ludvig 1684-1754 .... **LC 6**
See also DLB 300; RGWL 2, 3
Holcroft, Thomas 1745-1809 .... **NCLC 85**
See also DLB 39, 89, 158; RGEL 2
Holden, Ursula 1921- .... **CLC 18**
See also CA 101; CAAS 8; CANR 22
Holderlin, (Johann Christian) Friedrich
1770-1843 .... **NCLC 16; PC 4**
See also CDWLB 2; DLB 90; EW 5; RGWL 2, 3
Holdstock, Robert
See Holdstock, Robert P.

Holdstock, Robert P. 1948- .... **CLC 39**
See also CA 131; CANR 81; DLB 261; FANT; HGG; SFW 4; SUFW 2
Holinshed, Raphael fl. 1580- .... **LC 69**
See also DLB 167; RGEL 2
Holland, Isabelle (Christian)
1920-2002 .... **CLC 21**
See also AAYA 11, 64; CA 21-24R; 205; CAAE 181; CANR 10, 25, 47; CLR 57; CWRI 5; JRDA; LAIT 4; MAICYA 1, 2; SATA 8, 70; SATA-Essay 103; SATA-Obit 132; WYA
Holland, Marcus
See Caldwell, (Janet Miriam) Taylor (Holland)
Hollander, John 1929- .... **CLC 2, 5, 8, 14**
See also CA 1-4R; CANR 1, 52, 136; CP 1, 2, 3, 4, 5, 6, 7; DLB 5; MAL 5; SATA 13
Hollander, Paul
See Silverberg, Robert
Holleran, Andrew .... **CLC 38**
See Garber, Eric
See also CA 144; GLL 1
Holley, Marietta 1836(?)-1926 .... **TCLC 99**
See also CA 118; DLB 11; FL 1:3
Hollinghurst, Alan 1954- .... **CLC 55, 91**
See also BRWS 10; CA 114; CN 5, 6, 7; DLB 207; GLL 1
Hollis, Jim
See Summers, Hollis (Spurgeon, Jr.)
Holly, Buddy 1936-1959 .... **TCLC 65**
See also CA 213
Holmes, Gordon
See Shiel, M(atthew) P(hipps)
Holmes, John
See Souster, (Holmes) Raymond
Holmes, John Clellon 1926-1988 ...... **CLC 56**
See also BG 1:2; CA 9-12R; 125; CANR 4; CN 1, 2, 3, 4; DLB 16, 237
Holmes, Oliver Wendell, Jr.
1841-1935 .... **TCLC 77**
See also CA 114; 186
Holmes, Oliver Wendell
1809-1894 .... **NCLC 14, 81; PC 71**
See also AMWS 1; CDALB 1640-1865; DLB 1, 189, 235; EXPP; RGAL 4; SATA 34
Holmes, Raymond
See Souster, (Holmes) Raymond
Holt, Victoria
See Hibbert, Eleanor Alice Burford
See also BPFB 2
Holub, Miroslav 1923-1998 .... **CLC 4**
See also CA 21-24R; 169; CANR 10; CDWLB 4; CWW 2; DLB 232; EWL 3; RGWL 3
Holz, Detlev
See Benjamin, Walter
Homer c. 8th cent. B.C.- .... **CMLC 1, 16, 61; PC 23; WLCS**
See also AW 1; CDWLB 1; DA; DA3; DAB; DAC; DAM MST, POET; DLB 176; EFS 1; LAIT 1; LMFS 1; RGWL 2, 3; TWA; WP
Hongo, Garrett Kaoru 1951- .... **PC 23**
See also CA 133; CAAS 22; CP 7; DLB 120, 312; EWL 3; EXPP; RGAL 4
Honig, Edwin 1919- .... **CLC 33**
See also CA 5-8R; CAAS 8; CANR 4, 45, 144; CP 1, 2, 3, 4, 5, 6, 7; DLB 5
Hood, Hugh (John Blagdon) 1928- . **CLC 15, 28; SSC 42**
See also CA 49-52; CAAS 17; CANR 1, 33, 87; CN 1, 2, 3, 4, 5, 6, 7; DLB 53; RGSF 2
Hood, Thomas 1799-1845 .... **NCLC 16**
See also BRW 4; DLB 96; RGEL 2

Hooker, (Peter) Jeremy 1941- .... **CLC 43**
See also CA 77-80; CANR 22; CP 2, 3, 4, 5, 6, 7; DLB 40
Hooker, Richard 1554-1600 .... **LC 95**
See also BRW 1; DLB 132; RGEL 2
hooks, bell
See Watkins, Gloria Jean
Hope, A(lec) D(erwent) 1907-2000 .... **CLC 3, 51; PC 56**
See also BRWS 7; CA 21-24R; 188; CANR 33, 74; CP 1, 2, 3, 4; DLB 289; EWL 3; MTCW 1, 2; MTFW 2005; PFS 8; RGEL 2
Hope, Anthony 1863-1933 .... **TCLC 83**
See also CA 157; DLB 153, 156; RGEL 2; RHW
Hope, Brian
See Creasey, John
Hope, Christopher (David Tully)
1944- .... **CLC 52**
See also AFW; CA 106; CANR 47, 101; CN 4, 5, 6, 7; DLB 225; SATA 62
Hopkins, Gerard Manley
1844-1889 .... **NCLC 17; PC 15; WLC**
See also BRW 5; BRWR 2; CDBLB 1890-1914; DA; DA3; DAB; DAC; DAM MST, POET; DLB 35, 57; EXPP; PAB; RGEL 2; TEA; WP
Hopkins, John (Richard) 1931-1998 .. **CLC 4**
See also CA 85-88; 169; CBD; CD 5, 6
Hopkins, Pauline Elizabeth
1859-1930 .... **BLC 2; TCLC 28**
See also AFAW 2; BW 2, 3; CA 141; CANR 82; DAM MULT; DLB 50
Hopkinson, Francis 1737-1791 .... **LC 25**
See also DLB 31; RGAL 4
Hopley-Woolrich, Cornell George 1903-1968
See Woolrich, Cornell
See also CA 13-14; CANR 58; CAP 1; CMW 4; DLB 226; MTCW 2
Horace 65B.C.-8B.C. .... **CMLC 39; PC 46**
See also AW 2; CDWLB 1; DLB 211; RGWL 2, 3
Horatio
See Proust, (Valentin-Louis-George-Eugene) Marcel
Horgan, Paul (George Vincent O'Shaughnessy) 1903-1995 .. **CLC 9, 53**
See also BPFB 2; CA 13-16R; 147; CANR 9, 35; CN 1, 2, 3, 4, 5; DAM NOV; DLB 102, 212; DLBY 1985; INT CANR-9; MTCW 1, 2; MTFW 2005; SATA 13; SATA-Obit 84; TCWW 1, 2
Horkheimer, Max 1895-1973 .... **TCLC 132**
See also CA 216; 41-44R; DLB 296
Horn, Peter
See Kuttner, Henry
Horne, Frank (Smith) 1899-1974 .... **HR 1:2**
See also BW 1; CA 125; 53-56; DLB 51; WP
Horne, Richard Henry Hengist
1802(?)-1884 .... **NCLC 127**
See also DLB 32; SATA 29
Hornem, Horace Esq.
See Byron, George Gordon (Noel)
Horney, Karen (Clementine Theodore Danielsen) 1885-1952 .... **TCLC 71**
See also CA 114; 165; DLB 246; FW
Hornung, E(rnest) W(illiam)
1866-1921 .... **TCLC 59**
See also CA 108; 160; CMW 4; DLB 70
Horovitz, Israel (Arthur) 1939- .... **CLC 56**
See also CA 33-36R; CAD; CANR 46, 59; CD 5, 6; DAM DRAM; DLB 7; MAL 5
Horton, George Moses
1797(?)-1883(?) .... **NCLC 87**
See also DLB 50

Horvath, odon von 1901-1938
See von Horvath, Odon
See also EWL 3

Horvath, Oedoen von -1938
See von Horvath, Odon

Horwitz, Julius 1920-1986 .... **CLC 14**
See also CA 9-12R; 119; CANR 12

Hospital, Janette Turner 1942- .... **CLC 42, 145**
See also CA 108; CANR 48; CN 5, 6, 7; DLBY 2002; RGSF 2

Hostos, E. M. de
See Hostos (y Bonilla), Eugenio Maria de

Hostos, Eugenio M. de
See Hostos (y Bonilla), Eugenio Maria de

Hostos, Eugenio Maria
See Hostos (y Bonilla), Eugenio Maria de

Hostos (y Bonilla), Eugenio Maria de 1839-1903 .... **TCLC 24**
See also CA 123; 131; HW 1

Houdini
See Lovecraft, H(oward) P(hillips)

Houellebecq, Michel 1958- .... **CLC 179**
See also CA 185; CANR 140; MTFW 2005

Hougan, Carolyn 1943- .... **CLC 34**
See also CA 139

Household, Geoffrey (Edward West) 1900-1988 .... **CLC 11**
See also CA 77-80; 126; CANR 58; CMW 4; CN 1, 2, 3, 4; DLB 87; SATA 14; SATA-Obit 59

Housman, A(lfred) E(dward) 1859-1936 .... **PC 2, 43; TCLC 1, 10; WLCS**
See also AAYA 66; BRW 6; CA 104; 125; DA; DA3; DAB; DAC; DAM MST, POET; DLB 19, 284; EWL 3; EXPP; MTCW 1, 2; MTFW 2005; PAB; PFS 4, 7; RGEL 2; TEA; WP

Housman, Laurence 1865-1959 .... **TCLC 7**
See also CA 106; 155; DLB 10; FANT; RGEL 2; SATA 25

Houston, Jeanne (Toyo) Wakatsuki 1934- .... **AAL**
See also AAYA 49; CA 103, 232; CAAE 232; CAAS 16; CANR 29, 123; LAIT 4; SATA 78

Howard, Elizabeth Jane 1923- ..... **CLC 7, 29**
See also BRWS 11; CA 5-8R; CANR 8, 62, 146; CN 1, 2, 3, 4, 5, 6, 7

Howard, Maureen 1930- .... **CLC 5, 14, 46, 151**
See also CA 53-56; CANR 31, 75, 140; CN 4, 5, 6, 7; DLBY 1983; INT CANR-31; MTCW 1, 2; MTFW 2005

Howard, Richard 1929- .... **CLC 7, 10, 47**
See also AITN 1; CA 85-88; CANR 25, 80; CP 1, 2, 3, 4, 5, 6, 7; DLB 5; INT CANR-25; MAL 5

Howard, Robert E(rvin) 1906-1936 .... **TCLC 8**
See also BPFB 2; BYA 5; CA 105; 157; FANT; SUFW 1; TCWW 1, 2

Howard, Warren F.
See Pohl, Frederik

Howe, Fanny (Quincy) 1940- .... **CLC 47**
See also CA 117; 187; CAAE 187; CAAS 27; CANR 70, 116; CP 7; CWP; SATA-Brief 52

Howe, Irving 1920-1993 .... **CLC 85**
See also AMWS 6; CA 9-12R; 141; CANR 21, 50; DLB 67; EWL 3; MAL 5; MTCW 1, 2; MTFW 2005

Howe, Julia Ward 1819-1910 .... **TCLC 21**
See also CA 117; 191; DLB 1, 189, 235; FW

Howe, Susan 1937- .... **CLC 72, 152; PC 54**
See also AMWS 4; CA 160; CP 7; CWP; DLB 120; FW; RGAL 4

Howe, Tina 1937- .... **CLC 48**
See also CA 109; CAD; CANR 125; CD 5, 6; CWD

Howell, James 1594(?)-1666 .... **LC 13**
See also DLB 151

Howells, W. D.
See Howells, William Dean

Howells, William D.
See Howells, William Dean

Howells, William Dean 1837-1920 ... **SSC 36; TCLC 7, 17, 41**
See also AMW; CA 104; 134; CDALB 1865-1917; DLB 12, 64, 74, 79, 189; LMFS 1; MAL 5; MTCW 2; RGAL 4; TUS

Howes, Barbara 1914-1996 .... **CLC 15**
See also CA 9-12R; 151; CAAS 3; CANR 53; CP 1, 2, 3, 4; SATA 5; TCLE 1:1

Hrabal, Bohumil 1914-1997 ...... **CLC 13, 67; TCLC 155**
See also CA 106; 156; CAAS 12; CANR 57; CWW 2; DLB 232; EWL 3; RGSF 2

Hrabanus Maurus 776(?)-856 .... **CMLC 78**
See also DLB 148

Hrotsvit of Gandersheim c. 935-c. 1000 .... **CMLC 29**
See also DLB 148

Hsi, Chu 1130-1200 .... **CMLC 42**

Hsun, Lu
See Lu Hsun

Hubbard, L(afayette) Ron(ald) 1911-1986 .... **CLC 43**
See also AAYA 64; CA 77-80; 118; CANR 52; CPW; DA3; DAM POP; FANT; MTCW 2; MTFW 2005; SFW 4

Huch, Ricarda (Octavia) 1864-1947 .... **TCLC 13**
See Hugo, Richard
See also CA 111; 189; DLB 66; EWL 3

Huddle, David 1942- .... **CLC 49**
See also CA 57-60; CAAS 20; CANR 89; DLB 130

Hudson, Jeffrey
See Crichton, (John) Michael

Hudson, W(illiam) H(enry) 1841-1922 .... **TCLC 29**
See also CA 115; 190; DLB 98, 153, 174; RGEL 2; SATA 35

Hueffer, Ford Madox
See Ford, Ford Madox

Hughart, Barry 1934- .... **CLC 39**
See also CA 137; FANT; SFW 4; SUFW 2

Hughes, Colin
See Creasey, John

Hughes, David (John) 1930-2005 ..... **CLC 48**
See also CA 116; 129; 238; CN 4, 5, 6, 7; DLB 14

Hughes, Edward James
See Hughes, Ted
See also DA3; DAM MST, POET

Hughes, (James Mercer) Langston 1902-1967 ..... **BLC 2; CLC 1, 5, 10, 15, 35, 44, 108; DC 3; HR 1:2; PC 1, 53; SSC 6, 90; WLC**
See also AAYA 12; AFAW 1, 2; AMWR 1; AMWS 1; BW 1, 3; CA 1-4R; 25-28R; CANR 1, 34, 82; CDALB 1929-1941; CLR 17; DA; DA3; DAB; DAC; DAM DRAM, MST, MULT, POET; DFS 6, 18; DLB 4, 7, 48, 51, 86, 228, 315; EWL 3; EXPP; EXPS; JRDA; LAIT 3; LMFS 2; MAICYA 1, 2; MAL 5; MTCW 1, 2; MTFW 2005; NFS 21; PAB; PFS 1, 3, 6, 10, 15; RGAL 4; RGSF 2; SATA 4, 33; SSFS 4, 7; TUS; WCH; WP; YAW

Hughes, Richard (Arthur Warren) 1900-1976 .... **CLC 1, 11**
See also CA 5-8R; 65-68; CANR 4; CN 1, 2; DAM NOV; DLB 15, 161; EWL 3; MTCW 1; RGEL 2; SATA 8; SATA-Obit 25

Hughes, Ted 1930-1998 . **CLC 2, 4, 9, 14, 37, 119; PC 7**
See Hughes, Edward James
See also BRWC 2; BRWS 1; CA 1-4R; 171; CANR 1, 33, 66, 108; CLR 3; CP 1, 2, 3, 4, 5, 6; DAB; DAC; DLB 40, 161; EWL 3; EXPP; MAICYA 1, 2; MTCW 1, 2; MTFW 2005; PAB; PFS 4, 19; RGEL 2; SATA 49; SATA-Brief 27; SATA-Obit 107; TEA; YAW

Hugo, Richard
See Huch, Ricarda (Octavia)
See also MAL 5

Hugo, Richard F(ranklin) 1923-1982 .... **CLC 6, 18, 32; PC 68**
See also AMWS 6; CA 49-52; 108; CANR 3; CP 1, 2, 3; DAM POET; DLB 5, 206; EWL 3; PFS 17; RGAL 4

Hugo, Victor (Marie) 1802-1885 .... **NCLC 3, 10, 21, 161; PC 17; WLC**
See also AAYA 28; DA; DA3; DAB; DAC; DAM DRAM, MST, NOV, POET; DLB 119, 192, 217; EFS 2; EW 6; EXPN; GFL 1789 to the Present; LAIT 1, 2; NFS 5, 20; RGWL 2, 3; SATA 47; TWA

Huidobro, Vicente
See Huidobro Fernandez, Vicente Garcia
See also DLB 283; EWL 3; LAW

Huidobro Fernandez, Vicente Garcia 1893-1948 .... **TCLC 31**
See Huidobro, Vicente
See also CA 131; HW 1

Hulme, Keri 1947- .... **CLC 39, 130**
See also CA 125; CANR 69; CN 4, 5, 6, 7; CP 7; CWP; EWL 3; FW; INT CA-125

Hulme, T(homas) E(rnest) 1883-1917 .... **TCLC 21**
See also BRWS 6; CA 117; 203; DLB 19

Humboldt, Wilhelm von 1767-1835 .... **NCLC 134**
See also DLB 90

Hume, David 1711-1776 .... **LC 7, 56**
See also BRWS 3; DLB 104, 252; LMFS 1; TEA

Humphrey, William 1924-1997 .... **CLC 45**
See also AMWS 9; CA 77-80; 160; CANR 68; CN 1, 2, 3, 4, 5, 6; CSW; DLB 6, 212, 234, 278; TCWW 1, 2

Humphreys, Emyr Owen 1919- .... **CLC 47**
See also CA 5-8R; CANR 3, 24; CN 1, 2, 3, 4, 5, 6, 7; DLB 15

Humphreys, Josephine 1945- ...... **CLC 34, 57**
See also CA 121; 127; CANR 97; CSW; DLB 292; INT CA-127

Huneker, James Gibbons 1860-1921 .... **TCLC 65**
See also CA 193; DLB 71; RGAL 4

Hungerford, Hesba Fay
See Brinsmead, H(esba) F(ay)

Hungerford, Pixie
See Brinsmead, H(esba) F(ay)

Hunt, E(verette) Howard, (Jr.) 1918- .... **CLC 3**
See also AITN 1; CA 45-48; CANR 2, 47, 103; CMW 4

Hunt, Francesca
See Holland, Isabelle (Christian)

Hunt, Howard
See Hunt, E(verette) Howard, (Jr.)

Hunt, Kyle
See Creasey, John

Hunt, (James Henry) Leigh
1784-1859 .... **NCLC 1, 70**
See also DAM POET; DLB 96, 110, 144; RGEL 2; TEA

Hunt, Marsha 1946- .... **CLC 70**
See also BW 2, 3; CA 143; CANR 79

Hunt, Violet 1866(?)-1942 .... **TCLC 53**
See also CA 184; DLB 162, 197

Hunter, E. Waldo
See Sturgeon, Theodore (Hamilton)

Hunter, Evan 1926-2005 .... **CLC 11, 31**
See McBain, Ed
See also AAYA 39; BPFB 2; CA 5-8R; 241; CANR 5, 38, 62, 97; CMW 4; CN 1, 2, 3, 4, 5, 6, 7; CPW; DAM POP; DLB 306; DLBY 1982; INT CANR-5; MSW; MTCW 1; SATA 25; SFW 4

Hunter, Kristin
See Lattany, Kristin (Elaine Eggleston) Hunter
See also CN 1, 2, 3, 4, 5, 6

Hunter, Mary
See Austin, Mary (Hunter)

Hunter, Mollie 1922- .... **CLC 21**
See McIlwraith, Maureen Mollie Hunter
See also AAYA 13; BYA 6; CANR 37, 78; CLR 25; DLB 161; JRDA; MAICYA 1, 2; SAAS 7; SATA 54, 106, 139; SATA-Essay 139; WYA; YAW

Hunter, Robert (?)-1734 .... **LC 7**

Hurston, Zora Neale 1891-1960 .... **BLC 2; CLC 7, 30, 61; DC 12; HR 1:2; SSC 4, 80; TCLC 121, 131; WLCS**
See also AAYA 15; AFAW 1, 2; AMWS 6; BW 1, 3; BYA 12; CA 85-88; CANR 61; CDALBS; DA; DA3; DAC; DAM MST, MULT, NOV; DFS 6; DLB 51, 86; EWL 3; EXPN; EXPS; FL 1:6; FW; LAIT 3; LATS 1:1; LMFS 2; MAL 5; MAWW; MTCW 1, 2; MTFW 2005; NFS 3; RGAL 4; RGSF 2; SSFS 1, 6, 11, 19, 21; TUS; YAW

Husserl, E. G.
See Husserl, Edmund (Gustav Albrecht)

Husserl, Edmund (Gustav Albrecht)
1859-1938 .... **TCLC 100**
See also CA 116; 133; DLB 296

Huston, John (Marcellus)
1906-1987 .... **CLC 20**
See also CA 73-76; 123; CANR 34; DLB 26

Hustvedt, Siri 1955- .... **CLC 76**
See also CA 137

Hutten, Ulrich von 1488-1523 .... **LC 16**
See also DLB 179

Huxley, Aldous (Leonard)
1894-1963 .... **CLC 1, 3, 4, 5, 8, 11, 18, 35, 79; SSC 39; WLC**
See also AAYA 11; BPFB 2; BRW 7; CA 85-88; CANR 44, 99; CDBLB 1914-1945; DA; DA3; DAB; DAC; DAM MST, NOV; DLB 36, 100, 162, 195, 255; EWL 3; EXPN; LAIT 5; LMFS 2; MTCW 1, 2; MTFW 2005; NFS 6; RGEL 2; SATA 63; SCFW 1, 2; SFW 4; TEA; YAW

Huxley, T(homas) H(enry)
1825-1895 .... **NCLC 67**
See also DLB 57; TEA

Huygens, Constantijn 1596-1687 .... **LC 114**
See also RGWL 2, 3

Huysmans, Joris-Karl 1848-1907 ... **TCLC 7, 69**
See also CA 104; 165; DLB 123; EW 7; GFL 1789 to the Present; LMFS 2; RGWL 2, 3

Hwang, David Henry 1957- .... **CLC 55, 196; DC 4, 23**
See also CA 127; 132; CAD; CANR 76, 124; CD 5, 6; DA3; DAM DRAM; DFS 11, 18; DLB 212, 228, 312; INT CA-132; MAL 5; MTCW 2; MTFW 2005; RGAL 4

Hyde, Anthony 1946- .... **CLC 42**
See Chase, Nicholas
See also CA 136; CCA 1

Hyde, Margaret O(ldroyd) 1917- ..... **CLC 21**
See also CA 1-4R; CANR 1, 36, 137; CLR 23; JRDA; MAICYA 1, 2; SAAS 8; SATA 1, 42, 76, 139

Hynes, James 1956(?)- .... **CLC 65**
See also CA 164; CANR 105

Hypatia c. 370-415 .... **CMLC 35**

Ian, Janis 1951- .... **CLC 21**
See also CA 105; 187

Ibanez, Vicente Blasco
See Blasco Ibanez, Vicente
See also DLB 322

Ibarbourou, Juana de
1895(?)-1979 .... **HLCS 2**
See also DLB 290; HW 1; LAW

Ibarguengoitia, Jorge 1928-1983 ..... **CLC 37; TCLC 148**
See also CA 124; 113; EWL 3; HW 1

Ibn Battuta, Abu Abdalla
1304-1368(?) .... **CMLC 57**
See also WLIT 2

Ibn Hazm 994-1064 .... **CMLC 64**

Ibsen, Henrik (Johan) 1828-1906 .... **DC 2; TCLC 2, 8, 16, 37, 52; WLC**
See also AAYA 46; CA 104; 141; DA; DA3; DAB; DAC; DAM DRAM, MST; DFS 1, 6, 8, 10, 11, 15, 16; EW 7; LAIT 2; LATS 1:1; MTFW 2005; RGWL 2, 3

Ibuse, Masuji 1898-1993 .... **CLC 22**
See Ibuse Masuji
See also CA 127; 141; MJW; RGWL 3

Ibuse Masuji
See Ibuse, Masuji
See also CWW 2; DLB 180; EWL 3

Ichikawa, Kon 1915- .... **CLC 20**
See also CA 121

Ichiyo, Higuchi 1872-1896 .... **NCLC 49**
See also MJW

Idle, Eric 1943- .... **CLC 21**
See Monty Python
See also CA 116; CANR 35, 91

Idris, Yusuf 1927-1991 .... **SSC 74**
See also AFW; EWL 3; RGSF 2, 3; RGWL 3; WLIT 2

Ignatow, David 1914-1997 .... **CLC 4, 7, 14, 40; PC 34**
See also CA 9-12R; 162; CAAS 3; CANR 31, 57, 96; CP 1, 2, 3, 4, 5, 6; DLB 5; EWL 3; MAL 5

Ignotus
See Strachey, (Giles) Lytton

Ihimaera, Witi (Tame) 1944- .... **CLC 46**
See also CA 77-80; CANR 130; CN 2, 3, 4, 5, 6, 7; RGSF 2; SATA 148

Ilf, Ilya .... **TCLC 21**
See Fainzilberg, Ilya Arnoldovich
See also EWL 3

Illyes, Gyula 1902-1983 .... **PC 16**
See also CA 114; 109; CDWLB 4; DLB 215; EWL 3; RGWL 2, 3

Imalayen, Fatima-Zohra
See Djebar, Assia

Immermann, Karl (Lebrecht)
1796-1840 .... **NCLC 4, 49**
See also DLB 133

Ince, Thomas H. 1882-1924 .... **TCLC 89**
See also IDFW 3, 4

Inchbald, Elizabeth 1753-1821 .... **NCLC 62**
See also DLB 39, 89; RGEL 2

Inclan, Ramon (Maria) del Valle
See Valle-Inclan, Ramon (Maria) del

Infante, G(uillermo) Cabrera
See Cabrera Infante, G(uillermo)

Ingalls, Rachel (Holmes) 1940- .... **CLC 42**
See also CA 123; 127

Ingamells, Reginald Charles
See Ingamells, Rex

Ingamells, Rex 1913-1955 .... **TCLC 35**
See also CA 167; DLB 260

Inge, William (Motter) 1913-1973 ..... **CLC 1, 8, 19**
See also CA 9-12R; CAD; CDALB 1941-1968; DA3; DAM DRAM; DFS 1, 3, 5, 8; DLB 7, 249; EWL 3; MAL 5; MTCW 1, 2; MTFW 2005; RGAL 4; TUS

Ingelow, Jean 1820-1897 .... **NCLC 39, 107**
See also DLB 35, 163; FANT; SATA 33

Ingram, Willis J.
See Harris, Mark

Innaurato, Albert (F.) 1948(?)- ... **CLC 21, 60**
See also CA 115; 122; CAD; CANR 78; CD 5, 6; INT CA-122

Innes, Michael
See Stewart, J(ohn) I(nnes) M(ackintosh)
See also DLB 276; MSW

Innis, Harold Adams 1894-1952 .... **TCLC 77**
See also CA 181; DLB 88

Insluis, Alanus de
See Alain de Lille

Iola
See Wells-Barnett, Ida B(ell)

Ionesco, Eugene 1912-1994 ... **CLC 1, 4, 6, 9, 11, 15, 41, 86; DC 12; WLC**
See also CA 9-12R; 144; CANR 55, 132; CWW 2; DA; DA3; DAB; DAC; DAM DRAM, MST; DFS 4, 9; DLB 321; EW 13; EWL 3; GFL 1789 to the Present; LMFS 2; MTCW 1, 2; MTFW 2005; RGWL 2, 3; SATA 7; SATA-Obit 79; TWA

Iqbal, Muhammad 1877-1938 .... **TCLC 28**
See also CA 215; EWL 3

Ireland, Patrick
See O'Doherty, Brian

Irenaeus St. 130- .... **CMLC 42**

Irigaray, Luce 1930- .... **CLC 164**
See also CA 154; CANR 121; FW

Iron, Ralph
See Schreiner, Olive (Emilie Albertina)

Irving, John (Winslow) 1942- ... **CLC 13, 23, 38, 112, 175**
See also AAYA 8, 62; AMWS 6; BEST 89:3; BPFB 2; CA 25-28R; CANR 28, 73, 112, 133; CN 3, 4, 5, 6, 7; CPW; DA3; DAM NOV, POP; DLB 6, 278; DLBY 1982; EWL 3; MAL 5; MTCW 1, 2; MTFW 2005; NFS 12, 14; RGAL 4; TUS

Irving, Washington 1783-1859 . **NCLC 2, 19, 95; SSC 2, 37; WLC**
See also AAYA 56; AMW; CDALB 1640-1865; CLR 97; DA; DA3; DAB; DAC; DAM MST; DLB 3, 11, 30, 59, 73, 74, 183, 186, 250, 254; EXPS; GL 2; LAIT 1; RGAL 4; RGSF 2; SSFS 1, 8, 16; SUFW 1; TUS; WCH; YABC 2

Irwin, P. K.
See Page, P(atricia) K(athleen)

Isaacs, Jorge Ricardo 1837-1895 ... **NCLC 70**
See also LAW

Isaacs, Susan 1943- .... **CLC 32**
See also BEST 89:1; BPFB 2; CA 89-92; CANR 20, 41, 65, 112, 134; CPW; DA3; DAM POP; INT CANR-20; MTCW 1, 2; MTFW 2005

Isherwood, Christopher (William Bradshaw)
1904-1986 .... **CLC 1, 9, 11, 14, 44; SSC 56**
See also AMWS 14; BRW 7; CA 13-16R; 117; CANR 35, 97, 133; CN 1, 2, 3; DA3; DAM DRAM, NOV; DLB 15, 195; DLBY 1986; EWL 3; IDTP; MTCW 1, 2; MTFW 2005; RGAL 4; RGEL 2; TUS; WLIT 4

Ishiguro, Kazuo 1954- . **CLC 27, 56, 59, 110, 219**
See also AAYA 58; BEST 90:2; BPFB 2; BRWS 4; CA 120; CANR 49, 95, 133; CN 5, 6, 7; DA3; DAM NOV; DLB 194; EWL 3; MTCW 1, 2; MTFW 2005; NFS 13; WLIT 4; WWE 1

Ishikawa, Hakuhin
See Ishikawa, Takuboku

Ishikawa, Takuboku 1886(?)-1912 ..... **PC 10; TCLC 15**
See Ishikawa Takuboku
See also CA 113; 153; DAM POET

Iskander, Fazil (Abdulovich) 1929- .. **CLC 47**
See Iskander, Fazil' Abdulevich
See also CA 102; EWL 3

Iskander, Fazil' Abdulevich
See Iskander, Fazil (Abdulovich)
See also DLB 302

Isler, Alan (David) 1934- .... **CLC 91**
See also CA 156; CANR 105

Ivan IV 1530-1584 .... **LC 17**

Ivanov, Vyacheslav Ivanovich 1866-1949 .... **TCLC 33**
See also CA 122; EWL 3

Ivask, Ivar Vidrik 1927-1992 .... **CLC 14**
See also CA 37-40R; 139; CANR 24

Ives, Morgan
See Bradley, Marion Zimmer
See also GLL 1

Izumi Shikibu c. 973-c. 1034 .... **CMLC 33**

J. R. S.
See Gogarty, Oliver St. John

Jabran, Kahlil
See Gibran, Kahlil

Jabran, Khalil
See Gibran, Kahlil

Jackson, Daniel
See Wingrove, David (John)

Jackson, Helen Hunt 1830-1885 .... **NCLC 90**
See also DLB 42, 47, 186, 189; RGAL 4

Jackson, Jesse 1908-1983 .... **CLC 12**
See also BW 1; CA 25-28R; 109; CANR 27; CLR 28; CWRI 5; MAICYA 1, 2; SATA 2, 29; SATA-Obit 48

Jackson, Laura (Riding) 1901-1991 .... **PC 44**
See Riding, Laura
See also CA 65-68; 135; CANR 28, 89; DLB 48

Jackson, Sam
See Trumbo, Dalton

Jackson, Sara
See Wingrove, David (John)

Jackson, Shirley 1919-1965 . **CLC 11, 60, 87; SSC 9, 39; WLC**
See also AAYA 9; AMWS 9; BPFB 2; CA 1-4R; 25-28R; CANR 4, 52; CDALB 1941-1968; DA; DA3; DAC; DAM MST; DLB 6, 234; EXPS; HGG; LAIT 4; MAL 5; MTCW 2; MTFW 2005; RGAL 4; RGSF 2; SATA 2; SSFS 1; SUFW 1, 2

Jacob, (Cyprien-)Max 1876-1944 .... **TCLC 6**
See also CA 104; 193; DLB 258; EWL 3; GFL 1789 to the Present; GLL 2; RGWL 2, 3

Jacobs, Harriet A(nn) 1813(?)-1897 .... **NCLC 67, 162**
See also AFAW 1, 2; DLB 239; FL 1:3; FW; LAIT 2; RGAL 4

Jacobs, Jim 1942- .... **CLC 12**
See also CA 97-100; INT CA-97-100

Jacobs, W(illiam) W(ymark) 1863-1943 .... **SSC 73; TCLC 22**
See also CA 121; 167; DLB 135; EXPS; HGG; RGEL 2; RGSF 2; SSFS 2; SUFW 1

Jacobsen, Jens Peter 1847-1885 .... **NCLC 34**

Jacobsen, Josephine (Winder) 1908-2003 .... **CLC 48, 102; PC 62**
See also CA 33-36R; 218; CAAS 18; CANR 23, 48; CCA 1; CP 2, 3, 4, 5, 6, 7; DLB 244; PFS 23; TCLE 1:1

Jacobson, Dan 1929- .... **CLC 4, 14**
See also AFW; CA 1-4R; CANR 2, 25, 66; CN 1, 2, 3, 4, 5, 6, 7; DLB 14, 207, 225, 319; EWL 3; MTCW 1; RGSF 2

Jacqueline
See Carpentier (y Valmont), Alejo

Jacques de Vitry c. 1160-1240 .... **CMLC 63**
See also DLB 208

Jagger, Michael Philip
See Jagger, Mick

Jagger, Mick 1943- .... **CLC 17**
See also CA 239

Jahiz, al- c. 780-c. 869 .... **CMLC 25**
See also DLB 311

Jakes, John (William) 1932- .... **CLC 29**
See also AAYA 32; BEST 89:4; BPFB 2; CA 57-60, 214; CAAE 214; CANR 10, 43, 66, 111, 142; CPW; CSW; DA3; DAM NOV, POP; DLB 278; DLBY 1983; FANT; INT CANR-10; MTCW 1, 2; MTFW 2005; RHW; SATA 62; SFW 4; TCWW 1, 2

James I 1394-1437 .... **LC 20**
See also RGEL 2

James, Andrew
See Kirkup, James

James, C(yril) L(ionel) R(obert) 1901-1989 .... **BLCS; CLC 33**
See also BW 2; CA 117; 125; 128; CANR 62; CN 1, 2, 3, 4; DLB 125; MTCW 1

James, Daniel (Lewis) 1911-1988
See Santiago, Danny
See also CA 174; 125

James, Dynely
See Mayne, William (James Carter)

James, Henry Sr. 1811-1882 .... **NCLC 53**

James, Henry 1843-1916 .... **SSC 8, 32, 47; TCLC 2, 11, 24, 40, 47, 64, 171; WLC**
See also AMW; AMWC 1; AMWR 1; BPFB 2; BRW 6; CA 104; 132; CDALB 1865-1917; DA; DA3; DAB; DAC; DAM MST, NOV; DLB 12, 71, 74, 189; DLBD 13; EWL 3; EXPS; GL 2; HGG; LAIT 2; MAL 5; MTCW 1, 2; MTFW 2005; NFS 12, 16, 19; RGAL 4; RGEL 2; RGSF 2; SSFS 9; SUFW 1; TUS

James, M. R.
See James, Montague (Rhodes)
See also DLB 156, 201

James, Montague (Rhodes) 1862-1936 .... **SSC 16; TCLC 6**
See James, M. R.
See also CA 104; 203; HGG; RGEL 2; RGSF 2; SUFW 1

James, P. D. .... **CLC 18, 46, 122**
See White, Phyllis Dorothy James
See also BEST 90:2; BPFB 2; BRWS 4; CDBLB 1960 to Present; CN 4, 5, 6; DLB 87, 276; DLBD 17; MSW

James, Philip
See Moorcock, Michael (John)

James, Samuel
See Stephens, James

James, Seumas
See Stephens, James

James, Stephen
See Stephens, James

James, William 1842-1910 .... **TCLC 15, 32**
See also AMW; CA 109; 193; DLB 270, 284; MAL 5; NCFS 5; RGAL 4

Jameson, Anna 1794-1860 .... **NCLC 43**
See also DLB 99, 166

Jameson, Fredric (R.) 1934- .... **CLC 142**
See also CA 196; DLB 67; LMFS 2

James VI of Scotland 1566-1625 .... **LC 109**
See also DLB 151, 172

Jami, Nur al-Din 'Abd al-Rahman 1414-1492 .... **LC 9**

Jammes, Francis 1868-1938 .... **TCLC 75**
See also CA 198; EWL 3; GFL 1789 to the Present

Jandl, Ernst 1925-2000 .... **CLC 34**
See also CA 200; EWL 3

Janowitz, Tama 1957- .... **CLC 43, 145**
See also CA 106; CANR 52, 89, 129; CN 5, 6, 7; CPW; DAM POP; DLB 292; MTFW 2005

Japrisot, Sebastien 1931- .... **CLC 90**
See Rossi, Jean-Baptiste
See also CMW 4; NFS 18

Jarrell, Randall 1914-1965 .... **CLC 1, 2, 6, 9, 13, 49; PC 41; TCLC 177**
See also AMW; BYA 5; CA 5-8R; 25-28R; CABS 2; CANR 6, 34; CDALB 1941-1968; CLR 6; CWRI 5; DAM POET; DLB 48, 52; EWL 3; EXPP; MAICYA 1, 2; MAL 5; MTCW 1, 2; PAB; PFS 2; RGAL 4; SATA 7

Jarry, Alfred 1873-1907 .... **SSC 20; TCLC 2, 14, 147**
See also CA 104; 153; DA3; DAM DRAM; DFS 8; DLB 192, 258; EW 9; EWL 3; GFL 1789 to the Present; RGWL 2, 3; TWA

Jarvis, E. K.
See Ellison, Harlan (Jay)

Jawien, Andrzej
See John Paul II, Pope

Jaynes, Roderick
See Coen, Ethan

Jeake, Samuel, Jr.
See Aiken, Conrad (Potter)

Jean Paul 1763-1825 .... **NCLC 7**

Jefferies, (John) Richard 1848-1887 .... **NCLC 47**
See also DLB 98, 141; RGEL 2; SATA 16; SFW 4

Jeffers, (John) Robinson 1887-1962 .. **CLC 2, 3, 11, 15, 54; PC 17; WLC**
See also AMWS 2; CA 85-88; CANR 35; CDALB 1917-1929; DA; DAC; DAM MST, POET; DLB 45, 212; EWL 3; MAL 5; MTCW 1, 2; MTFW 2005; PAB; PFS 3, 4; RGAL 4

Jefferson, Janet
See Mencken, H(enry) L(ouis)

Jefferson, Thomas 1743-1826 . **NCLC 11, 103**
See also AAYA 54; ANW; CDALB 1640-1865; DA3; DLB 31, 183; LAIT 1; RGAL 4

Jeffrey, Francis 1773-1850 .... **NCLC 33**
See Francis, Lord Jeffrey

Jelakowitch, Ivan
See Heijermans, Herman

Jelinek, Elfriede 1946- .... **CLC 169**
See also AAYA 68; CA 154; DLB 85; FW

Jellicoe, (Patricia) Ann 1927- .... **CLC 27**
See also CA 85-88; CBD; CD 5, 6; CWD; CWRI 5; DLB 13, 233; FW

Jelloun, Tahar ben 1944- .... **CLC 180**
See Ben Jelloun, Tahar
See also CA 162; CANR 100

Jemyma
See Holley, Marietta

Jen, Gish .... **AAL; CLC 70, 198**
See Jen, Lillian
See also AMWC 2; CN 7; DLB 312

Jen, Lillian 1955-
See Jen, Gish
See also CA 135; CANR 89, 130

Jenkins, (John) Robin 1912- .... **CLC 52**
See also CA 1-4R; CANR 1, 135; CN 1, 2, 3, 4, 5, 6, 7; DLB 14, 271

Jennings, Elizabeth (Joan)
1926-2001 .... **CLC 5, 14, 131**
See also BRWS 5; CA 61-64; 200; CAAS 5; CANR 8, 39, 66, 127; CP 1, 2, 3, 4, 5, 6, 7; CWP; DLB 27; EWL 3; MTCW 1; SATA 66

Jennings, Waylon 1937-2002 .... **CLC 21**

Jensen, Johannes V(ilhelm)
1873-1950 .... **TCLC 41**
See also CA 170; DLB 214; EWL 3; RGWL 3

Jensen, Laura (Linnea) 1948- .... **CLC 37**
See also CA 103

Jerome, Saint 345-420 .... **CMLC 30**
See also RGWL 3

Jerome, Jerome K(lapka)
1859-1927 .... **TCLC 23**
See also CA 119; 177; DLB 10, 34, 135; RGEL 2

Jerrold, Douglas William
1803-1857 .... **NCLC 2**
See also DLB 158, 159; RGEL 2

Jewett, (Theodora) Sarah Orne
1849-1909 .... **SSC 6, 44; TCLC 1, 22**
See also AMW; AMWC 2; AMWR 2; CA 108; 127; CANR 71; DLB 12, 74, 221; EXPS; FL 1:3; FW; MAL 5; MAWW; NFS 15; RGAL 4; RGSF 2; SATA 15; SSFS 4

Jewsbury, Geraldine (Endsor)
1812-1880 .... **NCLC 22**
See also DLB 21

Jhabvala, Ruth Prawer 1927- . **CLC 4, 8, 29, 94, 138**
See also BRWS 5; CA 1-4R; CANR 2, 29, 51, 74, 91, 128; CN 1, 2, 3, 4, 5, 6, 7; DAB; DAM NOV; DLB 139, 194; EWL 3; IDFW 3, 4; INT CANR-29; MTCW 1, 2; MTFW 2005; RGSF 2; RGWL 2; RHW; TEA

Jibran, Kahlil
See Gibran, Kahlil

Jibran, Khalil
See Gibran, Kahlil

Jiles, Paulette 1943- .... **CLC 13, 58**
See also CA 101; CANR 70, 124; CWP

Jimenez (Mantecon), Juan Ramon
1881-1958 .... **HLC 1; PC 7; TCLC 4**
See also CA 104; 131; CANR 74; DAM MULT, POET; DLB 134; EW 9; EWL 3; HW 1; MTCW 1, 2; MTFW 2005; RGWL 2, 3

Jimenez, Ramon
See Jimenez (Mantecon), Juan Ramon

Jimenez Mantecon, Juan
See Jimenez (Mantecon), Juan Ramon

Jin, Ha .... **CLC 109**
See Jin, Xuefei
See also CA 152; DLB 244, 292; SSFS 17

Jin, Xuefei 1956-
See Jin, Ha
See also CANR 91, 130; MTFW 2005; SSFS 17

Jodelle, Etienne 1532-1573 .... **LC 119**
See also GFL Beginnings to 1789

Joel, Billy .... **CLC 26**
See Joel, William Martin

Joel, William Martin 1949-
See Joel, Billy
See also CA 108

John, Saint 10(?)-100 .... **CMLC 27, 63**

John of Salisbury c. 1115-1180 ..... **CMLC 63**

John of the Cross, St. 1542-1591 .... **LC 18**
See also RGWL 2, 3

John Paul II, Pope 1920-2005 .... **CLC 128**
See also CA 106; 133; 238

Johnson, B(ryan) S(tanley William)
1933-1973 .... **CLC 6, 9**
See also CA 9-12R; 53-56; CANR 9; CN 1; CP 1, 2; DLB 14, 40; EWL 3; RGEL 2

Johnson, Benjamin F., of Boone
See Riley, James Whitcomb

Johnson, Charles (Richard) 1948- .... **BLC 2; CLC 7, 51, 65, 163**
See also AFAW 2; AMWS 6; BW 2, 3; CA 116; CAAS 18; CANR 42, 66, 82, 129; CN 5, 6, 7; DAM MULT; DLB 33, 278; MAL 5; MTCW 2; MTFW 2005; RGAL 4; SSFS 16

Johnson, Charles S(purgeon)
1893-1956 .... **HR 1:3**
See also BW 1, 3; CA 125; CANR 82; DLB 51, 91

Johnson, Denis 1949- . **CLC 52, 160; SSC 56**
See also CA 117; 121; CANR 71, 99; CN 4, 5, 6, 7; DLB 120

Johnson, Diane 1934- .... **CLC 5, 13, 48**
See also BPFB 2; CA 41-44R; CANR 17, 40, 62, 95; CN 4, 5, 6, 7; DLBY 1980; INT CANR-17; MTCW 1

Johnson, E(mily) Pauline 1861-1913 . **NNAL**
See also CA 150; CCA 1; DAC; DAM MULT; DLB 92, 175; TCWW 2

Johnson, Eyvind (Olof Verner)
1900-1976 .... **CLC 14**
See also CA 73-76; 69-72; CANR 34, 101; DLB 259; EW 12; EWL 3

Johnson, Fenton 1888-1958 .... **BLC 2**
See also BW 1; CA 118; 124; DAM MULT; DLB 45, 50

Johnson, Georgia Douglas (Camp)
1880-1966 .... **HR 1:3**
See also BW 1; CA 125; DLB 51, 249; WP

Johnson, Helene 1907-1995 .... **HR 1:3**
See also CA 181; DLB 51; WP

Johnson, J. R.
See James, C(yril) L(ionel) R(obert)

Johnson, James Weldon 1871-1938 .. **BLC 2; HR 1:3; PC 24; TCLC 3, 19, 175**
See also AFAW 1, 2; BW 1, 3; CA 104; 125; CANR 82; CDALB 1917-1929; CLR 32; DA3; DAM MULT, POET; DLB 51; EWL 3; EXPP; LMFS 2; MAL 5; MTCW 1, 2; MTFW 2005; NFS 22; PFS 1; RGAL 4; SATA 31; TUS

Johnson, Joyce 1935- .... **CLC 58**
See also BG 1:3; CA 125; 129; CANR 102

Johnson, Judith (Emlyn) 1936- .... **CLC 7, 15**
See Sherwin, Judith Johnson
See also CA 25-28R; 153; CANR 34; CP 7

Johnson, Lionel (Pigot)
1867-1902 .... **TCLC 19**
See also CA 117; 209; DLB 19; RGEL 2

Johnson, Marguerite Annie
See Angelou, Maya

Johnson, Mel
See Malzberg, Barry N(athaniel)

Johnson, Pamela Hansford
1912-1981 .... **CLC 1, 7, 27**
See also CA 1-4R; 104; CANR 2, 28; CN 1, 2, 3; DLB 15; MTCW 1, 2; MTFW 2005; RGEL 2

Johnson, Paul (Bede) 1928- .... **CLC 147**
See also BEST 89:4; CA 17-20R; CANR 34, 62, 100

Johnson, Robert .... **CLC 70**

Johnson, Robert 1911(?)-1938 .... **TCLC 69**
See also BW 3; CA 174

Johnson, Samuel 1709-1784 .... **LC 15, 52; WLC**
See also BRW 3; BRWR 1; CDBLB 1660-1789; DA; DAB; DAC; DAM MST; DLB 39, 95, 104, 142, 213; LMFS 1; RGEL 2; TEA

Johnson, Uwe 1934-1984 .. **CLC 5, 10, 15, 40**
See also CA 1-4R; 112; CANR 1, 39; CDWLB 2; DLB 75; EWL 3; MTCW 1; RGWL 2, 3

Johnston, Basil H. 1929- .... **NNAL**
See also CA 69-72; CANR 11, 28, 66; DAC; DAM MULT; DLB 60

Johnston, George (Benson) 1913- .... **CLC 51**
See also CA 1-4R; CANR 5, 20; CP 1, 2, 3, 4, 5, 6, 7; DLB 88

Johnston, Jennifer (Prudence)
1930- .... **CLC 7, 150**
See also CA 85-88; CANR 92; CN 4, 5, 6, 7; DLB 14

Joinville, Jean de 1224(?)-1317 ..... **CMLC 38**

Jolley, (Monica) Elizabeth 1923- ...... **CLC 46; SSC 19**
See also CA 127; CAAS 13; CANR 59; CN 4, 5, 6, 7; EWL 3; RGSF 2

Jones, Arthur Llewellyn 1863-1947
See Machen, Arthur
See also CA 104; 179; HGG

Jones, D(ouglas) G(ordon) 1929- ...... **CLC 10**
See also CA 29-32R; CANR 13, 90; CP 1, 2, 3, 4, 5, 6, 7; DLB 53

Jones, David (Michael) 1895-1974 .... **CLC 2, 4, 7, 13, 42**
See also BRW 6; BRWS 7; CA 9-12R; 53-56; CANR 28; CDBLB 1945-1960; CP 1, 2; DLB 20, 100; EWL 3; MTCW 1; PAB; RGEL 2

Jones, David Robert 1947-
See Bowie, David
See also CA 103; CANR 104

Jones, Diana Wynne 1934- .... **CLC 26**
See also AAYA 12; BYA 6, 7, 9, 11, 13, 16; CA 49-52; CANR 4, 26, 56, 120; CLR 23; DLB 161; FANT; JRDA; MAICYA 1, 2; MTFW 2005; SAAS 7; SATA 9, 70, 108, 160; SFW 4; SUFW 2; YAW

Jones, Edward P. 1950- .... **CLC 76**
See also BW 2, 3; CA 142; CANR 79, 134; CSW; MTFW 2005

Jones, Gayl 1949- .... **BLC 2; CLC 6, 9, 131**
See also AFAW 1, 2; BW 2, 3; CA 77-80; CANR 27, 66, 122; CN 4, 5, 6, 7; CSW; DA3; DAM MULT; DLB 33, 278; MAL 5; MTCW 1, 2; MTFW 2005; RGAL 4

Jones, James 1921-1977 .... **CLC 1, 3, 10, 39**
See also AITN 1, 2; AMWS 11; BPFB 2; CA 1-4R; 69-72; CANR 6; CN 1, 2; DLB 2, 143; DLBD 17; DLBY 1998; EWL 3; MAL 5; MTCW 1; RGAL 4

Jones, John J.
See Lovecraft, H(oward) P(hillips)

Jones, LeRoi .... **CLC 1, 2, 3, 5, 10, 14**
See Baraka, Amiri
See also CN 1, 2; CP 1, 2, 3; MTCW 2

Jones, Louis B. 1953- .... **CLC 65**
See also CA 141; CANR 73

Jones, Madison (Percy, Jr.) 1925- .... **CLC 4**
See also CA 13-16R; CAAS 11; CANR 7, 54, 83; CN 1, 2, 3, 4, 5, 6, 7; CSW; DLB 152

Jones, Mervyn 1922- .... **CLC 10, 52**
See also CA 45-48; CAAS 5; CANR 1, 91; CN 1, 2, 3, 4, 5, 6, 7; MTCW 1

Jones, Mick 1956(?)- .... **CLC 30**

Jones, Nettie (Pearl) 1941- .... **CLC 34**
See also BW 2; CA 137; CAAS 20; CANR 88

Jones, Peter 1802-1856 .... **NNAL**

Jones, Preston 1936-1979 .... **CLC 10**
See also CA 73-76; 89-92; DLB 7

Jones, Robert F(rancis) 1934-2003 .... **CLC 7**
See also CA 49-52; CANR 2, 61, 118

Jones, Rod 1953- .... **CLC 50**
See also CA 128**

Jones, Terence Graham Parry
1942- .... **CLC 21**
See Jones, Terry; Monty Python
See also CA 112; 116; CANR 35, 93; INT CA-116; SATA 127

Jones, Terry
See Jones, Terence Graham Parry
See also SATA 67; SATA-Brief 51

Jones, Thom (Douglas) 1945(?)- ..... **CLC 81; SSC 56**
See also CA 157; CANR 88; DLB 244

Jong, Erica 1942- .... **CLC 4, 6, 8, 18, 83**
See also AITN 1; AMWS 5; BEST 90:2; BPFB 2; CA 73-76; CANR 26, 52, 75, 132; CN 3, 4, 5, 6, 7; CP 2, 3, 4, 5, 6, 7; CPW; DA3; DAM NOV, POP; DLB 2, 5, 28, 152; FW; INT CANR-26; MAL 5; MTCW 1, 2; MTFW 2005

Jonson, Ben(jamin) 1572(?)-1637 . **DC 4; LC 6, 33, 110; PC 17; WLC**
See also BRW 1; BRWC 1; BRWR 1; CDBLB Before 1660; DA; DAB; DAC; DAM DRAM, MST, POET; DFS 4, 10; DLB 62, 121; LMFS 1; PFS 23; RGEL 2; TEA; WLIT 3

Jordan, June (Meyer)
1936-2002 .. **BLCS; CLC 5, 11, 23, 114; PC 38**
See also AAYA 2, 66; AFAW 1, 2; BW 2, 3; CA 33-36R; 206; CANR 25, 70, 114; CLR 10; CP 3, 4, 5, 6, 7; CWP; DAM MULT, POET; DLB 38; GLL 2; LAIT 5; MAICYA 1, 2; MTCW 1; SATA 4, 136; YAW

Jordan, Neil (Patrick) 1950- .... **CLC 110**
See also CA 124; 130; CANR 54; CN 4, 5, 6, 7; GLL 2; INT CA-130

Jordan, Pat(rick M.) 1941- .... **CLC 37**
See also CA 33-36R; CANR 121

Jorgensen, Ivar
See Ellison, Harlan (Jay)

Jorgenson, Ivar
See Silverberg, Robert

Joseph, George Ghevarughese .... **CLC 70**

Josephson, Mary
See O'Doherty, Brian

Josephus, Flavius c. 37-100 .... **CMLC 13**
See also AW 2; DLB 176

Josiah Allen's Wife
See Holley, Marietta

Josipovici, Gabriel (David) 1940- ...... **CLC 6, 43, 153**
See also CA 37-40R; 224; CAAE 224; CAAS 8; CANR 47, 84; CN 3, 4, 5, 6, 7; DLB 14, 319

Joubert, Joseph 1754-1824 .... **NCLC 9**

Jouve, Pierre Jean 1887-1976 .... **CLC 47**
See also CA 65-68; DLB 258; EWL 3

Jovine, Francesco 1902-1950 .... **TCLC 79**
See also DLB 264; EWL 3

Joyce, James (Augustine Aloysius)
1882-1941 .... **DC 16; PC 22; SSC 3, 26, 44, 64; TCLC 3, 8, 16, 35, 52, 159; WLC**
See also AAYA 42; BRW 7; BRWC 1; BRWR 1; BYA 11, 13; CA 104; 126; CDBLB 1914-1945; DA; DA3; DAB; DAC; DAM MST, NOV, POET; DLB 10, 19, 36, 162, 247; EWL 3; EXPN; EXPS; LAIT 3; LMFS 1, 2; MTCW 1, 2; MTFW 2005; NFS 7; RGSF 2; SSFS 1, 19; TEA; WLIT 4

Jozsef, Attila 1905-1937 .... **TCLC 22**
See also CA 116; 230; CDWLB 4; DLB 215; EWL 3

Juana Ines de la Cruz, Sor
1651(?)-1695 ...... **HLCS 1; LC 5; PC 24**
See also DLB 305; FW; LAW; RGWL 2, 3; WLIT 1

Juana Inez de La Cruz, Sor
See Juana Ines de la Cruz, Sor

Judd, Cyril
See Kornbluth, C(yril) M.; Pohl, Frederik

Juenger, Ernst 1895-1998 .... **CLC 125**
See Junger, Ernst
See also CA 101; 167; CANR 21, 47, 106; DLB 56

Julian of Norwich 1342(?)-1416(?) . **LC 6, 52**
See also DLB 146; LMFS 1

Julius Caesar 100B.C.-44B.C.
See Caesar, Julius
See also CDWLB 1; DLB 211

Junger, Ernst
See Juenger, Ernst
See also CDWLB 2; EWL 3; RGWL 2, 3

Junger, Sebastian 1962- .... **CLC 109**
See also AAYA 28; CA 165; CANR 130; MTFW 2005

Juniper, Alex
See Hospital, Janette Turner

Junius
See Luxemburg, Rosa

Junzaburo, Nishiwaki
See Nishiwaki, Junzaburo
See also EWL 3

Just, Ward (Swift) 1935- .... **CLC 4, 27**
See also CA 25-28R; CANR 32, 87; CN 6, 7; INT CANR-32

Justice, Donald (Rodney)
1925-2004 .... **CLC 6, 19, 102; PC 64**
See also AMWS 7; CA 5-8R; 230; CANR 26, 54, 74, 121, 122; CP 1, 2, 3, 4, 5, 6, 7; CSW; DAM POET; DLBY 1983; EWL 3; INT CANR-26; MAL 5; MTCW 2; PFS 14; TCLE 1:1

Juvenal c. 60-c. 130 .... **CMLC 8**
See also AW 2; CDWLB 1; DLB 211; RGWL 2, 3

Juvenis
See Bourne, Randolph S(illiman)

K., Alice
See Knapp, Caroline

Kabakov, Sasha .... **CLC 59**

Kabir 1398(?)-1448(?) .... **LC 109; PC 56**
See also RGWL 2, 3

Kacew, Romain 1914-1980
See Gary, Romain
See also CA 108; 102

Kadare, Ismail 1936- .... **CLC 52, 190**
See also CA 161; EWL 3; RGWL 3

Kadohata, Cynthia (Lynn)
1956(?)- .... **CLC 59, 122**
See also CA 140; CANR 124; SATA 155

Kafka, Franz 1883-1924 ... **SSC 5, 29, 35, 60; TCLC 2, 6, 13, 29, 47, 53, 112; WLC**
See also AAYA 31; BPFB 2; CA 105; 126; CDWLB 2; DA; DA3; DAB; DAC; DAM MST, NOV; DLB 81; EW 9; EWL 3; EXPS; LATS 1:1; LMFS 2; MTCW 1, 2; MTFW 2005; NFS 7; RGSF 2; RGWL 2, 3; SFW 4; SSFS 3, 7, 12; TWA

Kahanovitsch, Pinkhes
See Der Nister

Kahn, Roger 1927- .... **CLC 30**
See also CA 25-28R; CANR 44, 69; DLB 171; SATA 37

Kain, Saul
See Sassoon, Siegfried (Lorraine)

Kaiser, Georg 1878-1945 .... **TCLC 9**
See also CA 106; 190; CDWLB 2; DLB 124; EWL 3; LMFS 2; RGWL 2, 3

Kaledin, Sergei .... **CLC 59**

Kaletski, Alexander 1946- .... **CLC 39**
See also CA 118; 143

Kalidasa fl. c. 400-455 .... **CMLC 9; PC 22**
See also RGWL 2, 3

Kallman, Chester (Simon)
1921-1975 .... **CLC 2**
See also CA 45-48; 53-56; CANR 3; CP 1, 2

Kaminsky, Melvin 1926-
See Brooks, Mel
See also CA 65-68; CANR 16; DFS 21

Kaminsky, Stuart M(elvin) 1934- ..... **CLC 59**
See also CA 73-76; CANR 29, 53, 89; CMW 4

Kamo no Chomei 1153(?)-1216 .... **CMLC 66**
See also DLB 203

Kamo no Nagaakira
See Kamo no Chomei

Kandinsky, Wassily 1866-1944 .... **TCLC 92**
See also AAYA 64; CA 118; 155

Kane, Francis
See Robbins, Harold

Kane, Henry 1918-
See Queen, Ellery
See also CA 156; CMW 4

Kane, Paul
See Simon, Paul (Frederick)

Kanin, Garson 1912-1999 .... **CLC 22**
See also AITN 1; CA 5-8R; 177; CAD; CANR 7, 78; DLB 7; IDFW 3, 4

Kaniuk, Yoram 1930- .... **CLC 19**
See also CA 134; DLB 299

Kant, Immanuel 1724-1804 ..... **NCLC 27, 67**
See also DLB 94

Kantor, MacKinlay 1904-1977 .... **CLC 7**
See also CA 61-64; 73-76; CANR 60, 63; CN 1, 2; DLB 9, 102; MAL 5; MTCW 2; RHW; TCWW 1, 2

Kanze Motokiyo
See Zeami

Kaplan, David Michael 1946- .... **CLC 50**
See also CA 187

Kaplan, James 1951- .... **CLC 59**
See also CA 135; CANR 121

Karadzic, Vuk Stefanovic
1787-1864 .... **NCLC 115**
See also CDWLB 4; DLB 147

Karageorge, Michael
See Anderson, Poul (William)

Karamzin, Nikolai Mikhailovich
1766-1826 .... **NCLC 3**
See also DLB 150; RGSF 2

Karapanou, Margarita 1946- .... **CLC 13**
See also CA 101

Karinthy, Frigyes 1887-1938 .... **TCLC 47**
See also CA 170; DLB 215; EWL 3

Karl, Frederick R(obert)
1927-2004 .... **CLC 34**
See also CA 5-8R; 226; CANR 3, 44, 143

Karr, Mary 1955- .... **CLC 188**
See also AMWS 11; CA 151; CANR 100; MTFW 2005; NCFS 5

Kastel, Warren
See Silverberg, Robert

Kataev, Evgeny Petrovich 1903-1942
See Petrov, Evgeny
See also CA 120

Kataphusin
See Ruskin, John

Katz, Steve 1935- .... **CLC 47**
See also CA 25-28R; CAAS 14, 64; CANR 12; CN 4, 5, 6, 7; DLBY 1983

Kauffman, Janet 1945- .... **CLC 42**
See also CA 117; CANR 43, 84; DLB 218; DLBY 1986

Kaufman, Bob (Garnell) 1925-1986 . **CLC 49**
See also BG 1:3; BW 1; CA 41-44R; 118; CANR 22; CP 1; DLB 16, 41

Kaufman, George S. 1889-1961 ...... **CLC 38; DC 17**
See also CA 108; 93-96; DAM DRAM; DFS 1, 10; DLB 7; INT CA 108; MTCW 2; MTFW 2005; RGAL 4; TUS

Kaufman, Moises 1964- .... **DC 26**
See also CA 211; DFS 22; MTFW 2005

Kaufman, Sue .... **CLC 3, 8**
See Barondess, Sue K(aufman)

Kavafis, Konstantinos Petrou 1863-1933
See Cavafy, C(onstantine) P(eter)
See also CA 104

Kavan, Anna 1901-1968 .... **CLC 5, 13, 82**
See also BRWS 7; CA 5-8R; CANR 6, 57; DLB 255; MTCW 1; RGEL 2; SFW 4

Kavanagh, Dan
See Barnes, Julian (Patrick)

Kavanagh, Julie 1952- .... **CLC 119**
See also CA 163

Kavanagh, Patrick (Joseph)
1904-1967 .... **CLC 22; PC 33**
See also BRWS 7; CA 123; 25-28R; DLB 15, 20; EWL 3; MTCW 1; RGEL 2

Kawabata, Yasunari 1899-1972 ..... **CLC 2, 5, 9, 18, 107; SSC 17**
See Kawabata Yasunari
See also CA 93-96; 33-36R; CANR 88; DAM MULT; MJW; MTCW 2; MTFW 2005; RGSF 2; RGWL 2, 3

Kawabata Yasunari
See Kawabata, Yasunari
See also DLB 180; EWL 3

Kaye, M(ary) M(argaret)
1908-2004 .... **CLC 28**
See also CA 89-92; 223; CANR 24, 60, 102, 142; MTCW 1, 2; MTFW 2005; RHW; SATA 62; SATA-Obit 152

Kaye, Mollie
See Kaye, M(ary) M(argaret)

Kaye-Smith, Sheila 1887-1956 .... **TCLC 20**
See also CA 118; 203; DLB 36

Kaymor, Patrice Maguilene
See Senghor, Leopold Sedar

Kazakov, Iurii Pavlovich
See Kazakov, Yuri Pavlovich
See also DLB 302

Kazakov, Yuri Pavlovich 1927-1982 . **SSC 43**
See Kazakov, Iurii Pavlovich; Kazakov, Yury
See also CA 5-8R; CANR 36; MTCW 1; RGSF 2

Kazakov, Yury
See Kazakov, Yuri Pavlovich
See also EWL 3

Kazan, Elia 1909-2003 .... **CLC 6, 16, 63**
See also CA 21-24R; 220; CANR 32, 78

Kazantzakis, Nikos 1883(?)-1957 .... **TCLC 2, 5, 33**
See also BPFB 2; CA 105; 132; DA3; EW 9; EWL 3; MTCW 1, 2; MTFW 2005; RGWL 2, 3

Kazin, Alfred 1915-1998 ..... **CLC 34, 38, 119**
See also AMWS 8; CA 1-4R; CAAS 7; CANR 1, 45, 79; DLB 67; EWL 3

Keane, Mary Nesta (Skrine) 1904-1996
See Keane, Molly
See also CA 108; 114; 151; RHW

Keane, Molly .... **CLC 31**
See Keane, Mary Nesta (Skrine)
See also CN 5, 6; INT CA-114; TCLE 1:1

Keates, Jonathan 1946(?)- .... **CLC 34**
See also CA 163; CANR 126

Keaton, Buster 1895-1966 .... **CLC 20**
See also CA 194

Keats, John 1795-1821 ...... **NCLC 8, 73, 121; PC 1; WLC**
See also AAYA 58; BRW 4; BRWR 1; CDBLB 1789 1832; DA; DA3; DAB; DAC; DAM MST, POET; DLB 96, 110; EXPP; LMFS 1; PAB; PFS 1, 2, 3, 9, 17; RGEL 2; TEA; WLIT 3; WP

Keble, John 1792-1866 .... **NCLC 87**
See also DLB 32, 55; RGEL 2

Keene, Donald 1922- .... **CLC 34**
See also CA 1-4R; CANR 5, 119

Keillor, Garrison .... **CLC 40, 115**
See Keillor, Gary (Edward)
See also AAYA 2, 62; BEST 89:3; BPFB 2; DLBY 1987; EWL 3; SATA 58; TUS

Keillor, Gary (Edward) 1942-
See Keillor, Garrison
See also CA 111; 117; CANR 36, 59, 124; CPW; DA3; DAM POP; MTCW 1, 2; MTFW 2005

Keith, Carlos
See Lewton, Val

Keith, Michael
See Hubbard, L(afayette) Ron(ald)

Keller, Gottfried 1819-1890 .... **NCLC 2; SSC 26**
See also CDWLB 2; DLB 129; EW; RGSF 2; RGWL 2, 3

Keller, Nora Okja 1965- .... **CLC 109**
See also CA 187

Kellerman, Jonathan 1949- .... **CLC 44**
See also AAYA 35; BEST 90:1; CA 106; CANR 29, 51; CMW 4; CPW; DA3; DAM POP; INT CANR-29

Kelley, William Melvin 1937- .... **CLC 22**
See also BW 1; CA 77-80; CANR 27, 83; CN 1, 2, 3, 4, 5, 6, 7; DLB 33; EWL 3

Kellogg, Marjorie 1922-2005 .... **CLC 2**
See also CA 81-84

Kellow, Kathleen
See Hibbert, Eleanor Alice Burford

Kelly, Lauren
See Oates, Joyce Carol

Kelly, M(ilton) T(errence) 1947- ...... **CLC 55**
See also CA 97-100; CAAS 22; CANR 19, 43, 84; CN 6

Kelly, Robert 1935- .... **SSC 50**
See also CA 17-20R; CAAS 19; CANR 47; CP 1, 2, 3, 4, 5, 6, 7; DLB 5, 130, 165

Kelman, James 1946- .... **CLC 58, 86**
See also BRWS 5; CA 148; CANR 85, 130; CN 5, 6, 7; DLB 194, 319; RGSF 2; WLIT 4

Kemal, Yasar
See Kemal, Yashar
See also CWW 2; EWL 3; WLIT 6

Kemal, Yashar 1923(?)- .... **CLC 14, 29**
See also CA 89-92; CANR 44

Kemble, Fanny 1809-1893 .... **NCLC 18**
See also DLB 32

Kemelman, Harry 1908-1996 .... **CLC 2**
See also AITN 1; BPFB 2; CA 9-12R; 155; CANR 6, 71; CMW 4; DLB 28

Kempe, Margery 1373(?)-1440(?) ... **LC 6, 56**
See also DLB 146; FL 1:1; RGEL 2

Kempis, Thomas a 1380-1471 .... **LC 11**

Kendall, Henry 1839-1882 .... **NCLC 12**
See also DLB 230

Keneally, Thomas (Michael) 1935- ... **CLC 5, 8, 10, 14, 19, 27, 43, 117**
See also BRWS 4; CA 85-88; CANR 10, 50, 74, 130; CN 1, 2, 3, 4, 5, 6, 7; CPW; DA3; DAM NOV; DLB 289, 299; EWL 3; MTCW 1, 2; MTFW 2005; NFS 17; RGEL 2; RHW

Kennedy, A(lison) L(ouise) 1965- ... **CLC 188**
See also CA 168, 213; CAAE 213; CANR 108; CD 5, 6; CN 6, 7; DLB 271; RGSF 2

Kennedy, Adrienne (Lita) 1931- .... **BLC 2; CLC 66; DC 5**
See also AFAW 2; BW 2, 3; CA 103; CAAS 20; CABS 3; CAD; CANR 26, 53, 82; CD 5, 6; DAM MULT; DFS 9; DLB 38; FW; MAL 5

Kennedy, John Pendleton
1795-1870 .... **NCLC 2**
See also DLB 3, 248, 254; RGAL 4

Kennedy, Joseph Charles 1929-
See Kennedy, X. J.
See also CA 1-4R, 201; CAAE 201; CANR 4, 30, 40; CWRI 5; MAICYA 2; MAICYAS 1; SATA 14, 86, 130; SATA-Essay 130

Kennedy, William (Joseph) 1928- ..... **CLC 6, 28, 34, 53**
See also AAYA 1; AMWS 7; BPFB 2; CA 85-88; CANR 14, 31, 76, 134; CN 4, 5, 6, 7; DA3; DAM NOV; DLB 143; DLBY 1985; EWL 3; INT CANR-31; MAL 5; MTCW 1, 2; MTFW 2005; SATA 57

Kennedy, X. J. .... **CLC 8, 42**
See Kennedy, Joseph Charles
See also AMWS 15; CAAS 9; CLR 27; CP 1, 2, 3, 4, 5, 6, 7; DLB 5; SAAS 22

Kenny, Maurice (Francis) 1929- ..... **CLC 87; NNAL**
See also CA 144; CAAS 22; CANR 143; DAM MULT; DLB 175

Kent, Kelvin
See Kuttner, Henry

Kenton, Maxwell
See Southern, Terry

Kenyon, Jane 1947-1995 .... **PC 57**
See also AAYA 63; AMWS 7; CA 118; 148; CANR 44, 69; CP 7; CWP; DLB 120; PFS 9, 17; RGAL 4

Kenyon, Robert O.
See Kuttner, Henry

Kepler, Johannes 1571-1630 .... **LC 45**

Ker, Jill
See Conway, Jill K(er)

Kerkow, H. C.
See Lewton, Val

Kerouac, Jack 1922-1969 ...... **CLC 1, 2, 3, 5, 14, 29, 61; TCLC 117; WLC**
See Kerouac, Jean-Louis Lebris de
See also AAYA 25; AMWC 1; AMWS 3; BG 3; BPFB 2; CDALB 1941-1968; CP 1; CPW; DLB 2, 16, 237; DLBD 3; DLBY 1995; EWL 3; GLL 1; LATS 1:2; LMFS 2; MAL 5; NFS 8; RGAL 4; TUS; WP

Kerouac, Jean-Louis Lebris de 1922-1969
See Kerouac, Jack
See also AITN 1; CA 5-8R; 25-28R; CANR 26, 54, 95; DA; DA3; DAB; DAC; DAM MST, NOV, POET, POP; MTCW 1, 2; MTFW 2005

Kerr, (Bridget) Jean (Collins)
1923(?)-2003 .... **CLC 22**
See also CA 5-8R; 212; CANR 7; INT CANR-7

Kerr, M. E. .... **CLC 12, 35**
See Meaker, Marijane (Agnes)
See also AAYA 2, 23; BYA 1, 7, 8; CLR 29; SAAS 1; WYA

Kerr, Robert .... **CLC 55**

Kerrigan, (Thomas) Anthony 1918- .. **CLC 4, 6**
See also CA 49-52; CAAS 11; CANR 4

Kerry, Lois
See Duncan, Lois

Kesey, Ken (Elton) 1935-2001 ... **CLC 1, 3, 6, 11, 46, 64, 184; WLC**
See also AAYA 25; BG 1:3; BPFB 2; CA 1-4R; 204; CANR 22, 38, 66, 124; CDALB 1968-1988; CN 1, 2, 3, 4, 5, 6, 7; CPW; DA; DA3; DAB; DAC; DAM

MST, NOV, POP; DLB 2, 16, 206; EWL 3; EXPN; LAIT 4; MAL 5; MTCW 1, 2; MTFW 2005; NFS 2; RGAL 4; SATA 66; SATA-Obit 131; TUS; YAW

Kesselring, Joseph (Otto) 1902-1967 .... **CLC 45**
See also CA 150; DAM DRAM, MST; DFS 20

Kessler, Jascha (Frederick) 1929- .... **CLC 4**
See also CA 17-20R; CANR 8, 48, 111; CP 1

Kettelkamp, Larry (Dale) 1933- .... **CLC 12**
See also CA 29-32R; CANR 16; SAAS 3; SATA 2

Key, Ellen (Karolina Sofia) 1849-1926 .... **TCLC 65**
See also DLB 259

Keyber, Conny
See Fielding, Henry

Keyes, Daniel 1927- .... **CLC 80**
See also AAYA 23; BYA 11; CA 17-20R, 181; CAAE 181; CANR 10, 26, 54, 74; DA; DA3; DAC; DAM MST, NOV; EXPN; LAIT 4; MTCW 2; MTFW 2005; NFS 2; SATA 37; SFW 4

Keynes, John Maynard 1883-1946 .... **TCLC 64**
See also CA 114; 162, 163; DLBD 10; MTCW 2; MTFW 2005

Khanshendel, Chiron
See Rose, Wendy

Khayyam, Omar 1048-1131 ... **CMLC 11; PC 8**
See Omar Khayyam
See also DA3; DAM POET; WLIT 6

Kherdian, David 1931- .... **CLC 6, 9**
See also AAYA 42; CA 21-24R, 192; CAAE 192; CAAS 2; CANR 39, 78; CLR 24; JRDA; LAIT 3; MAICYA 1, 2; SATA 16, 74; SATA-Essay 125

Khlebnikov, Velimir .... **TCLC 20**
See Khlebnikov, Viktor Vladimirovich
See also DLB 295; EW 10; EWL 3; RGWL 2, 3

Khlebnikov, Viktor Vladimirovich 1885-1922
See Khlebnikov, Velimir
See also CA 117; 217

Khodasevich, Vladislav (Felitsianovich) 1886-1939 .... **TCLC 15**
See also CA 115; DLB 317; EWL 3

Kielland, Alexander Lange 1849-1906 .... **TCLC 5**
See also CA 104

Kiely, Benedict 1919- ... **CLC 23, 43; SSC 58**
See also CA 1-4R; CANR 2, 84; CN 1, 2, 3, 4, 5, 6, 7; DLB 15, 319; TCLE 1:1

Kienzle, William X(avier) 1928-2001 .... **CLC 25**
See also CA 93-96; 203; CAAS 1; CANR 9, 31, 59, 111; CMW 4; DA3; DAM POP; INT CANR-31; MSW; MTCW 1, 2; MTFW 2005

Kierkegaard, Soren 1813-1855 ..... **NCLC 34, 78, 125**
See also DLB 300; EW 6; LMFS 2; RGWL 3; TWA

Kieslowski, Krzysztof 1941-1996 .... **CLC 120**
See also CA 147; 151

Killens, John Oliver 1916-1987 .... **CLC 10**
See also BW 2; CA 77-80; 123; CAAS 2; CANR 26; CN 1, 2, 3, 4; DLB 33; EWL 3

Killigrew, Anne 1660-1685 .... **LC 4, 73**
See also DLB 131

Killigrew, Thomas 1612-1683 .... **LC 57**
See also DLB 58; RGEL 2

Kim
See Simenon, Georges (Jacques Christian)

Kincaid, Jamaica 1949- ...... **BLC 2; CLC 43, 68, 137; SSC 72**
See also AAYA 13, 56; AFAW 2; AMWS 7; BRWS 7; BW 2, 3; CA 125; CANR 47, 59, 95, 133; CDALBS; CDWLB 3; CLR 63; CN 4, 5, 6, 7; DA3; DAM MULT, NOV; DLB 157, 227; DNFS 1; EWL 3; EXPS; FW; LATS 1:2; LMFS 2; MAL 5; MTCW 2; MTFW 2005; NCFS 1; NFS 3; SSFS 5, 7; TUS; WWE 1; YAW

King, Francis (Henry) 1923- .... **CLC 8, 53, 145**
See also CA 1-4R; CANR 1, 33, 86; CN 1, 2, 3, 4, 5, 6, 7; DAM NOV; DLB 15, 139; MTCW 1

King, Kennedy
See Brown, George Douglas

King, Martin Luther, Jr. 1929-1968 . **BLC 2; CLC 83; WLCS**
See also BW 2, 3; CA 25-28; CANR 27, 44; CAP 2; DA; DA3; DAB; DAC; DAM MST, MULT; LAIT 5; LATS 1:2; MTCW 1, 2; MTFW 2005; SATA 14

King, Stephen 1947- .... **CLC 12, 26, 37, 61, 113; SSC 17, 55**
See also AAYA 1, 17; AMWS 5; BEST 90:1; BPFB 2; CA 61-64; CANR 1, 30, 52, 76, 119, 134; CN 7; CPW; DA3; DAM NOV, POP; DLB 143; DLBY 1980; HGG; JRDA; LAIT 5; MTCW 1, 2; MTFW 2005; RGAL 4; SATA 9, 55, 161; SUFW 1, 2; WYAS 1; YAW

King, Stephen Edwin
See King, Stephen

King, Steve
See King, Stephen

King, Thomas 1943- .... **CLC 89, 171; NNAL**
See also CA 144; CANR 95; CCA 1; CN 6, 7; DAC; DAM MULT; DLB 175; SATA 96

Kingman, Lee .... **CLC 17**
See Natti, (Mary) Lee
See also CWRI 5; SAAS 3; SATA 1, 67

Kingsley, Charles 1819-1875 .... **NCLC 35**
See also CLR 77; DLB 21, 32, 163, 178, 190; FANT; MAICYA 2; MAICYAS 1; RGEL 2; WCH; YABC 2

Kingsley, Henry 1830-1876 .... **NCLC 107**
See also DLB 21, 230; RGEL 2

Kingsley, Sidney 1906-1995 .... **CLC 44**
See also CA 85-88; 147; CAD; DFS 14, 19; DLB 7; MAL 5; RGAL 4

Kingsolver, Barbara 1955- .... **CLC 55, 81, 130, 216**
See also AAYA 15; AMWS 7; CA 129; 134; CANR 60, 96, 133; CDALBS; CN 7; CPW; CSW; DA3; DAM POP; DLB 206; INT CA-134; LAIT 5; MTCW 2; MTFW 2005; NFS 5, 10, 12; RGAL 4; TCLE 1:1

Kingston, Maxine (Ting Ting) Hong 1940- ...... **AAL; CLC 12, 19, 58, 121; WLCS**
See also AAYA 8, 55; AMWS 5; BPFB 2; CA 69-72; CANR 13, 38, 74, 87, 128; CDALBS; CN 6, 7; DA3; DAM MULT, NOV; DLB 173, 212, 312; DLBY 1980; EWL 3; FL 1:6; FW; INT CANR-13; LAIT 5; MAL 5; MAWW; MTCW 1, 2; MTFW 2005; NFS 6; RGAL 4; SATA 53; SSFS 3; TCWW 2

Kinnell, Galway 1927- ..... **CLC 1, 2, 3, 5, 13, 29, 129; PC 26**
See also AMWS 3; CA 9-12R; CANR 10, 34, 66, 116, 138; CP 1, 2, 3, 4, 5, 6, 7; DLB 5; DLBY 1987; EWL 3; INT CANR-34; MAL 5; MTCW 1, 2; MTFW 2005; PAB; PFS 9; RGAL 4; TCLE 1:1; WP

Kinsella, Thomas 1928- .... **CLC 4, 19, 138; PC 69**
See also BRWS 5; CA 17-20R; CANR 15, 122; CP 1, 2, 3, 4, 5, 6, 7; DLB 27; EWL 3; MTCW 1, 2; MTFW 2005; RGEL 2; TEA

Kinsella, W(illiam) P(atrick) 1935- . **CLC 27, 43, 166**
See also AAYA 7, 60; BPFB 2; CA 97-100, 222; CAAE 222; CAAS 7; CANR 21, 35, 66, 75, 129; CN 4, 5, 6, 7; CPW; DAC; DAM NOV, POP; FANT; INT CANR-21; LAIT 5; MTCW 1, 2; MTFW 2005; NFS 15; RGSF 2

Kinsey, Alfred C(harles) 1894-1956 .... **TCLC 91**
See also CA 115; 170; MTCW 2

Kipling, (Joseph) Rudyard 1865-1936 . **PC 3; SSC 5, 54; TCLC 8, 17, 167; WLC**
See also AAYA 32; BRW 6; BRWC 1, 2; BYA 4; CA 105; 120; CANR 33; CDBLB 1890-1914; CLR 39, 65; CWRI 5; DA; DA3; DAB; DAC; DAM MST, POET; DLB 19, 34, 141, 156; EWL 3; EXPS; FANT; LAIT 3; LMFS 1; MAICYA 1, 2; MTCW 1, 2; MTFW 2005; NFS 21; PFS 22; RGEL 2; RGSF 2; SATA 100; SFW 4; SSFS 8, 21; SUFW 1; TEA; WCH; WLIT 4; YABC 2

Kircher, Athanasius 1602-1680 .... **LC 121**
See also DLB 164

Kirk, Russell (Amos) 1918-1994 .. **TCLC 119**
See also AITN 1; CA 1-4R; 145; CAAS 9; CANR 1, 20, 60; HGG; INT CANR-20; MTCW 1, 2

Kirkham, Dinah
See Card, Orson Scott

Kirkland, Caroline M. 1801-1864 . **NCLC 85**
See also DLB 3, 73, 74, 250, 254; DLBD 13

Kirkup, James 1918- .... **CLC 1**
See also CA 1-4R; CAAS 4; CANR 2; CP 1, 2, 3, 4, 5, 6, 7; DLB 27; SATA 12

Kirkwood, James 1930(?)-1989 .... **CLC 9**
See also AITN 2; CA 1-4R; 128; CANR 6, 40; GLL 2

Kirsch, Sarah 1935- .... **CLC 176**
See also CA 178; CWW 2; DLB 75; EWL 3

Kirshner, Sidney
See Kingsley, Sidney

Kis, Danilo 1935-1989 .... **CLC 57**
See also CA 109; 118; 129; CANR 61; CD-WLB 4; DLB 181; EWL 3; MTCW 1; RGSF 2; RGWL 2, 3

Kissinger, Henry A(lfred) 1923- ...... **CLC 137**
See also CA 1-4R; CANR 2, 33, 66, 109; MTCW 1

Kivi, Aleksis 1834-1872 .... **NCLC 30**

Kizer, Carolyn (Ashley) 1925- ... **CLC 15, 39, 80; PC 66**
See also CA 65-68; CAAS 5; CANR 24, 70, 134; CP 1, 2, 3, 4, 5, 6, 7; CWP; DAM POET; DLB 5, 169; EWL 3; MAL 5; MTCW 2; MTFW 2005; PFS 18; TCLE 1:1

Klabund 1890-1928 .... **TCLC 44**
See also CA 162; DLB 66

Klappert, Peter 1942- .... **CLC 57**
See also CA 33-36R; CSW; DLB 5

Klein, A(braham) M(oses) 1909-1972 .... **CLC 19**
See also CA 101; 37-40R; CP 1; DAB; DAC; DAM MST; DLB 68; EWL 3; RGEL 2

Klein, Joe
See Klein, Joseph

Klein, Joseph 1946- .... **CLC 154**
See also CA 85-88; CANR 55

Klein, Norma 1938-1989 .... **CLC 30**
See also AAYA 2, 35; BPFB 2; BYA 6, 7, 8; CA 41-44R; 128; CANR 15, 37; CLR 2, 19; INT CANR-15; JRDA; MAICYA 1, 2; SAAS 1; SATA 7, 57; WYA; YAW

Klein, T(heodore) E(ibon) D(onald)
1947- .... **CLC 34**
See also CA 119; CANR 44, 75; HGG

Kleist, Heinrich von 1777-1811 ...... **NCLC 2, 37; SSC 22**
See also CDWLB 2; DAM DRAM; DLB 90; EW 5; RGSF 2; RGWL 2, 3

Klima, Ivan 1931- .... **CLC 56, 172**
See also CA 25-28R; CANR 17, 50, 91; CDWLB 4; CWW 2; DAM NOV; DLB 232; EWL 3; RGWL 3

Klimentev, Andrei Platonovich
See Klimentov, Andrei Platonovich

Klimentov, Andrei Platonovich
1899-1951 .... **SSC 42; TCLC 14**
See Platonov, Andrei Platonovich; Platonov, Andrey Platonovich
See also CA 108; 232

Klinger, Friedrich Maximilian von
1752-1831 .... **NCLC 1**
See also DLB 94

Klingsor the Magician
See Hartmann, Sadakichi

Klopstock, Friedrich Gottlieb
1724-1803 .... **NCLC 11**
See also DLB 97; EW 4; RGWL 2, 3

Kluge, Alexander 1932- .... **SSC 61**
See also CA 81-84; DLB 75

Knapp, Caroline 1959-2002 .... **CLC 99**
See also CA 154; 207

Knebel, Fletcher 1911-1993 .... **CLC 14**
See also AITN 1; CA 1-4R; 140; CAAS 3; CANR 1, 36; CN 1, 2, 3, 4, 5; SATA 36; SATA-Obit 75

Knickerbocker, Diedrich
See Irving, Washington

Knight, Etheridge 1931-1991 ... **BLC 2; CLC 40; PC 14**
See also BW 1, 3; CA 21-24R; 133; CANR 23, 82; CP 1, 2, 3, 4; DAM POET; DLB 41; MTCW 2; MTFW 2005; RGAL 4; TCLE 1:1

Knight, Sarah Kemble 1666-1727 .... **LC 7**
See also DLB 24, 200

Knister, Raymond 1899-1932 .... **TCLC 56**
See also CA 186; DLB 68; RGEL 2

Knowles, John 1926-2001 ... **CLC 1, 4, 10, 26**
See also AAYA 10; AMWS 12; BPFB 2; BYA 3; CA 17-20R; 203; CANR 40, 74, 76, 132; CDALB 1968-1988; CLR 98; CN 1, 2, 3, 4, 5, 6, 7; DA; DAC; DAM MST, NOV; DLB 6; EXPN; MTCW 1, 2; MTFW 2005; NFS 2; RGAL 4; SATA 8, 89; SATA-Obit 134; YAW

Knox, Calvin M.
See Silverberg, Robert

Knox, John c. 1505-1572 .... **LC 37**
See also DLB 132

Knye, Cassandra
See Disch, Thomas M(ichael)

Koch, C(hristopher) J(ohn) 1932- .... **CLC 42**
See also CA 127; CANR 84; CN 3, 4, 5, 6, 7; DLB 289

Koch, Christopher
See Koch, C(hristopher) J(ohn)

Koch, Kenneth (Jay) 1925-2002 .... **CLC 5, 8, 44**
See also AMWS 15; CA 1-4R; 207; CAD; CANR 6, 36, 57, 97, 131; CD 5, 6; CP 1, 2, 3, 4, 5, 6, 7; DAM POET; DLB 5; INT CANR-36; MAL 5; MTCW 2; MTFW 2005; PFS 20; SATA 65; WP

Kochanowski, Jan 1530-1584 .... **LC 10**
See also RGWL 2, 3

Kock, Charles Paul de 1794-1871 . **NCLC 16**

Koda Rohan
See Koda Shigeyuki

Koda Rohan
See Koda Shigeyuki
See also DLB 180

Koda Shigeyuki 1867-1947 .... **TCLC 22**
See Koda Rohan
See also CA 121; 183

Koestler, Arthur 1905-1983 ... **CLC 1, 3, 6, 8, 15, 33**
See also BRWS 1; CA 1-4R; 109; CANR 1, 33; CDBLB 1945-1960; CN 1, 2, 3; DLBY 1983; EWL 3; MTCW 1, 2; MTFW 2005; NFS 19; RGEL 2

Kogawa, Joy Nozomi 1935- ...... **CLC 78, 129**
See also AAYA 47; CA 101; CANR 19, 62, 126; CN 6, 7; CP 1; CWP; DAC; DAM MST, MULT; FW; MTCW 2; MTFW 2005; NFS 3; SATA 99

Kohout, Pavel 1928- .... **CLC 13**
See also CA 45-48; CANR 3

Koizumi, Yakumo
See Hearn, (Patricio) Lafcadio (Tessima Carlos)

Kolmar, Gertrud 1894-1943 .... **TCLC 40**
See also CA 167; EWL 3

Komunyakaa, Yusef 1947- .. **BLCS; CLC 86, 94, 207; PC 51**
See also AFAW 2; AMWS 13; CA 147; CANR 83; CP 7; CSW; DLB 120; EWL 3; PFS 5, 20; RGAL 4

Konrad, George
See Konrad, Gyorgy

Konrad, Gyorgy 1933- .... **CLC 4, 10, 73**
See also CA 85-88; CANR 97; CDWLB 4; CWW 2; DLB 232; EWL 3

Konwicki, Tadeusz 1926- .... **CLC 8, 28, 54, 117**
See also CA 101; CAAS 9; CANR 39, 59; CWW 2; DLB 232; EWL 3; IDFW 3; MTCW 1

Koontz, Dean R. 1945- .... **CLC 78, 206**
See also AAYA 9, 31; BEST 89:3, 90:2; CA 108; CANR 19, 36, 52, 95, 138; CMW 4; CPW; DA3; DAM NOV, POP; DLB 292; HGG; MTCW 1; MTFW 2005; SATA 92, 165; SFW 4; SUFW 2; YAW

Koontz, Dean Ray
See Koontz, Dean R.

Koontz, Dean Ray
See Koontz, Dean R.

Kopernik, Mikolaj
See Copernicus, Nicolaus

Kopit, Arthur (Lee) 1937- ...... **CLC 1, 18, 33**
See also AITN 1; CA 81-84; CABS 3; CAD; CD 5, 6; DAM DRAM; DFS 7, 14; DLB 7; MAL 5; MTCW 1; RGAL 4

Kopitar, Jernej (Bartholomaus)
1780-1844 .... **NCLC 117**

Kops, Bernard 1926- .... **CLC 4**
See also CA 5-8R; CANR 84; CBD; CN 1, 2, 3, 4, 5, 6, 7; CP 1, 2, 3, 4, 5, 6, 7; DLB 13

Kornbluth, C(yril) M. 1923-1958 .... **TCLC 8**
See also CA 105; 160; DLB 8; SCFW 1, 2; SFW 4

Korolenko, V. G.
See Korolenko, Vladimir Galaktionovich

Korolenko, Vladimir
See Korolenko, Vladimir Galaktionovich

Korolenko, Vladimir G.
See Korolenko, Vladimir Galaktionovich

Korolenko, Vladimir Galaktionovich
1853-1921 .... **TCLC 22**
See also CA 121; DLB 277

Korzybski, Alfred (Habdank Skarbek)
1879-1950 .... **TCLC 61**
See also CA 123; 160

Kosinski, Jerzy (Nikodem)
1933-1991 .... **CLC 1, 2, 3, 6, 10, 15, 53, 70**
See also AMWS 7; BPFB 2; CA 17-20R; 134; CANR 9, 46; CN 1, 2, 3, 4; DA3; DAM NOV; DLB 2, 299; DLBY 1982; EWL 3; HGG; MAL 5; MTCW 1, 2; MTFW 2005; NFS 12; RGAL 4; TUS

Kostelanetz, Richard (Cory) 1940- .. **CLC 28**
See also CA 13-16R; CAAS 8; CANR 38, 77; CN 4, 5, 6; CP 2, 3, 4, 5, 6, 7

Kostrowitzki, Wilhelm Apollinaris de
1880-1918
See Apollinaire, Guillaume
See also CA 104

Kotlowitz, Robert 1924- .... **CLC 4**
See also CA 33-36R; CANR 36

Kotzebue, August (Friedrich Ferdinand) von
1761-1819 .... **NCLC 25**
See also DLB 94

Kotzwinkle, William 1938- ...... **CLC 5, 14, 35**
See also BPFB 2; CA 45-48; CANR 3, 44, 84, 129; CLR 6; CN 7; DLB 173; FANT; MAICYA 1, 2; SATA 24, 70, 146; SFW 4; SUFW 2; YAW

Kowna, Stancy
See Szymborska, Wislawa

Kozol, Jonathan 1936- .... **CLC 17**
See also AAYA 46; CA 61-64; CANR 16, 45, 96; MTFW 2005

Kozoll, Michael 1940(?)- .... **CLC 35**

Kramer, Kathryn 19(?)- .... **CLC 34**

Kramer, Larry 1935- .... **CLC 42; DC 8**
See also CA 124; 126; CANR 60, 132; DAM POP; DLB 249; GLL 1

Krasicki, Ignacy 1735-1801 .... **NCLC 8**

Krasinski, Zygmunt 1812-1859 .... **NCLC 4**
See also RGWL 2, 3

Kraus, Karl 1874-1936 .... **TCLC 5**
See also CA 104; 216; DLB 118; EWL 3

Kreve (Mickevicius), Vincas
1882-1954 .... **TCLC 27**
See also CA 170; DLB 220; EWL 3

Kristeva, Julia 1941- .... **CLC 77, 140**
See also CA 154; CANR 99; DLB 242; EWL 3; FW; LMFS 2

Kristofferson, Kris 1936- .... **CLC 26**
See also CA 104

Krizanc, John 1956- .... **CLC 57**
See also CA 187

Krleza, Miroslav 1893-1981 .... **CLC 8, 114**
See also CA 97-100; 105; CANR 50; CDWLB 4; DLB 147; EW 11; RGWL 2, 3

Kroetsch, Robert (Paul) 1927- .... **CLC 5, 23, 57, 132**
See also CA 17-20R; CANR 8, 38; CCA 1; CN 2, 3, 4, 5, 6, 7; CP 7; DAC; DAM POET; DLB 53; MTCW 1

Kroetz, Franz
See Kroetz, Franz Xaver

Kroetz, Franz Xaver 1946- .... **CLC 41**
See also CA 130; CANR 142; CWW 2; EWL 3

Kroker, Arthur (W.) 1945- .... **CLC 77**
See also CA 161

Kroniuk, Lisa
See Berton, Pierre (Francis de Marigny)

Kropotkin, Peter (Alekseievich)
1842-1921 .... **TCLC 36**
See Kropotkin, Petr Alekseevich
See also CA 119; 219

Kropotkin, Petr Alekseevich
See Kropotkin, Peter (Alekseievich)
See also DLB 277

Krotkov, Yuri 1917-1981 .... **CLC 19**
See also CA 102

Krumb
See Crumb, R(obert)

Krumgold, Joseph (Quincy)
1908-1980 .... **CLC 12**
See also BYA 1, 2; CA 9-12R; 101; CANR 7; MAICYA 1, 2; SATA 1, 48; SATA-Obit 23; YAW

Krumwitz
See Crumb, R(obert)

Krutch, Joseph Wood 1893-1970 ..... **CLC 24**
See also ANW; CA 1-4R; 25-28R; CANR 4; DLB 63, 206, 275

Krutzch, Gus
See Eliot, T(homas) S(tearns)

Krylov, Ivan Andreevich
1768(?)-1844 .... **NCLC 1**
See also DLB 150

Kubin, Alfred (Leopold Isidor)
1877-1959 .... **TCLC 23**
See also CA 112; 149; CANR 104; DLB 81

Kubrick, Stanley 1928-1999 .... **CLC 16; TCLC 112**
See also AAYA 30; CA 81-84; 177; CANR 33; DLB 26

Kumin, Maxine (Winokur) 1925- ..... **CLC 5, 13, 28, 164; PC 15**
See also AITN 2; AMWS 4; ANW; CA 1-4R; CAAS 8; CANR 1, 21, 69, 115, 140; CP 2, 3, 4, 5, 6, 7; CWP; DA3; DAM POET; DLB 5; EWL 3; EXPP; MTCW 1, 2; MTFW 2005; PAB; PFS 18; SATA 12

Kundera, Milan 1929- . **CLC 4, 9, 19, 32, 68, 115, 135; SSC 24**
See also AAYA 2, 62; BPFB 2; CA 85-88; CANR 19, 52, 74, 144; CDWLB 4; CWW 2; DA3; DAM NOV; DLB 232; EW 13; EWL 3; MTCW 1, 2; MTFW 2005; NFS 18; RGSF 2; RGWL 3; SSFS 10

Kunene, Mazisi (Raymond) 1930- ... **CLC 85**
See also BW 1, 3; CA 125; CANR 81; CP 1, 7; DLB 117

Kung, Hans .... **CLC 130**
See Kung, Hans

Kung, Hans 1928-
See Kung, Hans
See also CA 53-56; CANR 66, 134; MTCW 1, 2; MTFW 2005

Kunikida Doppo 1869(?)-1908
See Doppo, Kunikida
See also DLB 180; EWL 3

Kunitz, Stanley (Jasspon) 1905- .. **CLC 6, 11, 14, 148; PC 19**
See also AMWS 3; CA 41-44R; CANR 26, 57, 98; CP 1, 2, 3, 4, 5, 6, 7; DA3; DLB 48; INT CANR-26; MAL 5; MTCW 1, 2; MTFW 2005; PFS 11; RGAL 4

Kunze, Reiner 1933- .... **CLC 10**
See also CA 93-96; CWW 2; DLB 75; EWL 3

Kuprin, Aleksander Ivanovich
1870-1938 .... **TCLC 5**
See Kuprin, Aleksandr Ivanovich; Kuprin, Alexandr Ivanovich
See also CA 104; 182

Kuprin, Aleksandr Ivanovich
See Kuprin, Aleksander Ivanovich
See also DLB 295

Kuprin, Alexandr Ivanovich
See Kuprin, Aleksander Ivanovich
See also EWL 3

Kureishi, Hanif 1954- .. **CLC 64, 135; DC 26**
See also BRWS 11; CA 139; CANR 113; CBD; CD 5, 6; CN 6, 7; DLB 194, 245; GLL 2; IDFW 4; WLIT 4; WWE 1

Kurosawa, Akira 1910-1998 ..... **CLC 16, 119**
See also AAYA 11, 64; CA 101; 170; CANR 46; DAM MULT

Kushner, Tony 1956- .... **CLC 81, 203; DC 10**
See also AAYA 61; AMWS 9; CA 144; CAD; CANR 74, 130; CD 5, 6; DA3; DAM DRAM; DFS 5; DLB 228; EWL 3; GLL 1; LAIT 5; MAL 5; MTCW 2; MTFW 2005; RGAL 4; SATA 160

Kuttner, Henry 1915-1958 .... **TCLC 10**
See also CA 107; 157; DLB 8; FANT; SCFW 1, 2; SFW 4

Kutty, Madhavi
See Das, Kamala

Kuzma, Greg 1944- .... **CLC 7**
See also CA 33-36R; CANR 70

Kuzmin, Mikhail (Alekseevich)
1872(?)-1936 .... **TCLC 40**
See also CA 170; DLB 295; EWL 3

Kyd, Thomas 1558-1594 .. **DC 3; LC 22, 125**
See also BRW 1; DAM DRAM; DFS 21; DLB 62; IDTP; LMFS 1; RGEL 2; TEA; WLIT 3

Kyprianos, Iossif
See Samarakis, Antonis

L. S.
See Stephen, Sir Leslie

La3amon
See Layamon
See also DLB 146

Labe, Louise 1521-1566 .... **LC 120**

Labrunie, Gerard
See Nerval, Gerard de

La Bruyere, Jean de 1645-1696 .... **LC 17**
See also DLB 268; EW 3; GFL Beginnings to 1789

Lacan, Jacques (Marie Emile)
1901-1981 .... **CLC 75**
See also CA 121; 104; DLB 296; EWL 3; TWA

Laclos, Pierre-Ambroise Francois
1741-1803 .... **NCLC 4, 87**
See also DLB 313; EW 4; GFL Beginnings to 1789; RGWL 2, 3

Lacolere, Francois
See Aragon, Louis

La Colere, Francois
See Aragon, Louis

La Deshabilleuse
See Simenon, Georges (Jacques Christian)

Lady Gregory
See Gregory, Lady Isabella Augusta (Persse)

Lady of Quality, A
See Bagnold, Enid

La Fayette, Marie-(Madelaine Pioche de la Vergne) 1634-1693 .... **LC 2**
See Lafayette, Marie-Madeleine
See also GFL Beginnings to 1789; RGWL 2, 3

Lafayette, Marie-Madeleine
See La Fayette, Marie-(Madelaine Pioche de la Vergne)
See also DLB 268

Lafayette, Rene
See Hubbard, L(afayette) Ron(ald)

La Flesche, Francis 1857(?)-1932 .... **NNAL**
See also CA 144; CANR 83; DLB 175

La Fontaine, Jean de 1621-1695 .... **LC 50**
See also DLB 268; EW 3; GFL Beginnings to 1789; MAICYA 1, 2; RGWL 2, 3; SATA 18

Laforet, Carmen 1921-2004 .... **CLC 219**
See also CWW 2; DLB 322; EWL 3

Laforgue, Jules 1860-1887 . **NCLC 5, 53; PC 14; SSC 20**
See also DLB 217; EW 7; GFL 1789 to the Present; RGWL 2, 3

Lagerkvist, Paer (Fabian)
1891-1974 ..... **CLC 7, 10, 13, 54; TCLC 144**
See Lagerkvist, Par
See also CA 85-88; 49-52; DA3; DAM DRAM, NOV; MTCW 1, 2; MTFW 2005; TWA

Lagerkvist, Par .... **SSC 12**
See Lagerkvist, Paer (Fabian)
See also DLB 259; EW 10; EWL 3; RGSF 2; RGWL 2, 3

Lagerloef, Selma (Ottiliana Lovisa)
.... **TCLC 4, 36**
See Lagerlof, Selma (Ottiliana Lovisa)
See also CA 108; MTCW 2

Lagerlof, Selma (Ottiliana Lovisa)
1858-1940
See Lagerloef, Selma (Ottiliana Lovisa)
See also CA 188; CLR 7; DLB 259; RGWL 2, 3; SATA 15; SSFS 18

La Guma, (Justin) Alex(ander)
1925-1985 . **BLCS; CLC 19; TCLC 140**
See also AFW; BW 1, 3; CA 49-52; 118; CANR 25, 81; CDWLB 3; CN 1, 2, 3; CP 1; DAM NOV; DLB 117, 225; EWL 3; MTCW 1, 2; MTFW 2005; WLIT 2; WWE 1

Laidlaw, A. K.
See Grieve, C(hristopher) M(urray)

Lainez, Manuel Mujica
See Mujica Lainez, Manuel
See also HW 1

Laing, R(onald) D(avid) 1927-1989 . **CLC 95**
See also CA 107; 129; CANR 34; MTCW 1

Laishley, Alex
See Booth, Martin

Lamartine, Alphonse (Marie Louis Prat) de
1790-1869 .... **NCLC 11; PC 16**
See also DAM POET; DLB 217; GFL 1789 to the Present; RGWL 2, 3

Lamb, Charles 1775-1834 ..... **NCLC 10, 113; WLC**
See also BRW 4; CDBLB 1789-1832; DA; DAB; DAC; DAM MST; DLB 93, 107, 163; RGEL 2; SATA 17; TEA

Lamb, Lady Caroline 1785-1828 ... **NCLC 38**
See also DLB 116

Lamb, Mary Ann 1764-1847 .... **NCLC 125**
See also DLB 163; SATA 17

Lame Deer 1903(?)-1976 .... **NNAL**
See also CA 69-72

Lamming, George (William) 1927- ... **BLC 2; CLC 2, 4, 66, 144**
See also BW 2, 3; CA 85-88; CANR 26, 76; CDWLB 3; CN 1, 2, 3, 4, 5, 6, 7; CP 1; DAM MULT; DLB 125; EWL 3; MTCW 1, 2; MTFW 2005; NFS 15; RGEL 2

L'Amour, Louis (Dearborn)
1908-1988 .... **CLC 25, 55**
See also AAYA 16; AITN 2; BEST 89:2; BPFB 2; CA 1-4R; 125; CANR 3, 25, 40; CPW; DA3; DAM NOV, POP; DLB 206; DLBY 1980; MTCW 1, 2; MTFW 2005; RGAL 4; TCWW 1, 2

Lampedusa, Giuseppe (Tomasi) di
.... **TCLC 13**
See Tomasi di Lampedusa, Giuseppe
See also CA 164; EW 11; MTCW 2; MTFW 2005; RGWL 2, 3

Lampman, Archibald 1861-1899 ... **NCLC 25**
See also DLB 92; RGEL 2; TWA

Lancaster, Bruce 1896-1963 .... **CLC 36**
See also CA 9-10; CANR 70; CAP 1; SATA 9

Lanchester, John 1962- .... **CLC 99**
See also CA 194; DLB 267

Landau, Mark Alexandrovich
See Aldanov, Mark (Alexandrovich)

Landau-Aldanov, Mark Alexandrovich
See Aldanov, Mark (Alexandrovich)
Landis, Jerry
See Simon, Paul (Frederick)
Landis, John 1950- .... **CLC 26**
See also CA 112; 122; CANR 128
Landolfi, Tommaso 1908-1979 .... **CLC 11, 49**
See also CA 127; 117; DLB 177; EWL 3
Landon, Letitia Elizabeth
1802-1838 .... **NCLC 15**
See also DLB 96
Landor, Walter Savage
1775-1864 .... **NCLC 14**
See also BRW 4; DLB 93, 107; RGEL 2
Landwirth, Heinz 1927-
See Lind, Jakov
See also CA 9-12R; CANR 7
Lane, Patrick 1939- .... **CLC 25**
See also CA 97-100; CANR 54; CP 3, 4, 5, 6, 7; DAM POET; DLB 53; INT CA-97-100
Lane, Rose Wilder 1887-1968 ...... **TCLC 177**
See also CA 102; CANR 63; SATA 28, 29; TCWW 2
Lang, Andrew 1844-1912 .... **TCLC 16**
See also CA 114; 137; CANR 85; CLR 101; DLB 98, 141, 184; FANT; MAICYA 1, 2; RGEL 2; SATA 16; WCH
Lang, Fritz 1890-1976 .... **CLC 20, 103**
See also AAYA 65; CA 77-80; 69-72; CANR 30
Lange, John
See Crichton, (John) Michael
Langer, Elinor 1939- .... **CLC 34**
See also CA 121
Langland, William 1332(?)-1400(?) .... **LC 19, 120**
See also BRW 1; DA; DAB; DAC; DAM MST, POET; DLB 146; RGEL 2; TEA; WLIT 3
Langstaff, Launcelot
See Irving, Washington
Lanier, Sidney 1842-1881 . **NCLC 6, 118; PC 50**
See also AMWS 1; DAM POET; DLB 64; DLBD 13; EXPP; MAICYA 1; PFS 14; RGAL 4; SATA 18
Lanyer, Aemilia 1569-1645 .... **LC 10, 30, 83; PC 60**
See also DLB 121
Lao Tzu c. 6th cent. B.C.-3rd cent. B.C. .... **CMLC 7**
Lao-Tzu
See Lao Tzu
Lapine, James (Elliot) 1949- .... **CLC 39**
See also CA 123; 130; CANR 54, 128; INT CA-130
Larbaud, Valery (Nicolas)
1881-1957 .... **TCLC 9**
See also CA 106; 152; EWL 3; GFL 1789 to the Present
Lardner, Ring
See Lardner, Ring(gold) W(ilmer)
See also BPFB 2; CDALB 1917-1929; DLB 11, 25, 86, 171; DLBD 16; RGAL 4; RGSF 2
Lardner, Ring W., Jr.
See Lardner, Ring(gold) W(ilmer)
Lardner, Ring(gold) W(ilmer)
1885-1933 .... **SSC 32; TCLC 2, 14**
See Lardner, Ring
See also AMW; CA 104; 131; MAL 5; MTCW 1, 2; MTFW 2005; TUS
Laredo, Betty
See Codrescu, Andrei
Larkin, Maia
See Wojciechowska, Maia (Teresa)

Larkin, Philip (Arthur) 1922-1985 ... **CLC 3, 5, 8, 9, 13, 18, 33, 39, 64; PC 21**
See also BRWS 1; CA 5-8R; 117; CANR 24, 62; CDBLB 1960 to Present; CP 1, 2, 3, 4; DA3; DAB; DAM MST, POET; DLB 27; EWL 3; MTCW 1, 2; MTFW 2005; PFS 3, 4, 12; RGEL 2
La Roche, Sophie von
1730-1807 .... **NCLC 121**
See also DLB 94
La Rochefoucauld, Francois
1613-1680 .... **LC 108**
Larra (y Sanchez de Castro), Mariano Jose de 1809-1837 .... **NCLC 17, 130**
Larsen, Eric 1941- .... **CLC 55**
See also CA 132
Larsen, Nella 1893(?)-1963 .... **BLC 2; CLC 37; HR 1:3**
See also AFAW 1, 2; BW 1; CA 125; CANR 83; DAM MULT; DLB 51; FW; LATS 1:1; LMFS 2
Larson, Charles R(aymond) 1938- ... **CLC 31**
See also CA 53-56; CANR 4, 121
Larson, Jonathan 1960-1996 .... **CLC 99**
See also AAYA 28; CA 156; MTFW 2005
La Sale, Antoine de c. 1386-1460(?) . **LC 104**
See also DLB 208
Las Casas, Bartolome de
1474-1566 .... **HLCS; LC 31**
See Casas, Bartolome de las
See also DLB 318; LAW
Lasch, Christopher 1932-1994 .... **CLC 102**
See also CA 73-76; 144; CANR 25, 118; DLB 246; MTCW 1, 2; MTFW 2005
Lasker-Schueler, Else 1869-1945 ... **TCLC 57**
See Lasker-Schuler, Else
See also CA 183; DLB 66, 124
Lasker-Schuler, Else
See Lasker-Schueler, Else
See also EWL 3
Laski, Harold J(oseph) 1893-1950 . **TCLC 79**
See also CA 188
Latham, Jean Lee 1902-1995 .... **CLC 12**
See also AITN 1; BYA 1; CA 5-8R; CANR 7, 84; CLR 50; MAICYA 1, 2; SATA 2, 68; YAW
Latham, Mavis
See Clark, Mavis Thorpe
Lathen, Emma .... **CLC 2**
See Hennissart, Martha; Latsis, Mary J(ane)
See also BPFB 2; CMW 4; DLB 306
Lathrop, Francis
See Leiber, Fritz (Reuter, Jr.)
Latsis, Mary J(ane) 1927-1997
See Lathen, Emma
See also CA 85-88; 162; CMW 4
Lattany, Kristin
See Lattany, Kristin (Elaine Eggleston) Hunter
Lattany, Kristin (Elaine Eggleston) Hunter
1931- .... **CLC 35**
See Hunter, Kristin
See also AITN 1; BW 1; BYA 3; CA 13-16R; CANR 13, 108; CLR 3; CN 7; DLB 33; INT CANR-13; MAICYA 1, 2; SAAS 10; SATA 12, 132; YAW
Lattimore, Richmond (Alexander)
1906-1984 .... **CLC 3**
See also CA 1-4R; 112; CANR 1; CP 1, 2, 3; MAL 5
Laughlin, James 1914-1997 .... **CLC 49**
See also CA 21-24R; 162; CAAS 22; CANR 9, 47; CP 1, 2, 3, 4; DLB 48; DLBY 1996, 1997

Laurence, (Jean) Margaret (Wemyss)
1926-1987 . **CLC 3, 6, 13, 50, 62; SSC 7**
See also BYA 13; CA 5-8R; 121; CANR 33; CN 1, 2, 3, 4; DAC; DAM MST; DLB 53; EWL 3; FW; MTCW 1, 2; MTFW 2005; NFS 11; RGEL 2; RGSF 2; SATA-Obit 50; TCWW 2
Laurent, Antoine 1952- .... **CLC 50**
Lauscher, Hermann
See Hesse, Hermann
Lautreamont 1846-1870 .. **NCLC 12; SSC 14**
See Lautreamont, Isidore Lucien Ducasse
See also GFL 1789 to the Present; RGWL 2, 3
Lautreamont, Isidore Lucien Ducasse
See Lautreamont
See also DLB 217
Lavater, Johann Kaspar
1741-1801 .... **NCLC 142**
See also DLB 97
Laverty, Donald
See Blish, James (Benjamin)
Lavin, Mary 1912-1996 . **CLC 4, 18, 99; SSC 4, 67**
See also CA 9-12R; 151; CANR 33; CN 1, 2, 3, 4, 5, 6; DLB 15, 319; FW; MTCW 1; RGEL 2; RGSF 2
Lavond, Paul Dennis
See Kornbluth, C(yril) M.; Pohl, Frederik
Lawes, Henry 1596-1662 .... **LC 113**
See also DLB 126
Lawler, Ray
See Lawler, Raymond Evenor
See also DLB 289
Lawler, Raymond Evenor 1922- .... **CLC 58**
See Lawler, Ray
See also CA 103; CD 5, 6; RGEL 2
Lawrence, D(avid) H(erbert Richards)
1885-1930 .... **PC 54; SSC 4, 19, 73; TCLC 2, 9, 16, 33, 48, 61, 93; WLC**
See Chambers, Jessie
See also BPFB 2; BRW 7; BRWR 2; CA 104; 121; CANR 131; CDBLB 1914-1945; DA; DA3; DAB; DAC; DAM MST, NOV, POET; DLB 10, 19, 36, 98, 162, 195; EWL 3; EXPP; EXPS; LAIT 2, 3; MTCW 1, 2; MTFW 2005; NFS 18; PFS 6; RGEL 2; RGSF 2; SSFS 2, 6; TEA; WLIT 4; WP
Lawrence, T(homas) E(dward)
1888-1935 .... **TCLC 18**
See Dale, Colin
See also BRWS 2; CA 115; 167; DLB 195
Lawrence of Arabia
See Lawrence, T(homas) E(dward)
Lawson, Henry (Archibald Hertzberg)
1867-1922 .... **SSC 18; TCLC 27**
See also CA 120; 181; DLB 230; RGEL 2; RGSF 2
Lawton, Dennis
See Faust, Frederick (Schiller)
Layamon fl. c. 1200- .... **CMLC 10**
See Laȝamon
See also DLB 146; RGEL 2
Laye, Camara 1928-1980 ..... **BLC 2; CLC 4, 38**
See Camara Laye
See also AFW; BW 1; CA 85-88; 97-100; CANR 25; DAM MULT; MTCW 1, 2; WLIT 2
Layton, Irving 1912-2006 ...... **CLC 2, 15, 164**
See also CA 1-4R; CANR 2, 33, 43, 66, 129; CP 1, 2, 3, 4, 5, 6, 7; DAC; DAM MST, POET; DLB 88; EWL 3; MTCW 1, 2; PFS 12; RGEL 2
Layton, Irving Peter
See Layton, Irving

Lazarus, Emma 1849-1887 ...... **NCLC 8, 109**
Lazarus, Felix
　See Cable, George Washington
Lazarus, Henry
　See Slavitt, David R(ytman)
Lea, Joan
　See Neufeld, John (Arthur)
Leacock, Stephen (Butler)
　1869-1944 .... **SSC 39; TCLC 2**
　See also CA 104; 141; CANR 80; DAC; DAM MST; DLB 92; EWL 3; MTCW 2; MTFW 2005; RGEL 2; RGSF 2
Lead, Jane Ward 1623-1704 .... **LC 72**
　See also DLB 131
Leapor, Mary 1722-1746 .... **LC 80**
　See also DLB 109
Lear, Edward 1812-1888 ..... **NCLC 3; PC 65**
　See also AAYA 48; BRW 5; CLR 1, 75; DLB 32, 163, 166; MAICYA 1, 2; RGEL 2; SATA 18, 100; WCH; WP
Lear, Norman (Milton) 1922- .... **CLC 12**
　See also CA 73-76
Leautaud, Paul 1872-1956 .... **TCLC 83**
　See also CA 203; DLB 65; GFL 1789 to the Present
Leavis, F(rank) R(aymond)
　1895-1978 .... **CLC 24**
　See also BRW 7; CA 21-24R; 77-80; CANR 44; DLB 242; EWL 3; MTCW 1, 2; RGEL 2
Leavitt, David 1961- .... **CLC 34**
　See also CA 116; 122; CANR 50, 62, 101, 134; CPW; DA3; DAM POP; DLB 130; GLL 1; INT CA-122; MAL 5; MTCW 2; MTFW 2005
Leblanc, Maurice (Marie Emile)
　1864-1941 .... **TCLC 49**
　See also CA 110; CMW 4
Lebowitz, Fran(ces Ann) 1951(?)- ... **CLC 11, 36**
　See also CA 81-84; CANR 14, 60, 70; INT CANR-14; MTCW 1
Lebrecht, Peter
　See Tieck, (Johann) Ludwig
le Carré, John .... **CLC 3, 5, 9, 15, 28, 220**
　See Cornwell, David John Moore
　See also AAYA 42; BEST 89:4; BPFB 2; BRWS 2; CDBLB 1960 to Present; CMW 4; CN 1, 2, 3, 4, 5, 6, 7; CPW; DLB 87; EWL 3; MSW; MTCW 2; RGEL 2; TEA
Le Clezio, J(ean) M(arie) G(ustave)
　1940- .... **CLC 31, 155**
　See also CA 116; 128; CWW 2; DLB 83; EWL 3; GFL 1789 to the Present; RGSF 2
Leconte de Lisle, Charles-Marie-Rene
　1818-1894 .... **NCLC 29**
　See also DLB 217; EW 6; GFL 1789 to the Present
Le Coq, Monsieur
　See Simenon, Georges (Jacques Christian)
Leduc, Violette 1907-1972 .... **CLC 22**
　See also CA 13-14; 33-36R; CANR 69; CAP 1; EWL 3; GFL 1789 to the Present; GLL 1
Ledwidge, Francis 1887(?)-1917 .... **TCLC 23**
　See also CA 123; 203; DLB 20
Lee, Andrea 1953- .... **BLC 2; CLC 36**
　See also BW 1, 3; CA 125; CANR 82; DAM MULT
Lee, Andrew
　See Auchincloss, Louis (Stanton)
Lee, Chang-rae 1965- .... **CLC 91**
　See also CA 148; CANR 89; CN 7; DLB 312; LATS 1:2
Lee, Don L. .... **CLC 2**
　See Madhubuti, Haki R.
　See also CP 2, 3, 4

Lee, George W(ashington)
　1894-1976 .... **BLC 2; CLC 52**
　See also BW 1; CA 125; CANR 83; DAM MULT; DLB 51
Lee, (Nelle) Harper 1926- . **CLC 12, 60, 194; WLC**
　See also AAYA 13; AMWS 8; BPFB 2; BYA 3; CA 13-16R; CANR 51, 128; CDALB 1941-1968; CSW; DA; DA3; DAB; DAC; DAM MST, NOV; DLB 6; EXPN; LAIT 3; MAL 5; MTCW 1, 2; MTFW 2005; NFS 2; SATA 11; WYA; YAW
Lee, Helen Elaine 1959(?)- .... **CLC 86**
　See also CA 148
Lee, John .... **CLC 70**
Lee, Julian
　See Latham, Jean Lee
Lee, Larry
　See Lee, Lawrence
Lee, Laurie 1914-1997 .... **CLC 90**
　See also CA 77-80; 158; CANR 33, 73; CP 1, 2, 3, 4; CPW; DAB; DAM POP; DLB 27; MTCW 1; RGEL 2
Lee, Lawrence 1941-1990 .... **CLC 34**
　See also CA 131; CANR 43
Lee, Li-Young 1957- .... **CLC 164; PC 24**
　See also AMWS 15; CA 153; CANR 118; CP 7; DLB 165, 312; LMFS 2; PFS 11, 15, 17
Lee, Manfred B(ennington)
　1905-1971 .... **CLC 11**
　See Queen, Ellery
　See also CA 1-4R; 29-32R; CANR 2; CMW 4; DLB 137
Lee, Nathaniel 1645(?)-1692 .... **LC 103**
　See also DLB 80; RGEL 2
Lee, Shelton Jackson 1957(?)- .. **BLCS; CLC 105**
　See Lee, Spike
　See also BW 2, 3; CA 125; CANR 42; DAM MULT
Lee, Spike
　See Lee, Shelton Jackson
　See also AAYA 4, 29
Lee, Stan 1922- .... **CLC 17**
　See also AAYA 5, 49; CA 108; 111; CANR 129; INT CA-111; MTFW 2005
Lee, Tanith 1947- .... **CLC 46**
　See also AAYA 15; CA 37-40R; CANR 53, 102, 145; DLB 261; FANT; SATA 8, 88, 134; SFW 4; SUFW 1, 2; YAW
Lee, Vernon .... **SSC 33; TCLC 5**
　See Paget, Violet
　See also DLB 57, 153, 156, 174, 178; GLL 1; SUFW 1
Lee, William
　See Burroughs, William S(eward)
　See also GLL 1
Lee, Willy
　See Burroughs, William S(eward)
　See also GLL 1
Lee-Hamilton, Eugene (Jacob)
　1845-1907 .... **TCLC 22**
　See also CA 117; 234
Leet, Judith 1935- .... **CLC 11**
　See also CA 187
Le Fanu, Joseph Sheridan
　1814-1873 .... **NCLC 9, 58; SSC 14, 84**
　See also CMW 4; DA3; DAM POP; DLB 21, 70, 159, 178; GL 3; HGG; RGEL 2; RGSF 2; SUFW 1
Leffland, Ella 1931- .... **CLC 19**
　See also CA 29-32R; CANR 35, 78, 82; DLBY 1984; INT CANR-35; SATA 65
Leger, Alexis
　See Leger, (Marie-Rene Auguste) Alexis Saint-Leger

Leger, (Marie-Rene Auguste) Alexis Saint-Leger 1887-1975 .. **CLC 4, 11, 46; PC 23**
　See Perse, Saint-John; Saint-John Perse
　See also CA 13-16R; 61-64; CANR 43; DAM POET; MTCW 1
Leger, Saintleger
　See Leger, (Marie-Rene Auguste) Alexis Saint-Leger
Le Guin, Ursula K(roeber) 1929- ...... **CLC 8, 13, 22, 45, 71, 136; SSC 12, 69**
　See also AAYA 9, 27; AITN 1; BPFB 2; BYA 5, 8, 11, 14; CA 21-24R; CANR 9, 32, 52, 74, 132; CDALB 1968-1988; CLR 3, 28, 91; CN 2, 3, 4, 5, 6, 7; CPW; DA3; DAB; DAC; DAM MST, POP; DLB 8, 52, 256, 275; EXPS; FANT; FW; INT CANR-32; JRDA; LAIT 5; MAICYA 1, 2; MAL 5; MTCW 1, 2; MTFW 2005; NFS 6, 9; SATA 4, 52, 99, 149; SCFW 1, 2; SFW 4; SSFS 2; SUFW 1, 2; WYA; YAW
Lehmann, Rosamond (Nina)
　1901-1990 .... **CLC 5**
　See also CA 77-80; 131; CANR 8, 73; CN 1, 2, 3, 4; DLB 15; MTCW 2; RGEL 2; RHW
Leiber, Fritz (Reuter, Jr.)
　1910-1992 .... **CLC 25**
　See also AAYA 65; BPFB 2; CA 45-48; 139; CANR 2, 40, 86; CN 2, 3, 4, 5; DLB 8; FANT; HGG; MTCW 1, 2; MTFW 2005; SATA 45; SATA-Obit 73; SCFW 1, 2; SFW 4; SUFW 1, 2
Leibniz, Gottfried Wilhelm von
　1646-1716 .... **LC 35**
　See also DLB 168
Leimbach, Martha 1963-
　See Leimbach, Marti
　See also CA 130
Leimbach, Marti .... **CLC 65**
　See Leimbach, Martha
Leino, Eino .... **TCLC 24**
　See Lonnbohm, Armas Eino Leopold
　See also EWL 3
Leiris, Michel (Julien) 1901-1990 ..... **CLC 61**
　See also CA 119; 128; 132; EWL 3; GFL 1789 to the Present
Leithauser, Brad 1953- .... **CLC 27**
　See also CA 107; CANR 27, 81; CP 7; DLB 120, 282
le Jars de Gournay, Marie
　See de Gournay, Marie le Jars
Lelchuk, Alan 1938- .... **CLC 5**
　See also CA 45-48; CAAS 20; CANR 1, 70; CN 3, 4, 5, 6, 7
Lem, Stanislaw 1921- ...... **CLC 8, 15, 40, 149**
　See also CA 105; CAAS 1; CANR 32; CWW 2; MTCW 1; SCFW 1, 2; SFW 4
Lemann, Nancy (Elise) 1956- .... **CLC 39**
　See also CA 118; 136; CANR 121
Lemonnier, (Antoine Louis) Camille
　1844-1913 .... **TCLC 22**
　See also CA 121
Lenau, Nikolaus 1802-1850 .... **NCLC 16**
L'Engle, Madeleine (Camp Franklin)
　1918- .... **CLC 12**
　See also AAYA 28; AITN 2; BPFB 2; BYA 2, 5, 7; CA 1-4R; CANR 3, 21, 39, 66, 107; CLR 1, 14, 57; CPW; CWRI 5; DA3; DAM POP; DLB 52; JRDA; MAICYA 1, 2; MTCW 1, 2; MTFW 2005; SAAS 15; SATA 1, 27, 75, 128; SFW 4; WYA; YAW
Lengyel, Jozsef 1896-1975 .... **CLC 7**
　See also CA 85-88; 57-60; CANR 71; RGSF 2
Lenin 1870-1924
　See Lenin, V. I.
　See also CA 121; 168

Lenin, V. I. .... **TCLC 67**
See Lenin

Lennon, John (Ono) 1940-1980 .. **CLC 12, 35**
See also CA 102; SATA 114

Lennox, Charlotte Ramsay
1729(?)-1804 .... **NCLC 23, 134**
See also DLB 39; RGEL 2

Lentricchia, Frank, (Jr.) 1940- ...... **CLC 34**
See also CA 25-28R; CANR 19, 106; DLB 246

Lenz, Gunter .... **CLC 65**

Lenz, Jakob Michael Reinhold
1751-1792 .... **LC 100**
See also DLB 94; RGWL 2, 3

Lenz, Siegfried 1926- .... **CLC 27; SSC 33**
See also CA 89-92; CANR 80; CWW 2; DLB 75; EWL 3; RGSF 2; RGWL 2, 3

Leon, David
See Jacob, (Cyprien-)Max

Leonard, Elmore (John, Jr.) 1925- . **CLC 28, 34, 71, 120**
See also AAYA 22, 59; AITN 1; BEST 89:1, 90:4; BPFB 2; CA 81-84; CANR 12, 28, 53, 76, 96, 133; CMW 4; CN 5, 6, 7; CPW; DA3; DAM POP; DLB 173, 226; INT CANR-28; MSW; MTCW 1, 2; MTFW 2005; RGAL 4; SATA 163; TCWW 1, 2

Leonard, Hugh .... **CLC 19**
See Byrne, John Keyes
See also CBD; CD 5, 6; DFS 13; DLB 13

Leonov, Leonid (Maximovich)
1899-1994 .... **CLC 92**
See Leonov, Leonid Maksimovich
See also CA 129; CANR 76; DAM NOV; EWL 3; MTCW 1, 2; MTFW 2005

Leonov, Leonid Maksimovich
See Leonov, Leonid (Maximovich)
See also DLB 272

Leopardi, (Conte) Giacomo
1798-1837 .... **NCLC 22, 129; PC 37**
See also EW 5; RGWL 2, 3; WLIT 7; WP

Le Reveler
See Artaud, Antonin (Marie Joseph)

Lerman, Eleanor 1952- .... **CLC 9**
See also CA 85-88; CANR 69, 124

Lerman, Rhoda 1936- .... **CLC 56**
See also CA 49-52; CANR 70

Lermontov, Mikhail Iur'evich
See Lermontov, Mikhail Yuryevich
See also DLB 205

Lermontov, Mikhail Yuryevich
1814-1841 .... **NCLC 5, 47, 126; PC 18**
See Lermontov, Mikhail Iur'evich
See also EW 6; RGWL 2, 3; TWA

Leroux, Gaston 1868-1927 .... **TCLC 25**
See also CA 108; 136; CANR 69; CMW 4; MTFW 2005; NFS 20; SATA 65

Lesage, Alain-Rene 1668-1747 .... **LC 2, 28**
See also DLB 313; EW 3; GFL Beginnings to 1789; RGWL 2, 3

Leskov, N(ikolai) S(emenovich) 1831-1895
See Leskov, Nikolai (Semyonovich)

Leskov, Nikolai (Semyonovich)
1831-1895 .... **NCLC 25; SSC 34**
See Leskov, Nikolai Semenovich

Leskov, Nikolai Semenovich
See Leskov, Nikolai (Semyonovich)
See also DLB 238

Lesser, Milton
See Marlowe, Stephen

Lessing, Doris (May) 1919- ... **CLC 1, 2, 3, 6, 10, 15, 22, 40, 94, 170; SSC 6, 61; WLCS**
See also AAYA 57; AFW; BRWS 1; CA 9-12R; CAAS 14; CANR 33, 54, 76, 122; CBD; CD 5, 6; CDBLB 1960 to Present; CN 1, 2, 3, 4, 5, 6, 7; CWD; DA; DA3; DAB; DAC; DAM MST, NOV; DFS 20; DLB 15, 139; DLBY 1985; EWL 3; EXPS; FL 1:6; FW; LAIT 4; MTCW 1, 2; MTFW 2005; RGEL 2; RGSF 2; SFW 4; SSFS 1, 12, 20; TEA; WLIT 2, 4

Lessing, Gotthold Ephraim
1729-1781 .... **DC 26; LC 8, 124**
See also CDWLB 2; DLB 97; EW 4; RGWL 2, 3

Lester, Richard 1932- .... **CLC 20**

Levenson, Jay .... **CLC 70**

Lever, Charles (James)
1806-1872 .... **NCLC 23**
See also DLB 21; RGEL 2

Leverson, Ada Esther
1862(?)-1933(?) .... **TCLC 18**
See Elaine
See also CA 117; 202; DLB 153; RGEL 2

Levertov, Denise 1923-1997 .. **CLC 1, 2, 3, 5, 8, 15, 28, 66; PC 11**
See also AMWS 3; CA 1-4R; 178; 163; CAAE 178; CAAS 19; CANR 3, 29, 50, 108; CDALBS; CP 1, 2, 3, 4, 5, 6; CWP; DAM POET; DLB 5, 165; EWL 3; EXPP; FW; INT CANR-29; MAL 5; MTCW 1, 2; PAB; PFS 7, 17; RGAL 4; TUS; WP

Levi, Carlo 1902-1975 .... **TCLC 125**
See also CA 65-68; 53-56; CANR 10; EWL 3; RGWL 2, 3

Levi, Jonathan .... **CLC 76**
See also CA 197

Levi, Peter (Chad Tigar)
1931-2000 .... **CLC 41**
See also CA 5-8R; 187; CANR 34, 80; CP 1, 2, 3, 4, 5, 6, 7; DLB 40

Levi, Primo 1919-1987 ...... **CLC 37, 50; SSC 12; TCLC 109**
See also CA 13-16R; 122; CANR 12, 33, 61, 70, 132; DLB 177, 299; EWL 3; MTCW 1, 2; MTFW 2005; RGWL 2, 3; WLIT 7

Levin, Ira 1929- .... **CLC 3, 6**
See also CA 21-24R; CANR 17, 44, 74, 139; CMW 4; CN 1, 2, 3, 4, 5, 6, 7; CPW; DA3; DAM POP; HGG; MTCW 1, 2; MTFW 2005; SATA 66; SFW 4

Levin, Meyer 1905-1981 .... **CLC 7**
See also AITN 1; CA 9-12R; 104; CANR 15; CN 1, 2, 3; DAM POP; DLB 9, 28; DLBY 1981; MAL 5; SATA 21; SATA-Obit 27

Levine, Norman 1923-2005 .... **CLC 54**
See also CA 73-76; 240; CAAS 23; CANR 14, 70; CN 1, 2, 3, 4, 5, 6; CP 1; DLB 88

Levine, Norman Albert
See Levine, Norman

Levine, Philip 1928- .. **CLC 2, 4, 5, 9, 14, 33, 118; PC 22**
See also AMWS 5; CA 9-12R; CANR 9, 37, 52, 116; CP 1, 2, 3, 4, 5, 6, 7; DAM POET; DLB 5; EWL 3; MAL 5; PFS 8

Levinson, Deirdre 1931- .... **CLC 49**
See also CA 73-76; CANR 70

Levi-Strauss, Claude 1908- .... **CLC 38**
See also CA 1-4R; CANR 6, 32, 57; DLB 242; EWL 3; GFL 1789 to the Present; MTCW 1, 2; TWA

Levitin, Sonia (Wolff) 1934- .... **CLC 17**
See also AAYA 13, 48; CA 29-32R; CANR 14, 32, 79; CLR 53; JRDA; MAICYA 1, 2; SAAS 2; SATA 4, 68, 119, 131; SATA-Essay 131; YAW

Levon, O. U.
See Kesey, Ken (Elton)

Levy, Amy 1861-1889 .... **NCLC 59**
See also DLB 156, 240

Lewes, George Henry 1817-1878 ... **NCLC 25**
See also DLB 55, 144

Lewis, Alun 1915-1944 .... **SSC 40; TCLC 3**
See also BRW 7; CA 104; 188; DLB 20, 162; PAB; RGEL 2

Lewis, C. Day
See Day Lewis, C(ecil)
See also CN 1

Lewis, C(live) S(taples) 1898-1963 .... **CLC 1, 3, 6, 14, 27, 124; WLC**
See also AAYA 3, 39; BPFB 2; BRWS 3; BYA 15, 16; CA 81-84; CANR 33, 71, 132; CDBLB 1945-1960; CLR 3, 27; CWRI 5; DA; DA3; DAB; DAC; DAM MST, NOV, POP; DLB 15, 100, 160, 255; EWL 3; FANT; JRDA; LMFS 2; MAI-CYA 1, 2; MTCW 1, 2; MTFW 2005; RGEL 2; SATA 13, 100; SCFW 1, 2; SFW 4; SUFW 1; TEA; WCH; WYA; YAW

Lewis, Cecil Day
See Day Lewis, C(ecil)

Lewis, Janet 1899-1998 .... **CLC 41**
See Winters, Janet Lewis
See also CA 9-12R; 172; CANR 29, 63; CAP 1; CN 1, 2, 3, 4, 5, 6; DLBY 1987; RHW; TCWW 2

Lewis, Matthew Gregory
1775-1818 .... **NCLC 11, 62**
See also DLB 39, 158, 178; GL 3; HGG; LMFS 1; RGEL 2; SUFW

Lewis, (Harry) Sinclair 1885-1951 . **TCLC 4, 13, 23, 39; WLC**
See also AMW; AMWC 1; BPFB 2; CA 104; 133; CANR 132; CDALB 1917-1929; DA; DA3; DAB; DAC; DAM MST, NOV; DLB 9, 102, 284; DLBD 1; EWL 3; LAIT 3; MTCW 1, 2; MTFW 2005; NFS 15, 19, 22; RGAL 4; TUS

Lewis, (Percy) Wyndham
1884(?)-1957 .. **SSC 34; TCLC 2, 9, 104**
See also BRW 7; CA 104; 157; DLB 15; EWL 3; FANT; MTCW 2; MTFW 2005; RGEL 2

Lewisohn, Ludwig 1883-1955 .... **TCLC 19**
See also CA 107; 203; DLB 4, 9, 28, 102; MAL 5

Lewton, Val 1904-1951 .... **TCLC 76**
See also CA 199; IDFW 3, 4

Leyner, Mark 1956- .... **CLC 92**
See also CA 110; CANR 28, 53; DA3; DLB 292; MTCW 2; MTFW 2005

Lezama Lima, Jose 1910-1976 .... **CLC 4, 10, 101; HLCS 2**
See also CA 77-80; CANR 71; DAM MULT; DLB 113, 283; EWL 3; HW 1, 2; LAW; RGWL 2, 3

L'Heureux, John (Clarke) 1934- ...... **CLC 52**
See also CA 13-16R; CANR 23, 45, 88; CP 1, 2, 3, 4; DLB 244

Li Ch'ing-chao 1081(?)-1141(?) .... **CMLC 71**

Liddell, C. H.
See Kuttner, Henry

Lie, Jonas (Lauritz Idemil)
1833-1908(?) .... **TCLC 5**
See also CA 115

Lieber, Joel 1937-1971 .... **CLC 6**
See also CA 73-76; 29-32R

Lieber, Stanley Martin
See Lee, Stan

Lieberman, Laurence (James)
1935- .... **CLC 4, 36**
See also CA 17-20R; CANR 8, 36, 89; CP 1, 2, 3, 4, 5, 6, 7

Lieh Tzu fl. 7th cent. B.C.-5th cent. B.C. .... **CMLC 27**

Lieksman, Anders
See Haavikko, Paavo Juhani

Li Fei-kan 1904-
See Pa Chin
See also CA 105; TWA

Lifton, Robert Jay 1926- .... **CLC 67**
See also CA 17-20R; CANR 27, 78; INT CANR-27; SATA 66

Lightfoot, Gordon 1938- .... **CLC 26**
See also CA 109

Lightman, Alan P(aige) 1948- .... **CLC 81**
See also CA 141; CANR 63, 105, 138; MTFW 2005

Ligotti, Thomas (Robert) 1953- ...... **CLC 44; SSC 16**
See also CA 123; CANR 49, 135; HGG; SUFW 2

Li Ho 791-817 .... **PC 13**

Li Ju-chen c. 1763-c. 1830 .... **NCLC 137**

Lilar, Francoise
See Mallet-Joris, Francoise

Liliencron, (Friedrich Adolf Axel) Detlev von 1844-1909 .... **TCLC 18**
See also CA 117

Lille, Alain de
See Alain de Lille

Lilly, William 1602-1681 .... **LC 27**

Lima, Jose Lezama
See Lezama Lima, Jose

Lima Barreto, Afonso Henrique de 1881-1922 .... **TCLC 23**
See Lima Barreto, Afonso Henriques de
See also CA 117; 181; LAW

Lima Barreto, Afonso Henriques de
See Lima Barreto, Afonso Henriques de
See also DLB 307

Limonov, Eduard
See Limonov, Edward
See also DLB 317

Limonov, Edward 1944- .... **CLC 67**
See Limonov, Eduard
See also CA 137

Lin, Frank
See Atherton, Gertrude (Franklin Horn)

Lin, Yutang 1895-1976 .... **TCLC 149**
See also CA 45-48; 65-68; CANR 2; RGAL 4

Lincoln, Abraham 1809-1865 .... **NCLC 18**
See also LAIT 2

Lind, Jakov .... **CLC 1, 2, 4, 27, 82**
See Landwirth, Heinz
See also CAAS 4; DLB 299; EWL 3

Lindbergh, Anne (Spencer) Morrow 1906-2001 .... **CLC 82**
See also BPFB 2; CA 17-20R; 193; CANR 16, 73; DAM NOV; MTCW 1, 2; MTFW 2005; SATA 33; SATA-Obit 125; TUS

Lindsay, David 1878(?)-1945 .... **TCLC 15**
See also CA 113; 187; DLB 255; FANT; SFW 4; SUFW 1

Lindsay, (Nicholas) Vachel 1879-1931 .... **PC 23; TCLC 17; WLC**
See also AMWS 1; CA 114; 135; CANR 79; CDALB 1865-1917; DA; DA3; DAC; DAM MST, POET; DLB 54; EWL 3; EXPP; MAL 5; RGAL 4; SATA 40; WP

Linke-Poot
See Doeblin, Alfred

Linney, Romulus 1930- .... **CLC 51**
See also CA 1-4R; CAD; CANR 40, 44, 79; CD 5, 6; CSW; RGAL 4

Linton, Eliza Lynn 1822-1898 .... **NCLC 41**
See also DLB 18

Li Po 701-763 .... **CMLC 2; PC 29**
See also PFS 20; WP

Lipsius, Justus 1547-1606 .... **LC 16**

Lipsyte, Robert (Michael) 1938- ...... **CLC 21**
See also AAYA 7, 45; CA 17-20R; CANR 8, 57; CLR 23, 76; DA; DAC; DAM MST, NOV; JRDA; LAIT 5; MAICYA 1, 2; SATA 5, 68, 113, 161; WYA; YAW

Lish, Gordon (Jay) 1934- ..... **CLC 45; SSC 18**
See also CA 113; 117; CANR 79; DLB 130; INT CA-117

Lispector, Clarice 1925(?)-1977 .... **CLC 43; HLCS 2; SSC 34**
See also CA 139; 116; CANR 71; CDWLB 3; DLB 113, 307; DNFS 1; EWL 3; FW; HW 2; LAW; RGSF 2; RGWL 2, 3; WLIT 1

Littell, Robert 1935(?)- .... **CLC 42**
See also CA 109; 112; CANR 64, 115; CMW 4

Little, Malcolm 1925-1965
See Malcolm X
See also BW 1, 3; CA 125; 111; CANR 82; DA; DA3; DAB; DAC; DAM MST, MULT; MTCW 1, 2; MTFW 2005

Littlewit, Humphrey Gent.
See Lovecraft, H(oward) P(hillips)

Litwos
See Sienkiewicz, Henryk (Adam Alexander Pius)

Liu, E. 1857-1909 .... **TCLC 15**
See also CA 115; 190

Lively, Penelope 1933- .... **CLC 32, 50**
See also BPFB 2; CA 41-44R; CANR 29, 67, 79, 131; CLR 7; CN 5, 6, 7; CWRI 5; DAM NOV; DLB 14, 161, 207; FANT; JRDA; MAICYA 1, 2; MTCW 1, 2; MTFW 2005; SATA 7, 60, 101, 164; TEA

Lively, Penelope Margaret
See Lively, Penelope

Livesay, Dorothy (Kathleen) 1909-1996 .... **CLC 4, 15, 79**
See also AITN 2; CA 25-28R; CAAS 8; CANR 36, 67; CP 1, 2, 3, 4; DAC; DAM MST, POET; DLB 68; FW; MTCW 1; RGEL 2; TWA

Livy c. 59B.C.-c. 12 .... **CMLC 11**
See also AW 2; CDWLB 1; DLB 211; RGWL 2, 3

Lizardi, Jose Joaquin Fernandez de 1776-1827 .... **NCLC 30**
See also LAW

Llewellyn, Richard
See Llewellyn Lloyd, Richard Dafydd Vivian
See also DLB 15

Llewellyn Lloyd, Richard Dafydd Vivian 1906-1983 .... **CLC 7, 80**
See Llewellyn, Richard
See also CA 53-56; 111; CANR 7, 71; SATA 11; SATA-Obit 37

Llosa, (Jorge) Mario (Pedro) Vargas
See Vargas Llosa, (Jorge) Mario (Pedro)
See also RGWL 3

Llosa, Mario Vargas
See Vargas Llosa, (Jorge) Mario (Pedro)

Lloyd, Manda
See Mander, (Mary) Jane

Lloyd Webber, Andrew 1948-
See Webber, Andrew Lloyd
See also AAYA 1, 38; CA 116; 149; DAM DRAM; SATA 56

Llull, Ramon c. 1235-c. 1316 .... **CMLC 12**

Lobb, Ebenezer
See Upward, Allen

Locke, Alain (Le Roy) 1886-1954 .... **BLCS; HR 1:3; TCLC 43**
See also AMWS 14; BW 1, 3; CA 106; 124; CANR 79; DLB 51; LMFS 2; MAL 5; RGAL 4

Locke, John 1632-1704 .... **LC 7, 35**
See also DLB 31, 101, 213, 252; RGEL 2; WLIT 3

Locke-Elliott, Sumner
See Elliott, Sumner Locke

Lockhart, John Gibson 1794-1854 .. **NCLC 6**
See also DLB 110, 116, 144

Lockridge, Ross (Franklin), Jr. 1914-1948 .... **TCLC 111**
See also CA 108; 145; CANR 79; DLB 143; DLBY 1980; MAL 5; RGAL 4; RHW

Lockwood, Robert
See Johnson, Robert

Lodge, David (John) 1935- .... **CLC 36, 141**
See also BEST 90:1; BRWS 4; CA 17-20R; CANR 19, 53, 92, 139; CN 1, 2, 3, 4, 5, 6, 7; CPW; DAM POP; DLB 14, 194; EWL 3; INT CANR-19; MTCW 1, 2; MTFW 2005

Lodge, Thomas 1558-1625 .... **LC 41**
See also DLB 172; RGEL 2

Loewinsohn, Ron(ald William) 1937- .... **CLC 52**
See also CA 25-28R; CANR 71; CP 1, 2, 3, 4

Logan, Jake
See Smith, Martin Cruz

Logan, John (Burton) 1923-1987 .... **CLC 5**
See also CA 77-80; 124; CANR 45; CP 1, 2, 3, 4; DLB 5

Lo Kuan-chung 1330(?)-1400(?) .... **LC 12**

Lombard, Nap
See Johnson, Pamela Hansford

Lombard, Peter 1100(?)-1160(?) ... **CMLC 72**

London, Jack 1876-1916 .. **SSC 4, 49; TCLC 9, 15, 39; WLC**
See London, John Griffith
See also AAYA 13; AITN 2; AMW; BPFB 2; BYA 4, 13; CDALB 1865-1917; DLB 8, 12, 78, 212; EWL 3; EXPS; LAIT 3; MAL 5; NFS 8; RGAL 4; RGSF 2; SATA 18; SFW 4; SSFS 7; TCWW 1, 2; TUS; WYA; YAW

London, John Griffith 1876-1916
See London, Jack
See also CA 110; 119; CANR 73; DA; DA3; DAB; DAC; DAM MST, NOV; JRDA; MAICYA 1, 2; MTCW 1, 2; MTFW 2005; NFS 19

Long, Emmett
See Leonard, Elmore (John, Jr.)

Longbaugh, Harry
See Goldman, William (W.)

Longfellow, Henry Wadsworth 1807-1882 .... **NCLC 2, 45, 101, 103; PC 30; WLCS**
See also AMW; AMWR 2; CDALB 1640-1865; CLR 99; DA; DA3; DAB; DAC; DAM MST, POET; DLB 1, 59, 235; EXPP; PAB; PFS 2, 7, 17; RGAL 4; SATA 19; TUS; WP

Longinus c. 1st cent. - .... **CMLC 27**
See also AW 2; DLB 176

Longley, Michael 1939- .... **CLC 29**
See also BRWS 8; CA 102; CP 1, 2, 3, 4, 5, 6, 7; DLB 40

Longstreet, Augustus Baldwin 1790-1870 .... **NCLC 159**
See also DLB 3, 11, 74, 248; RGAL 4

Longus fl. c. 2nd cent. - .... **CMLC 7**

Longway, A. Hugh
See Lang, Andrew

Lonnbohm, Armas Eino Leopold 1878-1926
See Leino, Eino
See also CA 123

Lonnrot, Elias 1802-1884 .... **NCLC 53**
See also EFS 1

Lonsdale, Roger ed. .... **CLC 65**

Lopate, Phillip 1943- .... **CLC 29**
See also CA 97-100; CANR 88; DLBY 1980; INT CA-97-100

Lopez, Barry (Holstun) 1945- .... **CLC 70**
See also AAYA 9, 63; ANW; CA 65-68; CANR 7, 23, 47, 68, 92; DLB 256, 275; INT CANR-7, -23; MTCW 1; RGAL 4; SATA 67

Lopez de Mendoza, Inigo
See Santillana, Inigo Lopez de Mendoza, Marques de
Lopez Portillo (y Pacheco), Jose
1920-2004 .... **CLC 46**
See also CA 129; 224; HW 1
Lopez y Fuentes, Gregorio
1897(?)-1966 .... **CLC 32**
See also CA 131; EWL 3; HW 1
Lorca, Federico Garcia
See Garcia Lorca, Federico
See also DFS 4; EW 11; PFS 20; RGWL 2, 3; WP
Lord, Audre
See Lorde, Audre (Geraldine)
See also EWL 3
Lord, Bette Bao 1938- .... **AAL; CLC 23**
See also BEST 90:3; BPFB 2; CA 107; CANR 41, 79; INT CA-107; SATA 58
Lord Auch
See Bataille, Georges
Lord Brooke
See Greville, Fulke
Lord Byron
See Byron, George Gordon (Noel)
Lorde, Audre (Geraldine)
1934-1992 .... **BLC 2; CLC 18, 71; PC 12; TCLC 173**
See Domini, Rey; Lord, Audre
See also AFAW 1, 2; BW 1, 3; CA 25-28R; 142; CANR 16, 26, 46, 82; CP 2, 3, 4; DA3; DAM MULT, POET; DLB 41; FW; MAL 5; MTCW 1, 2; MTFW 2005; PFS 16; RGAL 4
Lord Houghton
See Milnes, Richard Monckton
Lord Jeffrey
See Jeffrey, Francis
Loreaux, Nichol .... **CLC 65**
Lorenzini, Carlo 1826-1890
See Collodi, Carlo
See also MAICYA 1, 2; SATA 29, 100
Lorenzo, Heberto Padilla
See Padilla (Lorenzo), Heberto
Loris
See Hofmannsthal, Hugo von
Loti, Pierre .... **TCLC 11**
See Viaud, (Louis Marie) Julien
See also DLB 123; GFL 1789 to the Present
Lou, Henri
See Andreas-Salome, Lou
Louie, David Wong 1954- .... **CLC 70**
See also CA 139; CANR 120
Louis, Adrian C. .... **NNAL**
See also CA 223
Louis, Father M.
See Merton, Thomas (James)
Louise, Heidi
See Erdrich, (Karen) Louise
Lovecraft, H(oward) P(hillips)
1890-1937 .... **SSC 3, 52; TCLC 4, 22**
See also AAYA 14; BPFB 2; CA 104; 133; CANR 106; DA3; DAM POP; HGG; MTCW 1, 2; MTFW 2005; RGAL 4; SCFW 1, 2; SFW 4; SUFW
Lovelace, Earl 1935- .... **CLC 51**
See also BW 2; CA 77-80; CANR 41, 72, 114; CD 5, 6; CDWLB 3; CN 1, 2, 3, 4, 5, 6, 7; DLB 125; EWL 3; MTCW 1
Lovelace, Richard 1618-1657 . **LC 24; PC 69**
See also BRW 2; DLB 131; EXPP; PAB; RGEL 2
Lowe, Pardee 1904- .... **AAL**
Lowell, Amy 1874-1925 ... **PC 13; TCLC 1, 8**
See also AAYA 57; AMW; CA 104; 151; DAM POET; DLB 54, 140; EWL 3; EXPP; LMFS 2; MAL 5; MAWW; MTCW 2; MTFW 2005; RGAL 4; TUS

Lowell, James Russell 1819-1891 ... **NCLC 2, 90**
See also AMWS 1; CDALB 1640-1865; DLB 1, 11, 64, 79, 189, 235; RGAL 4
Lowell, Robert (Traill Spence, Jr.)
1917-1977 .... **CLC 1, 2, 3, 4, 5, 8, 9, 11, 15, 37, 124; PC 3; WLC**
See also AMW; AMWC 2; AMWR 2; CA 9-12R; 73-76; CABS 2; CAD; CANR 26, 60; CDALBS; CP 1, 2; DA; DA3; DAB; DAC; DAM MST, NOV; DLB 5, 169; EWL 3; MAL 5; MTCW 1, 2; MTFW 2005; PAB; PFS 6, 7; RGAL 4; WP
Lowenthal, Michael (Francis)
1969- .... **CLC 119**
See also CA 150; CANR 115
Lowndes, Marie Adelaide (Belloc)
1868-1947 .... **TCLC 12**
See also CA 107; CMW 4; DLB 70; RHW
Lowry, (Clarence) Malcolm
1909-1957 .... **SSC 31; TCLC 6, 40**
See also BPFB 2; BRWS 3; CA 105; 131; CANR 62, 105; CDBLB 1945-1960; DLB 15; EWL 3; MTCW 1, 2; MTFW 2005; RGEL 2
Lowry, Mina Gertrude 1882-1966
See Loy, Mina
See also CA 113
Loxsmith, John
See Brunner, John (Kilian Houston)
Loy, Mina .... **CLC 28; PC 16**
See Lowry, Mina Gertrude
See also DAM POET; DLB 4, 54; PFS 20
Loyson-Bridet
See Schwob, Marcel (Mayer Andre)
Lucan 39-65 .... **CMLC 33**
See also AW 2; DLB 211; EFS 2; RGWL 2, 3
Lucas, Craig 1951- .... **CLC 64**
See also CA 137; CAD; CANR 71, 109, 142; CD 5, 6; GLL 2; MTFW 2005
Lucas, E(dward) V(errall)
1868-1938 .... **TCLC 73**
See also CA 176; DLB 98, 149, 153; SATA 20
Lucas, George 1944- .... **CLC 16**
See also AAYA 1, 23; CA 77-80; CANR 30; SATA 56
Lucas, Hans
See Godard, Jean-Luc
Lucas, Victoria
See Plath, Sylvia
Lucian c. 125-c. 180 .... **CMLC 32**
See also AW 2; DLB 176; RGWL 2, 3
Lucilius c. 180 B.C.-c. 101-02 B.C. .... **CMLC 82**
See also DLB 211
Lucretius c. 94B.C.-c. 49B.C. .... **CMLC 48**
See also AW 2; CDWLB 1; DLB 211; EFS 2; RGWL 2, 3
Ludlam, Charles 1943-1987 .... **CLC 46, 50**
See also CA 85-88; 122; CAD; CANR 72, 86; DLB 266
Ludlum, Robert 1927-2001 .... **CLC 22, 43**
See also AAYA 10, 59; BEST 89:1, 90:3; BPFB 2; CA 33-36R; 195; CANR 25, 41, 68, 105, 131; CMW 4; CPW; DA3; DAM NOV, POP; DLBY 1982; MSW; MTCW 1, 2; MTFW 2005
Ludwig, Ken 1950- .... **CLC 60**
See also CA 195; CAD; CD 6
Ludwig, Otto 1813-1865 .... **NCLC 4**
See also DLB 129
Lugones, Leopoldo 1874-1938 .... **HLCS 2; TCLC 15**
See also CA 116; 131; CANR 104; DLB 283; EWL 3; HW 1; LAW

Lu Hsun .... **SSC 20; TCLC 3**
See Shu-Jen, Chou
See also EWL 3
Lukacs, George .... **CLC 24**
See Lukacs, Gyorgy (Szegeny von)
Lukacs, Gyorgy (Szegeny von) 1885-1971
See Lukacs, George
See also CA 101; 29-32R; CANR 62; CDWLB 4; DLB 215, 242; EW 10; EWL 3; MTCW 1, 2
Luke, Peter (Ambrose Cyprian)
1919-1995 .... **CLC 38**
See also CA 81-84; 147; CANR 72; CBD; CD 5, 6; DLB 13
Lunar, Dennis
See Mungo, Raymond
Lurie, Alison 1926- ..... **CLC 4, 5, 18, 39, 175**
See also BPFB 2; CA 1-4R; CANR 2, 17, 50, 88; CN 1, 2, 3, 4, 5, 6, 7; DLB 2; MAL 5; MTCW 1; SATA 46, 112; TCLE 1:1
Lustig, Arnost 1926- .... **CLC 56**
See also AAYA 3; CA 69-72; CANR 47, 102; CWW 2; DLB 232, 299; EWL 3; SATA 56
Luther, Martin 1483-1546 .... **LC 9, 37**
See also CDWLB 2; DLB 179; EW 2; RGWL 2, 3
Luxemburg, Rosa 1870(?)-1919 ..... **TCLC 63**
See also CA 118
Luzi, Mario (Egidio Vincenzo)
1914-2005 .... **CLC 13**
See also CA 61-64; 236; CANR 9, 70; CWW 2; DLB 128; EWL 3
L'vov, Arkady .... **CLC 59**
Lydgate, John c. 1370-1450(?) .... **LC 81**
See also BRW 1; DLB 146; RGEL 2
Lyly, John 1554(?)-1606 .... **DC 7; LC 41**
See also BRW 1; DAM DRAM; DLB 62, 167; RGEL 2
L'Ymagier
See Gourmont, Remy(-Marie-Charles) de
Lynch, B. Suarez
See Borges, Jorge Luis
Lynch, David (Keith) 1946- ...... **CLC 66, 162**
See also AAYA 55; CA 124; 129; CANR 111
Lynch, James
See Andreyev, Leonid (Nikolaevich)
Lyndsay, Sir David 1485-1555 .... **LC 20**
See also RGEL 2
Lynn, Kenneth S(chuyler)
1923-2001 .... **CLC 50**
See also CA 1-4R; 196; CANR 3, 27, 65
Lynx
See West, Rebecca
Lyons, Marcus
See Blish, James (Benjamin)
Lyotard, Jean-Francois
1924-1998 .... **TCLC 103**
See also DLB 242; EWL 3
Lyre, Pinchbeck
See Sassoon, Siegfried (Lorraine)
Lytle, Andrew (Nelson) 1902-1995 ... **CLC 22**
See also CA 9-12R; 150; CANR 70; CN 1, 2, 3, 4, 5, 6; CSW; DLB 6; DLBY 1995; RGAL 4; RHW
Lyttelton, George 1709-1773 .... **LC 10**
See also RGEL 2
Lytton of Knebworth, Baron
See Bulwer-Lytton, Edward (George Earle Lytton)
Maas, Peter 1929-2001 .... **CLC 29**
See also CA 93-96; 201; INT CA-93-96; MTCW 2; MTFW 2005
Mac A'Ghobhainn, Iain
See Smith, Iain Crichton
Macaulay, Catherine 1731-1791 .... **LC 64**
See also DLB 104

Macaulay, (Emilie) Rose
1881(?)-1958 .... **TCLC 7, 44**
See also CA 104; DLB 36; EWL 3; RGEL 2; RHW

Macaulay, Thomas Babington
1800-1859 .... **NCLC 42**
See also BRW 4; CDBLB 1832-1890; DLB 32, 55; RGEL 2

MacBeth, George (Mann)
1932-1992 .... **CLC 2, 5, 9**
See also CA 25-28R; 136; CANR 61, 66; CP 1, 2, 3, 4; DLB 40; MTCW 1; PFS 8; SATA 4; SATA-Obit 70

MacCaig, Norman (Alexander)
1910-1996 .... **CLC 36**
See also BRWS 6; CA 9-12R; CANR 3, 34; CP 1, 2, 3, 4; DAB; DAM POET; DLB 27; EWL 3; RGEL 2

MacCarthy, Sir (Charles Otto) Desmond
1877-1952 .... **TCLC 36**
See also CA 167

MacDiarmid, Hugh .... **CLC 2, 4, 11, 19, 63; PC 9**
See Grieve, C(hristopher) M(urray)
See also CDBLB 1945-1960; CP 1, 2; DLB 20; EWL 3; RGEL 2

MacDonald, Anson
See Heinlein, Robert A(nson)

Macdonald, Cynthia 1928- .... **CLC 13, 19**
See also CA 49-52; CANR 4, 44, 146; DLB 105

MacDonald, George 1824-1905 .... **TCLC 9, 113**
See also AAYA 57; BYA 5; CA 106; 137; CANR 80; CLR 67; DLB 18, 163, 178; FANT; MAICYA 1, 2; RGEL 2; SATA 33, 100; SFW 4; SUFW; WCH

Macdonald, John
See Millar, Kenneth

MacDonald, John D(ann)
1916-1986 .... **CLC 3, 27, 44**
See also BPFB 2; CA 1-4R; 121; CANR 1, 19, 60; CMW 4; CPW; DAM NOV, POP; DLB 8, 306; DLBY 1986; MSW; MTCW 1, 2; MTFW 2005; SFW 4

Macdonald, John Ross
See Millar, Kenneth

Macdonald, Ross ..... **CLC 1, 2, 3, 14, 34, 41**
See Millar, Kenneth
See also AMWS 4; BPFB 2; CN 1, 2, 3; DLBD 6; MSW; RGAL 4

MacDougal, John
See Blish, James (Benjamin)

MacDougal, John
See Blish, James (Benjamin)

MacDowell, John
See Parks, Tim(othy Harold)

MacEwen, Gwendolyn (Margaret)
1941-1987 .... **CLC 13, 55**
See also CA 9-12R; 124; CANR 7, 22; CP 1, 2, 3, 4; DLB 53, 251; SATA 50; SATA-Obit 55

Macha, Karel Hynek 1810-1846 .... **NCLC 46**

Machado (y Ruiz), Antonio
1875-1939 .... **TCLC 3**
See also CA 104; 174; DLB 108; EW 9; EWL 3; HW 2; PFS 23; RGWL 2, 3

Machado de Assis, Joaquim Maria
1839-1908 ..... **BLC 2; HLCS 2; SSC 24; TCLC 10**
See also CA 107; 153; CANR 91; DLB 307; LAW; RGSF 2; RGWL 2, 3; TWA; WLIT 1

Machaut, Guillaume de c.
1300-1377 .... **CMLC 64**
See also DLB 208

Machen, Arthur .... **SSC 20; TCLC 4**
See Jones, Arthur Llewellyn
See also CA 179; DLB 156, 178; RGEL 2; SUFW 1

Machiavelli, Niccolo 1469-1527 ... **DC 16; LC 8, 36; WLCS**
See also AAYA 58; DA; DAB; DAC; DAM MST; EW 2; LAIT 1; LMFS 1; NFS 9; RGWL 2, 3; TWA; WLIT 7

MacInnes, Colin 1914-1976 .... **CLC 4, 23**
See also CA 69-72; 65-68; CANR 21; CN 1, 2; DLB 14; MTCW 1, 2; RGEL 2; RHW

MacInnes, Helen (Clark)
1907-1985 .... **CLC 27, 39**
See also BPFB 2; CA 1-4R; 117; CANR 1, 28, 58; CMW 4; CN 1, 2; CPW; DAM POP; DLB 87; MSW; MTCW 1, 2; MTFW 2005; SATA 22; SATA-Obit 44

Mackay, Mary 1855-1924
See Corelli, Marie
See also CA 118; 177; FANT; RHW

Mackay, Shena 1944- .... **CLC 195**
See also CA 104; CANR 88, 139; DLB 231, 319; MTFW 2005

Mackenzie, Compton (Edward Montague)
1883-1972 .... **CLC 18; TCLC 116**
See also CA 21-22; 37-40R; CAP 2; CN 1; DLB 34, 100; RGEL 2

Mackenzie, Henry 1745-1831 .... **NCLC 41**
See also DLB 39; RGEL 2

Mackey, Nathaniel (Ernest) 1947- .... **PC 49**
See also CA 153; CANR 114; CP 7; DLB 169

MacKinnon, Catharine A. 1946- .... **CLC 181**
See also CA 128; 132; CANR 73, 140; FW; MTCW 2; MTFW 2005

Mackintosh, Elizabeth 1896(?)-1952
See Tey, Josephine
See also CA 110; CMW 4

MacLaren, James
See Grieve, C(hristopher) M(urray)

MacLaverty, Bernard 1942- .... **CLC 31**
See also CA 116; 118; CANR 43, 88; CN 5, 6, 7; DLB 267; INT CA-118; RGSF 2

MacLean, Alistair (Stuart)
1922(?)-1987 .... **CLC 3, 13, 50, 63**
See also CA 57-60; 121; CANR 28, 61; CMW 4; CP 2, 3, 4, 5, 6, 7; CPW; DAM POP; DLB 276; MTCW 1; SATA 23; SATA-Obit 50; TCWW 2

Maclean, Norman (Fitzroy)
1902-1990 .... **CLC 78; SSC 13**
See also AMWS 14; CA 102; 132; CANR 49; CPW; DAM POP; DLB 206; TCWW 2

MacLeish, Archibald 1892-1982 ... **CLC 3, 8, 14, 68; PC 47**
See also AMW; CA 9-12R; 106; CAD; CANR 33, 63; CDALBS; CP 1, 2; DAM POET; DFS 15; DLB 4, 7, 45; DLBY 1982; EWL 3; EXPP; MAL 5; MTCW 1, 2; MTFW 2005; PAB; PFS 5; RGAL 4; TUS

MacLennan, (John) Hugh
1907-1990 .... **CLC 2, 14, 92**
See also CA 5-8R; 142; CANR 33; CN 1, 2, 3, 4; DAC; DAM MST; DLB 68; EWL 3; MTCW 1, 2; MTFW 2005; RGEL 2; TWA

MacLeod, Alistair 1936- .. **CLC 56, 165; SSC 90**
See also CA 123; CCA 1; DAC; DAM MST; DLB 60; MTCW 2; MTFW 2005; RGSF 2; TCLE 1:2

Macleod, Fiona
See Sharp, William
See also RGEL 2; SUFW

MacNeice, (Frederick) Louis
1907-1963 .... **CLC 1, 4, 10, 53; PC 61**
See also BRW 7; CA 85-88; CANR 61; DAB; DAM POET; DLB 10, 20; EWL 3; MTCW 1, 2; MTFW 2005; RGEL 2

MacNeill, Dand
See Fraser, George MacDonald

Macpherson, James 1736-1796 .... **LC 29**
See Ossian
See also BRWS 8; DLB 109; RGEL 2

Macpherson, (Jean) Jay 1931- .... **CLC 14**
See also CA 5-8R; CANR 90; CP 1, 2, 3, 4, 5, 6, 7; CWP; DLB 53

Macrobius fl. 430- .... **CMLC 48**

MacShane, Frank 1927-1999 .... **CLC 39**
See also CA 9-12R; 186; CANR 3, 33; DLB 111

Macumber, Mari
See Sandoz, Mari(e Susette)

Madach, Imre 1823-1864 .... **NCLC 19**

Madden, (Jerry) David 1933- .... **CLC 5, 15**
See also CA 1-4R; CAAS 3; CANR 4, 45; CN 3, 4, 5, 6, 7; CSW; DLB 6; MTCW 1

Maddern, Al(an)
See Ellison, Harlan (Jay)

Madhubuti, Haki R. 1942- ... **BLC 2; CLC 6, 73; PC 5**
See Lee, Don L.
See also BW 2, 3; CA 73-76; CANR 24, 51, 73, 139; CP 5, 6, 7; CSW; DAM MULT, POET; DLB 5, 41; DLBD 8; EWL 3; MAL 5; MTCW 2; MTFW 2005; RGAL 4

Madison, James 1751-1836 .... **NCLC 126**
See also DLB 37

Maepenn, Hugh
See Kuttner, Henry

Maepenn, K. H.
See Kuttner, Henry

Maeterlinck, Maurice 1862-1949 ..... **TCLC 3**
See also CA 104; 136; CANR 80; DAM DRAM; DLB 192; EW 8; EWL 3; GFL 1789 to the Present; LMFS 2; RGWL 2, 3; SATA 66; TWA

Maginn, William 1794-1842 .... **NCLC 8**
See also DLB 110, 159

Mahapatra, Jayanta 1928- .... **CLC 33**
See also CA 73-76; CAAS 9; CANR 15, 33, 66, 87; CP 4, 5, 6, 7; DAM MULT

Mahfouz, Naguib (Abdel Aziz Al-Sabilgi)
1911(?)- .... **CLC 153; SSC 66**
See Mahfuz, Najib (Abdel Aziz al-Sabilgi)
See also AAYA 49; BEST 89:2; CA 128; CANR 55, 101; DA3; DAM NOV; MTCW 1, 2; MTFW 2005; RGWL 2, 3; SSFS 9

Mahfuz, Najib (Abdel Aziz al-Sabilgi)
.... **CLC 52, 55**
See Mahfouz, Naguib (Abdel Aziz Al-Sabilgi)
See also AFW; CWW 2; DLBY 1988; EWL 3; RGSF 2; WLIT 6

Mahon, Derek 1941- .... **CLC 27; PC 60**
See also BRWS 6; CA 113; 128; CANR 88; CP 1, 2, 3, 4, 5, 6, 7; DLB 40; EWL 3

Maiakovskii, Vladimir
See Mayakovski, Vladimir (Vladimirovich)
See also IDTP; RGWL 2, 3

Mailer, Norman (Kingsley) 1923- . **CLC 1, 2, 3, 4, 5, 8, 11, 14, 28, 39, 74, 111**
See also AAYA 31; AITN 2; AMW; AMWC 2; AMWR 2; BPFB 2; CA 9-12R; CABS 1; CANR 28, 74, 77, 130; CDALB 1968-1988; CN 1, 2, 3, 4, 5, 6, 7; CPW; DA; DA3; DAB; DAC; DAM MST, NOV, POP; DLB 2, 16, 28, 185, 278; DLBD 3; DLBY 1980, 1983; EWL 3; MAL 5; MTCW 1, 2; MTFW 2005; NFS 10; RGAL 4; TUS

Maillet, Antoine 1929- .... **CLC 54, 118**
See also CA 115; 120; CANR 46, 74, 77, 134; CCA 1; CWW 2; DAC; DLB 60; INT CA-120; MTCW 2; MTFW 2005

Maimonides, Moses 1135-1204 ..... **CMLC 76**
See also DLB 115

Mais, Roger 1905-1955 .... **TCLC 8**
See also BW 1, 3; CA 105; 124; CANR 82; CDWLB 3; DLB 125; EWL 3; MTCW 1; RGEL 2

Maistre, Joseph 1753-1821 .... **NCLC 37**
See also GFL 1789 to the Present

Maitland, Frederic William 1850-1906 .... **TCLC 65**

Maitland, Sara (Louise) 1950- .... **CLC 49**
See also BRWS 11; CA 69-72; CANR 13, 59; DLB 271; FW

Major, Clarence 1936- ... **BLC 2; CLC 3, 19, 48**
See also AFAW 2; BW 2, 3; CA 21-24R; CAAS 6; CANR 13, 25, 53, 82; CN 3, 4, 5, 6, 7; CP 2, 3, 4, 5, 6, 7; CSW; DAM MULT; DLB 33; EWL 3; MAL 5; MSW

Major, Kevin (Gerald) 1949- .... **CLC 26**
See also AAYA 16; CA 97-100; CANR 21, 38, 112; CLR 11; DAC; DLB 60; INT CANR-21; JRDA; MAICYA 1, 2; MAICYAS 1; SATA 32, 82, 134; WYA; YAW

Maki, James
See Ozu, Yasujiro

Makine, Andrei 1957- .... **CLC 198**
See also CA 176; CANR 103; MTFW 2005

Malabaila, Damiano
See Levi, Primo

Malamud, Bernard 1914-1986 .. **CLC 1, 2, 3, 5, 8, 9, 11, 18, 27, 44, 78, 85; SSC 15; TCLC 129; WLC**
See also AAYA 16; AMWS 1; BPFB 2; BYA 15; CA 5-8R; 118; CABS 1; CANR 28, 62, 114; CDALB 1941-1968; CN 1, 2, 3, 4; CPW; DA; DA3; DAB; DAC; DAM MST, NOV, POP; DLB 2, 28, 152; DLBY 1980, 1986; EWL 3; EXPS; LAIT 4; LATS 1:1; MAL 5; MTCW 1, 2; MTFW 2005; NFS 4, 9; RGAL 4; RGSF 2; SSFS 8, 13, 16; TUS

Malan, Herman
See Bosman, Herman Charles; Bosman, Herman Charles

Malaparte, Curzio 1898-1957 .... **TCLC 52**
See also DLB 264

Malcolm, Dan
See Silverberg, Robert

Malcolm, Janet 1934- .... **CLC 201**
See also CA 123; CANR 89; NCFS 1

Malcolm X .... **BLC 2; CLC 82, 117; WLCS**
See Little, Malcolm
See also LAIT 5; NCFS 3

Malherbe, Francois de 1555-1628 .... **LC 5**
See also GFL Beginnings to 1789

Mallarme, Stephane 1842-1898 ...... **NCLC 4, 41; PC 4**
See also DAM POET; DLB 217; EW 7; GFL 1789 to the Present; LMFS 2; RGWL 2, 3; TWA

Mallet-Joris, Francoise 1930- .... **CLC 11**
See also CA 65-68; CANR 17; CWW 2; DLB 83; EWL 3; GFL 1789 to the Present

Malley, Ern
See McAuley, James Phillip

Mallon, Thomas 1951- .... **CLC 172**
See also CA 110; CANR 29, 57, 92

Mallowan, Agatha Christie
See Christie, Agatha (Mary Clarissa)

Maloff, Saul 1922- .... **CLC 5**
See also CA 33-36R

Malone, Louis
See MacNeice, (Frederick) Louis

Malone, Michael (Christopher) 1942- .... **CLC 43**
See also CA 77-80; CANR 14, 32, 57, 114

Malory, Sir Thomas 1410(?)-1471(?) . **LC 11, 88; WLCS**
See also BRW 1; BRWR 2; CDBLB Before 1660; DA; DAB; DAC; DAM MST; DLB 146; EFS 2; RGEL 2; SATA 59; SATA-Brief 33; TEA; WLIT 3

Malouf, (George Joseph) David 1934- .... **CLC 28, 86**
See also CA 124; CANR 50, 76; CN 3, 4, 5, 6, 7; CP 1, 3, 4, 5, 6, 7; DLB 289; EWL 3; MTCW 2; MTFW 2005

Malraux, (Georges-)Andre 1901-1976 .... **CLC 1, 4, 9, 13, 15, 57**
See also BPFB 2; CA 21-22; 69-72; CANR 34, 58; CAP 2; DA3; DAM NOV; DLB 72; EW 12; EWL 3; GFL 1789 to the Present; MTCW 1, 2; MTFW 2005; RGWL 2, 3; TWA

Malthus, Thomas Robert 1766-1834 .... **NCLC 145**
See also DLB 107, 158; RGEL 2

Malzberg, Barry N(athaniel) 1939- ... **CLC 7**
See also CA 61-64; CAAS 4; CANR 16; CMW 4; DLB 8; SFW 4

Mamet, David (Alan) 1947- .. **CLC 9, 15, 34, 46, 91, 166; DC 4, 24**
See also AAYA 3, 60; AMWS 14; CA 81-84; CABS 3; CAD; CANR 15, 41, 67, 72, 129; CD 5, 6; DA3; DAM DRAM; DFS 2, 3, 6, 12, 15; DLB 7; EWL 3; IDFW 4; MAL 5; MTCW 1, 2; MTFW 2005; RGAL 4

Mamoulian, Rouben (Zachary) 1897-1987 .... **CLC 16**
See also CA 25-28R; 124; CANR 85

Mandelshtam, Osip
See Mandelstam, Osip (Emilievich)
See also EW 10; EWL 3; RGWL 2, 3

Mandelstam, Osip (Emilievich) 1891(?)-1943(?) .... **PC 14; TCLC 2, 6**
See Mandelshtam, Osip
See also CA 104; 150; MTCW 2; TWA

Mander, (Mary) Jane 1877-1949 ... **TCLC 31**
See also CA 162; RGEL 2

Mandeville, Bernard 1670-1733 .... **LC 82**
See also DLB 101

Mandeville, Sir John fl. 1350- ...... **CMLC 19**
See also DLB 146

Mandiargues, Andre Pieyre de .... **CLC 41**
See Pieyre de Mandiargues, Andre
See also DLB 83

Mandrake, Ethel Belle
See Thurman, Wallace (Henry)

Mangan, James Clarence 1803-1849 .... **NCLC 27**
See also RGEL 2

Maniere, J.-E.
See Giraudoux, Jean(-Hippolyte)

Mankiewicz, Herman (Jacob) 1897-1953 .... **TCLC 85**
See also CA 120; 169; DLB 26; IDFW 3, 4

Manley, (Mary) Delariviere 1672(?)-1724 .... **LC 1, 42**
See also DLB 39, 80; RGEL 2

Mann, Abel
See Creasey, John

Mann, Emily 1952- .... **DC 7**
See also CA 130; CAD; CANR 55; CD 5, 6; CWD; DLB 266

Mann, (Luiz) Heinrich 1871-1950 ... **TCLC 9**
See also CA 106; 164, 181; DLB 66, 118; EW 8; EWL 3; RGWL 2, 3

Mann, (Paul) Thomas 1875-1955 . **SSC 5, 80, 82; TCLC 2, 8, 14, 21, 35, 44, 60, 168; WLC**
See also BPFB 2; CA 104; 128; CANR 133; CDWLB 2; DA; DA3; DAB; DAC; DAM MST, NOV; DLB 66; EW 9; EWL 3; GLL 1; LATS 1:1; LMFS 1; MTCW 1, 2; MTFW 2005; NFS 17; RGSF 2; RGWL 2, 3; SSFS 4, 9; TWA

Mannheim, Karl 1893-1947 .... **TCLC 65**
See also CA 204

Manning, David
See Faust, Frederick (Schiller)

Manning, Frederic 1882-1935 .... **TCLC 25**
See also CA 124; 216; DLB 260

Manning, Olivia 1915-1980 .... **CLC 5, 19**
See also CA 5-8R; 101; CANR 29; CN 1, 2; EWL 3; FW; MTCW 1; RGEL 2

Mano, D. Keith 1942- .... **CLC 2, 10**
See also CA 25-28R; CAAS 6; CANR 26, 57; DLB 6

Mansfield, Katherine .... **SSC 9, 23, 38, 81; TCLC 2, 8, 39, 164; WLC**
See Beauchamp, Kathleen Mansfield
See also BPFB 2; BRW 7; DAB; DLB 162; EWL 3; EXPS; FW; GLL 1; RGEL 2; RGSF 2; SSFS 2, 8, 10, 11; WWE 1

Manso, Peter 1940- .... **CLC 39**
See also CA 29-32R; CANR 44

Mantecon, Juan Jimenez
See Jimenez (Mantecon), Juan Ramon

Mantel, Hilary (Mary) 1952- .... **CLC 144**
See also CA 125; CANR 54, 101; CN 5, 6, 7; DLB 271; RHW

Manton, Peter
See Creasey, John

Man Without a Spleen, A
See Chekhov, Anton (Pavlovich)

Manzano, Juan Franciso 1797(?)-1854 .... **NCLC 155**

Manzoni, Alessandro 1785-1873 ... **NCLC 29, 98**
See also EW 5; RGWL 2, 3; TWA; WLIT 7

Map, Walter 1140-1209 .... **CMLC 32**

Mapu, Abraham (ben Jekutiel) 1808-1867 .... **NCLC 18**

Mara, Sally
See Queneau, Raymond

Maracle, Lee 1950- .... **NNAL**
See also CA 149

Marat, Jean Paul 1743-1793 .... **LC 10**

Marcel, Gabriel Honore 1889-1973 . **CLC 15**
See also CA 102; 45-48; EWL 3; MTCW 1, 2

March, William .... **TCLC 96**
See Campbell, William Edward March
See also CA 216; DLB 9, 86, 316; MAL 5

Marchbanks, Samuel
See Davies, (William) Robertson
See also CCA 1

Marchi, Giacomo
See Bassani, Giorgio

Marcus Aurelius
See Aurelius, Marcus
See also AW 2

Marguerite
See de Navarre, Marguerite

Marguerite d'Angouleme
See de Navarre, Marguerite
See also GFL Beginnings to 1789

Marguerite de Navarre
See de Navarre, Marguerite
See also RGWL 2, 3

Margulies, Donald 1954- .... **CLC 76**
See also AAYA 57; CA 200; CD 6; DFS 13; DLB 228

Marie de France c. 12th cent. - ...... **CMLC 8; PC 22**
See also DLB 208; FW; RGWL 2, 3

Marie de l'Incarnation 1599-1672 ...... **LC 10**
Marier, Captain Victor
    See Griffith, D(avid Lewelyn) W(ark)
Mariner, Scott
    See Pohl, Frederik
Marinetti, Filippo Tommaso
    1876-1944 .... **TCLC 10**
    See also CA 107; DLB 114, 264; EW 9;
    EWL 3; WLIT 7
Marivaux, Pierre Carlet de Chamblain de
    1688-1763 .... **DC 7; LC 4, 123**
    See also DLB 314; GFL Beginnings to
    1789; RGWL 2, 3; TWA
Markandaya, Kamala .... **CLC 8, 38**
    See Taylor, Kamala (Purnaiya)
    See also BYA 13; CN 1, 2, 3, 4, 5, 6, 7;
    EWL 3
Markfield, Wallace (Arthur)
    1926-2002 .... **CLC 8**
    See also CA 69-72; 208; CAAS 3; CN 1, 2,
    3, 4, 5, 6, 7; DLB 2, 28; DLBY 2002
Markham, Edwin 1852-1940 .... **TCLC 47**
    See also CA 160; DLB 54, 186; MAL 5;
    RGAL 4
Markham, Robert
    See Amis, Kingsley (William)
Markoosie .... **NNAL**
    See Patsauq, Markoosie
    See also CLR 23; DAM MULT
Marks, J.
    See Highwater, Jamake (Mamake)
Marks, J
    See Highwater, Jamake (Mamake)
Marks-Highwater, J
    See Highwater, Jamake (Mamake)
Marks-Highwater, J.
    See Highwater, Jamake (Mamake)
Markson, David M(errill) 1927- .... **CLC 67**
    See also CA 49-52; CANR 1, 91; CN 5, 6
Marlatt, Daphne (Buckle) 1942- .... **CLC 168**
    See also CA 25-28R; CANR 17, 39; CN 6,
    7; CP 4, 5, 6, 7; CWP; DLB 60; FW
Marley, Bob .... **CLC 17**
    See Marley, Robert Nesta
Marley, Robert Nesta 1945-1981
    See Marley, Bob
    See also CA 107; 103
Marlowe, Christopher 1564-1593 .. **DC 1; LC 22, 47, 117; PC 57; WLC**
    See also BRW 1; BRWR 1; CDBLB Before
    1660; DA; DA3; DAB; DAC; DAM
    DRAM, MST; DFS 1, 5, 13, 21; DLB 62;
    EXPP; LMFS 1; PFS 22; RGEL 2; TEA;
    WLIT 3
Marlowe, Stephen 1928- .... **CLC 70**
    See Queen, Ellery
    See also CA 13-16R; CANR 6, 55; CMW
    4; SFW 4
Marmion, Shakerley 1603-1639 .... **LC 89**
    See also DLB 58; RGEL 2
Marmontel, Jean-Francois 1723-1799 .. **LC 2**
    See also DLB 314
Maron, Monika 1941- .... **CLC 165**
    See also CA 201
Marquand, John P(hillips)
    1893-1960 .... **CLC 2, 10**
    See also AMW; BPFB 2; CA 85-88; CANR
    73; CMW 4; DLB 9, 102; EWL 3; MAL
    5; MTCW 2; RGAL 4
Marques, Rene 1919-1979 .. **CLC 96; HLC 2**
    See also CA 97-100; 85-88; CANR 78;
    DAM MULT; DLB 305; EWL 3; HW 1,
    2; LAW; RGSF 2
Marquez, Gabriel (Jose) Garcia
    See Garcia Marquez, Gabriel (Jose)
Marquis, Don(ald Robert Perry)
    1878-1937 .... **TCLC 7**
    See also CA 104; 166; DLB 11, 25; MAL
    5; RGAL 4

Marquis de Sade
    See Sade, Donatien Alphonse Francois
Marric, J. J.
    See Creasey, John
    See also MSW
Marryat, Frederick 1792-1848 .... **NCLC 3**
    See also DLB 21, 163; RGEL 2; WCH
Marsden, James
    See Creasey, John
Marsh, Edward 1872-1953 .... **TCLC 99**
Marsh, (Edith) Ngaio 1895-1982 .. **CLC 7, 53**
    See also CA 9-12R; CANR 6, 58; CMW 4;
    CN 1, 2, 3; CPW; DAM POP; DLB 77;
    MSW; MTCW 1, 2; RGEL 2; TEA
Marshall, Allen
    See Westlake, Donald E(dwin)
Marshall, Garry 1934- .... **CLC 17**
    See also AAYA 3; CA 111; SATA 60
Marshall, Paule 1929- .. **BLC 3; CLC 27, 72; SSC 3**
    See also AFAW 1, 2; AMWS 11; BPFB 2;
    BW 2, 3; CA 77-80; CANR 25, 73, 129;
    CN 1, 2, 3, 4, 5, 6, 7; DA3; DAM MULT;
    DLB 33, 157, 227; EWL 3; LATS 1:2;
    MAL 5; MTCW 1, 2; MTFW 2005;
    RGAL 4; SSFS 15
Marshallik
    See Zangwill, Israel
Marsten, Richard
    See Hunter, Evan
Marston, John 1576-1634 .... **LC 33**
    See also BRW 2; DAM DRAM; DLB 58,
    172; RGEL 2
Martel, Yann 1963- .... **CLC 192**
    See also AAYA 67; CA 146; CANR 114;
    MTFW 2005
Martens, Adolphe-Adhemar
    See Ghelderode, Michel de
Martha, Henry
    See Harris, Mark
Marti, Jose
    See Marti (y Perez), Jose (Julian)
    See also DLB 290
Marti (y Perez), Jose (Julian)
    1853-1895 .... **HLC 2; NCLC 63**
    See Marti, Jose
    See also DAM MULT; HW 2; LAW; RGWL
    2, 3; WLIT 1
Martial c. 40-c. 104 .... **CMLC 35; PC 10**
    See also AW 2; CDWLB 1; DLB 211;
    RGWL 2, 3
Martin, Ken
    See Hubbard, L(afayette) Ron(ald)
Martin, Richard
    See Creasey, John
Martin, Steve 1945- .... **CLC 30, 217**
    See also AAYA 53; CA 97-100; CANR 30,
    100, 140; DFS 19; MTCW 1; MTFW
    2005
Martin, Valerie 1948- .... **CLC 89**
    See also BEST 90:2; CA 85-88; CANR 49,
    89
Martin, Violet Florence 1862-1915 .. **SSC 56; TCLC 51**
Martin, Webber
    See Silverberg, Robert
Martindale, Patrick Victor
    See White, Patrick (Victor Martindale)
Martin du Gard, Roger
    1881-1958 .... **TCLC 24**
    See also CA 118; CANR 94; DLB 65; EWL
    3; GFL 1789 to the Present; RGWL 2, 3
Martineau, Harriet 1802-1876 .... **NCLC 26, 137**
    See also DLB 21, 55, 159, 163, 166, 190;
    FW; RGEL 2; YABC 2
Martines, Julia
    See O'Faolain, Julia

Martinez, Enrique Gonzalez
    See Gonzalez Martinez, Enrique
Martinez, Jacinto Benavente y
    See Benavente (y Martinez), Jacinto
Martinez de la Rosa, Francisco de Paula
    1787-1862 .... **NCLC 102**
    See also TWA
Martinez Ruiz, Jose 1873-1967
    See Azorin; Ruiz, Jose Martinez
    See also CA 93-96; HW 1
Martinez Sierra, Gregorio
    1881-1947 .... **TCLC 6**
    See also CA 115; EWL 3
Martinez Sierra, Maria (de la O'LeJarraga)
    1874-1974 .... **TCLC 6**
    See also CA 115; EWL 3
Martinsen, Martin
    See Follett, Ken(neth Martin)
Martinson, Harry (Edmund)
    1904-1978 .... **CLC 14**
    See also CA 77-80; CANR 34, 130; DLB
    259; EWL 3
Martyn, Edward 1859-1923 .... **TCLC 131**
    See also CA 179; DLB 10; RGEL 2
Marut, Ret
    See Traven, B.
Marut, Robert
    See Traven, B.
Marvell, Andrew 1621-1678 .... **LC 4, 43; PC 10; WLC**
    See also BRW 2; BRWR 2; CDBLB 1660-
    1789; DA; DA3; DAB; DAC; DAM MST,
    POET; DLB 131; EXPP; PFS 5; RGEL 2;
    TEA; WP
Marx, Karl (Heinrich)
    1818-1883 .... **NCLC 17, 114**
    See also DLB 129; LATS 1:1; TWA
Masaoka, Shiki -1902 .... **TCLC 18**
    See Masaoka, Tsunenori
    See also RGWL 3
Masaoka, Tsunenori 1867-1902
    See Masaoka, Shiki
    See also CA 117; 191; TWA
Masefield, John (Edward)
    1878-1967 .... **CLC 11, 47**
    See also CA 19-20; 25-28R; CANR 33;
    CAP 2; CDBLB 1890-1914; DAM POET;
    DLB 10, 19, 153, 160; EWL 3; EXPP;
    FANT; MTCW 1, 2; PFS 5; RGEL 2;
    SATA 19
Maso, Carole (?)- .... **CLC 44**
    See also CA 170; CN 7; GLL 2; RGAL 4
Mason, Bobbie Ann 1940- ... **CLC 28, 43, 82, 154; SSC 4**
    See also AAYA 5, 42; AMWS 8; BPFB 2;
    CA 53-56; CANR 11, 31, 58, 83, 125;
    CDALBS; CN 5, 6, 7; CSW; DA3; DLB
    173; DLBY 1987; EWL 3; EXPS; INT
    CANR-31; MAL 5; MTCW 1, 2; MTFW
    2005; NFS 4; RGAL 4; RGSF 2; SSFS 3,
    8, 20; TCLE 1:2; YAW
Mason, Ernst
    See Pohl, Frederik
Mason, Hunni B.
    See Sternheim, (William Adolf) Carl
Mason, Lee W.
    See Malzberg, Barry N(athaniel)
Mason, Nick 1945- .... **CLC 35**
Mason, Tally
    See Derleth, August (William)
Mass, Anna .... **CLC 59**
Mass, William
    See Gibson, William
Massinger, Philip 1583-1640 .... **LC 70**
    See also BRWS 11; DLB 58; RGEL 2
Master Lao
    See Lao Tzu

MASTERS

Masters, Edgar Lee 1868-1950 ...... **PC 1, 36; TCLC 2, 25; WLCS**
See also AMWS 1; CA 104; 133; CDALB 1865-1917; DA; DAC; DAM MST, POET; DLB 54; EWL 3; EXPP; MAL 5; MTCW 1, 2; MTFW 2005; RGAL 4; TUS; WP

Masters, Hilary 1928- .... **CLC 48**
See also CA 25-28R, 217; CAAE 217; CANR 13, 47, 97; CN 6, 7; DLB 244

Mastrosimone, William 1947- .... **CLC 36**
See also CA 186; CAD; CD 5, 6

Mathe, Albert
See Camus, Albert

Mather, Cotton 1663-1728 .... **LC 38**
See also AMWS 2; CDALB 1640-1865; DLB 24, 30, 140; RGAL 4; TUS

Mather, Increase 1639-1723 .... **LC 38**
See also DLB 24

Matheson, Richard (Burton) 1926- .. **CLC 37**
See also AAYA 31; CA 97-100; CANR 88, 99; DLB 8, 44; HGG; INT CA-97-100; SCFW 1, 2; SFW 4; SUFW 2

Mathews, Harry (Burchell) 1930- ..... **CLC 6, 52**
See also CA 21-24R; CAAS 6; CANR 18, 40, 98; CN 5, 6, 7

Mathews, John Joseph 1894-1979 .. **CLC 84; NNAL**
See also CA 19-20; 142; CANR 45; CAP 2; DAM MULT; DLB 175; TCWW 1, 2

Mathias, Roland (Glyn) 1915- .... **CLC 45**
See also CA 97-100; CANR 19, 41; CP 1, 2, 3, 4, 5, 6, 7; DLB 27

Matsuo Basho 1644(?)-1694 ...... **LC 62; PC 3**
See Basho, Matsuo
See also DAM POET; PFS 2, 7, 18

Mattheson, Rodney
See Creasey, John

Matthews, (James) Brander 1852-1929 .... **TCLC 95**
See also CA 181; DLB 71, 78; DLBD 13

Matthews, Greg 1949- .... **CLC 45**
See also CA 135

Matthews, William (Procter III) 1942-1997 .... **CLC 40**
See also AMWS 9; CA 29-32R; CAAS 18; CANR 12, 57; CP 2, 3, 4; DLB 5

Matthias, John (Edward) 1941- .... **CLC 9**
See also CA 33-36R; CANR 56; CP 4, 5, 6, 7

Matthiessen, F(rancis) O(tto) 1902-1950 .... **TCLC 100**
See also CA 185; DLB 63; MAL 5

Matthiessen, Peter 1927- ... **CLC 5, 7, 11, 32, 64**
See also AAYA 6, 40; AMWS 5; ANW; BEST 90:4; BPFB 2; CA 9-12R; CANR 21, 50, 73, 100, 138; CN 1, 2, 3, 4, 5, 6, 7; DA3; DAM NOV; DLB 6, 173, 275; MAL 5; MTCW 1, 2; MTFW 2005; SATA 27

Maturin, Charles Robert 1780(?)-1824 .... **NCLC 6**
See also BRWS 8; DLB 178; GL 3; HGG; LMFS 1; RGEL 2; SUFW

Matute (Ausejo), Ana Maria 1925- .. **CLC 11**
See also CA 89-92; CANR 129; CWW 2; DLB 322; EWL 3; MTCW 1; RGSF 2

Maugham, W. S.
See Maugham, W(illiam) Somerset

Maugham, W(illiam) Somerset 1874-1965 .. **CLC 1, 11, 15, 67, 93; SSC 8; WLC**
See also AAYA 55; BPFB 2; BRW 6; CA 5-8R; 25-28R; CANR 40, 127; CDBLB 1914-1945; CMW 4; DA; DA3; DAB; DAC; DAM DRAM, MST, NOV; DFS 22; DLB 10, 36, 77, 100, 162, 195; EWL 3; LAIT 3; MTCW 1, 2; MTFW 2005; RGEL 2; RGSF 2; SATA 54; SSFS 17

Maugham, William Somerset
See Maugham, W(illiam) Somerset

Maupassant, (Henri Rene Albert) Guy de 1850-1893 . **NCLC 1, 42, 83; SSC 1, 64; WLC**
See also BYA 14; DA; DA3; DAB; DAC; DAM MST; DLB 123; EW 7; EXPS; GFL 1789 to the Present; LAIT 2; LMFS 1; RGSF 2; RGWL 2, 3; SSFS 4, 21; SUFW; TWA

Maupin, Armistead (Jones, Jr.) 1944- .... **CLC 95**
See also CA 125; 130; CANR 58, 101; CPW; DA3; DAM POP; DLB 278; GLL 1; INT CA-130; MTCW 2; MTFW 2005

Maurhut, Richard
See Traven, B.

Mauriac, Claude 1914-1996 .... **CLC 9**
See also CA 89-92; 152; CWW 2; DLB 83; EWL 3; GFL 1789 to the Present

Mauriac, Francois (Charles) 1885-1970 .... **CLC 4, 9, 56; SSC 24**
See also CA 25-28; CAP 2; DLB 65; EW 10; EWL 3; GFL 1789 to the Present; MTCW 1, 2; MTFW 2005; RGWL 2, 3; TWA

Mavor, Osborne Henry 1888-1951
See Bridie, James
See also CA 104

Maxwell, William (Keepers, Jr.) 1908-2000 .... **CLC 19**
See also AMWS 8; CA 93-96; 189; CANR 54, 95; CN 1, 2, 3, 4, 5, 6, 7; DLB 218, 278; DLBY 1980; INT CA-93-96; SATA-Obit 128

May, Elaine 1932- .... **CLC 16**
See also CA 124; 142; CAD; CWD; DLB 44

Mayakovski, Vladimir (Vladimirovich) 1893-1930 .... **TCLC 4, 18**
See Maiakovskii, Vladimir; Mayakovsky, Vladimir
See also CA 104; 158; EWL 3; MTCW 2; MTFW 2005; SFW 4; TWA

Mayakovsky, Vladimir
See Mayakovski, Vladimir (Vladimirovich)
See also EW 11; WP

Mayhew, Henry 1812-1887 .... **NCLC 31**
See also DLB 18, 55, 190

Mayle, Peter 1939(?)- .... **CLC 89**
See also CA 139; CANR 64, 109

Maynard, Joyce 1953- .... **CLC 23**
See also CA 111; 129; CANR 64

Mayne, William (James Carter) 1928- .... **CLC 12**
See also AAYA 20; CA 9-12R; CANR 37, 80, 100; CLR 25; FANT; JRDA; MAICYA 1, 2; MAICYAS 1; SAAS 11; SATA 6, 68, 122; SUFW 2; YAW

Mayo, Jim
See L'Amour, Louis (Dearborn)

Maysles, Albert 1926- .... **CLC 16**
See also CA 29-32R

Maysles, David 1932-1987 .... **CLC 16**
See also CA 191

Mazer, Norma Fox 1931- .... **CLC 26**
See also AAYA 5, 36; BYA 1, 8; CA 69-72; CANR 12, 32, 66, 129; CLR 23; JRDA; MAICYA 1, 2; SAAS 1; SATA 24, 67, 105; WYA; YAW

Mazzini, Guiseppe 1805-1872 .... **NCLC 34**

McAlmon, Robert (Menzies) 1895-1956 .... **TCLC 97**
See also CA 107; 168; DLB 4, 45; DLBD 15; GLL 1

CUMULATIVE AUTHOR INDEX

McAuley, James Phillip 1917-1976 .. **CLC 45**
See also CA 97-100; CP 1, 2; DLB 260; RGEL 2

McBain, Ed
See Hunter, Evan
See also MSW

McBrien, William (Augustine) 1930- .... **CLC 44**
See also CA 107; CANR 90

McCabe, Patrick 1955- .... **CLC 133**
See also BRWS 9; CA 130; CANR 50, 90; CN 6, 7; DLB 194

McCaffrey, Anne 1926- .... **CLC 17**
See also AAYA 6, 34; AITN 2; BEST 89:2; BPFB 2; BYA 5; CA 25-28R, 227; CAAE 227; CANR 15, 35, 55, 96; CLR 49; CPW; DA3; DAM NOV, POP; DLB 8; JRDA; MAICYA 1, 2; MTCW 1, 2; MTFW 2005; SAAS 11; SATA 8, 70, 116, 152; SATA-Essay 152; SFW 4; SUFW 2; WYA; YAW

McCaffrey, Anne Inez
See McCaffrey, Anne

McCall, Nathan 1955(?)- .... **CLC 86**
See also AAYA 59; BW 3; CA 146; CANR 88

McCann, Arthur
See Campbell, John W(ood, Jr.)

McCann, Edson
See Pohl, Frederik

McCarthy, Charles, Jr. 1933-
See McCarthy, Cormac
See also CANR 42, 69, 101; CPW; CSW; DA3; DAM POP; MTCW 2; MTFW 2005

McCarthy, Cormac .... **CLC 4, 57, 101, 204**
See McCarthy, Charles, Jr.
See also AAYA 41; AMWS 8; BPFB 2; CA 13-16R; CANR 10; CN 6, 7; DLB 6, 143, 256; EWL 3; LATS 1:2; MAL 5; TCLE 1:2; TCWW 2

McCarthy, Mary (Therese) 1912-1989 .. **CLC 1, 3, 5, 14, 24, 39, 59; SSC 24**
See also AMW; BPFB 2; CA 5-8R; 129; CANR 16, 50, 64; CN 1, 2, 3, 4; DA3; DLB 2; DLBY 1981; EWL 3; FW; INT CANR-16; MAL 5; MAWW; MTCW 1, 2; MTFW 2005; RGAL 4; TUS

McCartney, (James) Paul 1942- . **CLC 12, 35**
See also CA 146; CANR 111

McCauley, Stephen (D.) 1955- .... **CLC 50**
See also CA 141

McClaren, Peter .... **CLC 70**

McClure, Michael (Thomas) 1932- ... **CLC 6, 10**
See also BG 1:3; CA 21-24R; CAD; CANR 17, 46, 77, 131; CD 5, 6; CP 1, 2, 3, 4, 5, 6, 7; DLB 16; WP

McCorkle, Jill (Collins) 1958- .... **CLC 51**
See also CA 121; CANR 113; CSW; DLB 234; DLBY 1987

McCourt, Frank 1930- .... **CLC 109**
See also AAYA 61; AMWS 12; CA 157; CANR 97, 138; MTFW 2005; NCFS 1

McCourt, James 1941- .... **CLC 5**
See also CA 57-60; CANR 98

McCourt, Malachy 1931- .... **CLC 119**
See also SATA 126

McCoy, Horace (Stanley) 1897-1955 .... **TCLC 28**
See also AMWS 13; CA 108; 155; CMW 4; DLB 9

McCrae, John 1872-1918 .... **TCLC 12**
See also CA 109; DLB 92; PFS 5

McCreigh, James
See Pohl, Frederik

McCullers, (Lula) Carson (Smith)
1917-1967 .... **CLC 1, 4, 10, 12, 48, 100; SSC 9, 24; TCLC 155; WLC**
See also AAYA 21; AMW; AMWC 2; BPFB 2; CA 5-8R; 25-28R; CABS 1, 3; CANR 18, 132; CDALB 1941-1968; DA; DA3; DAB; DAC; DAM MST, NOV; DFS 5, 18; DLB 2, 7, 173, 228; EWL 3; EXPS; FW; GLL 1; LAIT 3, 4; MAL 5; MAWW; MTCW 1, 2; MTFW 2005; NFS 6, 13; RGAL 4; RGSF 2; SATA 27; SSFS 5; TUS; YAW

McCulloch, John Tyler
See Burroughs, Edgar Rice

McCullough, Colleen 1937- ...... **CLC 27, 107**
See also AAYA 36; BPFB 2; CA 81-84; CANR 17, 46, 67, 98, 139; CPW; DA3; DAM NOV, POP; MTCW 1, 2; MTFW 2005; RHW

McCunn, Ruthanne Lum 1946- .... **AAL**
See also CA 119; CANR 43, 96; DLB 312; LAIT 2; SATA 63

McDermott, Alice 1953- .... **CLC 90**
See also CA 109; CANR 40, 90, 126; CN 7; DLB 292; MTFW 2005

McElroy, Joseph (Prince) 1930- ... **CLC 5, 47**
See also CA 17-20R; CN 3, 4, 5, 6, 7

McEwan, Ian (Russell) 1948- .... **CLC 13, 66, 169**
See also BEST 90:4; BRWS 4; CA 61-64; CANR 14, 41, 69, 87, 132; CN 3, 4, 5, 6, 7; DAM NOV; DLB 14, 194, 319; HGG; MTCW 1, 2; MTFW 2005; RGSF 2; SUFW 2; TEA

McFadden, David 1940- .... **CLC 48**
See also CA 104; CP 1, 2, 3, 4, 5, 6, 7; DLB 60; INT CA-104

McFarland, Dennis 1950- .... **CLC 65**
See also CA 165; CANR 110

McGahern, John 1934- ... **CLC 5, 9, 48, 156; SSC 17**
See also CA 17-20R; CANR 29, 68, 113; CN 1, 2, 3, 4, 5, 6, 7; DLB 14, 231, 319; MTCW 1

McGinley, Patrick (Anthony) 1937- . **CLC 41**
See also CA 120; 127; CANR 56; INT CA-127

McGinley, Phyllis 1905-1978 .... **CLC 14**
See also CA 9-12R; 77-80; CANR 19; CP 1, 2; CWRI 5; DLB 11, 48; MAL 5; PFS 9, 13; SATA 2, 44; SATA-Obit 24

McGinniss, Joe 1942- .... **CLC 32**
See also AITN 2; BEST 89:2; CA 25-28R; CANR 26, 70; CPW; DLB 185; INT CANR-26

McGivern, Maureen Daly
See Daly, Maureen

McGrath, Patrick 1950- .... **CLC 55**
See also CA 136; CANR 65; CN 5, 6, 7; DLB 231; HGG; SUFW 2

McGrath, Thomas (Matthew)
1916-1990 .... **CLC 28, 59**
See also AMWS 10; CA 9-12R; 132; CANR 6, 33, 95; CP 1, 2, 3, 4; DAM POET; MAL 5; MTCW 1; SATA 41; SATA-Obit 66

McGuane, Thomas (Francis III)
1939- .... **CLC 3, 7, 18, 45, 127**
See also AITN 2; BPFB 2; CA 49-52; CANR 5, 24, 49, 94; CN 2, 3, 4, 5, 6, 7; DLB 2, 212; DLBY 1980; EWL 3; INT CANR-24; MAL 5; MTCW 1; MTFW 2005; TCWW 1, 2

McGuckian, Medbh 1950- .... **CLC 48, 174; PC 27**
See also BRWS 5; CA 143; CP 4, 5, 6, 7; CWP; DAM POET; DLB 40

McHale, Tom 1942(?)-1982 .... **CLC 3, 5**
See also AITN 1; CA 77-80; 106; CN 1, 2, 3

McHugh, Heather 1948- .... **PC 61**
See also CA 69-72; CANR 11, 28, 55, 92; CP 4, 5, 6, 7; CWP

McIlvanney, William 1936- .... **CLC 42**
See also CA 25-28R; CANR 61; CMW 4; DLB 14, 207

McIlwraith, Maureen Mollie Hunter
See Hunter, Mollie
See also SATA 2

McInerney, Jay 1955- .... **CLC 34, 112**
See also AAYA 18; BPFB 2; CA 116; 123; CANR 45, 68, 116; CN 5, 6, 7; CPW; DA3; DAM POP; DLB 292; INT CA-123; MAL 5; MTCW 2; MTFW 2005

McIntyre, Vonda N(eel) 1948- .... **CLC 18**
See also CA 81-84; CANR 17, 34, 69; MTCW 1; SFW 4; YAW

McKay, Claude .... **BLC 3; HR 1:3; PC 2; TCLC 7, 41; WLC**
See McKay, Festus Claudius
See also AFAW 1, 2; AMWS 10; DAB; DLB 4, 45, 51, 117; EWL 3; EXPP; GLL 2; LAIT 3; LMFS 2; MAL 5; PAB; PFS 4; RGAL 4; WP

McKay, Festus Claudius 1889-1948
See McKay, Claude
See also BW 1, 3; CA 104; 124; CANR 73; DA; DAC; DAM MST, MULT, NOV, POET; MTCW 1, 2; MTFW 2005; TUS

McKuen, Rod 1933- .... **CLC 1, 3**
See also AITN 1; CA 41-44R; CANR 40; CP 1

McLoughlin, R. B.
See Mencken, H(enry) L(ouis)

McLuhan, (Herbert) Marshall
1911-1980 .... **CLC 37, 83**
See also CA 9-12R; 102; CANR 12, 34, 61; DLB 88; INT CANR-12; MTCW 1, 2; MTFW 2005

McManus, Declan Patrick Aloysius
See Costello, Elvis

McMillan, Terry (L.) 1951- . **BLCS; CLC 50, 61, 112**
See also AAYA 21; AMWS 13; BPFB 2; BW 2, 3; CA 140; CANR 60, 104, 131; CN 7; CPW; DA3; DAM MULT, NOV, POP; MAL 5; MTCW 2; MTFW 2005; RGAL 4; YAW

McMurtry, Larry 1936- .... **CLC 2, 3, 7, 11, 27, 44, 127**
See also AAYA 15; AITN 2; AMWS 5; BEST 89:2; BPFB 2; CA 5-8R; CANR 19, 43, 64, 103; CDALB 1968-1988; CN 2, 3, 4, 5, 6, 7; CPW; CSW; DA3; DAM NOV, POP; DLB 2, 143, 256; DLBY 1980, 1987; EWL 3; MAL 5; MTCW 1, 2; MTFW 2005; RGAL 4; TCWW 1, 2

McNally, T. M. 1961- .... **CLC 82**

McNally, Terrence 1939- ... **CLC 4, 7, 41, 91; DC 27**
See also AAYA 62; AMWS 13; CA 45-48; CAD; CANR 2, 56, 116; CD 5, 6; DA3; DAM DRAM; DFS 16, 19; DLB 7, 249; EWL 3; GLL 1; MTCW 2; MTFW 2005

McNamer, Deirdre 1950- .... **CLC 70**

McNeal, Tom .... **CLC 119**

McNeile, Herman Cyril 1888-1937
See Sapper
See also CA 184; CMW 4; DLB 77

McNickle, (William) D'Arcy
1904-1977 .... **CLC 89; NNAL**
See also CA 9-12R; 85-88; CANR 5, 45; DAM MULT; DLB 175, 212; RGAL 4; SATA-Obit 22; TCWW 1, 2

McPhee, John (Angus) 1931- .... **CLC 36**
See also AAYA 61; AMWS 3; ANW; BEST 90:1; CA 65-68; CANR 20, 46, 64, 69, 121; CPW; DLB 185, 275; MTCW 1, 2; MTFW 2005; TUS

McPherson, James Alan 1943- . **BLCS; CLC 19, 77**
See also BW 1, 3; CA 25-28R; CAAS 17; CANR 24, 74, 140; CN 3, 4, 5, 6; CSW; DLB 38, 244; EWL 3; MTCW 1, 2; MTFW 2005; RGAL 4; RGSF 2

McPherson, William (Alexander)
1933- .... **CLC 34**
See also CA 69-72; CANR 28; INT CANR-28

McTaggart, J. McT. Ellis
See McTaggart, John McTaggart Ellis

McTaggart, John McTaggart Ellis
1866-1925 .... **TCLC 105**
See also CA 120; DLB 262

Mead, George Herbert 1863-1931 . **TCLC 89**
See also CA 212; DLB 270

Mead, Margaret 1901-1978 .... **CLC 37**
See also AITN 1; CA 1-4R; 81-84; CANR 4; DA3; FW; MTCW 1, 2; SATA-Obit 20

Meaker, Marijane (Agnes) 1927-
See Kerr, M. E.
See also CA 107; CANR 37, 63, 145; INT CA-107; JRDA; MAICYA 1, 2; MAICYAS 1; MTCW 1, 2; SATA 20, 61, 99, 160; SATA-Essay 111; YAW

Medoff, Mark (Howard) 1940- .... **CLC 6, 23**
See also AITN 1; CA 53-56; CAD; CANR 5; CD 5, 6; DAM DRAM; DFS 4; DLB 7; INT CANR-5

Medvedev, P. N.
See Bakhtin, Mikhail Mikhailovich

Meged, Aharon
See Megged, Aharon

Meged, Aron
See Megged, Aharon

Megged, Aharon 1920- .... **CLC 9**
See also CA 49-52; CAAS 13; CANR 1, 140; EWL 3

Mehta, Deepa 1950- .... **CLC 208**

Mehta, Gita 1943- .... **CLC 179**
See also CA 225; CN 7; DNFS 2

Mehta, Ved (Parkash) 1934- .... **CLC 37**
See also CA 1-4R, 212; CAAE 212; CANR 2, 23, 69; MTCW 1; MTFW 2005

Melanchthon, Philipp 1497-1560 .... **LC 90**
See also DLB 179

Melanter
See Blackmore, R(ichard) D(oddridge)

Meleager c. 140B.C.-c. 70B.C. ...... **CMLC 53**

Melies, Georges 1861-1938 .... **TCLC 81**

Melikow, Loris
See Hofmannsthal, Hugo von

Melmoth, Sebastian
See Wilde, Oscar (Fingal O'Flahertie Wills)

Melo Neto, Joao Cabral de
See Cabral de Melo Neto, Joao
See also CWW 2; EWL 3

Meltzer, Milton 1915- .... **CLC 26**
See also AAYA 8, 45; BYA 2, 6; CA 13-16R; CANR 38, 92, 107; CLR 13; DLB 61; JRDA; MAICYA 1, 2; SAAS 1; SATA 1, 50, 80, 128; SATA-Essay 124; WYA; YAW

Melville, Herman 1819-1891 ..... **NCLC 3, 12, 29, 45, 49, 91, 93, 123, 157; SSC 1, 17, 46; WLC**
See also AAYA 25; AMW; AMWR 1; CDALB 1640-1865; DA; DA3; DAB; DAC; DAM MST, NOV; DLB 3, 74, 250, 254; EXPN; EXPS; GL 3; LAIT 1, 2; NFS 7, 9; RGAL 4; RGSF 2; SATA 59; SSFS 3; TUS

Members, Mark
See Powell, Anthony (Dymoke)

Membreno, Alejandro .... **CLC 59**

Menand, Louis 1952- .... **CLC 208**
See also CA 200

Menander c. 342B.C.-c. 293B.C. .... **CMLC 9, 51; DC 3**
See also AW 1; CDWLB 1; DAM DRAM; DLB 176; LMFS 1; RGWL 2, 3

Menchu, Rigoberta 1959- .. **CLC 160; HLCS 2**
See also CA 175; CANR 135; DNFS 1; WLIT 1

Mencken, H(enry) L(ouis) 1880-1956 .... **TCLC 13**
See also AMW; CA 105; 125; CDALB 1917-1929; DLB 11, 29, 63, 137, 222; EWL 3; MAL 5; MTCW 1, 2; MTFW 2005; NCFS 4; RGAL 4; TUS

Mendelsohn, Jane 1965- .... **CLC 99**
See also CA 154; CANR 94

Mendoza, Inigo Lopez de
See Santillana, Inigo Lopez de Mendoza, Marques de

Menton, Francisco de
See Chin, Frank (Chew, Jr.)

Mercer, David 1928-1980 .... **CLC 5**
See also CA 9-12R; 102; CANR 23; CBD; DAM DRAM; DLB 13, 310; MTCW 1; RGEL 2

Merchant, Paul
See Ellison, Harlan (Jay)

Meredith, George 1828-1909 .. **PC 60; TCLC 17, 43**
See also CA 117; 153; CANR 80; CDBLB 1832-1890; DAM POET; DLB 18, 35, 57, 159; RGEL 2; TEA

Meredith, William (Morris) 1919- .... **CLC 4, 13, 22, 55; PC 28**
See also CA 9-12R; CAAS 14; CANR 6, 40, 129; CP 1, 2, 3, 4, 5, 6, 7; DAM POET; DLB 5; MAL 5

Merezhkovsky, Dmitrii Sergeevich
See Merezhkovsky, Dmitry Sergeyevich
See also DLB 295

Merezhkovsky, Dmitry Sergeevich
See Merezhkovsky, Dmitry Sergeyevich
See also EWL 3

Merezhkovsky, Dmitry Sergeyevich 1865-1941 .... **TCLC 29**
See Merezhkovsky, Dmitrii Sergeevich; Merezhkovsky, Dmitry Sergeevich
See also CA 169

Merimee, Prosper 1803-1870 ... **NCLC 6, 65; SSC 7, 77**
See also DLB 119, 192; EW 6; EXPS; GFL 1789 to the Present; RGSF 2; RGWL 2, 3; SSFS 8; SUFW

Merkin, Daphne 1954- .... **CLC 44**
See also CA 123

Merleau-Ponty, Maurice 1908-1961 .... **TCLC 156**
See also CA 114; 89-92; DLB 296; GFL 1789 to the Present

Merlin, Arthur
See Blish, James (Benjamin)

Mernissi, Fatima 1940- .... **CLC 171**
See also CA 152; FW

Merrill, James (Ingram) 1926-1995 .. **CLC 2, 3, 6, 8, 13, 18, 34, 91; PC 28; TCLC 173**
See also AMWS 3; CA 13-16R; 147; CANR 10, 49, 63, 108; CP 1, 2, 3, 4; DA3; DAM POET; DLB 5, 165; DLBY 1985; EWL 3; INT CANR-10; MAL 5; MTCW 1, 2; MTFW 2005; PAB; PFS 23; RGAL 4

Merriman, Alex
See Silverberg, Robert

Merriman, Brian 1747-1805 .... **NCLC 70**

Merritt, E. B.
See Waddington, Miriam

Merton, Thomas (James) 1915-1968 . **CLC 1, 3, 11, 34, 83; PC 10**
See also AAYA 61; AMWS 8; CA 5-8R; 25-28R; CANR 22, 53, 111, 131; DA3; DLB 48; DLBY 1981; MAL 5; MTCW 1, 2; MTFW 2005

Merwin, W(illiam) S(tanley) 1927- ... **CLC 1, 2, 3, 5, 8, 13, 18, 45, 88; PC 45**
See also AMWS 3; CA 13-16R; CANR 15, 51, 112, 140; CP 1, 2, 3, 4, 5, 6, 7; DA3; DAM POET; DLB 5, 169; EWL 3; INT CANR-15; MAL 5; MTCW 1, 2; MTFW 2005; PAB; PFS 5, 15; RGAL 4

Metastasio, Pietro 1698-1782 .... **LC 115**
See also RGWL 2, 3

Metcalf, John 1938- .... **CLC 37; SSC 43**
See also CA 113; CN 4, 5, 6, 7; DLB 60; RGSF 2; TWA

Metcalf, Suzanne
See Baum, L(yman) Frank

Mew, Charlotte (Mary) 1870-1928 .. **TCLC 8**
See also CA 105; 189; DLB 19, 135; RGEL 2

Mewshaw, Michael 1943- .... **CLC 9**
See also CA 53-56; CANR 7, 47; DLBY 1980

Meyer, Conrad Ferdinand 1825-1898 .... **NCLC 81; SSC 30**
See also DLB 129; EW; RGWL 2, 3

Meyer, Gustav 1868-1932
See Meyrink, Gustav
See also CA 117; 190

Meyer, June
See Jordan, June (Meyer)

Meyer, Lynn
See Slavitt, David R(ytman)

Meyers, Jeffrey 1939- .... **CLC 39**
See also CA 73-76; 186; CAAE 186; CANR 54, 102; DLB 111

Meynell, Alice (Christina Gertrude Thompson) 1847-1922 .... **TCLC 6**
See also CA 104; 177; DLB 19, 98; RGEL 2

Meyrink, Gustav .... **TCLC 21**
See Meyer, Gustav
See also DLB 81; EWL 3

Michaels, Leonard 1933-2003 ..... **CLC 6, 25; SSC 16**
See also CA 61-64; 216; CANR 21, 62, 119; CN 3, 45, 6, 7; DLB 130; MTCW 1; TCLE 1:2

Michaux, Henri 1899-1984 .... **CLC 8, 19**
See also CA 85-88; 114; DLB 258; EWL 3; GFL 1789 to the Present; RGWL 2, 3

Micheaux, Oscar (Devereaux) 1884-1951 .... **TCLC 76**
See also BW 3; CA 174; DLB 50; TCWW 2

Michelangelo 1475-1564 .... **LC 12**
See also AAYA 43

Michelet, Jules 1798-1874 .... **NCLC 31**
See also EW 5; GFL 1789 to the Present

Michels, Robert 1876-1936 .... **TCLC 88**
See also CA 212

Michener, James A(lbert) 1907(?)-1997 .. **CLC 1, 5, 11, 29, 60, 109**
See also AAYA 27; AITN 1; BEST 90:1; BPFB 2; CA 5-8R; 161; CANR 21, 45, 68; CN 1, 2, 3, 4, 5, 6; CPW; DA3; DAM NOV, POP; DLB 6; MAL 5; MTCW 1, 2; MTFW 2005; RHW; TCWW 1, 2

Mickiewicz, Adam 1798-1855 . **NCLC 3, 101; PC 38**
See also EW 5; RGWL 2, 3

Middleton, (John) Christopher 1926- .... **CLC 13**
See also CA 13-16R; CANR 29, 54, 117; CP 1, 2, 3, 4, 5, 6, 7; DLB 40

Middleton, Richard (Barham) 1882-1911 .... **TCLC 56**
See also CA 187; DLB 156; HGG

Middleton, Stanley 1919- .... **CLC 7, 38**
See also CA 25-28R; CAAS 23; CANR 21, 46, 81; CN 1, 2, 3, 4, 5, 6, 7; DLB 14

Middleton, Thomas 1580-1627 ...... **DC 5; LC 33, 123**
See also BRW 2; DAM DRAM, MST; DFS 18, 22; DLB 58; RGEL 2

Migueis, Jose Rodrigues 1901-1980 . **CLC 10**
See also DLB 287

Mikszath, Kalman 1847-1910 .... **TCLC 31**
See also CA 170

Miles, Jack .... **CLC 100**
See also CA 200

Miles, John Russiano
See Miles, Jack

Miles, Josephine (Louise) 1911-1985 .... **CLC 1, 2, 14, 34, 39**
See also CA 1-4R; 116; CANR 2, 55; CP 1, 2, 3, 4; DAM POET; DLB 48; MAL 5; TCLE 1:2

Militant
See Sandburg, Carl (August)

Mill, Harriet (Hardy) Taylor 1807-1858 .... **NCLC 102**
See also FW

Mill, John Stuart 1806-1873 .... **NCLC 11, 58**
See also CDBLB 1832-1890; DLB 55, 190, 262; FW 1; RGEL 2; TEA

Millar, Kenneth 1915-1983 .... **CLC 14**
See Macdonald, Ross
See also CA 9-12R; 110; CANR 16, 63, 107; CMW 4; CPW; DA3; DAM POP; DLB 2, 226; DLBD 6; DLBY 1983; MTCW 1, 2; MTFW 2005

Millay, E. Vincent
See Millay, Edna St. Vincent

Millay, Edna St. Vincent 1892-1950 ..... **PC 6, 61; TCLC 4, 49, 169; WLCS**
See Boyd, Nancy
See also AMW; CA 104; 130; CDALB 1917-1929; DA; DA3; DAB; DAC; DAM MST, POET; DLB 45, 249; EWL 3; EXPP; FL 1:6; MAL 5; MAWW; MTCW 1, 2; MTFW 2005; PAB; PFS 3, 17; RGAL 4; TUS; WP

Miller, Arthur 1915-2005 ..... **CLC 1, 2, 6, 10, 15, 26, 47, 78, 179; DC 1; WLC**
See also AAYA 15; AITN 1; AMW; AMWC 1; CA 1-4R; 236; CABS 3; CAD; CANR 2, 30, 54, 76, 132; CD 5, 6; CDALB 1941-1968; DA; DA3; DAB; DAC; DAM DRAM, MST; DFS 1, 3, 8; DLB 7, 266; EWL 3; LAIT 1, 4; LATS 1:2; MAL 5; MTCW 1, 2; MTFW 2005; RGAL 4; TUS; WYAS 1

Miller, Henry (Valentine) 1891-1980 .... **CLC 1, 2, 4, 9, 14, 43, 84; WLC**
See also AMW; BPFB 2; CA 9-12R; 97-100; CANR 33, 64; CDALB 1929-1941; CN 1, 2; DA; DA3; DAB; DAC; DAM MST, NOV; DLB 4, 9; DLBY 1980; EWL 3; MAL 5; MTCW 1, 2; MTFW 2005; RGAL 4; TUS

Miller, Hugh 1802-1856 .... **NCLC 143**
See also DLB 190

Miller, Jason 1939(?)-2001 .... **CLC 2**
See also AITN 1; CA 73-76; 197; CAD; CANR 130; DFS 12; DLB 7

Miller, Sue 1943- .... **CLC 44**
See also AMWS 12; BEST 90:3; CA 139; CANR 59, 91, 128; DA3; DAM POP; DLB 143

Miller, Walter M(ichael, Jr.) 1923-1996 .... **CLC 4, 30**
See also BPFB 2; CA 85-88; CANR 108; DLB 8; SCFW 1, 2; SFW 4

Millett, Kate 1934- .... **CLC 67**
See also AITN 1; CA 73-76; CANR 32, 53, 76, 110; DA3; DLB 246; FW; GLL 1; MTCW 1, 2; MTFW 2005

Millhauser, Steven (Lewis) 1943- .... **CLC 21, 54, 109; SSC 57**
See also CA 110; 111; CANR 63, 114, 133; CN 6, 7; DA3; DLB 2; FANT; INT CA-111; MAL 5; MTCW 2; MTFW 2005

Millin, Sarah Gertrude 1889-1968 ... **CLC 49**
See also CA 102; 93-96; DLB 225; EWL 3

Milne, A(lan) A(lexander) 1882-1956 .... **TCLC 6, 88**
See also BRWS 5; CA 104; 133; CLR 1, 26; CMW 4; CWRI 5; DA3; DAB; DAC; DAM MST; DLB 10, 77, 100, 160; FANT; MAICYA 1, 2; MTCW 1, 2; MTFW 2005; RGEL 2; SATA 100; WCH; YABC 1

Milner, Ron(ald) 1938-2004 ..... **BLC 3; CLC 56**
See also AITN 1; BW 1; CA 73-76; 230; CAD; CANR 24, 81; CD 5, 6; DAM MULT; DLB 38; MAL 5; MTCW 1

Milnes, Richard Monckton 1809-1885 .... **NCLC 61**
See also DLB 32, 184

Milosz, Czeslaw 1911-2004 .... **CLC 5, 11, 22, 31, 56, 82; PC 8; WLCS**
See also AAYA 62; CA 81-84; 230; CANR 23, 51, 91, 126; CDWLB 4; CWW 2; DA3; DAM MST, POET; DLB 215; EW 13; EWL 3; MTCW 1, 2; MTFW 2005; PFS 16; RGWL 2, 3

Milton, John 1608-1674 ..... **LC 9, 43, 92; PC 19, 29; WLC**
See also AAYA 65; BRW 2; BRWR 2; CD-BLB 1660-1789; DA; DA3; DAB; DAC; DAM MST, POET; DLB 131, 151, 281; EFS 1; EXPP; LAIT 1; PAB; PFS 3, 17; RGEL 2; TEA; WLIT 3; WP

Min, Anchee 1957- .... **CLC 86**
See also CA 146; CANR 94, 137; MTFW 2005

Minehaha, Cornelius
See Wedekind, (Benjamin) Frank(lin)

Miner, Valerie 1947- .... **CLC 40**
See also CA 97-100; CANR 59; FW; GLL 2

Minimo, Duca
See D'Annunzio, Gabriele

Minot, Susan (Anderson) 1956- ...... **CLC 44, 159**
See also AMWS 6; CA 134; CANR 118; CN 6, 7

Minus, Ed 1938- .... **CLC 39**
See also CA 185

Mirabai 1498(?)-1550(?) .... **PC 48**

Miranda, Javier
See Bioy Casares, Adolfo
See also CWW 2

Mirbeau, Octave 1848-1917 .... **TCLC 55**
See also CA 216; DLB 123, 192; GFL 1789 to the Present

Mirikitani, Janice 1942- .... **AAL**
See also CA 211; DLB 312; RGAL 4

Mirk, John (?)-c. 1414 .... **LC 105**
See also DLB 146

Miro (Ferrer), Gabriel (Francisco Victor) 1879-1930 .... **TCLC 5**
See also CA 104; 185; DLB 322; EWL 3

Misharin, Alexandr .... **CLC 59**

Mishima, Yukio ... **CLC 2, 4, 6, 9, 27; DC 1; SSC 4; TCLC 161**
See Hiraoka, Kimitake
See also AAYA 50; BPFB 2; GLL 1; MJW; RGSF 2; RGWL 2, 3; SSFS 5, 12

Mistral, Frederic 1830-1914 .... **TCLC 51**
See also CA 122; 213; GFL 1789 to the Present

Mistral, Gabriela
See Godoy Alcayaga, Lucila
See also DLB 283; DNFS 1; EWL 3; LAW; RGWL 2, 3; WP

Mistry, Rohinton 1952- ... **CLC 71, 196; SSC 73**
See also BRWS 10; CA 141; CANR 86, 114; CCA 1; CN 6, 7; DAC; SSFS 6

Mitchell, Clyde
See Ellison, Harlan (Jay)

Mitchell, Emerson Blackhorse Barney 1945- .... **NNAL**
See also CA 45-48

Mitchell, James Leslie 1901-1935
See Gibbon, Lewis Grassic
See also CA 104; 188; DLB 15

Mitchell, Joni 1943- .... **CLC 12**
See also CA 112; CCA 1

Mitchell, Joseph (Quincy) 1908-1996 .... **CLC 98**
See also CA 77-80; 152; CANR 69; CN 1, 2, 3, 4, 5, 6; CSW; DLB 185; DLBY 1996

Mitchell, Margaret (Munnerlyn) 1900-1949 .... **TCLC 11, 170**
See also AAYA 23; BPFB 2; BYA 1; CA 109; 125; CANR 55, 94; CDALBS; DA3; DAM NOV, POP; DLB 9; LAIT 2; MAL 5; MTCW 1, 2; MTFW 2005; NFS 9; RGAL 4; RHW; TUS; WYAS 1; YAW

Mitchell, Peggy
See Mitchell, Margaret (Munnerlyn)

Mitchell, S(ilas) Weir 1829-1914 .... **TCLC 36**
See also CA 165; DLB 202; RGAL 4

Mitchell, W(illiam) O(rmond) 1914-1998 .... **CLC 25**
See also CA 77-80; 165; CANR 15, 43; CN 1, 2, 3, 4, 5, 6; DAC; DAM MST; DLB 88; TCLE 1:2

Mitchell, William (Lendrum) 1879-1936 .... **TCLC 81**
See also CA 213

Mitford, Mary Russell 1787-1855 ... **NCLC 4**
See also DLB 110, 116; RGEL 2

Mitford, Nancy 1904-1973 .... **CLC 44**
See also BRWS 10; CA 9-12R; CN 1; DLB 191; RGEL 2

Miyamoto, (Chujo) Yuriko 1899-1951 .... **TCLC 37**
See Miyamoto Yuriko
See also CA 170, 174

Miyamoto Yuriko
See Miyamoto, (Chujo) Yuriko
See also DLB 180

Miyazawa, Kenji 1896-1933 .... **TCLC 76**
See Miyazawa Kenji
See also CA 157; RGWL 3

Miyazawa Kenji
See Miyazawa, Kenji
See also EWL 3

Mizoguchi, Kenji 1898-1956 .... **TCLC 72**
See also CA 167

Mo, Timothy (Peter) 1950- .... **CLC 46, 134**
See also CA 117; CANR 128; CN 5, 6, 7; DLB 194; MTCW 1; WLIT 4; WWE 1

Modarressi, Taghi (M.) 1931-1997 ... **CLC 44**
See also CA 121; 134; INT CA-134

Modiano, Patrick (Jean) 1945- .... **CLC 18, 218**
See also CA 85-88; CANR 17, 40, 115; CWW 2; DLB 83, 299; EWL 3

Mofolo, Thomas (Mokopu) 1875(?)-1948 .... **BLC 3; TCLC 22**
See also AFW; CA 121; 153; CANR 83; DAM MULT; DLB 225; EWL 3; MTCW 2; MTFW 2005; WLIT 2

Mohr, Nicholasa 1938- .... **CLC 12; HLC 2**
See also AAYA 8, 46; CA 49-52; CANR 1, 32, 64; CLR 22; DAM MULT; DLB 145; HW 1, 2; JRDA; LAIT 5; LLW; MAICYA 2; MAICYAS 1; RGAL 4; SAAS 8; SATA 8, 97; SATA-Essay 113; WYA; YAW

Moi, Toril 1953- .... **CLC 172**
See also CA 154; CANR 102; FW

Mojtabai, A(nn) G(race) 1938- ...... **CLC 5, 9, 15, 29**
See also CA 85-88; CANR 88

Moliere 1622-1673 ..... **DC 13; LC 10, 28, 64, 125; WLC**
See also DA; DA3; DAB; DAC; DAM DRAM, MST; DFS 13, 18, 20; DLB 268; EW 3; GFL Beginnings to 1789; LATS 1:1; RGWL 2, 3; TWA

Molin, Charles
See Mayne, William (James Carter)

Molnar, Ferenc 1878-1952 .... **TCLC 20**
See also CA 109; 153; CANR 83; CDWLB 4; DAM DRAM; DLB 215; EWL 3; RGWL 2, 3

Momaday, N(avarre) Scott 1934- ...... **CLC 2, 19, 85, 95, 160; NNAL; PC 25; WLCS**
See also AAYA 11, 64; AMWS 4; ANW; BPFB 2; BYA 12; CA 25-28R; CANR 14, 34, 68, 134; CDALBS; CN 2, 3, 4, 5, 6, 7; CPW; DA; DA3; DAB; DAC; DAM MST, MULT, NOV, POP; DLB 143, 175, 256; EWL 3; EXPP; INT CANR-14; LAIT 4; LATS 1:2; MAL 5; MTCW 1, 2; MTFW 2005; NFS 10; PFS 2, 11; RGAL 4; SATA 48; SATA-Brief 30; TCWW 1, 2; WP; YAW

Monette, Paul 1945-1995 .... **CLC 82**
See also AMWS 10; CA 139; 147; CN 6; GLL 1

Monroe, Harriet 1860-1936 .... **TCLC 12**
See also CA 109; 204; DLB 54, 91

Monroe, Lyle
See Heinlein, Robert A(nson)

Montagu, Elizabeth 1720-1800 .... **NCLC 7, 117**
See also FW

Montagu, Mary (Pierrepont) Wortley 1689-1762 .... **LC 9, 57; PC 16**
See also DLB 95, 101; FL 1:1; RGEL 2

Montagu, W. H.
See Coleridge, Samuel Taylor

Montague, John (Patrick) 1929- ..... **CLC 13, 46**
See also CA 9-12R; CANR 9, 69, 121; CP 1, 2, 3, 4, 5, 6, 7; DLB 40; EWL 3; MTCW 1; PFS 12; RGEL 2; TCLE 1:2

Montaigne, Michel (Eyquem) de 1533-1592 .... **LC 8, 105; WLC**
See also DA; DAB; DAC; DAM MST; EW 2; GFL Beginnings to 1789; LMFS 1; RGWL 2, 3; TWA

Montale, Eugenio 1896-1981 ... **CLC 7, 9, 18; PC 13**
See also CA 17-20R; 104; CANR 30; DLB 114; EW 11; EWL 3; MTCW 1; PFS 22; RGWL 2, 3; TWA; WLIT 7

Montesquieu, Charles-Louis de Secondat 1689-1755 .... **LC 7, 69**
See also DLB 314; EW 3; GFL Beginnings to 1789; TWA

Montessori, Maria 1870-1952 .... **TCLC 103**
See also CA 115; 147

Montgomery, (Robert) Bruce 1921(?)-1978
See Crispin, Edmund
See also CA 179; 104; CMW 4

Montgomery, L(ucy) M(aud) 1874-1942 .... **TCLC 51, 140**
See also AAYA 12; BYA 1; CA 108; 137; CLR 8, 91; DA3; DAC; DAM MST; DLB 92; DLBD 14; JRDA; MAICYA 1, 2; MTCW 2; MTFW 2005; RGEL 2; SATA 100; TWA; WCH; WYA; YABC 1

Montgomery, Marion H., Jr. 1925- .... **CLC 7**
See also AITN 1; CA 1-4R; CANR 3, 48; CSW; DLB 6

Montgomery, Max
See Davenport, Guy (Mattison, Jr.)

Montherlant, Henry (Milon) de
1896-1972 .... **CLC 8, 19**
See also CA 85-88; 37-40R; DAM DRAM; DLB 72, 321; EW 11; EWL 3; GFL 1789 to the Present; MTCW 1

Monty Python
See Chapman, Graham; Cleese, John (Marwood); Gilliam, Terry (Vance); Idle, Eric; Jones, Terence Graham Parry; Palin, Michael (Edward)
See also AAYA 7

Moodie, Susanna (Strickland)
1803-1885 .... **NCLC 14, 113**
See also DLB 99

Moody, Hiram (F. III) 1961-
See Moody, Rick
See also CA 138; CANR 64, 112; MTFW 2005

Moody, Minerva
See Alcott, Louisa May

Moody, Rick .... **CLC 147**
See Moody, Hiram (F. III)

Moody, William Vaughan
1869-1910 .... **TCLC 105**
See also CA 110; 178; DLB 7, 54; MAL 5; RGAL 4

Mooney, Edward 1951-
See Mooney, Ted
See also CA 130

Mooney, Ted .... **CLC 25**
See Mooney, Edward

Moorcock, Michael (John) 1939- ...... **CLC 5, 27, 58**
See Bradbury, Edward P.
See also AAYA 26; CA 45-48; CAAS 5; CANR 2, 17, 38, 64, 122; CN 5, 6, 7; DLB 14, 231, 261, 319; FANT; MTCW 1, 2; MTFW 2005; SATA 93; SCFW 1, 2; SFW 4; SUFW 1, 2

Moore, Brian 1921-1999 ... **CLC 1, 3, 5, 7, 8, 19, 32, 90**
See Bryan, Michael
See also BRWS 9; CA 1-4R; 174; CANR 1, 25, 42, 63; CCA 1; CN 1, 2, 3, 4, 5, 6; DAB; DAC; DAM MST; DLB 251; EWL 3; FANT; MTCW 1, 2; MTFW 2005; RGEL 2

Moore, Edward
See Muir, Edwin
See also RGEL 2

Moore, G. E. 1873-1958 .... **TCLC 89**
See also DLB 262

Moore, George Augustus
1852-1933 .... **SSC 19; TCLC 7**
See also BRW 6; CA 104; 177; DLB 10, 18, 57, 135; EWL 3; RGEL 2; RGSF 2

Moore, Lorrie .... **CLC 39, 45, 68**
See Moore, Marie Lorena
See also AMWS 10; CN 5, 6, 7; DLB 234; SSFS 19

Moore, Marianne (Craig)
1887-1972 .... **CLC 1, 2, 4, 8, 10, 13, 19, 47; PC 4, 49; WLCS**
See also AMW; CA 1-4R; 33-36R; CANR 3, 61; CDALB 1929-1941; CP 1; DA; DA3; DAB; DAC; DAM MST, POET; DLB 45; DLBD 7; EWL 3; EXPP; FL 1:6; MAL 5; MAWW; MTCW 1, 2; MTFW 2005; PAB; PFS 14, 17; RGAL 4; SATA 20; TUS; WP

Moore, Marie Lorena 1957- .... **CLC 165**
See Moore, Lorrie
See also CA 116; CANR 39, 83, 139; DLB 234; MTFW 2005

Moore, Michael 1954- .... **CLC 218**
See also AAYA 53; CA 166

Moore, Thomas 1779-1852 ...... **NCLC 6, 110**
See also DLB 96, 144; RGEL 2

Moorhouse, Frank 1938- .... **SSC 40**
See also CA 118; CANR 92; CN 3, 4, 5, 6, 7; DLB 289; RGSF 2

Mora, Pat(ricia) 1942- .... **HLC 2**
See also AMWS 13; CA 129; CANR 57, 81, 112; CLR 58; DAM MULT; DLB 209; HW 1, 2; LLW; MAICYA 2; MTFW 2005; SATA 92, 134

Moraga, Cherrie 1952- ...... **CLC 126; DC 22**
See also CA 131; CANR 66; DAM MULT; DLB 82, 249; FW; GLL 1; HW 1, 2; LLW

Morand, Paul 1888-1976 .... **CLC 41; SSC 22**
See also CA 184; 69-72; DLB 65; EWL 3

Morante, Elsa 1918-1985 .... **CLC 8, 47**
See also CA 85-88; 117; CANR 35; DLB 177; EWL 3; MTCW 1, 2; MTFW 2005; RGWL 2, 3; WLIT 7

Moravia, Alberto .... **CLC 2, 7, 11, 27, 46; SSC 26**
See Pincherle, Alberto
See also DLB 177; EW 12; EWL 3; MTCW 2; RGSF 2; RGWL 2, 3; WLIT 7

More, Hannah 1745-1833 ...... **NCLC 27, 141**
See also DLB 107, 109, 116, 158; RGEL 2

More, Henry 1614-1687 .... **LC 9**
See also DLB 126, 252

More, Sir Thomas 1478(?)-1535 .... **LC 10, 32**
See also BRWC 1; BRWS 7; DLB 136, 281; LMFS 1; RGEL 2; TEA

Moreas, Jean .... **TCLC 18**
See Papadiamantopoulos, Johannes
See also GFL 1789 to the Present

Moreton, Andrew Esq.
See Defoe, Daniel

Morgan, Berry 1919-2002 .... **CLC 6**
See also CA 49-52; 208; DLB 6

Morgan, Claire
See Highsmith, (Mary) Patricia
See also GLL 1

Morgan, Edwin (George) 1920- .... **CLC 31**
See also BRWS 9; CA 5-8R; CANR 3, 43, 90; CP 1, 2, 3, 4, 5, 6, 7; DLB 27

Morgan, (George) Frederick
1922-2004 .... **CLC 23**
See also CA 17-20R; 224; CANR 21, 144; CP 2, 3, 4, 5, 6, 7

Morgan, Harriet
See Mencken, H(enry) L(ouis)

Morgan, Jane
See Cooper, James Fenimore

Morgan, Janet 1945- .... **CLC 39**
See also CA 65-68

Morgan, Lady 1776(?)-1859 .... **NCLC 29**
See also DLB 116, 158; RGEL 2

Morgan, Robin (Evonne) 1941- .... **CLC 2**
See also CA 69-72; CANR 29, 68; FW; GLL 2; MTCW 1; SATA 80

Morgan, Scott
See Kuttner, Henry

Morgan, Seth 1949(?)-1990 .... **CLC 65**
See also CA 185; 132

Morgenstern, Christian (Otto Josef Wolfgang) 1871-1914 .... **TCLC 8**
See also CA 105; 191; EWL 3

Morgenstern, S.
See Goldman, William (W.)

Mori, Rintaro
See Mori Ogai
See also CA 110

Mori, Toshio 1910-1980 .... **SSC 83**
See also CA 116; DLB 312; RGSF 2

Moricz, Zsigmond 1879-1942 .... **TCLC 33**
See also CA 165; DLB 215; EWL 3

Morike, Eduard (Friedrich)
1804-1875 .... **NCLC 10**
See also DLB 133; RGWL 2, 3

Mori Ogai 1862-1922 .... **TCLC 14**
See Ogai
See also CA 164; DLB 180; EWL 3; RGWL 3; TWA

Moritz, Karl Philipp 1756-1793 .... **LC 2**
See also DLB 94

Morland, Peter Henry
See Faust, Frederick (Schiller)

Morley, Christopher (Darlington)
1890-1957 .... **TCLC 87**
See also CA 112; 213; DLB 9; MAL 5; RGAL 4

Morren, Theophil
See Hofmannsthal, Hugo von

Morris, Bill 1952- .... **CLC 76**
See also CA 225

Morris, Julian
See West, Morris L(anglo)

Morris, Steveland Judkins 1950(?)-
See Wonder, Stevie
See also CA 111

Morris, William 1834-1896 . **NCLC 4; PC 55**
See also BRW 5; CDBLB 1832-1890; DLB 18, 35, 57, 156, 178, 184; FANT; RGEL 2; SFW 4; SUFW

Morris, Wright (Marion) 1910-1998 . **CLC 1, 3, 7, 18, 37; TCLC 107**
See also AMW; CA 9-12R; 167; CANR 21, 81; CN 1, 2, 3, 4, 5, 6; DLB 2, 206, 218; DLBY 1981; EWL 3; MAL 5; MTCW 1, 2; MTFW 2005; RGAL 4; TCWW 1, 2

Morrison, Arthur 1863-1945 .... **SSC 40; TCLC 72**
See also CA 120; 157; CMW 4; DLB 70, 135, 197; RGEL 2

Morrison, Chloe Anthony Wofford
See Morrison, Toni

Morrison, James Douglas 1943-1971
See Morrison, Jim
See also CA 73-76; CANR 40

Morrison, Jim .... **CLC 17**
See Morrison, James Douglas

Morrison, Toni 1931- ...... **BLC 3; CLC 4, 10, 22, 55, 81, 87, 173, 194**
See also AAYA 1, 22, 61; AFAW 1, 2; AMWC 1; AMWS 3; BPFB 2; BW 2, 3; CA 29-32R; CANR 27, 42, 67, 113, 124; CDALB 1968-1988; CLR 99; CN 3, 4, 5, 6, 7; CPW; DA; DA3; DAB; DAC; DAM MST, MULT, NOV, POP; DLB 6, 33, 143; DLBY 1981; EWL 3; EXPN; FL 1:6; FW; GL 3; LAIT 2, 4; LATS 1:2; LMFS 2; MAL 5; MAWW; MTCW 1, 2; MTFW 2005; NFS 1, 6, 8, 14; RGAL 4; RHW; SATA 57, 144; SSFS 5; TCLE 1:2; TUS; YAW

Morrison, Van 1945- .... **CLC 21**
See also CA 116; 168

Morrissy, Mary 1957- .... **CLC 99**
See also CA 205; DLB 267

Mortimer, John (Clifford) 1923- ...... **CLC 28, 43**
See also CA 13-16R; CANR 21, 69, 109; CBD; CD 5, 6; CDBLB 1960 to Present; CMW 4; CN 5, 6, 7; CPW; DA3; DAM DRAM, POP; DLB 13, 245, 271; INT CANR-21; MSW; MTCW 1, 2; MTFW 2005; RGEL 2

Mortimer, Penelope (Ruth)
1918-1999 .... **CLC 5**
See also CA 57-60; 187; CANR 45, 88; CN 1, 2, 3, 4, 5, 6

Mortimer, Sir John
See Mortimer, John (Clifford)

Morton, Anthony
See Creasey, John

Morton, Thomas 1579(?)-1647(?) .... **LC 72**
See also DLB 24; RGEL 2

Mosca, Gaetano 1858-1941 .... **TCLC 75**

Moses, Daniel David 1952- .... **NNAL**
See also CA 186

Mosher, Howard Frank 1943- .... **CLC 62**
See also CA 139; CANR 65, 115

Mosley, Nicholas 1923- .... **CLC 43, 70**
See also CA 69-72; CANR 41, 60, 108; CN 1, 2, 3, 4, 5, 6, 7; DLB 14, 207

Mosley, Walter 1952- .... **BLCS; CLC 97, 184**
See also AAYA 57; AMWS 13; BPFB 2; BW 2; CA 142; CANR 57, 92, 136; CMW 4; CN 7; CPW; DA3; DAM MULT, POP; DLB 306; MSW; MTCW 2; MTFW 2005

Moss, Howard 1922-1987 . **CLC 7, 14, 45, 50**
See also CA 1-4R; 123; CANR 1, 44; CP 1, 2, 3, 4; DAM POET; DLB 5

Mossgiel, Rab
See Burns, Robert

Motion, Andrew (Peter) 1952- .... **CLC 47**
See also BRWS 7; CA 146; CANR 90, 142; CP 4, 5, 6, 7; DLB 40; MTFW 2005

Motley, Willard (Francis)
1909-1965 .... **CLC 18**
See also BW 1; CA 117; 106; CANR 88; DLB 76, 143

Motoori, Norinaga 1730-1801 .... **NCLC 45**

Mott, Michael (Charles Alston)
1930- .... **CLC 15, 34**
See also CA 5-8R; CAAS 7; CANR 7, 29

Mountain Wolf Woman 1884-1960 . **CLC 92; NNAL**
See also CA 144; CANR 90

Moure, Erin 1955- .... **CLC 88**
See also CA 113; CP 7; CWP; DLB 60

Mourning Dove 1885(?)-1936 .... **NNAL**
See also CA 144; CANR 90; DAM MULT; DLB 175, 221

Mowat, Farley (McGill) 1921- .... **CLC 26**
See also AAYA 1, 50; BYA 2; CA 1-4R; CANR 4, 24, 42, 68, 108; CLR 20; CPW; DAC; DAM MST; DLB 68; INT CANR-24; JRDA; MAICYA 1, 2; MTCW 1, 2; MTFW 2005; SATA 3, 55; YAW

Mowatt, Anna Cora 1819-1870 ...... **NCLC 74**
See also RGAL 4

Moyers, Bill 1934- .... **CLC 74**
See also AITN 2; CA 61-64; CANR 31, 52

Mphahlele, Es'kia
See Mphahlele, Ezekiel
See also AFW; CDWLB 3; CN 4, 5, 6; DLB 125, 225; RGSF 2; SSFS 11

Mphahlele, Ezekiel 1919- ... **BLC 3; CLC 25, 133**
See Mphahlele, Es'kia
See also BW 2, 3; CA 81-84; CANR 26, 76; CN 1, 2, 3; DA3; DAM MULT; EWL 3; MTCW 2; MTFW 2005; SATA 119

Mqhayi, S(amuel) E(dward) K(rune Loliwe)
1875-1945 .... **BLC 3; TCLC 25**
See also CA 153; CANR 87; DAM MULT

Mrozek, Slawomir 1930- .... **CLC 3, 13**
See also CA 13-16R; CAAS 10; CANR 29; CDWLB 4; CWW 2; DLB 232; EWL 3; MTCW 1

Mrs. Belloc-Lowndes
See Lowndes, Marie Adelaide (Belloc)

Mrs. Fairstar
See Horne, Richard Henry Hengist

M'Taggart, John M'Taggart Ellis
See McTaggart, John McTaggart Ellis

Mtwa, Percy (?)- .... **CLC 47**
See also CD 6

Mueller, Lisel 1924- .... **CLC 13, 51; PC 33**
See also CA 93-96; CP 7; DLB 105; PFS 9, 13

Muggeridge, Malcolm (Thomas)
1903-1990 .... **TCLC 120**
See also AITN 1; CA 101; CANR 33, 63; MTCW 1, 2

Muhammad 570-632 .... **WLCS**
See also DA; DAB; DAC; DAM MST; DLB 311

Muir, Edwin 1887-1959 . **PC 49; TCLC 2, 87**
See also BRWS 6; CA 104; 193; DLB 20, 100, 191; EWL 3; RGEL 2

Muir, John 1838-1914 .... **TCLC 28**
See also AMWS 9; ANW; CA 165; DLB 186, 275

Mujica Lainez, Manuel 1910-1984 ... **CLC 31**
See Lainez, Manuel Mujica
See also CA 81-84; 112; CANR 32; EWL 3; HW 1

Mukherjee, Bharati 1940- ..... **AAL; CLC 53, 115; SSC 38**
See also AAYA 46; BEST 89:2; CA 107, 232; CAAE 232; CANR 45, 72, 128; CN 5, 6, 7; DAM NOV; DLB 60, 218; DNFS 1, 2; EWL 3; FW; MAL 5; MTCW 1, 2; MTFW 2005; RGAL 4; RGSF 2; SSFS 7; TUS; WWE 1

Muldoon, Paul 1951- .... **CLC 32, 72, 166**
See also BRWS 4; CA 113; 129; CANR 52, 91; CP 2, 3, 4, 5, 6, 7; DAM POET; DLB 40; INT CA-129; PFS 7, 22; TCLE 1:2

Mulisch, Harry (Kurt Victor)
1927- .... **CLC 42**
See also CA 9-12R; CANR 6, 26, 56, 110; CWW 2; DLB 299; EWL 3

Mull, Martin 1943- .... **CLC 17**
See also CA 105

Muller, Wilhelm .... **NCLC 73**

Mulock, Dinah Maria
See Craik, Dinah Maria (Mulock)
See also RGEL 2

Multatuli 1820-1887 .... **NCLC 165**
See also RGWL 2, 3

Munday, Anthony 1560-1633 .... **LC 87**
See also DLB 62, 172; RGEL 2

Munford, Robert 1737(?)-1783 .... **LC 5**
See also DLB 31

Mungo, Raymond 1946- .... **CLC 72**
See also CA 49-52; CANR 2

Munro, Alice (Anne) 1931- .... **CLC 6, 10, 19, 50, 95; SSC 3; WLCS**
See also AITN 2; BPFB 2; CA 33-36R; CANR 33, 53, 75, 114; CCA 1; CN 1, 2, 3, 4, 5, 6, 7; DA3; DAC; DAM MST, NOV; DLB 53; EWL 3; MTCW 1, 2; MTFW 2005; RGEL 2; RGSF 2; SATA 29; SSFS 5, 13, 19; TCLE 1:2; WWE 1

Munro, H(ector) H(ugh) 1870-1916 .... **WLC**
See Saki
See also AAYA 56; CA 104; 130; CANR 104; CDBLB 1890-1914; DA; DA3; DAB; DAC; DAM MST, NOV; DLB 34, 162; EXPS; MTCW 1, 2; MTFW 2005; RGEL 2; SSFS 15

Murakami, Haruki 1949- .... **CLC 150**
See Murakami Haruki
See also CA 165; CANR 102, 146; MJW; RGWL 3; SFW 4

Murakami Haruki
See Murakami, Haruki
See also CWW 2; DLB 182; EWL 3

Murasaki, Lady
See Murasaki Shikibu

Murasaki Shikibu 978(?)-1026(?) .. **CMLC 1, 79**
See also EFS 2; LATS 1:1; RGWL 2, 3

Murdoch, (Jean) Iris 1919-1999 ... **CLC 1, 2, 3, 4, 6, 8, 11, 15, 22, 31, 51; TCLC 171**
See also BRWS 1; CA 13-16R; 179; CANR 8, 43, 68, 103, 142; CBD; CDBLB 1960 to Present; CN 1, 2, 3, 4, 5, 6; CWD; DA3; DAB; DAC; DAM MST, NOV; DLB 14, 194, 233; EWL 3; INT CANR-8; MTCW 1, 2; MTFW 2005; NFS 18; RGEL 2; TCLE 1:2; TEA; WLIT 4

Murfree, Mary Noailles 1850-1922 .. **SSC 22; TCLC 135**
See also CA 122; 176; DLB 12, 74; RGAL 4

Murnau, Friedrich Wilhelm
See Plumpe, Friedrich Wilhelm

Murphy, Richard 1927- .... **CLC 41**
See also BRWS 5; CA 29-32R; CP 1, 2, 3, 4, 5, 6, 7; DLB 40; EWL 3

Murphy, Sylvia 1937- .... **CLC 34**
See also CA 121

Murphy, Thomas (Bernard) 1935- ... **CLC 51**
See Murphy, Tom
See also CA 101

Murphy, Tom
See Murphy, Thomas (Bernard)
See also DLB 310

Murray, Albert L. 1916- .... **CLC 73**
See also BW 2; CA 49-52; CANR 26, 52, 78; CN 7; CSW; DLB 38; MTFW 2005

Murray, James Augustus Henry
1837-1915 .... **TCLC 117**

Murray, Judith Sargent
1751-1820 .... **NCLC 63**
See also DLB 37, 200

Murray, Les(lie Allan) 1938- .... **CLC 40**
See also BRWS 7; CA 21-24R; CANR 11, 27, 56, 103; CP 1, 2, 3, 4, 5, 6, 7; DAM POET; DLB 289; DLBY 2001; EWL 3; RGEL 2

Murry, J. Middleton
See Murry, John Middleton

Murry, John Middleton
1889-1957 .... **TCLC 16**
See also CA 118; 217; DLB 149

Musgrave, Susan 1951- .... **CLC 13, 54**
See also CA 69-72; CANR 45, 84; CCA 1; CP 2, 3, 4, 5, 6, 7; CWP

Musil, Robert (Edler von)
1880-1942 .... **SSC 18; TCLC 12, 68**
See also CA 109; CANR 55, 84; CDWLB 2; DLB 81, 124; EW 9; EWL 3; MTCW 2; RGSF 2; RGWL 2, 3

Muske, Carol .... **CLC 90**
See Muske-Dukes, Carol (Anne)

Muske-Dukes, Carol (Anne) 1945-
See Muske, Carol
See also CA 65-68, 203; CAAE 203; CANR 32, 70; CWP

Musset, (Louis Charles) Alfred de
1810-1857 .... **DC 27; NCLC 7, 150**
See also DLB 192, 217; EW 6; GFL 1789 to the Present; RGWL 2, 3; TWA

Mussolini, Benito (Amilcare Andrea)
1883-1945 .... **TCLC 96**
See also CA 116

Mutanabbi, Al-
See al-Mutanabbi, Ahmad ibn al-Husayn Abu al-Tayyib al-Jufi al-Kindi
See also WLIT 6

My Brother's Brother
See Chekhov, Anton (Pavlovich)

Myers, L(eopold) H(amilton)
1881-1944 .... **TCLC 59**
See also CA 157; DLB 15; EWL 3; RGEL 2

Myers, Walter Dean 1937- .. **BLC 3; CLC 35**
See also AAYA 4, 23; BW 2; BYA 6, 8, 11; CA 33-36R; CANR 20, 42, 67, 108; CLR 4, 16, 35; DAM MULT, NOV; DLB 33;

INT CANR-20; JRDA; LAIT 5; MAICYA 1, 2; MAICYAS 1; MTCW 2; MTFW 2005; SAAS 2; SATA 41, 71, 109, 157; SATA-Brief 27; WYA; YAW

Myers, Walter M.
See Myers, Walter Dean

Myles, Symon
See Follett, Ken(neth Martin)

Nabokov, Vladimir (Vladimirovich) 1899-1977 .... **CLC 1, 2, 3, 6, 8, 11, 15, 23, 44, 46, 64; SSC 11, 86; TCLC 108; WLC**
See also AAYA 45; AMW; AMWC 1; AMWR 1; BPFB 2; CA 5-8R; 69-72; CANR 20, 102; CDALB 1941-1968; CN 1, 2; CP 2; DA; DA3; DAB; DAC; DAM MST, NOV; DLB 2, 244, 278, 317; DLBD 3; DLBY 1980, 1991; EWL 3; EXPS; LATS 1:2; MAL 5; MTCW 1, 2; MTFW 2005; NCFS 4; NFS 9; RGAL 4; RGSF 2; SSFS 6, 15; TUS

Naevius c. 265B.C.-201B.C. .... **CMLC 37**
See also DLB 211

Nagai, Kafu .... **TCLC 51**
See Nagai, Sokichi
See also DLB 180

Nagai, Sokichi 1879-1959
See Nagai, Kafu
See also CA 117

Nagy, Laszlo 1925-1978 .... **CLC 7**
See also CA 129; 112

Naidu, Sarojini 1879-1949 .... **TCLC 80**
See also EWL 3; RGEL 2

Naipaul, Shiva(dhar Srinivasa) 1945-1985 .... **CLC 32, 39; TCLC 153**
See also CA 110; 112; 116; CANR 33; CN 2, 3; DA3; DAM NOV; DLB 157; DLBY 1985; EWL 3; MTCW 1, 2; MTFW 2005

Naipaul, V(idiadhar) S(urajprasad) 1932- .... **CLC 4, 7, 9, 13, 18, 37, 105, 199; SSC 38**
See also BPFB 2; BRWS 1; CA 1-4R; CANR 1, 33, 51, 91, 126; CDBLB 1960 to Present; CDWLB 3; CN 1, 2, 3, 4, 5, 6, 7; DA3; DAB; DAC; DAM MST, NOV; DLB 125, 204, 207; DLBY 1985, 2001; EWL 3; LATS 1:2; MTCW 1, 2; MTFW 2005; RGEL 2; RGSF 2; TWA; WLIT 4; WWE 1

Nakos, Lilika 1903(?)-1989 .... **CLC 29**

Napoleon
See Yamamoto, Hisaye

Narayan, R(asipuram) K(rishnaswami) 1906-2001 .... **CLC 7, 28, 47, 121, 211; SSC 25**
See also BPFB 2; CA 81-84; 196; CANR 33, 61, 112; CN 1, 2, 3, 4, 5, 6, 7; DA3; DAM NOV; DNFS 1; EWL 3; MTCW 1, 2; MTFW 2005; RGEL 2; RGSF 2; SATA 62; SSFS 5; WWE 1

Nash, (Frediric) Ogden 1902-1971 . **CLC 23; PC 21; TCLC 109**
See also CA 13-14; 29-32R; CANR 34, 61; CAP 1; CP 1; DAM POET; DLB 11; MAICYA 1, 2; MAL 5; MTCW 1, 2; RGAL 4; SATA 2, 46; WP

Nashe, Thomas 1567-1601(?) .... **LC 41, 89**
See also DLB 167; RGEL 2

Nathan, Daniel
See Dannay, Frederic

Nathan, George Jean 1882-1958 .... **TCLC 18**
See Hatteras, Owen
See also CA 114; 169; DLB 137; MAL 5

Natsume, Kinnosuke
See Natsume, Soseki

Natsume, Soseki 1867-1916 .... **TCLC 2, 10**
See Natsume Soseki; Soseki
See also CA 104; 195; RGWL 2, 3; TWA

Natsume Soseki
See Natsume, Soseki
See also DLB 180; EWL 3

Natti, (Mary) Lee 1919-
See Kingman, Lee
See also CA 5-8R; CANR 2

Navarre, Marguerite de
See de Navarre, Marguerite

Naylor, Gloria 1950- ..... **BLC 3; CLC 28, 52, 156; WLCS**
See also AAYA 6, 39; AFAW 1, 2; AMWS 8; BW 2, 3; CA 107; CANR 27, 51, 74, 130; CN 4, 5, 6, 7; CPW; DA; DA3; DAC; DAM MST, MULT, NOV, POP; DLB 173; EWL 3; FW; MAL 5; MTCW 1, 2; MTFW 2005; NFS 4, 7; RGAL 4; TCLE 1:2; TUS

Neal, John 1793-1876 .... **NCLC 161**
See also DLB 1, 59, 243; FW; RGAL 4

Neff, Debra .... **CLC 59**

Neihardt, John Gneisenau 1881-1973 .... **CLC 32**
See also CA 13-14; CANR 65; CAP 1; DLB 9, 54, 256; LAIT 2; TCWW 1, 2

Nekrasov, Nikolai Alekseevich 1821-1878 .... **NCLC 11**
See also DLB 277

Nelligan, Emile 1879-1941 .... **TCLC 14**
See also CA 114; 204; DLB 92; EWL 3

Nelson, Willie 1933- .... **CLC 17**
See also CA 107; CANR 114

Nemerov, Howard (Stanley) 1920-1991 .... **CLC 2, 6, 9, 36; PC 24; TCLC 124**
See also AMW; CA 1-4R; 134; CABS 2; CANR 1, 27, 53; CN 1, 2, 3; CP 1, 2, 3, 4; DAM POET; DLB 5, 6; DLBY 1983; EWL 3; INT CANR-27; MAL 5; MTCW 1, 2; MTFW 2005; PFS 10, 14; RGAL 4

Neruda, Pablo 1904-1973 .. **CLC 1, 2, 5, 7, 9, 28, 62; HLC 2; PC 4, 64; WLC**
See also CA 19-20; 45-48; CANR 131; CAP 2; DA; DA3; DAB; DAC; DAM MST, MULT, POET; DLB 283; DNFS 2; EWL 3; HW 1; LAW; MTCW 1, 2; MTFW 2005; PFS 11; RGWL 2, 3; TWA; WLIT 1; WP

Nerval, Gerard de 1808-1855 ... **NCLC 1, 67; PC 13; SSC 18**
See also DLB 217; EW 6; GFL 1789 to the Present; RGSF 2; RGWL 2, 3

Nervo, (Jose) Amado (Ruiz de) 1870-1919 .... **HLCS 2; TCLC 11**
See also CA 109; 131; DLB 290; EWL 3; HW 1; LAW

Nesbit, Malcolm
See Chester, Alfred

Nessi, Pio Baroja y
See Baroja (y Nessi), Pio

Nestroy, Johann 1801-1862 .... **NCLC 42**
See also DLB 133; RGWL 2, 3

Netterville, Luke
See O'Grady, Standish (James)

Neufeld, John (Arthur) 1938- .... **CLC 17**
See also AAYA 11; CA 25-28R; CANR 11, 37, 56; CLR 52; MAICYA 1, 2; SAAS 3; SATA 6, 81, 131; SATA-Essay 131; YAW

Neumann, Alfred 1895-1952 .... **TCLC 100**
See also CA 183; DLB 56

Neumann, Ferenc
See Molnar, Ferenc

Neville, Emily Cheney 1919- .... **CLC 12**
See also BYA 2; CA 5-8R; CANR 3, 37, 85; JRDA; MAICYA 1, 2; SAAS 2; SATA 1; YAW

Newbound, Bernard Slade 1930-
See Slade, Bernard
See also CA 81-84; CANR 49; CD 5; DAM DRAM

Newby, P(ercy) H(oward) 1918-1997 .... **CLC 2, 13**
See also CA 5-8R; 161; CANR 32, 67; CN 1, 2, 3, 4, 5, 6; DAM NOV; DLB 15; MTCW 1; RGEL 2

Newcastle
See Cavendish, Margaret Lucas

Newlove, Donald 1928- .... **CLC 6**
See also CA 29-32R; CANR 25

Newlove, John (Herbert) 1938- .... **CLC 14**
See also CA 21-24R; CANR 9, 25; CP 1, 2, 3, 4, 5, 6, 7

Newman, Charles (Hamilton) 1938- . **CLC 2, 8**
See also CA 21-24R; CANR 84; CN 3, 4, 5, 6

Newman, Edwin (Harold) 1919- ...... **CLC 14**
See also AITN 1; CA 69-72; CANR 5

Newman, John Henry 1801-1890 . **NCLC 38, 99**
See also BRWS 7; DLB 18, 32, 55; RGEL 2

Newton, (Sir) Isaac 1642-1727 ...... **LC 35, 53**
See also DLB 252

Newton, Suzanne 1936- .... **CLC 35**
See also BYA 7; CA 41-44R; CANR 14; JRDA; SATA 5, 77

New York Dept. of Ed. .... **CLC 70**

Nexo, Martin Andersen 1869-1954 .... **TCLC 43**
See also CA 202; DLB 214; EWL 3

Nezval, Vitezslav 1900-1958 .... **TCLC 44**
See also CA 123; CDWLB 4; DLB 215; EWL 3

Ng, Fae Myenne 1957(?)- .... **CLC 81**
See also BYA 11; CA 146

Ngema, Mbongeni 1955- .... **CLC 57**
See also BW 2; CA 143; CANR 84; CD 5, 6

Ngugi, James T(hiong'o) . **CLC 3, 7, 13, 182**
See Ngugi wa Thiong'o
See also CN 1, 2

Ngugi wa Thiong'o
See Ngugi wa Thiong'o
See also CD 3, 4, 5, 6, 7; DLB 125; EWL 3

Ngugi wa Thiong'o 1938- ... **BLC 3; CLC 36, 182**
See Ngugi, James T(hiong'o); Ngugi wa Thiong'o
See also AFW; BRWS 8; BW 2; CA 81-84; CANR 27, 58; CDWLB 3; DAM MULT, NOV; DNFS 2; MTCW 1, 2; MTFW 2005; RGEL 2; WWE 1

Niatum, Duane 1938- .... **NNAL**
See also CA 41-44R; CANR 21, 45, 83; DLB 175

Nichol, B(arrie) P(hillip) 1944-1988 . **CLC 18**
See also CA 53-56; CP 1, 2, 3, 4; DLB 53; SATA 66

Nicholas of Cusa 1401-1464 .... **LC 80**
See also DLB 115

Nichols, John (Treadwell) 1940- .... **CLC 38**
See also AMWS 13; CA 9-12R, 190; CAAE 190; CAAS 2; CANR 6, 70, 121; DLBY 1982; LATS 1:2; MTFW 2005; TCWW 1, 2

Nichols, Leigh
See Koontz, Dean R.

Nichols, Peter (Richard) 1927- .... **CLC 5, 36, 65**
See also CA 104; CANR 33, 86; CBD; CD 5, 6; DLB 13, 245; MTCW 1

Nicholson, Linda ed. .... **CLC 65**

Ni Chuilleanain, Eilean 1942- .... **PC 34**
See also CA 126; CANR 53, 83; CP 7; CWP; DLB 40

Nicolas, F. R. E.
See Freeling, Nicolas

Niedecker, Lorine 1903-1970 ..... **CLC 10, 42; PC 42**
See also CA 25-28; CAP 2; DAM POET; DLB 48

Nietzsche, Friedrich (Wilhelm) 1844-1900 .... **TCLC 10, 18, 55**
See also CA 107; 121; CDWLB 2; DLB 129; EW 7; RGWL 2, 3; TWA

Nievo, Ippolito 1831-1861 .... **NCLC 22**

Nightingale, Anne Redmon 1943-
See Redmon, Anne
See also CA 103

Nightingale, Florence 1820-1910 ... **TCLC 85**
See also CA 188; DLB 166

Nijo Yoshimoto 1320-1388 .... **CMLC 49**
See also DLB 203

Nik. T. O.
See Annensky, Innokenty (Fyodorovich)

Nin, Anais 1903-1977 ..... **CLC 1, 4, 8, 11, 14, 60, 127; SSC 10**
See also AITN 2; AMWS 10; BPFB 2; CA 13-16R; 69-72; CANR 22, 53; CN 1, 2; DAM NOV, POP; DLB 2, 4, 152; EWL 3; GLL 2; MAL 5; MAWW; MTCW 1, 2; MTFW 2005; RGAL 4; RGSF 2

Nisbet, Robert A(lexander) 1913-1996 .... **TCLC 117**
See also CA 25-28R; 153; CANR 17; INT CANR-17

Nishida, Kitaro 1870-1945 .... **TCLC 83**

Nishiwaki, Junzaburo 1894-1982 .... **PC 15**
See Junzaburo, Nishiwaki
See also CA 194; 107; MJW; RGWL 3

Nissenson, Hugh 1933- .... **CLC 4, 9**
See also CA 17-20R; CANR 27, 108; CN 5, 6; DLB 28

Nister, Der
See Der Nister
See also EWL 3

Niven, Larry .... **CLC 8**
See Niven, Laurence Van Cott
See also AAYA 27; BPFB 2; BYA 10; DLB 8; SCFW 1, 2

Niven, Laurence Van Cott 1938-
See Niven, Larry
See also CA 21-24R, 207; CAAE 207; CAAS 12; CANR 14, 44, 66, 113; CPW; DAM POP; MTCW 1, 2; SATA 95; SFW 4

Nixon, Agnes Eckhardt 1927- .... **CLC 21**
See also CA 110

Nizan, Paul 1905-1940 .... **TCLC 40**
See also CA 161; DLB 72; EWL 3; GFL 1789 to the Present

Nkosi, Lewis 1936- .... **BLC 3; CLC 45**
See also BW 1, 3; CA 65-68; CANR 27, 81; CBD; CD 5, 6; DAM MULT; DLB 157, 225; WWE 1

Nodier, (Jean) Charles (Emmanuel) 1780-1844 .... **NCLC 19**
See also DLB 119; GFL 1789 to the Present

Noguchi, Yone 1875-1947 .... **TCLC 80**

Nolan, Christopher 1965- .... **CLC 58**
See also CA 111; CANR 88

Noon, Jeff 1957- .... **CLC 91**
See also CA 148; CANR 83; DLB 267; SFW 4

Norden, Charles
See Durrell, Lawrence (George)

Nordhoff, Charles Bernard 1887-1947 .... **TCLC 23**
See also CA 108; 211; DLB 9; LAIT 1; RHW 1; SATA 23

Norfolk, Lawrence 1963- .... **CLC 76**
See also CA 144; CANR 85; CN 6, 7; DLB 267

Norman, Marsha (Williams) 1947- . **CLC 28, 186; DC 8**
See also CA 105; CABS 3; CAD; CANR 41, 131; CD 5, 6; CSW; CWD; DAM DRAM; DFS 2; DLB 266; DLBY 1984; FW; MAL 5

Normyx
See Douglas, (George) Norman

Norris, (Benjamin) Frank(lin, Jr.) 1870-1902 .... **SSC 28; TCLC 24, 155**
See also AAYA 57; AMW; AMWC 2; BPFB 2; CA 110; 160; CDALB 1865-1917; DLB 12, 71, 186; LMFS 2; NFS 12; RGAL 4; TCWW 1, 2; TUS

Norris, Leslie 1921- .... **CLC 14**
See also CA 11-12; CANR 14, 117; CAP 1; CP 1, 2, 3, 4, 5, 6, 7; DLB 27, 256

North, Andrew
See Norton, Andre

North, Anthony
See Koontz, Dean R.

North, Captain George
See Stevenson, Robert Louis (Balfour)

North, Captain George
See Stevenson, Robert Louis (Balfour)

North, Milou
See Erdrich, (Karen) Louise

Northrup, B. A.
See Hubbard, L(afayette) Ron(ald)

North Staffs
See Hulme, T(homas) E(rnest)

Northup, Solomon 1808-1863 ...... **NCLC 105**

Norton, Alice Mary
See Norton, Andre
See also MAICYA 1; SATA 1, 43

Norton, Andre 1912-2005 .... **CLC 12**
See Norton, Alice Mary
See also AAYA 14; BPFB 2; BYA 4, 10, 12; CA 1-4R; 237; CANR 68; CLR 50; DLB 8, 52; JRDA; MAICYA 2; MTCW 1; SATA 91; SUFW 1, 2; YAW

Norton, Caroline 1808-1877 .... **NCLC 47**
See also DLB 21, 159, 199

Norway, Nevil Shute 1899-1960
See Shute, Nevil
See also CA 102; 93-96; CANR 85; MTCW 2

Norwid, Cyprian Kamil 1821-1883 .... **NCLC 17**
See also RGWL 3

Nosille, Nabrah
See Ellison, Harlan (Jay)

Nossack, Hans Erich 1901-1978 .... **CLC 6**
See also CA 93-96; 85-88; DLB 69; EWL 3

Nostradamus 1503-1566 .... **LC 27**

Nosu, Chuji
See Ozu, Yasujiro

Notenburg, Eleanora (Genrikhovna) von
See Guro, Elena (Genrikhovna)

Nova, Craig 1945- .... **CLC 7, 31**
See also CA 45-48; CANR 2, 53, 127

Novak, Joseph
See Kosinski, Jerzy (Nikodem)

Novalis 1772-1801 .... **NCLC 13**
See also CDWLB 2; DLB 90; EW 5; RGWL 2, 3

Novick, Peter 1934- .... **CLC 164**
See also CA 188

Novis, Emile
See Weil, Simone (Adolphine)

Nowlan, Alden (Albert) 1933-1983 ... **CLC 15**
See also CA 9-12R; CANR 5; CP 1, 2, 3; DAC; DAM MST; DLB 53; PFS 12

Noyes, Alfred 1880-1958 ...... **PC 27; TCLC 7**
See also CA 104; 188; DLB 20; EXPP; FANT; PFS 4; RGEL 2

Nugent, Richard Bruce 1906(?)-1987 .... **HR 1:3**
See also BW 1; CA 125; DLB 51; GLL 2

Nunn, Kem .... **CLC 34**
See also CA 159

Nussbaum, Martha Craven 1947- .. **CLC 203**
See also CA 134; CANR 102

Nwapa, Flora (Nwanzuruaha) 1931-1993 .... **BLCS; CLC 133**
See also BW 2; CA 143; CANR 83; CDWLB 3; CWRI 5; DLB 125; EWL 3; WLIT 2

Nye, Robert 1939- .... **CLC 13, 42**
See also BRWS 10; CA 33-36R; CANR 29, 67, 107; CN 1, 2, 3, 4, 5, 6, 7; CP 1, 2, 3, 4, 5, 6, 7; CWRI 5; DAM NOV; DLB 14, 271; FANT; HGG; MTCW 1; RHW; SATA 6

Nyro, Laura 1947-1997 .... **CLC 17**
See also CA 194

Oates, Joyce Carol 1938- ... **CLC 1, 2, 3, 6, 9, 11, 15, 19, 33, 52, 108, 134; SSC 6, 70; WLC**
See also AAYA 15, 52; AITN 1; AMWS 2; BEST 89:2; BPFB 2; BYA 11; CA 5-8R; CANR 25, 45, 74, 113, 129; CDALB 1968-1988; CN 1, 2, 3, 4, 5, 6, 7; CP 7; CPW; CWP; DA; DA3; DAB; DAC; DAM MST, NOV, POP; DLB 2, 5, 130; DLBY 1981; EWL 3; EXPS; FL 1:6; FW; GL 3; HGG; INT CANR-25; LAIT 4; MAL 5; MAWW; MTCW 1, 2; MTFW 2005; NFS 8; RGAL 4; RGSF 2; SATA 159; SSFS 1, 8, 17; SUFW 2; TUS

O'Brian, E. G.
See Clarke, Arthur C(harles)

O'Brian, Patrick 1914-2000 .... **CLC 152**
See also AAYA 55; CA 144; 187; CANR 74; CPW; MTCW 2; MTFW 2005; RHW

O'Brien, Darcy 1939-1998 .... **CLC 11**
See also CA 21-24R; 167; CANR 8, 59

O'Brien, Edna 1932- ...... **CLC 3, 5, 8, 13, 36, 65, 116; SSC 10, 77**
See also BRWS 5; CA 1-4R; CANR 6, 41, 65, 102; CDBLB 1960 to Present; CN 1, 2, 3, 4, 5, 6, 7; DA3; DAM NOV; DLB 14, 231, 319; EWL 3; FW; MTCW 1, 2; MTFW 2005; RGSF 2; WLIT 4

O'Brien, Fitz-James 1828-1862 ...... **NCLC 21**
See also DLB 74; RGAL 4; SUFW

O'Brien, Flann .... **CLC 1, 4, 5, 7, 10, 47**
See O Nuallain, Brian
See also BRWS 2; DLB 231; EWL 3; RGEL 2

O'Brien, Richard 1942- .... **CLC 17**
See also CA 124

O'Brien, (William) Tim(othy) 1946- . **CLC 7, 19, 40, 103, 211; SSC 74**
See also AAYA 16; AMWS 5; CA 85-88; CANR 40, 58, 133; CDALBS; CN 5, 6, 7; CPW; DA3; DAM POP; DLB 152; DLBD 9; DLBY 1980; LATS 1:2; MAL 5; MTCW 2; MTFW 2005; RGAL 4; SSFS 5, 15; TCLE 1:2

Obstfelder, Sigbjoern 1866-1900 .... **TCLC 23**
See also CA 123

O'Casey, Sean 1880-1964 .... **CLC 1, 5, 9, 11, 15, 88; DC 12; WLCS**
See also BRW 7; CA 89-92; CANR 62; CBD; CDBLB 1914-1945; DA3; DAB; DAC; DAM DRAM, MST; DFS 19; DLB 10; EWL 3; MTCW 1, 2; MTFW 2005; RGEL 2; TEA; WLIT 4

O'Cathasaigh, Sean
See O'Casey, Sean

Occom, Samson 1723-1792 .... **LC 60; NNAL**
See also DLB 175

Ochs, Phil(ip David) 1940-1976 .... **CLC 17**
See also CA 185; 65-68

O'Connor, Edwin (Greene)
1918-1968 .... **CLC 14**
See also CA 93-96; 25-28R; MAL 5

O'Connor, (Mary) Flannery
1925-1964 .... **CLC 1, 2, 3, 6, 10, 13, 15, 21, 66, 104; SSC 1, 23, 61, 82; TCLC 132; WLC**
See also AAYA 7; AMW; AMWR 2; BPFB 3; BYA 16; CA 1-4R; CANR 3, 41; CDALB 1941-1968; DA; DA3; DAB; DAC; DAM MST, NOV; DLB 2, 152; DLBD 12; DLBY 1980; EWL 3; EXPS; LAIT 5; MAL 5; MAWW; MTCW 1, 2; MTFW 2005; NFS 3, 21; RGAL 4; RGSF 2; SSFS 2, 7, 10, 19; TUS

O'Connor, Frank .... **CLC 23; SSC 5**
See O'Donovan, Michael Francis
See also DLB 162; EWL 3; RGSF 2; SSFS 5

O'Dell, Scott 1898-1989 .... **CLC 30**
See also AAYA 3, 44; BPFB 3; BYA 1, 2, 3, 5; CA 61-64; 129; CANR 12, 30, 112; CLR 1, 16; DLB 52; JRDA; MAICYA 1, 2; SATA 12, 60, 134; WYA; YAW

Odets, Clifford 1906-1963 ..... **CLC 2, 28, 98; DC 6**
See also AMWS 2; CA 85-88; CAD; CANR 62; DAM DRAM; DFS 3, 17, 20; DLB 7, 26; EWL 3; MAL 5; MTCW 1, 2; MTFW 2005; RGAL 4; TUS

O'Doherty, Brian 1928- .... **CLC 76**
See also CA 105; CANR 108

O'Donnell, K. M.
See Malzberg, Barry N(athaniel)

O'Donnell, Lawrence
See Kuttner, Henry

O'Donovan, Michael Francis
1903-1966 .... **CLC 14**
See O'Connor, Frank
See also CA 93-96; CANR 84

Oe, Kenzaburo 1935- .. **CLC 10, 36, 86, 187; SSC 20**
See Oe Kenzaburo
See also CA 97-100; CANR 36, 50, 74, 126; DA3; DAM NOV; DLB 182; DLBY 1994; LATS 1:2; MJW; MTCW 1, 2; MTFW 2005; RGSF 2; RGWL 2, 3

Oe Kenzaburo
See Oe, Kenzaburo
See also CWW 2; EWL 3

O'Faolain, Julia 1932- .... **CLC 6, 19, 47, 108**
See also CA 81-84; CAAS 2; CANR 12, 61; CN 2, 3, 4, 5, 6, 7; DLB 14, 231, 319; FW; MTCW 1; RHW

O'Faolain, Sean 1900-1991 ...... **CLC 1, 7, 14, 32, 70; SSC 13; TCLC 143**
See also CA 61-64; 134; CANR 12, 66; CN 1, 2, 3, 4; DLB 15, 162; MTCW 1, 2; MTFW 2005; RGEL 2; RGSF 2

O'Flaherty, Liam 1896-1984 .... **CLC 5, 34; SSC 6**
See also CA 101; 113; CANR 35; CN 1, 2, 3; DLB 36, 162; DLBY 1984; MTCW 1, 2; MTFW 2005; RGEL 2; RGSF 2; SSFS 5, 20

Ogai
See Mori Ogai
See also MJW

Ogilvy, Gavin
See Barrie, J(ames) M(atthew)

O'Grady, Standish (James)
1846-1928 .... **TCLC 5**
See also CA 104; 157

O'Grady, Timothy 1951- .... **CLC 59**
See also CA 138

O'Hara, Frank 1926-1966 .... **CLC 2, 5, 13, 78; PC 45**
See also CA 9-12R; 25-28R; CANR 33; DA3; DAM POET; DLB 5, 16, 193; EWL 3; MAL 5; MTCW 1, 2; MTFW 2005; PFS 8, 12; RGAL 4; WP

O'Hara, John (Henry) 1905-1970 . **CLC 1, 2, 3, 6, 11, 42; SSC 15**
See also AMW; BPFB 3; CA 5-8R; 25-28R; CANR 31, 60; CDALB 1929-1941; DAM NOV; DLB 9, 86; DLBD 2; EWL 3; MAL 5; MTCW 1, 2; MTFW 2005; NFS 11; RGAL 4; RGSF 2

O Hehir, Diana 1922- .... **CLC 41**
See also CA 93-96

Ohiyesa
See Eastman, Charles A(lexander)

Okada, John 1923-1971 .... **AAL**
See also BYA 14; CA 212; DLB 312

Okigbo, Christopher (Ifenayichukwu)
1932-1967 .. **BLC 3; CLC 25, 84; PC 7; TCLC 171**
See also AFW; BW 1, 3; CA 77-80; CANR 74; CDWLB 3; DAM MULT, POET; DLB 125; EWL 3; MTCW 1, 2; MTFW 2005; RGEL 2

Okri, Ben 1959- .... **CLC 87**
See also AFW; BRWS 5; BW 2, 3; CA 130; 138; CANR 65, 128; CN 5, 6, 7; DLB 157, 231, 319; EWL 3; INT CA-138; MTCW 2; MTFW 2005; RGEL 2; RGSF 2; SSFS 20; WLIT 2; WWE 1

Olds, Sharon 1942- .. **CLC 32, 39, 85; PC 22**
See also AMWS 10; CA 101; CANR 18, 41, 66, 98, 135; CP 7; CPW; CWP; DAM POET; DLB 120; MAL 5; MTCW 2; MTFW 2005; PFS 17

Oldstyle, Jonathan
See Irving, Washington

Olesha, Iurii
See Olesha, Yuri (Karlovich)
See also RGWL 2

Olesha, Iurii Karlovich
See Olesha, Yuri (Karlovich)
See also DLB 272

Olesha, Yuri (Karlovich) 1899-1960 . **CLC 8; SSC 69; TCLC 136**
See Olesha, Iurii; Olesha, Iurii Karlovich; Olesha, Yury Karlovich
See also CA 85-88; EW 11; RGWL 3

Olesha, Yury Karlovich
See Olesha, Yuri (Karlovich)
See also EWL 3

Oliphant, Mrs.
See Oliphant, Margaret (Oliphant Wilson)
See also SUFW

Oliphant, Laurence 1829(?)-1888 .. **NCLC 47**
See also DLB 18, 166

Oliphant, Margaret (Oliphant Wilson)
1828-1897 .... **NCLC 11, 61; SSC 25**
See Oliphant, Mrs.
See also BRWS 10; DLB 18, 159, 190; HGG; RGEL 2; RGSF 2

Oliver, Mary 1935- .... **CLC 19, 34, 98**
See also AMWS 7; CA 21-24R; CANR 9, 43, 84, 92, 138; CP 4, 5, 6, 7; CWP; DLB 5, 193; EWL 3; MTCW 2; MTFW 2005; PFS 15

Olivier, Laurence (Kerr) 1907-1989 . **CLC 20**
See also CA 111; 150; 129

Olsen, Tillie 1912- ... **CLC 4, 13, 114; SSC 11**
See also AAYA 51; AMWS 13; BYA 11; CA 1-4R; CANR 1, 43, 74, 132; CDALBS; CN 2, 3, 4, 5, 6, 7; DA; DA3; DAB; DAC; DAM MST; DLB 28, 206; DLBY 1980; EWL 3; EXPS; FW; MAL 5; MTCW 1, 2; MTFW 2005; RGAL 4; RGSF 2; SSFS 1; TCLE 1:2; TCWW 2; TUS

Olson, Charles (John) 1910-1970 .. **CLC 1, 2, 5, 6, 9, 11, 29; PC 19**
See also AMWS 2; CA 13-16; 25-28R; CABS 2; CANR 35, 61; CAP 1; CP 1; DAM POET; DLB 5, 16, 193; EWL 3; MAL 5; MTCW 1, 2; RGAL 4; WP

Olson, Toby 1937- .... **CLC 28**
See also CA 65-68; CANR 9, 31, 84; CP 3, 4, 5, 6, 7

Olyesha, Yuri
See Olesha, Yuri (Karlovich)

Olympiodorus of Thebes c. 375-c.
430 .... **CMLC 59**

Omar Khayyam
See Khayyam, Omar
See also RGWL 2, 3

Ondaatje, (Philip) Michael 1943- .... **CLC 14, 29, 51, 76, 180; PC 28**
See also AAYA 66; CA 77-80; CANR 42, 74, 109, 133; CN 5, 6, 7; CP 1, 2, 3, 4, 5, 6, 7; DA3; DAB; DAC; DAM MST; DLB 60; EWL 3; LATS 1:2; LMFS 2; MTCW 2; MTFW 2005; PFS 8, 19; TCLE 1:2; TWA; WWE 1

Oneal, Elizabeth 1934-
See Oneal, Zibby
See also CA 106; CANR 28, 84; MAICYA 1, 2; SATA 30, 82; YAW

Oneal, Zibby .... **CLC 30**
See Oneal, Elizabeth
See also AAYA 5, 41; BYA 13; CLR 13; JRDA; WYA

O'Neill, Eugene (Gladstone)
1888-1953 ... **DC 20; TCLC 1, 6, 27, 49; WLC**
See also AAYA 54; AITN 1; AMW; AMWC 1; CA 110; 132; CAD; CANR 131; CDALB 1929-1941; DA; DA3; DAB; DAC; DAM DRAM, MST; DFS 2, 4, 5, 6, 9, 11, 12, 16, 20; DLB 7; EWL 3; LAIT 3; LMFS 2; MAL 5; MTCW 1, 2; MTFW 2005; RGAL 4; TUS

Onetti, Juan Carlos 1909-1994 ... **CLC 7, 10; HLCS 2; SSC 23; TCLC 131**
See also CA 85-88; 145; CANR 32, 63; CDWLB 3; CWW 2; DAM MULT, NOV; DLB 113; EWL 3; HW 1, 2; LAW; MTCW 1, 2; MTFW 2005; RGSF 2

O Nuallain, Brian 1911-1966
See O'Brien, Flann
See also CA 21-22; 25-28R; CAP 2; DLB 231; FANT; TEA

Ophuls, Max 1902-1957 .... **TCLC 79**
See also CA 113

Opie, Amelia 1769-1853 .... **NCLC 65**
See also DLB 116, 159; RGEL 2

Oppen, George 1908-1984 ..... **CLC 7, 13, 34; PC 35; TCLC 107**
See also CA 13-16R; 113; CANR 8, 82; CP 1, 2, 3; DLB 5, 165

Oppenheim, E(dward) Phillips
1866-1946 .... **TCLC 45**
See also CA 111; 202; CMW 4; DLB 70

Opuls, Max
See Ophuls, Max

Orage, A(lfred) R(ichard)
1873-1934 .... **TCLC 157**
See also CA 122

Origen c. 185-c. 254 .... **CMLC 19**

Orlovitz, Gil 1918-1973 .... **CLC 22**
See also CA 77-80; 45-48; CN 1; CP 1, 2; DLB 2, 5

O'Rourke, P(atrick) J(ake) 1947- .. **CLC 209**
See also CA 77-80; CANR 13, 41, 67, 111; CPW; DAM POP; DLB 185

Orris
See Ingelow, Jean

Ortega y Gasset, Jose 1883-1955 .... **HLC 2; TCLC 9**
See also CA 106; 130; DAM MULT; EW 9; EWL 3; HW 1, 2; MTCW 1, 2; MTFW 2005

Ortese, Anna Maria 1914-1998 .... **CLC 89**
See also DLB 177; EWL 3

Ortiz, Simon J(oseph) 1941- ... **CLC 45, 208; NNAL; PC 17**
See also AMWS 4; CA 134; CANR 69, 118; CP 3, 4, 5, 6, 7; DAM MULT, POET; DLB 120, 175, 256; EXPP; MAL 5; PFS 4, 16; RGAL 4; TCWW 2

Orton, Joe ...... **CLC 4, 13, 43; DC 3; TCLC 157**
See Orton, John Kingsley
See also BRWS 5; CBD; CDBLB 1960 to Present; DFS 3, 6; DLB 13, 310; GLL 1; RGEL 2; TEA; WLIT 4

Orton, John Kingsley 1933-1967
See Orton, Joe
See also CA 85-88; CANR 35, 66; DAM DRAM; MTCW 1, 2; MTFW 2005

Orwell, George ...... **SSC 68; TCLC 2, 6, 15, 31, 51, 128, 129; WLC**
See Blair, Eric (Arthur)
See also BPFB 3; BRW 7; BYA 5; CDBLB 1945-1960; CLR 68; DAB; DLB 15, 98, 195, 255; EWL 3; EXPN; LAIT 4, 5; LATS 1:1; NFS 3, 7; RGEL 2; SCFW 1, 2; SFW 4; SSFS 4; TEA; WLIT 4; YAW

Osborne, David
See Silverberg, Robert

Osborne, George
See Silverberg, Robert

Osborne, John (James) 1929-1994 .... **CLC 1, 2, 5, 11, 45; TCLC 153; WLC**
See also BRWS 1; CA 13-16R; 147; CANR 21, 56; CBD; CDBLB 1945-1960; DA; DAB; DAC; DAM DRAM, MST; DFS 4, 19; DLB 13; EWL 3; MTCW 1, 2; MTFW 2005; RGEL 2

Osborne, Lawrence 1958- .... **CLC 50**
See also CA 189

Osbourne, Lloyd 1868-1947 .... **TCLC 93**

Osgood, Frances Sargent 1811-1850 .... **NCLC 141**
See also DLB 250

Oshima, Nagisa 1932- .... **CLC 20**
See also CA 116; 121; CANR 78

Oskison, John Milton 1874-1947 .... **NNAL; TCLC 35**
See also CA 144; CANR 84; DAM MULT; DLB 175

Ossian c. 3rd cent. - .... **CMLC 28**
See Macpherson, James

Ossoli, Sarah Margaret (Fuller) 1810-1850 .... **NCLC 5, 50**
See Fuller, Margaret; Fuller, Sarah Margaret
See also CDALB 1640-1865; FW; LMFS 1; SATA 25

Ostriker, Alicia (Suskin) 1937- .... **CLC 132**
See also CA 25-28R; CAAS 24; CANR 10, 30, 62, 99; CWP; DLB 120; EXPP; PFS 19

Ostrovsky, Aleksandr Nikolaevich
See Ostrovsky, Alexander
See also DLB 277

Ostrovsky, Alexander 1823-1886 .. **NCLC 30, 57**
See Ostrovsky, Aleksandr Nikolaevich

Otero, Blas de 1916-1979 .... **CLC 11**
See also CA 89-92; DLB 134; EWL 3

O'Trigger, Sir Lucius
See Horne, Richard Henry Hengist

Otto, Rudolf 1869-1937 .... **TCLC 85**

Otto, Whitney 1955- .... **CLC 70**
See also CA 140; CANR 120

Otway, Thomas 1652-1685 ... **DC 24; LC 106**
See also DAM DRAM; DLB 80; RGEL 2

Ouida .... **TCLC 43**
See De la Ramee, Marie Louise (Ouida)
See also DLB 18, 156; RGEL 2

Ouologuem, Yambo 1940- .... **CLC 146**
See also CA 111; 176

Ousmane, Sembene 1923- ... **BLC 3; CLC 66**
See Sembene, Ousmane
See also BW 1, 3; CA 117; 125; CANR 81; CWW 2; MTCW 1

Ovid 43B.C.-17 .... **CMLC 7; PC 2**
See also AW 2; CDWLB 1; DA3; DAM POET; DLB 211; PFS 22; RGWL 2, 3; WP

Owen, Hugh
See Faust, Frederick (Schiller)

Owen, Wilfred (Edward Salter) 1893-1918 ... **PC 19; TCLC 5, 27; WLC**
See also BRW 6; CA 104; 141; CDBLB 1914-1945; DA; DAB; DAC; DAM MST, POET; DLB 20; EWL 3; EXPP; MTCW 2; MTFW 2005; PFS 10; RGEL 2; WLIT 4

Owens, Louis (Dean) 1948-2002 .... **NNAL**
See also CA 137, 179; 207; CAAE 179; CAAS 24; CANR 71

Owens, Rochelle 1936- .... **CLC 8**
See also CA 17-20R; CAAS 2; CAD; CANR 39; CD 5, 6; CP 1, 2, 3, 4, 5, 6, 7; CWD; CWP

Oz, Amos 1939- ...... **CLC 5, 8, 11, 27, 33, 54; SSC 66**
See also CA 53-56; CANR 27, 47, 65, 113, 138; CWW 2; DAM NOV; EWL 3; MTCW 1, 2; MTFW 2005; RGSF 2; RGWL 3; WLIT 6

Ozick, Cynthia 1928- .... **CLC 3, 7, 28, 62, 155; SSC 15, 60**
See also AMWS 5; BEST 90:1; CA 17-20R; CANR 23, 58, 116; CN 3, 4, 5, 6, 7; CPW; DA3; DAM NOV, POP; DLB 28, 152, 299; DLBY 1982; EWL 3; EXPS; INT CANR-23; MAL 5; MTCW 1, 2; MTFW 2005; RGAL 4; RGSF 2; SSFS 3, 12

Ozu, Yasujiro 1903-1963 .... **CLC 16**
See also CA 112

Pabst, G. W. 1885-1967 .... **TCLC 127**

Pacheco, C.
See Pessoa, Fernando (Antonio Nogueira)

Pacheco, Jose Emilio 1939- .... **HLC 2**
See also CA 111; 131; CANR 65; CWW 2; DAM MULT; DLB 290; EWL 3; HW 1, 2; RGSF 2

Pa Chin .... **CLC 18**
See Li Fei-kan
See also EWL 3

Pack, Robert 1929- .... **CLC 13**
See also CA 1-4R; CANR 3, 44, 82; CP 1, 2, 3, 4, 5, 6, 7; DLB 5; SATA 118

Padgett, Lewis
See Kuttner, Henry

Padilla (Lorenzo), Heberto 1932-2000 .... **CLC 38**
See also AITN 1; CA 123; 131; 189; CWW 2; EWL 3; HW 1

Page, James Patrick 1944-
See Page, Jimmy
See also CA 204

Page, Jimmy 1944- .... **CLC 12**
See Page, James Patrick

Page, Louise 1955- .... **CLC 40**
See also CA 140; CANR 76; CBD; CD 5, 6; CWD; DLB 233

Page, P(atricia) K(athleen) 1916- .... **CLC 7, 18; PC 12**
See Cape, Judith
See also CA 53-56; CANR 4, 22, 65; CP 1, 2, 3, 4, 5, 6, 7; DAC; DAM MST; DLB 68; MTCW 1; RGEL 2

Page, Stanton
See Fuller, Henry Blake

Page, Stanton
See Fuller, Henry Blake

Page, Thomas Nelson 1853-1922 .... **SSC 23**
See also CA 118; 177; DLB 12, 78; DLBD 13; RGAL 4

Pagels, Elaine Hiesey 1943- .... **CLC 104**
See also CA 45-48; CANR 2, 24, 51; FW; NCFS 4

Paget, Violet 1856-1935
See Lee, Vernon
See also CA 104; 166; GLL 1; HGG

Paget-Lowe, Henry
See Lovecraft, H(oward) P(hillips)

Paglia, Camille (Anna) 1947- .... **CLC 68**
See also CA 140; CANR 72, 139; CPW; FW; GLL 2; MTCW 2; MTFW 2005

Paige, Richard
See Koontz, Dean R.

Paine, Thomas 1737-1809 .... **NCLC 62**
See also AMWS 1; CDALB 1640-1865; DLB 31, 43, 73, 158; LAIT 1; RGAL 4; RGEL 2; TUS

Pakenham, Antonia
See Fraser, Antonia (Pakenham)

Palamas, Costis
See Palamas, Kostes

Palamas, Kostes 1859-1943 .... **TCLC 5**
See Palamas, Kostis
See also CA 105; 190; RGWL 2, 3

Palamas, Kostis
See Palamas, Kostes
See also EWL 3

Palazzeschi, Aldo 1885-1974 .... **CLC 11**
See also CA 89-92; 53-56; DLB 114, 264; EWL 3

Pales Matos, Luis 1898-1959 .... **HLCS 2**
See Pales Matos, Luis
See also DLB 290; HW 1; LAW

Paley, Grace 1922- .. **CLC 4, 6, 37, 140; SSC 8**
See also AMWS 6; CA 25-28R; CANR 13, 46, 74, 118; CN 2, 3, 4, 5, 6, 7; CPW; DA3; DAM POP; DLB 28, 218; EWL 3; EXPS; FW; INT CANR-13; MAL 5; MAWW; MTCW 1, 2; MTFW 2005; RGAL 4; RGSF 2; SSFS 3, 20

Palin, Michael (Edward) 1943- .... **CLC 21**
See Monty Python
See also CA 107; CANR 35, 109; SATA 67

Palliser, Charles 1947- .... **CLC 65**
See also CA 136; CANR 76; CN 5, 6, 7

Palma, Ricardo 1833-1919 .... **TCLC 29**
See also CA 168; LAW

Pamuk, Orhan 1952- .... **CLC 185**
See also CA 142; CANR 75, 127; CWW 2; WLIT 6

Pancake, Breece Dexter 1952-1979
See Pancake, Breece D'J
See also CA 123; 109

Pancake, Breece D'J .... **CLC 29; SSC 61**
See Pancake, Breece Dexter
See also DLB 130

Panchenko, Nikolai .... **CLC 59**

Pankhurst, Emmeline (Goulden) 1858-1928 .... **TCLC 100**
See also CA 116; FW

Panko, Rudy
See Gogol, Nikolai (Vasilyevich)

Papadiamantis, Alexandros 1851-1911 .... **TCLC 29**
See also CA 168; EWL 3

Papadiamantopoulos, Johannes 1856-1910
See Moreas, Jean
See also CA 117

Papini, Giovanni 1881-1956 .... **TCLC 22**
See also CA 121; 180; DLB 264

Paracelsus 1493-1541 .... **LC 14**
See also DLB 179

Parasol, Peter
See Stevens, Wallace

Pardo Bazan, Emilia 1851-1921 .... **SSC 30**
See also EWL 3; FW; RGSF 2; RGWL 2, 3

Pareto, Vilfredo 1848-1923 .... **TCLC 69**
See also CA 175

Paretsky, Sara 1947- .... **CLC 135**
See also AAYA 30; BEST 90:3; CA 125; 129; CANR 59, 95; CMW 4; CPW; DA3; DAM POP; DLB 306; INT CA-129; MSW; RGAL 4

Parfenie, Maria
See Codrescu, Andrei

Parini, Jay (Lee) 1948- .... **CLC 54, 133**
See also CA 97-100, 229; CAAE 229; CAAS 16; CANR 32, 87

Park, Jordan
See Kornbluth, C(yril) M.; Pohl, Frederik

Park, Robert E(zra) 1864-1944 ..... **TCLC 73**
See also CA 122; 165

Parker, Bert
See Ellison, Harlan (Jay)

Parker, Dorothy (Rothschild)
1893-1967 . **CLC 15, 68; PC 28; SSC 2; TCLC 143**
See also AMWS 9; CA 19-20; 25-28R; CAP 2; DA3; DAM POET; DLB 11, 45, 86; EXPP; FW; MAL 5; MAWW; MTCW 1, 2; MTFW 2005; PFS 18; RGAL 4; RGSF 2; TUS

Parker, Robert B(rown) 1932- .... **CLC 27**
See also AAYA 28; BEST 89:4; BPFB 3; CA 49-52; CANR 1, 26, 52, 89, 128; CMW 4; CPW; DAM NOV, POP; DLB 306; INT CANR-26; MSW; MTCW 1; MTFW 2005

Parkin, Frank 1940- .... **CLC 43**
See also CA 147

Parkman, Francis, Jr. 1823-1893 .. **NCLC 12**
See also AMWS 2; DLB 1, 30, 183, 186, 235; RGAL 4

Parks, Gordon (Alexander Buchanan)
1912- .... **BLC 3; CLC 1, 16**
See also AAYA 36; AITN 2; BW 2, 3; CA 41-44R; CANR 26, 66, 145; DA3; DAM MULT; DLB 33; MTCW 2; MTFW 2005; SATA 8, 108

Parks, Suzan-Lori 1964(?)- .... **DC 23**
See also AAYA 55; CA 201; CAD; CD 5, 6; CWD; DFS 22; RGAL 4

Parks, Tim(othy Harold) 1954- ...... **CLC 147**
See also CA 126; 131; CANR 77, 144; CN 7; DLB 231; INT CA-131

Parmenides c. 515B.C.-c.
450B.C. .... **CMLC 22**
See also DLB 176

Parnell, Thomas 1679-1718 .... **LC 3**
See also DLB 95; RGEL 2

Parr, Catherine c. 1513(?)-1548 .... **LC 86**
See also DLB 136

Parra, Nicanor 1914- ... **CLC 2, 102; HLC 2; PC 39**
See also CA 85-88; CANR 32; CWW 2; DAM MULT; DLB 283; EWL 3; HW 1; LAW; MTCW 1

Parra Sanojo, Ana Teresa de la
1890-1936 .... **HLCS 2**
See de la Parra, (Ana) Teresa (Sonojo)
See also LAW

Parrish, Mary Frances
See Fisher, M(ary) F(rances) K(ennedy)

Parshchikov, Aleksei 1954- .... **CLC 59**
See Parshchikov, Aleksei Maksimovich

Parshchikov, Aleksei Maksimovich
See Parshchikov, Aleksei
See also DLB 285

Parson, Professor
See Coleridge, Samuel Taylor

Parson Lot
See Kingsley, Charles

Parton, Sara Payson Willis
1811-1872 .... **NCLC 86**
See also DLB 43, 74, 239

Partridge, Anthony
See Oppenheim, E(dward) Phillips

Pascal, Blaise 1623-1662 .... **LC 35**
See also DLB 268; EW 3; GFL Beginnings to 1789; RGWL 2, 3; TWA

Pascoli, Giovanni 1855-1912 .... **TCLC 45**
See also CA 170; EW 7; EWL 3

Pasolini, Pier Paolo 1922-1975 .. **CLC 20, 37, 106; PC 17**
See also CA 93-96; 61-64; CANR 63; DLB 128, 177; EWL 3; MTCW 1; RGWL 2, 3

Pasquini
See Silone, Ignazio

Pastan, Linda (Olenik) 1932- .... **CLC 27**
See also CA 61-64; CANR 18, 40, 61, 113; CP 3, 4, 5, 6, 7; CSW; CWP; DAM POET; DLB 5; PFS 8

Pasternak, Boris (Leonidovich)
1890-1960 ...... **CLC 7, 10, 18, 63; PC 6; SSC 31; WLC**
See also BPFB 3; CA 127; 116; DA; DA3; DAB; DAC; DAM MST, NOV, POET; DLB 302; EW 10; MTCW 1, 2; MTFW 2005; RGSF 2; RGWL 2, 3; TWA; WP

Patchen, Kenneth 1911-1972 .... **CLC 1, 2, 18**
See also BG 1:3; CA 1-4R; 33-36R; CANR 3, 35; CN 1; CP 1; DAM POET; DLB 16, 48; EWL 3; MAL 5; MTCW 1; RGAL 4

Pater, Walter (Horatio) 1839-1894 . **NCLC 7, 90, 159**
See also BRW 5; CDBLB 1832-1890; DLB 57, 156; RGEL 2; TEA

Paterson, A(ndrew) B(arton)
1864-1941 .... **TCLC 32**
See also CA 155; DLB 230; RGEL 2; SATA 97

Paterson, Banjo
See Paterson, A(ndrew) B(arton)

Paterson, Katherine (Womeldorf)
1932- .... **CLC 12, 30**
See also AAYA 1, 31; BYA 1, 2, 7; CA 21-24R; CANR 28, 59, 111; CLR 7, 50; CWRI 5; DLB 52; JRDA; LAIT 4; MAICYA 1, 2; MAICYAS 1; MTCW 1; SATA 13, 53, 92, 133; WYA; YAW

Patmore, Coventry Kersey Dighton
1823-1896 .... **NCLC 9; PC 59**
See also DLB 35, 98; RGEL 2; TEA

Paton, Alan (Stewart) 1903-1988 ...... **CLC 4, 10, 25, 55, 106; TCLC 165; WLC**
See also AAYA 26; AFW; BPFB 3; BRWS 2; BYA 1; CA 13-16; 125; CANR 22; CAP 1; CN 1, 2, 3, 4; DA; DA3; DAB; DAC; DAM MST, NOV; DLB 225; DLBD 17; EWL 3; EXPN; LAIT 4; MTCW 1, 2; MTFW 2005; NFS 3, 12; RGEL 2; SATA 11; SATA-Obit 56; TWA; WLIT 2; WWE 1

Paton Walsh, Gillian 1937- .... **CLC 35**
See Paton Walsh, Jill; Walsh, Jill Paton
See also AAYA 11; CANR 38, 83; CLR 2, 65; DLB 161; JRDA; MAICYA 1, 2; SAAS 3; SATA 4, 72, 109; YAW

Paton Walsh, Jill
See Paton Walsh, Gillian
See also AAYA 47; BYA 1, 8

Patterson, (Horace) Orlando (Lloyd)
1940- .... **BLCS**
See also BW 1; CA 65-68; CANR 27, 84; CN 1, 2, 3, 4, 5, 6

Patton, George S(mith), Jr.
1885-1945 .... **TCLC 79**
See also CA 189

Paulding, James Kirke 1778-1860 ... **NCLC 2**
See also DLB 3, 59, 74, 250; RGAL 4

Paulin, Thomas Neilson 1949-
See Paulin, Tom
See also CA 123; 128; CANR 98

Paulin, Tom .... **CLC 37, 177**
See Paulin, Thomas Neilson
See also CP 3, 4, 5, 6, 7; DLB 40

Pausanias c. 1st cent. - .... **CMLC 36**

Paustovsky, Konstantin (Georgievich)
1892-1968 .... **CLC 40**
See also CA 93-96; 25-28R; DLB 272; EWL 3

Pavese, Cesare 1908-1950 .... **PC 13; SSC 19; TCLC 3**
See also CA 104; 169; DLB 128, 177; EW 12; EWL 3; PFS 20; RGSF 2; RGWL 2, 3; TWA; WLIT 7

Pavic, Milorad 1929- .... **CLC 60**
See also CA 136; CDWLB 4; CWW 2; DLB 181; EWL 3; RGWL 3

Pavlov, Ivan Petrovich 1849-1936 . **TCLC 91**
See also CA 118; 180

Pavlova, Karolina Karlovna
1807-1893 .... **NCLC 138**
See also DLB 205

Payne, Alan
See Jakes, John (William)

Payne, Rachel Ann
See Jakes, John (William)

Paz, Gil
See Lugones, Leopoldo

Paz, Octavio 1914-1998 . **CLC 3, 4, 6, 10, 19, 51, 65, 119; HLC 2; PC 1, 48; WLC**
See also AAYA 50; CA 73-76; 165; CANR 32, 65, 104; CWW 2; DA; DA3; DAB; DAC; DAM MST, MULT, POET; DLB 290; DLBY 1990, 1998; DNFS 1; EWL 3; HW 1, 2; LAW; LAWS 1; MTCW 1, 2; MTFW 2005; PFS 18; RGWL 2, 3; SSFS 13; TWA; WLIT 1

p'Bitek, Okot 1931-1982 .... **BLC 3; CLC 96; TCLC 149**
See also AFW; BW 2, 3; CA 124; 107; CANR 82; CP 1, 2, 3; DAM MULT; DLB 125; EWL 3; MTCW 1, 2; MTFW 2005; RGEL 2; WLIT 2

Peacham, Henry 1578-1644(?) .... **LC 119**
See also DLB 151

Peacock, Molly 1947- .... **CLC 60**
See also CA 103; CAAS 21; CANR 52, 84; CP 7; CWP; DLB 120, 282

Peacock, Thomas Love
1785-1866 .... **NCLC 22**
See also BRW 4; DLB 96, 116; RGEL 2; RGSF 2

Peake, Mervyn 1911-1968 .... **CLC 7, 54**
See also CA 5-8R; 25-28R; CANR 3; DLB 15, 160, 255; FANT; MTCW 1; RGEL 2; SATA 23; SFW 4

Pearce, Philippa
See Christie, Philippa
See also CA 5-8R; CANR 4, 109; CWRI 5; FANT; MAICYA 2

Pearl, Eric
See Elman, Richard (Martin)

Pearson, T(homas) R(eid) 1956- .... **CLC 39**
See also CA 120; 130; CANR 97; CSW; INT CA-130

Peck, Dale 1967- .... **CLC 81**
See also CA 146; CANR 72, 127; GLL 2

Peck, John (Frederick) 1941- .... **CLC 3**
See also CA 49-52; CANR 3, 100; CP 4, 5, 6, 7

Peck, Richard (Wayne) 1934- .... **CLC 21**
See also AAYA 1, 24; BYA 1, 6, 8, 11; CA 85-88; CANR 19, 38, 129; CLR 15; INT CANR-19; JRDA; MAICYA 1, 2; SAAS 2; SATA 18, 55, 97, 110, 158; SATA-Essay 110; WYA; YAW

Peck, Robert Newton 1928- .... **CLC 17**
See also AAYA 3, 43; BYA 1, 6; CA 81-84, 182; CAAE 182; CANR 31, 63, 127; CLR 45; DA; DAC; DAM MST; JRDA; LAIT 3; MAICYA 1, 2; SAAS 1; SATA 21, 62, 111, 156; SATA-Essay 108; WYA; YAW

Peckinpah, (David) Sam(uel)
1925-1984 .... **CLC 20**
See also CA 109; 114; CANR 82

Pedersen, Knut 1859-1952
See Hamsun, Knut
See also CA 104; 119; CANR 63; MTCW 1, 2

Peele, George 1556-1596 .... **DC 27; LC 115**
See also BRW 1; DLB 62, 167; RGEL 2

Peeslake, Gaffer
See Durrell, Lawrence (George)

Peguy, Charles (Pierre)
1873-1914 .... **TCLC 10**
See also CA 107; 193; DLB 258; EWL 3; GFL 1789 to the Present

Peirce, Charles Sanders
1839-1914 .... **TCLC 81**
See also CA 194; DLB 270

Pellicer, Carlos 1897(?)-1977 .... **HLCS 2**
See also CA 153; 69-72; DLB 290; EWL 3; HW 1

Pena, Ramon del Valle y
See Valle-Inclan, Ramon (Maria) del

Pendennis, Arthur Esquir
See Thackeray, William Makepeace

Penn, Arthur
See Matthews, (James) Brander

Penn, William 1644-1718 .... **LC 25**
See also DLB 24

PEPECE
See Prado (Calvo), Pedro

Pepys, Samuel 1633-1703 ... **LC 11, 58; WLC**
See also BRW 2; CDBLB 1660-1789; DA; DA3; DAB; DAC; DAM MST; DLB 101, 213; NCFS 4; RGEL 2; TEA; WLIT 3

Percy, Thomas 1729-1811 .... **NCLC 95**
See also DLB 104

Percy, Walker 1916-1990 .... **CLC 2, 3, 6, 8, 14, 18, 47, 65**
See also AMWS 3; BPFB 3; CA 1-4R; 131; CANR 1, 23, 64; CN 1, 2, 3, 4; CPW; CSW; DA3; DAM NOV, POP; DLB 2; DLBY 1980, 1990; EWL 3; MAL 5; MTCW 1, 2; MTFW 2005; RGAL 4; TUS

Percy, William Alexander
1885-1942 .... **TCLC 84**
See also CA 163; MTCW 2

Perec, Georges 1936-1982 .... **CLC 56, 116**
See also CA 141; DLB 83, 299; EWL 3; GFL 1789 to the Present; RGWL 2

Pereda (y Sanchez de Porrua), Jose Maria de 1833-1906 .... **TCLC 16**
See also CA 117

Pereda y Porrua, Jose Maria de
See Pereda (y Sanchez de Porrua), Jose Maria de

Peregoy, George Weems
See Mencken, H(enry) L(ouis)

Perelman, S(idney) J(oseph)
1904-1979 .. **CLC 3, 5, 9, 15, 23, 44, 49; SSC 32**
See also AITN 1, 2; BPFB 3; CA 73-76; 89-92; CANR 18; DAM DRAM; DLB 11, 44; MTCW 1, 2; MTFW 2005; RGAL 4

Peret, Benjamin 1899-1959 .... **PC 33; TCLC 20**
See also CA 117; 186; GFL 1789 to the Present

Peretz, Isaac Leib
See Peretz, Isaac Loeb
See also CA 201

Peretz, Isaac Loeb 1851(?)-1915 ...... **SSC 26; TCLC 16**
See Peretz, Isaac Leib
See also CA 109

Peretz, Yitzkhok Leibush
See Peretz, Isaac Loeb

Perez Galdos, Benito 1843-1920 ..... **HLCS 2; TCLC 27**
See Galdos, Benito Perez
See also CA 125; 153; EWL 3; HW 1; RGWL 2, 3

Peri Rossi, Cristina 1941- .. **CLC 156; HLCS 2**
See also CA 131; CANR 59, 81; CWW 2; DLB 145, 290; EWL 3; HW 1, 2

Perlata
See Peret, Benjamin

Perloff, Marjorie G(abrielle)
1931- .... **CLC 137**
See also CA 57-60; CANR 7, 22, 49, 104

Perrault, Charles 1628-1703 .... **LC 2, 56**
See also BYA 4; CLR 79; DLB 268; GFL Beginnings to 1789; MAICYA 1, 2; RGWL 2, 3; SATA 25; WCH

Perry, Anne 1938- .... **CLC 126**
See also CA 101; CANR 22, 50, 84; CMW 4; CN 6, 7; CPW; DLB 276

Perry, Brighton
See Sherwood, Robert E(mmet)

Perse, St.-John
See Leger, (Marie-Rene Auguste) Alexis Saint-Leger

Perse, Saint-John
See Leger, (Marie-Rene Auguste) Alexis Saint-Leger
See also DLB 258; RGWL 3

Persius 34-62 .... **CMLC 74**
See also AW 2; DLB 211; RGWL 2, 3

Perutz, Leo(pold) 1882-1957 .... **TCLC 60**
See also CA 147; DLB 81

Peseenz, Tulio F.
See Lopez y Fuentes, Gregorio

Pesetsky, Bette 1932- .... **CLC 28**
See also CA 133; DLB 130

Peshkov, Alexei Maximovich 1868-1936
See Gorky, Maxim
See also CA 105; 141; CANR 83; DA; DAC; DAM DRAM, MST, NOV; MTCW 2; MTFW 2005

Pessoa, Fernando (Antonio Nogueira)
1888-1935 ..... **HLC 2; PC 20; TCLC 27**
See also CA 125; 183; DAM MULT; DLB 287; EW 10; EWL 3; RGWL 2, 3; WP

Peterkin, Julia Mood 1880-1961 .... **CLC 31**
See also CA 102; DLB 9

Peters, Joan K(aren) 1945- .... **CLC 39**
See also CA 158; CANR 109

Peters, Robert L(ouis) 1924- .... **CLC 7**
See also CA 13-16R; CAAS 8; CP 1, 7; DLB 105

Petofi, Sandor 1823-1849 .... **NCLC 21**
See also RGWL 2, 3

Petrakis, Harry Mark 1923- .... **CLC 3**
See also CA 9-12R; CANR 4, 30, 85; CN 1, 2, 3, 4, 5, 6, 7

Petrarch 1304-1374 .... **CMLC 20; PC 8**
See also DA3; DAM POET; EW 2; LMFS 1; RGWL 2, 3; WLIT 7

Petronius c. 20-66 .... **CMLC 34**
See also AW 2; CDWLB 1; DLB 211; RGWL 2, 3

Petrov, Evgeny .... **TCLC 21**
See Kataev, Evgeny Petrovich

Petry, Ann (Lane) 1908-1997 .. **CLC 1, 7, 18; TCLC 112**
See also AFAW 1, 2; BPFB 3; BW 1, 3; BYA 2; CA 5-8R; 157; CAAS 6; CANR 4, 46; CLR 12; CN 1, 2, 3, 4, 5, 6; DLB 76; EWL 3; JRDA; LAIT 1; MAICYA 1, 2; MAICYAS 1; MTCW 1; RGAL 4; SATA 5; SATA-Obit 94; TUS

Petursson, Halligrimur 1614-1674 .... **LC 8**

Peychinovich
See Vazov, Ivan (Minchov)

Phaedrus c. 15B.C.-c. 50 .... **CMLC 25**
See also DLB 211

Phelps (Ward), Elizabeth Stuart
See Phelps, Elizabeth Stuart
See also FW

Phelps, Elizabeth Stuart
1844-1911 .... **TCLC 113**
See Phelps (Ward), Elizabeth Stuart
See also DLB 74

Philips, Katherine 1632-1664 . **LC 30; PC 40**
See also DLB 131; RGEL 2

Philipson, Morris H. 1926- .... **CLC 53**
See also CA 1-4R; CANR 4

Phillips, Caryl 1958- .... **BLCS; CLC 96**
See also BRWS 5; BW 2; CA 141; CANR 63, 104, 140; CBD; CD 5, 6; CN 5, 6, 7; DA3; DAM MULT; DLB 157; EWL 3; MTCW 2; MTFW 2005; WLIT 4; WWE 1

Phillips, David Graham
1867-1911 .... **TCLC 44**
See also CA 108; 176; DLB 9, 12, 303; RGAL 4

Phillips, Jack
See Sandburg, Carl (August)

Phillips, Jayne Anne 1952- .... **CLC 15, 33, 139; SSC 16**
See also AAYA 57; BPFB 3; CA 101; CANR 24, 50, 96; CN 4, 5, 6, 7; CSW; DLBY 1980; INT CANR-24; MTCW 1, 2; MTFW 2005; RGAL 4; RGSF 2; SSFS 4

Phillips, Richard
See Dick, Philip K(indred)

Phillips, Robert (Schaeffer) 1938- .... **CLC 28**
See also CA 17-20R; CAAS 13; CANR 8; DLB 105

Phillips, Ward
See Lovecraft, H(oward) P(hillips)

Philostratus, Flavius c. 179-c. 244 .... **CMLC 62**

Piccolo, Lucio 1901-1969 .... **CLC 13**
See also CA 97-100; DLB 114; EWL 3

Pickthall, Marjorie L(owry) C(hristie)
1883-1922 .... **TCLC 21**
See also CA 107; DLB 92

Pico della Mirandola, Giovanni
1463-1494 .... **LC 15**
See also LMFS 1

Piercy, Marge 1936- .... **CLC 3, 6, 14, 18, 27, 62, 128; PC 29**
See also BPFB 3; CA 21-24R, 187; CAAE 187; CAAS 1; CANR 13, 43, 66, 111; CN 3, 4, 5, 6, 7; CP 1, 2, 3, 4, 5, 6, 7; CWP; DLB 120, 227; EXPP; FW; MAL 5; MTCW 1, 2; MTFW 2005; PFS 9, 22; SFW 4

Piers, Robert
See Anthony, Piers

Pieyre de Mandiargues, Andre 1909-1991
See Mandiargues, Andre Pieyre de
See also CA 103; 136; CANR 22, 82; EWL 3; GFL 1789 to the Present

Pilnyak, Boris 1894-1938 . **SSC 48; TCLC 23**
See Vogau, Boris Andreyevich
See also EWL 3

Pinchback, Eugene
See Toomer, Jean

Pincherle, Alberto 1907-1990 ...... **CLC 11, 18**
See Moravia, Alberto
See also CA 25-28R; 132; CANR 33, 63, 142; DAM NOV; MTCW 1; MTFW 2005

Pinckney, Darryl 1953- .... **CLC 76**
See also BW 2, 3; CA 143; CANR 79

Pindar 518(?)B.C.-438(?)B.C. .... **CMLC 12; PC 19**
See also AW 1; CDWLB 1; DLB 176; RGWL 2

Pineda, Cecile 1942- .... **CLC 39**
See also CA 118; DLB 209

Pinero, Arthur Wing 1855-1934 .... **TCLC 32**
See also CA 110; 153; DAM DRAM; DLB 10; RGEL 2

Pinero, Miguel (Antonio Gomez) 1946-1988 .... **CLC 4, 55**
See also CA 61-64; 125; CAD; CANR 29, 90; DLB 266; HW 1; LLW

Pinget, Robert 1919-1997 .... **CLC 7, 13, 37**
See also CA 85-88; 160; CWW 2; DLB 83; EWL 3; GFL 1789 to the Present

Pink Floyd
See Barrett, (Roger) Syd; Gilmour, David; Mason, Nick; Waters, Roger; Wright, Rick

Pinkney, Edward 1802-1828 .... **NCLC 31**
See also DLB 248

Pinkwater, D. Manus
See Pinkwater, Daniel Manus

Pinkwater, Daniel
See Pinkwater, Daniel Manus

Pinkwater, Daniel M.
See Pinkwater, Daniel Manus

Pinkwater, Daniel Manus 1941- .... **CLC 35**
See also AAYA 1, 46; BYA 9; CA 29-32R; CANR 12, 38, 89, 143; CLR 4; CSW; FANT; JRDA; MAICYA 1, 2; SAAS 3; SATA 8, 46, 76, 114, 158; SFW 4; YAW

Pinkwater, Manus
See Pinkwater, Daniel Manus

Pinsky, Robert 1940- .... **CLC 9, 19, 38, 94, 121, 216; PC 27**
See also AMWS 6; CA 29-32R; CAAS 4; CANR 58, 97, 138; CP 3, 4, 5, 6, 7; DA3; DAM POET; DLBY 1982, 1998; MAL 5; MTCW 2; MTFW 2005; PFS 18; RGAL 4; TCLE 1:2

Pinta, Harold
See Pinter, Harold

Pinter, Harold 1930- .. **CLC 1, 3, 6, 9, 11, 15, 27, 58, 73, 199; DC 15; WLC**
See also BRWR 1; BRWS 1; CA 5-8R; CANR 33, 65, 112, 145; CBD; CD 5, 6; CDBLB 1960 to Present; CP 1; DA; DA3; DAB; DAC; DAM DRAM, MST; DFS 3, 5, 7, 14; DLB 13, 310; EWL 3; IDFW 3, 4; LMFS 2; MTCW 1, 2; MTFW 2005; RGEL 2; TEA

Piozzi, Hester Lynch (Thrale) 1741-1821 .... **NCLC 57**
See also DLB 104, 142

Pirandello, Luigi 1867-1936 .. **DC 5; SSC 22; TCLC 4, 29, 172; WLC**
See also CA 104; 153; CANR 103; DA; DA3; DAB; DAC; DAM DRAM, MST; DFS 4, 9; DLB 264; EW 8; EWL 3; MTCW 2; MTFW 2005; RGSF 2; RGWL 2, 3; WLIT 7

Pirsig, Robert M(aynard) 1928- ... **CLC 4, 6, 73**
See also CA 53-56; CANR 42, 74; CPW 1; DA3; DAM POP; MTCW 1, 2; MTFW 2005; SATA 39

Pisarev, Dmitrii Ivanovich
See Pisarev, Dmitry Ivanovich
See also DLB 277

Pisarev, Dmitry Ivanovich 1840-1868 .... **NCLC 25**
See Pisarev, Dmitrii Ivanovich

Pix, Mary (Griffith) 1666-1709 .... **LC 8**
See also DLB 80

Pixerecourt, (Rene Charles) Guilbert de 1773-1844 .... **NCLC 39**
See also DLB 192; GFL 1789 to the Present

Plaatje, Sol(omon) T(shekisho) 1878-1932 .... **BLCS; TCLC 73**
See also BW 2, 3; CA 141; CANR 79; DLB 125, 225

Plaidy, Jean
See Hibbert, Eleanor Alice Burford

Planche, James Robinson 1796-1880 .... **NCLC 42**
See also RGEL 2

Plant, Robert 1948- .... **CLC 12**

Plante, David (Robert) 1940- . **CLC 7, 23, 38**
See also CA 37-40R; CANR 12, 36, 58, 82; CN 2, 3, 4, 5, 6, 7; DAM NOV; DLBY 1983; INT CANR-12; MTCW 1

Plath, Sylvia 1932-1963 ..... **CLC 1, 2, 3, 5, 9, 11, 14, 17, 50, 51, 62, 111; PC 1, 37; WLC**
See also AAYA 13; AMWR 2; AMWS 1; BPFB 3; CA 19-20; CANR 34, 101; CAP 2; CDALB 1941-1968; DA; DA3; DAB; DAC; DAM MST, POET; DLB 5, 6, 152; EWL 3; EXPN; EXPP; FL 1:6; FW; LAIT 4; MAL 5; MAWW; MTCW 1, 2; MTFW 2005; NFS 1; PAB; PFS 1, 15; RGAL 4; SATA 96; TUS; WP; YAW

Plato c. 428B.C.-347B.C. .... **CMLC 8, 75; WLCS**
See also AW 1; CDWLB 1; DA; DA3; DAB; DAC; DAM MST; DLB 176; LAIT 1; LATS 1:1; RGWL 2, 3

Platonov, Andrei
See Klimentov, Andrei Platonovich

Platonov, Andrei Platonovich
See Klimentov, Andrei Platonovich
See also DLB 272

Platonov, Andrey Platonovich
See Klimentov, Andrei Platonovich
See also EWL 3

Platt, Kin 1911- .... **CLC 26**
See also AAYA 11; CA 17-20R; CANR 11; JRDA; SAAS 17; SATA 21, 86; WYA

Plautus c. 254B.C.-c. 184B.C. .... **CMLC 24; DC 6**
See also AW 1; CDWLB 1; DLB 211; RGWL 2, 3

Plick et Plock
See Simenon, Georges (Jacques Christian)

Plieksans, Janis
See Rainis, Janis

Plimpton, George (Ames) 1927-2003 .... **CLC 36**
See also AITN 1; CA 21-24R; 224; CANR 32, 70, 103, 133; DLB 185, 241; MTCW 1, 2; MTFW 2005; SATA 10; SATA-Obit 150

Pliny the Elder c. 23-79 .... **CMLC 23**
See also DLB 211

Pliny the Younger c. 61-c. 112 .... **CMLC 62**
See also AW 2; DLB 211

Plomer, William Charles Franklin 1903-1973 .... **CLC 4, 8**
See also AFW; BRWS 11; CA 21-22; CANR 34; CAP 2; CN 1; CP 1, 2; DLB 20, 162, 191, 225; EWL 3; MTCW 1; RGEL 2; RGSF 2; SATA 24

Plotinus 204-270 .... **CMLC 46**
See also CDWLB 1; DLB 176

Plowman, Piers
See Kavanagh, Patrick (Joseph)

Plum, J.
See Wodehouse, P(elham) G(renville)

Plumly, Stanley (Ross) 1939- .... **CLC 33**
See also CA 108; 110; CANR 97; CP 3, 4, 5, 6, 7; DLB 5, 193; INT CA-110

Plumpe, Friedrich Wilhelm 1888-1931 .... **TCLC 53**
See also CA 112

Plutarch c. 46-c. 120 .... **CMLC 60**
See also AW 2; CDWLB 1; DLB 176; RGWL 2, 3; TWA

Po Chu-i 772-846 .... **CMLC 24**

Podhoretz, Norman 1930- .... **CLC 189**
See also AMWS 8; CA 9-12R; CANR 7, 78, 135

Poe, Edgar Allan 1809-1849 ..... **NCLC 1, 16, 55, 78, 94, 97, 117; PC 1, 54; SSC 1, 22, 34, 35, 54, 88; WLC**
See also AAYA 14; AMW; AMWC 1; AMWR 2; BPFB 3; BYA 5, 11; CDALB 1640-1865; CMW 4; DA; DA3; DAB; DAC; DAM MST, POET; DLB 3, 59, 73, 74, 248, 254; EXPP; EXPS; GL 3; HGG; LAIT 2; LATS 1:1; LMFS 1; MSW; PAB; PFS 1, 3, 9; RGAL 4; RGSF 2; SATA 23; SCFW 1, 2; SFW 4; SSFS 2, 4, 7, 8, 16; SUFW; TUS; WP; WYA

Poet of Titchfield Street, The
See Pound, Ezra (Weston Loomis)

Poggio Bracciolini, Gian Francesco 1380-1459 .... **LC 125**

Pohl, Frederik 1919- .... **CLC 18; SSC 25**
See also AAYA 24; CA 61-64, 188; CAAE 188; CAAS 1; CANR 11, 37, 81, 140; CN 1, 2, 3, 4, 5, 6; DLB 8; INT CANR-11; MTCW 1; MTFW 2005; SATA 24; SCFW 1, 2; SFW 4

Poirier, Louis 1910-
See Gracq, Julien
See also CA 122; 126; CANR 141

Poitier, Sidney 1927- .... **CLC 26**
See also AAYA 60; BW 1; CA 117; CANR 94

Pokagon, Simon 1830-1899 .... **NNAL**
See also DAM MULT

Polanski, Roman 1933- .... **CLC 16, 178**
See also CA 77-80

Poliakoff, Stephen 1952- .... **CLC 38**
See also CA 106; CANR 116; CBD; CD 5, 6; DLB 13

Police, The
See Copeland, Stewart (Armstrong); Summers, Andrew James

Polidori, John William 1795-1821 . **NCLC 51**
See also DLB 116; HGG

Poliziano, Angelo 1454-1494 .... **LC 120**
See also WLIT 7

Pollitt, Katha 1949- .... **CLC 28, 122**
See also CA 120; 122; CANR 66, 108; MTCW 1, 2; MTFW 2005

Pollock, (Mary) Sharon 1936- .... **CLC 50**
See also CA 141; CANR 132; CD 5; CWD; DAC; DAM DRAM, MST; DFS 3; DLB 60; FW

Pollock, Sharon 1936- .... **DC 20**
See also CD 6

Polo, Marco 1254-1324 .... **CMLC 15**
See also WLIT 7

Polonsky, Abraham (Lincoln) 1910-1999 .... **CLC 92**
See also CA 104; 187; DLB 26; INT CA-104

Polybius c. 200B.C.-c. 118B.C. .... **CMLC 17**
See also AW 1; DLB 176; RGWL 2, 3

Pomerance, Bernard 1940- .... **CLC 13**
See also CA 101; CAD; CANR 49, 134; CD 5, 6; DAM DRAM; DFS 9; LAIT 2

Ponge, Francis 1899-1988 .... **CLC 6, 18**
See also CA 85-88; 126; CANR 40, 86; DAM POET; DLBY 2002; EWL 3; GFL 1789 to the Present; RGWL 2, 3

Poniatowska, Elena 1933- .... **CLC 140; HLC 2**
See also CA 101; CANR 32, 66, 107; CD-WLB 3; CWW 2; DAM MULT; DLB 113; EWL 3; HW 1, 2; LAWS 1; WLIT 1

Pontoppidan, Henrik 1857-1943 .... **TCLC 29**
See also CA 170; DLB 300

Ponty, Maurice Merleau
See Merleau-Ponty, Maurice

Poole, Josephine .... **CLC 17**
See Helyar, Jane Penelope Josephine
See also SAAS 2; SATA 5

Popa, Vasko 1922-1991 . **CLC 19; TCLC 167**
See also CA 112; 148; CDWLB 4; DLB 181; EWL 3; RGWL 2, 3

Pope, Alexander 1688-1744 ...... **LC 3, 58, 60, 64; PC 26; WLC**
See also BRW 3; BRWC 1; BRWR 1; CD-BLB 1660-1789; DA; DA3; DAB; DAC; DAM MST, POET; DLB 95, 101, 213; EXPP; PAB; PFS 12; RGEL 2; WLIT 3; WP

Popov, Evgenii Anatol'evich
See Popov, Yevgeny
See also DLB 285

Popov, Yevgeny .... **CLC 59**
See Popov, Evgenii Anatol'evich

Poquelin, Jean-Baptiste
See Moliere

Porete, Marguerite (?)-1310 .... **CMLC 73**
See also DLB 208

Porphyry c. 233-c. 305 .... **CMLC 71**

Porter, Connie (Rose) 1959(?)- .... **CLC 70**
See also AAYA 65; BW 2, 3; CA 142; CANR 90, 109; SATA 81, 129

Porter, Gene(va Grace) Stratton .. **TCLC 21**
See Stratton-Porter, Gene(va Grace)
See also BPFB 3; CA 112; CWRI 5; RHW

Porter, Katherine Anne 1890-1980 ... **CLC 1, 3, 7, 10, 13, 15, 27, 101; SSC 4, 31, 43**
See also AAYA 42; AITN 2; AMW; BPFB 3; CA 1-4R; 101; CANR 1, 65; CDALBS; CN 1, 2; DA; DA3; DAB; DAC; DAM MST, NOV; DLB 4, 9, 102; DLBD 12; DLBY 1980; EWL 3; EXPS; LAIT 3; MAL 5; MAWW; MTCW 1, 2; MTFW 2005; NFS 14; RGAL 4; RGSF 2; SATA 39; SATA-Obit 23; SSFS 1, 8, 11, 16; TCWW 2; TUS

Porter, Peter (Neville Frederick) 1929- .... **CLC 5, 13, 33**
See also CA 85-88; CP 1, 2, 3, 4, 5, 6, 7; DLB 40, 289; WWE 1

Porter, William Sydney 1862-1910
See Henry, O.
See also CA 104; 131; CDALB 1865-1917; DA; DA3; DAB; DAC; DAM MST; DLB 12, 78, 79; MAL 5; MTCW 1, 2; MTFW 2005; TUS; YABC 2

Portillo (y Pacheco), Jose Lopez
See Lopez Portillo (y Pacheco), Jose

Portillo Trambley, Estela 1927-1998 .. **HLC 2**
See Trambley, Estela Portillo
See also CANR 32; DAM MULT; DLB 209; HW 1

Posey, Alexander (Lawrence) 1873-1908 .... **NNAL**
See also CA 144; CANR 80; DAM MULT; DLB 175

Posse, Abel .... **CLC 70**

Post, Melville Davisson 1869-1930 .... **TCLC 39**
See also CA 110; 202; CMW 4

Potok, Chaim 1929-2002 ... **CLC 2, 7, 14, 26, 112**
See also AAYA 15, 50; AITN 1, 2; BPFB 3; BYA 1; CA 17-20R; 208; CANR 19, 35, 64, 98; CLR 92; CN 4, 5, 6; DA3; DAM NOV; DLB 28, 152; EXPN; INT CANR-19; LAIT 4; MTCW 1, 2; MTFW 2005; NFS 4; SATA 33, 106; SATA-Obit 134; TUS; YAW

Potok, Herbert Harold -2002
See Potok, Chaim

Potok, Herman Harold
See Potok, Chaim

Potter, Dennis (Christopher George) 1935-1994 .... **CLC 58, 86, 123**
See also BRWS 10; CA 107; 145; CANR 33, 61; CBD; DLB 233; MTCW 1

Pound, Ezra (Weston Loomis) 1885-1972 .. **CLC 1, 2, 3, 4, 5, 7, 10, 13, 18, 34, 48, 50, 112; PC 4; WLC**
See also AAYA 47; AMW; AMWR 1; CA 5-8R; 37-40R; CANR 40; CDALB 1917-1929; CP 1; DA; DA3; DAB; DAC; DAM MST, POET; DLB 4, 45, 63; DLBD 15; EFS 2; EWL 3; EXPP; LMFS 2; MAL 5; MTCW 1, 2; MTFW 2005; PAB; PFS 2, 8, 16; RGAL 4; TUS; WP

Povod, Reinaldo 1959-1994 .... **CLC 44**
See also CA 136; 146; CANR 83

Powell, Adam Clayton, Jr. 1908-1972 .... **BLC 3; CLC 89**
See also BW 1, 3; CA 102; 33-36R; CANR 86; DAM MULT

Powell, Anthony (Dymoke) 1905-2000 .... **CLC 1, 3, 7, 9, 10, 31**
See also BRW 7; CA 1-4R; 189; CANR 1, 32, 62, 107; CDBLB 1945-1960; CN 1, 2, 3, 4, 5, 6; DLB 15; EWL 3; MTCW 1, 2; MTFW 2005; RGEL 2; TEA

Powell, Dawn 1896(?)-1965 .... **CLC 66**
See also CA 5-8R; CANR 121; DLBY 1997

Powell, Padgett 1952- .... **CLC 34**
See also CA 126; CANR 63, 101; CSW; DLB 234; DLBY 01

Powell, (Oval) Talmage 1920-2000
See Queen, Ellery
See also CA 5-8R; CANR 2, 80

Power, Susan 1961- .... **CLC 91**
See also BYA 14; CA 160; CANR 135; NFS 11

Powers, J(ames) F(arl) 1917-1999 ..... **CLC 1, 4, 8, 57; SSC 4**
See also CA 1-4R; 181; CANR 2, 61; CN 1, 2, 3, 4, 5, 6; DLB 130; MTCW 1; RGAL 4; RGSF 2

Powers, John J(ames) 1945-
See Powers, John R.
See also CA 69-72

Powers, John R. .... **CLC 66**
See Powers, John J(ames)

Powers, Richard (S.) 1957- .... **CLC 93**
See also AMWS 9; BPFB 3; CA 148; CANR 80; CN 6, 7; MTFW 2005; TCLE 1:2

Pownall, David 1938- .... **CLC 10**
See also CA 89-92; 180; CAAS 18; CANR 49, 101; CBD; CD 5, 6; CN 4, 5, 6, 7; DLB 14

Powys, John Cowper 1872-1963 ... **CLC 7, 9, 15, 46, 125**
See also CA 85-88; CANR 106; DLB 15, 255; EWL 3; FANT; MTCW 1, 2; MTFW 2005; RGEL 2; SUFW

Powys, T(heodore) F(rancis) 1875-1953 .... **TCLC 9**
See also BRWS 8; CA 106; 189; DLB 36, 162; EWL 3; FANT; RGEL 2; SUFW

Pozzo, Modesta
See Fonte, Moderata

Prado (Calvo), Pedro 1886-1952 ... **TCLC 75**
See also CA 131; DLB 283; HW 1; LAW

Prager, Emily 1952- .... **CLC 56**
See also CA 204

Pratchett, Terry 1948- .... **CLC 197**
See also AAYA 19, 54; BPFB 3; CA 143; CANR 87, 126; CLR 64; CN 6, 7; CPW; CWRI 5; FANT; MTFW 2005; SATA 82, 139; SFW 4; SUFW 2

Pratolini, Vasco 1913-1991 .... **TCLC 124**
See also CA 211; DLB 177; EWL 3; RGWL 2, 3

Pratt, E(dwin) J(ohn) 1883(?)-1964 . **CLC 19**
See also CA 141; 93-96; CANR 77; DAC; DAM POET; DLB 92; EWL 3; RGEL 2; TWA

Premchand .... **TCLC 21**
See Srivastava, Dhanpat Rai
See also EWL 3

Prescott, William Hickling 1796-1859 .... **NCLC 163**
See also DLB 1, 30, 59, 235

Preseren, France 1800-1849 .... **NCLC 127**
See also CDWLB 4; DLB 147

Preussler, Otfried 1923- .... **CLC 17**
See also CA 77-80; SATA 24

Prevert, Jacques (Henri Marie) 1900-1977 .... **CLC 15**
See also CA 77-80; 69-72; CANR 29, 61; DLB 258; EWL 3; GFL 1789 to the Present; IDFW 3, 4; MTCW 1; RGWL 2, 3; SATA-Obit 30

Prevost, (Antoine Francois) 1697-1763 .... **LC 1**
See also DLB 314; EW 4; GFL Beginnings to 1789; RGWL 2, 3

Price, (Edward) Reynolds 1933- ... **CLC 3, 6, 13, 43, 50, 63, 212; SSC 22**
See also AMWS 6; CA 1-4R; CANR 1, 37, 57, 87, 128; CN 1, 2, 3, 4, 5, 6, 7; CSW; DAM NOV; DLB 2, 218, 278; EWL 3; INT CANR-37; MAL 5; MTCW 2; MTFW 2005; NFS 18

Price, Richard 1949- .... **CLC 6, 12**
See also CA 49-52; CANR 3; CN 7; DLBY 1981

Prichard, Katharine Susannah 1883-1969 .... **CLC 46**
See also CA 11-12; CANR 33; CAP 1; DLB 260; MTCW 1; RGEL 2; RGSF 2; SATA 66

Priestley, J(ohn) B(oynton) 1894-1984 .... **CLC 2, 5, 9, 34**
See also BRW 7; CA 9-12R; 113; CANR 33; CDBLB 1914-1945; CN 1, 2, 3; DA3; DAM DRAM, NOV; DLB 10, 34, 77, 100, 139; DLBY 1984; EWL 3; MTCW 1, 2; MTFW 2005; RGEL 2; SFW 4

Prince 1958- .... **CLC 35**
See also CA 213

Prince, F(rank) T(empleton) 1912-2003 .... **CLC 22**
See also CA 101; 219; CANR 43, 79; CP 1, 2, 3, 4, 5, 6, 7; DLB 20

Prince Kropotkin
See Kropotkin, Peter (Alekseievich)

Prior, Matthew 1664-1721 .... **LC 4**
See also DLB 95; RGEL 2

Prishvin, Mikhail 1873-1954 .... **TCLC 75**
See Prishvin, Mikhail Mikhailovich

Prishvin, Mikhail Mikhailovich
See Prishvin, Mikhail
See also DLB 272; EWL 3

Pritchard, William H(arrison) 1932- .... **CLC 34**
See also CA 65-68; CANR 23, 95; DLB 111

Pritchett, V(ictor) S(awdon) 1900-1997 ... **CLC 5, 13, 15, 41; SSC 14**
See also BPFB 3; BRWS 3; CA 61-64; 157; CANR 31, 63; CN 1, 2, 3, 4, 5, 6; DA3; DAM NOV; DLB 15, 139; EWL 3; MTCW 1, 2; MTFW 2005; RGEL 2; RGSF 2; TEA

Private 19022
See Manning, Frederic
Probst, Mark 1925- .... **CLC 59**
See also CA 130
Procaccino, Michael
See Cristofer, Michael
Proclus c. 412-485 .... **CMLC 81**
Prokosch, Frederic 1908-1989 ...... **CLC 4, 48**
See also CA 73-76; 128; CANR 82; CN 1, 2, 3, 4; CP 1, 2, 3, 4; DLB 48; MTCW 2
Propertius, Sextus c. 50B.C.-c. 16B.C. .... **CMLC 32**
See also AW 2; CDWLB 1; DLB 211; RGWL 2, 3
Prophet, The
See Dreiser, Theodore (Herman Albert)
Prose, Francine 1947- .... **CLC 45**
See also CA 109; 112; CANR 46, 95, 132; DLB 234; MTFW 2005; SATA 101, 149
Proudhon
See Cunha, Euclides (Rodrigues Pimenta) da
Proulx, Annie
See Proulx, E. Annie
Proulx, E. Annie 1935- .... **CLC 81, 158**
See also AMWS 7; BPFB 3; CA 145; CANR 65, 110; CN 6, 7; CPW 1; DA3; DAM POP; MAL 5; MTCW 2; MTFW 2005; SSFS 18
Proulx, Edna Annie
See Proulx, E. Annie
Proust, (Valentin-Louis-George-Eugene) Marcel 1871-1922 ..... **SSC 75; TCLC 7, 13, 33; WLC**
See also AAYA 58; BPFB 3; CA 104; 120; CANR 110; DA; DA3; DAB; DAC; DAM MST, NOV; DLB 65; EW 8; EWL 3; GFL 1789 to the Present; MTCW 1, 2; MTFW 2005; RGWL 2, 3; TWA
Prowler, Harley
See Masters, Edgar Lee
Prudentius, Aurelius Clemens 348-c. 405 .... **CMLC 78**
See also EW 1; RGWL 2, 3
Prus, Boleslaw 1845-1912 .... **TCLC 48**
See also RGWL 2, 3
Pryor, Richard (Franklin Lenox Thomas) 1940-2005 .... **CLC 26**
See also CA 122; 152
Przybyszewski, Stanislaw 1868-1927 .... **TCLC 36**
See also CA 160; DLB 66; EWL 3
Pteleon
See Grieve, C(hristopher) M(urray)
See also DAM POET
Puckett, Lute
See Masters, Edgar Lee
Puig, Manuel 1932-1990 .... **CLC 3, 5, 10, 28, 65, 133; HLC 2**
See also BPFB 3; CA 45-48; CANR 2, 32, 63; CDWLB 3; DA3; DAM MULT; DLB 113; DNFS 1; EWL 3; GLL 1; HW 1, 2; LAW; MTCW 1, 2; MTFW 2005; RGWL 2, 3; TWA; WLIT 1
Pulitzer, Joseph 1847-1911 .... **TCLC 76**
See also CA 114; DLB 23
Purchas, Samuel 1577(?)-1626 .... **LC 70**
See also DLB 151
Purdy, A(lfred) W(ellington) 1918-2000 .... **CLC 3, 6, 14, 50**
See also CA 81-84; 189; CAAS 17; CANR 42, 66; CP 1, 2, 3, 4, 5, 6, 7; DAC; DAM MST, POET; DLB 88; PFS 5; RGEL 2
Purdy, James (Amos) 1923- .... **CLC 2, 4, 10, 28, 52**
See also AMWS 7; CA 33-36R; CAAS 1; CANR 19, 51, 132; CN 1, 2, 3, 4, 5, 6, 7; DLB 2, 218; EWL 3; INT CANR-19; MAL 5; MTCW 1; RGAL 4

Pure, Simon
See Swinnerton, Frank Arthur
Pushkin, Aleksandr Sergeevich
See Pushkin, Alexander (Sergeyevich)
See also DLB 205
Pushkin, Alexander (Sergeyevich) 1799-1837 .... **NCLC 3, 27, 83; PC 10; SSC 27, 55; WLC**
See Pushkin, Aleksandr Sergeevich
See also DA; DA3; DAB; DAC; DAM DRAM, MST, POET; EW 5; EXPS; RGSF 2; RGWL 2, 3; SATA 61; SSFS 9; TWA
P'u Sung-ling 1640-1715 .... **LC 49; SSC 31**
Putnam, Arthur Lee
See Alger, Horatio, Jr.
Puttenham, George 1529(?)-1590 .... **LC 116**
See also DLB 281
Puzo, Mario 1920-1999 .... **CLC 1, 2, 6, 36, 107**
See also BPFB 3; CA 65-68; 185; CANR 4, 42, 65, 99, 131; CN 1, 2, 3, 4, 5, 6; CPW; DA3; DAM NOV, POP; DLB 6; MTCW 1, 2; MTFW 2005; NFS 16; RGAL 4
Pygge, Edward
See Barnes, Julian (Patrick)
Pyle, Ernest Taylor 1900-1945
See Pyle, Ernie
See also CA 115; 160
Pyle, Ernie .... **TCLC 75**
See Pyle, Ernest Taylor
See also DLB 29; MTCW 2
Pyle, Howard 1853-1911 .... **TCLC 81**
See also AAYA 57; BYA 2, 4; CA 109; 137; CLR 22; DLB 42, 188; DLBD 13; LAIT 1; MAICYA 1, 2; SATA 16, 100; WCH; YAW
Pym, Barbara (Mary Crampton) 1913-1980 .... **CLC 13, 19, 37, 111**
See also BPFB 3; BRWS 2; CA 13-14; 97-100; CANR 13, 34; CAP 1; DLB 14, 207; DLBY 1987; EWL 3; MTCW 1, 2; MTFW 2005; RGEL 2; TEA
Pynchon, Thomas (Ruggles, Jr.) 1937- .... **CLC 2, 3, 6, 9, 11, 18, 33, 62, 72, 123, 192, 213; SSC 14, 84; WLC**
See also AMWS 2; BEST 90:2; BPFB 3; CA 17-20R; CANR 22, 46, 73, 142; CN 1, 2, 3, 4, 5, 6, 7; CPW 1; DA; DA3; DAB; DAC; DAM MST, NOV, POP; DLB 2, 173; EWL 3; MAL 5; MTCW 1, 2; MTFW 2005; RGAL 4; SFW 4; TCLE 1:2; TUS
Pythagoras c. 582B.C.-c. 507B.C. . **CMLC 22**
See also DLB 176
Q
See Quiller-Couch, Sir Arthur (Thomas)
Qian, Chongzhu
See Ch'ien, Chung-shu
Qian, Sima 145B.C.-c. 89B.C. .... **CMLC 72**
Qian Zhongshu
See Ch'ien, Chung-shu
See also CWW 2
Qroll
See Dagerman, Stig (Halvard)
Quarles, Francis 1592-1644 .... **LC 117**
See also DLB 126; RGEL 2
Quarrington, Paul (Lewis) 1953- ..... **CLC 65**
See also CA 129; CANR 62, 95
Quasimodo, Salvatore 1901-1968 .... **CLC 10; PC 47**
See also CA 13-16; 25-28R; CAP 1; DLB 114; EW 12; EWL 3; MTCW 1; RGWL 2, 3
Quatermass, Martin
See Carpenter, John (Howard)
Quay, Stephen 1947- .... **CLC 95**
See also CA 189
Quay, Timothy 1947- .... **CLC 95**
See also CA 189

Queen, Ellery .... **CLC 3, 11**
See Dannay, Frederic; Davidson, Avram (James); Deming, Richard; Fairman, Paul W.; Flora, Fletcher; Hoch, Edward D(entinger); Kane, Henry; Lee, Manfred B(ennington); Marlowe, Stephen; Powell, (Oval) Talmage; Sheldon, Walter J(ames); Sturgeon, Theodore (Hamilton); Tracy, Don(ald Fiske); Vance, John Holbrook
See also BPFB 3; CMW 4; MSW; RGAL 4
Queen, Ellery, Jr.
See Dannay, Frederic; Lee, Manfred B(ennington)
Queneau, Raymond 1903-1976 ..... **CLC 2, 5, 10, 42**
See also CA 77-80; 69-72; CANR 32; DLB 72, 258; EW 12; EWL 3; GFL 1789 to the Present; MTCW 1, 2; RGWL 2, 3
Quevedo, Francisco de 1580-1645 .... **LC 23**
Quiller-Couch, Sir Arthur (Thomas) 1863-1944 .... **TCLC 53**
See also CA 118; 166; DLB 135, 153, 190; HGG; RGEL 2; SUFW 1
Quin, Ann (Marie) 1936-1973 .... **CLC 6**
See also CA 9-12R; 45-48; CN 1; DLB 14, 231
Quincey, Thomas de
See De Quincey, Thomas
Quindlen, Anna 1953- .... **CLC 191**
See also AAYA 35; CA 138; CANR 73, 126; DA3; DLB 292; MTCW 2; MTFW 2005
Quinn, Martin
See Smith, Martin Cruz
Quinn, Peter 1947- .... **CLC 91**
See also CA 197
Quinn, Simon
See Smith, Martin Cruz
Quintana, Leroy V. 1944- ...... **HLC 2; PC 36**
See also CA 131; CANR 65, 139; DAM MULT; DLB 82; HW 1, 2
Quintilian c. 40-c. 100 .... **CMLC 77**
See also AW 2; DLB 211; RGWL 2, 3
Quintillian 0035-0100 .... **CMLC 77**
Quiroga, Horacio (Sylvestre) 1878-1937 ... **HLC 2; SSC 89; TCLC 20**
See also CA 117; 131; DAM MULT; EWL 3; HW 1; LAW; MTCW 1; RGSF 2; WLIT 1
Quoirez, Francoise 1935-2004 .... **CLC 9**
See Sagan, Francoise
See also CA 49-52; 231; CANR 6, 39, 73; MTCW 1, 2; MTFW 2005; TWA
Raabe, Wilhelm (Karl) 1831-1910 . **TCLC 45**
See also CA 167; DLB 129
Rabe, David (William) 1940- .. **CLC 4, 8, 33, 200; DC 16**
See also CA 85-88; CABS 3; CAD; CANR 59, 129; CD 5, 6; DAM DRAM; DFS 3, 8, 13; DLB 7, 228; EWL 3; MAL 5
Rabelais, Francois 1494-1553 .... **LC 5, 60; WLC**
See also DA; DAB; DAC; DAM MST; EW 2; GFL Beginnings to 1789; LMFS 1; RGWL 2, 3; TWA
Rabinovitch, Sholem 1859-1916
See Aleichem, Sholom
See also CA 104
Rabinyan, Dorit 1972- .... **CLC 119**
See also CA 170
Rachilde
See Vallette, Marguerite Eymery; Vallette, Marguerite Eymery
See also EWL 3
Racine, Jean 1639-1699 .... **LC 28, 113**
See also DA3; DAB; DAM MST; DLB 268; EW 3; GFL Beginnings to 1789; LMFS 1; RGWL 2, 3; TWA

Radcliffe, Ann (Ward) 1764-1823 ... **NCLC 6, 55, 106**
See also DLB 39, 178; GL 3; HGG; LMFS 1; RGEL 2; SUFW; WLIT 3

Radclyffe-Hall, Marguerite
See Hall, (Marguerite) Radclyffe

Radiguet, Raymond 1903-1923 ...... **TCLC 29**
See also CA 162; DLB 65; EWL 3; GFL 1789 to the Present; RGWL 2, 3

Radnoti, Miklos 1909-1944 .... **TCLC 16**
See also CA 118; 212; CDWLB 4; DLB 215; EWL 3; RGWL 2, 3

Rado, James 1939- .... **CLC 17**
See also CA 105

Radvanyi, Netty 1900-1983
See Seghers, Anna
See also CA 85-88; 110; CANR 82

Rae, Ben
See Griffiths, Trevor

Raeburn, John (Hay) 1941- .... **CLC 34**
See also CA 57-60

Ragni, Gerome 1942-1991 .... **CLC 17**
See also CA 105; 134

Rahv, Philip .... **CLC 24**
See Greenberg, Ivan
See also DLB 137; MAL 5

Raimund, Ferdinand Jakob 1790-1836 .... **NCLC 69**
See also DLB 90

Raine, Craig (Anthony) 1944- .. **CLC 32, 103**
See also CA 108; CANR 29, 51, 103; CP 3, 4, 5, 6, 7; DLB 40; PFS 7

Raine, Kathleen (Jessie) 1908-2003 .. **CLC 7, 45**
See also CA 85-88; 218; CANR 46, 109; CP 1, 2, 3, 4, 5, 6, 7; DLB 20; EWL 3; MTCW 1; RGEL 2

Rainis, Janis 1865-1929 .... **TCLC 29**
See also CA 170; CDWLB 4; DLB 220; EWL 3

Rakosi, Carl .... **CLC 47**
See Rawley, Callman
See also CA 228; CAAS 5; CP 1, 2, 3, 4, 5, 6, 7; DLB 193

Ralegh, Sir Walter
See Raleigh, Sir Walter
See also BRW 1; RGEL 2; WP

Raleigh, Richard
See Lovecraft, H(oward) P(hillips)

Raleigh, Sir Walter 1554(?)-1618 .... **LC 31, 39; PC 31**
See Ralegh, Sir Walter
See also CDBLB Before 1660; DLB 172; EXPP; PFS 14; TEA

Rallentando, H. P.
See Sayers, Dorothy L(eigh)

Ramal, Walter
See de la Mare, Walter (John)

Ramana Maharshi 1879-1950 .... **TCLC 84**

Ramoacn y Cajal, Santiago 1852-1934 .... **TCLC 93**

Ramon, Juan
See Jimenez (Mantecon), Juan Ramon

Ramos, Graciliano 1892-1953 .... **TCLC 32**
See also CA 167; DLB 307; EWL 3; HW 2; LAW; WLIT 1

Rampersad, Arnold 1941- .... **CLC 44**
See also BW 2, 3; CA 127; 133; CANR 81; DLB 111; INT CA-133

Rampling, Anne
See Rice, Anne
See also GLL 2

Ramsay, Allan 1686(?)-1758 .... **LC 29**
See also DLB 95; RGEL 2

Ramsay, Jay
See Campbell, (John) Ramsey

Ramuz, Charles-Ferdinand 1878-1947 .... **TCLC 33**
See also CA 165; EWL 3

Rand, Ayn 1905-1982 ...... **CLC 3, 30, 44, 79; WLC**
See also AAYA 10; AMWS 4; BPFB 3; BYA 12; CA 13-16R; 105; CANR 27, 73; CDALBS; CN 1, 2, 3; CPW; DA; DA3; DAC; DAM MST, NOV, POP; DLB 227, 279; MTCW 1, 2; MTFW 2005; NFS 10, 16; RGAL 4; SFW 4; TUS; YAW

Randall, Dudley (Felker) 1914-2000 . **BLC 3; CLC 1, 135**
See also BW 1, 3; CA 25-28R; 189; CANR 23, 82; CP 1, 2, 3, 4; DAM MULT; DLB 41; PFS 5

Randall, Robert
See Silverberg, Robert

Ranger, Ken
See Creasey, John

Rank, Otto 1884-1939 .... **TCLC 115**

Ransom, John Crowe 1888-1974 .. **CLC 2, 4, 5, 11, 24; PC 61**
See also AMW; CA 5-8R; 49-52; CANR 6, 34; CDALBS; CP 1, 2; DA3; DAM POET; DLB 45, 63; EWL 3; EXPP; MAL 5; MTCW 1, 2; MTFW 2005; RGAL 4; TUS

Rao, Raja 1909- .... **CLC 25, 56**
See also CA 73-76; CANR 51; CN 1, 2, 3, 4, 5, 6; DAM NOV; EWL 3; MTCW 1, 2; MTFW 2005; RGEL 2; RGSF 2

Raphael, Frederic (Michael) 1931- ... **CLC 2, 14**
See also CA 1-4R; CANR 1, 86; CN 1, 2, 3, 4, 5, 6, 7; DLB 14, 319; TCLE 1:2

Ratcliffe, James P.
See Mencken, H(enry) L(ouis)

Rathbone, Julian 1935- .... **CLC 41**
See also CA 101; CANR 34, 73

Rattigan, Terence (Mervyn) 1911-1977 .... **CLC 7; DC 18**
See also BRWS 7; CA 85-88; 73-76; CBD; CDBLB 1945-1960; DAM DRAM; DFS 8; DLB 13; IDFW 3, 4; MTCW 1, 2; MTFW 2005; RGEL 2

Ratushinskaya, Irina 1954- .... **CLC 54**
See also CA 129; CANR 68; CWW 2

Raven, Simon (Arthur Noel) 1927-2001 .... **CLC 14**
See also CA 81-84; 197; CANR 86; CN 1, 2, 3, 4, 5, 6; DLB 271

Ravenna, Michael
See Welty, Eudora (Alice)

Rawley, Callman 1903-2004
See Rakosi, Carl
See also CA 21-24R; 228; CANR 12, 32, 91

Rawlings, Marjorie Kinnan 1896-1953 .... **TCLC 4**
See also AAYA 20; AMWS 10; ANW; BPFB 3; BYA 3; CA 104; 137; CANR 74; CLR 63; DLB 9, 22, 102; DLBD 17; JRDA; MAICYA 1, 2; MAL 5; MTCW 2; MTFW 2005; RGAL 4; SATA 100; WCH; YABC 1; YAW

Ray, Satyajit 1921-1992 .... **CLC 16, 76**
See also CA 114; 137; DAM MULT

Read, Herbert Edward 1893-1968 ..... **CLC 4**
See also BRW 6; CA 85-88; 25-28R; DLB 20, 149; EWL 3; PAB; RGEL 2

Read, Piers Paul 1941- .... **CLC 4, 10, 25**
See also CA 21-24R; CANR 38, 86; CN 2, 3, 4, 5, 6, 7; DLB 14; SATA 21

Reade, Charles 1814-1884 .... **NCLC 2, 74**
See also DLB 21; RGEL 2

Reade, Hamish
See Gray, Simon (James Holliday)

Reading, Peter 1946- .... **CLC 47**
See also BRWS 8; CA 103; CANR 46, 96; CP 7; DLB 40

Reaney, James 1926- .... **CLC 13**
See also CA 41-44R; CAAS 15; CANR 42; CD 5, 6; CP 1, 2, 3, 4, 5, 6, 7; DAC; DAM MST; DLB 68; RGEL 2; SATA 43

Rebreanu, Liviu 1885-1944 .... **TCLC 28**
See also CA 165; DLB 220; EWL 3

Rechy, John (Francisco) 1934- ...... **CLC 1, 7, 14, 18, 107; HLC 2**
See also CA 5-8R, 195; CAAE 195; CAAS 4; CANR 6, 32, 64; CN 1, 2, 3, 4, 5, 6, 7; DAM MULT; DLB 122, 278; DLBY 1982; HW 1, 2; INT CANR-6; LLW; MAL 5; RGAL 4

Redcam, Tom 1870-1933 .... **TCLC 25**

Reddin, Keith 1956- .... **CLC 67**
See also CAD; CD 6

Redgrove, Peter (William) 1932-2003 .... **CLC 6, 41**
See also BRWS 6; CA 1-4R; 217; CANR 3, 39, 77; CP 1, 2, 3, 4, 5, 6, 7; DLB 40; TCLE 1:2

Redmon, Anne .... **CLC 22**
See Nightingale, Anne Redmon
See also DLBY 1986

Reed, Eliot
See Ambler, Eric

Reed, Ishmael (Scott) 1938- . **BLC 3; CLC 2, 3, 5, 6, 13, 32, 60, 174; PC 68**
See also AFAW 1, 2; AMWS 10; BPFB 3; BW 2, 3; CA 21-24R; CANR 25, 48, 74, 128; CN 1, 2, 3, 4, 5, 6, 7; CP 1, 2, 3, 4, 5, 6, 7; CSW; DA3; DAM MULT; DLB 2, 5, 33, 169, 227; DLBD 8; EWL 3; LMFS 2; MAL 5; MSW; MTCW 1, 2; MTFW 2005; PFS 6; RGAL 4; TCWW 2

Reed, John (Silas) 1887-1920 .... **TCLC 9**
See also CA 106; 195; MAL 5; TUS

Reed, Lou .... **CLC 21**
See Firbank, Louis

Reese, Lizette Woodworth 1856-1935 . **PC 29**
See also CA 180; DLB 54

Reeve, Clara 1729-1807 .... **NCLC 19**
See also DLB 39; RGEL 2

Reich, Wilhelm 1897-1957 .... **TCLC 57**
See also CA 199

Reid, Christopher (John) 1949- .... **CLC 33**
See also CA 140; CANR 89; CP 4, 5, 6, 7; DLB 40; EWL 3

Reid, Desmond
See Moorcock, Michael (John)

Reid Banks, Lynne 1929-
See Banks, Lynne Reid
See also AAYA 49; CA 1-4R; CANR 6, 22, 38, 87; CLR 24; CN 1, 2, 3, 7; JRDA; MAICYA 1, 2; SATA 22, 75, 111, 165; YAW

Reilly, William K.
See Creasey, John

Reiner, Max
See Caldwell, (Janet Miriam) Taylor (Holland)

Reis, Ricardo
See Pessoa, Fernando (Antonio Nogueira)

Reizenstein, Elmer Leopold
See Rice, Elmer (Leopold)
See also EWL 3

Remarque, Erich Maria 1898-1970 . **CLC 21**
See also AAYA 27; BPFB 3; CA 77-80; 29-32R; CDWLB 2; DA; DA3; DAB; DAC; DAM MST, NOV; DLB 56; EWL 3; EXPN; LAIT 3; MTCW 1, 2; MTFW 2005; NFS 4; RGWL 2, 3

Remington, Frederic S(ackrider) 1861-1909 .... **TCLC 89**
See also CA 108; 169; DLB 12, 186, 188; SATA 41; TCWW 2

Remizov, A.
See Remizov, Aleksei (Mikhailovich)

Remizov, A. M.
   See Remizov, Aleksei (Mikhailovich)
Remizov, Aleksei (Mikhailovich)
   1877-1957 .... **TCLC 27**
   See Remizov, Alexey Mikhaylovich
   See also CA 125; 133; DLB 295
Remizov, Alexey Mikhaylovich
   See Remizov, Aleksei (Mikhailovich)
   See also EWL 3
Renan, Joseph Ernest 1823-1892 . **NCLC 26, 145**
   See also GFL 1789 to the Present
Renard, Jules(-Pierre) 1864-1910 .. **TCLC 17**
   See also CA 117; 202; GFL 1789 to the Present
Renault, Mary .... **CLC 3, 11, 17**
   See Challans, Mary
   See also BPFB 3; BYA 2; CN 1, 2, 3; DLBY 1983; EWL 3; GLL 1; LAIT 1; RGEL 2; RHW
Rendell, Ruth (Barbara) 1930- .. **CLC 28, 48**
   See Vine, Barbara
   See also BPFB 3; BRWS 9; CA 109; CANR 32, 52, 74, 127; CN 5, 6, 7; CPW; DAM POP; DLB 87, 276; INT CANR-32; MSW; MTCW 1, 2; MTFW 2005
Renoir, Jean 1894-1979 .... **CLC 20**
   See also CA 129; 85-88
Resnais, Alain 1922- .... **CLC 16**
Revard, Carter (Curtis) 1931- .... **NNAL**
   See also CA 144; CANR 81; PFS 5
Reverdy, Pierre 1889-1960 .... **CLC 53**
   See also CA 97-100; 89-92; DLB 258; EWL 3; GFL 1789 to the Present
Rexroth, Kenneth 1905-1982 .... **CLC 1, 2, 6, 11, 22, 49, 112; PC 20**
   See also BG 1:3; CA 5-8R; 107; CANR 14, 34, 63; CDALB 1941-1968; CP 1, 2, 3; DAM POET; DLB 16, 48, 165, 212; DLBY 1982; EWL 3; INT CANR-14; MAL 5; MTCW 1, 2; MTFW 2005; RGAL 4
Reyes, Alfonso 1889-1959 .... **HLCS 2; TCLC 33**
   See also CA 131; EWL 3; HW 1; LAW
Reyes y Basoalto, Ricardo Eliecer Neftali
   See Neruda, Pablo
Reymont, Wladyslaw (Stanislaw)
   1868(?)-1925 .... **TCLC 5**
   See also CA 104; EWL 3
Reynolds, John Hamilton
   1794-1852 .... **NCLC 146**
   See also DLB 96
Reynolds, Jonathan 1942- .... **CLC 6, 38**
   See also CA 65-68; CANR 28
Reynolds, Joshua 1723-1792 .... **LC 15**
   See also DLB 104
Reynolds, Michael S(hane)
   1937-2000 .... **CLC 44**
   See also CA 65-68; 189; CANR 9, 89, 97
Reznikoff, Charles 1894-1976 .... **CLC 9**
   See also AMWS 14; CA 33-36; 61-64; CAP 2; CP 1, 2; DLB 28, 45; WP
Rezzori (d'Arezzo), Gregor von
   1914-1998 .... **CLC 25**
   See also CA 122; 136; 167
Rhine, Richard
   See Silverstein, Alvin; Silverstein, Virginia B(arbara Opshelor)
Rhodes, Eugene Manlove
   1869-1934 .... **TCLC 53**
   See also CA 198; DLB 256; TCWW 1, 2
R'hoone, Lord
   See Balzac, Honore de
Rhys, Jean 1890-1979 .... **CLC 2, 4, 6, 14, 19, 51, 124; SSC 21, 76**
   See also BRWS 2; CA 25-28R; 85-88; CANR 35, 62; CDBLB 1945-1960; CDWLB 3; CN 1, 2; DA3; DAM NOV; DLB 36, 117, 162; DNFS 2; EWL 3; LATS 1:1; MTCW 1, 2; MTFW 2005; NFS 19; RGEL 2; RGSF 2; RHW; TEA; WWE 1
Ribeiro, Darcy 1922-1997 .... **CLC 34**
   See also CA 33-36R; 156; EWL 3
Ribeiro, Joao Ubaldo (Osorio Pimentel)
   1941- .... **CLC 10, 67**
   See also CA 81-84; CWW 2; EWL 3
Ribman, Ronald (Burt) 1932- .... **CLC 7**
   See also CA 21-24R; CAD; CANR 46, 80; CD 5, 6
Ricci, Nino (Pio) 1959- .... **CLC 70**
   See also CA 137; CANR 130; CCA 1
Rice, Anne 1941- .... **CLC 41, 128**
   See Rampling, Anne
   See also AAYA 9, 53; AMWS 7; BEST 89:2; BPFB 3; CA 65-68; CANR 12, 36, 53, 74, 100, 133; CN 6, 7; CPW; CSW; DA3; DAM POP; DLB 292; GL 3; GLL 2; HGG; MTCW 2; MTFW 2005; SUFW 2; YAW
Rice, Elmer (Leopold) 1892-1967 ...... **CLC 7, 49**
   See Reizenstein, Elmer Leopold
   See also CA 21-22; 25-28R; CAP 2; DAM DRAM; DFS 12; DLB 4, 7; IDTP; MAL 5; MTCW 1, 2; RGAL 4
Rice, Tim(othy Miles Bindon)
   1944- .... **CLC 21**
   See also CA 103; CANR 46; DFS 7
Rich, Adrienne (Cecile) 1929- ... **CLC 3, 6, 7, 11, 18, 36, 73, 76, 125; PC 5**
   See also AMWR 2; AMWS 1; CA 9-12R; CANR 20, 53, 74, 128; CDALBS; CP 1, 2, 3, 4, 5, 6, 7; CSW; CWP; DA3; DAM POET; DLB 5, 67; EWL 3; EXPP; FL 1:6; FW; MAL 5; MAWW; MTCW 1, 2; MTFW 2005; PAB; PFS 15; RGAL 4; WP
Rich, Barbara
   See Graves, Robert (von Ranke)
Rich, Robert
   See Trumbo, Dalton
Richard, Keith .... **CLC 17**
   See Richards, Keith
Richards, David Adams 1950- .... **CLC 59**
   See also CA 93-96; CANR 60, 110; CN 7; DAC; DLB 53; TCLE 1:2
Richards, I(vor) A(rmstrong)
   1893-1979 .... **CLC 14, 24**
   See also BRWS 2; CA 41-44R; 89-92; CANR 34, 74; CP 1, 2; DLB 27; EWL 3; MTCW 2; RGEL 2
Richards, Keith 1943-
   See Richard, Keith
   See also CA 107; CANR 77
Richardson, Anne
   See Roiphe, Anne (Richardson)
Richardson, Dorothy Miller
   1873-1957 .... **TCLC 3**
   See also CA 104; 192; DLB 36; EWL 3; FW; RGEL 2
Richardson (Robertson), Ethel Florence Lindesay 1870-1946
   See Richardson, Henry Handel
   See also CA 105; 190; DLB 230; RHW
Richardson, Henry Handel .... **TCLC 4**
   See Richardson (Robertson), Ethel Florence Lindesay
   See also DLB 197; EWL 3; RGEL 2; RGSF 2
Richardson, John 1796-1852 .... **NCLC 55**
   See also CCA 1; DAC; DLB 99
Richardson, Samuel 1689-1761 ...... **LC 1, 44; WLC**
   See also BRW 3; CDBLB 1660-1789; DA; DAB; DAC; DAM MST, NOV; DLB 39; RGEL 2; TEA; WLIT 3
Richardson, Willis 1889-1977 .... **HR 1:3**
   See also BW 1; CA 124; DLB 51; SATA 60
Richler, Mordecai 1931-2001 .... **CLC 3, 5, 9, 13, 18, 46, 70, 185**
   See also AITN 1; CA 65-68; 201; CANR 31, 62, 111; CCA 1; CLR 17; CN 1, 2, 3, 4, 5, 7; CWRI 5; DAC; DAM MST, NOV; DLB 53; EWL 3; MAICYA 1, 2; MTCW 1, 2; MTFW 2005; RGEL 2; SATA 44, 98; SATA-Brief 27; TWA
Richter, Conrad (Michael)
   1890-1968 .... **CLC 30**
   See also AAYA 21; BYA 2; CA 5-8R; 25-28R; CANR 23; DLB 9, 212; LAIT 1; MAL 5; MTCW 1, 2; MTFW 2005; RGAL 4; SATA 3; TCWW 1, 2; TUS; YAW
Ricostranza, Tom
   See Ellis, Trey
Riddell, Charlotte 1832-1906 .... **TCLC 40**
   See Riddell, Mrs. J. H.
   See also CA 165; DLB 156
Riddell, Mrs. J. H.
   See Riddell, Charlotte
   See also HGG; SUFW
Ridge, John Rollin 1827-1867 ...... **NCLC 82; NNAL**
   See also CA 144; DAM MULT; DLB 175
Ridgeway, Jason
   See Marlowe, Stephen
Ridgway, Keith 1965- .... **CLC 119**
   See also CA 172; CANR 144
Riding, Laura .... **CLC 3, 7**
   See Jackson, Laura (Riding)
   See also CP 1, 2, 3, 4; RGAL 4
Riefenstahl, Berta Helene Amalia 1902-2003
   See Riefenstahl, Leni
   See also CA 108; 220
Riefenstahl, Leni .... **CLC 16, 190**
   See Riefenstahl, Berta Helene Amalia
Riffe, Ernest
   See Bergman, (Ernst) Ingmar
Riggs, (Rolla) Lynn
   1899-1954 .... **NNAL; TCLC 56**
   See also CA 144; DAM MULT; DLB 175
Riis, Jacob A(ugust) 1849-1914 .... **TCLC 80**
   See also CA 113; 168; DLB 23
Riley, James Whitcomb 1849-1916 .... **PC 48; TCLC 51**
   See also CA 118; 137; DAM POET; MAICYA 1, 2; RGAL 4; SATA 17
Riley, Tex
   See Creasey, John
Rilke, Rainer Maria 1875-1926 .... **PC 2; TCLC 1, 6, 19**
   See also CA 104; 132; CANR 62, 99; CDWLB 2; DA3; DAM POET; DLB 81; EW 9; EWL 3; MTCW 1, 2; MTFW 2005; PFS 19; RGWL 2, 3; TWA; WP
Rimbaud, (Jean Nicolas) Arthur
   1854-1891 ... **NCLC 4, 35, 82; PC 3, 57; WLC**
   See also DA; DA3; DAB; DAC; DAM MST, POET; DLB 217; EW 7; GFL 1789 to the Present; LMFS 2; RGWL 2, 3; TWA; WP
Rinehart, Mary Roberts
   1876-1958 .... **TCLC 52**
   See also BPFB 3; CA 108; 166; RGAL 4; RHW
Ringmaster, The
   See Mencken, H(enry) L(ouis)
Ringwood, Gwen(dolyn Margaret) Pharis
   1910-1984 .... **CLC 48**
   See also CA 148; 112; DLB 88
Rio, Michel 1945(?)- .... **CLC 43**
   See also CA 201
Rios, Alberto (Alvaro) 1952- .... **PC 57**
   See also AAYA 66; AMWS 4; CA 113; CANR 34, 79, 137; CP 7; DLB 122; HW 2; MTFW 2005; PFS 11

Ritsos, Giannes
See Ritsos, Yannis
Ritsos, Yannis 1909-1990 .... **CLC 6, 13, 31**
See also CA 77-80; 133; CANR 39, 61; EW 12; EWL 3; MTCW 1; RGWL 2, 3
Ritter, Erika 1948(?)- .... **CLC 52**
See also CD 5, 6; CWD
Rivera, Jose Eustasio 1889-1928 ... **TCLC 35**
See also CA 162; EWL 3; HW 1, 2; LAW
Rivera, Tomas 1935-1984 .... **HLCS 2**
See also CA 49-52; CANR 32; DLB 82; HW 1; LLW; RGAL 4; SSFS 15; TCWW 2; WLIT 1
Rivers, Conrad Kent 1933-1968 .... **CLC 1**
See also BW 1; CA 85-88; DLB 41
Rivers, Elfrida
See Bradley, Marion Zimmer
See also GLL 1
Riverside, John
See Heinlein, Robert A(nson)
Rizal, Jose 1861-1896 .... **NCLC 27**
Roa Bastos, Augusto (Jose Antonio) 1917-2005 .... **CLC 45; HLC 2**
See also CA 131; 238; CWW 2; DAM MULT; DLB 113; EWL 3; HW 1; LAW; RGSF 2; WLIT 1
Robbe-Grillet, Alain 1922- .... **CLC 1, 2, 4, 6, 8, 10, 14, 43, 128**
See also BPFB 3; CA 9-12R; CANR 33, 65, 115; CWW 2; DLB 83; EW 13; EWL 3; GFL 1789 to the Present; IDFW 3, 4; MTCW 1, 2; MTFW 2005; RGWL 2, 3; SSFS 15
Robbins, Harold 1916-1997 .... **CLC 5**
See also BPFB 3; CA 73-76; 162; CANR 26, 54, 112; DA3; DAM NOV; MTCW 1, 2
Robbins, Thomas Eugene 1936-
See Robbins, Tom
See also CA 81-84; CANR 29, 59, 95, 139; CN 7; CPW; CSW; DA3; DAM NOV, POP; MTCW 1, 2; MTFW 2005
Robbins, Tom .... **CLC 9, 32, 64**
See Robbins, Thomas Eugene
See also AAYA 32; AMWS 10; BEST 90:3; BPFB 3; CN 3, 4, 5, 6, 7; DLBY 1980
Robbins, Trina 1938- .... **CLC 21**
See also AAYA 61; CA 128
Roberts, Charles G(eorge) D(ouglas) 1860-1943 .... **TCLC 8**
See also CA 105; 188; CLR 33; CWRI 5; DLB 92; RGEL 2; RGSF 2; SATA 88; SATA-Brief 29
Roberts, Elizabeth Madox 1886-1941 .... **TCLC 68**
See also CA 111; 166; CLR 100; CWRI 5; DLB 9, 54, 102; RGAL 4; RHW; SATA 33; SATA-Brief 27; TCWW 2; WCH
Roberts, Kate 1891-1985 .... **CLC 15**
See also CA 107; 116; DLB 319
Roberts, Keith (John Kingston) 1935-2000 .... **CLC 14**
See also BRWS 10; CA 25-28R; CANR 46; DLB 261; SFW 4
Roberts, Kenneth (Lewis) 1885-1957 .... **TCLC 23**
See also CA 109; 199; DLB 9; MAL 5; RGAL 4; RHW
Roberts, Michele (Brigitte) 1949- .... **CLC 48, 178**
See also CA 115; CANR 58, 120; CN 6, 7; DLB 231; FW
Robertson, Ellis
See Ellison, Harlan (Jay); Silverberg, Robert
Robertson, Thomas William 1829-1871 .... **NCLC 35**
See Robertson, Tom
See also DAM DRAM

Robertson, Tom
See Robertson, Thomas William
See also RGEL 2
Robeson, Kenneth
See Dent, Lester
Robinson, Edwin Arlington 1869-1935 .... **PC 1, 35; TCLC 5, 101**
See also AMW; CA 104; 133; CDALB 1865-1917; DA; DAC; DAM MST, POET; DLB 54; EWL 3; EXPP; MAL 5; MTCW 1, 2; MTFW 2005; PAB; PFS 4; RGAL 4; WP
Robinson, Henry Crabb 1775-1867 .... **NCLC 15**
See also DLB 107
Robinson, Jill 1936- .... **CLC 10**
See also CA 102; CANR 120; INT CA-102
Robinson, Kim Stanley 1952- .... **CLC 34**
See also AAYA 26; CA 126; CANR 113, 139; CN 6, 7; MTFW 2005; SATA 109; SCFW 2; SFW 4
Robinson, Lloyd
See Silverberg, Robert
Robinson, Marilynne 1944- ...... **CLC 25, 180**
See also CA 116; CANR 80, 140; CN 4, 5, 6, 7; DLB 206; MTFW 2005
Robinson, Mary 1758-1800 .... **NCLC 142**
See also DLB 158; FW
Robinson, Smokey .... **CLC 21**
See Robinson, William, Jr.
Robinson, William, Jr. 1940-
See Robinson, Smokey
See also CA 116
Robison, Mary 1949- .... **CLC 42, 98**
See also CA 113; 116; CANR 87, CN 4, 5, 6, 7; DLB 130; INT CA-116; RGSF 2
Roches, Catherine des 1542-1587 ...... **LC 117**
Rochester
See Wilmot, John
See also RGEL 2
Rod, Edouard 1857-1910 .... **TCLC 52**
Roddenberry, Eugene Wesley 1921-1991
See Roddenberry, Gene
See also CA 110; 135; CANR 37; SATA 45; SATA-Obit 69
Roddenberry, Gene .... **CLC 17**
See Roddenberry, Eugene Wesley
See also AAYA 5; SATA-Obit 69
Rodgers, Mary 1931- .... **CLC 12**
See also BYA 5; CA 49-52; CANR 8, 55, 90; CLR 20; CWRI 5; INT CANR-8; JRDA; MAICYA 1, 2; SATA 8, 130
Rodgers, W(illiam) R(obert) 1909-1969 .... **CLC 7**
See also CA 85-88; DLB 20; RGEL 2
Rodman, Eric
See Silverberg, Robert
Rodman, Howard 1920(?)-1985 .... **CLC 65**
See also CA 118
Rodman, Maia
See Wojciechowska, Maia (Teresa)
Rodo, Jose Enrique 1871(?)-1917 .... **HLCS 2**
See also CA 178; EWL 3; HW 2; LAW
Rodolph, Utto
See Ouologuem, Yambo
Rodriguez, Claudio 1934-1999 .... **CLC 10**
See also CA 188; DLB 134
Rodriguez, Richard 1944- .... **CLC 155; HLC 2**
See also AMWS 14; CA 110; CANR 66, 116; DAM MULT; DLB 82, 256; HW 1, 2; LAIT 5; LLW; MTFW 2005; NCFS 3; WLIT 1
Roelvaag, O(le) E(dvart) 1876-1931
See Rolvaag, O(le) E(dvart)
See also CA 117; 171

Roethke, Theodore (Huebner) 1908-1963 .... **CLC 1, 3, 8, 11, 19, 46, 101; PC 15**
See also AMW; CA 81-84; CABS 2; CDALB 1941-1968; DA3; DAM POET; DLB 5, 206; EWL 3; EXPP; MAL 5; MTCW 1, 2; PAB; PFS 3; RGAL 4; WP
Rogers, Carl R(ansom) 1902-1987 .... **TCLC 125**
See also CA 1-4R; 121; CANR 1, 18; MTCW 1
Rogers, Samuel 1763-1855 .... **NCLC 69**
See also DLB 93; RGEL 2
Rogers, Thomas Hunton 1927- .... **CLC 57**
See also CA 89-92; INT CA-89-92
Rogers, Will(iam Penn Adair) 1879-1935 .... **NNAL; TCLC 8, 71**
See also CA 105; 144; DA3; DAM MULT; DLB 11; MTCW 2
Rogin, Gilbert 1929- .... **CLC 18**
See also CA 65-68; CANR 15
Rohan, Koda
See Koda Shigeyuki
Rohlfs, Anna Katharine Green
See Green, Anna Katharine
Rohmer, Eric .... **CLC 16**
See Scherer, Jean-Marie Maurice
Rohmer, Sax .... **TCLC 28**
See Ward, Arthur Henry Sarsfield
See also DLB 70; MSW; SUFW
Roiphe, Anne (Richardson) 1935- .. **CLC 3, 9**
See also CA 89-92; CANR 45, 73, 138; DLBY 1980; INT CA-89-92
Rojas, Fernando de 1475-1541 ... **HLCS 1, 2; LC 23**
See also DLB 286; RGWL 2, 3
Rojas, Gonzalo 1917- .... **HLCS 2**
See also CA 178; HW 2; LAWS 1
Roland (de la Platiere), Marie-Jeanne 1754-1793 .... **LC 98**
See also DLB 314
Rolfe, Frederick (William Serafino Austin Lewis Mary) 1860-1913 .... **TCLC 12**
See Al Siddik
See also CA 107; 210; DLB 34, 156; RGEL 2
Rolland, Romain 1866-1944 .... **TCLC 23**
See also CA 118; 197; DLB 65, 284; EWL 3; GFL 1789 to the Present; RGWL 2, 3
Rolle, Richard c. 1300-c. 1349 .... **CMLC 21**
See also DLB 146; LMFS 1; RGEL 2
Rolvaag, O(le) E(dvart) .... **TCLC 17**
See Roelvaag, O(le) E(dvart)
See also DLB 9, 212; MAL 5; NFS 5; RGAL 4
Romain Arnaud, Saint
See Aragon, Louis
Romains, Jules 1885-1972 .... **CLC 7**
See also CA 85-88; CANR 34; DLB 65, 321; EWL 3; GFL 1789 to the Present; MTCW 1
Romero, Jose Ruben 1890-1952 .... **TCLC 14**
See also CA 114; 131; EWL 3; HW 1; LAW
Ronsard, Pierre de 1524-1585 . **LC 6, 54; PC 11**
See also EW 2; GFL Beginnings to 1789; RGWL 2, 3; TWA
Rooke, Leon 1934- .... **CLC 25, 34**
See also CA 25-28R; CANR 23, 53; CCA 1; CPW; DAM POP
Roosevelt, Franklin Delano 1882-1945 .... **TCLC 93**
See also CA 116; 173; LAIT 3
Roosevelt, Theodore 1858-1919 ..... **TCLC 69**
See also CA 115; 170; DLB 47, 186, 275
Roper, William 1498-1578 .... **LC 10**
Roquelaure, A. N.
See Rice, Anne

Rosa, Joao Guimaraes 1908-1967 ... **CLC 23; HLCS 1**
See Guimaraes Rosa, Joao
See also CA 89-92; DLB 113, 307; EWL 3; WLIT 1

Rose, Wendy 1948- . **CLC 85; NNAL; PC 13**
See also CA 53-56; CANR 5, 51; CWP; DAM MULT; DLB 175; PFS 13; RGAL 4; SATA 12

Rosen, R. D.
See Rosen, Richard (Dean)

Rosen, Richard (Dean) 1949- .... **CLC 39**
See also CA 77-80; CANR 62, 120; CMW 4; INT CANR-30

Rosenberg, Isaac 1890-1918 .... **TCLC 12**
See also BRW 6; CA 107; 188; DLB 20, 216; EWL 3; PAB; RGEL 2

Rosenblatt, Joe .... **CLC 15**
See Rosenblatt, Joseph
See also CP 3, 4, 5, 6, 7

Rosenblatt, Joseph 1933-
See Rosenblatt, Joe
See also CA 89-92; CP 1, 2; INT CA-89-92

Rosenfeld, Samuel
See Tzara, Tristan

Rosenstock, Sami
See Tzara, Tristan

Rosenstock, Samuel
See Tzara, Tristan

Rosenthal, M(acha) L(ouis)
1917-1996 .... **CLC 28**
See also CA 1-4R; 152; CAAS 6; CANR 4, 51; CP 1, 2, 3, 4; DLB 5; SATA 59

Ross, Barnaby
See Dannay, Frederic

Ross, Bernard L.
See Follett, Ken(neth Martin)

Ross, J. H.
See Lawrence, T(homas) E(dward)

Ross, John Hume
See Lawrence, T(homas) E(dward)

Ross, Martin 1862-1915
See Martin, Violet Florence
See also DLB 135; GLL 2; RGEL 2; RGSF 2

Ross, (James) Sinclair 1908-1996 ... **CLC 13; SSC 24**
See also CA 73-76; CANR 81; CN 1, 2, 3, 4, 5, 6; DAC; DAM MST; DLB 88; RGEL 2; RGSF 2; TCWW 1, 2

Rossetti, Christina 1830-1894 ... **NCLC 2, 50, 66; PC 7; WLC**
See also AAYA 51; BRW 5; BYA 4; DA; DA3; DAB; DAC; DAM MST, POET; DLB 35, 163, 240; EXPP; FL 1:3; LATS 1:1; MAICYA 1, 2; PFS 10, 14; RGEL 2; SATA 20; TEA; WCH

Rossetti, Christina Georgina
See Rossetti, Christina

Rossetti, Dante Gabriel 1828-1882 . **NCLC 4, 77; PC 44; WLC**
See also AAYA 51; BRW 5; CDBLB 1832-1890; DA; DAB; DAC; DAM MST, POET; DLB 35; EXPP; RGEL 2; TEA

Rossi, Cristina Peri
See Peri Rossi, Cristina

Rossi, Jean-Baptiste 1931-2003
See Japrisot, Sebastien
See also CA 201; 215

Rossner, Judith (Perelman) 1935- . **CLC 6, 9, 29**
See also AITN 2; BEST 90:3; BPFB 3; CA 17-20R; CANR 18, 51, 73; CN 4, 5, 6, 7; DLB 6; INT CANR-18; MAL 5; MTCW 1, 2; MTFW 2005

Rostand, Edmond (Eugene Alexis)
1868-1918 .... **DC 10; TCLC 6, 37**
See also CA 104; 126; DA; DA3; DAB; DAC; DAM DRAM, MST; DFS 1; DLB 192; LAIT 1; MTCW 1; RGWL 2, 3; TWA

Roth, Henry 1906-1995 ..... **CLC 2, 6, 11, 104**
See also AMWS 9; CA 11-12; 149; CANR 38, 63; CAP 1; CN 1, 2, 3, 4, 5, 6; DA3; DLB 28; EWL 3; MAL 5; MTCW 1, 2; MTFW 2005; RGAL 4

Roth, (Moses) Joseph 1894-1939 ... **TCLC 33**
See also CA 160; DLB 85; EWL 3; RGWL 2, 3

Roth, Philip (Milton) 1933- ... **CLC 1, 2, 3, 4, 6, 9, 15, 22, 31, 47, 66, 86, 119, 201; SSC 26; WLC**
See also AAYA 67; AMWR 2; AMWS 3; BEST 90:3; BPFB 3; CA 1-4R; CANR 1, 22, 36, 55, 89, 132; CDALB 1968-1988; CN 3, 4, 5, 6, 7; CPW 1; DA; DA3; DAB; DAC; DAM MST, NOV, POP; DLB 2, 28, 173; DLBY 1982; EWL 3; MAL 5; MTCW 1, 2; MTFW 2005; RGAL 4; RGSF 2; SSFS 12, 18; TUS

Rothenberg, Jerome 1931- .... **CLC 6, 57**
See also CA 45-48; CANR 1, 106; CP 1, 2, 3, 4, 5, 6, 7; DLB 5, 193

Rotter, Pat ed. .... **CLC 65**

Roumain, Jacques (Jean Baptiste)
1907-1944 .... **BLC 3; TCLC 19**
See also BW 1; CA 117; 125; DAM MULT; EWL 3

Rourke, Constance Mayfield
1885-1941 .... **TCLC 12**
See also CA 107; 200; MAL 5; YABC 1

Rousseau, Jean-Baptiste 1671-1741 ...... **LC 9**

Rousseau, Jean-Jacques 1712-1778 .... **LC 14, 36, 122; WLC**
See also DA; DA3; DAB; DAC; DAM MST; DLB 314; EW 4; GFL Beginnings to 1789; LMFS 1; RGWL 2, 3; TWA

Roussel, Raymond 1877-1933 .... **TCLC 20**
See also CA 117; 201; EWL 3; GFL 1789 to the Present

Rovit, Earl (Herbert) 1927- .... **CLC 7**
See also CA 5-8R; CANR 12

Rowe, Elizabeth Singer 1674-1737 ..... **LC 44**
See also DLB 39, 95

Rowe, Nicholas 1674-1718 .... **LC 8**
See also DLB 84; RGEL 2

Rowlandson, Mary 1637(?)-1678 .... **LC 66**
See also DLB 24, 200; RGAL 4

Rowley, Ames Dorrance
See Lovecraft, H(oward) P(hillips)

Rowley, William 1585(?)-1626 ... **LC 100, 123**
See also DFS 22; DLB 58; RGEL 2

Rowling, J. K. 1966- .... **CLC 137, 217**
See also AAYA 34; BYA 11, 13, 14; CA 173; CANR 128; CLR 66, 80; MAICYA 2; MTFW 2005; SATA 109; SUFW 2

Rowling, Joanne Kathleen
See Rowling, J.K.

Rowson, Susanna Haswell
1762(?)-1824 .... **NCLC 5, 69**
See also AMWS 15; DLB 37, 200; RGAL 4

Roy, Arundhati 1960(?)- .... **CLC 109, 210**
See also CA 163; CANR 90, 126; CN 7; DLBY 1997; EWL 3; LATS 1:2; MTFW 2005; NFS 22; WWE 1

Roy, Gabrielle 1909-1983 .... **CLC 10, 14**
See also CA 53-56; 110; CANR 5, 61; CCA 1; DAB; DAC; DAM MST; DLB 68; EWL 3; MTCW 1; RGWL 2, 3; SATA 104; TCLE 1:2

Royko, Mike 1932-1997 .... **CLC 109**
See also CA 89-92; 157; CANR 26, 111; CPW

Rozanov, Vasilii Vasil'evich
See Rozanov, Vassili
See also DLB 295

Rozanov, Vasily Vasilyevich
See Rozanov, Vassili
See also EWL 3

Rozanov, Vassili 1856-1919 .... **TCLC 104**
See Rozanov, Vasilii Vasil'evich; Rozanov, Vasily Vasilyevich

Rozewicz, Tadeusz 1921- ...... **CLC 9, 23, 139**
See also CA 108; CANR 36, 66; CWW 2; DA3; DAM POET; DLB 232; EWL 3; MTCW 1, 2; MTFW 2005; RGWL 3

Ruark, Gibbons 1941- .... **CLC 3**
See also CA 33-36R; CAAS 23; CANR 14, 31, 57; DLB 120

Rubens, Bernice (Ruth) 1923-2004 . **CLC 19, 31**
See also CA 25-28R; 232; CANR 33, 65, 128; CN 1, 2, 3, 4, 5, 6, 7; DLB 14, 207; MTCW 1

Rubin, Harold
See Robbins, Harold

Rudkin, (James) David 1936- .... **CLC 14**
See also CA 89-92; CBD; CD 5, 6; DLB 13

Rudnik, Raphael 1933- .... **CLC 7**
See also CA 29-32R

Ruffian, M.
See Hasek, Jaroslav (Matej Frantisek)

Ruiz, Jose Martinez .... **CLC 11**
See Martinez Ruiz, Jose

Ruiz, Juan c. 1283-c. 1350 .... **CMLC 66**

Rukeyser, Muriel 1913-1980 . **CLC 6, 10, 15, 27; PC 12**
See also AMWS 6; CA 5-8R; 93-96; CANR 26, 60; CP 1, 2, 3; DA3; DAM POET; DLB 48; EWL 3; FW; GLL 2; MAL 5; MTCW 1, 2; PFS 10; RGAL 4; SATA-Obit 22

Rule, Jane (Vance) 1931- .... **CLC 27**
See also CA 25-28R; CAAS 18; CANR 12, 87; CN 4, 5, 6, 7; DLB 60; FW

Rulfo, Juan 1918-1986 .. **CLC 8, 80; HLC 2; SSC 25**
See also CA 85-88; 118; CANR 26; CDWLB 3; DAM MULT; DLB 113; EWL 3; HW 1, 2; LAW; MTCW 1, 2; RGSF 2; RGWL 2, 3; WLIT 1

Rumi, Jalal al-Din 1207-1273 ...... **CMLC 20; PC 45**
See also AAYA 64; RGWL 2, 3; WLIT 6; WP

Runeberg, Johan 1804-1877 .... **NCLC 41**

Runyon, (Alfred) Damon
1884(?)-1946 .... **TCLC 10**
See also CA 107; 165; DLB 11, 86, 171; MAL 5; MTCW 2; RGAL 4

Rush, Norman 1933- .... **CLC 44**
See also CA 121; 126; CANR 130; INT CA-126

Rushdie, (Ahmed) Salman 1947- .... **CLC 23, 31, 55, 100, 191; SSC 83; WLCS**
See also AAYA 65; BEST 89:3; BPFB 3; BRWS 4; CA 108; 111; CANR 33, 56, 108, 133; CN 4, 5, 6, 7; CPW 1; DA3; DAB; DAC; DAM MST, NOV, POP; DLB 194; EWL 3; FANT; INT CA-111; LATS 1:2; LMFS 2; MTCW 1, 2; MTFW 2005; NFS 22; RGEL 2; RGSF 2; TEA; WLIT 4

Rushforth, Peter (Scott) 1945- .... **CLC 19**
See also CA 101

Ruskin, John 1819-1900 .... **TCLC 63**
See also BRW 5; BYA 5; CA 114; 129; CDBLB 1832-1890; DLB 55, 163, 190; RGEL 2; SATA 24; TEA; WCH

Russ, Joanna 1937- .... **CLC 15**
See also BPFB 3; CA 25-28; CANR 11, 31, 65; CN 4, 5, 6, 7; DLB 8; FW; GLL 1; MTCW 1; SCFW 1, 2; SFW 4

Russ, Richard Patrick
See O'Brian, Patrick

Russell, George William 1867-1935
See A.E.; Baker, Jean H.
See also BRWS 8; CA 104; 153; CDBLB 1890-1914; DAM POET; EWL 3; RGEL 2

Russell, Jeffrey Burton 1934- .... **CLC 70**
See also CA 25-28R; CANR 11, 28, 52

Russell, (Henry) Ken(neth Alfred) 1927- .... **CLC 16**
See also CA 105

Russell, William Martin 1947-
See Russell, Willy
See also CA 164; CANR 107

Russell, Willy .... **CLC 60**
See Russell, William Martin
See also CBD; CD 5, 6; DLB 233

Russo, Richard 1949- .... **CLC 181**
See also AMWS 12; CA 127; 133; CANR 87, 114

Rutherford, Mark .... **TCLC 25**
See White, William Hale
See also DLB 18; RGEL 2

Ruyslinck, Ward .... **CLC 14**
See Belser, Reimond Karel Maria de

Ryan, Cornelius (John) 1920-1974 ..... **CLC 7**
See also CA 69-72; 53-56; CANR 38

Ryan, Michael 1946- .... **CLC 65**
See also CA 49-52; CANR 109; DLBY 1982

Ryan, Tim
See Dent, Lester

Rybakov, Anatoli (Naumovich) 1911-1998 .... **CLC 23, 53**
See Rybakov, Anatolii (Naumovich)
See also CA 126; 135; 172; SATA 79; SATA-Obit 108

Rybakov, Anatolii (Naumovich)
See Rybakov, Anatoli (Naumovich)
See also DLB 302

Ryder, Jonathan
See Ludlum, Robert

Ryga, George 1932-1987 .... **CLC 14**
See also CA 101; 124; CANR 43, 90; CCA 1; DAC; DAM MST; DLB 60

S. H.
See Hartmann, Sadakichi

S. S.
See Sassoon, Siegfried (Lorraine)

Sa'adawi, al- Nawal
See El Saadawi, Nawal
See also AFW; EWL 3

Saadawi, Nawal El
See El Saadawi, Nawal
See also WLIT 2

Saba, Umberto 1883-1957 .... **TCLC 33**
See also CA 144; CANR 79; DLB 114; EWL 3; RGWL 2, 3

Sabatini, Rafael 1875-1950 .... **TCLC 47**
See also BPFB 3; CA 162; RHW

Sabato, Ernesto (R.) 1911- .... **CLC 10, 23; HLC 2**
See also CA 97-100; CANR 32, 65; CDWLB 3; CWW 2; DAM MULT; DLB 145; EWL 3; HW 1, 2; LAW; MTCW 1, 2; MTFW 2005

Sa-Carneiro, Mario de 1890-1916 . **TCLC 83**
See also DLB 287; EWL 3

Sacastru, Martin
See Bioy Casares, Adolfo
See also CWW 2

Sacher-Masoch, Leopold von 1836(?)-1895 .... **NCLC 31**

Sachs, Hans 1494-1576 .... **LC 95**
See also CDWLB 2; DLB 179; RGWL 2, 3

Sachs, Marilyn 1927- .... **CLC 35**
See also AAYA 2; BYA 6; CA 17-20R; CANR 13, 47; CLR 2; JRDA; MAICYA 1, 2; SAAS 2; SATA 3, 68, 164; SATA-Essay 110; WYA; YAW

Sachs, Marilyn Stickle
See Sachs, Marilyn

Sachs, Nelly 1891-1970 .... **CLC 14, 98**
See also CA 17-18; 25-28R; CANR 87; CAP 2; EWL 3; MTCW 2; MTFW 2005; PFS 20; RGWL 2, 3

Sackler, Howard (Oliver) 1929-1982 .... **CLC 14**
See also CA 61-64; 108; CAD; CANR 30; DFS 15; DLB 7

Sacks, Oliver (Wolf) 1933- .... **CLC 67, 202**
See also CA 53-56; CANR 28, 50, 76; CPW; DA3; INT CANR-28; MTCW 1, 2; MTFW 2005

Sackville, Thomas 1536-1608 .... **LC 98**
See also DAM DRAM; DLB 62, 132; RGEL 2

Sadakichi
See Hartmann, Sadakichi

Sa'dawi, Nawal al-
See El Saadawi, Nawal
See also CWW 2

Sade, Donatien Alphonse Francois 1740-1814 .... **NCLC 3, 47**
See also DLB 314; EW 4; GFL Beginnings to 1789; RGWL 2, 3

Sade, Marquis de
See Sade, Donatien Alphonse Francois

Sadoff, Ira 1945- .... **CLC 9**
See also CA 53-56; CANR 5, 21, 109; DLB 120

Saetone
See Camus, Albert

Safire, William 1929- .... **CLC 10**
See also CA 17-20R; CANR 31, 54, 91

Sagan, Carl (Edward) 1934-1996 .... **CLC 30, 112**
See also AAYA 2, 62; CA 25-28R; 155; CANR 11, 36, 74; CPW; DA3; MTCW 1, 2; MTFW 2005; SATA 58; SATA-Obit 94

Sagan, Francoise .... **CLC 3, 6, 9, 17, 36**
See Quoirez, Francoise
See also CWW 2; DLB 83; EWL 3; GFL 1789 to the Present; MTCW 2

Sahgal, Nayantara (Pandit) 1927- .... **CLC 41**
See also CA 9-12R; CANR 11, 88; CN 1, 2, 3, 4, 5, 6, 7

Said, Edward W. 1935-2003 .... **CLC 123**
See also CA 21-24R; 220; CANR 45, 74, 107, 131; DLB 67; MTCW 2; MTFW 2005

Saint, H(arry) F. 1941- .... **CLC 50**
See also CA 127

St. Aubin de Teran, Lisa 1953-
See Teran, Lisa St. Aubin de
See also CA 118; 126; CN 6, 7; INT CA-126

Saint Birgitta of Sweden c. 1303-1373 .... **CMLC 24**

Saint Gregory of Nazianzus 329-389 .... **CMLC 82**

Sainte-Beuve, Charles Augustin 1804-1869 .... **NCLC 5**
See also DLB 217; EW 6; GFL 1789 to the Present

Saint-Exupery, Antoine (Jean Baptiste Marie Roger) de 1900-1944 .... **TCLC 2, 56, 169; WLC**
See also AAYA 63; BPFB 3; BYA 3; CA 108; 132; CLR 10; DA3; DAM NOV; DLB 72; EW 12; EWL 3; GFL 1789 to the Present; LAIT 3; MAICYA 1, 2; MTCW 1, 2; MTFW 2005; RGWL 2, 3; SATA 20; TWA

St. John, David
See Hunt, E(verette) Howard, (Jr.)

St. John, J. Hector
See Crevecoeur, Michel Guillaume Jean de

Saint-John Perse
See Leger, (Marie-Rene Auguste) Alexis Saint-Leger
See also EW 10; EWL 3; GFL 1789 to the Present; RGWL 2

Saintsbury, George (Edward Bateman) 1845-1933 .... **TCLC 31**
See also CA 160; DLB 57, 149

Sait Faik .... **TCLC 23**
See Abasiyanik, Sait Faik

Saki .... **SSC 12; TCLC 3**
See Munro, H(ector) H(ugh)
See also BRWS 6; BYA 11; LAIT 2; RGEL 2; SSFS 1; SUFW

Sala, George Augustus 1828-1895 . **NCLC 46**

Saladin 1138-1193 .... **CMLC 38**

Salama, Hannu 1936- .... **CLC 18**
See also EWL 3

Salamanca, J(ack) R(ichard) 1922- .. **CLC 4, 15**
See also CA 25-28R, 193; CAAE 193

Salas, Floyd Francis 1931- .... **HLC 2**
See also CA 119; CAAS 27; CANR 44, 75, 93; DAM MULT; DLB 82; HW 1, 2; MTCW 2; MTFW 2005

Sale, J. Kirkpatrick
See Sale, Kirkpatrick

Sale, Kirkpatrick 1937- .... **CLC 68**
See also CA 13-16R; CANR 10

Salinas, Luis Omar 1937- ... **CLC 90; HLC 2**
See also AMWS 13; CA 131; CANR 81; DAM MULT; DLB 82; HW 1, 2

Salinas (y Serrano), Pedro 1891(?)-1951 .... **TCLC 17**
See also CA 117; DLB 134; EWL 3

Salinger, J(erome) D(avid) 1919- .. **CLC 1, 3, 8, 12, 55, 56, 138; SSC 2, 28, 65; WLC**
See also AAYA 2, 36; AMW; AMWC 1; BPFB 3; CA 5-8R; CANR 39, 129; CDALB 1941-1968; CLR 18; CN 1, 2, 3, 4, 5, 6, 7; CPW 1; DA; DA3; DAB; DAC; DAM MST, NOV, POP; DLB 2, 102, 173; EWL 3; EXPN; LAIT 4; MAICYA 1, 2; MAL 5; MTCW 1, 2; MTFW 2005; NFS 1; RGAL 4; RGSF 2; SATA 67; SSFS 17; TUS; WYA; YAW

Salisbury, John
See Caute, (John) David

Sallust c. 86B.C.-35B.C. .... **CMLC 68**
See also AW 2; CDWLB 1; DLB 211; RGWL 2, 3

Salter, James 1925- .. **CLC 7, 52, 59; SSC 58**
See also AMWS 9; CA 73-76; CANR 107; DLB 130

Saltus, Edgar (Everton) 1855-1921 . **TCLC 8**
See also CA 105; DLB 202; RGAL 4

Saltykov, Mikhail Evgrafovich 1826-1889 .... **NCLC 16**
See also DLB 238:

Saltykov-Shchedrin, N.
See Saltykov, Mikhail Evgrafovich

Samarakis, Andonis
See Samarakis, Antonis
See also EWL 3

Samarakis, Antonis 1919-2003 .... **CLC 5**
See Samarakis, Andonis
See also CA 25-28R; 224; CAAS 16; CANR 36

Sanchez, Florencio 1875-1910 .... **TCLC 37**
See also CA 153; DLB 305; EWL 3; HW 1; LAW

Sanchez, Luis Rafael 1936- .... **CLC 23**
See also CA 128; DLB 305; EWL 3; HW 1; WLIT 1

Sanchez, Sonia 1934- .... **BLC 3; CLC 5, 116, 215; PC 9**
See also BW 2, 3; CA 33-36R; CANR 24, 49, 74, 115; CLR 18; CP 2, 3, 4, 5, 6, 7; CSW; CWP; DA3; DAM MULT; DLB 41; DLBD 8; EWL 3; MAICYA 1, 2; MAL 5; MTCW 1, 2; MTFW 2005; SATA 22, 136; WP

Sancho, Ignatius 1729-1780 .... **LC 84**

Sand, George 1804-1876 ..... **NCLC 2, 42, 57; WLC**
See also DA; DA3; DAB; DAC; DAM MST, NOV; DLB 119, 192; EW 6; FL 1:3; FW; GFL 1789 to the Present; RGWL 2, 3; TWA

Sandburg, Carl (August) 1878-1967 . **CLC 1, 4, 10, 15, 35; PC 2, 41; WLC**
See also AAYA 24; AMW; BYA 1, 3; CA 5-8R; 25-28R; CANR 35; CDALB 1865-1917; CLR 67; DA; DA3; DAB; DAC; DAM MST, POET; DLB 17, 54, 284; EWL 3; EXPP; LAIT 2; MAICYA 1, 2; MAL 5; MTCW 1, 2; MTFW 2005; PAB; PFS 6, 12; RGAL 4; SATA 8; TUS; WCH; WP; WYA

Sandburg, Charles
See Sandburg, Carl (August)

Sandburg, Charles A.
See Sandburg, Carl (August)

Sanders, (James) Ed(ward) 1939- .... **CLC 53**
See Sanders, Edward
See also BG 1:3; CA 13-16R; CAAS 21; CANR 13, 44, 78; CP 1, 2, 3, 4, 5, 6, 7; DAM POET; DLB 16, 244

Sanders, Edward
See Sanders, (James) Ed(ward)
See also DLB 244

Sanders, Lawrence 1920-1998 .... **CLC 41**
See also BEST 89:4; BPFB 3; CA 81-84; 165; CANR 33, 62; CMW 4; CPW; DA3; DAM POP; MTCW 1

Sanders, Noah
See Blount, Roy (Alton), Jr.

Sanders, Winston P.
See Anderson, Poul (William)

Sandoz, Mari(e Susette) 1900-1966 .. **CLC 28**
See also CA 1-4R; 25-28R; CANR 17, 64; DLB 9, 212; LAIT 2; MTCW 1, 2; SATA 5; TCWW 1, 2

Sandys, George 1578-1644 .... **LC 80**
See also DLB 24, 121

Saner, Reg(inald Anthony) 1931- .... **CLC 9**
See also CA 65-68; CP 3, 4, 5, 6, 7

Sankara 788-820 .... **CMLC 32**

Sannazaro, Jacopo 1456(?)-1530 .... **LC 8**
See also RGWL 2, 3; WLIT 7

Sansom, William 1912-1976 . **CLC 2, 6; SSC 21**
See also CA 5-8R; 65-68; CANR 42; CN 1, 2; DAM NOV; DLB 139; EWL 3; MTCW 1; RGEL 2; RGSF 2

Santayana, George 1863-1952 .... **TCLC 40**
See also AMW; CA 115; 194; DLB 54, 71, 246, 270; DLBD 13; EWL 3; MAL 5; RGAL 4; TUS

Santiago, Danny .... **CLC 33**
See James, Daniel (Lewis)
See also DLB 122

Santillana, Inigo Lopez de Mendoza, Marques de 1398-1458 .... **LC 111**
See also DLB 286

Santmyer, Helen Hooven 1895-1986 .... **CLC 33; TCLC 133**
See also CA 1-4R; 118; CANR 15, 33; DLBY 1984; MTCW 1; RHW

Santoka, Taneda 1882-1940 .... **TCLC 72**

Santos, Bienvenido N(uqui) 1911-1996 ... **AAL; CLC 22; TCLC 156**
See also CA 101; 151; CANR 19, 46; CP 1; DAM MULT; DLB 312; EWL; RGAL 4; SSFS 19

Sapir, Edward 1884-1939 .... **TCLC 108**
See also CA 211; DLB 92

Sapper .... **TCLC 44**
See McNeile, Herman Cyril

Sapphire
See Sapphire, Brenda

Sapphire, Brenda 1950- .... **CLC 99**

Sappho fl. 6th cent. B.C.- ... **CMLC 3, 67; PC 5**
See also CDWLB 1; DA3; DAM POET; DLB 176; FL 1:1; PFS 20; RGWL 2, 3; WP

Saramago, Jose 1922- ..... **CLC 119; HLCS 1**
See also CA 153; CANR 96; CWW 2; DLB 287; EWL 3; LATS 1:2

Sarduy, Severo 1937-1993 .... **CLC 6, 97; HLCS 2; TCLC 167**
See also CA 89-92; 142; CANR 58, 81; CWW 2; DLB 113; EWL 3; HW 1, 2; LAW

Sargeson, Frank 1903-1982 .... **CLC 31**
See also CA 25-28R; 106; CANR 38, 79; CN 1, 2, 3; EWL 3; GLL 2; RGEL 2; RGSF 2; SSFS 20

Sarmiento, Domingo Faustino 1811-1888 .... **HLCS 2**
See also LAW; WLIT 1

Sarmiento, Felix Ruben Garcia
See Dario, Ruben

Saro-Wiwa, Ken(ule Beeson) 1941-1995 .... **CLC 114**
See also BW 2; CA 142; 150; CANR 60; DLB 157

Saroyan, William 1908-1981 ... **CLC 1, 8, 10, 29, 34, 56; SSC 21; TCLC 137; WLC**
See also AAYA 66; CA 5-8R; 103; CAD; CANR 30; CDALBS; CN 1, 2; DA; DA3; DAB; DAC; DAM DRAM, MST, NOV; DFS 17; DLB 7, 9, 86; DLBY 1981; EWL 3; LAIT 4; MAL 5; MTCW 1, 2; MTFW 2005; RGAL 4; RGSF 2; SATA 23; SATA-Obit 24; SSFS 14; TUS

Sarraute, Nathalie 1900-1999 .... **CLC 1, 2, 4, 8, 10, 31, 80; TCLC 145**
See also BPFB 3; CA 9-12R; 187; CANR 23, 66, 134; CWW 2; DLB 83, 321; EW 12; EWL 3; GFL 1789 to the Present; MTCW 1, 2; MTFW 2005; RGWL 2, 3

Sarton, (Eleanor) May 1912-1995 .... **CLC 4, 14, 49, 91; PC 39; TCLC 120**
See also AMWS 8; CA 1-4R; 149; CANR 1, 34, 55, 116; CN 1, 2, 3, 4, 5, 6; CP 1, 2, 3, 4; DAM POET; DLB 48; DLBY 1981; EWL 3; FW; INT CANR-34; MAL 5; MTCW 1, 2; MTFW 2005; RGAL 4; SATA 36; SATA-Obit 86; TUS

Sartre, Jean-Paul 1905-1980 . **CLC 1, 4, 7, 9, 13, 18, 24, 44, 50, 52; DC 3; SSC 32; WLC**
See also AAYA 62; CA 9-12R; 97-100; CANR 21; DA; DA3; DAB; DAC; DAM DRAM, MST, NOV; DFS 5; DLB 72, 296, 321; EW 12; EWL 3; GFL 1789 to the Present; LMFS 2; MTCW 1, 2; MTFW 2005; NFS 21; RGSF 2; RGWL 2, 3; SSFS 9; TWA

Sassoon, Siegfried (Lorraine) 1886-1967 .... **CLC 36, 130; PC 12**
See also BRW 6; CA 104; 25-28R; CANR 36; DAB; DAM MST, NOV, POET; DLB 20, 191; DLBD 18; EWL 3; MTCW 1, 2; MTFW 2005; PAB; RGEL 2; TEA

Satterfield, Charles
See Pohl, Frederik

Satyremont
See Peret, Benjamin

Saul, John (W. III) 1942- .... **CLC 46**
See also AAYA 10, 62; BEST 90:4; CA 81-84; CANR 16, 40, 81; CPW; DAM NOV, POP; HGG; SATA 98

Saunders, Caleb
See Heinlein, Robert A(nson)

Saura (Atares), Carlos 1932-1998 .... **CLC 20**
See also CA 114; 131; CANR 79; HW 1

Sauser, Frederic Louis
See Sauser-Hall, Frederic

Sauser-Hall, Frederic 1887-1961 ...... **CLC 18**
See Cendrars, Blaise
See also CA 102; 93-96; CANR 36, 62; MTCW 1

Saussure, Ferdinand de 1857-1913 .... **TCLC 49**
See also DLB 242

Savage, Catharine
See Brosman, Catharine Savage

Savage, Richard 1697(?)-1743 .... **LC 96**
See also DLB 95; RGEL 2

Savage, Thomas 1915-2003 .... **CLC 40**
See also CA 126; 132; 218; CAAS 15; CN 6, 7; INT CA-132; SATA-Obit 147; TCWW 2

Savan, Glenn 1953-2003 .... **CLC 50**
See also CA 225

Sax, Robert
See Johnson, Robert

Saxo Grammaticus c. 1150-c. 1222 .... **CMLC 58**

Saxton, Robert
See Johnson, Robert

Sayers, Dorothy L(eigh) 1893-1957 . **SSC 71; TCLC 2, 15**
See also BPFB 3; BRWS 3; CA 104; 119; CANR 60; CDBLB 1914-1945; CMW 4; DAM POP; DLB 10, 36, 77, 100; MSW; MTCW 1, 2; MTFW 2005; RGEL 2; SSFS 12; TEA

Sayers, Valerie 1952- .... **CLC 50, 122**
See also CA 134; CANR 61; CSW

Sayles, John (Thomas) 1950- .... **CLC 7, 10, 14, 198**
See also CA 57-60; CANR 41, 84; DLB 44

Scammell, Michael 1935- .... **CLC 34**
See also CA 156

Scannell, Vernon 1922- .... **CLC 49**
See also CA 5-8R; CANR 8, 24, 57, 143; CN 1, 2; CP 1, 2, 3, 4, 5, 6, 7; CWRI 5; DLB 27; SATA 59

Scarlett, Susan
See Streatfeild, (Mary) Noel

Scarron 1847-1910
See Mikszath, Kalman

Scarron, Paul 1610-1660 .... **LC 116**
See also GFL Beginnings to 1789; RGWL 2, 3

Schaeffer, Susan Fromberg 1941- ..... **CLC 6, 11, 22**
See also CA 49-52; CANR 18, 65; CN 4, 5, 6, 7; DLB 28, 299; MTCW 1, 2; MTFW 2005; SATA 22

Schama, Simon (Michael) 1945- ...... **CLC 150**
See also BEST 89:4; CA 105; CANR 39, 91

Schary, Jill
See Robinson, Jill

Schell, Jonathan 1943- .... **CLC 35**
See also CA 73-76; CANR 12, 117

Schelling, Friedrich Wilhelm Joseph von
1775-1854 .... **NCLC 30**
See also DLB 90

Scherer, Jean-Marie Maurice 1920-
See Rohmer, Eric
See also CA 110

Schevill, James (Erwin) 1920- .... **CLC 7**
See also CA 5-8R; CAAS 12; CAD; CD 5, 6; CP 1, 2, 3, 4

Schiller, Friedrich von 1759-1805 ...... **DC 12; NCLC 39, 69**
See also CDWLB 2; DAM DRAM; DLB 94; EW 5; RGWL 2, 3; TWA

Schisgal, Murray (Joseph) 1926- .... **CLC 6**
See also CA 21-24R; CAD; CANR 48, 86; CD 5, 6; MAL 5

Schlee, Ann 1934- .... **CLC 35**
See also CA 101; CANR 29, 88; SATA 44; SATA-Brief 36

Schlegel, August Wilhelm von
1767-1845 .... **NCLC 15, 142**
See also DLB 94; RGWL 2, 3

Schlegel, Friedrich 1772-1829 .... **NCLC 45**
See also DLB 90; EW 5; RGWL 2, 3; TWA

Schlegel, Johann Elias (von)
1719(?)-1749 .... **LC 5**

Schleiermacher, Friedrich
1768-1834 .... **NCLC 107**
See also DLB 90

Schlesinger, Arthur M(eier), Jr.
1917- .... **CLC 84**
See also AITN 1; CA 1-4R; CANR 1, 28, 58, 105; DLB 17; INT CANR-28; MTCW 1, 2; SATA 61

Schlink, Bernhard 1944- .... **CLC 174**
See also CA 163; CANR 116

Schmidt, Arno (Otto) 1914-1979 ...... **CLC 56**
See also CA 128; 109; DLB 69; EWL 3

Schmitz, Aron Hector 1861-1928
See Svevo, Italo
See also CA 104; 122; MTCW 1

Schnackenberg, Gjertrud (Cecelia)
1953- .... **CLC 40; PC 45**
See also AMWS 15; CA 116; CANR 100; CP 7; CWP; DLB 120, 282; PFS 13

Schneider, Leonard Alfred 1925-1966
See Bruce, Lenny
See also CA 89-92

Schnitzler, Arthur 1862-1931 ..... **DC 17; SSC 15, 61; TCLC 4**
See also CA 104; CDWLB 2; DLB 81, 118; EW 8; EWL 3; RGSF 2; RGWL 2, 3

Schoenberg, Arnold Franz Walter
1874-1951 .... **TCLC 75**
See also CA 109; 188

Schonberg, Arnold
See Schoenberg, Arnold Franz Walter

Schopenhauer, Arthur 1788-1860 . **NCLC 51, 157**
See also DLB 90; EW 5

Schor, Sandra (M.) 1932(?)-1990 ...... **CLC 65**
See also CA 132

Schorer, Mark 1908-1977 .... **CLC 9**
See also CA 5-8R; 73-76; CANR 7; CN 1, 2; DLB 103

Schrader, Paul (Joseph) 1946- . **CLC 26, 212**
See also CA 37-40R; CANR 41; DLB 44

Schreber, Daniel 1842-1911 .... **TCLC 123**

Schreiner, Olive (Emilie Albertina)
1855-1920 .... **TCLC 9**
See also AFW; BRWS 2; CA 105; 154; DLB 18, 156, 190, 225; EWL 3; FW; RGEL 2; TWA; WLIT 2; WWE 1

Schulberg, Budd (Wilson) 1914- .. **CLC 7, 48**
See also BPFB 1; CA 25-28R; CANR 19, 87; CN 1, 2, 3, 4, 5, 6, 7; DLB 6, 26, 28; DLBY 1981, 2001; MAL 5

Schulman, Arnold
See Trumbo, Dalton

Schulz, Bruno 1892-1942 .. **SSC 13; TCLC 5, 51**
See also CA 115; 123; CANR 86; CDWLB 4; DLB 215; EWL 3; MTCW 2; MTFW 2005; RGSF 2; RGWL 2, 3

Schulz, Charles M. 1922-2000 .... **CLC 12**
See also AAYA 39; CA 9-12R; 187; CANR 6, 132; INT CANR-6; MTFW 2005; SATA 10; SATA-Obit 118

Schulz, Charles Monroe
See Schulz, Charles M.

Schumacher, E(rnst) F(riedrich)
1911-1977 .... **CLC 80**
See also CA 81-84; 73-76; CANR 34, 85

Schumann, Robert 1810-1856 .... **NCLC 143**

Schuyler, George Samuel 1895-1977 . **HR 1:3**
See also BW 2; CA 81-84; 73-76; CANR 42; DLB 29, 51

Schuyler, James Marcus 1923-1991 .. **CLC 5, 23**
See also CA 101; 134; CP 1, 2, 3, 4; DAM POET; DLB 5, 169; EWL 3; INT CA-101; MAL 5; WP

Schwartz, Delmore (David)
1913-1966 ... **CLC 2, 4, 10, 45, 87; PC 8**
See also AMWS 2; CA 17-18; 25-28R; CANR 35; CAP 2; DLB 28, 48; EWL 3; MAL 5; MTCW 1, 2; MTFW 2005; PAB; RGAL 4; TUS

Schwartz, Ernst
See Ozu, Yasujiro

Schwartz, John Burnham 1965- .... **CLC 59**
See also CA 132; CANR 116

Schwartz, Lynne Sharon 1939- .... **CLC 31**
See also CA 103; CANR 44, 89; DLB 218; MTCW 2; MTFW 2005

Schwartz, Muriel A.
See Eliot, T(homas) S(tearns)

Schwarz-Bart, Andre 1928- .... **CLC 2, 4**
See also CA 89-92; CANR 109; DLB 299

Schwarz-Bart, Simone 1938- . **BLCS; CLC 7**
See also BW 2; CA 97-100; CANR 117; EWL 3

Schwerner, Armand 1927-1999 .... **PC 42**
See also CA 9-12R; 179; CANR 50, 85; CP 2, 3, 4; DLB 165

Schwitters, Kurt (Hermann Edward Karl
Julius) 1887-1948 .... **TCLC 95**
See also CA 158

Schwob, Marcel (Mayer Andre)
1867-1905 .... **TCLC 20**
See also CA 117; 168; DLB 123; GFL 1789 to the Present

Sciascia, Leonardo 1921-1989 .. **CLC 8, 9, 41**
See also CA 85-88; 130; CANR 35; DLB 177; EWL 3; MTCW 1; RGWL 2, 3

Scoppettone, Sandra 1936- .... **CLC 26**
See Early, Jack
See also AAYA 11, 65; BYA 8; CA 5-8R; CANR 41, 73; GLL 1; MAICYA 2; MAICYAS 1; SATA 9, 92; WYA; YAW

Scorsese, Martin 1942- .... **CLC 20, 89, 207**
See also AAYA 38; CA 110; 114; CANR 46, 85

Scotland, Jay
See Jakes, John (William)

Scott, Duncan Campbell
1862-1947 .... **TCLC 6**
See also CA 104; 153; DAC; DLB 92; RGEL 2

Scott, Evelyn 1893-1963 .... **CLC 43**
See also CA 104; 112; CANR 64; DLB 9, 48; RHW

Scott, F(rancis) R(eginald)
1899-1985 .... **CLC 22**
See also CA 101; 114; CANR 87; CP 1, 2, 3, 4; DLB 88; INT CA-101; RGEL 2

Scott, Frank
See Scott, F(rancis) R(eginald)

Scott, Joan .... **CLC 65**

Scott, Joanna 1960- .... **CLC 50**
See also CA 126; CANR 53, 92

Scott, Paul (Mark) 1920-1978 ...... **CLC 9, 60**
See also BRWS 1; CA 81-84; 77-80; CANR 33; CN 1, 2; DLB 14, 207; EWL 3; MTCW 1; RGEL 2; RHW; WWE 1

Scott, Ridley 1937- .... **CLC 183**
See also AAYA 13, 43

Scott, Sarah 1723-1795 .... **LC 44**
See also DLB 39

Scott, Sir Walter 1771-1832 .... **NCLC 15, 69, 110; PC 13; SSC 32; WLC**
See also AAYA 22; BRW 4; BYA 2; CDBLB 1789-1832; DA; DAB; DAC; DAM MST, NOV, POET; DLB 93, 107, 116, 144, 159; GL 3; HGG; LAIT 1; RGEL 2; RGSF 2; SSFS 10; SUFW 1; TEA; WLIT 3; YABC 2

Scribe, (Augustin) Eugene 1791-1861 . **DC 5; NCLC 16**
See also DAM DRAM; DLB 192; GFL 1789 to the Present; RGWL 2, 3

Scrum, R.
See Crumb, R(obert)

Scudery, Georges de 1601-1667 .... **LC 75**
See also GFL Beginnings to 1789

Scudery, Madeleine de 1607-1701 .. **LC 2, 58**
See also DLB 268; GFL Beginnings to 1789

Scum
See Crumb, R(obert)

Scumbag, Little Bobby
See Crumb, R(obert)

Seabrook, John
See Hubbard, L(afayette) Ron(ald)

Seacole, Mary Jane Grant
1805-1881 .... **NCLC 147**
See also DLB 166

Sealy, I(rwin) Allan 1951- .... **CLC 55**
See also CA 136; CN 6, 7

Search, Alexander
See Pessoa, Fernando (Antonio Nogueira)

Sebald, W(infried) G(eorg)
1944-2001 .... **CLC 194**
See also BRWS 8; CA 159; 202; CANR 98; MTFW 2005

Sebastian, Lee
See Silverberg, Robert

Sebastian Owl
See Thompson, Hunter S(tockton)

Sebestyen, Igen
See Sebestyen, Ouida

Sebestyen, Ouida 1924- .... **CLC 30**
See also AAYA 8; BYA 7; CA 107; CANR 40, 114; CLR 17; JRDA; MAICYA 1, 2; SAAS 10; SATA 39, 140; WYA; YAW

Sebold, Alice 1963(?)- .... **CLC 193**
See also AAYA 56; CA 203; MTFW 2005

Second Duke of Buckingham
See Villiers, George

Secundus, H. Scriblerus
See Fielding, Henry

Sedges, John
See Buck, Pearl S(ydenstricker)

Sedgwick, Catharine Maria
1789-1867 .... **NCLC 19, 98**
See also DLB 1, 74, 183, 239, 243, 254; FL 1:3; RGAL 4

Seelye, John (Douglas) 1931- .... **CLC 7**
See also CA 97-100; CANR 70; INT CA-97-100; TCWW 1, 2

Seferiades, Giorgos Stylianou 1900-1971
See Seferis, George
See also CA 5-8R; 33-36R; CANR 5, 36; MTCW 1

Seferis, George .... CLC 5, 11; PC 66
See Seferiades, Giorgos Stylianou
See also EW 12; EWL 3; RGWL 2, 3

Segal, Erich (Wolf) 1937- .... CLC 3, 10
See also BEST 89:1; BPFB 3; CA 25-28R; CANR 20, 36, 65, 113; CPW; DAM POP; DLBY 1986; INT CANR-20; MTCW 1

Seger, Bob 1945- .... CLC 35

Seghers, Anna .... CLC 7
See Radvanyi, Netty
See also CDWLB 2; DLB 69; EWL 3

Seidel, Frederick (Lewis) 1936- .... CLC 18
See also CA 13-16R; CANR 8, 99; CP 1, 2, 3, 4, 5, 6, 7; DLBY 1984

Seifert, Jaroslav 1901-1986 . CLC 34, 44, 93; PC 47
See also CA 127; CDWLB 4; DLB 215; EWL 3; MTCW 1, 2

Sei Shonagon c. 966-1017(?) .... CMLC 6

Sejour, Victor 1817-1874 .... DC 10
See also DLB 50

Sejour Marcou et Ferrand, Juan Victor
See Sejour, Victor

Selby, Hubert, Jr. 1928-2004 ..... CLC 1, 2, 4, 8; SSC 20
See also CA 13-16R; 226; CANR 33, 85; CN 1, 2, 3, 4, 5, 6, 7; DLB 2, 227; MAL 5

Selzer, Richard 1928- .... CLC 74
See also CA 65-68; CANR 14, 106

Sembene, Ousmane
See Ousmane, Sembene
See also AFW; EWL 3; WLIT 2

Senancour, Etienne Pivert de 1770-1846 .... NCLC 16
See also DLB 119; GFL 1789 to the Present

Sender, Ramon (Jose) 1902-1982 ...... CLC 8; HLC 2; TCLC 136
See also CA 5-8R; 105; CANR 8; DAM MULT; DLB 322; EWL 3; HW 1; MTCW 1; RGWL 2, 3

Seneca, Lucius Annaeus c. 4B.C.-c. 65 .... CMLC 6; DC 5
See also AW 2; CDWLB 1; DAM DRAM; DLB 211; RGWL 2, 3; TWA

Senghor, Leopold Sedar 1906-2001 ... BLC 3; CLC 54, 130; PC 25
See also AFW; BW 2; CA 116; 125; 203; CANR 47, 74, 134; CWW 2; DAM MULT, POET; DNFS 2; EWL 3; GFL 1789 to the Present; MTCW 1, 2; MTFW 2005; TWA

Senior, Olive (Marjorie) 1941- .... SSC 78
See also BW 3; CA 154; CANR 86, 126; CN 6; CP 7; CWP; DLB 157; EWL 3; RGSF 2

Senna, Danzy 1970- .... CLC 119
See also CA 169; CANR 130

Serling, (Edward) Rod(man) 1924-1975 .... CLC 30
See also AAYA 14; AITN 1; CA 162; 57-60; DLB 26; SFW 4

Serna, Ramon Gomez de la
See Gomez de la Serna, Ramon

Serpieres
See Guillevic, (Eugene)

Service, Robert
See Service, Robert W(illiam)
See also BYA 4; DAB; DLB 92

Service, Robert W(illiam) 1874(?)-1958 ... PC 70; TCLC 15; WLC
See Service, Robert
See also CA 115; 140; CANR 84; DA; DAC; DAM MST, POET; PFS 10; RGEL 2; SATA 20

Seth, Vikram 1952- .... CLC 43, 90
See also BRWS 10; CA 121; 127; CANR 50, 74, 131; CN 6, 7; CP 7; DA3; DAM MULT; DLB 120, 271, 282; EWL 3; INT CA-127; MTCW 2; MTFW 2005; WWE 1

Seton, Cynthia Propper 1926-1982 .. CLC 27
See also CA 5-8R; 108; CANR 7

Seton, Ernest (Evan) Thompson 1860-1946 .... TCLC 31
See also ANW; BYA 3; CA 109; 204; CLR 59; DLB 92; DLBD 13; JRDA; SATA 18

Seton-Thompson, Ernest
See Seton, Ernest (Evan) Thompson

Settle, Mary Lee 1918-2005 .... CLC 19, 61
See also BPFB 3; CA 89-92; CAAS 1; CANR 44, 87, 126; CN 6, 7; CSW; DLB 6; INT CA-89-92

Seuphor, Michel
See Arp, Jean

Sevigne, Marie (de Rabutin-Chantal) 1626-1696 .... LC 11
See Sevigne, Marie de Rabutin Chantal
See also GFL Beginnings to 1789; TWA

Sevigne, Marie de Rabutin Chantal
See Sevigne, Marie (de Rabutin-Chantal)
See also DLB 268

Sewall, Samuel 1652-1730 .... LC 38
See also DLB 24; RGAL 4

Sexton, Anne (Harvey) 1928-1974 ..... CLC 2, 4, 6, 8, 10, 15, 53, 123; PC 2; WLC
See also AMWS 2; CA 1-4R; 53-56; CABS 2; CANR 3, 36; CDALB 1941-1968; CP 1, 2; DA; DA3; DAB; DAC; DAM MST, POET; DLB 5, 169; EWL 3; EXPP; FL 1:6; FW; MAL 5; MAWW; MTCW 1, 2; MTFW 2005; PAB; PFS 4, 14; RGAL 4; SATA 10; TUS

Shaara, Jeff 1952- .... CLC 119
See also CA 163; CANR 109; CN 7; MTFW 2005

Shaara, Michael (Joseph, Jr.) 1929-1988 .... CLC 15
See also AITN 1; BPFB 3; CA 102; 125; CANR 52, 85; DAM POP; DLBY 1983; MTFW 2005

Shackleton, C. C.
See Aldiss, Brian W(ilson)

Shacochis, Bob .... CLC 39
See Shacochis, Robert G.

Shacochis, Robert G. 1951-
See Shacochis, Bob
See also CA 119; 124; CANR 100; INT CA-124

Shadwell, Thomas 1641(?)-1692 .... LC 114
See also DLB 80; IDTP; RGEL 2

Shaffer, Anthony (Joshua) 1926-2001 .... CLC 19
See also CA 110; 116; 200; CBD; CD 5, 6; DAM DRAM; DFS 13; DLB 13

Shaffer, Peter (Levin) 1926- .. CLC 5, 14, 18, 37, 60; DC 7
See also BRWS 1; CA 25-28R; CANR 25, 47, 74, 118; CBD; CD 5, 6; CDBLB 1960 to Present; DA3; DAB; DAM DRAM, MST; DFS 5, 13; DLB 13, 233; EWL 3; MTCW 1, 2; MTFW 2005; RGEL 2; TEA

Shakespeare, William 1564-1616 .... WLC
See also AAYA 35; BRW 1; CDBLB Before 1660; DA; DA3; DAB; DAC; DAM DRAM, MST, POET; DFS 20, 21; DLB 62, 172, 263; EXPP; LAIT 1; LATS 1:1; LMFS 1; PAB; PFS 1, 2, 3, 4, 5, 8, 9; RGEL 2; TEA; WLIT 3; WP; WS; WYA

Shakey, Bernard
See Young, Neil

Shalamov, Varlam (Tikhonovich) 1907-1982 .... CLC 18
See also CA 129; 105; DLB 302; RGSF 2

Shamloo, Ahmad
See Shamlu, Ahmad

Shamlou, Ahmad
See Shamlu, Ahmad

Shamlu, Ahmad 1925-2000 .... CLC 10
See also CA 216; CWW 2

Shammas, Anton 1951- .... CLC 55
See also CA 199

Shandling, Arline
See Berriault, Gina

Shange, Ntozake 1948- ... BLC 3; CLC 8, 25, 38, 74, 126; DC 3
See also AAYA 9, 66; AFAW 1, 2; BW 2; CA 85-88; CABS 3; CAD; CANR 27, 48, 74, 131; CD 5, 6; CP 7; CWD; CWP; DA3; DAM DRAM, MULT; DFS 2, 11; DLB 38, 249; FW; LAIT 4, 5; MAL 5; MTCW 1, 2; MTFW 2005; NFS 11; RGAL 4; SATA 157; YAW

Shanley, John Patrick 1950- .... CLC 75
See also AMWS 14; CA 128; 133; CAD; CANR 83; CD 5, 6

Shapcott, Thomas W(illiam) 1935- .. CLC 38
See also CA 69-72; CANR 49, 83, 103; CP 1, 2, 3, 4, 5, 6, 7; DLB 289

Shapiro, Jane 1942- .... CLC 76
See also CA 196

Shapiro, Karl (Jay) 1913-2000 ...... CLC 4, 8, 15, 53; PC 25
See also AMWS 2; CA 1-4R; 188; CAAS 6; CANR 1, 36, 66; CP 1, 2, 3, 4, 5, 6; DLB 48; EWL 3; EXPP; MAL 5; MTCW 1, 2; MTFW 2005; PFS 3; RGAL 4

Sharp, William 1855-1905 .... TCLC 39
See Macleod, Fiona
See also CA 160; DLB 156; RGEL 2

Sharpe, Thomas Ridley 1928-
See Sharpe, Tom
See also CA 114; 122; CANR 85; INT CA-122

Sharpe, Tom .... CLC 36
See Sharpe, Thomas Ridley
See also CN 4, 5, 6, 7; DLB 14, 231

Shatrov, Mikhail .... CLC 59

Shaw, Bernard
See Shaw, George Bernard
See also DLB 10, 57, 190

Shaw, G. Bernard
See Shaw, George Bernard

Shaw, George Bernard 1856-1950 ..... DC 23; TCLC 3, 9, 21, 45; WLC
See Shaw, Bernard
See also AAYA 61; BRW 6; BRWC 1; BRWR 2; CA 104; 128; CDBLB 1914-1945; DA; DA3; DAB; DAC; DAM DRAM, MST; DFS 1, 3, 6, 11, 19, 22; EWL 3; LAIT 3; LATS 1:1; MTCW 1, 2; MTFW 2005; RGEL 2; TEA; WLIT 4

Shaw, Henry Wheeler 1818-1885 .. NCLC 15
See also DLB 11; RGAL 4

Shaw, Irwin 1913-1984 .... CLC 7, 23, 34
See also AITN 1; BPFB 3; CA 13-16R; 112; CANR 21; CDALB 1941-1968; CN 1, 2, 3; CPW; DAM DRAM, POP; DLB 6, 102; DLBY 1984; MAL 5; MTCW 1, 21; MTFW 2005

Shaw, Robert (Archibald) 1927-1978 .... CLC 5
See also AITN 1; CA 1-4R; 81-84; CANR 4; CN 1, 2; DLB 13, 14

Shaw, T. E.
See Lawrence, T(homas) E(dward)

Shawn, Wallace 1943- .... CLC 41
See also CA 112; CAD; CD 5, 6; DLB 266

Shchedrin, N.
See Saltykov, Mikhail Evgrafovich

Shea, Lisa 1953- .... CLC 86
See also CA 147

Sheed, Wilfrid (John Joseph) 1930- . **CLC 2, 4, 10, 53**
See also CA 65-68; CANR 30, 66; CN 1, 2, 3, 4, 5, 6, 7; DLB 6; MAL 5; MTCW 1, 2; MTFW 2005

Sheehy, Gail 1937- .... **CLC 171**
See also CA 49-52; CANR 1, 33, 55, 92; CPW; MTCW 1

Sheldon, Alice Hastings Bradley 1915(?)-1987
See Tiptree, James, Jr.
See also CA 108; 122; CANR 34; INT CA-108; MTCW 1

Sheldon, John
See Bloch, Robert (Albert)

Sheldon, Walter J(ames) 1917-1996
See Queen, Ellery
See also AITN 1; CA 25-28R; CANR 10

Shelley, Mary Wollstonecraft (Godwin) 1797-1851 ...... **NCLC 14, 59, 103; WLC**
See also AAYA 20; BPFB 3; BRW 3; BRWC 2; BRWS 3; BYA 5; CDBLB 1789-1832; DA; DA3; DAB; DAC; DAM MST, NOV; DLB 110, 116, 159, 178; EXPN; FL 1:3; GL 3; HGG; LAIT 1; LMFS 1, 2; NFS 1; RGEL 2; SATA 29; SCFW 1, 2; SFW 4; TEA; WLIT 3

Shelley, Percy Bysshe 1792-1822 .. **NCLC 18, 93, 143; PC 14, 67; WLC**
See also AAYA 61; BRW 4; BRWR 1; CDBLB 1789-1832; DA; DA3; DAB; DAC; DAM MST, POET; DLB 96, 110, 158; EXPP; LMFS 1; PAB; PFS 2; RGEL 2; TEA; WLIT 3; WP

Shepard, James R. .... **CLC 36**
See also CA 137; CANR 59, 104; SATA 90, 164

Shepard, Jim
See Shepard, James R.

Shepard, Lucius 1947- .... **CLC 34**
See also CA 128; 141; CANR 81, 124; HGG; SCFW 2; SFW 4; SUFW 2

Shepard, Sam 1943- .... **CLC 4, 6, 17, 34, 41, 44, 169; DC 5**
See also AAYA 1, 58; AMWS 3; CA 69-72; CABS 3; CAD; CANR 22, 120, 140; CD 5, 6; DA3; DAM DRAM; DFS 3, 6, 7, 14; DLB 7, 212; EWL 3; IDFW 3, 4; MAL 5; MTCW 1, 2; MTFW 2005; RGAL 4

Shepherd, Jean Parker 1921-1999 .... **TCLC 177**
See also AITN 2; CA 77-80, 187

Shepherd, Michael
See Ludlum, Robert

Sherburne, Zoa (Lillian Morin) 1912-1995 .... **CLC 30**
See also AAYA 13; CA 1-4R; 176; CANR 3, 37; MAICYA 1, 2; SAAS 18; SATA 3; YAW

Sheridan, Frances 1724-1766 .... **LC 7**
See also DLB 39, 84

Sheridan, Richard Brinsley 1751-1816 .... **DC 1; NCLC 5, 91; WLC**
See also BRW 3; CDBLB 1660-1789; DA; DAB; DAC; DAM DRAM, MST; DFS 15; DLB 89; WLIT 3

Sherman, Jonathan Marc 1968- .... **CLC 55**
See also CA 230

Sherman, Martin 1941(?)- .... **CLC 19**
See also CA 116; 123; CAD; CANR 86; CD 5, 6; DFS 20; DLB 228; GLL 1; IDTP

Sherwin, Judith Johnson
See Johnson, Judith (Emlyn)
See also CANR 85; CP 2, 3, 4; CWP

Sherwood, Frances 1940- .... **CLC 81**
See also CA 146; 220; CAAE 220

Sherwood, Robert E(mmet) 1896-1955 .... **TCLC 3**
See also CA 104; 153; CANR 86; DAM DRAM; DFS 11, 15, 17; DLB 7, 26, 249; IDFW 3, 4; MAL 5; RGAL 4

Shestov, Lev 1866-1938 .... **TCLC 56**

Shevchenko, Taras 1814-1861 .... **NCLC 54**

Shiel, M(atthew) P(hipps) 1865-1947 .... **TCLC 8**
See Holmes, Gordon
See also CA 106; 160; DLB 153; HGG; MTCW 2; MTFW 2005; SCFW 1, 2; SFW 4; SUFW

Shields, Carol (Ann) 1935-2003 ...... **CLC 91, 113, 193**
See also AMWS 7; CA 81-84; 218; CANR 51, 74, 98, 133; CCA 1; CN 6, 7; CPW; DA3; DAC; MTCW 2; MTFW 2005

Shields, David (Jonathan) 1956- .... **CLC 97**
See also CA 124; CANR 48, 99, 112

Shiga, Naoya 1883-1971 .... **CLC 33; SSC 23; TCLC 172**
See Shiga Naoya
See also CA 101; 33-36R; MJW; RGWL 3

Shiga Naoya
See Shiga, Naoya
See also DLB 180; EWL 3; RGWL 3

Shilts, Randy 1951-1994 .... **CLC 85**
See also AAYA 19; CA 115; 127; 144; CANR 45; DA3; GLL 1; INT CA-127; MTCW 2; MTFW 2005

Shimazaki, Haruki 1872-1943
See Shimazaki Toson
See also CA 105; 134; CANR 84; RGWL 3

Shimazaki Toson .... **TCLC 5**
See Shimazaki, Haruki
See also DLB 180; EWL 3

Shirley, James 1596-1666 .... **DC 25; LC 96**
See also DLB 58; RGEL 2

Sholokhov, Mikhail (Aleksandrovich) 1905-1984 .... **CLC 7, 15**
See also CA 101; 112; DLB 272; EWL 3; MTCW 1, 2; MTFW 2005; RGWL 2, 3; SATA-Obit 36

Shone, Patric
See Hanley, James

Showalter, Elaine 1941- .... **CLC 169**
See also CA 57-60; CANR 58, 106; DLB 67; FW; GLL 2

Shreve, Susan
See Shreve, Susan Richards

Shreve, Susan Richards 1939- .... **CLC 23**
See also CA 49-52; CAAS 5; CANR 5, 38, 69, 100; MAICYA 1, 2; SATA 46, 95, 152; SATA-Brief 41

Shue, Larry 1946-1985 .... **CLC 52**
See also CA 145; 117; DAM DRAM; DFS 7

Shu-Jen, Chou 1881-1936
See Lu Hsun
See also CA 104

Shulman, Alix Kates 1932- .... **CLC 2, 10**
See also CA 29-32R; CANR 43; FW; SATA 7

Shuster, Joe 1914-1992 .... **CLC 21**
See also AAYA 50

Shute, Nevil .... **CLC 30**
See Norway, Nevil Shute
See also BPFB 3; DLB 255; NFS 9; RHW; SFW 4

Shuttle, Penelope (Diane) 1947- .... **CLC 7**
See also CA 93-96; CANR 39, 84, 92, 108; CP 3, 4, 5, 6, 7; CWP; DLB 14, 40

Shvarts, Elena 1948- .... **PC 50**
See also CA 147

Sidhwa, Bapsi
See Sidhwa, Bapsi (N.)
See also CN 6, 7

Sidhwa, Bapsy (N.) 1938- .... **CLC 168**
See Sidhwa, Bapsi
See also CA 108; CANR 25, 57; FW

Sidney, Mary 1561-1621 .... **LC 19, 39**
See Sidney Herbert, Mary

Sidney, Sir Philip 1554-1586 . **LC 19, 39; PC 32**
See also BRW 1; BRWR 2; CDBLB Before 1660; DA; DA3; DAB; DAC; DAM MST, POET; DLB 167; EXPP; PAB; RGEL 2; TEA; WP

Sidney Herbert, Mary
See Sidney, Mary
See also DLB 167

Siegel, Jerome 1914-1996 .... **CLC 21**
See Siegel, Jerry
See also CA 116; 169; 151

Siegel, Jerry
See Siegel, Jerome
See also AAYA 50

Sienkiewicz, Henryk (Adam Alexander Pius) 1846-1916 .... **TCLC 3**
See also CA 104; 134; CANR 84; EWL 3; RGSF 2; RGWL 2, 3

Sierra, Gregorio Martinez
See Martinez Sierra, Gregorio

Sierra, Maria (de la O'LeJarraga) Martinez
See Martinez Sierra, Maria (de la O'LeJarraga)

Sigal, Clancy 1926- .... **CLC 7**
See also CA 1-4R; CANR 85; CN 1, 2, 3, 4, 5, 6, 7

Siger of Brabant 1240(?)-1284(?) . **CMLC 69**
See also DLB 115

Sigourney, Lydia H.
See Sigourney, Lydia Howard (Huntley)
See also DLB 73, 183

Sigourney, Lydia Howard (Huntley) 1791-1865 .... **NCLC 21, 87**
See Sigourney, Lydia H.; Sigourney, Lydia Huntley
See also DLB 1

Sigourney, Lydia Huntley
See Sigourney, Lydia Howard (Huntley)
See also DLB 42, 239, 243

Siguenza y Gongora, Carlos de 1645-1700 .... **HLCS 2; LC 8**
See also LAW

Sigurjonsson, Johann
See Sigurjonsson, Johann

Sigurjonsson, Johann 1880-1919 ... **TCLC 27**
See also CA 170; DLB 293; EWL 3

Sikelianos, Angelos 1884-1951 .... **PC 29; TCLC 39**
See also EWL 3; RGWL 2, 3

Silkin, Jon 1930-1997 .... **CLC 2, 6, 43**
See also CA 5-8R; CAAS 5; CANR 89; CP 1, 2, 3, 4, 5, 6; DLB 27

Silko, Leslie (Marmon) 1948- .... **CLC 23, 74, 114, 211; NNAL; SSC 37, 66; WLCS**
See also AAYA 14; AMWS 4; ANW; BYA 12; CA 115; 122; CANR 45, 65, 118; CN 4, 5, 6, 7; CP 4, 5, 6, 7; CPW 1; CWP; DA; DA3; DAC; DAM MST, MULT, POP; DLB 143, 175, 256, 275; EWL 3; EXPP; EXPS; LAIT 4; MAL 5; MTCW 2; MTFW 2005; NFS 4; PFS 9, 16; RGAL 4; RGSF 2; SSFS 4, 8, 10, 11; TCWW 1, 2

Sillanpaa, Frans Eemil 1888-1964 ... **CLC 19**
See also CA 129; 93-96; EWL 3; MTCW 1

Sillitoe, Alan 1928- .. **CLC 1, 3, 6, 10, 19, 57, 148**
See also AITN 1; BRWS 5; CA 9-12R, 191; CAAE 191; CAAS 2; CANR 8, 26, 55, 139; CDBLB 1960 to Present; CN 1, 2, 3, 4, 5, 6; CP 1, 2, 3, 4; DLB 14, 139; EWL 3; MTCW 1, 2; MTFW 2005; RGEL 2; RGSF 2; SATA 61

Silone, Ignazio 1900-1978 .... **CLC 4**
See also CA 25-28; 81-84; CANR 34; CAP 2; DLB 264; EW 12; EWL 3; MTCW 1; RGSF 2; RGWL 2, 3

Silone, Ignazione
See Silone, Ignazio

Silver, Joan Micklin 1935- .... **CLC 20**
See also CA 114; 121; INT CA-121

Silver, Nicholas
See Faust, Frederick (Schiller)

Silverberg, Robert 1935- .... **CLC 7, 140**
See also AAYA 24; BPFB 3; BYA 7, 9; CA 1-4R, 186; CAAE 186; CAAS 3; CANR 1, 20, 36, 85, 140; CLR 59; CN 6, 7; CPW; DAM POP; DLB 8; INT CANR-20; MAICYA 1, 2; MTCW 1, 2; MTFW 2005; SATA 13, 91; SATA-Essay 104; SCFW 1, 2; SFW 4; SUFW 2

Silverstein, Alvin 1933- .... **CLC 17**
See also CA 49-52; CANR 2; CLR 25; JRDA; MAICYA 1, 2; SATA 8, 69, 124

Silverstein, Shel(don Allan)
1932-1999 .... **PC 49**
See also AAYA 40; BW 3; CA 107; 179; CANR 47, 74, 81; CLR 5, 96; CWRI 5; JRDA; MAICYA 1, 2; MTCW 2; MTFW 2005; SATA 33, 92; SATA-Brief 27; SATA-Obit 116

Silverstein, Virginia B(arbara Opshelor)
1937- .... **CLC 17**
See also CA 49-52; CANR 2; CLR 25; JRDA; MAICYA 1, 2; SATA 8, 69, 124

Sim, Georges
See Simenon, Georges (Jacques Christian)

Simak, Clifford D(onald) 1904-1988 . **CLC 1, 55**
See also CA 1-4R; 125; CANR 1, 35; DLB 8; MTCW 1; SATA-Obit 56; SCFW 1, 2; SFW 4

Simenon, Georges (Jacques Christian)
1903-1989 .... **CLC 1, 2, 3, 8, 18, 47**
See also BPFB 3; CA 85-88; 129; CANR 35; CMW 4; DA3; DAM POP; DLB 72; DLBY 1989; EW 12; EWL 3; GFL 1789 to the Present; MSW; MTCW 1, 2; MTFW 2005; RGWL 2, 3

Simic, Charles 1938- .... **CLC 6, 9, 22, 49, 68, 130; PC 69**
See also AMWS 8; CA 29-32R; CAAS 4; CANR 12, 33, 52, 61, 96, 140; CP 2, 3, 4, 5, 6, 7; DA3; DAM POET; DLB 105; MAL 5; MTCW 2; MTFW 2005; PFS 7; RGAL 4; WP

Simmel, Georg 1858-1918 .... **TCLC 64**
See also CA 157; DLB 296

Simmons, Charles (Paul) 1924- .... **CLC 57**
See also CA 89-92; INT CA-89-92

Simmons, Dan 1948- .... **CLC 44**
See also AAYA 16, 54; CA 138; CANR 53, 81, 126; CPW; DAM POP; HGG; SUFW 2

Simmons, James (Stewart Alexander)
1933- .... **CLC 43**
See also CA 105; CAAS 21; CP 1, 2, 3, 4, 5, 6, 7; DLB 40

Simms, William Gilmore
1806-1870 .... **NCLC 3**
See also DLB 3, 30, 59, 73, 248, 254; RGAL 4

Simon, Carly 1945- .... **CLC 26**
See also CA 105

Simon, Claude 1913-2005 ... **CLC 4, 9, 15, 39**
See also CA 89-92; 241; CANR 33, 117; CWW 2; DAM NOV; DLB 83; EW 13; EWL 3; GFL 1789 to the Present; MTCW 1

Simon, Claude Eugene Henri
See Simon, Claude

Simon, Claude Henri Eugene
See Simon, Claude

Simon, Myles
See Follett, Ken(neth Martin)

Simon, (Marvin) Neil 1927- ... **CLC 6, 11, 31, 39, 70; DC 14**
See also AAYA 32; AITN 1; AMWS 4; CA 21-24R; CAD; CANR 26, 54, 87, 126; CD 5, 6; DA3; DAM DRAM; DFS 2, 6, 12, 18; DLB 7, 266; LAIT 4; MAL 5; MTCW 1, 2; MTFW 2005; RGAL 4; TUS

Simon, Paul (Frederick) 1941(?)- ..... **CLC 17**
See also CA 116; 153

Simonon, Paul 1956(?)- .... **CLC 30**

Simonson, Rick ed. .... **CLC 70**

Simpson, Harriette
See Arnow, Harriette (Louisa) Simpson

Simpson, Louis (Aston Marantz)
1923- .... **CLC 4, 7, 9, 32, 149**
See also AMWS 9; CA 1-4R; CAAS 4; CANR 1, 61, 140; CP 1, 2, 3, 4, 5, 6, 7; DAM POET; DLB 5; MAL 5; MTCW 1, 2; MTFW 2005; PFS 7, 11, 14; RGAL 4

Simpson, Mona (Elizabeth) 1957- ... **CLC 44, 146**
See also CA 122; 135; CANR 68, 103; CN 6, 7; EWL 3

Simpson, N(orman) F(rederick)
1919- .... **CLC 29**
See also CA 13-16R; CBD; DLB 13; RGEL 2

Sinclair, Andrew (Annandale) 1935- . **CLC 2, 14**
See also CA 9-12R; CAAS 5; CANR 14, 38, 91; CN 1, 2, 3, 4, 5, 6, 7; DLB 14; FANT; MTCW 1

Sinclair, Emil
See Hesse, Hermann

Sinclair, Iain 1943- .... **CLC 76**
See also CA 132; CANR 81; CP 7; HGG

Sinclair, Iain MacGregor
See Sinclair, Iain

Sinclair, Irene
See Griffith, D(avid Lewelyn) W(ark)

Sinclair, Mary Amelia St. Clair 1865(?)-1946
See Sinclair, May
See also CA 104; HGG; RHW

Sinclair, May .... **TCLC 3, 11**
See Sinclair, Mary Amelia St. Clair
See also CA 166; DLB 36, 135; EWL 3; RGEL 2; SUFW

Sinclair, Roy
See Griffith, D(avid Lewelyn) W(ark)

Sinclair, Upton (Beall) 1878-1968 ..... **CLC 1, 11, 15, 63; TCLC 160; WLC**
See also AAYA 63; AMWS 5; BPFB 3; BYA 2; CA 5-8R; 25-28R; CANR 7; CDALB 1929-1941; DA; DA3; DAB; DAC; DAM MST, NOV; DLB 9; EWL 3; INT CANR-7; LAIT 3; MAL 5; MTCW 1, 2; MTFW 2005; NFS 6; RGAL 4; SATA 9; TUS; YAW

Singe, (Edmund) J(ohn) M(illington)
1871-1909 .... **WLC**

Singer, Isaac
See Singer, Isaac Bashevis

Singer, Isaac Bashevis 1904-1991 .. **CLC 1, 3, 6, 9, 11, 15, 23, 38, 69, 111; SSC 3, 53, 80; WLC**
See also AAYA 32; AITN 1, 2; AMW; AMWR 2; BPFB 3; BYA 1, 4; CA 1-4R; 134; CANR 1, 39, 106; CDALB 1941-1968; CLR 1; CN 1, 2, 3, 4; CWRI 5; DA; DA3; DAB; DAC; DAM MST, NOV; DLB 6, 28, 52, 278; DLBY 1991; EWL 3; EXPS; HGG; JRDA; LAIT 3; MAICYA 1, 2; MAL 5; MTCW 1, 2; MTFW 2005; RGAL 4; RGSF 2; SATA 3, 27; SATA-Obit 68; SSFS 2, 12, 16; TUS; TWA

Singer, Israel Joshua 1893-1944 .... **TCLC 33**
See also CA 169; EWL 3

Singh, Khushwant 1915- .... **CLC 11**
See also CA 9-12R; CAAS 9; CANR 6, 84; CN 1, 2, 3, 4, 5, 6, 7; EWL 3; RGEL 2

Singleton, Ann
See Benedict, Ruth (Fulton)

Singleton, John 1968(?)- .... **CLC 156**
See also AAYA 50; BW 2, 3; CA 138; CANR 67, 82; DAM MULT

Siniavskii, Andrei
See Sinyavsky, Andrei (Donatevich)
See also CWW 2

Sinjohn, John
See Galsworthy, John

Sinyavsky, Andrei (Donatevich)
1925-1997 .... **CLC 8**
See Siniavskii, Andrei; Sinyavsky, Andrey Donatovich; Tertz, Abram
See also CA 85-88; 159

Sinyavsky, Andrey Donatovich
See Sinyavsky, Andrei (Donatevich)
See also EWL 3

Sirin, V.
See Nabokov, Vladimir (Vladimirovich)

Sissman, L(ouis) E(dward)
1928-1976 .... **CLC 9, 18**
See also CA 21-24R; 65-68; CANR 13; CP 2; DLB 5

Sisson, C(harles) H(ubert)
1914-2003 .... **CLC 8**
See also BRWS 11; CA 1-4R; 220; CAAS 3; CANR 3, 48, 84; CP 1, 2, 3, 4, 5, 6, 7; DLB 27

Sitting Bull 1831(?)-1890 .... **NNAL**
See also DA3; DAM MULT

Sitwell, Dame Edith 1887-1964 ..... **CLC 2, 9, 67; PC 3**
See also BRW 7; CA 9-12R; CANR 35; CDBLB 1945-1960; DAM POET; DLB 20; EWL 3; MTCW 1, 2; MTFW 2005; RGEL 2; TEA

Siwaarmill, H. P.
See Sharp, William

Sjoewall, Maj 1935- .... **CLC 7**
See Sjowall, Maj
See also CA 65-68; CANR 73

Sjowall, Maj
See Sjoewall, Maj
See also BPFB 3; CMW 4; MSW

Skelton, John 1460(?)-1529 ..... **LC 71; PC 25**
See also BRW 1; DLB 136; RGEL 2

Skelton, Robin 1925-1997 .... **CLC 13**
See Zuk, Georges
See also AITN 2; CA 5-8R; 160; CAAS 5; CANR 28, 89; CCA 1; CP 1, 2, 3, 4; DLB 27, 53

Skolimowski, Jerzy 1938- .... **CLC 20**
See also CA 128

Skram, Amalie (Bertha)
1847-1905 .... **TCLC 25**
See also CA 165

Skvorecky, Josef (Vaclav) 1924- ...... **CLC 15, 39, 69, 152**
See also CA 61-64; CAAS 1; CANR 10, 34, 63, 108; CDWLB 4; CWW 2; DA3; DAC; DAM NOV; DLB 232; EWL 3; MTCW 1, 2; MTFW 2005

Slade, Bernard 1930- .... **CLC 11, 46**
See Newbound, Bernard Slade
See also CAAS 9; CCA 1; CD 6; DLB 53

Slaughter, Carolyn 1946- .... **CLC 56**
See also CA 85-88; CANR 85; CN 5, 6, 7

Slaughter, Frank G(ill) 1908-2001 ... **CLC 29**
See also AITN 2; CA 5-8R; 197; CANR 5, 85; INT CANR-5; RHW

Slavitt, David R(ytman) 1935- ..... **CLC 5, 14**
See also CA 21-24R; CAAS 3; CANR 41, 83; CN 1, 2; CP 1, 2, 3, 4, 5, 6, 7; DLB 5, 6

Slesinger, Tess 1905-1945 .... **TCLC 10**
See also CA 107; 199; DLB 102

Slessor, Kenneth 1901-1971 .... **CLC 14**
See also CA 102; 89-92; DLB 260; RGEL 2

Slowacki, Juliusz 1809-1849 .... **NCLC 15**
See also RGWL 3

Smart, Christopher 1722-1771 . **LC 3; PC 13**
See also DAM POET; DLB 109; RGEL 2

Smart, Elizabeth 1913-1986 .... **CLC 54**
See also CA 81-84; 118; CN 4; DLB 88

Smiley, Jane (Graves) 1949- ...... **CLC 53, 76, 144**
See also AAYA 66; AMWS 6; BPFB 3; CA 104; CANR 30, 50, 74, 96; CN 6, 7; CPW 1; DA3; DAM POP; DLB 227, 234; EWL 3; INT CANR-30; MAL 5; MTFW 2005; SSFS 19

Smith, A(rthur) J(ames) M(arshall) 1902-1980 .... **CLC 15**
See also CA 1-4R; 102; CANR 4; CP 1, 2, 3; DAC; DLB 88; RGEL 2

Smith, Adam 1723(?)-1790 .... **LC 36**
See also DLB 104, 252; RGEL 2

Smith, Alexander 1829-1867 .... **NCLC 59**
See also DLB 32, 55

Smith, Anna Deavere 1950- .... **CLC 86**
See also CA 133; CANR 103; CD 5, 6; DFS 2, 22

Smith, Betty (Wehner) 1904-1972 .... **CLC 19**
See also BPFB 3; BYA 3; CA 5-8R; 33-36R; DLBY 1982; LAIT 3; RGAL 4; SATA 6

Smith, Charlotte (Turner) 1749-1806 .... **NCLC 23, 115**
See also DLB 39, 109; RGEL 2; TEA

Smith, Clark Ashton 1893-1961 .... **CLC 43**
See also CA 143; CANR 81; FANT; HGG; MTCW 2; SCFW 1, 2; SFW 4; SUFW

Smith, Dave .... **CLC 22, 42**
See Smith, David (Jeddie)
See also CAAS 7; CP 3, 4, 5, 6, 7; DLB 5

Smith, David (Jeddie) 1942-
See Smith, Dave
See also CA 49-52; CANR 1, 59, 120; CSW; DAM POET

Smith, Florence Margaret 1902-1971
See Smith, Stevie
See also CA 17-18; 29-32R; CANR 35; CAP 2; DAM POET; MTCW 1, 2; TEA

Smith, Iain Crichton 1928-1998 .... **CLC 64**
See also BRWS 9; CA 21-24R; 171; CN 1, 2, 3, 4, 5; CP 1, 2, 3, 4; DLB 40, 139, 319; RGSF 2

Smith, John 1580(?)-1631 .... **LC 9**
See also DLB 24, 30; TUS

Smith, Johnston
See Crane, Stephen (Townley)

Smith, Joseph, Jr. 1805-1844 .... **NCLC 53**

Smith, Lee 1944- .... **CLC 25, 73**
See also CA 114; 119; CANR 46, 118; CN 7; CSW; DLB 143; DLBY 1983; EWL 3; INT CA-119; RGAL 4

Smith, Martin
See Smith, Martin Cruz

Smith, Martin Cruz 1942- .. **CLC 25; NNAL**
See also BEST 89:4; BPFB 3; CA 85-88; CANR 6, 23, 43, 65, 119; CMW 4; CPW; DAM MULT, POP; HGG; INT CANR-23; MTCW 2; MTFW 2005; RGAL 4

Smith, Patti 1946- .... **CLC 12**
See also CA 93-96; CANR 63

Smith, Pauline (Urmson) 1882-1959 .... **TCLC 25**
See also DLB 225; EWL 3

Smith, Rosamond
See Oates, Joyce Carol

Smith, Sheila Kaye
See Kaye-Smith, Sheila

Smith, Stevie .... **CLC 3, 8, 25, 44; PC 12**
See Smith, Florence Margaret
See also BRWS 2; CP 1; DLB 20; EWL 3; PAB; PFS 3; RGEL 2

Smith, Wilbur (Addison) 1933- .... **CLC 33**
See also CA 13-16R; CANR 7, 46, 66, 134; CPW; MTCW 1, 2; MTFW 2005

Smith, William Jay 1918- .... **CLC 6**
See also AMWS 13; CA 5-8R; CANR 44, 106; CP 1, 2, 3, 4, 5, 6, 7; CSW; CWRI 5; DLB 5; MAICYA 1, 2; SAAS 22; SATA 2, 68, 154; SATA-Essay 154; TCLE 1:2

Smith, Woodrow Wilson
See Kuttner, Henry

Smith, Zadie 1976- .... **CLC 158**
See also AAYA 50; CA 193; MTFW 2005

Smolenskin, Peretz 1842-1885 .... **NCLC 30**

Smollett, Tobias (George) 1721-1771 ... **LC 2, 46**
See also BRW 3; CDBLB 1660-1789; DLB 39, 104; RGEL 2; TEA

Snodgrass, W(illiam) D(e Witt) 1926- .... **CLC 2, 6, 10, 18, 68**
See also AMWS 6; CA 1-4R; CANR 6, 36, 65, 85; CP 1, 2, 3, 4, 5, 6, 7; DAM POET; DLB 5; MAL 5; MTCW 1, 2; MTFW 2005; RGAL 4; TCLE 1:2

Snorri Sturluson 1179-1241 .... **CMLC 56**
See also RGWL 2, 3

Snow, C(harles) P(ercy) 1905-1980 ... **CLC 1, 4, 6, 9, 13, 19**
See also BRW 7; CA 5-8R; 101; CANR 28; CDBLB 1945-1960; CN 1, 2; DAM NOV; DLB 15, 77; DLBD 17; EWL 3; MTCW 1, 2; MTFW 2005; RGEL 2; TEA

Snow, Frances Compton
See Adams, Henry (Brooks)

Snyder, Gary (Sherman) 1930- . **CLC 1, 2, 5, 9, 32, 120; PC 21**
See also AMWS 8; ANW; BG 1:3; CA 17-20R; CANR 30, 60, 125; CP 1, 2, 3, 4, 5, 6, 7; DA3; DAM POET; DLB 5, 16, 165, 212, 237, 275; EWL 3; MAL 5; MTCW 2; MTFW 2005; PFS 9, 19; RGAL 4; WP

Snyder, Zilpha Keatley 1927- .... **CLC 17**
See also AAYA 15; BYA 1; CA 9-12R; CANR 38; CLR 31; JRDA; MAICYA 1, 2; SAAS 2; SATA 1, 28, 75, 110, 163; SATA-Essay 112, 163; YAW

Soares, Bernardo
See Pessoa, Fernando (Antonio Nogueira)

Sobh, A.
See Shamlu, Ahmad

Sobh, Alef
See Shamlu, Ahmad

Sobol, Joshua 1939- .... **CLC 60**
See Sobol, Yehoshua
See also CA 200

Sobol, Yehoshua 1939-
See Sobol, Joshua
See also CWW 2

Socrates 470B.C.-399B.C. .... **CMLC 27**

Soderberg, Hjalmar 1869-1941 .... **TCLC 39**
See also DLB 259; EWL 3; RGSF 2

Soderbergh, Steven 1963- .... **CLC 154**
See also AAYA 43

Sodergran, Edith (Irene) 1892-1923
See Soedergran, Edith (Irene)
See also CA 202; DLB 259; EW 11; EWL 3; RGWL 2, 3

Soedergran, Edith (Irene) 1892-1923 .... **TCLC 31**
See Sodergran, Edith (Irene)

Softly, Edgar
See Lovecraft, H(oward) P(hillips)

Softly, Edward
See Lovecraft, H(oward) P(hillips)

Sokolov, Alexander V(sevolodovich) 1943-
See Sokolov, Sasha
See also CA 73-76

Sokolov, Raymond 1941- .... **CLC 7**
See also CA 85-88

Sokolov, Sasha .... **CLC 59**
See Sokolov, Alexander V(sevolodovich)
See also CWW 2; DLB 285; EWL 3; RGWL 2, 3

Solo, Jay
See Ellison, Harlan (Jay)

Sologub, Fyodor .... **TCLC 9**
See Teternikov, Fyodor Kuzmich
See also EWL 3

Solomons, Ikey Esquir
See Thackeray, William Makepeace

Solomos, Dionysios 1798-1857 .... **NCLC 15**

Solwoska, Mara
See French, Marilyn

Solzhenitsyn, Aleksandr I(sayevich) 1918- .. **CLC 1, 2, 4, 7, 9, 10, 18, 26, 34, 78, 134; SSC 32; WLC**
See Solzhenitsyn, Aleksandr Isaevich
See also AAYA 49; AITN 1; BPFB 3; CA 69-72; CANR 40, 65, 116; DA; DA3; DAB; DAC; DAM MST, NOV; DLB 302; EW 13; EXPS; LAIT 4; MTCW 1, 2; MTFW 2005; NFS 6; RGSF 2; RGWL 2, 3; SSFS 9; TWA

Solzhenitsyn, Aleksandr Isaevich
See Solzhenitsyn, Aleksandr I(sayevich)
See also CWW 2; EWL 3

Somers, Jane
See Lessing, Doris (May)

Somerville, Edith Oenone 1858-1949 .... **SSC 56; TCLC 51**
See also CA 196; DLB 135; RGEL 2; RGSF 2

Somerville & Ross
See Martin, Violet Florence; Somerville, Edith Oenone

Sommer, Scott 1951- .... **CLC 25**
See also CA 106

Sommers, Christina Hoff 1950- .... **CLC 197**
See also CA 153; CANR 95

Sondheim, Stephen (Joshua) 1930- . **CLC 30, 39, 147; DC 22**
See also AAYA 11, 66; CA 103; CANR 47, 67, 125; DAM DRAM; LAIT 4

Sone, Monica 1919- .... **AAL**
See also DLB 312

Song, Cathy 1955- .... **AAL; PC 21**
See also CA 154; CANR 118; CWP; DLB 169, 312; EXPP; FW; PFS 5

Sontag, Susan 1933-2004 ... **CLC 1, 2, 10, 13, 31, 105, 195**
See also AMWS 3; CA 17-20R; 234; CANR 25, 51, 74, 97; CN 1, 2, 3, 4, 5, 6, 7; CPW; DA3; DAM POP; DLB 2, 67; EWL 3; MAL 5; MAWW; MTCW 1, 2; MTFW 2005; RGAL 4; RHW; SSFS 10

Sophocles 496(?)B.C.-406(?)B.C. .... **CMLC 2, 47, 51; DC 1; WLCS**
See also AW 1; CDWLB 1; DA; DA3; DAB; DAC; DAM DRAM, MST; DFS 1, 4, 8; DLB 176; LAIT 1; LATS 1:1; LMFS 1; RGWL 2, 3; TWA

Sordello 1189-1269 .... **CMLC 15**

Sorel, Georges 1847-1922 .... **TCLC 91**
See also CA 118; 188

Sorel, Julia
See Drexler, Rosalyn

Sorokin, Vladimir .... **CLC 59**
See Sorokin, Vladimir Georgievich

Sorokin, Vladimir Georgievich
See Sorokin, Vladimir
See also DLB 285
Sorrentino, Gilbert 1929- .. **CLC 3, 7, 14, 22, 40**
See also CA 77-80; CANR 14, 33, 115; CN 3, 4, 5, 6, 7; CP 1, 2, 3, 4, 5, 6, 7; DLB 5, 173; DLBY 1980; INT CANR-14
Soseki
See Natsume, Soseki
See also MJW
Soto, Gary 1952- ... **CLC 32, 80; HLC 2; PC 28**
See also AAYA 10, 37; BYA 11; CA 119; 125; CANR 50, 74, 107; CLR 38; CP 4, 5, 6, 7; DAM MULT; DLB 82; EWL 3; EXPP; HW 1, 2; INT CA-125; JRDA; LLW; MAICYA 2; MAICYAS 1; MAL 5; MTCW 2; MTFW 2005; PFS 7; RGAL 4; SATA 80, 120; WYA; YAW
Soupault, Philippe 1897-1990 .... **CLC 68**
See also CA 116; 147; 131; EWL 3; GFL 1789 to the Present; LMFS 2
Souster, (Holmes) Raymond 1921- .... **CLC 5, 14**
See also CA 13-16R; CAAS 14; CANR 13, 29, 53; CP 1, 2, 3, 4, 5, 6, 7; DA3; DAC; DAM POET; DLB 88; RGEL 2; SATA 63
Southern, Terry 1924(?)-1995 .... **CLC 7**
See also AMWS 11; BPFB 3; CA 1-4R; 150; CANR 1, 55, 107; CN 1, 2, 3, 4, 5, 6; DLB 2; IDFW 3, 4
Southerne, Thomas 1660-1746 .... **LC 99**
See also DLB 80; RGEL 2
Southey, Robert 1774-1843 .... **NCLC 8, 97**
See also BRW 4; DLB 93, 107, 142; RGEL 2; SATA 54
Southwell, Robert 1561(?)-1595 .... **LC 108**
See also DLB 167; RGEL 2; TEA
Southworth, Emma Dorothy Eliza Nevitte 1819-1899 .... **NCLC 26**
See also DLB 239
Souza, Ernest
See Scott, Evelyn
Soyinka, Wole 1934- .. **BLC 3; CLC 3, 5, 14, 36, 44, 179; DC 2; WLC**
See also AFW; BW 2, 3; CA 13-16R; CANR 27, 39, 82, 136; CD 5, 6; CDWLB 3; CN 6, 7; CP 1, 2, 3, 4, 5, 6 ,7; DA; DA3; DAB; DAC; DAM DRAM, MST, MULT; DFS 10; DLB 125; EWL 3; MTCW 1, 2; MTFW 2005; RGEL 2; TWA; WLIT 2; WWE 1
Spackman, W(illiam) M(ode) 1905-1990 .... **CLC 46**
See also CA 81-84; 132
Spacks, Barry (Bernard) 1931- .... **CLC 14**
See also CA 154; CANR 33, 109; CP 3, 4, 5, 6, 7; DLB 105
Spanidou, Irini 1946- .... **CLC 44**
See also CA 185
Spark, Muriel (Sarah) 1918- ..... **CLC 2, 3, 5, 8, 13, 18, 40, 94; SSC 10**
See also BRWS 1; CA 5-8R; CANR 12, 36, 76, 89, 131; CDBLB 1945-1960; CN 1, 2, 3, 4, 5, 6, 7; CP 1, 2, 3, 4, 5, 6, 7; DA3; DAB; DAC; DAM MST, NOV; DLB 15, 139; EWL 3; FW; INT CANR-12; LAIT 4; MTCW 1, 2; MTFW 2005; NFS 22; RGEL 2; TEA; WLIT 4; YAW
Spaulding, Douglas
See Bradbury, Ray (Douglas)
Spaulding, Leonard
See Bradbury, Ray (Douglas)
Speght, Rachel 1597-c. 1630 .... **LC 97**
See also DLB 126
Spence, J. A. D.
See Eliot, T(homas) S(tearns)

Spencer, Anne 1882-1975 .... **HR 1:3**
See also BW 2; CA 161; DLB 51, 54
Spencer, Elizabeth 1921- .... **CLC 22; SSC 57**
See also CA 13-16R; CANR 32, 65, 87; CN 1, 2, 3, 4, 5, 6, 7; CSW; DLB 6, 218; EWL 3; MTCW 1; RGAL 4; SATA 14
Spencer, Leonard G.
See Silverberg, Robert
Spencer, Scott 1945- .... **CLC 30**
See also CA 113; CANR 51; DLBY 1986
Spender, Stephen (Harold) 1909-1995 .. **CLC 1, 2, 5, 10, 41, 91; PC 71**
See also BRWS 2; CA 9-12R; 149; CANR 31, 54; CDBLB 1945-1960; CP 1, 2, 3, 4; DA3; DAM POET; DLB 20; EWL 3; MTCW 1, 2; MTFW 2005; PAB; PFS 23; RGEL 2; TEA
Spengler, Oswald (Arnold Gottfried) 1880-1936 .... **TCLC 25**
See also CA 118; 189
Spenser, Edmund 1552(?)-1599 ...... **LC 5, 39, 117; PC 8, 42; WLC**
See also AAYA 60; BRW 1; CDBLB Before 1660; DA; DA3; DAB; DAC; DAM MST, POET; DLB 167; EFS 2; EXPP; PAB; RGEL 2; TEA; WLIT 3; WP
Spicer, Jack 1925-1965 .... **CLC 8, 18, 72**
See also BG 1:3; CA 85-88; DAM POET; DLB 5, 16, 193; GLL 1; WP
Spiegelman, Art 1948- .... **CLC 76, 178**
See also AAYA 10, 46; CA 125; CANR 41, 55, 74, 124; DLB 299; MTCW 2; MTFW 2005; SATA 109, 158; YAW
Spielberg, Peter 1929- .... **CLC 6**
See also CA 5-8R; CANR 4, 48; DLBY 1981
Spielberg, Steven 1947- .... **CLC 20, 188**
See also AAYA 8, 24; CA 77-80; CANR 32; SATA 32
Spillane, Frank Morrison 1918-
See Spillane, Mickey
See also CA 25-28R; CANR 28, 63, 125; DA3; MTCW 1, 2; MTFW 2005; SATA 66
Spillane, Mickey .... **CLC 3, 13**
See Spillane, Frank Morrison
See also BPFB 3; CMW 4; DLB 226; MSW
Spinoza, Benedictus de 1632-1677 .. **LC 9, 58**
Spinrad, Norman (Richard) 1940- ...... **CLC 46**
See also BPFB 3; CA 37-40R, 233; CAAE 233; CAAS 19; CANR 20, 91; DLB 8; INT CANR-20; SFW 4
Spitteler, Carl (Friedrich Georg) 1845-1924 .... **TCLC 12**
See also CA 109; DLB 129; EWL 3
Spivack, Kathleen (Romola Drucker) 1938- .... **CLC 6**
See also CA 49-52
Spofford, Harriet (Elizabeth) Prescott 1835-1921 .... **SSC 87**
See also CA 201; DLB 74, 221
Spoto, Donald 1941- .... **CLC 39**
See also CA 65-68; CANR 11, 57, 93
Springsteen, Bruce (F.) 1949- .... **CLC 17**
See also CA 111
Spurling, Hilary 1940- .... **CLC 34**
See also CA 104; CANR 25, 52, 94
Spurling, Susan Hilary
See Spurling, Hilary
Spyker, John Howland
See Elman, Richard (Martin)
Squared, A.
See Abbott, Edwin A.
Squires, (James) Radcliffe 1917-1993 .... **CLC 51**
See also CA 1-4R; 140; CANR 6, 21; CP 1, 2, 3, 4

Srivastava, Dhanpat Rai 1880(?)-1936
See Premchand
See also CA 118; 197
Stacy, Donald
See Pohl, Frederik
Stael
See Stael-Holstein, Anne Louise Germaine Necker
See also EW 5; RGWL 2, 3
Stael, Germaine de
See Stael-Holstein, Anne Louise Germaine Necker
See also DLB 119, 192; FL 1:3; FW; GFL 1789 to the Present; TWA
Stael-Holstein, Anne Louise Germaine Necker 1766-1817 .... **NCLC 3, 91**
See Stael; Stael, Germaine de
Stafford, Jean 1915-1979 .. **CLC 4, 7, 19, 68; SSC 26, 86**
See also CA 1-4R; 85-88; CANR 3, 65; CN 1, 2; DLB 2, 173; MAL 5; MTCW 1, 2; MTFW 2005; RGAL 4; RGSF 2; SATA-Obit 22; SSFS 21; TCWW 1, 2; TUS
Stafford, William (Edgar) 1914-1993 .... **CLC 4, 7, 29; PC 71**
See also AMWS 11; CA 5-8R; 142; CAAS 3; CANR 5, 22; CP 1, 2, 3, 4; DAM POET; DLB 5, 206; EXPP; INT CANR-22; MAL 5; PFS 2, 8, 16; RGAL 4; WP
Stagnelius, Eric Johan 1793-1823 . **NCLC 61**
Staines, Trevor
See Brunner, John (Kilian Houston)
Stairs, Gordon
See Austin, Mary (Hunter)
Stalin, Joseph 1879-1953 .... **TCLC 92**
Stampa, Gaspara c. 1524-1554 .. **LC 114; PC 43**
See also RGWL 2, 3; WLIT 7
Stampflinger, K. A.
See Benjamin, Walter
Stancykowna
See Szymborska, Wislawa
Standing Bear, Luther 1868(?)-1939(?) .... **NNAL**
See also CA 113; 144; DAM MULT
Stanislavsky, Konstantin (Sergeivich) 1863(?)-1938 .... **TCLC 167**
See also CA 118
Stannard, Martin 1947- .... **CLC 44**
See also CA 142; DLB 155
Stanton, Elizabeth Cady 1815-1902 .... **TCLC 73**
See also CA 171; DLB 79; FL 1:3; FW
Stanton, Maura 1946- .... **CLC 9**
See also CA 89-92; CANR 15, 123; DLB 120
Stanton, Schuyler
See Baum, L(yman) Frank
Stapledon, (William) Olaf 1886-1950 .... **TCLC 22**
See also CA 111; 162; DLB 15, 255; SCFW 1, 2; SFW 4
Starbuck, George (Edwin) 1931-1996 .... **CLC 53**
See also CA 21-24R; 153; CANR 23; CP 1, 2, 3, 4; DAM POET
Stark, Richard
See Westlake, Donald E(dwin)
Staunton, Schuyler
See Baum, L(yman) Frank
Stead, Christina (Ellen) 1902-1983 ... **CLC 2, 5, 8, 32, 80**
See also BRWS 4; CA 13-16R; 109; CANR 33, 40; CN 1, 2, 3; DLB 260; EWL 3; FW; MTCW 1, 2; MTFW 2005; RGEL 2; RGSF 2; WWE 1
Stead, William Thomas 1849-1912 .... **TCLC 48**
See also CA 167

Stebnitsky, M.
See Leskov, Nikolai (Semyonovich)

Steele, Richard 1672-1729 .... **LC 18**
See also BRW 3; CDBLB 1660-1789; DLB 84, 101; RGEL 2; WLIT 3

Steele, Timothy (Reid) 1948- .... **CLC 45**
See also CA 93-96; CANR 16, 50, 92; CP 7; DLB 120, 282

Steffens, (Joseph) Lincoln
1866-1936 .... **TCLC 20**
See also CA 117; 198; DLB 303; MAL 5

Stegner, Wallace (Earle) 1909-1993 .. **CLC 9, 49, 81; SSC 27**
See also AITN 1; AMWS 4; ANW; BEST 90:3; BPFB 3; CA 1-4R; 141; CAAS 9; CANR 1, 21, 46; CN 1, 2, 3, 4, 5; DAM NOV; DLB 9, 206, 275; DLBY 1993; EWL 3; MAL 5; MTCW 1, 2; MTFW 2005; RGAL 4; TCWW 1, 2; TUS

Stein, Gertrude 1874-1946 .... **DC 19; PC 18; SSC 42; TCLC 1, 6, 28, 48; WLC**
See also AAYA 64; AMW; AMWC 2; CA 104; 132; CANR 108; CDALB 1917-1929; DA; DA3; DAB; DAC; DAM MST, NOV, POET; DLB 4, 54, 86, 228; DLBD 15; EWL 3; EXPS; FL 1:6; GLL 1; MAL 5; MAWW; MTCW 1, 2; MTFW 2005; NCFS 4; RGAL 4; RGSF 2; SSFS 5; TUS; WP

Steinbeck, John (Ernst) 1902-1968 ... **CLC 1, 5, 9, 13, 21, 34, 45, 75, 124; SSC 11, 37, 77; TCLC 135; WLC**
See also AAYA 12; AMW; BPFB 3; BYA 2, 3, 13; CA 1-4R; 25-28R; CANR 1, 35; CDALB 1929-1941; DA; DA3; DAB; DAC; DAM DRAM, MST, NOV; DLB 7, 9, 212, 275, 309; DLBD 2; EWL 3; EXPS; LAIT 3; MAL 5; MTCW 1, 2; MTFW 2005; NFS 1, 5, 7, 17, 19; RGAL 4; RGSF 2; RHW; SATA 9; SSFS 3, 6; TCWW 1, 2; TUS; WYA; YAW

Steinem, Gloria 1934- .... **CLC 63**
See also CA 53-56; CANR 28, 51, 139; DLB 246; FW; MTCW 1, 2; MTFW 2005

Steiner, George 1929- .... **CLC 24, 221**
See also CA 73-76; CANR 31, 67, 108; DAM NOV; DLB 67, 299; EWL 3; MTCW 1, 2; MTFW 2005; SATA 62

Steiner, K. Leslie
See Delany, Samuel R(ay), Jr.

Steiner, Rudolf 1861-1925 .... **TCLC 13**
See also CA 107

Stendhal 1783-1842 .. **NCLC 23, 46; SSC 27; WLC**
See also DA; DA3; DAB; DAC; DAM MST, NOV; DLB 119; EW 5; GFL 1789 to the Present; RGWL 2, 3; TWA

Stephen, Adeline Virginia
See Woolf, (Adeline) Virginia

Stephen, Sir Leslie 1832-1904 .... **TCLC 23**
See also BRW 5; CA 123; DLB 57, 144, 190

Stephen, Sir Leslie
See Stephen, Sir Leslie

Stephen, Virginia
See Woolf, (Adeline) Virginia

Stephens, James 1882(?)-1950 .... **SSC 50; TCLC 4**
See also CA 104; 192; DLB 19, 153, 162; EWL 3; FANT; RGEL 2; SUFW

Stephens, Reed
See Donaldson, Stephen R(eeder)

Stephenson, Neal 1959- .... **CLC 220**
See also AAYA 38; CA 122; CANR 88, 138; CN 7; MTCW 2005; SFW 4

Steptoe, Lydia
See Barnes, Djuna
See also GLL 1

Sterchi, Beat 1949- .... **CLC 65**
See also CA 203

Sterling, Brett
See Bradbury, Ray (Douglas); Hamilton, Edmond

Sterling, Bruce 1954- .... **CLC 72**
See also CA 119; CANR 44, 135; CN 7; MTFW 2005; SCFW 2; SFW 4

Sterling, George 1869-1926 .... **TCLC 20**
See also CA 117; 165; DLB 54

Stern, Gerald 1925- .... **CLC 40, 100**
See also AMWS 9; CA 81-84; CANR 28, 94; CP 3, 4, 5, 6, 7; DLB 105; RGAL 4

Stern, Richard (Gustave) 1928- ... **CLC 4, 39**
See also CA 1-4R; CANR 1, 25, 52, 120; CN 1, 2, 3, 4, 5, 6, 7; DLB 218; DLBY 1987; INT CANR-25

Sternberg, Josef von 1894-1969 .... **CLC 20**
See also CA 81-84

Sterne, Laurence 1713-1768 .... **LC 2, 48; WLC**
See also BRW 3; BRWC 1; CDBLB 1660-1789; DA; DAB; DAC; DAM MST, NOV; DLB 39; RGEL 2; TEA

Sternheim, (William Adolf) Carl
1878-1942 .... **TCLC 8**
See also CA 105; 193; DLB 56, 118; EWL 3; IDTP; RGWL 2, 3

Stevens, Margaret Dean
See Aldrich, Bess Streeter

Stevens, Mark 1951- .... **CLC 34**
See also CA 122

Stevens, Wallace 1879-1955 . **PC 6; TCLC 3, 12, 45; WLC**
See also AMW; AMWR 1; CA 104; 124; CDALB 1929-1941; DA; DA3; DAB; DAC; DAM MST, POET; DLB 54; EWL 3; EXPP; MAL 5; MTCW 1, 2; PAB; PFS 13, 16; RGAL 4; TUS; WP

Stevenson, Anne (Katharine) 1933- .. **CLC 7, 33**
See also BRWS 6; CA 17-20R; CAAS 9; CANR 9, 33, 123; CP 3, 4, 5, 6, 7; CWP; DLB 40; MTCW 1; RHW

Stevenson, Robert Louis (Balfour)
1850-1894 .... **NCLC 5, 14, 63; SSC 11, 51; WLC**
See also AAYA 24; BPFB 3; BRW 5; BRWC 1; BRWR 1; BYA 1, 2, 4, 13; CDBLB 1890-1914; CLR 10, 11; DA; DA3; DAB; DAC; DAM MST, NOV; DLB 18, 57, 141, 156, 174; DLBD 13; GL 3; HGG; JRDA; LAIT 1, 3; MAICYA 1, 2; NFS 11, 20; RGEL 2; RGSF 2; SATA 100; SUFW; TEA; WCH; WLIT 4; WYA; YABC 2; YAW

Stewart, J(ohn) I(nnes) M(ackintosh)
1906-1994 .... **CLC 7, 14, 32**
See Innes, Michael
See also CA 85-88; 147; CAAS 3; CANR 47; CMW 4; CN 1, 2, 3, 4, 5; MTCW 1, 2

Stewart, Mary (Florence Elinor)
1916- .... **CLC 7, 35, 117**
See also AAYA 29; BPFB 3; CA 1-4R; CANR 1, 59, 130; CMW 4; CPW; DAB; FANT; RHW; SATA 12; YAW

Stewart, Mary Rainbow
See Stewart, Mary (Florence Elinor)

Stifle, June
See Campbell, Maria

Stifter, Adalbert 1805-1868 .. **NCLC 41; SSC 28**
See also CDWLB 2; DLB 133; RGSF 2; RGWL 2, 3

Still, James 1906-2001 .... **CLC 49**
See also CA 65-68; 195; CAAS 17; CANR 10, 26; CSW; DLB 9; DLBY 01; SATA 29; SATA-Obit 127

Sting 1951-
See Sumner, Gordon Matthew
See also CA 167

Stirling, Arthur
See Sinclair, Upton (Beall)

Stitt, Milan 1941- .... **CLC 29**
See also CA 69-72

Stockton, Francis Richard 1834-1902
See Stockton, Frank R.
See also AAYA 68; CA 108; 137; MAICYA 1, 2; SATA 44; SFW 4

Stockton, Frank R. .... **TCLC 47**
See Stockton, Francis Richard
See also BYA 4, 13; DLB 42, 74; DLBD 13; EXPS; SATA-Brief 32; SSFS 3; SUFW; WCH

Stoddard, Charles
See Kuttner, Henry

Stoker, Abraham 1847-1912
See Stoker, Bram
See also CA 105; 150; DA; DA3; DAC; DAM MST, NOV; HGG; MTFW 2005; SATA 29

Stoker, Bram . **SSC 62; TCLC 8, 144; WLC**
See Stoker, Abraham
See also AAYA 23; BPFB 3; BRWS 3; BYA 5; CDBLB 1890-1914; DAB; DLB 304; GL 3; LATS 1:1; NFS 18; RGEL 2; SUFW; TEA; WLIT 4

Stolz, Mary (Slattery) 1920- .... **CLC 12**
See also AAYA 8; AITN 1; CA 5-8R; CANR 13, 41, 112; JRDA; MAICYA 1, 2; SAAS 3; SATA 10, 71, 133; YAW

Stone, Irving 1903-1989 .... **CLC 7**
See also AITN 1; BPFB 3; CA 1-4R; 129; CAAS 3; CANR 1, 23; CN 1, 2, 3, 4; CPW; DA3; DAM POP; INT CANR-23; MTCW 1, 2; MTFW 2005; RHW; SATA 3; SATA-Obit 64

Stone, Oliver (William) 1946- .... **CLC 73**
See also AAYA 15, 64; CA 110; CANR 55, 125

Stone, Robert (Anthony) 1937- ... **CLC 5, 23, 42, 175**
See also AMWS 5; BPFB 3; CA 85-88; CANR 23, 66, 95; CN 4, 5, 6, 7; DLB 152; EWL 3; INT CANR-23; MAL 5; MTCW 1; MTFW 2005

Stone, Ruth 1915- .... **PC 53**
See also CA 45-48; CANR 2, 91; CP 7; CSW; DLB 105; PFS 19

Stone, Zachary
See Follett, Ken(neth Martin)

Stoppard, Tom 1937- ... **CLC 1, 3, 4, 5, 8, 15, 29, 34, 63, 91; DC 6; WLC**
See also AAYA 63; BRWC 1; BRWR 2; BRWS 1; CA 81-84; CANR 39, 67, 125; CBD; CD 5, 6; CDBLB 1960 to Present; DA; DA3; DAB; DAC; DAM DRAM, MST, NOV; DFS 2, 5, 8, 11, 13, 16; DLB 13, 233; DLBY 1985; EWL 3; LATS 1:2; MTCW 1, 2; MTFW 2005; RGEL 2; TEA; WLIT 4

Storey, David (Malcolm) 1933- . **CLC 2, 4, 5, 8**
See also BRWS 1; CA 81-84; CANR 36; CBD; CD 5, 6; CN 1, 2, 3, 4, 5, 6; DAM DRAM; DLB 13, 14, 207, 245; EWL 3; MTCW 1; RGEL 2

Storm, Hyemeyohsts 1935- ... **CLC 3; NNAL**
See also CA 81-84; CANR 45; DAM MULT

Storm, (Hans) Theodor (Woldsen)
1817-1888 .... **NCLC 1; SSC 27**
See also CDWLB 2; DLB 129; EW; RGSF 2; RGWL 2, 3

Storni, Alfonsina 1892-1938 . **HLC 2; PC 33; TCLC 5**
See also CA 104; 131; DAM MULT; DLB 283; HW 1; LAW

Stoughton, William 1631-1701 .... **LC 38**
See also DLB 24

417

Stout, Rex (Todhunter) 1886-1975 ..... **CLC 3**
See also AITN 2; BPFB 3; CA 61-64; CANR 71; CMW 4; CN 2; DLB 306; MSW; RGAL 4

Stow, (Julian) Randolph 1935- ... **CLC 23, 48**
See also CA 13-16R; CANR 33; CN 1, 2, 3, 4, 5, 6, 7; CP 1, 2, 3, 4; DLB 260; MTCW 1; RGEL 2

Stowe, Harriet (Elizabeth) Beecher 1811-1896 .... **NCLC 3, 50, 133; WLC**
See also AAYA 53; AMWS 1; CDALB 1865-1917; DA; DA3; DAB; DAC; DAM MST, NOV; DLB 1, 12, 42, 74, 189, 239, 243; EXPN; FL 1:3; JRDA; LAIT 2; MAICYA 1, 2; NFS 6; RGAL 4; TUS; YABC 1

Strabo c. 64B.C.-c. 25 .... **CMLC 37**
See also DLB 176

Strachey, (Giles) Lytton 1880-1932 .... **TCLC 12**
See also BRWS 2; CA 110; 178; DLB 149; DLBD 10; EWL 3; MTCW 2; NCFS 4

Stramm, August 1874-1915 .... **PC 50**
See also CA 195; EWL 3

Strand, Mark 1934- .. **CLC 6, 18, 41, 71; PC 63**
See also AMWS 4; CA 21-24R; CANR 40, 65, 100; CP 1, 2, 3, 4, 5, 6, 7; DAM POET; DLB 5; EWL 3; MAL 5; PAB; PFS 9, 18; RGAL 4; SATA 41; TCLE 1:2

Stratton-Porter, Gene(va Grace) 1863-1924
See Porter, Gene(va Grace) Stratton
See also ANW; CA 137; CLR 87; DLB 221; DLBD 14; MAICYA 1, 2; SATA 15

Straub, Peter (Francis) 1943- ... **CLC 28, 107**
See also BEST 89:1; BPFB 3; CA 85-88; CANR 28, 65, 109; CPW; DAM POP; DLBY 1984; HGG; MTCW 1, 2; MTFW 2005; SUFW 2

Strauss, Botho 1944- .... **CLC 22**
See also CA 157; CWW 2; DLB 124

Strauss, Leo 1899-1973 .... **TCLC 141**
See also CA 101; 45-48; CANR 122

Streatfeild, (Mary) Noel 1897(?)-1986 .... **CLC 21**
See also CA 81-84; 120; CANR 31; CLR 17, 83; CWRI 5; DLB 160; MAICYA 1, 2; SATA 20; SATA-Obit 48

Stribling, T(homas) S(igismund) 1881-1965 .... **CLC 23**
See also CA 189; 107; CMW 4; DLB 9; RGAL 4

Strindberg, (Johan) August 1849-1912 ... **DC 18; TCLC 1, 8, 21, 47; WLC**
See also CA 104; 135; DA; DA3; DAB; DAC; DAM DRAM, MST; DFS 4, 9; DLB 259; EW 7; EWL 3; IDTP; LMFS 2; MTCW 2; MTFW 2005; RGWL 2, 3; TWA

Stringer, Arthur 1874-1950 .... **TCLC 37**
See also CA 161; DLB 92

Stringer, David
See Roberts, Keith (John Kingston)

Stroheim, Erich von 1885-1957 ..... **TCLC 71**

Strugatskii, Arkadii (Natanovich) 1925-1991 .... **CLC 27**
See Strugatsky, Arkadii (Natanovich)
See also CA 106; 135; SFW 4

Strugatskii, Boris (Natanovich) 1933- .... **CLC 27**
See Strugatsky, Boris (Natanovich)
See also CA 106; SFW 4

Strugatsky, Arkadii Natanovich
See Strugatskii, Arkadii (Natanovich)
See also DLB 302

Strugatsky, Boris (Natanovich)
See Strugatskii, Boris (Natanovich)
See also DLB 302

Strummer, Joe 1952-2002 .... **CLC 30**

Strunk, William, Jr. 1869-1946 ...... **TCLC 92**
See also CA 118; 164; NCFS 5

Stryk, Lucien 1924- .... **PC 27**
See also CA 13-16R; CANR 10, 28, 55, 110; CP 1, 2, 3, 4, 5, 6, 7

Stuart, Don A.
See Campbell, John W(ood, Jr.)

Stuart, Ian
See MacLean, Alistair (Stuart)

Stuart, Jesse (Hilton) 1906-1984 ... **CLC 1, 8, 11, 14, 34; SSC 31**
See also CA 5-8R; 112; CANR 31; CN 1, 2, 3; DLB 9, 48, 102; DLBY 1984; SATA 2; SATA-Obit 36

Stubblefield, Sally
See Trumbo, Dalton

Sturgeon, Theodore (Hamilton) 1918-1985 .... **CLC 22, 39**
See Queen, Ellery
See also AAYA 51; BPFB 3; BYA 9, 10; CA 81-84; 116; CANR 32, 103; DLB 8; DLBY 1985; HGG; MTCW 1, 2; MTFW 2005; SCFW 4; SFW 4; SUFW

Sturges, Preston 1898-1959 .... **TCLC 48**
See also CA 114; 149; DLB 26

Styron, William 1925- .... **CLC 1, 3, 5, 11, 15, 60; SSC 25**
See also AMW; AMWC 2; BEST 90:4; BPFB 3; CA 5-8R; CANR 6, 33, 74, 126; CDALB 1968-1988; CN 1, 2, 3, 4, 5, 6, 7; CPW; CSW; DA3; DAM NOV, POP; DLB 2, 143, 299; DLBY 1980; EWL 3; INT CANR-6; LAIT 2; MAL 5; MTCW 1, 2; MTFW 2005; NCFS 1; NFS 22; RGAL 4; RHW; TUS

Su, Chien 1884-1918
See Su Man-shu
See also CA 123

Suarez Lynch, B.
See Bioy Casares, Adolfo; Borges, Jorge Luis

Suassuna, Ariano Vilar 1927- .... **HLCS 1**
See also CA 178; DLB 307; HW 2; LAW

Suckert, Kurt Erich
See Malaparte, Curzio

Suckling, Sir John 1609-1642 . **LC 75; PC 30**
See also BRW 2; DAM POET; DLB 58, 126; EXPP; PAB; RGEL 2

Suckow, Ruth 1892-1960 .... **SSC 18**
See also CA 193; 113; DLB 9, 102; RGAL 4; TCWW 2

Sudermann, Hermann 1857-1928 .. **TCLC 15**
See also CA 107; 201; DLB 118

Sue, Eugene 1804-1857 .... **NCLC 1**
See also DLB 119

Sueskind, Patrick 1949- .... **CLC 44, 182**
See Suskind, Patrick

Suetonius c. 70-c. 130 .... **CMLC 60**
See also AW 2; DLB 211; RGWL 2, 3

Sukenick, Ronald 1932-2004 ..... **CLC 3, 4, 6, 48**
See also CA 25-28R; 209; 229; CAAE 209; CAAS 8; CANR 32, 89; CN 3, 4, 5, 6, 7; DLB 173; DLBY 1981

Suknaski, Andrew 1942- .... **CLC 19**
See also CA 101; CP 3, 4, 5, 6, 7; DLB 53

Sullivan, Vernon
See Vian, Boris

Sully Prudhomme, Rene-Francois-Armand 1839-1907 .... **TCLC 31**
See also GFL 1789 to the Present

Su Man-shu .... **TCLC 24**
See Su, Chien
See also EWL 3

Sumarokov, Aleksandr Petrovich 1717-1777 .... **LC 104**
See also DLB 150

Summerforest, Ivy B.
See Kirkup, James

Summers, Andrew James 1942- .... **CLC 26**

Summers, Andy
See Summers, Andrew James

Summers, Hollis (Spurgeon, Jr.) 1916- .... **CLC 10**
See also CA 5-8R; CANR 3; CN 1, 2, 3; CP 1, 2, 3, 4; DLB 6; TCLE 1:2

Summers, (Alphonsus Joseph-Mary Augustus) Montague 1880-1948 .... **TCLC 16**
See also CA 118; 163

Sumner, Gordon Matthew .... **CLC 26**
See Police, The; Sting

Sun Tzu c. 400B.C.-c. 320B.C. ...... **CMLC 56**

Surrey, Henry Howard 1517-1574 ... **LC 121; PC 59**
See also BRW 1; RGEL 2

Surtees, Robert Smith 1805-1864 .. **NCLC 14**
See also DLB 21; RGEL 2

Susann, Jacqueline 1921-1974 .... **CLC 3**
See also AITN 1; BPFB 3; CA 65-68; 53-56; MTCW 1, 2

Su Shi
See Su Shih
See also RGWL 2, 3

Su Shih 1036-1101 .... **CMLC 15**
See Su Shi

Suskind, Patrick .... **CLC 182**
See Sueskind, Patrick
See also BPFB 3; CA 145; CWW 2

Sutcliff, Rosemary 1920-1992 .... **CLC 26**
See also AAYA 10; BYA 1, 4; CA 5-8R; 139; CANR 37; CLR 1, 37; CPW; DAB; DAC; DAM MST, POP; JRDA; LATS 1:1; MAICYA 1, 2; MAICYAS 1; RHW; SATA 6, 44, 78; SATA-Obit 73; WYA; YAW

Sutro, Alfred 1863-1933 .... **TCLC 6**
See also CA 105; 185; DLB 10; RGEL 2

Sutton, Henry
See Slavitt, David R(ytman)

Suzuki, D. T.
See Suzuki, Daisetz Teitaro

Suzuki, Daisetz T.
See Suzuki, Daisetz Teitaro

Suzuki, Daisetz Teitaro 1870-1966 .... **TCLC 109**
See also CA 121; 111; MTCW 1, 2; MTFW 2005

Suzuki, Teitaro
See Suzuki, Daisetz Teitaro

Svevo, Italo .... **SSC 25; TCLC 2, 35**
See Schmitz, Aron Hector
See also DLB 264; EW 8; EWL 3; RGWL 2, 3; WLIT 7

Swados, Elizabeth (A.) 1951- .... **CLC 12**
See also CA 97-100; CANR 49; INT CA-97-100

Swados, Harvey 1920-1972 .... **CLC 5**
See also CA 5-8R; 37-40R; CANR 6; CN 1; DLB 2; MAL 5

Swan, Gladys 1934- .... **CLC 69**
See also CA 101; CANR 17, 39; TCLE 1:2

Swanson, Logan
See Matheson, Richard (Burton)

Swarthout, Glendon (Fred) 1918-1992 .... **CLC 35**
See also AAYA 55; CA 1-4R; 139; CANR 1, 47; CN 1, 2, 3, 4, 5; LAIT 5; SATA 26; TCWW 1, 2; YAW

Swedenborg, Emanuel 1688-1772 ..... **LC 105**

Sweet, Sarah C.
See Jewett, (Theodora) Sarah Orne

Swenson, May 1919-1989 ...... **CLC 4, 14, 61, 106; PC 14**
See also AMWS 4; CA 5-8R; 130; CANR 36, 61, 131; CP 1, 2, 3, 4; DA; DAB; DAC; DAM MST, POET; DLB 5; EXPP; GLL 2; MAL 5; MTCW 1, 2; MTFW 2005; PFS 16; SATA 15; WP

Swift, Augustus
See Lovecraft, H(oward) P(hillips)

Swift, Graham (Colin) 1949- ...... **CLC 41, 88**
See also BRWS 2; BRWS 5; CA 117; 122; CANR 46, 71, 128; CN 4, 5, 6, 7; DLB 194; MTCW 2; MTFW 2005; NFS 18; RGSF 2

Swift, Jonathan 1667-1745 ..... **LC 1, 42, 101; PC 9; WLC**
See also AAYA 41; BRW 3; BRWC 1; BRWR 1; BYA 5, 14; CDBLB 1660-1789; CLR 53; DA; DA3; DAB; DAC; DAM MST, NOV, POET; DLB 39, 95, 101; EXPN; LAIT 1; NFS 6; RGEL 2; SATA 19; TEA; WCH; WLIT 3

Swinburne, Algernon Charles 1837-1909 ...... **PC 24; TCLC 8, 36; WLC**
See also BRW 5; CA 105; 140; CDBLB 1832-1890; DA; DA3; DAB; DAC; DAM MST, POET; DLB 35, 57; PAB; RGEL 2; TEA

Swinfen, Ann .... **CLC 34**
See also CA 202

Swinnerton, Frank (Arthur) 1884-1982 .... **CLC 31**
See also CA 202; 108; CN 1, 2, 3; DLB 34

Swinnerton, Frank Arthur 1884-1982 .... **CLC 31**
See also CA 108; DLB 34

Swithen, John
See King, Stephen

Sylvia
See Ashton-Warner, Sylvia (Constance)

Symmes, Robert Edward
See Duncan, Robert (Edward)

Symonds, John Addington 1840-1893 .... **NCLC 34**
See also DLB 57, 144

Symons, Arthur 1865-1945 .... **TCLC 11**
See also CA 107; 189; DLB 19, 57, 149; RGEL 2

Symons, Julian (Gustave) 1912-1994 .... **CLC 2, 14, 32**
See also CA 49-52; 147; CAAS 3; CANR 3, 33, 59; CMW 4; CN 1, 2, 3, 4, 5; CP 1, 3, 4; DLB 87, 155; DLBY 1992; MSW; MTCW 1

Synge, (Edmund) J(ohn) M(illington) 1871-1909 .... **DC 2; TCLC 6, 37**
See also BRW 6; BRWR 1; CA 104; 141; CDBLB 1890-1914; DAM DRAM; DFS 18; DLB 10, 19; EWL 3; RGEL 2; TEA; WLIT 4

Syruc, J.
See Milosz, Czeslaw

Szirtes, George 1948- .... **CLC 46; PC 51**
See also CA 109; CANR 27, 61, 117; CP 4, 5, 6, 7

Szymborska, Wislawa 1923- ... **CLC 99, 190; PC 44**
See also CA 154; CANR 91, 133; CDWLB 4; CWP; CWW 2; DA3; DLB 232; DLBY 1996; EWL 3; MTCW 2005; PFS 15; RGWL 3

T. O., Nik
See Annensky, Innokenty (Fyodorovich)

Tabori, George 1914- .... **CLC 19**
See also CA 49-52; CANR 4, 69; CBD; CD 5, 6; DLB 245

Tacitus c. 55-c. 117 .... **CMLC 56**
See also AW 2; CDWLB 1; DLB 211; RGWL 2, 3

Tagore, Rabindranath 1861-1941 .... **PC 8; SSC 48; TCLC 3, 53**
See also CA 104; 120; DA3; DAM DRAM, POET; EWL 3; MTCW 1, 2; MTFW 2005; PFS 18; RGEL 2; RGSF 2; RGWL 2, 3; TWA

Taine, Hippolyte Adolphe 1828-1893 .... **NCLC 15**
See also EW 7; GFL 1789 to the Present

Talayesva, Don C. 1890-(?) .... **NNAL**

Talese, Gay 1932- .... **CLC 37**
See also AITN 1; CA 1-4R; CANR 9, 58, 137; DLB 185; INT CANR-9; MTCW 1, 2; MTFW 2005

Tallent, Elizabeth (Ann) 1954- .... **CLC 45**
See also CA 117; CANR 72; DLB 130

Tallmountain, Mary 1918-1997 .... **NNAL**
See also CA 146; 161; DLB 193

Tally, Ted 1952- .... **CLC 42**
See also CA 120; 124; CAD; CANR 125; CD 5, 6; INT CA-124

Talvik, Heiti 1904-1947 .... **TCLC 87**
See also EWL 3

Tamayo y Baus, Manuel 1829-1898 .... **NCLC 1**

Tammsaare, A(nton) H(ansen) 1878-1940 .... **TCLC 27**
See also CA 164; CDWLB 4; DLB 220; EWL 3

Tam'si, Tchicaya U
See Tchicaya, Gerald Felix

Tan, Amy (Ruth) 1952- . **AAL; CLC 59, 120, 151**
See also AAYA 9, 48; AMWS 10; BEST 89:3; BPFB 3; CA 136; CANR 54, 105, 132; CDALBS; CN 6, 7; CPW 1; DA3; DAM MULT, NOV, POP; DLB 173, 312; EXPN; FL 1:6; FW; LAIT 3, 5; MAL 5; MTCW 2; MTFW 2005; NFS 1, 13, 16; RGAL 4; SATA 75; SSFS 9; YAW

Tandem, Felix
See Spitteler, Carl (Friedrich Georg)

Tanizaki, Jun'ichiro 1886-1965 ... **CLC 8, 14, 28; SSC 21**
See Tanizaki Jun'ichiro
See also CA 93-96; 25-28R; MJW; MTCW 2; MTFW 2005; RGSF 2; RGWL 2

Tanizaki Jun'ichiro
See Tanizaki, Jun'ichiro
See also DLB 180; EWL 3

Tannen, Deborah F(rances) 1945- .. **CLC 206**
See also CA 118; CANR 95

Tanner, William
See Amis, Kingsley (William)

Tao Lao
See Storni, Alfonsina

Tapahonso, Luci 1953- .... **NNAL; PC 65**
See also CA 145; CANR 72, 127; DLB 175

Tarantino, Quentin (Jerome) 1963- .... **CLC 125**
See also AAYA 58; CA 171; CANR 125

Tarassoff, Lev
See Troyat, Henri

Tarbell, Ida M(inerva) 1857-1944 . **TCLC 40**
See also CA 122; 181; DLB 47

Tarkington, (Newton) Booth 1869-1946 .... **TCLC 9**
See also BPFB 3; BYA 3; CA 110; 143; CWRI 5; DLB 9, 102; MAL 5; MTCW 2; RGAL 4; SATA 17

Tarkovskii, Andrei Arsen'evich
See Tarkovsky, Andrei (Arsenyevich)

Tarkovsky, Andrei (Arsenyevich) 1932-1986 .... **CLC 75**
See also CA 127

Tartt, Donna 1964(?)- .... **CLC 76**
See also AAYA 56; CA 142; CANR 135; MTFW 2005

Tasso, Torquato 1544-1595 .... **LC 5, 94**
See also EFS 2; EW 2; RGWL 2, 3; WLIT 7

Tate, (John Orley) Allen 1899-1979 .. **CLC 2, 4, 6, 9, 11, 14, 24; PC 50**
See also AMW; CA 5-8R; 85-88; CANR 32, 108; CN 1, 2; CP 1, 2; DLB 4, 45, 63; DLBD 17; EWL 3; MAL 5; MTCW 1, 2; MTFW 2005; RGAL 4; RHW

Tate, Ellalice
See Hibbert, Eleanor Alice Burford

Tate, James (Vincent) 1943- ...... **CLC 2, 6, 25**
See also CA 21-24R; CANR 29, 57, 114; CP 1, 2, 3, 4, 5, 6, 7; DLB 5, 169; EWL 3; PFS 10, 15; RGAL 4; WP

Tate, Nahum 1652(?)-1715 .... **LC 109**
See also DLB 80; RGEL 2

Tauler, Johannes c. 1300-1361 .... **CMLC 37**
See also DLB 179; LMFS 1

Tavel, Ronald 1940- .... **CLC 6**
See also CA 21-24R; CAD; CANR 33; CD 5, 6

Taviani, Paolo 1931- .... **CLC 70**
See also CA 153

Taylor, Bayard 1825-1878 .... **NCLC 89**
See also DLB 3, 189, 250, 254; RGAL 4

Taylor, C(ecil) P(hilip) 1929-1981 .... **CLC 27**
See also CA 25-28R; 105; CANR 47; CBD

Taylor, Edward 1642(?)-1729 . **LC 11; PC 63**
See also AMW; DA; DAB; DAC; DAM MST, POET; DLB 24; EXPP; RGAL 4; TUS

Taylor, Eleanor Ross 1920- .... **CLC 5**
See also CA 81-84; CANR 70

Taylor, Elizabeth 1912-1975 ..... **CLC 2, 4, 29**
See also CA 13-16R; CANR 9, 70; CN 1, 2; DLB 139; MTCW 1; RGEL 2; SATA 13

Taylor, Frederick Winslow 1856-1915 .... **TCLC 76**
See also CA 188

Taylor, Henry (Splawn) 1942- .... **CLC 44**
See also CA 33-36R; CAAS 7; CANR 31; CP 7; DLB 5; PFS 10

Taylor, Kamala (Purnaiya) 1924-2004
See Markandaya, Kamala
See also CA 77-80; 227; MTFW 2005; NFS 13

Taylor, Mildred D(elois) 1943- .... **CLC 21**
See also AAYA 10, 47; BW 1; BYA 3, 8; CA 85-88; CANR 25, 115, 136; CLR 9, 59, 90; CSW; DLB 52; JRDA; LAIT 3; MAICYA 1, 2; MTFW 2005; SAAS 5; SATA 135; WYA; YAW

Taylor, Peter (Hillsman) 1917-1994 .. **CLC 1, 4, 18, 37, 44, 50, 71; SSC 10, 84**
See also AMWS 5; BPFB 3; CA 13-16R; 147; CANR 9, 50; CN 1, 2, 3, 4, 5; CSW; DLB 218, 278; DLBY 1981, 1994; EWL 3; EXPS; INT CANR-9; MAL 5; MTCW 1, 2; MTFW 2005; RGSF 2; SSFS 9; TUS

Taylor, Robert Lewis 1912-1998 .... **CLC 14**
See also CA 1-4R; 170; CANR 3, 64; CN 1, 2; SATA 10; TCWW 1, 2

Tchekhov, Anton
See Chekhov, Anton (Pavlovich)

Tchicaya, Gerald Felix 1931-1988 .. **CLC 101**
See Tchicaya U Tam'si
See also CA 129; 125; CANR 81

Tchicaya U Tam'si
See Tchicaya, Gerald Felix
See also EWL 3

Teasdale, Sara 1884-1933 .... **PC 31; TCLC 4**
See also CA 104; 163; DLB 45; GLL 1; PFS 14; RGAL 4; SATA 32; TUS

Tecumseh 1768-1813 .... **NNAL**
See also DAM MULT

Tegner, Esaias 1782-1846 .... **NCLC 2**
Teilhard de Chardin, (Marie Joseph) Pierre
 1881-1955 .... **TCLC 9**
 See also CA 105; 210; GFL 1789 to the Present
Temple, Ann
 See Mortimer, Penelope (Ruth)
Tennant, Emma (Christina) 1937- .. **CLC 13, 52**
 See also BRWS 9; CA 65-68; CAAS 9; CANR 10, 38, 59, 88; CN 3, 4, 5, 6, 7; DLB 14; EWL 3; SFW 4
Tenneshaw, S. M.
 See Silverberg, Robert
Tenney, Tabitha Gilman
 1762-1837 .... **NCLC 122**
 See also DLB 37, 200
Tennyson, Alfred 1809-1892 ... **NCLC 30, 65, 115; PC 6; WLC**
 See also AAYA 50; BRW 4; CDBLB 1832-1890; DA; DA3; DAB; DAC; DAM MST, POET; DLB 32; EXPP; PAB; PFS 1, 2, 4, 11, 15, 19; RGEL 2; TEA; WLIT 4; WP
Teran, Lisa St. Aubin de .... **CLC 36**
 See St. Aubin de Teran, Lisa
Terence c. 184B.C.-c. 159B.C. ...... **CMLC 14; DC 7**
 See also AW 1; CDWLB 1; DLB 211; RGWL 2, 3; TWA
Teresa de Jesus, St. 1515-1582 .... **LC 18**
Teresa of Avila, St.
 See Teresa de Jesus, St.
Terkel, Louis 1912-
 See Terkel, Studs
 See also CA 57-60; CANR 18, 45, 67, 132; DA3; MTCW 1, 2; MTFW 2005
Terkel, Studs .... **CLC 38**
 See Terkel, Louis
 See also AAYA 32; AITN 1; MTCW 2; TUS
Terry, C. V.
 See Slaughter, Frank G(ill)
Terry, Megan 1932- .... **CLC 19; DC 13**
 See also CA 77-80; CABS 3; CAD; CANR 43; CD 5, 6; CWD; DFS 18; DLB 7, 249; GLL 2
Tertullian c. 155-c. 245 .... **CMLC 29**
Tertz, Abram
 See Sinyavsky, Andrei (Donatevich)
 See also RGSF 2
Tesich, Steve 1943(?)-1996 .... **CLC 40, 69**
 See also CA 105; 152; CAD; DLBY 1983
Tesla, Nikola 1856-1943 .... **TCLC 88**
Teternikov, Fyodor Kuzmich 1863-1927
 See Sologub, Fyodor
 See also CA 104
Tevis, Walter 1928-1984 .... **CLC 42**
 See also CA 113; SFW 4
Tey, Josephine .... **TCLC 14**
 See Mackintosh, Elizabeth
 See also DLB 77; MSW
Thackeray, William Makepeace
 1811-1863 .... **NCLC 5, 14, 22, 43; WLC**
 See also BRW 5; BRWC 2; CDBLB 1832-1890; DA; DA3; DAB; DAC; DAM MST, NOV; DLB 21, 55, 159, 163; NFS 13; RGEL 2; SATA 23; TEA; WLIT 3
Thakura, Ravindranatha
 See Tagore, Rabindranath
Thames, C. H.
 See Marlowe, Stephen
Tharoor, Shashi 1956- .... **CLC 70**
 See also CA 141; CANR 91; CN 6, 7
Thelwall, John 1764-1834 .... **NCLC 162**
 See also DLB 93, 158
Thelwell, Michael Miles 1939- .... **CLC 22**
 See also BW 2; CA 101
Theobald, Lewis, Jr.
 See Lovecraft, H(oward) P(hillips)

Theocritus c. 310B.C.- .... **CMLC 45**
 See also AW 1; DLB 176; RGWL 2, 3
Theodorescu, Ion N. 1880-1967
 See Arghezi, Tudor
 See also CA 116
Theriault, Yves 1915-1983 .... **CLC 79**
 See also CA 102; CCA 1; DAC; DAM MST; DLB 88; EWL 3
Theroux, Alexander (Louis) 1939- ..... **CLC 2, 25**
 See also CA 85-88; CANR 20, 63; CN 4, 5, 6, 7
Theroux, Paul (Edward) 1941- ..... **CLC 5, 8, 11, 15, 28, 46**
 See also AAYA 28; AMWS 8; BEST 89:4; BPFB 3; CA 33-36R; CANR 20, 45, 74, 133; CDALBS; CN 1, 2, 3, 4, 5, 6, 7; CP 1; CPW 1; DA3; DAM POP; DLB 2, 218; EWL 3; HGG; MAL 5; MTCW 1, 2; MTFW 2005; RGAL 4; SATA 44, 109; TUS
Thesen, Sharon 1946- .... **CLC 56**
 See also CA 163; CANR 125; CP 7; CWP
Thespis fl. 6th cent. B.C.- .... **CMLC 51**
 See also LMFS 1
Thevenin, Denis
 See Duhamel, Georges
Thibault, Jacques Anatole Francois
 1844-1924
 See France, Anatole
 See also CA 106; 127; DA3; DAM NOV; MTCW 1, 2; TWA
Thiele, Colin (Milton) 1920- .... **CLC 17**
 See also CA 29-32R; CANR 12, 28, 53, 105; CLR 27; CP 1, 2; DLB 289; MAICYA 1, 2; SAAS 2; SATA 14, 72, 125; YAW
Thistlethwaite, Bel
 See Wetherald, Agnes Ethelwyn
Thomas, Audrey (Callahan) 1935- .... **CLC 7, 13, 37, 107; SSC 20**
 See also AITN 2; CA 21-24R, 237; CAAE 237; CAAS 19; CANR 36, 58; CN 2, 3, 4, 5, 6, 7; DLB 60; MTCW 1; RGSF 2
Thomas, Augustus 1857-1934 .... **TCLC 97**
 See also MAL 5
Thomas, D(onald) M(ichael) 1935- . **CLC 13, 22, 31, 132**
 See also BPFB 3; BRWS 4; CA 61-64; CAAS 11; CANR 17, 45, 75; CDBLB 1960 to Present; CN 4, 5, 6, 7; CP 1, 2, 3, 4, 5, 6, 7; DA3; DLB 40, 207, 299; HGG; INT CANR-17; MTCW 1, 2; MTFW 2005; SFW 4
Thomas, Dylan (Marlais) 1914-1953 .... **PC 2, 52; SSC 3, 44; TCLC 1, 8, 45, 105; WLC**
 See also AAYA 45; BRWS 1; CA 104; 120; CANR 65; CDBLB 1945-1960; DA; DA3; DAB; DAC; DAM DRAM, MST, POET; DLB 13, 20, 139; EWL 3; EXPP; LAIT 3; MTCW 1, 2; MTFW 2005; PAB; PFS 1, 3, 8; RGEL 2; RGSF 2; SATA 60; TEA; WLIT 4; WP
Thomas, (Philip) Edward 1878-1917 . **PC 53; TCLC 10**
 See also BRW 6; BRWS 3; CA 106; 153; DAM POET; DLB 19, 98, 156, 216; EWL 3; PAB; RGEL 2
Thomas, Joyce Carol 1938- .... **CLC 35**
 See also AAYA 12, 54; BW 2, 3; CA 113; 116; CANR 48, 114, 135; CLR 19; DLB 33; INT CA-116; JRDA; MAICYA 1, 2; MTCW 1, 2; MTFW 2005; SAAS 7; SATA 40, 78, 123, 137; SATA-Essay 137; WYA; YAW
Thomas, Lewis 1913-1993 .... **CLC 35**
 See also ANW; CA 85-88; 143; CANR 38, 60; DLB 275; MTCW 1, 2

Thomas, M. Carey 1857-1935 .... **TCLC 89**
 See also FW
Thomas, Paul
 See Mann, (Paul) Thomas
Thomas, Piri 1928- .... **CLC 17; HLCS 2**
 See also CA 73-76; HW 1; LLW
Thomas, R(onald) S(tuart)
 1913-2000 .... **CLC 6, 13, 48**
 See also CA 89-92; 189; CAAS 4; CANR 30; CDBLB 1960 to Present; CP 1, 2, 3, 4, 5, 6, 7; DAB; DAM POET; DLB 27; EWL 3; MTCW 1; RGEL 2
Thomas, Ross (Elmore) 1926-1995 .. **CLC 39**
 See also CA 33-36R; 150; CANR 22, 63; CMW 4
Thompson, Francis (Joseph)
 1859-1907 .... **TCLC 4**
 See also BRW 5; CA 104; 189; CDBLB 1890-1914; DLB 19; RGEL 2; TEA
Thompson, Francis Clegg
 See Mencken, H(enry) L(ouis)
Thompson, Hunter S(tockton)
 1937(?)-2005 .... **CLC 9, 17, 40, 104**
 See also AAYA 45; BEST 89:1; BPFB 3; CA 17-20R; 236; CANR 23, 46, 74, 77, 111, 133; CPW; CSW; DA3; DAM POP; DLB 185; MTCW 1, 2; MTFW 2005; TUS
Thompson, James Myers
 See Thompson, Jim (Myers)
Thompson, Jim (Myers)
 1906-1977(?) .... **CLC 69**
 See also BPFB 3; CA 140; CMW 4; CPW; DLB 226; MSW
Thompson, Judith (Clare Francesca)
 1954- .... **CLC 39**
 See also CA 143; CD 5, 6; CWD; DFS 22
Thomson, James 1700-1748 ..... **LC 16, 29, 40**
 See also BRWS 3; DAM POET; DLB 95; RGEL 2
Thomson, James 1834-1882 .... **NCLC 18**
 See also DAM POET; DLB 35; RGEL 2
Thoreau, Henry David 1817-1862 .. **NCLC 7, 21, 61, 138; PC 30; WLC**
 See also AAYA 42; AMW; ANW; BYA 3; CDALB 1640-1865; DA; DA3; DAB; DAC; DAM MST; DLB 1, 183, 223, 270, 298; LAIT 2; LMFS 1; NCFS 3; RGAL 4; TUS
Thorndike, E. L.
 See Thorndike, Edward L(ee)
Thorndike, Edward L(ee)
 1874-1949 .... **TCLC 107**
 See also CA 121
Thornton, Hall
 See Silverberg, Robert
Thorpe, Adam 1956- .... **CLC 176**
 See also CA 129; CANR 92; DLB 231
Thubron, Colin (Gerald Dryden)
 1939- .... **CLC 163**
 See also CA 25-28R; CANR 12, 29, 59, 95; CN 5, 6, 7; DLB 204, 231
Thucydides c. 455B.C.-c. 395B.C. . **CMLC 17**
 See also AW 1; DLB 176; RGWL 2, 3
Thumboo, Edwin Nadason 1933- .... **PC 30**
 See also CA 194; CP 1
Thurber, James (Grover)
 1894-1961 .. **CLC 5, 11, 25, 125; SSC 1, 47**
 See also AAYA 56; AMWS 1; BPFB 3; BYA 5; CA 73-76; CANR 17, 39; CDALB 1929-1941; CWRI 5; DA; DA3; DAB; DAC; DAM DRAM, MST, NOV; DLB 4, 11, 22, 102; EWL 3; EXPS; FANT; LAIT 3; MAICYA 1, 2; MAL 5; MTCW 1, 2; MTFW 2005; RGAL 4; RGSF 2; SATA 13; SSFS 1, 10, 19; SUFW; TUS

Thurman, Wallace (Henry)
1902-1934 ..... **BLC 3; HR 1:3; TCLC 6**
See also BW 1, 3; CA 104; 124; CANR 81; DAM MULT; DLB 51

Tibullus c. 54B.C.-c. 18B.C. .... **CMLC 36**
See also AW 2; DLB 211; RGWL 2, 3

Ticheburn, Cheviot
See Ainsworth, William Harrison

Tieck, (Johann) Ludwig
1773-1853 .... **NCLC 5, 46; SSC 31**
See also CDWLB 2; DLB 90; EW 5; IDTP; RGSF 2; RGWL 2, 3; SUFW

Tiger, Derry
See Ellison, Harlan (Jay)

Tilghman, Christopher 1946- .... **CLC 65**
See also CA 159; CANR 135; CSW; DLB 244

Tillich, Paul (Johannes)
1886-1965 .... **CLC 131**
See also CA 5-8R; 25-28R; CANR 33; MTCW 1, 2

Tillinghast, Richard (Williford)
1940- .... **CLC 29**
See also CA 29-32R; CAAS 23; CANR 26, 51, 96; CP 2, 3, 4, 5, 6, 7; CSW

Timrod, Henry 1828-1867 .... **NCLC 25**
See also DLB 3, 248; RGAL 4

Tindall, Gillian (Elizabeth) 1938- ...... **CLC 7**
See also CA 21-24R; CANR 11, 65, 107; CN 1, 2, 3, 4, 5, 6, 7

Tiptree, James, Jr. .... **CLC 48, 50**
See Sheldon, Alice Hastings Bradley
See also DLB 8; SCFW 1, 2; SFW 4

Tirone Smith, Mary-Ann 1944- ...... **CLC 39**
See also CA 118; 136; CANR 113; SATA 143

Tirso de Molina 1580(?)-1648 .... **DC 13; HLCS 2; LC 73**
See also RGWL 2, 3

Titmarsh, Michael Angelo
See Thackeray, William Makepeace

Tocqueville, Alexis (Charles Henri Maurice Clerel Comte) de 1805-1859 .. **NCLC 7, 63**
See also EW 6; GFL 1789 to the Present; TWA

Toer, Pramoedya Ananta 1925- ...... **CLC 186**
See also CA 197; RGWL 3

Toffler, Alvin 1928- .... **CLC 168**
See also CA 13-16R; CANR 15, 46, 67; CPW; DAM POP; MTCW 1, 2

Toibin, Colm 1955- .... **CLC 162**
See also CA 142; CANR 81; CN 7; DLB 271

Tolkien, J(ohn) R(onald) R(euel)
1892-1973 .... **CLC 1, 2, 3, 8, 12, 38; TCLC 137; WLC**
See also AAYA 10; AITN 1; BPFB 3; BRWC 2; BRWS 2; CA 17-18; 45-48; CANR 36, 134; CAP 2; CDBLB 1914-1945; CLR 56; CN 1; CPW 1; CWRI 5; DA; DA3; DAB; DAC; DAM MST, NOV, POP; DLB 15, 160, 255; EFS 2; EWL 3; FANT; JRDA; LAIT 1:2; LMFS 2; MAICYA 1, 2; MTCW 1, 2; MTFW 2005; NFS 8; RGEL 2; SATA 2, 32, 100; SATA-Obit 24; SFW 4; SUFW; TEA; WCH; WYA; YAW

Toller, Ernst 1893-1939 .... **TCLC 10**
See also CA 107; 186; DLB 124; EWL 3; RGWL 2, 3

Tolson, M. B.
See Tolson, Melvin B(eaunorus)

Tolson, Melvin B(eaunorus)
1898(?)-1966 .... **BLC 3; CLC 36, 105**
See also AFAW 1, 2; BW 1, 3; CA 124; 89-92; CANR 80; DAM MULT, POET; DLB 48, 76; MAL 5; RGAL 4

Tolstoi, Aleksei Nikolaevich
See Tolstoy, Alexey Nikolaevich

Tolstoi, Lev
See Tolstoy, Leo (Nikolaevich)
See also RGSF 2; RGWL 2, 3

Tolstoy, Aleksei Nikolaevich
See Tolstoy, Alexey Nikolaevich
See also DLB 272

Tolstoy, Alexey Nikolaevich
1882-1945 .... **TCLC 18**
See Tolstoi, Aleksei Nikolaevich
See also CA 107; 158; EWL 3; SFW 4

Tolstoy, Leo (Nikolaevich)
1828-1910 . **SSC 9, 30, 45, 54; TCLC 4, 11, 17, 28, 44, 79, 173; WLC**
See Tolstoi, Lev
See also AAYA 56; CA 104; 123; DA; DA3; DAB; DAC; DAM MST, NOV; DLB 238; EFS 2; EW 7; EXPS; IDTP; LAIT 2; LATS 1:1; LMFS 1; NFS 10; SATA 26; SSFS 5; TWA

Tolstoy, Count Leo
See Tolstoy, Leo (Nikolaevich)

Tomalin, Claire 1933- .... **CLC 166**
See also CA 89-92; CANR 52, 88; DLB 155

Tomasi di Lampedusa, Giuseppe 1896-1957
See Lampedusa, Giuseppe (Tomasi) di
See also CA 111; DLB 177; EWL 3; WLIT 7

Tomlin, Lily .... **CLC 17**
See Tomlin, Mary Jean

Tomlin, Mary Jean 1939(?)-
See Tomlin, Lily
See also CA 117

Tomline, F. Latour
See Gilbert, W(illiam) S(chwenck)

Tomlinson, (Alfred) Charles 1927- .... **CLC 2, 4, 6, 13, 45; PC 17**
See also CA 5-8R; CANR 33; CP 1, 2, 3, 4, 5, 6, 7; DAM POET; DLB 40; TCLE 1:2

Tomlinson, H(enry) M(ajor)
1873-1958 .... **TCLC 71**
See also CA 118; 161; DLB 36, 100, 195

Tonna, Charlotte Elizabeth
1790-1846 .... **NCLC 135**
See also DLB 163

Tonson, Jacob fl. 1655(?)-1736 .... **LC 86**
See also DLB 170

Toole, John Kennedy 1937-1969 ..... **CLC 19, 64**
See also BPFB 3; CA 104; DLBY 1981; MTCW 2; MTFW 2005

Toomer, Eugene
See Toomer, Jean

Toomer, Eugene Pinchback
See Toomer, Jean

Toomer, Jean 1894-1967 .. **BLC 3; CLC 1, 4, 13, 22; HR 1:3; PC 7; SSC 1, 45; TCLC 172; WLCS**
See also AFAW 1, 2; AMWS 3, 9; BW 1; CA 85-88; CDALB 1917-1929; DA3; DAM MULT; DLB 45, 51; EWL 3; EXPP; EXPS; LMFS 2; MAL 5; MTCW 1, 2; MTFW 2005; NFS 11; RGAL 4; RGSF 2; SSFS 5

Toomer, Nathan Jean
See Toomer, Jean

Toomer, Nathan Pinchback
See Toomer, Jean

Torley, Luke
See Blish, James (Benjamin)

Tornimparte, Alessandra
See Ginzburg, Natalia

Torre, Raoul della
See Mencken, H(enry) L(ouis)

Torrence, Ridgely 1874-1950 .... **TCLC 97**
See also DLB 54, 249; MAL 5

Torrey, E(dwin) Fuller 1937- .... **CLC 34**
See also CA 119; CANR 71

Torsvan, Ben Traven
See Traven, B.

Torsvan, Benno Traven
See Traven, B.

Torsvan, Berick Traven
See Traven, B.

Torsvan, Berwick Traven
See Traven, B.

Torsvan, Bruno Traven
See Traven, B.

Torsvan, Traven
See Traven, B.

Tourneur, Cyril 1575(?)-1626 .... **LC 66**
See also BRW 2; DAM DRAM; DLB 58; RGEL 2

Tournier, Michel (Edouard) 1924- .... **CLC 6, 23, 36, 95; SSC 88**
See also CA 49-52; CANR 3, 36, 74; CWW 2; DLB 83; EWL 3; GFL 1789 to the Present; MTCW 1, 2; SATA 23

Tournimparte, Alessandra
See Ginzburg, Natalia

Towers, Ivar
See Kornbluth, C(yril) M.

Towne, Robert (Burton) 1936(?)- ...... **CLC 87**
See also CA 108; DLB 44; IDFW 3, 4

Townsend, Sue .... **CLC 61**
See Townsend, Susan Lilian
See also AAYA 28; CA 119; 127; CANR 65, 107; CBD; CD 5, 6; CPW; CWD; DAB; DAC; DAM MST; DLB 271; INT CA-127; SATA 55, 93; SATA-Brief 48; YAW

Townsend, Susan Lilian 1946-
See Townsend, Sue

Townshend, Pete
See Townshend, Peter (Dennis Blandford)

Townshend, Peter (Dennis Blandford)
1945- .... **CLC 17, 42**
See also CA 107

Tozzi, Federigo 1883-1920 .... **TCLC 31**
See also CA 160; CANR 110; DLB 264; EWL 3; WLIT 7

Tracy, Don(ald Fiske) 1905-1970(?)
See Queen, Ellery
See also CA 1-4R; 176; CANR 2

Trafford, F. G.
See Riddell, Charlotte

Traherne, Thomas 1637(?)-1674 .. **LC 99; PC 70**
See also BRW 2; BRWS 11; DLB 131; PAB; RGEL 2

Traill, Catharine Parr 1802-1899 .. **NCLC 31**
See also DLB 99

Trakl, Georg 1887-1914 .... **PC 20; TCLC 5**
See also CA 104; 165; EW 10; EWL 3; LMFS 2; MTCW 2; RGWL 2, 3

Trambley, Estela Portillo .... **TCLC 163**
See Portillo Trambley, Estela
See also CA 77-80; RGAL 4

Tranquilli, Secondino
See Silone, Ignazio

Transtroemer, Tomas Gosta
See Transtromer, Tomas (Goesta)

Transtromer, Tomas (Gosta)
See Transtromer, Tomas (Goesta)
See also CWW 2

Transtromer, Tomas (Goesta)
1931- .... **CLC 52, 65**
See Transtromer, Tomas (Gosta)
See also CA 117; 129; CAAS 17; CANR 115; DAM POET; DLB 257; EWL 3; PFS 21

Transtromer, Tomas Gosta
See Transtromer, Tomas (Goesta)

Traven, B. 1882(?)-1969 .... **CLC 8, 11**
See also CA 19-20; 25-28R; CAP 2; DLB 9, 56; EWL 3; MTCW 1; RGAL 4

Trediakovsky, Vasilii Kirillovich
1703-1769 .... **LC 68**
See also DLB 150

Treitel, Jonathan 1959- .... **CLC 70**
See also CA 210; DLB 267

Trelawny, Edward John
1792-1881 .... **NCLC 85**
See also DLB 110, 116, 144

Tremain, Rose 1943- .... **CLC 42**
See also CA 97-100; CANR 44, 95; CN 4, 5, 6, 7; DLB 14, 271; RGSF 2; RHW

Tremblay, Michel 1942- .... **CLC 29, 102**
See also CA 116; 128; CCA 1; CWW 2; DAC; DAM MST; DLB 60; EWL 3; GLL 1; MTCW 1, 2; MTFW 2005

Trevanian .... **CLC 29**
See Whitaker, Rod(ney)

Trevor, Glen
See Hilton, James

Trevor, William .. **CLC 7, 9, 14, 25, 71, 116; SSC 21, 58**
See Cox, William Trevor
See also BRWS 4; CBD; CD 5, 6; CN 1, 2, 3, 4, 5, 6, 7; DLB 14, 139; EWL 3; LATS 1:2; RGEL 2; RGSF 2; SSFS 10; TCLE 1:2

Trifonov, Iurii (Valentinovich)
See Trifonov, Yuri (Valentinovich)
See also DLB 302; RGWL 2, 3

Trifonov, Yuri (Valentinovich)
1925-1981 .... **CLC 45**
See Trifonov, Iurii (Valentinovich); Trifonov, Yury Valentinovich
See also CA 126; 103; MTCW 1

Trifonov, Yury Valentinovich
See Trifonov, Yuri (Valentinovich)
See also EWL 3

Trilling, Diana (Rubin) 1905-1996 . **CLC 129**
See also CA 5-8R; 154; CANR 10, 46; INT CANR-10; MTCW 1, 2

Trilling, Lionel 1905-1975 ..... **CLC 9, 11, 24; SSC 75**
See also AMWS 3; CA 9-12R; 61-64; CANR 10, 105; CN 1, 2; DLB 28, 63; EWL 3; INT CANR-10; MAL 5; MTCW 1, 2; RGAL 4; TUS

Trimball, W. H.
See Mencken, H(enry) L(ouis)

Tristan
See Gomez de la Serna, Ramon

Tristram
See Housman, A(lfred) E(dward)

Trogdon, William (Lewis) 1939-
See Heat-Moon, William Least
See also AAYA 66; CA 115; 119; CANR 47, 89; CPW; INT CA-119

Trollope, Anthony 1815-1882 .... **NCLC 6, 33, 101; SSC 28; WLC**
See also BRW 5; CDBLB 1832-1890; DA; DA3; DAB; DAC; DAM MST, NOV; DLB 21, 57, 159; RGEL 2; RGSF 2; SATA 22

Trollope, Frances 1779-1863 .... **NCLC 30**
See also DLB 21, 166

Trollope, Joanna 1943- .... **CLC 186**
See also CA 101; CANR 58, 95; CN 7; CPW; DLB 207; RHW

Trotsky, Leon 1879-1940 .... **TCLC 22**
See also CA 118; 167

Trotter (Cockburn), Catharine
1679-1749 .... **LC 8**
See also DLB 84, 252

Trotter, Wilfred 1872-1939 .... **TCLC 97**

Trout, Kilgore
See Farmer, Philip Jose

Trow, George W. S. 1943- .... **CLC 52**
See also CA 126; CANR 91

Troyat, Henri 1911- .... **CLC 23**
See also CA 45-48; CANR 2, 33, 67, 117; GFL 1789 to the Present; MTCW 1

Trudeau, G(arretson) B(eekman) 1948-
See Trudeau, Garry B.
See also AAYA 60; CA 81-84; CANR 31; SATA 35

Trudeau, Garry B. .... **CLC 12**
See Trudeau, G(arretson) B(eekman)
See also AAYA 10; AITN 2

Truffaut, Francois 1932-1984 ... **CLC 20, 101**
See also CA 81-84; 113; CANR 34

Trumbo, Dalton 1905-1976 .... **CLC 19**
See also CA 21-24R; 69-72; CANR 10; CN 1, 2; DLB 26; IDFW 3, 4; YAW

Trumbull, John 1750-1831 .... **NCLC 30**
See also DLB 31; RGAL 4

Trundlett, Helen B.
See Eliot, T(homas) S(tearns)

Truth, Sojourner 1797(?)-1883 .... **NCLC 94**
See also DLB 239; FW; LAIT 2

Tryon, Thomas 1926-1991 .... **CLC 3, 11**
See also AITN 1; BPFB 3; CA 29-32R; 135; CANR 32, 77; CPW; DA3; DAM POP; HGG; MTCW 1

Tryon, Tom
See Tryon, Thomas

Ts'ao Hsueh-ch'in 1715(?)-1763 .... **LC 1**

Tsushima, Shuji 1909-1948
See Dazai Osamu
See also CA 107

Tsvetaeva (Efron), Marina (Ivanovna)
1892-1941 .... **PC 14; TCLC 7, 35**
See also CA 104; 128; CANR 73; DLB 295; EW 11; MTCW 1, 2; RGWL 2, 3

Tuck, Lily 1938- .... **CLC 70**
See also CA 139; CANR 90

Tu Fu 712-770 .... **PC 9**
See Du Fu
See also DAM MULT; TWA; WP

Tunis, John R(oberts) 1889-1975 ...... **CLC 12**
See also BYA 1; CA 61-64; CANR 62; DLB 22, 171; JRDA; MAICYA 1, 2; SATA 37; SATA-Brief 30; YAW

Tuohy, Frank .... **CLC 37**
See Tuohy, John Francis
See also CN 1, 2, 3, 4, 5, 6, 7; DLB 14, 139

Tuohy, John Francis 1925-
See Tuohy, Frank
See also CA 5-8R; 178; CANR 3, 47

Turco, Lewis (Putnam) 1934- ..... **CLC 11, 63**
See also CA 13-16R; CAAS 22; CANR 24, 51; CP 1, 2, 3, 4, 5, 6, 7; DLBY 1984; TCLE 1:2

Turgenev, Ivan (Sergeevich)
1818-1883 ...... **DC 7; NCLC 21, 37, 122; SSC 7, 57; WLC**
See also AAYA 58; DA; DAB; DAC; DAM MST, NOV; DFS 6; DLB 238, 284; EW 6; LATS 1:1; NFS 16; RGSF 2; RGWL 2, 3; TWA

Turgot, Anne-Robert-Jacques
1727-1781 .... **LC 26**
See also DLB 314

Turner, Frederick 1943- .... **CLC 48**
See also CA 73-76, 227; CAAE 227; CAAS 10; CANR 12, 30, 56; DLB 40, 282

Turton, James
See Crace, Jim

Tutu, Desmond M(pilo) 1931- .. **BLC 3; CLC 80**
See also BW 1, 3; CA 125; CANR 67, 81; DAM MULT

Tutuola, Amos 1920-1997 ..... **BLC 3; CLC 5, 14, 29**
See also AFW; BW 2, 3; CA 9-12R; 159; CANR 27, 66; CDWLB 3; CN 1, 2, 3, 4, 5, 6; DA3; DAM MULT; DLB 125; DNFS 2; EWL 3; MTCW 1, 2; MTFW 2005; RGEL 2; WLIT 2

Twain, Mark .... **SSC 6, 26, 34, 87; TCLC 6, 12, 19, 36, 48, 59, 161; WLC**
See Clemens, Samuel Langhorne
See also AAYA 20; AMW; AMWC 1; BPFB 3; BYA 2, 3, 11, 14; CLR 58, 60, 66; DLB 11; EXPN; EXPS; FANT; LAIT 2; MAL 5; NCFS 4; NFS 1, 6; RGAL 4; RGSF 2; SFW 4; SSFS 1, 7, 16, 21; SUFW; TUS; WCH; WYA; YAW

Tyler, Anne 1941- . **CLC 7, 11, 18, 28, 44, 59, 103, 205**
See also AAYA 18, 60; AMWS 4; BEST 89:1; BPFB 3; BYA 12; CA 9-12R; CANR 11, 33, 53, 109, 132; CDALBS; CN 1, 2, 3, 4, 5, 6, 7; CPW; CSW; DAM NOV, POP; DLB 6, 143; DLBY 1982; EWL 3; EXPN; LATS 1:2; MAL 5; MAWW; MTCW 1, 2; MTFW 2005; NFS 2, 7, 10; RGAL 4; SATA 7, 90; SSFS 17; TCLE 1:2; TUS; YAW

Tyler, Royall 1757-1826 .... **NCLC 3**
See also DLB 37; RGAL 4

Tynan, Katharine 1861-1931 .... **TCLC 3**
See also CA 104; 167; DLB 153, 240; FW

Tyndale, William c. 1484-1536 .... **LC 103**
See also DLB 132

Tyutchev, Fyodor 1803-1873 .... **NCLC 34**

Tzara, Tristan 1896-1963 .... **CLC 47; PC 27; TCLC 168**
See also CA 153; 89-92; DAM POET; EWL 3; MTCW 2

Uchida, Yoshiko 1921-1992 .... **AAL**
See also AAYA 16; BYA 2, 3; CA 13-16R; 139; CANR 6, 22, 47, 61; CDALBS; CLR 6, 56; CWRI 5; DLB 312; JRDA; MAICYA 1, 2; MTCW 1, 2; MTFW 2005; SAAS 1; SATA 1, 53; SATA-Obit 72

Udall, Nicholas 1504-1556 .... **LC 84**
See also DLB 62; RGEL 2

Ueda Akinari 1734-1809 .... **NCLC 131**

Uhry, Alfred 1936- .... **CLC 55**
See also CA 127; 133; CAD; CANR 112; CD 5, 6; CSW; DA3; DAM DRAM, POP; DFS 11, 15; INT CA-133; MTFW 2005

Ulf, Haerved
See Strindberg, (Johan) August

Ulf, Harved
See Strindberg, (Johan) August

Ulibarri, Sabine R(eyes)
1919-2003 .... **CLC 83; HLCS 2**
See also CA 131; 214; CANR 81; DAM MULT; DLB 82; HW 1, 2; RGSF 2

Unamuno (y Jugo), Miguel de
1864-1936 .. **HLC 2; SSC 11, 69; TCLC 2, 9, 148**
See also CA 104; 131; CANR 81; DAM MULT, NOV; DLB 108, 322; EW 8; EWL 3; HW 1, 2; MTCW 1, 2; MTFW 2005; RGSF 2; RGWL 2, 3; SSFS 20; TWA

Uncle Shelby
See Silverstein, Shel(don Allan)

Undercliffe, Errol
See Campbell, (John) Ramsey

Underwood, Miles
See Glassco, John

Undset, Sigrid 1882-1949 ..... **TCLC 3; WLC**
See also CA 104; 129; DA; DA3; DAB; DAC; DAM MST, NOV; DLB 293; EW 9; EWL 3; FW; MTCW 1, 2; MTFW 2005; RGWL 2, 3

Ungaretti, Giuseppe 1888-1970 ... **CLC 7, 11, 15; PC 57**
See also CA 19-20; 25-28R; CAP 2; DLB 114; EW 10; EWL 3; PFS 20; RGWL 2, 3; WLIT 7

Unger, Douglas 1952- .... **CLC 34**
See also CA 130; CANR 94

Unsworth, Barry (Forster) 1930- .... **CLC 76, 127**
See also BRWS 7; CA 25-28R; CANR 30, 54, 125; CN 6, 7; DLB 194

Updike, John (Hoyer) 1932- . **CLC 1, 2, 3, 5, 7, 9, 13, 15, 23, 34, 43, 70, 139, 214; SSC 13, 27; WLC**
See also AAYA 36; AMW; AMWC 1; AMWR 1; BPFB 3; BYA 12; CA 1-4R; CABS 1; CANR 4, 33, 51, 94, 133; CDALB 1968-1988; CN 1, 2, 3, 4, 5, 6, 7; CP 1, 2, 3, 4, 5, 6, 7; CPW 1; DA; DA3; DAB; DAC; DAM MST, NOV, POET, POP; DLB 2, 5, 143, 218, 227; DLBD 3; DLBY 1980, 1982, 1997; EWL 3; EXPP; HGG; MAL 5; MTCW 1, 2; MTFW 2005; NFS 12; RGAL 4; RGSF 2; SSFS 3, 19; TUS

Upshaw, Margaret Mitchell
See Mitchell, Margaret (Munnerlyn)

Upton, Mark
See Sanders, Lawrence

Upward, Allen 1863-1926 .... **TCLC 85**
See also CA 117; 187; DLB 36

Urdang, Constance (Henriette) 1922-1996 .... **CLC 47**
See also CA 21-24R; CANR 9, 24; CP 1, 2, 3, 4; CWP

Uriel, Henry
See Faust, Frederick (Schiller)

Uris, Leon (Marcus) 1924-2003 ... **CLC 7, 32**
See also AITN 1, 2; BEST 89:2; BPFB 3; CA 1-4R; 217; CANR 1, 40, 65, 123; CN 1, 2, 3, 4, 5, 6; CPW 1; DA3; DAM NOV, POP; MTCW 1, 2; MTFW 2005; SATA 49; SATA-Obit 146

Urista (Heredia), Alberto (Baltazar) 1947- .... **HLCS 1**
See Alurista
See also CA 182; CANR 2, 32; HW 1

Urmuz
See Codrescu, Andrei

Urquhart, Guy
See McAlmon, Robert (Menzies)

Urquhart, Jane 1949- .... **CLC 90**
See also CA 113; CANR 32, 68, 116; CCA 1; DAC

Usigli, Rodolfo 1905-1979 .... **HLCS 1**
See also CA 131; DLB 305; EWL 3; HW 1; LAW

Usk, Thomas (?)-1388 .... **CMLC 76**
See also DLB 146

Ustinov, Peter (Alexander) 1921-2004 .... **CLC 1**
See also AITN 1; CA 13-16R; 225; CANR 25, 51; CBD; CD 5, 6; DLB 13; MTCW 2

U Tam'si, Gerald Felix Tchicaya
See Tchicaya, Gerald Felix

U Tam'si, Tchicaya
See Tchicaya, Gerald Felix

Vachss, Andrew (Henry) 1942- .... **CLC 106**
See also CA 118, 214; CAAE 214; CANR 44, 95; CMW 4

Vachss, Andrew H.
See Vachss, Andrew (Henry)

Vaculik, Ludvik 1926- .... **CLC 7**
See also CA 53-56; CANR 72; CWW 2; DLB 232; EWL 3

Vaihinger, Hans 1852-1933 .... **TCLC 71**
See also CA 116; 166

Valdez, Luis (Miguel) 1940- ..... **CLC 84; DC 10; HLC 2**
See also CA 101; CAD; CANR 32, 81; CD 5, 6; DAM MULT; DFS 5; DLB 122; EWL 3; HW 1; LAIT 4; LLW

Valenzuela, Luisa 1938- .... **CLC 31, 104; HLCS 2; SSC 14, 82**
See also CA 101; CANR 32, 65, 123; CDWLB 3; CWW 2; DAM MULT; DLB 113; EWL 3; FW; HW 1, 2; LAW; RGSF 2; RGWL 3

Valera y Alcala-Galiano, Juan 1824-1905 .... **TCLC 10**
See also CA 106

Valerius Maximus fl. 20- .... **CMLC 64**
See also DLB 211

Valery, (Ambroise) Paul (Toussaint Jules) 1871-1945 .... **PC 9; TCLC 4, 15**
See also CA 104; 122; DA3; DAM POET; DLB 258; EW 8; EWL 3; GFL 1789 to the Present; MTCW 1, 2; MTFW 2005; RGWL 2, 3; TWA

Valle-Inclan, Ramon (Maria) del 1866-1936 .... **HLC 2; TCLC 5**
See del Valle-Inclan, Ramon (Maria)
See also CA 106; 153; CANR 80; DAM MULT; DLB 134; EW 8; EWL 3; HW 2; RGSF 2; RGWL 2, 3

Vallejo, Antonio Buero
See Buero Vallejo, Antonio

Vallejo, Cesar (Abraham) 1892-1938 .... **HLC 2; TCLC 3, 56**
See also CA 105; 153; DAM MULT; DLB 290; EWL 3; HW 1; LAW; RGWL 2, 3

Valles, Jules 1832-1885 .... **NCLC 71**
See also DLB 123; GFL 1789 to the Present

Vallette, Marguerite Eymery 1860-1953 .... **TCLC 67**
See Rachilde
See also CA 182; DLB 123, 192

Valle Y Pena, Ramon del
See Valle-Inclan, Ramon (Maria) del

Van Ash, Cay 1918-1994 .... **CLC 34**
See also CA 220

Vanbrugh, Sir John 1664-1726 .... **LC 21**
See also BRW 2; DAM DRAM; DLB 80; IDTP; RGEL 2

Van Campen, Karl
See Campbell, John W(ood, Jr.)

Vance, Gerald
See Silverberg, Robert

Vance, Jack .... **CLC 35**
See Vance, John Holbrook
See also DLB 8; FANT; SCFW 1, 2; SFW 4; SUFW 1, 2

Vance, John Holbrook 1916-
See Queen, Ellery; Vance, Jack
See also CA 29-32R; CANR 17, 65; CMW 4; MTCW 1

Van Den Bogarde, Derek Jules Gaspard Ulric Niven 1921-1999 .... **CLC 14**
See Bogarde, Dirk
See also CA 77-80; 179

Vandenburgh, Jane .... **CLC 59**
See also CA 168

Vanderhaeghe, Guy 1951- .... **CLC 41**
See also BPFB 3; CA 113; CANR 72, 145; CN 7

van der Post, Laurens (Jan) 1906-1996 .... **CLC 5**
See also AFW; CA 5-8R; 155; CANR 35; CN 1, 2, 3, 4, 5, 6; DLB 204; RGEL 2

van de Wetering, Janwillem 1931- ... **CLC 47**
See also CA 49-52; CANR 4, 62, 90; CMW 4

Van Dine, S. S. .... **TCLC 23**
See Wright, Willard Huntington
See also DLB 306; MSW

Van Doren, Carl (Clinton) 1885-1950 .... **TCLC 18**
See also CA 111; 168

Van Doren, Mark 1894-1972 .... **CLC 6, 10**
See also CA 1-4R; 37-40R; CANR 3; CN 1; CP 1; DLB 45, 284; MAL 5; MTCW 1, 2; RGAL 4

Van Druten, John (William) 1901-1957 .... **TCLC 2**
See also CA 104; 161; DLB 10; MAL 5; RGAL 4

Van Duyn, Mona (Jane) 1921-2004 .. **CLC 3, 7, 63, 116**
See also CA 9-12R; 234; CANR 7, 38, 60, 116; CP 1, 2, 3, 4, 5, 6, 7; CWP; DAM POET; DLB 5; MAL 5; MTFW 2005; PFS 20

Van Dyne, Edith
See Baum, L(yman) Frank

van Itallie, Jean-Claude 1936- .... **CLC 3**
See also CA 45-48; CAAS 2; CAD; CANR 1, 48; CD 5, 6; DLB 7

Van Loot, Cornelius Obenchain
See Roberts, Kenneth (Lewis)

van Ostaijen, Paul 1896-1928 .... **TCLC 33**
See also CA 163

Van Peebles, Melvin 1932- .... **CLC 2, 20**
See also BW 2, 3; CA 85-88; CANR 27, 67, 82; DAM MULT

van Schendel, Arthur(-Francois-Emile) 1874-1946 .... **TCLC 56**
See also EWL 3

Vansittart, Peter 1920- .... **CLC 42**
See also CA 1-4R; CANR 3, 49, 90; CN 4, 5, 6, 7; RHW

Van Vechten, Carl 1880-1964 ... **CLC 33; HR 1:3**
See also AMWS 2; CA 183; 89-92; DLB 4, 9, 51; RGAL 4

van Vogt, A(lfred) E(lton) 1912-2000 . **CLC 1**
See also BPFB 3; BYA 13, 14; CA 21-24R; 190; CANR 28; DLB 8, 251; SATA 14; SATA-Obit 124; SCFW 1, 2; SFW 4

Vara, Madeleine
See Jackson, Laura (Riding)

Varda, Agnes 1928- .... **CLC 16**
See also CA 116; 122

Vargas Llosa, (Jorge) Mario (Pedro) 1936- .... **CLC 3, 6, 9, 10, 15, 31, 42, 85, 181; HLC 2**
See Llosa, (Jorge) Mario (Pedro) Vargas
See also BPFB 3; CA 73-76; CANR 18, 32, 42, 67, 116, 140; CDWLB 3; CWW 2; DA; DA3; DAB; DAC; DAM MST, MULT, NOV; DLB 145; DNFS 2; EWL 3; HW 1, 2; LAIT 5; LATS 1:2; LAW; LAWS 1; MTCW 1, 2; MTFW 2005; RGWL 2; SSFS 14; TWA; WLIT 1

Varnhagen von Ense, Rahel 1771-1833 .... **NCLC 130**
See also DLB 90

Vasari, Giorgio 1511-1574 .... **LC 114**

Vasiliu, George
See Bacovia, George

Vasiliu, Gheorghe
See Bacovia, George
See also CA 123; 189

Vassa, Gustavus
See Equiano, Olaudah

Vassilikos, Vassilis 1933- .... **CLC 4, 8**
See also CA 81-84; CANR 75; EWL 3

Vaughan, Henry 1621-1695 .... **LC 27**
See also BRW 2; DLB 131; PAB; RGEL 2

Vaughn, Stephanie .... **CLC 62**

Vazov, Ivan (Minchov) 1850-1921 . **TCLC 25**
See also CA 121; 167; CDWLB 4; DLB 147

Veblen, Thorstein B(unde)
1857-1929 .... **TCLC 31**
See also AMWS 1; CA 115; 165; DLB 246; MAL 5

Vega, Lope de 1562-1635 .. **HLCS 2; LC 23, 119**
See also EW 2; RGWL 2, 3

Vendler, Helen (Hennessy) 1933- ... **CLC 138**
See also CA 41-44R; CANR 25, 72, 136; MTCW 1, 2; MTFW 2005

Venison, Alfred
See Pound, Ezra (Weston Loomis)

Ventsel, Elena Sergeevna 1907-2002
See Grekova, I.
See also CA 154

Verdi, Marie de
See Mencken, H(enry) L(ouis)

Verdu, Matilde
See Cela, Camilo Jose

Verga, Giovanni (Carmelo)
1840-1922 .... **SSC 21, 87; TCLC 3**
See also CA 104; 123; CANR 101; EW 7; EWL 3; RGSF 2; RGWL 2, 3; WLIT 7

Vergil 70B.C.-19B.C. ... **CMLC 9, 40; PC 12; WLCS**
See Virgil
See also AW 2; DA; DA3; DAB; DAC; DAM MST, POET; EFS 1; LMFS 1

Vergil, Polydore c. 1470-1555 .... **LC 108**
See also DLB 132

Verhaeren, Emile (Adolphe Gustave)
1855-1916 .... **TCLC 12**
See also CA 109; EWL 3; GFL 1789 to the Present

Verlaine, Paul (Marie) 1844-1896 .. **NCLC 2, 51; PC 2, 32**
See also DAM POET; DLB 217; EW 7; GFL 1789 to the Present; LMFS 2; RGWL 2, 3; TWA

Verne, Jules (Gabriel) 1828-1905 ... **TCLC 6, 52**
See also AAYA 16; BYA 4; CA 110; 131; CLR 88; DA3; DLB 123; GFL 1789 to the Present; JRDA; LAIT 2; LMFS 2; MAICYA 1, 2; MTFW 2005; RGWL 2, 3; SATA 21; SCFW 1, 2; SFW 4; TWA; WCH

Verus, Marcus Annius
See Aurelius, Marcus

Very, Jones 1813-1880 .... **NCLC 9**
See also DLB 1, 243; RGAL 4

Vesaas, Tarjei 1897-1970 .... **CLC 48**
See also CA 190; 29-32R; DLB 297; EW 11; EWL 3; RGWL 3

Vialis, Gaston
See Simenon, Georges (Jacques Christian)

Vian, Boris 1920-1959(?) .... **TCLC 9**
See also CA 106; 164; CANR 111; DLB 72, 321; EWL 3; GFL 1789 to the Present; MTCW 2; RGWL 2, 3

Viaud, (Louis Marie) Julien 1850-1923
See Loti, Pierre
See also CA 107

Vicar, Henry
See Felsen, Henry Gregor

Vicente, Gil 1465-c. 1536 .... **LC 99**
See also DLB 318; IDTP; RGWL 2, 3

Vicker, Angus
See Felsen, Henry Gregor

Vidal, (Eugene Luther) Gore 1925- .. **CLC 2, 4, 6, 8, 10, 22, 33, 72, 142**
See Box, Edgar
See also AAYA 64; AITN 1; AMWS 4; BEST 90:2; BPFB 3; CA 5-8R; CAD; CANR 13, 45, 65, 100, 132; CD 5, 6; CDALBS; CN 1, 2, 3, 4, 5, 6, 7; CPW; DA3; DAM NOV, POP; DFS 2; DLB 6, 152; EWL 3; INT CANR-13; MAL 5; MTCW 1, 2; MTFW 2005; RGAL 4; RHW; TUS

Viereck, Peter (Robert Edwin)
1916- .... **CLC 4; PC 27**
See also CA 1-4R; CANR 1, 47; CP 1, 2, 3, 4, 5, 6, 7; DLB 5; MAL 5; PFS 9, 14

Vigny, Alfred (Victor) de
1797-1863 .... **NCLC 7, 102; PC 26**
See also DAM POET; DLB 119, 192, 217; EW 5; GFL 1789 to the Present; RGWL 2, 3

Vilakazi, Benedict Wallet
1906-1947 .... **TCLC 37**
See also CA 168

Villa, Jose Garcia 1908-1997 ... **AAL; PC 22, TCLC 176**
See also CA 25-28R; CANR 12, 118; CP 1, 2, 3, 4; DLB 312; EWL 3; EXPP

Villard, Oswald Garrison
1872-1949 .... **TCLC 160**
See also CA 113; 162; DLB 25, 91

Villarreal, Jose Antonio 1924- .... **HLC 2**
See also CA 133; CANR 93; DAM MULT; DLB 82; HW 1; LAIT 4; RGAL 4

Villaurrutia, Xavier 1903-1950 ...... **TCLC 80**
See also CA 192; EWL 3; HW 1; LAW

Villaverde, Cirilo 1812-1894 .... **NCLC 121**
See also LAW

Villehardouin, Geoffroi de
1150(?)-1218(?) .... **CMLC 38**

Villiers, George 1628-1687 .... **LC 107**
See also DLB 80; RGEL 2

Villiers de l'Isle Adam, Jean Marie Mathias Philippe Auguste 1838-1889 ... **NCLC 3; SSC 14**
See also DLB 123, 192; GFL 1789 to the Present; RGSF 2

Villon, Francois 1431-1463(?) . **LC 62; PC 13**
See also DLB 208; EW 2; RGWL 2, 3; TWA

Vine, Barbara .... **CLC 50**
See Rendell, Ruth (Barbara)
See also BEST 90:4

Vinge, Joan (Carol) D(ennison)
1948- .... **CLC 30; SSC 24**
See also AAYA 32; BPFB 3; CA 93-96; CANR 72; SATA 36, 113; SFW 4; YAW

Viola, Herman J(oseph) 1938- .... **CLC 70**
See also CA 61-64; CANR 8, 23, 48, 91; SATA 126

Violis, G.
See Simenon, Georges (Jacques Christian)

Viramontes, Helena Maria 1954- .... **HLCS 2**
See also CA 159; DLB 122; HW 2; LLW

Virgil
See Vergil
See also CDWLB 1; DLB 211; LAIT 1; RGWL 2, 3; WP

Visconti, Luchino 1906-1976 .... **CLC 16**
See also CA 81-84; 65-68; CANR 39

Vitry, Jacques de
See Jacques de Vitry

Vittorini, Elio 1908-1966 .... **CLC 6, 9, 14**
See also CA 133; 25-28R; DLB 264; EW 12; EWL 3; RGWL 2, 3

Vivekananda, Swami 1863-1902 .... **TCLC 88**

Vizenor, Gerald Robert 1934- .... **CLC 103; NNAL**
See also CA 13-16R, 205; CAAE 205; CAAS 22; CANR 5, 21, 44, 67; DAM MULT; DLB 175, 227; MTCW 2; MTFW 2005; TCWW 2

Vizinczey, Stephen 1933- .... **CLC 40**
See also CA 128; CCA 1; INT CA-128

Vliet, R(ussell) G(ordon)
1929-1984 .... **CLC 22**
See also CA 37-40R; 112; CANR 18; CP 2, 3

Vogau, Boris Andreyevich 1894-1938
See Pilnyak, Boris
See also CA 123; 218

Vogel, Paula A(nne) 1951- ... **CLC 76; DC 19**
See also CA 108; CAD; CANR 119, 140; CD 5, 6; CWD; DFS 14; MTFW 2005; RGAL 4

Voigt, Cynthia 1942- .... **CLC 30**
See also AAYA 3, 30; BYA 1, 3, 6, 7, 8; CA 106; CANR 18, 37, 40, 94, 145; CLR 13, 48; INT CANR-18; JRDA; LAIT 5; MAICYA 1, 2; MAICYAS 1; MTFW 2005; SATA 48, 79, 116, 160; SATA-Brief 33; WYA; YAW

Voigt, Ellen Bryant 1943- .... **CLC 54**
See also CA 69-72; CANR 11, 29, 55, 115; CP 7; CSW; CWP; DLB 120; PFS 23

Voinovich, Vladimir (Nikolaevich)
1932- .... **CLC 10, 49, 147**
See also CA 81-84; CAAS 12; CANR 33, 67; CWW 2; DLB 302; MTCW 1

Vollmann, William T. 1959- .... **CLC 89**
See also CA 134; CANR 67, 116; CN 7; CPW; DA3; DAM NOV, POP; MTCW 2; MTFW 2005

Voloshinov, V. N.
See Bakhtin, Mikhail Mikhailovich

Voltaire 1694-1778 . **LC 14, 79, 110; SSC 12; WLC**
See also BYA 13; DA; DA3; DAB; DAC; DAM DRAM, MST; DLB 314; EW 4; GFL Beginnings to 1789; LATS 1:1; LMFS 1; NFS 7; RGWL 2, 3; TWA

von Aschendrof, Baron Ignatz
See Ford, Ford Madox

von Chamisso, Adelbert
See Chamisso, Adelbert von

von Daeniken, Erich 1935- .... **CLC 30**
See also AITN 1; CA 37-40R; CANR 17, 44

von Daniken, Erich
See von Daeniken, Erich

von Hartmann, Eduard
1842-1906 .... **TCLC 96**

von Hayek, Friedrich August
See Hayek, F(riedrich) A(ugust von)

von Heidenstam, (Carl Gustaf) Verner
See Heidenstam, (Carl Gustaf) Verner von

von Heyse, Paul (Johann Ludwig)
See Heyse, Paul (Johann Ludwig von)

von Hofmannsthal, Hugo
See Hofmannsthal, Hugo von

von Horvath, Odon
See von Horvath, Odon

von Horvath, Odon
See von Horvath, Odon

von Horvath, Odon 1901-1938 .... **TCLC 45**
See von Horvath, Oedoen
See also CA 118; 194; DLB 85, 124; RGWL 2, 3

von Horvath, Oedoen
See von Horvath, Odon
See also CA 184

von Kleist, Heinrich
See Kleist, Heinrich von

von Liliencron, (Friedrich Adolf Axel) Detlev
See Liliencron, (Friedrich Adolf Axel) Detlev von

Vonnegut, Kurt, Jr. 1922- . **CLC 1, 2, 3, 4, 5, 8, 12, 22, 40, 60, 111, 212; SSC 8; WLC**
See also AAYA 6, 44; AITN 1; AMWS 2; BEST 90:4; BPFB 3; BYA 3, 14; CA 1-4R; CANR 1, 25, 49, 75, 92; CDALB

1968-1988; CN 1, 2, 3, 4, 5, 6, 7; CPW 1; DA; DA3; DAB; DAC; DAM MST, NOV, POP; DLB 2, 8, 152; DLBD 3; DLBY 1980; EWL 3; EXPN; EXPS; LAIT 4; LMFS 2; MAL 5; MTCW 1, 2; MTFW 2005; NFS 3; RGAL 4; SCFW; SFW 4; SSFS 5; TUS; YAW

Von Rachen, Kurt
See Hubbard, L(afayette) Ron(ald)

von Rezzori (d'Arezzo), Gregor
See Rezzori (d'Arezzo), Gregor von

von Sternberg, Josef
See Sternberg, Josef von

Vorster, Gordon 1924- .... **CLC 34**
See also CA 133

Vosce, Trudie
See Ozick, Cynthia

Voznesensky, Andrei (Andreievich) 1933- .... **CLC 1, 15, 57**
See Voznesensky, Andrey
See also CA 89-92; CANR 37; CWW 2; DAM POET; MTCW 1

Voznesensky, Andrey
See Voznesensky, Andrei (Andreievich)
See also EWL 3

Wace, Robert c. 1100-c. 1175 .... **CMLC 55**
See also DLB 146

Waddington, Miriam 1917-2004 .... **CLC 28**
See also CA 21-24R; 225; CANR 12, 30; CCA 1; CP 1, 2, 3, 4, 5, 6, 7; DLB 68

Wagman, Fredrica 1937- .... **CLC 7**
See also CA 97-100; INT CA-97-100

Wagner, Linda W.
See Wagner-Martin, Linda (C.)

Wagner, Linda Welshimer
See Wagner-Martin, Linda (C.)

Wagner, Richard 1813-1883 ..... **NCLC 9, 119**
See also DLB 129; EW 6

Wagner-Martin, Linda (C.) 1936- .... **CLC 50**
See also CA 159; CANR 135

Wagoner, David (Russell) 1926- .... **CLC 3, 5, 15; PC 33**
See also AMWS 9; CA 1-4R; CAAS 3; CANR 2, 71; CN 1, 2, 3, 4, 5, 6, 7; CP 1, 2, 3, 4, 5, 6, 7; DLB 5, 256; SATA 14; TCWW 1, 2

Wah, Fred(erick James) 1939- .... **CLC 44**
See also CA 107; 141; CP 1, 7; DLB 60

Wahloo, Per 1926-1975 .... **CLC 7**
See also BPFB 3; CA 61-64; CANR 73; CMW 4; MSW

Wahloo, Peter
See Wahloo, Per

Wain, John (Barrington) 1925-1994 . **CLC 2, 11, 15, 46**
See also CA 5-8R; 145; CAAS 4; CANR 23, 54; CDBLB 1960 to Present; CN 1, 2, 3, 4, 5; CP 1, 2, 3, 4; DLB 15, 27, 139, 155; EWL 3; MTCW 1, 2; MTFW 2005

Wajda, Andrzej 1926- .... **CLC 16, 219**
See also CA 102

Wakefield, Dan 1932- .... **CLC 7**
See also CA 21-24R; 211; CAAE 211; CAAS 7; CN 4, 5, 6, 7

Wakefield, Herbert Russell 1888-1965 .... **TCLC 120**
See also CA 5-8R; CANR 77; HGG; SUFW

Wakoski, Diane 1937- .... **CLC 2, 4, 7, 9, 11, 40; PC 15**
See also CA 13-16R, 216; CAAE 216; CAAS 1; CANR 9, 60, 106; CP 1, 2, 3, 4, 5, 6, 7; CWP; DAM POET; DLB 5; INT CANR-9; MAL 5; MTCW 2; MTFW 2005

Wakoski-Sherbell, Diane
See Wakoski, Diane

Walcott, Derek (Alton) 1930- ... **BLC 3; CLC 2, 4, 9, 14, 25, 42, 67, 76, 160; DC 7; PC 46**
See also BW 2; CA 89-92; CANR 26, 47, 75, 80, 130; CBD; CD 5, 6; CDWLB 3; CP 1, 2, 3, 4, 5, 6, 7; DA3; DAB; DAC; DAM MST, MULT, POET; DLB 117; DLBY 1981; DNFS 1; EFS 1; EWL 3; LMFS 2; MTCW 1, 2; MTFW 2005; PFS 6; RGEL 2; TWA; WWE 1

Waldman, Anne (Lesley) 1945- .... **CLC 7**
See also BG 1:3; CA 37-40R; CAAS 17; CANR 34, 69, 116; CP 1, 2, 3, 4, 5, 6, 7; CWP; DLB 16

Waldo, E. Hunter
See Sturgeon, Theodore (Hamilton)

Waldo, Edward Hamilton
See Sturgeon, Theodore (Hamilton)

Walker, Alice (Malsenior) 1944- .... **BLC 3; CLC 5, 6, 9, 19, 27, 46, 58, 103, 167; PC 30; SSC 5; WLCS**
See also AAYA 3, 33; AFAW 1, 2; AMWS 3; BEST 89:4; BPFB 3; BW 2, 3; CA 37-40R; CANR 9, 27, 49, 66, 82, 131; CDALB 1968-1988; CN 4, 5, 6, 7; CPW; CSW; DA; DA3; DAB; DAC; DAM MST, MULT, NOV, POET, POP; DLB 6, 33, 143; EWL 3; EXPN; EXPS; FL 1:6; FW; INT CANR-27; LAIT 3; MAL 5; MAWW; MTCW 1, 2; MTFW 2005; NFS 5; RGAL 4; RGSF 2; SATA 31; SSFS 2, 11; TUS; YAW

Walker, David Harry 1911-1992 .... **CLC 14**
See also CA 1-4R; 137; CANR 1; CN 1, 2; CWRI 5; SATA 8; SATA-Obit 71

Walker, Edward Joseph 1934-2004
See Walker, Ted
See also CA 21-24R; 226; CANR 12, 28, 53

Walker, George F(rederick) 1947- .. **CLC 44, 61**
See also CA 103; CANR 21, 43, 59; CD 5, 6; DAB; DAC; DAM MST; DLB 60

Walker, Joseph A. 1935-2003 .... **CLC 19**
See also BW 1, 3; CA 89-92; CAD; CANR 26, 143; CD 5, 6; DAM DRAM, MST; DFS 12; DLB 38

Walker, Margaret (Abigail) 1915-1998 .... **BLC; CLC 1, 6; PC 20; TCLC 129**
See also AFAW 1, 2; BW 2, 3; CA 73-76; 172; CANR 26, 54, 76, 136; CN 1, 2, 3, 4, 5, 6; CP 1, 2, 3, 4; CSW; DAM MULT; DLB 76, 152; EXPP; FW; MAL 5; MTCW 1, 2; MTFW 2005; RGAL 4; RHW

Walker, Ted .... **CLC 13**
See Walker, Edward Joseph
See also CP 1, 2, 3, 4, 5, 6, 7; DLB 40

Wallace, David Foster 1962- ... **CLC 50, 114; SSC 68**
See also AAYA 50; AMWS 10; CA 132; CANR 59, 133; CN 7; DA3; MTCW 2; MTFW 2005

Wallace, Dexter
See Masters, Edgar Lee

Wallace, (Richard Horatio) Edgar 1875-1932 .... **TCLC 57**
See also CA 115; 218; CMW 4; DLB 70; MSW; RGEL 2

Wallace, Irving 1916-1990 .... **CLC 7, 13**
See also AITN 1; BPFB 3; CA 1-4R; 132; CAAS 1; CANR 1, 27; CPW; DAM NOV, POP; INT CANR-27; MTCW 1, 2

Wallant, Edward Lewis 1926-1962 ... **CLC 5, 10**
See also CA 1-4R; CANR 22; DLB 2, 28, 143, 299; EWL 3; MAL 5; MTCW 1, 2; RGAL 4

Wallas, Graham 1858-1932 .... **TCLC 91**

Waller, Edmund 1606-1687 .... **LC 86**
See also BRW 2; DAM POET; DLB 126; PAB; RGEL 2

Walley, Byron
See Card, Orson Scott

Walpole, Horace 1717-1797 .... **LC 2, 49**
See also BRW 3; DLB 39, 104, 213; GL 3; HGG; LMFS 1; RGEL 2; SUFW 1; TEA

Walpole, Hugh (Seymour) 1884-1941 .... **TCLC 5**
See also CA 104; 165; DLB 34; HGG; MTCW 2; RGEL 2; RHW

Walrond, Eric (Derwent) 1898-1966 . **HR 1:3**
See also BW 1; CA 125; DLB 51

Walser, Martin 1927- .... **CLC 27, 183**
See also CA 57-60; CANR 8, 46, 145; CWW 2; DLB 75, 124; EWL 3

Walser, Robert 1878-1956 ..... **SSC 20; TCLC 18**
See also CA 118; 165; CANR 100; DLB 66; EWL 3

Walsh, Gillian Paton
See Paton Walsh, Gillian

Walsh, Jill Paton .... **CLC 35**
See Paton Walsh, Gillian
See also CLR 2, 65; WYA

Walter, Villiam Christian
See Andersen, Hans Christian

Walters, Anna L(ee) 1946- .... **NNAL**
See also CA 73-76

Walther von der Vogelweide c. 1170-1228 .... **CMLC 56**

Walton, Izaak 1593-1683 .... **LC 72**
See also BRW 2; CDBLB Before 1660; DLB 151, 213; RGEL 2

Wambaugh, Joseph (Aloysius), Jr. 1937- .... **CLC 3, 18**
See also AITN 1; BEST 89:3; BPFB 3; CA 33-36R; CANR 42, 65, 115; CMW 4; CPW; DA3; DAM NOV, POP; DLB 6; DLBY 1983; MSW; MTCW 1, 2

Wang Wei 699(?)-761(?) .... **PC 18**
See also TWA

Warburton, William 1698-1779 .... **LC 97**
See also DLB 104

Ward, Arthur Henry Sarsfield 1883-1959
See Rohmer, Sax
See also CA 108; 173; CMW 4; HGG

Ward, Douglas Turner 1930- .... **CLC 19**
See also BW 1; CA 81-84; CAD; CANR 27; CD 5, 6; DLB 7, 38

Ward, E. D.
See Lucas, E(dward) V(errall)

Ward, Mrs. Humphry 1851-1920
See Ward, Mary Augusta
See also RGEL 2

Ward, Mary Augusta 1851-1920 ... **TCLC 55**
See Ward, Mrs. Humphry
See also DLB 18

Ward, Nathaniel 1578(?)-1652 .... **LC 114**
See also DLB 24

Ward, Peter
See Faust, Frederick (Schiller)

Warhol, Andy 1928(?)-1987 .... **CLC 20**
See also AAYA 12; BEST 89:4; CA 89-92; 121; CANR 34

Warner, Francis (Robert le Plastrier) 1937- .... **CLC 14**
See also CA 53-56; CANR 11; CP 1, 2, 3, 4

Warner, Marina 1946- .... **CLC 59**
See also CA 65-68; CANR 21, 55, 118; CN 5, 6, 7; DLB 194; MTFW 2005

Warner, Rex (Ernest) 1905-1986 ...... **CLC 45**
See also CA 89-92; 119; CN 1, 2, 3, 4; CP 1, 2, 3, 4; DLB 15; RGEL 2; RHW

Warner, Susan (Bogert) 1819-1885 .... **NCLC 31, 146**
See also DLB 3, 42, 239, 250, 254

Warner, Sylvia (Constance) Ashton
See Ashton-Warner, Sylvia (Constance)

Warner, Sylvia Townsend
1893-1978 .. **CLC 7, 19; SSC 23; TCLC 131**
See also BRWS 7; CA 61-64; 77-80; CANR 16, 60, 104; CN 1, 2; DLB 34, 139; EWL 3; FANT; FW; MTCW 1, 2; RGEL 2; RGSF 2; RHW

Warren, Mercy Otis 1728-1814 ..... **NCLC 13**
See also DLB 31, 200; RGAL 4; TUS

Warren, Robert Penn 1905-1989 .. **CLC 1, 4, 6, 8, 10, 13, 18, 39, 53, 59; PC 37; SSC 4, 58; WLC**
See also AITN 1; AMW; AMWC 2; BPFB 3; BYA 1; CA 13-16R; 129; CANR 10, 47; CDALB 1968-1988; CN 1, 2, 3, 4; CP 1, 2, 3, 4; DA; DA3; DAB; DAC; DAM MST, NOV, POET; DLB 2, 48, 152, 320; DLBY 1980, 1989; EWL 3; INT CANR-10; MAL 5; MTCW 1, 2; MTFW 2005; NFS 13; RGAL 4; RGSF 2; RHW; SATA 46; SATA-Obit 63; SSFS 8; TUS

Warrigal, Jack
See Furphy, Joseph

Warshofsky, Isaac
See Singer, Isaac Bashevis

Warton, Joseph 1722-1800 .... **NCLC 118**
See also DLB 104, 109; RGEL 2

Warton, Thomas 1728-1790 .... **LC 15, 82**
See also DAM POET; DLB 104, 109; RGEL 2

Waruk, Kona
See Harris, (Theodore) Wilson

Warung, Price .... **TCLC 45**
See Astley, William
See also DLB 230; RGEL 2

Warwick, Jarvis
See Garner, Hugh
See also CCA 1

Washington, Alex
See Harris, Mark

Washington, Booker T(aliaferro)
1856-1915 .... **BLC 3; TCLC 10**
See also BW 1; CA 114; 125; DA3; DAM MULT; LAIT 2; RGAL 4; SATA 28

Washington, George 1732-1799 .... **LC 25**
See also DLB 31

Wassermann, (Karl) Jakob
1873-1934 .... **TCLC 6**
See also CA 104; 163; DLB 66; EWL 3

Wasserstein, Wendy 1950-2006 . **CLC 32, 59, 90, 183; DC 4**
See also AMWS 15; CA 121; 129; CABS 3; CAD; CANR 53, 75, 128; CD 5, 6; CWD; DA3; DAM DRAM; DFS 5, 17; DLB 228; EWL 3; FW; INT CA-129; MAL 5; MTCW 2; MTFW 2005; SATA 94

Waterhouse, Keith (Spencer) 1929- . **CLC 47**
See also CA 5-8R; CANR 38, 67, 109; CBD; CD 6; CN 1, 2, 3, 4, 5, 6, 7; DLB 13, 15; MTCW 1, 2; MTFW 2005

Waters, Frank (Joseph) 1902-1995 .. **CLC 88**
See also CA 5-8R; 149; CAAS 13; CANR 3, 18, 63, 121; DLB 212; DLBY 1986; RGAL 4; TCWW 1, 2

Waters, Mary C. .... **CLC 70**

Waters, Roger 1944- .... **CLC 35**

Watkins, Frances Ellen
See Harper, Frances Ellen Watkins

Watkins, Gerrold
See Malzberg, Barry N(athaniel)

Watkins, Gloria Jean 1952(?)- .... **CLC 94**
See also BW 2; CA 143; CANR 87, 126; DLB 246; MTCW 2; MTFW 2005; SATA 115

Watkins, Paul 1964- .... **CLC 55**
See also CA 132; CANR 62, 98

Watkins, Vernon Phillips
1906-1967 .... **CLC 43**
See also CA 9-10; 25-28R; CAP 1; DLB 20; EWL 3; RGEL 2

Watson, Irving S.
See Mencken, H(enry) L(ouis)

Watson, John H.
See Farmer, Philip Jose

Watson, Richard F.
See Silverberg, Robert

Watts, Ephraim
See Horne, Richard Henry Hengist

Watts, Isaac 1674-1748 .... **LC 98**
See also DLB 95; RGEL 2; SATA 52

Waugh, Auberon (Alexander)
1939-2001 .... **CLC 7**
See also CA 45-48; 192; CANR 6, 22, 92; CN 1, 2, 3; DLB 14, 194

Waugh, Evelyn (Arthur St. John)
1903-1966 .. **CLC 1, 3, 8, 13, 19, 27, 44, 107; SSC 41; WLC**
See also BPFB 3; BRW 7; CA 85-88; 25-28R; CANR 22; CDBLB 1914-1945; DA; DA3; DAB; DAC; DAM MST, NOV, POP; DLB 15, 162, 195; EWL 3; MTCW 1, 2; MTFW 2005; NFS 13, 17; RGEL 2; RGSF 2; TEA; WLIT 4

Waugh, Harriet 1944- .... **CLC 6**
See also CA 85-88; CANR 22

Ways, C. R.
See Blount, Roy (Alton), Jr.

Waystaff, Simon
See Swift, Jonathan

Webb, Beatrice (Martha Potter)
1858-1943 .... **TCLC 22**
See also CA 117; 162; DLB 190; FW

Webb, Charles (Richard) 1939- .... **CLC 7**
See also CA 25-28R; CANR 114

Webb, Frank J. .... **NCLC 143**
See also DLB 50

Webb, James H(enry), Jr. 1946- ...... **CLC 22**
See also CA 81-84

Webb, Mary Gladys (Meredith)
1881-1927 .... **TCLC 24**
See also CA 182; 123; DLB 34; FW

Webb, Mrs. Sidney
See Webb, Beatrice (Martha Potter)

Webb, Phyllis 1927- .... **CLC 18**
See also CA 104; CANR 23; CCA 1; CP 1, 2, 3, 4, 5, 6, 7; CWP; DLB 53

Webb, Sidney (James) 1859-1947 .. **TCLC 22**
See also CA 117; 163; DLB 190

Webber, Andrew Lloyd .... **CLC 21**
See Lloyd Webber, Andrew
See also DFS 7

Weber, Lenora Mattingly
1895-1971 .... **CLC 12**
See also CA 19-20; 29-32R; CAP 1; SATA 2; SATA-Obit 26

Weber, Max 1864-1920 .... **TCLC 69**
See also CA 109; 189; DLB 296

Webster, John 1580(?)-1634(?) .... **DC 2; LC 33, 84, 124; WLC**
See also BRW 2; CDBLB Before 1660; DA; DAB; DAC; DAM DRAM, MST; DFS 17, 19; DLB 58; IDTP; RGEL 2; WLIT 3

Webster, Noah 1758-1843 .... **NCLC 30**
See also DLB 1, 37, 42, 43, 73, 243

Wedekind, (Benjamin) Frank(lin)
1864-1918 .... **TCLC 7**
See also CA 104; 153; CANR 121, 122; CDWLB 2; DAM DRAM; DLB 118; EW 8; EWL 3; LMFS 2; RGWL 2, 3

Wehr, Demaris .... **CLC 65**

Weidman, Jerome 1913-1998 .... **CLC 7**
See also AITN 2; CA 1-4R; 171; CAD; CANR 1; CD 1, 2, 3, 4, 5; DLB 28

Weil, Simone (Adolphine)
1909-1943 .... **TCLC 23**
See also CA 117; 159; EW 12; EWL 3; FW; GFL 1789 to the Present; MTCW 2

Weininger, Otto 1880-1903 .... **TCLC 84**

Weinstein, Nathan
See West, Nathanael

Weinstein, Nathan von Wallenstein
See West, Nathanael

Weir, Peter (Lindsay) 1944- .... **CLC 20**
See also CA 113; 123

Weiss, Peter (Ulrich) 1916-1982 .. **CLC 3, 15, 51; TCLC 152**
See also CA 45-48; 106; CANR 3; DAM DRAM; DFS 3; DLB 69, 124; EWL 3; RGWL 2, 3

Weiss, Theodore (Russell)
1916-2003 .... **CLC 3, 8, 14**
See also CA 9-12R; 189; 216; CAAE 189; CAAS 2; CANR 46, 94; CP 1, 2, 3, 4, 5, 6, 7; DLB 5; TCLE 1:2

Welch, (Maurice) Denton
1915-1948 .... **TCLC 22**
See also BRWS 8, 9; CA 121; 148; RGEL 2

Welch, James (Phillip) 1940-2003 ..... **CLC 6, 14, 52; NNAL; PC 62**
See also CA 85-88; 219; CANR 42, 66, 107; CN 5, 6, 7; CP 2, 3, 4, 5, 6, 7; CPW; DAM MULT, POP; DLB 175, 256; LATS 1:1; RGAL 4; TCWW 1, 2

Weldon, Fay 1931- . **CLC 6, 9, 11, 19, 36, 59, 122**
See also BRWS 4; CA 21-24R; CANR 16, 46, 63, 97, 137; CDBLB 1960 to Present; CN 3, 4, 5, 6, 7; CPW; DAM POP; DLB 14, 194, 319; EWL 3; FW; HGG; INT CANR-16; MTCW 1, 2; MTFW 2005; RGEL 2; RGSF 2

Wellek, Rene 1903-1995 .... **CLC 28**
See also CA 5-8R; 150; CAAS 7; CANR 8; DLB 63; EWL 3; INT CANR-8

Weller, Michael 1942- .... **CLC 10, 53**
See also CA 85-88; CAD; CD 5, 6

Weller, Paul 1958- .... **CLC 26**

Wellershoff, Dieter 1925- .... **CLC 46**
See also CA 89-92; CANR 16, 37

Welles, (George) Orson 1915-1985 .. **CLC 20, 80**
See also AAYA 40; CA 93-96; 117

Wellman, John McDowell 1945-
See Wellman, Mac
See also CA 166; CD 5

Wellman, Mac .... **CLC 65**
See Wellman, John McDowell; Wellman, John McDowell
See also CAD; CD 6; RGAL 4

Wellman, Manly Wade 1903-1986 ... **CLC 49**
See also CA 1-4R; 118; CANR 6, 16, 44; FANT; SATA 6; SATA-Obit 47; SFW 4; SUFW

Wells, Carolyn 1869(?)-1942 .... **TCLC 35**
See also CA 113; 185; CMW 4; DLB 11

Wells, H(erbert) G(eorge) 1866-1946 . **SSC 6, 70; TCLC 6, 12, 19, 133; WLC**
See also AAYA 18; BPFB 3; BRW 6; CA 110; 121; CDBLB 1914-1945; CLR 64; DA; DA3; DAB; DAC; DAM MST, NOV, DLB 34, 70, 156, 178; EWL 3; EXPS; HGG; LAIT 3; LMFS 2; MTCW 1, 2; MTFW 2005; NFS 17, 20; RGEL 2; RGSF 2; SATA 20; SCFW 1, 2; SFW 4; SSFS 3; SUFW; TEA; WCH; WLIT 4; YAW

Wells, Rosemary 1943- .... **CLC 12**
See also AAYA 13; BYA 7, 8; CA 85-88; CANR 48, 120; CLR 16, 69; CWRI 5; MAICYA 1, 2; SAAS 1; SATA 18, 69, 114, 156; YAW

Wells-Barnett, Ida B(ell)
1862-1931 .... **TCLC 125**
See also CA 182; DLB 23, 221

Welsh, Irvine 1958- .... **CLC 144**
See also CA 173; CANR 146; CN 7; DLB 271

Welty, Eudora (Alice) 1909-2001 .. **CLC 1, 2, 5, 14, 22, 33, 105, 220; SSC 1, 27, 51; WLC**
See also AAYA 48; AMW; AMWR 1; BPFB 3; CA 9-12R; 199; CABS 1; CANR 32, 65, 128; CDALB 1941-1968; CN 1, 2, 3, 4, 5, 6, 7; CSW; DA; DA3; DAB; DAC; DAM MST, NOV; DLB 2, 102, 143; DLBD 12; DLBY 1987, 2001; EWL 3; EXPS; HGG; LAIT 3; MAL 5; MAWW; MTCW 1, 2; MTFW 2005; NFS 13, 15; RGAL 4; RGSF 2; RHW; SSFS 2, 10; TUS

Wen I-to 1899-1946 .... **TCLC 28**
See also EWL 3

Wentworth, Robert
See Hamilton, Edmond

Werfel, Franz (Viktor) 1890-1945 ... **TCLC 8**
See also CA 104; 161; DLB 81, 124; EWL 3; RGWL 2, 3

Wergeland, Henrik Arnold
1808-1845 .... **NCLC 5**

Wersba, Barbara 1932- .... **CLC 30**
See also AAYA 2, 30; BYA 6, 12, 13; CA 29-32R, 182; CAAE 182; CANR 16, 38; CLR 3, 78; DLB 52; JRDA; MAICYA 1, 2; SAAS 2; SATA 1, 58; SATA-Essay 103; WYA; YAW

Wertmueller, Lina 1928- .... **CLC 16**
See also CA 97-100; CANR 39, 78

Wescott, Glenway 1901-1987 .. **CLC 13; SSC 35**
See also CA 13-16R; 121; CANR 23, 70; CN 1, 2, 3, 4; DLB 4, 9, 102; MAL 5; RGAL 4

Wesker, Arnold 1932- .... **CLC 3, 5, 42**
See also CA 1-4R; CAAS 7; CANR 1, 33; CBD; CD 5, 6; CDBLB 1960 to Present; DAB; DAM DRAM; DLB 13, 310, 319; EWL 3; MTCW 1; RGEL 2; TEA

Wesley, John 1703-1791 .... **LC 88**
See also DLB 104

Wesley, Richard (Errol) 1945- .... **CLC 7**
See also BW 1; CA 57-60; CAD; CANR 27; CD 5, 6; DLB 38

Wessel, Johan Herman 1742-1785 .... **LC 7**
See also DLB 300

West, Anthony (Panther)
1914-1987 .... **CLC 50**
See also CA 45-48; 124; CANR 3, 19; CN 1, 2, 3, 4; DLB 15

West, C. P.
See Wodehouse, P(elham) G(renville)

West, Cornel (Ronald) 1953- .... **BLCS; CLC 134**
See also CA 144; CANR 91; DLB 246

West, Delno C(loyde), Jr. 1936- .... **CLC 70**
See also CA 57-60

West, Dorothy 1907-1998 ...... **HR 1:3; TCLC 108**
See also BW 2; CA 143; 169; DLB 76

West, (Mary) Jessamyn 1902-1984 ... **CLC 7, 17**
See also CA 9-12R; 112; CANR 27; CN 1, 2, 3; DLB 6; DLBY 1984; MTCW 1, 2; RGAL 4; RHW; SATA-Obit 37; TCWW 2; TUS; YAW

West, Morris L(anglo) 1916-1999 ..... **CLC 6, 33**
See also BPFB 3; CA 5-8R; 187; CANR 24, 49, 64; CN 1, 2, 3, 4, 5, 6; CPW; DLB 289; MTCW 1, 2; MTFW 2005

West, Nathanael 1903-1940 .. **SSC 16; TCLC 1, 14, 44**
See also AMW; AMWR 2; BPFB 3; CA 104; 125; CDALB 1929-1941; DA3; DLB 4, 9, 28; EWL 3; MAL 5; MTCW 1, 2; MTFW 2005; NFS 16; RGAL 4; TUS

West, Owen
See Koontz, Dean R.

West, Paul 1930- .... **CLC 7, 14, 96**
See also CA 13-16R; CAAS 7; CANR 22, 53, 76, 89, 136; CN 1, 2, 3, 4, 5, 6, 7; DLB 14; INT CANR-22; MTCW 2; MTFW 2005

West, Rebecca 1892-1983 ... **CLC 7, 9, 31, 50**
See also BPFB 3; BRWS 3; CA 5-8R; 109; CANR 19; CN 1, 2, 3; DLB 36; DLBY 1983; EWL 3; FW; MTCW 1, 2; MTFW 2005; NCFS 4; RGEL 2; TEA

Westall, Robert (Atkinson)
1929-1993 .... **CLC 17**
See also AAYA 12; BYA 2, 6, 7, 8, 9, 15; CA 69-72; 141; CANR 18, 68; CLR 13; FANT; JRDA; MAICYA 1, 2; MAICYAS 1; SAAS 2; SATA 23, 69; SATA-Obit 75; WYA; YAW

Westermarck, Edward 1862-1939 . **TCLC 87**

Westlake, Donald E(dwin) 1933- . **CLC 7, 33**
See also BPFB 3; CA 17-20R; CAAS 13; CANR 16, 44, 65, 94, 137; CMW 4; CPW; DAM POP; INT CANR-16; MSW; MTCW 2; MTFW 2005

Westmacott, Mary
See Christie, Agatha (Mary Clarissa)

Weston, Allen
See Norton, Andre

Wetcheek, J. L.
See Feuchtwanger, Lion

Wetering, Janwillem van de
See van de Wetering, Janwillem

Wetherald, Agnes Ethelwyn
1857-1940 .... **TCLC 81**
See also CA 202; DLB 99

Wetherell, Elizabeth
See Warner, Susan (Bogert)

Whale, James 1889-1957 .... **TCLC 63**

Whalen, Philip (Glenn) 1923-2002 .... **CLC 6, 29**
See also BG 1:3; CA 9-12R; 209; CANR 5, 39; CP 1, 2, 3, 4, 5, 6, 7; DLB 16; WP

Wharton, Edith (Newbold Jones)
1862-1937 ... **SSC 6, 84; TCLC 3, 9, 27, 53, 129, 149; WLC**
See also AAYA 25; AMW; AMWC 2; AMWR 1; BPFB 3; CA 104; 132; CDALB 1865-1917; DA; DA3; DAB; DAC; DAM MST, NOV; DLB 4, 9, 12, 78, 189; DLBD 13; EWL 3; EXPS; FL 1:6; GL 3; HGG; LAIT 2, 3; LATS 1:1; MAL 5; MAWW; MTCW 1, 2; MTFW 2005; NFS 5, 11, 15, 20; RGAL 4; RGSF 2; RHW; SSFS 6, 7; SUFW; TUS

Wharton, James
See Mencken, H(enry) L(ouis)

Wharton, William (a pseudonym)
1925- .... **CLC 18, 37**
See also CA 93-96; CN 4, 5, 6, 7; DLBY 1980; INT CA-93-96

Wheatley (Peters), Phillis
1753(?)-1784 ... **BLC 3; LC 3, 50; PC 3; WLC**
See also AFAW 1, 2; CDALB 1640-1865; DA; DA3; DAC; DAM MST, MULT, POET; DLB 31, 50; EXPP; FL 1:1; PFS 13; RGAL 4

Wheelock, John Hall 1886-1978 .... **CLC 14**
See also CA 13-16R; 77-80; CANR 14; CP 1, 2; DLB 45; MAL 5

Whim-Wham
See Curnow, (Thomas) Allen (Monro)

White, Babington
See Braddon, Mary Elizabeth

White, E(lwyn) B(rooks)
1899-1985 .... **CLC 10, 34, 39**
See also AAYA 62; AITN 2; AMWS 1; CA 13-16R; 116; CANR 16, 37; CDALBS; CLR 1, 21; CPW; DA3; DAM POP; DLB 11, 22; EWL 3; FANT; MAICYA 1, 2; MAL 5; MTCW 1, 2; MTFW 2005; NCFS 5; RGAL 4; SATA 2, 29, 100; SATA-Obit 44; TUS

White, Edmund (Valentine III)
1940- .... **CLC 27, 110**
See also AAYA 7; CA 45-48; CANR 3, 19, 36, 62, 107, 133; CN 5, 6, 7; DA3; DAM POP; DLB 227; MTCW 1, 2; MTFW 2005

White, Hayden V. 1928- .... **CLC 148**
See also CA 128; CANR 135; DLB 246

White, Patrick (Victor Martindale)
1912-1990 ...... **CLC 3, 4, 5, 7, 9, 18, 65, 69; SSC 39, TCLC 176**
See also BRWS 1; CA 81-84; 132; CANR 43; CN 1, 2, 3, 4; DLB 260; EWL 3; MTCW 1; RGEL 2; RGSF 2; RHW; TWA; WWE 1

White, Phyllis Dorothy James 1920-
See James, P. D.
See also CA 21-24R; CANR 17, 43, 65, 112; CMW 4; CN 7; CPW; DA3; DAM POP; MTCW 1, 2; MTFW 2005; TEA

White, T(erence) H(anbury)
1906-1964 .... **CLC 30**
See also AAYA 22; BPFB 3; BYA 4, 5; CA 73-76; CANR 37; DLB 160; FANT; JRDA; LAIT 1; MAICYA 1, 2; RGEL 2; SATA 12; SUFW 1; YAW

White, Terence de Vere 1912-1994 ... **CLC 49**
See also CA 49-52; 145; CANR 3

White, Walter
See White, Walter F(rancis)

White, Walter F(rancis) 1893-1955 ... **BLC 3; HR 1:3; TCLC 15**
See also BW 1; CA 115; 124; DAM MULT; DLB 51

White, William Hale 1831-1913
See Rutherford, Mark
See also CA 121; 189

Whitehead, Alfred North
1861-1947 .... **TCLC 97**
See also CA 117; 165; DLB 100, 262

Whitehead, E(dward) A(nthony)
1933- .... **CLC 5**
See Whitehead, Ted
See also CA 65-68; CANR 58, 118; CBD; CD 5; DLB 310

Whitehead, Ted
See Whitehead, E(dward) A(nthony)
See also CD 6

Whiteman, Roberta J. Hill 1947- ...... **NNAL**
See also CA 146

Whitemore, Hugh (John) 1936- .... **CLC 37**
See also CA 132; CANR 77; CBD; CD 5, 6; INT CA-132

Whitman, Sarah Helen (Power)
1803-1878 .... **NCLC 19**
See also DLB 1, 243

Whitman, Walt(er) 1819-1892 .. **NCLC 4, 31, 81; PC 3; WLC**
See also AAYA 42; AMW; AMWR 1; CDALB 1640-1865; DA; DA3; DAB; DAC; DAM MST, POET; DLB 3, 64, 224, 250; EXPP; LAIT 2; LMFS 1; PAB; PFS 2, 3, 13, 22; RGAL 4; SATA 20; TUS; WP; WYAS 1

Whitney, Phyllis A(yame) 1903- .... **CLC 42**
See also AAYA 36; AITN 2; BEST 90:3; CA 1-4R; CANR 3, 25, 38, 60; CLR 59; CMW 4; CPW; DA3; DAM POP; JRDA; MAICYA 1, 2; MTCW 2; RHW; SATA 1, 30; YAW

Whittemore, (Edward) Reed, Jr.
1919- .... **CLC 4**
See also CA 9-12R, 219; CAAE 219; CAAS 8; CANR 4, 119; CP 1, 2, 3, 4, 5, 6, 7; DLB 5; MAL 5

Whittier, John Greenleaf
1807-1892 .... **NCLC 8, 59**
See also AMWS 1; DLB 1, 243; RGAL 4

Whittlebot, Hernia
See Coward, Noel (Peirce)

Wicker, Thomas Grey 1926-
See Wicker, Tom
See also CA 65-68; CANR 21, 46, 141

Wicker, Tom .... **CLC 7**
See Wicker, Thomas Grey

Wideman, John Edgar 1941- .. **BLC 3; CLC 5, 34, 36, 67, 122; SSC 62**
See also AFAW 1, 2; AMWS 10; BPFB 4; BW 2, 3; CA 85-88; CANR 14, 42, 67, 109, 140; CN 4, 5, 6, 7; DAM MULT; DLB 33, 143; MAL 5; MTCW 2; MTFW 2005; RGAL 4; RGSF 2; SSFS 6, 12; TCLE 1:2

Wiebe, Rudy (Henry) 1934- .. **CLC 6, 11, 14, 138**
See also CA 37-40R; CANR 42, 67, 123; CN 1, 2, 3, 4, 5, 6, 7; DAC; DAM MST; DLB 60; RHW; SATA 156

Wieland, Christoph Martin
1733-1813 .... **NCLC 17**
See also DLB 97; EW 4; LMFS 1; RGWL 2, 3

Wiene, Robert 1881-1938 .... **TCLC 56**

Wieners, John 1934- .... **CLC 7**
See also BG 1:3; CA 13-16R; CP 1, 2, 3, 4, 5, 6, 7; DLB 16; WP

Wiesel, Elie(zer) 1928- .... **CLC 3, 5, 11, 37, 165; WLCS**
See also AAYA 7, 54; AITN 1; CA 5-8R; CAAS 4; CANR 8, 40, 65, 125; CDALBS; CWW 2; DA; DA3; DAB; DAC; DAM MST, NOV; DLB 83, 299; DLBY 1987; EWL 3; INT CANR-8; LAIT 4; MTCW 1, 2; MTFW 2005; NCFS 4; NFS 4; RGWL 3; SATA 56; YAW

Wiggins, Marianne 1947- .... **CLC 57**
See also BEST 89:3; CA 130; CANR 60, 139; CN 7

Wigglesworth, Michael 1631-1705 .... **LC 106**
See also DLB 24; RGAL 4

Wiggs, Susan .... **CLC 70**
See also CA 201

Wight, James Alfred 1916-1995
See Herriot, James
See also CA 77-80; SATA 55; SATA-Brief 44

Wilbur, Richard (Purdy) 1921- ...... **CLC 3, 6, 9, 14, 53, 110; PC 51**
See also AMWS 3; CA 1-4R; CABS 2; CANR 2, 29, 76, 93, 139; CDALBS; CP 1, 2, 3, 4, 5, 6, 7; DA; DAB; DAC; DAM MST, POET; DLB 5, 169; EWL 3; EXPP; INT CANR-29; MAL 5; MTCW 1, 2; MTFW 2005; PAB; PFS 11, 12, 16; RGAL 4; SATA 9, 108; WP

Wild, Peter 1940- .... **CLC 14**
See also CA 37-40R; CP 1, 2, 3, 4, 5, 6, 7; DLB 5

Wilde, Oscar (Fingal O'Flahertie Wills)
1854(?)-1900 .... **DC 17; SSC 11, 77; TCLC 1, 8, 23, 41, 175; WLC**
See also AAYA 49; BRW 5; BRWC 1, 2; BRWR 2; BYA 15; CA 104; 119; CANR 112; CDBLB 1890-1914; DA; DA3; DAB; DAC; DAM DRAM, MST, NOV; DFS 4, 8, 9, 21; DLB 10, 19, 34, 57, 141, 156, 190; EXPS; FANT; GL 3; LATS 1:1; NFS 20; RGEL 2; RGSF 2; SATA 24; SSFS 7; SUFW; TEA; WCH; WLIT 4

Wilder, Billy .... **CLC 20**
See Wilder, Samuel
See also AAYA 66; DLB 26

Wilder, Samuel 1906-2002
See Wilder, Billy
See also CA 89-92; 205

Wilder, Stephen
See Marlowe, Stephen

Wilder, Thornton (Niven)
1897-1975 .. **CLC 1, 5, 6, 10, 15, 35, 82; DC 1, 24; WLC**
See also AAYA 29; AITN 2; AMW; CA 13-16R; 61-64; CAD; CANR 40, 132; CDALBS; CN 1, 2; DA; DA3; DAB; DAC; DAM DRAM, MST, NOV; DFS 1, 4, 16; DLB 4, 7, 9, 228; DLBY 1997; EWL 3; LAIT 3; MAL 5; MTCW 1, 2; MTFW 2005; RGAL 4; RHW; WYAS 1

Wilding, Michael 1942- ...... **CLC 73; SSC 50**
See also CA 104; CANR 24, 49, 106; CN 4, 5, 6, 7; RGSF 2

Wiley, Richard 1944- .... **CLC 44**
See also CA 121; 129; CANR 71

Wilhelm, Kate .... **CLC 7**
See Wilhelm, Katie (Gertrude)
See also AAYA 20; BYA 16; CAAS 5; DLB 8; INT CANR-17; SCFW 2

Wilhelm, Katie (Gertrude) 1928-
See Wilhelm, Kate
See also CA 37-40R; CANR 17, 36, 60, 94; MTCW 1; SFW 4

Wilkins, Mary
See Freeman, Mary E(leanor) Wilkins

Willard, Nancy 1936- .... **CLC 7, 37**
See also BYA 5; CA 89-92; CANR 10, 39, 68, 107; CLR 5; CP 2, 3, 4; CWP; CWRI 5; DLB 5, 52; FANT; MAICYA 1, 2; MTCW 1; SATA 37, 71, 127; SATA-Brief 30; SUFW 2; TCLE 1:2

William of Malmesbury c. 1090B.C.-c.
1140B.C. .... **CMLC 57**

William of Ockham 1290-1349 ..... **CMLC 32**

Williams, Ben Ames 1889-1953 ..... **TCLC 89**
See also CA 183; DLB 102

Williams, C(harles) K(enneth)
1936- .... **CLC 33, 56, 148**
See also CA 37-40R; CAAS 26; CANR 57, 106; CP 1, 2, 3, 4, 5, 6, 7; DAM POET; DLB 5; MAL 5

Williams, Charles
See Collier, James Lincoln

Williams, Charles (Walter Stansby)
1886-1945 .... **TCLC 1, 11**
See also BRWS 9; CA 104; 163; DLB 100, 153, 255; FANT; RGEL 2; SUFW 1

Williams, Ella Gwendolen Rees
See Rhys, Jean

Williams, (George) Emlyn
1905-1987 .... **CLC 15**
See also CA 104; 123; CANR 36; DAM DRAM; DLB 10, 77; IDTP; MTCW 1

Williams, Hank 1923-1953 .... **TCLC 81**
See Williams, Hiram King

Williams, Helen Maria
1761-1827 .... **NCLC 135**
See also DLB 158

Williams, Hiram Hank
See Williams, Hank

Williams, Hiram King
See Williams, Hank
See also CA 188

Williams, Hugo (Mordaunt) 1942- ... **CLC 42**
See also CA 17-20R; CANR 45, 119; CP 1, 2, 3, 4, 5, 6, 7; DLB 40

Williams, J. Walker
See Wodehouse, P(elham) G(renville)

Williams, John A(lfred) 1925- . **BLC 3; CLC 5, 13**
See also AFAW 2; BW 2, 3; CA 53-56, 195; CAAE 195; CAAS 3; CANR 6, 26, 51, 118; CN 1, 2, 3, 4, 5, 6, 7; CSW; DAM MULT; DLB 2, 33; EWL 3; INT CANR-6; MAL 5; RGAL 4; SFW 4

Williams, Jonathan (Chamberlain)
1929- .... **CLC 13**
See also CA 9-12R; CAAS 12; CANR 8, 108; CP 1, 2, 3, 4, 5, 6, 7; DLB 5

Williams, Joy 1944- .... **CLC 31**
See also CA 41-44R; CANR 22, 48, 97

Williams, Norman 1952- .... **CLC 39**
See also CA 118

Williams, Sherley Anne 1944-1999 ... **BLC 3; CLC 89**
See also AFAW 2; BW 2, 3; CA 73-76; 185; CANR 25, 82; DAM MULT, POET; DLB 41; INT CANR-25; SATA 78; SATA-Obit 116

Williams, Shirley
See Williams, Sherley Anne

Williams, Tennessee 1911-1983 . **CLC 1, 2, 5, 7, 8, 11, 15, 19, 30, 39, 45, 71, 111; DC 4; SSC 81; WLC**
See also AAYA 31; AITN 1, 2; AMW; AMWC 1; CA 5-8R; 108; CABS 3; CAD; CANR 31, 132; CDALB 1941-1968; CN 1, 2, 3; DA; DA3; DAB; DAC; DAM DRAM, MST; DFS 17; DLB 7; DLBD 4; DLBY 1983; EWL 3; GLL 1; LAIT 4; LATS 1:2; MAL 5; MTCW 1, 2; MTFW 2005; RGAL 4; TUS

Williams, Thomas (Alonzo)
1926-1990 .... **CLC 14**
See also CA 1-4R; 132; CANR 2

Williams, William C.
See Williams, William Carlos

Williams, William Carlos
1883-1963 .... **CLC 1, 2, 5, 9, 13, 22, 42, 67; PC 7; SSC 31**
See also AAYA 46; AMW; AMWR 1; CA 89-92; CANR 34; CDALB 1917-1929; DA; DA3; DAB; DAC; DAM MST, POET; DLB 4, 16, 54, 86; EWL 3; EXPP; MAL 5; MTCW 1, 2; MTFW 2005; NCFS 4; PAB; PFS 1, 6, 11; RGAL 4; RGSF 2; TUS; WP

Williamson, David (Keith) 1942- ...... **CLC 56**
See also CA 103; CANR 41; CD 5, 6; DLB 289

Williamson, Ellen Douglas 1905-1984
See Douglas, Ellen
See also CA 17-20R; 114; CANR 39

Williamson, Jack .... **CLC 29**
See Williamson, John Stewart
See also CAAS 8; DLB 8; SCFW 1, 2

Williamson, John Stewart 1908-
See Williamson, Jack
See also CA 17-20R; CANR 23, 70; SFW 4

Willie, Frederick
See Lovecraft, H(oward) P(hillips)

Willingham, Calder (Baynard, Jr.)
1922-1995 .... **CLC 5, 51**
See also CA 5-8R; 147; CANR 3; CN 1, 2, 3, 4, 5; CSW; DLB 2, 44; IDFW 3, 4; MTCW 1

Willis, Charles
See Clarke, Arthur C(harles)

Willy
See Colette, (Sidonie-Gabrielle)

Willy, Colette
See Colette, (Sidonie-Gabrielle)
See also GLL 1

Wilmot, John 1647-1680 .... **LC 75; PC 66**
See Rochester
See also BRW 2; DLB 131; PAB

Wilson, A(ndrew) N(orman) 1950- .. **CLC 33**
See also BRWS 6; CA 112; 122; CN 4, 5, 6, 7; DLB 14, 155, 194; MTCW 2

Wilson, Angus (Frank Johnstone)
1913-1991. **CLC 2, 3, 5, 25, 34; SSC 21**
See also BRWS 1; CA 5-8R; 134; CANR 21; CN 1, 2, 3, 4; DLB 15, 139, 155; EWL 3; MTCW 1, 2; MTFW 2005; RGEL 2; RGSF 2

Wilson, August 1945-2005 .. **BLC 3; CLC 39, 50, 63, 118; DC 2; WLCS**
See also AAYA 16; AFAW 2; AMWS 8; BW 2, 3; CA 115; 122; CAD; CANR 42, 54, 76, 128; CD 5, 6; DA; DA3; DAB; DAC; DAM DRAM, MST, MULT; DFS 3, 7, 15, 17; DLB 228; EWL 3; LAIT 4; LATS 1:2; MAL 5; MTCW 1, 2; MTFW 2005; RGAL 4

Wilson, Brian 1942- .... **CLC 12**

Wilson, Colin (Henry) 1931- .... **CLC 3, 14**
See also CA 1-4R; CAAS 5; CANR 1, 22, 33, 77; CMW 4; CN 1, 2, 3, 4, 5, 6; DLB 14, 194; HGG; MTCW 1; SFW 4

Wilson, Dirk
See Pohl, Frederik

Wilson, Edmund 1895-1972 .. **CLC 1, 2, 3, 8, 24**
See also AMW; CA 1-4R; 37-40R; CANR 1, 46, 110; CN 1; DLB 63; EWL 3; MAL 5; MTCW 1, 2; MTFW 2005; RGAL 4; TUS

Wilson, Ethel Davis (Bryant)
1888(?)-1980 .... **CLC 13**
See also CA 102; CN 1, 2; DAC; DAM POET; DLB 68; MTCW 1; RGEL 2

Wilson, Harriet
See Wilson, Harriet E. Adams
See also DLB 239

Wilson, Harriet E.
See Wilson, Harriet E. Adams
See also DLB 243

Wilson, Harriet E. Adams
1827(?)-1863(?) .... **BLC 3; NCLC 78**
See Wilson, Harriet; Wilson, Harriet E.
See also DAM MULT; DLB 50

Wilson, John 1785-1854 .... **NCLC 5**

Wilson, John (Anthony) Burgess 1917-1993
See Burgess, Anthony
See also CA 1-4R; 143; CANR 2, 46; DA3; DAC; DAM NOV; MTCW 1, 2; MTFW 2005; NFS 15; TEA

Wilson, Lanford 1937- .. **CLC 7, 14, 36, 197; DC 19**
See also CA 17-20R; CABS 3; CAD; CANR 45, 96; CD 5, 6; DAM DRAM; DFS 4, 9, 12, 16, 20; DLB 7; EWL 3; MAL 5; TUS

Wilson, Robert M. 1941- .... **CLC 7, 9**
See also CA 49-52; CAD; CANR 2, 41; CD 5, 6; MTCW 1

Wilson, Robert McLiam 1964- .... **CLC 59**
See also CA 132; DLB 267

Wilson, Sloan 1920-2003 .... **CLC 32**
See also CA 1-4R; 216; CANR 1, 44; CN 1, 2, 3, 4, 5, 6

Wilson, Snoo 1948- .... **CLC 33**
See also CA 69-72; CBD; CD 5, 6

Wilson, William S(mith) 1932- .... **CLC 49**
See also CA 81-84

Wilson, (Thomas) Woodrow
1856-1924 .... **TCLC 79**
See also CA 166; DLB 47

Wilson and Warnke eds. .... **CLC 65**

Winchilsea, Anne (Kingsmill) Finch
1661-1720
See Finch, Anne
See also RGEL 2

Windham, Basil
See Wodehouse, P(elham) G(renville)

Wingrove, David (John) 1954- .... **CLC 68**
See also CA 133; SFW 4

Winnemucca, Sarah 1844-1891 .... **NCLC 79; NNAL**
See also DAM MULT; DLB 175; RGAL 4

Winstanley, Gerrard 1609-1676 .... **LC 52**

Wintergreen, Jane
See Duncan, Sara Jeannette

Winters, Arthur Yvor
See Winters, Yvor

Winters, Janet Lewis .... **CLC 41**
See Lewis, Janet
See also DLBY 1987

Winters, Yvor 1900-1968 .... **CLC 4, 8, 32**
See also AMWS 2; CA 11-12; 25-28R; CAP 1; DLB 48; EWL 3; MAL 5; MTCW 1; RGAL 4

Winterson, Jeanette 1959- .... **CLC 64, 158**
See also BRWS 4; CA 136; CANR 58, 116; CN 5, 6, 7; CPW; DA3; DAM POP; DLB 207, 261; FANT; FW; GLL 1; MTCW 2; MTFW 2005; RHW

Winthrop, John 1588-1649 .... **LC 31, 107**
See also DLB 24, 30

Wirth, Louis 1897-1952 .... **TCLC 92**
See also CA 210

Wiseman, Frederick 1930- .... **CLC 20**
See also CA 159

Wister, Owen 1860-1938 .... **TCLC 21**
See also BPFB 3; CA 108; DLB 9, 78, 186; RGAL 4; SATA 62; TCWW 1, 2

Wither, George 1588-1667 .... **LC 96**
See also DLB 121; RGEL 2

Witkacy
See Witkiewicz, Stanislaw Ignacy

Witkiewicz, Stanislaw Ignacy
1885-1939 .... **TCLC 8**
See also CA 105; 162; CDWLB 4; DLB 215; EW 10; EWL 3; RGWL 2, 3; SFW 4

Wittgenstein, Ludwig (Josef Johann)
1889-1951 .... **TCLC 59**
See also CA 113; 164; DLB 262; MTCW 2

Wittig, Monique 1935-2003 .... **CLC 22**
See also CA 116; 135; 212; CANR 143; CWW 2; DLB 83; EWL 3; FW; GLL 1

Wittlin, Jozef 1896-1976 .... **CLC 25**
See also CA 49-52; 65-68; CANR 3; EWL 3

Wodehouse, P(elham) G(renville)
1881-1975 . **CLC 1, 2, 5, 10, 22; SSC 2; TCLC 108**
See also AAYA 65; AITN 2; BRWS 3; CA 45-48; 57-60; CANR 3, 33; CDBLB 1914-1945; CN 1, 2; CPW 1; DA3; DAB; DAC; DAM NOV; DLB 34, 162; EWL 3; MTCW 1, 2; MTFW 2005; RGEL 2; RGSF 2; SATA 22; SSFS 10

Woiwode, L.
See Woiwode, Larry (Alfred)

Woiwode, Larry (Alfred) 1941- ... **CLC 6, 10**
See also CA 73-76; CANR 16, 94; CN 3, 4, 5, 6, 7; DLB 6; INT CANR-16

Wojciechowska, Maia (Teresa)
1927-2002 .... **CLC 26**
See also AAYA 8, 46; BYA 3; CA 9-12R, 183; 209; CAAE 183; CANR 4, 41; CLR 1; JRDA; MAICYA 1, 2; SAAS 1; SATA 1, 28, 83; SATA-Essay 104; SATA-Obit 134; YAW

Wojtyla, Karol (Jozef)
See John Paul II, Pope

Wojtyla, Karol (Josef)
See John Paul II, Pope

Wolf, Christa 1929- .... **CLC 14, 29, 58, 150**
See also CA 85-88; CANR 45, 123; CDWLB 2; CWW 2; DLB 75; EWL 3; FW; MTCW 1; RGWL 2, 3; SSFS 14

Wolf, Naomi 1962- .... **CLC 157**
See also CA 141; CANR 110; FW; MTFW 2005

Wolfe, Gene 1931- .... **CLC 25**
See also AAYA 35; CA 57-60; CAAS 9; CANR 6, 32, 60; CPW; DAM POP; DLB 8; FANT; MTCW 2; MTFW 2005; SATA 118, 165; SCFW 2; SFW 4; SUFW 2

Wolfe, Gene Rodman
See Wolfe, Gene

Wolfe, George C. 1954- .... **BLCS; CLC 49**
See also CA 149; CAD; CD 5, 6

Wolfe, Thomas (Clayton)
1900-1938 .... **SSC 33; TCLC 4, 13, 29, 61; WLC**
See also AMW; BPFB 3; CA 104; 132; CANR 102; CDALB 1929-1941; DA; DA3; DAB; DAC; DAM MST, NOV; DLB 9, 102, 229; DLBD 2, 16; DLBY 1985, 1997; EWL 3; MAL 5; MTCW 1, 2; NFS 18; RGAL 4; SSFS 18; TUS

Wolfe, Thomas Kennerly, Jr.
1931- .... **CLC 147**
See Wolfe, Tom
See also CA 13-16R; CANR 9, 33, 70, 104; DA3; DAM POP; DLB 185; EWL 3; INT CANR-9; MTCW 1, 2; MTFW 2005; TUS

Wolfe, Tom .... **CLC 1, 2, 9, 15, 35, 51**
See Wolfe, Thomas Kennerly, Jr.
See also AAYA 8, 67; AITN 2; AMWS 3; BEST 89:1; BPFB 3; CN 5, 6, 7; CPW; CSW; DLB 152; LAIT 5; RGAL 4

Wolff, Geoffrey (Ansell) 1937- .... **CLC 41**
See also CA 29-32R; CANR 29, 43, 78

Wolff, Sonia
See Levitin, Sonia (Wolff)

Wolff, Tobias (Jonathan Ansell)
1945- .... **CLC 39, 64, 172; SSC 63**
See also AAYA 16; AMWS 7; BEST 90:2; BYA 12; CA 114; 117; CAAS 22; CANR 54, 76, 96; CN 5, 6, 7; CSW; DA3; DLB 130; EWL 3; INT CA-117; MTCW 2; MTFW 2005; RGAL 4; RGSF 2; SSFS 4, 11

Wolfram von Eschenbach c. 1170-c. 1220 .... **CMLC 5**
See Eschenbach, Wolfram von
See also CDWLB 2; DLB 138; EW 1; RGWL 2

Wolitzer, Hilma 1930- .... **CLC 17**
See also CA 65-68; CANR 18, 40; INT CANR-18; SATA 31; YAW

Wollstonecraft, Mary 1759-1797 .... **LC 5, 50, 90**
See also BRWS 3; CDBLB 1789-1832; DLB 39, 104, 158, 252; FL 1:1; FW; LAIT 1; RGEL 2; TEA; WLIT 3

Wonder, Stevie .... **CLC 12**
See Morris, Steveland Judkins

Wong, Jade Snow 1922- .... **CLC 17**
See also CA 109; CANR 91; SATA 112

Woodberry, George Edward
1855-1930 .... **TCLC 73**
See also CA 165; DLB 71, 103

Woodcott, Keith
See Brunner, John (Kilian Houston)

Woodruff, Robert W.
See Mencken, H(enry) L(ouis)

Woolf, (Adeline) Virginia 1882-1941 .. **SSC 7, 79; TCLC 1, 5, 20, 43, 56, 101, 123, 128; WLC**
See also AAYA 44; BPFB 3; BRW 7; BRWC 2; BRWR 1; CA 104; 130; CANR 64, 132; CDBLB 1914-1945; DA; DA3; DAB; DAC; DAM MST, NOV; DLB 36, 100, 162; DLBD 10; EWL 3; EXPS; FL 1:6; FW; LAIT 3; LATS 1:1; LMFS 2; MTCW 1, 2; MTFW 2005; NCFS 2; NFS 8, 12; RGEL 2; RGSF 2; SSFS 4, 12; TEA; WLIT 4

Woollcott, Alexander (Humphreys)
1887-1943 .... **TCLC 5**
See also CA 105; 161; DLB 29

Woolrich, Cornell .... **CLC 77**
See Hopley-Woolrich, Cornell George
See also MSW

Woolson, Constance Fenimore
1840-1894 .... **NCLC 82; SSC 90**
See also DLB 12, 74, 189, 221; RGAL 4

Wordsworth, Dorothy 1771-1855 . **NCLC 25, 138**
See also DLB 107

Wordsworth, William 1770-1850 .. **NCLC 12, 38, 111; PC 4, 67; WLC**
See also BRW 4; BRWC 1; CDBLB 1789-1832; DA; DA3; DAB; DAC; DAM MST, POET; DLB 93, 107; EXPP; LATS 1:1; LMFS 1; PAB; PFS 2; RGEL 2; TEA; WLIT 3; WP

Wotton, Sir Henry 1568-1639 .... **LC 68**
See also DLB 121; RGEL 2

Wouk, Herman 1915- .... **CLC 1, 9, 38**
See also BPFB 2, 3; CA 5-8R; CANR 6, 33, 67, 146; CDALBS; CN 1, 2, 3, 4, 5, 6; CPW; DA3; DAM NOV, POP; DLBY 1982; INT CANR-6; LAIT 4; MAL 5; MTCW 1, 2; MTFW 2005; NFS 7; TUS

Wright, Charles (Penzel, Jr.) 1935- .. **CLC 6, 13, 28, 119, 146**
See also AMWS 5; CA 29-32R; CAAS 7; CANR 23, 36, 62, 88, 135; CP 3, 4, 5, 6, 7; DLB 165; DLBY 1982; EWL 3; MTCW 1, 2; MTFW 2005; PFS 10

Wright, Charles Stevenson 1932- ..... **BLC 3; CLC 49**
See also BW 1; CA 9-12R; CANR 26; CN 1, 2, 3, 4, 5, 6, 7; DAM MULT, POET; DLB 33

Wright, Frances 1795-1852 .... **NCLC 74**
See also DLB 73

Wright, Frank Lloyd 1867-1959 .... **TCLC 95**
See also AAYA 33; CA 174

Wright, Jack R.
See Harris, Mark

Wright, James (Arlington)
1927-1980 .... **CLC 3, 5, 10, 28; PC 36**
See also AITN 2; AMWS 3; CA 49-52; 97-100; CANR 4, 34, 64; CDALBS; CP 1, 2; DAM POET; DLB 5, 169; EWL 3; EXPP; MAL 5; MTCW 1, 2; MTFW 2005; PFS 7, 8; RGAL 4; TUS; WP

Wright, Judith (Arundell)
1915-2000 .... **CLC 11, 53; PC 14**
See also CA 13-16R; 188; CANR 31, 76, 93; CP 1, 2, 3, 4, 5, 6, 7; CWP; DLB 260; EWL 3; MTCW 1, 2; MTFW 2005; PFS 8; RGEL 2; SATA 14; SATA-Obit 121

Wright, L(aurali) R. 1939- .... **CLC 44**
See also CA 138; CMW 4

Wright, Richard (Nathaniel)
1908-1960 ... **BLC 3; CLC 1, 3, 4, 9, 14, 21, 48, 74; SSC 2; TCLC 136; WLC**
See also AAYA 5, 42; AFAW 1, 2; AMW; BPFB 3; BW 1; BYA 2; CA 108; CANR 64; CDALB 1929-1941; DA; DA3; DAB; DAC; DAM MULT, NOV; DLB 76, 102; DLBD 2; EWL 3; EXPN; LAIT 3, 4; MAL 5; MTCW 1, 2; MTFW 2005; NCFS 1; NFS 1, 7; RGAL 4; RGSF 2; SSFS 3, 9, 15, 20; TUS; YAW

Wright, Richard B(ruce) 1937- .... **CLC 6**
See also CA 85-88; CANR 120; DLB 53

Wright, Rick 1945- .... **CLC 35**

Wright, Rowland
See Wells, Carolyn

Wright, Stephen 1946- .... **CLC 33**
See also CA 237

Wright, Willard Huntington 1888-1939
See Van Dine, S. S.
See also CA 115; 189; CMW 4; DLBD 16

Wright, William 1930- .... **CLC 44**
See also CA 53-56; CANR 7, 23

Wroth, Lady Mary 1587-1653(?) .... **LC 30; PC 38**
See also DLB 121

Wu Ch'eng-en 1500(?)-1582(?) .... **LC 7**

Wu Ching-tzu 1701-1754 .... **LC 2**

Wulfstan c. 10th cent. -1023 .... **CMLC 59**

Wurlitzer, Rudolph 1938(?)- .... **CLC 2, 4, 15**
See also CA 85-88; CN 4, 5, 6, 7; DLB 173

Wyatt, Sir Thomas c. 1503-1542 . **LC 70; PC 27**
See also BRW 1; DLB 132; EXPP; RGEL 2; TEA

Wycherley, William 1640-1716 .... **LC 8, 21, 102**
See also BRW 2; CDBLB 1660-1789; DAM DRAM; DLB 80; RGEL 2

Wyclif, John c. 1330-1384 .... **CMLC 70**
See also DLB 146

Wylie, Elinor (Morton Hoyt)
1885-1928 .... **PC 23; TCLC 8**
See also AMWS 1; CA 105; 162; DLB 9, 45; EXPP; MAL 5; RGAL 4

Wylie, Philip (Gordon) 1902-1971 ... **CLC 43**
See also CA 21-22; 33-36R; CAP 2; CN 1; DLB 9; SFW 4

Wyndham, John .... **CLC 19**
See Harris, John (Wyndham Parkes Lucas) Beynon
See also DLB 255; SCFW 1, 2

Wyss, Johann David Von
1743-1818 .... **NCLC 10**
See also CLR 92; JRDA; MAICYA 1, 2; SATA 29; SATA-Brief 27

Xenophon c. 430B.C.-c. 354B.C. ... **CMLC 17**
See also AW 1; DLB 176; RGWL 2, 3

Xingjian, Gao 1940-
See Gao Xingjian
See also CA 193; DFS 21; RGWL 3

Yakamochi 718-785 .... **CMLC 45; PC 48**

Yakumo Koizumi
See Hearn, (Patricio) Lafcadio (Tessima Carlos)

Yamada, Mitsuye (May) 1923- .... **PC 44**
See also CA 77-80

Yamamoto, Hisaye 1921- .... **AAL; SSC 34**
See also CA 214; DAM MULT; DLB 312; LAIT 4; SSFS 14

Yamauchi, Wakako 1924- .... **AAL**
See also CA 214; DLB 312

Yanez, Jose Donoso
See Donoso (Yanez), Jose

Yanovsky, Basile S.
See Yanovsky, V(assily) S(emenovich)

Yanovsky, V(assily) S(emenovich)
1906-1989 .... **CLC 2, 18**
See also CA 97-100; 129

Yates, Richard 1926-1992 .... **CLC 7, 8, 23**
See also AMWS 11; CA 5-8R; 139; CANR 10, 43; CN 1, 2, 3, 4, 5; DLB 2, 234; DLBY 1981, 1992; INT CANR-10

Yau, John 1950- .... **PC 61**
See also CA 154; CANR 89; CP 4, 5, 6, 7; DLB 234, 312

Yeats, W. B.
See Yeats, William Butler

Yeats, William Butler 1865-1939 . **PC 20, 51; TCLC 1, 11, 18, 31, 93, 116; WLC**
See also AAYA 48; BRW 6; BRWR 1; CA 104; 127; CANR 45; CDBLB 1890-1914; DA; DA3; DAB; DAC; DAM DRAM, MST, POET; DLB 10, 19, 98, 156; EWL 3; EXPP; MTCW 1, 2; MTFW 2005; NCFS 3; PAB; PFS 1, 2, 5, 7, 13, 15; RGEL 2; TEA; WLIT 4; WP

Yehoshua, A(braham) B. 1936- .. **CLC 13, 31**
See also CA 33-36R; CANR 43, 90, 145; CWW 2; EWL 3; RGSF 2; RGWL 3; WLIT 6

Yellow Bird
See Ridge, John Rollin

Yep, Laurence Michael 1948- .... **CLC 35**
See also AAYA 5, 31; BYA 7; CA 49-52; CANR 1, 46, 92; CLR 3, 17, 54; DLB 52, 312; FANT; JRDA; MAICYA 1, 2; MAICYAS 1; SATA 7, 69, 123; WYA; YAW

Yerby, Frank G(arvin) 1916-1991 ...... **BLC 3; CLC 1, 7, 22**
See also BPFB 3; BW 1, 3; CA 9-12R; 136; CANR 16, 52; CN 1, 2, 3, 4, 5; DAM MULT; DLB 76; INT CANR-16; MTCW 1; RGAL 4; RHW

Yesenin, Sergei Alexandrovich
See Esenin, Sergei (Alexandrovich)

Yesenin, Sergey
See Esenin, Sergei (Alexandrovich)
See also EWL 3

Yevtushenko, Yevgeny (Alexandrovich)
1933- .... **CLC 1, 3, 13, 26, 51, 126; PC 40**
See Evtushenko, Evgenii Aleksandrovich
See also CA 81-84; CANR 33, 54; DAM POET; EWL 3; MTCW 1

Yezierska, Anzia 1885(?)-1970 .... **CLC 46**
See also CA 126; 89-92; DLB 28, 221; FW; MTCW 1; RGAL 4; SSFS 15

Yglesias, Helen 1915- .... **CLC 7, 22**
See also CA 37-40R; CAAS 20; CANR 15, 65, 95; CN 4, 5, 6, 7; INT CANR-15; MTCW 1

Yokomitsu, Riichi 1898-1947 .... **TCLC 47**
See also CA 170; EWL 3

Yonge, Charlotte (Mary)
1823-1901 .... **TCLC 48**
See also CA 109; 163; DLB 18, 163; RGEL 2; SATA 17; WCH

York, Jeremy
See Creasey, John

York, Simon
See Heinlein, Robert A(nson)

Yorke, Henry Vincent 1905-1974 ..... **CLC 13**
See Green, Henry
See also CA 85-88; 49-52

Yosano Akiko 1878-1942 .... **PC 11; TCLC 59**
See also CA 161; EWL 3; RGWL 3

Yoshimoto, Banana .... **CLC 84**
See Yoshimoto, Mahoko
See also AAYA 50; NFS 7

Yoshimoto, Mahoko 1964-
See Yoshimoto, Banana
See also CA 144; CANR 98; SSFS 16

Young, Al(bert James) 1939- ... **BLC 3; CLC 19**
See also BW 2, 3; CA 29-32R; CANR 26, 65, 109; CN 2, 3, 4, 5, 6, 7; CP 1, 2, 3, 4, 5, 6, 7; DAM MULT; DLB 33

Young, Andrew (John) 1885-1971 ...... **CLC 5**
See also CA 5-8R; CANR 7, 29; CP 1; RGEL 2

Young, Collier
See Bloch, Robert (Albert)

Young, Edward 1683-1765 .... **LC 3, 40**
See also DLB 95; RGEL 2

Young, Marguerite (Vivian)
1909-1995 .... **CLC 82**
See also CA 13-16; 150; CAP 1; CN 1, 2, 3, 4, 5, 6

Young, Neil 1945- .... **CLC 17**
See also CA 110; CCA 1

Young Bear, Ray A. 1950- ... **CLC 94; NNAL**
See also CA 146; DAM MULT; DLB 175; MAL 5

Yourcenar, Marguerite 1903-1987 ... **CLC 19, 38, 50, 87**
See also BPFB 3; CA 69-72; CANR 23, 60, 93; DAM NOV; DLB 72; DLBY 1988; EW 12; EWL 3; GFL 1789 to the Present; GLL 1; MTCW 1, 2; MTFW 2005; RGWL 2, 3

Yuan, Chu 340(?)B.C.-278(?)B.C. . **CMLC 36**

Yurick, Sol 1925- .... **CLC 6**
See also CA 13-16R; CANR 25; CN 1, 2, 3, 4, 5, 6, 7; MAL 5

Zabolotsky, Nikolai Alekseevich 1903-1958 .... **TCLC 52**
See Zabolotsky, Nikolay Alekseevich
See also CA 116; 164

Zabolotsky, Nikolay Alekseevich
See Zabolotsky, Nikolay Alekseevich
See also EWL 3

Zagajewski, Adam 1945- .... **PC 27**
See also CA 186; DLB 232; EWL 3

Zalygin, Sergei -2000 .... **CLC 59**

Zalygin, Sergei (Pavlovich) 1913-2000 .... **CLC 59**
See also DLB 302

Zamiatin, Evgenii
See Zamyatin, Evgeny Ivanovich
See also RGSF 2; RGWL 2, 3

Zamiatin, Evgenii Ivanovich
See Zamyatin, Evgeny Ivanovich
See also DLB 272

Zamiatin, Yevgenii
See Zamyatin, Evgeny Ivanovich

Zamora, Bernice (B. Ortiz) 1938- .. **CLC 89; HLC 2**
See also CA 151; CANR 80; DAM MULT; DLB 82; HW 1, 2

Zamyatin, Evgeny Ivanovich 1884-1937 .... **SSC 89; TCLC 8, 37**
See Zamiatin, Evgenii; Zamiatin, Evgenii Ivanovich; Zamyatin, Yevgeny Ivanovich
See also CA 105; 166; SFW 4

Zamyatin, Yevgeny Ivanovich
See Zamyatin, Evgeny Ivanovich
See also EW 10; EWL 3

Zangwill, Israel 1864-1926 ... **SSC 44; TCLC 16**
See also CA 109; 167; CMW 4; DLB 10, 135, 197; RGEL 2

Zanzotto, Andrea 1921- .... **PC 65**
See also CA 208; CWW 2; DLB 128; EWL 3

Zappa, Francis Vincent, Jr. 1940-1993
See Zappa, Frank
See also CA 108; 143; CANR 57

Zappa, Frank .... **CLC 17**
See Zappa, Francis Vincent, Jr.

Zaturenska, Marya 1902-1982 ..... **CLC 6, 11**
See also CA 13-16R; 105; CANR 22; CP 1, 2, 3

Zayas y Sotomayor, Maria de 1590-c. 1661 .... **LC 102**
See also RGSF 2

Zeami 1363-1443 .... **DC 7; LC 86**
See also DLB 203; RGWL 2, 3

Zelazny, Roger (Joseph) 1937-1995 . **CLC 21**
See also AAYA 7, 68; BPFB 3; CA 21-24R; 148; CANR 26, 60; CN 6; DLB 8; FANT; MTCW 1, 2; MTFW 2005; SATA 57; SATA-Brief 39; SCFW 1, 2; SFW 4; SUFW 1, 2

Zhang Ailing
See Chang, Eileen
See also CWW 2; RGSF 2

Zhdanov, Andrei Alexandrovich 1896-1948 .... **TCLC 18**
See also CA 117; 167

Zhukovsky, Vasilii Andreevich
See Zhukovsky, Vasily (Andreevich)
See also DLB 205

Zhukovsky, Vasily (Andreevich) 1783-1852 .... **NCLC 35**
See Zhukovsky, Vasilii Andreevich

Ziegenhagen, Eric .... **CLC 55**

Zimmer, Jill Schary
See Robinson, Jill

Zimmerman, Robert
See Dylan, Bob

Zindel, Paul 1936-2003 ...... **CLC 6, 26; DC 5**
See also AAYA 2, 37; BYA 2, 3, 8, 11, 14; CA 73-76; 213; CAD; CANR 31, 65, 108; CD 5, 6; CDALBS; CLR 3, 45, 85; DA; DA3; DAB; DAC; DAM DRAM, MST, NOV; DFS 12; DLB 7, 52; JRDA; LAIT 5; MAICYA 1, 2; MTCW 1, 2; MTFW 2005; NFS 14; SATA 16, 58, 102; SATA-Obit 142; WYA; YAW

Zinn, Howard 1922- .... **CLC 199**
See also CA 1-4R; CANR 2, 33, 90

Zinov'Ev, A. A.
See Zinoviev, Alexander (Aleksandrovich)

Zinov'ev, Aleksandr (Aleksandrovich)
See Zinoviev, Alexander (Aleksandrovich)
See also DLB 302

Zinoviev, Alexander (Aleksandrovich) 1922- .... **CLC 19**
See Zinov'ev, Aleksandr (Aleksandrovich)
See also CA 116; 133; CAAS 10

Zizek, Slavoj 1949- .... **CLC 188**
See also CA 201; MTFW 2005

Zoilus
See Lovecraft, H(oward) P(hillips)

Zola, Emile (Edouard Charles Antoine) 1840-1902 ...... **TCLC 1, 6, 21, 41; WLC**
See also CA 104; 138; DA; DA3; DAB; DAC; DAM MST, NOV; DLB 123; EW 7; GFL 1789 to the Present; IDTP; LMFS 1, 2; RGWL 2; TWA

Zoline, Pamela 1941- .... **CLC 62**
See also CA 161; SFW 4

Zoroaster 628(?)B.C.-551(?)B.C. ... **CMLC 40**

Zorrilla y Moral, Jose 1817-1893 .... **NCLC 6**

Zoshchenko, Mikhail (Mikhailovich) 1895-1958 .... **SSC 15; TCLC 15**
See also CA 115; 160; EWL 3; RGSF 2; RGWL 3

Zuckmayer, Carl 1896-1977 .... **CLC 18**
See also CA 69-72; DLB 56, 124; EWL 3; RGWL 2, 3

Zuk, Georges
See Skelton, Robin
See also CCA 1

Zukofsky, Louis 1904-1978 ... **CLC 1, 2, 4, 7, 11, 18; PC 11**
See also AMWS 3; CA 9-12R; 77-80; CANR 39; CP 1, 2; DAM POET; DLB 5, 165; EWL 3; MAL 5; MTCW 1; RGAL 4

Zweig, Paul 1935-1984 .... **CLC 34, 42**
See also CA 85-88; 113

Zweig, Stefan 1881-1942 .... **TCLC 17**
See also CA 112; 170; DLB 81, 118; EWL 3

Zwingli, Huldreich 1484-1531 .... **LC 37**
See also DLB 179

Literary Criticism Series
Cumulative Topic Index

This index lists all topic entries in Thompson Gale's *Children's Literature Review* (CLR), *Classical and Medieval Literature Criticism* (CMLC), *Contemporary Literary Criticism* (CLC), *Drama Criticism* (DC), *Literature Criticism from 1400 to 1800* (LC), *Nineteenth-Century Literature Criticism* (NCLC), *Short Story Criticism* (SSC), and *Twentieth-Century Literary Criticism* (TCLC). The index also lists topic entries in the Gale Critical Companion Collection, which includes the following publications: *The Beat Generation* (BG), *Feminism in Literature* (FL), *Gothic Literature* (GL), and *Harlem Renaissance* (HR).

Abbey Theatre in the Irish Literary Renaissance TCLC 154: 1-114
    origins and development, 2-14
    major figures, 14-30
    plays and controversies, 30-59
    artistic vision and significance, 59-114

Abolitionist Literature of Cuba and Brazil, Nineteenth-Century NCLC 132: 1-94
    overviews, 2-11
    origins and development, 11-23
    sociopolitical concerns, 23-39
    poetry, 39-47
    prose, 47-93

The Aborigine in Nineteenth-Century Australian Literature NCLC 120: 1-88
    overviews, 2-27
    representations of the Aborigine in Australian literature, 27-58
    Aboriginal myth, literature, and oral tradition, 58-88

The Aesopic Fable LC 51: 1-100
    the British Aesopic Fable, 1-54
    the Aesopic tradition in non-English-speaking cultures, 55-66
    political uses of the Aesopic fable, 67-88
    the evolution of the Aesopic fable, 89-99

African-American Folklore and Literature TCLC 126: 1-67
    African-American folk tradition, 1-16
    representative writers, 16-34
    hallmark works, 35-48
    the study of African-American literature and folklore, 48-64

Age of al-Andalus CMLC 81: 1-174
    overviews, 1-48
    history, society, and culture, 48-127
    Andalusī poetry, 127-73

Age of Johnson LC 15: 1-87
    Johnson's London, 3-15
    aesthetics of neoclassicism, 15-36
    "age of prose and reason," 36-45
    clubmen and bluestockings, 45-56
    printing technology, 56-62
    periodicals: "a map of busy life," 62-74
    transition, 74-86

The Age of King Alfred the Great CMLC 79: 1-141
    overviews and historical background, 4-17
    the Alfredian translations, 17-43
    King Alfred's prefaces, 43-84
    Alfred and Boethius, 84-140

Age of Spenser LC 39: 1-70
    overviews and general studies, 2-21
    literary style, 22-34
    poets and the crown, 34-70

AIDS in Literature CLC 81: 365-416

Alcohol and Literature TCLC 70: 1-58
    overview, 2-8
    fiction, 8-48
    poetry and drama, 48-58

American Abolitionism NCLC 44: 1-73
    overviews and general studies, 2-26
    abolitionist ideals, 26-46
    the literature of abolitionism, 46-72

American Autobiography TCLC 86: 1-115
    overviews and general studies, 3-36
    American authors and autobiography, 36-82
    African-American autobiography, 82-114

American Black Humor Fiction TCLC 54: 1-85
    characteristics of black humor, 2-13
    origins and development, 13-38
    black humor distinguished from related literary trends, 38-60
    black humor and society, 60-75
    black humor reconsidered, 75-83

American Civil War in Literature NCLC 32: 1-109
    overviews and general studies, 2-20
    regional perspectives, 20-54
    fiction popular during the war, 54-79
    the historical novel, 79-108

American Frontier in Literature NCLC 28: 1-103
    definitions, 2-12
    development, 12-17
    nonfiction writing about the frontier, 17-30
    frontier fiction, 30-45
    frontier protagonists, 45-66
    portrayals of Native Americans, 66-86
    feminist readings, 86-98
    twentieth-century reaction against frontier literature, 98-100

American Humor Writing NCLC 52: 1-59
    overviews and general studies, 2-12
    the Old Southwest, 12-42
    broader impacts, 42-5
    women humorists, 45-58

American Naturalism in Short Fiction SSC 77: 1-103
    overviews and general studies, 2-30
    major authors of American literary Naturalism, 30-102
        Ambrose Bierce, 30
        Stephen Crane, 30-53
        Theodore Dreiser, 53-65
        Jack London, 65-80
        Frank Norris, 80-9
        Edith Wharton, 89-102

American Novel of Manners TCLC 130: 1-42
    history of the Novel of Manners in America, 4-10
    representative writers, 10-18
    relevancy of the Novel of Manners, 18-24
    hallmark works in the Novel of Manners, 24-36
    Novel of Manners and other media, 36-40

American Mercury, **The** TCLC 74: 1-80

American Popular Song, Golden Age of TCLC 42: 1-49
    background and major figures, 2-34
    the lyrics of popular songs, 34-47

American Proletarian Literature TCLC 54: 86-175
    overviews and general studies, 87-95
    American proletarian literature and the American Communist Party, 95-111
    ideology and literary merit, 111-17
    novels, 117-36
    Gastonia, 136-48
    drama, 148-54
    journalism, 154-9
    proletarian literature in the United States, 159-74

American Realism NCLC 120: 89-246
    overviews, 91-112
    background and sources, 112-72
    social issues, 172-223
    women and realism, 223-45

American Renaissance SSC 64: 46-193
    overviews and general studies, 47-103
    major authors of short fiction, 103-92

American Romanticism NCLC 44: 74-138
  overviews and general studies, 74-84
  sociopolitical influences, 84-104
  Romanticism and the American frontier, 104-15
  thematic concerns, 115-37

American Western Literature TCLC 46: 1-100
  definition and development of American Western literature, 2-7
  characteristics of the Western novel, 8-23
  Westerns as history and fiction, 23-34
  critical reception of American Western literature, 34-41
  the Western hero, 41-73
  women in Western fiction, 73-91
  later Western fiction, 91-9

American Writers in Paris TCLC 98: 1-156
  overviews and general studies, 2-155

Anarchism NCLC 84: 1-97
  overviews and general studies, 2-23
  the French anarchist tradition, 23-56
  Anglo-American anarchism, 56-68
  anarchism: incidents and issues, 68-97

Angry Young Men TCLC 166: 1-80
  overviews, 2-18
  major figures, 18-58
  themes and style, 58-79

Animals in Literature TCLC 106: 1-120
  overviews and general studies, 2-8
  animals in American literature, 8-45
  animals in Canadian literature, 45-57
  animals in European literature, 57-100
  animals in Latin American literature, 100-06
  animals in women's literature, 106-20

Antebellum South, Literature of the NCLC 112:1-188
  overviews, 4-55
  culture of the Old South, 55-68
  antebellum fiction: pastoral and heroic romance, 68-120
  role of women: a subdued rebellion, 120-59
  slavery and the slave narrative, 159-85

Anti-Americanism TCLC 158: 1-98
  overviews and general studies, 3-18
  literary and intellectual perspectives, 18-36
  social and political reactions, 36-98

Anti-Apartheid TCLC 162: 1-121
  overviews, 3-45
  major authors, 45-74
  anti-apartheid literature and the liberal tradition, 74-101
  writing under apartheid: historical views, 101-20

The Apocalyptic Movement TCLC 106: 121-69

Aristotle CMLC 31:1-397
  philosophy, 3-100
  poetics, 101-219
  rhetoric, 220-301
  science, 302-397

Art and Literature TCLC 54: 176-248
  overviews and general studies, 176-93
  definitions, 193-219
  influence of visual arts on literature, 219-31
  spatial form in literature, 231-47

Arthurian Literature CMLC 10: 1-127
  historical context and literary beginnings, 2-27
  development of the legend through Malory, 27-64
  development of the legend from Malory to the Victorian Age, 65-81
  themes and motifs, 81-95
  principal characters, 95-125

Arthurian Revival NCLC 36: 1-77
  overviews and general studies, 2-12
  Tennyson and his influence, 12-43
  other leading figures, 43-73
  the Arthurian legend in the visual arts, 73-6

The Audience and Nineteenth-Century Literature NCLC 160: 1-158
  overviews, 3-35
  race, class, gender, 35-89
  America, 89-102
  Britain and Europe, 102-30
  genre and audience, 130-57

Australian Cultural Identity in Nineteenth-Century Literature NCLC 124: 1-164
  overviews and general studies, 4-22
  poetry, 22-67
  fiction, 67-135
  role of women writers, 135-64

Australian Literature TCLC 50: 1-94
  origins and development, 2-21
  characteristics of Australian literature, 21-33
  historical and critical perspectives, 33-41
  poetry, 41-58
  fiction, 58-76
  drama, 76-82
  Aboriginal literature, 82-91

Aztec Myths and Literature LC 122: 1-182
  Overviews and General Studies, 3-68
  Cosmology, 68-136
  Language and Literature, 136-81

The Beat Generation BG 1:1-562
  the Beat Generation: an overview, 1-137
    primary sources, 3-32
    overviews and general studies, 32-47
    Beat Generation as a social phenomenon, 47-65
    drugs, inspiration, and the Beat Generation, 65-92
    religion and the Beat Generation, 92-124
    women of the Beat Generation, 124-36
  Beat "scene": East and West, 139-259
    primary sources, 141-77
    Beat scene in the East, 177-218
    Beat scene in the West, 218-59
  Beat Generation publishing: periodicals, small presses, and censorship, 261-349
    primary sources, 263-74
    overview, 274-88
    Beat periodicals: "little magazines," 288-311
    Beat publishing: small presses, 311-24
    Beat battles with censorship, 324-49
  performing arts and the Beat Generation, 351-417
    primary sources, 353-58
    Beats and film, 358-81
    Beats and music, 381-415
  visual arts and the Beat Generation, 419-91
    primary sources, 421-24
    critical commentary, 424-90

Beat Generation, Literature of the TCLC 42: 50-102
  overviews and general studies, 51-9
  the Beat generation as a social phenomenon, 59-62
  development, 62-5
  Beat literature, 66-96
  influence, 97-100

The Bell Curve Controversy CLC 91: 281-330

Bildungsroman in Nineteenth-Century Literature NCLC 20: 92-168
  surveys, 93-113
  in Germany, 113-40
  in England, 140-56
  female *Bildungsroman*, 156-67
  NCLC 152: 1-129
    overview, 3-16
    definition and issues, 16-52
    female *Bildungsromane*, 52-83
    ideology and nationhood, 83-128

Black Humor, Contemporary CLC 196: 1-128
  overviews and general studies, 2-18
  black humor in American fiction, 18-28
  development and history, 29-62
  major authors, 62-115
  technique and narrative, 115-127

Bloomsbury Group TCLC 34: 1-73
  history and major figures, 2-13
  definitions, 13-7
  influences, 17-27
  thought, 27-40
  prose, 40-52
  and literary criticism, 52-4
  political ideals, 54-61
  response to, 61-71

The Bloomsbury Group TCLC 138: 1-59
  representative members of the Bloomsbury Group, 9-24
  literary relevance of the Bloomsbury Group, 24-36
  Bloomsbury's hallmark works, 36-48
  other modernists studied with the Bloomsbury Group, 48-54

The Blues in Literature TCLC 82: 1-71

Bly, Robert, *Iron John: A Book about Men and Men's Work* CLC 70: 414-62

The Book of J CLC 65: 289-311

The Book of Common Prayer LC 118: 1-76
  overviews, 2-43
  translation and diffusion, 44-63
  influence of the Prayer Book, 63-76

Brazilian Literature TCLC 134: 1-126
  overviews and general studies, 3-33
  Brazilian poetry, 33-48
  contemporary Brazilian writing, 48-76
  culture, politics, and race in Brazilian writing, 76-100
  modernism and postmodernism in Brazil, 100-25

British Ephemeral Literature LC 59: 1-70
  overviews and general studies, 1-9
  broadside ballads, 10-40
  chapbooks, jestbooks, pamphlets, and newspapers, 40-69

Buddhism and Literature TCLC 70: 59-164
  eastern literature, 60-113
  western literature, 113-63

Buddhism in the Nineteenth-Century Western World NCLC 164: 1-88
  overviews, 3-47
  Buddhism and Western Philosophers, 47-74
  Buddhism in Western Literature, 74-88

The *Bulletin* and the Rise of Australian Literary Nationalism NCLC 116: 1-121
  overviews, 3-32
  legend of the nineties, 32-55
  Bulletin style, 55-71
  Australian literary nationalism, 71-98
  myth of the bush, 98-120

Businessman in American Literature TCLC 26: 1-48
  portrayal of the businessman, 1-32
  themes and techniques in business fiction, 32-47

The Calendar LC 55: 1-92
  overviews and general studies, 2-19
  measuring time, 19-28
  calendars and culture, 28-60
  calendar reform, 60-92

Captivity Narratives LC 82: 71-172
  overviews, 72-107
  captivity narratives and Puritanism, 108-34

captivity narratives and Native Americans, 134-49
influence on American literature, 149-72

Caribbean Literature TCLC 138: 60-135
overviews and general studies, 61-9
ethnic and national identity, 69-107
expatriate Caribbean literature, 107-23
literary histoiography, 123-35

Catholicism in Nineteenth-Century American Literature NCLC 64: 1-58
overviews, 3-14
polemical literature, 14-46
Catholicism in literature, 47-57

Cavalier Poetry and Drama LC 107: 1-71
overviews, 2-36
Cavalier drama, 36-48
major figures, 48-70

Celtic Mythology CMLC 26: 1-111
overviews and general studies, 2-22
Celtic myth as literature and history, 22-48
Celtic religion: Druids and divinities, 48-80
Fionn MacCuhaill and the Fenian cycle, 80-111

Celtic Twilight See Irish Literary Renaissance

Censorship and Contemporary World Literature CLC 194: 1-80
overviews and general studies, 2-19
notorious cases, 19-59
censorship in the global context, 59-79

Censorship of the Press in the Nineteenth Century NCLC 156: 1-133
overviews, 3-29
censorship in Austria, Germany, and Russia, 29-87
censorship in France and Spain, 87-120
censorship in England and America, 120-33

Censorship in Twentieth-Century Literature TCLC 154: 115-238
overviews and general studies, 117-25
censorship and obscenity trials, 125-61
censorship and sexual politics, 161-81
censorship and war, 181-207
political censorship and the state, 207-28
censorship and the writer, 228-38

The Chartist Movement and Literature NCLC 60: 1-84
overview: nineteenth-century working-class fiction, 2-19
Chartist fiction and poetry, 19-73
the Chartist press, 73-84

The Chicago Renaissance TCLC 154: 239-341
overviews and general studies, 240-60
definitions and growth, 260-82
the language debate, 282-318
major authors, 318-40

Chicano/a Literature, Contemporary CLC 205: 82-181
overviews, 84-124
Chicana studies, 124-40
some representative works, 140-80

Chick-Lit and Lad-Lit CLC 210: 115-64
overviews, 117-25
the debate over Chick Lit, 125-46
representative authors, 146-64

Child Labor in Nineteenth-Century Literature NCLC 108: 1-133
overviews, 3-10
climbing boys and chimney sweeps, 10-16
the international traffic in children, 16-45
critics and reformers, 45-82
fictional representations of child laborers, 83-132

Children's Literature, Nineteenth-Century NCLC 52: 60-135
overviews and general studies, 61-72
moral tales, 72-89
fairy tales and fantasy, 90-119
making men/making women, 119-34

Christianity in Twentieth-Century Literature TCLC 110: 1-79
overviews and general studies, 2-31
Christianity in twentieth-century fiction, 31-78

Chronicle Plays LC 89: 1-106
development of the genre, 2-33
historiography and literature, 33-56
genre and performance, 56-88
politics and ideology, 88-106

The City and Literature TCLC 90: 1-124
overviews and general studies, 2-9
the city in American literature, 9-86
the city in European literature, 86-124

City Comedy LC 118: 77-211
origins and development, 79-113
economic issues, 113-32
women and city comedy, 132-82
the plays of Thomas Middleton, 182-211

Civic Critics, Russian NCLC 20: 402-46
principal figures and background, 402-9
and Russian Nihilism, 410-6
aesthetic and critical views, 416-45

The Cockney School NCLC 68: 1-64
overview, 2-7
Blackwood's Magazine and the contemporary critical response, 7-24
the political and social import of the Cockneys and their critics, 24-63

Colonial America: The Intellectual Background LC 25: 1-98
overviews and general studies, 2-17
philosophy and politics, 17-31
early religious influences in Colonial America, 31-60
consequences of the Revolution, 60-78
religious influences in post-revolutionary America, 78-87
colonial literary genres, 87-97

Colonialism in Victorian English Literature NCLC 56: 1-77
overviews and general studies, 2-34
colonialism and gender, 34-51
monsters and the occult, 51-76

Columbus, Christopher, Books on the Quincentennial of His Arrival in the New World CLC 70: 329-60

Comic Books TCLC 66: 1-139
historical and critical perspectives, 2-48
superheroes, 48-67
underground comix, 67-88
comic books and society, 88-122
adult comics and graphic novels, 122-36

Comedy of Manners LC 92: 1-75
overviews, 2-21
comedy of manners and society, 21-47
comedy of manners and women, 47-74

Commedia dell'Arte LC 83: 1-147
overviews, 2-7
origins and development, 7-23
characters and actors, 23-45
performance, 45-62
texts and authors, 62-100
influence in Europe, 100-46

Conduct Books in Nineteenth-Century Literature NCLC 152: 130-229
women's education, 131-68
feminist revisions, 168-82
American behavioral literature: cultivating national identity, 182-209
English behavioral literature: defining a middle class, 209-27

Connecticut Wits NCLC 48: 1-95
overviews and general studies, 2-40
major works, 40-76
intellectual context, 76-95

Crime Fiction, Contemporary CLC 209: 34-192
overviews, 37-61
ethnicity and race in crime fiction, 61-105
literary traditions and crime fiction, 105-43
themes, 143-81
representative authors, 181-92

Crime in Literature TCLC 54: 249-307
evolution of the criminal figure in literature, 250-61
crime and society, 261-77
literary perspectives on crime and punishment, 277-88
writings by criminals, 288-306

Crime-Mystery-Detective Stories SSC 59:89-226
overviews and general studies, 90-140
origins and early masters of the crime-mystery-detective story, 140-73
hard-boiled crime-mystery-detective fiction, 173-209
diversity in the crime-mystery-detective story, 210-25

The Crusades CMLC 38: 1-144
history of the Crusades, 3-60
literature of the Crusades, 60-116
the Crusades and the people: attitudes and influences, 116-44

Cuban Exile Literature, Contemporary CLC 207: 1-100
overviews, 2-20
Cubana writers and exile, 20-48
some representative works, 48-100

Cyberpunk TCLC 106: 170-366
overviews and general studies, 171-88
feminism and cyberpunk, 188-230
history and cyberpunk, 230-70
sexuality and cyberpunk, 270-98
social issues and cyberpunk, 299-366

Cyberpunk Short Fiction SSC 60: 44-108
overviews and general studies, 46-78
major writers of cyberpunk fiction, 78-81
sexuality and cyberpunk fiction, 81-97
additional pieces, 97-108

Czechoslovakian Literature of the Twentieth Century TCLC 42:103-96
through World War II, 104-35
de-Stalinization, the Prague Spring, and contemporary literature, 135-72
Slovak literature, 172-85
Czech science fiction, 185-93

Dadaism TCLC 46: 101-71
background and major figures, 102-16
definitions, 116-26
manifestos and commentary by Dadaists, 126-40
theater and film, 140-58
nature and characteristics of Dadaist writing, 158-70

Danish Literature See Twentieth-Century Danish Literature

Darwinism and Literature NCLC 32: 110-206
background, 110-31
direct responses to Darwin, 131-71
collateral effects of Darwinism, 171-205

Death in American Literature NCLC 92: 1-170
overviews and general studies, 2-32
death in the works of Emily Dickinson, 32-72

death in the works of Herman Melville, 72-101
death in the works of Edgar Allan Poe, 101-43
death in the works of Walt Whitman, 143-70

Death in Nineteenth-Century British Literature NCLC 68: 65-142
overviews and general studies, 66-92
responses to death, 92-102
feminist perspectives, 103-17
striving for immortality, 117-41

Death in Literature TCLC 78: 1-183
fiction, 2-115
poetry, 115-46
drama, 146-81

Decadence in Nineteenth-Century Literature NCLC 164: 90-191
overviews, 90-132
Decadent literary subjects, 132-44
Decadence in British literature, 144-57
Decadence in French literature, 158-79
women writers and Decadence, 179-90

Deconstruction TCLC 138: 136-256
overviews and general studies, 137-83
deconstruction and literature, 183-221
deconstruction in philosophy and history, 221-56

de Man, Paul, Wartime Journalism of CLC 55: 382-424

Depictions of Islam in Modern Literature TCLC 166: 81-198
overviews, 82-115
literature in the Muslim world, 115-56
Western interpretations, 156-82
women, Islam, and literature, 182-97

Detective Fiction, Nineteenth-Century NCLC 36: 78-148
origins of the genre, 79-100
history of nineteenth-century detective fiction, 101-33
significance of nineteenth-century detective fiction, 133-46
NCLC 148: 1-161
overviews, 3-26
origins and influences, 26-63
major authors, 63-134
Freud and detective fiction, 134-59

Detective Fiction, Twentieth-Century TCLC 38: 1-96
genesis and history of the detective story, 3-22
defining detective fiction, 22-32
evolution and varieties, 32-77
the appeal of detective fiction, 77-90

Detective Story See Crime-Mystery-Detective Stories

Dime Novels NCLC 84: 98-168
overviews and general studies, 99-123
popular characters, 123-39
major figures and influences, 139-52
socio-political concerns, 152-167

Disease and Literature TCLC 66: 140-283
overviews and general studies, 141-65
disease in nineteenth-century literature, 165-81
tuberculosis and literature, 181-94
women and disease in literature, 194-221
plague literature, 221-53
AIDS in literature, 253-82

El Dorado, The Legend of See The Legend of El Dorado

The Double in Nineteenth-Century Literature NCLC 40: 1-95
genesis and development of the theme, 2-15
the double and Romanticism, 16-27
sociological views, 27-52
psychological interpretations, 52-87
philosophical considerations, 87-95

Dramatic Realism NCLC 44: 139-202
overviews and general studies, 140-50
origins and definitions, 150-66
impact and influence, 166-93
realist drama and tragedy, 193-201

Drugs and Literature TCLC 78: 184-282
overviews and general studies, 185-201
pre-twentieth-century literature, 201-42
twentieth-century literature, 242-82

Dystopias in Contemporary Literature CLC 168: 1-91
overviews and general studies, 2-52
dystopian views in Margaret Atwood's *The Handmaid's Tale* (1985), 52-71
feminist readings of dystopias, 71-90

Eastern Mythology CMLC 26: 112-92
heroes and kings, 113-51
cross-cultural perspective, 151-69
relations to history and society, 169-92

Ecocriticism and Nineteenth-Century Literature NCLC 140: 1-168
overviews, 3-20
American literature: Romantics and Realists, 20-76
American explorers and naturalists, 76-123
English literature: Romantics and Victorians, 123-67

Ecofeminism and Nineteenth-Century Literature NCLC 136: 1-110
overviews, 2-24
the local landscape, 24-72
travel writing, 72-109

Eighteenth-Century British Periodicals LC 63: 1-123
rise of periodicals, 2-31
impact and influence of periodicals, 31-64
periodicals and society, 64-122

Eighteenth-Century Travel Narratives LC 77: 252-355
overviews and general studies, 254-79
eighteenth-century European travel narratives, 279-334
non-European eighteenth-century travel narratives, 334-55

Electronic "Books": Hypertext and Hyperfiction CLC 86: 367-404
books vs. CD-ROMS, 367-76
hypertext and hyperfiction, 376-95
implications for publishing, libraries, and the public, 395-403

Eliot, T. S., Centenary of Birth CLC 55: 345-75

Elizabethan Drama LC 22: 140-240
origins and influences, 142-67
characteristics and conventions, 167-83
theatrical production, 184-200
histories, 200-12
comedy, 213-20
tragedy, 220-30

Elizabethan Prose Fiction LC 41: 1-70
overviews and general studies, 1-15
origins and influences, 15-43
style and structure, 43-69

The Emergence of the Short Story in the Nineteenth Century NCLC 140: 169-279
overviews, 171-74
the American short story, 174-214
the short story in Great Britain and Ireland, 214-235
stories by women in English, 235-45
the short story in France and Russia, 245-66
the Latin American short story, 266-77

Enclosure of the English Common NCLC 88: 1-57
overviews and general studies, 1-12
early reaction to enclosure, 12-23
nineteenth-century reaction to enclosure, 23-56

The Encyclopedists LC 26: 172-253
overviews and general studies, 173-210
intellectual background, 210-32
views on esthetics, 232-41
views on women, 241-52

English Abolitionist Literature of the Nineteenth Century NCLC 136: 111-235
overview, 112-35
origins and development, 135-42
poetry, 142-58
prose, 158-80
sociopolitical concerns, 180-95
English abolitionist literature and feminism, 195-233

English Caroline Literature LC 13: 221-307
background, 222-41
evolution and varieties, 241-62
the Cavalier mode, 262-75
court and society, 275-91
politics and religion, 291-306

English Decadent Literature of the 1890s NCLC 28: 104-200
fin de siècle: the Decadent period, 105-19
definitions, 120-37
major figures: "the tragic generation," 137-50
French literature and English literary Decadence, 150-7
themes, 157-61
poetry, 161-82
periodicals, 182-96

English Emblem Books LC 125: 1-99
overviews, 2-27
background and contexts, 27-63
major emblem writers, 63-83
religion and emblem books, 83-99

English Essay, Rise of the LC 18: 238-308
definitions and origins, 236-54
influence on the essay, 254-69
historical background, 269-78
the essay in the seventeenth century, 279-93
the essay in the eighteenth century, 293-307

English Mystery Cycle Dramas LC 34: 1-88
overviews and general studies, 1-27
the nature of dramatic performances, 27-42
the medieval worldview and the mystery cycles, 43-67
the doctrine of repentance and the mystery cycles, 67-76
the fall from grace in the mystery cycles, 76-88

The English Realist Novel, 1740-1771 LC 51: 102-98
overviews and general studies, 103-22
from Romanticism to Realism, 123-58
women and the novel, 159-175
the novel and other literary forms, 176-197

English Revolution, Literature of the LC 43: 1-58
overviews and general studies, 2-24
pamphlets of the English Revolution, 24-38
political sermons of the English Revolution, 38-48
poetry of the English Revolution, 48-57

English Romantic Hellenism NCLC 68: 143-250
overviews and general studies, 144-69
historical development of English Romantic Hellenism, 169-91
influence of Greek mythology on the Romantics, 191-229

influence of Greek literature, art, and culture on the Romantics, 229-50

English Romantic Poetry NCLC 28: 201-327
  overviews and reputation, 202-37
  major subjects and themes, 237-67
  forms of Romantic poetry, 267-78
  politics, society, and Romantic poetry, 278-99
  philosophy, religion, and Romantic poetry, 299-324

The Epistolary Novel LC 59: 71-170
  overviews and general studies, 72-96
  women and the Epistolary novel, 96-138
  principal figures: Britain, 138-53
  principal figures: France, 153-69

Espionage Literature TCLC 50: 95-159
  overviews and general studies, 96-113
  espionage fiction/formula fiction, 113-26
  spies in fact and fiction, 126-38
  the female spy, 138-44
  social and psychological perspectives, 144-58

European Debates on the Conquest of the Americas LC 67: 1-129
  overviews and general studies, 3-56
  major Spanish figures, 56-98
  English perceptions of Native Americans, 98-129

European Romanticism NCLC 36: 149-284
  definitions, 149-77
  origins of the movement, 177-82
  Romantic theory, 182-200
  themes and techniques, 200-23
  Romanticism in Germany, 223-39
  Romanticism in France, 240-61
  Romanticism in Italy, 261-4
  Romanticism in Spain, 264-8
  impact and legacy, 268-82

Exile in Literature TCLC 122: 1-129
  overviews and general studies, 2-33
  exile in fiction, 33-92
  German literature in exile, 92-129

Existentialism and Literature TCLC 42: 197-268
  overviews and definitions, 198-209
  history and influences, 209-19
  Existentialism critiqued and defended, 220-35
  philosophical and religious perspectives, 235-41
  Existentialist fiction and drama, 241-67

Ezra Pound Controversy TCLC 150: 1-132
  politics of Ezra Pound, 3-42
  anti-semitism of Ezra Pound, 42-57
  the Bollingen Award controversy, 57-76
  Pound's later writing, 76-104
  criticism of *The Pisan Cantos,* 104-32

Familiar Essay NCLC 48: 96-211
  definitions and origins, 97-130
  overview of the genre, 130-43
  elements of form and style, 143-59
  elements of content, 159-73
  the Cockneys: Hazlitt, Lamb, and Hunt, 173-91
  status of the genre, 191-210

Fantasy in Contemporary Literature CLC 193: 137-250
  overviews and general studies, 139-57
  language, form, and theory, 157-91
  major writers, 191-230
  women writers and fantasy, 230-50

Fashion in Nineteenth-Century Literature NCLC 128: 104-93
  overviews and general studies, 105-38
  fashion and American literature, 138-46
  fashion and English literature, 146-74
  fashion and French literature, 174-92

The Faust Legend LC 47: 1-117

Fear in Literature TCLC 74: 81-258
  overviews and general studies, 81
  pre-twentieth-century literature, 123
  twentieth-century literature, 182

Feminism in the 1990s: Commentary on Works by Naomi Wolf, Susan Faludi, and Camille Paglia CLC 76: 377-415

Feminist Criticism, Contemporary CLC 180: 1-103
  overviews and general studies, 2-59
  modern French feminist theory, 59-102

Feminist Criticism in 1990 CLC 65: 312-60

Feminism in Literature FL 1: 1-279; 2: 1-295; 4: 1-626
  women and women's writings from antiquity through the middle ages, 1:1-99
    primary sources, 1:4-12
    women in the ancient world, 1:12-34
    women in the medieval world, 1:34-56
    women in classical art and literature, 1:56-74
    classical and medieval women writers, 1:74-96
  women in the 16th, 17th, and 18th centuries: an overview, 1:101-91
    primary sources, 1:104-11
    overviews, 1:112-32
    society, 1:132-64
    politics, 1:164-77
    women in literature, 1:177-90
  women's literature in the 16th, 17th, and 18th centuries 1:193-279
    primary sources, 1:195-201
    overviews, 1:202-39
    women's literature in the 16th, 17th, and 18th centuries, 1:239-78
  women in the 19th century: an overview, 2:1-88
    primary sources, 2:3-15
    overviews, 2:15-50
    early feminists, 2:50-67
    representations of women in literature and art in the 19th century, 2:67-86
  women's literature in the 19th century, 2:89-206
    primary sources, 2:91-9
    overviews, 2:99-140
    American women writers, 2:141-77
    British women writers, 2:177-204
  United States suffrage movement in the 19th century, 2:207-95
    primary sources, 2:209-29
    overviews, 2:229-39
    the civil war and its effect on suffrage, 2:239-53
    suffrage: issues and individuals, 2:253-94
  women in the early to mid-20th century (1900-1960): an overview, 4:1-126
    primary sources, 4:1-14
    overviews, 4:14-48
    social and economic conditions, 4:48-67
    women and the arts, 4:67-125
  suffrage in the 20th century, 4:127-234
    primary sources, 4:129-36
    overviews, 4:136-77
    major figures and organizations, 4:177-214
    women and law, 4:214-32
  women's literature from 1900 to 1960, 4:235-344
    primary sources, 4:238-41
    overviews, 4:241-61
    impact of the world wars, 4:261-304
    women and the dramatic tradition, 4:304-39
    Asian American influences, 4:339-42
  the feminist movement in the 20th century, 4:345-443
    primary sources, 4:347-58
    overviews, 4:358-403
    feminist legal battles, 4:403-34
    third-wave feminism, 4:434-42
  women's literature from 1960 to the present, 4:445-536
    primary sources, 4:448-60
    overviews, 4:460-83
    women authors of color, 4:483-97
    feminist literary theory, 4:497-511
    modern lesbian literature, 4:511-534

Fifteenth-Century English Literature LC 17: 248-334
  background, 249-72
  poetry, 272-315
  drama, 315-23
  prose, 323-33

Fifteenth-Century Spanish Poetry LC 100:82-173
  overviews and general studies, 83-101
  the Cancioneros, 101-57
  major figures, 157-72

Film and Literature TCLC 38: 97-226
  overviews and general studies, 97-119
  film and theater, 119-34
  film and the novel, 134-45
  the art of the screenplay, 145-66
  genre literature/genre film, 167-79
  the writer and the film industry, 179-90
  authors on film adaptations of their works, 190-200
  fiction into film: comparative essays, 200-23

Finance and Money as Represented in Nineteenth-Century Literature NCLC 76: 1-69
  historical perspectives, 2-20
  the image of money, 20-37
  the dangers of money, 37-50
  women and money, 50-69

Folklore and Literature TCLC 86: 116-293
  overviews and general studies, 118-144
  Native American literature, 144-67
  African-American literature, 167-238
  folklore and the American West, 238-57
  modern and postmodern literature, 257-91

Food in Literature TCLC 114: 1-133
  food and children's literature, 2-14
  food as a literary device, 14-32
  rituals invloving food, 33-45
  food and social and ethnic identity, 45-90
  women's relationship with food, 91-132

Food in Nineteenth-Century Literature NCLC 108: 134-288
  overviews, 136-74
  food and social class, 174-85
  food and gender, 185-219
  food and love, 219-31
  food and sex, 231-48
  eating disorders, 248-70
  vegetarians, carnivores, and cannibals, 270-87

French Drama in the Age of Louis XIV LC 28: 94-185
  overview, 95-127
  tragedy, 127-46
  comedy, 146-66
  tragicomedy, 166-84

French Enlightenment LC 14: 81-145
  the question of definition, 82-9
  le siècle des lumières, 89-94
  women and the salons, 94-105
  censorship, 105-15
  the philosophy of reason, 115-31
  influence and legacy, 131-44

French New Novel TCLC 98: 158-234
  overviews and general studies, 158-92
  influences, 192-213
  themes, 213-33

French Realism NCLC 52: 136-216
  origins and definitions, 137-70
  issues and influence, 170-98
  realism and representation, 198-215

French Revolution and English Literature
NCLC 40: 96-195
  history and theory, 96-123
  romantic poetry, 123-50
  the novel, 150-81
  drama, 181-92
  children's literature, 192-5

French Symbolist Poetry NCLC 144: 1-107
  overviews, 2-14
  Symbolist aesthetics, 14-47
  the Symbolist lyric, 47-60
  history and influence, 60-105

Futurism TCLC 166: 199-338
  overviews, 200-10
  poetry, 210-23
  theater, 223-32
  music, 232-46
  Futurism and Fascism, 246-312
  women Futurist writers, 312-37

Futurism, Italian TCLC 42: 269-354
  principles and formative influences, 271-9
  manifestos, 279-88
  literature, 288-303
  theater, 303-19
  art, 320-30
  music, 330-6
  architecture, 336-9
  and politics, 339-46
  reputation and significance, 346-51

Gaelic Revival See Irish Literary Renaissance

Gates, Henry Louis, Jr., and African-American Literary Criticism CLC 65: 361-405

Gaucho Literature TCLC 158: 99-195
  overviews and general studies, 101-43
  major works, 143-95

Gambling in Nineteenth-Century Literature
NCLC 168: 1-84
  overview, 2-7
  gambling in American literature, 7-39
  gambling in British literature, 39-57
  gambling in Russian literature, 57-84

Gay and Lesbian Literature CLC 76: 416-39

Gay and Lesbian Literature, Contemporary
CLC 171: 1-130
  overviews and general studies, 2-43
  contemporary gay literature, 44-95
  lesbianism in contemporary literature, 95-129

Gender in Nineteenth-Century Literature
NCLC 168: 192-352
  overviews, 195-256
  gender and race, 256-83
  gender and men, 283-309
  gender and class, 309-20
  gender and the text, 320-51

Generation of 1898 Short Fiction SSC 75: 182-287
  overviews and general studies, 182-210
  major short story writers of the Generation of 1898, 210-86
    Azorín, 210-16
    Emilia Pardo Bazán, 216-34
    Vicente Blasco Ibáñez, 234-36
    Gabriel Miró, 236-43
    Miguel de Unamuno, 243-68
    Ramon del Valle-Inclán, 268-86

German Exile Literature TCLC 30: 1-58
  the writer and the Nazi state, 1-10
  definition of, 10-4
  life in exile, 14-32
  surveys, 32-50
  Austrian literature in exile, 50-2
  German publishing in the United States, 52-7

German Expressionism TCLC 34: 74-160
  history and major figures, 76-85
  aesthetic theories, 85-109
  drama, 109-26
  poetry, 126-38
  film, 138-42
  painting, 142-7
  music, 147-53
  and politics, 153-8

The Ghost Story SSC 58: 1-142
  overviews and general studies, 1-21
  the ghost story in American literature, 21-49
  the ghost story in Asian literature, 49-53
  the ghost story in European and English literature, 54-89
  major figures, 89-141

The Gilded Age NCLC 84: 169-271
  popular themes, 170-90
  Realism, 190-208
  Aestheticism, 208-26
  socio-political concerns, 226-70

***Glasnost* and Contemporary Soviet Literature** CLC 59: 355-97

***Gone with the Wind* as Cultural Phenomenon**
TCLC 170: 1-103
  overviews, 2-60
  race, gender, and class in *Gone with the Wind*, 60-102

Gothic Drama NCLC 132: 95-198
  overviews, 97-125
  sociopolitical contexts, 125-58
  Gothic playwrights, 158-97

Gothic Literature GL 1: 1-577
  Gothic Literature: an overview, 1-106
    primary sources, 4-16
    overviews, 16-40
    origins of the Gothic, 40-57
    American Gothic, 57-74
    European Gothic, 74-104
  society, culture, and the Gothic, 107-229
    primary sources, 110-27
    overviews, 127-80
    race and the Gothic, 180-210
    women and the Gothic, 210-28
  gothic themes, settings, and figures, 231-387
    primary sources, 236-49
    overviews, 249-64
    haunted dwellings and the supernatural, 264-301
    psychology and the Gothic, 301-42
    vampires, 342-85
  performing arts and the Gothic, 389-474
    primary sources, 394-401
    drama, 401-15
    film, 415-52
    television, 452-60
    music, 461-73
  visual arts and the Gothic, 475-526
    primary sources, 477-80
    overviews, 480-86
    architecture, 486-506
    art, 506-525

Gothic Novel NCLC 28: 328-402
  development and major works, 328-34
  definitions, 334-50
  themes and techniques, 350-78
  in America, 378-85
  in Scotland, 385-91
  influence and legacy, 391-400

The Governess in Nineteenth-Century Literature NCLC 104: 1-131
  overviews and general studies, 3-28
  social roles and economic conditions, 28-86
  fictional governesses, 86-131

The Grail Theme in Twentieth-Century Literature TCLC 142: 1-89
  overviews and general studies, 2-20
  major works, 20-89

Graphic Narratives CLC 86: 405-32
  history and overviews, 406-21
  the "Classics Illustrated" series, 421-2
  reviews of recent works, 422-32

Graphic Novels CLC 177: 163-299
  overviews and general studies, 165-198
  critical readings of major works, 198-286
  reviews of recent graphic novels, 286-299

Graveyard Poets LC 67: 131-212
  origins and development, 131-52
  major figures, 152-75
  major works, 175-212

Greek Historiography CMLC 17: 1-49

Greek Lyric Poetry, The Rise of CMLC 77: 226-329
  overviews, 229-46
  literary history, 246-72
  themes and style, 272-302
  representative authors, 302-28

Greek Mythology CMLC 26: 193-320
  overviews and general studies, 194-209
  origins and development of Greek mythology, 209-29
  cosmogonies and divinities in Greek mythology, 229-54
  heroes and heroines in Greek mythology, 254-80
  women in Greek mythology, 280-320

Greek Theater CMLC 51: 1-58
  criticism, 2-58

Hard-Boiled Fiction TCLC 118: 1-109
  overviews and general studies, 2-39
  major authors, 39-76
  women and hard-boiled fiction, 76-109

The Harlem Renaissance HR 1: 1-563
  overviews and general studies of the Harlem Renaissance, 1-137
    primary sources, 3-12
    overviews, 12-38
    background and sources of the Harlem Renaissance, 38-56
    the New Negro aesthetic, 56-91
    patrons, promoters, and the New York Public Library, 91-121
    women of the Harlem Renaissance, 121-37
  social, economic, and political factors that influenced the Harlem Renaissance, 139-240
    primary sources, 141-53
    overviews, 153-87
    social and economic factors, 187-213
    Black intellectual and political thought, 213-40
  publishing and periodicals during the Harlem Renaissance, 243-339
    primary sources, 246-52
    overviews, 252-68
    African American writers and mainstream publishers, 268-91
    anthologies: *The New Negro* and others, 291-309
    African American periodicals and the Harlem Renaissance, 309-39
  performing arts during the Harlem Renaissance, 341-465
    primary sources, 343-48
    overviews, 348-64
    drama of the Harlem Renaissance, 364-92
    influence of music on Harlem Renaissance writing, 437-65

visual arts during the Harlem Renaissance, 467-563
- primary sources, 470-71
- overviews, 471-517
- painters, 517-36
- sculptors, 536-58
- photographers, 558-63

Harlem Renaissance TCLC 26: 49-125
- principal issues and figures, 50-67
- the literature and its audience, 67-74
- theme and technique in poetry, fiction, and drama, 74-115
- and American society, 115-21
- achievement and influence, 121-2

Havel, Václav, Playwright and President CLC 65: 406-63

Heroic Drama LC 91: 249-373
- definitions and overviews, 251-78
- politics and heroic drama, 278-303
- early plays: Dryden and Orrery, 303-51
- later plays: Lee and Otway, 351-73

Historical Fiction, Nineteenth-Century NCLC 48: 212-307
- definitions and characteristics, 213-36
- Victorian historical fiction, 236-65
- American historical fiction, 265-88
- realism in historical fiction, 288-306

Hollywood and Literature TCLC 118: 110-251
- overviews and general studies, 111-20
- adaptations, 120-65
- socio-historical and cultural impact, 165-206
- theater and hollywood, 206-51

Holocaust and the Atomic Bomb: Fifty Years Later CLC 91: 331-82
- the Holocaust remembered, 333-52
- Anne Frank revisited, 352-62
- the atomic bomb and American memory, 362-81

Holocaust Denial Literature TCLC 58: 1-110
- overviews and general studies, 1-30
- Robert Faurisson and Noam Chomsky, 30-52
- Holocaust denial literature in America, 52-71
- library access to Holocaust denial literature, 72-5
- the authenticity of Anne Frank's diary, 76-90
- David Irving and the "normalization" of Hitler, 90-109

Holocaust, Literature of the TCLC 42: 355-450
- historical overview, 357-61
- critical overview, 361-70
- diaries and memoirs, 370-95
- novels and short stories, 395-425
- poetry, 425-41
- drama, 441-8

Homosexuality in Nineteenth-Century Literature NCLC 56: 78-182
- defining homosexuality, 80-111
- Greek love, 111-44
- trial and danger, 144-81

Humors Comedy LC 85: 194-324
- overviews, 195-251
- major figures: Ben Jonson, 251-93
- major figures: William Shakespeare, 293-324

Hungarian Literature of the Twentieth Century TCLC 26: 126-88
- surveys of, 126-47
- *Nyugat* and early twentieth-century literature, 147-56
- mid-century literature, 156-68
- and politics, 168-78
- since the 1956 revolt, 178-87

Hysteria in Nineteenth-Century Literature NCLC 64: 59-184
- the history of hysteria, 60-75
- the gender of hysteria, 75-103
- hysteria and women's narratives, 103-57
- hysteria in nineteenth-century poetry, 157-83

Image of the Noble Savage in Literature LC 79: 136-252
- overviews and development, 136-76
- the Noble Savage in the New World, 176-221
- Rousseau and the French Enlightenment's view of the noble savage, 221-51

Imagism TCLC 74: 259-454
- history and development, 260
- major figures, 288
- sources and influences, 352
- Imagism and other movements, 397
- influence and legacy, 431

Immigrants in Nineteenth-Century Literature, Representation of NCLC 112: 188-298
- overview, 189-99
- immigrants in America, 199-223
- immigrants and labor, 223-60
- immigrants in England, 260-97

Incest in Nineteenth-Century American Literature NCLC 76: 70-141
- overview, 71-88
- the concern for social order, 88-117
- authority and authorship, 117-40

Incest in Victorian Literature NCLC 92: 172-318
- overviews and general studies, 173-85
- novels, 185-276
- plays, 276-84
- poetry, 284-318

Indian Literature in English TCLC 54: 308-406
- overview, 309-13
- origins and major figures, 313-25
- the Indo-English novel, 325-55
- Indo-English poetry, 355-67
- Indo-English drama, 367-72
- critical perspectives on Indo-English literature, 372-80
- modern Indo-English literature, 380-9
- Indo-English authors on their work, 389-404

The Industrial Revolution in Literature NCLC 56: 183-273
- historical and cultural perspectives, 184-201
- contemporary reactions to the machine, 201-21
- themes and symbols in literature, 221-73

The Influence of Ernest Hemingway TCLC 162: 122-259
- overviews, 123-43
- writers on Hemingway, 143-58
- Hemingway's evocation of place, 158-84
- gender and identity, 184-229
- Hemingway and the quest for meaning, 229-58

The Influence of William Faulkner TCLC 170: 104-255
- overviews, 105-16
- Faulkner and narrative, 116-60
- Faulkner and psychology, 160-80
- Faulkner and race, 180-219
- impact on contemporary culture, 219-43
- Faulkner and women, 243-54

The Irish Famine as Represented in Nineteenth-Century Literature NCLC 64: 185-261
- overviews and general studies, 187-98
- historical background, 198-212
- famine novels, 212-34
- famine poetry, 234-44
- famine letters and eye-witness accounts, 245-61

Irish Literary Renaissance TCLC 46: 172-287
- overview, 173-83
- development and major figures, 184-202
- influence of Irish folklore and mythology, 202-22
- Irish poetry, 222-34
- Irish drama and the Abbey Theatre, 234-56
- Irish fiction, 256-86

Irish Nationalism and Literature NCLC 44: 203-73
- the Celtic element in literature, 203-19
- anti-Irish sentiment and the Celtic response, 219-34
- literary ideals in Ireland, 234-45
- literary expressions, 245-73

The Irish Novel NCLC 80: 1-130
- overviews and general studies, 3-9
- principal figures, 9-22
- peasant and middle class Irish novelists, 22-76
- aristocratic Irish and Anglo-Irish novelists, 76-129

Israeli Literature TCLC 94: 1-137
- overviews and general studies, 2-18
- Israeli fiction, 18-33
- Israeli poetry, 33-62
- Israeli drama, 62-91
- women and Israeli literature, 91-112
- Arab characters in Israeli literature, 112-36

Italian Futurism See **Futurism, Italian**

Italian Humanism LC 12: 205-77
- origins and early development, 206-18
- revival of classical letters, 218-23
- humanism and other philosophies, 224-39
- humanism and humanists, 239-46
- the plastic arts, 246-57
- achievement and significance, 258-76

Italian Romanticism NCLC 60: 85-145
- origins and overviews, 86-101
- Italian Romantic theory, 101-25
- the language of Romanticism, 125-45

Jacobean Drama LC 33: 1-37
- the Jacobean worldview: an era of transition, 2-14
- the moral vision of Jacobean drama, 14-22
- Jacobean tragedy, 22-3
- the Jacobean masque, 23-36

Jazz and Literature TCLC 102: 3-124

Jewish-American Fiction TCLC 62: 1-181
- overviews and general studies, 2-24
- major figures, 24-48
- Jewish writers and American life, 48-78
- Jewish characters in American fiction, 78-108
- themes in Jewish-American fiction, 108-43
- Jewish-American women writers, 143-59
- the Holocaust and Jewish-American fiction, 159-81

Jews in Literature TCLC 118: 252-417
- overviews and general studies, 253-97
- representing the Jew in literature, 297-351
- the Holocaust in literature, 351-416

The Journals of Lewis and Clark NCLC 100: 1-88
- overviews and general studies, 4-30
- journal-keeping methods, 30-46
- Fort Mandan, 46-51

the Clark journal, 51-65
the journals as literary texts, 65-87

Kabuki LC 73: 118-232
overviews and general studies, 120-40
the development of Kabuki, 140-65
major works, 165-95
Kabuki and society, 195-231

King Alfred the Great, The Age of See The Age of King Alfred the Great

The Kit-Kat Club LC 71: 66-112
overviews and general studies, 67-88
major figures, 88-107
attacks on the Kit-Kat Club, 107-12

The Knickerbocker Group NCLC 56: 274-341
overviews and general studies, 276-314
Knickerbocker periodicals, 314-26
writers and artists, 326-40

Künstlerroman TCLC 150: 133-260
overviews and general studies, 135-51
major works, 151-212
feminism in the *Künstlerroman*, 212-49
minority *Künstlerroman*, 249-59

The Lake Poets NCLC 52: 217-304
characteristics of the Lake Poets and their works, 218-27
literary influences and collaborations, 227-66
defining and developing Romantic ideals, 266-84
embracing Conservatism, 284-303

Language Poets TCLC 126: 66-172
overviews and general studies, 67-122
selected major figures in language poetry, 122-72

Larkin, Philip, Controversy CLC 81: 417-64

Latin American Literature, Twentieth-Century TCLC 58: 111-98
historical and critical perspectives, 112-36
the novel, 136-45
the short story, 145-9
drama, 149-60
poetry, 160-7
the writer and society, 167-86
Native Americans in Latin American literature, 186-97

Law and Literature TCLC 126: 173-347
overviews and general studies, 174-253
fiction critiquing the law, 253-88
literary responses to the law, 289-346

The Legend of El Dorado LC 74: 248-350
overviews, 249-308
major explorations for El Dorado, 308-50

The Legend of Pope Joan LC 123: 1-88
overviews and general studies, 3-87

The Levellers LC 51: 200-312
overviews and general studies, 201-29
principal figures, 230-86
religion, political philosophy, and pamphleteering, 287-311

The Lilith Legend in Modern Literature TCLC 170: 256-319
overviews, 257-67
historical and literary background, 267-89
the Lilith legend in twentieth-century literature, 289-319

Literary Criticism in the Nineteenth Century, American NCLC 128: 1-103
overviews and general studies, 2-44
the trancendentalists, 44-65
"young America," 65-71
James Russell Lowell, 71-9
Edgar Allan Poe, 79-97
Walt Whitman, 97-102

Literary Expressionism TCLC 142: 90-185
overviews and general studies, 91-138
themes in literary expressionism, 138-61
expressionism in Germany, 161-84

The Literary Marketplace Nineteenth-Century NCLC 128: 194-368
overviews and general studies, 197-228
British literary marketplace, 228-66
French literary marketplace, 266-82
American literary marketplace, 282-323
Women in the literary marketplace, 323-67

Literary Prizes TCLC 122: 130-203
overviews and general studies, 131-34
the Nobel Prize in Literature, 135-83
the Pulitzer Prize, 183-203

Literature and Millenial Lists CLC 119: 431-67
The Modern Library list, 433
The Waterstone list, 438-439

Literature in Response to the September 11 Attacks CLC 174: 1-46
Major works about September 11, 2001, 2-22
Critical, artistic, and journalistic responses, 22-45

Literature of the American Cowboy NCLC 96: 1-60
overview, 3-20
cowboy fiction, 20-36
cowboy poetry and songs, 36-59

Literature of the California Gold Rush NCLC 92: 320-85
overviews and general studies, 322-24
early California Gold Rush fiction, 324-44
Gold Rush folklore and legend, 344-51
the rise of Western local color, 351-60
social relations and social change, 360-385

Literature of the Counter-Reformation LC 109: 213-56
overviews and general studies, 214-33
influential figures, 233-56

The Living Theatre DC 16: 154-214

Luddism in Nineteenth-Century Literature NCLC 140: 280-365
overviews, 281-322
the literary response, 322-65

Lynching in Nineteenth-Century Literature NCLC 148: 162-247
lynching in literature and music, 163-92
Ida B. Wells-Barnett and the anti-lynching movement, 192-221
resistance to lynching in society and the press, 221-46

Madness in Nineteenth-Century Literature NCLC 76: 142-284
overview, 143-54
autobiography, 154-68
poetry, 168-215
fiction, 215-83

Madness in Twentieth-Century Literature TCLC 50: 160-225
overviews and general studies, 161-71
madness and the creative process, 171-86
suicide, 186-91
madness in American literature, 191-207
madness in German literature, 207-13
madness and feminist artists, 213-24

Magic Realism TCLC 110: 80-327
overviews and general studies, 81-94
magic realism in African literature, 95-110
magic realism in American literature, 110-32
magic realism in Canadian literature, 132-46
magic realism in European literature, 146-66
magic realism in Asian literature, 166-79
magic realism in Latin-American literature, 179-223
magic realism in Israeli literature and the novels of Salman Rushdie, 223-38
magic realism in literature written by women, 239-326

The Martin Marprelate Tracts LC 101: 165-240
criticism, 166-240

Marxist Criticism TCLC 134: 127-57
overviews and general studies, 128-67
Marxist interpretations, 167-209
cultural and literary Marxist theory, 209-49
Marxism and feminist critical theory, 250-56

The Masque LC 63: 124-265
development of the masque, 125-62
sources and structure, 162-220
race and gender in the masque, 221-64

Medical Writing LC 55: 93-195
colonial America, 94-110
enlightenment, 110-24
medieval writing, 124-40
sexuality, 140-83
vernacular, 185-95

Memoirs of Trauma CLC 109: 419-466
overview, 420
criticism, 429

Metafiction TCLC 130: 43-228
overviews and general studies, 44-85
Spanish metafiction, 85-117
studies of metafictional authors and works, 118-228

Metaphysical Poets LC 24: 356-439
early definitions, 358-67
surveys and overviews, 367-92
cultural and social influences, 392-406
stylistic and thematic variations, 407-38

Missionaries in the Nineteenth-Century, Literature of NCLC 112: 299-392
history and development, 300-16
uses of ethnography, 316-31
sociopolitical concerns, 331-82
David Livingstone, 382-91

The Modern Essay TCLC 58: 199-273
overview, 200-7
the essay in the early twentieth century, 207-19
characteristics of the modern essay, 219-32
modern essayists, 232-45
the essay as a literary genre, 245-73

Modern French Literature TCLC 122: 205-359
overviews and general studies, 207-43
French theater, 243-77
gender issues and French women writers, 277-315
ideology and politics, 315-24
modern French poetry, 324-41
resistance literature, 341-58

Modern Irish Literature TCLC 102: 125-321
overview, 129-44
dramas, 144-70
fiction, 170-247
poetry, 247-321

Modern Japanese Literature TCLC 66: 284-389
poetry, 285-305
drama, 305-29
fiction, 329-61
western influences, 361-87

Modernism TCLC 70: 165-275
definitions, 166-84
Modernism and earlier influences, 184-200
stylistic and thematic traits, 200-29

poetry and drama, 229-42
redefining Modernism, 242-75

Monasticism and Literature CMLC 74: 88-294
major figures, 89-132
secular influences, 132-54
monastic principles and literary practices, 154-232
women and monasticism, 232-93

Muckraking Movement in American Journalism TCLC 34: 161-242
development, principles, and major figures, 162-70
publications, 170-9
social and political ideas, 179-86
targets, 186-208
fiction, 208-19
decline, 219-29
impact and accomplishments, 229-40

Multiculturalism CLC 189: 167-254
overviews and general studies, 168-93
the effects of multiculturalism on global literature, 193-213
multicultural themes in specific contemporary works, 213-53

Multiculturalism in Literature and Education CLC 70: 361-413

Music and Modern Literature TCLC 62: 182-329
overviews and general studies, 182-211
musical form/literary form, 211-32
music in literature, 232-50
the influence of music on literature, 250-73
literature and popular music, 273-303
jazz and poetry, 303-28

Mystery Story See Crime-Mystery-Detective Stories

Native American Literature CLC 76: 440-76

Natural School, Russian NCLC 24: 205-40
history and characteristics, 205-25
contemporary criticism, 225-40

Naturalism NCLC 36: 285-382
definitions and theories, 286-305
critical debates on Naturalism, 305-16
Naturalism in theater, 316-32
European Naturalism, 332-61
American Naturalism, 361-72
the legacy of Naturalism, 372-81

Negritude TCLC 50: 226-361
origins and evolution, 227-56
definitions, 256-91
Negritude in literature, 291-343
Negritude reconsidered, 343-58

Negritude TCLC 158: 196-280
overviews and general studies, 197-208
major figures, 208-25
Negritude and humanism, 225-29
poetry of Negritude, 229-47
politics of Negritude, 247-68
the Negritude debate, 268-79

New Criticism TCLC 34: 243-318
development and ideas, 244-70
debate and defense, 270-99
influence and legacy, 299-315

TCLC 146: 1-108
overviews and general studies, 3-19
defining New Criticism, 19-28
place in history, 28-51
poetry and New Criticism, 51-78
major authors, 78-108

The New Humanists TCLC 162: 260-341
overviews, 261-92
major figures, 292-310
New Humanism in education and literature, 310-41

New South, Literature of the NCLC 116: 122-240
overviews, 124-66
the novel in the New South, 166-209
myth of the Old South in the New, 209-39

The New Woman in Nineteenth-Century Literature NCLC 156: 134-281
overview, 136-39
historical and social context, 139-57
contemporary descriptions of the new woman, 157-65
the new woman and popular fiction, 165-86
the new woman and the decadents, 187-207
the new woman and the theater, 207-48
Henry James, Bram Stoker, and Others, 248-80

The New World in Renaissance Literature LC 31: 1-51
overview, 1-18
utopia vs. terror, 18-31
explorers and Native Americans, 31-51

New York Intellectuals and *Partisan Review* TCLC 30: 117-98
development and major figures, 118-28
influence of Judaism, 128-39
Partisan Review, 139-57
literary philosophy and practice, 157-75
political philosophy, 175-87
achievement and significance, 187-97

The New Yorker TCLC 58: 274-357
overviews and general studies, 274-95
major figures, 295-304
New Yorker style, 304-33
fiction, journalism, and humor at *The New Yorker,* 333-48
the new *New Yorker,* 348-56

Newgate Novel NCLC 24: 166-204
development of Newgate literature, 166-73
Newgate Calendar, 173-7
Newgate fiction, 177-95
Newgate drama, 195-204

New Zealand Literature TCLC 134: 258-368
overviews and general studies, 260-300
Maori literature, 300-22
New Zealand drama, 322-32
New Zealand fiction, 332-51
New Zealand poetry, 351-67

Nigerian Literature of the Twentieth Century TCLC 30: 199-265
surveys of, 199-227
English language and African life, 227-45
politics and the Nigerian writer, 245-54
Nigerian writers and society, 255-62

Nihilism and Literature TCLC 110: 328-93
overviews and general studies, 328-44
European and Russian nihilism, 344-73
nihilism in the works of Albert Camus, Franz Kafka, and John Barth, 373-92

Nineteenth-Century Captivity Narratives NCLC 80:131-218
overview, 132-37
the political significance of captivity narratives, 137-67
images of gender, 167-96
moral instruction, 197-217

Nineteenth-Century Euro-American Literary Representations of Native Americans NCLC 104: 132-264
overviews and general studies, 134-53
Native American history, 153-72
the Indians of the Northeast, 172-93
the Indians of the Southeast, 193-212
the Indians of the West, 212-27
Indian-hater fiction, 227-43
the Indian as exhibit, 243-63

Nineteenth-Century Native American Autobiography NCLC 64: 262-389
overview, 263-8
problems of authorship, 268-81
the evolution of Native American autobiography, 281-304
political issues, 304-15
gender and autobiography, 316-62
autobiographical works during the turn of the century, 362-88

Nineteenth-Century Pornography NCLC 144: 108-202
nineteenth-century pornographers, 110-64
pornography and literature, 164-91
pornography and censorship, 191-201

Nineteenth-Century Western Literature in Japan NCLC 156: 282-352
overviews, 283-305
European literature in Japan, 305-28
American literature in Japan, 328-52

Noh Drama LC 103: 189-270
overviews, 190-94
origins and development, 194-214
structure, 214-28
types of plays, 228-45
masks in Noh drama, 245-57
Noh drama and the audience, 257-69

Norse Mythology CMLC 26: 321-85
history and mythological tradition, 322-44
Eddic poetry, 344-74
Norse mythology and other traditions, 374-85

Northern Humanism LC 16: 281-356
background, 282-305
precursor of the Reformation, 305-14
the Brethren of the Common Life, the Devotio Moderna, and education, 314-40
the impact of printing, 340-56

The Novel of Manners NCLC 56: 342-96
social and political order, 343-53
domestic order, 353-73
depictions of gender, 373-83
the American novel of manners, 383-95

Novels of the Ming and Early Ch'ing Dynasties LC 76: 213-356
overviews and historical development, 214-45
major works—overview, 245-85
genre studies, 285-325
cultural and social themes, 325-55

Nuclear Literature: Writings and Criticism in the Nuclear Age TCLC 46: 288-390
overviews and general studies, 290-301
fiction, 301-35
poetry, 335-8
nuclear war in Russo-Japanese literature, 338-55
nuclear war and women writers, 355-67
the nuclear referent and literary criticism, 367-88

Occultism in Modern Literature TCLC 50: 362-406
influence of occultism on literature, 363-72
occultism, literature, and society, 372-87
fiction, 387-96
drama, 396-405

Opium and the Nineteenth-Century Literary Imagination NCLC 20:250-301
original sources, 250-62
historical background, 262-71
and literary society, 271-9
and literary creativity, 279-300

Orientalism NCLC 96: 149-364
overviews and general studies, 150-98
Orientalism and imperialism, 198-229
Orientalism and gender, 229-59

Orientalism and the nineteenth-century novel, 259-321
Orientalism in nineteenth-century poetry, 321-63

The Oxford Movement NCLC 72: 1-197
overviews and general studies, 2-24
background, 24-59
and education, 59-69
religious responses, 69-128
literary aspects, 128-178
political implications, 178-196

The Parnassian Movement NCLC 72: 198-241
overviews and general studies, 199-231
and epic form, 231-38
and positivism, 238-41

Pastoral Literature of the English Renaissance LC 59: 171-282
overviews and general studies, 172-214
principal figures of the Elizabethan period, 214-33
principal figures of the later Renaissance, 233-50
pastoral drama, 250-81

Periodicals, Nineteenth-Century American NCLC 132: 199-374
overviews, chronology, and development, 200-41
literary periodicals, 241-83
regional periodicals, 283-317
women's magazines and gender issues, 317-47
minority periodicals, 347-72

Periodicals, Nineteenth-Century British NCLC 24: 100-65
overviews and general studies, 100-30
in the Romantic Age, 130-41
in the Victorian era, 142-54
and the reviewer, 154-64

Picaresque Literature of the Sixteenth and Seventeenth Centuries LC 78: 223-355
context and development, 224-71
genre, 271-98
the picaro, 299-326
the picara, 326-53

Plath, Sylvia, and the Nature of Biography CLC 86: 433-62
the nature of biography, 433-52
reviews of *The Silent Woman,* 452-61

Political Theory from the 15th to the 18th Century LC 36: 1-55
overview, 1-26
natural law, 26-42
empiricism, 42-55

Polish Romanticism NCLC 52: 305-71
overviews and general studies, 306-26
major figures, 326-40
Polish Romantic drama, 340-62
influences, 362-71

Politics and Literature TCLC 94: 138-61
overviews and general studies, 139-96
Europe, 196-226
Latin America, 226-48
Africa and the Caribbean, 248-60

Popular Literature TCLC 70: 279-382
overviews and general studies, 280-324
"formula" fiction, 324-336
readers of popular literature, 336-351
evolution of popular literature, 351-382

The Portrayal of Jews in Nineteenth-Century English Literature NCLC 72: 242-368
overviews and general studies, 244-77
Anglo-Jewish novels, 277-303
depictions by non-Jewish writers, 303-44
Hebraism versus Hellenism, 344-67

The Portrayal of Mormonism NCLC 96: 61-148
overview, 63-72
early Mormon literature, 72-100
Mormon periodicals and journals, 100-10
women writers, 110-22
Mormonism and nineteenth-century literature, 122-42
Mormon poetry, 142-47

Post-apartheid Literature CLC 187: 284-382
overviews and general studies, 286-318
the post-apartheid novel, 318-65
post-apartheid drama, 365-81

Postcolonial African Literature TCLC 146: 110-239
overviews and general studies, 111-45
ideology and theory, 145-62
postcolonial testimonial literature, 162-99
major authors, 199-239

Postcolonialism TCLC 114: 134-239
overviews and general studies, 135-153
African postcolonial writing, 153-72
Asian/Pacific literature, 172-78
postcolonial literary theory, 178-213
postcolonial women's writing, 213-38

Postmodernism TCLC 90:125-307
overview, 126-166
criticism, 166-224
fiction, 224-282
poetry, 282-300
drama, 300-307

Pragmatism in Nineteenth-Century Literature NCLC 168: 85-209
overviews, 86-133
pragmatism and literature, 133-52
Charles Sanders Peirce, 152-65
William James, 165-208

Pre-Raphaelite Movement NCLC 20: 302-401
overview, 302-4
genesis, 304-12
Germ and *Oxford and Cambridge Magazine,* 312-20
Robert Buchanan and the "Fleshly School of Poetry," 320-31
satires and parodies, 331-4
surveys, 334-51
aesthetics, 351-75
sister arts of poetry and painting, 375-94
influence, 394-9

Pre-romanticism LC 40: 1-56
overviews and general studies, 2-14
defining the period, 14-23
new directions in poetry and prose, 23-45
the focus on the self, 45-56

The Presentation of Literature in the Nineteenth Century NCLC 160: 159-226
book design, 160-71
gift books, 172-91
serial novels, 191-214
dime novels, 214-226

Pre-Socratic Philosophy CMLC 22: 1-56
overviews and general studies, 3-24
the Ionians and the Pythagoreans, 25-35
Heraclitus, the Eleatics, and the Atomists, 36-47
the Sophists, 47-55

The Prison in Nineteenth-Century Literature NCLC 116: 241-357
overview, 242-60
romantic prison, 260-78
domestic prison, 278-316
America as prison, 316-24
physical prisons and prison authors, 324-56

Protestant Hagiography and Martyrology LC 84: 106-217
overview, 106-37
John Foxe's *Book of Martyrs,* 137-97
martyrology and the feminine perspective, 198-216

Protestant Reformation, Literature of the LC 37: 1-83
overviews and general studies, 1-49
humanism and scholasticism, 49-69
the reformation and literature, 69-82

Psychoanalysis and Literature TCLC 38: 227-338
overviews and general studies, 227-46
Freud on literature, 246-51
psychoanalytic views of the literary process, 251-61
psychoanalytic theories of response to literature, 261-88
psychoanalysis and literary criticism, 288-312
psychoanalysis as literature/literature as psychoanalysis, 313-34

The Quarrel between the Ancients and the Moderns LC 63: 266-381
overviews and general studies, 267-301
Renaissance origins, 301-32
Quarrel between the Ancients and the Moderns in France, 332-58
Battle of the Books in England, 358-80

Racism in Literature TCLC 138: 257-373
overviews and general studies, 257-326
racism and literature by and about African Americans, 292-326
theme of racism in literature, 326-773

Rap Music CLC 76: 477-50

Reader-Response Criticism TCLC 146: 240-357
overviews and general studies, 241-88
critical approaches to reader response, 288-342
reader-response interpretation, 342-57

Realism in Short Fiction SSC 63: 128-57
overviews and general studies, 129-37
realist short fiction in France, 137-62
realist short fiction in Russia, 162-215
realist short fiction in England, 215-31
realist short fiction in the United States, 231-56

Regionalism and Local Color in Short Fiction SSC 65: 160-289
overviews and general studies, 163-205
regionalism/local color fiction of the west, 205-42
regionalism/local color fiction of the midwest, 242-57
regionalism/local color fiction of the south, 257-88

Renaissance Natural Philosophy LC 27: 201-87
cosmology, 201-28
astrology, 228-54
magic, 254-86

Representations of Africa in Nineteenth-Century Literature NCLC 148: 248-351
overview, 251-66
Northeast and Central Africa, 266-76
South Africa, 276-301
West Africa, 301-49

Representations of the Devil in Nineteenth-Century Literature NCLC 100: 89-223
overviews and general studies, 90-115
the Devil in American fiction, 116-43
English Romanticism: the satanic school, 143-89
Luciferian discourse in European literature, 189-222

Restoration Drama LC 21: 184-275
general overviews and general studies, 185-230

Jeremy Collier stage controversy, 230-9
other critical interpretations, 240-75

Revenge Tragedy LC 71: 113-242
overviews and general studies, 113-51
Elizabethan attitudes toward revenge, 151-88
the morality of revenge, 188-216
reminders and remembrance, 217-41

Revising the Literary Canon CLC 81: 465-509

Revising the Literary Canon TCLC 114: 240-84
overviews and general studies, 241-85
canon change in American literature, 285-339
gender and the literary canon, 339-59
minority and third-world literature and the canon, 359-84

Revolutionary Astronomers LC 51: 314-65
overviews and general studies, 316-25
principal figures, 325-51
Revolutionary astronomical models, 352-64

Robin Hood, Legend of LC 19: 205-58
origins and development of the Robin Hood legend, 206-20
representations of Robin Hood, 220-44
Robin Hood as hero, 244-56

Romance Fiction, Contemporary CLC 206: 178-271
overviews, 180-93
literary conventions, 193-215
opposing viewpoints, 215-20
reader response to Romance literature, 220-37
Romance literature in the world, 237-70

Romantic Literary Criticism NCLC 144: 203-357
background and overviews, 205-30
literary reviews, 230-38
the German Romantics, 238-81
Wordsworth and Coleridge, 281-326
variations on Romantic critical theory, 326-56

Rushdie, Salman, *Satanic Verses* **Controversy** CLC 55: 214-63; 59:404-56

Russian Nihilism NCLC 28: 403-47
definitions and overviews, 404-17
women and Nihilism, 417-27
literature as reform: the Civic Critics, 427-33
Nihilism and the Russian novel: Turgenev and Dostoevsky, 433-47

Russian Thaw TCLC 26: 189-247
literary history of the period, 190-206
theoretical debate of socialist realism, 206-11
Novy Mir, 211-7
Literary Moscow, 217-24
Pasternak, *Zhivago*, and the Nobel prize, 224-7
poetry of liberation, 228-31
Brodsky trial and the end of the Thaw, 231-6
achievement and influence, 236-46

Salem Witch Trials LC 38: 1-145
overviews and general studies, 2-30
historical background, 30-65
judicial background, 65-78
the search for causes, 78-115
the role of women in the trials, 115-44

Salinger, J. D., Controversy Surrounding *In Search of J. D. Salinger* CLC 55: 325-44

Samizdat Literature TCLC 150: 261-342
overviews and general studies, 262-64
history and development, 264-309
politics and Samizdat, 309-22
voices of Samizdat, 322-42

Sanitation Reform, Nineteenth-Century NCLC 124: 165-257
overviews and general studies, 166
primary texts, 186-89
social context, 189-221
public health in literature, 221-56

Science and Modern Literature TCLC 90: 308-419
overviews and general studies, 295-333
fiction, 333-95
poetry, 395-405
drama, 405-19

Science in Nineteenth-Century Literature NCLC 100: 224-366
overviews and general studies, 225-65
major figures, 265-336
sociopolitical concerns, 336-65

Science Fiction, Nineteenth-Century NCLC 24: 241-306
background, 242-50
definitions of the genre, 251-56
representative works and writers, 256-75
themes and conventions, 276-305

Scottish Chaucerians LC 20: 363-412

Scottish Poetry, Eighteenth-Century LC 29: 95-167
overviews and general studies, 96-114
the Scottish Augustans, 114-28
the Scots Vernacular Revival, 132-63
Scottish poetry after Burns, 163-66

The Sea in Literature TCLC 82: 72-191
drama, 73-9
poetry, 79-119
fiction, 119-91

The Sea in Nineteenth-Century English and American Literature NCLC 104: 265-362
overviews and general studies, 267-306
major figures in American sea fiction—Cooper and Melville, 306-29
American sea poetry and short stories, 329-45
English sea literature, 345-61

The Sensation Novel NCLC 80: 219-330
overviews and general studies, 221-46
principal figures, 246-62
nineteenth-century reaction, 262-91
feminist criticism, 291-329

The Sentimental Novel NCLC 60: 146-245
overviews and general studies, 147-58
the politics of domestic fiction, 158-79
a literature of resistance and repression, 179-212
the reception of sentimental fiction, 213-44

September 11 Attacks See Literature in Response to the September 11 Attacks

Sex and Literature TCLC 82: 192-434
overviews and general studies, 193-216
drama, 216-63
poetry, 263-87
fiction, 287-431

Sherlock Holmes Centenary TCLC 26: 248-310
Doyle's life and the composition of the Holmes stories, 248-59
life and character of Holmes, 259-78
method, 278-79
Holmes and the Victorian world, 279-92
Sherlockian scholarship, 292-301
Doyle and the development of the detective story, 301-07
Holmes's continuing popularity, 307-09

Short Science Fiction, Golden Age of, 1938-1950 SSC 73: 1-145
overviews and general studies, 3-48
publishing history of Golden Age Short Science Fiction, 48-65
major Golden Age Short Science Fiction authors and editors
Isaac Asimov, 65-77
Ray Bradbury, 77-92
John W. Campbell, 92-106
Arthur C. Clarke, 106-15
Robert A. Heinlein, 115-29
Damon Knight, 129-40
Frederik Pohl, 141-43

Short-Short Fiction SSC 61: 311-36
overviews and general studies, 312-19
major short-short fiction writers, 319-35

The Silver Fork Novel NCLC 88: 58-140
criticism, 59-139

Slave Narratives, American NCLC 20: 1-91
background, 2-9
overviews and general studies, 9-24
contemporary responses, 24-7
language, theme, and technique, 27-70
historical authenticity, 70-5
antecedents, 75-83
role in development of Black American literature, 83-8

The Slave Trade in British and American Literature LC 59: 283-369
overviews and general studies, 284-91
depictions by white writers, 291-331
depictions by former slaves, 331-67

Social Conduct Literature LC 55: 196-298
overviews and general studies, 196-223
prescriptive ideology in other literary forms, 223-38
role of the press, 238-63
impact of conduct literature, 263-87
conduct literature and the perception of women, 287-96
women writing for women, 296-98

Social Protest Literature of Victorian England NCLC 160: 227-359
overviews: protest in Victorian literature, 229-62
woman question, 262-304
condition-of-England novel, 304-58

Social Protest Literature Outside England, Nineteenth-Century NCLC 124: 258-350
overviews and general studies, 259-72
oppression revealed, 272-306
literature to incite or prevent reform, 306-50

Socialism NCLC 88: 141-237
origins, 142-54
French socialism, 154-83
Anglo-American socialism, 183-205
Socialist-Feminism, 205-36

Southern Gothic Literature TCLC 142: 186-270
overviews and general studies, 187-97
major authors in southern Gothic literature, 197-230
structure and technique in southern Gothic literature, 230-50
themes in southern Gothic literature, 250-70

Southern Literature, Contemporary CLC 167: 1-132
criticism, 2-131

Southern Literature of the Reconstruction NCLC 108: 289-369
overview, 290-91
reconstruction literature: the consequences of war, 291-321
old south to new: continuities in southern culture, 321-68

Southwestern Humor SSC 81: 105-248
overviews, 106-83
Mark Twain, 183-97

George Washington Harris, 197-208
other major figures, 208-46

Spanish Civil War Literature TCLC 26: 311-85
topics in, 312-33
British and American literature, 333-59
French literature, 359-62
Spanish literature, 362-73
German literature, 373-75
political idealism and war literature, 375-83

Spanish Golden Age Literature LC 23: 262-332
overviews and general studies, 263-81
verse drama, 281-304
prose fiction, 304-19
lyric poetry, 319-31

Sparta in Literature CMLC 70: 145-271
overviews, 147-61
Spartan poetry, 161-72
the Spartan myth, 172-200
historical background, 200-27
Spartan society and culture, 227-69

Spasmodic School of Poetry NCLC 24: 307-52
history and major figures, 307-21
the Spasmodics on poetry, 321-7
Firmilian and critical disfavor, 327-39
theme and technique, 339-47
influence, 347-51

Sports in Literature TCLC 86: 294-445
overviews and general studies, 295-324
major writers and works, 324-402
sports, literature, and social issues, 402-45

Steinbeck, John, Fiftieth Anniversary of *The Grapes of Wrath* CLC 59: 311-54

Sturm und Drang NCLC 40: 196-276
definitions, 197-238
poetry and poetics, 238-58
drama, 258-75

Supernatural Fiction in the Nineteenth Century NCLC 32: 207-87
major figures and influences, 208-35
the Victorian ghost story, 236-54
the influence of science and occultism, 254-66
supernatural fiction and society, 266-86

Supernatural Fiction, Modern TCLC 30: 59-116
evolution and varieties, 60-74
"decline" of the ghost story, 74-86
as a literary genre, 86-92
technique, 92-101
nature and appeal, 101-15

Surrealism TCLC 30: 334-406
history and formative influences, 335-43
manifestos, 343-54
philosophic, aesthetic, and political principles, 354-75
poetry, 375-81
novel, 381-6
drama, 386-92
film, 392-8
painting and sculpture, 398-403
achievement, 403-5

Surrealism in Children's Literature CLR 103: 127-200
overviews and general studies, 130-52
critical analysis of surrealist children's authors and works, 152-99

Sylvia Beach and Company TCLC 158: 281-370
overviews and general studies, 282-97
Shakespeare and Company, 297-314
the business of publishing, 315-40
Sylvia Beach and James Joyce, 341-70

Symbolism, Russian TCLC 30: 266-333
doctrines and major figures, 267-92
theories, 293-8
and French Symbolism, 298-310
themes in poetry, 310-4
theater, 314-20
and the fine arts, 320-32

Symbolist Movement, French NCLC 20: 169-249
background and characteristics, 170-86
principles, 186-91
attacked and defended, 191-7
influences and predecessors, 197-211
and Decadence, 211-6
theater, 216-26
prose, 226-33
decline and influence, 233-47

Television and Literature TCLC 78: 283-426
television and literacy, 283-98
reading vs. watching, 298-341
adaptations, 341-62
literary genres and television, 362-90
television genres and literature, 390-410
children's literature/children's television, 410-25

Theater of the Absurd TCLC 38: 339-415
"The Theater of the Absurd," 340-7
major plays and playwrights, 347-58
and the concept of the absurd, 358-86
theatrical techniques, 386-94
predecessors of, 394-402
influence of, 402-13

Tin Pan Alley See American Popular Song, Golden Age of

Tobacco Culture LC 55: 299-366
social and economic attitudes toward tobacco, 299-344
tobacco trade between the old world and the new world, 344-55
tobacco smuggling in Great Britain, 355-66

Transcendentalism, American NCLC 24: 1-99
overviews and general studies, 3-23
contemporary documents, 23-41
theological aspects of, 42-52
and social issues, 52-74
literature of, 74-96

Travel Narratives in Contemporary Literature CLC 204: 260-351
overviews, 261-76
major authors, 276-311
modern travel writing, 311-31
women writers and travel, 331-51

Travel Writing in the Nineteenth Century NCLC 44: 274-392
the European grand tour, 275-303
the Orient, 303-47
North America, 347-91
NCLC 168: 210-347
overviews, 212-43
women's travel writing, 243-311
other notable travel writers and their works, 312-47

Travel Writing in the Twentieth Century TCLC 30: 407-56
conventions and traditions, 407-27
and fiction writing, 427-43
comparative essays on travel writers, 443-54

Treatment of Death in Children's Literature CLR 101: 152-201
overviews and general studies, 155-80
analytical and bibliographical reviews of death in children's literature, 180-97
death of animals in children's literature, 197-200

Tristan and Isolde Legend CMLC 42: 311-404

Troubadours CMLC 66: 244-383
overviews, 245-91

politics, economics, history, and the troubadours, 291-344
troubadours and women, 344-82

True-Crime Literature CLC 99: 333-433
history and analysis, 334-407
reviews of true-crime publications, 407-23
writing instruction, 424-29
author profiles, 429-33

Twentieth-Century Danish Literature TCLC 142: 271-344
major works, 272-84
major authors, 284-344

***Ulysses* and the Process of Textual Reconstruction** TCLC 26:386-416
evaluations of the new *Ulysses*, 386-94
editorial principles and procedures, 394-401
theoretical issues, 401-16

Unconventional Family in Children's Literature CLR 102: 146-213
overviews and general studies, 149-79
analytical and bibliographical reviews, 179-97
types of unconventional families: foster, adopted, homosexual, 197-212

Utilitarianism NCLC 84: 272-340
J. S. Mill's Utilitarianism: liberty, equality, justice, 273-313
Jeremy Bentham's Utilitarianism: the science of happiness, 313-39

Utopianism NCLC 88: 238-346
overviews: Utopian literature, 239-59
Utopianism in American literature, 259-99
Utopianism in British literature, 299-311
Utopianism and Feminism, 311-45

Utopian Literature, Nineteenth-Century NCLC 24: 353-473
definitions, 354-74
overviews and general studies, 374-88
theory, 388-408
communities, 409-26
fiction, 426-53
women and fiction, 454-71

Utopian Literature, Renaissance LC 32: 1-63
overviews and general studies, 2-25
classical background, 25-33
utopia and the social contract, 33-9
origins in mythology, 39-48
utopia and the Renaissance country house, 48-52
influence of millenarianism, 52-62

Vampire in Literature TCLC 46: 391-454
origins and evolution, 392-412
social and psychological perspectives, 413-44
vampire fiction and science fiction, 445-53

Vernacular Bibles LC 67: 214-388
overviews and general studies, 215-59
the English Bible, 259-355
the German Bible, 355-88

Victorian Autobiography NCLC 40: 277-363
development and major characteristics, 278-88
themes and techniques, 289-313
the autobiographical tendency in Victorian prose and poetry, 313-47
Victorian women's autobiographies, 347-62
NCLC 152: 230-365
overviews and general studies, 232-61
autobiography and the self, 261-93
autobiography and gender, 293-307
autobiography and class, 307-36
autobiography and fiction, 336-64

Victorian Critical Theory NCLC 136: 236-379
overviews and general studies, 237-86
Matthew Arnold, 286-324

Walter Pater and aestheticism, 324-36
other Victorian critics, 336-78

Victorian Fantasy Literature NCLC 60: 246-384
overviews and general studies, 247-91
major figures, 292-366
women in Victorian fantasy literature, 366-83

Victorian Hellenism NCLC 68: 251-376
overviews and general studies, 252-78
the meanings of Hellenism, 278-335
the literary influence, 335-75

Victorian Illustrated Fiction NCLC 120: 247-356
overviews and development, 128-76
technical and material aspects of book illustration, 276-84
Charles Dickens and his illustrators, 284-320
William Makepeace Thackeray, 320-31
George Eliot and Frederic Leighton, 331-51
Lewis Carroll and John Tenniel, 351-56

Victorian Novel NCLC 32: 288-454
development and major characteristics, 290-310
themes and techniques, 310-58
social criticism in the Victorian novel, 359-97
urban and rural life in the Victorian novel, 397-406
women in the Victorian novel, 406-25
Mudie's Circulating Library, 425-34
the late-Victorian novel, 434-51

Vietnamese Literature TCLC 102: 322-386

Vietnam War in Literature and Film CLC 91: 383-437
overview, 384-8
prose, 388-412
film and drama, 412-24
poetry, 424-35

The Vietnam War in Short Fiction SSC 79: 83-177
overviews and general studies, 84-93
women authors of Vietnam War short fiction, 93-116
Robert Olen Butler: *A Good Scent from a Strange Mountain* (1992), 116-31
Barry Hannah: *Airships* (1978), 131-50
Tim O'Brien: *The Things They Carried* (1990), 150-65
Tobias Wolff: *Back in the World* (1985), 165-69
other authors and works, 169-76

Violence in Literature TCLC 98: 235-358
overviews and general studies, 236-74
violence in the works of modern authors, 274-358

Vorticism TCLC 62: 330-426
Wyndham Lewis and Vorticism, 330-8
characteristics and principles of Vorticism, 338-65
Lewis and Pound, 365-82
Vorticist writing, 382-416
Vorticist painting, 416-26

The Well-Made Play NCLC 80: 331-370
overviews and general studies, 332-45
Scribe's style, 345-56
the influence of the well-made play, 356-69

Women's Autobiography, Nineteenth Century NCLC 76: 285-368
overviews and general studies, 287-300
autobiographies concerned with religious and political issues, 300-15
autobiographies by women of color, 315-38
autobiographies by women pioneers, 338-51
autobiographies by women of letters, 351-68

Women's Diaries, Nineteenth-Century NCLC 48: 308-54
overview, 308-13
diary as history, 314-25
sociology of diaries, 325-34
diaries as psychological scholarship, 334-43
diary as autobiography, 343-8
diary as literature, 348-53

Women in Modern Literature TCLC 94: 262-425
overviews and general studies, 263-86
American literature, 286-304
other national literatures, 304-33
fiction, 333-94
poetry, 394-407
drama, 407-24

Women Writers, Seventeenth-Century LC 30: 2-58
overview, 2-15
women and education, 15-9
women and autobiography, 19-31
women's diaries, 31-9
early feminists, 39-58

World War I Literature TCLC 34: 392-486
overview, 393-403
English, 403-27
German, 427-50
American, 450-66
French, 466-74
and modern history, 474-82

World War I Short Fiction SSC 71: 187-347
overviews and general studies, 187-206
female short fiction writers of World War I, 206-36
Central Powers
  Czechoslovakian writers of short fiction, 236-44
  German writers of short fiction, 244-61
Entente/Allied Alliance
  Australian writers of short fiction, 261-73
  English writers of short fiction, 273-305
  French writers of short fiction, 305-11
Associated Power: American writers of short fiction, 311-46

Yellow Journalism NCLC 36: 383-456
overviews and general studies, 384-96
major figures, 396-413

Yiddish Literature TCLC 130: 229-364
overviews and general studies, 230-54
major authors, 254-305
Yiddish literature in America, 305-34
Yiddish and Judaism, 334-64

Young Playwrights Festival
1988 CLC 55: 376-81
1989 CLC 59: 398-403
1990 CLC 65: 444-8

TCLC Cumulative Nationality Index

AMERICAN

Abbey, Edward **160**
Adams, Andy **56**
Adams, Brooks **80**
Adams, Henry (Brooks) **4, 52**
Addams, Jane **76**
Agee, James (Rufus) **1, 19**
Aldrich, Bess (Genevra) Streeter **125**
Allen, Fred **87**
Anderson, Maxwell **2, 144**
Anderson, Sherwood **1, 10, 24, 123**
Anthony, Susan B(rownell) **84**
Atherton, Gertrude (Franklin Horn) **2**
Austin, Mary (Hunter) **25**
Baker, Ray Stannard **47**
Baker, Carlos (Heard) **119**
Bambara, Toni Cade **116**
Barry, Philip **11**
Baum, L(yman) Frank **7, 132**
Beard, Charles A(ustin) **15**
Becker, Carl (Lotus) **63**
Belasco, David **3**
Bell, James Madison **43**
Benchley, Robert (Charles) **1, 55**
Benedict, Ruth (Fulton) **60**
Benét, Stephen Vincent **7**
Benét, William Rose **28**
Bettelheim, Bruno **143**
Bierce, Ambrose (Gwinett) **1, 7, 44**
Biggers, Earl Derr **65**
Bishop, Elizabeth **121**
Bishop, John Peale **103**
Black Elk **33**
Boas, Franz **56**
Bodenheim, Maxwell **44**
Bok, Edward W. **101**
Bourne, Randolph S(illiman) **16**
Boyd, James **115**
Boyd, Thomas (Alexander) **111**
Bradford, Gamaliel **36**
Brautigan, Richard **133**
Brennan, Christopher John **17**
Brennan, Maeve **124**
Brodkey, Harold (Roy) **123**
Bromfield, Louis (Brucker) **11**
Broun, Heywood **104**
Bryan, William Jennings **99**
Burroughs, Edgar Rice **2, 32**
Burroughs, William S(eward) **121**
Cabell, James Branch **6**
Cable, George Washington **4**
Cahan, Abraham **71**
Caldwell, Erskine (Preston) **117**
Campbell, Joseph **140**
Capote, Truman **164**
Cardozo, Benjamin N(athan) **65**
Carnegie, Dale **53**
Cather, Willa (Sibert) **1, 11, 31, 99, 132, 152**
Chambers, Robert W(illiam) **41**
Chambers, (David) Whittaker **129**
Chandler, Raymond (Thornton) **1, 7**
Chapman, John Jay **7**
Chase, Mary Ellen **124**
Chesnutt, Charles W(addell) **5, 39**
Childress, Alice **116**
Chopin, Katherine **5, 14, 127**
Cobb, Irvin S(hrewsbury) **77**
Coffin, Robert P(eter) Tristram **95**
Cohan, George M(ichael) **60**
Comstock, Anthony **13**
Cotter, Joseph Seamon Sr. **28**
Cram, Ralph Adams **45**
Crane, (Harold) Hart **2, 5, 80**
Crane, Stephen (Townley) **11, 17, 32**
Crawford, F(rancis) Marion **10**
Crothers, Rachel **19**
Cullen, Countée **4, 37**
Cummings, E. E. **137**
Darrow, Clarence (Seward) **81**
Davis, Rebecca (Blaine) Harding **6**
Davis, Richard Harding **24**
Day, Clarence (Shepard Jr.) **25**
Dent, Lester **72**
De Voto, Bernard (Augustine) **29**
Dewey, John **95**
Dickey, James **151**
Dixon, Thomas, Jr. **163**
di Donato, Pietro **159**
Dreiser, Theodore (Herman Albert) **10, 18, 35, 83**
Du Bois, W. E. B. **169**
Dulles, John Foster **72**
Dunbar, Paul Laurence **2, 12**
Duncan, Isadora **68**
Dunne, Finley Peter **28**
Eastman, Charles A(lexander) **55**
Eddy, Mary (Ann Morse) Baker **71**
Einstein, Albert **65**
Erskine, John **84**
Faulkner, William **141**
Faust, Frederick (Schiller) **49**
Fenollosa, Ernest (Francisco) **91**
Fields, W. C. **80**
Fisher, Dorothy (Frances) Canfield **87**
Fisher, Rudolph **11**
Fisher, Vardis **140**
Fitzgerald, F(rancis) Scott (Key) **1, 6, 14, 28, 55, 157**
Fitzgerald, Zelda (Sayre) **52**
Fletcher, John Gould **35**
Foote, Mary Hallock **108**
Ford, Henry **73**
Forten, Charlotte L. **16**
Freeman, Douglas Southall **11**
Freeman, Mary E(leanor) Wilkins **9**
Fuller, Henry Blake **103**
Futrelle, Jacques **19**
Gale, Zona **7**
Garland, (Hannibal) Hamlin **3**
Gilman, Charlotte (Anna) Perkins (Stetson) **9, 37, 117**
Ginsberg, Allen **120**
Glasgow, Ellen (Anderson Gholson) **2, 7**
Glaspell, Susan **55, 175**
Goldman, Emma **13**
Green, Anna Katharine **63**
Grey, Zane **6**
Griffith, D(avid Lewelyn) W(ark) **68**
Griggs, Sutton (Elbert) **77**
Guest, Edgar A(lbert) **95**
Guiney, Louise Imogen **41**
Haley, Alex **147**
Hall, James Norman **23**
Handy, W(illiam) C(hristopher) **97**
Harper, Frances Ellen Watkins **14**
Harris, Joel Chandler **2**
Harte, (Francis) Bret(t) **1, 25**
Hartmann, Sadakichi **73**
Hatteras, Owen **18**
Hawthorne, Julian **25**
Hearn, (Patricio) Lafcadio (Tessima Carlos) **9**
Hecht, Ben **101**
Heller, Joseph **131, 151**
Hellman, Lillian (Florence) **119**
Hemingway, Ernest (Miller) **115**
Henry, O. **1, 19**
Hergesheimer, Joseph **11**
Heyward, (Edwin) DuBose **59**
Higginson, Thomas Wentworth **36**
Himes, Chester **139**
Holley, Marietta **99**
Holly, Buddy **65**
Holmes, Oliver Wendell Jr. **77**
Hopkins, Pauline Elizabeth **28**
Horney, Karen (Clementine Theodore Danielsen) **71**
Howard, Robert E(rvin) **8**
Howe, Julia Ward **21**
Howells, William Dean **7, 17, 41**
Huneker, James Gibbons **65**
Hurston, Zora Neale **121, 131**
Ince, Thomas H. **89**
James, Henry **2, 11, 24, 40, 47, 64, 171**
James, William **15, 32**
Jarrell, Randall **177**
Jewett, (Theodora) Sarah Orne **1, 22**
Johnson, James Weldon **3, 19, 175**
Johnson, Robert **69**
Kerouac, Jack **117**
Kinsey, Alfred C(harles) **91**
Kirk, Russell (Amos) **119**
Kornbluth, C(yril) M. **8**
Korzybski, Alfred (Habdank Skarbek) **61**
Kubrick, Stanley **112**
Kuttner, Henry **10**
Lane, Rose Wilder **177**
Lardner, Ring(gold) W(ilmer) **2, 14**
Lewis, (Harry) Sinclair **4, 13, 23, 39**
Lewisohn, Ludwig **19**
Lewton, Val **76**
Lindsay, (Nicholas) Vachel **17**
Locke, Alain (Le Roy) **43**
Lockridge, Ross (Franklin) Jr. **111**
London, Jack **9, 15, 39**
Lorde, Audre **173**
Lovecraft, H(oward) P(hillips) **4, 22**
Lowell, Amy **1, 8**
Malamud, Bernard **129**

447

Mankiewicz, Herman (Jacob) **85**
March, William **96**
Markham, Edwin **47**
Marquis, Don(ald Robert Perry) **7**
Masters, Edgar Lee **2, 25**
Matthews, (James) Brander **95**
Matthiessen, F(rancis) O(tto) **100**
McAlmon, Robert (Menzies) **97**
McCoy, Horace (Stanley) **28**
McCullers, Carson **155**
Mead, George Herbert **89**
Mencken, H(enry) L(ouis) **13**
Merrill, James **173**
Micheaux, Oscar (Devereaux) **76**
Millay, Edna St. Vincent **4, 49, 169**
Mitchell, Margaret (Munnerlyn) **11**
Mitchell, S(ilas) Weir **36**
Mitchell, William **81**
Monroe, Harriet **12**
Moody, William Vaughan **105**
Morley, Christopher (Darlington) **87**
Morris, Wright **107**
Muir, John **28**
Murfree, Mary Noailles **135**
Nash, (Frediric) Ogden **109**
Nathan, George Jean **18**
Nemerov, Howard (Stanley) **124F**
Neumann, Alfred **100**
Nisbet, Robert A(lexander) **117**
Nordhoff, Charles (Bernard) **23**
Norris, (Benjamin) Frank(lin Jr.) **24, 155**
O'Connor, Flannery **132**
O'Neill, Eugene (Gladstone) **1, 6, 27, 49**
Oppen, George **107**
Osbourne, Lloyd **93**
Oskison, John Milton **35**
Park, Robert E(zra) **73**
Parker, Dorothy **143**
Patton, George S(mith) Jr. **79**
Peirce, Charles Sanders **81**
Percy, William Alexander **84**
Petry, Ann (Lane) **112**
Phelps, Elizabeth Stuart **113**
Phillips, David Graham **44**
Portillo Trambley, Estela **163**
Post, Melville Davisson **39**
Pulitzer, Joseph **76**
Pyle, Ernie **75**
Pyle, Howard **81**
Rawlings, Marjorie Kinnan **4**
Reed, John (Silas) **9**
Reich, Wilhelm **57**
Remington, Frederic **89**
Rhodes, Eugene Manlove **53**
Riggs, (Rolla) Lynn **56**
Riis, Jacob A(ugust) **80**
Riley, James Whitcomb **51**
Rinehart, Mary Roberts **52**
Roberts, Elizabeth Madox **68**
Roberts, Kenneth (Lewis) **23**
Robinson, Edwin Arlington **5, 101**
Rogers, Carl **125**
Rogers, Will(iam Penn Adair) **8, 71**
Roosevelt, Franklin Delano **93**
Roosevelt, Theodore **69**
Rourke, Constance (Mayfield) **12**
Runyon, (Alfred) Damon **10**
Saltus, Edgar (Everton) **8**
Santayana, George **40**
Santmyer, Helen Hooven **133**
Santos, Bienvenido N. **156**
Sapir, Edward **108**
Saroyan, William **137**
Schoenberg, Arnold Franz Walter **75**
Shepherd, Jean **177**
Sherwood, Robert E(mmet) **3**
Sinclair, Upton **160**
Slesinger, Tess **10**
Stanton, Elizabeth Cady **73**
Steffens, (Joseph) Lincoln **20**
Stein, Gertrude **1, 6, 28, 48**
Steinbeck, John **135**

Sterling, George **20**
Stevens, Wallace **3, 12, 45**
Stockton, Frank R. **47**
Stroheim, Erich von **71**
Strunk, William Jr. **92**
Sturges, Preston **48**
Tarbell, Ida M(inerva) **40**
Tarkington, (Newton) Booth **9**
Taylor, Frederick Winslow **76**
Teasdale, Sara **4**
Tesla, Nikola **88**
Thomas, Augustus **97**
Thomas, M. Carey **89**
Thorndike, Edward L(ee) **107**
Thurman, Wallace (Henry) **6**
Toomer, Jean **172**
Torrence, Ridgely **97**
Twain, Mark **6, 12, 19, 36, 48, 59, 161**
Van Doren, Carl (Clinton) **18**
Veblen, Thorstein B(unde) **31**
Villard, Oswald Garrison **160**
Walker, Margaret **129**
Washington, Booker T(aliaferro) **10**
Wells, Carolyn **35**
Wells-Barnett, Ida B(ell) **125**
West, Dorothy **108**
West, Nathanael **1, 14, 44**
Whale, James **63**
Wharton, Edith (Newbold Jones) **3, 9, 27, 53, 129, 149**
White, Walter F(rancis) **15**
Williams, Ben Ames **89**
Williams, Hank **81**
Wilson, (Thomas) Woodrow **79**
Wirth, Louis **92**
Wister, Owen **21**
Wolfe, Thomas (Clayton) **4, 13, 29, 61**
Woodberry, George Edward **73**
Woollcott, Alexander (Humphreys) **5**
Wright, Frank Lloyd **95**
Wright, Richard **136**
Wylie, Elinor (Morton Hoyt) **8**

ARGENTINIAN

Arlt, Roberto (Godofredo Christophersen) **29**
Borges, Jorge Luis **109**
Güiraldes, Ricardo (Guillermo) **39**
Hudson, W(illiam) H(enry) **29**
Lugones, Leopoldo **15**
Storni, Alfonsina **5**

AUSTRALIAN

Baynton, Barbara **57**
Franklin, (Stella Maria Sarah) Miles (Lampe) **7**
Furphy, Joseph **25**
Ingamells, Rex **35**
Lawson, Henry (Archibald Hertzberg) **27**
Paterson, A(ndrew) B(arton) **32**
Warung, Price **45**
White, Patrick **176**

AUSTRIAN

Beer-Hofmann, Richard **60**
Bernhard, Thomas **165**
Broch, Hermann **20**
Brod, Max **115**
Freud, Sigmund **52**
Hayek, F(riedrich) A(ugust von) **109**
Hofmannsthal, Hugo von **11**
Kafka, Franz **2, 6, 13, 29, 47, 53, 112**
Kraus, Karl **5**
Kubin, Alfred (Leopold Isidor) **23**
Meyrink, Gustav **21**
Musil, Robert (Edler von) **12, 68**
Pabst, G. W. **127**
Perutz, Leo(pold) **60**
Rank, Otto **115**
Roth, (Moses) Joseph **33**
Schnitzler, Arthur **4**
Steiner, Rudolf **13**

Stroheim, Erich von **71**
Trakl, Georg **5**
Weininger, Otto **84**
Werfel, Franz (Viktor) **8**
Zweig, Stefan **17**

BELGIAN

Bosschere, Jean de **19**
Lemonnier, (Antoine Louis) Camille **22**
Maeterlinck, Maurice **3**
Sarton, May (Eleanor) **120**
van Ostaijen, Paul **33**
Verhaeren, Émile (Adolphe Gustave) **12**

BRAZILIAN

Cunha, Euclides (Rodrigues Pimenta) da **24**
Drummond de Andrade, Carlos **139**
Lima Barreto, Afonso Henrique de **23**
Machado de Assis, Joaquim Maria **10**
Ramos, Graciliano **32**

BULGARIAN

Vazov, Ivan (Minchov) **25**

CANADIAN

Campbell, Wilfred **9**
Carman, (William) Bliss **7**
Carr, Emily **32**
Connor, Ralph **31**
Drummond, William Henry **25**
Duncan, Sara Jeannette **60**
Engel, Marian **137**
Frye, Northrup **165**
Garneau, (Hector de) Saint-Denys **13**
Innis, Harold Adams **77**
Knister, Raymond **56**
Leacock, Stephen (Butler) **2**
Lewis, (Percy) Wyndham **2, 9, 104**
McCrae, John **12**
Montgomery, L(ucy) M(aud) **51, 140**
Nelligan, Emile **14**
Pickthall, Marjorie L(owry) C(hristie) **21**
Roberts, Charles G(eorge) D(ouglas) **8**
Scott, Duncan Campbell **6**
Service, Robert W(illiam) **15**
Seton, Ernest (Evan) Thompson **31**
Stringer, Arthur **37**
Wetherald, Agnes Ethelwyn **81**

CHILEAN

Donoso, José **133**
Godoy Alcayaga, Lucila **2**
Huidobro Fernandez, Vicente Garcia **31**
Prado (Calvo), Pedro **75**

CHINESE

Lin, Yutang **149**
Liu, E. **15**
Lu Hsun **3**
Su Man-shu **24**
Wen I-to **28**

COLOMBIAN

Rivera, José Eustasio **35**

CUBAN

Sarduy, Servero **167**

CZECH

Brod, Max **115**
Chapek, Karel **6, 37**
Freud, Sigmund **52**
Hasek, Jaroslav (Matej Frantisek) **4**
Hrabal, Bohumil **155**
Kafka, Franz **2, 6, 13, 29, 47, 53, 112**
Nezval, Vitezslav **44**

DANISH

Brandes, Georg (Morris Cohen) **10**
Hansen, Martin A(lfred) **32**
Jensen, Johannes V. **41**
Nexo, Martin Andersen **43**
Pontoppidan, Henrik **29**

DUTCH

Bok, Edward W. **101**
Couperus, Louis (Marie Anne) **15**
Heijermans, Herman **24**
Hillesum, Etty **49**
van Schendel, Arthur(-Francois-Émile) **56**

ENGLISH

Abbott, Edwin **139**
Abercrombie, Lascelles **141**
Alexander, Samuel **77**
Barbellion, W. N. P. **24**
Baring, Maurice **8**
Baring-Gould, Sabine **88**
Beerbohm, (Henry) Max(imilian) **1, 24**
Bell, Gertrude (Margaret Lowthian) **67**
Belloc, (Joseph) Hilaire (Pierre Sebastien Rene Swanton) **7, 18**
Bennett, (Enoch) Arnold **5, 20**
Benson, A.C. **123**
Benson, E(dward) F(rederic) **27**
Benson, Stella **17**
Bentley, E(dmund) C(lerihew) **12**
Beresford, J(ohn) D(avys) **81**
Besant, Annie (Wood) **9**
Blackmore, R(ichard) D(oddridge) **27**
Blackwood, Algernon (Henry) **5**
Bolt, Robert **175**
Bottomley, Gordon **107**
Bowen, Elizabeth **148**
Braddon, Mary Elizabeth **111**
Bramah, Ernest **72**
Bridges, Robert (Seymour) **1**
Brooke, Rupert (Chawner) **2, 7**
Buchanan, Robert **107**
Burke, Thomas **63**
Butler, Samuel **1, 33**
Butts, Mary **77**
Byron, Robert **67**
Caine, Hall **97**
Carpenter, Edward **88**
Carter, Angela **139**
Chesterton, G(ilbert) K(eith) **1, 6, 64**
Childers, (Robert) Erskine **65**
Churchill, Winston (Leonard Spencer) **113**
Clark, Kenneth Mackenzie **147**
Coleridge, Mary E(lizabeth) **73**
Collier, John **127**
Collingwood, R(obin) G(eorge) **67**
Conrad, Joseph **1, 6, 13, 25, 43, 57**
Coppard, A(lfred) E(dgar) **5**
Corelli, Marie **51**
Crofts, Freeman Wills **55**
Crowley, Aleister **7**
Dahl, Roald **173**
Dale, Colin **18**
Davies, William Henry **5**
Delafield, E. M. **61**
de la Mare, Walter (John) **4, 53**
Dobson, Austin **79**
Doughty, Charles M(ontagu) **27**
Douglas, Keith (Castellain) **40**
Dowson, Ernest (Christopher) **4**
Doyle, Arthur Conan **7**
Drinkwater, John **57**
Dunsany **2, 59**
Eddison, E(ric) R(ucker) **15**
Elaine **18**
Elizabeth **41**
Ellis, (Henry) Havelock **14**
Firbank, (Arthur Annesley) Ronald **1**
Flecker, (Herman) James Elroy **43**
Ford, Ford Madox **1, 15, 39, 57, 172**
Forester, C(ecil) S(cott) **152**
Forster, E(dward) M(organ) **125**
Freeman, R(ichard) Austin **21**
Galsworthy, John **1, 45**
Gilbert, W(illiam) S(chwenck) **3**
Gill, Eric **85**
Gissing, George (Robert) **3, 24, 47**
Glyn, Elinor **72**
Gosse, Edmund (William) **28**
Grahame, Kenneth **64, 136**
Granville-Barker, Harley **2**
Gray, John (Henry) **19**
Gurney, Ivor (Bertie) **33**
Haggard, H(enry) Rider **11**
Hall, (Marguerite) Radclyffe **12**
Hardy, Thomas **4, 10, 18, 32, 48, 53, 72, 143, 153**
Henley, William Ernest **8**
Hilton, James **21**
Hodgson, William Hope **13**
Hope, Anthony **83**
Housman, A(lfred) E(dward) **1, 10**
Housman, Laurence **7**
Hudson, W(illiam) H(enry) **29**
Hulme, T(homas) E(rnest) **21**
Hunt, Violet **53**
Jacobs, W(illiam) W(ymark) **22**
James, Montague (Rhodes) **6**
Jerome, Jerome K(lapka) **23**
Johnson, Lionel (Pigot) **19**
Kaye-Smith, Sheila **20**
Keynes, John Maynard **64**
Kipling, (Joseph) Rudyard **8, 17, 167**
Laski, Harold J(oseph) **79**
Lawrence, D(avid) H(erbert Richards) **2, 9, 16, 33, 48, 61, 93**
Lawrence, T(homas) E(dward) **18**
Lee, Vernon **5**
Lee-Hamilton, Eugene (Jacob) **22**
Leverson, Ada **18**
Lindsay, David **15**
Lowndes, Marie Adelaide (Belloc) **12**
Lowry, (Clarence) Malcolm **6, 40**
Lucas, E(dward) V(errall) **73**
Macaulay, (Emilie) Rose **7, 44**
MacCarthy, (Charles Otto) Desmond **36**
Mackenzie, Compton (Edward Montague) **116**
Maitland, Frederic William **65**
Manning, Frederic **25**
Marsh, Edward **99**
McTaggart, John McTaggart Ellis **105**
Meredith, George **17, 43**
Mew, Charlotte (Mary) **8**
Meynell, Alice (Christina Gertrude Thompson) **6**
Middleton, Richard (Barham) **56**
Milne, A(lan) A(lexander) **6, 88**
Moore, G. E. **89**
Morrison, Arthur **72**
Muggeridge, Thomas (Malcom) **120**
Murdoch, Iris **171**
Murry, John Middleton **16**
Myers, L(eopold) H(amilton) **59**
Nightingale, Florence **85**
Naipaul, Shiva(dhar) (Srinivasa) **153**
Noyes, Alfred **7**
Oppenheim, E(dward) Phillips **45**
Orage, Alfred Richard **157**
Orton, Joe **157**
Orwell, George **2, 6, 15, 31, 51, 128, 129**
Osborne, John **153**
Owen, Wilfred (Edward Salter) **5, 27**
Pankhurst, Emmeline (Goulden) **100**
Pinero, Arthur Wing **32**
Powys, T(heodore) F(rancis) **9**
Quiller-Couch, Arthur (Thomas) **53**
Richardson, Dorothy Miller **3**
Rolfe, Frederick (William Serafino Austin Lewis Mary) **12**
Rosenberg, Isaac **12**
Ruskin, John **20**
Sabatini, Rafael **47**
Saintsbury, George (Edward Bateman) **31**
Sapper **44**
Sayers, Dorothy L(eigh) **2, 15**
Shiel, M(atthew) P(hipps) **8**
Sinclair, May **3, 11**
Stapledon, (William) Olaf **22**
Stead, William Thomas **48**
Stephen, Leslie **23**
Strachey, (Giles) Lytton **12**
Summers, (Alphonsus Joseph-Mary Augustus) Montague **16**
Sutro, Alfred **6**
Swinburne, Algernon Charles **8, 36**
Symons, Arthur **11**
Thomas, (Philip) Edward **10**
Thompson, Francis (Joseph) **4**
Tolkien, J. R. R. **137**
Tomlinson, H(enry) M(ajor) **71**
Trotter, Wilfred **97**
Upward, Allen **85**
Van Druten, John (William) **2**
Wakefield, Herbert (Russell) **120**
Wallace, (Richard Horatio) Edgar **57**
Wallas, Graham **91**
Walpole, Hugh (Seymour) **5**
Ward, Mary Augusta **55**
Warner, Sylvia Townsend **131**
Warung, Price **45**
Webb, Mary Gladys (Meredith) **24**
Webb, Sidney (James) **22**
Welch, (Maurice) Denton **22**
Wells, H(erbert) G(eorge) **6, 12, 19, 133**
Whitehead, Alfred North **97**
Williams, Charles (Walter Stansby) **1, 11**
Wodehouse, P(elham) G(renville) **108**
Woolf, (Adeline) Virginia **1, 5, 20, 43, 56, 101, 128**
Yonge, Charlotte (Mary) **48**
Zangwill, Israel **16**

ESTONIAN

Talvik, Heiti **87**
Tammsaare, A(nton) H(ansen) **27**

FILIPINO

Villa, José García **176**

FINNISH

Leino, Eino **24**
Soedergran, Edith (Irene) **31**
Westermarck, Edward **87**

FRENCH

Alain **41**
Apollinaire, Guillaume **3, 8, 51**
Arp, Jean **115**
Artaud, Antonin (Marie Joseph) **3, 36**
Bachelard, Gaston **128**
Barbusse, Henri **5**
Barrès, (Auguste-)Maurice **47**
Barthes, Roland **135**
Bataille, Georges **155**
Benda, Julien **60**
Bergson, Henri(-Louis) **32**
Bernanos, (Paul Louis) Georges **3**
Bernhardt, Sarah (Henriette Rosine) **75**
Bloy, Léon **22**
Bourget, Paul (Charles Joseph) **12**
Claudel, Paul (Louis Charles Marie) **2, 10**
Cocteau, Jean (Maurice Eugene Clement) **119**
Colette, (Sidonie-Gabrielle) **1, 5, 16**
Coppee, Francois **25**
Crevel, Rene **112**
Daumal, Rene **14**
Deleuze, Gilles **116**
Desnos, Robert **22**
Drieu la Rochelle, Pierre(-Eugène) **21**
Dujardin, Edouard (Emile Louis) **13**
Durkheim, Emile **55**
Epstein, Jean **92**

Fargue, Leon-Paul **11**
Feydeau, Georges (Léon Jules Marie) **22**
Fondane, Benjamin **159**
Genet, Jean **128**
Gide, André (Paul Guillaume) **5, 12, 36, 177**
Giono, Jean **124**
Giraudoux, Jean(-Hippolyte) **2, 7**
Gourmont, Remy(-Marie-Charles) de **17**
Halévy, Elie **104**
Huysmans, Joris-Karl **7, 69**
Jacob, (Cyprien-)Max **6**
Jammes, Francis **75**
Jarry, Alfred **2, 14, 147**
Larbaud, Valery (Nicolas) **9**
Léautaud, Paul **83**
Leblanc, Maurice (Marie Emile) **49**
Leroux, Gaston **25**
Lyotard, Jean-François **103**
Martin du Gard, Roger **24**
Melies, Georges **81**
Merlau-Ponty, Maurice **156**
Mirbeau, Octave **55**
Mistral, Frédéric **51**
Nizan, Paul **40**
Péguy, Charles (Pierre) **10**
Péret, Benjamin **20**
Proust, (Valentin-Louis-George-Eugène-)Marcel **7, 13, 33, 161**
Radiguet, Raymond **29**
Renard, Jules **17**
Rolland, Romain **23**
Rostand, Edmond (Eugene Alexis) **6, 37**
Roussel, Raymond **20**
Saint-Exupéry, Antoine (Jean Baptiste Marie Roger) de **2, 56, 169**
Schwob, Marcel (Mayer André) **20**
Sorel, Georges **91**
Sully Prudhomme, René-François-Armand **31**
Teilhard de Chardin, (Marie Joseph) Pierre **9**
Tzara, Tristan **168**
Valéry, (Ambroise) Paul (Toussaint Jules) **4, 15**
Vallette, Marguerite Eymery **67**
Verne, Jules (Gabriel) **6, 52**
Vian, Boris **9**
Weil, Simone (Adolphine) **23**
Zola, Émile (Édouard Charles Antoine) **1, 6, 21, 41**

GERMAN

Adorno, Theodor W(iesengrund) **111**
Andreas-Salome, Lou **56**
Arp, Jean **115**
Auerbach, Erich **43**
Ball, Hugo **104**
Barlach, Ernst (Heinrich) **84**
Benjamin, Walter **39**
Benn, Gottfried **3**
Borchert, Wolfgang **5**
Brecht, (Eugen) Bertolt (Friedrich) **1, 6, 13, 35, 169**
Carossa, Hans **48**
Cassirer, Ernst **61**
Doeblin, Alfred **13**
Einstein, Albert **65**
Ewers, Hanns Heinz **12**
Feuchtwanger, Lion **3**
Frank, Bruno **81**
George, Stefan (Anton) **2, 14**
Goebbels, (Paul) Joseph **68**
Haeckel, Ernst Heinrich (Philipp August) **83**
Hauptmann, Gerhart (Johann Robert) **4**
Heym, Georg (Theodor Franz Arthur) **9**
Heyse, Paul (Johann Ludwig von) **8**
Hitler, Adolf **53**
Horkheimer, Max **132**
Horney, Karen (Clementine Theodore Danielsen) **71**
Huch, Ricarda (Octavia) **13**
Husserl, Edmund (Gustav Albrecht) **100**
Kaiser, Georg **9**
Klabund **44**
Kolmar, Gertrud **40**
Lasker-Schueler, Else **57**
Liliencron, (Friedrich Adolf Axel) Detlev von **18**
Luxemburg, Rosa **63**
Mann, (Luiz) Heinrich **9**
Mann, (Paul) Thomas **2, 8, 14, 21, 35, 44, 60, 168**
Mannheim, Karl **65**
Michels, Robert **88**
Morgenstern, Christian (Otto Josef Wolfgang) **8**
Neumann, Alfred **100**
Nietzsche, Friedrich (Wilhelm) **10, 18, 55**
Ophuls, Max **79**
Otto, Rudolf **85**
Plumpe, Friedrich Wilhelm **53**
Raabe, Wilhelm (Karl) **45**
Rilke, Rainer Maria **1, 6, 19**
Schreber, Daniel Paul **123**
Schwitters, Kurt (Hermann Edward Karl Julius) **95**
Simmel, Georg **64**
Spengler, Oswald (Arnold Gottfried) **25**
Sternheim, (William Adolf) Carl **8**
Strauss, Leo **141**
Sudermann, Hermann **15**
Toller, Ernst **10**
Vaihinger, Hans **71**
von Hartmann, Eduard **96**
Wassermann, (Karl) Jakob **6**
Weber, Max **69**
Wedekind, (Benjamin) Frank(lin) **7**
Wiene, Robert **56**

GHANIAN

Casely-Hayford, J(oseph) E(phraim) **24**

GREEK

Cavafy, C(onstantine) P(eter) **2, 7**
Kazantzakis, Nikos **2, 5, 33**
Palamas, Kostes **5**
Papadiamantis, Alexandros **29**
Sikelianos, Angelos **39**

HAITIAN

Roumain, Jacques (Jean Baptiste) **19**

HUNGARIAN

Ady, Endre **11**
Babits, Mihaly **14**
Csath, Geza **13**
Herzl, Theodor **36**
Horváth, Ödön von **45**
Jozsef, Attila **22**
Karinthy, Frigyes **47**
Mikszath, Kalman **31**
Molnár, Ferenc **20**
Moricz, Zsigmond **33**
Radnóti, Miklós **16**

ICELANDIC

Sigurjonsson, Johann **27**

INDIAN

Chatterji, Saratchandra **13**
Dasgupta, Surendranath **81**
Gandhi, Mohandas Karamchand **59**
Ghose, Aurabinda **63**
Iqbal, Muhammad **28**
Naidu, Sarojini **80**
Premchand **21**
Ramana Maharshi **84**
Tagore, Rabindranath **3, 53**
Vivekananda, Swami **88**

INDONESIAN

Anwar, Chairil **22**

IRANIAN

Hedabayat, Sādeq **21**

IRISH

A.E. **3, 10**
Baker, Jean H. **3, 10**
Cary, (Arthur) Joyce (Lunel) **1, 29**
Gogarty, Oliver St. John **15**
Gregory, Isabella Augusta (Persse) **1, 176**
Harris, Frank **24**
Joyce, James (Augustine Aloysius) **3, 8, 16, 35, 52, 159**
Ledwidge, Francis **23**
Martin, Violet Florence **51**
Martyn, Edward **131**
Moore, George Augustus **7**
Murdoch, Iris **171**
O'Faolain, Sean **143**
O'Grady, Standish (James) **5**
Shaw, George Bernard **3, 9, 21, 45**
Somerville, Edith Oenone **51**
Stephens, James **4**
Stoker, Bram **8, 144**
Synge, (Edmund) J(ohn) M(illington) **6, 37**
Tynan, Katharine **3**
Wilde, Oscar (Fingal O'Flahertie Wills) **1, 8, 23, 41, 175**
Yeats, William Butler **1, 11, 18, 31, 93, 116**

ISRAELI

Agnon, S(hmuel) Y(osef Halevi) **151**

ITALIAN

Alvaro, Corrado **60**
Betti, Ugo **5**
Brancati, Vitaliano **12**
Campana, Dino **20**
Carducci, Giosuè (Alessandro Giuseppe) **32**
Croce, Benedetto **37**
D'Annunzio, Gabriele **6, 40**
de Filippo, Eduardo **127**
Deledda, Grazia (Cosima) **23**
Gadda, Carlo Emilio **144**
Gentile, Giovanni **96**
Giacosa, Giuseppe **7**
Ginzburg, Natalia **156**
Jovine, Francesco **79**
Levi, Carlo **125**
Levi, Primo **109**
Malaparte, Curzio **52**
Marinetti, Filippo Tommaso **10**
Montessori, Maria **103**
Mosca, Gaetano **75**
Mussolini, Benito (Amilcare Andrea) **96**
Papini, Giovanni **22**
Pareto, Vilfredo **69**
Pascoli, Giovanni **45**
Pavese, Cesare **3**
Pirandello, Luigi **4, 29, 172**
Protolini, Vasco **124**
Saba, Umberto **33**
Tozzi, Federigo **31**
Verga, Giovanni (Carmelo) **3**

JAMAICAN

De Lisser, H(erbert) G(eorge) **12**
Garvey, Marcus (Moziah Jr.) **41**
Mais, Roger **8**
Redcam, Tom **25**

JAPANESE

Abé, Kōbō **131**
Akutagawa Ryunosuke **16**
Dazai Osamu **11**
Endō, Shūsaku **152**
Futabatei, Shimei **44**
Hagiwara, Sakutaro **60**
Hayashi, Fumiko **27**
Ishikawa, Takuboku **15**
Kunikida, Doppo **99**

Masaoka, Shiki **18**
Mishima, Yukio **161**
Miyamoto, (Chujo) Yuriko **37**
Miyazawa, Kenji **76**
Mizoguchi, Kenji **72**
Mori Ogai **14**
Nagai, Kafu **51**
Nishida, Kitaro **83**
Noguchi, Yone **80**
Santoka, Taneda **72**
Shiga, Naoya **172**
Shimazaki Toson **5**
Suzuki, Daisetz Teitaro **109**
Yokomitsu, Riichi **47**
Yosano Akiko **59**

LATVIAN

Berlin, Isaiah **105**
Rainis, Jānis **29**

LEBANESE

Gibran, Kahlil **1, 9**

LESOTHAN

Mofolo, Thomas (Mokopu) **22**

LITHUANIAN

Kreve (Mickevicius), Vincas **27**

MEXICAN

Azuela, Mariano **3**
Gamboa, Federico **36**
Garro, Elena **153**
Gonzalez Martinez, Enrique **72**
Ibargüengoitia, Jorge **148**
Nervo, (Jose) Amado (Ruiz de) **11**
Reyes, Alfonso **33**
Romero, José Rubén **14**
Villaurrutia, Xavier **80**

NEPALI

Devkota, Laxmiprasad **23**

NEW ZEALANDER

Mander, (Mary) Jane **31**
Mansfield, Katherine **2, 8, 39, 164**

NICARAGUAN

Darío, Rubén **4**

NIGERIAN

Okigbo, Christopher **171**

NORWEGIAN

Bjoernson, Bjoernstjerne (Martinius) **7, 37**
Bojer, Johan **64**
Grieg, (Johan) Nordahl (Brun) **10**
Hamsun, Knut **151**
Ibsen, Henrik (Johan) **2, 8, 16, 37, 52**
Kielland, Alexander Lange **5**
Lie, Jonas (Lauritz Idemil) **5**
Obstfelder, Sigbjoern **23**
Skram, Amalie (Bertha) **25**
Undset, Sigrid **3**

PAKISTANI

Iqbal, Muhammad **28**

PERUVIAN

Arguedas, José María **147**
Palma, Ricardo **29**
Vallejo, César (Abraham) **3, 56**

POLISH

Asch, Sholem **3**
Borowski, Tadeusz **9**
Conrad, Joseph **1, 6, 13, 25, 43, 57**
Herbert, Zbigniew **168**
Peretz, Isaac Loeb **16**
Prus, Boleslaw **48**
Przybyszewski, Stanislaw **36**
Reymont, Wladyslaw (Stanislaw) **5**
Schulz, Bruno **5, 51**
Sienkiewicz, Henryk (Adam Alexander Pius) **3**
Singer, Israel Joshua **33**
Witkiewicz, Stanislaw Ignacy **8**

PORTUGUESE

Pessoa, Fernando (António Nogueira) **27**
Sa-Carniero, Mario de **83**

PUERTO RICAN

Hostos (y Bonilla), Eugenio Maria de **24**

ROMANIAN

Bacovia, George **24**
Caragiale, Ion Luca **76**
Rebreanu, Liviu **28**

RUSSIAN

Aldanov, Mark (Alexandrovich) **23**
Andreyev, Leonid (Nikolaevich) **3**
Annensky, Innokenty (Fyodorovich) **14**
Artsybashev, Mikhail (Petrovich) **31**
Babel, Isaak (Emmanuilovich) **2, 13, 171**
Bagritsky, Eduard **60**
Bakhtin, Mikhail **160**
Balmont, Konstantin (Dmitriyevich) **11**
Bely, Andrey **7**
Berdyaev, Nikolai (Aleksandrovich) **67**
Bergelson, David **81**
Blok, Alexander (Alexandrovich) **5**
Bryusov, Valery Yakovlevich **10**
Bulgakov, Mikhail (Afanas'evich) **2, 16, 159**
Bulgya, Alexander Alexandrovich **53**
Bunin, Ivan Alexeyevich **6**
Chekhov, Anton (Pavlovich) **3, 10, 31, 55, 96, 163**
Der Nister **56**
Eisenstein, Sergei (Mikhailovich) **57**
Esenin, Sergei (Alexandrovich) **4**
Fadeyev, Alexander **53**
Gladkov, Fyodor (Vasilyevich) **27**
Gumilev, Nikolai (Stepanovich) **60**
Gurdjieff, G(eorgei) I(vanovich) **71**
Guro, Elena **56**
Hippius, Zinaida **9**
Ilf, Ilya **21**
Ivanov, Vyacheslav Ivanovich **33**
Kandinsky, Wassily **92**
Khlebnikov, Velimir **20**
Khodasevich, Vladislav (Felitsianovich) **15**
Klimentov, Andrei Platonovich **14**
Korolenko, Vladimir Galaktionovich **22**
Kropotkin, Peter (Aleksieevich) **36**
Kuprin, Aleksander Ivanovich **5**
Kuzmin, Mikhail **40**
Lenin, V. I. **67**
Mandelstam, Osip (Emilievich) **2, 6**
Mayakovski, Vladimir (Vladimirovich) **4, 18**
Merezhkovsky, Dmitry Sergeyevich **29**
Nabokov, Vladimir (Vladimirovich) **108**
Olesha, Yuri **136**
Pavlov, Ivan Petrovich **91**
Petrov, Evgeny **21**
Pilnyak, Boris **23**
Prishvin, Mikhail **75**
Remizov, Aleksei (Mikhailovich) **27**
Rozanov, Vassili **104**
Shestov, Lev **56**
Sologub, Fyodor **9**
Stalin, Joseph **92**
Stanislavsky, Konstantin **167**
Tolstoy, Alexey Nikolaevich **18**
Tolstoy, Leo (Nikolaevich) **4, 11, 17, 28, 44, 79, 173**
Trotsky, Leon **22**
Tsvetaeva (Efron), Marina (Ivanovna) **7, 35**
Zabolotsky, Nikolai Alekseevich **52**
Zamyatin, Evgeny Ivanovich **8, 37**
Zhdanov, Andrei Alexandrovich **18**
Zoshchenko, Mikhail (Mikhailovich) **15**

SCOTTISH

Barrie, J(ames) M(atthew) **2, 164**
Brown, George Douglas **28**
Buchan, John **41**
Cunninghame Graham, Robert (Gallnigad) Bontine **19**
Davidson, John **24**
Doyle, Arthur Conan **7**
Frazer, J(ames) G(eorge) **32**
Lang, Andrew **16**
MacDonald, George **9, 113**
Muir, Edwin **2, 87**
Murray, James Augustus Henry **117**
Sharp, William **39**
Tey, Josephine **14**

SLOVENIAN

Cankar, Ivan **105**

SOUTH AFRICAN

Bosman, Herman Charles **49**
Campbell, (Ignatius) Roy (Dunnachie) **5**
La Guma, Alex **140**
Mqhayi, S(amuel) E(dward) K(rune Loliwe) **25**
Paton, Alan **165**
Plaatje, Sol(omon) T(shekisho) **73**
Schreiner, Olive (Emilie Albertina) **9**
Smith, Pauline (Urmson) **25**
Vilakazi, Benedict Wallet **37**

SPANISH

Alas (y Urena), Leopoldo (Enrique Garcia) **29**
Aleixandre, Vicente **113**
Barea, Arturo **14**
Baroja (y Nessi), Pio **8**
Benavente (y Martinez), Jacinto **3**
Blasco Ibáñez, Vicente **12**
Echegaray (y Eizaguirre), Jose (Maria Waldo) **4**
García Lorca, Federico **1, 7, 49**
Jiménez (Mantecón), Juan Ramón **4**
Machado (y Ruiz), Antonio **3**
Martinez Sierra, Gregorio **6**
Martinez Sierra, Maria (de la O'LeJarraga) **6**
Miro (Ferrer), Gabriel (Francisco Victor) **5**
Onetti, Juan Carlos **131**
Ortega y Gasset, José **9**
Pereda (y Sanchez de Porrua), Jose Maria de **16**
Pérez Galdós, Benito **27**
Ramoacn y Cajal, Santiago **93**
Salinas (y Serrano), Pedro **17**
Sender, Ramón **136**
Unamuno (y Jugo), Miguel de **2, 9, 148**
Valera y Alcala-Galiano, Juan **10**
Valle-Inclán, Ramón (Maria) del **5**

SWEDISH

Bengtsson, Frans (Gunnar) **48**
Dagerman, Stig (Halvard) **17**
Ekelund, Vilhelm **75**
Heidenstam, (Carl Gustaf) Verner von **5**
Key, Ellen (Karolina Sofia) **65**
Lagerkvist, Pär **144**
Lagerloef, Selma (Ottiliana Lovisa) **4, 36**
Söderberg, Hjalmar **39**
Strindberg, (Johan) August **1, 8, 21, 47**
Weiss, Peter **152**

SWISS

Canetti, Elias **157**
Frisch, Max (Rudolf) **121**
Hesse, Herman **148**
Ramuz, Charles-Ferdinand **33**
Rod, Edouard **52**
Saussure, Ferdinand de **49**
Spitteler, Carl (Friedrich Georg) **12**
Walser, Robert **18**

SYRIAN

Gibran, Kahlil **1, 9**

TURKISH

Sait Faik **23**

UKRAINIAN

Aleichem, Sholom **1, 35**
Bialik, Chaim Nachman **25**

UGANDAN

p'Bitek, Okot **149**

URUGUAYAN

Quiroga, Horacio (Sylvestre) **20**
Sánchez, Florencio **37**

WELSH

Dahl, Roald **173**
Davies, William Henry **5**
Evans, Caradoc **85**
Lewis, Alun **3**
Thomas, Dylan (Marlais) **1, 8, 45, 105**

YUGOSLAVIAN

Andrić, Ivo **135**
Popa, Vasko **167**

TCLC-177 Title Index

"1914" (Jarrell) **177**:192
"1945: The Death of the Gods" (Jarrell) **177**:195, 239
"90 North" (Jarrell) **177**:170, 172, 174, 176-77, 214, 220, 222, 224, 228, 232
"About Popular Culture" (Jarrell) **177**:222
"Absent Without Leave" (Jarrell) **177**:193-94
"Against Abstract Expressionism" (Jarrell) **177**:190, 240
"The Age of Criticism" (Jarrell) **177**:184
The America of George Ade (Shepherd) **177**:293, 295, 298, 302
"Americans and Their Cars" (Shepherd) **177**:316
"The Angels at Hamburg" (Jarrell) **177**:195
The Animal Family (Jarrell) **177**:153, 155-58, 210
"At Home in the Ozarks" (Lane) **177**:282
"At the End of the Rainbow" (Jarrell) **177**:173
"The Augsburg Adoration" (Jarrell) **177**:162
"A & W Root Beer Stand" (Shepherd) **177**:316
"The Bad Music" (Jarrell) **177**:155, 222
"Bamberg" (Jarrell) **177**:143, 162
The Bat-Poet (Jarrell) **177**:152-56, 159
"The Bat-Poet" (Jarrell) **177**:153
"La Belle au Bois Dorman" (Jarrell) **177**:128
"The Bird of Night" (Jarrell) **177**:154-55, 158
"The Black Swan" (Jarrell) **177**:125, 131, 152, 177
Blood for a Stranger (Jarrell) **177**:138, 154-55, 163, 189
"Bombers" (Jarrell) **177**:192
"The Boyg, Peer Gynt, The One Only One" (Jarrell) **177**:127
"The Breath of Night" (Jarrell) **177**:155
"The Bronze David of Donatello" (Jarrell) **177**:162, 211
"Burning the Letters" (Jarrell) **177**:126, 129, 170, 176-77, 193, 195
Les Cahiers d'André Walter (Gide) **177**:12, 82, 91
"A Camp in the Prussian Forest" (Jarrell) **177**:126, 176, 258
"Camps and Fields" (Jarrell) **177**:193
Caractères (Gide) **177**:46
"The Carnegie Library, Juvenile Division" (Jarrell) **177**:129, 152, 169
"Carrier" (Jarrell) **177**:193
Les Caves du Vatican (Gide) **177**:5, 35, 73
"Changes of Attitude and Rhetoric in Auden's Poetry" (Jarrell) **177**:187
"Children and Civilians" (Jarrell) **177**:195
"Children Selecting Books in a Library" (Jarrell) **177**:138-40, 157, 169, 231
"Children's Arms" (Jarrell) **177**:181
"The Christmas Roses" (Jarrell) **177**:214-15, 224-26
A Christmas Story (Shepherd) **177**:315
"Cinderella" (Jarrell) **177**:152-53
"The Collected Poems of Wallace Stevens" (Jarrell) **177**:176, 186
"Come to the Stone" (Jarrell) **177**:173

The Complete Poems (Jarrell) **177**:145-50, 154, 157-59, 162, 164, 172, 219-31, 239, 241-42, 259
"Considérations sur la mythologie grecque" (Gide) **177**:8786
"A Conversation with the Devil" (Jarrell) **177**:129, 172, 231, 242
Corydon (Gide) **177**:102, 111
The Counterfeiters (Gide)
See *Les Faux monnayeurs*
"A Country Life" (Jarrell) **177**:127
"Courage" (Lane) **177**:284
"Credo" (Lane) **177**:273, 275, 286
"The Dead in Melanesia" (Jarrell) **177**:127, 195
"The Dead Wingman" (Jarrell) **177**:193, 223-24, 227
"The Death of the Ball Turret Gunner" (Jarrell) **177**:126, 131, 134, 136, 176, 194, 196, 205, 243-48
"Deutsch durch Freud" (Jarrell) **177**:152
The Discovery of Freedom (Lane) **177**:270
Diverging Roads (Lane) **177**:279
"Don't Send Your Son to College" (Lane) **177**:286
"Don't Try to Account for Anything" (Shepherd) **177**:296
"Dreams" (Jarrell) **177**:155
"Duel in the Snow" (Shepherd) **177**:293
L'école des femmes (Gide) **177**:102
"Eighth Air Force" (Jarrell) **177**:126, 129, 149, 172, 176, 191-94, 245, 248
"The Elementary scene" (Jarrell) **177**:219
"The End of the Line" (Jarrell) **177**:175, 178, 215, 220-21
"The End of the Rainbow" (Jarrell) **177**:152, 158-59, 162, 170, 172, 175, 177, 215-16, 218, 226
"An English Garden in Austria" (Jarrell) **177**:127, 196
"The English in England" (Jarrell) **177**:186
"Esthetic Theories: Art as Expression" (Jarrell) **177**:221
"The Face" (Jarrell) **177**:140, 175, 207, 214
"Fake Shepherds" (Shepherd) **177**:317
Les Faux monnayeurs (Gide) **177**:10, 35, 46, 73, 102
The Ferrari in the Bedroom (Shepherd) **177**:296-97, 299, 315, 319
"A Field Hospital" (Jarrell) **177**:195
"Fifty Years of American Poetry" (Jarrell) **177**:179, 183, 188-89
"First New Suit Out of the Army" (Shepherd) **177**:316
"First Shaves" (Shepherd) **177**:316
A Fistful of Fig Newtons (Shepherd) **177**:303, 315
Fly by Night (Jarrell) **177**:157-59
"For an Emigrant" (Jarrell) **177**:214, 251
"The Forgotten Man" (Lane) **177**:276
Free Land (Lane) **177**:266-67, 270-71, 273-80, 286-87
"Freud to Paul: The Stages of Auden's Ideology" (Jarrell) **177**:187

"From the Kingdom of Necessity" (Jarrell) **177**:244
"A Front" (Jarrell) **177**:126, 129, 193-94, 223, 227
Fruits of the Earth (Gide)
See *Les Nourritures Terrestres*
"A Game at Salzburg" (Jarrell) **177**:125, 129, 196, 216-17
"A Ghost, a Real Ghost" (Jarrell) **177**:140
"A Ghost Story" (Jarrell) **177**:155
The Gingerbread Rabbit (Jarrell) **177**:155
"The Girl Dreams that She Is Giselle" (Jarrell) **177**:152
"A Girl in a Library" (Jarrell) **177**:131-32, 140, 143, 155, 169, 172, 176, 178-79, 207, 216, 218, 254
Give Me Liberty (Lane) **177**:286
"Give Me Liberty" (Lane) **177**:275
"Gleaning" (Jarrell) **177**:177-78
"Go, Man, Go!" (Jarrell) **177**:239
The Golden Bird and Other Tales from Grimm (Jarrell) **177**:153
"The Grandstand Passion Play of Delbert and the Bumpus Hounds" (Shepherd) **177**:305
"Gunner" (Jarrell) **177**:176
El Hadj (Gide) **177**:35
"Hairy Gertz and the Forty-Seven Crappies" (Shepherd) **177**:294, 297
"Hamburger Binge" (Shepherd) **177**:316
"Harold's Super Service" (Shepherd) **177**:299
"The Head of Wisdom" (Jarrell) **177**:162
"Hohensalzburg: Fantastic Variations on a Theme of Romantic Character" (Jarrell) **177**:152, 155, 159, 196, 208
"Hope" (Jarrell) **177**:145-46, 148, 155, 206
"The House in the Wood" (Jarrell) **177**:134-36, 209-10
"A Hunt in the Black Forest" (Jarrell) **177**:134, 145, 147
"If I Could Live My Life Over Again" (Lane) **177**:282
If It Die (Gide)
See *Si le grain ne meurt*
The Immoralist (Gide) **177**:1-121
"In Galleries" (Jarrell) **177**:162, 229-30
In God We Trust, All Others Pay Cash (Shepherd) **177**:292-95, 298, 300, 304, 310, 315, 319
"In Nature There Is Neither Right nor Left nor Wrong" (Jarrell) **177**:218
"In the Vernacular" (Jarrell) **177**:185
"In the Ward: The Sacred Wood" (Jarrell) **177**:125, 127, 129, 176
"The Indy 500" (Shepherd) **177**:299
"Innocence" (Lane) **177**:277
"The Intellectual in America" (Jarrell) **177**:190
Isabelle (Gide) **177**:9, 31
"Jamestown" (Jarrell) **177**:162, 172, 228
Jean Shepherd's America (Shepherd) **177**:298, 304, 311, 314
"Jerome" (Jarrell) **177**:162-64, 167, 170, 173
"Jews at Haifa" (Jarrell) **177**:251
"John Ransom's Poetry" (Jarrell) **177**:199

"Jonah" (Jarrell) **177**:127, 152, 156
Journal 1889-1939 (Gide) **177**:25-26, 28, 30, 51
"Junk in the Basement" (Shepherd) **177**:316
Kipling, Auden & Co.: Essays and Reviews (Jarrell) **177**:183, 185, 187, 190, 220-22, 231, 241, 245-47
"The Knight, Death, and the Devil" (Jarrell) **177**:162, 167
"Lady Bates" (Jarrell) **177**:129, 155, 159, 172, 224
"Leave" (Jarrell) **177**:194
Let the Hurricane Roar (Lane) **177**:266-67, 271-75, 278, 284-87
"Letters à Angèle" (Gide) **177**:27, 100
"Les Limited de l'art" (Gide) **177**:49
"The Lines" (Jarrell) **177**:195
"The Little Cars" (Jarrell) **177**:239
Little Friend, Little Friend (Jarrell) **177**:138, 176, 194
"A Little Poem" (Jarrell) **177**:138
"London" (Jarrell) **177**:147
"The Lonely Man" (Jarrell) **177**:226
Losses (Jarrell) **177**:138
"Losses" (Jarrell) **177**:127, 152, 176, 192, 194, 219, 247
"Lost at C" (Shepherd) **177**:299-300
"The Lost Children" (Jarrell) **177**:177, 207, 218
The Lost World (Jarrell) **177**:130, 137, 140, 144, 155, 162, 165, 173, 175-77, 179-80, 193, 212, 218, 238
"The Lost World" (Jarrell) **177**:129, 132-34, 136, 143, 145, 158, 172-74, 176-77, 179-82, 191, 201, 204-5, 207, 211
"Love at the USO" (Shepherd) **177**:316
"A Lullaby" (Jarrell) **177**:193
"The Machine Gun" (Jarrell) **177**:214
"Mail Call" (Jarrell) **177**:193
"A Man Meets a Woman in the Street" (Jarrell) **177**:150, 158, 172, 174, 176, 228-29, 231
"The Märchen" (Jarrell) **177**:134, 155, 169, 205
"The Meteorite" (Jarrell) **177**:228
"Midwestern Drugstores and Drive-Ins" (Shepherd) **177**:316
"Money" (Jarrell) **177**:172
"Mother, Said the Child" (Jarrell) **177**:155
"Moving" (Jarrell) **177**:127, 224
Narcissus (Gide)
  See *Le traité du Narcisse*
"Nestus Gurley" (Jarrell) **177**:152, 173
New Faces of 1962 (Shepherd) **177**:311
"New Georgia" (Jarrell) **177**:149, 195
"The New Ghost" (Jarrell) **177**:177
"Next Day" (Jarrell) **177**:140, 172, 176-77, 199-201, 207, 211, 219, 222-24, 226, 231-32
"Nice Old Lady" (Lane) **177**:268
"The Night before the Night before Christmas" (Jarrell) **177**:125, 148, 159, 170-72, 177, 204-5, 211, 216-18, 224, 226
"The Night People vs. Creeping Meatballism" (Shepherd) **177**:314
"A Night with Lions" (Jarrell) **177**:180-81
"Nollekans" (Jarrell) **177**:127, 162
The Notebooks of André Walter (Gide)
  See *Les cahiers d'André Walter*
Les Nourritures terrestres (Gide) **177**:4, 7, 12-16, 25-26, 31, 34, 48, 78, 81, 84, 93, 99, 115
"The Obscurity of the Poet" (Jarrell) **177**:154, 157, 222, 238, 240, 242
Oedipe (Gide) **177**:86
Oeuvres complètes d'André (Gide) **177**:14, 25-28, 34, 39, 46, 48-50, 61, 73, 100
"The Old and the New Masters" (Jarrell) **177**:156, 162, 164, 167, 240-41
Old Home Town (Lane) **177**:266-70, 272, 282
"Old Maid" (Lane) **177**:267-68
"On Preparing to Read Kipling" (Jarrell) **177**:185
"On the Railway Platform" (Jarrell) **177**:138

"The One Who Was Different" (Jarrell) **177**:133, 222
"Orestes at Tauris" (Jarrell) **177**:145
"The Orient Express" (Jarrell) **177**:129, 196, 230
"The Other Frost" (Jarrell) **177**:186
"The Owl's Bedtime Story" (Jarrell) **177**:159
Paludes (Gide) **177**:34-35, 67
The Pastoral Symphony (Gide)
  See *La Symphonie pastorale*
"A Perfectly Free Association" (Jarrell) **177**:227
Phantom of the Open Hearth (Shepherd) **177**:304
"The Phantom of the Open Hearth" (Shepherd) **177**:298-99
Philoctète (Gide) **177**:105
Pictures from an Institution (Jarrell) **177**:169, 172, 190, 230
"A Pilot from the Carrier" (Jarrell) **177**:192, 204-5, 210, 223
"Pilots, Man Your Planes" (Jarrell) **177**:192
"The Player Piano" (Jarrell) **177**:149, 155, 174, 176, 178, 222
Poetry and the Age (Jarrell) **177**:143, 154, 179, 183-84, 186-87, 190, 221-22, 239-40, 242, 245-46, 248
"Poetry and the Age" (Jarrell) **177**:172
"Poets, Critics, and Readers" (Jarrell) **177**:182
"Port of Embarkation" (Jarrell) **177**:195
La Porte étroite (Gide) **177**:31, 36, 46, 102
"The Prince" (Jarrell) **177**:145-46, 177
Le Prométhée mal enchaîé (Gide) **177**:34, 46
Prometheus Illbound (Gide)
  See *Le Prométhée mal enchaîé*
Proserpine (Gide) **177**:107
"Protocols" (Jarrell) **177**:147, 177, 195, 222, 258
"A Quilt Pattern" (Jarrell) **177**:125, 128-29, 147-48, 196, 205-8
The Rage for the Lost Penny (Jarrell) **177**:137-38, 213-14
Randall Jarrell's Letters (Jarrell) **177**:191, 193-94, 222, 224, 228-29, 237
"The Range in the Desert" (Jarrell) **177**:194
"Reflections on Wallace Stevens" (Jarrell) **177**:186
"The Refugees" (Jarrell) **177**:251, 253-58
Le Retour de l'enfant prodigue (Gide) **177**:46
"The Return of the Native to the Indiana Mill Town" (Shepherd) **177**:293
The Return of the Prodigal (Gide)
  See *Le retour de l'enfant prodigue*
"The Return of the Smiling Wimpy Doll" (Shepherd) **177**:295, 309
"A Rhapsody on Irish Themes" (Jarrell) **177**:172
"The Rising Sun" (Jarrell) **177**:155
Le Roi Candaule (Gide) **177**:105, 107
Romans, récits et soties (Gide) **177**:99-101
"Rude Noises in Company K" (Shepherd) **177**:316
A Sad Heart at the Supermarket (Jarrell) **177**:153, 179, 183, 185, 190, 223, 231-32, 239
"A Sad Heart at the Supermarket" (Jarrell) **177**:172, 177, 231-32, 239-40
Saül (Gide) **177**:30, 105-6, 108
The School for Wives (Gide)
  See *L'école des femmes*
"Scut Farkas and the Murderous Mariah" (Shepherd) **177**:306
"Sears Roebuck" (Jarrell) **177**:172
"Second Air Force" (Jarrell) **177**:126, 141, 194
"See Through X-Ray Eyes" (Shepherd) **177**:316
"Seele im Raum" (Jarrell) **177**:129, 138, 140-43, 170, 172-73, 177, 180, 196, 229-31
Selected Poems (Jarrell) **177**:125-27, 130, 138, 140, 195-96, 210, 218, 222, 244
The Seven-League Crutches (Jarrell) **177**:132, 139, 162, 176, 194, 196, 217-18, 229
Shepherd's Pie (Shepherd) **177**:304, 311
"Shoplifting" (Shepherd) **177**:316
Si le grain ne meurt (Gide) **177**:51, 102

"A Sick Child" (Jarrell) **177**:127, 143, 152, 172
"The Sick Nought" (Jarrell) **177**:178, 194, 223, 225, 232
"Siegfried" (Jarrell) **177**:149, 170, 172, 192-93
"The Sleeping Beauty: Variation of the Prince" (Jarrell) **177**:125, 129, 152
"Slobbus Americanus in the Cultural Vanguard" (Shepherd) **177**:299, 302
"The Smell of Homes" (Shepherd) **177**:316
"The Smiling Wimpy Doll" (Shepherd) **177**:310
"The Snow Leopard" (Jarrell) **177**:127
"The Soldier Walks Under the Trees of the University" (Jarrell) **177**:221
"Soldiers" (Jarrell) **177**:195
"Some Lines from Whitman" (Jarrell) **177**:139
"Song: Not There" (Jarrell) **177**:127
"A Soul" (Jarrell) **177**:152, 157, 196
"The Star-Crossed Romance of Josephine Cosnowski" (Shepherd) **177**:308
"The State" (Jarrell) **177**:146, 173, 177
"Stories" (Jarrell) **177**:169, 172
"A Story" (Jarrell) **177**:172, 174, 176, 177, 213-14
Straight is the Gate (Gide)
  See *La porte étroite*
"A Street off Sunset" (Jarrell) **177**:146, 176, 180-81
"The Survivor among Graves" (Jarrell) **177**:195
La Symphonie pastorale (Gide) **177**:31, 45, 49, 58-59
"The Taste of the Age" (Jarrell) **177**:239
"Tennis Date with First Love" (Shepherd) **177**:316
Théâtre (Gide) **177**:106
Thésée (Gide) **177**:35, 46, 78, 87
"Thinking of the Lost World" (Jarrell) **177**:136, 141, 145, 154, 170, 173-74, 210, 218-19, 226
The Third Book of Criticism (Jarrell) **177**:183, 186, 188, 190, 221
"Three bills" (Jarrell) **177**:178
"The Times Worsen" (Jarrell) **177**:238
"To Be Dead" (Jarrell) **177**:215
"The Tower" (Jarrell) **177**:221
"The Trades" (Jarrell) **177**:194
Le Traité du Narcisse (Gide) **177**:35
"Transient Barracks" (Jarrell) **177**:192, 225-28
"The Truth" (Jarrell) **177**:176, 195, 222, 225-26
"Un Esprit non prévenu" (Gide) **177**:98
"Unison" (Jarrell) **177**:195
Urien's Voyage (Gide)
  See *Le voyage d'Urien*
"Variations III" (Jarrell) **177**:147
"Variations" (Jarrell) **177**:147
The Vatican Swindle (Gide)
  See *Les caves du Vatican*
"The Venetian Blind" (Jarrell) **177**:224
Voice in the Night (Shepherd) **177**:312
Le Voyage d'Urien (Gide) **177**:4, 12
Wanda Hickey's Night of Golden Memories, and Other Disasters (Shepherd) **177**:295-96, 299, 304-5, 315
"Wanda Hickey's Night of Golden Memories" (Shepherd) **177**:304, 308
"A War" (Jarrell) **177**:195
"A Ward in the States" (Jarrell) **177**:155
"Washing" (Jarrell) **177**:149
"A Well-to-do Invalid" (Jarrell) **177**:132, 178
"Well Water" (Jarrell) **177**:157
"Why I'm Such a Sorehead" (Shepherd) **177**:316
"Why Particulars Are So Much More Effective Than Generalities" (Jarrell) **177**:225
"The Wide Prospect" (Jarrell) **177**:195
"Windows" (Jarrell) **177**:155
The Woman at the Washington Zoo (Jarrell) **177**:131, 139-40, 162, 173, 176-77, 193, 215
"The Woman at the Washington Zoo" (Jarrell) **177**:125, 132, 141, 152, 159, 170, 172-73, 175-77, 181, 183, 207, 211, 218-19, 231-32

ISBN 0-7876-8931-9